Magill's Cinema Annual 2018

Magill's Cinema Annual 2018

37th Edition
A Survey of the films of 2017

Brian Tallerico, Editor

A VideoHound® Reference

GALE
A Cengage Company
Farmington Hills, Mich • San Francisco • New York • Waterville, Maine
Meriden, Conn • Mason, Ohio • Chicago

GALE
A Cengage Company

Magill's Cinema Annual 2018

Brian Tallerico, Editor

Senior Content Developer: Michael J. Tyrkus

Editorial Support Services: Wayne Fong

Composition and Electronic Prepress: Amy Darga, Evi Seoud

Manufacturing: Rita Wimberley

Gale, a Cengage Company
27500 Drake Rd.
Farmington Hills, MI, 48331-3535

ISBN-13: 978-1-4103-2416-0

ISSN: 0739-2141

This title is also available as an e-book.
ISBN-13: 978-1-4103-3464-0
Contact your Gale sales representative for ordering information.

Printed in Mexico
1 2 3 4 5 6 7 22 21 20 19 18

Contents

Preface	VII
Introduction	IX
Contributing Reviewers	XI
User's Guide	XIII
The Films of 2017	1
List of Awards	443
Obituaries	445
Selected Film Books of 2017	459
Director Index	465
Screenwriter Index	471
Cinematographer Index	477
Editor Index	481
Art Director Index	487
Music Director Index	491
Performer Index	495
Subject Index	511
Title Index	525

Preface

Magill's Cinema Annual 2018 continues the fine film reference tradition that defines the VideoHound® series of entertainment industry products published by Gale. The thirty-seventh annual volume in a series that developed from the twenty-one-volume core set, *Magill's Survey of Cinema,* the *Annual* was formerly published by Salem Press. Gale's twenty-fourth volume, as with the previous Salem volumes, contains essay-reviews of significant domestic and foreign films released in the United States during the preceding year.

The *Magill's* editorial staff at Gale, A Cengage Company, comprising the VideoHound® team and a host of *Magill's* contributors, continues to provide the enhancements that were added to the *Annual* when Gale acquired the line. These features include:

- More essay-length reviews of significant films released during the year
- Obituaries and book review sections
- Trivia and &ldquof;un facts" about the reviewed movies, their stars, the crew, and production
- Quotes and dialogue "soundbites" from reviewed movies, or from stars and crew about the film
- More complete awards and nominations listings, including the American Academy Awards®, the Golden Globes, and others (see the User's Guide for more information on awards coverage)
- Box office grosses, including year-end and other significant totals
- Publicity taglines featured in film reviews and advertisements

In addition to those listed above, *Magill's Cinema Annual 2018* still continues to feature the following additional elements and enhancements:

- An obituaries section profiling major contributors to the film industry who died in 2017
- An annotated list of selected film books published in 2017
- Nine indexes: Director, Screenwriter, Cinematographer, Editor, Art Director, Music Director, Performer, Subject, and Title (now cumulative)

COMPILATION METHODS

The *Magill's* editorial staff reviews a variety of entertainment industry publications, including trade magazines and newspapers, as well as online sources, on a daily and weekly basis to select significant films for review in *Magill's Cinema Annual. Magill's* staff and other contributing reviewers, including film scholars and university faculty, write the reviews included in the *Annual.*

MAGILL'S CINEMA ANNUAL: A VIDEOHOUND® REFERENCE

The *Magill's Survey of Cinema* series, now supplemented by the *Annual,* is the recipient of the Reference Book of the Year Award in Fine Arts by the American Library Association. Gale, an award-winning publisher of reference products, is proud to offer *Magill's Cinema Annual* as part of its popular VideoHound® product line, which includes *VideoHound®'s Golden Movie Retriever.* Other Gale film-related products include the four-volume *International Dictionary of Films and Filmmakers, Women Filmmakers & Their Films, The Video Source Book,* the *Contemporary Theatre, Film, and Television* series, the four-volume *Schirmer Encyclopedia of Film,* and the *Books to Film: Cinematic Adaptation of Literary Works* series.

ACKNOWLEDGMENTS

The writing staff of *Magill's Cinema Annual 2018,* which consists of publishing professionals, freelance writers, and paid film critics, has given their all to this year's remarkable edition. Together, we work to create a comprehensive, critical view of the year in film. The staff continues to impress with their knowledge, dedication, and abilities, as they analyze film not merely from the standpoint of a viewer but as experts in their field. They bring a wide variety of background and personalities together to support one purpose.

Magill's Cinema Annual 2018 was truly a collaboratively created work and would be nothing without, not only the support of the writers assigned to it, but the friends and family who so completely back its editor in every capacity. He would particularly like to thank those who inspire him professionally, including Chaz Ebert, Matt Zoller Seitz, Dann Gire, and David Fear. He would also like to dedicate this edition to Roger Ebert, a mentor and role model to this day. Most of all, this book isn't possible without the consistent support of Lauren Tallerico and the remarkable spirit of Lucas, Miles, and Noah Tallerico. They are the stars in my sky.

We at *Magill's* look forward to another exciting year in film and preparing the next edition of *Magill's Cinema Annual.* As always, we invite your comments, questions, and suggestions. Please direct them to:

Editor, *Magill's Cinema Annual*
Gale, A Cengage Company
27500 Drake Road
Farmington Hills, MI 48331-3535
Phone: (248) 699-8552
Toll-Free: (800) 347-GALE (4253)
Fax: (248) 699-8865

The Year in Film 2017: An Introduction

This past year was one of the most tumultuous years in the history of Hollywood, reflected most prominently in the cascade of accusations against its power structure that emerged in the wake of the truth about how Miramax head Harvey Weinstein had been acting for decades as more and more of his victims came forward every week, including actresses Ashley Judd, Mira Sorvino, and Annabella Sciorra. It reached to a level in which campaigns under the hashtags #MeToo and #TimesUp became shorthand for a revolution, a change in the way business is done in Hollywood. And Weinstein wasn't alone. Accusations against James Toback, Brett Ratner, Kevin Spacey, Jeffrey Tambor, and more followed, resulting in an actual movement that felt, at the end of the year, like it would result in notable change. Not only did people lose their jobs—Spacey was noticeably recast in Ridley Scott's *All the Money in the World* after he had shot all of his scenes and Tambor was booted from Amazon's *Transparent*—but calls for equal pay and on-set representation grew too loud for Hollywood to ignore. Will this all result in better films? It almost certainly will, given the culture of fear it's replacing, but only time will tell.

The year 2017 will also be remembered as the first of the Trump administration, and filmmakers began addressing the national anxiety caused by the 45th President through their art, although that's likely to only increase as films in production this year get released in 2018 and beyond. It's likely a trend only getting started, but films like *Get Out* and *The Shape of Water* felt more cutting than they would have under a different administration that cared more about racial harmony and the plight of immigrants. Whether Trump attacked Hollywood directly, by calling out Meryl Streep for an awards speech or mocking *Saturday Night Live* on Twitter, as he continues to challenge human liberties and rights, the film world is certain to respond.

Perhaps because they were so bombarded with the real horrors of the world, from the possible war with North Korea to an increasingly depressing slate of school shootings, people wanted to escape when they went to the multiplex. As they have for three years running, ticket buyers made a Lucasfilm product the highest-grossing movie of the year, as *Star Wars: The Last Jedi* topped the box-office charts despite a loud backlash against its perceived failings in some online circles. Superheroes continued to be one of the most profitable professions in the film world, but it was a somewhat surprising hero that would lead them this year, given she's a part of the DC Universe and not Marvel, and given she's, well, a she. Patty Jenkins's *Wonder Woman* was the highest-grossing superhero movie of the year, leading a crew that included an amazing SIX other superhero flicks in the top twenty: *Guardians of the Galaxy, Vol. 2, Spider-Man: Homecoming, Thor: Ragnarok, Justice League, Logan,* and *The LEGO Batman Movie.*

Most of all, ticket buyers proved how much they like familiarity. Every single film in the top ten of the year in terms of box office was either a sequel or derived from a familiar source material (as in the case of *Wonder Woman*). It was, however, refreshing to see a few original concepts connect with audiences enough to land in the next ten spots, including Pixar's *Coco,* Christopher Nolan's *Dunkirk,* and Jordan Peele's Oscar®-winning *Get Out.*

Peele's and Nolan's films were the two most popular to win Oscars® this year. They were joined by a more unusual crew of critical darlings than we've seen in years, including a gay romance, a monster movie, the story of a perfectionist fashion designer, and a biting black comedy about the American South written by an Irishman. *Dunkirk* and *Get Out* were both nominated for Best Picture and Best Director, and they were joined in the big category of the night by *Call Me by Your Name, Darkest Hour, Lady Bird, Phantom Thread, Three Billboards outside Ebbing, Missouri,* and the winner for Picture and Director, Guillermo del Toro's *The Shape of Water.* Unlike a lot of years, the Academy spread the wealth around, giving two acting awards to *Billboards* (Sam Rockwell and Frances McDormand), and one each to *Darkest Hour* (Gary Oldman) and *I, Tonya* (Allison Janney). *Get Out* and *Call Me by Your Name* took home Oscars® for screenwriting, a first for the legendary James Ivory and a first for the Academy when Peele became the only African American to win for screenwriting, and he did so with his debut film.

Other critical darlings reflected through awards season but not necessarily on Oscar® night included Sean Baker's *The Florida Project,* Kogonada's *Columbus,* Yorgos Lanthimos's *The Killing of a Sacred Deer,* David Lowery's *A Ghost Story,* Terence Davies's *A Quiet Passion, James Franco's The Disaster Artist,* and a trio of films that premiered not in theaters but on the online service Netflix: *Mudbound, Okja,* and *The Meyerowitz Stories (New and Selected).* Taken as a whole, the year in acclaimed films shows a wide variety of genres, styles, and creative voices. In short, it was a very good year for film.

Where does Hollywood go from here? Does the trend to recognize creative voices who aren't only white men (Peele and Del Toro being good examples of people who used their backgrounds and cultural identities to great impact in their 2017 films) continue or does the industry go back to playing it safe? It feels, more than ever, that a door has been opened that cannot be closed again. There will be no need for campaigns like #OscarsSoWhite in the future and it's difficult to think that #TimesUp won't have a similar impact on the industry. Women still only direct 11% of films but the success of films like *Wonder Woman* and *Lady Bird* seem certain to push that number upwards. Hopefully, the #MeToo movement will result in women in more powerful positions across the industry, not only in the director's chair.

Ultimately, 2017 felt like a watershed, industry-redefining year but in ways that we won't fully be able to realize or discuss until we see what happens next. Will we get more directors who are non-white men? Will we see artists responding to Trump's administration more fervently through their filmmaking? And, will we continue to seek comfort in the familiar arms of Marvel, Star Wars, Disney, and sequels? The answer to these questions is, almost certainly, yes, but only time will tell. Harvey Weinstein may have damaged Hollywood in a shocking way but the inspirational refusal to let him hurt it forever will lead to healing. And hopefully some truly great movies too.

Brian Tallerico
Chicago, Illinois

Contributing Reviewers

Nick Allen
Professional Film Critic

David L. Boxerbaum
Freelance Reviewer

Tom Burns
Freelance Reviewer

David Canfield
Professional Film Critic

Erik Childress
Professional Film Critic

Mark Dujsik
Professional Film Critic

Odie Henderson
Professional Film Critic

Don Lewis
Professional Film Critic

Jacob Oller
Professional Film Critic

Matt Pais
Professional Film Critic

Brent Simon
Professional Film Critic

Michael Snydel
Professional Film Critic

Peter Sobczynski
Professional Film Critic

Collin Souter
Professional Film Critic

Scout Tafoya
Freelance Reviewer

Brian Tallerico
Professional Film Critic

Michael J. Tyrkus
Professional Film Critic

User's Guide

ALPHABETIZATION

Film titles and reviews are arranged on a word-by-word basis, including articles and prepositions. English leading articles (A, An, The) are ignored, as are foreign leading articles (El, Il, La, Las, Le, Les, Los). Other considerations:

- Acronyms appear alphabetically as if regular words.
- Common abbreviations in titles file as if they are spelled out, so *Mr. Death* will be found as if it was spelled *Mister Death.*
- Proper names in titles are alphabetized beginning with the individual's first name, for instance, *Gloria* will be found under "G."
- Titles with numbers, for instance, *200 Cigarettes,* are alphabetized as if the numbers were spelled out, in this case, "Two-Hundred." When numeric titles gather in close proximity to each other, the titles will be arranged in a low-to-high numeric sequence.

SPECIAL SECTIONS

The following sections that are designed to enhance the reader's examination of film are arranged alphabetically; they include:

- *List of Awards.* An annual list of awards bestowed upon the year's films by the following: Academy of Motion Picture Arts and Sciences, British Academy of Film and Television Arts Awards, Directors Guild of America Awards, Golden Globe Awards, Golden Raspberry Awards, Independent Spirit Awards, the Screen Actors Guild Awards, and the Writer's Guild Awards.
- *Obituaries.* Profiles major contributors to the film industry who died in 2017.
- *Selected Film Books of 2017.* An annotated list of selected film books published in 2017.

INDEXES

Film titles and artists are separated into nine indexes, allowing the reader to effectively approach a film from any one of several directions, including not only its credits but its subject matter.

- *Director, Screenwriter, Cinematographer, Editor, Art Director, Music Director,* and *Performer* indexes are arranged alphabetically according to artists appearing in this volume, followed by a list of the films on which they worked. In the *Performer* index, a (V) beside a movie title indicates voice-only work and an (N) beside a movie title indicates work as narrator.
- *Subject Index.* Films may be categorized under several of the subject terms arranged alphabetically in this section.
- *Title Index.* The title index is a cumulative alphabetical list of films covered in the thirty volumes of the *Magill's Cinema Annual,* including the films covered in this volume. Films reviewed in past volumes are cited with the year in which the film appeared in the *Annual*; films reviewed in this volume are cited with the film title and this year's edition in boldface. Original and alternate titles are cross-referenced to the American release title in the Title Index. Titles of retrospective films are followed by the year, in brackets, of their original release.

SAMPLE REVIEW

Each *Magill's* review contains up to sixteen items of information. A fictionalized composite sample review containing all the elements of information that may be included in a full-length review follows the outline on the facing page. The circled number following each element in the sample review designates an item of information that is explained in the outline.

1. **Title:** Film title as it was released in the United States.
2. **Foreign or alternate title(s):** The film's original title or titles as released outside the United States, or alternate film title or titles. Foreign and alternate titles also appear in the Title Index to facilitate user access.
3. **Taglines:** Up to ten publicity taglines for the film from advertisements or reviews.
4. **Box office information:** Year-end or other box office domestic revenues for the film.
5. **Film review:** A signed review of the film, including an analytic overview of the film and its critical reception.
6. **Reviewer byline:** The name of the reviewer who wrote the full-length review. A complete list of this volume's contributors appears in the "Contributing Reviewers" section which follows the Introduction.
7. **Principal characters:** Listings of the film's principal characters and the names of the actors who play them in the film.
8. **Country of origin:** The film's country or countries of origin and the languages featured in the film.
9. **Release date:** The year of the film's first general release.
10. **Production information:** This section typically includes the name(s) of the film's producer(s), production company, and distributor; director(s); screenwriter(s); cinematographer(s); editor(s); art director(s); production designer(s); music composer(s); and other credits such as visual effects, sound, costume design, and song(s) and songwriter(s).
11. **MPAA rating:** The film's rating by the Motion Picture Association of America. If there is no rating given, the line will read, "Unrated."
12. **Running time:** The film's running time in minutes.
13. **Reviews:** A list of brief citations of major newspaper and journal reviews of the film, including author, publication title, and date of review.
14. **Film quotes:** Memorable dialogue directly from the film, attributed to the character who spoke it, or comment from cast or crew members or reviewers about the film.
15. **Film trivia:** Interesting tidbits about the film, its cast, or production crew.
16. **Awards information:** Awards won by the film, followed by category and name of winning cast or crew member. Listings of the film's nominations follow the wins on a separate line for each award. Awards are arranged alphabetically. Information is listed for films that won or were nominated for the following awards: American Academy Awards®, British Academy of Film and Television Arts Awards, Directors Guild of America Awards, Golden Globe Awards, Golden Raspberry Awards, Independent Spirit Awards, the Screen Actors Guild Awards, and the Writers Guild of America Awards.

THE GUMP DIARIES ①

(Los Diarios del Gump) ②

Love means never having to say you're stupid.

—Movie tagline ③

Box Office: $10 million④

In writer/director Robert Zemeckis' *Back to the Future* trilogy (1985, 1989, 1990), Marty McFly (Michael J. Fox) and his scientist sidekick Doc Brown (Christopher Lloyd) journey backward and forward in time, attempting to smooth over some rough spots in their personal histories in order to remain true to their individual destinies. Throughout their time-travel adventures, Doc Brown insists that neither he nor Marty influence any major historical events, believing that to do so would result in catastrophic changes in humankind's ultimate destiny. By the end of the trilogy, however, Doc Brown has revised his thinking and tells Marty that, "Your future hasn't been written yet. No one's has. Your future is whatever you make it. So make it a good one."

In *Forrest Gump,* Zemeckis once again explores the theme of personal destiny and how an individual's life affects and is affected by his historical time period. This time, however, Zemeckis and screenwriter Eric Roth chronicle the life of a character who does nothing but meddle in the historical events of his time without even trying to do so. By the film's conclusion, however, it has become apparent that Zemeckis' main concern is something more than merely having fun with four decades of American history. In the process of re-creating significant moments in time, he has captured on celluloid something eternal and timeless—the soul of humanity personified by a nondescript simpleton from the deep South.

The film begins following the flight of a seemingly insignificant feather as it floats down from the sky and brushes against various objects and people before finally coming to rest at the feet of Forrest Gump (Tom Hanks). Forrest, who is sitting on a bus-stop bench, reaches down and picks up the feather, smooths it out, then opens his traveling case and carefully places the feather between the pages of his favorite book, *Curious George.*

In this simple but hauntingly beautiful opening scene, the filmmakers illustrate the film's principal concern: Is life a series of random events over which a person has no control, or is there an underlying order to things that leads to the fulfillment of an individual's destiny? The rest of the film is a humorous and moving attempt to prove that, underlying the random, chaotic events that make up a person's life, there exists a benign and simple order.

Forrest sits on the bench throughout most of the film, talking about various events of his life to others who happen to sit down next to him. It does not take long, however, for the audience to realize that Forrest's seemingly random chatter to a parade of strangers has a perfect chronological order to it. He tells his first story after looking down at the feet of his first bench partner and observing, "Mama always said that you can tell a lot about a person by the shoes they wear." Then, in a voice-over narration, Forrest begins the story of his life, first by telling about the first pair of shoes he can remember wearing.

The action shifts to the mid-1950s with Forrest as a young boy (Michael Humphreys) being fitted with leg braces to correct a curvature in his spine. Despite this traumatic handicap, Forrest remains unaffected, thanks to his mother (Sally Field) who reminds him on more than one occasion that he is no different from anyone else. Although this and most of Mrs. Gump's other words of advice are in the form of hackneyed cliches, Forrest, whose intelligence quotient is below normal, sincerely believes every one of them, namely because he instinctively knows they are sincere expressions of his mother's love and fierce devotion. ⑤

John Byline ⑥

CREDITS ⑦

Forrest Gump: Tom Hanks
Forrest's Mother: Sally Field
Young Forrest: Michael Humphreys
Origin: United States ⑧
Language: English, Spanish
Released: 1994 ⑨
Production: Liz Heller, John Manulis; New Line Cinema; released by Island Pictures ⑩
Directed by: Robert Zemeckis
Written by: Eric Roth
Cinematography by: David Phillips
Music by: Graeme Revell
Editing: Dana Congdon
Production Design: Danny Nowak
Sound: David Sarnoff
Costumes: David Robinson
MPAA rating: R ⑪
Running time: 102 minutes ⑫

REVIEWS ⑬

Doe, Jane. *Los Angeles Times.* July 6, 1994.
Doe, John. *Entertainment Weekly.* July 15, 1994.
Reviewer, Paul. *Hollywood Reporter.* June 29, 1994.
Writer, Zach. *New York Times Online.* July 15, 1994.

QUOTES ⑭

Forrest Gump (Tom Hanks): "The state of existence may be likened unto a receptacle containing cocoa-based confections, in that one may never predict that which one may receive."

TRIVIA ⑮

Hanks was the first actor since Spencer Tracy to win back-to-back Oscars® for Best Actor. Hanks received the award in 1993 for his performance in *Philadelphia.* Tracy won Oscars® in 1937 for *Captains Courageous* and in 1938 for *Boys Town.*

AWARDS ⑯

Academy Awards 1994: Film, Actor (Hanks), Special Effects, Cinematography

Nomination:

Golden Globes 1994: Film, Actor (Hanks), Supporting Actress (Field), Music.

A

ABACUS: SMALL ENOUGH TO JAIL

Box Office: $113,278

Prolific documentarian Steve James trades on the popular wave of true-crime procedurals by mixing the genre's inherent drama with the economic outrage permeating a post-recession America. With *Abacus: Small Enough to Jail,* James recounts the story of the solitary bank to be indicted over the 2008 financial crisis. Abacus Federal Savings Bank in the heart of New York City's Chinatown, a family-run institution that caters to Chinese immigrants, operates primarily on an honor and cash basis. The Sung family, led by patriarch Thomas who is bolstered by his stalwart wife Hwei Lin and four daughters, oversee the bank and its operations in different roles. But when a rogue employee solicits bribes for loans, giving the Manhattan District Attorney ample ammunition to crucify the bank in the national post-crash rage, the entire family becomes implicated in the crime.

James' strength at finding hope in his documentary subjects warms an otherwise icy financial crime thriller with the heartbreak, struggle, and personality of those who have found themselves betrayed. Yes, betrayed because the film makes clear over a series of chronological interviews with lawyers, defendants, prosecutors, and community activists that the tradition of this bank was to bridge the cultural and economic gap from China to the U.S. They are a bastion of their neighborhood, helping people fulfill the American Dream. The institution of the bank is—at its purest idealism—a great elevator, a machine for upward mobility. But here, in this time period, we have learned to loathe banks while the government bails them out.

Abacus: Small Enough to Jail drills down into this anger to find the hopeful core stoking the fire. What the film finds is that while certain banks were too big to fail, the history of economic discrimination against small businesses in this country, along with its systemic racism, leads to the film's conclusion being tied up in its bleakly appropriate subtitle.

The film is most exciting as a court drama, the documents appearing, the law mistreating employees like nothing the media had ever seen. Clips of the paraded Abacus employees, linked together by handcuffs in a chain gang, imply the unthinkable translation of treatment to white bankers at the large banks. An example is being made here, one by the government and one by the documentary itself. However, the strongest material in the film is its establishment of a community. The prosecutorial detail, background work, and touching interviews with the Sung daughters paint an elaborate portrait of a community built on the trust of a handshake and a common outsider status. That this is taken advantage of by an unscrupulous employee in the most capitalist of capitalist institutions is unsurprising, but more than its share of heartbreaking thanks to James' thorough exploration of the people affected by the case.

Triumphant closure is usually withheld for war dramas and sports documentaries, but like the Sung household favorite *It's a Wonderful Life* (1946), the thriving community builds to as satisfying a conclusion as the results of the legal battle. Immigrants coming together, helping each other aspire to greater things through cultural support or the simple economic boost of a loan, are the backbone of what America should be. The film centers itself around the Sung family not just as the victims of an injustice, but as the pinnacle of citizenry. That the injustice happens to them is another bitter irony to swallow—thankfully washed down with the sweet relationship between family members.

The Sungs are entertaining enough to hold their own sitcom if they had not been embroiled in a corruption scandal that threw decades of unspoken Chinatown culture clash into the courtroom-sketched spotlight. They thrive with each other, bouncing off one another with the onscreen electricity shared only by highly-trained actors and completely untrained laymen. The closeness allowed to James, in both the camera's framing and the director's relationship to the family, is stunningly effective at getting across just how sweet this family is and how cruel their persecution. The film never devolves into witchhunts or propaganda, showing interview footage from both sides of the trial and allowing its subjects to wrestle with the guilt of poor oversight, but it can feel a bit too set on retrofitting an underdog moniker on a family, and community, whose situation is far more complex.

Jacob Oller

CREDITS

Origin: United States

Language: English

Released: 2017

Production: Mark Mitten, Julie Goldman; Blue Ice Films, Kartemquin Films Ltd., Mitten Media, Motto Pictures; released by PBS Distribution

Directed by: Steve James

Cinematography by: Tom Bergmann

Music by: Joshua Adams

Editing: John Farbrother; David E. Simpson

MPAA rating: Unrated

Running time: 88 minutes

REVIEWS

Bailey, Jason. *Flavorwire.* September 18, 2016.

Charity, Tom. *Sight and Sound.* September 23, 2016.

Grierson, Tim. *Screen International.* May 15, 2017.

Jenkins, Mark. *NPR.* May 18, 2017.

Kim, Yoonsoo. *Village Voice.* May 17, 2017.

Kenigsberg, Ben. *New York Times.* May 18, 2017.

Nakhnikian, Elise. *Slant Magazine.* October 3, 2016.

Phipps, Keith. *Uproxx.* June 15, 2017.

Seitz, Matt Zoller. *RogerEbert.com.* May 19, 2017.

Wilner, Norman. *NOW Toronto.* October 14, 2016.

AWARDS

Nominations:

Oscars 2017: Feature Doc.

Directors Guild 2017: Documentary Director (James)

AFTER THE STORM

(Umi yori mo mada fukaku)

Box Office: $272,132

The "Storm" that is being referred to in *After the Storm* is a typhoon on its way to Japan that will arrive in a few days. The characters in the film know about the storm, but are too consumed in their own personal dramas to fully acknowledge it, as anyone would probably be. The best most people can do is take precautions, hunker down and hope for the best. It takes an adult mindset to make adjustments to one's life when dealing with natural elements that are over-powering. There is a kind of metaphor in this scenario that is not lost on writer-director Hirokazu Kore-eda as he tells the story of a man who has lost that adult way of thinking when it comes to his personal life. When a storm comes, he runs away (figuratively speaking) when he knows full well that he should have prepared. Every day, this man has to weather something that he is not cut out for and the people around him all know it and try to tell him.

The man is Ryôta (Hiroshi Abe), an award-winning novelist who has yet to write anything of substance since his novel, *The Empty Table.* He currently makes money as a private investigator at the Yamabe Detective Agency, spying on cheating husbands and the like. He insists to everyone that he is doing research for his next novel, but he spends much of his money at the racetrack, often losing. The novel he alludes to seems to be just a deflection against anyone who tries to criticize him for his life choices; it probably does not exist in any form. At one point, he gets an offer to write a story for a manga, which he feels is demeaning to him. He tells the editor, "I'm trying to finish my new novel in a hurry," to which the editor replies "Well, I wouldn't want to get in the way of that."

Ryôta's main problem, though, is his inability to pay child support for his only son, Shingo (Taiyô Yoshizawa), a 12-year-old who lives with his mother, Kyôko (Yôko Maki). Ryôta has been using his experience on the job as a detective to spy on his ex-wife and kid. He sees that she has started seeing another man.

When he sees his son during his monthly visit, he insists that Shingo ask his mom about her intentions with this new man and report back on her answers. He does so and her answers are understandably vague, much to Ryôta's frustration. Shingo, though, knows his father all too well and returns the favor of putting him in a difficult situation by asking Ryôta if he has paid child support, a question he wants to avoid as much as possible. To him, it is one thing to lie to an ex-wife, but something else entirely when he has to look his own son in the eye and stumble for an answer he can live with.

The film opens with a report of the pending storm on the radio, but instead of dwelling on that or even introducing Ryôta, Kyôko, or Shingo, Kore-eda instead opens with a lengthy scene between Ryôta's sister Chinatsu (Satomi Kobayashi) and mother, Kyoko (Kirin Kiki). They talk about the loss of the family patriarch and how Kyoko needs to get out more so she does not become senile. Ryôta gets introduced later as the son who visits Kyoko and has an even longer scene with her before his ex-wife and kid are introduced into the narrative. Kore-eda is careful to make sure no character in this piece disappear into the background when Ryôta's story takes over. Every character deals with a tragedy, big or small, and all are grappling with the people they are becoming in the face of these situations. As Ryôta says at one point, "Listen, it's not that easy to grow up to be the man you want to be."

Therein lies the main theme of the piece, the theme of aging successfully as a human being. Ryôta, forever with a five o'clock shadow and messy hair, has become what his mother feared he would—his father. Unfit for the responsibilities of parenthood in every way, Ryôta's actions have always been at odds with his words. Abe's performance is wonderful in conveying this inner battle without ever succumbing to any melodrama. The scene in which he tries to connect with his son in his mom's house during the storm in the later half of the film is both touching and deeply tragic. Shingo is playing the board game "Life" with Chinatsu (a metaphor that may be a little too on-target), but nobody wants to play it with Ryôta, try as he may to be a fun person to be around. Abe's performance shows all the layers of desperation, longing, and pain that Ryôta takes with him every day into his own game of life.

Comparisons between Kore-eda and Yasujiro Ozu have been made regularly and it is easy to see why. Kore-eda is deeply in touch with each and every one of his characters and is wise not to overwrite or over-explain anything. Even the young Shingo has been smartly written, with great attention to how kids talk, think, and behave, particularly children of divorce. A lesser writer would have had Shingo confront his father in a way that would have sounded phony, but Kore-eda has such a delicate touch in his directing that one feels they are eavesdropping on these characters. The scenes with Kyôko seem to linger even more. Maki's performance as the matriarch of this family has elements of warmth, understanding, and deep pain as she sees her son flailing in his adult responsibilities. She really becomes the second main character here.

After the Storm continues Kore-eda's fascinating career as a director of family dramas that have authenticity, tragedy, humor, and heart. The typhoon the story promises time and again does come about, but its existence is simply a means to which the characters can come together in one place. The storm passes, but instead of taking shelter at one's own home, Ryôta takes shelter first with his mother, then in a playground structure his father used to take him to when he was younger. Eventually, though, the storm must end and the characters, who have finally all come clean about their intentions and their lot in life, have to clean up and move on. After the storm, what's left?

Collin Souter

CREDITS

Shinoda Ryôta: Hiroshi Abe
Shiraishi Kyôko: Yoko Maki
Shinoda Yoshiko: Kirin Kiki
Yamabe Koichiro: Riri Furanki
Chinatsu Nakashima: Satomi Kobayashi
Origin: United States
Language: Japanese
Released: 2017
Production: Tsugihiko Fujiwara, Takashi Ishihara, Kazumi Kawashiro, Kaoru Matsuzaki, Hijiri Taguchi, Tatsumi Yoda, Akihiko Yose; Aoi Promotion, Bandai Visual Company Ltd., GAGA; released by Film Movement
Directed by: Hirokazu Kore-eda
Written by: Hirokazu Kore-eda
Cinematography by: Yutaka Yamazaki
Editing: Hirokazu Kore-eda
Art Direction: Keiko Mitsumatsu
Costumes: Kazuko Kurosawa
MPAA rating: Unrated
Running time: 117 minutes

REVIEWS

Brody, Richard. *New Yorker.* March 27, 2017.
Burr, Ty. *Boston Globe.* April 6, 2017.
Chang, Justin. *Lost Angeles Times.* March 16, 2017.
Ebiri, Bilge. *Village Voice.* March 14, 2017.
Ehrlich, David. *IndieWire.* March 17, 2017.

Kenny, Glenn. *New York Times.* March 15, 2017.
Long, Tom. *Detroit News.* April 7, 2017.
MacDonald, Moira. *Seattle Times.* June 15, 2017.
Morgenstern, Joe. *Washington Post.* March 16, 2017.
Pickett, Leah. *Chicago Reader.* October 20, 2016.

TRIVIA

Although released later, *After the Storm* wrapped earlier than director Hirokazu Koreeda's previous work *Our Little Sister* (2015). Filming of *After the Storm* took place starting in May 2014, during production of *Our Little Sister*, which was shot throughout that year.

ALIEN: COVENANT

The path to paradise begins in hell.
—Movie tagline

Box Office: $74.3 Million

In 2012, Ridley Scott returned to the world he created in the breakthrough, landmark *Alien* (1979) for the first time in nearly 35 years, and audiences were notably torn about the results. On one hand, *Prometheus* (2012) displayed Scott's signature stunning craftsmanship, but it also altered the canon of a beloved property, and that never goes down well with serious fans. Somehow, messing with what happened before Ellen Ripley met that alien on the Nostromo was tantamount to heresy in the eyes of some serious sci-fi lovers and *Prometheus* was greeted with significant disdain in genre circles. Part of the problem was that it introduced so much new mythology about creators and biblical allegories without giving viewers the hardcore, acid-spitting action they were expecting. "It was an *Alien* movie with barely any aliens," was a common complaint. And so Scott inserted the key word into the title of his next movie in the franchise, and upped the ante in terms of "alien action," but the film was much closer in tone and style to his 2012 offering than the 1979 one, dividing audiences yet again. Make no mistake, *Alien: Covenant* is a gorgeous film, complete with stunning production design and brilliant visual compositions. Mileage will vary in terms of its storytelling, but it's one of the best-looking sci-fi films of all time, and people should not be so quick to dismiss that as if it's easy or common.

Alien: Covenant opens by tying it directly to a pair of characters from *Prometheus*—business leader Peter Weyland (Guy Pearce) and an android named David (Michael Fassbender). It's a gorgeous scene under which to set the credits and cements a theme of the film to follow: evolution and the search for a Creator. Almost immediately, David figures out that Weyland built him, but asks then who built Weyland? And, almost immediately, David senses that he is another evolutionary step: a creation that knows its creator. What would we do if we were introduced to God on our first day of existence? These are the kind of deep, philosophical questions that Scott and screenwriters John Logan and Dante Harper will ask amidst the chaos of facesuckers and chestbursters.

Cut to 2104, 11 years after the action of *Prometheus*. A ship named Covenant is headed to a planet called Origae-6 with a crew of 15 active members and hundreds of colonists in stasis and human embryos. They are going to build a civilization. While the crew sleeps, an android modeled on the same human form as David named Walter (think of it as David 2.0, and he's also played by Fassbender) is monitoring the ship. A burst of energy damages the ship and kills the captain (played in a flashback cameo by James Franco). The death of the leader of this group of colonists is important because it leaves them adrift and uncertain. And so they make the classic mistake of sci-fi films and ignore the genre's cardianl rule: never answer a distress signal.

The group of the Covenant is now led by Chris Oram (Billy Crudup), a man of faith who clashes with Branson's widow Daniels (Katherine Waterston). Scott and his screenwriters populate their film with couples and doppelgangers. Of course, there are the two identical androids. Chief pilot Tennessee (Danny McBride) has a wife in Faris (Amy Seimetz). Oram has a wife in Karine (Carmen Ejogo). The Covenant's navigator Ricks (Jussie Smollett) too has a wife in Upworth (Callie Hernandez). But Daniels is widowed, making her a lone wolf, and the de facto leader because of how she's going to remind viewers of Ripley in that sense.

The Covenant team lands on the planet that has been emitting the distress signal and are attacked relatively quickly. Before the crew really knows what's happening, spores are entering their bodies and breeding, while others are dying on the ship. The terrified survivors huddle in what look like ancient ruins, where they meet David, who has apparently been there since arriving with Elizabeth Shaw after the conclusion of events depicted in *Prometheus*. We learn that David has been on this planet, essentially bioengineering what will come to be the alien creature from the 1979 classic. He manipulates those around him, including Oram and Walter, into being a part of his grand experiment to play God.

Shot by Dariusz Wolski (*Dark City* [1998], *The Martian* [2015]), *Alien: Covenant* looks stunning. Whether they are charting the interior of the Covenant, terrifying viewers with a great night attack sequence, or maneuvering the halls of David's home for the last decade, the camerawork here is fluid and mesmerizing, more so than nearly any Hollywood blockbuster of 2017. Scott has always been a master craftsman but his skill in that department has somehow seemed to improve in recent years, as his work is always some of the most gorgeous in cinema. Credit should also go to the production design team, who beautifully blend classic imagery of timeless ruins with their vision of the future on the planet. It is the look of an archaeological dig that happened to find something horrifying.

While scenes of Fassbender playing flute with his clone may not have been what audiences were looking for after *Prometheus,* there's no denying that this film provides more "typical Alien" action than the previous installment. However, the lack of a traditional hero—one could argue that Scott identifies more with David as his protagonist than Daniels—and a film that works better in a philosophical register than as an action movie made this one divisive too. There was even talk that Scott would not finish the story continued here after the film failed to gross even $75 domestically, not even meeting its budget. However, another $165 million worldwide likely made that a moot point. As Scott almost miraculously seems to be entering the most prolific phase of his career in his eighties (he also directed *All the Money in the World* this year), one hopes that he makes at least one more of these before his career ends. Maybe two.

Brian Tallerico

CREDITS

David/Walter: Michael Fassbender
Daniels: Katherine Waterston
Oram: Billy Crudup
Tennessee: Danny McBride
Lope: Demian Bichir
Origin: United States
Language: English
Released: 2017
Production: David Giler, Walter Hill, Mark Huffam, Michael Schaefer, Ridley Scott; Brandywine Productions, Scott Free Productions; released by Twentieth Century Fox Film Corp.
Directed by: Ridley Scott
Written by: John Logan; Dante Harper
Cinematography by: Dariusz Wolski
Music by: Jed Kurzel
Sound: Oliver Tarney
Editing: Pietro Scalia
Art Direction: Ian Gracie
Costumes: Janty Yates
Production Design: Chris Seagers
MPAA rating: R
Running time: 122 minutes

REVIEWS

Burr, Ty. *Boston Globe.* May 17, 2017.
LaSalle, Mick. *San Francisco Chronicle.* May 17, 2017.
McCarthy, Todd. *Hollywood Reporter.* May 6, 2017.
Nicholson, Amy. *MTV News.* May 22, 2017.
Roeper, Richard. *Chicago Sun-Times.* May 17, 2017.
Seitz, Matt Zoller. *RogerEbert.com.* May 16, 2017.
Stewart, Sara. *New York Post.* May 18, 2017.
Sullivan, Kevin P. *Entertainment Weekly.* May 6, 2017.
Travers, Peter. *Rolling Stone.* May 17, 2017.
Vishnevetsky, Ignatiy. *The A.V. Club.* May 15, 2017.

QUOTES

Walter: "One wrong note eventually ruins the entire symphony."

TRIVIA

For the first time since *Alien 3* (1992), an alien's point of view is shown. However, in this film, we also see the alien's visual spectrum.

ALL EYEZ ON ME

Legends never die.
—Movie tagline

Box Office: $45 Million

All Eyez on Me does not illuminate the life or work of Tupac Shakur, except in the way it casts the popular rapper and actor in a saintly glow. By the time of his death, at the age of 25, he had recorded five studio albums (including the double album from which the movie has borrowed its title) and appeared in seven feature films. The text coda for this biographical movie provides this and additional trivia about Shakur's accomplishments, which is an appropriate ending for a movie that plays like a dramatized checklist of the major details of the man's life.

This is a movie loaded with information yet possessing very little insight. It is both rushed—in the way the screenplay (written by Jeremy Haft, Eddie Gonzalez, and Steven Bagatourian) moves from event to event—and dull—in the way it moves without pausing to examine these events in any context beyond the fact that they happened. There is no sense of momentum to Shakur's life in the movie—no appreciation for how each accomplishment and obstruction may have affected the trajectory of his career. He comes across as destined for fame and blameless in any action that resulted in the infamy that shadowed him during the final years of his life.

This attitude would make for a simplistic portrait of anyone, let alone a public figure like Shakur, whose life was, to put it mildly, controversial, and whose death—six days after being shot in Las Vegas on September 7, 1996—remains a mystery, which has served as fodder for a wealth of conspiracy theories. If the movie's version of Shakur is close to that of a saint, then his death in the movie is that of a martyr, with director Benny Boom (a veteran of television and music videos, although, based on the evidence here, one would not know the latter, since the movie's musical performances are uniformly bland) focusing on the iconography of Shakur's shooting, while providing a gospel-choir farewell in the movie's final minutes. As for what cause, other than his own fame, Shakur is a martyr within the movie's vision, that remains unclear.

Demetrius Shipp Jr. plays Tupac with, perhaps, the correct combination of charm and naïve innocence for the movie's portrayal of the character. It opens with Tupac in prison in 1995, following a sexual abuse conviction that the screenplay argues against by means of the character's ignorance of his accuser's case. A documentarian (played by Hill Harper) interviewing the incarcerated rapper provides an excuse to go through Tupac's childhood, raised by his mother Afeni (Danai Gurira), a member of the Black Panther Party, to note racial injustice.

If there is a conflict here, it is in the way Tupac rises through the hip-hop scene by bringing attention to those injustices, fighting with record executives about the importance of a song like "Brenda's Got a Baby," while becoming complacent in his artistic vision after achieving a certain level of fame. Since the movie is hesitant to portray its subject in any way approaching a negative light, though, that apparent hypocrisy is offset by a vast conspiracy of politicians (then-Vice President Dan Quayle goes on a minor crusade against hip hop, with Tupac's lyrics being specifically targeted for their antagonism toward the police) and within the legal system (Tupac is presented as the victim in the aforementioned sexual assault case), as well as becoming caught up in an East Coast-West Coast rivalry.

The most dominant presence in that rivalry is Biggie Smalls (Jamal Woolard), aka The Notorious B.I.G., who releases a song that Tupac interprets as an admission of guilt in a 1994 armed robbery, which resulted in Tupac being shot five times. Meanwhile, Suge Knight (Dominic L. Santana), the infamous record executive who is portrayed here as an almost gangster-like figure (although the movie comes close to justifying his strong-armed, occasionally violent tactics), seems to treat the competition between the coastal factions of hip-hop artists more as a publicity stunt.

An objective look at all of these events—which is the only way to view what happens, since the movie provides no thematic through line for the narrative—suggests that Tupac is a man always looking for a cause in which to fight. His downfall, then, is becoming too involved in a professional rivalry that is not as real as he imagines. Neither the screenplay nor Boom implies this, of course, since the filmmakers have little interest in examining their subject as a man capable of making errors in judgment. Things simply happen to Tupac here, from his rise after an "incident" that resulted in the death of a 6-year-old boy (the movie conveniently ignores that Shakur's gun was the weapon) to his own fatal shooting, immediately following an attack on a local gang member.

No one involved seems to understand that saints can be boring, and the movie itself does a poor job of convincing that Shakur was a saint by any definition of the word, which is not, obviously, a condemnation of the man. *All Eyez on Me* seems incapable of such nuance.

Mark Dujsik

CREDITS

Tupac Shakur: Demetrius Shipp, Jr.
Afeni Shakur: Danai Gurira
Jada Pinkett: Kat Graham
Journalist: Hill Harper
Kidada Jones: Annie Ilonzeh
Origin: United States
Language: English
Released: 2017
Production: L.T. Hutton, David Robinson, James G. Robinson; Morgan Creek Productions Inc., Program Pictures, Voltage Pictures; released by Codeblack Films, Lionsgate
Directed by: Benny Boom
Written by: Jeremy Haft; Eddie Gonzalez; Steven Bagatourian
Cinematography by: Peter Menzies, Jr.
Music by: John Paesano
Sound: William R. Dean; Craig Mann
Music Supervisor: Trygge Toven
Editing: Joel Cox
Art Direction: John Richardson
Costumes: Francine Jamison-Tanchuck
Production Design: Derek R. Hill
MPAA rating: R
Running time: 139 minutes

REVIEWS

Allen, Nick. *RogerEbert.com.* June 16, 2017.

Cabrera, Marcos. *Village Voice*. June 16, 2017.
Guzmán, Rafer. *Newsday*. June 15, 2017.
Harris, Aisha. *Slate*. June 16, 2017.
Kenny, Glenn. *New York Times*. June 15, 2017.
Macfarlane, Steve. *Slant Magazine*. June 16, 2017.
Orndorf, Brian. *Blu-Ray.com*. June 16, 2017.
Suzanne-Mayer, Dominick. *Consequence of Sound*. June 16, 2017.
Westhoff, Ben. *Village Voice*. June 20, 2017.
Yoshida, Emily. *Vulture*. June 16, 2017.

QUOTES

Mutulu: "You must stand for something, you must live for something! And you must be willing to die for something!"

TRIVIA

Filmmaker John Singleton was originally attached to direct this film, but he and the studio disagreed on how Tupac should be portrayed. Singleton eventually left the project but has since stated that he still hopes to make his own Tupac film one day, on his own terms. He was also the only director to have Afeni Shakur's full blessing to tell her son's story.

ALL I SEE IS YOU

Box Office: $217,644

The problems of *All I See Is You* are apparent from an early reflective action showing the central character, Gina (Blake Lively), alone on her terrace, furtively enjoying a cigarette. What should be a quick, throwaway gesture is treated as mighty and monumental. The director, Marc Forster, works in tight close up on her face, with the camera all voluptuous and emphatic. The overt stylization converts the objects into a particular fetish.

The manner in which Lively pulls on her cigarette seems meant to give off an erotic charge, the scene shot like a high-end perfume advertisement. The off-scale and absurdity of the situation only highlights the failure of the larger work. Everything feels italicized, draining the work of any discovery or greater sense of revelation. The movie is too pumped up and adrenalized. It is a movie about stimuli, of imagery and sound that is turned inside out, a self-exposure revealing the emptiness of its ideas. The movie has some potentially interesting parts, but it has no center or a larger point of view to play off. What becomes clear is just how amorphous and inchoate the work is.

The German-born Forster has worked on a diversified range of ambitious literary projects like *Stranger Than Fiction* (2006), *The Kite Runner* (2007), and *World War Z* (2013). He also made a James Bond film, *Quantum of Solace* (2008). He made his early reputation with his adroit direction of women, orchestrating Halle Berry's Academy Award-winning turn in *Monster's Ball* (2001).

The film that made his Hollywood career possible was his deeply compelling second feature, *Everything Put Together* (2000). The movie featured a brilliant, striking turn by Radha Mitchell as a young woman coping with the devastating loss of a child. Aided by Mitchell's great performance, Forster worked out an expressive visual design with a deeply unsettling use of the subjective camera in dramatically exploring the harsh manner Mitchell was cut off from her intimate circle of friends. The movie remains the director's most coherent and artistically satisfying work, its strongest moments echoing the works of Roman Polanski, like *Repulsion* (1965) and *Rosemary's Baby* (1968).

All I See Is You plays off the works of Polanski and Luis Buñuel. It also limns the fractured interior consciousness of a young woman shaped emotionally by bereavement and loss. She is an American expatriate who lives with her husband, James (Jason Clarke), in Bangkok, Thailand. As a teenager she was blinded from a car accident that killed her parents.

The movie's subject is instability. Forster and his cinematographer, Matthias Königswieser, work hard to find a visual equivalent of violence and breakdown, streaking lights, distortions, and pointillist flares. The work is a whirl of a fractured visual syntax marked by dreams, hallucinations, and recovered historical trauma. Gina is able to distinguish certain colors, patterns, and shapes. Like Buñuel's *Belle de Jour* (1967), the movie opens with an elaborate sexual fantasy with Gina being sexually consumed in an orgy.

At the start, there's a tenderness, even love, between her husband, but it is mixed with a certain dread and shame at not being able to conceive a child. Everything changes after she undergoes a radical experimental corneal transplant that restores sight to her right eye. Her doctor (Danny Huston) says that with steroid treatments she is likely to achieve a complete recovery.

The premise of a woman borne anew is rife with opportunities, but the mannered direction and the mediocre script quickly nullify the possibilities. During a trip to Spain, the couple's erotic rebirth points instead to a rupture. Echoing the opening scene, now aboard a train cutting through the beautiful landscape, the couple plays out their own elaborate sexual game of bondage and control that achieves the opposite result. Visiting her bohemian sister, Carla (Ahna O'Reilly) and her artist husband, Miguel (Miguel Fernández), in Barcelona, Gina is avid for excitement and adventure. Stalking the back alley of a Barcelona red light district, she even takes in a live sex show.

As conceived and written, the character of Gina becomes increasingly less interesting and overtly more controlling and manipulative and her liberation yields a particularly harsh and sorrow register. *All I See Is You* becomes like two foundational works of modernist cinema, *Voyage to Italy* (1954) and *Contempt* (1963), a portrait of a marriage.

It proves particularly bleak. The story is as jittery and unmoored as the camera. Once the central characters return to Bangkok, the plot takes over to absurd and increasingly unsettling degrees, encompassing various infidelities and personal acts of humiliation. Forster is fatally unsure about what the movie wants to say, devolving into bleak caricature of damaged masculinity as Clarke's character is emasculated and Gina is driven to greater acts of selfishness.

The movie has no rhythm or forward momentum, mutating from moment to moment. Forster wrote the script with Sean Conway, and from the start something seems amiss. As narrative the film makes little psychological sense or gives an emotionally plausible reason for the couple's connection to its setting and place. James, it is revealed, works in insurance. That vagueness is not an insurmountable hurdle as much as an unfortunate emblem of unconscious racism, like an ugly scene at a nightclub where Gina is harassed by a group of young Thai partygoers. The white Westerners, like Huston's doctor, are saviors, the rest foreign objects.

The whole film is built on naïve foundations, of Gina's need to be rescued at the start and James falling sideways into inconsequence once she achieves greater independence. The movie not only has no characters to speak of though projects an utter loathing of them. For instance, James obsessively replays a 360-degree video of their night on the train, an abject reminder of his own failure to perform.

The movie is too serious to work as trash and too poorly conceived to work as drama. The actors are game though given few opportunities. Like Scarlett Johansson, Lively is probably too astoundingly beautiful to ever get her just due as an actress. With a few exceptions, like Rebecca Miller's *The Private Lives of Pippa Lee* (2009), Lively has not really been tasked with too demanding or emotionally intricate work. Her male directors show remarkably little faith in her abilities.

It is deeply unfortunate because she is, on occasion, able to radiate a sense of thrill, pleasure, or wonder. In *All I See Is You*, she remains distressingly out of sight.

Patrick Z. McGavin

CREDITS

Gina: Blake Lively
James: Jason Clarke
Carla: Ahna O'Reilly
Karen: Yvonne Strahovski
Daniel: Wes Chatham
Origin: United States
Language: English
Released: 2017
Production: Craig Baumgarten, Michael Selby, Marc Forster; LINK Entertainment, Wing and a Prayer Pictures; released by Open Road Films
Directed by: Marc Forster
Written by: Marc Forster; Sean Conway
Cinematography by: Matthias Koenigwieser
Music by: Marc Streitenfeld
Music Supervisor: Mathieu Schreyer
Editing: Hughes Winborne
Costumes: Frank Fleming
Production Design: Jennifer Williams
MPAA rating: R
Running time: 110 minutes

REVIEWS

Anderson, Soren. *Seattle Times*. October 26, 2017.
Catsoulis, Jeannette. *New York Times*. October 26, 2017.
Cordova, Randy. *Arizona Republic*. October 26, 2017.
Hassenger, Jesse. *The A.V. Club*. October 24, 2017.
Keough, Peter. *Boston Globe*. October 25, 2017.
O'Sullivan, Michael. *Washington Post*. October 26, 2017.
Walsh, Katie. *Chicago Tribune*. October 26, 2017.
White, Danielle. *Austin Chronicle*. October 25, 2017.
Wolfe, April. *Village Voice*. October 24, 2017.
Yoshida, Emily. *New York Magazine*. October 24, 2017.

TRIVIA

This film premiered at the 2016 Toronto International Film Festival.

ALL THE MONEY IN THE WORLD

J. Paul Getty had a fortune. Everyone else paid the price.
—Movie tagline

Box Office: $24.6 Million

Films, of course, can and do exist as stand-alone works of art. But given the cost of major studio releases and the fact that they are subject to external market forces, more than a few get locked into a narrative that develops around them—hence the reputations of certain movies as everything from a "box office flop" to a critically praised, commercial under-performer that was "ahead of its time."

Occasionally, however, pre-release news reaches such a critical mass that it is virtually impossible, at least in the lifetimes of the primary parties involved, to judge a film entirely separate and distinct from the events that have propelled it into the mainstream news cycle. Perhaps the most recent highest-profile instance of this involved *Mr. & Mrs. Smith* (2005), which starred Brad Pitt and Angelina Jolie. Released in the wake of Pitt's divorce from Jennifer Aniston, another huge star, and at a time when his off-screen relationship with Jolie was still nascent, it sparked both tabloid allegations of on-set infidelity (denied by both parties) and major newspaper think-pieces about workplace attraction, flirting, and boundaries. A timeline to rival the Kennedy assassination was debated, opposing "Team Angelina" and "Team Jennifer" T-shirts were manufactured, and the entire theatrical release was somehow turned into a gender-charged referendum on romance, femininity, and faithfulness in the 21st century.

A similar fate befalls the crime thriller *All the Money in the World*, which details the fallout from the 1973 kidnapping of the teenage grandson of oil tycoon John Paul Getty, but finds itself instead caught up in the undertow of the Harvey Weinstein sexual harassment and assault scandal that engulfed Hollywood in 2017, and will forevermore be known as the movie from which Kevin Spacey was excised. Following allegations against Spacey that first surfaced on October 29, and in the ensuing days mushroomed to reveal a pattern of abusive behavior spanning many years, director Ridley Scott faced a tough decision about the December 22 release of his film, and one with seemingly no good options. After huddling with producer Dan Friedkin and Sony Pictures higher-ups, on November 8, Scott made the decision to recast Spacey's key supporting role with Christopher Plummer and commence nine days of emergency re-shoots in late November, while still aiming to keep the film's theatrical calendar date.

Ultimately released on Christmas Day, *All the Money in the World* finished seventh during its opening weekend with $5.6 million—top among new releases, but still far behind the biggest holdover hits of the holiday period, *Star Wars: The Last Jedi*, *Jumanji: Welcome to the Jungle*, and *Coco*.

Adapted by David Scarpa from John Pearson's 1995 book *Painfully Rich: The Outrageous Fortunes and Misfortunes of the Heirs of J. Paul Getty*, the film opens in the summer of 1973, before flashing back to earlier days—both in the life of oil magnate John Paul Getty (Plummer), and the domestic existence of the adult son he never met, John Paul Getty, Jr. (Andrew Buchan), and the latter's wife Gail (Michelle Williams). Getty gives John a job, which of course opens the door to an instantly transformed and elevated lifestyle for the young man.

Things go sideways when 16-year-old John Paul Getty III (Charlie Plummer, no relation), known as Paul, is kidnapped in Italy. Gail desperately tries to convince her son's billionaire, namesake grandfather, at the time by far the richest person in the world, to pay the demanded ransom of $17 million. Getty refuses, however, setting up a stalemate with the kidnappers, nominally headed up by Cinquanta (Romain Duris). Unbeknownst to Gail, Getty also tasks his personal security advisor Fletcher Chase (Mark Wahlberg), a former CIA operative, with keeping discrete tabs on the Italian police inquiry—and eventually even investigating whether Paul had something to do with his own disappearance, in an attempt to make some easy money.

As weeks go by without the ransom being paid, impatience blooms and arguments break out amongst the kidnappers. When one of them accidentally reveals his face to Paul, it leads to a flash of violence in which he is killed by another kidnapper. Later, the contract for Paul is essentially sold off to another criminal syndicate, and Cinquanta finds himself in the position of having to implement the more gruesome demands of his new boss, Mammoliti (Marco Leonardi), who simply wants to bring a resolution to what he essentially views as a devalued investment. Getty, by this point, is more amenable to shelling out a ransom, but, to Gail's horror, he still balks at paying anything close to full price.

All the Money in the World is an interesting film, but what ultimately keeps it a bit locked in the narrative starter's block—and perhaps makes its subject matter a better exploration for the first season of the new television series *Trust* (2018)—is its dogged devotion to conventionality. Class distinction and elitism are certainly predominant among the film's themes—they are interwoven throughout, and present right from the start, with voiceover narration that characterizes the experience of being as rich as John Paul Getty as being "from another planet, where the force of gravity bends light." There is also a nice speech in which Getty himself waxes rhapsodic about how being rich is different than getting rich, and how that informs one's worldview.

Yet one wishes Scott's movie delved a bit deeper, exploring not just Gail's outsider status as someone who married into the family, but also the fractional splintering of Fletcher's disillusion with Getty's miserly manipulation—the movie gives Wahlberg a nice kiss-off monologue at a certain point, but it seems undermotivated.

Additionally, there is an interesting parallelism to be found in Gail's phone relationship with Cinquanta, when late in the standoff he tries to counsel her and says, "You think you're the only one fighting an empire? I just want Paul to live." That he could feel sympathy for her plight, and efforts to pry open her father-in-law's wallet would seem to provide contrast and connect the film a bit more readily to the current zeitgeist of the times, and the study of a man so infatuated with his own wealth, and projection and protection of same, that it warps his ability to form genuine human connections. Alas, Scarpa's script is more streamlined, and not built to really explore its characters with much psychological depth.

The film is instead a very well rendered chronicling of its ensemble players each playing their part in trying to resolve the kidnap scenario—but a chronicling with, oddly, little native sense of ticking-clock tension. The middle Getty, son to the patriarch and father to Paul, falls out of the film for a long time, and Paul (real-life father to Balthazar Getty) is a bedraggled cipher stuck under one of the worst cinematic hairdos of the year. Time spent with him is a drag.

On a technical level, *All the Money in the World* represents Scott's characteristic accomplished professionalism—which is to say that, whatever one thinks of it, there is definitely a unifying aesthetic. Composer Daniel Pemberton delivers an evocative score, while cinematographer Dariusz Wolski imprints a cool, grey-slate of gloominess on the movie that seems to mirror the emptiness of Getty's inner life.

Any appraisal of the performances in *All the Money in the World* is understandably filtered first and foremost through the elder Plummer, and he delivers wonderfully, capturing the emotionally withholding instincts of Getty. While the footage of Spacey in make-up that was part of the film's first trailer looked incredible, Plummer (who is 30 years older) more closely resembles the actual age of Getty during the events depicted throughout most of the film.

Wahlberg turns in stalwart work, projecting at least a minor chord of moral awakening as a man who learns to redirect his professional energies in service of the better angels of his nature. Williams, however, does not quite earn the bulk of the plaudits she has received for her work here. While she brings a resolute tenacity to her characterization of Gail, her cultured, upper-crust accent comes and goes—both in certain scenes with Getty and others which ostensibly would not have been part of the reshoots. This, plus a tendency to lean into all the most obvious emotional moments of the script, renders her characterization functional but hardly revelatory or haunting.

The film's technical precision and distinctive mood—in an era where so many studio movies lack individual personality—and certainly the sheer bravura accomplishment of Scott's dumping of Spacey and daring, deadline-defying do-over all feed an instinct to grade *All the Money in the World* on a curve, an instinct many reviewers apparently could not entirely resist. Still, at 132 minutes, this stylishly composed drama is too sluggish to call great. It is not the first time that the flash of money has trumped reason, however, and it likely will not be the last.

Brent Simon

CREDITS

Gail Harris: Michelle Williams
J. Paul Getty: Christopher Plummer
Fletcher Chase: Mark Wahlberg
Cinquata: Romain Duris
John Paul Getty III: Charlie Plummer
Origin: United States
Language: English
Released: 2017
Production: Chris Clark, Quentin Curtis, Dan Friedkin, Mark Huffam, Bradley Thomas, Kevin J. Walsh, Ridley Scott; Imperative Entertainment, Panorama Films, Red Rum Films, Scott Free Productions; released by Tri-Star Pictures Inc.
Directed by: Ridley Scott
Written by: David Scarpa
Cinematography by: Dariusz Wolski
Music by: Daniel Pemberton
Sound: Oliver Tarney
Editing: Claire Simpson
Art Direction: Cristina Onori
Production Design: Arthur Max
MPAA rating: R
Running time: 132 minutes

REVIEWS

Dargis, Manohla. *New York Times*. December 24, 2017.
Debruge, Peter. *Variety*. December 20, 2017.
LaSalle, Mick. *San Francisco Chronicle*. December 22, 2017.
McCarthy, Todd. *Hollywood Reporter*. December 19, 2017.
Persall, Steve. *Tampa Bay Times*. December 21, 2017.
Seitz, Matt Zoller. *RogerEbert.com*. December 23, 2017.
Sims, David. *The Atlantic*. January 4, 2018.
Smith, Kyle. *National Review*. December 23, 2017.

Taylor, Ella. *NPR.* December 21, 2017.
Wilson, Calvin. *St. Louis Post Dispatch.* December 25, 2017.

TRIVIA

Actor Jack Nicholson was originally offered the role of Jean Paul Getty. but declined.

AWARDS

Nominations:

Oscars 2017: Actor--Supporting (Plummer)

British Acad. 2017: Actor--Supporting (Plummer)

Golden Globes 2018: Actor--Supporting (Plummer), Actress--Drama (Williams), Director (Scott)

AMERICAN ASSASSIN

Assassins aren't born. They're made.
—Movie tagline

Box Office: $36.2 Million

Cinemagoers have long been conditioned to associate the world of secret agents with the most recognizable character in the business—James Bond. The modern equivalent of Jason Bourne was an asset in the dark recesses of the intelligence community; the kind that would get us neuralyzed by the Men in Black so we could live our lives under the blanket of ignorance and plausible deniability. Yet maybe going back to our days playing Hide and Seek, there is something fascinating about spies, hidden identities and top-secret missions. The movies are more likely to take the Bond approach than that of George Smiley or Alec Leamas, though even reduced to the title of just another assassin comes with its own set of rules, scruples, and coldness. Done right, you get *The Day of the Jackal* (1973) or *Munich* (2005). Done wrong and you get the character at the center of *American Assassin,* a name not even worth mentioning since it will be forgotten by the end of these 112 minutes if not the second syllable of the film's Script.

Mitch Rapp is his name and he is played by Dylan O'Brien as a man who would happily say it loud before he killed you to make a point. That would be getting ahead of his story though which began in Vince Flynn's book series with *Transfer of Power* in 1999; itself already ahead of Mitch's origin story which would take place within the eleventh book in the series published in 2010. Rapp was once just an ordinary guy on vacation in Ibiza with his girlfriend—whom he is about to propose to—when a group of jihadists storm the beach and massacre nearly everyone. Over the next few years he sets out on a quest to locate the mastermind behind the attack. This involves growing a beard, training in combat, watching some ISIS videos, and just becoming generally unpleasant.

When his international vigilantism is thwarted by the CIA, he is brought in and recognized as one of those few good men with the skills necessary for the "good" fight. He is introduced to Stan Hurley (Michael Keaton), a former Navy SEAL who now trains soldiers for the special unit known as Orion. Apparently, it does not take much training other than a few fights in the woods before Mitch is quickly made a part of Hurley's team despite the cloud of a vendetta that still clearly compromises his ability to play nice with others. On Rapp's first mission, Orion is tracking the sale of Russian nuclear material to a group of Iranians. But the man who may be orchestrating the whole plan is a former member of the team (Taylor Kitsch) still holding his own grudge over the man in charge.

Here a classic conflict is established. A chief protagonist turned into a rage-fueled machine against the forces of evil is thrust into a battle against an antagonist who once fought for good but was compromised by his own vendetta against the government and the agent who made him. Two ideologies wading in the same grey area of justice can fulfill a narrative purpose that helps defines these characters as something more than just X's and O's on a tracking device. The screenplay, credited to four writers, seems to actively resist the notion that any such grey area even exists. Bad guy has nuke. Good guy wants to kill bad guy. Case closed. That is fine when there is an established hero such as James Bond but while it is easy to sympathize with Rapp's tragedy, it remains to be seen whether we want him on our team.

Following the rules has often led to the legal entanglements that set bad people free, so fiction has often catered to the layman's thirst for justice in an unjust world. But at what cost? Throw any moral complications and false intelligence out the window, not because the *American Assassin* is never confronted with even the remote possibility but because he compromises the one rule any soldier knows the moment they blanket themselves in even the metaphorical uniform. Mitch Rapp is not a faceless blip because of the cold compromise a professional killer must make to justify what they are doing. He is just written with all the depth of a bored kid locked in his room, charging into the breach during a game of *Halo.* Mitch is not concerned about his team or even winning the game. He just wants to stack up the most points and O'Brien's one-dimensional performance is devoid of charisma, nuance, or, frankly, menace. The visceral impact of his loss is felt in the opening scene, but beyond that he is always just one moment away from pulling his weapon to win a staring contest.

Michael Cuesta has cut his teeth more in the television arena than film, even despite a few well-acclaimed films like *L.I.E.* (2001) and *Kill the Messenger* (2014). His work from 2011-12 on television's *Homeland* is a clear influence on what becomes the most generic episode of a show that occasional got too ridiculous for its "realistic" view of international terrorist affairs but could always fall back on some strong performances to pull viewers through. With O'Brien and Kitsch fighting over who can be blander or louder, it is left to Keaton find a bridge between subtlety and being more demonstrative when faced with the same torture that spy George Clooney went through in *Syriana* (2005). "The enemy dresses like a deer and he kills like a lion and that's what we gotta do. We just gotta do it better," says Keaton's Hurley, which should have been the cue for a fifth screenwriter to take a crack.

By the end of *American Assassin* and its winking nudge towards a sequel, it is hard to look at it as anything but a cynical attempt to jump-start another franchise. Lacking anything past the same cinematic palettes of control stations, dark hotel rooms, and substitute Middle Eastern locations, Cuesta's film would not pass muster on the small screen where tech credits have risen in the high-definition era. It's action scenes are quick and forgettable save for the climactic boat battle that ups the stakes by driving unattended through a series of occasional waves making our combatants more liable to contract seasickness rather than harm from the nuclear device on board. Filmmakers may have conceded that audiences would rather see Officer Callahan from *Dirty Harry* (1971) than Mitchell Gant from *Firefox* (1982). But that hardly made John Malkovich's talky ex-CIA assassin from *In the Line of Fire* (1993) any less compelling. Any hope that Keaton and O'Brien would develop the kind of mentored relationship between Robert Redford and Brad Pitt in *Spy Game* (2001) is lost before their first mission. Any similar belief that Rapp and Hurley would develop a rapport with an audience in search of another hero is lost the moment those elevator doors close.

Erik Childress

CREDITS

Mitch Rapp: Dylan O'Brien
Stan Hurley: Michael Keaton
Irene Kennedy: Sanaa Lathan
Ghost: Taylor Kitsch
Annika: Shiva Negar
Origin: United States
Language: English, Italian, Arabic, Polish, Turkish, Persian
Released: 2017
Production: Lorenzo di Bonaventura, Nick Wechsler; Lionsgate; released by CBS Films Inc.
Directed by: Michael Cuesta
Written by: Stephen Schiff; Michael Finch; Edward Zwick; Marshall Herskovitz
Cinematography by: Enrique Chediak
Music by: Steven Price
Music Supervisor: Chris Seefried
Editing: Conrad Buff, IV
Art Direction: Matthew Gray; Gianpaolo Rifino
Costumes: Anna B. Sheppard
Production Design: Andrew Laws
MPAA rating: R
Running time: 112 minutes

REVIEWS

Baumgarten, Marjorie. *Austin Chronicle.* September 21, 2017.
Bell, Josh. *Las Vegas Weekly.* September 14, 2017.
Berardinelli, James. *ReelViews.* September 17, 2017.
Gronvall, Andrea. *ReelViews.* September 14, 2017.
Johanson, MaryAnn. *Flick Filosopher.* September 17, 2017.
Judy, Jim. *ScreenIt.* September 15, 2017.
Nicholson, Amy. *Variety.* September 13, 2017.
Phillips, Michael. *Chicago Tribune.* September 14, 2017.
Seitz, Matt Zoller. *RogerEbert.com.* September 16, 2017.
Turan, Kenneth. *ReelViews.* September 14, 2017.

TRIVIA

At one point, actor Bruce Willis was attached to play Mitch Rapp's mentor.

AMERICAN MADE

The sky is never the limit.
—Movie tagline

Box Office: $51.3 Million

There are numerous high-powered weapons on display during the rollicking course of *American Made* that are aiming to make the people before them come around to a desired point of view. Notable among them is that long-familiar, potently-ingratiating, and gleaming grin of its star, Tom Cruise. When faced with the high-wattage charm exuded by those choppers, filmmaker Doug Liman obviously felt almost as confident as Cruise's cocky pilot protagonist that viewers would see things his way during this "fun lie based upon a true story." Moviegoers would surely feel compelled to turn at least one blind eye to the shadiness of the man behind those shades, sunglasses that are reminiscent of those donned by a prior audacious aviator fans fondly recall from early in Cruise's career, namely "Maverick" Mitchell from *Top Gun* (1986). The many shots of Cruise at the controls in *American Made* (the actor did his own flying) only emphasize that he is also expertly in control of this vehicle and its viewers.

The actor portrays Barry Seal, a highly-restless TWA ace who traded in the rote transporting of people for exhilaratingly-challenging, tantalizingly-lucrative opportunities purportedly presented to him by employers ranging from the U.S. Government to Columbia's Medellin drug cartel. For the former, Seal agreed to secretly transport guns down to Nicaragua that might help topple its Sandinista regime, and then vowed to smuggle in cocaine for the latter on the return trip. While he appears to have been quite comfortable with both tasks, more than a few audience members certainly felt very uncomfortable about the illicit importing of drugs that went on to kill his own countrymen. Nevertheless, both Liman and Cruise empathetically expressed an understanding of Barry, sizing him up as a flawed fellow one cannot help but love anyway as a gutsily-adventurous, charismatically-amiable guy, compellingly-brimming with brio and can-do American spirit. Seal claimed that his brain contained no regrets, right up until the day it was resultantly filled with bullets. His portrayer, at least, continues to fly high, a 57-year-old, well-established movie star still capable of captivating audiences so that they will go along for a wild ride.

The ride a bored Barry provides Trans World ticket-buyers in 1978 (after an era-establishing opening) is certainly a turbulent one, as he livens things up with a little controlled chaos that is capable of bringing a look of satisfaction to his own face and one of confusion and alarm to those of the people seated in both the plane and theaters. The scene foreshadows the story's subsequent tumultuousness that is also largely of the man's own making, unable to rein in his reckless, risky response to the allure of craved fun and funds. The pilot may calmly and dexterously press things on the instrument panel before him, but the CIA's Schafer (Domhnall Gleeson) obviously knows precisely what buttons to push when it comes to Seal. Schafer offers the hotshot a chance to earn more than a little cold cash by taking reconnaissance photos above Central American unrest, making Barry feel indispensably, singularly skilled and delighting him further with a sure-to-be-irresistible offer to try out the world's fastest twin engine. It is plain that thrill-seeking is in Barry's blood, with adrenaline levels soaring even before his gleeful ascent. As for what was—or should have been—going on in his head: Seal barely pauses to utilize what intelligence he personally possesses therein before agreeing to gather the kind wanted by the government. "I do tend to leap before I look," Barry admits as he directly addresses the audience in one of the periodic helpings of videotaped hindsight interspersed throughout. "Maybe I should have asked a few more questions." As for *American Made,* it also proceeds in a hurried, devil-may-care manner, likely to prevent pondering about such things as the degree to which liberties were taken with the facts in creating an entertaining experience.

Cruise's physique is one obvious falsehood, as the real Seal was no matinee idol. Barry was balding and similarly-proportioned to the potbellied passenger he tells members of the burgeoning Medellin cartel led by Pablo Escobar (Mauricio Mejía) would disastrously strain his plane already burdened with blow and ready to go. (Seal was given the Spanish sobriquet "El Gordo," or "The Fat One.") While bets are taken as to whether he will survive a daring attempt to take off at the forested end of a too-short runway (even without the aforementioned portly man's poundage), Seal manifestly means to prove himself by proving the odds wrong, and rises to the occasion. Things do not go off without a hitch, however, as he imperfectly eludes the outstretched branches of the treetops, like his amazing ability to repeatedly free himself from the grasp of those out to stop his seemingly-overconfident undertakings. Cinematographer César Charlone provides numerous aerial shots of breathtakingly-lush landscapes, even greener than the bills Barry perpetually has in mind and that soon seem to rival the leaves below with their plentitude upon payment. They come to cascade out of a closet, and are surreptitiously planted like seed money for his family's future upon government-gifted arboreal acreage in Arkansas, always available for a shovel-expedited woodsy withdrawal. Disaster ensues for no-account brother-in-law JB (well-played by Caleb Landry Jones), upon unscrupulously unearthing some to benefit himself.

American Made would have benefitted from more and deeper digging into Barry. Efforts are made to advance an affectionate affinity for Seal in scenes revealing an admirable desire to live up to his responsibilities as provider for his worried-but-won-over-by-wealth wife Lucy (lovely Sarah Wright) and small children. Speaking of kids, one could not help but think of a certain nursery rhyme at one point: like Little Jack Horner, who stuck in his thumb, pulled out a plum, and said "What a good boy am I," Barry, who notes that he seemingly wound up having "fingers in every pie on the rack," is put forth here, simply but not completely convincingly, as a roguishly-rebellious, Louisianan good ol' boy who got his hands on plum assignments enticingly served up to him by others. How, the film seems to ask, could he be expected to resist such temptation? It is also made to seem as if his heart was in the right place when he shoos children away from his car in case it had been wired to explode by the Medellin men he had double-crossed. One is left to wonder: Was Seal himself wired in such a way that he really never felt any responsibility for the countless young people snuffed out instead by the drugs he delivered? Seal's culpability is nowhere near as easily wiped away as the raindrops upon his windshield just seconds before he is wiped out within the car by an assassin.

Those responsible for *American Made* could feel proud about what they had delivered to the public, and the $50 million-budgeted film grossed over $134 million worldwide amidst generally-favorable reviews. Arthur Liman, the director's father, served as chief counsel to the 1987 Senate Committee investigating the subsequent Iran-Contra fiasco, and his son's film makes the point in its waning frames that our government, like Barry, seems to have an absurd, irrepressible impulse-control problem when it comes to ill-considered secret schemes, the kind of foolhardy foreign finessing that has tended to lead only to American-made messes. When Seal pays the ultimate price for his own such pursuits, one of his videos freezes, and then his image slowly fades away. One is reminded of Lewis Carroll's Cheshire Cat, as what lingered most for many after leaving theaters were Cruise's purposefully-transfixing showings of shining teeth.

David L. Boxerbaum

CREDITS

Barry Seal: Tom Cruise
Monty "Schafer": Domhnall Gleeson
Lucy Seal: Sarah Wright
Sheriff Downing: Jesse Plemons
JB: Caleb Landry Jones
Origin: United States
Language: English, Spanish
Released: 2017
Production: Ray Angelic, Doug Davison, Brian Grazer, Brian Oliver, Kim Roth, Tyler Thompson; Cross Creek Pictures, Imagine Entertainment; released by Universal Pictures Inc.
Directed by: Doug Liman
Written by: Gary Spinelli
Cinematography by: Cesar Charlone
Music by: Christophe Beck
Sound: Ron Bochar; Philip Stockton
Music Supervisor: Gabe Hilfer; Julianne Jordan
Editing: Andrew Mondshein
Art Direction: Elizabeth Cummings
Costumes: Jenny Gering
Production Design: Dan Weil
MPAA rating: R
Running time: 115 minutes

REVIEWS

Anderson, John. *Wall Street Journal.* September 28, 2017.
Burr, Ty. *Boston Globe.* September 27, 2017.
Dargis, Manohla. *New York Times.* September 28, 2017.
Felperin, Leslie. *Hollywood Reporter.* August 17, 2017.
Lane, Anthony. *New Yorker.* September 25, 2017.
Lodge, Guy. *Variety.* August 17, 2017.
Nashawaty, Chris. *Entertainment Weekly.* September 26, 2017.
O'Sullivan, Michael. *Washington Post.* September 28, 2017.
Phillips, Michael. *Chicago Tribune.* September 28, 2017.
Rainer, Peter. *Christian Science Monitor.* September 29, 2017.

QUOTES

Barry Seal: "The problem isn't the room. It's weight."

TRIVIA

This is actor Tom Cruise's first R-rated film in nine years (since the 2008 film *Tropic Thunder*).

ANNABELLE: CREATION

You don't know the real story.
—Movie tagline

Box Office: $102.1 Million

When director James Wan first brought *The Conjuring* (2013) to audiences, it could hardly be predicted that the film would spawn a billion dollar franchise of spinoffs, sequels, and prequels. Perhaps even less likely is that four films in, the franchise would continue to be producing quality horror entertainment. *Annabelle: Creation* is actually the best of these continuations, and certainly the scariest.

The film begins in the early 1940s as Samuel Mullins (Anthony LaPaglia) and his wife Esther (Miranda Otto) grieve the loss of their young daughter Bee/Annabelle (Samara Lee). Desperate to reconnect with her, they are fooled by a demon posing as Annabelle into an occult ritual which traps the demon in one of Samuel's beautiful handmade porcelain dolls. Once they realize their horrifying mistake, they quickly enlist a priest who blesses the house as they seal the doll up in their daughter's bedroom closet in an effort to keep the demon from finding a human host.

A dozen years pass, and, though their grief remains as strong as ever, the couple have opened their home to a group of orphans. Led by Sister Charlotte (Stephanie Sigman), the girls excitedly settle in, but, later that night, Janice (Talitha Eliana Bateman), who has been crippled by polio, hears noises coming from the room they have been told not enter and discovers the door unlocked. Once inside, she finds a key that opens the closet where the doll resides. No longer in hiding, the demon begins to exert its influence over Janice until it fully possesses her, continuing to torment the other girls. Frightened by the changes in her best friend, Linda (Lulu Wilson) confesses to Samuel what she knows about Janice and the doll, leading the demon to murder Samuel. Sister Charlotte confronts Esther in her sickbed demanding to know the truth and realizes the demon means to kill them all. Before she can gather the girls, she and Linda find themselves in a deadly battle with a possessed Janice, barely escaping with their lives as they lock both Janice and the doll back in the closet.

This is scary stuff. Director David F. Sandberg shows a continued flair for horror having helmed last year's excellent *Lights Out* (2016). Following the example laid out by the franchise producer James Wan, Sandberg has crafted suspense sequences that generate serious chills. Wan's work has often been called a tribute to Mario Bava, and his horrific female monsters have certainly called to mind the entities in the *Black Sabbath* (*I tre volti della paura*, 1963) segment "A Drop Of Water" ("La goccia d?acqua"). But Wan has been equally at home using images of the demonic and Sandberg knows exactly how to light such grotesques in the most disturbing ways possible. When they do slink back into the shadows, such as in the expertly-crafted scene of Janice trying to escape the demon in a stair lift, they become even more unbearable. Plain and simple, *Annabelle: Creation* is the stuff of which nightmares are made.

Casting Anthony LaPaglia and Miranda Otto as Mr. and Mrs. Mullins is overkill in terms of the script's needs for their characters, but they exert perfect control over the pathos the script calls on them to deliver. It's fun to see Lulu Wilson here as the character Linda. Her turn in *Ouija: Origin of Evil* (2016), also a prequel film, was stunning. She's equally good here, though not the lead. That role belongs to young Talitha Eliana Bateman as Janice. Bateman is as good in her part as anyone around her, even when the script has her doing things that characters only do in horror movies. This is perhaps the film's biggest flaw. Characters are always walking into dark forbidden areas, or losing their footing to help create the tension. Sandberg clearly reveals he can do without such stuff. The murder of Samuel takes place in in a cheerily lit dining room and is a stunning example of how good he is at getting his audience to follow him into harm's way.

One thing Sandberg stays away from is Annabelle herself. The doll is creepy to be sure but not a true major character in the film at least not in the sense that say Fats is in the movie *Magic* (1978) or Talking Tina is in the classic *Twilight Zone* episode, "Living Doll" (1963). Annabelle makes key appearances but does her evil work largely through others. It makes for some complicated mythology since it begs the question of how Annabelle, the doll, becomes possessed once again since Janice has fled. Perhaps *The Nun* will answer such questions. *Annabelle: Creation* does a fine job of fleshing out another great character for the "Conjuring" universe.

Dave Canfield

CREDITS

Samuel Mullins: Anthony LaPaglia
Bee: Samara Lee
Esther Mullins: Miranda Otto
Victor Palmeri: Brad Greenquist
Linda: Lulu Wilson
Origin: United States
Language: English
Released: 2017
Production: Peter Safran, James Wan; Atomic Monster, New Line Cinema L.L.C., RatPac-Dune Entertainment, The Safron Company; released by Warner Bros. Entertainment Inc.
Directed by: David F. Sandberg
Written by: Gary Dauberman
Cinematography by: Maxime Alexandre
Music by: Benjamin Wallfisch
Sound: William R. Dean
Editing: Michel Aller
Art Direction: Jason Garner
Costumes: Leah Butler
Production Design: Jennifer Spence
MPAA rating: R
Running time: 109 minutes

REVIEWS

Abele, Robert. *TheWrap*. June 20, 2017.
Boo, Bernard. *PopMatters*. August 11, 2017.
Brayton, Tim. *Alternate Ending*. August 25, 2017.
Catsoulis, Jeannette. *New York Times*. August 10, 2017.
Chang, Justin. *Los Angeles Times*. August 10, 2017.
Daniell, Mark. *Toronto Sun*. August 10, 2017.
Debruge, Peter. *Variety*. June 20, 2017.
Dowd, A.O. *The A.V. Club*. August 10, 2017.
Feldberg, Isaac. *Boston Globe*. August 10, 2017.
O'Sullivan, Michael. *Washington Post*. August 10, 2017.

QUOTES

Janice: "Forgive me, Father, for I am about to sin."

TRIVIA

The bulk of the film takes place in 1955, twelve years before the events of the first film.

ATOMIC BLONDE

Box Office: $51.7 Million

On paper, at least, *Atomic Blonde* is a film that sounds as if it could not possibly fail to deliver the action movie goods. It has been produced in the most super-stylish manner imaginable, it features star/co-producer Charlize Theron in prime ass-kicking mode and it contains the requisite amount of sex, violence, and dazzling set-pieces, including one jaw-dropping how-did-they-do-that sequence that has been deemed an instant classic by connoisseurs of the genre. And yet, while it has so many individual elements that do work, the film as a whole never quite comes together into a satisfying whole in the manner of the Jason Bourne films or *John Wick* (2014) to name the most obvious of its numerous antecedents. The result is one of those movies where one can watch it and be vaguely entertained on some basic fundamental level while thinking at the same time that it should be a lot better.

Set in 1989, during the waning days of the Cold War, the film stars Theron as MI6 agent Lorraine Broughton. As it opens, she is being debriefed by her superior (Toby Jones) and a CIA Chief (John Goodman) regarding her activities in Berlin over the previous ten days, the flashback of which takes up the bulk of the narrative. After the murder of a British agent results in the disappearance of a list of the names and locations of all members of British intelligence in the field, Lorraine is sent in to track down and retrieve it. After arriving in West Berlin (where she is almost instantly ambushed by a couple of attackers that she fends off with the help of one of her stylish high heels), she makes contact with David Percival (James McAvoy), a onetime Berlin bureau chief who now makes a dubious living selling booze and clothes on the black market. She does not entirely trust David, but he does contribute two vital elements to her cause—a connection to a Stasi agent (Eddie Marsan) who has committed the list to memory and is willing to turn it over in exchange for helping him; and a warning that there is a double agent, known only as Satchel, who may be coming after her.

Although the screenplay by Kurt Johnstad, based on Antony Johnston's graphic novel *The Coldest City*, is filled with any number of curveballs and complications—the most welcome being Sofia Boutella as a novice French agent who quickly finds herself being seduced James Bond-stye by Lorraine and the most bewildering being Til Schweiger as a character whose presence is never quite adequately explained—there really isn't much more to the actual plot than what has already been described. The ingredients are there for a nifty retro-style spy thriller, but it soon becomes apparent that the narrative is little more than a laundry line designed solely as a way of hanging together the various action beats. The flashback structure also works against it because on the rare occasions when the story seems to be building up a head of dramatic steam, the story cuts back to Lorraine recounting the events to her superiors and everything gets set back to square one. This particular approach has no obvious benefit—the final punchline to this element is not worth it—and seems to have been added in order to distract viewers from noticing that the story does not really go anywhere, the bad guys are a disappointment, and Lorraine, for all of her vaunted espionage skills, doesn't really do much of anything other than deliver savage beatdowns of anyone crossing her path, more often than not to the accompaniment of a well-chosen soundtrack of 1980s-era favorites.

One key reason that *Atomic Blonde* almost works, or at least creates the illusion that it does for a time, is because those beatdowns have been expertly conceived and executed with enough impact to thrill even the most hardcore of action movie junkies. The film was directed by David Leitch, who previously co-directed *John Wick* and who clearly knows how to do action properly on-screen. Of these exquisitely choreographed set pieces, there are two that especially stand out. In one, Lorraine is pursued by a couple of KGB agents who follow her into a screening of *Stalker* (1979), leading to a striking moment in which the formal beauty of Andrei Tarkovsky's imagery serves as ironic juxtaposition to the brutality unfolding in front of it. The second, one that was greeted with delight even by those who otherwise had no use for the film as a whole, comes when Lorraine and the defecting agent are ambushed in the streets and forced to take cover inside a nearby building, kicking off an increasingly astonishing sequence in which she single-handedly fights off waves of bad guys up and down the various floors, using weapons ranging from guns to furniture to her bare hands, before eventually fleeing the building and hopping into a car for a chase—all of which is presented as a seemingly seamless five minute-plus chunk of film without a single obvious cut of notice. The end result is one of those increasingly rare action scenes that demands to be seen twice—once simply to luxuriate in the genuine thrills and excitement that it manages to generate and again to be able to look at it closer and be astonished by the incredible technical effort that presumably went into making it all come off as well as it does.

The other reason, of course, is the indomitable presence of Theron as Lorraine. Having already established her action film bona fides with her instantly iconic turn as Imperator Furiosa in *Mad Max: Fury Road* (2015), it is perhaps not exactly surprising to see her dominate the proceedings here as well. However, her performance works for reasons other than the thoroughly convincing ferocity that she brings to the scenes in which she shoots, stabs, strangles, and slams countless bad guys. That stuff is easy enough but even though both the body count and the storyline threaten to spiral into pure cartoonishness, she finds ways of keeping Lorraine at least somewhat grounded in something vaguely resembling reality. She dishes out a lot of punishment, for example, but receives plenty of it in return and the way that she suggests the lingering aftereffects of said skirmishes that are only partially quelled by what appears to be her all-Stoli diet adds a rare human element to the proceedings. And while she may appear to be some kind of ice queen throughout (and not just because of her tendency to take ice baths to help the recuperation process), she demonstrates some genuine heat in her scenes with Boutella, which are the best non-action (okay, a different kind of action) beats in the film, and which ultimately work because of the chemistry the two develop between each other and not just because of any cheap titillation. (She demonstrates far less chemistry in her scenes with McAvoy but, to be fair, that may be the point.)

Because the action scenes are so impressive and because Theron makes such an impact, one is almost tempted to come away from *Atomic Blonde* thinking that it is better than it really is. And yet, it never quite manages to click in the way that it clearly should have thanks to a number of key conceptual failures on the part of the screenplay. That said, this is the rare not-so-good movie where a sequel might actually be a welcome thing—if the filmmakers could bring Theron and Leitch back into the fold, and this time give them a screenplay that was up to snuff, there is every reason to believe that the end result could indeed be the action classic that the film desperately wants to be but which it ultimately fails at becoming.

Peter Sobczynski

CREDITS

Lorraine Broughton: Charlize Theron
David Percival: James McAvoy
Spyglass: Eddie Marsan
Emmett Kurzfeld: John Goodman
Eric Gray: Toby Jones
Origin: United States
Language: English, German, Russian, Swedish
Released: 2017
Production: A.J. Dix, Eric Gitter, Beth Kono, Kelly McCormick, Peter Schwerin, Charlize Theron; 87Eleven, Closed on Mondays Entertainment, Denver and Delilah Productions, T.G.I.M Films; released by Focus Features L.L.C.
Directed by: David Leitch
Written by: Kurt Johnstad
Cinematography by: Jonathan Sela
Music by: Tyler Bates
Sound: Thomas Huhn; Nicklas Lindh
Music Supervisor: John Houlihan
Editing: Elisabet Ronaldsdottir
Art Direction: Zsuzsa Kismarty-Lechner
Costumes: Cindy Evans
Production Design: David Scheunemann
MPAA rating: R
Running time: 115 minutes

REVIEWS

Anderson, Melissa. *Village Voice.* July 27, 2017.
Barker, Andrew. *Variety.* March 13, 2017.
Brody, Richard. *New Yorker.* July 24, 2017.
Burr, Ty. *Boston Globe.* July 27, 2017.
Chang, Justin. *Los Angeles Times.* July 27, 2017.
Dargis, Manohla. *New York Times.* July 27, 2017.
DeFore, John. *Hollywood Reporter.* March 13, 2017.
Kohn, Eric. *IndieWIRE.* March 15, 2017.
O'Sullivan, Michael. *Washington Post.* July 27, 2017.
Zacharek, Stephanie. *Time.* July 27, 2017.

QUOTES

Lorraine Broughton: "I'm my own bitch now!"

TRIVIA

Actress Charlize Theron said that the success of *Mad Max: Fury Road* (2015) helped with the development of this film.

B

THE B-SIDE: ELSA DORFMAN'S PORTRAIT PHOTOGRAPHY

The camera is magic. (September 2, 2015)
—Movie tagline

Box Office: $125,227

Cultural anthropologist, journalist, and filmmaker Errol Morris makes documentaries as found art, engrossing and fascinating inquiries into the nature of truth as they celebrate and tangle with a particular American characteristic of eccentricity and flamboyantly imaginative personalities.

His stylized and intricate portraits include some of the most famous, powerful, and influential figures in politics, science, and art. He has also explored the forlorn or unknown without changing his style or technique. Morris's defining trait is that he is indefatigable, intelligent, funny, and inclusive. He weaves the camera, intimate and catching, like his own personal instrument. His best films are hypnotic, relentless though clear-eyed and highly sophisticated.

Morris's funny and revealing debut, *Gates of Heaven* (1978), about the proprietors of two pet cemeteries in Northern California, revealed a fully-formed voice and style, a probing and restless intelligence who demonstrated a natural rapport and interest in the Americana. The director's third feature, *The Thin Blue Line* (1988), about the killing of a Dallas police officer and the attendant miscarriage of justice, resulted in the release of a death row inmate and a confession from the actual killer.

He subsequently found interesting ways to push the envelope stylistically and open up his films. One of his greatest works, *Fast, Cheap & Out of Control* (1997), brilliantly intercuts among its four principal characters, the rhythms yielding a singular and transcendent study of obsession. His film, *The Fog of War* (2003), which won the Academy Award for Best Documentary, was a confrontation, or masterly duel if you will, where this skilled and talented interlocutor addressed the controversial life and legacy of Robert McNamara, the architect of the American military buildup in Vietnam.

His most disturbing work is probably *Mr. Death* (1999), laconic and eerie, in relating the story of an engineer who designed an electric chair for capital punishment and through a strange confluence of events became an outspoken proponent in the Holocaust denial movement. "I'm a Jewish guy from Long Island, and I always wanted to make a movie about the Holocaust," Morris once said. "The more ill-advised a project is, the more someone tells me this can't possibly work or shouldn't work, the more I want to do it."

Morris has also expanded the scope of nonfiction possibilities, though sometimes to questionable or problematic ends. He directed one fiction film, the mystery thriller *The Dark Wind* (1991). Many of his non-fiction films are laced with fiction techniques, the most conscious is his extensive use of re-enactments in movies like *The Thin Blue Line.* His movies are very cinematic in their use of landscape, objects and forms, and his terrific use of music, especially the films featuring the exquisitely minimalist compositions of Philip Glass.

Morris's new film, *The B-Side*, works out some interesting corollaries to his other films, the nature of process and art, like *Fast, Cheap & Out of Control.* It is a quieter and more wistful work, lovely, unforced, and direct in its simplicity and engagement with the subject. It is a portrait of the artist, rendered in his own sly way, elegant, quiet and deeply confident.

The movie's subtitle, *Elsa Dorfman's Portrait Photography*, lays out both the subject and style. Like Morris, Dorfman is a cultural fixture in Cambridge, Massachusetts. The nature of their interaction is necessarily warm and tender and what emerges through their conversations is a vibrant personal history, of artists, writers, poets, photography, and the form itself.

Dorfman, who is now 80-years old, has a remarkable story. Whether luck, habit or providence, she had an unerring ability of being at the center of some extraordinary cultural movements. "This nice Jewish girl," as she deprecatingly calls herself in the interview sessions, was very attuned to the moment and had the eye and the sensibility to give it depth and perspective.

Her first job out of college in New York at the vital independent publisher Grove Press produced a funny and accidental encounter with the great Beat poet Allen Ginsberg. His early New York Jewish humor startled her and her savvy and grace likewise struck a chord, cementing the start of a lifelong and passionate friendship.

Adrift in New York, where the publishing gig did not really pan out to her liking, Dorfman returned home to her middle-class Jewish Boston family. She caught a break and was hired to work in a lab at the Massachusetts Institute of Technology (MIT). She showed a great eye, a deft sensitivity for the texture and lines of faces. Friends like Ginsberg helped her get phenomenal access, like intimate backstage photographs of Bob Dylan.

She was fearless and uninhibited, crafting lovely and startlingly intimate nudes of her friends like Ginsberg but also her own family, her husband and her son. She even published a book about her family life. *The B-Side* collates memoir to a colorful social and cultural history. Its hidden subject is obsolescence, or what technology has done to the art and meaning of photographic representation.

At the very moment the advent of digital threatened to change her work, Dorfman went bigger. The balance of the film is how Dorfman became a specialist in the large-format twenty-four-by-twenty-four inch Polaroid portraits she shot primarily at her studio. Curiously, the process became more industrial, with the fixed perspective of the camera and careful way she arranged her subjects.

What emerges in Morris's telling is her extraordinary empathy and insight into her subjects. As the portraits take shape the very different personalities, styles, and personal temperament of the individuals and their families on view achieve an incredible clarity and physical density.

The movie is not a major work by Morris, as it is deliberately conceived and shot in a much quieter register. At just 76 minutes, it lacks the depth and elasticity necessary of a great documentary. The movie lacks the tension, volatility, and formal elegance of his best work. Even some of the home movie nature of the filmmaking becomes haphazard, in the scattered framing.

Finally, the niggling hardly seems to matter. *The B-Side* is really a portrait of friendship, of the director's to his own subject. Morris's friendship perhaps made him reluctant to probe deeper than normal. The movie is definitely frustrating in that regard.

The wider friendship of photographer and poet yields some of the most beautiful, touching and finally deeply emotional passages as Dorfman reveals her friendship with Ginsberg (1926-1997) and his partner, Peter Orlovsky. A sequence where she plays back many years later the final phone messages Ginsberg left with her are quite devastating.

Late in the film, Dorfman says the opportunity to work out her ideas of portraiture, photography, and art fulfilled a lifetime ambition of attaining the offbeat and spontaneous and outside normal boundaries. In that regard, she personifies the exuberant individualism of the classic Errol Morris subject.

Patrick Z. McGavin

CREDITS

Herself: Elsa Dorfman
Origin: United States
Language: English
Released: 2017
Production: Steven Hathaway; Fourth Floor Productions, Moxie Pictures; released by Neon
Directed by: Errol Morris
Cinematography by: Nathan Swingle; Nathan Allen Swingle
Music by: Paul-Leonard Morgan
Sound: Joel Dougherty
Editing: Steven Hathaway
Art Direction: Eugenia Magann Haynes
MPAA rating: R
Running time: 66 minutes

REVIEWS

Abele, Robert. *Los Angeles Times.* June 29, 2017.
Barker, Andrew. *Variety.* April 24, 2017.
Baumgarten, Marjorie. *Austin Chronicle.* July 19, 2017.

Bowen, Chuck. *Slant Magazine.* May 30, 2017.
D'Angelo, Mike. *The A.V. Club.* June 28, 2017.
Grierson, Tim. *Paste Magazine.* June 26, 2017.
Kenny, Glenn. *New York Times.* June 29, 2017.
Lee, Benjamin. *The Guardian.* April 21, 2017.
Morgenstern, Joe. *Wall Street Journal.* June 29, 2017.
O'Sullivan, Michael. *Washington Post.* July 13, 2017.

BABY DRIVER

All you need is one killer track.
—Movie tagline

Box Office: $107.8 Million

Baby Driver is the culmination of every daydreamer's music video fantasies, the car radio thrumming is the heartbeat of an action scene and every measure as epic as your imagination promised. Edgar Wright, the film's writer and director, cements himself with this film not only as the king of tongue-in-cheek genre fare, but of earnestly referential, inventive cinema. This heist movie, Wright's first non-comedy, focuses on the getaway driver Baby (Ansel Elgort) who effectively stars in a series of music videos over the course of the film. Baby suffers from tinnitus thanks to a childhood accident and incessantly listens to music so he can exist in the world (and do his job) painlessly.

Baby lip syncs and dances along with the film's continuous, diegetic soundtrack piped in through his ever-present earbuds, making a modern jukebox musical (one with a delicious cameo by Paul Williams) out of everyday activities like picking up coffee or making a sandwich. Wright utilizes his skills with meticulous background gags and pinpoint edits to great effect here, implementing lyrics and credits in symbiotic form with their surroundings. The film's most effective musical character moments are like those with which it opens: a guy singing along in a car. The movie uses "Bellbottoms" by The Jon Spencer Blues Explosion to explain an entire character. Baby, waiting on his heist-mates, rocks out like most criminals do not. He flails his arms, beats the dashboard, and flicks the wipers. He honks the horn—a dangerous, cocky celebration coming from a bank robber. It's unironic, unself-conscious bliss. A man lives in a fantasy that promises he is as cool as he thinks he is, so he can go do something as cool as the things we all wish we did: drive fast to beat the system.

This system is one of family, owned and embodied by the two sides of Baby's family. On one hand, Baby's adoptive father has a similarly complicated relationship with sound but an uncomplicated relationship with the law. Joseph (CJ Jones, the rare and wonderful case of a deaf actor playing a deaf character) adopted Baby after his tinnitus-inducing accident. His communication with his son is clipped, caring, and kinetic, a physical extension of the film's thrumming motion where its signature sound cannot penetrate. Their relationship is sweet and simple, save for Baby's illicit activities.

This leads to Baby's other adoptive father, the one that introduced him to crime, who directs his actions with the overarching paternalism of classic kingpin omniscience. This is Doc (Kevin Spacey, sinister and caring in equal measure). Doc puts these heists together, setting the thieving machinery in motion. He recruits the best and never repeats a crew. Yuppie couple Buddy (Jon Hamm, more powerful the sleazier he's allowed to be) and Darling (Eiza González, shallow and indicative of Wright's struggles writing female characters after his trilogy's foray into male friendship) are the Clyde and Bonnie of this circle, while Bats (Jamie Foxx) rounds out the gang that collectively has the most screentime. Together with Baby, the crooks conspire to rob banks, Post Offices, and more in tightly choreographed heists and even tighter escapes when things inevitably go wrong.

The pleasures of this movie come from synchronicity. Its funky soundtrack alone would be wasted, but with all the perfect timing of the action, it's like watching a finely oiled machine churn its gears for an onlooker's amusement at a World's Fair. This type of mechanical movement, either properly or in rebellion, makes everything more visually interesting. Take the classic examples of Freder working almost literally around the clock in *Metropolis* (1927) or Charlie Chaplin being defeated by assembly lines in *Modern Times* (1936). The machinery, the choreography, the practiced motion of a human body—it all serves to equalize the process and blur the line between organic and inorganic, perfection, and imperfection. In the previous examples it can make humans seem more fallible, but industrialization isn't the sole use for this visual toolbox. The same effect happens when a person is in a car, though Wright utilizes it for the opposite purpose on the ego. When Elgort flips on the windshield wipers, he's doing a wave. When he pounds on the side of the door or slaps the steering wheel, it's an extension of hamboning on his body. When he mouths the words to the song in his rearview mirror, he sees the reflection of a rock star looking back at him. Not so in historic films. Their sweeping gestures make the film funny, cartoonish, and exaggerated but the context of the factory brings them back down to a defeatable, fallible humanity. They are simply men lost in a metal jungle. Here, Baby is always in control, though in accordance with this philosophy, he becomes far more human once he loses it.

The film leans not into pastiche like Wright's previous work, but is an entry full of the genre's hallmarks all with a twist befitting an obsessive like the auteur. This means, of course, that one last job goes awry. Unsurprisingly, this comes after Baby has met someone and they become entwined, giving him something to lose. This someone is Debora (Lily James, delivering a solid performance with a thin character) whose main contribution to the film is a great joke about the band T. Rex. Her presence is the weakest element of the film, because here even the music can't help power through the slushy, unfocused writing. Weaker female characters are as indicative of Wright's usually impressive work as his constant in-jokes and references, only here they are central to a plot no longer focused exclusively on the specific relationships between men. Another key difference is that this is his first film set in America.

Baby Driver seems inherently American, because nowhere else do people fetishize their cars so strongly as extensions of their masculinity. Americans strap a lot of personal worth to their cars—especially men. This association stems from geography and historical patriarchy. America's so vast that having a car means freedom and freedom for one's family. This freedom calls to Baby and Debora alike, the seduction of the open road a sweet song whose call is muffled overseas. It is a calling empty of cold irony, one that runs hot and fast on diesel and style.

Baby's stunts are successes because he taps into a source of modern invincibility, the heightened combination of motion and sound. *Baby Driver* is a success for the same reason. There are depths of meaning, of American history, of masculinity, of desire and criminality, layered underneath the flashy exterior like lyrics ripe with metaphor. That it comes in a package almost too zippy for its own good only makes the reward riskier and, as Baby and Doc would attest to, all the sweeter.

Jacob Oller

CREDITS

Baby: Ansel Elgort
Doc: Kevin Spacey
Debora: Lily James
Darling: Eiza González
Buddy: Jon Hamm
Bats: Jamie Foxx
Origin: United States
Language: English, Sign languages
Released: 2017
Production: Tim Bevan, Eric Fellner, Nira Park; Double Negative, Media Rights Capital L.P.; released by TriStar Pictures Inc.
Directed by: Edgar Wright
Written by: Edgar Wright
Cinematography by: Bill Pope
Music by: Steven Price
Sound: Julian Slater
Music Supervisor: Kirsten Lane
Editing: Jonathan Amos; Paul Machliss
Art Direction: Nigel Churcher
Costumes: Courtney Hoffman
Production Design: Marcus Rowland
MPAA rating: R
Running time: 112 minutes

REVIEWS

Bailey, Jason. *Flavorwire*. June 26, 2017.
Borders, Meredith. *Birth.Movies.Death*. March 12, 2017.
Burr, Ty. *Boston Globe*. June 28, 2017.
Cole, Jake. *Slant Magazine*. June 24, 2017.
Chang, Justin. *Los Angeles Times*. June 27, 2017.
Ebiri, Bilge. *L.A. Weekly*. June 26, 2017.
Hornaday, Ann. *Washington Post*. June 27, 2017.
Murthi, Vikram. *The A.V. Club*. June 29, 2017.
Orr, Christopher. *The Atlantic*. June 28, 2017.
Phillips, Michael. *Chicago Tribune*. June 27, 2017.

QUOTES

Bats: "The moment you catch feelings is the moment you catch a bullet."

TRIVIA

Actor Jon Hamm's role was written specifically for him, and he is the only actor from the first table read of the script to be included in the final film.

AWARDS

British Acad. 2017: Film Editing
Nominations:
Oscars 2017: Film Editing, Sound, Sound FX Editing
British Acad. 2017: Sound
Golden Globes 2018: Actor--Mus./Comedy (Elgort)

THE BAD BATCH

Box Office: $180,851

The young director Ana Lily Amirpour is a punk aesthete blessed with a restless intelligence and a striking compositional eye. Her terrific debut, the Persian-language *A Girl Walks Home Alone at Night* (2014), was a nervy feminist vampire movie shot in sinuously cool black and white that demonstrated distinctive formal energies.

Her follow up, *The Bad Batch*, is another postmodern genre pastiche, that yokes together the feminist revenge thriller, the post-apocalyptic Western, and the poetic fatalism of the classic film noir. Amirpour, like Kathryn Bigelow, has a flair for visceral, kinetic movement and is unafraid to explore the moral consequences of violence and loss. Her movie is violent and ugly and unsettling in its racial ideas. It's a flawed work, of conception and character. Unfortunately, the writing never reaches the same level as the eerie and suggestive imagery. Even in its highly imperfect, uneven form, the movie is a thrilling showcase of a young director's voice and talent.

The dystopian thriller summons a perverse and hardscrabble future society in the vast expanse of the southwest. The undesirable, the so-called "bad batch," the criminals, loners and outcasts, are rounded up and tattooed (echoes of the Holocaust), at a Texas outsourcing facility and left to fend for themselves in a lawless zone outside. That is the fate, at the start, of Arlen (Suki Waterhouse). Armed with a couple of essentials, like a jug of water, she takes her rejection from the mainstream in stride, a defiant symbol of her looming independence and freedom.

She is soon disabused of her idealism. The brutal landscape outside the border fence has cleaved into two dominant societies of warriors, scavengers, and survivalists. Arlen is trapped in the more malevolent one made up of fascist body builders and cannibals. Moving in this desert wilderness, Arlen tries to elude her captors but is quickly apprehended by two people who chase her down from the back of a tricked-out golf cart. Arlen is drugged, tortured, and horribly mutilated, with her right arm severed below the elbow and her right leg dismembered.

Her survival instincts kick in and she escapes her tormentors and orchestrates her own plot for revenge. After a mysterious figure intervenes on her behalf, Arlen finds safe haven at an alternate makeshift society called Comfort, a neon-lit fortified compound run by a dissolute philosopher king named the Dream (Keanu Reeves), a wealthy polygamist and drug trafficker who lords over a group of concubines. These women, willowy models, most of them pregnant and deeply loyal to him, live in a walled-in commune and enforce his rule as members of a heavily armed private militia.

The action then fast-forwards five months. Arlen, her strength recovered and given a prosthetic leg, is now caught between extremes, eager to reclaim her honor and some degree of humanity by meting out her vengeance against the nihilists who attacked her. In a confrontation at a detritus-marked junkyard frequented by the cannibals, Arlen kills a young woman named Maria (Yolanda Ross) and takes possession of her child, Honey (Jayda Fink). Returning to Comfort, Arlen leaves the child with the privileged sanctum of the concubines.

If the cannibals' redoubt marked one kind of extreme, Comfort is the more open and sybaritic playground fueled by its own pleasure principle of music and drugs. Arlen is intoxicated by the possibilities. At a rave she drops acid and becomes unmoored as she wanders into the iridescent desert. After the hallucinogens wear off, she is nearly violated during an encounter the following day until another mysterious figure intervenes.

The stranger, known as the Miami Man (Jason Momoa), the letters inked on his chest, is putatively a member of the cannibal clan. Of greater priority is finding his daughter. He is significantly the father of Honey, the child Arlen abducted and placed under the privileged female order community ruling Comfort. Arlen deftly finds another mysterious figure who shoots Miami Man and allows her to regain her freedom and return to Comfort.

Amirpour is an emerging stylist who has the natural, evocative ability to think visually. The movie is loaded with knockout images, a motorcyclist cutting through the jangled night landscape or the evocative and lyrical motion inside a protective canopy shielding two people from the same brutally harsh desert terrain.

The language and ideas are not as innovative, revealing or successfully integrated, either contextually or dramatically. The cannibal society, for instance, is indifferently detailed. Working for the first time in English, Amirpour is certainly an unpredictable director of actors, privileging the mannered and bizarrely idiosyncratic. An unrecognizable Jim Carrey, as the Hermit, brings a charge of unpredictability and nerve with his furious, unhinged activity and highly inflected speech rhythms. (Giovanni Ribisi and Diego Luna, going full method, are far less interesting in secondary parts.)

Reeves, detached, outrageous, is not only unafraid to come off as preposterous, but his line readings veer from underplayed to the ridiculous, a man in flight from his own femininity, who if nothing, is certainly never dull. Momoa is a physical and charged actor suffused with vulnerability and loss. He does what he can with a mostly unplayable part. His big character reveal, that he was a Cuban migrant who was exiled for being undocumented, has political shading.

A former model, Waterhouse is more of a presence than a natural actor. She lacks the technical skill. Her Texas twang wavers, for instance, without shape or authenticity. Strangely, the inchoate nature of the part is oddly suiting. Waterhouse is still finding her range and voice. What she brings to the part is a sensuous immediacy. Even when the dialogue is, quite frankly, terrible, like an almost laughable crucial part opposite Momoa, where she says, plaintively, "Do you want to hang out?" there is something direct, even feral in her playing, a stripped down intensity and quickness that is deeply satisfying.

She flits between identities, avenging angel and frightened innocent. With her developing conscience, of her culpability of Honey being sequestered at Comfort, she undertakes a mission with Miami Man to bring about the young girl's release. The director's treatment of violence is harsh, unyielding, and terrifying, without closure or release. The gifted cinematographer Lyle Vincent, who also photographed *A Girl Walks Home Alone at Night*, has a fast and immersive style that in its purest state is quite electric. The sun-drenched color is unsettling, even apocalyptic. The opening passages, done almost without any dialogue, are particularly entrancing that conjure a vision of cruelty and rebirth.

At times, Amirpour goes too far (the lack of feeling directed at non-white casualties, for instance). Rather than simply poach other films, like the Mad Max titles, for their iconography and style, Amirpour locates her own vision. Her talent cannot transcend the limitations of her ideas or associations. *The Bad Batch* is the work of a director with her own vision, who knows what she wants to say, on her terms and in her own impressive style.

Patrick Z. McGavin

CREDITS

Arlen: Suki Waterhouse
Miami Man: Jason Momoa
The Dream: Keanu Reeves
Maria: Yolonda Ross
The Screamer: Giovanni Ribisi
Hermit: Jim Carrey
Origin: United States
Language: English
Released: 2017
Production: Megan Ellison, Danny Gabai, Sina Sayyah; Annapurna Productions, LLC, Human Stew Factory, Vice Films; released by Neon
Directed by: Ana Lily Amirpour
Written by: Ana Lily Amirpour
Cinematography by: Lyle Vincent
Sound: Chris Terhune
Music Supervisor: Andrea von Foerster
Editing: Alex O'Flinn
Art Direction: Sean Brennan
Costumes: Natalie O'Brien
Production Design: Brandon Tonner-Connolly
MPAA rating: R
Running time: 118 minutes

REVIEWS

Brody, Richard. *The New Yorker*. June 27, 2017.
Chang, Justin. *Los Angeles Times*. June 22, 2017.
Kiang, Jessica. *The Playlist*. September 6, 2016.
Kohn, Eric. *IndieWire*. September 6, 2016.
Kupecki, Josh. *Austin Chronicle*. June 21, 2017.
Lodge, Guy. *Variety*. September 6, 2016.
Nicholson, Amy. *MTV News*. June 22, 2017.
Rife, Katie. *The A.V. Club*. June 21, 2017.
Rooney, David. *The Hollywood Reporter*. September 6, 2016.
Scott, A.O. *New York Times*. June 22, 2017.

QUOTES

Arlen: "Strange isn't it? Here we are. In the darkest corner of this Earth. And we're afraid of our own kind."

TRIVIA

No soundstage shoots were utilized during production. The entire film was filmed in extreme locations; primarily outdoors in high heat.

A BAD MOMS CHRISTMAS

Celebrate the holidays like a mother.
—Movie tagline

Box Office: $72.1 Million

Bad Moms was the definition of "sleeper hit" when released in August 2016, while adding itself to an unofficial canon of "bad" people movies—*Bad Santa* (2003), *Bad Teacher* (2011), *Bad Grandpa* (2013). Having grossed a worldwide total of nearly $184 million and becoming a hit for rising distribution company STX Entertainment, a sequel was inevitable, but few could have predicted that it would come so quickly. Released just fourteen months later with interest in a sugary booze drink of holiday respite, *A Bad Moms Christmas* proves to be one of the most hollow of assembly-line comedies, in which any time for effort likely could not have salvaged a movie of such shallow comedic values.

Mila Kunis, Kristen Bell, and Kathryn Hahn return as the rambunctious titular characters, taking their penchant for debauchery from beyond parent parties, as in the first film, to the busiest time of the year. Their efforts to survive the holiday season are challenged by the arrival of their own mothers, which provides a type of backstory for how these women became who they are.

Amy (Kunis) has her own interest in creating a traditional Christmas challenged by her type-A, extremely wealthy yet selfish mother Ruth (Christine Baranski), who constantly upstages her daughter and becomes a terror in the process. Kristen Bell's Kiki character, as plucky as she is, is revealed to have an even more positively intense mother in the shape of Sandy (Cheryl Hines), who brings up the question of how overbearing parents can be, with loving intentions, before it's too late (Sandy spontaneously buys a house next to Kiki's as a surprise, for one). Ragtag Bad Mom Carla (Kathryn Hahn) has her own dysfunctional relationship with her free-spirited mother Isis (Susan Sarandon, intentionally cast for her rebellious presence but gravely underused), who may just be back in Carla's life merely to get money, and is even less responsible than Carla is.

Written and directed by Scott Moore and Jon Lucas, this is the latest in their batch of party comedies (which includes the screenplay for *The Hangover* [2009], their directorial debut *21 & Over* [2013]), in which liberated, immature shenanigans are cut between a desire to feign some type of heart. With this film, it leads to numerous scenes that are eye-rolling, whether of the forced comedy or drama variety, with the mothers owning the title designation by getting drunk, smoking weed, destroying things, and then reconciling their own stresses of being mothers in the next scene.

Yet as the movie lacks much charisma with its shoehorned, over-drawn comedy, the relationships it shows on the mend become all the more tedious, especially when the cartoonish characteristics of the new moms prove to have little behind them as well. Lucas and Moore work with very broad, universal topics (motherhood, the stresses of the holidays), and offer basic food for thought about what is most important for both, but the sentiment is as thin as a greeting card with a naughty word in it.

As was the case with the original film, the most valuable player here is Hahn, who is able to play raucous but heartfelt with an archetypical character. While the script does her few favors throughout, she does have a great scene with a male stripper named Ty (Justin Hartley) at her waxing job, making a meet-cute that is a rare spark for Lucas and Moore's script. The two play flirtatious yet innocent as she waxes his nether regions, and Hahn's ability to provide nuance to a character initially thought to be a mere clown shines yet again.

The now-franchise's idea of fun is sporadic sequences set to aggressive rock or rap music, often within malls or distinctive stores, or other places where moms are expected to be "good." Slow-motion is used for emphasis on the purportedly wacky physical comedy, but its repetitive nature makes it seem like it is also being used to expand the film's running time. Like with *Bad Moms*, the goofiness plays out like music videos, its holiday antics never one to resist product placement. An entire bonding sequence with all of the moms and children is even set inside a trampoline factory, with Sarandon later wearing a baseball cap brandishing the logo.

There is a complete lack of edge to a movie like *A Bad Moms Christmas*, its naughty fun leading to a tame R-rated debauchery. Viewers offended by jokes about sex or explicit words, or those shocked at the idea of women cutting loose in public, may find the movie a bit more liberated. But even with its usage of bad language, milking every swear as if it were skateboarding on the sidewalk, is old hat in the scheme of various non-extreme "bad" movies. A movie can only be so "bad" when its largest antics involve stealing a Christmas tree from a Foot Locker.

Nick Allen

CREDITS

Amy: Mila Kunis
Kiki: Kristen Bell
Carla: Kathryn Hahn
Ruth: Christine Baranski
Isis: Susan Sarandon
Origin: United States
Language: English
Released: 2017
Production: Suzanne Todd; Huayi Brothers Media; released by STX Entertainment
Directed by: Jon Lucas; Scott Moore
Written by: Jon Lucas; Scott Moore
Cinematography by: Mitchell Amundsen
Music by: Christopher Lennertz
Sound: Kami Asgar; Erin Oakley
Music Supervisor: Julia Michels
Editing: James Thomas
Costumes: Julia Caston
Production Design: Marcia Hinds
MPAA rating: R
Running time: 104 minutes

REVIEWS

Catsoulis, Jeannette. *New York Times.* November 2, 2017.
Erbland, Kate. *IndieWire.* November 1, 2017.
Frosch, Jon. *Hollywood Reporter.* November 1, 2017.
Greenblatt, Leah. *Entertainment Weekly.* November 1, 2017.
MacDonald, Moira. *Seattle Times.* November 1, 2017.
Merry, Stephanie. *Washington Post.* November 1, 2017.

Nicholson, Amy. *Uproxx*. November 1, 2017.
Noveck, Jocelyn. *Associated Press*. November 3, 2017.
Walsh, Katie. *Tribune News Service*. November 1, 2017.
Yoshida, Emily. *New York Magazine/Vulture*. October 31, 2017.

QUOTES

Carla (to Ty): "Put a baby in me Santa number two!"

TRIVIA

This is the first sequel for a movie in which she appeared in the original that Mila Kunis has made; she played the lead in *American Psycho II: All American Girl* (2002), but wasn't in the original film.

AWARDS

Nominations:

Golden Raspberries 2017: Worst Support. Actress (Sarandon)

THE BALLAD OF LEFTY BROWN

Box Office: $7,856

"This is the West," says the newspaper editor at the end of John Ford's great film, *The Man Who Shot Liberty Valance* (1962). "When the legend becomes fact, print the legend." No other art form is so central to American ideas, and informed by psychology, character, and action. The matter of authenticity, a divide between the real and the self-declared, is also fundamental to any telling. The Western touches all sides and moves in any direction, revival, revisionist, theatrical, or the wholly made up.

The very title, *The Ballad of Lefty Brown*, acknowledges a narrative history both defiant and open-ended. The film is archetype or song, a special telling or re-imagining of personality standing astride a specific history. This second feature by the young American director Jared Moshé is a tribute to the great works that preceded it. Peter Fonda, for instance, has a small though vital part as an idealistic frontiersman. His presence and his remarkable physical and vocal resemblance to his father, Henry Fonda, instinctively summon the great Westerns that Henry Fonda made with John Ford, like *My Darling Clementine* (1946).

The director's first film, *Dead Man's Burden* (2012), was a post-Civil War Western set on the New Mexico frontier. Both of his films are taken from his own scripts. His new movie conforms to the requirements of the form—painterly shots of vistas, open landscapes and movement. The deeper question is whether the filmmaker is willing to either undercut or deepen his own ideas and find something different to tell. That very history is also a terrible burden for any director. Inviting comparisons to some of the greatest films ever made sets up a pattern of expectations virtually impossible to meet. *The Ballad of Lefty Brown* works best when it moves against the grain, upending expectation and finding its own variations on themes and style.

The movie is set in Montana, in 1899, as the territories are being formally incorporated into becoming the 41st state. In the early movements, Moshé maps out an interesting in-between state, a society in transition between a brutal past and encroaching modernization. Lefty Brown (Bill Pullman), trusted sidekick with a colorful past as a soldier and cowboy, accompanies his friend, Edward Johnson (Peter Fonda), in carrying out his particular brand of Old Testament-inflected frontier justice against a killer.

Johnson is preparing to embark on a career as a newly-elected senator and official government representative. A skilled capitalist rancher who operates a massive spread with his wife, Laura (Kathy Baker), Johnson is also an idealist ready to challenge the system. Rustlers ambush the two friends, Lefty and Johnson, as the pair share a final moment of reminiscence. Guilt ridden over his failure to protect his friend, Lefty sets out to track the killers.

In its own manner, *The Ballad of Lefty Brown* is an anti-Western given how the point of view shifts from the stoic and skilled lawman to his shambling sideman, modeled on the sort Walter Brennan specialized in Howard Hawks' great *Rio Bravo* (1959), the type who speaks softly, inelegantly, and works in a seemingly passive register and continually undermines the very notion of authority or direct action.

Moshé works hard to invigorate the traditional chase and pursuit pattern. The director has a good feel for character, best represented with the introduction of the fresh-faced and itinerant kid, Jeremiah (Diego Josef) Lefty takes in. The kid has natural instincts and moxie, if not exactly the kind of experience necessary for the job. He has a conception, or idea, more than a concrete feeling for the specifics of the West, shaped by his incessant reading of dime store novels, the very stories that Lefty was a participant in. "That there is why you are never going to be written about in any of these books," Jeremiah says just as they corner the men responsible, thinking Lefty's plan lacks initiative.

These moments show the film off to its best advantage. Josef is a talented young actor and Pullman is an old pro, grizzled, craggy, and avuncular. The back and forth between the two has a quiet and touching vulnerability that brings a sharp range of humor, feeling, and warmth.

Moshé is also a decent visual stylist who is aided immeasurably by a very fine cinematographer, David McFarland. The movie develops a sharp contrast between the open vistas and Big Mountain landscape and the more claustrophobic, fragmentary bursts captured in the shootout between Lefty and the killers. The soundtrack is also skillfully assembled, a tight and expressive blending of noise, fear, and the sense of violation. Up to this point *The Ballad of Lefty Brown* seems a superior example of its kind, in part because of how skillfully it acknowledges and plays off its own archetypes. The rhythms are more secure, flavorful, and interesting in the first half.

The second half is becomes more beholden to those received ideas rather than trying to find something fresh to say. Moshé works through but never quite satisfactorily deepens the tonal changes by the major plot revelation, the realization that Johnson's death was a political assassination possibly reaching to the highest levels of local government.

The themes of paranoia and suspicion align with the anti- or revisionist Western motifs in the first half. It also shows how the modernist flair, a critique of capitalism, a pervading sense of corruption and self-dealing, are poorly developed or feel out of place. Moshé slowly surrenders control as the demands of plot suffocate the movie's second and least interesting part, as Lefty must prove his innocence after he is framed for the killing. Making matters worse, the director's native talent for set pieces and action scenes is undone by the preposterousness of the set-up. This yields a drawn out and drab showdown with the governor (Jim Caviezel) at the center of the dark and treacherous network of activity.

In language, thought, even the evocative character touches, *The Ballad of Lefty Brown* evokes a privileged past that also illustrates something vital missing from its center.

Patrick Z. McGavin

CREDITS

Lefty Brown: Bill Pullman
Edward Johnson: Peter Fonda
Oak: Joseph Lee Anderson
Biscuit: Michael Spears
Laura Johnson: Kathy Baker
Origin: United States
Language: English
Released: 2017
Production: Neda Armian, Dan Burks, Edward Parks, Jared Moshe; Armian Pictures, Higher Content, Om Films; released by A24 Films LLC
Directed by: Jared Moshe
Written by: Jared Moshe
Cinematography by: David McFarland
Music by: H. Scott Salinas
Sound: Bryan Parker
Editing: Terel Gibson
Costumes: Jonny Pray
Production Design: Eve McCarney
MPAA rating: Unrated
Running time: 111 minutes

REVIEWS

Dargis, Manohla. *New York Times.* December 14, 2017.
DeFore, John. *Hollywood Reporter.* October 20, 2017.
Kenny, Glenn. *RogerEbert.com.* December 15, 2017.
King, Danny. *Village Voice.* December 21, 2017.
Kohn, Eric. *IndieWire.* April 14, 2017.
Leydon, Joe. *Variety.* April 14, 2017.
Lund, Carson. *Slant Magazine.* December 16, 2017.
Solzman, Danielle. *Consequence of Sound.* May 26, 2017.
Turan, Kenneth. *Los Angeles Times.* December 14, 2017.
Vishnevetsky, Ignatiy. *The A.V. Club.* December 12, 2017.

BAND AID

Misery loves accompaniment.
—Movie tagline

Box Office: $248,370

The actor, playwright, and director Zoe Lister-Jones has a disarmingly droll, though bracing, delivery that hits like a dart. In her debut feature, *Band Aid*, which she wrote, directed, and stars in, Lister-Jones shows an unflappable style and cutting wit. Even when throwing off zingers, she remains uncommonly cool. In one wonderful scene, visiting the home of her neighbor, a recovering sex addict, the Lister-Jones's character happens upon one of several beautiful, wayward women seemingly using the space as a private sanctuary and asks: "Are you here of your own free will?"

It is a sharp moment—sly, funny, and observant, and Lister-Jones infuses the exchange with a great aplomb and nerve. The story plays out in the radiant Southern California light, but the humor and rhythms are New York and Jewish. It's seemingly self-deprecatingly and deadpan, but it is also barbed and aggressive. The movie plays off a deeply secular Jewish idea, that everything is performance, or material. The notion of a bickering couple that uses music as a means of reconciliation is a natural outgrowth.

At its best, the movie is fast and quick and comes at unsuspecting angles. The particular tone is signaled immediately, with the central couple, Anna (Lister-Jones) and her husband, Ben (Adam Pally), introduced in a quickly escalating argument inside their kitchen. He wants her to be more open and generous about their sex life; she wants him to be more responsible, like doing the dishes. They know each other's weaknesses and pressure points. No area, seemingly, is taboo or out-of-bounds, even in one riotous early joke about Holocaust survivors.

The movie is a comedy of manners about the most redoubtable of institutions, a portrait of a marriage seemingly on the verge of collapse. Young, smart, and attractive, the couple seems engaged in a mode of open warfare, perpetually on edge and given little room or opportunity to just live in the moment. Lister-Jones works in her own idiom, loose and spontaneous. She finds her own vernacular, a hipster stoner married couple comedy.

The conflict is sharpened with them, into heartbreak and disgust, since it appears they are only truly alive and uninhibited when they are at each other's throats. The vicissitudes, compromises, and struggles of the creative life have wiped them out and shuttered them emotionally. Amy demonstrated great promise and talent as a writer, but now that part of her life is a cruel and bitter memory signified by her cancelled book contract.

Now she works as a driver for Uber. (The promised autonomy of the digital economy, she discovers, in a hilarious and discomfiting montage, is just more of the same, being subjected to outrageous displays of male privilege and self-regard). At least the job provides some distance from Ben, who has also succumbed to the path of least resistance. His talent for graphic design and visual artist is now wasted as he barely musters the time, energy, or inspiration to turn out corporate logos. Most days, it appears, he barely has the motivation to get out of his bathrobe.

Lister-Jones is also highly attuned to a natural fact of all marriages. They are bound not simply by the emotional, sexual, or personal dynamics of the individuals though further stressed by complications brought out by nexus of family and friends. The imposition of Ben's mother, for instance, with her intimate inquiries into the most personal of subjects, for instance, feels particularly intrusive for Anna. The early sections are wired and whip smart, because the jokes go either way, from the personal to the political. Even the couple's therapist (Retta) is exasperated, though impressed, by the acuity and intelligence of their put-downs.

At a kids' birthday party, the level of discomfort occasionally cuts too close for comfort. A quiet moment of improvisation messing around with some children's musical instruments (and the influence of weed) is just the inspiration Anna needs to redraw the terms of their relationship. She wants to start a band as a way to mediate their conflict and pain by liberating themselves creatively, returning to zero, as it were, of their youth and idealism.

Anna dusts off an old bass and guitar and two go to work riffing with each other, drawing on the particulars of their arguments and the simplicity, power, and freedom unleashed by their creative energy to soften the pain and torment. The playing of music becomes a way for the two to talk back and forth, in lyrics, notes, and sound rather than out of anger or defensiveness. Right from the start, playing in their garage, the two achieve a kind of delicate balance, of warmth, compromise, and subtlety of expression. Musically they are accomplished amateurs, bristling with energy and individual flourishes.

Things turn up a perverse notch by the wild card, dramatically, in the serendipitous appearance of the couple's peculiar next-door neighbor, Dave (Fred Armisen). His studied weirdness and apparent kink notwithstanding, he is a gifted drummer and the couple recruit him into the act.

Lister-Jones is doing a lot here (she even wrote the lyrics, with Kyle Forester). Her directing style is clean, observant, and direct without ever being derivative. Significantly, the primary technical collaborators are mostly women. The cinematographer, Hillary Spera, has a fluent and easy style. The light is often lyrical but the colors are muted, even shaded. The night photography, especially the Los Angeles clubs where the trio, under name Dirty Dishes perform, is rhapsodic. Libby Cuenin's editing is also fast and persuasive. The songs are both oblique and direct (including titles like "Love is Lying" and "Mood"). They are not profound or memorable, but that is precisely the point.

That tension or vulnerability Lister-Jones conjures is more potent given how fully she is in control of her own image, her own ideas, as an actor and director. She is sexy and beautiful enough to play the romantic lead, but she is also very good at sublimating her feelings and ideas. There is a plaintive sadness, a melancholy, even when the humor is screamingly funny. The dramatic revelation of the deeply personal incident of loss that colors and frames her actions is not surprising, but her underplaying remains deeply moving. Pally is also a compelling presence, mercurial and funny but also withholding in a way that deepens the performance. Armisen is a singular and daft performer, with his contorted body language and eerie vocal pitch.

If anything, Lister-Jones is almost too much of a good thing. *Band Aid* has the typical imperfections and occasional flatness endemic to a first film. At times, Lister-Jones is playing to the crowd, with some of the raunchier moments. Structurally the last third has probably too many reversals and shifts to fully assimilate. *Band Aid* is small and self-contained, but its pleasures are deep.

Patrick Z. McGavin

CREDITS

Anna: Zoe Lister-Jones
Ben: Adam Pally
Dave: Fred Armisen
Shirley: Susie Essman
Grace: Hannah Simone
Origin: United States
Language: English
Released: 2017
Production: Natalia Anderson, Zoe Lister-Jones; Mister Lister Films, QC Entertainment; released by IFC Films
Directed by: Zoe Lister-Jones
Written by: Zoe Lister-Jones
Cinematography by: Hillary Spera
Music by: Lucius
Sound: Penny Harold
Music Supervisor: Alison Rosenfeld
Editing: Libby Cuenin
Costumes: Sarah Fleming
Production Design: Hillary Gurtler
MPAA rating: R
Running time: 91 minutes

REVIEWS

Barker, Andrew. *Variety.* March 24, 2017.
Dowd, A.A. *The A.V. Club.* June 1, 2017.
Goodykoontz, Bill. *Arizona Republic.* June 15, 2017.
Kenigsberg, Ben. *New York Times.* June 1, 2017.
LaSalle, Mick. *San Francisco Chronicle.* June 7, 2017.
Linden, Sheri. *Hollywood Reporter.* March 24, 2017.
O'Sullivan, Michael. *Washington Post.* June 8, 2017.
Walsh, Katie. *Los Angeles Times.* June 1, 2017.
Wilson, Calvin. *St. Louis Post-Dispatch.* June 15, 2017.
Wolfe, April. *Village Voice.* May 31, 2017.

QUOTES

Ben: "The sensation I get from sex and the sensation I get from eating pizza, it's like, interchangeable for me at this point."

TRIVIA

Actors Colin Hanks, Zoe Lister-Jones, and Angelique Cabral all star together in the sitcom *Life in Pieces.*

BATTLE OF THE SEXES

He made a bet. She made history.
—Movie tagline

Box Office: $12.6 Million

Two-thousand seventeen became a year in which unheard people, particularly women and African Americans, were increasingly vocal in their demand for change. Co-directors Jonathan Dayton and Valerie Faris's wonderful *Battle of the Sexes,* which, on the surface, details a man vs. woman tennis match between world class tennis champion Billie Jean King and former men's tennis great Bobby Riggs in 1977, couldn't seem more timely. Yet, for as excellent as the film is (and it's one of the best of the year) one cannot help but feel chagrined that the white patriarchal heteronormativity on display throughout the film does not feel at all removed from where people are today in the viewpoint of those upholding the gross and outdated ideals in "Trump's America."

Battle of the Sexes has been promoted as a biopic detailing a wildly-hyped tennis match between self-proclaimed "Male Chauvinist Pig" Bobby Riggs (Steve Carell) and "Women's Libber" Billie Jean King (Emma Stone). But the film really only uses the tennis match as a kind of shelf to place a very well-told story about Billie Jean King, a woman who was not only one of the finest tennis players ever, but also a righteous woman who put her own career and legend at stake to fight for women's rights. It's a shame more people in modern society aren't aware of what King did to try and fix the disparity between equal pay between genders. Perhaps *Battle of the Sexes* will help shed some light on her truly brave and boundary-pushing life.

In many ways, *Battle of the Sexes* is a biopic about Billie Jean King. Or, perhaps it just feels that way as Bobby Riggs is a bit of an empty suit both onscreen and apparently in real life. Well-known in the 1970s as a gambler, ham, and hustler, Carell's interpretation of the pro-tennis hall of famer does not leave much room for empathy as the film opens with him daydreaming in a stuffy office job, mentally rehashing days of old on the court. Always looking for an angle, a light bulb goes off when he sees a television news snippet wherein King, after winning a major championship, speaks out about the fact that women make less than men on the pro-circuit. While viewers know what Riggs will ultimately do (challenge King to a man versus woman tennis match, designed to "put women back in their place"), the filmmakers don't really do much with Riggs aside from set him on a collision course with King. Yet, this isn't really a complaint as the story of Billie Jean King is much more compelling than that of her competitor.

As King, Stone completely embodies the character without feeling like an imitation. Her vocal inflections and body language portray King exactly as remembered in her 1970s heyday. After winning a major tennis open, King is invited to defend her title at another big event. Realizing her position of power, she goes toe to toe with

Jack Kramer (Bill Pullman), the head of the United Lawn Tennis Association, demanding as much money as the professional men's tennis players receive. In a rebuttal that feels straight out of the mouth of a 2017 Trump-supporting male chauvinist, Kramer denies the pay boost for a variety of paltry excuses, thus forcing King, alongside her longtime secretary Marilyn Barnett (Sarah Silverman), to form their own professional women's tennis circuit. It's an incredibly bold move that ultimately pays off not just for King and her fellow women tennis players, but also financially as sponsors begin coming in, including cigarette manufacturer Phillip-Morris who ironically use the events to promote ladies cigarette Virginia Slims. Yet what makes *Battle of the Sexes* a top-notch biopic isn't just a fascinating true story with excellent performances, it's the way the film feels like it plopped into the modern day multiplex straight out of a 1977 movie theater.

A heated debate is currently underway in the world of cinema and it concerns the use of nostalgia on-screen. Long story short, many feel that big-budget blockbusters like the *Star Wars* franchise and Netflix's hugely popular *Stranger Things* series (by ways of example) are relying on shots, graphics, color palettes, and characterizations that are meant to play on the emotions of the viewers who are psychologically attached to older material without really giving them anything new. The issue therein for many is that these nostalgia-based films and series are merely a paint-by-numbers recreation of previously loved material, thus making them a recreation rather than a new work. What makes *Battle of the Sexes* dip a toe into this nostalgia-based arena but then ultimately move past it is the clever and keen vision of directors Dayton and Faris, as realized via cinematographer Linus Sandgren, who is quickly establishing himself as a major name in filmmaking with *American Hustle* (2013) and *La La Land* (2016), which won him Oscar gold. But again, *Battle of the Sexes* doesn't marinate in nostalgic-looking 1970s cinema just for the sake of doing so, it flat out steals from it with such a depth of detail it develops its own look entirely.

Film historians and mere fans of the form will love seeing the janky, awkward edits so reminiscent of 1970s cinema as it grew away from the studio system, thus forging a more raw and unpolished look. Wonky, warbling sound also imbues *Battle of the Sexes* with a delightful sense of old cinema rendered new. Also impressive is the way the film's aged looking film stock isn't afraid to get into a near extreme close-up on a character's face as truths are being revealed about things like Riggs' inferiority complex or King's previously (at least in terms of the film) unknown attraction to women. As is common knowledge now and, of somewhat greater acceptance, Billie Jean King would later come out as a lesbian after being "outed" in 1981. However, in *Battle of the Sexes*, her choice of partners is merely blossoming as she begins a secretive affair with a free-spirited hairdresser named Marilyn Barnett (Andrea Riseborough). This plot point is at once handled in a sweet, delicate way that also allows for harsh realities such as the fact King is married to a man (Austin Stowell) and there's a large chunk of potentially lost advertising and marketing should the world know King is gay.

Yet what makes *Battle of the Sexes* so masterful and compelling is the way the film maintains a sort of seventies sweetness while still revealing unfair sexual politics as dictated by aging white men who are very bad at concealing their fear of women rising. And again, making this even more upsetting is how much many of these men and their opinions are still the "norm" these days, even as women have proven themselves to be equal in every sense of the word. Another area *Battle of the Sexes* excels in is hitting viewers with hard truths while not feeling condescending or as if they are shouting for equality. Throughout the film, one never feels as though Riggs truly believes the chauvinism he's espousing but rather, he's cashing in or playing on the antiquated, shortsighted ideals of those who seek to deny women their equality. King's sexuality is also handled in a delicate yet honest way that really makes one believe in the burgeoning love affair between King and Barnett. Also interesting to note is the fact many who lived through the much buzzed about Riggs-King tennis match or saw the fairly recent ESPN "30 for 30" film *The Match Maker* (2013) still can't remember how the whole match shook out. Therefore the tennis match itself becomes compelling as viewers sit courtside, willing King, and moreso all women, to victory.

Don R. Lewis

CREDITS

Billie Jean King: Emma Stone

Bobby Riggs: Steve Carell

Marilyn Barnett: Andrea Riseborough

Rosie Casals: Natalie Morales

Gladys Heldman: Sarah Silverman

Origin: United States

Language: English

Released: 2017

Production: Danny Boyle, Christian Colson, Robert Graf; Cloud Eight Films, Decibel Films, TSG Entertainment; released by Fox Searchlight Pictures

Directed by: Jonathan Dayton; Valerie Faris

Written by: Simon Beaufoy

Cinematography by: Linus Sandgren

Music by: Nicholas Britell
Sound: Mildred Iatrou; Ai-Ling Lee
Editing: Pamela Martin
Art Direction: Alexander Wei
Costumes: Mary Zophres
Production Design: Judy Becker
MPAA rating: PG-13
Running time: 121 minutes

REVIEWS

Ehrlich, David. *IndieWire.* September 2, 2017.
Gray, Christopher. *Slant Magazine.* September 28, 2017.
Greenblatt, Leah. *Entertainment Weekly.* September 21, 2017.
Lane, Anthony. *New Yorker.* September 18, 2017.
LaSalle, Mick. *San Francisco Chronicle.* September 21, 2017.
McCarthy, Todd. *Hollywood Reporter.* September 10, 2017.
McDonald, Moira. *Seattle Times.* September 27, 2017.
Smith, Anna. *Time Out New York.* September 23, 2017.
Wilkinson, Alissa. *Vox.* September 28, 2017.
Wolfe, April. *Village Voice.* September 28, 2017.

TRIVIA

In 1973, Billie Jean King was 29 and Bobby Riggs was 55. At the time of filming, actress Emma Stone was 28 and actor Steve Carell was 54.

AWARDS

Nominations:

Golden Globes 2018: Actor--Mus./Comedy (Carell), Actress--Mus./Comedy (Stone)

Screen Actors Guild 2017: Actor--Supporting (Carell)

BAYWATCH

Go ahead and stare.
—Movie tagline

Beaches ain't ready,
—Movie tagline

Don't worry, summer is coming.
—Movie tagline

Get your guard on.
—Movie tagline

Box Office: $58.1 Million

Perhaps at some point converting the television drama *Baywatch* (1989-2001) into an R-rated comedy with traces of *21 Jump Street* (2012) seemed like a good idea. It would allow the material to reference its own silliness and maybe even amp up the sexuality of the series that made Pamela Anderson a star and taught viewers worldwide about the importance of slow-motion running on the beach.

It is safe to say, however, that any notions of an inspired, sequel-generating adaptation deflated about twelve minutes into the studio's first viewing of the movie as inexplicable lifeguard candidate Ronnie Greenbaum (Jon Bass) finds his genitalia stuck in a chair. If this were a quick, unfunny cutaway gag, executives might have groaned and still hoped for the best. Yet director Seth Gordon, whose career after the spectacular documentary *The King of Kong: A Fistful of Quarters* (2007) contains awful, mean-spirited comedies like *Horrible Bosses* (2011) and *Identity Thief* (2013), allows this sequence to drag on. And on. And on. Not only is the set piece taken from the very bottom of the Farrelly brothers' garbage can, but it is the sort of awful attempt at humor that pretty much guarantees a very long two hours ahead.

Even more astonishing, however, is how quickly this exhausting and pointless exercise in raunch and snark deprives the effortlessly appealing Dwayne Johnson of his charm. Instead of just allowing top dog lifeguard Mitch Buchannon (Johnson) and his 500 career saves to exude warmth and authority, writers Damian Shannon and Mark Swift (whose experience on *Freddy vs. Jason* [2003] and the remake of *Friday the 13th* [2009] really should not have landed them this job) force him to spout out insults that would not have worked for Dr. Cox (John C. McGinley) on *Scrubs* (2001-2010). Attempting to cut dishonored Olympic gold medalist and wannabe lifeguard Matt Brody (Zac Efron) down to size, Mitch resorts to really sharp material like calling him One Direction, New Kids on the Block, and 'NSync—all in the same scene. Later, he refers to him as Justin Bieber and *High School Musical* (2006), wink wink. It cannot be overstated how little thought seems to have been put into the entirety of *Baywatch*, from these obnoxious one-liners to the one-dimensional subplot of a blatantly villainous real estate magnate (Priyanka Chopra) who may also be a drug dealer.

Plus, it is not as if those elements were shrugged off in favor of heart-pounding action sequences or camaraderie among the cast. Gordon utilizes slow motion whenever possible, effectively taking away the urgency of lifeguard rescues and fawning over the saviors (Michael Bay would have had more fun worshiping the heroes and drawn a little more drama from the victims as well). Meanwhile, each mini-drama fails to coalesce into any type of whole. This includes Mitch and Matt's bickering; Matt's attempted flirtation with Summer Quinn (Alexandra Daddario), another lifeguard-in-training; and Ronnie's inability to form words in the presence of CJ

Parker (Kelly Rohrbach), a lifeguard who shows him sweetness no matter how many times he really, really, really does not deserve it.

Considering how little prior knowledge of the property is required, it would not have been hard for a *Baywatch* revival to provide escapist entertainment and, despite being a reboot, stand out from its superhero-driven summer competition. Yet, much like recent adaptations of *The Smurfs* (2011), *Entourage* (2015), and *Chips* (2017), *Baywatch* lacks ideas, sharpness, and an ability to harness what made the source material successful in the first place. Sure, corny jokes and cleavage are on-brand, but the movie's blend of underdog sheepishness and muscular bro culture makes for an awkward blend of 1980s, 1990s, and 2000s and unfolds like a trailer for itself. *Pain and Gain* (2013) knew how to have fun with sharp physiques and weak minds; *Baywatch* provides no effort and then tries too hard, like the first-time marathon runner who does not train, immediately breaks an ankle, and then keeps on hobbling along.

That means a scene in which Mitch giggles while telling Matt to inspect a dead man's genitals in the morgue and jokes whose punch lines reference Stevie Wonder and Stephen Hawking. (Two other memorable abominations: Mitch declaring, "You're going night-night, bitch," and "Bath time, shithead" when a guy with a diaper pail on his head falls in a pool.) Victoria Leeds (Chopra) responds to Matt calling her crazy by saying, "If I was a man you'd call me driven," an odd line for a movie that makes sure to ogle Rohrbach whenever possible. Surprisingly enough, she's the cast member who emerges cleanest, perhaps because the *Sports Illustrated* swimsuit model benefits from low expectations, or because she acquits herself well to CJ's genuine goodness (despite the movie treating her purely as a fantasy object to be obtained) or because anyone would look professional next to Bass's knockoff Josh Gad routine. Which is excruciating enough when Gad does it.

There is merit in the mystique of the lifeguard, and an early moment when two young guys claim they heard Mitch invented Google and cured the common cold speak to the potential for connecting the iconic lifesavers to the community they support. Not surprisingly, that quickly falls down the list of priorities that give primary attention to the professional and romantic fates of the hotshot white guy and the dweeby white guy. The abundance of people who define the world that way in 2017 only reinforce how much movies, including a piece of childish nostalgia like *Baywatch*, need to look ahead, even when mining the past for ideas and especially when the target audience is young men who see themselves as the sharks and everyone else as the sand.

Matt Pais

CREDITS

Mitch Buchannon: Dwayne "The Rock" Johnson
Matt Brody: Zac Efron
Victoria Leeds: Priyanka Chopra
Summer Quinn: Alexandra Daddario
CJ Parker: Kelly Rohrbach
Origin: United States
Language: English
Released: 2017
Production: Michael Berk, Gregory J. Bonann, Beau Flynn, Ivan Reitman, Douglas Schwartz; Huahua Media, Shanghai Film Group Corp, Uncharted; released by Paramount Pictures Corp.
Directed by: Seth Gordon
Written by: Damian Shannon; Mark Swift
Cinematography by: Eric Steelberg
Music by: Christopher Lennertz
Sound: Elmo Weber
Music Supervisor: Todd Bozung
Editing: Peter S. Elliott
Art Direction: Tom Frohling
Costumes: Dayna Pink
Production Design: Shepherd Frankel
MPAA rating: R
Running time: 116 minutes

REVIEWS

Duralde, Alonso. *TheWrap*. May 23, 2017.
Kenny, Glenn. *RogerEbert.com*. May 24, 2017.
Mecca, Dan. *The Film Stage*. May 24, 2017.
Merry, Stephanie. *Washington Post*. May 25, 2017.
Mondello, Bob. *NPR*. May 27, 2017.
Phillips, Michael. *Chicago Tribune*. May 24, 2017.
Roeper, Richard. *Chicago Sun-Times*. May 24, 2017.
Rose, Steve. *The Guardian*. May 23, 2017.
Smith, Patrick. *The Telegraph*. May 23, 2017.
Stevens, Dana. *Slate*. May 25, 2017.

QUOTES

Mitch Buchannon: "There's your cot, don't jack off on my sheets."

TRIVIA

Zac Efron supplied Dwayne Johnson with all the names to call him in the movie, like "One Direction" and "Bieber."

AWARDS

Nominations:

Golden Raspberries 2017: Worst Actor (Efron), Worst Picture, Worst Remake/Sequel, Worst Screenplay

BEACH RATS

Box Office: $473,771

There's a good reason no one much invokes the name Pier Paolo Pasolini in modern film criticism. Too few people capture half of what he was good at, let alone all of it. Eliza Hittman, in her second feature, no less, has made a film worthy of Pasolini at his best. She has his ability to poetically reframe neorealist story tropes as a mythic, romantic spiral towards the abyss. She shifts his chosen milieu (rotting seaside Italian villages and near-deserted country towns) to Coney Island without losing any of the depressing specificity. Both places feel almost biblical in their housing the search for dignity through self-annihilation. You could picture *Beach Rats* transpiring beat for beat with Pasolini's sweaty, sensual holy fools with unibrows and nothing at all would be lost. She's made a film that achieves a sort of temporal transcendence through commitment to place and bodies.

Beach Rats concerns Frankie (Harris Dickinson), a closeted gay man who has not quite reached adulthood. College is never brought up, and it's summertime so his mother, Donna (Kate Hodge) does not mention pending responsibilities. Frankie's routine is aimless but steady. He hangs out with his three closest friends—Nick (Frank Hakaj), Alexei (David Ivanov), and Jesse (Anton Selyaninov)—who seem similarly unmoored from responsibility and their own families. He argues with his sister Carla (Nicole Flyus), cannot quite come to terms with his invalid father dying from his sickbed in the small living room of the family's cramped apartment, and spends his nights locked in his bedroom cruising a gay men's webcam chat site. Frankie has not come out of the closet, and indeed if he knows his own sexuality, he's choosing not to be honest about it with himself or anyone else. By chance, he meets a local girl named Simone (Madeline Weinstein) under the weekly fireworks display on the Coney Island boardwalk. He flirts with her and takes her home, but his mind is on the bare shoulders of his friends and the opportunity to get high and clam up. Frankie botches their moment of intimacy but comes crawling back for forgiveness the following day because he realizes how important it is to appear to have a female romantic interest in his tiny, traditional community. He keeps Simone happy and even feigns sexual interest in her to keep their relationship appear alive. Not that this stops him from taking increasingly big risks with the men he meets online. What begins as flirtations and coy talk turns into seaside hook-ups and motel room trysts. The various fraying threads of Frankie's life come together in a violent way when he decides he cannot keep from being himself when his friends and family alike put pressure on him to be their version of himself.

Beach Rats is a sublime gaze at flowering, yet imprisoned sexuality. Hittman and cinematographer Hélène Louvart fix their patient, open camera at the many bodies on display and find the beauty of everybody who passes before them. There's the faded but potent glamour of Donna, who has passed on her smoking and her reticence to her Adonis-like son. Frankie carries himself with less certainty than his mother, but it's made clear that he owes his mix of introvert tendencies and commanding shyness to her. Hittman never underlines anything because she does such a fine job establishing the boundaries she then blurs over the film's fleet and sexy 96 minute running time. Everyone, from the drifters Frankie has sex with to the young men who call him friend but would judge him if they knew his secret to the young women who float past without ever arousing Frankie's interest—everyone is given a sensual inner life and a sexual exterior. Their humanity comes from their mutual desire. Frankie's sexual attention, positive or negative, grounds them. He cannot measure up in some encounters, and in others he can become a lonely man's whole world. Harris Dickinson's lonely eyes and hangdog expression show off every hurtful word and tossed off insult he's endured in his short life. His neediness, his unwillingness to let anyone walk away from him or stop an online flirtation before its time, is a plain extension of the parental dynamic with which he grew up. The knowledge that his true self is so close to the surface turns every scene into a maelstrom of passion and discovery. Hittman and Louvart film Frankie's beach-set brief encounters with a deliberately shaky light source, as if we in the audience are spying on the men in darkness, a trick borrowed from David Lynch's *Twin Peaks: Fire Walk With Me* (1992). It contrasts magnificently with the neon shapes captured on the boardwalks at night, the smoke from the boys vape pens, and the stern figures in the home Frankie occupies with his family.

The way Hittman watches Frankie and company get high and have sex in their rust-flecked, salt-licked, and sunburnt corner of New York resembles nothing in modern American cinema. It is only the likes of Pasolini or Bernardo Bertolucci, whose earliest films *Accattone* (1961) and *The Grim Reaper* (1962), respectively also watched hopeless men tie themselves in violent knots avoiding the truths in their hearts and souls. Like those Italian modernists, Hittman is not interested in conventional morality, but in seeing how the godless are bent out of shape in traditionally moral, religious environments. Frankie's experience in church, during his father's funeral, sees him quiet and inarticulate in the face of his loss. It's only during sex with older men that he begins to loosen up and articulate some of what he keeps silent everyday. The drugs he uses with his friends and sex with women he does not find attractive are tools for burying his true self that ultimately lead him closer to his identity. The harder he works to conceal this identity, the clearer it becomes that he is not who he pretends to be. Destroying the self can only mean the parts left over are everything you are not. Hittman never overplays her hand, patiently taking in the voluptuous vices Frankie contends with, and waiting for him, and her audience, to come to their own sense of self. Her film is similarly most impressive because of what it's not as well as what it is. It isn't a typical coming-of-age story, nor is it a rote replaying of 1960s world cinema tropes. It's a confident, beautiful, and wholly singular work about identity and community.

Scout Tafoya

CREDITS

Frankie: Harris Dickinson
Simone: Madeline Weinstein
Donna: Kate Hodge
Joe: Neal Huff
Carla: Nicole Flyus
Origin: United States
Language: English
Released: 2017
Production: Brad Becker-Parton, Andrew Goldman, Drew P. Houpt, Paul Mezey; Animal Kingdom, Cinereach, Secret Engine; released by Neon
Directed by: Eliza Hittman
Written by: Eliza Hittman
Cinematography by: Helene Louvart
Music by: Nicholas Leone
Sound: Chris Foster
Music Supervisor: Melissa Chapman; Annie Pearlman
Editing: Scott Cummings; Joe Murphy
Costumes: Olga Mill
Production Design: Grace Yun
MPAA rating: R
Running time: 98 minutes

REVIEWS

Chang, Justin. *Los Angeles Times*. August 24, 2017.
Fujishima, Kenji. *Paste Magazine*. August 24, 2017.
Kenigsberg, Ben. *New York Times*. August 24, 2017.
Lodge, Guy. *Variety*. January 25, 2017.
Nordine, Michael. *TheWrap*. January 25, 2017.
O'Malley, Sheila. *RogerEbert.com*. August 25, 2017.
Rothlopf, Joshua *Time Out New York*. August 23, 2017.
Vishnevetsky, Ignatiy. *The A.V. Club*. August 23, 2017.
Wolfe, April. *The Village Voice*. August 24, 2017.
Zacharek, Stephanie. *Time*. August 24, 2017.

AWARDS

Nominations:

Ind. Spirit 2018: Actor (Dickinson), Cinematog.

BEATRIZ AT DINNER

She was invited, but she's not welcome.
—Movie tagline

Box Office: $7.1 Million

Beatriz at Dinner is bracketed by languorous, idyllically-lovely images depicting a canoe's navigation of a waterway lined with thick, healthy masses of mangroves. These shots are actually assuaging if bittersweet trips back in time and back to Mexico within the world-weary mind of the titular protagonist (Salma Hayek), journeys that are achingly propelled by elegiac longing as much as that paddle. The first precedes her waking to start a day that she eventually chooses to make her last, and the second is just before she enters into eternal—and much-needed—rest. Beatriz had long ago been forced by crushing circumstance to immigrate to America from Tlaltechutli, a fictional village that Aztec aficionados will recognize is named after the ancient civilization's Earth Goddess. That she sprang from there is apt, as this woman who spends part of her time de-stressing the shoulders of others carries the world upon her own, wracked by a deeply-rooted, grave concern for the well-being of both the planet and the overwhelming overabundance of pained living things struggling upon it. Having Beatriz, who is as laudably-intentioned as the film itself, lose her own struggle is quite shocking and yet not at all surprising, as she is like an all-too-absorbent empathetic sponge that is profoundly and permanently weighed-down with worry, strung out because she cannot be wrung out. That Beatriz ultimately gives up is definitely not uplifting, and yet the filmmakers were apparently striving to use this cinematic act of hopelessness as a stimulus to bring about real-life reason to hope.

On the opposite coast of Mexico from nostalgically-glimpsed Guererro sits the world's largest gulf, and while it is never depicted here, what is on display is a different sizable gulf that exists between people of different economic classes, races, political beliefs, and values. Director Miguel Arteta and screenwriter Mike White, who previously collaborated on *Chuck & Buck* (2000) and *The Good Girl* (2002), evidently aimed to rouse a frightfully-polarized populace that seems to care so little about each other and the planet they share. Maybe they can be jolted awake and into taking corrective action like Beatriz at the outset, humanely shushing her adored, bedroom-ensconced pet goat's blaring bleating, lest her neighbor hear and heartlessly silence the animal like he did the angelically-white one whose demise horribly haunts her. While the credits claim that "any similarity to actual persons...is purely coincidental," Beatriz's most shamelessly opposite-opinioned fellow diner is unabashedly reminiscent of what some regard as a similarly-loudmouthed but far-less-cuddly old goat, one currently dwelling within a Washington, D.C., house that is much grander than this lady's modest abode.

Beatriz is positioned on the far side of the aforementioned figurative expanse of troubled water from smugly-surnamed Doug Strutt (a charming/chilling John Lithgow), his initials a mere letter away from those of the 45th president. She is a short, quietly-dedicated Latina immigrant who toils as a holistic healer, and is brimmingly-full of the milk of human kindness. Beatriz palpably stews about mankind's poor stewardship of nature. Doug, in every sense a towering figure and always the charismatic center of attention, is a white, wealthy, native-born, and blithely-voracious developer notoriously-known for his blasé insensitivity and questionable integrity. The only time he wants to get closer to nature is if it will enable him to get off a better shot and guarantee a big-game trophy to go with his trophy (third) wife. Strutt is manifestly full of himself and, well, something else. Thus, when Beatriz, inconsolably-devastated since her hometown was destroyed and her family displaced by a comparably-capitalizing capitalist, keeps staring at this man and expressing a nagging, wary feeling that she recognizes him, many viewers felt a similar sensation.

The person that they could not stop looking at was actually Hayek's Beatriz, suspensefully holding her tongue until too much wine fatefully passes and loosens her lips and enables her to open her mouth and administer an earnest tongue-lashing. Assisted by Arteta's scrutinizing closeups, the decidedly-deglamorized actress is mesmerizing right from Beatriz's intriguingly-inscrutable beginnings. The spiritual character appears to seek consolation from both the Virgin Mary and Buddha, but her own countenance is markedly unlike that of the latter, eternally-beaming religious icon as she contemplates the cancer that is killing a young patient or the pollution that is also slowly but surely exterminating the environment. Apparently, these higher powers have not been able to make her feel less powerless. Beatriz is soon sharply contrasted with the powerful and largely happy-go-lucky upon taking a juxtaposing jaunt down the coast and upscale to give a massage to well-meaning lady of the manse Kathy (effective Connie Britton) in monied Newport Beach, which is ironic since Beatriz, declared by the grateful client to be not just a friend but a saint for wonders once worked upon her chemo-depleted daughter, is the one far more in need of being deeply soothed. The miracle-worker's departure is prevented when her car conks out, and thus an invitation is extended to include her at a dinner given by Kathy and her husband Grant (David Warshofsky) to celebrate a business boon. By the time she does leave, Beatriz herself has also broken down.

The guest list had been comprised of Doug and his comparatively-better half Jeana (Amy Landecker), as well as cunning legal eagle Alex (a jovially-jerky Jay Duplass) and his equally-social-climbing spouse Shannon (Chloë Sevigny). To say that Beatriz will now be included is shown to not be quite accurate. This socially-awkward plain Jane's outsider status is further emphasized when her dressed-up, made-up counterparts (or, more accurately, counterpoints) fail to acknowledge her presence as they walk by, when she is positioned toward one side of the frame while the cattily-cackling other women are grouped toward the other, or when sensibly-soled Beatriz seems even more diminutive and different in the shadow of that in-every-way-well-heeled clique. Doug's assumption that she must be a servant was guaranteed to make viewers wince and squirm.

When dinner is served, one expects that things would get almost as acutely—but far more enjoyably—uncomfortable as the kidney stones discussed here, creating anxious anticipation of a delightfully-painful outcome in which this out-of-place protagonist pointedly puts this cluelessly-condescending lot in theirs. The guests are not the only ones who are provided with a lot to chew on, and there are unquestionably moments that are as delicious for the audience to take in as anything served up at the table. However, things never get as entertainingly excruciating as they should. Doug certainly feels discomfort when an unravelling Beatriz briefly appears to take a literal stab at what might be viewed as fantasized class-action retribution on behalf of those perpetually pained by the president, not actually but aptly taking a letter opener to a cutthroat pain in the neck. (How one is supposed to feel about any vicarious, perverse thrill or subsequent disappointment is worth pondering.) Beatriz does actual harm to Doug's phone upon hurling it at him along with her outraged disdain. She has made a barely perceptible crack in it, and it does not seem that she has more than slightly broken through to give its owner or the other's more than a moment's pause.

Feeling bleak and burnt out, Beatriz is finally and fully extinguished with her death dive into the Pacific while the carefree one-percenters back at the dinner send gaily-glowing wish lanterns up into the night's sky and appallingly boast about having enough legal firepower to defend themselves should a destructive conflagration resultantly ensue in the surrounding environs. Where is the hope in that? "If you actually care about the world, there's no place for you in it," Arteta rather alarming asserted. "The movie is lamenting that." His disconcertingly-dark declaration is almost enough to make one feel like following his forlorn character's extreme example. However, the reaction this worthwhile, critically-praised indie (which barely widened beyond its initial limited release) is likely meant to elicit is not our opting to resignedly head down into the depths of an ocean of despair, but to instead ignite an aspiration to start a conversation—across the table, the political aisle, or whatever divides us—and come up with solutions for what presently plagues and polarizes. Otherwise, akin to those images cited at the outset, we may someday find ourselves collectively up a creek—but without a paddle.

David L. Boxerbaum

CREDITS

Beatriz: Salma Hayek
Doug: John Lithgow
Kathy: Connie Britton
Alex: Jay Duplass
Jeana: Amy Landecker
Shannon: Chloe Sevigny
Origin: United States
Language: English, Spanish
Released: 2017
Production: Aaron L. Gilbert, David Hinojosa, Pamela Koffler, Christine Vachon; Bron Studios, Killer Films; released by FilmNation Entertainment, Roadside Attractions
Directed by: Miguel Arteta
Written by: Mike White
Cinematography by: Wyatt Garfield
Music by: Mark Mothersbaugh
Sound: Dan Snow
Music Supervisor: Margaret Yen
Editing: Jay Deuby
Costumes: Christina Blackaller
Production Design: Ashley Fenton
MPAA rating: R
Running time: 82 minutes

REVIEWS

Burr, Ty. *Boston Globe.* June 14, 2017.
Chang, Justin. *Los Angeles Times.* June 8, 2017.
Gleiberman, Owen. *Variety.* January 25, 2017.
Hornaday, Ann. *Washington Post.* June 15, 2017.
Lane, Anthony. *New Yorker.* June 12, 2017.
Phillips, Michael. *Chicago Tribune.* June 15, 2017.
Roeper, Richard. *Chicago Sun-Times.* June 15, 2017.
Scott, A.O. *New York Times.* June 8, 2017.
Travers, Peter. *Rolling Stone.* June 8, 2017.
Zacharek, Stephanie. *Time.* June 8, 2017.

QUOTES

Beatriz: "All tears flow from the same source."

TRIVIA

This is Mike White and Miguel Arteta's third film together, having previously made *Chuck and Buck* (2000) and *The Good Girl* (2002).

AWARDS

Nominations:

Ind. Spirit 2018: Actress (Hayek), Screenplay

BEAUTY AND THE BEAST

Be our guest.
—Movie tagline

Box Office: $504 Million

There are two scenes in *Beauty and the Beast,* Disney's live-action, CGI-imbued remake of their much-loved 1991 cartoon classic, during which both titular characters undergo a refashioning that fails to turn out quite right. Belle (lovely Emma Watson) is overly outfitted in an elaborate pink ensemble befitting a princess, but not her—the enthusiastic dresser being a wardrobe named Madame de Garderobe (top-drawer vocalist/actress Audra McDonald). This excessive getup designed with gusto by the prima donna-turned-piece-of-furniture just does not make for the best possible presentation. Belle's beastly captor (Dan Stevens), the thoroughly-hirsute suitor with whom she gets tangled up, becomes hairier still with a wig that looks even more ridiculous than hers, and the white powder puffed upon his face looks like an unsightly skin condition in need of a physician (or is it a vet?). This does nothing to enhance his animal magnetism. Too often in this film, it seems as if its animated antecedent has been given the same sort of treatment—a similarly well-intentioned but misguided "more is more" makeover.

This "tale as old as time" (or at least 1740) about Belle and the Beast is presented with too many bells and whistles, admittedly entertaining yet with an excess of extras. It was told far better and more economically twenty-six years ago; the additional forty-five minutes does not add the same amount of enchantment. To utilize lyrics from its title track, the film satisfies most whenever it reverentially tries to seem "ever just the same." However, is there ever a surprise that one will recall happily ever after? Not really. A nostalgic pull is counted upon to help fill theater seats for these Disney do-overs. However, the wistfulness of those watching can just as easily become a hindrance if they are then filled with dissatisfaction every time the remake suffers by comparison to its predecessor—in this case, the first animated feature to be nominated for the Best Picture Academy Award. The well-remembered "Be Our Guest" sequence is here again to speak of fare that is never less than first rate (although its dramatically-pumped-up kineticism almost calls for Dramamine), but what this latest adaptation brings to the table is often either tepidly reheated or overcooked. It is unquestionably "second best," and if one adds Jean Cocteau's *La Belle et la Bete* (1946) to the menu, this version slips further still. As in the scenes referred to at the outset, things really were better off left as they were.

"Oh how divine! Glamour music and magic combine!" Garderobe sings near the beginning in her pre-furnishing finery. "What a display! What a breathtaking, thrilling array! Let us sing with gusto fit to bust!" It is as if director Bill Condon is describing the manner in which he aims to convey the material. He begins his version with the lavish, swirling spectacle of an opulent ball thrown by a profligate prince who has adorned the surface of his superficial, selfish self. After his dismissal of an unexpectedly-powerful old crone, the ugliness of his own exterior comes to match that of his interior until the day his empty heart is filled up with transformative true love. Unfortunately, the movie itself remains hollow.

Belle is given even more cause this time to longingly sing about leaving the staid sameness of life in her 18th century provincial French village, her beloved escapade-filled books still affording the sole means of thrilling escape. Her reason to want to sally forth: local brutally-backward thinking. In the original, the character had merely shared her love of reading with some page-nibbling sheep, but there are much greater ramifications to chew upon here. Watson's Belle, clearly taking a dim view of the town sending solely the boys marching off to school and bright futures, has taken matters into her own hands to make that situation a thing of the past. She has devised a precursor of the washing machine that might help get rid of both ground-in dirt and long-entrenched sexist diminution, a contraption that will free up the laundering lasses for some learning. Here, Belle is shown teaching a lovely little lamb of the human variety, and small-town small-mindedness does not just lead to the singing with benign bemusement of her being "a most peculiar Mademoiselle," but also the viewing of her à la Typhoid Mary as a potentially-dangerous Literacy Belle, infecting with her intellect. There is an attempt to stymie her with the smashing of this imaginative invention, an act that is also meant to break her spirit. There is purposely more potency (and poignancy) this time when she sings, "I want so much more than they've got planned." This girl, one is to sense, may very well have the gumption to someday have everyone singing a very different tune. The character has thus been given a 21st-century feminist-fueled boost up from amongst the pedestrian throng and onto a pedestal. While slight of build, this actress of *Harry Potter* fame imbues her Belle with brainy and brave Hermione heft, as well as the actress' own real-life activist push for equality.

One is to note the pluck of this Belle after her tenderheartedly-devoted father (a nicely-understated Kevin Kline) picks her one of the Beast's roses and is imprisoned within his castle; how she does not wait for the creature to step into the light and reveal his hideousness but has the courage to step towards him instead. The film's own approach to the Beast is unfortunately less praiseworthy: once both unnerving and endearing, he is now less scary, tiresomely morose, petulant, and all too charmless. He is about as forbiddingly chilly and gloomy as the curse-induced conditions outside the castle. As the rose petals ominously fall, one senses a rather leaden rapport developing but not palpable love blooming between he and Belle, certainly nothing captivatingly lovely or sweetly sigh-inducing. Here the two not only bond over The Bard but also through the hardships revealed in explanatory backstories few yearned to have told, which include the tragic, early loss of both their mothers. Belle's heartstring-tugging history comes to light within the dark of a Paris loft to which the odd couple travel back in time via a bewitched book. The tome is the only thing here that is truly transporting.

Despite being a live-action version boasting a Belle with more verve (if less voice), the busyness of its distractingly-decorative décor, or all the swooping, spinning camera movements, things seemed more delightfully alive in the original captivating animated cartoon. Compare the CGI depictions here of Lumiere (an accent-challenged Ewan McGregor), Cogsworth (Ian McKellen), or Mrs. Potts (Emma Thompson) with their animated anthropomorphized alter egos, and there is now a decided deficiency of expressiveness and irresistible appeal. Cogsworth catches a glimpse of his fishwife near the end and wishes over and over that he could turn back into a clock. Although this $160 million-budgeted remake grossed more than a billion dollars worldwide, some fans of the original found themselves sitting in theaters and repeatedly making a similarly-worded wish: to turn back the clock to 1991.

David L. Boxerbaum

CREDITS

Belle: Emma Watson
Beast: Dan Stevens
Gaston: Luke Evans
Lumiere: Ewan McGregor
Maurice: Kevin Kline
Le Fou: Josh Gad
Origin: United States
Language: English
Released: 2017
Production: Don Hahn, David Hoberman, Todd Lieberman; Mandeville Films; released by Walt Disney Pictures
Directed by: Bill Condon
Written by: Evan Spiliotopoulos; Stephen Chbosky
Cinematography by: Tobias A. Schliessler
Music by: Alan Menken
Music Supervisor: Matthew Rush Sullivan
Editing: Virginia Katz
Costumes: Jacqueline Durran
Production Design: Sarah Greenwood
MPAA rating: PG

REVIEWS

Burr, Ty. *Boston Globe.* March 16, 2017.
Chang, Justin. *Los Angeles Times.* March 14, 2017.
Felperin, Leslie. *Hollywood Reporter.* March 3, 2017.
Gleiberman, Owen. *Variety.* March 3, 2017.
Hornaday, Ann. *Washington Post.* March 16, 2017.
Lane, Anthony. *The New Yorker.* March 20, 2017.
Morgenstern, Joe. *Wall Street Journal.* March 16, 2017.
Nashawaty, Chris. *Entertainment Weekly.* March 3, 2017.
Phillips, Michael. *Chicago Tribune.* March 16, 2017.
Scott, A.O. *New York Times.* March 3, 2017.

QUOTES

Lumière: "What if she is the one? The one who will break the spell?"

TRIVIA

Actor Ryan Gosling was originally offered the role of the Beast, but turned it down to appear in *La La Land* (2016) instead. Similarly, actress Emma Watson was offered the lead role in that film, but turned that down to make this one.

AWARDS

Nominations:

Oscars 2017: Costume Des., Production Design
British Acad. 2017: Costume Des., Production Design

BEFORE I FALL

You won't know what happens until it's too late.
—Movie tagline

Box Office: $12.2 Million

On paper, "*Groundhog Day* (1993)-meets-*Mean Girls* (2004)" absolutely could have worked. The sense of endlessness during high school, and how many flawed behaviors might change given the perspective of daily repetition, create an opportunity to explore something fascinating about teenage identity. Who would change, who would not, and does that indicate anything about who these people really are, or only at this time?

Before I Fall, universally and accurately regarded as a dramatic mash-up of these two beloved comedies, has neither fun nor insight to draw from the concept. Instead of a blackly funny examination of adolescent impulses seen through the lens of a time warp, the film, adapted by Maria Maggenti from Lauren Oliver's novel, takes an approach both sanctimonious and simple. Almost instantly upon realizing that she is reliving the same day over and over again, Sam (Zoey Deutch) reevaluates her life choices and decides to become the moral voice of her group of friends, inevitably her school's snotty queen bees who, critically, are not actually bad people but just insecure kids ripe for a lesson about being nice.

Making things worse is cringe-inducing dialogue that just sounds like how an adult guesses that kids talk (Maggenti is in her fifties). "At least we did it right," Lindsay (Halston Sage, looking eerily like a younger version of *Mean Girls* star Rachel McAdams), the group's version of Regina George, says as she reflects on their high school experience. "Kissed the hottest boys, went to the sickest parties." Ouch. That is almost as bad as "Lindsay doesn't do cute; it's not in her lexicon," which sounds like the rare line deemed too phony even for *Dawson's Creek* (1998-2003). (Side note: No one has ever treated "Cupid Day," whatever that is, like it was a national holiday.) Still, even worse is the painfully narrow-minded characterizations surrounding the circle of popular girls, from the grouchy, bullied lesbian ("I'm in hetero-normative hell") to the clique's object of ridicule (played by Elena Kampouris, who, along with *My Big Fat Greek Wedding 2* [2016], *The Cobbler* [2014], *Men, Women and Children* [2014], and *Labor Day* [2013], is racking up an epically terrible filmography) just having stringy hair to Kent (Logan Miller), the nice guy with a crush on Sam. His interactions with the main character are among the most troubling scenes in a film full of them.

Kent is positioned as the alternative to Sam's boyfriend, Rob (Kian Lawley), whose character is presented with really subtle and precise details like a backward hat, a nose ring and a fondness for sitting with his foot on the table. Kent does not possess any of these traits. Yet his controlling, obsessive attention toward Sam is far creepier than it is meant to be. He sends her notes saying "I see you" and "This isn't you" as an attempt to save Sam from the cruelty of her friends, which would seem condescending from anyone and especially strange from someone whom she has not had much interaction with for a decade. Kent is apparently such a saint/dope that ever since Sam did something nice for him when they were kids he has had feelings for her and is sure that the kind girl he remembers is still in there underneath the awful follower she has become as a young adult.

Once again, there could be some tension drawn from Kent's idealistic perception and the more complicated wrinkles in Sam. Except director Ry Russo-Young gets little from Deutch, whose collection of roles in a short window of time seems more a product of being the daughter of Lea Thompson and director Howard Deutch than actually having the talents of a justifiably rising actress. Deutch was dreadful in *Vampire Academy* (2014) and forgettable in the fantastic *Everybody Wants Some!!* (2016), and in *Before I Fall* she sinks to the material's level. At no point does Sam possess the dimensions of a multi-layered teenager going through both common stresses and a very extreme situation, which happens to cycle back to the beginning of each day just after a near-death experience. It is a lot for a young woman to handle, to say nothing of the way the story mangles the butterfly effect and shoehorns in an unnecessary and unfair example of martyrdom. Meanwhile, Sam, who provides horrendous voiceover like "Maybe for you there's a tomorrow...so much time you can bathe in it...but for me there's only today," transitions from off-putting and mean to blandly saved, and Deutch fails to explore the gap in between.

There is merit in presenting high school like a horror movie, with nasty agendas and confused people doing the best they can to survive or die. But *Before I Fall* is not *Heathers* (1988) or *Carrie* (1976). It is a lot closer to *If I Stay,* another excruciating, young adult novel-based hypothetical about death. It has a painfully basic view of Sam's experience, as if not only is this extremely unpleasant person only one day from achieving enlightenment but it would happen right away in the face of an unthinkable situation like living the same day ad nauseum. The film at least could have considered that maybe Sam would try to exploit the opportunity to test her limits a little bit. Or that Juliet (Kampouris) would have prepared a slightly sharper burn of her enemies than just "You're a bitch" if she were planning to take her life that night.

That, however, would require containing anything of substance outside the theoretical benefit of someone bad realizing that actions and words have consequences and turning into someone good at the drop of a hat. Just because the message is right does not prevent everything else from being wrong.

Matt Pais

CREDITS

Samantha Kingston: Zoey Deutch
Lindsay Edgecomb: Halston Sage
Kent McFuller: Logan Miller
Rob Cokran: Kian Lawley
Juliet Sykes: Elena Kampouris
Origin: United States
Language: English
Released: 2017
Production: Matt Kaplan, Brian Robbins, Jonathan Shestack; Awesomeness Films, Jon Shestack Productions; released by Open Road Films
Directed by: Ry Russo-Young
Written by: Maria Maggenti
Cinematography by: Michael Fimognari
Music by: Adam Taylor
Sound: Lewis Goldstein
Music Supervisor: Howard Paar
Editing: Joe Landauer
Costumes: Eilidh McAllister
Production Design: Paul Joyal
MPAA rating: PG-13
Running time: 98 minutes

REVIEWS

Chang, Justin. *Los Angeles Times.* March 2, 2017.
Debruge, Peter. *Variety.* January 23, 2017.
Dowd, A.A. *The A.V. Club.* March 1, 2017.
Ehrlich, David. *IndieWire.* February 27, 2017.
Felperin, Leslie. *Hollywood Reporter.* January 23, 2017.
Macdonald, Moira. *Seattle Times.* March 2, 2017.
Nicholson, Amy. *MTV News.* March 9, 2017.

Russo, Tom. *Boston Globe.* March 2, 2017.
Scott, A.O. *New York Times.* March 1, 2017.
Truitt, Brian. *USA Today.* March 2, 2017.

QUOTES

Samantha Kingston: "How is it possible to change so much and not be able to change anything at all?"

TRIVIA

The film was shot in only twenty-four days.

THE BEGUILED

Innocent, until betrayed.
—Movie tagline

Box Office: $10.7 Million

When it was announced that Sofia Coppola's next film project was going to be a remake of *The Beguiled* (1971), Don Siegel's psycho-sexual exercise in Civil War-era Gothic horror, many eyebrows were raised in curiosity. This response had less to do with Coppola herself, who had long since proven herself to be one of the most fascinating and distinct American filmmakers of her generation with such acclaimed works as *Lost in Translation* (2003), *Marie Antoinette* (2006), and *The Bling Ring* (2013), as to her particular choice of material. How would her dreamy and languid cinematic approach, one that favored character and atmosphere to narrative, blend with the lurid thrills that Siegel and star Clint Eastwood mined with their unabashedly pulpy and occasionally misogynistic take on Thomas P. Cullinan's 1966 novel *A Painted Devil*? Rather than just being an instantly forgettable rehash of familiar material in the manner of so many of the other cinematic remakes that clogged multiplexes in 2017, Coppola, who won the Best Director prize at Cannes for her efforts, took the basic premise and, by making a key shift in its narrative perspective, has managed to turn it into a fresh and vital work that not only is of a piece with the rest of her unique filmography but is one of the years very best (and most timely, as it would eventually turn out) films to boot.

Set in 1864, the story takes place entirely in and around a nearly-abandoned Virginia-based girls school that is within earshot of the still-raging Civil War and currently populated only by headmistress Martha Farnsworth (Nicole Kidman), teacher Edwina Morrow (Kirsten Dunst), and five students. One day, while out in the nearby woods in search of mushrooms, young student Amy (Oona Laurence) stumbles across John McBurney (Colin Farrell), a corporal in the Union Army who is on the run for desertion and suffering from a badly wounded leg. Taking sympathy on him, Amy brings him back to the school, where he promptly passes out due to his injuries. The women debate whether to take him in or to give him up to the Confederate soldiers who occasionally pass by their doors, but Martha decides that the most Christian thing to do would be to take him in and nurse him back to health before deciding whether to give him up or not. She begins tending to his wounds and when the soldiers do come by to check in on her and the others, no mention is made of McBurney.

Not surprisingly, the arrival of a handsome and charming male stranger has an immediate effect on all of the women at the school and they begin competing amongst themselves for his attentions. Knowing a good thing when he sees it and having no desire to be turned over, McBurney encourages and returns those affections, especially towards Martha and Edwina. And when he is well enough to move, he begins helping out in the garden in an obvious attempt to extend his stay. When Martha does announce that he is healthy enough to leave in a few days, he tries to convince her to keep him on as a gardener and further tries to solidify his position by confessing his love for Edwina, who is the one most clearly besotted by him and who looks at him as her only means of escape from a life of loneliness that, in her mind, is embodied by Martha. One evening, Edwina is expecting McBurney to visit her room after everyone has gone to bed but when she hears a strange noise, she investigates and finds him canoodling in bed with Alicia (Elle Fanning), the oldest and most rebellious of the students. This discovery kicks off a series of shocking events in which McBurney's charm mutates into something much uglier and the women demonstrate that they are more than capable of taking care of themselves after all.

From a plot perspective, Coppola's take on *The Beguiled* is not markedly dissimilar from Siegel's. There has been some streamlining here and there—some of it welcome (there is no longer any hint of Martha's incestuous relationship with her brother that played a prominent part the first time around) and some of it the source of controversy (the elimination of a slave character, a move that some critics took Coppola to task for what they considered to be a whitewashing of the realities of the era, essentially suggesting that she was nowhere near as woke as Siegel). In terms of approach, however, the two takes could not be more dissimilar. Siegel presented his version as a sort of deranged "Penthouse Forum" saga in which a hunky stud, who finds himself all alone in a house filled with sex-crazed women in need of the satisfaction that he is all too happy to give them, only to turn into murderous harpies when he tries to assert some kind of control over the situation. The end result was essentially an extended castration nightmare and while it was reasonably fun in a trashy sort of way—especially in the way that it played with Eastwood's image as a big screen stud—viewers did not exactly come away from it with an enlightened view with regards to gender politics. (If one were to make a list of bad first-date movies, it would probably rank near the top.)

While retaining the bones of the story, Coppola has rejiggered the material in ways that have transformed the lurid into the languid in a manner more befitting her general approach as a filmmaker. Part of this is due to her stylistic approach that combines a dreamy visual presentation from cinematographer Philippe Le Sourd, stunning production design by Anne Ross and a spare but effective score by Phoenix into a package that is both gorgeous and vaguely unsettling. More importantly, she has shifted the focus of the story from McBurney to the female characters and has dialed way back on the more over-the-top elements. Martha, for example, is no longer the "Unsatisfied Spinster From Hell," but a woman who is compassionate and holds certain yearnings, to be sure, but who will come down hard on anyone who tries to mess with her or her charges. As for the other female characters, Coppola develops them more fully as well and gives them some unexpected shadings—there is a lot more going on with Edwina than immediately meets the mind and even Alicia is portrayed in a more sympathetic manner as a girl who is less a slut and more someone who is bored out of her mind and desperate for any form of excitement to liven things up. Even McBurney is painted in more human terms as well—instead of Eastwood's predatory cad, this version is one who is driven to do what he does almost entirely by his desire to avoid returning to the horrors of the battlefield and who is as surprised as anyone else when things begin to spin out of control.

While some fans of the original may be taken aback at the notion of a version that downplays the sleazier elements and is firmly on the side of the women, others, especially those who have previously found favor with Coppola's often-polarizing filmmaking style, are likely to find it fascinating. From the opening frames, she creates an atmosphere of beauty and dread that is so vivid that viewers can practically smell both the woods and the gunpowder wafting in the air just beyond the shuttered gates of the school. The performances from the entire cast are excellent—the only one who doesn't quite outdo their predecessor is Farrell, who is very good but who is not quite as instantly captivating as Eastwood (though it could be argued that is exactly the point)—and in chronicling the interactions of the denizens of the school, Coppola once again reminds us that she is one of the most deft filmmakers around today in terms of presenting the intricacies of female relationships of all stripes. When the story shifts from the dreamy to something more narratively driven than she is usually known for, Coppola proves to be equal to the task by proving herself to be adept at presenting both suspense, albeit in a low-key manner, and a welcome strain of dark humor that drives the closing scenes in a most appealing manner.

Like its predecessor, *The Beguiled* did not prove to be a big box-office success—though one wonders how it might have fared if it had been delayed from its summer release date to the fall, where a tale of female empowerment might have found a more receptive audience in the wake of the numerous sexual abuse scandals that rocked the film industry at the time. However, with its combination of strong acting, black humor, striking atmosphere, and quiet eroticism, all conducted by a top filmmaker at the peak of her talents, it is a film that will almost certainly be rediscovered at some point down the line and have its considerable achievements receive the appreciation that they so fully deserve. In transcending its pulpy underpinnings for something fuller, smarter, and deeper, Coppola has made one of the most striking films of the year, one that demonstrates that a remake is not necessarily a bad thing as long as there are real ideas governing its existence other than the hopes of exploiting a familiar title for some easy cash. Of course, there are those that may disagree and to them, all I can do is suggest that they try the mushrooms.

Peter Sobczynski

CREDITS

Corporal McBurney: Colin Farrell
Miss Martha: Nicole Kidman
Edwina: Kirsten Dunst
Alicia: Elle Fanning
Amy: Oona Laurence
Origin: United States
Language: English, French
Released: 2017
Production: Youree Henley, Sofia Coppola; American Zoetrope, FR Productions; released by Focus Features L.L.C.
Directed by: Sofia Coppola
Written by: Sofia Coppola
Cinematography by: Philippe Le Sourd
Music by: Phoenix
Editing: Sarah Flack
Art Direction: Jennifer Dehghan
Costumes: Stacey Battat
Production Design: Anne Ross

MPAA rating: R
Running time: 93 minutes

REVIEWS

Chang, Justin. *Los Angeles Times.* June 22, 2017.
Ebiri, Bilge. *Village Voice.* May 25, 2017.
Gleiberman, Owen. *Variety.* May 24, 2017.
Lane, Anthony. *New Yorker.* June 19, 2017.
McCarthy, Todd. *Hollywood Reporter.* May 24, 2017.
Scott, A.O. *New York Times.* June 22, 2017.
Stevens, Dana. *Slate.* June 21, 2017.
Yoshida, Emily. *New York Magazine/Vulture.* May 24, 2017.
Zacharek, Stephanie. *Time.* May 25, 2017.

QUOTES

Martha Farnsworth: "It's seems the enemy...it's not what we believed."

TRIVIA

During rehearsals, a civil war re-enactor instructed Nicole Kidman on medical procedures of the time.

THE BELKO EXPERIMENT

Box Office: $10.2 Million

Greg McLean's latest social experiment is about as reliable and efficient as the average corporate drone, but it also plays like a downsized version of what it might have been. If only director McLean or writer James Gunn had been more experimental, *The Belko Experiment* might have yielded more compelling results. Instead, it borrows an idea from Kinji Fukasaku's satiric horror masterpiece *Battle Royale* (2000) without doing anything interesting with it.

Belko Enterprises is a non-profit organization operating out of a remote office building in Bogota, Columbia. Employees have chips implanted in their necks on their first day of work so that they can be tracked in case of kidnapping, a big problem in the area. One day, as people begin arriving for work, a new security detail takes over. Just as everyone settles in, a voice delivers an ultimatum via the intercom. They must kill three of their fellow employees in a specified amount of time or employees will be chosen at random and killed. Steel shutters descend along every possible escape route and point of contact with the outside world. As time runs out, the voice ups the ante by detonating the tracking chips in the heads of six employees.

The film progresses in the expected manner with various predictable factions forming, all of whom have their own ideas about who should live and who should die. The voice keeps demanding more human sacrifices and the tension between groups leads to a bloodbath.

Fukasaku's film featured high school students being made examples of by the government as a warning to the rest of the rebellious youth in a future Japan. But all *The Belko Experiment* really does is change the students to office workers and hide the reason the slaughter is taking place. To be fair, the film does make some effort to deal with the human condition. Barry the company's CEO, played to amoral perfection by Tony Goldwyn, immediately takes the lead, commandeering weapons from the security locker and taking a group of faithful company men to separate the employees according to who he thinks should live or die. Employee Mike Milch (John Gallagher, Jr.) does everything he can to stand in Tony's way, and leads his own group to a different part of the building.

Though the film signals its intention to use the rest of the cast for cannon fodder pretty early on there are a few notable turns. John C. McGinley plays Wendell, a misogynistic brute all too happy to have a chance to be in charge. Like all the would-be judges in the film, Wendell is ultimately a coward, but, in McGinley's hands, the character is just human enough for audiences to imagine Wendell haunted years later by his decisions here. Too bad his character arc gives the audience a far more paltry payoff.

Sean Gunn plays Marty, a stoner and conspiratorially-minded burn out who comes up with the brilliant idea of cutting unexploded chips out of people's heads to use as a makeshift bomb. His character exists mainly for comic relief, however dark the film's sense of humor may be. In one great scene, Marty, convinced this whole thing must be an illusion, watches as the heads of thirty people around him are systematically detonated. Melonie Diaz plays Dany, a first-day employee, whose fight to simply survive the chaos ends up giving her story some unexpected weight.

Unlike great horror films such as the aforementioned *Battle Royale* or *Dawn of the Dead* (1978) that are tonally consistent and use humor to reinforce their satiric message, *The Belko Experiment* seems scattered and uncertain of what part humor plays in this narrative. It seems a shame since writer James Gunn has handled genre so well before in *Slither* (2006) and *Super* (2010). Perhaps director Greg McLean, whose best work is the heavy-handed suspense horror film *Wolf Creek* (2005) simply lacks a light enough touch. If one observation could suffice as a review it might be that *The Belko Experiment* is neither as scary or satirically observant as it needs to be.

The film ends as a lone survivor discovers there are similar experiments going on simultaneously all over the world. The shadowy organization that runs them is a weak throwback to the government conspiracies that have dominated genre films since the mid-seventies. *The Belko Experiment* does take a small risk by attempting to reveal the men behind the curtain but, again, a comparison to *Battle Royale* is helpful. In Fukasaku's film, the hypocrisy of those running the experiment is exposed. In *The Belko Experiment,* only the weaknesses of the script are.

So, though a strong cast makes *The Belko Experiment* worth seeing, especially for horror fans and there are a few strong set pieces, there are also a lot of moments where the temptation to shout advice to the characters will remind even stalwart genre fans that *The Belko Experiment* sat around on a shelf for a good long while before finally being released this year.

Dave Canfield

CREDITS

Mike Milch: John Gallagher, Jr.

Barry Norris: Tony Goldwyn

Leandra Florez: Adria Arjona

Wendell Dukes: John C. McGinley

Dany Wilkins: Melonie Diaz

Origin: United States

Language: English

Released: 2017

Production: Peter Safran, James Gunn; Blumhouse Productions, LLC., Metro-Goldwyn-Mayer Pictures, Orion Pictures, Safran Co.; released by BH Tilt

Directed by: Greg McLean

Written by: James Gunn

Cinematography by: Luis David Sansans

Music by: Tyler Bates

Sound: Trevor Gates

Editing: Julia Wong

Art Direction: César Montoya

Production Design: Carlos Osorio

MPAA rating: R

Running time: 89 minutes

REVIEWS

Abele, Robert. *TheWrap*. March 15, 2017.

DeFore, John. *Hollywood Reporter*. March 17, 2017.

Dowd A.A. *The A.V. Club*. March 16, 2017.

Guzman, Rafer. *Newsday*. March 16, 2017.

Harvey, Dennis. *Variety*. September 12, 2016.

Hertz, Barry. *Globe and Mail*. May 12, 2017.

Hewitt, Chris. *Empire Magazine*. April 18, 2017.

Kenny, Glenn. *New York Times*. March 15, 2017.

Scherstuhl, Alan. *Village Voice*. March 15, 2017.

Yoshida, Emily. *New York Magazine/Vulture*. March 15, 2017.

QUOTES

Leandra Florez: "At the end of the day people are out for themselves."

TRIVIA

Actor John Gallagher Jr. had previously auditioned for a role in a film directed by James Gunn, but wasn't right for the part. Gunn, however, thought Gallagher was the best actor he'd seen in an audition and vowed to work with him.

THE BIG SICK

An awkward true story.
—Movie tagline

Box Office: $42.9 Million

Judd Apatow lets his comedies "graze." Whether as a writer/director (*This is 40* [2012], *Funny People* [2009]) or producer (*The Five-Year Engagement* [2012], *Forgetting Sarah Marshall* [2008]), the comedy influencer's name has become synonymous with a gentle sort of bloat. It is often a tired-but-fair criticism: comedy, even the sort of vulnerability-based, redemption-of-a-schlub character comedy Apatow often deals with, thrives on sharpness, and the movies' extended running times have a tendency to dilute their joy without deepening the feeling. More improvisation, yes, but also a sense of how more is not always more when it comes to jokes. Keep the best ones, cut the next tier down and maximize the consistency.

In the case of *The Big Sick*, though, the extra minutes that may as well be called the "Apatow 15" find an appropriate thematic use. This is not to say that this is the first time he has dealt with painful situations in which the characters would feel like every second was an hour. (It is worth mentioning *Forgetting Sarah Marshall* again here.) Or that the arguably superfluous time in the two-hour *The Big Sick* results in a high percentage of additional laughs. It does not; in fact, the movie grows a bit repetitive, especially in terms of a few different recurring scenes (comedians hanging out, a mother's attempted fix-ups for her son) that do not necessarily grow funnier over time.

Yet, maybe for the first time, the material emotionally connects with the sluggishness because, as opposed to a (usually male) character struggling to grow up, this is not a story about something so basic. Telling a mostly-true version of their relationship that was nearly, and tragically, cut short by a medically induced coma, Kumail Nanjiani (who stars as himself) and Emily V. Gordon (played in the movie by Zoe Kazan) deal with nothing less than the fear of a loved one dying and difficult questions about familial expectations and forgiveness. When estranged from somebody, or waiting to find out if an important person is going to survive, time moves slowly. The viewer's impatience to the movie's pace is nothing compared to the characters' frustration at the slow-moving world around them.

The nature of the coma-related plot has the impact of cutting the film in half into B.C. and A.C. (Before and After Coma). In the first part, Kumail and Emily meet when she winningly heckles one of his stand-up performances—actually, she screams "Woo!" and learns that commentary does not have to be negative to count as heckling; it just has to be a distraction—and she distinguishes herself by not falling for his go-to move of writing her name in Urdu. They quickly develop a rapport that resonates throughout the movie, which is not about love as fire but a steady, amusing warmth. These two have fun together, and that is enough, until Emily stumbles onto the cigar box where Kumail collects photos of the women his mom, Sharmeen (Zenobia Shroff), brings to their house to meet him. They may live in Chicago, but according to Kumail's parents, a proper Pakistani son marries a Pakistani woman, which he neither agrees with nor has the courage to fully confront.

He declines to tell his parents (Anupam Kher plays Kumail's father, Azmat) about Emily and they break up after a big fight rooted in his struggles in the face of history-based expectations. In real life, Kumail and Emily did not break up before she became sick and was put in a medically-induced coma, and the forced nature of this conflict fittingly rings a bit false. It does, however, create new stakes for the period after Emily gets sick, with Kumail summoned to the hospital to support her even though they are no longer dating. There, he meets her parents, Beth (Holly Hunter) and Terry (Ray Romano), who mostly see him as an unwelcome nuisance because of how he hurt their daughter.

Yet the movie hinges on Kumail, inevitably returning to the hospital even after Emily's parents ask him to leave, developing a bond with these people, the three of them united in love and worry. Though Nanjiani and Gordon's script also invents infidelity between Terry and Beth that is not taken from real life, they could not feel more authentic as people and the film is an incredible showcase for Hunter and Romano. She's extraordinary, whether bubbling over with frustration and insisting Emily should move to a better hospital or standing up to a heckler at Kumail's show. He's heartbreaking and emotional without overplaying anything as Terry attempts to share insights without realizing that, in the midst of continuous fear and sadness, he is not entirely sure what he has learned other than how painful it can be to love someone.

There are many well-observed moments like this throughout *The Big Sick*. That ranges from Khadija (Vella Lovell), one of the women hand-selected for Kumail to date, expressing how hollow it feels to constantly be told that she deserves better, to Kumail and his brother, Naveed (Adeel Akhtar), reassuring white customers at a restaurant that they should not fear them because they also hate terrorists. Kumail and Terry also have a great scene in the hospital when he tries to express that he wants to talk to a Muslim about 9/11 but winds up suggesting he has never talked to anyone about 9/11. The film has a light touch in approaching difficult material, and it is no small feat to deal honestly with racism and death and still go down easy.

So it is a shame that the film also has so many places it could use refinement. Nanjiani acquits himself fine in his first starring role, and Kazan is excellent as Emily, but the bond between them never lives up to the supposed depth of their connection. Thus, for too long his presence at the hospital feels more like obligation and regret than big feelings. It is also odd that an adaptation written by both Nanjiani and Gordon seems so weighted toward him. This is exacerbated by the sense that Emily helps Kumail open up (particularly regarding his one-man show) and Beth enlivens Terry's life, but it is debatable if the men reciprocate what they receive. In addition, Kumail's pressure from his parents fails to distinguish itself from similar plotlines in many other movies and shows, including the recent season of Aziz Ansari's *Master of None*, and director Michael Showalter, who wraps things up on a painfully conventional note, struggles to create a sense of place in Chicago. Overall, things are rarely funny or affecting enough to resonate as better than good.

Of course, the general pleasantness is also why the overuse of Kumail's comedian friends (including Bo Burnham and Aidy Bryant) remains palatable. (Not the same for his annoying, mediocre comedian roommate played by Ed Herbstman.) *The Big Sick* earns its generosity of spirit through characters that are flawed but appealing and trying to make decisions to do right by themselves and others. With more stories and people like this, the romantic comedy label might not seem like an insult anymore.

Matt Pais

CREDITS

Kumail: Kumail Nanjiani
Emily: Zoe Kazan
Beth: Holly Hunter
Terry: Ray Romano
Azmat: Anupam Kher
Origin: United States
Language: English, Urdu
Released: 2017
Production: Judd Apatow, Barry Mendel; Apatow Productions, FilmNation Entertainment; released by Lionsgate
Directed by: Michael Showalter
Written by: Kumail Nanjiani; Emily V. Gordon
Cinematography by: Brian Burgoyne
Music by: Michael Andrews
Sound: Tom Paul
Music Supervisor: Joe Rudge
Editing: Robert Nassau
Art Direction: Andy Eklund
Costumes: Sarah Mae Burton
Production Design: Brandon Tonner-Connolly
MPAA rating: R
Running time: 120 minutes

REVIEWS

Burr, Ty. *Boston Globe.* June 28, 2017.
Cea, Max. *Salon.com.* June 27, 2017.
Chang, Justin. *Los Angeles Times.* June 22, 2017.
Dowd, A.A. *The A.V. Club.* June 21, 2017.
Ebiri, Bilge. *Village Voice.* January 24, 2017.
Goldberg, Peter. *Slant Magazine.* June 19, 2017.
Persall, Steve. *Tampa Bay Times.* July 5, 2017.
Roeper, Richard. *Chicago Sun-Times.* June 29, 2017.
Stevens, Dana. *Slate.* June 15, 2017.
Zacharek, Stephanie. *Time.* June 23, 2017.

QUOTES

Chris: "You know, it might be a good thing. Like, she might wake up with a new skill. Like, my cousin, blacked out once, and then, when he came to, he thought he knew a different language."
CJ: "Did he?"
Chris: "No. Apparently, it was...it was just gibberish that he made up. It was brain damage."

TRIVIA

The decision to include real-life photos of Emily and Kumail during the end credits was suggested by actress Leslie Mann after seeing an early cut of the film.

AWARDS

Ind. Spirit 2018: First Screenplay
Nominations:
Oscars 2017: Orig. Screenplay
Ind. Spirit 2018: Actress--Supporting (Hunter)
Screen Actors Guild 2017: Actress--Supporting (Hunter), Cast
Writers Guild 2017: Orig. Screenplay

BITTER HARVEST

Soviet Union. 1933. Stalin's tyranny could destroy their country. But not their love.
—Movie tagline

Box Office: $557,241

Bitter Harvest, which took nearly 10 years to produce and subsequently release, starts with a faux-poetic passage about young love and ends with figures about deaths under Stalin's regime, but don't be fooled by its pretensions towards importance. This film is as rote, soulless, boringly didactic, and predictable as any Hollywood movie from the 1950s about the Roman Empire. That comparison is not idly chosen: like those films, historical figures make pointless cameos in the lives of the central functionary lovers, and the genocide depicted is just window dressing for a fantastically dull and ordinary story of a young man at a crossroads in life, making his way back to his one true love. Georgian director George Mendeluk, a B-movie director attempting to go legit, and his co-writer Richard Bachynsky Hoover, a day player turned first-time scribe, have clearly seen enough historical epics to know the expected beats they have to hit between the opening and closing credits. What these element lack here is a reason to exist. Anyone wanting insight into life in Ukraine under Stalin won't find any insight at which they couldn't have blindly guessed. Anyone looking for a movie worth an hour and forty minutes of their time will have to look elsewhere.

Yuri (Max Irons) is a painter and the son of a farmer/soldier, Yaroslav (Barry Pepper), in a wealthy part of the Ukrainian countryside. He's loved Natalka (Samantha Barks) all his life, and now that they are old enough to be wed, he has to decide whether to leave for the cities with his friends, or stay and wait for her to allow him to marry her. She finally acquiesces but their wedding day is marred by tragedy. Stalin (Gary Oliver) has sent his troops to Ukrainian villages like this one to integrate all their farming and production into his collectivist government. The troops nearly kill Natalka's mother riding into town and then they hang Yuri's father. Property is seized, farmers arrested, women are forced to marry Russian officials, and chaos generally reigns. Which means that Yuri picks a swell time to try to make his fortune outside the city, leaving Natalka in the care of elderly firebrand Ivan (Terence Stamp). Naturally, it's only a few months until Natalka miscarries the baby she and Yuri conceived before his departure and she's forced to marry the worst of the Russian troops to stay alive.

In Kiev, Yuri finds himself tangentially involved in the anti-Bolshevik resistance, but his connection to the movement kills himself when he discovers he's being followed and then Yuri accidentally murders a soldier at his funeral. In prison with no hope of getting back to Natalka and the child he doesn't know was killed before it was born, Yuri begins plotting an escape. He impresses a guard (Richard Brake) with his ability to sketch Natalka's visage on the wall of his cell, so much so that the guard agrees to be Yuri's next subject. A sharpened paint brush to the throat allows Yuri to kill the vain guard and escape into the harsh winter outside, wending his way back to his hometown to rescue Natalka from her hideous new circumstances. This means contending with the Red Army contingent that's still camped out in his hometown, which he's only too happy to do.

Bitter Harvest has both too much plot and too little investment in any one detail for this film to have been anything but a failure. Natalka, who we are told in the opening minutes of the film, is the love of Yuri's life, is easily abandoned (along with her point of view) when Yuri heeds the siren call of Kiev and the possibility it affords him to become a respected artist. How we are meant to sympathize with him when he chooses his terrible, anonymous paintings over his girlfriend and her dying mother is a hurdle that even a much better film couldn't clear. That this film uses it for a completely clichéd long distance love arc is pretty offensive and it would unseat *Bitter Harvest* completely if any sympathy or momentum had been generated by that point.

Little missteps prevent that, such as Max Irons's utter blandness as a leading man, the anachronistic costuming, the preposterous haircut given only to Barry Pepper, the randomly chosen expressionistic color palette that has to be thrown away minutes later when the famine sets in. The film is careless to an inexcusable degree. Mendeluk and Hoover plainly wanted this film to tell the complete history of Ukraine, but they couldn't even tell the whole story of one hapless lovelorn fool without detouring into dinner parties with Joseph Stalin. Playing Stalin as a moustache-twirling super-villain does not count as much of a choice, because the man is historically synonymous with moustache twirling super-villainry. He's not actually a part of Yuri's story, except as the accidental grand architect of his fate. Showing him cursing the Ukrainians up and down allows no fact or idea that even a pre-teen viewer would have divined. Of course, Stalin was evil, showing him and his cronies as thoughtless raping and pillaging machines may be historically accurate but it's dramatically inert and narratively fatal. Naturally, Yuri has to survive to kill them all (Stalin excepted) because Mendeluk naively imagines there can be a happy ending to a story like this. Shambolically stylistic and sleep-inducing every minute Richard Brake isn't on screen providing his oily, one-of-a-kind character actor electricity, *Bitter Harvest* is best summed up by Yuri's own criticism of the collectivist art he sees taking over the museums in Kiev. "This isn't art." Quite.

Scout Tafoya

CREDITS

Yuri: Max Irons

Medved: Richard Brake

Ivan: Terence Stamp

Natalka: Samantha Barks

Mykola: Aneurin Barnard

Origin: United States

Language: English, Russian

Released: 2017

Production: Chad Barager, Jaye Gazeley, Ian Ihnatowycz, Stuart Baird; Devil's Harvest Production, Tell Me A Storey; released by Roadside Attractions

Directed by: George Mendeluk

Written by: George Mendeluk; Richard Bachynsky Hoover

Cinematography by: Douglas Milsome

Music by: Benjamin Wallfisch

Sound: Dane A. Davis

Editing: Stuart Baird; Lenka Svab

Costumes: Tatyana Fedotova; Galina Otenko; Aleksandra Stepina

Production Design: George Mendeluk; Martin Hitchcock; Vladimir Radlinski

MPAA rating: R

Running time: 103 minutes

REVIEWS

Clarke, Cath. *Time Out London*. February 22, 2017.

Catsoulis, Jeannette. *New York Times*. February 23, 2017.

Cheshire, Godfrey. *RogerEbert.com*. February 24, 2017.

Debruge, Peter. *Variety*. February 23, 2017.

Felperin, Leslie. *The Guardian*. February 23, 2017.

Ivanov, Oleg. *Slant Magazine*. February 21, 2017.

Keogh, Tom. *Seattle Times*. February 22, 2017.

Linden, Sheri. *Los Angeles Times*. February 23, 2017.

Vishnevetsky, Ignatiy. *The A.V. Club*. February 22, 2017.

Vonder Haar, Pete. *Village Voice*. February 22, 2017.

QUOTES

Yuri: "My Ukraine was a world where legend lived and anything was possible."

TRIVIA

Actors Max Irons and Aneurrin Barnard played brothers Edward IV and Richard III, respectively in *The White Queen* (2013).

BLADE OF THE IMMORTAL

(Mugen no junin)

To save her life he will take a thousand others.
—Movie tagline

There is redemption in vengeance.
—Movie tagline

His path is paved in blood.
—Movie tagline

Evil has an undying enemy.
—Movie tagline

Box Office: $150,532

Touted as the 100th film by legendary modern director Takashi Miike, *Blade of the Immortal* (*Mugen no jûnin*) is probably the most perfect entryway into the prolific philosopher-filmmakers' oeuvre. It's got his trademark extreme violence, but it doesn't revel in it the way of a lot of his earlier work, namely provocations like 2001's *Visitor Q* and *Ichi the Killer* or 2006's *Imprint*. It's focused on a man lost in a complex mythology, stuck thanks to a set of supernatural circumstances and an ingrown sense of honor that's frequently as much of a crutch as it is a benefit. It's filled with colorful supporting characters and concerns itself with their infighting and shifting allegiances. Lastly, and perhaps most importantly, its central concern is with the body's threshold for pain. *Blade of the Immortal* has just about every one of Miike's touchstones and obsessions, but overall comes across as a much more gentle and approachable work, despite a spectacular body count.

Manji (Takua Kimura) is an angry, angsty swordsman cursed by two painful memories that occurred during the Tokugawa Shogunate period in Japan. The first is the murder of his sister Machi (Hana Sugisaki), who was killed as punishment for Manji's murder of a corrupt lord. Manji managed to kill every member of the gang responsible for her murder, but not before he sustained a grievous, potentially fatal injury. As fortune would have it, a nun named Yaobikuni (Yôko Yamamoto) finds him during what should be his last moments on earth and infects him with "sacred blood worms," a species that reconstruct dead tissue and replenish red blood cells at an alarming rate. The result is that as long as the blood worms live inside Manji's body, he will never die, at least not from any injury he could sustain in a sword fight.

Manji's legend grows over the next fifty years as his existential dread mounts and he retreats into a quiet country life hoping to live under the radar of civilization, lest anyone else attempt to put his immortality to the test. So he's less than sympathetic when a woman named Rin Asano (also Hana Sugisaki) seeks him out. Her father was murdered by a swordsman called Anotsu Kagehisa (Sôta Fukushi), the head of a gang called the Itto-ryu, and she wants revenge that only someone like Manji could help her exast. Manji initially isn't thrilled at the prospect of killing anybody else, but between Rin Asano's uncanny resemblance to his sister, and, at the very least, her genuine need for some protection, he lets her hang around him while he decides what to do with her. It isn't long before opponents start falling out of the woodwork, attempting to quell Rin's bloodlust now that she has an immortal sell-sword on her side.

Manji starts regularly having to fend off members of the Itto-ryu, but as a consequence, grows to learn more about them. Their fight is with the local government, spurred by an old blood feud begun by Rin Asano's grandfather when he insulted the honor of Kagehisa's grandfather, a fact that's been kept secret from the public. A rival gang, the Mugai-ryu, appear out of nowhere offering to help Manji kill the members of the Itto-ryu, but there seems to be something off about them. They're even more bloodthirsty and sadistic than any of the Itto-ryu, and they don't seem to care who's killed as a consequence of their actions. Manji suspects that this plot is a little too big for him to solve by himself, but by now the local lords have mobilized a hundred men to deal with the remaining Itto-ryu members as well as Rin and Manji.

The plot of *Blade of the Immortal* comes from a popular manga series, which accounts for the baroque chain of events and the incredible, distinct character designs. The ornate robes, flamboyant make-up and hair styles, and the complicated backstory are presented matter-of-factly by Miike, who never lets fantasy get in the way of his true aims as a storyteller and thinker. He has never taken a beat to admire his own work, never asked you to be awed or wowed by the incredible fantasy and choreography he pulls off with what appears to be little effort, even though he works harder than just about any filmmaker on earth. He used to make anywhere from three to six films a year, though he's slowed his pace since 2008, now only making two or three. The extra time has opened him up to more deliberate story beats and allowing for a greater depth of character than ever interested him before. His characters used to be sketched just a little more hastily in order to launch into the main action. Lately he's clearly enjoyed getting to know his characters through their exposure to pain and the ever-thickening plot over longer periods of time.

Blade of the Immortal, like other recent Miike efforts such as *Hara-Kiri: Death of a Samurai* (2011) and *Shield of Straw* (2013) tapers its conventional thrills with an air of melancholy and lost purpose. Miike's flirted with immortality before in the grueling and fascinating *Izo* (2004), and this film plays like its more emotional sequel. Manji's plight is inherently tragic because he cannot die and will have to watch whoever he gets close to perish. The parallels between Rin and Machi bring out in him a sense of resignation to fate's abjectly cruel design for him. He'll never get to live or die the way he wants to. Rin Asano meanwhile is merely looking for an outlet for her grief, which is complicated by her inability to fend for herself, let alone handle someone as skilled as Kagehisa in battle, and the growing realization that her foe is as driven by grief as she is. Kagehisa is provoked by a battle that was begun before his birth, and his slippery legacy has hardened his spirit. He may be even more fatalistic and depressive than Manji, and that's before the government enacts one final betrayal against his clan. This is a film about survivors who aren't sure what they'll do if they ever achieve their goals. Miike films them with dignity, frequently losing their fierce figures in crowds of nameless opponents, only to discover them, covered in blood, death scrawled all over their faces, the will to move slowly draining away from them. The final battle is a psychological marvel as each remaining combatant has to destroy hundreds of soldiers in order to meet again, and with each blow of their sword, they erase a small part of their purpose. In between its fantastically staged combat scenes, *Blade of the Immortal* asks who we are when our personal wars have ended and the smoke has cleared.

Scout Tafoya

CREDITS

Manji: Takuya Kimura
Rin Asano/Machi, Manji's sister: Hana Sugisaki
Anotsu Kagehisa: Sota Fukushi
Shira: Hayato Ichihara
Makie Otono-Tachibana: Erika Toda
Origin: United States
Language: Japanese
Released: 2017
Production: Misako Saka, Jeremy Thomas, Shigeji Maeda; Warner Bros. Entertainment Inc.; released by Magnet Releasing
Directed by: Takashi Miike
Written by: Tetsuya Oishi
Cinematography by: Nobuyasu Kita
Music by: Koji Endo
Sound: Masatoshi Katsumata
Editing: Kenji Yamashita
Costumes: Yuya Maeda
Production Design: Toshiyuki Matsumiya
MPAA rating: R
Running time: 140 minutes

REVIEWS

Bowen, Chuck. *Slant.* October 31, 2017.
Catsoulis, Jeannette. *New York Times.* November 2, 2017.
De Semlyen, Phil. *Time Out.* December 5, 2017.
Hoffman, Jordan. *The Guardian.* May 24, 2017.
Lee, Maggie. *Variety.* May 24, 2017.
Murray, Noel. *Los Angeles Times.* October 31, 2017.
Phipps, Keith. *Uproxx.* December 4, 2017.
Rife, Katie. *The A.V. Club.* November 2, 2017.
Robey, Tim *The Telegraph.* December 11, 2017.
Vestby, Ethan. *The Film Stage.* November 6, 2017.

QUOTES

Rin Asano: "But do right and wrong matter when it's for people you love?"

TRIVIA

This is Takashi Miike's 100th film.

BLADE RUNNER 2049

Box Office: $92 Million

Film noir is a genre, style, or mood that is drenched in lonesomeness. A single detective, lost in a world he no longer understands, struggles to find meaning through a plot often designed to give none. *Blade Runner 2049,* following in the hybrid science fiction footsteps of its predecessor, embraces the cynicism of solitary pursuits as a great, beautiful piece of neo-noir. Where the first film watched as Rick Deckard (Harrison Ford) worked as a solo Blade Runner to round up and kill a team of bio-engineered replicants, only to question his own humanity as his pursuit went on, the sequel—set thirty years in the future and released thirty-five years after the original—offers opposite plot implications.

K (Ryan Gosling) is introduced as a replicant with the same job Deckard used to have, but through his slow, meandering pursuit of a series of cover-ups, he begins to face questions about his personhood as well. After a routine run-in with a rogue replicant (Dave Bautista, whose meticulous and soft gestures contrast brilliantly with his hulking savagery), K uncovers the beginnings of a mystery that threatens to rattle the core of his society's system.

In this system, replicants are second-class citizens to the degree that they are executed if their programming does not fall in line during regular check-ups. Deviancy is a death sentence. The only reason these cybernetic creations do not rebel against the humans is that they are manufactured by a monopolistic company (led by a CEO played by Jared Leto) in such quantities to ensure control.

Control and power, especially when considering an individual's place in context of these two, rattle throughout the film. K bows to his lieutenant (Robin Wright) up until the moment when he suspects something. There is a beautiful singularity that grows from the plot into Roger Deakins's isolating cinematography. K is alone in his pursuit of the truth, fighting against those who wish to conceal it, and he is often framed alone, wandering through hazy orange landscapes of emptiness and decay. These vistas promise nothing but disappointment and ruin, the same fate for the truth that they suffered at the hands of mankind. Every shot is delicate and destructive, a depth charge one cannot fully appreciate when in the midst of it. Rainy streets and long, dark drives have been replaced with dusty flights and cavernous factories-turned-orphanages. Science fiction's future embodies noir's pulpy past thanks to Deakins and director Denis Villeneuve's ominous, observational hand. K enters these locations of his own will, but it never feels anything but predetermined.

This predetermination comes from the fable-like story woven by writers Hampton Fancher and Michael Green, who manage to extract hope from a well-worn and cynical structure full of detectives and cyber prostitutes with hard drives of gold. Hallmarks of noir add color to the deadened plods of the plot's procession, peppering in strange characters played by actors like Barkhad Abdi, Lennie James, and Hiam Abbass in bit parts. They inform the world. The dialogue operates similarly, being sparse yet implying the huge, sprawling and complex caverns of history and culture underneath 2049 Los Angeles just as the slangs and nuances of 1940s detective stories attempted to capture the corrupt bubbles of Chicago or New York.

The spectacularly ambitious film spared no expense in finding a separation from its predecessor. It tells the story of Los Angeles in the future's future, where a future has aged and changed. It plays on its audience's own maturation since the original film. The production team crafted a world that was both full of relics and yet even more advanced than before—both in terms of technology and apocalyptic degradation. Background props, aged sets, and costume details perform science fiction magic so perfectly that their illusions go unnoticed and their presentation becomes reality. Surrounding the actors with such spectacle allows them to effectively undersell their performances, finding a more real, beaten-down quietness among the film's wonder.

Blade Runner 2049 may be a film of loneliness, seen again when K meets a quarantined dreamcrafter (Carla Juri, light and engaging) who weaves the neural implants acting as memories for the replicants, but the bonds between its characters are what make the movie more than a grimy detective story. Gosling, complex and quiet, forces the reconstruction of internal conversations just from a hard gaze into the middle distance. His puzzled look, often masking anguish behind his eyes, encourages watchers to consider the plot up to this point—and what it means for K. Stoic performances, in the right story, allow time to understand and contextualize.

His quietness furthers the film's subversiveness. *Blade Runner 2049* dismantles the hero complex present in most contemporary fiction with misdirection and heart. K meets Deckard (Ford, subtle and damaged), thinking that they are key pieces to the mystery. They, along with K's hologram girlfriend Joi (Ana de Armas), are on the run from the CEO's replicant enforcer (Sylvia Hoeks, giving an equally emotionless counterpart to Gosling's performance). Of course they must be onto something and of course these men must be the center of the story.

A winning performance by de Armas seems to confirm this, all of her charm and helplessness wedged into a program built to please men, but then these expectations crumble as rapidly and intensely as the derelict environments in which they occur. As in the first film, where Deckard's solitude came from his (and the audience's) reckoning of where he stood in the replicant/human divide, the second entry poses a similar supposition for its audience to follow throughout the film. When the bait part is over and it becomes time for the switch, there is no resentment of being tricked because the trick is part of the point.

Understanding how the trick was so easily executed makes the impact of the truth vindication rather than damnation. From a genre standpoint, the film is at the intersection where science fiction and neo-noir wish to tear each other apart, yet it still dares to hope. Finding meaning in convolution follows the appearance of neo-noir—winding an audience and protagonist around endless loops to show the world's utter apathy—but with a sci-fi kicker. That *Blade Runner 2049* is able to pull off such an ambitious trick is impressive, but its beauty and detail ensure that its trick will be a pleasure to fall for over and over again.

Jacob Oller

CREDITS

K: Ryan Gosling

Rick Deckard: Harrison Ford

Joi: Ana de Armas

Luv: Sylvia Hoeks

Lieutenant Joshi: Robin Wright

Origin: Canada, United Kingdom, United States

Language: English
Released: 2017
Production: Broderick Johnson, Andrew A. Kosove, Cynthia Sikes, Bud Yorkin; 16:14 Entertainment, Alcon Entertainment, Columbia Pictures, Scott Free Productions, Torridon Films; released by Warner Bros. Pictures
Directed by: Denis Villeneuve
Written by: Hampton Fancher; Michael Green
Cinematography by: Roger Deakins
Music by: Benjamin Wallfisch; Hans Zimmer
Sound: Mark A. Mangini
Music Supervisor: Deva Anderson
Editing: Joe Walker
Art Direction: Paul Inglis
Costumes: Renee April
Production Design: Dennis Gassner
MPAA rating: R
Running time: 164 minutes

REVIEWS

Anderson, Soren. *Seattle Times*. October 4, 2017.
Bastién, Angelica. *Vulture*. October 11, 2017.
Burr, Ty. *Boston Globe*. October 5, 2017.
Dowd, A.A. *The A.V. Club*. September 29, 2017.
Ebiri, Bilge. *Village Voice*. September 29, 2017.
Greenblatt, Leah. *Entertainment Weekly*. September 29, 2017.
Kohn, Eric. *IndieWire*. September 29, 2017.
McCarthy, Todd. *Hollywood Reporter*. September 29, 2017.
Phillips, Michael. *Chicago Tribune*. August 16, 2017.
Willmore, Alison. *Buzzfeed News*. September 29, 2017.

QUOTES

Wallace: "Pain reminds you the joy you felt was real."

TRIVIA

Actor/singer David Bowie was director Denis Villeneuve's first choice for the role of Niander Wallace, but Bowie passed away before filming began.

AWARDS

Oscars 2017: Cinematog., Visual FX
British Acad. 2017: Cinematog., Visual FX
Nominations:
Oscars 2017: Production Design, Sound, Sound FX Editing
British Acad. 2017: Film Editing, Makeup, Orig. Score, Production Design, Sound
British Acad. 2018: Director (Villeneuve)

BOO 2! A MADEA HALLOWEEN

(Tyler Perry's Boo 2! A Madea Halloween)

Box Office: $47.3 Million

The Tyler Perry film has become an annual staple of the American movie landscape, both as a reliable cash cow for the studio (Lionsgate) and a punchline for any joke involving a horrible movie. Perry created a marketplace all his own with the Madea films, and even his non-Madea films, connecting with a predominantly African American female Christian audience. His films mix broad humor with a faith-based message that is often brought about in a sermon from one of the main characters (usually Madea) that in no way bears any resemblance to real life. Sometimes, as in the case of *Tyler Perry's Boo 2! A Madea Halloween*, the message is not born out of Christian values, but out of everyday common sense. By the end of this particular film, the message is all about divorced parents needing to "co-parent" in order to bring up a well-rounded kid.

One does not actively watch this particular Tyler Perry movie, so much as stare at it. It is the work of a performer who has lost all manner of inspiration. If his films were ever good, they certainly have lost whatever goodwill they had once had to try and attract viewers. Perry seems satisfied enough with just turning on the camera while he gets into costume and mugs his way through one tedious scene after another. This will come as no surprise to anyone who has watched more than four or five of his films between, say, 2012 and 2017, but for someone looking to see if Perry had indeed grown as a filmmaker since working with David Fincher (he famously said in an interview after giving a very good supporting performance in Fincher's *Gone Girl* [2014]), they will see that no such jump in quality exists anywhere. If anything, he has forgotten everything ever told to him about craft, character, and storytelling.

The fact that it is a sequel does not help. It is bad enough Perry is putting on the Madea dress once again, but now he has to conjure up another storyline that will tie his brand of nonsense into the Halloween season. His attempts at delivering scares and laughs simultaneously amount to little more than everyone screaming at each other while also screaming at whatever is chasing them. It also does not help that whatever is chasing them—a faceless guy with a chainsaw—is not all that menacing. He actually seems very forgiving and willing to let the slowest of cars outrun him. There is a reason for that that cannot be revealed, but no spoiler will go so far as to ruin a movie that has been ruined already just by having Perry show up, first at the keyboard to write it, then to his studio to produce it, and, finally, on set to direct and star in it.

After Perry's name scrolls across the screen no less than five times before the actual credits roll (Tyler Perry Films presents a Tyler Perry Production), the story begins. The film brings back characters from the first *Tyler Perry's Boo! A Madea Halloween* (2016) and begins at a prep school where teenage Tiffany (Diamond White) and Gabriella (Inanna Sarkis) are hoping to attend a frat house Halloween party nearby. Tiffany's dad, Brian (Perry), shows up on her birthday to give her a lame present (headphones) while her mom, Debrah (Taja V. Simpson), gets her a car. Her divorced parents cannot agree on how to raise Tiffany. Brian cannot see her as anything but a child and Debrah has lost all forms of basic parenting skills, choosing instead to spoil her and say yes to her every request.

This conflict eventually results in the Tiffany and Gabriella attending the party, which has been moved from the frat house (thanks to the shenanigans that occurred in the last film) to Lake Derrick, where, apparently, many kids have been killed in the past and nobody has yet been apprehended. Once Brian gets wind of this, he partners up with Gabriella's dad, Victor (Tito Ortiz), to try and find them and bring them home. Brian's relatives—his father Joe (Perry), Aunt Madea (Perry), Aunt Bam (Cassi Davis), and Hattie (Patrice Lovely)—also want to help out after Madea conveniently overhears every detail about his party from Tiffany. The four of them hop in a car and make their way out to Camp Derrick, where mayhem eventually ensues in the form of a ghoulish girl and chainsaw-wielding maniacs.

It takes about an hour before all that occurs because Perry is so wrapped up in long, tedious back-and-forths between himself as Brian and the myriad of other characters he portrays. Early in the film, when Brian enters his house and finds his relatives sitting in the living room, he stands there as they argue with each other, not at all acknowledging that he is there. Why not just leave the room then? Because Perry wants to show off how he can play three characters in one scene while making it look effortless. Instead, it looks very much effort-full. Instead of trying for a single master shot in which all three characters appear, Perry settles on lazily cutting between them with little silences between the lines. No flair, no reliance on timing or nuance. Every scene is punctuated by a tired temp score that sounds left in out of spite. Every comedic scene is just one character contradicting another character, ad nauseum.

The best that can be said is that it is not all Perry's show, as it was in the beginning of his career. By employing Davis and Lovely in roles that require as much broad gestures and make-up as Perry gives to himself, he at least shows an interest in sharing screen time with people who can liven up the place. Also, Perry leaves out the usual, awkwardly-inserted Christian message this time. Aside from a couple "Praise Jesus!" lines and Gabriella's acknowledging of being a Christian, there is little here for anyone hoping for (or dreading) the big sermon. Still, this is amateurish and undisciplined filmmaking on every level, which his fan base does not seem to mind or notice. As long as Perry's name remains above, below, and on either side of the title, he will always have that fan base to give his films the #1 spot on the box office charts in their opening week, which happened with both *Boo!* films. It keeps working, which is why he keeps working. But that is what this looks and feels like for everyone involved: Work, which is death for a comedy.

Collin Souter

CREDITS

Madea/Joe/Brian: Tyler Perry
Aunt Bam: Cassi Davis
Hattie: Patrice Lovely
Jonathan: Yousef Erakat
Tiffany: Diamond White
Origin: United States
Language: English
Released: 2017
Production: Ozzie Areu, Will Areu, Mark Swinton, Tyler Perry; Tyler Perry Co.; released by Lionsgate
Directed by: Tyler Perry
Written by: Tyler Perry
Cinematography by: Richard J. Vialet
Music by: Philip White
Music Supervisor: Joel C. High
Editing: Larry Sexton
Costumes: Crystal Hayslett
Production Design: Paul Wonsek
MPAA rating: PG-13
Running time: 101 minutes

REVIEWS

Bramesco, Charles. *The A.V. Club*. October 23, 2017.
DeFore, John. *Hollywood Reporter*. October 20, 2017.
Duralde, Alonso. *TheWrap*. October 20, 2017.
Gibron, Bill. *Film Racket*. October 20, 2017.
Gleiberman, Owen. *Variety*. October 20, 2017.
Henderson, odie. *RogerEbert.com*. October 20, 2017.
Kenny, Glenn. *New York Times*. October 20, 2017.
Myers, Kimber. *Los Angeles Times*. October 20, 2017.
Orndorf, Brian. *Blu-Ray.com*. October 20, 2017.
Schwerdtfeger, Conner. *CinemaBlend.com*. October 20, 2017.

TRIVIA

At the trailer event, Tyler Perry stated that every time the movie was sent to Lionsgate, it was returned with an R-rating, which led to material being cut to garner a a PG-13 rating.

AWARDS

Golden Raspberries 2017: Worst Actress (Perry)

Nominations:

Golden Raspberries 2017: Worst Remake/Sequel

THE BOOK OF HENRY

Never leave things undone.
—Movie tagline

Box Office: $4.5 Million

The Book of Henry plays like somebody stole an unproduced script from the 1980s (think Amblin Entertainment) and decided to kill the best character off during a rewrite. This is a movie that panders and it is cliché-ridden enough that it commits an even bigger sin: *The Book of Henry* is boring.

Henry Carpenter (Jaeden Lieberher), is a boy genius. When not tinkering with his Rube Goldberg type inventions, he spends his time protecting his younger brother Peter (Jacob Tremblay) from bullies, encouraging his single mom Susan (Naomi Watts) to take her idea of writing kids' books more seriously, and dabbles in investments smartly enough to have accumulated a decent nest egg for his family. In short, his life is more or less about taking care of others. When he sees Christina (Maddie Ziegler), his friend next door being abused by her dad Glenn (Dean Norris), a policeman, he lets people know, including his school principal Mrs. Wilder (Tonya Pinkins). When he realizes no one wants to challenge Glenn because of his connections, he launches his own plan, writing the details down in a notebook.

But a sudden seizure leads doctors to diagnose Henry with a brain tumor. Before going into surgery, he makes his brother promise to let their mother know about the book. In a matter of days, Henry dies. Susan, completely distraught, decides to focus on Henry's step-by-step plan, which involves assassinating Glenn, complete with an ironclad alibi. But just as Susan is about to pull the trigger her conscience forces her to confront Glenn who scoffs and reminds her no one will believe her word against his. Glenn calls the police to pick Susan up but, unbeknownst to him, Mrs. Wilder who, moved by Christina's situation, calls social services to launch an investigation. Glenn finds out the police are on the way to his house and kills himself. Susan adopts Christina and finally writers her children's book.

Everyone in this mess deserves better than Gregg Hurwitz's manipulative screenplay, but, to his credit, it could be noted that director Colin Trevorrow read an early version that was basically a black comedy and took a pass. Both should have left well enough alone. No way it was worse than this. Trevorrow has made some good stuff. His debut, the sci-fi romantic comedy *Safety Not Guaranteed* (2012), was hard to pigeonhole but full of heart and was entertaining. His follow-up, *Jurassic World* (2015), was a solid entry in that franchise. But this film sets up a larger-than-life character in Henry, complete with unlikely steampunk aesthetic and then tries to plunk him down into the real world. His idea to kill Glenn is a horrible one that no adult would take seriously enough to actually implement. The script surrounds the family with the sassy waitress, the good natured but ineffective bureaucrats, and other stock characters, but they have nothing to do but go through the paces. In fact, no one in this movie acts like a real person. At one point, the bullies bothering Peter spare him because, as they point out to Henry, "You're smart at least."

The efforts of a fine cast, set in motion by Jaeden Lieberher, whose portrayal of Henry should earn him a career, account for almost any fun viewers are likely to have here. Naomi Watts is fine, but then she almost always elevates any part. It could be remarked that her recent involvement in the rebirth of *Twin Peaks* has come at a good time since she seems to be stuck in some pretty forgettable big screen projects lately. But the one cast member that should definitely have more to do is Maddie Ziegler in her big screen debut as Christina. Despite her centrality to the plot, Christina is largely silent, something to be acted on. In a film this tonally inconsistent, it is difficult to excuse and only underlines the lack of focus in the writing. Ironically, when dealing with subjects like death and grief the movie has its best moments. A better story where Henry carries out his own plan is easy to imagine and might have even supported the weird mix of light-hearted child-in-all-of-us energy and attempts at dark Hitchcockian suspense.

In the end, *The Book of Henry* is likely darker than anyone intended. Kids see the world in black and white, especially the world of crime and punishment. No one learns anything about that here. But they do get the dubious satisfaction of imagining how great it would be to murder the right person. The script gives them a literal blueprint and, until near the end, tacit permission to enjoy it.

Dave Canfield

CREDITS

Susan Carpenter: Naomi Watts
Henry Carpenter: Jaeden Lieberher
Peter Carpenter: Jacob Tremblay
Sheila: Sarah Silverman
Glenn Sickleman: Dean Norris
Origin: United States

Language: English
Released: 2017
Production: Sidney Kimmel, Adam Richman, Gregg Hurwitz; Double Nickel Entertainment, Sidney Kimmel Entertainment; released by Focus Features L.L.C.
Directed by: Colin Trevorrow
Written by: Gregg Hurwitz
Cinematography by: John Schwartzman
Music by: Michael Giacchino
Sound: Al Nelson
Editing: Kevin Stitt
Art Direction: Derek Wang
Costumes: Melissa Toth
Production Design: Kalina Ivanov
MPAA rating: PG-13
Running time: 105 minutes

REVIEWS

Addiego, Walter V. *San Francisco Chronicle.* June 14, 2017.
Burr, Ty. *Boston Globe.* June 15, 2017.
Callahan, Dan. *TheWrap.* June 14, 2017.
Chang, Justin. *Los Angeles Times.* June 15, 2017.
Dargis, Manohla. *New York Times.* June 15, 2017.
Dudley, Joshua. *New York Observer.* June 18, 2017.
Gleiberman, Owen. *Variety.* June 15, 2017.
Kohn, Eric. *IndieWire.* June 15, 2017.
O'Sullivan. *Washington Post.* June 15, 2017.
Yoshida, Emily. *New York Magazine/Vulture.* June 15, 2017.

QUOTES

Susan Carpenter: "I didn't want things to get violent."
Henry Carpenter: "Violence isn't the worst thing in the world."

TRIVIA

The film was shot in thirty-six days.

THE BOSS BABY

Ruthless and toothless!
—Movie tagline

Box Office: $175 Million

"Oh, that Boss Baby is just too much!" is an approving appraisal that understandably went through many moviegoers' minds while chuckling yet again at this DreamWorks production's humorously-tart-tongued and tyrannical titular tyke, actually an undercover, quite-junior executive who is provided here with the well-honed acidic articulation of Alec Baldwin. Unfortunately, it was just as understandable if viewers ultimately uttered the exact same sentence in a less complimentary sense when referring to the film itself, as those responsible for this adaptation of the simple, charming, and widely-relatable 2010 picture book by writer/illustrator Marla Frazee have poured too much of their own creativity into the voluminous additions of confusion-inducing overcomplication and chaos. It is rather like when the adorable face of this tiny-suited hoot of a head honcho is slathered with a sickly shade of makeup so that he can convincingly spew a vacuum-full of fake vomit, or when the features of quite-endearing pseudo-sibling Tim Templeton (well-cast Miles Bakshi, grandson of animation legend Ralph) are totally obscured by a real-food cascade from the baby's countenance, except not only the audience but the film itself come to temporarily lose sight of what had heretofore been so engagingly identifiable, and it is scarcely a laughing matter as things became generally buried beneath a lot of less-than-appealing stuff.

No matter how sapped newbie moms and dads feel after the branching-out and blossoming upon their family tree, Frazee's book provided a reassuring reminder that the resulting apple of their eye is, despite any evidence seemingly to the contrary, predominantly sweet. If there are other fruits of one's loins already present, the ultimate comforting uplift of this message will surely also resonate with children filled with fret-fueled jealousy, sure that the family's latest addition is being disgustingly spoiled rotten, often smells that way too, and should therefore be thrown out post-haste.

It was fresh musings about kid coping that led to the tri-membered family Frazee had created gaining a seven-year-old boy through the process of cinematic adaptation and not adoption, and the focus was thus shifted to fraternal friction that would eventually spark brotherly love. The film is framed with voiceover from an adult Tim (Tobey Maguire) harking back to halcyon days before the hostile household takeover perpetrated by a monopolizing, corporate-speaking, deceptively-angel-faced hellion with both pacifier and portfolio. As the mature-voiced Tim notes early-on that his parents (Lisa Kudrow and Jimmy Kimmel) always said he had an "overactive imagination." With the first few of many delightfully-depicted childhood adventure fantasies in which things sometimes get even hairier than the big, blue gorilla young Tim initially battles, it is clear that the "Boss Baby" is a creative reconfiguration of reality. He springs from grown-up Tim's still-fertile mind, a new madcap metaphorical embellishment about his brother's real arrival that the ending confirms he has purposefully created to help his own offspring-about-to-become-a-sibling, a daughter currently struggling with the same anticipatory anxiety that he once felt.

Many in the audience understood the difficulty of dealing with such displacement, empathizing with Tim when the three's-company bliss he was enjoying with his parents is fouled up as if "out of nowhere" (he failed to comprehend that noticeable baby bump) by a fourth that quickly seems to be crowding him entirely out of both his accustomed place as the sole center of attention and his mother and father's heretofore wholly-devoted hearts. The pint-sized usurper certainly had little trouble commanding the attention and affections of viewers, the intriguingly-sneaky and irrepressibly-cheeky cherub's not only being in every sense (including winsomely) big-headed, but also possessing expression-enhancing oversized baby blues (Tim even more so), reminding one of the peepers that peered out of the waif portraits in *Big Eyes* (2014). As for the character's big mouth: Director Tom McGrath revealed that he sold The Powers That Be on the film by showing them clips of the baby from his *Megamind* (2010) and adding snippets of Baldwin's Jack Donaghy dialogue from NBC's *30 Rock*, and having the actor's highly-recognizable voice cuttingly coming from the tiniest of chops does loom large here. (While many took this small-in-many-ways, autocratic bully of a businessman as an oh-so-timely, sly skewering of the current president that Baldwin has already been so famously and devilishly depicting on *Saturday Night Live*, McGrath pointed out that characterization and casting decisions were largely made years before Donald Trump became affront and center in the political arena.)

Adults likely also chortled when this top-dog tot barked "Cookies are for closers!"—an alteration of the actor's frequently-quoted line from *Glengarry Glen Ross* (1992). They probably enjoyed other retro references, including the variously-stylized and sometimes briefly-nightmarish daydream sequences that pay homage to iconic animators like Looney Tunes legend Chuck Jones and fellow Warner Bros. wonders Maurice Noble and Tex Avery, the singing of "Blackbird" by The Beatles (at least the first few of too many times), and the sight of numerous imagination-enhancing playthings wistfully recalled from the simpler time of their own childhoods. However, there is soon nothing simple about *The Boss Baby*, and while the toy train of one scene never derails, the film, increasingly overloaded and hurtling at an ever-escalating rate of speed, soon arrives at a perplexingly-twisty stretch upon which it temporarily does just that.

It is noted at one point in Frazee's book that the Boss Baby was not saying a word that made any sense "but that didn't stop him," and many moviegoers may begin to feel the same about the film amidst eruptions of excessive, hard-to-follow exposition about the convoluted, vengeful plot of dastardly PuppyCo. CEO Francis Francis (Steve Buscemi, as the former Super Colossal Big Fat Boss Baby). The climax of the film involves the worldwide dissemination via a rocket ship launched from downtown Las Vegas of perma-puppies meant to corner the market on cuteness, as well as The Boss Baby and Tim's frenetic race by bike, a plane filled with Elvis impersonators, and a vehicle filled with adoring bimbos to ensure the future of the aforementioned other type of lovable babes. It is ultimately worth it for any temporarily-nonplussed audience members to stick around for the satisfyingly-touching togetherness of *The Boss Baby*'s finale, which includes the assurance of there always being plenty of love to go around. As the $125 million film grossed around a half-billion worldwide, it also seems assured that there will be plenty of money around to make its hinted-at sequel.

David L. Boxerbaum

CREDITS

Boss Baby: Alec Baldwin
Francis Francis: Steve Buscemi
Dad: Jimmy Kimmel
Mom: Lisa Kudrow
Adult Tim: Tobey Maguire
Tim: Miles Christopher Bakshi
Origin: United States
Language: English
Released: 2017
Production: Ramsey Naito; DreamWorks Animation L.L.C.; released by Twentieth Century Fox Film Corp.
Directed by: Tom McGrath
Written by: Michael McCullers
Music by: Steve Mazzaro; Hans Zimmer
Sound: Paul N.J. Ottosson
Editing: James Ryan
MPAA rating: PG
Running time: 97 minutes

REVIEWS

Chang, Justin. *Los Angeles Times*. March 30, 2017.
Franich, Darren. *Entertainment Weekly*. March 30, 2017.
Genzlinger, Neil. *New York Times*. March 30, 2017.
Gleiberman, Owen. *Variety*. March 12, 2017.
Padua, Pat. *Washington Post*. March 30, 2017.
Rechtshaffen, Michael. *Hollywood Reporter*. March 12, 2017.
Russo, Tom. *Boston Globe*. March 30, 2017.
Walsh, Katie. *Chicago Tribune*. March 30, 2017.
Zwecker, Bill. *Chicago Sun-Times*. March 30, 2017.

QUOTES

Tim [about "Blackbird"]: "That's my special song! My parents wrote it just for me."
Boss Baby: "Your parents are Lennon and McCartney?"

TRIVIA

The first trailer for the film was released on National Boss's Day.

AWARDS

Nominations:

Oscars 2017: Animated Film

Golden Globes 2018: Animated Film

BPM (BEATS PER MINUTE)

(120 battements par minute)

Box Office: $100,072

In Robin Campillo's enthralling French drama *BPM (Beats Per Minute)*, the political is deeply personal, beautifully illustrated by the movie's dynamic mix of feeling and purpose. It's also captured in a mélange of styles that suggestively intertwines agitprop with radical group theater. This movie is haunted by a specter of breakdown and death but also furiously alive to possibility.

The movie's full English title means "beats per minute," connoting a heartbeat. It also touches on consciousness and desire, freedom and movement. Set in the early 1990s, the story is about the formation of the Paris chapter of ACT Up, an AIDS-advocacy group. The movie charts how the organization developed various political provocations and street demonstrations in demanding a more aggressive response from the government and pharmaceutical companies in combating the rising AIDS pandemic.

Campillo also wrote the film with Philippe Mangeot. He also served as one of the three editors. His versatility has been one of his most distinctive and exciting qualities. He was a crucial collaborator, as writer and editor, on the superb early films of Laurent Cantet, *Human Resources* (1999); *Time Out* (2001); and the Cannes prizewinner, *The Class* (2008). *BPM* is his third feature as a director, and the film's particular energy and vibrancy springs from his deep personal connection, with much of the material shaped by his own experiences as a young activist in Paris ACT Up.

The movie is also a French analog to David France's excellent American documentary, *How to Survive a Plague* (2012). *BPM* is a deeply French film, given that much of the first half is structured around the weekly Tuesday night meetings held at a university lecture hall where the group members, primarily young gay men, meet to discuss policy, adapt new slogans, and devise strategy initiatives.

The meetings are conducted as almost parliamentary procedures, with double speakers who argue dialectically opposing positions. The group's leaders are Thibault (Antoine Reinartz), a pragmatist who is distrusted by some for his slick ability to play both sides. His nervy top organizer, Sophie (Adèle Haenel), is blessed with a more revolutionary, confrontational genius for political stunts and shock tactics. At that first meeting, the newcomers learn about a delicious twist to the proceedings, of approval conveyed through the snapping of their fingers. That peculiar sound, of the staccato, almost nervous rhyming, is a jolt.

As the primary editor, Campillo also fractures the chronology, starting the movie by cutting back and forth between a public revolt and the group's first meeting. The film begins as the members interrupt a lecture by a government health minister by staging his mock arrest, then handcuffing and dousing him with a balloon of fake red blood. Campillo's cutting links policy to action, reinforcing the group's notion that engagement and action necessarily trumps decorum and formal pleasantries. Rather than being pedantic, these moments have a jolting humor and thrill, like a follow-up demonstration at the corporate offices of a powerful pharmaceutical company where activists initially target the wrong department, or another impromptu gathering at a neighborhood school to inform a group of school-aged kids about the dangers of needle sharing. As one member gives out practical lessons about safe sex, the teacher cuts in to say, "Don't forget about your maps for next week."

The humor humanizes the characters, as does their quest to balance their activism with more recognizable forms of release and thrill. Even as the movie argues for action in the face of institutional indifference, Campillo breaks up the rhythm of the group meetings and political stunts with colorful, pungent reminders of an individual need for social connection and sexual expression. Campillo punctuates these erotic reveries with a series of scenes set inside a dance club, with neon-sculpted throb lights and disco music. If these young warriors are engaged in one particular kind of battle, they are nevertheless eager to give into the demands of the flesh, of companionship and love, even for those who are HIV-positive and must constantly track their T-cell counts.

If the first half of *BPM* is a charged social history, the second half is quieter, more reflective, and emotionally devastating. Having mapped out his characters and their various dilemmas, showing their struggle to achieve their ends and maintain some public symphony in discovering how to mediate action with compromise, Campillo narrows his focus and concentrates on the specific human and personal consequences of the struggle as played out in the relationship of Sean (Nahuel Pérez Biscayart) and Nathan (Arnaud Valois).

The political theater marches go on, like a brilliantly staged mass death scene rendered through some striking overhead shots. Increasingly, a larger human question takes precedence. Many of the dominant characters from the first half shift over to the margins. The concentration deepens. *BPM* moves beautifully, tenderly toward something ever more beautiful, romantic, and evanescent. Campillo handles the transition wonderfully. The very talented cinematographer Jeanne Lapoirie achieves some remarkable visual power, moving gracefully from the throbbing, kinetic actions of the street theater with the more plaintive, intimate exchanges of the two lovers. An excellent example is one of the most unforgettable images in the film of the two men shown in long shot at the beach, their bodies tiny, as they approach the edge of the shore as the swells and waves crash at their feet. The water practically taunts them. In another scene, Nathan and Sean share an intense intimate moment inside a hospital room, a playful and erotic assertion of healing and rebirth.

As a work of art, *BPM* is frequently a sobering, bracing act of defiance. Even as it meditates on memory and time, the movie privileges a specific kind of vitality, sexually, politically, even if, as happens throughout the body ultimately gives in and fails. An important point is made, that ACT Up fought for not only just for the gay community but the other high-risk groups like drugs addicts and prostitutes ostracized by the wider society.

Emotionally, the movie is volatile and headstrong, eruptive, angry, and mournful. *BPM* fits a mood and captures a time. The movie is long but never indulgent or slack. By the end it is exquisitely sad, overpowering. One of the main characters, his body wasting away and his breathing labored, has a fantastic, chilling vision of a blood-drenched Seine. Always a symbol of birth and cleansing, the water imagery is now a harbinger of death. Thanks to his radical action, a death sentence no longer hangs over an entire community. Life in all of its permutations moves on.

Patrick Z. McGavin

CREDITS

Sean Dalmazo: Nahuel Perez Biscayart
Nathan: Arnaud Valois
Sophie: Adele Haenel
Max: Felix Maritaud
Germain: Mehdi Toure
Origin: United States
Language: French
Released: 2017
Production: Hugues Charbonneau, Marie-Ange Luciani; Les Films de Pierre; released by The Orchard
Directed by: Robin Campillo
Written by: Robin Campillo
Cinematography by: Jeanne Lapoirie
Music by: Arnaud Rebotini
Sound: Valerie Deloof
Editing: Robin Campillo; Stephanie Leger; Anita Roth
Costumes: Isabelle Pannetier
MPAA rating: Unrated
Running time: 140 minutes

REVIEWS

Baumgarten, Marjorie. *Austin Chronicle.* January 25, 2018.
Burr, Ty. *Boston Globe.* January 31, 2018.
Chang, Justin. *Los Angeles Times.* October 26, 2017.
Dowd, A.A. *The A.V. Club.* October 26, 2017.
Edelstein, David. *New York Magazine.* October 25, 2017.
Greenblatt, Leah. *Entertainment Weekly.* October 20, 2017.
Jenkins, Mark. *Washington Post.* November 16, 2017.
LaSalle, Mick. *San Francisco Chronicle.* November 9, 2017.
Scott, A.O. *New York Times.* October 19, 2017.
Wolfe, April. *Village Voice.* October 19, 2017.

TRIVIA

The name of the production company "Les films de Pierre" of Hugues Charbonneau and Marie-Ange Luciani is an homage to Pierre Bergé.

AWARDS

Nominations:

Ind. Spirit 2018: Foreign Film

BRAD'S STATUS

Box Office: $2.1 Million

Writer-director Mike White has developed into a unique voice for middle-class malaise and those who experience an existential crisis of sorts. His characters often come from a good place, but have failed to reach either a potential greatness or an epiphany that will lead to a more satisfying outlook on their lives. More recently, he has focused on the role activism plays in the lives of his troubled protagonists. In *Year of the Dog* (2007), the character of Peggy (Molly Shannon) finds fulfillment in rescuing animals after the death of her dog. In the HBO series *Enlightened*, Amy Jellicoe (Laura Dern) also finds fulfillment in trying to do the right thing for others, but at the expense of everyone around her. Her activism leads to catastrophe, more often than not. Now, with *Brad's Status*, White centers on a white male who has lived his life trying to raise money for good causes while all his friends from college have taken money for themselves and have lived lives of luxury.

Watching his old friends from afar on social media is keeping Brad (Ben Stiller) up at nights. Money problems have been constantly rattling through his mind as he lies awake wondering if he made the right choices in life by trying to be a good person instead of a success. Lately, to him, these virtues are mutually exclusive. He resorts to flippantly asking his wife, Melanie (Jenna Fischer), "Who gets your parents' house after they die?" He sees his employees, many of whom are at least twenty years younger than him, quitting the job to pursue careers that have a better chance at being lucrative. He loves his wife, but questions whether or not her own idealism kept him from selling out. "Maybe her contentment undermined my ambition," he ponders, via voice-over.

Now, his son Troy (Austin Abrams) has been granted an interview at Harvard University and could very well get in. This latest development has him lying awake at night with even more anxiety. The two of them fly out to Harvard as well as Tufts University where he also has an appointment. They have a healthy and honest relationship and Troy can often see right through his father. When they get to Harvard. Troy realizes he got the appointment date wrong and Brad confronts the department heads and tries to convince them to let his son have the interview anyway, all the while Troy begs him to let it go and not cause a scene, which he knows is coming and will be detrimental to him if he does get into Harvard. Being a teenager, he feels he will always be looked at as the kid with the annoying father.

Brad calls Melanie and asks, "Who do we know at Harvard?" They know one of Brad's older, more successful friends, Craig (Michael Sheen). Brad would rather not call on Craig, a former staffer at the White House and now a successful author. He does so anyway and Craig comes through. Troy, a music prodigy who knows little about the real world, lands the interviews he needs and is beaming with joy once again. When Brad calls on Craig, though, he learns that he was never invited to another friend's wedding, a friend who was recently on the cover of *Architecture Digest* magazine. Apparently, everyone from his old group of friends attended except him. Perhaps, his status as the head of a non-profit keeps him from getting invited to high-profile events for fear of being asked to donate money.

White is careful not to beg the audience for their sympathy for Brad. Middle-aged white male malaise has fallen out of fashion as a narrative in so many ways over the years that a film like *Brad's Status* could be seen as culturally out of step from the first page of the script onwards. White's film, though, is about that very awareness of being out of step. At one point in the film, Brad and Troy meet up with an older friend of Troy's a female student at Harvard named Ananya (Shazi Raja), who later hears Brad listing all his personal problems and general dissatisfaction in life. "You're lucky," she tells him. "You're fifty and you still think the world is made for you." She calls him out on his white privilege and asks him not to ask her to feel sorry for him. The audience will have the same sentiments early on, but it would be a mistake to approach White's film as any kind of statement on Millennials v. Generation X. *Brad's Status* centers on a more universal theme of aging, past failures, and perspective on the haves and have-nots.

In a way, that is also a problem with White's script. It becomes pretty clear early on that the more successful people in the film—from Billy (Jemaine Clemente), who lives a life of luxury and has already retired, to Jason (Luke Wilson), a businessman with a private jet—will be the source of quiet mockery. Brad and Melanie have a solid marriage and have a most ideal son. It is hard to feel sorry for Brad, so the realization he comes to when he figures out how blessed his life has been in contrast with the shallowness of his rich friends is something that the audience can feel a little too early in the proceedings. Brad comes to this realization long before the film ends and White seems to be reiterating it with every phone call Brad has to any one of the people from his past. By the end, there is little left to say.

White is so good at nailing every moment and every bit of humor that the film maintains a nice fluidity and remains engaging, in spite of this flaw. Stiller has always been at his best when he is in a darker place and he is the perfect surrogate here. His scenes with Abrams are warm and very believable. White closes the film, typically, with an inner monologue that ends with a declarative conclusion, which makes it the connective tissue between this and his other films. At the end of *The Good Girl* (2002), Justine (Jennifer Aniston) finally says, "I have problems." *Year of the Dog* (2007) concludes with Peggy stating, in so many words, "I am fulfilled." Here, Brad simply says that he "is alive" and that that might have to be good enough. It may not seem like much of a sentiment in the moment, but in the context of White's body of work, it makes for a compelling piece of a bigger whole.

Collin Souter

CREDITS

Brad Sloan: Ben Stiller
Troy Sloan: Austin Abrams
Melanie Sloan: Jenna Fischer
Craig Fisher: Michael Sheen
Billy Wearslter: Jemaine Clement
Jason Hatfield: Luke Wilson
Origin: United States
Language: English
Released: 2017
Production: David Bernad, Dede Gardner, Sidney Kimmel, Brad Pitt, Mike White; Amazon Studios, Plan B Entertainment, Sidney Kimmel Entertainment; released by Annapurna Pictures
Directed by: Mike White
Written by: Mike White
Cinematography by: Xavier Perez Grobet
Music by: Mark Mothersbaugh
Sound: Bryan Parker
Editing: Heather Persons
Art Direction: Zoe Sakellaropoulo
Costumes: Alex Bovaird
Production Design: Richard Hoover
MPAA rating: R
Running time: 102 minutes

REVIEWS

Abele, Robert. *TheWrap*. September 11, 2017.
Chang, Justin. *Los Angeles Times*. September 14, 2017.
D'Angelo, Mike. *The A.V. Club*. September 13, 2017.
Eagan, Daniel. *Film Journal International*. September 13, 2017.
Kohn, Eric. *IndieWire*. September 11, 2017.
Lemire, Christy. *RogerEbert.com*. September 14, 2017.
Schumacher, Allison. *Consequence of Sound*. September 14, 2017.
Scott, A.O. *New York Times*. September 14, 2017.
Stewart, Sara. *New York Post*. September 14, 2017.
Taylor, Kate. *Globe and Mail*. September 11, 2017.

QUOTES

Brad Sloan: "I'm alive."

TRIVIA

Director Mike White has a cameo in the film, playing Nick.

BRAWL IN CELL BLOCK 99

S. Craig Zahler makes slow-burn films that deconstruct macho male archetypes. His harrowing Western *Bone Tomahawk* (2015) felt like a relatively standard genre entry until it exploded in a horrific final act that would make Eli Roth cover his eyes. Similarly, *Brawl in Cell Block 99* is a relatively straightforward prison drama about a man who digs himself deeper and deeper into an inescapable hole, which also culminates in tarrying violence. With just these two films, Zahler has already announced himself as a talented director to watch, not only for his unique sense of pacing but for the performances he can draw from square-jawed actors like his leading man here, Vince Vaughn, doing arguably the best work of his career.

Vaughn stars as Bradley Thomas, an everyman who is about to have a very bad day. First, he loses his job at an auto repair shop, leading him to come home early, where he catches his wife, Lauren (Jennifer Carpenter), having an illicit conversation in her car in the driveway. He then notices signs of an affair on her neck and Lauren admits that she's been cheating on Bradley, leading the hulking man to literally tear apart her car with his bare hands. It's a crazy, extended sequence in which Bradley rips apart a car piece by piece, wrenching free its hood and mirrors, etc. It's a way for Zahler to foreshadow violence and extreme acts of strength. This kind of anger is within Bradley Thomas and could be inspired to be unleashed. Bradley then decides to forgive Lauren, and Zahler drops a few interesting elements into the background of this couple's story, including a fight with alcoholism and an unborn child they lost. This day is just another roadblock which they will overcome, but Zahler has defined their relationship as well as the fact that Bradley now has to go back to working in the criminal underworld to make ends meet.

A year and a half later and Bradley is working for Gil (Marc Blucas), who introduces him to Eleazar (Dion Mucciacito) and gives him a new assignment—to pick up a delivery of crystal meth with two of Eleazar's men. Bradley is hesitant about running a dangerous job with two shady strangers, but Gil convinces him with an offer of three months paternity leave. Bradley's loyalty to family and his wife will become a theme throughout the film. Bradley insists that he's in charge and that the other men must follow his orders. Of course, they do not, and things go very wrong, ending in a shootout with police. Even though Bradley intervenes in a way that captures his cohorts and saves the lives of several policemen, he gets seven years in prison for his efforts.

While Bradley is in jail, Lauren is kidnapped by Eleazar's men. The next day, Bradley is visited by someone credited only as the Placid Man (the eternal Udo Kier), who tells him that Bradley must assassinate an inmate named Christopher Bridges or Lauren's child will be brutally, and forcefully aborted. Bridges is not at the medium-security prison at which Bradley resides—he is at a maximum one called Redleaf, in the titular cell block 99. Bradley breaks a guard's arm, ensuring his transfer to Redleaf, where he discovers what Zahler basically films like a circle of hell.

There are few rules at Redleaf but the ones there are happen to be enforced by Warden Tuggs (Don Johnson), a sadistic monster who throws Bradley in a cell filled with feces. And this is just the start of Bradley's journey, which eventually starts to feel like Dante going deeper and deeper into the underworld. By the end, Bradley is speaking to the devil himself, Eleazar, who has entrapped Bradley into ruining his life and going on this nightmarish journey. With Zahler's intense style, there is the sense long before the film is over that Bradley is not going to escape this hellscape and live a happy life with his wife and child. The best he can do is ensure their safety. And he may have to smash a few heads to do just that.

Brawl in Cell Block 99 is a visceral, brutal film that starts off like a relatively routine story of an everyman succumbing to the criminal underworld to keep his family together but becomes something much darker and far more insane. Just as Zahler found cannibalism and brutality in the old west, he looks under the surface of the prison drama and finds human excrement and bloody violence. It's a fascinating journey into the heart of darkness that starts to echo that Joseph Conrad novel in its increasingly nightmarish, dreamlike visuals. There are parts of cell block 99 that don't feel human, as if a demon could come around a corner and it would fit snugly into the narrative.

Zahler's confident storytelling is probably the best thing about *Brawl in Cell Block 99* but none of it works without Vince Vaughn's committed performance. Finally escaping the man-children he played for too long in bad comedies, Vaughn has recast himself as a very intriguing dramatic actor on HBO's *True Detective,* Mel Gibson's *Hacksaw Ridge* (2016), and this film. His square-jawed, all-American looks fit perfectly in these stories of men beset by violence who find their own anger and their own salvation. It's possibly the best work of his career and leads one to anticipate what he does next. Hopefully it's another film with S. Craig Zahler.

Brian Tallerico

CREDITS

Bradley Thomas: Vince Vaughn
Lauren Thomas: Jennifer Carpenter
Warden Tuggs: Don Johnson
Placid Man: Udo Kier
Gil: Marc Blucas
Origin: United States
Language: English
Released: 2017
Production: Jack Heller, Dallas Sonnier; Assemble Media, Caliber Media Co., Cinestate, IMG Films, Nasser Group, Realmbuilders Productions, XYZ Films; released by RLJ Entertainment Inc.
Directed by: S. Craig Zahler
Written by: S. Craig Zahler
Cinematography by: Benji Bakshi
Music by: S. Craig Zahler; Jeff Herriott
Sound: Craig Kyllonen
Editing: Greg D'Auria
Art Direction: Max Wixom
Costumes: Megan Stark Evans
Production Design: Freddy Waff
MPAA rating: Unrated
Running time: 132 minutes

REVIEWS

Abele, Robert. *TheWrap*. October 5, 2017.
Abrams, Simon. *RogerEbert.com*. October 6, 2017.
Catsoulis, Jeannette. *New York Times*. October 5, 2017.
Chang, Justin. *Los Angeles Times*. October 5, 2017.
D'Angelo, Mike. *The A.V. Club*. October 4, 2017.
Fear, David. *Rolling Stone*. October 5, 2017.
Jenkins, Mark. *Washington Post*. October 12, 2017.
Kohn, Eric. *IndieWire*. September 14, 2017.
Packham, Chris. *Village Voice*. October 4, 2017.
Rothkopf, Joshua. *Time Out*. October 6, 2017.

TRIVIA

During the Toronto International Film Festival, producers commented that the destruction of the car was indeed done by Vince Vaughn himself.

THE BREADWINNER

Box Office: $256,205

When the 2018 Academy Award® nominations were announced, a little animated film from a company called Cartoon Saloon beat out several options from major companies, including a Warner Bros' entry (*The LEGO Batman Movie* [2017]), a monster of a box-office hit from Universal (*Despicable Me 3* [2017]), and even a Pixar sequel (*Cars 3* [2017]). Further exacerbating the surprise factor at the nomination was the subject matter of *The Breadwinner,* and the fact that it carried a PG-13 rating. This story is decidedly not for children, at least not for the littlest ones, and it deals with subject matter that would be absolutely terrifying and heartbreaking were it a live-action film. That it does so with tenderness and truth is why it was nominated over Lightning McQueen and the Minions, and why Cartoon Saloon, who also made Oscar® nominees *The Secret of Kells* (2009) and *Song of the Sea* (2014), is increasingly being taken seriously as an animation powerhouse.

Saara Chaudry elegantly voices Parvana, an unforgettable heroine in a part of the world that does not encourage or support 11-year-old girls who are forced to become heroic. In Kabul, girls are not allowed in the marketplace, but Parvana gets around this because she's needed to accompany and aide her father (Ali Badshah), as he only has one leg. It is not just the presence of a girl in the bazaar that upsets the misogynistic Taliban members who patrol it, but Parvana's father aggravates by his very presence as the professor represents a brand of intellectualism that always challenges those in power. And Parvana's already-fragile world shatters completely when Taliban members drag her father away, and imprison him, leaving only the girl with a baby brother and a sick mother. How could they possibly provide and survive when women are not even allowed to leave the home to get water or see Parvana's father? Director Nora Twomey, working from the book by Deborah Ellis, deftly conveys the true danger of their predicament without feeling manipulative or exploitative.

Parvana has to grow up quickly, becoming a de facto provider for her family and keeping their spirits up as their situation worsens. First, she becomes what her father likely was for her at some point, a storyteller—she calms her brother by relaying the fable of a boy who stood up to the power structure around her, "The Elephant King," which Twomey renders in a style different from the rest of the film. Then Parvana runs into a classmate who has cut her hair and is pretending to be her brother, giving her the idea to do the same. As a boy, Parvana can move around the city and provide for her family. Of course, she becomes the titular breadwinner, but the danger of the world around her is never far from the front of the narrative, especially as she works to free her father.

In an era that focuses more heavily than ever on gender rights, the story of a young girl who confronts violent misogyny head-on has international value. Parvana's story becomes a lesson for young ladies who face patriarchies and sexism in any culture, although that's not to imply that the film softens the specific difficulties of being a girl in a Taliban-run country for some sort of perceived universalism, as children's films so often do. On the contrary, it feels very specific to its region, beautifully balancing the inherent danger of a violent, misogynistic culture with Parvana's hope and optimism.

The technical elements on display are top-notch throughout, particularly the various animated styles and the score by Jeff and Mychael Danna, which recalls music of the area in which the film is set but also has own unique flavor. It's a much less visually vibrant film when compared to the aforementioned *The Secret of Kells* and *Song of the Sea*—both of which pulsed with the green colors of their Irish heritage and setting—and yet it achieves its own beauty. Certain studios start to take on visual consistencies in their work in that one can typically tell when a film comes from Pixar or Studio Ghibli, for example. *The Breadwinner* looks different than the last two Cartoon Saloon hits in that it uses brown more than green, but also feels of a piece visually at the same time with its emphasis on what can be conveyed through human eyes.

Animation is at a unique place in its history in that the Davids and Goliaths of the form seem to be growing further and further apart in terms of international prominence and financial success. *The Boss Baby* (2017) made the entirety of the gross of *The Breadwinner* in its first few hours of release. Families still tend to go to safe, familiar product when they are looking to spend money on seeing a movie, which is understandable given the dire state of the world. People want escapism through animation more than cultural commentary. And yet films like *The Breadwinner* inevitably find their audience (and the Oscar® nomination will surely help). Just as "serious" animated fare like *Grave of the Fireflies* (1988), *Persepolis* (2007), or *Mary and Max* (2009) eventually got to the people who would appreciate them, *The Breadwinner* will find its way. But, just like Parvana's journey, it may take a little more effort than it should have to.

Brian Tallerico

CREDITS

Voice of Parvana: Saara Chaudry
Voice of Shauzia: Soma Bhatia
Voice of Idrees/Sulayman: Noorin Gulamgaus
Voice of Fattema: Laara Sadiq
Voice of Nurullah: Ali Badshah
Origin: United States
Language: English
Released: 2017
Production: Angelina Jolie, Anthony Leo, Tomm Moore, Andrew Rosen, Paul Young; Aircraft Pictures, Cartoon Saloon, Gaia Entertainment, Guru Animation, Jolie Pas Productions, Mélusine Productions; released by GKIDS
Directed by: Nora Twomey

Written by: Anita Doron; Deborah Ellis
Music by: Jeff Danna; Mychael Danna
Sound: J.R. Fountain
Editing: Darragh Byrne
Art Direction: Ciaran Duffy; Reza Riahi
MPAA rating: PG-13
Running time: 94 minutes

REVIEWS

Addiego, Walter. *San Francisco Chronicle.* November 29, 2017.
Connelly, Sherilyn. *Village Voice.* November 16, 2017.
Ehrlich, David. *IndieWire.* November 20, 2017.
Kenny, Glenn. *New York Times.* November 16. 2017.
Larsen, Vanessa H. *Washington Post.* November 22, 2017.
Linden, Sheri. *Hollywood Reporter.* October 29, 2017.
Mobarak, Jared. *The Film Stage.* October 29, 2017.
Sobczynski, Peter. *RogerEbert.com.* November 17, 2017.
Turan, Kenneth. *Los Angeles Times.* November 16, 2017.
White, Danielle. *Austin Chronicle.* November 30, 2017.

TRIVIA

This is the first feature film project for Guru Studio as well as the first time distributor GKIDS is executive producing a film.

AWARDS

Nominations:

Oscars 2017: Animated Film
Golden Globes 2018: Animated Film

BREATHE

An inspiration love story.
—Movie tagline
With her love, he lived.
—Movie tagline

Box Office: $490,131

The directorial debut of Andy Serkis, *Breathe* may not exactly breathe new life into the biographical drama genre, but it does tell a compelling story in an engaging, if somewhat broad-strokes, fashion. Anchored by sensitive, finely-tuned work from Andrew Garfield and Netflix's *The Crown* star Claire Foy, this true-life story will have fans of romantic period pieces reaching for Kleenex, or at least burrowing in empathetic identification deeper into their couch pillows—which is the setting where they are likely to experience first contact with this tale. After debuting at the Toronto Film Festival in September 2017, *Breathe* went on to receive a boutique autumnal theatrical release via indie distributor Bleecker Street, but only grossed around $500,000 domestically.

Strongly reminiscent of *The Theory of Everything* (2014), which told another time-spanning, real-life love story about a quadriplegic man, *Breathe* focuses on Robin Cavendish (Garfield), a British soldier and explorer turned businessman who in the late 1950s contracts polio at 28 years of age. In an instant, this vital, athletic young man is struck down—paralyzed below the neck, incapable of breathing without a machine, and unable even to speak for a brief period of time. The future looks bleak, and Robin even pleads with his wife, Diana Blacker (Foy), to let him die.

Diana, however, is pregnant, and refuses to give in to Robin's negativity. Despite the doctor's prognosis of only three months to live, Robin defies the odds, and is further bolstered in spirit when he and Diana make the decision to leave the hospital—a decision unheard of at the time. Connected to a respirator at home, Robin finds himself surrounded by an extended network of family and friends—including brothers-in-law Bloggs and David (both played by Tom Hollander), and Oxford University professor Teddy Hall (Hugh Bonneville), who eventually develops and builds a wheelchair with a built-in, mobile respirator in order to give Robin freedom from the dreary confines of life in bed. Over the ensuing years, spanning more than two decades, Robin and Diana continue to live as full of a shared life as possible, raising their son Jonathan and even traveling abroad.

While it is certainly very emotionally heavy subject matter, *Breathe* pushes past the darkness to a place infused with a sense of humanity—and even an easygoing sense of self-effacing playfulness for long stretches of time. Gratifyingly, Serkis shows that even in moments of despair and depression, the best of us do not lose the essential compass of our personality. In Robin's case, that character and disposition is of a man who is loving, giving, intellectually curious, and desirous of new experiences. A focus on these qualities provides some welcome levity, and helps the tears arrive more naturally during the movie's emotional passages, a handful of which seem programmatic or at least familiar.

Breathe would perhaps connect a bit more robustly if it focused on Robin and Diana's advocacy for other paralyzed individuals. The screenplay, by William Nicholson, alights on this development briefly, and features the couple both returning to the hospital with Robin in his wheelchair and visiting a medical facility and conference for care of the disabled in Germany. But the film's inability to sketch with much depth any other paralyzed character (who could thus provide significant comparison and contrast to Robin) gives these passages a bit of a perfunctory feeling.

Sometimes, too, *Breathe* skips or glosses over small details, like how or why Robin and Diana would be allowed to just take his respirator and other presumably costly equipment with him as he leaves the hospital. If, in fact, there sometimes seems like an overall lack of perspective or outside complications, it is perhaps with good reason, since Jonathan Cavendish actually serves as a producer on the movie.

On the technical side, while Serkis is well known as an actor for his motion-capture work in the big-budget *Planet of the Apes* and *The Lord of the Rings* franchises, *Breathe* evinces an affection for classical dramatic storytelling, and the embrace of a sensible tool kit to boot. Eschewing flashiness, Serkis opts for simple, effective framing and sentiment, as with a scene where newborn Jonathan is merely held to the side of Robin's face. One of the high points of the movie is undeniably Robert Richardson's cinematography, burnished with warm orange hues in its outdoor travel sequences, in order to contrast with some of the cooler color palettes of the disinfected rooms and spaces in which Robin is trapped. Composer Nitin Sawhney's evocative score also connects in forthright fashion.

Mostly, though, *Breathe* is just a wonderful showcase for Garfield and Foy, who possess a pleasant chemistry with one another and each deliver wonderful performances. Foy brings a sensitivity to Diana, while also getting to very much reveal her to be the ballast of the story. Garfield, meanwhile, impressively makes viewers feel the oppressiveness of his condition through a constricted voice. Through it all, Serkis and his collaborators present a believably loving relationship, and not one dictated merely by duty or routine. It is this quality, of a fully lived and shared life, that injects the characters with a multi-dimensionality, and gives *Breathe* the sort of emotional punching power and conventional uplift that many viewers crave.

Brent Simon

CREDITS

Robin Cavendish: Andrew Garfield
Diana Cavendish: Claire Foy
Lady Neville: Diana Rigg
Mary Dawney: Miranda Raison
Jonathan age 22: Dean-Charles Chapman
Origin: United Kingdom
Language: English
Released: 2017
Production: Jonathan Cavendish; Imaginarium Inc.; released by Bleecker Street Media
Directed by: Andy Serkis
Written by: William Nicholson
Cinematography by: Robert Richardson
Music by: Nitin Sawhney
Sound: Becki Ponting
Music Supervisor: Ian Neil
Editing: Masahiro Hirakubo
Costumes: Charlotte Walter
Production Design: James Merifield
MPAA rating: PG-13
Running time: 117 minutes

REVIEWS

Catsoulis, Jeannette. *New York Times.* October 12, 2017.
Cordova, Randy. *Arizona Republic.* October 19, 2017.
Ide, Wendy. *Screen International.* September 11, 2017.
LaSalle, Mick. *San Francisco Chronicle.* October 18, 2017.
Lodge, Guy. *Variety.* September 11, 2017.
Nolfi, Joey. *Entertainment Weekly.* October 12, 2017.
Smith, Derek. *Slant.* October 9, 2017.
Tallerico, Brian. *RogerEbert.com.* September 12, 2017.
Verniere, James. *Boston Herald.* October 20, 2017.
Zacharek, Stephanie. *Time.* October 20, 2017.

TRIVIA

Andrew Garfield, Diana Rigg, Miranda Raison, Roger Ashton-Griffiths, and Hugh Bonneville have all appeared as guest stars on *Doctor Who.*

BRIGHT

Bright is a film that comes from the imagination of a 32-year-old man even if it feels like the ramblings of a child who knows the names of his action figures but could not hold their parent's attention beyond six minutes of knocking each one of them over. The writer in question is Max Landis, son of filmmaker John Landis who in-between some classic comedies tried mixing them with even more outlandish, and gory, horror elements in films like *An American Werewolf in London* (1981) and *Innocent Blood* (1992). Max has cut his teeth here mostly blending fantasy and violence, though he could certainly take a few paternal lessons in what constitutes comedy. It has been a downhill slope for the writer since the breakout success of the teen superhero saga, *Chronicle* (2012) and the changing landscape of film distribution, led by the online streaming service Netflix, was banking on him to usher in an attempt at high-concept filmmaking that would never see the darkened inside of a movie theater. This proved to be a gift for movie lovers. Just not in the traditional sense.

In an alternate reality, human beings co-exist with creatures of the Nine Races. More specifically from what you may have read in Tolkien or seen brought to life by Peter Jackson in one of the more extraordinary examples of epic fantasy filmmaking ever in his (first) *Lord of the Rings* trilogy (2001-2003). Namely orcs, the seemingly low-intelligent minions forged in darkness to become armies for more powerful masters. One of those orcs has now become a member of the Los Angeles Police Department. Nick Jakoby (Joel Edgerton) is not well-accepted by his fellow officers and is deemed a traitor by his orc race; all of whom have apparently become gang-bangers and layabouts. His partner, Daryl Ward (Will Smith) fares no better, at least with his daughter who says, "Why do you have to be a policeman? Everyone hates policemen." This could set the stage for a potentially interesting take on racially-stoked power dynamics but that goes out the window the moment Ward beats a fairy—yes, an actual fairy—to death under the cloud of the dialogue, "Fairy lives don't matter today."

During one of their investigations, Jakoby becomes privy to a prophecy that involves both himself and his partner. A Dark Lord is coming, and a group of militant orcs are searching for a source of magic that can be used to defeat it. What better source than a wand? "Who owns a wand," one character asks? "A bright," is the answer. Landis's script is content to just leave the definition as vague as someone who can touch a wand and wield its power without getting all Gollum about it. Leilah (Noomi Rapace, who looks born for this role as an elf) is the owner of the wand in question, but it is the spry Tikka (Lucy Fry) who possesses it. Everybody, including local human and orc gangs alike, want the wand to either heal their wounds or become all-powerful, and it is up to Jakoby and Ward to keep it safe by fleeing into the night never getting the kind of backup one might see in Los Angeles for a traffic stop, let alone multiple gun battles and explosions.

Bright is so painfully unaware of its own senselessness that it is impossible to lodge any of it under the column of fun. Landis's comedy stylings are so off the mark in the opening scenes that it immediately cloaks our heroes with, perhaps an unintended cloud of homophobia masked as comic entendres. "I'm straight. I don't need no physical love" is Ward's response to his concerned partner's query about his marriage. Their relationship is reduced to Smith doing his tired shtick of apparent streetwise quips that would not be edgy even on a very special episode of *The Fresh Prince of Bel-Air.* Their lack of chemistry or genuine friction provides nobody to root for or find common ground with. The only sympathy reserved for Jakoby is that the actor underneath (who is trying to find a character) had to endure countless hours of makeup while nobody suggested to give Will Smith a touchup to play anyone but the same egocentric action hero version of himself that he's been playing for over two decades. At one point, Ward sprays mace directly into the camera and it is tempting to lean into the frame yourself to receive the benefits of being blinded halfway through this boorish fanboy mash-up under the tattered guise of social commentary.

Landis may have watched *Lord of the Rings* as a teenager or possibly stumbled upon *Alien Nation* (1988) some night on cable but having distanced himself from the final version at least some of the fault must lay with its director. Before (and even after) venturing behind the camera, Ayer's propensity for his two-guys-in-a-car screenwriting did not go unnoticed. For a while it worked too with films like *Training Day* (2001), *Harsh Times* (2005), and *End of Watch* (2012). His attention shift from the law to the ne'er-do-wells of society (including the worst demons of law enforcement) has not suited him well from ugly trash like *Sabotage* (2014) to one of the worst comic book adaptations ever in *Suicide Squad* (2016), also featuring Smith as a character distinguishable from Ward only by a single skill and his haircut. An occasional action beat works momentarily, which is more than can be said about *Suicide Squad,* but it still leads to another climax where magical women hold up shiny objects while less interesting men in power try to take it away from them. This may be reading way further into an unfortunate social connection that really is not there nor in Ayer's heart, but any viewer's attempt to insert anything into this narrative instantly makes it more interesting than it ever is.

Erik Childress

CREDITS

Daryl Ward: Will Smith

Nick Jakoby: Joel Edgerton

Leilah: Noomi Rapace

Kandomere: Edgar Ramirez

Tikka: Lucy Fry

Origin: United States

Language: English, Spanish

Released: 2017

Production: Eric Newman, Ted Sarandos, Bryan Unkeless, David Ayer; Clubhouse Pictures, Overbrook Entertainment; released by Netflix Inc.

Directed by: David Ayer

Written by: Max Landis

Cinematography by: Roman Vasyanov

Music by: David Sardy

Sound: Piero Mura

Music Supervisor: Gabe Hilfer; Season Kent

Editing: Aaron Brock; Geoffrey O'Brien; Michael Tronick
Art Direction: Christopher Brown; Kasra Farahani; Bradley Rubin
Costumes: Kelli Jones
Production Design: Andrew Menzies
MPAA rating: Unrated
Running time: 117 minutes

REVIEWS

DeBruge, Peter. *Variety*. December 20, 2017.
Hunter, Rob. *Film School Rejects*. December 22, 2017.
Klimek, Chris. *Lainey Gossip*. December 21, 2017.
Marrs, Sarah. *Lainey Gossip*. December 27, 2017.
Mayer, Dominick. *Consequence of Sound*. December 23, 2017.
Orndorf, Brian. *Blu-ray.com*. December 28, 2017.
Roeper, Richard. *Chicago Sun-Times*. December 26, 2017.
Stern, Marlow. *The Daily Beast*. December 26, 2017.
Swietek, Frank. *One Guy's Opinion*. December 26, 2017.
Singer, Matt. *ScreenCrush*. December 22, 2017.

QUOTES

Nick Jakoby: "I think we might be in a prophecy."
Daryl Ward: "We're not in a Prophecy, all right?"
Nick Jakoby: "How do you know?"
Daryl Ward: "We're in a stolen Toyota Corolla."

TRIVIA

This is the first Netflix Original movie to have a sequel. In fact, the deal for the second movie was signed before the first film was released.

THE BYE BYE MAN

Don't think it. Don't say it. Don't think it. Don't say it. Don't think it. Don't say it. Don't think it. Don't say it. Don't think it. Don't say it. Don't think it. Don't say it.
—Movie tagline

The evil behind the most unspeakable acts has a name
—Movie tagline

Box Office: $22.4 Million

From the ashes of *Candyman* (1992) or their shared origin in the childhood legend of Bloody Mary, *The Bye Bye Man*'s mantra of "Don't think it, don't say it" rises. Intended to set up multiple iterations of teen-slaying flicks, the proto-franchise horror film creates its onomastically-powered ghoul to be as replicable as possible for the future. The problem is that to enjoy that potential for expansion, the derivative film's creativity must suffer. The protagonist teens must avoid saying or thinking the titular supernatural baddie's name or else he gains influence over their minds as he approaches closer and closer. While his victims hallucinate, unable to remove the name from their attention like a particular image someone tells you not to think about, they near a murderous madness with a lack of logic that is comparable to that of the film's narrative.

Elliot (Douglas Smith), his girlfriend Sasha (Cressida Bonas), and their friend John (Lucien Laviscount, the most dramatically game of the leads) move into a home that's not quite haunted, but certainly touched with a certain otherworldliness. Unexplained coins drop from nightstands while a growling at midnight somehow leaves scratch marks on their fencing. After finding a clue (a hidden name carved into a desk drawer) the housemates host a house-party-turned-seance led by one of the new-wave "sensitive" teen hippie attendees (Jenna Kanell). There's nothing original about these plot beats, which makes it even more frustrating that the film fails to acknowledge its own monotony. The residents begin seeing things that aren't there and investigating vague search terms in a library, desperately seeking the origin story of evil and the loopholes that typically come with it.

The tension that seems implicit in a small group of people whose linguistic virality could spread a demon's evil with a simple slip of the tongue simply is not present. Character interactions never have the time nor pacing to develop a sense of danger or fear, as they try to cram so much into each conversation. Lines break under the weight of their whiplashing intent, either setting up supernatural fear or oddly-pitched sexual tension between Sasha and the promiscuous John. Bonas spends so much of her energy fruitlessly trying to pass as American (the hard consonants at the ends of her words fading out due to her natural British cadence), that there's none left over to use on chemistry with Laviscount. What's more, the delicate social fear of cuckoldry simply has no time to grow in a film that struggles with far less complicated jump scares.

The slovenly direction by Stacy Title damns the film on a technical level. Potentially suspenseful key shots of the cramped home's interior are poorly chosen and the lighting is so inconsistent that some scenes look more like evenly-bright sitcoms than the moody shadows of the rest of the film. Title cannot help her actors either, provoking or failing to restrain their hokiness. Horror acting is already a difficult task, finding a balance of emoting that does not feel overwhelming or too heightened for the film's tone, but characters reduced to gibbering madmen almost never fare well.

Repetitive incantations require big performances, so big that they are very hard to fit into a movie attempting small-scale homey scares. Even in more intensely stylized films like *The Number 23* (2007) or *1408* (2007), seasoned actors Jim Carrey and John Cusack fail to effectively pull off spooky chanting. In *The Bye Bye Man*, this duty falls to Smith, whose tired eyes have endlessly expressive potential, but must shout something as mundane as "Don't think it, don't say it" over and over again. It's hard to avoid the realm of mockery—especially if the rest of the film's unintentional campiness fights against any sort of earnest tonal establishment.

These tonal problems appear in its most vital elements. Namely, its demonic villain. Under his hooded cowl, the Bye Bye Man (Doug Jones) wears a simple henley and well-pressed pants. Jones' mime-like mastery over his thin body is swallowed up by the underwhelming normalcy of his clothing. His CGI zombie mutt has the same outdated effect as video games from the late 1990s while his ominous pointing never projects the kind of creeping horror it attempts. His aesthetic, coupled with the circumstances of his summoning, make the Bye Bye Man too goofy to frighten.

When approached with a silly rule in a horror movie, audiences are almost begged to speculate about ways to get around it, almost like a science fiction film's piquing of various physical or chemical curiosities in its viewers. Why the film's protagonists never decide to use synonyms or euphemisms for the phrase "The Bye Bye Man," so they avoid using his proper name, is never discussed, but this is only one flaw of many in the ramshackle film.

The Bye Bye Man is not scary, but, even worse, it also is not any fun. Despite all the narrative detours, the film never seems aware of its own silliness. Even when Faye Dunaway's oddball widow appears with a handgun and a repertoire of puffy dialogue, it is only a frustrating digression not nearly hallucinatory enough to justify the film's sloppy laboriousness.

Jacob Oller

CREDITS

Sasha: Cressida Bonas
John: Lucien Laviscount
Bye Bye Man: Doug Jones
Detective Shaw: Carrie-Anne Moss
Widow Redmon: Faye Dunaway
Origin: United States
Language: English, Spanish
Released: 2017
Production: Simon Horsman, Trevor Macy, Jeffrey Soros; Huayi Brothers Media, Intrepid Pictures; released by STX Entertainment
Directed by: Stacy Title
Written by: Jonathan Penner
Cinematography by: James Kniest
Music by: The Newton Brothers
Sound: Kelly Cabral
Music Supervisor: James Curd
Editing: Ken Blackwell
Art Direction: Jason Garner
Costumes: Leah Butler
Production Design: Jennifer Spence
MPAA rating: PG-13
Running time: 97 minutes

REVIEWS

Abele, Robert. *TheWrap.* January 12, 2017.
Crump, Andy. *Paste Magazine.* January 18, 2017.
Fear, David. *Rolling Stone.* January 12, 2017.
Graham, Adam. *Detroit News.* January 13, 2017.
Grierson, Tim. *Screen International.* January 12, 2017.
Keough, Peter. *Boston Globe.* January 12, 2017.
Larson, Richard. *Slant Magazine.* January 12, 2017.
Merry, Stephanie. *Washington Post.* January 12, 2017.
Pickett, Leah. *Chicago Reader.* January 19, 2017.
Sobczynski, Peter. *RogerEbert.com.* January 13, 2017.

QUOTES

Detective Shaw: "What happened? You're gonna tell me, you know what?"
Elliot: "Please don't make me say it. Don't say it, don't think it. If I tell you about him, you and your kids...You're all dead. I'm afraid of putting this into your head."
Detective Shaw: "Tell me."
Elliot: "The Bye Bye Man."

TRIVIA

This is the second collaboration between Carrie-Anne Moss and Douglas Smith. They previously appeared together in *Treading Water.*

C

CALL ME BY YOUR NAME

Box Office: $11.3 Million

Summer romances should embrace the lightheadedness that goes along with spending too much time in anything as radiant as the sun or a new love. Finding the dizziness in the pursuit, the intoxication of the guessing game, is as delicate a procedure as the detective-like prowess needed to determine the mutuality of a crush. Especially if it's between two men in the 1980s, as it is in director Luca Guadagnino's humid *Call Me by Your Name*.

The film, adapted from André Aciman's sumptuous debut 2007 novel about love and loss, restrains some of the book's insight into its main character's psyche to better muddy its romantic waters. Elio (Timothée Chalamet), a 17-year-old American-Italian Jewish boy, and his family summer in a small town in Italy each year. They take in a doctoral student each year to help his professor father (Michael Stuhlbarg) with academic goings-on in the world of art history. This year is different. This year they get cocksure American Oliver (Armie Hammer). The student stays in Elio's room each year, kicking him out and laying the groundwork for the identity-blending obsession that is this film's beloved metaphor for passionate romance.

Sayombhu Mukdeeprom's lazy camera drifts up and away after watching its protagonists bike along a grassy meadow path, almost bored with the mundanity of it all, until it trains its steady laser focus on the small moments of intimacy (a grabbed forearm, a massaged shoulder) that could mean everything. The camera is a nervous, erotic device that watches dancing with as much personal interest as professional and Hammer makes its job easy. His short-shorted costumes and unbuttoned shirts fetishize every inch of his large frame, and his easy-breezy performance lends a bored athleticism to his movements inside of the bright, warm color palette. Sometimes achingly slow, the film's love of music—including original songs composed seemingly of orchestral sunlight by Sufjan Stevens—keeps things moving when the films nods off in the heat. This only happens near the beginning, because once Oliver and Elio begin their interactions in earnest, the plot is as enthralling as a bonfire.

The introvert and extrovert tug-of-war each other towards their social comfort zone, obviously finding affinity with each other through music (Elio is a composer) and the classics. Oliver is instantly everyone's favorite, winning over Elio's parents as quickly as the Italian girls in the village. The budding relationship between the two first appears as jealousy, then manifests as the kind of life-taking fetishism found in films like *Black Swan* (2010), though this film embraces a more positive psychology towards the attraction phenomenon. As the pair continue to share time with one another, details like their Judaism and their cultural intellect bind them after the initial teasing and competitiveness of a crush.

This becomes infatuation, as Oliver's hints drive Elio to the point of fantasy—capturing the insurrectionary feeling of discovering shared passion, especially at a time (1983, to be exact) when this passion is still considered deviant. The sexuality in the film is the same as the love—brisk, delicate, and mostly delivered in suggestions and hints. James Ivory—prolific adaptor as he is—penned a creative and delicate script allowing one to lose himself in the Italian countryside and the small, intense romance blooming onscreen without vulgarity. Ivory and Guadagnino choice to do away with the protagonist's verbose interiority rather than lean on voiceover, creates a film relying on subtext and glances. Very few explicit scenes, and none with anything like the nudity women perform in their love stories, culminate in a stymied film content to bottle its build-up as a torturous continuation of its story's slow edge. However, a soon-to-be-infamous scene with a cut peach gives *American Pie* (1999) a run for its money for the best food-based representation of over-abundant sexuality.

Call Me by Your Name understands the youthful urge towards sex as extremely personal rather than purely physical (though the film too is concerned about the male body, not just ogling its stars, but a history of eroticism in Greek statues and classical forms). Sex becomes a catalyst for shame, self-doubt, self-expression, and the intimacy of a relationship. If one cannot be with the one they love, who do they turn to—and how does this frustration affect them? More importantly, this film understands that the truly important part of this immature display is the person used for nothing more than a substitute, as is local girl Marzia (Esther Garrel) for Elio. There could be something there, if Elio ever saw her as a person.

Recognizing its characters flaws, the things they shove aside for their all-encompassing affection of one season, the film can smartly maneuver towards the name-sharing, clothes-sharing, life-sharing relationship that would take over its characters' lives if external forces didn't enter the equation. Whether noon or night in a daylit attic or a twilight tree branch, the inseparability and unspoken intimacy displayed by Hammer and Chalamet carry the film with the discomfort associated with staring too long at a loving couple in public. It is far too private to be displayed and then, becomes far too private to exist at all. Oliver returns home and Elio returns to his bedroom, now empty of Oliver's belongings.

Elio has a discussion with his father that allows Stuhlbarg to deliver one of the greatest speeches ever to respond to the uncomfortable outing of an offspring. He approves. Not only does he approve of the friendship (with plenty of winks) but he approves of Elio. He approves of the luck he has had to be as open and honest with himself as he is at such a young age. It is the most verbose scene in the film and hits like a waterfall. Stuhlbarg, in a film with two of the best male performances of the year, distinguishes himself with a single scene—a quiet scene delivered in a close hum, on a shared couch, with nothing more fancy than a reverse shot distracting from his words.

As quickly as this cascades over Elio, it still does nothing to assuage his romantic loss. The ending, which uses the credits to great formal effect, is one of the best acting moments of the year, allowing Chalamet ample time to process and grieve memories after a movie spent watching him mature. In this moment, the film finally feels as if it has reached its present, as if the previous few hours were nothing but the pleasant recollections of an old sentimental fool that loved once, if only for a moment.

Jacob Oller

CREDITS

Oliver: Armie Hammer

Elio: Timothée Chalamet

Mr. Perlman: Michael Stuhlbarg

Annella: Amira Casar

Marzia: Esther Garrel

Origin: United States

Language: English, Italian, French, German

Released: 2017

Production: Emilie Georges, Marco Morabito, Howard Rosenman, Peter Spears, Rodrigo Teixeira, Luca Guadagnino, James Ivory; Frenesy Film Company, La Cinéfacture, M.Y.R.A. Entertainment, Memento Films International, RT Features, Water's End Productions; released by Sony Pictures Classics

Directed by: Luca Guadagnino

Written by: James Ivory

Cinematography by: Sayombhu Mukdeeprom

Music Supervisor: Robin Urdang

Editing: Walter Fasano

Art Direction: Roberta Federico

Costumes: Giulia Piersanti

Production Design: Samuel Deshors

MPAA rating: R

Running time: 132 minutes

REVIEWS

Borders, Meredith. *Birth.Movies.Death.* January 24, 2017.

Chang, Justin. *Los Angeles Times.* January 25, 2017.

Dowd, A.A. *The A.V. Club.* January 24, 2017.

Debruge, Peter. *Variety.* January 23, 2017.

Fujishima, Kenji. *Slant Magazine.* February 14, 2017.

Han, Angie *Slashfilm.* June 13, 2017.

Lawson, Richard. *Vanity Fair.* January 26, 2017.

Raup, Jordan. *The Film Stage.* January 25, 2017.

Slater-Williams, Josh. *The Skinny.* October 18, 2017.

Woodward, Adam. *Little White Lies.* October 25, 2017.

QUOTES

Mr. Perlman: "Nature has cunning ways of finding our weakest spot."

TRIVIA

On its premiere night at the New York Film Festival, this film received a ten-minute standing ovation—the longest standing ovation ever at the festival.

AWARDS

Oscars 2017: Adapt. Screenplay
British Acad. 2017: Adapt. Screenplay
Ind. Spirit 2018: Actor (Chalamet), Cinematog.
Writers Guild 2017: Adapt. Screenplay

Nominations:

Oscars 2017: Actor (Chalamet), Film, Orig. Song Score and/or Adapt. ("Mystery of Love")
British Acad. 2017: Actor (Chalamet), Film
British Acad. 2018: Director (Guadagnino)
Golden Globes 2018: Actor--Drama (Chalamet), Actor--Supporting (Hammer), Film--Drama
Ind. Spirit 2018: Actor--Supporting (Hammer), Director (Guadagnino), Film, Film Editing
Screen Actors Guild 2017: Actor (Chalamet)

CAPTAIN UNDERPANTS: THE FIRST EPIC MOVIE

You've seen Britain, you've seen France...But you've never seen anyone like this guy.
—Movie tagline

Box Office: $73.9 Million

Dav Pilkey's book series *The Adventures of Captain Underpants* has become an industry unto itself in its two decades of existence, so a film adaptation seemed inevitable. Luckily, the DreamWorks-funded project is no mere cash grab, reflecting the creative spirit of the source material in nearly every scene instead of just trying to serve as a marketing tie-in to an already-successful property. So many films aimed at children take their intelligence and artistic spirit for granted, but Nicholas Stoller's script for *Captain Underpants: The First Epic Movie* respects both, and gets in a few good bits of silly physical humor to boot. It's a clever, sweet, and inspirational tale of friendship, creativity, and a superhero who runs around in his tighty whities.

George Beard (Kevin Hart) and Harold Hutchins (Thomas Middleditch) are best friends, next-door neighbors, and fourth-graders. They also happen to the resident pranksters at Jerome Horwitz Element School. They prank whenever they see the chance, and the target of their pranks is typically Principal Krupp (Ed Helms), a figure of authority and the villain of creativity in their lives. In their copious free time, George and Harold write their own comic book, Captain Underpants, with a hero who's relatively self-explanatory—he fights crime in his underpants (then again, so do most superheroes).

Everything changes for George and Harold after one of their pranks gets caught on video. The boys tamper with an invention at a school assembly called the Turbo Toilet 2000, and school nerd/snitch Melvin Sneedley (Jordan Peele) catches them. Principal Krupp threatens to break the boys up, putting them in separate classes, and destroying their friendship. George and Harold move to stop this catastrophe by using a 3D Hypno Ring that they found in a cereal box, thereby turning Krupp into their character, Captain Underpants. Suddenly, their principal is jumping around town in his underwear, but the boys learn that they can turn him on and off by snapping their fingers and splashing water on his face. They basically implant their superhero in the principal role and think life can go on as normal.

Of course, every superhero movie needs a supervillain, and this story's arrives in the form of the wonderfully-named (and even more wonderfully-voiced by Nick Kroll) Professor Pee-Pee Diarrheastein Poopypants. "Professor P." is the new teacher at the school, but he's got a secret mission to eliminate laughter, a natural obsession after decades of people mocking his name. He recruits Melvin just as the boys are separated into different classrooms after Principal Krupp returns to his alter ego form just as a school carnival is going hysterically awry. Professor Poopypants develops a giant version of a Turbo Toilet 2000 that turns children into humorless zombies. Can George and Harold reunite in time to return their Principal to superhero form and save the day? Of course, they can.

Clearly, the plot of *Captain Underpants* is not Pixar-level brilliant, but it's the execution and spirit of David Soren's film that allows it to soar. Most importantly, Stoller's script embraces the creativity of Pilkey's books, which often broke in style and form. For example, one of Pilkey's books would break the story to turn into a flip book, forcing the reader to turn the pages quickly to see a piece of animation. The books are constantly changing their very structure to encourage the creativity of the reader and Soren's film often does the same, allowing for fourth-wall breaks from the characters and change-ups in the style of animation. It makes for a film that's never stale—like so many by-the-numbers kids' movies—and that hurtles through its brief running time (89 minutes). The film arguably pushes the threshold of "potty humor," but it's designed to be the creative product of a couple of nine-year-olds and, well, kids that age like that kind of thing. And it takes a surprising degree of intelligence to make an entertaining film that features things that are this dumb.

It helps to have a voice cast as completely committed as the group assembled here. Hart and Middleditch are convincing as young friends, but it's the out-there turns from Helms and, especially, Kroll that really elevate the experience. Kroll has been a gifted comedian for years, particularly on his *The Kroll Show*, and this is another great, underrated performance.

Sadly, there's not a lot of space in the American film market for unestablished animated franchises lately. Unless it bears the Pixar/Disney brand or features minions, it's hard to make a lot of money, and *Captain Underpants* only mustered around $74 million domestically, despite garnering strong reviews. With solid international returns and a low budget, it's possible that another adventure of the underwear-donning principal and his two creators could eventually be greenlit, but that feels unlikely. Viewers will have to settle for this one shining moment when a fat man in his tighty-whities streaked across the sky, ready to save us all from humorless monsters.

Brian Tallerico

CREDITS

George: Kevin Hart (Voice)
Mr. Krupp/Captain Underpants: Ed Helms (Voice)
Professor Poopypants: Nick Kroll (Voice)
Harold: Thomas Middleditch (Voice)
Melvin: Jordan Peele (Voice)
Origin: United States
Language: English
Released: 2017
Production: Mireille Soria, Mark Swift; DreamWorks Animation L.L.C.; released by Twentieth Century Fox Film Corp.
Directed by: David Soren
Written by: Nicholas Stoller
Music by: Theodore Shapiro
Sound: Michael Babcock
Editing: Matt(hew) Landon
Production Design: Nate Wragg
MPAA rating: PG
Running time: 89 minutes

REVIEWS

Anderson, Soren. *Seattle Times.* June 1, 2017.
Duralde, Alonso. *TheWrap.* June 1, 2017.
Greenblatt, Leah. *Entertainment Weekly.* June 2, 2017.
Robey, Tim. *The Telegraph.* August 3, 2017.
Russo, Tom. *Boston Globe.* May 31, 2017.
Seitz, Matt Zoller. *RogerEbert.com.* June 2, 2017.
Vishnevetsky, Ignatiy. *The A.V. Club.* May 31, 2017.
Walsh, Katie. *Los Angeles Times.* June 1, 2017.
Watson, Keith. *Slant Magazine.* June 1, 2017.
Welch, Alex. *IGN.* June 1, 2017.

QUOTES

Professor Poopypants: "Hiyah class, I'm your cool new teacher, not some scary guy with a secret evil agenda."

TRIVIA

In the first book, one of the pranks that George and Harold pull is having "Weird Al" play over the school PA system for six hours. This film's theme song is performed by "Weird Al" Yankovic.

CARS 3

From this moment, everything will change.
—Movie tagline

It's not over until lightning strikes.
—Movie tagline

One last chance, One last dream.
—Movie tagline

It's on.
—Movie tagline

Box Office: $152.9 Million

The *Cars* movies occupy a questionable place in the history of Pixar. The groundbreaking animation studio has possibly won as much critical and popular acclaim as Walt Disney in his heyday—leading to Disney acquiring the studio in 2006—and animation fans have almost uniformly embraced every film they have released. However, there have been a few exceptions to that rule, and the biggest one has to be this turbo-charged franchise. While children and grown-ups alike have lauded Pixar movies like *Toy Story* (1995), *Monsters Inc.* (2001), and *Inside Out* (2015), there is something about the *Cars* movies that make adults groan and roll their eyes. They don't tap into the same cross-generational appeal as the rest of Pixar's back catalog, which is odd because, at their core, the *Cars* movies are the most dated, derivative, and old-fashioned stories that Pixar has ever presented.

Cars (2006) was pleasantly (if not passionately) received by audiences, even though the down-home story of a race car, Lightning McQueen (Owen Wilson), learning to love small-town America did not really offer anything new. (Some have argued that the film is essentially a long-in-the-tooth retelling of the Michael J. Fox vehicle *Doc Hollywood* [1991].) In fact, the major story surrounding *Cars* upon its release was not the film's cinematic merits, but rather how much merchandising money it made for Disney. A sequel emerged five years later, *Cars 2* (2006), which made the *Gremlins 2*-esque decision to explore a completely different film genre. *Cars 2* abandoned the unrepentant Americana of the original film and instead placed Mater (Larry the Cable Guy), Lightning McQueen's dim-witted tow truck best friend, into an international spy spoof à la Austin Powers. This experiment inspired the lowest critical rating of any Pixar movie to date.

So perhaps it was not surprising that *Cars 3* decided to go back to the well of the original movie. Unfortunately, while the first *Cars* was derivative of a selection of well-worn sports and small-town pride movies, *Cars 3* is simply derivative of *Cars* itself. One wonders how any race-car-loving six-year-old has the patience to sit through such a cloying, unoriginal redo of a movie they probably watched on their parents' iPad on the way to the theater.

There is nothing to *Cars 3*. It is a shockingly ephemeral movie. Watching it feels like going to a county fair to watch a long-forgotten classic rock band play a 30-minute set of only their hits. You know they are not in their prime, you suspect they are using backing tracks, and everyone present—band included—realizes that they are just there to collect a paycheck. Director Brian Fee definitely collected a paycheck for *Cars 3*—his last name delivering its own pun—but he didn't give his audience any substance or heart in return.

Cars 3 pretends *Cars 2* never happened. (The film is noticeably light on Mater. One wonders if this is because *Cars 2* proved that a little Mater goes a long way or because Disney worried that Larry the Cable Guy's increasingly conservative political statements might limit the movie's appeal.) *Cars 3* re-introduces us to Lightning McQueen, who has now won the Piston Cup he so coveted in the first *Cars* seven times. He's become a legitimate racing legend, though he still mourns the passing of his mentor, Doc Hudson (played by the late, great Paul Newman). The central conceit of *Cars 3* is introduced quickly—there is a new generation of uber-racers, led by Jackson Storm (Armie Hammer), that is threatening to make old-timers like McQueen obsolete.

McQueen gets into a massive accident while trying to compete against Storm for the Piston Cup and finds himself injured—both in body and pride. He mulls retirement, but his new sponsor instead sends him to an elite training facility (right out of *Rocky IV* [1985]) to train the same way that Jackson Storm does. McQueen's trainer is by-the-book female racer, Cruz Ramirez (Cristela Alonzo), who you can immediately tell will become his antagonist/eventual protégé. Cruz tries to train McQueen in "new racing" while McQueen instructs her in the down-home "Pepperidge Farm Remembers" school of racing that Doc Hudson introduced him to in the first film.

This all leads to a final confrontation with Storm—McQueen bets that, if he does not win an upcoming race, he will retire. The conclusion of the race might not be what your six-year-old expects, but it's so telegraphed that any adult who has seen a movie before will be able to see it coming from 400 laps away. Some critics have mistakenly labeled the ending as surprisingly "woke"—it introduces an aspect of gender politics hitherto unseen in the *Cars* universe—but, in reality, the ending just does what the *Cars* movies do best. It panders.

The *Cars* movies are the Pixar equivalent of those original Hallmark Christmas movies. Everyone knows that they are cheesy, sentimental, and unoriginal, but there's a segment of the population that revels in them, regarding them as a kind of pop culture comfort food. While *Cars 3* isn't as blatantly unfunny as *Cars 2*, it is still a syrupy, over-done rehash of a story you've already seen a million times before. Like a Hallmark movie, *Cars 3* might be worth watching on a basic cable channel on a lazy Sunday morning, but otherwise, there's no real reason why you should ever seek it out.

Tom Burns

CREDITS

Lightning McQueen: Owen Wilson (Voice)
Cruz Ramirez: Cristela Alonzo (Voice)
Smokey: Chris Cooper (Voice)
Sterling: Nathan Fillion (Voice)
Mater: Larry the Cable Guy (Voice)
Jackson Storm: Armie Hammer (Voice)
Origin: United States
Language: English
Released: 2017
Production: Kevin Reher; Pixar Animation Studios; released by Walt Disney Pictures
Directed by: Brian Fee
Written by: Keil Murray; Bob Peterson; Mike Rich
Music by: Randy Newman
Sound: Brian Chumney; Tom Myers
Editing: Jason Hudak
Production Design: William Cone
MPAA rating: G
Running time: 102 minutes

REVIEWS

Andersen, Soren. *Seattle Times*. June 13, 2017.
Feeney, Mark. *Boston Globe*. June 14, 2017.

Greenblatt, Leah. *Entertainment Weekly*. June 12, 2017.
Kenny, Glenn. *New York Times*. June 14, 2017.
Kohn, Eric. *IndieWire*. June 12, 2017.
O'Sullivan, Michael. *Washington Post*. June 15, 2017.
Seitz, Matt Zoller. *RogerEbert.com*. June 15, 2017.
Truitt, Brian. *USA Today*. June 12, 2017.
Turan, Kenneth. *Los Angeles Times*. June 15, 2017.
White, James. *Empire*. July 17, 2017.

QUOTES

Sally Carrera: "Don't fear failure. Be afraid of not having the chance, you have the chance!"

TRIVIA

Some of Paul Newman's voice recordings for Doc Hudson that were cut out of *Cars* (2006) were used for this film, making it the actor's first posthumous role in a movie nearly nine years after his death.

CHIPS

Chip happens.
—Movie tagline

Box Office: $18.6 Million

When *21 Jump Street* (2012) became an unexpected comedy hit, it was only a matter of time before the Hollywood wheel spun to a reboot of *CHiPs,* the 1977-83 hit series that turned Larry Wilcox and Erik Estrada into household names. That show's buddy comedy structure about a straitlaced officer in the California Highway Patrol (CHP, which gave the show its weird name) and his more devil-may-care partner has been transported to the 2010s relatively intact, although the congenial tone of the television series has been replaced with a shocking degree of homophobia and misogyny. The movie version of *CHiPs* wastes the talents of its cast on a horrible screenplay that's almost entirely bereft of actual humor and leaden direction from star Dax Shepard. The only nice thing anyone can say about *CHIPs* is that it made such a small impact on the pop culture scene that most people forgot it ever came out.

The generally likable Shepard also stars as Jon Baker, a man whose body has been destroyed by years of accidents as a stunt motorcycle driver. Baker is kind of a moron, but the likable kind, and he's honestly trying to do his best as a new member of the California Highway Patrol. Shepard is a car and motorcycle nut himself (something displayed in his previous film, *Hit and Run* [2012]) and so he does most of his own bike-riding here, however he seems to be having more fun than the audience. Shepard's general aw-shucks affability often goes a long way, but it's startlingly offset here by a script that's full of homophobic, sexist, and just generally bad jokes.

Another actor who's too often the best thing about bad movies, Michael Peña, co-stars as Frank Poncherello, this time imagined as an undercover FBI agent, working to flush out dirty cops within the CHP, a group led by a scenery-chewing Vincent D'Onofrio. Bafflingly, the dirty cop subplot of *CHIPs* is played relatively straight, as if Shepard is unsure of what kind of movie he's making. The "plot" of something like *21 Jump Street* was merely a skeleton on which to hang that film's far-superior sense of humor, but here it distracts more from the scenes that are meant to be funny, creating a movie that lurches and comes to a stop whenever the plot has to kick back in.

Part of the problem is that neither Shepard or Peña are playing anything approximating real people. Shepard's Baker has a wife (played by his real-life spouse Kristen Bell, slumming here in a movie she's far too good for) but that's just an excuse for sitcomish scenes about how whipped he is and how much "men" don't like therapy in Los Angeles. Baker also pops pills and eats junk food and lives on the edge. But he's a black hole of a character—one who feels designed to try to hit a punchline instead of anything genuine. If Shepard the filmmaker had gone true slapstick like a Zucker Brothers film then this approach might have worked, but the movie is too often grounded for that. And he doesn't have the comedic guts. Peña's exasperation at his moronic partner allows him to come out a bit better, but even this guy is a hornball cartoon. One can almost see the exhaustion on his face during a scene in which it actually makes contact with Shepard's testicles.

CHIPs is one of those movie's that's constantly winking at you, like the host of "The Chris Farley Show" from *Saturday Night Live*—"Remember this? Wasn't it awesome?" Making a reference to something is not the same thing as actually writing a joke, and when Shepard's film has to try to produce some laughs of its own, it gets dark and pretty gross, leaning on its R-rating in an attempt to shock people into laughter. The film never settles on a tone, dipping into some bizarrely grisly violence at times without ever establishing a sense of suspense or stakes for its characters, and becomes an increasingly gross experience as it rides along a highway to nowhere.

Luckily, the almost-worldwide dismissal of *CHIPs* by critics (a stunning 28/100 on Metacritic) extended to audiences too, and the film tanked at theaters, bringing in under $20 million domestically (compared to the $138 million of the first *21 Jump Street* and even the $58 million of the also-loathed *Baywatch* [2017]). What

Shepard and company learned with *CHIPs* is that just referencing something beloved in the past isn't going to make it beloved again. No one ever thought this would be said, but Erik Estrada deserved better.

Brian Tallerico

CREDITS

Jon Baker: Dax Shepard
Frank "Ponch" Poncherello: Michael Peña
Lindsey Taylor: Jessica McNamee
Clay Allen: Adam Brody
Brian Grieves: Ryan Hansen
Origin: United States
Language: English, Spanish
Released: 2017
Production: Ravi Mehta, Andrew Panay, Dax Shepard; Primate Pictures, RatPac-Dune Entertainment; released by Warner Bros. Entertainment Inc.
Directed by: Dax Shepard
Written by: Dax Shepard
Cinematography by: Mitchell Amundsen
Music by: Fil Eisler
Sound: Cameron Frankley; Jon Michaels
Music Supervisor: Jason Altshuler
Editing: Dan Lebental
Art Direction: Nick Ralbovsky
Costumes: Diane Crooke
Production Design: Maher Ahmad
MPAA rating: R
Running time: 100 minutes

REVIEWS

Abrams, Simon. *RogerEbert.com*. March 24, 2017.
Catsoulis, Jeanette. *New York Times*. March 23, 2017.
Gleiberman, Owen. *Variety*. March 23, 2017.
Goodykoontz, Bill. *Arizona Republic*. March 23, 2017.
Jones, Kimberley. *Austin Chronicle*. March 29, 2017.
Lindsey, Craig D. *Village Voice*. March 24, 2017.
Rife, Katie. *The A.V. Club*. March 23, 2017.
Scheck, Frank. *Hollywood Reporter*. March 23, 2017.
Semley, John. *Globe and Mail*. March 23, 2017.
Zacharek, Stephanie. *Time*. March 24, 2017.

QUOTES

Ponch: "Yoga pants!"

TRIVIA

Original television series star Erik Estrada has an uncredited cameo as a paramedic near the end of the film.

CHUCK

The untold story of the inspiration for Rocky Balboa.
—Movie tagline

Box Office: $320,725

From the sheer volume of them, it would appear as though the biopic business is booming. The only problem is that filmmakers are so desperate to get films financed that they will take just about any real-life story, so long as it's tangentially related to a well-known showbiz or historical incident or personality. On paper it might sound like an interesting idea to tell the true story of Chuck Wepner, the palooka boxer from New Jersey who inspired Sylvester Stallone to write *Rocky* (1976). But, in practice, the film feels like an exercise in opportunistic wheel spinning after the success of the sorta-sequel *Creed* (2015) turned the *Rocky* money machine back on. The film does not feel like it came from a place of empathy or of even genuine interest, but rather like Academy Award®-nominated director Philippe Falardeau wanted to make something, anything, and was handed this script. His aesthetic ideas halfway fit the period, but there is not a single moment of excitement generated by his impatient directing. One wonders why bother telling the real story of the man behind *Rocky* when the fictitious version is so much more interesting and cinematic?

Chuck Wepner (Liev Schreiber) is at the end of his career, boxing a grizzly bear as a cheap publicity stunt in the mood to recall his supposed glory days. In the 1960s, he became a regional heavyweight champion nicknamed The Bayonne Bleeder. He was content to coast, drinking and womanizing between bouts in the ring and with his long-suffering second wife Phyliss (Elisabeth Moss), with whom he has two children. In 1975, his fortunes changed for better, and worse, when fighting promoter Don King decides that he needs a gimmick for an upcoming Muhammad Ali (Pooch Hall) fight. King and Ali decide to hit the race angle hard, making the bout Black vs. White, and, being of the few white boxers in Ali's class, Wepner's name is drawn. Suddenly the Bayonne Bleeder is a cause célèbre in his hometown. He trains with Al Braverman (Ron Perlman) for weeks before the bout while also giving interviews and talking himself up at bars. The added fame the fight brings him puts even more strain on his marriage but when push comes to shove, Phyllis shows up to support him. The fight goes as well as can be expected—the match is stopped on a technicality just as Ali looked to be winning. Afterwards, Wepner is still treated like a champion—he lasted 15 rounds with the heavyweight champion of the world.

What Wepner does not count on is how hard it is to stay on top when you've become famous on a technicality. He does not take his fighting career seriously; he starts taking hard drugs; he tries and fails to strike up a relationship with his estranged brother John (Michael Rapaport); he alienates Phyliss entirely. He becomes something of a joke when in a fight with André the Giant, the wrestler throws him out of the ring. Wepner tries to become a talk show staple but that does not take. His only saving grace is when Sylvester Stallone (Morgan Spector) writes the movie *Rocky* based on his life. The extra fame goes right to his head, to the point where he spends months trying to track down Stallone to meet him. Like most of the gifts Wepner receives, their eventual meeting is a double-edged sword. Stallone, it turns out, has written Wepner a part in *Rocky II* (1979) and wants him to audition, but after an all-night bender with his close friend John (Jim Gaffigan) and a couple of girls, he shows up dazed and panicky and blows his audition. The only person in Chuck's life who brings him any stability or joy is Linda (Naomi Watts), the bartender who will eventually become his third wife.

The shapelessness of *Chuck* is one of its biggest problems. Like so many biopics, it's just a series of things happening to the same person, who does not grow or change, because the history has dictated they wouldn't. Schreiber's running voicever turns every event into a kind of wry joke. Every comment he offers of his descent into obscurity and pain seems to imply we in the audience shouldn't take it so seriously. He's laughing about it omnisciently from the fictitious present, so how bad could any of this be? It turns his cocaine benders and failed marriage into a funny little footnote on the road to having a useless biopic made about him. It's a bizarre, distancing strategy. Yes, the facts are for the most part accurate, the only thing this film has on *Rocky*, but not even the title character gets any enjoyment out of any of it. It doesn't seem interesting to anyone involved, on screen or behind the camera.

Veteran Canadian cinematographer Nicolas Bolduc gets the look of grainy, ugly 1970s film down perfectly, but that has the unwanted benefit of making everything feel smaller, less expansive, and less like the real world it's aiming to depict. Editor Richard Comeau does his best keeping up the Scorsese-inspired madness that most every filmmaker tries to achieve when telling historical, drug-fueled tales of this sort. But both the look and the momentum are distractions from the obviously tangential nature of the story. Wepner's story needn't have played like the story of a loser who was never even as exciting as Rocky Balboa, but in Bolduc and company's hands, that's how it feels. No one will ever recommend *Chuck* over *Rocky*. Stallone was wise to print the legend because the truth, as told here, just is not that compelling.

Scout Tafoya

CREDITS

Chuck Wepner: Liev Schreiber
Linda Wepner: Naomi Watts
Phyllis Wepner: Elisabeth Moss
Al Braverman: Ron Perlman
John Stoehr: Jim Gaffigan
Origin: United States
Language: English
Released: 2017
Production: Michael Tollin, Christa Campbell, Lati Grobman, Carl Hampe, Liev Schreiber; Campbell Grobman Films, Das Films, Jeff Rice Films, Mike Tollin Productions; released by IFC Films
Directed by: Philippe Falardeau
Written by: Liev Schreiber; Jeff Feuerzeig; Jerry Stahl; Michael Cristofer
Cinematography by: Nicolas Bolduc
Music by: Corey A. Jackson
Sound: Kris Casavant
Music Supervisor: Selena Arizanovic
Editing: Richard Comeau
Art Direction: Gonzalo Cordoba
Production Design: Inbal Weinberg
MPAA rating: R
Running time: 98 minutes

REVIEWS

Abele, Robert. *Los Angeles Times*. May 4, 2017.
Bowen, Chuck. *Slant Magazine*. May 2, 2017.
Callahan, Dan. *TheWrap*. April 28, 2017.
Dowd, A.A. *The A.V. Club*. May 9, 2017.
Kenny, Glenn. *New York Times*. May 4, 2017.
Kiang, Jessica. *The Playlist*. September 14, 2016.
Lodge, Guy *Variety* September 14, 2016.
Padua, Pat. *Washington Post* July 13, 2017.
Russo, Tom. *Boston, Globe*. May 10, 2017.
Wolfe, April. *Village Voice*. May 3, 2017.

TRIVIA

Was originally titles *The Bleeder* but changed due to viewers thinking it was a horror film as well as other movies having the same name.

CHURCHILL

No Lies. Just Leadership.
—Movie tagline

"You must look at facts because they look at you." - Winston Churchill
—Movie tagline

The icon you know. The man you don't.
—Movie tagline

Box Office: $1.3 Million

For the historically challenged, film can shed some light on a part of history that a viewer may not know much about. Yet at the end of the day, the film needs to succeed in and of itself as a good story—be well-told. *Churchill* features a solid performance by Brian Cox as the titular Winston Churchill, but the film itself fails due to an inability of what to make of the iconic British Prime Minister. As a result, audiences are left to wonder if the man was merely a drunken, ego-driven windbag who was only great at giving speeches and trying to maintain his popularity, or a good-hearted man of the people who's sworn duty was to protect and honor Britain. Obviously, the answer in real-life may be "both," but *Churchill* never chooses a side, and whenever it wanders towards one, it course corrects so dramatically, it takes viewers out of the moment.

Churchill opens just days before the planned D-Day Invasion at Normandy during World War II. Britain has already been at war for five years, and while most are weary of the non-stop battles, countrymen look to Churchill as a never wavering source of motivation. And he does supply a certain kind of staunch British "keep calm and carry on" attitude that still manages to hold the country together, morale wise at least. However, Churchill himself seems to be cracking at the seams as he wanders a mossy English beach that he soon sees turn red with the blood of dead soldiers. As if that weren't grotesque enough, his iconic hat blows off his head into the bloody sea and he waddles in to retrieve it. Yet Churchill has good reason to be wary as he saw the toll war took on his truly beloved country just decades before during World War I, and having been scarred by those heavy losses, he feels he needs to possibly stall or find a way to call off the planned D-Day invasion.

Enter the war room, in this case, a pleasant picnic in the British countryside with military officials where Churchill has honed an impassioned plea to rethink this massive invasion even though he had previously signed off on it. While it's an intriguing character trait to have a man of power kind of waffle on an already-planned invasion, the rest of the cast Cox has to interact with fall far behind his excellent performance. John Slattery was fantastic as smarmy-yet-charming Roger Sterling in the television show *Mad Men* (2007-2015) but his performance here as American General Dwight Eisenhower feels as though he's performing in a mediocre television miniseries from the 1990s. While he does indeed smoke cigarettes and have a silver fox look going, his acting chops leave much to be desired against Cox's bravura performance. This issue frequently arises as some of the largest plot points in *Churchill* involve Slattery and Cox going head-to-head and these scenes never come off as dramatic as probably intended as Cox outpaces Slattery in every way.

At times, director Jonathan Teplitzky and writer Alex von Tunzelmann portray Winston Churchill as a mere figurehead or cheerleader who was really a bullying, loose-cannon drunk, but then they seem to take it back and show he's really a passionate man of the people. The film succeeds in showing that he was indeed outflanked and outnumbered by true military men like Eisenhower and General Bernard Montgomery (Julian Wadham) but it fails to show his strengths. Thus, when Churchill is finally asked to stay out of it if he's not going to be supportive, his subsequent breakdown due to being reprimanded by King George VI (James Purefoy) after an exasperated Eisenhower goes behind Churchill's back to rat him out, it comes off like a tantrum by an old drunk fool. What follows then feels silly and tacked-on as Churchill seemingly realizes he still has a wife (a terribly underused Miranda Richardson), who, along with a female typist (Ella Purnell) he's spent the previous two-acts shouting at, talk some sense into him from a British woman's point of view. This all culminates in Churchill deciding to ditch hard liquor for a bit, pull up his knickers, and deliver the rousing "We Shall Fight on the Beaches" speech that fuels British troops jingoism into the launch of D-Day.

While indeed it's impossible to truly show who a person "is" in a film, *Churchill* uses the broadest strokes possible, all to its detriment. There are scenes of forced comedy that wither on the vine and worst of all, the film feels incredibly boring. This, for lack of a better term, is a real drag as Winston Churchill was such an iconic, bombastic figure and the film is dealing with feelings he had prior to a major turning point in world history. Yet, aside from a solid performance by Brian Cox, the film falls flat in every other way.

Don R. Lewis

CREDITS

Winston Churchill: Brian Cox
Clemmie Churchill: Miranda Richardson
Dwight Eisenhower: John Slattery
General Montgomery: Julian Wadham
Jan Smuts: Richard Durden
Origin: United States
Language: English
Released: 2017
Production: Claudia Bluemhuber, Nick Taussig, Piers Tempest, Paul Van Carter; Salon Pictures; released by Cohen Media Group
Directed by: Jonathan Teplitzky
Written by: Alex von Tunzelmann
Cinematography by: David Higgs

Music by: Lorne Balfe
Sound: Andy Shelley; Ian Wilson
Music Supervisor: Rupert Hollier
Editing: Chris Gill
Art Direction: Fiona Gavin
Costumes: Bartholomew Cariss
Production Design: Chris Roope
MPAA rating: PG
Running time: 105 minutes

REVIEWS

Baumgarten, Marjorie. *Austin Chronicle*. June 7, 2017.
Burr, Ty. *Boston Globe*. May 31, 2017.
Goldstein, Gary. *Los Angeles Times*. June 1, 2017.
Ide, Wendy. *Screen International*. May 29, 2017.
Kenny, Glenn. *New York Times*. June 1, 2017.
Moore, Roger. *Movie Nation*. June 7, 2017.
Pile, Jonathan. *Empire*. June 19, 2017.
Roeper, Richard. *Chicago Sun-Times*. June 1, 2017.
Taylor, Kate. *The Globe and Mail (Toronto)*. June 8, 2017.
Travers, Peter. *Rolling Stone*. June 1, 2017.

QUOTES

Winston Churchill: "I am choosing between trials and tribulations. Do stop adding to them."

TRIVIA

Actor Brian Cox gained twenty-two pounds for the role, not wanting to wear a fat suit and latex.

THE CIRCLE

Secrets are lies. Sharing is caring. Privacy is theft.
—Movie tagline

Knowing is good. Knowing everything is better.
—Movie tagline

Box Office: $20.5 Million

From the moment it surfaced in 2004 until now, a majority of those who have no desire to join the ubiquitous social media network Facebook have often said they have no desire to "let the world know what they're having for lunch." While that excuse is inherently short-sighted in terms of what social media can truly offer users, other, more thoughtful avoiders of the social network, take that idea a step further by seeing a major issue in giving up their right to privacy to a major corporation who are profiting off personal information. In fact, it could be said the greatest trick modern day social media, as well as technology, has played on users is that it's made it basically a non-issue to freely and openly give up personal information to a faceless Internet-based entity. From users constantly, willfully alerting "friends" to their whereabouts to location services on phones knowing exactly where they are to the many users of the iPhone who have their fingerprint set up as a log-in device, very few people actually think about their right to privacy in terms of these daily occurrences. This brings us to director James Ponsoldt's modern-day conspiracy thriller *The Circle,* which takes all of these privacy issues much deeper, and the result has one feeling it's all a bit too current and insightful for comfort.

Based on Dave Eggers's 2013 book of the same name (which Eggers also helped adapt alongside Ponsoldt) *The Circle* is a fictional, semi-dystopian tale based on a sort of Facebook-meets-Google-meets-Apple social media conglomerate (called The Circle) which has risen far past the heights of the aforementioned tech giants. The Circle is not only a place to connect with friends—old and never met before in real life—online, they also have hardware (computers and watches) which can track location, health and personal preferences. As *The Circle* opens, we meet young, hard-working Mae (Emma Watson), who is temping in customer service. She soon gets the call from Annie (Karen Gillan), a real-life friend and fast-rising employee at the Circle who has arranged for Mae to get an interview at the hi-tech campus in Silicon Valley. Before one can catch their breath, Mae is getting the lay of the amazing land and participating in a job interview that pushes boundaries as well as samples tastes in what is certainly some kind of crafty, algorithmic way of seeing if Mae will be a good fit for the company.

Apparently she is as Mae is quickly-promoted to the role of customer satisfaction clerk, a job fit for modern times with a fancy cubicle, full health coverage and an aforementioned cool watch that tracks health, location, and who knows what else. As it just so happens, the Circle also offers housing and encourages participation in countless classes like yoga and pottery, as well as lavish parties full of free drinks and food as well as popular rock stars of the day. Through the watch (and a menagerie of always-watching, platitude spewing Circle sycophants) the Circle knows where you are, what you're doing (or, not doing), how much you're drinking and all sorts of other personal behaviors and choices no corporation truly needs to know. This is where *The Circle* starts to really get interesting while also seriously creepy.

Through a somewhat poorly rendered and iffy sequence of events, the Circle ends up saving Mae's life. As she recovers, she finds herself face-to-face with the gregarious and hip head of the company, Eamon Bailey (Tom Hanks), who knows things about Mae she's never volunteered, including the fact that her father (Bill Paxton) suffers from debilitating multiple sclerosis and her mother (Glenne Headly) is barely able to keep him in decent health. In a rather Machiavellian quid-pro-quo, Bailey convinces Mae to agree to be the "face" of a new product from the Circle by becoming "transparent" via a wearable, nearly invisible HD video camera barely larger than a marble. The camera (cleverly called "See Change") is designed to give everyone the ability to share their life in real time. Be it the mundane, daily existence of a grocery clerk to the downtrodden minority citizen in a war torn country. An intriguing product for sure but again, everything seen and heard is transmitted through the Circle. In exchange for sharing herself with whoever wants to watch her, Mae's family is given premium healthcare and all sorts of Circle gadgets, love, and lack of privacy as their lives are now being filmed as well.

Almost immediately, Mae becomes an online celebrity as millions of daily viewers watch her go about her life. Yet, not everyone is impressed. Lifelong friend and avoider of all things tech Mercer (Ellar Coltrane) immediately sees the implications of what the Circle knows and how it not only detracts from personal moments and choices but also how anything too good to be true usually is. There's also former Circle ingénue Ty (John Boyega), who roams freely around campus, warning anyone who will listen about the dangers of unchecked power and information. These side characters are where *The Circle* falters a bit as it's incredibly hard to believe Ty is allowed to basically be a ghost on campus, able to go anywhere and do whatever he pleases unchecked as the Circle takes a perverse pride in monitoring and controlling their employees. It's also immediately clear to viewers that Mae is being killed with kindness and is getting set up for a major fall. Still, *The Circle* is clever and insightful on a number of other levels.

For one, *The Circle* is the first fictional film to really get into the unchecked power of mega-sites like Facebook and Google who traffic (and, profit hugely) off of personal information. The lack of films—fiction or non—thus far is surprising as Google's power has been massive and is still rising to this day almost without question from users, media, or even the government at large. While their motto "Don't be evil" seems like a fine idea when read, few people actually question the philosophical question of whose definition of evil one is talking about. *The Circle* cleverly gets to this idea and the one of transparency but not until late in the film. Still, it's a valuable question and situation worth personal examination and discussion. Also intriguing, the casting of Ellar Coltrane as proud luddite Mercer is rather humorous as his only other major role was that of the main character Mason in *Boyhood* (2014), Richard Linklater's brilliant experimental hit that followed Coltrane in real life for 13 years, filming a segment every summer. Viewers of that film literally follow Coltrane/Mason as he grows up, much as the Circle follows its users.

The Circle also marks a departure for writer/director Ponsoldt, who has crafted a solid career examining big, brilliant, and damaged people in films like *Smashed* (2012), *The Spectacular Now* (2013) and the semi-biopic on David Foster Wallace, *The End of the Tour* (2015). Ponsoldt has a way with big personalities and this meshes well here. Overall, *The Circle* is an imperfect-yet-timely film that posits many questions that need to be asked and discussed.

Don R. Lewis

CREDITS

Mae: Emma Watson
Bailey: Tom Hanks
Ty: John Boyega
Annie: Karen Gillan
Mercer: Ellar Coltrane
Origin: United States
Language: English
Released: 2017
Production: Anthony Bregman, Gary Goetzman, James Ponsoldt; 1978 Films, Imagenation Abu Dhabi FZ, Likely Story, Parkes+MacDonald Image Nation, Route One Entertainment, The Playtone Co.; released by STX Entertainment
Directed by: James Ponsoldt
Written by: James Ponsoldt; Dave Eggers
Cinematography by: Matthew Libatique
Music by: Danny Elfman
Sound: Dror Mohar
Music Supervisor: Tiffany Anders
Editing: Lisa Lassek; Franklin Peterson
Art Direction: Sarah M. Pott; Sebastian Schroder
Costumes: Emma Potter
Production Design: Gerald Sullivan
MPAA rating: PG
Running time: 110 minutes

REVIEWS

Burr, Ty. *Boston Globe*. April 28, 2017.
D'Arcy, David. *Screen International*. April 27, 2017.
DeFore, John. *Hollywood Reporter*. April 27, 2017.
Kenny, Glenn. *New York Times*. April 27, 2017.
LaSalle, Mick. *San Francisco Chronicle*. April 27, 2017.
Myers, Kimber. *The Playlist*. April 28, 2017.
Nakhnikian, Elise. *Slant Magazine*. April 28, 2017.
Seitz, Matt Zoller. *RogerEbert.com*. April 28, 2017.
Stewart, Sarah. *New York Post*. April 27, 2017.
Travers, Peter. *Rolling Stone*. April 28, 2017.

QUOTES

Eamon Bailey: "Knowing is good, but knowing everything is better."

TRIVIA

While actor Bill Paxton died shortly before the film's release, actress Glenne Headley, who played his wife in the film, died the same year just after the film's release.

AWARDS

Nominations:

Golden Raspberries 2017: Worst Actress (Watson)

COCO

Box Office: $202.9 Million

Can you make a family-friendly movie about death? That seems to have been one of Pixar's goals when they began the development of *Coco*, their nineteenth feature film. The movie wisely chooses to broach the topic of mortality by surrounding it in the sugar-shock colors and skulls of Mexico's Day of the Dead celebration, a seemingly ideal vehicle to make death palatable for young audiences. The animated *The Book of Life* (2014) used the same conceit with perhaps more visual flair—and less storytelling depth—than what Pixar attempts with *Coco*.

As a result, *Coco* feels more like *Inside Out* (2015) than any other Pixar movie. Both films created elaborate scenarios to bring abstract concepts to life. In *Inside Out,* it was the emotions of a young girl. In *Coco,* it's the weight of death and legacy on families. And, like *Inside Out, Coco* amazingly finds a way to make its abstract concepts powerfully resonate with audiences, young and old alike.

While *Coco* might not embody the same audacious originality of *Inside Out,* directors Lee Unkrich and Adrian Molina do find a way to tell a story with profound emotional depth, while at the same time, showing off the best that Pixar has to offer. The story borrows storytelling tropes from movies ranging from *Beetlejuice* (1988) to *Back to the Future* (1985), but it's also expertly crafted and painfully funny. The unsatisfying fart jokes of the *Cars* movies are nowhere to be found in the script by Molina and Matthew Aldrich, or the excellent songs by *Frozen*'s Robert Lopez and Kristen Anderson-Lopez. Instead, *Coco* is legitimately smart, clever, and silly—all in equal measure. This may be Pixar's funniest film to date, even though its third act takes great pains to pluck at the heartstrings.

Coco turns Mexico's traditional Day of the Dead into the backdrop for an Orpheus-esque fable about a boy trying to reconcile himself with his family's tragic past. (The film has already become the highest-grossing movie in Mexico's history.) The boy, Miguel Rivera (Anthony Gonzalez), loves music more than anything, but his family considers it a forbidden pleasure. According to legend, the father of his great-grandmother Coco (Ana Ofelia Murguía) left his family to pursue a career in music. After that, music was banned by the shoemaking Rivera family—a ban that has been passed down from generation to generation.

Miguel, who taught himself to play the guitar in secret, wants to convince his family to lift the ban by winning a local Day of the Dead talent show. However, after his grandmother Elena destroys his guitar, Miguel decides to sneak into the mausoleum of his idol, legendary singer Ernesto de la Cruz (Benjamin Bratt), and steal Ernesto's guitar to use in the show. However, this act of trespass curses Miguel, effectively making him invisible to the Land of the Living and granting him access to the Land of the Dead—a landscape that ranks as one of Pixar's most impressive design achievements to date. The multi-leveled cityscape of eye-popping colors and elaborately-designed skeletons is truly breathtaking in its beauty and depth.

To lift the curse, Miguel must receive forgiveness and blessing from a member of his deceased family, so, with the clock ticking, he disguises himself as a skeleton and ventures across the veil. Along the way, Miguel befriends a sly trickster Héctor (Gael García Bernal) who helps Miguel for a price—Héctor is desperate to deliver a photo to his still-living daughter so she won't forget him—learns the truth about his family history, and encounters his hero Ernesto, who, like all heroes, is never exactly what one would expect.

At worst, the storytelling in *Coco* is a bit more familiar than a Pixar fan might expect. There are third-act twists that are telegraphed far too early and Héctor's story—fighting against the fear of being forgotten forever—is more than a little similar to the arc of *Inside Out*'s Bing-Bong. (*Coco,* while one of Pixar's better films, simply can't compete with the gut-punch of Bing-Bong's final moments.)

But, despite treading a few well-worn story beats, *Coco* is an expertly-told tale, brimming with moments of invention and verve. We find ourselves legitimately caring about Miguel and the Rivera family. We are invested in their fate and, as the third act swells to a performance of a song called "Remember Me," our hearts ache for everything they feel and everything they have lost. Even if you're not won over by the wacky afterlife hi-jinks, the finale of *Coco* has an emotional heft that's almost impossible to ignore.

So, can you make a family-friendly movie about death? Apparently, the answer is yes. Because, even with all the set-dressings of wacky skulls and silly dog sidekicks, *Coco* still addresses the topic of death head-on. Fortunately, in the best tradition of Pixar, it does so with such humor, spirit, and truth that kids won't be traumatized and adults won't roll their eyes. *Coco* is a movie that will stick to your skeletal ribs long after you've left the theater, which is an amazing accomplishment for the nineteenth film from the studio that started with *Toy Story* (1995).

Despite their recent (and unfortunate) penchant for sequels, the folks at Pixar still know how to tell a story that touches on the bigger things in life. While *Coco* has its flaws, it still ranks amongst Pixar's most ambitious projects like *Ratatouille* (2007), *WALL-E* (2008), *Up* (2009), and *Inside Out*. It is a movie that wants us to think about things that aren't always easy to think about. That's a rare quality in a film—a quality that the studio will hopefully never lose.

Tom Burns

CREDITS

Voice of Chicarron: Edward James Olmos
Voice of Ernesto de la Cruz: Benjamin Bratt
Voice of Mama Imelda: Alanna Ubach
Voice of Hector: Gael Garcia Bernal
Voice: John Ratzenberger
Origin: United States
Language: English
Released: 2017
Production: Darla K. Anderson; Pixar Animation Studios; released by Walt Disney Pictures
Directed by: Lee Unkrich; Adriana Molina
Written by: Lee Unkrich; Adriana Molina; Matthew Aldrich
Music by: Michael Giacchino
Editing: Lee Unkrich; Steve Bloom
Production Design: Harley Jessup
MPAA rating: PG
Running time: 109 minutes

REVIEWS

Busis, Hillary. *Vanity Fair*. December 9, 2017.
Debruge, Peter. *Variety*. October 20, 2017.
de Semlyen, Phil. *Time Out*. November 20, 2017.
Hartlaub, Peter. *San Francisco Chronicle*. November 16, 2017.
Oleksinski, Johnny. *New York Post*. November 20, 2017.
Orr, Christopher. *The Atlantic*. January 9, 2018.
Rechtshaffen, Michael. *Hollywood Reporter*. October 20, 2017.
Scherstuhl, Alan. *Village Voice*. November 21, 2017.
Scott, A.O. *New York Times*. November 21, 2017.
Taylor, Drew. *The Playlist*. November 10, 2017.

QUOTES

Ernesto de la Cruz (from trailer): "I have to sing. It's not just 'in' me. It 'is' me."

TRIVIA

The film took six years to complete, more than any other Pixar film to date.

AWARDS

Oscars 2017: Animated Film, Orig. Song Score and/or Adapt. ("Remember Me")
British Acad. 2017: Animated Film
Golden Globes 2018: Animated Film
Nominations:
Golden Globes 2018: Song ("Remember Me")

COLLIDE

How far would you go for the one you love?
—Movie tagline

Box Office: $2.3 Million

Considering the exquisitely terrible lows the series has sunk to over its now decades-old history, it's still surprising that the *Fast and the Furious* movies have become a cultural phenomenon. The only franchises currently running that possess comparable economic staying power are the *Star Wars* films and the movies produced by Marvel and DC Comics. The runaway success of these deeply silly movies about drag racers who became international thieves and spies has led to an uptick in very silly, flamboyant movies about heists and car chases like *Contraband* (2012), *Safe House* (2015), *Faster* (2010), and *Need for Speed* (2014), to say nothing of the resurgence of movies starring Vin Diesel, including the return of his ridiculous *XXX* movies. The latest film to show the visible influence of the *Fast and the Furious* universe is the mostly forgettable *Collide*, which feels like a film made as quickly as possible so that it could beat *The Fate of the Furious* (2017) to theaters. British director Eran Creevy does not have much in the way of a personal style, but what little he possesses keeps the film moving at a quick enough clip that you reach the finish line without growing bored.

Casey Stein (Nicholas Hoult) is a smalltime drug dealer working for a dazed kingpin called Geran (Ben Kingsley) in Germany. He's happy enough coasting until he meets Juliette Marne (Felicity Jones), a fellow

American who catches his eye at the club he works one night. She's pretty and charismatic enough that, after one encounter, he decides to resign from his life of crime and go straight. Their life together is like a storybook until Marne passes out one night while on a date. Her kidney is failing and because she's not a German citizen, she does not qualify for a transplant. She has to consider moving back home to the States in order to get treatment because she cannot afford anything else. Backed into a corner, a lightbulb goes off over Casey's head. Maybe he can talk to his friend Matthias (Marwan Kenzari), still in Gerwan's employ, and figure out a way to skim something off the top of Germany's criminal underworld operations. Geran has a plan, it turns out, that fits the situation like a glove. They are going to rip off a big-time drug dealer named Hagen Kahl (Anthony Hopkins) using his truck-based transit system for his narcotics. The deal predictably goes awry almost immediately, setting off a chase across vast swathes of the German countryside. Casey has to stay one step ahead of Hagen's thugs before they either kill him or find Juliette. Once Hagen figures out that Geran is behind the disruption in his business, the stakes and the body count go up.

Creevy's previous film, the similarly forgettable neo-noir *Welcome to the Punch* (2013), had a kind of nervous energy and bleak amorality that made it engaging, if not essential. He got great performances from a rogue's gallery of British character actors and his neon-soaked London was a scary enough creation. Relegated to a more anonymous Germany (he doesn't have a feel for the location), all that remains is Creevy's intense stare, his competent handling of action sequences and his kindness towards actors. It's not exactly acuity, but he certainly loves and respects Kingsley and Hopkins enough to let them chew all the scenery they feel entitled to. Kingsley's basically fusing his two characters from *Iron Man 3* (2013) and is as entertaining as possible, given the boring character he's stuck playing. Hopkins is the hammiest he's been since *The Wolfman* (2010), taking a moment to misremember the day on which a pointless anecdote transpired. His abject over-acting is a non-stop delight and more than makes up for the comparably anemia of the two leads. Hopkins and Kingsley shooting it out in a German café isn't nearly as exciting as watching them try to out-act each other. Hoult is as fine and likable as ever but Jones can't possibly measure up to the film's implicit description of her as the kind of girl that would cause a drug dealer to go straight. She's meant to be a sort of naïve, Helen of Troy figure, but Jones' gift is her every-woman charisma. Asking her to be so radiant she would change the course of a man's life is not only bad screenwriting, but plays against her strengths—namely that she's an intelligent, normal person. Making things stranger still is the decision to make Hoult and Jones, both British, play Americans for no discernable reasons.

There's a chase on the Autobahn that, while exciting enough, is not the groundbreaking feat of action filmmaking it needed to be to justify the film's existence. There's simply no way that this enterprise was not sold on the promise of a pulse-racing car chase set on the most famous lawless highway in the world. Yes, it's exciting to watch and imagine how they planned the chase, but no, it's not quite enough to justify the existence of such a small-time action thriller.

Collide is slightly above average for a film that would have, in better days, gone straight to Redbox, but it's no wonder it basically skipped theatres. Creevy is not up to the challenge of making this kind of action thriller work. He does not have the patience to build a story around likable, lived-in characters, cutting too quickly to the action sequences, which do not have much weight because Casey and Juliette are cyphers through and through. *Collide* needed another draft and a more invested filmmaker to sell its paltry ideas and meager thrills.

Scout Tafoya

CREDITS

Casey Stein: Nicholas Hoult
Juliette Marne: Felicity Jones
Matthias: Marwan Kenzari
Geran: Ben Kingsley
Hagen Kahl: Anthony Hopkins
Origin: United States
Language: English
Released: 2017
Production: Ben Pugh, Joel Silver, Rory Aitken, Daniel Hetzer, Brian Kavanaugh-Jones; 42, Automatik Entertainment, DMG Entertainment and Media Company Ltd., Hands-on Producers, Silver Pictures Inc.; released by Open Road Films
Directed by: Eran Creevy
Written by: Eran Creevy; F. Scott Frazier
Cinematography by: Ed Wild
Music by: Ilan Eshkeri
Sound: Joakim Sundstrom
Music Supervisor: Ian Neil
Editing: Chris Gill
Art Direction: Robyn Paiba
Costumes: Sharon Gilham
Production Design: Joel Collins
MPAA rating: PG-13
Running time: 99 minutes

REVIEWS

Allen, Nick. *RogerEbert.com.* February 24, 2017.

Anderson, Jeffrey. *Common Sense Media.* February 25, 2017.
Moore, Roger. *Movie Nation.* February 25, 2017.
Murray, Noel. *Los Angeles Times.* February 24, 2017.
Savlov, Marc. *Austin Chronicle.* March 1, 2017.
Scheck, Frank. *Hollywood Reporter.* February 23, 2017.
Thomas, Rob. *Capital Times.* February 24, 2017.
Thompson, Luke. *Forbes.* February 24, 2017.
Vishnevetsky, Ignatiy. *The A.V. Club.* February 24, 2017.
Watson, Keith. *Slant Magazine.* February 23, 2017.

QUOTES

Casey Stein: "They're gonna kill the love of my life."

TRIVIA

Zac Efron and Amber Heard were originally cast in the lead roles.

AWARDS

Nominations:

Golden Raspberries 2017: Worst Support. Actor (Hopkins)

COLOSSAL

All she could do was save the world.
—Movie tagline
There's a monster in all of us.
—Movie tagline

Box Office: $3 Million

Rarely have kaiju been put to such good use than in *Colossal.* Writer/director Nacho Vigalondo comes close to creating a new genre with this deeply moving and wildly entertaining story that uses giant monsters, romantic comedy, and solidly-drawn, believable characters to surprisingly poignant ends.

Gloria (Anne Hathaway) has a drinking problem that has cost her job, her boyfriend Tim (Dan Stevens), and their shared big city apartment in New York. She decides to head back to her hometown and sort things out and almost immediately runs into Oscar (Jason Sudeikis), an old childhood friend who not only helps her settle in but offers her a job at his bar. Soon, she finds herself drinking after her shift well into the morning hours with Oscar and his pals, eccentric Garth (Tim Blake Nelson) and good-looking-but-innocent Joel (Austin Stowell) at the local playground.

One morning, after walking back home, she see a news report detailing the sudden appearance of a giant monster wreaking havoc in Seoul, South Korea. Within a few days, Gloria realizes that the monster is mimicking the movements she makes in the playground each morning. She drunkenly confides in her friends by demonstrating her power, only to wake up horrified the next morning when Oscar shows her a picture of a giant robot that he manifested as well with a similar pattern. Realizing death and destruction dog her movements when drunk and working with Oscar to minimize their impact, Gloria swears off liquor but appears in South Korea one more time to write an apology in the dirt. All seems well until she makes a decision to sneak off to Joel's house, angering Oscar, who has started showing up at the playground on his own. Soon, Oscar, drunk almost round the clock, demands that Gloria—who is now trying to keep him under control—get drunk with him, and, when she refuses, races off to the playground, forcing Gloria to pursue and physically fight him. The next morning, Oscar apologizes, but when Tim comes into town to try and bring Gloria back to New York, Oscar threatens to resume his monstrous activities at the playground unless she stays forever, setting the stage for an epic showdown that takes place across two continents.

Colossal is ample proof writer director Nacho Vigalondo is one of the most imaginative filmmakers working today. Since his striking debut, *Timecrimes* (2007), he has shown an indisputable knack for hanging interesting stories on the skeleton of well-realized genre conventions, using time travel, alien invasion, and now the kaiju film to make movies first and foremost about the desperate people caught up in his adventures. His plots go in unexpected directions but not out of showy cleverness. His stories are surprising because he has created characters that are surprising as well.

His casting of the film is adventurous and unexpected. While up and comer Dan Stevens is predictably and excellently self-absorbed as the big city boyfriend who wants to play savior, Tim Blake Nelson almost steals the show as the long suffering small-town Garth. What could have been a simple bit of comic relief emerges as an eccentric but strong character unwilling to bow down to Oscar's abuse.

But leads Anne Hathaway and especially Jason Sudeikis own their roles and this movie. Sudeikis offers a chilling but complex portrait of an abusive personality. Even when he stomps South Korea by proxy he never becomes a cartoon. Oscar not only seems like a genuinely nice guy at times but a deeply wounded one, ready and willing to apologize when his alcoholic behavior crosses the line. His increasingly violent and manipulative actions mask a real-world monster but also a pathetic excuse for a human being.

Hathaway is well-cast as a high-functioning alcoholic who has gotten by using her natural charm and likability. Her strong performance helps the film do its work of deconstructing what initially feels like a standard female romantic comedy character. Her story is actually all about becoming comfortable in her own skin and facing down her insecurities and fear.

Another reason to praise Vigalondo here is his ability to connect the events of the playground and South Korea. The special effects are well done but often Vigalondo uses only his camera to achieve powerful effects such as when he contrasts the size difference between Gloria and Sudeikis in the fight sequences. The design of the kaiju in the film is clever but only in retrospect. At first glance they appear to be merely leftover mock-ups from other franchise blockbusters but once the film reveals them to be psychic projections of cheap children's toys their appearance makes perfect sense.

Colossal embraces the idea that individual thoughts and actions not only matter but are what connect people to one another. But its empowerment goes further. *Colossal* suggests that heroism itself is something people can grow into despite the monstrous challenges that threaten to keep them mired in bitterness, anger, fear, or the comfortable places where they could hide from the work. We are monstrous in our power is its ultimate statement even as it ends on a note of beautiful humility.

Dave Canfield

CREDITS

Gloria: Anne Hathaway
Oscar: Jason Sudeikis
Joel: Austin Stowell
Tim: Dan Stevens
Origin: United States
Language: English
Released: 2017
Production: Zev Foreman, Nahikari Ipina, Russell Levine, Dominic Rustam; Brightlight Pictures, Legion M, Route One Entertainment, Toy Fight Productions; released by Neon
Directed by: Nacho Vigalondo
Written by: Nacho Vigalondo
Cinematography by: Eric Kress
Music by: Bear McCreary
Sound: Mark Gingras
Music Supervisor: Linda Cohen
Editing: Ben Baudhuin; Luke Doolan
Art Direction: Roger Fires
Costumes: Antoinette Messam
Production Design: Sue Chan
MPAA rating: R
Running time: 109 minutes

REVIEWS

Brody, Richard. *New Yorker*. April 10, 2017.
Burr, Ty. *Boston Globe*. April 13, 2017.
Han, Angie. *Slashfilm*. June 13, 2017.
Hornaday, Ann. *Washington Post*. April 13, 2017.
Howell, Peter. *Toronto Star*. April 20, 2017.
Huddleston, Tom. *Time Out*. September 11, 2016.
LaSalle, Mick. *San Francisco Chronicle*. April 12, 2017.
Ruiz, Nicolas. *Codigo espagueti*. July 24, 2017.
Scott, A.O. *New York Times*. April 6, 2017.
Willmore, Alison. *BuzzFeed News*. September 26, 2016.

QUOTES

Oscar: "So, you don't remember anything we talked about last night, huh?"
Gloria: "I got really melodramatic, didn't I?"

TRIVIA

Anne Hathaway was in the second trimester of her pregnancy while filming.

COLUMBUS

Box Office: $1 Million

Americans are not known for taking notice of the little things in life. This is especially true in 2017, from the stale-but-relevant recognition of superheroes/sequels/remakes/reboots dominating big screens to daily news of hate and nuclear weapons on small and smaller screens. So *Columbus*, a quiet and delicate work of thought and feeling, arrives at a time when nearly everything else seems huge and physical.

Yet the film does not need to stand as such a stark contrast against an onslaught of brawn to resonate as a lovely distillation of people's temporary occupation of space and what they do within it. The feature debut of South Korean-American director Kogonada, *Columbus* contains the type of economic and opportunity-based despair that informs other Midwestern festival fare like *Winter's Bone* (2010) but seen through an entirely different lens—aware of the world's purposeful designs and not just their absence.

In this restrained drama, Casey (Haley Lu Richardson) always meant to leave Columbus, Indiana. After enough time looking after her mother (Michelle Forbes), though, Casey has resigned herself toward acceptance, blurring should not and can not, as if the thing that life seemed to choose for her was what she wanted anyway. One day during her work at a library, Casey encounters a former high school classmate, who now lives in Los Angeles and recently traveled to Amsterdam. This other girl could not imagine living in Columbus anymore.

Without pushing too hard, and in one of many stunning, revealing moments from Richardson, Kogonada establishes a social hierarchy that appears familiar and yet a step past the conventional. There is observation in this kind of sadness, seen through Casey as she so frequently becomes lost among rows of books and enamored with the town's architecture, which maybe one day, or in another life, would be a profession and not a hobby.

Into the life of the girl who never left comes Jin (John Cho, effortless in an unusually dramatic starring role), who cannot wait to leave town. He has no idea when that will be, however, as he waits to find out when/if his father, a professor of architecture, will emerge from a coma. The two men were never close, and they have not spoken for more than a year. Jin resents the distraction from his work as a translator in Seoul, at least until he meets Casey. The two begin touring the local architectural highlights, for her it's a rare opportunity to share her passion and for him their relationship is a way to indirectly connect to his father without having to actually spend time with him.

The notion of a walk-and-talk intellectual romance may seem somewhere between the verbosity of *Before Sunrise* (1995) or the somewhat chaste temptation of *Liberal Arts* (2013). That surface reading obscures the very specific ache that exists for both and often wordlessly connects them. In a softly devastating scene in which Casey explains her relationship with her mom, Richardson is heartbreaking, her pain seeping out while still trying to keep it in. For a long time she has been very sad, close to breaking, and yet it is not a stretch to think that her bond with Jin may push her in a new direction, no matter how long they are in each other's lives. For him, Casey provides a certain lightness to a topic previously weighed down by his anger toward his father. When he challenges her to explain why a building moves her, and she later delights in him admitting to having studied up on the subject, there is a sense of them moving towards each other and yet remaining at a certain distance. It is if they know this friendship and moment may exist only now, but they do not have the energy to be bothered by that. There are too many other things to be sad about.

Meanwhile, Kogonada, in a more promising debut as a director than a writer, dares to open up this intimacy and also close it off, sometimes less interested in what is being said than the gestures happening in the meantime. He stages this rapport against the chirping of birds, the looming of buildings, and the sprinkling of water onto plants. In this scenery is the rare opportunity to process the world inside and outside the head, a daunting task on a hard day. Whether in a long shot of Casey exiting a long aisle after dropping off a job application or the adjacency of people and the structures they admire, the filmmaker creates questions of permanence and subjective impact, of who used to live in this house and travel on this road, of the possibility of being diminished by something that pulls you in. Seen through different, less patient eyes, the story would not have nearly the same weight.

At times, though, *Columbus* does struggle to match its tone to its language. A discussion between Casey and a colleague with a crush (Rory Culkin) is a bit too on the nose about different types of people's quantity of interest and attention span toward everyday life, and the film's ending goes a little easy in letting the central relationship off the hook. The conflict between them feels more inevitable than earned, and the history between Jin and his father lacks detail. As Jin's father's partner, Parker Posey never really gets the chance to establish the clarity of her co-stars.

Yet the film allows viewers to hear unarticulated questions and see feelings the characters attempt to hide. (A late shot of Casey coming to understand the degree to which she is mad, hurt, and regretful all at once is astonishing.) There is love here but no reason to believe anything will be done with it, not in this place where jobs are scarce and the beautiful imagery contrasts with most of the people who move among it. The age and cultural differences at work between Jin and Casey are neither relevant nor irrelevant. All they can do is appreciate the way they rejuvenate each other against the sadness of their families, providing a sense of choice in the shadow of obligation.

One night, Casey's mom says a dish needs more spice; Casey replies that she was going for subtle, allowing them to more clearly taste the food and experience a better aftertaste. It would be hard to find a more fitting summary for the confident, personal *Columbus*, and the way it lingers.

Matt Pais

CREDITS

Jin: John Cho
Casey: Haley Lu Richardson
Eleanor: Parker Posey
Gabriel: Rory Culkin
Maria: Michelle Forbes
Origin: United States
Language: English, Korean
Released: 2017
Production: Danielle Renfrew Behrens, Aaron Boyd, Giulia Caruso, Ki Jin Kim, Andrew Miano, Chris Weitz; Depth of Field, Nonetheless Productions; released by Superlative Films

Directed by: Kogonada
Written by: Kogonada
Cinematography by: Elisha Christian
Music by: Hammock
Sound: Andrea Gard
Editing: Kogonada
Art Direction: Adriaan Harsta
Costumes: Emily Moran
Production Design: Diana Rice
MPAA rating: Unrated
Running time: 104 minutes

REVIEWS

Bowen, Chuck. *Slant Magazine.* July 30, 2017.
Chang, Justin. *Los Angeles Times.* August 3, 2017.
Crump, Andrew. *Paste Magazine.* August 7, 2017.
Dowd, A.A. *The A.V. Club.* August 3, 2017.
Erbland, Kate. *IndieWire.* August 3, 2017.
Ebiri, Bilge. *Village Voice.* August 1, 2017.
Kang, Inkoo. *TheWrap.* August 4, 2017.
Merry, Stephanie. *Washington Post.* August 17, 2017.
O'Malley, Sheila. *RogerEbert.com.* August 4, 2017.
Raup, Jordan. *The Film Stage.* June 23, 2017.

TRIVIA

Columbus, Indiana is known as "The Athens on the Prarie."

AWARDS

Nominations:

Ind. Spirit 2018: Cinematog., First Screenplay

CROWN HEIGHTS

How far would you go for justice?
—Movie tagline

Box Office: $238,558

There is a decided lack of responsibility or accountability placed on any person, institution, or system in *Crown Heights*, a rushed and mostly hollow dramatization of the story of Colin Warner. The real Warner was arrested, tried, and convicted for the murder of someone whom he did not know, to whom he had never spoken, and whom he insisted he did not kill.

Warner spent almost 20 years in prison—not counting the two years during which he was incarcerated as his trial proceeded—despite the fact that another man, with whom Warner was tried, had confessed to the murder two years after being released on parole, following a seven-year sentence for second-degree murder. The confessed killer was a minor. Warner was not—hence the longer sentence.

Warner's story is an obvious case of failure on the part of the legal system, yet writer/director Matt Ruskin essentially has made a movie that sees all of this as some terrible and twisted accident. It happened, and it is a shame that it didn. That is about the extent of the filmmaker's understanding of how this injustice transpired and his outrage over the fact that it, in fact, did occur. The movie, based on Anya Bourg's two-part piece from *This American Life*, counts on the audience to fill in the blanks, and even then, Ruskin is hesitant to aid anyone watching this hastened account of Warner's 21-year ordeal in connecting how and why an innocent man went through this.

In the movie, Colin is played by Lakeith Stanfield, in a performance that has the additional weight of bearing almost the entirety of the movie's point upon it. Some introductory scenes point out that Colin is no saint: He steals a car, is involved in a black market enterprise for stolen vehicles, and gets away with his actual crimes.

The choice is a strange one on Ruskin's part, since there is no attempt to communicate anything else about this man before he is arrested for murder—apart from the fact that he is an immigrant from Trinidad. The detail of his criminal activity exists in a vacuum, since it has no narrative connection. The police do not suspect him of any crimes, let alone the ones he has actually committed, so it does not even serve as an excuse for how the detectives who arrest him decide upon doing so.

The arrest occurs because of an alleged witness, who is later revealed to have had his account coerced by the police. Colin is taken into custody, and sometime later, so, too, is the real killer, who refuses to confess, lest he take the brunt of the sentencing. Like the rest of the narrative, the process of the trial speeds past in brief glimpses, with the most noteworthy one, perhaps, coming after the verdict. The judge basically states that it is obvious that this is a miscarriage of justice (not enough of one, though, apparently, to override the verdict, as is a judge's prerogative in such a circumstance). The moment is noteworthy primarily because it amounts to the range of the movie's theme: This is bad, yet there is nothing that could have been done to stop it from happening.

A similar sentiment comes from Colin's best friend and, later, brother-in-law Carl "KC" King (Nnamdi Asomugha), who tells his wife, Colin's sister, Briana (Marsha Stephanie Blake) that it could have been him who was arrested—or could be arrested in the future. The notion of a justice system that is prejudicial on the basis of race is implied in only this moment (a few speeches from elected officials contain some undertones of prejudice, although their inclusion in the narrative is mostly to show the political atmosphere of a tough-on-crime sentiment running through the 1980s and 1990s). Other than that, Ruskin seems either unwilling to state the obvious or unable to explore the implications of such a system.

The story amounts to little more than a melodrama, in which the narrative cuts between Colin's time in prison—as he transforms from an innocent man into one who is hardened by his experience in prison and, from there, into someone who is willing to deny the possibility of his freedom, if it means having to show remorse for a crime he did not commit—and Carl's work to exonerate his friend/brother-in-law. For that, he enlists the help of a lawyer (played by character actor Bill Camp, who lends authenticity to a thankless role), begins investigating on his own time, and causes friction in his relationship with his wife (who is, again, Colin's sister—a fact that Ruskin almost appears to forget, given her dismissal of Carl's efforts). Colin has a letter-writing relationship with Antoinette (Natalie Paul), an old friend from the neighborhood, which becomes a romantic one.

Beyond telling a story that goes from hopelessness to a happy ending, Ruskin's intentions are never clear. Indeed, it is difficult to tell if the filmmaker possesses any significant thoughts on the subjects that are inherent to material such as this. *Crown Heights* merely portrays events—and, even then, does so with little sense of time passing. Within the bigger picture of a system that would allow and/or enable such injustice to happen, any context for those events is completely circumstantial.

Mark Dujsik

CREDITS

Colin Warner: Lakeith Stanfield
Carl "KC" King: Nnamdi Asomugha
Antoinette: Natalie Paul
Leon Grant: Amari Cheatom
Briana: Marsha Stephanie Blake
Origin: United States
Language: English
Released: 2017
Production: Nnamdi Asomugha, Matt Ruskin; Black Maple Films, Iam21 Entertainment, Washington Square Films; released by IFC Films
Directed by: Matt Ruskin
Written by: Matt Ruskin
Cinematography by: Ben Kutchins
Music by: Mark De Gli Antoni
Sound: Gregory King
Editing: Paul Greenhouse; Joe Hutshing
Art Direction: Joshua Petersen
Costumes: Meghan Kasperlik
Production Design: Kaet McAnneny
MPAA rating: R
Running time: 94 minutes

REVIEWS

Baumgarten, Marjorie. *Austin Chronicle*. September 8, 2017.
Duralde, Alonso. *TheWrap*. August 17, 2017.
Fujishima, Kenji. *Slant Magazine*. August 13, 2017.
Hartlaub, Peter. *San Francisco Chronicle*. August 29, 2017.
Hornaday, Ann. *Washington Post*. August 31, 2017.
King, Danny. *Village Voice*. August 22, 2017.
Phillips, Michael. *Chicago Tribune*. August 31, 2017.
Scott, A.O. *New York Times*. August 17, 2017.
Seitz, Matt Zoller. *RogerEbert.com*. August 18, 2017.
Yoshida, Emily. *Vulture*. August 17, 2017.

AWARDS

Nominations:

Ind. Spirit 2018: Actor--Supporting (Asomugha)

A CURE FOR WELLNESS

All of us are human. None of us are immune.
—Movie tagline

Box Office: $8.1 Million

Like *Rosemary's Baby* (1968) and *The Innocents* (1961), *A Cure for Wellness* starts with the sound of a child singing as a prelude to the awful things that lay ahead. The technique is quite effective, invoking innocence but also eeriness due to the mournful quality of the tunes chosen. But unlike either of those twisting and turning gothic horrors *A Cure for Wellness* heads exactly where viewers will expect, undercutting most of the impact its mystery plotting and stunning visuals could have had.

After starting with the sudden death of a middle-aged man in a large office complex, the film introduces a young executive from the same company named Lockhart (Dane DeHaan), who has recently attracted the attention of the front office through his highly profitable but ill-conceived financial fraud. Hoping to place the blame on the company boss, Pembroke (Harry Groener), the board sends Lockhart to retrieve the CEO from a beautiful but mysterious health spa in the Swiss Alps that utilizes its mysterious spring and the eels that live in it to cure the ills of wealthy patrons.

Upon arrival, Lockhart is given a polite but firm runaround by the staff, including the genteel Dr. Heinreich Volmer (Jason Isaacs). Deciding to leave and return later, Lockhart and his driver speed off, but have a serious auto accident. When Lockhart wakes up, he finds himself back in the spa with a broken leg. Assured by Volmer that his bosses back home have been informed of his need to recuperate, Lockhart sets about trying to find Pembroke and uncover what he can about the obvious conspiracy at work here. While there, he meets dozens of spa patrons, all wealthy and all possessed of a calmness that somehow fails to ring true.

During that time, he meets the ethereal Hannah (Mia Goth), a pale girl far younger than anyone else at the spa. Volmer later tells Lockhart that Hannah is different than the other guests, her health is in need of extra attention and Lockhart observes that Volmer feeds her drops from one of the little blue bottles which are found all over the estate. Lockhart also discovers that the spa was built on the ruins of a castle estate, which was burned down by villagers over 200 years ago. The baron had attempted to marry his own sister to keep his bloodline pure. He had also kidnapped and experimented on any number of villagers. After killing the baron, the villagers cut the baby out of the sister's womb and threw it into the water hoping to drown it. But the healing waters revived the infant and have been the source of the health spas reputation since.

Convinced that they are being held prisoner, Lockhart escapes the spa with Hannah by biking into the town at the foot of the mountain. While there he is told that that the spa treatments eventually lead to fatal dehydration despite the constant drinking of the spas healing waters. After he and Hannah are rescued by Volmer from the townsfolk who hate everyone from the mountain, Lockhart continues his investigation of the grounds eventually discovering that the experiments never ended.

The 146-minute runtime here is almost forgivable given how bright all the film's technical details shine. The cinematography successfully places the world of *A Cure for Wellness* in a gothic nether region, caught halfway between the real and the fantastic. Likewise, sets, costumes, special effects—all the technical elements—shine. Everything is in place for Verbinski to hang a great story on, but that potentially great tale gets lost in a screenplay centered on a less-than-compelling mystery and a lot of genre conventions that simply never come to life.

As for cast, DeHaan is a great choice for the role of Lockhart, a man who is initially thoroughly unlikeable but ultimately determined to undermine and overcome the conspiracy that holds himself and Hannah captive. Likewise, Mia Goth, whose sense of ethereality and ageless innocence seems effortless, delivers what's needed. But Jason Isaacs steals the film from both of them. Isaacs has always been a dynamic onscreen presence lending gravitas to even the simplest genre films. He creates a memorable villain in Volmer even when the script lets him down.

This brings the primary problem to the fore. The characters in this piece are, to a one, simple genre stereotypes, which would work if the screenplay were tighter and the dialogue punchier. But far too much time is wasted on a pair of ersatz mysteries that most viewers will have figured out long before the final confrontation. The first mystery is what part the water and the eels play in Volmer's scheme. But even here the film establishes too few rules. While it may be easy to accept that the idle rich would submit their existential crisis' to Volmer, the film never adequately explains why Lockhart does. As soon as the screenplay requires it, he goes from drinking a few glasses of water to being immersed in an airtight ominous-looking water filled drum as part of a series of treatments he has only agreed to in order to lull Volmer into a state of false security.

A Cure for Wellness is simply not as epic an arc as it wants to be. The sad thing is that Verbinski is telling a tale for the present times. Wellness, as defined in the film, is that state of being in which passive consumerism pacifies and anesthetizes until the consumer is consumed. By the time Lockhart is peddling madly away from burning ruins of his old worldview, perhaps mentally damaged forever, the audience should care more about not only his fate, but their own.

Dave Canfield

CREDITS

Lockhart: Dane DeHaan

Volmer: Jason Isaacs

Hannah: Mia Goth

Enrico: Ivo Nandi

Deputy Director: Adrian Schiller

Origin: United States

Language: English

Released: 2017

Production: David Crockett, Arnon Milchan; Regency Enterprises, TSG Entertainment; released by Twentieth Century Fox Film Corp.

Directed by: Gore Verbinski

Written by: Justin Haythe
Cinematography by: Bojan Bazelli
Music by: Benjamin Wallfisch
Sound: David Farmer; Douglas Murray
Editing: Pete Beaudreau; Lance Pereira
Art Direction: Grant Armstrong
Costumes: Jenny Beavan
Production Design: Eve Stewart
MPAA rating: R
Running time: 146 minutes

REVIEWS

Brody, Richard. *New Yorker.* February 20, 2017.
Chang, Justin. *Los Angeles Times.* February 16, 2017.
Donato, Matt. *We Got This Covered.* February 7, 2017.
Dowd, A.A. *The A.V. Club.* February 16, 2017.
Ehrlich, David. *IndieWire.* February 7, 2017.
Jones, Alan. *Radio Times.* February 23, 2017.
MacDonald, Moira. *Seattle Times.* February, 14, 2017.
Marsh, James. *South China Morning Post.* February 15, 2017.
Topel, Fred. *We Live Entertainment.* February 7, 2015.
Whitney, Erin. *ScreenCrush.* February 15, 2017.

QUOTES

Volmer: "Do you know what the cure for the human condition is? Disease. Because that's the only way one could hope for a cure."

TRIVIA

Although the story takes place in Switzerland, the film was shot in Hechingen, Germany.

D

DADDY'S HOME 2

More Daddies. More Problems.
—Movie tagline

Box Office: $103.8 Million

Before the cinematic extension of their *Saturday Night Live* partnership came full circle with their long-awaited sequel to *Anchorman* (2004), Adam McKay and Will Ferrell created an inspired partnership with Mark Wahlberg. After his Oscar® nomination for *The Departed* (2006), the actor was mired in a rut of mediocre dramas and even more forgettable action films. Along came the perfect marriage of *The Other Guys* (2010), a riff on buddy cop movies with each actor playing escalated versions of their own personalities but with an underlying counterbalance of dark pasts and insecurity. When Ferrell and Wahlberg reteamed for *Daddy's Home* (2015) what you expected was what you got in a more family-based comedy with the actors playing their types to a tee. The holiday release went on to be one of the biggest hits of both of their careers, leading to the inevitable sequel. While McKay is only a producing partner on these films, the follow-up once again boasts a pair of potentially funny casting decisions that never achieves its full potential thanks to a truly lazy effort that ramps up the slapstick and ignores the undercurrent of what these films are supposed to be about.

Whatever differences the competing fathers had during the first film has given way to a friendship where Brad (Ferrell, doing nothing new) is bringing Dusty (Wahlberg, doing even less) hot cocoa on his crossing guard detail. Having newly remarried to Karen (Alessandra Ambrosio) Dusty is now facing the prospect of being a stepdad himself to her daughter, Adrianna (Didi Costine), who is not interested in his attempts at affection. Brad's wife and Dusty's ex, Sara (Linda Cardellini) has her own jealousy over not just Karen's supermodel looks, but her own self-conscious feeling over whatever commentary the writer is putting in her little book. What better time to bring the family together for a single Christmas? Even the ones who invite themselves?

Dusty's father, Kurt (Mel Gibson), a no-nonsense, manly-man astronaut is coming to town. So is Brad's dad, Don (John Lithgow), a more joyful figure whose public display of affection towards his son runs counter to the distant but constantly challenged relationship between Dusty and his own. More offensive to Kurt is any arrangement whatsoever that allows Brad to take time away from Dusty and his kids. To dispel any confusion over which house this joint holiday will take place, Kurt rents a cabin for all of them and then casually hoping to drive a wedge between the co-dads.

The screenplay by John Morris and director Sean Anders (both co-authors of the first film along with Brian Burns) opens the door to the head-butting of different parenting styles that resulted in the soft and tough exteriors of our original combatants. Except here with one side showing a total lack of affection and no scruples in telling dirty jokes to children the script makes a more direct metaphor for its own inconsistencies and outright cowardice. Leaning the material in a family-friendly direction is one thing but Anders shows no curiosity nor leaves any room for the actors to improvise their way into even a comfortably funny interplay about one side making a fair point for their technique. They would rather have them fall on their face in a more traditional manner.

Daddy's Home 2 arguably features more sight gags, pratfalls, and whoopsie-daisy-look-how-stupid-I-am moments than most comedies in the modern age—just in the first 30 minutes. Given its holiday setting, Anders self-consciously appears to be trying to create some new perennial viewing by copying the Clark Griswold model of *National Lampoon's Christmas Vacation* (1989) including an out-of-control sledding sequence and a gag involving house lights. The latter may be the film's most inspired visual moment but without the proper setup feels like just another in a string of crashes, falls, and screw-ups involving injuries that only Looney Tunes characters would walk away from unscathed. How many times can the foibles of a parent trying to do good go disastrously wrong before a comedy resorts to one of them getting shot for their efforts? As much as this film can fit it in roughly 53 minutes.

The bare minimum requirement for this sequel to achieve is simply finding a new way to use the same old tricks with the additions meant to entice viewers to spend time with these characters again. There was nothing left unanswered in the original except for how the amusing cameo of John Cena as Dusty's new stepdad competition could fit in. The wrestler-turned-actor who once said, "I look like Mark Wahlberg ate Mark Wahlberg" in *Trainwreck* (2015) gets a late third act call to join the party but gets nary a line of dialogue even close to that. The real crime though is not just making Lithgow and Gibson mere doppelgangers as fathers, but the best Anders can muster up as a moment between them is a brief exchange in front of the urinals that has no ending. Except when it is reminding us how well some of its material worked when in the right hands—dealing with a drunk child in *The Landlord* short or Ferrell singing to bring the family together just like he did in *Step Brothers* (2008)—*Daddy's Home 2* is forgettable on every level.

Erik Childress

CREDITS

Brad: Will Ferrell
Dusty: Mark Wahlberg
Kurt: Mel Gibson
Don: John Lithgow
Sara: Linda Cardellini
Origin: United States
Language: English
Released: 2017
Production: Chris Henchy, Adam McKay, Kevin J. Messick, Will Ferrell, John Morris; Gary Sanchez Productions; released by Paramount Pictures Corp.
Directed by: Sean Anders
Written by: Sean Anders; John Morris
Cinematography by: Julio Macat
Music by: Michael Andrews
Sound: Andrew DeCristofaro; Darren "Sunny" Warkentin
Editing: Brad Wilhite
Art Direction: Rachel Block
Costumes: Carol Ramsey
Production Design: Clayton Hartley
MPAA rating: PG-13
Running time: 100 minutes

REVIEWS

Berardinelli, James. *ReelViews*. November 10, 2017.
Erhlich, David. *IndieWire*. November 10, 2017.
Gibron, Bill. *Film Racket*. November 14, 2017.
Johanson, MaryAnn. *Flick Filosopher*. November 28, 2017.
Kenigsberg, Ben. *New York Times*. November 9, 2017.
Kenny, Glenn. *RogerEbert.com*. November 10, 2017.
Lybarger, Dan. *Arkansas Democrat-Gazette*. November 10, 2017.
McGranaghan, Mike. *Aisle Seat*. November 10, 2017.
Nusair, David. *New York Magazine/Vulture*. December 10, 2017.
Orndorf, Brian. *Blu-ray.com*. November 10, 2017.

TRIVIA

This is the second time John Lithgow has played a character's father with the last name Whitaker; he also played Jerome Whitaker (Barney's father) on *How I Met Your Mother*.

AWARDS

Golden Raspberries 2017: Worst Support. Actor (Gibson)

Nominations:

Golden Raspberries 2017: Worst Actor (Wahlberg)

THE DARK TOWER

There are other worlds than these.
—Movie tagline

In a world of superheroes, there is only one gunslinger.
—Movie tagline

Box Office: $50.7 Million

The resulting adaptation of Stephen King's most prolific work, *The Dark Tower* is a curiosity of compromise. The brief action/adventure film addresses a vast Western-and-fantasy-influenced mythology spanning eight novels and supplementary materials with a strategy appropriate to its impossible task. The series is full of King hallmarks, like the gothic explorations of mystical childhood and the impacts of drug abuse told through both sprawling metaphor and realistically flawed characters. *The Dark Tower* discards many cinematic conventions in order to capture just a few of these flavorful characteristics in its own take on the story of the dimension-hopping Gunslinger, creating an entirely new amalgamation where a complete adaptation would be unfeasible.

This Gunslinger, Roland (Idris Elba), is the last of his kind—a Clint Eastwood second-stringer whose seriousness is as much his superpower as his godlike accuracy with a pistol. His goal is to defeat the Man in Black (Matthew McConaughey) who seeks to destroy the tower which is the center of every universe: his universe, Roland's universe, and the universe of Jake (Tom Taylor) the Earth boy. Eschewing all exposition, a risky decision signalling a filmmaker's trust in its audience. Director Nikolaj Arcel and his horde of co-writers allow the absurd narrative to wash over the film from the very beginning, developing the scenes not with location intertitles but with the jarring aesthetics of Terry Gilliam's *Time Bandits*. The film's other worlds are terrifying, uncanny, but not without their humor.

These other worlds come populated by the Man in Black's steampunk Trans Corporation employees, fake skin stretched over their alien rat faces, who are in the business of kidnapping and exploiting children for their psychic energy. This energy can damage the tower, which is how the three main characters collide. Jake is a powerful psychic, possessing the same "shine" as the characters in Stanley Kubrick's classic snowbound king adaptation. He sees these other worlds in his dreams, waking to a small-scale New York City that itches at its boundaries. Jake knows there is more than this and the film is intent on proving him correct. He escapes employees sent for him, meets up with Roland through a portal, and embarks on a quest to stop the Man in Black.

There are more details to the plot than this, but the specifics are contrary to the film's cause, which is simplification. Expecting an audience to understand the battle of good vs. evil and the existence of magic and gunslingers is ambitious, but meeting a film halfway is part of its pleasures. Actively suspending disbelief requires more moxie of a film than most have to give, which makes even the sloppy misfires much more engaging than rote mediocrity. This film, for all its compromise and speed, distills many of Stephen King's pet philosophies and themes into an enjoyable, quick piece of Young Adult action—even if some of it, especially a mid-movie fight scene with a demon, is completely incomprehensible and underlit.

Disposing of its epic aspirations, the plot's most effective parts concern the power of children. King, in many of his stories, uses childhood innocence to explain their closer relationship to the magic of the world. Mysticism and its fleeting relationship with people, leaving when they get too old to believe in it, is one of King's calling cards. Another is a penchant for intertextuality that allows the actors to embrace humor alongside their storybook moralities.

This is not a fantasy world that takes itself seriously. The specific writing—its situations, its physical comedy, its dialogue—makes up for its lackluster arcs by allowing its characters the room to embrace strangeness. Jake is an effective audience surrogate and an even more effective foil for his more seasoned co-stars. McConaughey embodies total evil, evil without purpose, in ways both spoken and seen. He slides through scenes like a man-sized oil slick, even when cooking chicken in an apron. The absurdity lightens the mood of a film that could've easily been bogged down with its own baggage while allowing its actors to play in the space of the fiction. Cruel evil and lawful good cannot help but feel out of place in the human world of gray areas and moral in-betweens.

The film's best sequences, those apart from the single successful action scene which fades the sound mix out to show Roland's masterful focus, are those of fish-out-of-water conversation. Elba lands each deadpan stronger than the last (until climaxing in a hilarious New York City hospital scene), balancing the proud stoic hero with an understated humor. His glowering gaze stabilizes the screen in a world of chaos, while McConaughey chews scenery by inflicting cartoonish cruelties. These are more than superheroes, they are pure moral forces. Thankfully their earnestness and the film's all-too-easy conclusion are tempered by the strange hints of a much larger world that put so much character into a film whose special effects and overall story would otherwise make for an outdated and generic tale.

There is a brief reference to Excalibur, an ancient structure (carnival ride) in Roland's world, and a demon made of a house. The speed with which these components blaze past makes them equal parts distracting and flavorful, the alien decorations of an unfamiliar world. This is another of the film's strong suits, as it sprinkles in details from the books while immersing the barrage of fantasy lore with self-effacing humor. However, its complete lack of lighting in its major action scenes and inconsistent editing leaves *The Dark Tower* in the awkward position of being an action film whose worst parts are its action. The adaptive process of compromise has left King's mythos almost completely lost in the summer tentpole solvent it has been forced inside.

Jacob Oller

CREDITS

Walter/Man in Black: Matthew McConaughey
Roland Deschain: Idris Elba
Jake: Tom Taylor
Steven: Dennis Haysbert
Soldier: Ben Gavin
Origin: United States
Language: English
Released: 2017
Production: Ron Howard, Erica Huggins, Akiva Goldsman; Imagine Entertainment, Media Rights Capital L.P., Sony Pictures Entertainment Inc., Weed Road Pictures; released by Columbia Pictures
Directed by: Nikolaj Arcel
Written by: Nikolaj Arcel; Akiva Goldsman; Jeff Pinkner; Anders Thomas Jensen
Cinematography by: Rasmus Videbaek
Music by: Junkie XL
Sound: Michael Babcock; Jeremy Peirson
Editing: Alan Edward Bell; Dan Zimmerman
Art Direction: Guy Potgieter; Brad Ricker
Costumes: Trish Summerville
Production Design: Christopher Glass; Oliver Scholl
MPAA rating: PG-13
Running time: 95 minutes

REVIEWS

Covert, Colin. *Minneapolis Star Tribune*. August 3, 2017.
Coyle, Jake. *Associated Press*. August 3, 2017.
Edelstein, David. *New York Magazine*. August 2, 2017.
Hassannia, Tina. *National Post*. August 3, 2017.
Hunter, Rob. *Film School Rejects*. August 3, 2017.
Lawson, Richard. *Vanity Fair*. August 3, 2017.
Tallerico, Brian. *RogerEbert.com*. August 4, 2017.
Vishnevetsky, Ignatiy. *The A.V. Club*. August 3, 2017.
Walsh, Katie. *Tribune News Service*. August 4, 2017.
Zacharek, Stephanie. *Time Magazine*. August 3, 2017.

QUOTES

Jake Chambers: "It's a hotdog."
Roland Deschain: "Savages. What breed?"

TRIVIA

Actors Daniel Craig, Christian Bale, Viggo Mortensen, Javier Bardem, and Mads Mikkelsen were all considered for the lead role before Idris Elba was cast.

DARKEST HOUR

Never, never, never surrender.
—Movie tagline

Never give up. Never give in.
—Movie tagline

A man with the heart of a nation.
—Movie tagline

Box Office: $45.8 Million

In one of the odder cinematic developments of 2017, the massive evacuation of thousands of Allied troops trapped on the beaches of Dunkirk, France in May of 1940 would prove to be a key element of a number of films that came out during the year. The most notable, of course, was *Dunkirk* (2017), Christopher Nolan's elaborately staged and visually stunning recreation of the rescue that became one of the most acclaimed films of the year. On a much smaller scale, the British romantic comedy *Their Finest* (2017) dealt in part with a group of government propaganda filmmakers charged with putting together a film about two sisters who helped take part in the rescue. By comparison, *Darkest Hour* serves as a sort of origin story for those other titles in that it chronicles the first decisive weeks of Winston Churchill's reign as Prime Minister of England. It is a potentially fascinating subject for the movie but for some reason, the film has no idea of what to do with it and winds up squandering it all on a surprisingly dull, long-winded, and one-note biopic that never feels as if it is about anything other than trying to earn Gary Oldman a long-overdue Oscar.

That becomes obvious right from the start as Churchill is deliberately kept off screen during an extended sequence of members of Parliament demanding the removal of Neville Chamberlain for being too soft on Hitler and his expansion through Europe. Everyone speaks of Churchill in hushed tones, especially the pro-Chamberlain Tories, who loathe Churchill's more hawkish attitude but are faced with the reality that the opposition has the votes and will accept no other candidate. Eventually, the film finally deigns to reveal him in all of his splendor in a sequence in which Churchill roams about his bedroom, artfully festooned with photogenic clouds of cigar smoke, chomping on his breakfast, and the scenery, doing a couple of glasses of booze and terrorizing unsuspecting new secretary Elizabeth Layton (Lily James). His wife, Clementine (Kristen Scott Thomas), is not quite as intimidated and knows exactly how to cut him down to size when his ego threatens to take over.

Although he was correct about the threat posed by Hitler, Churchill still has a number of political enemies dating back to the failed campaign at Gallipoli and while he is officially, though somewhat reluctantly, asked by King George VI to form a new government, his enemies in the cabinet begin a plot to simultaneously resign if he refuses to enter into negotiations with Germany, a move that could inspire a vote of no confidence that would lead to his replacement as Prime Minister with their preferred candidate, current Foreign Secretary Lord Halifax (Stephen Dillane). Their position is bolstered when Churchill's speech to Parliament does not go over well and he continues to refuse to negotiate a peace settlement with Germany. When word of the soldiers trapped at Dunkirk arrives, Churchill opts to override his cabinet and launch an attack in Calais that will distract the enemy enough to help pull off the Dunkirk evacuation. This works, but the eventual surrender of France and the inability of the United States to offer aid because of the Neutrality Act begin to weigh heavily on him and he is forced to decide whether to negotiate with Germany and save his position or act on his conscience and risk losing everything.

The period of history covered by *Darkest Hour* deals with any number of complex political and social events but you would not get any sense of that by watching it. Instead, director Joe Wright (whose *Atonement* (2007) also included a notable Dunkirk sequence—it's a small evacuation after all) and soreenwriter Anthony McCarten have created a tale that is so simplistic in its approach that the result is a film that could have easily been ground out by the propaganda creators of *Their Finest* (2016). Although Churchill would prove to be right, his opponents had perfectly legitimate reasons to oppose him—still reeling from the horrors of the World War I, they wanted to do anything within their power to avoid a second one. However, there is no sense of nuance here with regards to such a key point—when Churchill's foes insist on attempting peace negotiations, they are portrayed so cravenly that you can practically see them reaching for their Nazi armbands.

By comparison, Churchill is portrayed throughout as a ferocious grizzly bear when dealing with his political appointments and a big, lovable teddy bear in private. Despite having a checkered past in terms of wartimes engagements, we never get even the slightest flicker of self-doubt in his actions, the kind of thing that might have made him seem more like a real person and less like a symbol. Likewise, the film as a whole never stops to question or challenge his decisions, preferring an approach that stops just short of outright worship—he was a great man, no doubt, but the decision to portray him as such a flawless person short-circuits any possible dramatic tension and leads to a number of scenes in which Churchill pontificates endlessly while the music swells in the background and those on his side look on him adoringly. The worst of these scenes—one so bad that it teeters uneasily towards self-parody—comes during the one moment in the film where Churchill feels even the slightest inkling of doubt towards his hawkish attitude towards war. Instead of being driven in his car, he elects to ride the subway with the common people, who regard his presence with awe. When he asks them their feelings on going to war with Germany, everyone—even a little girl—backs him up 100

and, when it seems that the scene cannot possibly get any tackier, he begins reciting some inspiring poetry and the lone black guy on the train (and possibly the entire movie) joins in as well, moving him (and theoretically those in the audience) to tears over their support. The scene is a real embarrassment—a show-stopper in the worst sense of the word that even Churchill himself might have thought to be a bit over-the-top.

As for Gary Oldman, he is one of the finest actors working today and if there were any justice in the film world, he would already have a shelf full of Oscars® for his indelible performances in such films as *Sid and Nancy* (1986), *JFK* (1991), *The Contender* (2000), and *Tinker Tailor Soldier Spy* (2011) but it was only with the latter movie that he received his first nomination. As written, the role of Churchill is one that practically screams "Nominate Me!" in every single scene and Oldman makes sure that no one can possibly not notice his work. Ensconced in pounds of makeup and smoking cigar after cigar, he blusters through the material with all the bombast of an actor in a one-man show playing to the cheapest seats—he hits all of the broad strokes but, with the exception of his scenes with Kristen Scott Thomas that allow him to turn things down a notch, he never gives us any sense of who the man really was as he did when playing other real-life characters like Sid Vicious and Lee Harvey Oswald. It is an impersonation—and a pretty good one, as such things go—but it is nothing more than that and to see an actor as talented as Oldman blatantly angling for an Oscar® is a bit dispiriting. If he does win the award for *Darkest Hour* (at the time these words are being written, the nominations have not come out but he is still considered to be the front-runner), it will most likely be given to him as a tribute to his entire career rather than to celebrate his middling efforts here.

Peter Sobczynski

CREDITS

Winston Churchill: Gary Oldman
Elizabeth Layton: Lily James
King George VI: Ben Mendelsohn
Clementine Churchill: Kristin Scott Thomas
Viscount Halifax: Stephen (Dillon) Dillane
Origin: United States
Language: English
Released: 2017

Production: Tim Bevan, Lisa Bruce, Eric Fellner, Douglas Urbanski, Anthony McCarten; Perfect World Pictures, Working Title Films Ltd.; released by Focus Features L.L.C.
Directed by: Joe Wright
Written by: Anthony McCarten
Cinematography by: Bruno Delbonnel
Music by: Dario Marianelli
Sound: Craig Berkey; Becki Ponting
Music Supervisor: Maggie Rodford
Editing: Valerio Bonelli
Art Direction: Nick Gottschalk
Costumes: Jacqueline Durran
Production Design: Sarah Greenwood
MPAA rating: PG-13
Running time: 125 minutes

REVIEWS

Adams, Sam. *Slate.* November 22, 2017.
DeBruge, Peter. *Variety.* September 2, 2017.
Lawson, Richard. *Vanity Fair.* November 21, 2017.
McCarthy, Todd. *Hollywood Reporter.* September 2, 2017.
Powers, John. *Vogue.* September 12, 2017.
Reed, Rex. *New York Observer.* November 27, 2017.
Scherstuhl, Alan. *Village Voice.* November 21, 2017.
Sott, A.O. *New York Times.* November 21, 2017.
Turan, Kenneth. *Los Angeles Times.* November 21, 2017.
Yoshida, Emily. *New York Magazine/Vulture.* November 17, 2017.

QUOTES

Winston Churchill: "You cannot reason with a tiger when your head is in its mouth."

TRIVIA

Actor Gary Oldman is the fifth *Harry Potter* actor to portray Winston Churchill after Michael Gambon (Albus Dumbledore) in *Churchill's Secret* (2016), Timothy Spall (Peter Pettigrew) in *The King's Speech* (2010), Brendan Gleeson (Mad Eye Moody) in *Into the Storm* (2009), and Robert Hardy in *War and Remembrance* (1988) and *Bomber Harris* (1989).

AWARDS

Oscars 2017: Actor (Oldman), Makeup
British Acad. 2017: Actor (Oldman), Makeup
Golden Globes 2018: Actor--Drama (Oldman)
Screen Actors Guild 2017: Actor (Oldman)

Nominations:

Oscars 2017: Cinematog., Costume Des., Film, Production Design
British Acad. 2017: Actress--Supporting (Scott Thomas), Cinematog., Costume Des., Film, Orig. Score, Production Design

DESPICABLE ME 3

Oh brother.
—Movie tagline
Hard times ahead.
—Movie tagline

Box Office: $264.6 Million

At the end of *Minions* (2015), the film that precedes *Despicable Me 3* in this series, the lovable yellow minion creatures meet their current master, Gru. *Minions* takes place prior to the events of *Despicable Me* (2010), and its ending hinted that *Despicable Me 3* would continue the early exploits of Gru and his team. For continuity's sake, *Despicable Me 3* should have ended just before the events of the first movie, bringing the Gru Chronicles full circle. Instead, directors Kyle Balda, Pierre Coffin, and Eric Guillon disavow any knowledge of the prequel and continue where *Despicable Me 2* (2013) left off.

Fans of backstories will not be too disappointed, however, as *Despicable Me 3* introduces a heretofore unknown character into the mix. Supervillain-turned-good-guy Gru (voice of Steve Carell) discovers that he has an identical twin brother, Dru (also Carell). Dru is everything Gru is not: He's got a full head of luxurious hair, he's rich beyond measure, and he's in shape. In a twist as old as the Smothers Brothers' shtick, it's also clear that Dad liked Dru best. Gru's nameless, mean, old Mom (voice of Julie Andrews) explains that, upon divorcing, she and her ex-husband assumed sole custody of one of the twins. Dru appears to have gotten the better end of the deal, that is, a parent who loved him and a law-abiding road to financial success. But anything that looks this perfect will always disintegrate under scrutiny.

Before Gru and his family can travel to Dru's homeland of Freedonia, Gru must deal with the repercussions of an on-the-job mistake. After marrying Anti-Villain League (AVL) employee Lucy (voice of Kristen Wiig) at the end of *Despicable Me 2,* Gru joins her in bringing down bad guys. Their latest target is Balthazar Bratt (voice of Trey Parker), a has-been child star whose *Dennis the Menace* rip-off 1980s series, "Evil Bratt," was once the talk of TV. Once Bratt hit puberty, his career hit the skids. Like many 1980s child stars, Bratt became intimate with the wrong side of the law, though his biggest crimes warrant arrest only by the fashion police: Bratt's wardrobe remains as trapped in the 1980s as his damaged psyche.

Taking his TV show tagline "I've Been a Bad Boy!" to heart, Bratt tries to steal the world's largest diamond, only to be stopped by Gru and Lucy. Despite foiling the heist, Gru and Lucy are fired from the AVL for allowing Bratt to escape. By terminating her two best agents, the misguided new head of AVL, Valerie Da Vinci (voice of Jenny Slate), shoots herself in the foot; her actions allow Bratt to eventually steal the diamond. The gem will power a gigantic robot to take revenge on the entertainment industry that derailed Bratt's rise to superstardom.

As *Minions* revealed, the minions themselves exist solely to serve an evil master. Once it's clear that Gru is not returning to villainy, his assistants strike off on their own to find their next meal ticket. The minions are why the series has grossed almost $3 billion worldwide, yet *Despicable Me 3* can barely find anything for them to do. This is the first sign that the film is in trouble. The best the minions can do is get arrested, though their prison subplot culminates with their biggest musical number so far. Gilbert and Sullivan have never sounded better, but it's a case of too little, too late.

Meanwhile, in Freedonia, Gru learns that, despite striking it rich, Dru has always been a disappointment to their father. This is because Dad was, like Gru, a master villain. Since Dru never had the skill for the family business, he was deemed a failure. Despite being raised by the wrong parent, Gru still inherited his father's penchant for dastardly deeds. Now Dru wants to be schooled in the dark arts, but Gru refuses to regress to his former self. Eventually, Gru enlists Dru's help in stealing the giant diamond from Bratt, though unbeknownst to Dru, Gru plans to use it as a bargaining chip to get his job back at AVL. Once they retrieve the jewel, Dru becomes angry at Gru's noble intentions, and a rift develops between them.

Like the minions, Gru's lovely, adopted "gurls" (as he calls them) are pushed into a rather meaningless subplot. Agnes (voice of Nev Scharrel), the cutest of the bunch, overhears Dru's butler talking about the legend of a unicorn in the Freedonia forest. Agnes's obsession with unicorns is a series staple—her stuffed unicorn was the recipient of the series's best one-liner way back in *Despicable Me*—so she embarks on a search and retrieve mission with her sisters Edith (voice of Dana Gaier) and Margo (voice of Miranda Cosgrove). They find a one-horned goat which, despite Agnes's delight, is a real letdown for any viewer whose suspension of disbelief is big enough to accommodate minions and killer bubble gum.

Despicable Me 3's climax ropes in both the minions and the "gurls," the latter of which are kidnapped by Bratt. Bratt also manages to again steal the diamond, which forces Dru and Gru to work together to save the day. Gru's battle with Bratt involves bad fashion, break dancing, Madonna, and the evilest of all 1980s era instruments—the keytar. Bratt's obsession with the greatest decade of the twentieth century should be catnip for folks who grew up in the 1980s, but *Despicable Me 3* has traded the honest, sentimental emotions that ran through the prior installments for a self-sabotaging sense of irony and mean-spirited mockery.

Even when Gru was at his meanest (for example, when he attacks Margo's potential beau with a freeze gun in *Despicable Me 2*) he still managed to reveal a very effective softer side. As Gru grew emotionally in the first two films, the audience became more invested in his ragtag family unit. *Despicable Me 3* will have none of these mushy feelings; it's the surly teenager of the series, putting up walls and insults as a defense mechanism. Even poor Lucy, whose subplot deals with her trying to be maternal, can't conjure up much empathy because she's so underused.

Despicable Me 3 is the worst in the series, and though it made a ton of money at the box office, its haphazard plot and listless execution makes it hard to defend or enjoy. The ending paves the way for *Despicable Me 4*, but Universal might be wise to call it quits now. If they continue on this current sour trajectory, the presumed *Spy vs. Spy*-style plot may make the next movie actually despicable.

Odie Henderson

CREDITS

Gru/Dru: Steve Carell (Voice)

Lucy: Kristen Wiig (Voice)

Balthazar Bratt: Trey Parker (Voice)

Margo: Miranda Cosgrove (Voice)

Edith: Dana Gaier (Voice)

Origin: United States

Language: English

Released: 2017

Production: Janet Healy, Chris Meledandri; Illumination Entertainment; released by Universal Pictures Inc.

Directed by: Kyle Balda; Pierre Coffin

Written by: Cinco Paul; Ken Daurio

Music by: Pharrell Williams

Sound: Dennis Leonard; Timothy Nielsen

Editing: Claire Dodgson

MPAA rating: PG

Running time: 90 minutes

REVIEWS

Berardinelli, James. *ReelViews*. June 30, 2017.
Duralde, Alonso. *TheWrap*. June 29, 2017.
Mintzer, Jordan. *Hollywood Reporter*. June 14, 2017.
O'Sullivan, Michael. *Washington Post*. June 29, 2017.
Pulver, Andrew. *The Guardian*. June 26, 2017.
Russo, Tom. *Boston Globe*. June 29, 2017.
Sobczynski, Peter. *RogerEbert.com*. June 29, 2017.
Vishnevetsky, Ignatiy. *The A.V. Club*. June 28, 2017.
Webster, Andy. *New York Times*. June 29, 2017.
Whitty, Stephen. *New York Daily News*. June 26, 2017.

QUOTES

Gru's Mom: "Shortly after you and your brother were born, your father and I divorced, and we each took one son. Obviously, I got second pick."

TRIVIA

Steve Carell has said that although *Despicable Me 3* may be his last film as the voice of Gru, if he were asked to do a cameo in any future Minion sequels, he would do so happily.

DETROIT

It's time we knew.
—Movie tagline

Box Office: $16.8 Million

There may perhaps be no better film to signal the end of the presidency of Barrack Obama and the divisiveness surrounding the beginning of his successor's tenure as our nation's Commander in Chief than director Kathryn Bigelow's powerful depiction of the unrest that shook the Motor City amidst the racial divide that threatened to consume this country in July 1967—*Detroit*.

Detroit, the film, is a dramatic representation (with some considerable creative license taken) of events that erupted on the night of July 25, 1967 which ultimately became known to history as the Algiers Motel Incident. For those unfamiliar with the events—as civil unrest ran rampant across the country that summer, known as the "long, hot summer of 1967," riots motivated by race relations occurred in Atlanta, Boston, and Cincinnati in June. Then, with tensions escalating in cities like Chicago, Birmingham, and New York throughout July, the violence and unrest culminated with a riot in Newark, New Jersey and one in Detroit, Michigan that would ultimately become known as the "Twelfth Street Riot."

Believing there was a sniper somewhere in the Algiers Motel, three "white" Detroit police officers collected the occupants of the motel in the establishment's annex and proceeded to question them for hours in a gross display and misuse of authority over civil rights. In total, there were nine unarmed individuals at the motel. Most of them were black and were subsequently subjected to hours of brutality as the three aforementioned policemen questioned them using physical beatings and other terror tactics to extract the information they desired. Tragically, three of the young black men would die at the hands of the officers, who were ultimately acquitted by a jury of any wrongdoing.

Although the story is based on actual events, screenwriter Mark Boal (who also wrote the films *Zero Dark Thirty* [2012] and *The Hurt Locker* [2008] for Bigelow) does, as is revealed prior to the film's final credits, "lightly fictionalize" the facts of the incident for dramatic purposes. That being said, nothing that occurs throughout the film feels out of place or rings false. That is, this is not simply a case of using a historical event to comment on modern times—although the film does achieve that superbly. Instead, *Detroit* is a moody set piece that drives home again and again the fact that this country still has a long way to go to overcome the racial injustice that has befallen many of its citizens and still seems to be a way of life for many others—a fact keenly illustrated in the film's animated introductory sequence that, as Adam Graham wrote in the *Detroit News*, "briefly and succinctly explains the history of racial segregation in our nation's inner cities."

Bigelow, who has previously won a Best Director and Picture Oscar® for *The Hurt Locker* and earned a Best Picture nomination for *Zero Dark Thirty*, does a superlative job of creating tension amidst sparse locations and with relatively few actors. As the narrative unfurls, the film itself starts to feel like the exact event it is supposed to be depicting. There's a claustrophobic atmosphere that one wishes would just end and give the characters (and viewers) a reprieve from the atrocities unfolding onscreen, but *Detroit* proves far too engrossing to look away at any point. There's also a foreboding lesson within the narrative.

There's an artistic solemnness to *Detroit* that is present throughout but never overtakes the overall narrative, allowing the viewer to hold his or her own opinions towards the events depicted onscreen. As Michael Phillips wrote in the *Chicago Tribune*, "the film speaks to our present-day rage-fueled American divisions." Ultimately though, as history continues to remind us, it appears that even though we've come so far, we still have quite a long way to go.

Michael J. Tyrkus

CREDITS

Dismukes: John Boyega
Krauss: Will Poulter
Larry: Algee Smith
Carl: Jason Mitchell
Attorney Auerbach: John Krasinski
Origin: United States
Language: English
Released: 2017
Production: Matthew Budman, Megan Ellison, Colin Wilson, Kathryn Bigelow, Mark Boal; Annapurna Productions, LLC, First Light Productions, Page 1; released by Annapurna Distribution
Directed by: Kathryn Bigelow
Written by: Mark Boal
Cinematography by: Barry Ackroyd
Music by: James Newton Howard
Sound: Paul N.J. Ottosson
Music Supervisor: George Drakoulias; Randall Poster
Editing: William Goldenberg; Harry Yoon
Art Direction: Greg Berry
Costumes: Francine Jamison-Tanchuck
Production Design: Jeremy Hindle
MPAA rating: R
Running time: 143 minutes

REVIEWS

Burr, Ty. *Boston Globe*. August 2, 2017.
Gleiberman, Owen. *Variety*. July 23, 2017.
Graham, Adam. *Detroit News*. July 23, 2017.
Hornaday, Ann. *Washington Post*. July 28, 2017.
Macdonald, Moira. *Seattle Times*. August 2, 2017.
McCarthy, Todd. *Hollywood Reporter*. July 23, 2017.
Phillips, Michael. *Chicago Tribune*. July 27, 2017.
Scott, A.O. *New York Times*. July 26, 2017.
Travers, Peter. *Rolling Stone*. July 26, 2017.
Vishnevetsky, Ignatiy. *The A.V. Club*. July 27, 2017.

QUOTES

Krauss: "It's a war zone out there. They're destroying the city."

TRIVIA

Some scenes in the film were filmed in Hamtramck, Michigan, a city surrounded by Detroit.

DIARY OF A WIMPY KID: THE LONG HAUL

A wimp will rise.
—Movie tagline

Box Office: $20.7 Million

There is always the temptation for the critic faced with reviewing a film made expressly for younger viewers to go a little easier on it than they might under ordinary circumstances. After all, the kid-centric audience (and the parents or older siblings charged with taking them to the multiplex) tend to be less concerned with the subtler artistic qualities and more focused on whether they will be sufficiently entertained (or at least distracted) for 90 minutes or so and things like silly slapstick and ramshackle narratives tend to be forgiven or at least conveniently overlooked. That said, even the most lenient observer will find it impossible to give a pass to the borderline loathsome *Diary of a Wimpy Kind: The Long Haul*, the fourth entry in the film franchise based on the bestselling children's book series by Jeff Kinney and featuring an entirely new cast replacing the actors from previous installments. Those earlier films—*Diary of a Wimpy Kid* (2010), *Rodrick Rules* (2011), and *Dog Days* (2012)—were no masterpieces, but they displayed some traces of a genial charm that are completely absent from this ugly, mean-spirited, and surprisingly gross entry

As suggested by the title, *The Long Haul* deals with that most hallowed and potentially horrifying of family rituals—the road trip. This time around, the titular diarist, middle schooler Greg Heffley (Jason Drucker) and his family—overworked dad Frank (Tom Everett Scott), eccentric mom Susan (Alicia Silverstone), disgusting would-be rocker older brother Rodrick (Charlie Wright), and toddler Manny (Dylan and Wyatt Walters)—are heading off to Indiana for a party celebrating the 90th birthday of their Meemaw and have elected (okay, Mom elected) to drive instead of fly in order to bond as a family. This is bad enough, but the situation becomes intolerable for Greg when Mom unexpectedly announces that this will be a device-free trip, a decision that can only mean that she has slipped from eccentric to flat-out insane. The trip yields a number of unexpected complications, ranging from grungy motel rooms and lost luggage to Greg inadvertently antagonizing a bearded goon and his family who seem to turn up wherever the Heffley's visit a county fair where Rodrick consumes too much fried butter on a stick before hitting the rides and Manny wins a piglet that he does not want to give up.

For Greg, staying away from the Internet might not be such a bad idea since an escapade chasing after Manny in a ball pit went viral and left him with the nickname "Diaper Hands." When he discovers that one of his heroes, an obnoxious YouTube personality, is going to be appearing at a video game convention in Indianapolis at the same time his family is in the state, he and Rodrick scheme to slip away to it so that Greg can get a video that he can post online and erase all traces of "Diaper Hands." After all, the convention is only a couple of inches away from where they are supposed to be on the map they are using. How far away can that be? Shockingly, this interlude leads not only to the usual litany of public embarrassment—especially when the crowd realizes that "Diaper Hands" is in their midst—but disappointing Mom, who only wanted them to have a nice family trip.

With all of the stars of the previous films having been replaced for this go-around (the original child actors simply grew too old to play the parts), co-writers Kinney and David Bowers, the latter also serving as director, may have worried that the audiences that made those films into decent-sized hits might rebel over the changes and decided to shift the emphasis of the film away from the characters themselves as a way of covering their bases. Unfortunately, they have elected to go heavy on the broad, visual humor with a weirdly insistent emphasis on gross humor. Granted, the *Wimpy Kid* franchise was never shy about displaying goofy slapstick but this time around, fans are treated to long and loud depictions of vomiting (the aforementioned stuff with the fried butter), urination (Greg is forced to pee in a bottle while on the road), flatulence and the defecation habits of no fewer than three different species. Look, I know that kids like icky sight gags and stuff like that, but the sheer volume of gorge-inducing gags (no pun intended) on display here is enough to put the works of the Farrelly Brothers to shame.

As for the new cast, the results are pretty much a mixed bag. As Greg, Drucker does a fairly good job of filling the shoes of Zachary Gordon and shows an ability to play a normal, if perpetually mortified, kid that the film never takes advantage of. Viewers of a certain age may cringe at the notion of one-time teen screen siren Silverstone playing the mother of three kids but that is the most memorable thing about her work—she never quite manages to approximate the genial weirdness of her character. As for Tom Everett Scott as Dad, the most memorable thing about him is the odd happenstance that he is replacing Steve Zahn, his fellow former member of the fictional rock group The Wonders from *That Thing You Do!* (1996)—if the series continues, Jonathan Schaech is presumably waiting in the wings to take over when needed. Making far too much of an impression is Wright as Rodrick, who overplays the nasty older brother bit to such off-putting extremes that he seems to be auditioning for a road company version of *We Need to Talk About Kevin* (2011).

Diary of a Wimpy Kid: The Long Haul is an excruciating slog of a film that might momentarily distract younger viewers, though it will certainly not stick with them in the way that a good movie might, while utterly repelling anyone who is old enough to know better.

Peter Sobczynski

CREDITS

Greg Heffley: Jason Drucker
Susan Heffley: Alicia Silverstone
Frank Heffley: Tom Everett Scott
Rodrick Heffley: Charlie Wright
Rowley: Owen Asztalos
Origin: United States
Language: English
Released: 2017
Production: Nina Jacobson, Brad Simpson; Base Camp ATI, Color Force, TSG Entertainment; released by Twentieth Century Fox Film Corp.
Directed by: David Bowers
Written by: David Bowers; Jeff Kinney
Cinematography by: Anthony B. Richmond
Music by: Ed Shearmur
Sound: Wayne Lemmer
Music Supervisor: Julia Michels
Editing: Troy Takaki
Costumes: Mary Claire Hannan
Production Design: Aaron Osborne
MPAA rating: PG
Running time: 91 minutes

REVIEWS

Barnard, Linda. *Toronto Star*. May 18, 2017.
Davis, Steve. *Austin Chronicle*. May 18, 2017.
Fragoso, Sam. *TheWrap*. May 15, 2017.
Genzlinger, Neil. *New York Times*. May 17, 2017.
Graham, Adam. *Detroit News*. May 19, 2017.
Harvey, Dennis. *Variety*. May 15, 2017.
Horowitz, Jane. *Washington Post*. May 18, 2017.
Rechtshaffen, Michael. *Hollywood Reporter*. May 15, 2017.
Russo, Tom. *Boston Globe*. May 18, 2017.
Walsh, Katie. *Los Angeles Times*. May 22, 2017.

QUOTES

Susan Heffley: "Greg Heflley! You're grounded for life!"

TRIVIA

Tom Everett Scott plays Frank Heffley in the movie, a role was formerly portrayed by Steve Zahn. Both Zahn and Scott starred together in *That Thing You Do!* (1996).

DINA

Box Office: $90,503

From the start, she is exceptionally easy to identity with, like her way of admitting a weakness for sweets just as she is about to undergo a procedure at her dentist's office. Reality television is another of her guilty pleasures. Dina Buno is an outsized, even flamboyant personality, an indomitable woman who is forward, direct, and unvarnished. Even in her quiet moments, she is always on.

The intimate portrait, *Dina*, by the directors Antonio Santini and Dan Sickles, is a work of a vital spontaneity that in its psychological and human study becomes a revealing document about its own making. The 48-year old Dina is a low-level, highly functioning autistic, with emotional behavior consistent with Asperger syndrome, obsessive-compulsive disorder, and high-level anxiety. "You were never one thing," her hilariously dissembling mother remarks. The vulnerability or unease Dina projects is never for show.

Sickles, who has also worked as an actor, is a longtime friend of Dina, which no doubt explains the deep trust between filmmakers and subject on display throughout. *Dina* collapses most of the formal boundaries of cinéma vérité. The movie is colored by observation and capture. The filmmakers, for the most part, skillfully and aggressively shape the material in the composition and editing, incorporating techniques associated with fiction, like the contrapuntal use of music. The cinematographer Adam Uhl, who also photographed *The Death and Life of Martha P. Johnson* (2017), works from an intensely fixed perspective.

The movie has some very interesting uses of distance and point of view, like shooting Dina from across the street through the perspective of a window looking into her apartment. The editor, Sofia Subercaseaux, also works with very hard and sharp cuts, evident from an early moment between Dina and her fiancé, Scott Levin, as they eat at a restaurant before taking in a movie. This pronounced technique is the opposite of a clean or invisible style. The movie cuts dexterously between forms, of documentary and fiction.

Dina is the narrative catalyst. She admits her disability has sometimes rendered her socially invisible, a marginalized life exacerbated by class and her restricted social mobility. *Dina* is a cry to be heard and rewarded with the fullness of life, love, happiness, and the wider chance of fulfillment. The movie alludes to her past traumas, the death of her first husband, a violent encounter with a male acquaintance, the physical scars visible when she is seen changing in and out of her clothes. *Dina* is built around a different kind of self-assertion, about identity and the longing to love and be loved.

The movie, set in suburban Philadelphia, is framed around the events, activities, and rituals connected to her forthcoming wedding to Scott. He is her opposite in many regards, sweet and inward, almost childlike in his naiveté, particularly about sex. He suffers a more acute form of Asperger's, but he is fully functioning and communicative. Part of the joy of the movie is observing the ease of their social interactions, like Scott, taking the early morning bus in order to get to his work as a Wal-Mart door greeter, having a lovely small moment with another man about their shared connection with music. Scott currently lives at home with his parents, and is preparing to make the leap to moving in with Dina.

The couple has a strong network of friends and family, some of whom are also developmentally disabled. The naturalness and ease between the two is touching. But, every relationship has its own fissures and complications. In the movie's most remarkable sequence, during a trip on the promenade boardwalk in Ocean City, New Jersey, the late summer idyll is broken by their differences of experiences and temperament. "I've been around," Dina remarks, in giving him a special pre-wedding copy of *The Joy of Sex* (1972). Twelve million copies have been sold, he remarks. "I think I am more into this than you," she says. "I can learn," he responds. What follows is a remarkably rank exchange about sexual experimentation and self-pleasure.

Intimacy, in all its forms, is exceptionally difficult for Scott, obvious not just in his abstaining from premarital sex, but a deeper reluctance to reciprocate her tenderness, even returning a simple touch or caress. The differences are magnified in another fantastic sequence as Dina and female associates have a riotous and playful night with a male stripper at her bachelorette party contrasted against the men, who are seen in an emotionally muted night of bowling. *Dina* is loaded with such moments of dissonance, like their honeymoon, spent at what appears to be a miniature Playboy mansion, as the two take a swim in a custom designed bath shaped in the form of a massive champagne glass. What should be kitsch feels extraordinarily joyous.

All documentaries fundamentally pivot on the relationship of subjects and creators and *Dina* is no exception. As her female dissatisfaction ratchets up ("I wonder what a honeymoon is like for people who have passion," Dina says aloud), the sexual dissonance between the couple is a wedge. In one excruciating moment with his father, Scott admits to feeling a deeper sense of shame and inadequacy. The filmmakers have shown admirable tact, but these passages seem to go too far in pushing into extreme levels of discomfort.

It is part of the paradox of the film, the movie is sharper and less exploitative when positioned at a remove. It become more problematic in close-up. The point is sharply illustrated in the movie's big reveal, the playing of the 911 recording her "mentally damaged," in her words, assailant, made after stabbing her seven or eight times. The imagery is haunting, a long shot of a bench on a jutting hill as the sky transforms into the inky black night. The words are harrowing. "You are going to live, and I am going to die," the man is heard in the recording.

The movie shares some affinities with Crystal Moselle's prize-winning documentary, *The Wolfpack* (2015), about a group of brothers walled off from existence by their brutalist father who responded by taking refuge in their extreme isolation and remaking movies. Like that film, *Dina* won the top documentary prize of the Sundance Film Festival. As a consequence of their peculiar environment, the brothers are preternaturally self-aware, bright, and intellectually curious that underlines their particular resilience and courage to break free. Dina also has some sharpened qualities, and a lovely voice. As a movie and subject, *Dina* is tremendously sympathetic. She is never drawn as an object of pity.

The deeper portrait is unflinching and tough. During one contentious moment with her mother at the nail salon, in the lead up to the wedding, her mother interrupts her by snapping: "Maybe you're talking too much about yourself." Complications and imperfections aside, Dina has earned the right to rejoice.

Patrick Z. McGavin

CREDITS

Origin: United States
Language: English
Released: 2017
Production: Antonio Santini, Daniel Sickles; Cinereach, El Peligro, Killer Films; released by The Orchard
Directed by: Antonio Santini; Daniel Sickles
Cinematography by: Adam Uhl
Editing: Sofia Subercaseaux
MPAA rating: Unrated
Running time: 103 minutes

REVIEWS

Addlego, Walter. *San Francisco Chronicle.* October 18, 2017.
Coogan, Dean. *Entertainment Weekly.* October 7, 2017.
Goldstein, Gary. *Los Angeles Times.* October 12, 2017.
Gray, Christopher. *Slant Magazine.* October 4, 2017.
Hornaday, Ann. *Washington Post.* October 18, 2017.
Kenny, Glenn. *New York Times.* October 5, 2017.
Keough, Peter. *Boston Globe.* November 9, 2017.
Thompson, Gary. *Philadelphia Daily News.* October 12, 2017.
Wolfe, April. *Village Voice.* October 4, 2017.
Yoshida, Emily. *New York Magazine.* October 9, 2017.

THE DINNER

How far would you go...to save your children?
—Movie tagline

Box Office: $1.3 Million

When moviegoers were presented with the title *Guess Who's Coming to Dinner?* (1967) it was an invitation to discovery; one that may have included everyone's beliefs on race and tradition. *My Dinner with Andre* (1981) delivered exactly as promised with Wallace Shawn trading stories, both professional and personal, over the course of a couple hours and other courses as well. *The Dinner* hints in just a pair of words at something more definitive. Semantics aside, the gathering of four good actors airing their grievances over an inescapable table of food has the makings of claustrophobic drama that many fine playwrights have utilized to memorable effect. Oren Moverman's adaptation—a third of the Herman Koch novel—savagely undercuts the shifting morality of its players by embracing a timeline structure that removes any sense of satiric empathy or tension from the piece.

History teacher Paul Lohman (Steve Coogan) practices for his class lectures about the Civil War. Communicating with his son, Michael (Charlie Plummer), is another matter though. At first it appears to be just the normal growing pains—girls and the dangers of smoking—but there is something yet unclear about the awkwardness. Along with his wife, Claire (Laura Linney), they are meeting at an upscale eatery with Paul's brother, Stan (Richard Gere), and his wife, Katelyn (Rebecca Hall), whose body language in the car suggests something worrisome is on her mind too. It's their kids. Something has got to be done about their kids.

Stan makes it clear as they sit down that this is the night that they are going to put it all out on the table. Their boy, Rick (Seamus Davey-Fitzpatrick), along with Michael, was involved with an incident pertaining to an ATM and a homeless woman. The moment was caught on security cameras and though authorities cannot positively identify the two boys, another witness has posted footage of the incident online with a threat to reveal more in a sequel. Stan is running for Governor and has a bill in need of urgent attention this evening as well. Paul, meanwhile, does everything in his vocal power to change the subject—shifting focus to his disdain for his brother's pomposity and talking about anything but the incident. Turns out this is the film's plan as well.

The approach taken by the film is akin to someone trying to have a painful conversation but doing everything in their power to keep the talk alternately intellectual and light as a feather in the hopes of avoiding it as long as humanly possible. Viewers are the patient listeners attempting to be polite, yet aware that some sort of gut punch is lingering in the air and cannot help but yell out "GET ON WITH IT!" This is a dance *The Dinner* does not even take delight in having by teasing little bits of info in search of the ultimate truth. Before accusations are made or innuendos laid out—a half-hour into the film no less—we already bear witness to the bulk of the horrible incident. Frankly, enough is said in that moment without the ultimate escalation of its criminality.

Moverman's adaptation has loftier ambitions than the fate of a couple punk teenagers by putting the focus on Paul and how his son may have been emotionally affected as a boy by his behavior. Except this whole section is a fractured bust as well. Amusing as it may be to watch Coogan (with an American accent) give restaurant staff a hard time with his connection to Michael Winterbottom's "Trip" series, his abrasiveness comes off more as a boorish stall tactic rather than a by-product of self-aggrandized intelligentsia. Are we watching a deeply ill man or just an incredibly stubborn one? The exasperation of a man of such privilege comparing his own depression levels to that of Gettysburg is enough to make us not care what the answer really is.

"It doesn't matter what we teach. We learn nothing," Paul says in voiceover. About all we learn here is how long it takes one film to get to the cheese and dessert courses. Koch's book may have European roots but the bourgeois morality is as much an American staple and the decision to treat such a teeter-totter seriously rather than satirically leaves no wiggle room. Either offer a treatise on mental illness and the sins it unconsciously inspires or simply give us the dirt. The film finally begins to hum in the homestretch while Coogan remains quiet in the corner for an extended scene allowing Gere a chance to shine with authoritative charm when he appears to speak from the heart. While there are occasional nuggets of Paul's racist attitudes, *The Dinner* believes it is cozying up to ethical grey areas while never appearing to know the colors needed to forcefully mix up the fervor it should inspire. Ending the film with additional ambiguity after spelling out so much over the course of its intertwining flashbacks is enough to leave every guest to its table famished.

Erik Childress

CREDITS

Dylan Heinz: Michael Chernus
Kamryn Velez: Taylor Rae Almonte
Paul Lohman: Steve Coogan
Michael Lohman: Charlie Plummer
Rick Lohman: Seamus Davey-Fitzpatrick
Origin: United States
Language: English
Released: 2017
Production: Caldecott Chubb, Lawrence Inglee, Julia Lebedev, Eddie Vaisman; Blackbird, ChubbCo Film Co., Code Red; released by The Orchard
Directed by: Oren Moverman
Written by: Oren Moverman
Cinematography by: Bobby Bukowski
Sound: Tony Volante
Music Supervisor: Rachel Fox
Editing: Alex Hall
Art Direction: Gonzalo Cordoba
Costumes: Catherine George
Production Design: Kelly McGehee
MPAA rating: R
Running time: 120 minutes

REVIEWS

Bell, Josh. *Las Vegas Weekly.* May 4, 2017.
Chang, Justin. *Los Angeles Times.* May 4, 2017.
Dowd, A.A. *The A.V. Club.* May 4, 2017.
Fuijshima, Kenji. *Slant Magazine.* February 11, 2017.
Gire, Dann. *Daily Herald.* May 4, 2017.
Lodge, Guy. *Newsweek.* May 26, 2017.
Marks, Scott. *San Diego Reader.* May 5, 2017.
Puchko, Kristy. *Las Vegas Weekly.* May 2, 2017.
Roeper, Richard. *Chicago Sun-Times.* May 4, 2017.
Tobias, Scott. *NPR.* May 4, 2017.

TRIVIA

At one time, Cate Blanchett was attached to direct this film.

THE DISASTER ARTIST

Box Office: $20.9 Million

It takes true friendship to make a truly horrible movie. James Franco's *The Disaster Artist* chronicles the production of one of the most notoriously awful films of all time, Tommy Wiseau's *The Room* (2003), a low-budget drama that would have just disappeared into the bargain bin of cinematic history, but some films are simply too bad to be ignored. The legend of *The Room* started with a billboard. Just before the film's release in 2003, Wiseau took out a billboard with his giant face, with one eye half-blinking, advertising a film that no one had ever heard of and was not coming to a theater near most of America. The single billboard on Highland Avenue in Hollywood became something of a tourist attraction in itself due to its extreme oddity, and Wiseau would continue to pay to keep it up for five years (at a rumored cost of $5k a month). And then a few people actually saw the movie.

The Room opened in 2003 and was widely panned by the few Los Angeles critics who saw it, and reports were that most ticket buyers asked for their money back. It grossed a measly $1,800 during its two-week run, but it had started to form a cult just before that 14-day period ended. The story goes that the last show had 100 people, most of whom were openly laughing at and mocking the film. Wiseau received letters from fans who attended that screening and booked another one in 2004. All of this going down in Los Angeles helped greatly, as the film amassed a collection of celebrity fans, who helped its midnight cult movie status grow exponentially.

Franco opens his story of the making of *The Room* there, with actual celebrity fans speaking about how much they enjoy *The Room,* including Adam Scott, Kristen Bell, and several more. It's an odd choice to open the film but it sets a reverent tone—you are not going to just witness the making of any bad movie, you are going to witness the making of the King of Bad Movies.

From there, *The Disaster Artist* flashes back to the core of its narrative—or, at least, what should be the core—the friendship between Greg Sestero and Tommy Wiseau, played by real-life brothers Dave Franco and James Franco, respectively. Of course, there's something "meta" about casting actual brothers as Greg and Tommy that makes them feel more connected and tied than they otherwise would.

Greg meets Tommy at an acting class in San Francisco, and he's immediately drawn to Wiseau's fearlessness and, well, eccentricities. Tommy claims to be close to the same age as teenager Greg when, of course, he's not, and it's very unclear where his money comes from. He's a mysterious figure, and Franco and his screenwriters—Michael H. Weber and Scott Neustadter—lean into the mythology around Wiseau in that he's routinely lied about his background, age, and finances. Early on, it's already hard to tell if Franco wants viewers to laugh at Tommy Wiseau or just along with all his eccentricity. Whether or not Franco sees Wiseau as a clown, something to be mocked, is central to one's enjoyment of *The Disaster Artist,* and a difficult question to answer throughout the film. (And Franco calling Wiseau up to the stage when he won a Golden Globe for this film only to push him away without letting him speak added fuel to the theory that the actor/director is mocking/using Wiseau more than paying any sort of respectful homage to him.)

Greg and Tommy become best buddies, and the pair quickly move to Los Angeles to make their acting dreams come true. It's there that Greg meets a bartender named Amber (Alison Brie), and something of a love triangle forms, although sexual interest from Tommy to Greg is never explicitly portrayed. It's more that he does not like how much time Greg is spending with Amber instead of with him, or how much easier the pursuit of fame seems to be going for Greg, who gets an agent while Tommy does not. All of this feeds into Tommy's script for *The Room,* which is about a love triangle with Tommy playing a banker named Johnny and Greg playing his best friend Mark.

Production begins on *The Room* and the comedy aspect of *The Disaster Artist* kicks into high gear. Franco's friend and regular collaborator Seth Rogen appears as Sandy Schklair, the script supervisor who basically ended up directing *The Room* (and even fought for co-directing credit after the movie became an unexpected hit); Ari Graynor stars as the actress who played "Lisa" in the movie within a movie; Josh Hucherson the actor who played "Denny"; Jacki Weaver the actress who played "Claudette," who notoriously drops that she has breast cancer in one scene, only for that character detail to never return. Production of *The Room* is portrayed as a series of bad decisions and talentless mistakes, such as when Wiseau shoots himself in a scene and then keeps acting or basically brutalizes the cast with his naked ass. Wiseau's misogyny, both on-set and in the film, is only briefed touched upon.

Franco fills his cast for *The Disaster Artist* with former collaborators and friends like his brother, Rogen, and Brie. And he cleverly includes the trio behind the hilarious podcast "How Did This Get Made?"—Paul Scheer, Jason Mantzoukas, and June Diane Raphael—as a clever in-joke. Much of *The Disaster Artist* feels like an in-joke, and there's a sense that Franco's view of filmmaking as a collaborative process is one of the reasons he admires Wiseau's do-it-yourself fearlessness. Franco's complete lack of visual composition could be a subtle commentary on Wiseau's similar weaknesses or it could be indicative of the filmmaker's laziness. One has to wonder if a movie about a bad-looking film has to be so awful to look at itself, but *The Disaster Artist* is often a hideous movie visually with bizarrely asymmetrical shot compositions and lazy style choices.

Of course, fans will argue that *The Disaster Artist* doesn't need to look good because it lives or dies on the strength of James Franco's performance, and it really is the reason the movie works at all (the Oscar® nomination for best screenplay was particularly surprising as there were more deserving choices snubbed, and headlines were made when Franco himself, who won the Golden Globe, was snubbed for an expected Best Actor nomination on the heels of sexual assault accusations). *The Disaster Artist* hums along on the fearlessness of Franco's work, as he commits completely to the larger-than-life character that is Tommy Wiseau. The strange accent, the unique gait, the outbursts of anger, the unchecked ego—James Franco gets all of it. It's likely because he identifies, at least in part, with the passion that led Wiseau to become a cult icon. In another world, James Franco could have been Tommy Wiseau. And, at least in Tommy's mind, he could have been James Franco.

Brian Tallerico

CREDITS

Greg: Dave Franco
Tommy: James Franco
Sandy: Seth Rogen
Juliette: Ari Graynor
Amber: Alison Brie
Origin: United States
Language: English
Released: 2017
Production: Evan Goldberg, Vince Jolivette, James Weaver, James Franco, Seth Rogen; Good Universe, New Line Cinema L.L.C., Point Grey Pictures, Rabbit Bandini Productions, Ramona Films, RatPac-Dune Entertainment; released by A24 Films LLC
Directed by: James Franco
Written by: Scott Neustadter; Michael H. Weber
Cinematography by: Brandon Trost
Music by: Dave Porter
Sound: Christopher S. Aud
Music Supervisor: Gabe Hilfer
Editing: Stacey Schroeder
Art Direction: Rachel Rockstroh
Costumes: Brenda Abbandandolo
Production Design: Chris L. Spellman
MPAA rating: R
Running time: 104 minutes

REVIEWS

Allen, Nick. *RogerEbert.com.* December 1, 2017.
Childress, Erik. *The Playlist.* March 14, 2017.
Dargis, Manohla. *New York Times.* November 30, 2017.
Ebiri, Bilge. *Village Voice.* November 30, 2017.
Phillips, Michael. *Chicago Tribune.* November 30, 2017.
Rechtshaffen, Michael. *Hollywood Reporter.* March 13, 2017.
Rothkopf, Joshua. *Time Out.* November 20, 2017.
Stevens, Dana. *Slate.* December 7, 2017.
Travers, Peter. *Rolling Stone.* November 29, 2017.
Wilkinson, Alissa. *Vox.* December 7, 2017.

QUOTES

Greg Sestero: "Tommy, dude, this really isn't necessary."
Tommy Wiseau: "No, no! Very necessary. I need to show my ass to sell this picture."

TRIVIA

This film received a standing ovation after its premiere at the SXSW film festival in March 2017.

AWARDS

Golden Globes 2018: Actor--Mus./Comedy (Franco)
Nominations:
Oscars 2017: Adapt. Screenplay
Golden Globes 2018: Film--Mus./Comedy
Ind. Spirit 2018: Actor (Franco)
Screen Actors Guild 2017: Actor (Franco)
Writers Guild 2017: Adapt. Screenplay

A DOG'S PURPOSE

Every dog happens for a reason.
—Movie tagline
Some pets stay with you forever.
—Movie tagline

Box Office: $64.5 Million

The latest chapter of pet cinema comes with *A Dog's Purpose,* which has a unique mission. In this case, the consciousness of the title animal is provided by the likes of Josh Gad, who dazzled audiences by voicing sidekick Olaf in *Frozen* (2013) but is now left alone in the recording booth to provide the only animal voice in this movie. As Gad whimsically voices a Golden Retriever named Bailey, a German Shepherd named Ellie, a Corgi named Tino, and later a St. Bernard named Buddy, Gad offers what an intelligent dog might be thinking at different points, especially while experiencing reincarnation. It makes for a greeting card of a film that is sometimes amusing, and always kind of strange.

Based on the adored book by W. Bruce Cameron (who co-wrote this film adaptation), *A Dog's Purpose* has some yearning to get the viewer thinking as well. "What is the meaning of life?" is the film's opening line, with Gad born into a dog's body that is quickly off-screen euthanized, starting a rattling, low-key anxiety that this movie is about waiting for cute animals to eventually die. There are not many movies for the family set that begin with this type of question, so some kudos is warranted for director Lasse Hallström. He aims to make this movie a snack for thought, while still offering different shots of cute dogs, sometimes showing their literal point-of-view.

The main story concerns that of Bailey, Gad's second dog and the Golden Retriever who becomes our window into Americana, not unlike Skip in the movie *My Dog Skip* (2000). In a plot line that might be even more American than apple pie itself, Bailey comes into the life of a young boy named Ethan (played by Bryce Gheisar when eight years old) who adores the dog, growing up with him in a house with a loving mother (Juliet Rylance) and an alcoholic, paranoid father (Luke Kirby). Ethan eventually flowers into a strapping high school quarterback (now played by K.J. Apa), a pristine boyfriend (to Britt Robertson's Haley), and Bailey enjoys dog pleasures like dashing through fields and befriending a donkey. This harmony is destroyed in a way that directly challenges the film's uber-American values: Ethan loses a football scholarship when hurting his leg escaping, and the father disappears from the picture, changing the quaintness of their nuclear family. Eventually, Bailey himself too dies.

But life goes on for the soul of Bailey, which then appears in the body of a female German Shepard named Ellie, who works as a cop dog. John Ortiz provides a soulful performance as Carlos, a career-man of the badge who also lives alone, but learns to bond with the dog he helps catch criminals with. In a cheap attempt to add tension and heroism to the story, Ellie is shown saving Carlos' life taking a bullet for him, not before throwing herself into hectic waters (the sequence would later be put under scrutiny for possible animal abuse).

The next chapter is of more considerable lightness, as it portrays a young woman named Maya (Kirby Howell-Baptiste) with her Corgi named Tino. What starts as a tale of a young woman working hard at her studies (which is not given enough focus in film in general) then becomes a sweet, rejuvenating love story, in which Tino finds a mate with a large dog, and Maya falls in love with that dog's owner. Tino watches as Maya and Al (Pooch Hall) create a family, have energetic children. Soon enough, it is Tino's time to move into the ether.

All of this comes full circle when Bailey is born again as Buddy, a Saint Bernard-looking animal that experiences neglect when owned by a rowdy young couple. As the movie makes a point to present the different types of homes that pets are brought into, *A Dog's Purpose* shows the viewer in a time-lapse montage this adorable pup left outside, with no one to care for him. Buddy sees a brighter day when he comes back into the life of Ethan (now played by Dennis Quaid), recognizing the smells he did when he was known as Bailey. Quaid provides the movie with more dramatic legitimacy one may originally expect as he sells the story's idea of reincarnation, namely the spirit of Bailey returning in a different dog, decades later. His face of recognition when expressing such a bizarre emotion is unexpectedly warming.

The whole enterprise is captured with much manufactured quaintness, in spite of the film's conscious efforts to be slightly progressive with depictions of gender (Gad voicing a female dog) or race (as with Maya's love story). The obvious heart in the story would feel more immediate were it treated with more than its sweeping, wholesale Americana or numerous bloodless moments, however shiny things may look. Even its grappling of the afterlife, in which bubbles are used as visual transitions of Bailey's soul from one dog to the next, shows that the movie is more concerned with being gentle than interesting. That is of course relatively fair for its audience, but it creates a shallow effect for a story that wants to be full of philosophical kibble.

Budgeted at around $22 million, *A Dog's Purpose* was relatively successful in America, earning double its price tag domestically. However, a sequel became more guaranteed with the very curious foreign box office numbers, of which added $129 million to a worldwide gross of $194.2 million. Hallstrom's film was especially popular in China, where it grossed $88 million. Dogs may not serve a huge narrative purpose in Hollywood, but their effect on the box office guarantees audiences will always get to watch them.

Nick Allen

CREDITS

Adult Ethan: Dennis Quaid
Adult Hannah: Peggy Lipton
Teen Ethan: K.J. Apa
Teen Hannah: Britt Robertson
Bailey/Buddy/Tino/Ellie: Josh Gad (Voice)
Origin: United States
Language: English, French, Spanish
Released: 2017
Production: Gavin Polone; Amblin Partners L.L.C., Pariah Entertainment Group; released by Universal Pictures
Directed by: Lasse Hallstrom
Written by: W. Bruce Cameron; Cathryn Michon; Audrey Wells; Maya Forbes; Wally Wolodarsky
Cinematography by: Terry Stacey
Music by: Rachel Portman
Sound: Eliza Paley
Music Supervisor: Liza Richardson
Editing: Robert Leighton
Art Direction: Rejean Labrie; Larry Spittle
Costumes: Shay Cunliffe
Production Design: Michael Carlin
MPAA rating: PG
Running time: 100 minutes

REVIEWS

Barker, Andrew. *Variety*. January 24, 2017.

Dry, Jude. *IndieWire*. January 25, 2017.
Duralde, Alonso. *TheWrap*. January 24, 2017.
Genzlinger, Neil. *New York Times*. January 25, 2017.
Nehme, Farran Smith. *New York Magazine/Vulture*. January 30, 2017.
Pickett, Leah. *Chicago Reader*. January 26, 2017.
Rife, Katie. *The A.V. Club*. January 26, 2017.
Schenk, Frank. *Hollywood Reporter*. January 25, 2017.
Walsh, Katie. *Los Angeles Times*. February 2, 2017.
Zacharek, Stephanie. *Time*. January 26, 2017.

QUOTES

Bailey: "I had a purpose, I was needed again and again and again. With each new life I was learning a new lesson."

TRIVIA

During the Corgi segment of the film, the missing tail was humorous because some Welsh Corgis are born with their tails naturally short or missing, while others may have their tails docked between 2-5 days old due to historical tradition or as a measure of conformation to the breed standard.

DOWNSIZING

We are meant for something bigger.
—Movie tagline

Box Office: $24.4 Million

Writer/director Alexander Payne has always had a gift for taking a look at smaller, more mundane people in society and rendering them larger than life and more exciting. A seemingly small, moral conundrum tends to wreak havoc on everyman (or, everywoman) characters in Payne's films before audiences are taken on a journey that hopefully leaves them a bit wiser and more empathetic than they may have been before the film began. Starting with his common sense arguments for and against abortion in *Citizen Ruth* (1996), which put him on the map to arguably his best film, the high school election drama *Election* (1999), Payne has a knack for taking seemingly normal people and putting them in small yet explosive situations. He also wrote and directed two different road trip films featuring aging men in Jack Nicholson and Bruce Dern in *About Schmidt* (2002) and *Nebraska* (2013), respectively. His other road trip comedy *Sideways* (2004) was a surprise hit and that film, as well as the George Clooney starrer *The Descendants* (2011), won Oscars®. Clearly, Payne has been on a serious roll, and expectations for the science-fiction comedy-drama *Downsizing* (2017) were big, no pun intended. The concept for the film is high and reteams Payne with his co-Oscar® winner Jim Taylor which would all appear to be a slam-dunk for the studio as well as audiences. Alas, much like plot points in all of Payne's films, things don't always go as planned.

In *Downsizing*, audiences are introduced to a modern world where it's become possible to shrink human beings—as well as almost any material—down to a miniature scale. Normal, everyday people who are tired of living a life where they are struggling to succeed or make ends meet can voluntarily be shrunken down and live out their days out in a tiny resort-like city called "Leisure Land" with other small people. If you wanted, say, a pint of beer, it would take one drop to fill your tiny glass thus making the cost of said beer miniscule, to say the least. Garish-looking, working dollhouses where one could reside would cost a few hundred dollars as would cars and boats shrunken to a miniature size. These examples do not even touch upon the reduction of population size per square foot or the massive reduction in human waste that could seriously help the planet. These are all intriguing ideas as was casting Matt Damon in the lead as lovable loser Paul Safranek and comedy superstar Kristen Wiig as his tentative wife Audrey. Indeed, *Downsizing* has all the components of a great film and a real crowd pleaser which makes it all the more shocking when the entire affair falls completely flat due to uninteresting character development, lame plot turns, and the truly strange choice to play the story out in a totally "straight" fashion. *Downsizing* isn't a comedy even though it has humorous moments; it's a drama about tiny people, and, much like their pie-in-the-sky utopic lifestyle post-shrinkage, it doesn't work at all.

Damon's Safranek is a sweet, hardworking everyman who can barely make ends meet himself as an occupational therapist for a meat packing facility in Nebraska. While he and Audrey's house is nice and cozy, they want more, and, after many a night spent crunching the numbers, Paul realizes it's just not going to happen any time soon, if ever, on their budget. At a high school reunion, Paul and Audrey are stunned to see longtime friends Dave and Carol Johnson (Jason Sudeikis and Maribeth Monroe) have taken the plunge and "downsized" and are preaching the word to all their friends about how great it's been. The selling point is more time to do all the things one wishes they had time to do for a fraction of the cost. In fact, most small people no longer have a need for a job so inexpensive is their life, once their full-sized assets are liquidated. After much thought, Paul and Audrey decide that shrinking down to live the lives they want is the way to go and after selling everything they own, they are off to a clinic to be shrunk down to about five inches tall. After a lengthy and somewhat unnecessary sequence showing fellow "Downsizers" being shaven head to toe and having dental implants removed, the shrink is on and before he knows it, Paul is five inches tall and in a recovery room. However, it soon turns out that Audrey got cold feet and has not only decided to not join her husband, but she also soon files for divorce which is where the film vaults to in one of a few odd feeling, tacked on time jumps.

At this point, *Downsizing* has lost all of its comedic actors who featured prominently in the commercials for the film. Wiig's character is never heard from again and the Sudeikis character shows up once more during a boring party scene. While this isn't really a big deal as Damon is more than capable of carrying a film, it does feel like a bait and switch due to the fact that the film had been touted as a comedy featuring Wiig and Sudeikis. And as the runtime drags on, it's almost as if Payne and frequent collaborator Taylor realize this and decide to introduce a smarmy, Eurotrash upstairs neighbor named Dusan (Christoph Waltz) to lighten the mood. Dusan likes to smoke fancy cigars and party and he somehow convinces buttoned-up Paul to live it up a little and soon, Paul has taken Ecstasy and a derivative scene of him happily and dreamily hallucinating takes place. The scene isn't funny or interesting and, worse, Paul seemingly learns nothing from this sudden mood-enhancing drug. The scene does allow for the introduction of Ngoc Lan Tran (Hong Chau), a once strong and powerful Vietnamese dissident who gave a leg in her fight for her rights who is now reduced to the role of housekeeper in this truly modern society that's basically a heavy-handed example of white privilege. While, sure, anyone who can afford it can be shrunk down, society still needs marginalized people who will do the dirty work like cleaning houses, gardening, and all the menial day-to-day jobs that help even a "small" society function. These "minorities" are allowed to be small for a reduced rate but their lifestyle doesn't improve as they're relegated to manual labor and taking care of those who can afford to be small and not work.

Due to his ever-present niceness and desire to help, Paul decides he can help Tran with her cheaply made prosthetic leg. Shrill and sassy, Tran is standoffish towards Paul at first. But soon, she sees he has some expertise in the world of medicine (he attended medical school before dropping out to take care of his mother) and a terse friendship is formed. For the remainder of the film, Tran shrieks at Paul and forces him to help the sickly, poverty stricken residents just outside of the resort who live in cheap portable buildings where they're packed in like sardines and stacked in tiny rooms, endlessly piled high. From here *Downsizing* pivots from dull to a pretty sanctimonious, bummer of a movie wherein Paul and Tran try to help underserved and ill people before heading off to Norway to see Dr. Jorgen Asbjørnsen (Rolf Lassgård) who invented the whole "Downsizing" operation. Upon finding him, Paul, Tran, and Dusan discover he's not only reduced to overseeing a worshipful, cult-like village of tiny people, he also has very bad news for the planet at large. From here the film stumbles into a final act that is almost a complete 180 from where it started—in a bad way—before dragging on until graciously allowing audiences to be free of this strangely dull and tedious film.

Downsizing is indeed a boring, bad movie but it does have a few positives. It was refreshing to see an actress of Asian descent in Hong Chau as Tran be a character who doesn't feel like a prototypical cinematic Asian character. While she does have a bit of a clichéd tarnished, war-stricken backstory, she's very much of the "now" and Chau is a very fine actress. It's a shame she was written to be so shrill and unlikable. *Downsizing* also offers some intriguing ideas about how we treat our planet and the benefits of "going small," yet, in the end, the film suffers from taking itself much too seriously. While granted, going in thinking the film would be a light comedy only to have it be a kind of preachy, heavy-handed think piece makes such a genre switch difficult to parse, the film still should have been better considering the wealth of talent behind it. It's as if Payne has suddenly taken his gift for making a mundane story feel extraordinary and, when finally giving audiences an extraordinary story he (and Taylor) have managed to make it mundane.

Don R. Lewis

CREDITS

Paul Safranek: Matt Damon
Dusan Mirkovic: Christoph Waltz
Ngoc Lan Tran: Hong Chau
Audrey Safranek: Kristen Wiig
Dr. Jorgen Asbjornsen: Rolf Lassgard
Origin: United States
Language: English, Spanish, Icelandic, Norwegian
Released: 2017
Production: Jim Burke, Megan Ellison, Mark Johnson, Alexander Payne, Jim Taylor; Ad Hominem Enterprises; released by Paramount Pictures Corp.
Directed by: Alexander Payne
Written by: Alexander Payne; Jim Taylor
Cinematography by: Phedon Papamichael
Music by: Rolfe Kent
Editing: Kevin Tent
Art Direction: Kimberley Zaharko
Costumes: Wendy Chuck
Production Design: Stefania Cella

MPAA rating: R
Running time: 135 minutes

REVIEWS

Baumgarten, Marjorie. *Austin Chronicle.* December 21, 2017.
Brooks, Xan. *The Guardian.* August 30, 2017.
Chang, Justin. *Los Angeles Times.* December 21, 2017.
Hornaday, Ann. *Washington Post.* December 21, 2017.
Kiang, Jessica. *The Playlist.* August 30, 2017.
LaSalle, Mick. *San Francisco Chronicle.* December 20, 2017.
Marshall, Lee. *Screen International.* August 30, 2017.
O'Malley, Sheila. *RogerEbert.com.* December 22, 2017.
Travers, Peter. *Rolling Stone.* December 19, 2017.
Uhlich, Keith. *Slant Magazine.* September 10, 2017.

TRIVIA

This is the first film, since *Citizen Ruth,* that Alexander Payne has written that was not based on a book.

AWARDS

Nominations:

Golden Globes 2018: Actress--Supporting (Chau)
Screen Actors Guild 2017: Actress--Supporting (Chau)

DUNKIRK

The event that shaped our world.
—Movie tagline
At the point of crisis, at the point of annihilation, survival is victory.
—Movie tagline

Box Office: $188.4 Million

War has been explored every which way throughout cinema; a medium that François Truffaut famously said exalted the very concept of it. The filmmaker did not live long enough to see the battleground reduced to video game generals rushing in to save the day and rack up as many kills as possible. Every war and nearly every infamous battle has been recreated on film and television to tell tales of history, politics, and bravery. Casualties are a natural part of those narratives, each feeling more senseless than the next especially those on the side of good whose names we do not always remember. Christopher Nolan is a filmmaker who has been rightly championed over the course of a 20-year career that has produced nine previous features. Championed not for pushing the boundaries of new technologies or even just a self-proprietor against the rising antiquation of shooting on film, but for his prowess as a storyteller and the innovative ways he can find within the process to present big, even original, ideas to his audience. Who better than Nolan to take a major wartime event in history, untaught in most American schools, and use his unique narrative drive to tell the story of the all-too-many nameless soldiers whose accomplishment in survival may have helped save even more lives?

In 1940, during World War II, German forces had pushed Allied soldiers towards the port of Dunkirk. Surrounded by the Germans on one side and the water on the other, some 400,000 troops were left stranded and vulnerable, waiting for rescue efforts that were being thwarted from above and below. Tommy (Fionn Whitehead) narrowly escapes an ambush in town and finds himself on the beach looking for a way onto any available ship. Commander Bolton (Kenneth Branagh) opines that "home" is just on the other side of the water though with the shallowness of the mole's surroundings limiting such large vessel rescues moot, the soldiers are sitting ducks from any direction.

Across the channel, the Navy has commissioned civilians to use their own boats to help bring the soldiers back. Mr. Dawson (Mark Rylance) and his son, Peter (Tom Glynn-Carney) are among those to answer the call as is local boy, George (Barry Keoghan) who hops aboard hoping to do his part. Meanwhile, from the air, a group of Spitfires move towards France. Pilots Farrier (Tom Hardy) and Collins (Jack Lowden) are tasked to provide cover for those making their way from the beach as well as those incoming with little military experience and even less weaponry.

This crossroads of conflict is enough for any filmmaker to make a compelling war picture just on pure battle theatrics alone. Except Nolan chooses not to idly settle for a traditional narrative of heroes and villains. In the opening moments he slyly clues us into that by not just identifying where the peril exists ("The Mole," "The Sea," and "The Air") but the period of time (a week, a day, an hour) to which the soldiers, civilians, and pilots are ticking down, perhaps on their own lives.

This method plays right into Nolan's recurring exploration on the concept of time right down to his own pocket watch being incorporated into Hans Zimmer's score. *Memento* (2000) told its story backwards to put us into the fractured memory of its protagonist. The dream logic of *Inception* (2010) slowed down the mental acuity of the characters who tried to change their reality through a potentially endless fantasy. Then his sci-fi epic, *Interstellar* (2014), took it to a multi-galaxy scale where time showed us how inconsequential humans could be. Especially if they did nothing.

Leave it to the historians to debate whether the events of Dunkirk turned the tide of the war in any capacity. Nolan's film may end with the words of Winston Churchill—who was instrumental in the activation of Operation Dynamo—but it is primarily a call to action and a horrific testament to survival at all costs. The abject slaughter of soldiers in battle in films has gone a long way to counterpoint Truffaut's comments, but the absolute waste of human life without a fighting chance has rarely been depicted with such shocking intimacy. Nothing to do but duck and pray on the beach. Nowhere to go when the fortunate few to board a ship find it sinking as fast as it is struck by enemy fire. These are dead men walking, standing and swimming while the convergence of the stories only expedites the dread as well as the hope.

The minimum of dialogue may shift speculation that Nolan portrays these men as simple targets rather than flesh and blood; especially given the PG-13 level of carnage. However, his screenplay cleverly controls that debate by the depiction of Dawson's boat and their pickup of a shell-shocked soldier (Cillian Murphy). Time folding back upon himself shows this man as one in control of his leadership skills under the cover of darkness but a nerve-shattered mess the moment he discovers his rescuers were taking him right back into the hell he just narrowly survived. Who could blame him? Dawson and his son each have their own understanding on how best to handle a man not thinking clearly and the result of their actions is a representation of a two-sided principle. The first casualty of war may be truth to the members of government who too often send these boys to die but to those on the front lines it may indeed be innocence.

The human element is never to be ignored through every ticking second of *Dunkirk*, but it is also an extraordinary technical achievement. Recreation of imagery through archival photos is only a portion of the attention of detail that puts us right into the thick of the horror. The ripple effect of a piercing bullet in the opening scene follows us through the rest of the ordeal as we, like the soldiers, have no inclination of which direction the next will come from. The airborne sequences with its creaky craft and deafening engines are masterfully integrated to keep the non-linear structure clear to an audience who must seek out the geography of the vehicles on the water just as the pilots have to track their enemies in the sky. Zimmer's score, very much an integral character during *Inception*, again feels like a clock on a timebomb inside a beating heart all interwoven into an exponential conflation of the storylines collapsing into one another with a breathless ferocity that almost never lets up.

Criticism of Nolan over time of being a cold and humorless filmmaker is well-documented but one that should have faded by now. *Dunkirk* hardly leaves any room for laughter, let alone a smile save for an introverted admiration of his craft, though the prospect of giving a vocal cameo to Michael Caine (who played a spitfire pilot in *Battle of Britain* [1969]) and doubling down on Tom Hardy doing his dialogue behind another mask is good enough for a pair of winks. The emotional element that has only grown stronger with each passing film may only feel like an exhale at first. Escaping the barrage of trauma endured by even the characters we only know by uniform is a prelude to wanting to savor every bit of oxygen you can muster. It may only be after some distance from the battlefield and the calm gliding of that spitfire looking for a place to land can we establish the ability to be truly moved, not just by the survival but for how it was achieved with the collaboration of a sound strategist (only heard from in the closing moments) and the selflessness of ordinary people.

Dunkirk may represent the most heroic story ever about retreat; a distinction that in no way is defined by cowardice. Running from the past for a more hopeful tomorrow (even if occasionally seeking vengeance) is another staple of Nolan's films. He replays the key opening shot of *The Prestige* (2006) replicating a bygone era of top hats with the helmets left behind on the beach; no bodies to occupy them anymore. Like his interpretation of Batman, the more-than-300,000 that made it out of Dunkirk alive became a symbol of perseverance that did not need medals as a reward for many of the enemy they killed. "All we did was survive," one soldier says to a blind man who responds, "That's enough." The way Christopher Nolan presents it, it was more than enough.

Erik Childress

CREDITS

Tommy: Fionn Whitehead
Peter: Tom Glynn-Carney
Collins: Jack Lowden
Alex: Harry Styles
Gibson: Aneurin Barnard
Origin: United States
Language: English, French, German
Released: 2017
Production: Christopher Nolan; Dombey Street Productions, Kaap Holland Film, Syncopy; released by Warner Bros. Pictures
Directed by: Christopher Nolan
Written by: Christopher Nolan
Cinematography by: Hoyte Van Hoytema
Music by: Hans Zimmer
Sound: Richard King
Editing: Lee Smith
Art Direction: Kevin Ishioka; Eggert Ketilsson

Costumes: Jeffrey Kurland
Production Design: Nathan Crowley
MPAA rating: PG-13
Running time: 106 minutes

REVIEWS

Berardinelli, James. *ReelViews.* July 18, 2017.
Brody, Richard. *New Yorker.* July 28, 2017.
Cerny, Alan. *ComingSoon.net.* July 18, 2017.
Dargis, Manohla. *ReelViews.* July 20, 2017.
Johanson, MaryAnn. *Flick Filosopher.* July 19, 2017.
McGranaghan, Mike. *Aisle Seat.* July 21, 2017.
Morgenstern, Joe. *Wall Street Journal.* July 19, 2017.
Snider, Eric D. *EricDSnider.com.* July 20, 2017.
Turan, Kenneth. *ReelViews.* July 20, 2017.
Willmore, Allison. *BuzzFeed.* July 28, 2017.

QUOTES

Mr. Dawson: "Men my age dictate this war. Why should we be allowed to send our children to fight it?"

TRIVIA

After first-hand accounts of the Dunkirk evacuation revealed to director Christopher Nolan how young and inexperienced the soldiers were, he decided to cast unknown actors for the beach setting.

AWARDS

Oscars 2017: Film Editing, Sound

British Acad. 2017: Sound

Nominations:

Oscars 2017: Cinematog., Director (Nolan), Film, Orig. Score, Production Design

British Acad. 2017: Cinematog., Film, Film Editing, Orig. Score, Production Design, Visual FX

British Acad. 2018: Director (Nolan)

Directors Guild 2017: Director (Nolan)

Golden Globes 2018: Director (Nolan), Film--Drama, Orig. Score

E

THE EMOJI MOVIE

An adventure beyond words
—Movie tagline
Welcome to the secret world inside your phone.
—Movie tagline

Box Office: $86.1 Million

Arguably the most loathed film of 2017, Sony's *The Emoji Movie* was perceived almost as a personal attack by critics when it was released in the summer of this year. Metacritic, a site that aggregates film reviews to produce a single score, currently lists *The Emoji Movie* at a stunning 12 out of 100, indicating "overwhelming dislike." Alonso Duralde of *The Wrap* called it "a soul-crushing disaster"; Emily Yoshida of *New York Magazine* said it was "one of the darkest, most dismaying films" she had ever seen; and the *New York Post*'s Johnny Oleksinski simply said "Please restore my eyes to factory settings." Could it really be that bad? How could any piece of disposable animated entertainment produce such universal vitriol? By being a soulless cash grab that steals the template from Pixar's *Inside Out* (2015) and, ironically, drains it of all recognizable human emotion.

T.J. Miller voices Gene, a "meh" emoji who lives in Textopolis, the digital landscape inside of a smart phone, this one belonging to a young man named Alex (Jake T. Austin). Gene has two "meh" parents named Mel (Steven Wright) and Mary (Jennifer Coolidge), but he struggles when put on the spot, and can't make the expression his user demands of him. Alex receives a text from his crush Addie, and attempts to respond with a cavalier "meh," but Gene screws it up and makes a nonsensical face instead of that requested, which leads to the order that he be deleted. He escapes Textopolis before that can happen, and goes on a wacky adventure where he learns to be confident about himself, while kids get inundated with hollow product placement designed to eliminate their individuality at the same time.

As he's embarking on his adventure, Gene runs into Hi-5 (James Corden), an emoji who used to be popular but doesn't really get used anymore, who tells him that they can be fixed if they can only find a hacker, and escape the bots chasing them. While Alex thinks his phone needs to be repaired, leading to outright panic in Textopolis, Gene and Hi-5 find a hacker named Jailbreak (Anan Faris). She's less optimistic than her new friends, hoping to reach the Dropbox so she can go live in the cloud—whatever the heck that means. The bots come after all three of them, leading them to escape into Candy Crush, and any hope that *The Emoji Movie* might turn into something greater is killed like a deleted app.

From here, *The Emoji Movie* spirals into a series of product placement scenes that take place across apps like Instagram, Spotify, and Twitter. To suggest that this kind of timely advertisement is unlikely to age well is an understatement. It's about as disposable as a Geico commercial that makes a reference to a specific meme. It's not hard to believe that Spotify may not exist in a few years, and *The Emoji Movie* will get even more confusing and horrendous with time, if that's possible. This is about where plot recaps fall apart because, well, *The Emoji Movie* does not really have one. It's a series of nonsensical bits centered on apps. Yes, they have to escape the evil leader of Textopolis, named Smiler (Maya Rudolph), but it's nearly impossible to care. And, yes, of course, Gene eventually becomes comfortable with who he is in his heart, and everything is returned to order in emoji land.

The Emoji Movie does not have an original thought in its hideously designed head. The concept of something inhuman like emojis come to life has been cribbed from *Toy Story* (1995) and *Inside Out,* among other, better films. And the lack of creative energy seeps into every frame and line of the product—one is hesitant to call it a film because it barely qualifies. The dialogue is dull, even for children, partially because the line delivery is so lackluster that one can practically assume that the cast delivered it over the phone (with the exception of Rudolph, who gives her all to everything, even garbage like this). No one cares—not the writers, director, or cast. Why should viewers?

The grand tragedy of *The Emoji Movie* is not really that it's disposable trash—because it really is—but that kids and families around the world chose not to dispose of it. There are soulless animated films every year—*The Nut Job 2* (2017) and *Norm of the North* (2016) spring to mind—but they don't usually make a lot of money and disappear before kids can pester their parents to take them to the multiplex. This fate did not befall *The Emoji Movie,* which made over $200 million worldwide on a budget of around $50 million. That leads one to wonder if a sequel is not inevitably bound to be released. Like doomsday preppers planning for the end of the world, critics may want to get ready.

Brian Tallerico

CREDITS

Gene: T.J. Miller (Voice)
Hi-5: James Corden (Voice)
Jailbreak: Anna Faris (Voice)
Smiler: Maya Rudolph (Voice)
Mel Meh: Steven Wright (Voice)
Origin: United States
Language: English
Released: 2017
Production: Michelle Raimo; LStar Capital, Sony Pictures Animation; released by Columbia Pictures
Directed by: Tony Leondis
Written by: Tony Leondis; Eric Siegel; Mike White
Music by: Patrick Doyle
Music Supervisor: JoJo Villanueva
Editing: William Caparella
Art Direction: Ryan L. Carlson
Production Design: Carlos Zaragoza
MPAA rating: PG
Running time: 86 minutes

REVIEWS

Bramesco, Charles. *The Guardian.* July 28, 2017.
Ebiri, Bilge. *Village Voice.* July 31, 2017.
Ehrlich, David. *IndieWire.* July 27, 2017.
Grierson, Tim. *Screen International.* July 27, 2017.
Kenny, Glenn. *New York Times.* July 27, 2017.
Laffly, Tomris. *Time Out.* July 28, 2017.
Oleksinski, Johnny. *New York Post.* July 27, 2017.
Singer, Matt. *ScreenCrush.* July 27, 2017.
Sobczynski, Peter. *RogerEbert.com.* July 28, 2017.
Wilkinson, Alissa. *Vox.* July 27, 2017.

QUOTES

Hi-5: "Welcome to the Loser's Lounge, where the emojis who never get used hang out."

TRIVIA

According to actor T.J. Miller, this is the fastest produced animated film in history.

AWARDS

Golden Raspberries 2017: Worst Director (Leondis), Worst Picture, Worst Screenplay

EVERYTHING, EVERYTHING

Risk everything...for love.
—Movie tagline

Box Office: $34.1 Million

Combine the eroticism of *Twilight* (2008) with the wisdom of *Bubble Boy* (2001) and the result is *Everything, Everything*, a strong candidate for the year's least credible, worst-acted movie. Every moment is an appalling and pathetic display of amateurism to the degree that, despite the film's young adult (YA) pedigree, it is a bit shocking it was released in theaters at all.

Adapting Nicola Yoon's novel, director Stella Meghie displays not one capable instinct toward the work or her cast. In their biggest starring roles to date, Amandla Stenberg of *The Hunger Games* (2012) and Nick Robinson of *Jurassic World* (2015) appear to have been told to pretend that they are twinkling, defining chemistry as googly eyes instead of an actual, identifiable connection. She plays Maddy, who since birth has dealt with such a severe case of immunodeficiency that she has not left her Southern California house in 18 years. He is Olly, who moves in next door and is presented as a bad boy simply because he wears black

T-shirts, has longish hair, and has an abusive father. In reality, he's just as bland as Maddy. That means their forbidden love, built on gazes through the window and then texts and then a discovery that they actually can touch and Maddy's totally okay, is not a case of opposites attract so much as two dull people with limited opportunities leaning on each other and mistaking it for something substantial. Worse still is that most of the scenes unfold like rehearsals, adding an additional layer of phoniness to a story that is cutesy and manipulative and not in tune with its uncomfortable layers in the slightest.

Under the circumstances, Maddy should feel varying degrees of frustration and impatience toward her situation, mixed with hunger and fear once Olly comes into her life. Instead, she is one-dimensional, gawking simplicity, neither one of them expressing a lot of curiosity to know each other well and defaulting to maximum innocence. Even for 18-year-olds at the start of a relationship, the closeness just never materializes, partly because the story and resulting feelings are so woefully underwritten. It remains unclear how Olly feels about the new community when he is not around Maddy or what makes her special to him, not just a pretty girl who lives next door and provides an escape from an unhappy family life. Meanwhile, considering that in terrible voiceovers (sample line: "Why would anyone set themselves up for a broken heart?") she claims to pass her days partially through books and Internet videos, it seems fair to assume a reasonably healthy awareness of popular culture. Yet Maddy appears both pretty well adjusted for someone with virtually no social interaction ever (besides her mom [Anika Noni Rose], nurse [Ana de la Reguera], and the nurse's daughter [Danube Hermosillo]) and, besides for one line of *Moonstruck* (1987), not at all influenced by the content she has digested in her alone time. (Which explains why she does not recognize Olly's move bitten from *Love, Actually* [2003]). Furthermore, she never seems sick or to wonder at all about her condition or display any side effects from a life lived in indoor solitude. *Everything, Everything* repeatedly establishes the potential for drama only to look away.

This might be different—at least a palatable, off-brand *The Fault in Our Stars* (2014)—if Maddy and Olly were a little younger, or if Meghie, working from a script by J. Mills Goodloe (the creepy *The Age of Adaline* [2015] and goopy *The Best of Me* [2014]), gave the material any movement. Even arguments exist in a vacuum, though, with no emotional follow-through or recognizable human behavior. Maddy and Olly are so stiff that their attempts at wonder are cloying, and their claims about empowering each other feel unsupported. Lending voiceover to an email that he thinks could be their last communication, Robinson contributes not an ounce of passion or feeling, as if there actually is a shared history at stake.

It is okay for the participants in a romance, at any age, to seem naïve. But *Everything, Everything* comes off as a flat-out lie, all the way to a twist that reinforces the film's clumsy handling of child abuse and the responses of young adults. Meanwhile, the attempt to break away from onscreen texts by showing Maddy and Olly actually talking to each other is made even more stilted by repeated imagery of an astronaut, a symbol of Maddy's isolation. Once again, this brings the supposed love between 18-year-olds down to a 10-year-old's level, advanced by Maddy's painful niceness and the lack of psychology to anyone's difficult circumstances other than the aforementioned twist, which is insulting on multiple levels. Despite the parallels of a confined mother and child, this is a long, long way from the fantastically acted and insightful *Room* (2015).

The absence of both courage and talent is deadly for any movie, and *Everything, Everything* whiffs even in places it might have worked. "Princess Madeline and her glass castle," Olly notes when they finally have a chance to speak in the same room. "I'm not a princess," she responds, as if there will be an effort to make this feel like a modern relationship and not Rapunzel. "Good," he says, adding, "Because I'm not a prince." If anyone involved dared to pull back the layers of these people as flawed kids deciding to combine their islands, the film could have had a kind of sad charm. It certainly could have given Maddy a greater drive toward making the most of her situation and show that people who are dealt a difficult hand can still thrive.

Alas, this garbage refracts teenage heat and serious medical and familial issues into exchanges that barely qualify for a PG-13 rating. (That Maddy never feels sick until after sex is also a bizarre plea for abstinence, even though these two believe they're in love and at the time she thinks she may die soon. Come on.) This is a Disney movie in YA clothes, just another uninspired tale of a heroine who wants the one thing she cannot have and the dreamboat who comes along to help her get it. The whole, infuriating thing is a whisper, too stupid to recognize when it is time to scream.

Matt Pais

CREDITS

Maddy Whittier: Amandla Stenberg

Olly Bright: Nick Robinson

Pauline Whittier: Anika Noni Rose

Carla: Ana de la Reguera

Kayra: Taylor Hickson
Origin: United States
Language: English
Released: 2017
Production: Elysa Dutton, Leslie Morgenstein; Alloy Entertainment L.L.C.; released by MGM Studios Inc.
Directed by: Stella Meghie
Written by: J. Mills Goodloe
Cinematography by: Igor Jadue-Lillo
Music by: Ludwig Göransson
Music Supervisor: Kier Lehman
Editing: Nancy Richardson
Art Direction: David Clarke
Costumes: Avery Plewes
Production Design: Charisse Cardenas
MPAA rating: PG-13
Running time: 96 minutes

REVIEWS

Burr, Ty. *Boston Globe.* May 17, 2017.
Dry, Jude. *IndieWire.* May 22, 2017.
Henderson, Eric. *Slant Magazine.* May 18, 2017.
Leydon, Joe. *Variety.* May 18, 2017.
O'Sullivan, Michael. *Washington Post.* May 25, 2017.
Puig, Claudia. *TheWrap.* May 17, 2017.
Rife, Katie. *The A.V. Club.* May 18, 2017.
Roeper, Richard. *Chicago Sun-Times.* May 18, 2017.
Savlov, Marc. *Austin Chronicle.* May 17, 2017.
Stewart, Sara. *New York Post.* May 18, 2017.

QUOTES

Maddy Whittier: "I'm willing to sacrifice everything just to live one perfect day."

TRIVIA

Olly's life at home was a bigger focus in the book than in the film.

THE EXCEPTION

(The Kaiser's Last Kiss)

One duty. One desire. One decision.
—Movie tagline

Box Office: $708,973

Jai Courtney, after facing a few hiccups in his acting career, finds a niche that suits him well—the romantic lead in a Nazi drama. Its specificity is rare, but this is its strength. His performance in *The Exception* is a nuanced contrast to the schlocky action fare in which he has paid his dues since coming to American audiences from his native Australia. The film may be more than Courtney, but his performance is what makes it notable.

Based on Alan Judd's 2003 novel *The Kaiser's Last Kiss, The Exception*, set in a fictionalized World War II timeline (sure to frustrate European history scholars), follows German soldier Stefan Brandt (Courtney) on assignment to the personal detail of exiled Kaiser Wilhelm II (Christopher Plummer). He is to spy on the former monarch, on the pretext of serving as his bodyguard, to determine the Kaiser's allegiances to the Third Reich. Shortly after he arrives, Brandt learns that an unidentified British spy is snooping around the local village, evading the Germans, and complicating an already deliciously pulpy plot.

The soldier with a mysterious past, a Kaiser with a lifetime of bitterness, and a maid of indeterminate allegiance—all in an immaculately-set castle curated for its romance, on grounds striking in their pre-War beauty. Surrounded by spycraft, ulterior motives, and Nazi paranoia, emotions run hot. This maid, Mieke (Lily James), sparks a romance with Brandt begun with a series of lustful glances. The relative silence between the two early in their affair is frustrating and awkward yet winning—the burning wordlessness that only occurs in bad romance novels—because their chemistry is undeniably passionate.

This is thanks to David Leveaux, a British theater director making his film debut, who shows a steady hand with his actors and a commanding sense for camera placement. Leveaux instills paranoia and secrecy in scenes by having cinematographer Roman Osin angle his peering eye through windows and around corners. Different lighting tinges each scene with ambient tones (especially when using candlelight) and deft, ogling changes in the audience's perspective reflect the young romance's shifts in power dynamics. The camera becomes excited along with Leveaux's characters; it spins around Wilhelm to kinetically capture his freedom as he takes simple pleasure in something simple like feeding ducks, or, less innocently, focuses on its stars' disrobed bodies.

The Exception has an admirably egalitarian policy towards nudity, using it effectively with both its male and female stars. This is particularly effective with Courtney. The novelty of male full-frontal allows his character a much-needed vulnerability—revealing, among other things, a large abdominal scar from wartime shrapnel behind his Nazi greys. The film sometimes fades in and out to showcase Brandt's memories, his traumatic dreams of past wartime horrors, signifying guilt, fear, and self-loathing in a performance that is never too soft but never too stony. Mieke is a bit slight as a character, but James finds depth in her through a quiet, rushed desperation. Her hesitation as she admits to Brandt that she is Jewish is both completely endearing and troubling; in turn, their romance gains importance as something worthy of this trust.

The film's other romance, that between the Kaiser and his stolen homeland, is just as involved and complex. The Kaiser, whom Plummer fills with humor and gravitas, hates being reminded of the Germany that blamed, ousted, and forgot about him. He is endearing and scary, a character who has incredible potential for cruelty somehow humanized by Plummer. The Kaiser's wife, Princess Hermine Reuss of Greiz (Janet McTeer), doesn't get much to do until the surprise visit of Heinrich Himmler (a delightfully deadpan and evil Eddie Marsan), head of the SS, which the former royalty think is to confirm the monarchy will be restored. That McTeer's wild eyes and tittering body language finds a hopeful balance between pathetic and sweet is quite amazing when both sides, Nazis and monarchists, have a history of ruthless power.

Balancing this is the movie's true achievement. A well-edited film, *The Exception* always finds time to linger on brief breaths before the action begins and the moments of reflection after it ends, adding depth to an otherwise straightforward story. Editor Nicolas Gaster (who also served as the film's second unit director) is able to surmise the perfect length for each shot. Yet, the film never quite achieves the level of fevered hurry for which it aims—sometimes due to its often trite, on-the-nose dialogue and sometimes because of the stilted delivery of said dialogue. The explanations, admittances, and declarations uttered by the characters here need conversational groundwork before spewing forth as if from a burst pipe, and without that foundation, which *The Exception* can struggle to provide, they are jarring. Still, Leveaux's first film is a romantic and pleasantly small one about love in an era when love always contested with duty to something greater.

Jacob Oller

CREDITS

Mieke de Jong: Lily James
Stefan Brandt: Jai Courtney
Princess Hermine: Janet McTeer
Kaiser Wilhelm II: Christopher Plummer
Heinrich Himmler: Eddie Marsan
Origin: United States
Language: English
Released: 2017
Production: Lou Pitt, Judy Tossell; Alton Road Productions, Egoli Tossell Film, Egoli Tossell KLK, Ostar Productions, Umedia; released by A24 Films LLC
Directed by: David Leveaux
Written by: Simon Burke
Cinematography by: Roman Osin
Music by: Ilan Eshkeri
Sound: Francois Dumont
Editing: Nicolas Gaster
Costumes: Daniela Ciancio
Production Design: Hubert Pouille
MPAA rating: R
Running time: 107 minutes

REVIEWS

Covert, Colin. *Minneapolis Star Tribune*. June 22, 2017.
Coyle, Jake. *Associated Press*. June 1, 2017.
Debruge, Peter. *Variety*. June 2, 2017.
Edelstein, David. *New York Magazine*. June 1, 2017.
Eagan, Daniel. *Film Journal International*. June 1, 2017.
Lawson, Richard. *Vanity Fair*. September 16, 2016.
Merry, Stephanie. *Washington Post*. June 29, 2017.
Scott, A.O. *New York Times*. June 1, 2017.
Turan, Kenneth. *Los Angeles Times*. June 1, 2017.
Wloszczyna, Susan. *RogerEbert.com*. June 2, 2017.

QUOTES

Kaiser Wilhelm II: "I'm ashamed to say that before and after my first marriage I, myself, fathered at least two illegitimate children: one with an Austrian countess, another with a French prostitute who was known in court circles as Madame L'Amour. Both of them, incidentally, blackmailed me for huge sums of money, the Countess and the prostitute. I expected better of the prostitute."

TRIVIA

Was partly filmed at the real house of the Kaiser at Huize Doorn.

F

A FANTASTIC WOMAN

(Una Mujer Fantastica)

A compelling character study that proves politically necessary, co-writer/director Sebastián Lelio's *A Fantastic Woman* tells of the life of a Chilean trans woman named Marina (Daniela Vega, a transgender actress). The script details a particularly humiliating point in her life, of when she is not allowed to properly grieve her former lover, an older cisgender man named Orlando (Francisco Reyes), after he suddenly passes away. Orlando's family, including his wife and son, prevent her from attending the wake, the funeral, and do not give her the general courtesy of being able to grieve for Orlando publicly. Vega's performance, as unwavering as her character trying to navigate her place in an unfair world, is a surrogate into a societal tragedy. As Lelio's script becomes more than its goal to provide representation of a transgender person's experience and anxieties, *A Fantastic Woman* acutely reveals itself to be just another episode in the life of someone who unjustly seems so foreign to others.

There is a curious complication in this script from Lelio and Gonzalo Maza, as it takes a lead character in a very polarizing position—that of being the other woman—but proclaims that the animosity towards them is more than just their involvement with infidelity. Marina's complicated relationship with Orlando becomes a scapegoat for their pure dislike of Marina's sexuality. *A Fantastic Woman* raises questions about the privilege of occupying space both physically and emotionally, and details how there are people who are still provided neither, in spite of their own flesh and blood pain.

Delicacy is a defining currency with the spare events of this film as Lelio sharply creates the image of a loving relationship, showing the viewer Orlando, and then introducing them to Marina the way Orlando might have fallen for her: singing on a stage, commanding everyone's attention, radiating. In the acutely edited moments that follow, accompanied by a perfect soundtrack match—"Time" by the Alan Parsons Project—*A Fantastic Woman* creates a striking image of a pure, universal love: slow dancing, low-key birthday celebrations, passion of all forms.

This is a very tall emotional height from which Lelio drops the viewer, with many finely calibrated emotional scenes that follow. After Orlando has died and Marina has been left alone, Lelio lets the movie itself become a type of tragedy where compassion is in short supply. As Marina tries to communicate or even connect with members of Orlando's family, she is met with a vile hatred: her sexuality is insulted, and later she is physically assaulted after being kidnapped. Her choices with her body and identity are also questioned by nosy bureaucrats, like police officers. The amount of empathy that people have for her can seemingly be graded on a point scale, with Orlando's family having the lowest rankings: they do not recognize her as someone that Orlando loved, or as a fellow human being at all.

While Marina hits each tenuous interaction head-on, trying to shield her self-esteem in the process, Lelio makes numerous expressive but flat moments out of her daydreams; after Orlando passes, she sometimes sees him as if he were flesh-and-blood in the room, or later there's a mini dancing sequence that has her flying up to the ceiling right to the camera. Soundtrack cues can be hit and miss too, as when Lelio has Vega driving through

Santiago, listening to the chorus of "(You Make Me Feel Like) A Natural Woman" by Aretha Franklin. These directorial choices lean on how much Lelio's vision is not all that new itself aside from its heroic representation; even as a story about grief, *A Fantastic Woman* adds little to the visual storytelling of such a personal process.

But while the movie can run a bit thin as a character study, it has the talent in front of and behind the camera to make the movie more intricate than its obvious political stance. Vega is a magnetic presence as she deals with the grief as if she were completely alone in the world, while acting like a second-class citizen as if everyone else's needs were more important than hers. While Lelio rarely resists inserting a glaringly poetic situation (such as a tracking shot that has her almost being blown over by intense wind on a street), her performance is vividly internal, mixing sadness with anger as told with heartbreaking stoicism.

The gesture of representation of that of a trans woman's talent and perspective is a distinct pitch to be reckoned with; *A Fantastic Woman* entered the history books as soon as it was released given the way that it adds one more title to the minimal amount of movies like it. And encouragingly, the film received an Oscar® nomination in 2018 for Best Foreign Language Film. But in an arguably even bigger feat, Vega was chosen to speak at the very awards ceremony, a historical moment for transgender people to be seen and given that stage. She was the first openly transgender presenter for the ceremony, creating a factoid that was a long time coming. Fittingly, her star vehicle *A Fantastic Woman* notes how far all of world cinema has come in sharing the lives that are not just those of cisgender heterosexual white men, while grounded by its tragedy of a world without empathy.

Nick Allen

CREDITS

Marina Vidal: Daniela Vega
Orlando: Francisco Reyes
Gabo: Luis Gnecco
Sonia: Aline Kuppenheim
Bruno: Nicolas Saavedra
Origin: United States
Language: Spanish
Released: 2018
Production: Juan de Dios Larrain, Pablo Larrain, Sebastian Lelio, Gonzalo Maza; Fabula, Participant Media L.L.C.; released by Sony Pictures Classics
Directed by: Sebastian Lelio
Written by: Sebastian Lelio; Gonzalo Maza
Cinematography by: Benjamin Echazarreta
Music by: Matthew Herbert
Sound: Daniel Iribarren
Editing: Soledad Salfate
Costumes: Muriel Parra
Production Design: Estefania Larrain
MPAA rating: R
Running time: 100 minutes

REVIEWS

Bahr, Lindsey. *Associated Press.* January 31, 2018.
Chang, Justin. *Los Angeles Times.* November 15, 2017.
Greenblatt, Leah. *Entertainment Weekly.* January 26, 2017.
Hornaday, Ann. *Washington Post.* February 7, 2018.
Kang, Inkoo. *TheWrap.* January 31, 2018.
Lodge, Guy. *Variety.* October 11, 2017.
Taylor, Kate. *Globe and Mail.* February 9, 2018.
Vishnevetsky, Ignatiy. *The A.V. Club.* November 14, 2017.
Walsh, Katie. *Tribune News Service.* February 2, 2018.
Yoshida, Emily. *New York Magazine/Vulture.* November 14, 2017.

TRIVIA

This is Chile's submission to the Foreign Language Film Award of the 90th Annual Academy Awards.

AWARDS

Oscars 2017: Foreign Film
Ind. Spirit 2018: Foreign Film
Nominations:
Golden Globes 2018: Foreign Film

THE FATE OF THE FURIOUS

New roads ahead.
—Movie tagline
Family no more.
—Movie tagline
The ride isn't over.
—Movie tagline
Ride or die. Remember.
—Movie tagline

Box Office: $226 Million

The grandest image of any *Fast and Furious* movie can be found in the middle of the franchise's eighth installment, *The Fate of the Furious.* An endless amount of cars have been dumped from a multiple-story parking lot like crumbs swiped off a table, piling on top of each other and bursting into flames on the street below. The frame is filled with destroyed automobiles, some digitally added and some not, and the visual is akin to the expressive chaos of a Jackson Pollock painting. It is this type of commitment to chaos that has kept the franchise's thrills at full speed, and this very value that makes this seventh sequel such a blast.

Directed by F. Gary Gray, the movie begins with a sequence of similar ridiculousness, cluing viewers back into the type of world that many have imitated throughout the years but few have achieved. Vin Diesel returns as muscle head messiah Dom, the stone-faced, lunk-headed spiritual guide of the series. This time he is in Cuba, as if blessing them with their presence and exclaiming how great the people and its place are (the movie does have the honore of of being one of the first Hollywood productions in Cuba since the embargo). The sequence goes as one might expect—Dom wins a race by driving a flaming truck backwards before the makeshift bomb explodes—but it shows the type of iconography that Diesel has created for himself as someone who has long been the franchise, even when he was only a cameo in one of the installments (*The Fast and the Furious: Tokyo Drift* [2006]). In this movie, he reaches levels of self-piety that can only be equated to fellow action star Steven Seagal giving a long-winded speech about the environment in his directorial debut, *On Deadly Ground* (1994), and with the same corrosive lack of self-awareness.

Diesel takes that importance to his own arc in the story, which has him—gasp—going rogue against his small army of vehicle-driving friends, violating the franchise's bread and butter value of family. However, it is in the dumb brilliance of these movies that the reason he is turning against his family is indeed family, as his captor, Cipher (played by Charlize Theron, in not-so-menacing white dreadlocks), has kidnapped Dom's illegitimate son and his wife Elena (Elsa Pataky) and made Dom appear brainwashed to keep the baby boy alive. This twist proves to be a fine touch to this story and to the series, a massive twist that aligns to the series' goal of being a macho soap opera, where the storytelling has as much grease as the engines.

This betrayal is lumped in with Cipher's goal to attain some type of Doomsday device that has been lazily taken from the action villain handbook, including the God's Eye, a program that can seemingly hack everything. This includes cars both parked and with people inside them (as in that Pollock-esque carnage) and later on a dormant nuclear submarine, during a climax that continues the "how-did-they-produce-this" awe of the later franchise installments. There is a certain thrill in watching these movies and pondering the many steps of preproduction and production, and *The Fate of the Furious* achieves that with extensive sequences in New York City and in Siberia.

With Dom helping Cipher in her goal to become all-powerful, the franchise's team of road superheroes tries to stop them, with the help of an FBI agent named Mr. Nobody (Kurt Russell) and his constantly upstaged assistant, played by Scott Eastwood. Returning to the series are Michelle Rodriguez, Dwayne Johnson, Tyrese Gibson, Nathalie Emmanuel, and Jason Statham among others. As the most burly of the bunch, Johnson and Statham have a breakout from jail scene that proves to be a film highlight, carrying over the flipping-cameras and in-your-face fighting of James Wan's *Furious 7* (2015) while in the middle of a dubstep-scored prison riot. Not unlike the characters in *The Goonies* (1985), this batch of characters set out on an adventure that leaves them in the same state of awe as the audience, making it all the more believable when they are driving and smashing up parts of New York City, or racing a nuclear submarine in Siberia.

Gray steps into his largest action movie yet, though he has a history with the likes of *Set It Off* (1996), *The Italian Job* (2003), and *Law Abiding Citizen* (2009). Here, he continues the allegiance to the massive and relatively silly, but he does not have the same eye as his predecessor, Justin Lin (director of four previous films in the series). Gray is able to create scenarios that work within the logic of the series cars slingshotting at each other on New York City streets, that chase with a nuclear submarine—but there is a lack of tension to it. Gray has the right sensibilities but one wishes he pushed the spectacle a bit more, or did not align to use so much CGI with scenes that pop with practical destruction.

Still, there is an abundant amount of small thrills to be had in this story, which sees returning franchise screenwriter Chris Morgan whipping up more massive action set-pieces, and intentionally laugh-out-loud tacky dialogue. A few bits of pleasure: the on-screen emasculation of an actor descended from Clint Eastwood, Charlize Theron and her army of hackers looking like they all work at Starbucks, Helen Mirren getting the token PG-13 F-bomb, a crowd-pleasing sequence where Jason Statham carries a baby around a small plane while beating up bad guys. There is also a running theme of animal-based metaphors, with Cipher comically warning Dom at one point, "I'm the crocodile at the watering hole."

Creating comedy and thrills, often in the same sequence, the movie does err towards the gravity of irony, in that eventually ridiculousness can only be played for so long before everything must become sarcastic. Like the James Bond movies of the Roger

Moore era, the *Fast and Furious* films are quickly becoming cheeky and jokes of themselves, even more than they were with their frosted tips and rap-metal mise en scène in Rob Cohen's franchise starter, *The Fast and the Furious* (2001). This does not take away from the fun of the series, as the jokes are often amusing and the action scenes are indeed incredible, but it does bring to question sincerity to character and spectacle, which was the fuel injection that Lin brought into the movies, and changed the game in a way not much different than Christopher Nolan's take on Batman forever changed how people saw superhero films. *The Fate of the Furious* seems to be gloating that it is the goofiest movie to ever make a billion dollars.

As of this printing, the *Fast and Furious* franchise is working on a ninth film, of which director Justin Lin has heroically decided to return. Along with his efforts, the question always remains with these films of where they can go next. Outer space is often joked about as the final frontier for this franchise and its characters, but *The Fate of the Furious* proves the plausibility of such a concept. If the series can maintain its sincerity to its characters, and treat them with a sense of adventure that even they are surprised about, the possibilities are endless. Given the imagination the series has, along with its sense of humor, going to outer space seems like destiny for these characters.

Nick Allen

CREDITS

Dominic Toretto: Vin Diesel
Hobbs: Dwayne "The Rock" Johnson
Deckard Shaw: Jason Statham
Letty: Michelle Rodriguez
Roman Pearce: Tyrese Gibson
Origin: United States
Language: English, Russian
Released: 2017
Production: Michael Fottrell, Neal H. Moritz, Vin Diesel, Chris Morgan; One Race Films, Original Film; released by Universal Pictures Inc.
Directed by: F. Gary Gray
Written by: Chris Morgan
Cinematography by: Stephen Windon
Music by: Brian Tyler
Sound: Peter Brown; Mark P. Stoeckinger
Editing: Paul Rubell; Christian Wagner
Art Direction: Desma Murphy
Costumes: Sanja Milkovic Hays; Marlene Stewart
Production Design: Bill Brzeski
MPAA rating: PG-13
Running time: 136 minutes

REVIEWS

Adams, Sam. *Slate*. April 13, 2017.
Chang, Justin. *Los Angeles Times*. April 13, 2017.
Dargis, Manohla. *New York Times*. April 12, 2017.
Ehrlich, David. *IndieWire*. April 9, 2017.
Kim, Kristen Yoonsoo. *Village Voice*. April 13, 2017.
MacDonald, Moira. *Seattle Times*. April 12, 2017.
Merry, Stephanie. *Washington Post*. April 13, 2017.
Morgenstern, Joe. *Wall Street Journal*. April 13, 2017.
Vishnevetsky, Ignatiy. *The A.V. Club*. April 12, 2017.
Yoshida, Emily. *New York Magazine/Vulture*. April 12, 2017.

QUOTES

Hobbs: "With all due respect captain, when this whole thing is over, we're gonna find a location and I'm gonna knock your teeth so far down your throat you're gonna stick a toothbrush right up your a** to brush them."

TRIVIA

This is the first film in the franchise to include two Oscar winners--Helen Mirren (uncredited) and Charlize Theron.

FATHER FIGURES

The ultimate paternity quest.
—Movie tagline

Box Office: $17.4 Million

Justin Malen's screenplay for *Father Figures* wants to have it both ways. It wants to be a ribald, nothing-is-sacred comedy, and it wants to be a genuine, heartfelt look at the bond between a pair of brothers and the meaning of what truly makes a family. In what should fail to come as a surprise to anyone, the movie is a tonal mess that is neither funny nor sincere in its emotional payoff.

The plot is a routine road trip story, in which Ed Helms and Owen Wilson play brothers Peter and Kyle Reynolds, who are polar opposites in attitude, success, and outlook. Whatever could be mined from the central relationship is mostly dismissed for a string of gags, based on encounters with strangers and, more importantly, a series of men, whom the pair believe could be their biological father. The strangers and suspected fathers are extremes unto themselves—from a former professional football player, to a con man with a proclivity toward angry outbursts, to a veterinarian played by Christopher Walken.

Before any of this unfolds, though, there is the introduction to the fraternal twins. Peter is divorced and practically unwelcome in the lives of his family. He is a doctor by trade—a profession that he sought after learning that the man whom he believed was his father had died from colon cancer. Peter's first scene is of giving a patient a prostate examination, and it is not a good sign that Malen provides exactly every joke about the scene that an audience would expect.

Kyle caught a financial windfall by chance while walking the beach near his home in Hawaii. His figure adorns the labels of bottles of a successful brand of barbeque sauce. He does not have to work a regular job, and he has just become engaged to Kaylani (Jessica Gomes). She is pregnant, and Kyle tells the news to his and Peter's mother Helen (Glenn Close) by telling her that she is finally going to be a grandmother, even though she has been one for more a decade with Peter's son.

Peter discovers Helen's decades-old lie about the identity of the men's father (when he sees the allegedly dead man on his favorite TV show). That sends the brothers on a trip to Miami to see the man who probably is their actual father: former football player Terry Bradshaw (who plays himself).

One of the key running jokes of the movie involves Helen's sexual past, which means that just about every male character who talks about her ends up discussing her proclivities in bed. The judgment toward the character is at least offset by the awkwardness of having Bradshaw and, later, one of his friends (played by Ving Rhames) talk about a former lover's sexual performance to two complete strangers—only being ashamed of sharing such private matters when the two learn that they are speaking to the woman's sons.

For the most part, that is the central gag surrounding the brothers' encounter with Bradshaw, who realizes that he could not be their father after playing catch with Peter for a while. The next suspected father is Roland (J.K. Simmons), who points a gun at them—even after learning why they are visiting him—and framing them for an attempted car robbery. A diversion with a hitchhiker (played by Katt Williams, offering the dimmest of bright spots) makes it feel as if Malen has run out of ideas after the second suspected father, and the entire enterprise becomes discomforting when Peter and Kyle meet the third possible man. They arrive for his wake, and the movie spends an inordinate amount of time on the possibility that Peter has had sex with a woman (played by Kate Aselton) who might be his half-sister.

In between all of these contrived scenarios and half-baked gags, Malen and director Lawrence Sher attempt to develop the relationship between Peter and Kyle, since the movie's ultimate goal has little to do with humor (one could argue the rest of the movie has little to do with humor as well) and everything to do with that bond. One almost appreciates how the final encounter (with Walken's character, who is in a relationship with his much-younger assistant [played by Ali Wong]—that is the entirety of the joke, really) results in a complete about-face in the movie's tone and intentions.

One could appreciate it, if only the movie cared half as much about developing likeable, believable characters and jokes with actual punch lines (as well as setups, for that matter) as it did trying to milk its final revelation for unearned pathos. Nothing is earned in *Father Figures*, though, because its attempts at both humor and emotion are half-hearted at best.

Mark Dujsik

CREDITS

Mr. Jensen: Robert Jon Mello
Peter Reynolds: Ed Helms
Annie: Retta
Ethan: Zachary Haven
Katherine: Mary Grill
Origin: United States
Language: English
Released: 2017
Production: Ali Bell, Broderick Johnson, Andrew A. Kosove, Ivan Reitman; Alcon Entertainment L.L.C., DMG Entertainment and Media Company Ltd., Montecito Picture Co.; released by Warner Bros. Pictures
Directed by: Lawrence Sher
Written by: Justin Malen
Cinematography by: John Lindley
Music by: Rob Simonsen
Sound: Perry Robertson
Editing: Dana E. Glauberman
Art Direction: Jeremy Woolsey
Production Design: Stephen H. Carter
MPAA rating: R
Running time: 113 minutes

REVIEWS

Allen, Nick. *RogerEbert.com*. December 22, 2017.
DeFore, John. *Hollywood Reporter*. December 21, 2017.
Goodykoontz, Bill. *Arizona Republic*. December 21, 2017.
Hassenger, Jesse. *The A.V. Club*. December 21, 2017.
Henderson, Eric. *Slant Magazine*. December 22, 2017.
Kenigsberg, Ben. *New York Times*. December 21, 2017.
Meyer, Carla. *San Francisco Chronicle*. December 21, 2017.
Orndorf, Brian. *Blu-Ray.com*. December 22, 2017.
Walsh, Katie. *Chicago Tribune*. December 21, 2017.
Whittaker, Richard. *Austin Chronicle*. December 29, 2017.

TRIVIA

The original title os this film was *Bastards.*

FERDINAND

You will bullieve.
—Movie tagline
Built to fight. Born to love.
—Movie tagline

Box Office: $80.7 Million

In its most effective sections, it is clear that *Ferdinand* comes from a children's book. The book is the 1936 tale *The Story of Ferdinand,* written by Munro Leaf and illustrated by Robert Lawson, which was previously adapted as a short film, entitled *Ferdinand the Bull* (1938), from Walt Disney's animation house.

Simplicity is key to a good children's book and short film. The modern adaptation, a computer-animated feature from Blue Sky Studios and director Carlos Saldanha, begins and climaxes with relative simplicity. In between, the screenplay (by Robert L. Baird, Tim Federle, and Brad Copeland) overburdens the simple, straightforward story of a non-violent bull with far too many attempts to please and appease the movie's core audience.

The modest tale has been transformed into a generic comedy showcase for a string of eccentric side players and a few sequences of action—mainly an early chase sequence and another extended, four-tier one that leads up to the final standoff. Lost in all of these extraneous characters and action-driven diversions is the central figure, the pacifist bull named Ferdinand (voiced with surprising gentleness by former professional wrestler-turned-actor John Cena).

The character has been seen through a few lenses in the decades since the publication of Leaf and Lawson's book (an obviously pacifist response to mounting political tensions in the world at the time of its publication and, in more recent times, a subversive allegory about sexuality), yet the screenwriters and Saldanha simply take the character for what he is: a bull who refuses to fight, despite his substantial size and the social pressures placed upon him. There is nothing political or subversive about the movie's Ferdinand, except, perhaps, as a means to put an end to the "sport" of bullfighting, by way of a sympathetic figure and an unexpected acknowledgement of the practice's cruelty. It is still a regular occurrence in Spain, although one imagines a younger generation that sees this movie might contribute to the ever-dwindling crowds that view the violent blood sport in Spain these days.

The basic setup of the original story remains. The young Ferdinand (voice of Colin H. Murphy) smells and cares for flowers, while his fellow bull calves play by butting heads, imagining themselves growing up to become fearsome and fearless warriors in the "glory" of the bullfighting ring. The adult bulls do the same for the famous matador El Primero (voice of Miguel Ángel Silvestre), who arrives at the ranch looking for his next challenge. The bullfighter chooses Ferdinand's father (voice of Jeremy Sisto). In a moment that shows the filmmakers are capable of telling this story with a subtle touch, the fate of Ferdinand's father is revealed in a melancholy view of a returning trailer, empty of any sign of its former occupant.

Ferdinand runs away from the ranch (the first of the movie's several chase sequences), finds himself at a family farm, and is raised for a few years by Nina (voiced as a younger girl by Julia Saldanha [the director's daughter] and as an older one by Lily Day). In those years, he grows to a tremendous size, and after an unintentionally destructive incident during the nearby town's annual flower festival, Ferdinand is captured and returned to the ranch of his calf years.

At this point, the entire tone and purpose of the movie changes. Ferdinand's fellow calves at the ranch have grown, and as bulls, they possess easily identifiable and often comical personalities. Valiente (voice of Bobby Cannavale), like his father (also voiced by Cannavale), wants to become a champion bull in the ring and is antagonistic toward Ferdinand. Guapo (voice of retired football player Peyton Manning) becomes nauseated whenever he's under pressure, and Bones (voice of Anthony Anderson) is a scrawny bull. The newer bulls are Angus (voice of David Tennant), who possesses a thick Scottish brogue and cannot see anything through his thick hair, and Maquina (voice of Tim Nordquist), who may be a robot or may simply behave like one.

The rest of the ranch's characters are equally broad or broader. There are a trio of thieving hedgehogs (voiced by Gina Rodriguez, Daveed Diggs, and Gabriel Iglesias), a trio of German show horses (voiced by Flula Borg, Sally Phillips, and Boris Kodjoe) who dance on two legs, and one wildly peculiar "calming goat" named Lupe (voice of Kate McKinnon). McKinnon's vocal performance is up to the task, yet one constantly suspects that the additional comic sidekicks, comrades, and bit players are, at best, a distraction from the main story or, at worst, a calculated effort on the part of the filmmakers to appeal to children with a near-nonstop deluge of wackiness (the horse-bull dance-off is downright embarrassing in this regard).

The heart of the story is, not necessarily Ferdinand's dedication to non-violence, but his kindness toward all of these animals who either dislike him or look at him with confusion. After the long slog of shenanigans at the ranch and the lengthy chase sequence that follows—it starts on the ranch, arrives at a train station, and ends in the streets of Madrid, while having no purpose for the overall narrative—it comes as a surprise that the climax in the bullfighting ring (after Ferdinand learns the terrible truth of what happens to the bulls by seeing a wall lined and rowed with trophy horns) follows through on that thread, while still showing the brutality of bullfighting.

This is a tricky accomplishment, and like the movie's opening scenes, the sequence shows what *Ferdinand* could have been. Both sections trust the character, the simplicity of the foundational tale, and, most importantly, the audience. The rest of the movie displays little of that trust.

Mark Dujsik

CREDITS

Ferdinand: John Cena
Valiente's Father/Valiente: Bobby Cannavale
Voice of Moreno: Raul Esparza
Voice of Young Valiente: Jack Gore
Voice of Young Guapo: Jet Jurgensmeyer
Origin: United States
Language: English
Released: 2017
Production: Bruce Anderson, John Davis, Lori Forte, Lisa Stetler; Blue Sky Studios; released by Twentieth Century Fox Animation
Directed by: Carlos Saldanha
Written by: Robert L. Baird; Tim Federle; Brad Copeland
Cinematography by: Renato Falcao
Music by: John Powell
Sound: Randy Thom
Editing: Harry Hitner
Art Direction: Thomas Cardone
MPAA rating: PG
Running time: 108 minutes

REVIEWS

Bell, Josh. *Las Vegas Weekly.* December 14, 2017.
Henderson, Eric. *Slant Magazine.* December 13, 2017.
Ide, Wendy. *Screen International.* December 7, 2017.
Johanson, MaryAnn. *Flick Filosopher.* December 11, 2017.
Kenigsberg, Ben. *New York Times.* December 14, 2017.
Murthi, Vikram. *The A.V. Club.* December 13, 2017.
Savlov, Marc. *Austin Chronicle.* December 15, 2017.
Tobias, Scott. *NPR.* December 14, 2017.
Walsh, Katie. *Chicago Tribune.* December 15, 2017.
Wloszczyna, Susan. *RogerEbert.com.* December 15, 2017.

QUOTES

Lupe: "I can't wait to show you to the rest of the guys! They're gonna fertilize the yard."

TRIVIA

Despite being released in 3D, the film's first trailer nor it's poster mention a 3D release.

AWARDS

Nominations:

Oscars 2017: Animated Film
Golden Globes 2018: Animated Film, Song ("Home")

FIFTY SHADES DARKER

Every fairy tale has a dark side
—Movie tagline
Slip into something a shade darker.
—Movie tagline

Box Office: $114.6 Million

An observant filmmaker can use a narrative's pace and structure to mirror the trajectory of an intense physical and emotional experience. Consider how Adrian Lyne navigates curiosity that becomes different forms of fear in erotic thrillers like *Fatal Attraction* (1987), *Indecent Proposal* (1993), and *Unfaithful* (2002). The stories unfold in tandem with the characters' passions, heating or cooling, cascading and fraying. Nothing is simple or easily resolved.

Fifty Shades Darker, on the other hand, represents a parallel between narrative and sex in that the movie is all build-up and no payoff. Whether capturing supporting characters who generate tension only to disappear with stunning ease or drooling over intimate foreplay and then shrugging at what happens afterward, director James Foley, taking over for *Fifty Shades of Grey* (2015) helmer Sam Taylor-Johnson, seems remarkably disinterested in consequence. Of course, Niall Leonard's adaptation of E.L. James' novel largely hinges on wishy-washy mixed signals between its main characters, so perhaps the film's dismissive tendencies are a feeble effort not to overshadow the goop at its center. In other words, logic is beside the point when mediocre fodder better suited for the 1 a.m. slot on Showtime becomes an international phenomenon.

The original film focused on ashamed dominance aficionado Christian Grey (Jamie Dornan) pressuring

Anastasia Steele (Dakota Johnson) to sign a literal sexual contract, which might be the epitome of a turn-off. Daring to ask the not-at-all engrossing question "Will two people who already have had a bunch of sex have some more?" the sequel creates a revolving door of Anastasia suggesting she cannot be what Christian wants her to be, Christian saying he loves her more than his fetishes, Anastasia tiptoeing toward what he wants anyway and then pulling back, requiring him to profess his love even more. This is a good time to remember that James' books originally began as *Twilight* fan fiction. Arguably the most important parallel there is both series' emphasis on a bland female lead, identified as the target of a supposedly charismatic man's affections even though she possesses the personality of the grass surrounding the Space Needle in the film's Seattle setting. To capitalize on the, ahem, gray area in its characters's wants and needs and consider how sexual compatibility informs long-term connection, *Fifty Shades Darker* needs an understanding of what brings these two together outside of one's interest in spanking and the other's latent openness to being spanked.

Alas, conversation between these two complexity pits typically go like this: "What do you want, Anastasia? If we're going to communicate you have to tell me." / "I want you." Then, a very short time after, Christian seems to need more specific information, so he asks, "What do you want, Anastasia?" She responds, "I want all of you." Not that it was ever in doubt that these two want to spend some naked time together. The issue is that they have nothing else to say or do, and the pathetic attempts to create this bond, mostly through Christian addressing childhood trauma, still fail to remove these ice sculptures from their protective frozen casing. The film certainly does not do enough to convince that this is a traumatized man-baby given the freedom to feel only through an ideal partner who knows how to listen and possesses more substance than his past submissives.

Along with Christian's heartbroken ex-spanking receiver Leila (Bella Heathcote) and Anastasia's sexually harassing boss Jack (Eric Johnson), Elena represents one leg of the aforementioned tripod of cheap pot-stirrers, popping up occasionally to approximate drama with the subtlety of a paddle to the skin. If anyone involved in this installment believes these tangential and ultimately disposable people justify the "Darker" element of the title, perhaps they have not heard of the words "Duller" and "Drearier."

In isolated moments, the film threatens to work up a mild sweat. Christian observes Anastasia in lingerie, getting ready, and she asks, "You're just going to stand there gawking?" "Yeah," he responds. "I think I might." That is reasonably hot. She feels sexy. He wants her. That works. The same goes for the eroticism of his movement on a pommel horse, and Christian pretending to tie his shoes in an elevator and then running his hands up Anastasia's leg and under her dress in a public place. He forces her to contain herself, and the film understands the intensity of the sexual power dynamic at play.

Yet so much of this story comprises exchanges like her asking, "Why do you have my bank account details?" and then dropping it. The predatory nature of their relationship makes this not so much a "will they/won't they" as a case of "they should not and nobody wants them to." Consequently, Johnson seems more embarrassed to participate this time as she is supposed to pretend to be persuaded by Christian elaborating on his marriage proposal only with the cliché, "Because I want to spend every second of the rest of my life with you." First of all, the rest-of life-thing usually does come along with marriage. And even the most in-love couples know that every second is too much.

With even a low-to-moderate amount of maturity and intelligence, *Fifty Shades Darker* could have been a reasonably insightful, or at least honest and dramatically engaging portrait of fetishes and love operating together. How does what each of these characters will and will not do impact how they see each other? Does it, and does it have to, especially when dealing with the more mundane elements of daily life and commitment? After all, it is not as if theaters are full of domestically-set, studio-driven features that take a frank look at little-discussed elements of sexuality and apply those to long-term relationships.

Instead, it takes a simultaneously giggling and sex-negative approach to its indulgences, proud of going there but ultimately ashamed of the content. That is, however, perfectly encapsulated by the inclusion of a moody, female-led cover of Coldplay's "The Scientist," a song whose mood suggests it might be about something haunting and juicy, only to lead somewhere basic and boring.

Matt Pais

CREDITS

Anastasia Steele: Dakota Johnson
Christian Grey: Jamie Dornan
Jack Hyde: Eric Johnson
Kate Kavanagh: Eloise Mumford
Leila: Bella Heathcote
Elena Lincoln: Kim Basinger
Origin: United States
Language: English
Released: 2017

Production: Dana Brunetti, Michael De Luca, E.L. James, Marcus Viscidi; Perfect World Pictures; released by Universal Pictures Inc.
Directed by: James Foley
Written by: Niall Leonard
Cinematography by: John Schwartzman
Music by: Danny Elfman
Music Supervisor: Dana Sano
Editing: Richard Francis-Bruce
Art Direction: Jeremy Stanbridge
Costumes: Shay Cunliffe
Production Design: Nelson Coates
MPAA rating: R
Running time: 118 minutes

REVIEWS

Anderson, Melissa. *Village Voice.* February 10, 2017.
Bennett, Laura. *Slate.* February 16, 2017.
DeFore, John. *Hollywood Reporter.* February 9, 2017.
Gray, Christopher. *Slant Magazine.* February 9, 2017.
Macdonald, Moira. *Seattle Times.* February 9, 2017.
Rife, Katie. *The A.V. Club.* February 9, 2017.
Roeper, Richard. *Chicago Sun-Times.* February 9, 2017.
Truitt, Brian. *USA Today.* February 9, 2017.
Turan, Kenneth. *Los Angeles Times.* February 9, 2017.
Zacharek, Stephanie. *Time.* February 9, 2017.

QUOTES

Christian Grey: "I hope you're not a sore loser."
Anastasia Steele: "That depends on how hard you spank me."

TRIVIA

Ana's line, "I expect you to call me Ana. I don't expect you to fetch me coffee unless you're getting some for yourself, and the rest we'll just make up as we go along" is the same line spoken by Tess (Melanie Griffith, Dakota Johnson's mother) in *Working Girl* (1988).

AWARDS

Golden Raspberries 2017: Worst Remake/Sequel, Worst Support. Actress (Basinger)

Nominations:

Golden Raspberries 2017: Worst Actor (Dornan), Worst Actress (Johnson), Worst Director (Foley), Worst Picture, Worst Screenplay

FILM STARS DON'T DIE IN LIVERPOOL

Love, just like in the movies.
—Movie tagline

Box Office: $246,262

On paper, the notion of a film about the tumultuous life of actress Gloria Grahame would seem to be a no-brainer. Despite winning a Best Supporting Actress Oscar® for *The Bad and the Beautiful* (1952) and eventually becoming a cult favorite through her appearances in such film noir favorites as *Crossfire* (1947), *In a Lonely Place* (1950), *Sudden Fear* (1952), and *The Big Heat* (1953), Hollywood's unwillingness to see her as anything other than the prototypical tough broad (which intensified following criticism of her appearance as Ado Annie in the screen version of *Oklahoma!* (1955) and her tumultuous personal life that included four marriages—her second being to filmmaker Nicholas Ray and her fourth to Ray's son, with whom she reportedly began an affair when he was her 13-year-old stepson—pretty much derailed her career by the end of the Fifties and she spent the last two decades of her life grinding out a living via television, the stage and the occasional B movie. And yet, by reducing its focus to the last couple of years of her life and centering around her relationship with a struggling young British actor, *Film Stars Don't Die in Liverpool* reduces Grahame's life and work to the status of a bland and confusingly recounted romantic weepie—the kind of film that Grahame herself never appeared in—that is so innocuous and uninterested in her that she often comes across as an afterthought to what is theoretically meant to be her story.

The film opens in England in 1981 as Gloria (Annette Bening) is backstage preparing for a performance in *The Glass Menagerie* when she collapses in her dressing room. Instead of going to the hospital, she contacts aspiring young actor Peter Turner (Jamie Bell), with whom she began a passionate but short-lived romance after the two met when she was in town for another stage performance two years earlier, and asks if she can stay with his family in their ramshackle Liverpool home. Peter's mother and father (Julie Walters and Kenneth Cranham) are delighted to see Gloria again but it doesn't take them long to see what their son either cannot, or will not, acknowledge—that Gloria is suffering from something far worse than the attack of gas that she has claimed. The film then alternates between flashbacks of their earlier days together, culminating with the circumstances behind their breakup, with the present, in which Peter tries to help Gloria get through what are clearly her final days in the manner that she wishes.

The early scenes of *Film Stars Don't Die in Liverpool,* which has been adapted from Turner's book of the same name by Matt Greenhalgh, are the best. The opening bit showing Gloria going through her various pre-stage rituals is a fascinating glimpse of the preparations that an actor deploys in order to steel themselves for a night trodding the boards. The scenes chronicling the beginning of the relationship between her and Peter are also a lot of fun as well—there is an especially winning bit showing the two sitting in a packed movie theater watching *Alien* (1979) that leaves her cackling with glee and him squirming in his seat during the chest-burster scene. Unfortunately, all the excitement and energy drains out roughly a half-hour or so into the proceedings and the rest is just an increasingly turgid collection of soap opera clichés that alternates between the two fighting and making up in flashbacks and Peter helplessly watching Gloria suffer from the cancer and peritonitis that would eventually kill her. The switching back and forth between past and present doesn't help matters much either—partly because the jumps forward and backwards end up killing whatever dramatic tension might have been building and partly because the differences between 1981 and 1979 are too negligible to notice and occasionally inspire confusion.

The big problem with the film is that the film never really demonstrates any real interest in the particulars of Grahame's life. Oh sure, little bits of trivia and references to her past are doled out here and there (when asked if anyone has ever told her that she looks like Lauren Bacall when she smokes, she tartly replies "Yes—Humphrey Bogart.") but for the most part, the screenplay never gets around to exploring who Grahame was or what made her tick. There is one ugly scene involving her mother (a one-scene cameo from Vanessa Redgrave) and sister that seems to exist only to drop a clunky reference to the scandal involving her former stepson but other than that, we never get a sense of who she was as a person, on or off the stage, and since she comes across as a cipher for the most part, it is virtually impossible to work up much of an interest in her relationship with Peter, which is portrayed here only in the most generic of terms. There must have been some kind of spark that united the two—even something as simple as being two fellow actors—but there is no sense of it on display here: throughout the film, they always seem to be meeting for the very first time.

The best thing about *Film Stars Don't Die in Liverpool* is, not surprisingly, the performance by Annette Bening, whose first notable screen performance in *The Grifters* (1990) was an overt homage to the kind of characters that Grahame herself played in her heyday. She does not do a precise imitation of Grahame, per se, she instead conjures up the essence of what made her such a compelling screen presence and which merges surprising well with her own particular performance style. She rightly dominates the proceedings, as Grahame herself no doubt did in real life, but she doesn't simply trample over them in the manner of a typical overbearing star turn. The trouble is, she doesn't really have to do that much to dominate things because *Film Stars Don't Die in Liverpool* is such weak tea that even the mousiest wallflower could steamroller the material with relatively little effort. Gloria Grahame deserves much more than to have her life boiled down into a generic May-December romantic melodrama and Annette Bening deserves better than to have to embody those cliches when she is capable of doing so much more. There is a great movie to be made about Gloria Grahame with a juicy role for Annette Bening—this one just is not it.

Peter Sobczynski

CREDITS

Peter Turner: Jamie Bell
Gloria Grahame: Annette Bening
Bella Turner: Julie Walters
Jeanne McDougall: Vanessa Redgrave
Joe Turner, Jr.: Stephen Graham
Origin: United States
Language: English
Released: 2017
Production: Barbara Broccoli, Colin Vaines; Eon Productions, Synchronistic Pictures; released by Sony Pictures Classics
Directed by: Paul McGuigan
Written by: Matt Greenhalgh
Cinematography by: Urszula Pontikos
Music by: J. Ralph
Sound: Paul Davies
Music Supervisor: Ian Neil
Editing: Nick Emerson
Art Direction: Tom Weaving
Production Design: Eve Stewart
MPAA rating: R
Running time: 105 minutes

REVIEWS

Catsoulis, Jeanette. *New York Times*. December 27, 2017.
Debruge, Peter. *Variety*. September 3, 2017.
Farber, Stephen. *Hollywood Reporter*. September 2, 2017.
Kang, Inkoo. *TheWrap*. December 22, 2017.
Lane, Anthony. *New Yorker*. January 8, 2018.
Morgenstern, Joe. *Wall Street Journal*. December 25, 2017.
Powers, John. *Vogue*. December 13, 2017.
Scherstuhl, Alan. *Village Voice*. December 29, 2017.
Taylor, Ella. *NPR*. December 28, 2017.
Turan, Kenneth. *Los Angeles Times*. December 25, 2017.

QUOTES

Peter Turner: "Has anyone ever told you that you look like Lauren Bacall when you smoke?"
Gloria Grahame: "Humphrey Bogart. And I didn't like it then either."

TRIVIA

This is only the second non-James Bond movie produced by Eon Productions, the first was *Call Me Bwana* (1963).

AWARDS

Nominations:

British Acad. 2017: Actor (Bell), Actress (Bening), Adapt. Screenplay

FIST FIGHT

After school. Parking lot. It's on.
—Movie tagline

Box Office: $32.2 Million

Fist Fight is an adult remake of *Three O'Clock High*, the 1987 film about a terrified teenager awaiting his demise at the hands of the bully who challenges him to an afterschool fight.

As the clock slowly ticks toward the intended fight time in *Three O'Clock High*, the bullied teen, Jerry (Casey Siemaszko) does everything in his power to avoid his confrontation with his potential destroyer, Buddy Revell (Richard Tyson). Some of Jerry's actions are ethically questionable, but the last acts of desperate men are rarely righteous. Eventually, Jerry pays Buddy with ill-gotten gains to cancel the fight, but when Buddy challenges his masculinity, Jerry demands the fight go on as planned. Buddy is eventually knocked out with his own brass knuckles.

Reimagining this story with adult actors does little to undo the adolescent nature of the material; if anything, it makes *Fist Fight* more jarringly childish. An attempt is made to offset this by framing the story within the confines of a much larger societal issue: the corruption of the public-school system. This is a nod to the thinly veiled McCarthyism attack in this film's primary influence, *High Noon* (1952). By reinstating the allegorical modus operandi absent from *Three O'Clock High*, director Richie Keen and screenwriters Van Robichaux and Evan Susser make a valiant grab for the brass ring of maturity.

Unfortunately, *Fist Fight* pitches most of its satire at crotch level, opting for cheap, dirty laughs instead of the stinging commentary the material demands. The mean-spiritedness of the film's humor is quite often effective but only superficially. One longs for a more daring satirist like director Michael Ritchie at the helm, or more ambitiously, for the caustic brilliance that buoyed the dismantling of the medical profession in Paddy Chayefsky and Arthur Hiller's *The Hospital* (1971). Instead, a plethora of dick jokes uneasily co-exist with the message that schools are failing their students.

The battle royale unfolding at 3 P.M. is between English teacher Andy Campbell (Charlie Day) and history teacher Ron Strickland (Ice Cube). It's the last day of school at Roosevelt High, and while the seniors concern themselves with all manner of horrific senior pranks, the teachers worry about the rapidly swinging budgetary ax that will leave many of them unemployed. Campbell has an obnoxious, whiny middle-school aged daughter Ally (Alexa Nisenson) and a very pregnant wife, Maggie (JoAnna Garcia), so the specter of unemployment hangs more perilously over his head than his opponent's.

There's no information on the personal life of Strickland, but there are plenty of possibly apocryphal stories about his toughness. *Fist Fight* presents these tales in amusing vignettes that place actor Ice Cube in scenes reminiscent of his prior work in *Boyz n the Hood* (1991), *Three Kings* (1999), and Walter Hill's *Trespass* (1992). In the hallowed halls of beloved cinematic teachers, Strickland is much closer to Morgan Freeman's bat-wielding Joe Clark than Sidney Poitier's benevolent Sir. The students are afraid of Strickland, though not enough to resist pranking him during his history class.

Strickland's prank is the catalyst for his fight with Andy Campbell. Strickland scares Campbell into helping him deal with the antiquated audiovisual equipment he's using to show a Civil War documentary. The prank is that one of the students, Neil (Austin Zajur) is controlling the VCR with his phone, turning off the video at inopportune moments. Campbell rats Neil out, resulting in Strickland destroying the offending cell phone. But when Neil gets another phone and executes the prank again, Strickland goes ballistic, knocking over equipment and descending upon Neil's evacuated desk with a fire ax. The students run out screaming. Campbell and Strickland are sent to the office of their frazzled boss, Principal Tyler (Dean Norris).

Principal Tyler has no sympathy for the one prank played on Strickland, because the students have been pranking him all day. They've glued items to his desk and painted his car before parking it in the hallway. Since neither Strickland nor Neil will talk about the ax incident, Principal Tyler dangles the carrot of job security in front of the silent Campbell. In a panic, Campbell tattles on Strickland. Had Campbell been as knowledgeable about rap as his daughter, he'd know that "snitches get stitches." And Strickland is a master at sutures.

"I'm going to fight you!" Strickland tells Campbell after Principal Tyler fires the history teacher. "3 o'clock, outside!" The beatdown is another appointment in Campbell's already busy schedule. He has three prank-filled classes to teach throughout the day. He has his job meeting with the superintendent of schools (Dennis

Haysbert) at 2:15. Campbell also is performing a father-daughter song and dance at Ally's school at 2:30. The dance is set to "Seasons of Love" from *Rent,* but Ally wants to change it to a Big Sean song. The dance moves are the same; the lyrics are most certainly not. Big Sean's song has five-hundred twenty-five thousand six-hundred curse words, including the one in the title. Ally plans to level all those no-no words at her talent show rival, Tricia.

Strickland's a lone wolf, but Campbell has his own clique of teachers who try to advise him during this stressful day. There's incompetent Coach Crawford (Tracy Morgan), who can't stop sleeping with his students' parents and guidance counselor Miss Holly (Jillian Bell), who can't stop sleeping with her students. Crawford and Holly seem more than happy to wallow in the same juvenile sex-based humor *Fist Fight* reserves for the senior class members, yet they still come off as more affable characters than the milquetoast Campbell does.

In fact, as Campbell becomes more desperate, he becomes less likable. He bribes Neil with a MacBook Pro to contradict the story Campbell told Principal Tyler, and when that backfires, he tries to get Strickland arrested for drug possession by planting Molly in his bag. To *Fist Fight*'s credit, it is completely aware of the optics of a White teacher trying to frame a Black one. The film is also cognizant of how Ice Cube's anger is being presented, so it gives Strickland the higher moral ground. Sure, he's perpetually pissed, but he really is more invested in the students and the school than any other teacher, Campbell included. "I don't need to be liked," Strickland tells Campbell in an early scene. "I need to educate!"

The desire to be liked fills a chamber in the bitter, cynical heart of *Fist Fight,* and the film wears that beating organ on its sleeve as big as day. Its ultimate message is uttered, in the film's funniest scene, by the 911 Operator (Kym Wheatley) who takes Campbell's call for help. "You're a grown man!" she tells him. "Go on and take that ass whippin'!" Like Ally's rap-assisted cussing out of Tricia, Campbell going through with the fight is an appearances-only proposition. Tricia still wins the talent show, and Strickland still wins the fight. Yet the film treats Ally and Campbell's actions as some form of sacrificial nobility, which is as absurd as it is American.

At least in Campbell's case, there's an optimistic silver lining. His throwdown with Strickland brings awareness to the awful plight of public school funding and maintenance. *Fist Fight* ends with the two antagonists joining forces to whip the school and its students into shape. It feels like a betrayal of the film's cynicism until one realizes that the nice guy wins in the end by defying his nature and becoming an ass.

Odie Henderson

CREDITS

Ron Strickland: Ice Cube
Andy Campbell: Charlie Day
Coach Crawford: Tracy Morgan
Holly: Jillian Bell
Ms. Monet: Christina Hendricks
Mehar: Kumail Nanjiani
Chris Cornwell
Origin: United States
Language: English
Released: 2017
Production: Dan Cohen, Max Greenfield, Shawn Levy, John Rickard; New Line Cinema L.L.C., Van Brand, Wrigley Pictures; released by Warner Bros. Pictures
Directed by: Richie Keen
Written by: Van Robichaux; Evan Susser
Cinematography by: Eric Alan Edwards
Music by: Dominic Lewis
Music Supervisor: Kier Lehman
Editing: Matthew Freund
Costumes: Denise Wingate
MPAA rating: R
Running time: 91 minutes

REVIEWS

Debruge, Peter. *Variety.* February 16, 2017.
DeFore, John. *The Hollywood Reporter.* February 16, 2017.
Ebiri, Bilge. *Village Voice.* February 22, 2017.
Goldstein, Gary. *Los Angeles Times.* February 16, 2017.
Moore, Roger. *Movie Nation.* February 16, 2017.
Roeper, Richard. *Chicago Sun-Times.* February 16, 2017.
Scott, A.O. *New York Times.* February 16, 2017.
Suzanne-Mayer, Dominick. *Consequence of Sound.* February 16, 2017.
Travers, Peter. *Rolling Stone.* February 17, 2017.
Watson, Keith. *Slant Magazine.* February 16, 2017.

QUOTES

Strickland: "Snitches get stitches."

TRIVIA

Andy's reaction to Holly hitting him is the same as Brad Pitt's reaction to being hit in *Fight Club* (1999): "You got me in the ear."

FIVE CAME BACK

They showed the war to the world.
—Movie tagline

Five Came Back is an excellent documentary based on the 2014 book *Five Came Back: A Story of Hollywood and the Second World War* by one of the world's finest writers on cinema, Mark Harris. As our current news cycle is dominated by talk of the influence propaganda can have on world affairs, this documentary clearly comes at a remarkably timely time, detailing the American military's attempts to use the cinema as a way to positively sway American morale as World War II came to their doorstep.

Directed by Laurent Bouzereau, who has directed a staggering 299 "documentaries" on cinema in the form of specials, home entertainment disc extras, shorts, and features such as this one, *Five Came Back* features the talking heads of modern-day master directors with footage and interviews of the five classic master directors it profiles from the World War II era. These classic directors were some of the most important of their generation (as well as of all time), and each voluntarily joined the war effort in order to create American wartime propaganda as well as document American efforts in World War II. The modern directors guiding viewers on this journey are Guillermo del Toro, Steven Spielberg, Paul Greengrass, Lawrence Kasdan, and Francis Ford Coppola who all give thoughts on the wartime works of Frank Capra (the *Why We Fight* series [1943-1945]), John Ford (*The Battle of Midway* [1942]), John Huston, and William Wyler (who both directed quite a few WWII documentaries but are scarcely in the film), and George Stevens, who is perhaps the most intriguing storyline in the entire film. While *Five Came Back* is ostensibly an educational film for fans of cinema and wartime history, one simply cannot help but be sucked in by what these five filmmakers voluntarily gave up in order to help the American war effort by using their specialized skillsets. While indeed, all five came back, they were all irrevocable changed.

As mentioned, *Five Came Back* kind of glosses over the stories of John Huston and William Wyler. To be fair, the effect his time in overseas battle zones had on Huston seemed to later manifest in his already growing pre-war ability to offer depth and empathy to his difficult fictional characters. Yet Huston's wartime documentaries also had a major focus on veterans returning from war with severe issues that were clearly Post Traumatic Stress Disorder (PTSD) before that was a recognized diagnosis and obviously, emotionally damaged soldiers kind of fly in the face of wartime cheerleading propaganda. Thus the military suppressed these films for many years until they were recently made available on Blu-ray under the title *Let There Be Light: John Huston's Wartime Documentaries* (2016). Director Wyler definitely also did his part, but his films seemingly did not have the impact of his four counterparts, even though it's revealed the man gave up most of his hearing by flying in war planes without proper ear protection. Sacrifices like that truly seem awesome when one pauses to think of any American director today, including the ones in the film, jumping into wartime fray.

Previous to watching *Five Came Back*, Frank Capra's *Why We Fight* series is probably the most common example used in film school to talk about American cinematic war efforts. Yet *Five Came Back* smartly focuses on just how hard Capra struggled to bring this amazing series to light. Straddling a line similar to one John Ford faced, Capra was a staunch conservative but also, deeply humanitarian. Thus, he had trouble with the many nuances war brings in terms of country versus humanitarianism. *Five Came Back* wisely dives into this area rather than retreading the *Why We Fight* series, including visual propaganda cribbed from German propaganda master, Leni Riefenstahl, which is all well-treaded territory. Equally shown as divided, *Five Came Back* shows the bullish John Ford desperately wanting to fit in with the big time soldiers but instead coming off as a bit of a wannabe. Perhaps ironically, the male protagonists in Ford's many masterpieces show very manly men, these men also end up feeling a bit out of place in society. Almost inverting the idea of the "Ford Male Protagonist," *Five Came Back* shows Ford as boisterous and very "male" in terms of his bravado and machismo yet also intimates that his non-military status was a bit castrating, as was his reaction to witnessing a massacre first-hand. That moment resulted in Ford retreating into a five-day drunken bender before being unceremoniously sent home from the war.

Even though all of these storylines are intriguing in their own way, it turns out George Stevens's storyline is the most compelling. Leaving behind a loving wife and young son, Stevens clearly stands to lose the most when he enlists. His wartime efforts also stumble out of the gate when he arrives in Egypt a few days too late to film a major victory. Still, Stevens stays the course and tirelessly documents the day-to-day efforts of American soldiers. Spielberg really takes ownership of the Stevens storyline in *Five Came Back* and viewers see why many shots Stevens gets in his wartime footage are clearly inspiration for many of like-minded shots in Spielberg's own *Saving Private Ryan* (1998). In fact, Spielberg may have downright "borrowed" them for his film. Later, viewers truly feel the crushing terror Stevens must have felt in 1945 as he filmed troops liberating Dachau, the horrifying German Concentration Camp. In a truly human moment, *Five Came Back* explains that Stevens filmed hours of dead, tortured, and emaciated Jews in order to document what he saw so people would believe it yet, he never had the heart to watch the footage he took even as he did research for his adaptation of *The*

Diary of Anne Frank (1959). Even more poignantly, it's pointed out that before leaving for the war, Stevens was arguably the number one light-comedy director in Hollywood but upon returning from the war, he went on to make beautifully humanistic dramas such as *A Place in the Sun* (1951), *Shane* (1953), and *Giant* (1956), yet never again directed a comedy.

In fact, *Five Came Back* posits the notion that all five of the titular directors returned home from the war not only changed men but also upon return then made the "best" films of their career. From Huston's *The Treasure of the Sierra Madre* (1948), Ford's *My Darling Clementine* (1946), Wyler's *The Best Years of Our Lives* (1946), Capra's *It's a Wonderful Life* (1946), and Stevens's aforementioned *A Place in the Sun,* it's a pretty fair assessment.

All in all, *Five Came Back* is an intriguing, heady, inspiring, and educational look at the power of cinema. While it is unclear how well-received the film might be to those who aren't cinephiles or history aficionados, the film is still entertaining and highly watchable. Another issue is the lack of a female filmmaker perspective even though the film adds Meryl Streep as narrator. Yet perhaps the lack of a female on camera speaks more to the lack of female perspective in all of cinema. In any case, *Five Came Back* is a joy to watch and even if one isn't a war, film, or history buff can be a nice way to pique a thus far dormant interest in these areas.

Don R. Lewis

CREDITS

Himself: Francis Ford Coppola
Himself: Guillermo del Toro
Himself: Paul Greengrass
Himself: Lawrence Kasdan
Himself: Steven Spielberg
Origin: United States
Language: English
Released: 2017
Production: John Battsek, Laurent Bouzereau; Amblin Television, IACF Productions, Passion Pictures, Rock Paper Scissors Entertainment; released by Netflix Inc.
Directed by: Laurent Bouzereau
Written by: Mark Harris
Cinematography by: Sean Kirby
Music by: Jeremy Turner
Sound: Trip Brock; Bruce Stubblefield
Editing: Will Znidaric
Art Direction: Leanne Dare; Peggy Oei
MPAA rating: Unrated
Running time: 180 minutes

REVIEWS

Anderson, John. *Wall Street Journal.* March 30, 2017.
Bowen, Chuck. *Slant Magazine.* March 24, 2017.
Debruge, Peter. *Variety.* April 3, 2017.
Kenigsberg, Ben. *New York Times.* March 31, 2017.
Li, Shirley. *Entertainment Weekly.* March 24, 2017.
Lowman, Rob. *Los Angeles Daily News.* March 30, 2017.
Simms, David. *The Atlantic.* April 3, 2017.
Travers, Ben. *IndieWire.* March 31, 2017.
Turan, Kenneth. *Los Angeles Times.* April 3, 2017.
Zacharek, Stephanie. *Time.* April 3, 2017.

TRIVIA

The "Five" refers to John Huston, John Ford, Frank Capra, William Wyler, and George Stevens.

FLATLINERS

You haven't lived until you've died.
—Movie tagline

Box Office: $16.9 Million

Cinephiles for years have preached what they believe should be the golden rule about remakes. If it must be done, do not redo a film that got it right the first time. Take another shot at the ones that were failures. That is not to say to just remake any bad movie as a challenge but to focus on projects with good ideas that may have come up short. Joel Schumacher's *Flatliners* (1990) was certainly one of those, a visually rich, if thematically slight, horror film about medical students eager to explore the moments just after death by using themselves as guinea pigs. It was a premise that screamed originality with a great cast who could sell it until it slowly degenerated into a less interesting tale of haunted atonement. Niels Arden Oplev's 2017 edition is less of a remake and more a complete degeneration into borrowed shocks and a cast not engaged enough to sell just how moronic their characters really are.

Years prior to her medical residency, Courtney (Ellen Page) experienced a tragedy when she drove off a bridge and caused the death of her younger sister. In present day, as she and her fellow students are challenged by Dr. Barry Wolfson (Kiefer Sutherland) to expand on their knowledge, she entices Jamie (James Norton) with sex into the basement. As the staff's resident playboy—and a rich one to boot—Jamie cannot resist breaking another heart, although Courtney's true intention lies in stopping her own. After a minute of exploring, she expects him and her good friend, Sophia (Kiersey Clemons) to reverse the procedure and bring her back to life.

The experiment hardly goes off without a hitch prompting the involvement of former firefighter-turned-doctor-in-training, Ray (Diego Luna) and his competitor and soon-to-be-love-interest, Marlo (Nina Dobrev). Intrigued by the results in which Courtney appears to have gained knowledge after her trip into the unknown, all but Ray are eager to take a turn. Once the film quickly gets nearly all of them onto the same playing field—two of them go back-to-back in the same night—it is time for the afterlife to reveal its true price for window shopping and send its characters hurtling into true nothingness.

The 1990 screenplay by Peter Filardi serviced the idea that our souls may not be worthy of such a tour if our consciences were not clean. Suffice to say this cinematic limbo was not invested in original sin but each character's greatest encores to God's birthmark. Whether it was an absence of monogamy, the guilt of a father's suicide or the outright bullying shared by two of them, Schumacher handled these developments with at least enough personal fear and sensitivity to hold interest in the people if not the collapse of a promising premise. Ben Ripley's 2017 draft is not a variation on Filardi's themes but a cheap copy enabled by the director's sheer lack of curiosity and reliance on familiar tropes such as Courtney's sister becoming some half-hearted version of creepy Samira from *The Ring* (2002). Leaning on that scare tactic rather than focusing her as a genuine motivating character trait is precisely the kind of dodge you should expect from a film that could not even be bothered to utter the words heaven or hell.

If that is a decision to concentrate on the scientific side of the debate, so be it. Then again as one character says, "This isn't science. This is pseudo-science." But no one would be quick to dismiss some faith-leaning zealot when confronted with the alternative of letting one of these dim bulbs diagnose them. Courtney's entire plan is dependent on the guy who mistakenly (nearly) gives a patient a rectal exam and the friend who just told her the night prior that she could not remember all the medical terminology. Later when the group debates—rather than the amusing Name That Tune-like wagering the 1990 crew engaged in—that three minutes of death might be too long and result in brain damage seem to have already forgotten that Courtney's maiden voyage takes up at least five minutes of screen time. By the end, Sophia should at least be able to retain the fact that her colleagues have turned the term "flatlining" into a verb,

Whatever the endgame is for this remake it has nothing to do with science, faith or even simple visual stimuli. Schumacher and cinematographer Jan De Bont saved their mood lighting for the inner and outer corridors of Loyola University in Chicago, leaving the visions of their flatlining sessions more of a puzzle than an affirmative. The one opportunity Oplev had for a slam dunk with this project was to just go the full *Brainstorm* (1983) and present a portrait of wonder (or horror) interspersed with the suspense of bringing these explorers back to life. Courtney flies over campus like she is Ebenezer Scrooge in Robert Zemeckis' animated take on *A Christmas Carol* (2009) and Jamie takes some all-powerful motorcycle ride through an empty city. The remaining trips are even less memorable. Families who have experienced the real-life trauma or death-defying joy of a loved one returning with a great story may feel further disheartened that none of them came back like John Travolta in *Phenomenon* (1996) or George Costanza on a sexual fast. How come they can't recite rare medical conditions or become Seth Brundle in the sack? Any experimenter worth their salt would ask such questions. Except these are idiots.

"If you're willing to change an autopsy report...then maybe you shouldn't be a doctor," is one of the more on-point conclusions uttered by a member of our flatlining crew. If only they had a guiding mentor to help wipe the slate clean of their original sins and start fresh under their "do no harm" oath. Kiefer Sutherland must be here for a reason given it was his Nelson Wright that started it all with the words "Today's a good day to die." Despite interviews where he claimed to be playing Wright again the only possible allusion to it in the final film is his cane. So, either Sutherland is the character who got beaten within an inch of his life now under a different name or he's doing some tribute to Hugh Laurie's Dr. Gregory House.

In a film that should be extrapolating the virtue of cherishing every minute, the new *Flatliners* is a waste of time and brainwaves. Instead of focusing on the meaning of life (or death), maybe everyone should have been figuring out how to bring a great idea back to life instead of letting its final edit be so dead on arrival.

Erik Childress

CREDITS

Courtney: Ellen Page
Ray: Diego Luna
Marlo: Nina Dobrev
Jamie: James Norton
Sophia: Kiersey Clemons
Origin: United States
Language: English
Released: 2017
Production: Michael Douglas, Laurence Mark, Peter Safran; Cross Creek Pictures, Furthur Films Inc.; released by Columbia Pictures

Directed by: Niels Arden Oplev
Written by: Ben Ripley
Cinematography by: Eric Kress
Music by: Nathan Barr
Sound: Mandell Winter
Editing: Tom Elkins
Art Direction: Michaela Cheyne
Costumes: Jenny Gering
Production Design: Niels Sejer
MPAA rating: PG-13
Running time: 110 minutes

REVIEWS

Berardinelli, James. *ReelViews*. September 30, 2017.
D'Angelo, Mike. *The A.V. Club*. September 29, 2017.
Edelstein, David. *New York Magazine/Vulture*. September 29, 2017.
Erhlich, David. *IndieWire*. September 29, 2017.
Johanson, MaryAnn. *Flick Filosopher*. September 29, 2017.
Kenny, Glenn. *New York Times*. September 29, 2017.
Murray, Noel. *Los Angeles Times*. September 29, 2017.
Orndorf, Brian. *Blu-Ray.com*. September 29, 2017.
Robinson, Tasha. *The Verge*. October 2, 2017.
Seitz, Matt Zoller. *RogerEbert.com*. September 30, 2017.

QUOTES

Jamie: "It's a great day to die!"

THE FLORIDA PROJECT

Find your kingdom.
—Movie tagline
Welcome to a magical kingdom.
—Movie tagline

Box Office: $5.7 Million

The American independent filmmaker Sean Baker achieves breathtaking new heights with his extraordinary sixth feature, *The Florida Project*. His subject, the interior lives of children, is knotty and complex, and the filmmaker reveals the toughness and sensitivity of some of the best practitioners of the form, like the French director François Truffaut, who made his early reputation with his great short film, *Les mistons* (1957) and his autobiographical debut feature, *The 400 Blows* (1959).

Kids are a natural for film given their unpredictable behavior, avid sense for adventure, and their anarchic impulses. The line between realistic presentation and exploitation is exceptionally fine. One wrong move, and everything collapses. Baker makes his young players active collaborators in the process, and the results deepen the material emotionally. This movie is a particular fresco that combines the lyrical, impudent power of Jean Vigo's *Zero for Conduct* (1933) with the disturbing and stark realism of Luis Buñuel's *Los Olvidados* (1950). The movie is like found art. It is never a sentimental or glorified portrait. Just the opposite, a cruel menace seems to hang over much of *The Florida Project*.

Baker beautifully intertwines the kids' funky and exhilarating abandon against the more rueful, sad, and opportunistic actions of the adults. *The Florida Project* is really the third piece of Baker's loose trilogy about the tragic undertow of the American dream factory works that expose the illusion of the redemptive power of the make believe. In *Starlet* (2012), two women are wounded by their experiences in the adult film industry. In *Tangerine* (2015), the central friendship is played out between two transvestite prostitutes working a seedy off-Hollywood boulevard. Those films were fast and kinetic, the style sharply tailored to the subjects. *Tangerine* was particularly interesting visually. Baker shot the film with customized iPhone cameras fitted with special anamorphic lenses that yielded a transfixing lascivious quality.

The new film was written with Chris Bergoch, who previously worked with Baker on *Tangerine*. The setting is suburban Orlando on the underside of Disney World, a mostly disreputable mercantile stretch of strip clubs, fast food stores, gun shops, and architecturally surreal objects that rise off the sterile sun-streaked landscapes. Except for its remarkable closing section, *The Florida Project* was shot, on 35mm film stock, by the supremely gifted Alexis Zabe, the Mexican cinematographer of Carlos Reygadas' great *Silent Light* (2007). The grain has a powerful solidity and voluptuous shape, and the palette is deeper, richer and often unsettling.

The primary location, the Magic Castle, is a garish three-story, mauve-colored motel for the economically distressed. The firecracker at the center of the story is Moonee, a precocious and wildly inventive six-year old. She has a quicksilver wit, a disarming smile and an irrepressible guile. Moonee lives in unit 323, with her mother, Halley (Bria Vinaite), at a nightly cost of $38. Played by an assured and vibrant young actress named Brooklynn Prince, Moonee lets her imagination run wild. She turns the motel and its adjacent spaces into her own private kingdom.

The movie feels almost plotless, the incidents, actions, and developments pieced together as a series of thematically bound vignettes. Like *Tangerine*, Baker develops a fast and engaging rhythm that is often explosively funny and unpredictable. He also edits his own films, and the cutting here is fluid and striking.

Baker has a canny eye for movement and spontaneity, and the kids' actions, however irresponsible or selfish, have an unimpeachable logic.

Baker works in the vein of the Depression-era *Our Gang* comedies. With the start of her summer break Moonee has time to burn. The movie begins with a wail, or in this case, the first of a series of pincer attacks warding off the general boredom of a lazy summer afternoon. Moonee is a thrill-seeker of the first order, and charismatic enough to draw a crowd, like her sidekick Scooty (Christopher Rivera). The kids are merry pranksters, and their mischief is more a function of their natural ebullience and curiosity. They are quiet rebels against the rule-bound order imposed by adults.

Working in widescreen and typically foregrounding the kids against these absurd objects, Baker and Zabe photograph these looming emporiums and bric-a-brac with an alienating strangeness, like the great French director Jacques Tati, in *Playtime* (1967). Standing against the oblong dome shape of Orange World or the massive head of a wizard that adorns a second-hand novelty shop, the kids look like visitors from another planet. The effect is weirdly transfixing. Moonee, Scooty, and a new friend, Jancey (Valeria Cotto), are delightfully resourceful. Every person they encounter is a potential mark. "The doctor said we have asthma, and we have to have ice cream right away," Scooty tells one bystander, in an effort to extract the necessary money.

The first half is glancing and propulsive as the story progresses from the two very distinct divisions, the kids need for adventure and discovery against the adults struggle to maintain some semblance of normalcy. These kids, especially Moonee, are preternaturally aware of their surroundings, a natural byproduct of living in the shadow of Disney World. They seem deeply aware of the social divide. Taking Jancey on a tour of the motel, Moonee has a straightforward, blunt ability to assess character. "The man who lives in here gets arrested a lot," Moonee says. "The woman here thinks she is married to Jesus."

The most compassionate and fully drawn adult is Bobby (Willem Dafoe), the motel manager. He is in perpetual crisis mode, defusing one hot-button incident after another, with a quiet competence and low-key magnanimity. Bobby is the movie's conscience and moral center. As frustrated as he gets at the kids for their unruly antics, like shutting off the electricity in ruining three hours of his work, Bobby quietly revels in the attention and is deeply protective. In one troubling incident, when an older man suddenly hangs around the kids, Bobby comes to their rescue. Knowing the intimate particulars of their often-daily lives, Bobby understands, even sometimes facilitates, their need for diversions.

As a well-heeled foreign couple on their honeymoon discovers when they turn up at the motel by accident, the Magic Castle is a dreary place of last resort. Scooty lives with his mother, Ashley (Mela Murder), one floor below Moonee. Ashley works at a local waffle house and supplies the kids with the necessary food. Halley is, quite frankly, a mess. She is a child woman on the verge of a constant breakdown, drawing the ire of Bobby for repeated infractions, many minor, though some, like late rent payments, of a more serious nature. Moonee's father is never seen or talked about. A former stripper, Halley works various hustles to try and get by.

The contrast of the behavior only underscores the lack of responsibility and parental care, the kids mirth and colorful activity buoyant and freewheeling turning sad and desperate when performed by Halley, for instance trying to sell perfume at a nearby upscale hotel. Moonee is a skilled accomplice and she plays her part. "It will make the girls flirt with you," she tells one man. The episode ends in humiliation with a security guard ordering them off the property and Halley smashing the bottles in disgust and anger.

Baker works through spellbinding moods, tender and heartbreaking, voluble and melancholy. What is particularly shattering is that the movie has no protective distance. The kids are never shielded from the messy and harsh complications of adult life. More often than not they are thrown up against it. Their innocence only carries them so far. The narrative ruptures when their carelessness nearly causes a catastrophic accident in a nearby vacant lot. The fissures, of friendships and social connections, only deepen the vulnerability of Moonee and her mother. Ostracized by the community, Halley is forced into ever more dangerous and illegal activities.

Baker orchestrates the parts beautifully. For all of its brashness and personal flouting, *The Florida Project* has plenty of haunting moments, like Bobby in a furtive moment, standing astride the balcony, having a smoke in the twilight night. Dafoe has always been an interesting and versatile actor with a face that could go either way. His heavy and deep lined face here suggests an accumulated weariness, a man lost in space.

The other actors do not have the same technical range. They are almost uniformly sensational. Vinaite, whom Baker reportedly discovered on Instagram, is a revelation. With her piercings and her elaborately detailed tattoos, she projects a feral defensiveness that often turns into a vicious rage. Her movements are ferocious and quick.

The kids are heartbreaking but never sentimentalized. Brooklynn Prince floats and whirls in the imagination, but what makes the character so alive and distinctive is the lack of pretense. Her line readings fuse cruel observance with a lean sureness. "I can always tell when somebody is about to cry," she says during one devastating moment. The two other primary kids, Christopher Rivera and Valeria Cotto, also demonstrate steely nerves and an emotional alertness.

The ending, with its much different speed and visual style, is open to multiple interpretations, a daring escape, a new beginning, or a frightening emblem of a life ripped apart. By refusing to ignore the cruel aspects of American life and culture, Sean Baker has pushed his art forward and expanded on the promise and excitement of his earlier work. Those films were necessary step to this point. *The Florida Project* is startling, enthralling, and unforgettable.

Patrick Z. McGavin

CREDITS

Bobby: Willem Dafoe
Moonee: Brooklynn Prince
Halley: Bria Vinaite
Scooty: Christopher Rivera
Dicky: Aiden Malik
Origin: United States
Language: English, Spanish, Portuguese
Released: 2017
Production: Kevin Chinoy, Andrew Duncan, Alex Saks, Francesca Silvestri, Shih-Ching Tsou, Sean Baker, Chris Bergoch; Cre Film, Freestyle Picture Company, June Pictures, Sweet Tomato Films; released by A24 Films LLC
Directed by: Sean Baker
Written by: Sean Baker; Chris Bergoch
Cinematography by: Alexis Zabe
Music by: Lorne Balfe
Sound: Coll Anderson
Music Supervisor: Matthew Hearon-Smith
Editing: Sean Baker
Costumes: Fernando Rodriguez
Production Design: Stephonik Youth
MPAA rating: R
Running time: 115 minutes

REVIEWS

Burr, Ty. *Boston Globe.* October 11, 2017.
Chang, Justin. *Los Angeles Times.* October 5, 2017.
Dowd, A.A. *The A.V. Club.* October 5, 2017.
Morgenstern, Joe. *Wall Street Journal.* October 5, 2017.
Phillips, Michael. *Chicago Tribune* . October 12, 2017.
Rainer, Peter. *Christian Science Monitor* . October 7, 2017.
Rothkopf, Joshua. *Time Out New York.* October 6, 2017.
Scott, A.O. *New York Times.* October 5, 2017.
Stevens, Dana. *Slate.* October 12, 2017.
Zacharek, Stephanie. *Time Magazine.* October 5, 2017.

QUOTES

Moonee: "I can always tell when adults are about to cry."

TRIVIA

Actor Willem Dafoe spent a week living in area before filming started in order to immerse himself in the life of the characters and to master the nuances of the regional dialect.

AWARDS

Nominations:

Oscars 2017: Actor--Supporting (Dafoe)
British Acad. 2017: Actor--Supporting (Dafoe)
Golden Globes 2018: Actor--Supporting (Dafoe)
Ind. Spirit 2018: Director (Baker), Film
Screen Actors Guild 2017: Actor--Supporting (Dafoe)

THE FOREIGNER

Never push a good man too far.
—Movie tagline

Box Office: $34.4 Million

For over a decade, Martin Campbell made unpretentious crime and action films in America that somehow kept him off the radar of auteurist critics. A more buoyant, flashy alternative to peers like Tony Scott, Philip Noyce, Kathryn Bigelow, Paul Verhoeven, James Cameron, or Andrew Davis, Campbell dealt in big emotional beats, intricate plots, expressive but underplayed colors, expensive, clean action choreography and set pieces, and laughs that played to the back of the house. After reinventing the Bond films twice, first with *GoldenEye* (1995) and then with *Casino Royale* (2006), he found himself a little adrift in Hollywood. His one attempt at a superhero movie, *Green Lantern* (2011), fared poorly, and he retreated into TV for over five years. *The Foreigner,* his first theatrical release since then, is a return to form in many ways, though it's a little breathless for its own good, almost as if Campbell wanted to pack as much detail into the film as possible to keep himself occupied. There's as much intrigue and incident here for one of the mini-series—*Reilly: Ace of Spies* (1983) or *Edge of Darkness* (1985)—he started his career directing. It barely fits into the movie's two-hour runtime, but Campbell makes it hum along without any fuss.

Quan Ngoc Minh (Jackie Chan) is a single father who owns a Chinese restaurant in London. When dropping his daughter Fan (Katie Leung) off to shop one afternoon, a terrorist group sets off a bomb nearby and kills her and a dozen other people. A group calling itself the "Authentic IRA" claims responsibility, so the first phone call that the British make in the aftermath is to Liam Hennessey (Pierce Brosnan), a deputy minister in the Irish government who used to be a leader in the provisional IRA when they were still on the attack. Hennessey rounds up all his old IRA chums and shakes them down for information. If anyone knows anything about the attacks, he wants to know. He tells his contact in the British government, Katherine Davies (Lia Williams) that he will be able to get more information if he has a bargaining chip to bring back to his people; namely, the release of some IRA members still sitting in prison due to their violent actions in the 1990s.

Meanwhile, Quan is doing a little reconnaissance of his own. He looks into the old IRA and brings his findings to Richard Bromley (Ray Fearon) at Scotland Yard, who's in charge of the investigation. Bromley assures Quan he will let him know when he knows anything, but Quan is unmoved. He wants vengeance or justice, whichever's easiest. Quan sets off for Belfast, Ireland to pay Hennessey a visit at his house, planting a small bomb in the toilet of his offices and taking pictures of the minister with his mistress (Charlie Murphy). Hennessey takes his wife Mary (Orla Brady) and a huge contingent of bodyguards and retreats to his country estate. Though shaken, Hennessey still tries to keep up his bargaining with the British, which includes sending his nephew Sean (Rory Fleck Byrne) to Bromley with a new strategy. If Scotland Yard taps the phones of every potential splinter of the IRA and waits to hear a change in their code words when communicating with each other, they will know who in the government is aiding the Authentic IRA. The hitch is that the next bombing, of a London bus, happens without any code words. The only question is whether Quan, who makes short work of Hennessey's bodyguards, will kill or, at the very least, destroy the credibility of the minister before he has a chance to fully squeeze the British for the release of his political prisoners.

The above description does not include a third of the intrigue, double crosses, and treachery the film eventually gets around to revealing. It's to Campbell's credit that every new development, which hit every ten or fifteen minutes, flows perfectly into the narrative. We expect that this nest of vipers will continue to betray one another with ease, it's merely a matter of the design of those back-stabbings. The film only runs into trouble when it gets to the denouement and has to mete out punishment to its terrorists and politicians. Its treatment of both of the women in Hennessey's life is heinous. Despite everyone in the movie being an opportunist, liar, murderer, or some combination of the three (including melancholy Quan out for righteous revenge), it's the women who suffer the most. Hennessey's mistress is really working for the Authentic IRA and is sleeping with him to keep tabs on him. She's tortured and shot and in general treated the worst for her use of sex to gain the upper hand. A similar fate befalls Mary Hennessey, who's sleeping around as well. Her husband has his freedom stripped by the powers that be for his willingness to use violence for his own ends, but his wife, whose only crime is extra-marital sex and a wish for justice for her dead IRA gunman brother, is handed a much worse punishment. The gender imbalance makes the film's conclusion harder to enjoy, despite its satisfactory handling of most of the plot threads.

Of course, it isn't just the plot that satisfies. Campbell's blue-hued images of men fighting with words and fists are wholly engrossing. Campbell, who reintroduced old-fashioned swashbuckling to audiences with *The Mask of Zorro* (1998), does a great job capturing Jackie Chan's martial arts movements in spaces great and small. His escape from his hotel when Hennessey's bodyguards first locate him is a marvel of confident action staging, never losing track of anyone or any of Chan's still-impressive physicality. At 63, Chan still knows how to handle himself in a fight scene beautifully. Maybe even more impressive than that is the way he totally transforms himself into a grieving first generation father and craftsman. As Quan, he does not appear to be nimble, limber Jackie Chan for even a second, making his bursts of kinetic action play like a complete, if welcome, surprise. The sadness of loss and solitude infects his every movement, even as he's hunting people like animals in the wilderness. It's a command performance in the middle of an acre of conniving and double-dealing.

Scout Tafoya

CREDITS

Quan Ngoc Minh: Jackie Chan

Liam Hennessy: Pierce Brosnan

Bromley: Ray Fearon

Sean Morrison: Rory Fleck-Byrne

Christy Murphy: Stephen Hogan

Origin: United States

Language: English, Mandarin Chinese

Released: 2017

Production: Wayne Marc Godfrey, Claire Kupchak, Scott Lumpkin, Jianhong Qi, Arthur Sarkissian, Cathy Schulman, Jamie Marshall, Maojun Zeng, Jackie Chan; Huayi Brothers Media Company Ltd., Sparkle Roll Media Corp., Wanda Media Co.; released by STX Entertainment

Directed by: Martin Campbell
Written by: David Marconi
Cinematography by: David Tattersall
Music by: Cliff Martinez; Jason Markey
Sound: Dave McMoyler; Jon Title
Editing: Angela Catanzaro
Art Direction: Nick Dent
Costumes: Alex Bovaird
Production Design: Alex Cameron
MPAA rating: R
Running time: 113 minutes

REVIEWS

Berra, John. *Screen International.* October 10, 2017.
Debrudge, Peter. *Variety.* October 10, 2017.
Kenny, Glenn. *New York Times.* October 12, 2017.
LaSalle, Mick. *San Francisco Chronicle.* October 12, 2016.
Russo, Tom. *Boston Globe.* October 13, 2017.
Smith, Derek. *Slant Magazine.* October 12, 2017.
Tsui, Clarence. *Hollywood Reporter.* October 10, 2017.
Vishnevetsky, Ignatiy. *The A.V. Club.* October 13, 2017.
Walsh, Katie *Chicago Tribune.* October 12, 2016.
Worthington, Clint. *Consequence of Sound.* October 12, 2017.

QUOTES

Quan Ngoc Minh: "Politicians and terrorists, they are just 2 ends of the same snake."
Quan Ngoc Minh: "What's the difference?"
Liam Hennessy: "There is a difference."
Liam Hennessy: "One end bites and the other doesn't."

TRIVIA

Actors Jackie Chan and Pierce Brosnan have both starred in separate adaptations of *Around the World in 80 Days.* Chan appeared in the 2004 theatrical film while Brosnan starred in the 1989 television mini-series.

47 METERS DOWN

No help above, no hope below.
—Movie tagline

No way out. No way up. No chance in hell.
—Movie tagline

Stay out of the water.
—Movie tagline

How do you survive the world's greatest predators?
—Movie tagline

Box Office: $44.3 Million

Since *Jaws* (1975), there has been a perplexing double standard of sorts regarding shark movies. In theory, they should be a guaranteed box-office draw as the start of the concept of a summer blockbuster literally began with one when Steven Spielberg's big screen debut took the box office by storm. Since then, however, almost no shark movie has drawn the same interest from audiences or critics. Once you've seen one shark attack, it takes quite a bit of formal acuity and inventiveness to make another one seem fresh. Hot on the heels of 2016's masterfully directed box-office smash *The Shallows*, which all but does cartwheels to find a new way to pit one person against a bloodthirsty shark, comes Johannes Roberts's *47 Meters Down*. Nowhere near as inventive or daring, *47 Meters Down* dials back on ambition and goes longer on realism with mixed results. The film is an effective exercise in building tension and it's quite good fun, but that's about it.

Sisters Lisa (Mandy Moore) and Kate (Claire Holt) are on a vacation together in Mexico. Lisa's been keeping a big secret from Kate to try and preserve both of their moods but one day can no longer keep it to herself. Her longtime boyfriend has left her because she's too boring. And, as it must be in movies like this, Kate decides to remedy this with an old-fashioned, daringly stupid, and highly dangerous adventure. They meet two studs on the beach named Javier (Chris Johnson) and Louis (Yani Gellman), who have just the thing for a couple of rich white girls looking to go native. They have a friend named Captain Taylor (Matthew Modine) who runs a little diving operation off of his boat. He takes people into shark-infested waters so they can go cage diving. Kate thinks this sounds like a great idea and manages to browbeat Lisa into giving it a try over her objections.

Things go well for about ten seconds as they take in the horrifying majesty of the 20-foot sharks all around them, but the winch holding the cage in the water starts to fail and Lisa demands to be taken up. Taylor tries to lift them back into the boat but the winch breaks completely and the cage plummets to the ocean floor. There are, of course, several obstacles to their rescue. The girls are too far down for their radios to work, which means they have to swim in open water in order to make contact with the boat. They only have a limited supply of oxygen and panicking, which is the first thing Lisa does, only sucks it up faster. They can't swim to the surface without risk of getting the bends, and the crew of the boat doesn't know where they are exactly in order to lower a cable attached to a replacement winch. So, unless the girls take an active part in their own rescue, they are going to die in a hurry. But leaving the cage to do so puts them in range of at least three giant sharks.

There's something to be said for this kind of simple thriller. Two girls in a cage fighting for their lives; there isn't a lot to get wrong in that scenario. Lisa's backstory about being too boring is the only thematic idea that gets lip service paid to it, and not even cathartically. It's really just an excuse to get her in the cage with her sister. The film has nothing to say, which is perfectly fine, because anything grander would have been more than a modest thriller like this could reasonably sustain. This is purely a movie about problem solving while man-eating fish hover just out of sight waiting to catch the heroes if they slip up. Mark Silk's photography makes effective use of the darkness of the ocean around the girls (the movie never rises to the surface to check on the crew in the boat—it's all ocean floor from the minute the winch breaks). The dark blues of the deep present a frightening challenge for the viewer's eyes. Do you want to look into the abyss and see the shape of a shark or is darkness more comforting?

As a film about people of average intelligence solving high stakes puzzles while under just about the highest amount of pressure imaginable, *47 Meters Down* wants somewhat for inspiration and investment. The two girls look and sound alike, so it's difficult to remember who's in what particular danger at any given moment, and as the canvas is so small, the new problems have to pile up or boredom will set in. As that's the start and end of this film's modus operandi, it achieves everything it sets out to, which is not a terrible rubric to be judged on. In that way, it's not unlike the disreputable John Stockwell film *Turistas* (2006) or the excellently grim killer plant movie *The Ruins* (2008), which are also about beautiful tourists in a beautiful place trying to stay a step ahead of murder and disaster. Neither film will win awards or hang around in the cultural memory, but a solid thriller always has a place in the modern cinematic landscape.

Scout Tafoya

CREDITS

Kate: Claire Holt
Lisa: Mandy Moore
Javier: Chris Johnson
Louis: Yani Gellman
Captain Taylor: Matthew Modine
Origin: United States
Language: English
Released: 2017
Production: James Harris, Mark Lane; Tea Shop & Film Company, The Fyzz Facility; released by Entertainment Studios Motion Pictures
Directed by: Johannes Roberts
Written by: Johannes Roberts; Ernest Riera
Cinematography by: Mark Silk
Music by: tomandandy
Sound: Richard Kondal
Music Supervisor: Jen Moss; Chris Piccaro
Editing: Martin Brinkler
Costumes: Eleanor Baker
Production Design: David Bryan
MPAA rating: PG-13
Running time: 89 minutes

REVIEWS

Catsoulis, Jeannette. *New York Times.* June 15, 2017.
Duralde, Alonso. *TheWrap.* June 15, 2017.
Jolin, Dan. *Empire.* July 31, 2017.
Leydon, Joe. *Variety.* June 15, 2017.
Myers, Kimber. *The Playlist.* June 15, 2017.
Nordine, Michael. *IndieWire.* June 15, 2017.
Robey, Tim. *The Telegraph.* August 3, 2017.
Seymour, Tom. *Time Out London.* July 25, 2017.
Walsh, Katie. *Los Angeles Times.* June 16, 2017.
Zwecker, Bill. *Chicago Sun-Times.* June 16, 2017.

QUOTES

Sammie: "Oh it's like you're going to the zoo, except you're in the cage."

TRIVIA

At the depth the characters are supposedly at, experts suggest there would be about fifteen minutes of air for them.

THE FOUNDER

He took someone else's idea and America ate it up.
—Movie tagline

Box Office: $12.8 Million

Baseball, apple pie, and McDonald's—that may not be the exact ranking of quintessential American institutions, but it is hard to dispute how recognizable the sound of that name is to a country that has strived on capitalism and the dream of making it within that system. The golden arches that appears on practically every corner of the world are as synonymous with the franchise as one of the most famous brand names in history. Ray Kroc, the man behind what the fast food chain has become today, may be a legend to some but John Lee Hancock's film is determined to print the truth.

"Don't worry, it moves fast," a customer tells Kroc (Michael Keaton), as he stands in line at the original McDonald's. Up to that point he was just a salesman pitching multi-mixers to restaurants with the need to blend up more than one milkshake at a time. When he phones Dick McDonald (Nick Offerman) and hears his location needs eight of them, he drives out to pay them a visit. Once there, he gets a tour from Dick's brother, Mac (John Carroll Lynch), and sees an operation that is not just an assembly line that produces orders in seconds but feels like a community experience. Kroc refers to it as "the new American church" as he pitches every business' favorite "F" word to the brothers: franchise.

Dick and Mac are initially skeptical of the proposal. "It's better to have one great restaurant than fifty mediocre ones," they agree, but Kroc is persuasive enough to get them to give it a go and Mac, even with health issues, knows how much Dick wants the business to thrive. Then arrives the first scene with Kroc's wife, Ethel (Laura Dern), who throws cold water on this enterprising tale with the information that they are already well off; living beyond their means while Ray continues to chase the moving line of what is enough. "Schemes" is a word she casually throws at him. The expectation of a con man in our midst is a potentially fascinating direction for this story to turn on. Instead it stays the course of a typical rags-to-riches tale, only without the rags and the more interesting characters left behind.

Michael Keaton has played bad guys in movies before, most notably in *Beetlejuice* (1988) but to more of the psychopathic variety in *Pacific Heights* (1990) and *Desperate Measures* (1998). Ray Kroc, however, comes off as the most reprehensible of the bunch though simply for the normalcy of an evil this country perpetrated. Mild-mannered and even folksy, but duplicitous to the point of crushing the souls of a pair of dreamers who translated their ideas into hard work, Kroc represents the American way stolen through the contractual sleight of hand known as capitalism.

Exploring this angle as the overarching commentary of a reverse underdog story would make for a fresher and even darker perspective than what screenwriter Robert Siegel has in store for the film's less interesting second half. A personal touch to what really made Kroc tick would have at least presented a character study representative of those lost themes. Instead it is personal to a fault including an amiability transformed into outright dirty dealing that is seemingly influenced by a failing marriage and a wife swap that adds a borderline anti-woman sentiment suggesting McDonald's may have persevered under its original intent if not for those nagging ladies trying to carve out a little of their happiness. It allows an odd out for Kroc's behavior that is too damaging to simply be normalized as another guy who took advantage of an opportunity because he had the resources to do so.

As a history lesson into the actual foundation of the McDonalds' dream, Hancock momentarily takes a documentarian approach that would have ultimately served the film's goals to greater effect, especially when it wants to be an eye-opener into real estate technicalities. Offerman and Lynch are so wonderful together in these early scenes that the eventuality of their sad story is tempered by not making them the focus and reducing Kroc as the villainous outsider who thwarts their plans. Along with Keaton, the three make a wonderful team, so the film suffers when it moves to a solo act instead of the pluralized name synonymous with the golden arches. *The Founder* drifts from "this is probably the best hamburger I've ever tasted" to "we are not interested in a milkshake that contains no milk" too quickly. As metaphors for the film itself those two lines of dialogue are pretty apt.

Erik Childress

CREDITS

Ray Kroc: Michael Keaton
Dick McDonald: Nick Offerman
Mac McDonald: John Carroll Lynch
Joan Smith: Linda Cardellini
Harry J. Sonneborn: B.J. Novak
Ethel Kroc: Laura Dern
Origin: United States
Language: English
Released: 2017
Production: Don Handfield, Aaron Ryder; FilmNation Entertainment; released by The Weinstein Company
Directed by: John Lee Hancock
Written by: Robert Siegel
Cinematography by: John Schwartzman
Music by: Carter Burwell
Sound: Jon Johnson
Editing: Robert Frazen
Costumes: Daniel Orlandi
Production Design: Michael Corenblith
MPAA rating: PG-13
Running time: 115 minutes

REVIEWS

Brody, Richard. *The New Yorker*. January 23, 2017.
Cerny, Alan. *ComingSoon.net*. January 19, 2017.
Edelstein, David. *New York Magazine/Vulture*. January 19, 2017.

Gire, Dann. *Daily Herald.* January 19, 2017.
Minow, Nell. *Beliefnet.* January 20, 2017.
Nusair, David. *Reel Film Reviews.* January 23, 2017.
Orndorf, Brian. *Blu-ray.com.* January 26, 2017.
Phillips, Michael. *Chicago Tribune.* January 19, 2017.
Roeper, Richard. *Chicago Sun-Times.* January 19, 2017.
Sims, David. *The Atlantic.* February 9, 2017.

QUOTES

Ray Kroc: "If I saw a competitor drowning, I'd shove a hose down his throat."

TRIVIA

The company that Ray Kroc originally worked for prior to founding McDonald's, Prince Castle, still exists and supplies McDonald's with much of its equipment.

FOXTROT

Israel's submission for the 2017 Foreign Language Oscar®, *Foxtrot* is told in three parts—none completely earned. The beauty of Samuel Maoz's film is that, despite its narrative failings, the sheer chutzpah shown in its satirical defiance of the Israeli state makes its boldness commendable. The film centers around a family whose son Jonathan (Yonatan Shiray) is in the military and all the absurdist anxiety that comes along with that burden. The three narrative sections are split along lines in the son's life: the first when his parents are informed of his death, the second observing his time stationed at a remote desert checkpoint, and the third on the first birthday passing after his death. All sting with humor that threatens to flip into cruel mockery, but the emotional gut punches these deserve are all pulled because of the film's structural wonkiness.

Section by section, these are stunning short films of completely different tone. Together, they tell a disjointed story so relentlessly acidic that it cripples a viewer's ability to discern different flavors. Take the dark humor of the first section, where Jonathan's parents (played by Sarah Adler and Lior Ashkenazi) are informed by a group of military representatives that their son has fallen in the line of duty. This verbiage is extremely important to the proceedings, as political correctness and appearances are paramount in this time of grief. The mother spasms, then is knocked out by a tranquilizer, while the father silently seethes with all the suppressed emotions of a sitcom fifty-something.

It's not incompetently shot—with overhead drone shots effectively inducing the nausea such a shocking declaration would inevitably inflict—nor incompetently acted. Ashkenazi builds a silent fury with a bone-rattling intensity and hopelessness that takes all the nuance-driven neurosis of Larry David's *Curb Your Enthusiasm* and weaponizes it. Its brevity, however, and its assumption that its audience will be on board for this oddly-toned bout of narrative gymnastics makes the entire opening segment more an exercise in patience. Patience in the viewer, wondering where this will lead, and (perhaps too much) patience of the filmmaker building to the inevitable punchline that leads to the film's second act.

The second segment, which is by far its strongest, follows a similar joke structure, though its military setting already makes it strange that it is best interpreted as a comedy bit. Here, Jonathan and his squad of three other youths maintain the security of a road checkpoint so obscure and remote that their main traffic comes from a single indecisive camel. This section, with far more atmosphere and built-in characterization than the more tightly-shot apartment scenes, is ripe for a dry buddy comedy about the dreadfully dull tedium of the majority of military service. The meaninglessness of it all, in service of nationalism that the film argues is ultimately nowhere to be found, gets a few laughs as the soldiers trudge through mud and rain to shake down one or two cars a week.

Finding hope, humor, and valid criticism in the soldiers's monotonous days is far easier for the film than the ultra-cynical jokes shoehorned in as act transitions. After the font of world-building that was the checkpoint oasis, the return to Jonathan's parents's apartment is a downgrade in both aesthetic and thematic potency. While the chemistry between Adler and Ashkenazi is natural enough to explain the prickly development of their relationship, the large swathes of emotional development left offscreen stifles the characters rather than sets them free. Whether approaching the complexity of grief and the selfishness that comes with death or the futility of military service, *Foxtrot* is simply undone by Moaz's ambitious design. Creatively constructed and decently put together, the jokes fall as flat as the emotions because its scope is either too wide or too small, flailing in the void between.

Jacob Oller

CREDITS

Michael Feldmann: Lior Ashkenazi
Daphna Feldmann: Sarah Adler
Jonathan: Yonathan Shiray
Alma: Shira Haas
Death Notification Officer: Danny Isserles
Origin: United States

Language: Hebrew
Released: 2018
Production: Marc Baschet, Viola Fugen, Cedomir Kolar, Eitan Mansuri, Michel Merkt, Michael Weber; Bord Cadre Films; released by Sony Pictures Classics
Directed by: Samuel Maoz
Written by: Samuel Maoz
Cinematography by: Giora Bejach
Music by: Ophir Leibovitch; Amit Poznansky
Editing: Arik Leibovitch; Guy Nemesh
Art Direction: Eyal Elhadad; Francis Kiko Soeder
Production Design: Arad Sawat
MPAA rating: R
Running time: 114 minutes

REVIEWS

Brooks, Xan. *The Guardian*. September 4, 2017.
Brown, Hannah. *Jerusalem Post*. September 28, 2017.
Fainaru, Dan. *Screen International*. September 1, 2017.
Hoffman, Jordan. *Vanity Fair*. September 12, 2017.
Kohn, Eric. *IndieWire*. September 5, 2017.
O'Callaghan, Paul. *Sight and Sound*. September 12, 2017.
Ryder, Alistair. *Film Inquiry*. October 15, 2017.
Su, Zhuo-Ning. *The Film Stage*. September 12, 2017.
Weissberg, Jay. *Variety*. September 2, 2017.
Young, Deborah. *Hollywood Reporter*. September 1, 2017.

TRIVIA

Writer/director Samuel Maoz has described this film as a "philosophical puzzle."

FRANTZ

Box Office: $880,883

Francois Ozon's *Frantz* mediates on heavy, serious subjects—memory, guilt, inconsolable loss—in exploring the regret by the one who feels responsible contrasted against those trapped by the past or struggling in finding a way to push on.

Like much of the French director's work, the movie is a highly formidable physical work with its immaculate cinematography and vivid period reconstruction. Ozon has always been a terrific director of actors, and this film demonstrates that talent with acuity and grace as he showcases actors working in a range of styles and moods, articulating the pain and anguish in coping with the sorrow and loneliness.

At the same time Ozon has set himself with an impossibly unfair comparison. His movie is a reworking of a key work by one of the greatest directors who ever lived. Jean-Luc Godard's provocative take on the best way to criticize a movie is to remake it is here either audacious or marks the height of hubris.

The earlier film, *Broken Lullaby* (1932), by the peerless Ernst Lubitsch, was a peculiar work in that director's career, a dark and brooding anti-war adaptation, by his usual writer, Samson Raphaelson, from a play by Maurice Rostand, originally released as *The Man I Killed*—also the title of the play. The movie's reputation suffers in context with the radiant masterpieces like *Trouble in Paradise* (1932) Lubitsch made the same year. "Even hard-core Lubitsch aficionados have been known to run screaming from this film," the critic and historian Dave Kehr wrote. "I, however, find it sublime, one of the most piercing and cinematically supple of all of Lubitsch's films. His themes transfer cleanly from the comedies, and they are developed with unusual urgency."

Ozon has made sixteen features since his first full-length production, *Sitcom* (1998). The best said about his work is that it is never boring, static, or passive. His movies have crossed all sides, bridging concerns of money, class, culture, and (especially) sexuality. He has made films in French (primarily), English, and German. His poaching of Lubitsch follows a pattern of indebtedness to German directors; his first fully developed work, *Water Drops on Burning Rocks* (2000), was adapted from a play by Rainer Werner Fassbinder and his musical *8 Women* (2002) extensively referenced the films of Douglas Sirk.

Guilt and transgression are a constant, reflecting his fascination with power, authority, and relationships and underscoring the marked influence of Alfred Hitchcock and Claude Chabrol. Typically with Ozon, the kinkier the more interesting, as *Water Drops on Burning Rocks* showed or the opening moment of *Young & Beautiful* (2013), his beautiful and sexually coveted young protagonist (Marine Vacth) is viewed through a pair of binoculars, the watcher revealed to be her adolescent brother.

His tendency toward cultural appropriation signifies a deeper limitation and accounts for the unevenness of his movies. What is missing with Ozon is a dominant personality or point of view, making him a typically less interesting or dynamic filmmaker than Olivier Assayas, Arnaud Desplechin, or Leos Carax. If Ozon has never made a truly great film, he has certainly made movies, like *Frantz*, that linger in the imagination.

The strongest parts of *Frantz*—ruminative, mysterious, and studded with loss—link it with two of the director's most concentrated works, *Under the Sand* (2000) and *Time to Leave* (2005). Each of those is haunted by the specter of mortality or an irretrievable absence. Structurally the movie is bound by echoes and rhyming motifs of language, memory, and identity. The story has a two-part structure, each shaped around a stranger's odyssey to a foreign land that proves particularly effective in developing its themes and ideas.

Shot by Pascal Marti, who has photographed most of Ozon's recent work, *Frantz* opens with a burst of color, outlining a formal strategy of sometimes making a full transition to color to italicize dramatically significant moments—a crucial flashback, an idyll in the mountain landscapes, a nightmare. The majority of the film is rendered in a pristine chromatic black and white, aligned with the downbeat or restrained emotional rhythms.

The movie is set in the spring of 1919, just months after the armistice formally ended the bloody and catastrophic First World War (1914-1918). The first half of *Frantz*, set in the small German village of Quedlinburg, is structured around mourning. The beautiful and self-contained Anna (Paula Beer) grieves the death of her fiancé, Frantz Hoffmeister (Anton von Lucke), an infantryman killed in France. One day as she prepares her ritual of placing flowers at his grave, Anna notices another man also standing over the plot. The young man is disconsolate, nearing breakdown as he stands over the gravesite. She lives with Frantz's parents, the stern and proper town doctor, Hans (Ernst Stötzner) and stoic Magda (Marie Gruber).

Pierre Rivoire (Pierre Niney), the young French man, turns up at the practice of the doctor, who angrily refuses to see him. "Every Frenchman is my son's murderer," the doctor says. At Anna's intervention, the parents relent and the nervous, almost withdrawn Pierre relates the story of how the two met as students in Paris when Frantz was studying there before the war. They bonded over their passion for art and culture, with trips to the Louvre, and a shared affinity for the violin. Adrien played in the conservatory.

Pierre's warm and revealing tale brings solace to the parents and cements a more direct bond with Anna. Walking in the valleys of the bucolic mountain landscapes, Anna sketches ever-greater details about her fiancé. He was a passionate Francophile (the two often spoke French in secret). Frantz's mother had been tacitly orchestrating a relationship between the two. Anna's only other suitor is the much older and persistently glum Kreutz (Johann von Bülow), a fervent nationalist. Pierre accompanies Anna to the town's spring ball, creating difficulties for Doctor Hoffmeister, in his personal and professional associations.

Pierre is an enigma—especially to Anna. His tortured body language, difficulty expressing emotion, and elliptical comments suggest a significant missing part of his narrative. (This being an Ozon film, the possibility of a sexual relationship between the two men seems entirely possible.) The truth emerges after Pierre fails to turn up at the appointed hour for a dinner at the family's house. Knowing intimate details that unnerve Anna, Pierre breaks down and reveals his true identity as the enemy soldier who killed Frantz. He shot him at close range in a trench amid the confusion of a German ambush of his French unit. Frantz, a pacifist, stood unarmed, his weapon unloaded, when Pierre fired the mortal shot.

As Pierre attempts to expiate his perceived sins and returns home, Anna withholds the truth from Frantz's parents. Months later, a letter Anna writes to Frantz is returned without a forwarding address. Magda convinces Anna to travel to Paris to discover the fate of Pierre and her journey sets in motion the film's second movement. *Frantz* has a great deal to be impressed with—direction, evocative production details and the lyrical, pungent performances. Anna is the centerpiece, and Beer gives an intensely physical performance, never ostentatious, pared down, tremulous, and nervy.

The second half is more dependent on incident and story detail and not always to the film's advantage. Ozon also works a little too aggressively to create symmetry between the parts, like the singing in a German bar of a patriotic song that is repeated in a Paris cafe with a rendition of "La Marseillaise." Ozon is much more powerful working indirectly, glancing, like the most devastating image of the film, a reflection caught on the window of Anna's train of a devastated French landscape and city laying in ruins.

Dramatically, Anna is the more interesting character. The revelations following of Pierre's return to Paris lack the same weight of his earlier confession. Niney, who bears an uncanny resemblance to Adrien Brody, is a more passive, interior performer. It is a morally slippery performance, and Pierre remains too recessive to really make the material sing. That performance mirrors the larger creative enterprise. *Frantz* is solid, eerie though never transcendent or within reach of Ernst Lubitsch's original.

Patrick Z. McGavin

CREDITS

Adrien Rivoire: Pierre Niney
Anna: Paula Beer
Doktor Hans Hoffmeister: Ernst Stötzner
Magda Hoffmeister: Marie Gruber
Kreutz: Johann von Bülow
Origin: United States
Language: French, German
Released: 2017

Production: Eric Altmayer, Nicolas Altmayer, Stefan Arndt, Uwe Schott; Mandarin Films; released by Music Box Films
Directed by: Francois Ozon
Written by: Francois Ozon
Cinematography by: Pascal Marti
Music by: Philippe Rombi
Editing: Laure Gardette
Art Direction: Susanne Abel
Costumes: Pascaline Chavanne
Production Design: Michel Barthelemy
MPAA rating: PG-13
Running time: 113 minutes

REVIEWS

Anderson, Melissa. *Village Voice.* March 15, 2017.
Burr, Ty. *Boston Globe.* March 30, 2017.
Chang, Justin. *Los Angeles Times.* March 23, 2017.
D'Angelo, Mike. *The A.V. Club.* March 14, 2017.
Hoeij, Boyd van. *Hollywood Reporter.* September 16, 2016.
Holden, Stephen. *New York Times.* March 15, 2017.
Kupecki, Josh. *Austin Chronicle.* April 5, 2017.
Macdonald, Moira. *Seattle Times.* March 30, 2017.
Morgenstern, Joe. *Wall Street Journal.* March 23, 2017.
Nashawaty, Chris. *Entertainment Weekly.* March 15, 2017.
O'Sullivan, Michael. *Washington Post.* April 6, 2017.

TRIVIA

Based on *Broken Lullaby* (1932) by director Ernst Lubitsch.

FREE FIRE

All guns. No control.
—Movie tagline

Box Office: $1.8 Million

Free Fire is the slightest of Ben Wheatley's films but that hardly makes it any less enjoyable. It leans too much on its set-up, and the dialogue sometimes seems forced, but a fantastic cast at the top of their game bring all the bravado needed to support the film's central conceit: to make a movie that is essentially one giant gunfight. It also helps that Wheatley is clearly having the time of his life making it all work.

It is 1978. Two low-level hoods, Stevo (Sam Riley) and Bernie (Enzo Cilenti), are driving to meet their boss Frank (Michael Smiley) and his henchman Chris (Cillian Murphy), who the audience are led to believe are IRA members making a gun deal. During the ride, Stevo confides that he was beaten up by the cousin of a woman he abused at a nightclub. Upon arrival, the group meets with Justine (Brie Larson), the intermediary for the buy who connects them with Ord (Armie Hammer), the representative of arms dealer Vernon (Sharlto Copley) and his men: Martin (Babou Ceesay), Harry (Jack Reynor), and Gordon (Noah Taylor). Tensions rise when Vernon delivers the wrong weapons, but Chris urges Frank to go ahead with the deal so Stevo and Bernie secure the goods in their van. Suddenly, Stevo notices that Harry is the man who had beaten him the night before and as they argue a single shot is fired sparking off a lengthy gun battle that devolves into every man for himself and everyone for the money.

Free Fire falls comfortably into the category of a fun night at the movies. Wheatley could be forgiven for taking it a little easy after distilling J.G. Ballard's supposedly unfilmable novel *High-Rise* (2016) into a powerful visual satire on the haves and the have nots. It was complex heady stuff. Action choreography aside, *Free Fire* is not so much. Those hoping this would be an outrageous bullet ballet in the vein of *Shoot 'em Up* (2007), which is also essentially one, long gunfight might feel a little disappointed. While the bullets do fly furiously, the physics tend to stay grounded in at least semi-reality. Wheatley is a little more concerned with his characters. To that end, he assembles a cast of stellar character actors. Armie Hammer owns the role of Ord, a smooth charmer with a big mouth, a character who gives him a chance to exercise his exceptional sense of comic timing. Given his physicality, he could have simply played the part as a requisite crime boss, but Ord comes across far more eccentric and even fragile.

Another highlight is Sharlto Copley as the weaselly gun runner Vernon. Copley has been ill-used since his stunning debut in *District 9* (2009). *Free Fire* gives him a solid amount of screen time and a far better character to play with than the recent *Chappie* (2015) or *Hardcore Henry* (2015). Copley is also aware of his physicality and Vernon is a case study in overcompensation. Vernon's partner Martin is played in a more straightforward manner by a very capable Babou Ceesay and the dynamic between the two creates a sense of uncertainty regarding who is really in charge. One of Wheatley's regular players, the great Michael Smiley, gives Frank an air of seedy desperation, a man who cannot understand how he wound up stuck with idiots like Stevo and Bernie. But perhaps the most interesting characters are Chris (Cillian Murphy) and intermediary Justine (Brie Larson) who quickly emerge as the only reasonably sane presences at the meet and have a past that no one else knows about.

Setting the film in the 1970s gives Wheatley and longtime creative partner and co-writer Amy Jump a style to aim for and *Free Fire* certainly plays like a fast and loose 1970s exploiter at times. But the script just feels like everyone is trying too hard to sound tough,

"Hey, I like your cardboard armor." Harry says. "It's protection from infection." Vernon quips. With so many characters, the endless attempts at posturing fly by almost as fast as the ammo. And, while *Free Fire* is worth watching again to catch the ones missed the first time, the real salvation of the film is the editing, which not only keeps the mayhem in motion but makes it relatively easy to keep track of who is shooting at who. Audiences may even find themselves caring about the sad sack would-be criminal masterminds who end up determined to slaughter each other.

Since his debut film, *Down Terrace* (2009), Ben Wheatley has shown himself to be a master of the use of violence. Sometimes, as in *Kill List* (2011), the effect is at the service of pure horror. In *Sightseers* (2012), it was darkly comic. Here it almost plays like Edgar Wright-lite. This is unlikely to be Wheatley's breakthrough to mainstream larger budget projects but it stands alongside his other work as a nice diversion.

Dave Canfield

CREDITS

Bernie: Enzo Cilenti
Stevo: Sam Riley
Frank: Michael Smiley
Justine: Brie Larson
Chris: Cillian Murphy
Ord: Armie Hammer
Origin: United States
Language: English
Released: 2017
Production: Andrew Starke; Film 4, Protagonist Pictures, Rook Films; released by A24 Films LLC
Directed by: Ben Wheatley
Written by: Ben Wheatley; Amy Jump
Cinematography by: Laurie Rose
Music by: Geoff Barrow; Ben Salisbury
Sound: Martin Pavey
Music Supervisor: Ian Neil
Editing: Ben Wheatley; Amy Jump
Art Direction: Nigel Pollock
Costumes: Emma Fryer
Production Design: Paki Smith
MPAA rating: R
Running time: 91 minutes

REVIEWS

Dowd, A.A. *The A.V. Club*. April 20, 2017.
Guzman, Rafer. *Newsday*. April 20, 2017.
Hertz, Barry. *Globe and Mail*. April 21, 2017.
Kenny, Glenn. *New York Times*. April 20, 2017.
Kohn, Eric. *Indiewire*. September 12, 2017.
Medsker, David. *Bullz-Eye.com*. April 20, 2017.
Morris, Brogan. *Paste Magazine*. April 21, 2017.
Olsen, Mark. *Los Angeles Times*. April 20, 2017.
Rothkopf, Joshua. *Time Out*. April 21, 2017.
Savlov, Marc. *Austin Chronicle*. April 20, 2017.

QUOTES

Harry: "Hey, I like your cardboard armor."
Vernon: "It's protection from infection."

TRIVIA

While planning out the dimensions of the set, director Ben Wheatley built a scale replica of the film's warehouse using the video game *Minecraft*.

FRIEND REQUEST

Be careful who you click with.
—Movie tagline
Like. Comment. Kill.
—Movie tagline

Box Office: $3.8 Million

Considering its omnipresence in our daily lives and all the unspeakable things that can be found on it in real life with just a couple of keystrokes, the notion of creating a horror movie based around the Internet would seem to be an ideal method of playing with our fears of the still-developing technological age and our place in it. And yet, the majority of the attempts to do just that, including the likes of *Feardotcom* (2002), *Cry Wolf* (2005), *Untraceable* (2008), and *Unfriended* (2014) have been little more than disposable junk so utterly forgettable that it is unlikely that many of you reading this review recalled that they even existed until reading this sentence. The latest such film of this type is *Friend Request*, a broken link of a thriller that is so utterly bland, formless, and lacking in inspiration that the whole thing feels like a RickRoll sans the winning soundtrack. Not only are there cat videos out there that come closer to providing genuine scares than any of the would-be frights on display here, but one of them actually turns up in the film itself and supplies one of the only two moments that come close to inspiring actual terror.

Our heroine is Laura (Alycia Debnam-Carey), a college student who appears to have the perfect life—she is beautiful, smart, well-liked, and does charity work in her spare time. She also has friends aplenty, both in real life and, perhaps more importantly, online where her friend count on the hugely popular social networking site that she uses—which looks, sounds, and acts exactly like Facebook but is never referred to as such, presumably as the result of a lawyer's missive far more terrifying than the screenplay proper—counts more than 800 people following her every post. On the opposite end of the social stratum is Marina (Liesl Ahlers), a odd goth girl who wears nothing but black, sits by herself at lunch, and appears to not have a single friend to speak of, real or virtual. Taking pity on Marina, Laura accepts her friend request but quickly learns to regret having done so when Marina begins acting weird and possessive towards her. Eventually, even the saintly Laura reaches the limits of her patience and first lies about her upcoming birthday party to avoid inviting Marina—though she still posts dozens of photos of the event online for all to see—and then, following an ugly confrontation, commits the ultimate act of betrayal by unfriending her. Marina reacts to this in pretty much the expected manner—she not only commits suicide by simultaneously hanging and burning herself but does so in front of her computer in order to broadcast the act for all to see.

Laura feels guilty about Marina's suicide, but her sadness turns to horror when the video of the act mysteriously turns up on her "Fauxbook" page, resisting all attempts to remove it prove unsuccessful and her virtual followers, repulsed by what they believe to be her cruelty, begin unfriending her in droves. In a further blow to her status, all the friends who were at Laura's birthday celebration start dying in bizarre and gruesome ways with videos of those deaths turning up on Laura's feed as well. With her real and virtual friend counts both rapidly dwindling and her social status at pariah stage, Laura is determined to find Marina's body (oh yeah—the school and police immediately designated Marina a suicide despite never actually finding a body to prove that there was actually a death) and her research into her online tormentor reveals not just a bleak backstory but the possibility that bringing an end to everything may require her to confront forces even more powerful and evil than those found in a typical ISP provider.

The idea of a mad slasher movie in which the vast majority of the body count is digital in nature and where the loss of online friends is afforded as much, if not more, dramatic weight that the gory murders of actual flesh-and-blood people sounds like something that, in the right hands, could have been spun into a script plumbing the world of social media for both social satire and meta-horror thrills—it might have worked as an episode of *Black Mirror*, for example. Of course, to do this would require such things as talent and effort and so director Simon Verhoeven and co-writers Matthew Ballen and Phillip Koch instead elected to serve up an exceptionally bald retread of the American version of *The Ring* (2002) that has been updated from the world of VHS tapes to the smartphone era almost as incompetently as that film's actual contemporary reboot, *Rings* (2017). The scare scenes are as aimless and devoid of thrills as can be, despite the intense efforts by co-composers Gary Go and Martin Todsharow to goose things up with an amusingly overblown score. Neither Laura nor Marina register as particularly interesting characters and, as a result, it is impossible to feel much of anything towards them—Debnam-Carey and Ahlers presumably both had the same problem, to judge by their listless performances. As for the film's utterly perfunctory ending, it somehow pulls off the trick of coming across as both dully predictable and vaguely offensive though most viewers will have long since abandoned the film to check their phones and tablets to notice.

As it is unlikely that any sane and clear-headed person will ever voluntarily watch *Friend Request* in their lifetimes, perhaps the other moment of genuine terror that it displays can be divulged here. After Marina's video posts on Laura's feed to the consternation of her peers and the school faculty, she does everything that she can to try to remove it to no avail. Eventually, we see her enduring one of the most painful of modern-day tortures—being stuck on the phone with a customer service representative unsuccessfully trying to explain what her problem is and getting absolutely no help in return. It may not be much but my guess that it is the only point in this whole sorry exercise that viewers will actually respond to when they see it. As for the rest, it might be too much to suggest that spending 92 minutes on hold with customer service would provide more actual entertainment value that spending it watching *Friend Request* but the fact that anyone forced to choose between the two would be well advised to think that decision over very carefully should suggest just how crummy this film really is.

Peter Sobczynski

CREDITS

Laura: Alycia Debnam-Carey
Tyler: William Moseley
Kobe: Connor Paolo
Olivia: Brit Morgan
Isabel: Brooke Markham
Origin: United States
Language: English
Released: 2017

Production: Quirin Berg, Max Wiedemann; Seven Pictures, Two Oceans Production, Wiedemann & Berg Filmproduktion; released by Entertainment Studios Motion Pictures

Directed by: Simon Verhoeven

Written by: Simon Verhoeven; Matthew Ballen; Philip Koch

Cinematography by: Joe Heim

Music by: Gary Go; Martin Todsharow

Sound: Nico Krebs

Editing: Denis Bachter; Tom Seil

Costumes: Tatjana Brecht-Bergen; Wolfgang Ender; Reza Levy

Production Design: Sylvain Gingras; Tommy Starks

MPAA rating: R

Running time: 92 minutes

REVIEWS

Duralde, Alonso. *TheWrap*. September 22, 2017.

Horton, Robert. *Seattle Weekly*. September 22, 2017.

Kiang, Jessica. *Variety*. September 21, 2017.

Kupecki, Josh. *Austin Chronicle*. September 28, 2017.

Lloyd, Kate. *Time Out*. April 19, 2017.

MacDonald, Moira. *Seattle Times*. September 21, 2017.

Padua, Pat. *Washington Post*. September 21, 2017.

Righetti, Jamie. *IndieWire*. September 22, 2017.

Rozsa, Matthew. *Salon*. September 23, 2017.

Walsh, Katie. *Los Angeles Times*. September 22, 2017.

QUOTES

Evil is trending.

Young Marina: "I just want to be friends...best friends...forever."

TRIVIA

Even though the whole movie revolves around Facebook, the product is not explicity mentioned.

G

GEOSTORM

Brave the storm
—Movie tagline

Some things were never meant to be controlled... Heaven forbid those same things should ever control us.
—Movie tagline

Surf's up... WAY up.
—Movie tagline

Box Office: $33.7 Million

Cashing in on the geopolitical crisis that is global warming, *Geostorm* attempts to provide a science-fictional solution inside the framework of generic action thrills. A long and convoluted production—seeing the replacement of writer/director Dean Devlin by Danny Cannon and Laeta Kalogridis—is visible in every frame of the schlocky B-movie that is so unaware of itself that it cannot even find pleasures in its absurd levels of camp.

This theatrical ridiculousness comes from the high pressure front of the intense, labyrinthine plot and the low pressure front of stars Gerard Butler (playing Jake Lawson) and Jim Sturgess (playing Jake's brother, Max), which form a truly devastating cinematic storm cell. Jake is the lead architect of an international effort formed to combat rising instances of extreme weather events across the globe. To do so, they create a large network of interlinked satellites (physically interlinked, via large ropey CGI cables, to give the appearance of an atmospheric net) aimed to disrupt extreme events and modulate weather, thereby preventing the effects of global warming through technology rather than behavioral adaptation.

This fix-it plan mirrors the moral airbrushing undertaken by the film's script when it comes to Jake. Butler plays the swaggering scientist like a gruff alcoholic and the world seems constructed specifically to highlight his greatness in all things. People on the street swoon, curmudgeonly Senators are cowed, and other scientists are intellectually intimidated in his presence. Jake is, the movie asserts, a real American. He is so brusque and down-to-earth that he refuses to follow government guidelines and is fired, being promptly replaced as head of the satellite network (known as Dutch Boy, after the dike-plugging hero of the story-within-a-story in *Hans Brinker; or, the Silver Skates: A Story of Life in Holland*) by Max. Max is some sort of undersecretary in the State Department and seems to have no experience with anything but the Hollywood version of government work, which consists of wearing a suit and attending off-screen meetings.

After a three-year cut, something is amiss with Dutch Boy. Towns are being annihilated by blizzards that look like supervillain freeze rays and heat waves that look like volcanic eruptions. An inside job is suspected, and Jake is recruited to go to space, check out the operational base onboard the International Space Station, and solve the problem. The film, which had reshoots two years after initial photography, feels like two different productions. There is the action/disaster film, that prioritizes lackluster CGI in its one fun scene (a smart-car escape driven by Daniel Wu's Hong Kong scientist) and in countless boring ones, meshed together with a government procedural built around sniffing out a conspiracy. The latter is as well-conceived as the former is exciting, both failing at their genre conventions as conventionally as possible.

Geostorm is a confusion of stereotypes with the only consistency being its unrelenting determination that its lead be a perfect definition of old-school masculinity. Whether he is flying during a spacewalk to retrieve a door or fixing a solar panel (that he built) on his house (that he built), Jake is the action hero version of a scientist that went out of fashion in the late 1990s. As he stumbles his way through a boring space plot on hastily-dressed sets and Max walks down drab hallway after drab hallway sussing out the asinine political conspiracy, all that remains is the promise of the actual geostorm—a global storm combining the terrible super-weather.

That this promise ends in disappointment is one thing, but ending the same way it began—with overwritten voiceover delivered by a grating child (Talitha Bateman)—festoons this insipid film with bookends most akin to the warnings on packs of cigarettes. *Geostorm* may be dangerous for the mental health of the viewer, but at least it contains a countdown timer assuring you that it will soon come to a close.

Jacob Oller

CREDITS

Jake Lawson: Gerard Butler
Max Lawson: Jim Sturgess
Sarah Wilson: Abbie Cornish
Ute Fassbinder: Alexandra Maria Lara
Cheng Long: Daniel Wu
Origin: United States
Language: English
Released: 2017
Production: David Ellison, Dana Goldberg, Dean Devlin; Skydance Media, RatPac-Dune Entertainment, Stereo D, Twisted Media; released by Warner Bros. Pictures
Directed by: Dean Devlin
Written by: Dean Devlin; Paul Guyot
Cinematography by: Roberto Schaefer
Music by: Lorne Balfe
Sound: Cameron Frankley
Editing: Chris Lebenzon; John Refoua; Ron Rosen
Costumes: Susan Matheson
Production Design: Kirk M. Petruccelli
MPAA rating: PG-13
Running time: 109 minutes

REVIEWS

Abele, Robert. *TheWrap*. October 20, 2017.
Cordova, Randy. *Arizona Republic*. October 20, 2017.
D'Angelo, Mike. *The A.V. Club*. October 20, 2017.
Debruge, Peter. *Variety*. October 20, 2017.
DeFore, John. *Hollywood Reporter*. October 21, 2017.
Jones, J.R. *Chicago Reader*. October 26, 2017.
Rosen, Christopher. *Entertainment Weekly*. October 20, 2017.
Scott, A.O. *New York Times*. October 20, 2017.
Sobczynski, Peter. *RogerEbert.com*. October 20, 2017.
Smith, Anna. *Time Out*. October 20, 2017.

QUOTES

Leonard Dekkom: "How did you do that?"
President Andrew Palma: "Because I'm the g***amn President of the United States!"

TRIVIA

Several cast and crew (even the film's extras) noted that lead star/producer Gerard Butler kept forgetting all his lines.

GET OUT

Just because you're invited, doesn't mean you're welcome.
—Movie tagline

Box Office: $175.9 Million

In his debut film as writer/director, Jordan Peele (best known as half of the Comedy Central sketch comedy duo *Key & Peele*) has made one of the more legitimately frightening horror movies of the past decade, and he pulled off this feat by truly understanding where the "horror" in a horror movie should come from—reality. But that does not mean that *Get Out* aspires to be some hyper-real, documentary-esque reproduction of cruelty. Instead, Peele has created a film steeped in allegory that, in the tradition of the best works of filmmakers like George Romero, uses a fantastic situation to call out society's ugly truths that too often go unspoken.

In this case, those truths have a lot of say about the realities of being black in modern America. The film's central scenario feels like a twisted riff on *Guess Who's Coming to Dinner?* (1967). A young African-African photographer named Chris Washington (Daniel Kaluuya) is traveling to WASP-ish New England to spend the weekend with the affluent family of his white girlfriend, Rose Armitage (Allison Williams). However, once they arrive, it quickly becomes apparent that something sinister is seething beneath the genial demeanor of Rose's parents Dean and Missy (Bradley Whitford and Catherine Keener). The underlying sense of danger for Chris is firmly established by the film's opening scene in which a young black man, lost in upscale suburbia, finds himself being assaulted and kidnapped by a silent attacker wearing a medieval helmet. That scene stands as a chilling non-sequitur until much later in the film when we learn that the young man's fate is a disturbing precursor to what Chris has waiting for him on the other side of his weekend.

But this is so much more than an "uh oh, evil parents" movie. *Get Out* has two distinct qualities that helped turn it into a hit. The first is Peele's unique and brilliantly insightful perspective on race and the African-American experience. In an alternate universe, there is probably a much dumber and less effective version of *Get Out,* where Rose's parents are Confederate-flag-waving, banjo-playing rednecks who abduct black men because they see them as the "enemy." While that very binary "black and white" kind of racism does still exist today, Peele, rather smartly, went for a much less obvious choice and used the horror genre to call out the suffocating racism of appropriation. The villains of *Get Out* would never, ever admit to hating African Americans. Instead, they covet them. Rose's father claims he would have voted for Obama for a third term and he's being genuine. That being said, the faux-progressiveness that Chris encounters in the wilds of L.L. Bean New England is just as dehumanizing and sinister as anything he could encounter in the Deep South.

Rose's parents and their wealthy suburban brethren covet Chris, but by doing so, they reduce him to an object, a piece of meat. And the scenario that Peele creates—the evil Stepford Wives plot behind Chris' uncomfortable weekend—comes across as an almost Cronenbergian form of biological gentrification. Rose's parents idolize Chris' blackness to such a degree that they essentially deem him unworthy of it and make plans to move in and colonize it for themselves. And it's truly remarkable that Peele was able to use *Get Out* to call out that kind of smiling collegiate prejudice for what it is—a form of racism that is every bit as cruel (and probably more insidious) as any cross-burning hick.

The other distinct quality that made *Get Out* a success was how clearly Peele loves horror movies. It's remarkable that this is his first movie as a writer/director, because he plays with thriller tropes throughout the film like an established master. Working in collaboration with his cinematographer, Toby Oliver, and his editor, Gregory Plotkin, Peele expertly plays with every trick in the horror book. There are jump scares, tense walks through long hallways at night, freaky psychedelic nightmare sequences—the gang's all here. However, Peele bends over backwards to bring a new, fresh perspective to even the whoriest of horror clichés, indulging in each one with obvious glee, while working overtime to justify each moment on a story and character level.

Case in point, there is a moment in *Get Out* that you have seen in almost every horror movie. A character hits an evil character with a car, the evil person falls to the ground—presumably dead—but, rather than driving away, the heroic character goes back "just to make sure." Now, anyone who's ever seen a horror movie knows this is a terrible idea. The evil person obviously is still alive and going back to check on them is a painfully stupid thing to do. When I saw *Get Out* in the theater, the crowd started screaming at the screen, mocking the hero and imploring him to turn around. However, the genius thing about *Get Out* is that Peele actually built an honest, justified story reason for the hero to make that decision. Peele got to have his cake and eat it too. He crafted an iconic horror movie moment, but he did the heavy lifting to have that moment make psychological and emotional sense within the framework of the film.

The cast of *Get Out* is uniformly strong—Allison Williams stands out for her slow-burn creepiness—but the movie, as well made as it is, does have some flaws. There are a few logic gaps surrounding Chris' escape plans—cellphones have made plausible horror movie scenarios a lot tougher to craft these days and there are moments in the second act that start to drag as we move towards the inevitable conclusion. LilRel Howery absolutely kills it as Chris' best friend Rod (and the film's comedic relief), but there's an extended scene in the middle of the film, when Rod is trying to convince the police that Chris may be in trouble that strains for laughs and goes on far too long. (It's the only moment of the film that feels more like a weak *Key & Peele* skit rather than a virtuoso horror movie.)

But those complaints are few and far between. With *Get Out,* Jordan Peele has created a truly great horror movie, a film that understands that the best horror movies actually have some substance under their skin, rather than just blood and guts. This is a film that outscares *Alien: Covenant* (2017) and speaks about racism more eloquently than anything Kathryn Bigelow attempted in *Detroit* (2017). It's a remarkable achievement.

Tom Burns

CREDITS

Chris Washington: Daniel Kaluuya
Rose Armitage: Allison Williams
Missy Armitage: Catherine Keener
Dean Armitage: Bradley Whitford
Jeremy Armitage: Caleb Landry Jones
Origin: United States
Language: English
Released: 2017

Production: Edward H. Hamm, Jr., Sean McKittrick, Jason Blum, Jordan Peele; Blumhouse Productions, LLC., QC Entertainment; released by Universal Pictures
Directed by: Jordan Peele
Written by: Jordan Peele
Cinematography by: Toby Oliver
Music by: Michael Abels
Sound: Trevor Gates
Music Supervisor: Christopher Mollere
Editing: Gregory Plotkin
Art Direction: Chris Craine
Costumes: Nadine Haders
Production Design: Rusty Smith
MPAA rating: R
Running time: 104 minutes

REVIEWS

Bradshaw, Peter. *The Guardian*. March 20, 2017.
Brody, Richard. *The New Yorker*. February 22, 2017.
Dargis, Manohla. *New York Times*. February 23, 2017.
Harris, Aisha. *Slate*. February 23, 2017.
Morgenstern, Joe. *Wall Street Journal*. February 23, 2017.
Myers, Kimber. *The Playlist*. February 23, 2017.
Nicholson, Amy. *MTV News*. February 26, 2017.
Rainer, Peter. *Christian Science Monitor*. March 10, 2017.
Robinson, Tasha. *The Verge*. February 26, 2017.
Zacharek, Stephanie. *Time*. February 23, 2017.

QUOTES

Rod Williams: "Man, I told you not to go in that house."

TRIVIA

Jordan Peele directed scenes in the movie while doing impersonations of Tracy Morgan, Forest Whitaker, and Barack Obama.

AWARDS

Oscars 2017: Orig. Screenplay
Ind. Spirit 2018: Director (Peele), Film
Writers Guild 2017: Orig. Screenplay
Nominations:
Oscars 2017: Actor (Kaluuya), Director (Peele), Film
British Acad. 2017: Actor (Kaluuya), Orig. Screenplay
Directors Guild 2017: Director (Peele)
Golden Globes 2018: Actor--Mus./Comedy (Kaluuya), Film--Mus./Comedy
Ind. Spirit 2018: Actor (Kaluuya), Film Editing, Screenplay
Screen Actors Guild 2017: Actor (Kaluuya), Cast

GHOST IN THE SHELL

Box Office: $40.6 Million

As a critic, *Ghost in the Shell* is the kind of movie that brings out your inner Gene Shalit. It is such an inept, navel-gazing mess that it immediately makes you want to resort to hacky puns like "It's a shell of a movie!" or "There's not a ghost of a chance that you'll enjoy this film!" More than anything, *Ghost in the Shell* will probably stand as a testament to the fickle appeal of the live-action adaptation genre. While Disney's *Beauty and The Beast* (2017) adaptation brought in over a billion dollars at the international box office, *Ghost in the Shell*—a Western retelling of the popular Japanese manga—was both a critical and financial bomb.

Why did *Beauty and the Beast* thrive while *Ghost in the Shell* died on the vine? Both brought popular animated storylines to life using Hollywood actors and special effects, and both were met with a certain amount of fan-base skepticism when they were announced. So why did audiences reject one and embrace the other? Looking beyond Disney's unrivaled marketing prowess, the answer probably lies in what each project promised and what they delivered. The live action *Beauty and the Beast* sold itself as a loving companion and complimentary piece to the original, and nostalgic audiences flocked to it. While, on the other hand, the live action *Ghost in the Shell* took one of the most complex and beloved anime/manga properties that Japan has ever produced and found itself both disrespecting the source material and unable to bring any new ideas to the table at all. The end result is not a tribute or a derivative work, it was just a hollow shadow play, stealing snippets of cool anime images from CrunchyRoll and inch-deep philosophical ponderings from an undergrad film student's term paper on Ridley Scott's *Blade Runner* (1982).

Director Rupert Sanders brought a bit of panache to his directorial debut, *Snow White and the Huntsman* (2012), a forgettable film with a strong cast and an interesting visual palate, but it's hard to see what if anything he brought to *Ghost in the Shell.* Maybe the blame lies more with the screenwriters—Jamie Moss, William Wheeler, and Ehren Kruger—who had the entire library of *Ghost in the Shell* manga to work from and yet all they were able to pull out of that massive storytelling network was a tired old "Am I man or machine" storyline that was already showing its age back when *Robocop* debuted in 1987.

But, while there's plenty of creative blame to go around, one has to reserve a certain degree of sympathy for Scarlett Johansson, who plays the film's lead, Mira Killian ("The Major"), and has to spend a large portion of the film in perhaps the most unflattering nude body-suit in the history of cinema. Johansson is given nothing to play with in *Ghost in the Shell.* Her character is a cipher, she has no defining characteristics, no purpose. She's a character built to stomp through uninspired action scenes, pausing only for overly long, overly earnest philosophic musings.

The story that the screenwriters have cobbled together from the *Ghost in the Shell* lore is an origin story of sorts for The Major. In the future, corporations (and Japanese culture) have seemingly taken over the world, and human beings have begun regularly implanting technological "upgrades" into their bodies. After Mira Killian is injured in a terrorist explosion, which kills her family, the omnipresent Hanka Robotics corporation places her consciousness inside of a "shell" (i.e. an artificial robotic body). When the filmmakers were accused of white-washing their *Ghost in the Shell* adaptation by casting Johansson in a role typically depicted as Asian, they tried to justify the decision by claiming that the "shell" was Caucasian, but the consciousness inside the shell was still that of an Asian girl. This seems like a lame justification for the casting and also seems to suggest that *Ghost in the Shell* actually addresses race and racism in any way, which it really does not. (There is a plotline about the government marginalizing refugees, but the main refugee characters are played by Johansson and Michael Pitt, who are as Caucasian as they come.)

For whatever reason, Hanka Robotics decides to loan Killian out to an anti-terrorist group called Section 9, where she becomes known as The Major and regularly teams up with her partner Batou (Pilou Asbæk) to fight cyber-crime and battle rogue robo-geishas. After a corporate assassination attempt goes wrong, The Major learns that a hacker named Kuze is targeting executives from Hanka Robotics and, as she follows his path of destruction, she becomes more and more aware of a series of hallucinatory glitches that begin to make The Major question her memories and her grasp on reality.

Johansson finds herself playing a clueless character, desperate to solve a mystery that's obvious to anyone who's ever seen a movie before, which is a painfully thankless role for such a talented actress. Also, on a story level, it makes *Ghost in the Shell* a surprisingly difficult movie to sit through. Even though it clocks in at 106 minutes, the lack of narrative momentum makes the film feel twice as long.

Sanders makes a shallow attempt to mimic images and set pieces from the *Ghost in the Shell* manga and anime movies, but none of them feel vibrant or earned, coming across more like visual karaoke than anything else. Typically, big dystopian sci-fi movies like this live and die on their action and visuals. Unfortunately, Sanders cannot even deliver superficially, because there's simply nothing in his version of *Ghost in the Shell* that will catch your eye, even for a moment. Every vista looks familiar and clichéd. The action is trite, overly edited, and unoriginal. Even the visuals of the characters themselves look like uninspired cosplay.

Ultimately, there is no reason for this version of *Ghost in the Shell* to exist. It does not bring anything new to the table; it does not revel in the nostalgia of the source material. It is just a designer impostor, hoping that, if it smells enough like the original, people won't notice how cheap it is. Unfortunately, everything about the film stinks in such a way that it's the one aspect of the movie that's impossible to ignore.

Tom Burns

CREDITS

Major: Scarlett Johansson
Batou: Pilou Asbaek
Aramaki: Takeshi "Beat" Kitano
Dr. Ouelet: Juliette Binoche
Kuze: Michael Pitt
Origin: United States
Language: English, Japanese
Released: 2017
Production: Michael Costigan, Steven Paul; Dreamworks L.L.C., Reliance Entertainment; released by Paramount Pictures Corp.
Directed by: Rupert Sanders
Written by: Jamie Moss; William Wheeler; Ehren Kruger
Cinematography by: Jess Hall
Music by: Lorne Balfe; Clint Mansell
Sound: Per Hallberg
Editing: Billy Rich; Neil Smith
Art Direction: Richard L. Johnson
Costumes: Kurt and Bart
Production Design: Jan Roelfs
MPAA rating: PG-13
Running time: 107 minutes

REVIEWS

Andersen, Soren. *Seattle Times*. March 30, 2017.
Dargis, Manohla. *New York Times*. March 30, 2017.
Hornaday, Ann. *Washington Post*. March 30, 2017.
Mintzer, Jordan. *The Hollywood Reporter*. March 28, 2017.
Nesselson, Lisa. *Screen International*. March 28, 2017.
Opam, Kwame. *The Verge*. March 31, 2017.
Perez, Rodrigo. *The Playlist*. March 30, 2017.
Persall, Steve. *Tampa Bay Times*. March 30, 2017.
Rothkopf, Joshua. *Time Out/New York*. March 30, 2017.
Savlov, Marc. *Austin Chronicle*. April 5, 2017.

QUOTES

The Major: "They created me. But they cannot control me."

TRIVIA

For the Japanese release of this film, the voice actors from *Ghost in the Shell* (1995) all reprise their roles.

A GHOST STORY

It's all about time.
—Movie tagline

Box Office: $1.6 Million

David Lowery left his biggest film in terms of budget—2016's fantastic remake of Disney's *Pete's Dragon*—and reunited with his closest collaborators, including the two stars of his debut *Ain't Them Bodies Saints* (2013), for his smallest and best work to date. Shot almost entirely over a weekend in a small house in Texas for only around $100k, *A Ghost Story* is a meditative, hypnotic examination of the human distinction of being both minute in comparison to the grand scheme of history but also gigantic within the personal moment. Of course, when looked at against the fabric of time, a tiny piece of paper placed lovingly in a wall means almost nothing. And yet, to the individual who put it there and the emotion it expresses across realities, it is literally everything. Lowery's film is ambitious, mesmerizing, moving, and unlike anything else released in 2017. It is simply one of the year's best films.

From its opening scenes, Lowery is playing with time and audience expectations. An unnamed male character played by Casey Affleck and an unnamed female character played by Rooney Mara live together in a small house. With very little dialogue, Lowery presents a few shots of their humble, simple existence, including a scene in which they think they hear something in the living room late at night. Are they being haunted? Audiences are naturally going to bring that expectation into a film with a title like this, but Lowery doesn't deliver traditional jump scares or even supernatural mood-setters. There's an eerie sense that something "greater" is happening, but these lives are relatively average, as is their humble starter home.

Lowery takes his time in ways that indicate this will not be a predictably structured film. We watch the Woman take out the trash all the way down her driveway and then walk back again. It's the kind of shot that Lowery knows will make viewers question why it was even included, but it's indicative of how the filmmaker is constructing his film in a unique way. The small things matter, and, later, the big things will fly by in the blink of an eye. He's using cinematic time like an accordion, pushing and pulling against traditional pacing in a way that amplifies the film's themes.

Before Lowery can do that, the man dies. It's a car accident, off camera, and he's next seen on a gurney in a hospital with a sheet over his body. His wife leaves and Lowery's camera lingers for a long time before the man sits up, never removing the sheet from his body, making him a "ghost" in the old-fashioned way that viewers are used to seeing on Halloween or in community theater. He gets up and leaves the hospital, returning home, where he is often a background figure, watching his wife go about her life. He sees her eat a pie on the kitchen floor in an instantly-notorious scene given the time that Lowery takes with it, showing Mara's character consume the entire thing in one shot. It's kind of a make-or-break moment for the film with viewers. People are either with the experiment or not.

From here, Lowery starts playing with time with incredibly subtle edits and blocking. As the ghost moves about the house, life goes on around him. People will walk through doors indicating different days and experiences, but the ghost remains unmoved. Time, which Lowery has been deliberate about to this point, is speeding up. The ghost sees another ghost in the house next door and the two can communicate telepathically. Ultimately, the wife decides to move, placing a small note in a hole in the wall before she goes.

Time then speeds up even more. The ghost haunts other families that move into the house, and a party unfolds at which Will Oldham gives a controversial speech about the insignificance of a single lifetime (which only feels controversial if you believe Lowery implicitly agrees with the speech—because then it's a filmmaker "spelling out" his themes—however, a case can be made just as equally that *A Ghost Story* proves Oldham wrong.) The ghost exists well into the future. The house is destroyed, and *A Ghost Story* achieves near sci-fi classification as skyscrapers sprout up where the house used to be. Ultimately, the ghost falls from a high building, and essentially time loops in on itself. We see him back before the house was built, watching settlers build it and then get killed by Native Americans. And then *A Ghost Story* gets back to its opening scenes—revealing that the Man was, in a sense, actually haunting himself. And only when the ghost gets back to the note left by his wife, finally able to read it, does his journey end.

Framing it in a way that makes the film look like old photos—rounded edges and saturated colors—cinematographer Andrew Droz Palermo (*You're Next* [2011]) achieves a visual palette that perfectly accompanies Lowery's minimalist storytelling. It's also a deftly-edited film by Lowery himself, as the rhythm of the movie is essential for its success given its lack of traditional narrative thrust. It's a film that sometimes resembles a dream, and it requires the viewer to dismantle expectations of standard plot and three-act structure. It's so rare to see a movie that feels like work from a different template and uses a different cinematic language—one that's emotionally familiar but requires a new way of viewing by people who see it.

Ultimately, *A Ghost Story* becomes a masterpiece because of the emotional undercurrent that runs so strongly underneath it. In the end, it is a meditation on grief, which viewers have seen before in the supernatural arena, but it is unlike anything seen in an American cinema in generations—it has echoes more of European films about loss from the 1950s and 1960s than anything the horror genre has produced recently. With just three films, David Lowery has announced himself as one of the most important American filmmakers of his generation, whether he's working from a Disney budget or getting his friends together for a weekend to make a follow-up that's unforgettable.

Brian Tallerico

CREDITS

C: Casey Affleck
M: Rooney Mara
Little Boy: McColm Cephas, Jr.
Doctor: Kenneisha Thompson
Man in Wheelchair: Grover Coulson
Origin: United States
Language: English
Released: 2017
Production: Toby Halbrooks, James M. Johnston, Adam Donaghey; Ideaman Studios, Sailor Bear, Zero Trans Fat Productions; released by A24 Films LLC
Directed by: David Lowery
Written by: David Lowery
Cinematography by: Andrew Droz Palermo
Music by: Daniel Hart
Editing: David Lowery
Art Direction: David Pink
Costumes: Annell Brodeur
Production Design: Jade Healy; Tom Walker
MPAA rating: R
Running time: 92 minutes

REVIEWS

Chang, Justin. *Los Angeles Times.* July 6, 2017.
Dowd, A.A. *The A.V. Club.* July 5, 2017.
Grierson, Tim. *Screen International.* January 22, 2017.
Murray, Noel. *The Playlist.* January 22, 2017.
Phillips, Michael. *Chicago Tribune.* July 13, 2017.
Raup, Jordan. *The Film Stage.* January 22, 2017.
Scott, A.O. *New York Times.* July 6, 2017.
Seitz, Matt Zoller. *RogerEbert.com.* July 6, 2017.
Truitt, Brian. *USA Today.* July 5, 2017.
Wilkinson, Alissa. *Vox.* July 8, 2017.

QUOTES

Houseguest: "A writer writes a novel, a songwriter writes a song, we do what we can to endure."

TRIVIA

Was shot in Irving, Texas using profits from *Pete's Dragon* (2016).

GIFTED

How do you create an ordinary life for an extraordinary girl?
—Movie tagline

Box Office: $24.8 Million

Perhaps it is apt that this film about a prickly little mathematics prodigy is out to do quite a number on one's composure. During one of *Gifted*'s many tear-triggering scenes, the reunion of seven-year-old arithmetic ace Mary (McKenna Grace) and her ever-loving, ever-stubbled Uncle Frank (nicely-underplaying Chris Evans) aimed to make the audience awash with so much salt water that members might almost feel the need to climb up into one of the boats he repairs to avoid drowning in what ducts were dispensing. It was not a vessel but the characters and then viewers who did indeed break down in a different sense, with Mary and Frank clinging to each other as tightly as many moviegoers consequently gripped their Kleenexes. When the girl places a thumb in each corner of Frank's mouth and makes him smile with a purposeful push upward, her endeavor seems akin to this production's own ever-increasing manipulation.

"I thought I was bad for you," the pint-sized genius's once-and-future caretaking uncle laments, but then Frank continues that he "must be doing something right" because Mary is a possessor of commendable qualities. While Frank can never be considered to be detrimental, so much of the unabashed heartstring-tugging of this film is, and while *Gifted* may be "sweet," one of three adjectives he bestows upon his beloved braniac charge, the production is certainly not also worthy of being termed "amazing," nor is it as "smart" as she is. Yet, one has to admit that, like the well-meaning man responsible for Mary, those responsible for *Gifted* have done some things rather right.

They correctly solved the problem of selecting two worthwhile leads who would create appealing, palpably-believable chemistry. It is abundantly plain from the start how much Evans' character cares about Grace's gifted girl. Soon after Mary takes a seat in a prosaic first-grade classroom after previously being home-schooled by Frank, one notes that the intellectually-imperious and impatient youngster's social skills decidedly lag behind her highly-advanced ones relating to reckoning. She loudly and disrespectfully gives the principal a piece of her superior mind, and then a boy's nose is out of joint—quite literally—after she bashes it due to his derisiveness, both of which show that some essential things are simply not computing. Since Bonnie (Jenny Slate), her teacher and the obvious eventual (and rather imprudent) love interest of Frank, has to resort to a calculator in order to verify the answers astoundingly spouted by this mini human one, an accelerated education involving intense study at an exclusive prep school is recommended for Mary, fueled forward by a full-ride scholarship. However, the chance at a full life is what a sincerely-concerned Frank feels (for eventually-revealed, understandable reasons) that this girl with no similarly-aged friends needs most, learning how to be well-adjusted amongst the average-intelligenced folk with whom she will need to successfully interact during most of her time in life. He also wishes her to be one whiz kid who will not miss out on the matchless and precious fun of simply being a kid—before her youth all-too-quickly whizzes by.

This girl who Frank wants to be a well-rounded person is put forth in a well-rounded performance by Grace. There is, indeed, something about her Mary. She comes off as both recognizably real and engaging, managing to stay this side of grating (even if some may understandably feel that she periodically teeters on the brink). While her character is manifestly exceptional when it comes to knowing all the answers to equations, she is nevertheless quite unremarkable for her age in being endlessly full of questions. There is one rather lovely scene involving a Q and A between this high-IQ kid and her uncle, with Mary endearingly climbing upon Frank as the sassy little lass insistently asks about all sorts of things, an interlude bathed in a picturesque sunset's glow that quite pleasingly also conveys an additional kind of warmth.

The sun begins to set less attractively on the film, however, when focus on the distinctive, disarming give-and-take between this pair—featuring some sparkling sparking—is largely diverted to the more standard-issue interaction between Frank and his estranged British mum Evelyn (Lindsay Duncan), whose upper lip is by no means the only thing about her that is quite rigidly stiff. Evelyn suddenly rides in on her high horse and expresses her desire to raise Mary, to lift her up out of what she deems as neglectful normalcy and gallop back together toward Boston with a tunnel-visioned eye on higher learning. Will the highest thing perhaps turn out to be the cost to Mary, potentially traumatized upon leaving behind much-loved Frank, the landlady (Octavia Spencer) who is a stalwartly-concerned companion and source of unbridled fun, and Fred, the one-eyed cat that makes Evelyn sniff due to an allergy and not, for once, haughty disdain?

In that woman's day, she had apparently felt societal pressure to opt for matrimony and motherhood instead of sallying forth toward making her own mark in mathematics. A lingering frustration about her dreams meeting a premature dead-end seems inextricably linked to Evelyn's even-more-promising daughter (and Mary's mom), Dianne, meeting a far more regrettable one: isolated, undoubtedly feeling parental pressure, and depressed, the twenty-two-year-old's "rarer than radium" mind had chosen to commit suicide. Frank, revealed to be gifted himself, had apparently chosen a job with flexible hours so he could dutifully teach and take care of Mary in a manner of which his sister might approve, although at one point he gripes that playing Mr. Mom is cramping his style, depriving him of even "five minutes of my own life." Wanting to prevent lament from continuing on as a significant part of the family's lineage, Frank will fight for what he feels is in Mary's best interest, and a generally-less-than-gripping court battle ensues over the child's custody and the correct manner of intellectual cultivation.

Not in the best interests of the film is the increasing melodramatic manipulativeness that follows, which had some viewers looking down their noses à la Evelyn and sniffing due to scorn for the over-plotted script's machinations and their own allergic reaction to excessive schmaltz. Anyone who heard the promises to Mary that she need not worry about "going anywhere" and did not recognize them as glaringly-ominous foreshadowing need not bother ever applying to Mensa. With "Fly Away Little Pretty Bird" being sappily sung on the soundtrack, one would have to be a dodo to experience any shock during the film's biggest "We dare you not to blubber!" scene in which Frank walks away from Mary's meltdown upon being left with a foster family, the court's incredulity-testing choice of an unhappy medium. Then there is the dramatic reprieve that prevents poor Mary from almost also losing her cherished kitty, just a split-second before he is euthanized. Still, in spite of such things and more, it was not a furball but an emotion-induced lump in the throat that genuinely-moved moviegoers were feeling during the satisfying relief of Frank and Mary's aforementioned reunion. It leads to an ending where everyone finally uses their supposedly-brilliant heads to come up with a compromise that even cerebral slowpokes had likely thought of long before.

David L. Boxerbaum

CREDITS

Frank Adler: Chris Evans
Mary Adler: McKenna Grace
Evelyn: Lindsay Duncan

Bonnie: Jenny Slate
Roberta Taylor: Octavia Spencer
Origin: United States
Language: English
Released: 2017
Production: Andy Cohen, Karen Lunder; Dayday Films, FilmNation Entertainment, Grade A Entertainment; released by Fox Searchlight Pictures
Directed by: Marc Webb
Written by: Tom Flynn
Cinematography by: Stuart Dryburgh
Music by: Rob Simonsen
Sound: Ron Bochar
Music Supervisor: Meghan Currier
Editing: Bill Pankow
Costumes: Abby O'Sullivan
Production Design: Laura Fox
MPAA rating: PG-13
Running time: 101 minutes

REVIEWS

Chang, Justin. *Los Angeles Times*. April 5, 2017.
Gleiberman, Owen. *Variety*. March 30, 2017.
Herrington, Nicole. *New York Times*. April 6, 2017.
Nashawaty, Chris. *Entertainment Weekly*. April 6, 2017.
O'Sullivan, Michael. *Washington Post*. April 6, 2017.
Phillips, Michael. *Chicago Tribune*. April 6, 2017.
Roeper, Richard. *Chicago Sun-Times*. April 5, 2017.
Russo, Tom. *Boston Globe*. April 6, 2017.
Scheck, Frank. *Hollywood Reporter*. April 5, 2017.
Truitt, Brian. *USA Today*. April 5, 2017.

QUOTES

Mary Adler: "He's a good person. He wanted me before I was smart."

TRIVIA

After filming had ended, actors Chris Evans and Jenny Slate began a relationship and broke up almost a year later.

GIRLS TRIP

You'll be glad you came.
—Movie tagline

Box Office: $115.2 Million

Sometimes a comedy's laugh factor dominates everything else about it. Character development, logical story elements, and originality can be forgotten about entirely so long as the jokes and gags remain consistently funny. Judd Apatow's films, for instance, never aspire to be original or daring. *The 40-year-Old Virgin* (2005) had a storyline that was basically recycled from dozens of 1980s comedies about guys who wanted to get laid. But the characters had charm and wit, and Catherine Keener played a woman who had more than just a lovely physicality. That film also ran over two hours, which was quite a feat for a straight-up comedy. For the most part, the audience who made that film a hit did not seem to mind and it opened the door for more comedies (especially Apatow comedies) to push for more improv and sight gags to extend the running time and to let the story get pushed to the side. Comedies, though, run the risk of wearing out their welcome when they run over the standard 90-100 minutes.

That is certainly the case with *Girls Trip*, which may as well be called *Sex and the City 3* or *Bridesmaids 2*, but with an African American cast and even more juvenile gags. It is aimed squarely at African American females who have been craving a "raunch-mantic" comedy they can call their own in an age when the Apatow-based ensemble comedies have taken over the landscape. Things have fared better for women in this respect, at least in terms of quantity of films, if not quality. The same summer of *Girls Trip* also saw the female answer to *The Hangover* trilogy with *Rough Night* (2017). The all-female reboot of *Ghostbusters* (2016) the previous summer signaled a kind of movement within the industry to be more female-centric with their projects. Both films yielded mixed results and less-than-stellar box office returns. Now comes *Girls Trip*, a film with a similar kind of spirit as your average male driven raunch comedy, but also with the same level of base inanity.

The film centers on four college friends who have grown up and moved on from their days of drunken debauchery. Ryan (Regina Hall) has become a successful self-help author and is married to her college sweetheart, Stewart (Mike Colter). The two of them are a popular media couple on the verge of signing a lucrative deal to host a talk show together, so long as their marriage survives it. Sasha (Queen Latifah) graduated with a journalism degree, but has squandered it on a somewhat successful gossip blog called "Sasha's Secrets." Dina (Tiffany Haddish in a star-making performance) is the loud, obnoxious member of the group, the one who has been trouble with the law and who is quick to physically assault anyone who does her friends wrong. Of course, she is also the most sexually promiscuous. No group of this kind would be complete without the single parent of two who has since lost her outrageous side while dealing with more adult responsibilities. Lisa (Jada Pinkett Smith) is a nurse who shows up over-dressed for every occasion.

The occasion bringing these four friends together after all these years has to do with a festival in New Orleans called the Essence Festival, which celebrates black womanhood. Ryan and Stewart have been invited to attend and do some panels, so Ryan decides to invite her old friends as guests. Ryan and Stewart's marriage has been on the skids since his indiscretions. This accounts for some complications that ensue when the women arrive in New Orleans. When Stewart is seen sitting in a lobby with another woman, Dina verbally and physically assaults him (the woman turns out to be his Aunt). This gets the women kicked out of the posh hotel where they had a reservation. They end up at a seedy motel where an old man comes to the door and offers them money for services. The scene ends with him exposing his genitalia.

More complications arise when an intimate paparazzi picture of Stewart with an Instagram celebrity named Samone (Deborah Ayorinde) surfaces. Sasha, because of her website, gets a first look at the picture and there is a brief debate among the three women as to whether or not to show it to Ryan. Of course, Ryan finds out and, throughout the rest of the film, Ryan and Stewart struggle with whether or not to stay together so they can keep the aforementioned talk show deal. Sasha also has something to lose by possibly betraying her friend by selling the picture to *TMZ* so she can pay her rent. The other two characters have the typical friction that comes with either being the prude or the slutty member of the group. The prude eventually becomes the party girl she used to be and the slutty one pretty much stays the same. Saving the day at almost every turn is another old friend of theirs, Julian (Larenz Tate), who plays bass in a band performing at the festival that weekend.

The screenplay by Kenya Barris, Karen McCullah, Tracy Oliver, and Erica Rivinoja pays a lot of lip service to the idea of being "real" and "fake," but the movie itself has a problem maintaining any semblance of realism. A broad comedy never has to be nuanced and delicate with its characters, but when director Malcolm Lee throws in a brief time-lapse montage after a scene of the four women praying (sincerely) in a hotel room, the effect feels completely forced. Likewise, when the film feels like it finally has its ending, it goes on for another forty minutes with a long, drawn-out drama involving Ryan and Stewart as well as the four friends (nicknamed the Flossy Posse), who have a predictable falling out.

The comedy itself also has a dull predictability to it. For all its attempts at being outrageous, *Girls Trip* goes for all the obvious tropes of the modern-day R-rated comedy. Gratuitous male genitalia, fruit-based sex gags, urinating from a great height, scenes involving drinks spiked with hallucinogens, and a dance-off in a bar that results in a brawl. Lee cannot direct a single scene without an aggressive score underlining every gag that the viewer can see coming miles away. There will be many in the film's target audience who will not mind such contrivances and are willing to go along with the film's "anything goes" spirit. The likable cast appear to be having a great time and the film could have used more musical performances as relief from the tired comedy. Of course, there should be a raunchy comedy aimed at African American women, but like Ryan, they deserve better than this.

Collin Souter

CREDITS

Ryan Pierce: Regina Hall
Sasha Franklin: Queen Latifah
Lisa Cooper: Jada Pinkett Smith
Dina: Tiffany Haddish
Julian Stevens: Larenz Tate
Origin: United States
Language: English
Released: 2017
Production: William Packer, Malcolm Lee; Perfect World Pictures, Will Packer Productions; released by Universal Pictures Inc.
Directed by: Malcolm Lee
Written by: Kenya Barris; Tracy Oliver
Cinematography by: Greg Gardiner
Music by: David Newman
Sound: Lidia Tamplenizza
Editing: Paul Millspaugh
Art Direction: Jason Baldwin Stewart
Costumes: Danielle Hollowell
Production Design: Keith Brian Burns
MPAA rating: R
Running time: 122 minutes

REVIEWS

Anderson, Melissa. *Village Voice*. July 19, 2017.
Ao, Bethany. *Boston Globe*. July 20, 2017.
Chang, Justin. *Los Angeles Times*. July 20, 2017.
Demara, Bruce. *Toronto Star*. July 20, 2017.
Erbland, Kate. *IndieWire*. July 12, 2017.
Grovnall, Andrea. *Chicago Reader*. July 20, 2017.
Harris, Aisha. *Slate*. July 20, 2017.
Hassenger, Jesse. *The A.V. Club*. July 19, 2017.
MacDonald, Moira. *Seattle Times*. July 19, 2017.
Stewart, Sara. *New York Post*. July 20, 2017.

QUOTES

Ryan Pierce: "I am strong. I am powerful. I am beautiful."

TRIVIA

This is the first film produced, written, directed by, and starring African Americans to cross the $100 million mark.

THE GLASS CASTLE

Home goes wherever we go.
—Movie tagline

Box Office: $17.3 Million

It is astounding that the author of memoir-turned-movie *The Glass Castle* did not wind up permanently-shattered, or at least half-cracked. Jeannette Walls was let down more than brought up by a complicated couple of seemingly-mad nomads: a bohemian mother far more into painting than parenting, and a disconcertingly-fickle, force-of-nature father who was almost always into a bottle. Jeannette and the other three offspring of Rex and Rose Mary Walls gradually learned that they would largely need to fend for themselves, which at times included fending off sexual abuse from both relatives and strangers. They passed much of their chaotic formative years skipping town ahead of bill collectors and the law, getting by in a near-cross-country slew of ramshackle residences when they had any roof over their heads at all. It was a constant struggle to muddle through without electricity, heat, indoor plumbing, and, too often, food. Such things certainly do not make Jeannette's parents seem much like providers, and yet both she and this film based upon her bestselling work aimed to leave moviegoers with a decidedly-different perspective.

Ultimately coming to not only love and admire but understand and accept the duo as regrettably-damaged souls who likely did the best they were capable of doing, Jeannette has generously asserted with genuine gratitude that she did indeed receive things that have served her quite well from her ill-equipped parents, including intelligence, creativity, and experiences that have resulted in resilience and compassion—not to mention material that has benefitted the writer materially. Yes, it is all in how one chooses to look at things, as in the surprisingly-warm scene here in which a starry-eyed tween Jeannette (a promising, soulful Ella Anderson) and Rex (a wearyingly-potent Woody Harrelson) lay out in the Christmastime cold and, gazing upward, concentrate on what is buoyantly-bright amidst no lack of black. Unfortunately, more than a few moviegoers became too chilled as they stared with increasing, wide-eyed alarm at a degree of darkness up on the screen that made any light awfully tough to appreciatively perceive.

While Jeannette never suffered from a breakdown, healthfully processing her past between the covers of her evenhanded 2005 bestseller instead of upon a therapist's couch, this cinematic adaptation is detrimentally affected by the decision of screenwriters Destin Daniel Cretton and Andrew Lanham (the former also serving as director) to break it down into a choppy presentation of chunks. Their film (as many critics have complained) creates frustration as it forever flashes back and forth between various powerful points in her impoverished, unsettled, and unsettlingly youth and 1989, when things are far less gripping, but certainly not too shabby for an adult Jeanette, having risen to be a bigtime, New York gossip columnist with a Park Avenue apartment and a rather dull but dependable and wealthy fiancé (Max Greenfield), ironically digging up the secrets of other's lives while sheepishly taking care to keep her own buried. (She is played here by Brie Larson, who is so successful at getting across that Walls had put up sturdily-protective walls that it too often is a controlled-to-the-point-of-colorlessness performance.) The book had backed up only once after the cab in which she was riding pulled up next to a Lower East Side, disheveled dumpster diver who Jeannette was mortified to recognize as her mother, then proceeded in a chronological fashion to look at all she had yearned to exist solely in the rear-view mirror until coming both back to a "present" and resultantly to terms with her past. Just as errant dreamer Rex had only built castles in the sky and never the ever-promised, splendid home base he kept designing for his family, the film likewise lets viewers down, as any hoped-for momentum sadly also never materializes.

It was all too successful, however, in realizing a buildup of custodial consternation within its audiences' adults, the vividness provided by a visual representation of events magnifying their visceral impact and destroying the balance better achieved in Jeannette's prose. One's indignation aptly burned after self-absorbed painter Rose Mary (Naomi Watts in a sketchily-adapted role) grandiosely puts her artwork before the aching hunger of her children (paintings may have permanence, while all meals will indeed soon pass), leaving an endearingly-diminutive Jeanette (Chandler Head) to attempt to cook hot dogs on the stove by herself and resultantly catch on fire, ending up with permanent scars on her stomach instead of anything within it. Later on, Anderson's version of the character is almost done in by another classical element and the other parent, as reckless Rex thrice throws her into the deep water of a public pool for both a swimming and life lesson: "Sink or swim!" The distress and outrage of moviegoers was considerably heightened each time the camera submerged them along with a jolted Jeanette, forcing them to look on helplessly while she gasps and flails in terror and must rescue herself. "That was a shocker!" stressed the real Jeannette after viewing this impactful depiction, adding that she "wanted to rush at the screen." Some viewers likely felt like running the other way instead—doing "the skedaddle," as Rex routinely referred to the family's beating of a hasty retreat—when an understandably-trepidatious young Jeannette is incredibly asked to stitch up the bender brawl wounds of this father she would love to fix in general but cannot, and were themselves cut to the quick when the poor, pained thing makes a tremulous and quite touching request of her own in return that he save both himself and his family with a promise to never again partake. When a pool hall scheme involves sending off the teenaged fruit of his loins (played somewhat unconvincingly by late-twenties Larson) with a guy hornily hoping to satisfy his own, viewers felt like crowning Rex with a cue stick.

Nevertheless, there was a great desire here to have the audience sympathetically take into account that said head was already hurting. They were to understand how inaccurate it would be to ever say that this roaringly-destructive drunk was feeling no pain. In particular, it is intimated after Rex's elderly, oppressively-odious mother (an effective Robin Bartlett) is caught molesting Jeannette's kid brother Brian (Charlie Shotwell) that history was trying to ruinously repeat itself. In a final scene right from Jeanette's book but augmented here by a sappy score trying its darndest to make viewers well up along with it, the family gathers (significantly) for Thanksgiving and toasts dear, departed, complex Rex, laughing while assessing him with affectionate acceptance. Both the book and this film that has truncated it to largely hone in on the relationship between Jeannette and Rex share an overall aim to candidly reveal things in all their complexity, and there is an intriguingly-kaleidoscopic characterization of him as magnetic and repellent, humorous and no laughing matter, lovingly gentle and explosively brutal, encouraging and discouraging, insightful and shockingly blind to his destructiveness. During the aforementioned holiday hail, Rose Mary states that at least the kids' father did not bore. Yet here, he is, more than anything, difficult to bear—a mercurial monster. After what viewers have witnessed with their own eyes, many found that the forgiveness of this fête was significantly harder to swallow than the booze in those glasses raised with paradoxical pleasure to Rex. Jeannette has spoken of choosing to look at potentially-burdensome baggage handed to her by both parents and assessing those things instead as useful gifts—"some take more unwrapping than others," she admits—for those willing to accept them as such. However, such silver linings were awfully difficult to discern upon the silver screen.

David L. Boxerbaum

CREDITS

Jeannette: Brie Larson
Rex: Woody Harrelson
Rose Mary: Naomi Watts
Young Jeannette: Ella Anderson
Youngest Jeannette: Chandler Head
Origin: United States
Language: English
Released: 2017
Production: Ken Kao, Gil Netter; Netter Productions; released by Lionsgate
Directed by: Destin Daniel Cretton
Written by: Destin Daniel Cretton; Andrew Lanham
Cinematography by: Brett Pawlak
Music by: Joel P. West
Sound: Onnalee Blank; Branden Spencer
Music Supervisor: Joe Rudge
Editing: Nat Sanders
Art Direction: Nicolas Lepage
Costumes: Joy Cretton; Mirren Gordon-Crozier
Production Design: Sharon Seymour
MPAA rating: PG-13
Running time: 127 minutes

REVIEWS

Burr, Ty. *Boston Globe.* August 9, 2017.
Debruge, Peter. *Variety.* August 6, 2017.
Linden, Sheri. *Hollywood Reporter.* August 6, 2017.
McGovern, Joe. *Entertainment Weekly.* August 10, 2017.
Merry, Stephanie. *Washington Post.* August 10, 2017.
Phillips, Michael. *Chicago Tribune.* August 10, 2017.
Roeper, Richard. *Chicago Sun-Times.* August 10, 2017.
Scott, A.O. *New York Times.* August 10, 2017.
Truitt, Brian. *USA Today.* August 10, 2017.
Turan, Kenneth. *Los Angeles Times.* August 10, 2017.

TRIVIA

Jennifer Lawrence was attached to star and produce the movie for quite awhile, but eventually had to drop out and Brie Larson was subsequently cast.

GOING IN STYLE

You're never too old to get even.
—Movie tagline

Box Office: $45 Million

Zach Braff's *Going in Style* is a kinder, gentler remake of the 1979 dramedy that starred George Burns, Lee Strasberg, and Art Carney. As befitting 1970s-era cinema, writer-director Martin Brest's original ventured into dark places that Braff's version does not dare investigate: There's a bitterness about growing old that permeates every frame. Additionally, two of the main characters die, and Burns' character is imprisoned after the heist that anchors the film.

The current incarnation of *Going in Style* isn't out to rattle the viewer. It is firmly entrenched in the subgenre that birthed senior comedies like *Grumpy Old Men* (1993) and *Out to Sea* (1997). There will be no death nor incarceration for Braff's bank-robbing heroes Joe (Michael Caine), Willie (Morgan Freeman), and Albert (Alan Arkin). Rather than rage against the dying of the light, these characters seem merely annoyed that they can't change the bulb.

This is not necessarily a bad thing; different times beget different styles. The downer comedy has since found a home in the indie film market rather than in big-budget Hollywood. However, Theodore Melfi's script is self-aware enough to pay lip service to its predecessor's darkness before veering in the opposite direction. A scene that appears to be a eulogy for Albert turns out to be the best man's toast at his wedding. During the robbery, the heroes are fired upon with real ammunition at close range but are never hit.

And when it looks as if FBI Agent Arlen Hammer (Matt Dillon) has enough incontrovertible evidence to send Willie to jail, those plans are foiled by a cute little girl who's more than willing to lie to save a man she knows is guilty. This last development is certainly deus ex machina as comfort food, but 1970s era audiences would not have tolerated a lovable old codger being sent to the gallows by a kid either.

Loveable old codgers these gentlemen are, subsisting solely on the charms their portrayers can evoke in their sleep. This trio of Oscar winners are definitely earning a paycheck for not stretching their acting gifts too far. But *Going in Style* doesn't commit the sin of *Last Vegas* (2013), which featured a group of Oscar® winning old-timers (including Freeman) in an adventurous tale of camaraderie devoid of any believable notion that its characters could be friends. Even in antagonistic scenes, Caine, Freeman, and Arkin radiate warmth toward one another, creating a cohesive buddy unit that one cannot help but root for when the system does them wrong.

That system is the factory where Willie, Albert, and Joe have spent their entire careers. It has been sold to an international firm that skirts U.S. laws about pensions. As a result, retirees dependent on these payouts are suddenly without any measurable form of income. Even so, that money isn't enough for Joe to stay current on the mortgage payments on the DUMBO-area house he shares with his daughter and granddaughter. *Going in Style* opens with Joe at his bank arguing with the uncaring banker who sold him a predatory second mortgage. When that bank is successfully robbed by a tattoo-wearing bandit and his crew, Joe gets the idea that his gang can do the same. Joe's desire to hit his Williamsburg-based bank intensifies when he discovers it is in collusion with his former employer's pension drainage.

Naturally, Willie and his roommate, Albert think Joe is off his rocker. On the phone, they point out the age difference between them and the bank robbers, and also mention their lack of criminal experience. The split screens by which Braff shoots their group phone call is as old-school as the landline phones the trio are using; the scene evokes "The Telephone Song" number from *Bye Bye Birdie* (1963), which starred a much-younger version of Albert's love interest, Ann-Margret. Her character, Annie Santori, is given little to do here, though her charm and beauty are a welcome oasis in a desert of grizzled old men.

In a set piece that pays homage to the original movie's central idea of robbery just for the hell of it, Joe and company first target their local grocery store. While store employee Annie distracts Albert with her woo pitching, Joe and Willie attempt to shoplift ridiculous items like an entire pork loin and a bag of Gold Medal Flour. Here, Braff reminds his detractors that he's the king of cutesy underscoring of scenes with on-the-nose or inappropriate songs. Joe and Willie's unsuccessful getaway on a stolen Little Rascal scooter is set to a rap song by Mystikal that is censored to protect the PG-13 rating. (Don't worry—the Rascal's owner provides the requisite F-word allowed by the MPAA.)

Though it is funny, this entire sequence feels extraneous until its arresting security guard (Kenan Thompson) shows up later to accurately peg Albert as one of the bank robbers based on grocery store security footage. The botched robbery also convinces Joe that he needs an expert to help him take down Williamsburg Savings Bank. Enter Jesus (John Ortiz), a mastermind recommended to Joe by his weed-growing ex-son-in-law, Murphy (Peter Serafinowicz). Jesus will also serve as the temporary money-holder should the heist succeed. When none of the robbers can adhere to Jesus' strict timeline due to their inability to move like twentysomethings, Jesus mutters that "maybe the police will be late getting there."

The police are indeed late, so late that the ultimately successful robbery can accommodate aforementioned distractions like the real bullet spraying and that deceitful little girl. She shows sympathy for Willie who suffers a health scare while dressed in a Sammy Davis Jr. mask (the trio are disguised as The Rat Pack). Willie's temporary setback is due to his need for a kidney transplant, a secret he has hidden from his friends and the one thing that almost ruins the heist. When the girl removes Willie's mask, Agent Hammer gets a good look at half of Willie's face on the bank's surveillance video. As a result, she becomes Hammer's star witness and the surprise hero of *Going in Style.*

The never-in-doubt happy ending includes a wedding and a $2.3 million dollar payout. The money not only covers everyone's pension but also provides some financial independence for friends played by an unhinged Christopher Lloyd and August Wilson regular Anthony Chisholm. They round out a solid cast who keep *Going in Style* afloat even in its most absurdly coincidental moments. This is the kind of movie one watches on a rainy Sunday afternoon or at three o'clock in the morning on basic cable. It's charming enough to hold one's attention without demanding much heavy lifting on the viewer's part.

Odie Henderson

CREDITS

Willie: Morgan Freeman
Joe: Michael Caine
Albert: Alan Arkin
Annie: Ann-Margret
Brooklyn: Joey King
Origin: United States
Language: English
Released: 2017
Production: Donald De Line; De Line Pictures, New Line Cinema L.L.C., RatPac-Dune Entertainment, Village Roadshow Pictures; released by Warner Bros. Entertainment Inc.
Directed by: Zach Braff
Written by: Theodore Melfi
Cinematography by: Rodney Charters
Music by: Rob Simonsen
Sound: Michael J. Benavente; Ben Wilkins
Music Supervisor: Andrea von Foerster
Editing: Myron Kerstein
Art Direction: Laura Ballinger
Costumes: Gary Jones
Production Design: Anne Ross
MPAA rating: PG-13
Running time: 96 minutes

REVIEWS

Baumgarten, Marjorie. *Austin Chronicle.* April 5, 2017.
Burr, Ty. *Boston Globe.* April 6, 2017.
Dowd, A.A. *The A.V. Club.* April 6, 2017.
Henderson, Eric. *Slant Magazine.* April 6, 2017.
Hornaday, Ann. *Washington Post.* April 6, 2017.
Lemiere, Christy. *RogerEbert.com.* April 7, 2017.
MacDonald, Moira. *Seattle Times.* April 5, 2017.
Nashawathy, Chris. *Entertainment Weekly.* April 6, 2017.
Phillips, Michael. *Chicago Tribune.* April 6, 2017.
Zwecker, Bill. *Chicago Sun-Times.* April 6, 2017.

QUOTES

Joe: "These banks practically destroyed this country. They crushed a lot of people's dreams, and nothing ever happened to them. We three old guys, we hit a bank. We get away with it, we retire in dignity. Worst comes to the worst, we get caught, we get a bed, three meals a day, and better health care than we got now."

TRIVIA

The restaurant where Willie, Joe, and Albert meet for lunch is the same where Jimmy Conway (Robert De Niro) usually met with Henry Hill (Ray Liotta) in *Goodfellas* (1990).

GOLD

It was never about the money.
—Movie tagline
Prove 'em all wrong.
—Movie tagline
Based on a too good to be true story.
—Movie tagline

Box Office: $7.2 Million

Matthew McConaughey's transformation and performance in *Gold* are the most noteworthy elements of the movie. The actor first appears looking mostly as himself, albeit with a slightly receding hairline and some false teeth. After a brief prologue, the story picks up seven years later, and McConaughey's appearance has changed substantially. He is now bald and possesses a noticeable belly, while those teeth look even worse than before.

If this seems like a rather superficial point to highlight about the movie, given that so much of it is the work of makeup and hairstyling (as well as the gaining of extra weight on McConaughey's part), that is true. This fact is mostly a sign of how superficial the rest of the movie is. At least McConaughey's outward appearance has the foundation of the actor's fine performance beneath it. On the other hand, if there is a point to telling this story, Patrick Massett and John Zinman's screenplay does not find it.

The story is based on a scandal involving a Canadian mining company and a fraudulent gold claim in the

1990s. Massett and Zinman transplant the real-life events to the United States, shift the time period to 1988, and change the names of all the participants. The commonly used phrase, "Inspired by a true story," is accurately incorporated to open the story proper here. The underlying truth of the movie's story seems to be primary selling point for the screenwriters and director Stephen Gaghan.

McConaughey plays Kenny Wells, a higher-up at a Reno-based metal and mineral prospecting company called Washoe, which is owned and run by his father (played by Craig T. Nelson, in a brief appearance). Prospecting and mining have been a family business since Kenny's great-grandfather came to Nevada. In the seven years since his father's death, though, Kenny has more or less ruined the company—sending it into debt, failing to obtain investors for exploratory drilling campaigns, and running the operation of the business from a local a bar. He has lost his house and is now living with his perpetual girlfriend Kay (Bryce Dallas Howard), who exists in this story to be supportive and, ultimately, wronged—just to show how success destroys Kenny's good nature.

The success literally comes from a dream—of a promising area of land of Indonesia and a geologist named Michael Acosta (Édgar Ramírez). Michael became famous in the world of prospecting and mining for finding the largest copper deposit in history, but his luck has diminished since then. Kenny is drawn to him because of one the geologist's theories about a "ring of fire"—a motherlode of gold—in the mountains of Indonesia. Pawning anything of value he still possesses, Kenny buys a plane ticket to meet with Michael, and the two strike an agreement to find this gold, with Michael providing the expertise and Kenny raising the necessary funding.

After a lengthy expedition (which includes Kenny developing malaria and Michael bargaining with local workers to keep them on the job), Michael finds gold. For his part, Kenny is given the opportunity to wave his newfound yet still-untapped wealth in the faces of investors who turned him down in the past, others in the mining business, and the entirety of the Wall Street establishment. His key flaw, though, is that he is not in it for the money. Kenny wants his name attached to the largest gold find—worth about $30 billion—in history.

The most dramatically and thematically promising notion of this story is the fact that Kenny and Michael's entire enterprise is a lie. Strangely, this is the one detail that the screenplay keeps from the audience until the third act. The movie provides a hint that something is amiss, in flashes of scenes of Kenny being interviewed by an FBI agent (played by Toby Kebbell), yet the full brunt of the implications and consequences of the fraud at the heart of this story is saved as a cheap plot twist. Whatever could be culled from such an obvious metaphor is condensed into a monologue by Kenny, who says that the entire system of wealth and finance is based on a lie upon which everyone agrees.

Instead, the movie indulges in the strange particulars of this story (involving corporate sabotage and political palm-greasing) and in Kenny's broad character arc, as he transforms from a broke nobody with nothing into a proud, uncaring man, willing to sell his soul at the mere taste of fame and the promise of wealth. Much of his change involves the acquisition of material goods, and there is an undeniable quality of wish fulfillment here, with Kenny standing in as a symbol—the unlikely recipient of riches and success.

The ultimate lesson is, ostensibly, in the illusion of this fortune. That lesson is unconvincing, even beyond the way the movie's final note completely contradicts that moral. Worse, the narrative of *Gold* offers only general insights into the real scenario and characters upon which it is loosely based.

Mark Dujsik

CREDITS

Kenny Wells: Matthew McConaughey
Michael Acosta: Edgar Ramirez
Kay: Bryce Dallas Howard
Connie Wright: Macon Blair
Bobby Burns: Adam LeFevre
Origin: United States
Language: English
Released: 2016
Production: Michael Nozik, Teddy Schwarzman, Matthew McConaughey, Patrick Massett, John Zinman; Black Bear Pictures, Boies/Schiller Film Group, Hwy61, Living Films; released by TWC-Dimension
Directed by: Stephen Gagham
Written by: Patrick Massett; John Zinman
Cinematography by: Robert Elswit
Music by: Daniel Pemberton
MPAA rating: R
Running time: 120 minutes

REVIEWS

Abele, Robert. *Los Angeles Times*. January 26, 2017.
Baumgarten, Marjorie. *Austin Chronicle*. January 27, 2017.
Berardinelli, James. *ReelViews*. January 26, 2017.
Derakhshani, Tirdad. *Philadelphia Inquirer*. January 27, 2017.
Fujishima, Kenji. *Slant Magazine*. January 23, 2017.
Hassenger, Jesse. *The A.V. Club*. December 30, 2016.

Macdonald, Moira. *Seattle Times*. January 25, 2017.
Scott, A.O. *New York Times*. January 26, 2017.
Seitz, Matt Zoller. *RogerEbert.com*. January 26, 2017.
Walsh, Katie. *Chicago Tribune*. January 26, 2017.

QUOTES

Kenny Wells: "The guy who invented the hamburger was smart. But the guy who invented the cheeseburger...genius."

TRIVIA

Actor Matthew McConaughey shaved his head, gained 45 lbs by eating cheeseburgers and drinking beer and milkshakes in an effort to make the character less attractive.

AWARDS

Nominations:

Golden Globes 2017: Orig. Song Score and/or Adapt. ("Gold")

GOOD TIME

Box Office: $2 Million

Josh and Benny Safdie have lately emerged as the heirs apparent to 1970s New York City cinema of grime and grimness. From their early shorts and features, *The Pleasure of Being Robbed* (2008) and *Daddy Longlegs* (2009), they have expressed an interest in bodegas; back alleys; and bums, dreamers, and drifters long on ambition, short on sense and money. They took a turn for the extra rough with *Heaven Knows What* (2014), a true story based on lead actress Arielle Holmes's life as a heroin addict living in parks and on street corners in New York City. The brothers' combination of long lenses, handheld close-ups, angular electronic music on the score, and the lived-in details of life on the streets (dirty parkas, abandoned apartments, coarse, phlegmy diction) sought to reclaim the lost kingdom of 1970s filmmakers like William Friedkin, Jerry Schatzberg, Andrzej Zulawski, and John Cassavetes. The Safdie brothers have returned with a film that cements them as kings of a lone new wave, taking the reality of the slimy New York underbelly and wedding it to capital-A stars, proof that Hollywood likes what they are selling. *Good Time* may be their strongest work yet, their most kinetic, crazy, and, despite the film playing like a descent into the underworld, their most fun.

We first meet the Nikas brothers, Connie (Robert Pattinson) and Nick (co-director Benny Safdie) during the latter's psychiatric evaluation. His intelligence is barely that of a child and he requires clinical help and a supportive environment if he's ever going to do more than just survive. That's not what Connie, an inveterate grafter, user, and criminal, wants to hear. He's got a plan to get out of their Queens neighborhood for good, but it does not involve paying for full-time psychiatric help and medicine for his brother. Instead, he orchestrates a quick bank robbery and enlists Nick's help. Things go awry almost immediately, starting with the explosion of a red dye pack in the bag of money and ending with Nick falling through a plate glass door and getting arrested. While he languishes in Riker's Island, Connie throws himself into the task of raising the required bail money.

His first stop is his on-again-off-again girlfriend Corey (Jennifer Jason Leigh), who labors under the delusion that her handsome young paramour was robbing the bank to buy the two of them a place out of the city. He turns the charm on to get her to max out her mother's credit cards for the $10,000 he needs for bail. (Most of the money from the robbery cannot be used because it's still got the red dye all over it.) Corey's mother cancels her cards as soon as she realizes what's going on and Connie abandons her to move onto his next scheme. Nick is maced during a small scuffle on his first day inside and rushed to a hospital, giving Connie the opportunity to break him out. No sooner has he absconded with a wheelchair-bound, unconscious body, than he discovers that he's grabbed the wrong patient. Ray (Buddy Duress) is just some other poor fool from prison who was injured during his arrest. Turns out he was newly-paroled when a friend brought him along for an acid deal, during which he was busted anew. Connie decides to take the unscrupulous and confused Ray back to where he and his friends stashed their drugs before being arrested (Adventureland amusement park), find the drugs and sell them. This can only happen if Ray can find the missing merchandise, find a reliable seller, and not get caught by park security (Barkhad Abdi) or the police. The odds are against all of this, but Connie does not know how to slow down.

The Safdies and cinematographer Sean Price Williams have outdone themselves crafting *Good Time*. The interplay between the many shades of neon found in New York—from police lights to a Sprite bottle that acts as a third-act MacGuffin—and the darkness that follows Connie wherever he goes. The cold Queens streets he haunts like a tweaker poltergeist have an unsparing blue and black hue that seems to cut into his being. Connie's red jacket and bleach-blonde hair turn him into a bolt of human lightning cutting a path of destruction and privilege across the poor neighborhoods he thinks he's above. Williams films him with an almost gymnastic enthusiasm, switching from close-ups to thousand-yard zooms then to helicopter shots, keeping pace with Connie's own unstoppable rhythm and energy. The film rings with grammatical echoes of *The French Connection* (1971) *Scarecrow* (1973), and the confusion-heavy 1970s work of Cassavettes, but it moves so briskly that the reference points are unclear until after the credits have rolled. The film behaves likes its protagonist, sprinting through one nightmare scenario after another, finding the most charismatic angles and edits to keep Connie afloat.

In Pattinson, the Safdies have found an expressive, exciting lead who commits fully to the scuzzy milieu he commands. The young actor has proven himself a peerless, fearless chameleon, willing to splash around in the mire of humanity for his art. If the Safdies channel Jerry Schatzberg's 1971 study of heroin addicts *The Panic in Needle Park* (and their own heroin movie *Heaven Knows What* in 2014, says they do) then Pattinson is their Al Pacino, cunning, handsome, and feckless. With insomnia under his eyes, five o'clock shadow on his face, and lies on his tongue, it's impossible to look away from him. Of course he's only the ringleader of a hugely talented cast. Barkhad Abdi and Jennifer Jason Leigh have a small amount of screen time, but both sizzle enough for a whole film. Leigh's pathetic desperation as she devolves into shrieking hysteria is deeply effective and Abdi efficiently and hilarious tells his character's life story just through his posturing and lack of patience with the intruders at Adventureland. Duress, Safdie, and Taliah Webster as a girl roped into helping Connie, all shine just as brightly as Pattinson. Duress, whom the Safdies discovered and put in a plum supporting role in *Heaven Knows What*, is a riot, swearing and kicking his way through one disaster after another. His elongated vowels perfectly betray his utter cluelessness even as he imagines he sees two steps ahead of the world. Safdie nicely underplays Nick's handicap, relying on a speech impediment and a dead eyed stare instead of a showier, emotional approach to a character that does not fundamentally understand his circumstances. Webster is perfect as a teenager in over her head, just going with the flow because of a complete lack of productive adult supervision. She listens to Connie because he happens to be more persuasive than the grandmother who looks after her. And that's ultimately the biggest take away from *Good Time*. The film does not peddle a broad message about scrappers and strivers or the lengths we go for the ones we love. The Safdies know that Connie's love of Nick is all about pride, and that he would happily sell out dozens of people to loudly prove he loves anyone other than himself. It's the fastest and smoothest talker who survives in the Safdies's world and *Good Time* crowns Connie king, if only for one long night in Queens, New York.

Scout Tafoya

CREDITS

Connie Nikas: Robert Pattinson
Nick Nikas: Benny Safdie
Crystal: Taliah Webster
Corey Ellman: Jennifer Jason Leigh
Dash the Park Security Guard: Barkhad Abdi
Origin: United States
Language: English
Released: 2017
Production: Sebastian Bear-McClard, Oscar Boyson, Terry Douglas, Paris Kasidokostas Latsis; Elara Pictures, Rhea Films; released by A24 Films LLC
Directed by: Benny Safdie; Joshua Safdie
Written by: Benny Safdie; Joshua Safdie
Cinematography by: Sean Price Williams
Music by: Oneohtrix Point Never
Sound: Ryan M. Price
Music Supervisor: Oneohtrix Point Never
Editing: Benny Safdie; Ronald Bronstein
Costumes: Miyako Bellizzi; Mordechai Rubinstein
Production Design: Sam Lisenco
MPAA rating: R
Running time: 101 minutes

REVIEWS

Burr, Ty. *Boston Globe*. August 24, 2017.
Chang, Justin. *Los Angeles Times*. August 10, 2017.
Dowd, A.A. *The A.V. Club*. August 10, 2017.
Grierson, Tim. *Screen International*. May 25, 2017.
Hornaday, Ann. *Washington Post*. August 17, 2017.
Kiang, Jessica. *The Playlist*. May 25, 2017.
Lodge, Guy. *Variety*. May 25, 2017.
Robey, Tim. *The Telegraph*. May 25, 2017.
Scott, A.O. *New York Times*. August 10, 2017.
Stevens, Dana. *Slate*. August 17, 2017.

QUOTES

Connie Nikas: "I think something very important is happening and it's deeply connected to my purpose."

TRIVIA

Actors Robert Pattinson and Benny Safdie prepared for their roles by working at a car wash in Queens, New York.

AWARDS

Nominations:

Ind. Spirit 2018: Actor (Pattinson), Actor--Supporting (Safdie), Actress--Supporting (Webster), Director (Safdie), Director (Safdie), Film Editing

GOODBYE CHRISTOPHER ROBIN

Inspired by the true story.
—Movie tagline

Box Office: $1.7 Million

Everyone knows and most people love the adorable Winnie-the-Pooh and his quintessential cadre of animal pals; the authoritative Owl, the worrisome Piglet, the emo Eeyore, and, of course, the ADD-addled Tigger. They have been a part of most Anglo children's lives since they were created in 1926 by author and poet A.A. Milne. Yet few people know the origin of the stories nor much about author Milne. Judging by his Pooh stories, which are close to a century old, one might think he's an ongoing candidate for father of the year honors and his home is full of childlike whimsy and fun. However, after watching sluggish award season bait film *Goodbye Christopher Robin*, one quickly realizes Milne was not only a fairly absentee father but also an opportunistic bore, suffering from posttraumatic stress disorder way before that was a diagnosable issue.

As *Goodbye Christopher Robin* opens, a montage of Milne (Domhnall Gleeson) in the trenches of World War I combined with him attempting to adjust to life back in early 20th Century London quickly and dully plays out. Milne's socialite wife Daphne (Margot Robbie) has been anxiously awaiting his return so they can start a family and Milne can get back to authoring books that will add to the coffers that dwindled a bit during wartime. However, Milne is unhappy, depressive, and breaks down when he hears a loud noise or popping sound. Who knew early 1900s London has so many balloons? Thus, a move to the country is what A.A. desires and Daphne grudgingly obliges to. Once there, A.A. brightens a bit and a child is born unto them named, you guessed it, Christopher Robin.

Yet the life of a socialite and well-known author leaves little time for a child and even though the big move was ostensibly made in order to have a creative and familial nest for the Milnes a nanny named Olive (Kelly Macdonald) is quickly hired, and she is tasked with raising the child as his parents get on with their lives. This is shown in a cold-feeling montage of an ever-aging Christopher standing in an upper story window with Olive as his parents go off to a party. Although the Milne's seem happy-go-lucky, back at home, A.A. still suffers the effects of war both physically and mentally, and this takes a toll on his creativity. He is blocked and unable to write. This is bad for the family business, as Daphne is prone to point out. After reaching a boiling point, Daphne leaves her family for a few weeks in London to party it up, and nanny Olive's mother falls ill, leaving A.A. alone with his son, who he really doesn't know at all. This is where the film gets even more unlikable, detached, and awkward.

After a few false starts at father-son bonding, A.A. finally decides to let Christopher (Will Tilston) take the lead. Off the pair ventures into the heavily wooded area around their estate, searching for adventure, wild animals, and whatever else comes their way. Young Christopher particularly likes bears and his favorite toy is a stuffed bear he calls "Winnie" after a bear at the London Zoo named "Winnipeg" and the bear is at the center of each new daily adventure. Hmm, thinks the audience, as well as the creatively stymied A.A., who suddenly becomes very interested in the child he bore and essentially left with the hired help. Before long, A.A. calls in friend and artist E.H. Shepard (Stephen Campbell Moore), who sketches Christopher and Winnie in a variety of places and poses. These drawings soon begin to resemble the classic Winnie-the-Pooh drawings one recognizes from the books, before the more popularized Disney adaptation took hold, and the elder Milne is furiously writing again.

So, essentially at this point, the audience realizes Winnie-the-Pooh is a bit of collaboration between the author A.A. Milne and his son, the soon-to-be-famous-against-his-will Christopher Robin. Yet the collaboration is only authorized by the author and the young boy doesn't realize the "fun" he's having with his previously absentee father is actually a kind of creative headhunting being done in order for Milne to get back on top as an author. To its credit, wary (or cynical) audience members catch on to this fact before *Goodbye Christopher Robin* really takes the plot there, and, predictably, A.A. and Daphne go back to their highfalutin lifestyle, leaving young Christopher with nanny Olive to deal with the press and public pressures that have always plagued celebrities. These scenes are about as close to emotional as *Goodbye Christopher Robin* ever gets, but, even so, the scenes just don't work due to a lack of depth or warmth to the characters and a dull, straightforward way of shooting scenes. Also of no help to viewers is how cloyingly adorable Will Tilston is as Christopher Robin.

While the film does not gloss over the difficulties young Christopher is forced to face alone, it's still a lousy, selfish thing to do to a kid and when it's done by a bit of an empty vessel as A.A. Milne is, as played by Gleeson, one can't help but feel rather icky about the whole film. Perhaps a warmer, less staunch director than Simon Curtis (whose *My Week with Marilyn* [2011] suffered a similar fate and vibe) would allow the multifaceted layers of A.A. Milne some life. Yet instead *Goodbye Christopher Robin* feels stilted and boring, a fate not befitting the story of the creation of such a chubby little cubby all stuffed with fluff.

Don R. Lewis

CREDITS

A. A. Milne: Domhnall Gleeson
Daphne Milne: Margot Robbie

Olive: Kelly McDonald
Christopher Robin, aged 8: Will Tilston
Christopher Robin: Alex Lawther
Origin: United Kingdom
Language: English
Released: 2017
Production: Steve Christian, Damian Jones; DJ Films; released by Fox Searchlight Pictures
Directed by: Simon Curtis
Written by: Frank Cottrell Boyce; Simon Vaughan
Cinematography by: Ben Smithard
Music by: Carter Burwell
Music Supervisor: Sarah Bridge
Editing: Victoria Boydell
Costumes: Odile Dicks-Mireaux
Production Design: David Roger
MPAA rating: PG
Running time: 107 minutes

REVIEWS

Catsoulis, Jeannette. *New York Times*. October 11, 2017.
Chang, Justin. *Los Angeles Times*. October 12, 2017.
Ehrlich, David. *IndieWire*. September 22, 2017.
LaSalle, Mick. *San Francisco Chronicle*. October 18, 2017.
Linden, Sheri. *Hollywood Reporter*. September 20, 2017.
Macdonald, Moira. *Seattle Times*. October 19, 2017.
O'Hara, Helen. *The Telegraph*. September 20, 2017.
Pile, Jonathan. *Empire*. September 25, 2017.
Smith, Derek. *Slant Magazine*. September 30, 2017.
Wloszczyna, Susan. *RogerEbert.com*. October 13, 2017.

QUOTES

Christopher Robin (age 8): "Are you writing a book? I thought we were just having fun?"
Alan Milne: "We're writing a book and we're having fun."

TRIVIA

This film was shot on location in Oxfordshire, Surrey, East Sussex, and London.

GRADUATION

(Bacalaureat)

A father will do anything to save his daughter's future.
—Movie tagline

Box Office: $175,975

The director Cristian Mungiu is a key figure of the Romanian New Wave, a thrilling national film movement that has detonated critical consciousness over the last decade. Mungiu's breakthrough second feature, *4 Months, 3 Weeks and 2 Days* (2007), was an unflinching drama tracking the efforts of two young women, university students, trying to secure an illegal abortion. Set at the end of the repressive communist regime of the dictator Nicolae Ceausescu, the movie elevated Romanian cinema by winning the prestigious Palme d'Or at the Cannes Film Festival.

The movie also established the hallmarks of the movement: the moral rot of the Ceausescu period, one marked by compromise; a rigorous, deeply naturalistic visual syntax built on duration and unbroken takes; a stripped-down acting style drawn around themes of private anguish and breakdown. Mungiu's next feature, *Beyond the Hills* (2012), also explored the complicated, socially taboo relationship of two women. The tone was just as chilling and ice black in examining another sinister brand of institutional totalitarianism—the restrictive practices of the Orthodox church.

In the cinema of Cristian Mungiu, the notes are dark. The sensations are unnerving and pungent. The director's new film, *Graduation*, is another damning, emotionally devastating social portrait of moral unease and violation. Part of what makes Mungiu such a revealing director is his command of atmosphere, pace, and mood. He has a great, intuitive feel for character, showing people free falling through time and space, trapped by bureaucratic or social inertia. His visual style, unadorned, direct, carries a profound sense of entrapment and unease, of people feeling under constant surveillance.

"I have this feeling somebody's following me," says Romeo Aldea (Adrian Titieni), the movie's central character. He is a middle-aged doctor who lives in a nondescript provincial section of the country with his wife, Magda (Lia Bugnar), and 18-year old daughter, Eliza (Maria Dragus). Romeo lived abroad during the communist dictatorship and returned in 1991, hopeful that a new, better version of the country would emerge. Now this respected man, one of virtue and competence, is seemingly under attack. The movie opens with a rock smashing through a window of the family's apartment. Later on, his car is also vandalized.

The most damning attack happens to Eliza at the most critical juncture of her young life. On her way to school one morning, Eliza is abducted and attacked near a construction site. However, her assailant was thwarted in his attempt to sexually assault her. Eliza is left severely traumatized by the incident. Her badly injured right arm is set in a bulky cast. Eliza was completing her final exams, the final step for her to secure an academic scholarship to study in Cambridge. Romeo had orchestrated it all, setting up private English tutors and academic specialists. His plans for his daughter are now threatened.

Suspicion and surprise hover over everything. An exam proctor wonders whether Eliza is concealing information inside her cast. Romeo is a privileged authority figure though hardly a paragon of virtue. He is carrying out an affair with Sandra (Maline Manovici), a single mother with a young son. The flat, withering exchanges between Romeo and his wife Magda reveal just how indifferent they have become towards each other.

Romeo becomes further distressed after Eliza fails to finish two parts of her written exam, meaning she has to get a nearly perfect score on the final test. Convinced of his own rectitude, Romeo turns desperate and becomes exceedingly caught in a vice grip of his own petty amorality. He yields his own principles and ideas in his quixotic efforts to create a fail safe for Eliza and ensure she receives the scholarship by taking any measures necessary.

These middle sections are among the most magnetic in the film. With precision, Mungiu documents the doctor's downward spiral. His connections with a police commander (Vlad Ivanov) investigating the assault lead him to carry favor with a political fixer, Bulai (Petre Ciubotaru), who needs inside help securing a liver transplant. The political fixer's contacts provide access to a top-level exam board official (Gelu Colceag).

With his marriage dead now, Romeo has put all of his dreams on his daughter. He rationalizes, with his wife and lover, of the necessity of his deceit. "You avoid making clear decisions," Magda says. *Graduation* slowly, imperceptibly, evolves into a classic noir, Romanian-style, streaked in a mounting sense of dread and defeat in animating a man forced to reckon with his own perfidy and treachery. It is chilling, in these circles, how easily the corruption is maintained. "Don't tell me you live off of your salary?" one of the conspirators remarks to Romeo. The doctor's collapse and his developing realization at how deeply he is trapped in the Byzantine system is clear in the movie's most remarkable scene, a tense interview when two dogged members of the prosecution present him a clear moral choice of coming clean.

Mungiu is working with a new cinematographer, Tudor Vladimir Panduru. Like the director's two previous films, *Graduation* has an unblinking, punishing visual style conveying a comprehensive malaise. The moment is crystallized in one pensive sequence, a long shot of Romeo isolated in the frame, staring into the abject space while sitting alone on a swing at a children's park. His dawning powerlessness is also reinforced by another personal attack, the shattering of his car window as the car is parked and looking out a drab apartment complex with its Brutalist, low-slung Soviet-style architecture.

The question of guilt is permanently suspended over the drama. One of the movie's most compelling subplots develops from Romeo's almost violent indifference to Marius (Rares Andrici), Eliza's older, working-class boyfriend. In one electrifying scene, Romeo presses the young man with evidence that he had the chance to stop the attack on Eliza and that he either failed or lost his nerve to act. The sequence turns into a tense, fascinating discussion about honor. The scene underlines an essential skill of Mungiu in his sharp, provocative ability to dramatize abstract ideas and give them shape, dimension, and heft.

Like its immediate predecessors, *Graduation* is undoubtedly uncomfortable, even confrontational, about its wider social implications. It presents a society still at war with itself and unable to disentangle the sins of the past. Mungiu's films are not spontaneous and have little throwaway pleasures or enjoyable moments. Whatever humor exists provides for little release or escape. The moral inquiries the film poses, of the necessity of honor and trust, and how those principles are damaged by expediency or self-dealing, make for a heightened experience. At the strictest level, *Graduation* is unaccommodating, refusing to answer some essential questions, like the identity of Eliza's attacker, posed by the story. Mungiu is after something deeper, richer and harder to grasp. This essential movie gets there.

Patrick Z. McGavin

CREDITS

Romeo Aldea: Adrian Titieni

Eliza Aldea: Maria Dragus

Magda: Lia Bugnar

Sandra: Malina Manovici

Chief Inspector: Vlad Ivanov

Origin: United States

Language: Romanian

Released: 2017

Production: Cristian Mungiu; Canal+ Group, Ciné Plus, Eurimages, France 3 Cinema, France Televisions SA, Groupama Romania, Les Films du Fleuve, Mobra Films, Orange S.A., Why Not Productions, Wild Bunch; released by Sundance Selects

Directed by: Cristian Mungiu

Written by: Cristian Mungiu

Cinematography by: Tudor Vladimir Panduru

Editing: Mircea Olteanu

Costumes: Brandusa Ioan

Production Design: Simona Paduretu
MPAA rating: R
Running time: 128 minutes

REVIEWS

Burr, Ty. *Boston Globe.* May 31, 2017.
Chang, Justin. *Los Angeles Times.* April 13, 2017.
Dowd, A.A. *The A.V. Club.* April 5, 2017.
Hornaday, Ann. *Washington Post.* April 13, 2017.
Kiang, Jessica. *Playlist.* May 21, 2016.
LaSalle, Mick. *San Francisco Chronicle.* April 20, 2017.
Morgenstern, Joe. *Wall Street Journal.* September 21, 2017.
Phillips, Michael. *Chicago Tribune.* April 20, 2017.
Scott, A.O. *New York Times.* April 6, 2017.
Wilson, Calvin. *Austin Chronicle.* April 27, 2017.

QUOTES

Romeo: "Eliza, you have to do your best. It'd be a pity to miss this chance. Some important steps in life depend on small things. And some chances shouldn't be wasted."

TRIVIA

An alternative title that was considered for the film was *Recycled Feelings.*

THE GREAT WALL

Seventeen hundred years to build. Fifty-five hundred miles long. What were they trying to keep out?
—Movie tagline

Box Office: $45.5 Million

Zhang Yimou has set the pace for Chinese blockbusters and prestige pictures alike for over thirty years. The golden boy of the Fifth Generation (a group of Chinese filmmakers who got their start in the 1980s), Zhang has not only prospered abroad and at home, but risen to the level of cultural hero. In 2008, he was asked to orchestrate the now-famous opening ceremony of the Olympic Games, which are still talked about with reverence. There's a better than average chance it's his images, whether of the throngs of perfectly orchestrated digital armies in films like *Curse of the Golden Flower* (2006), the huge mass of dancers from the opening ceremony, the elastic marshal artists of *Hero* (2002) and *House of Flying Daggers* (2004), or the repressed heroines of *Red Sorghum* (1987), *Ju Dou* (1990), and *Raise the Red Lantern* (1991), that define the popular imagining of modern Chinese art.

So, when Legendary Pictures decided to produce a film about the Great Wall of China, hiring Zhang was a no-brainer. He had the filmmaking chops to bring a great big action film to life, and would have no trouble ticking off all the international co-production boxes. There are ties to the hugely popular *Game of Thrones* in the form of co-star Pedro Pascal and composer Ramin Djawadi, a big American movie star in lead Matt Damon, and tons of Chinese icons, old and new, all over the cast. The film did very little business in the States, but its global box office receipts came in at twice its $150 million dollar budget, which was the highest for any Chinese production to date. *The Great Wall* seemed like everything Zhang's career had been leading up to, from a historical standpoint, tackling the most famous Chinese icon in his oft-imitated but rarely eclipsed style.

Sometime during the second century, a group of European mercenaries are scouring China for the secret to gunpowder, of which they've only heard rumors. Their leader, William Garin (Damon), knows his mission has become a boondoggle, with most of his men unfit to continue traveling thanks to their exhaustion and injuries, but he will not give up so easily. That is, until the camp is attacked by a monster one night, leaving only himself and his deputy Pero Tovar (Pascal) alive. Their resolve is such that when they accidentally run into the Great Wall of China, and into the arms of the massive armed force that occupies it, they throw their weapons down and surrender. General Shao (Hanyu Zhang), Strategist Wang (Andy Lau) and Commanders Lin (Tian Jing), Wu (Eddie Peng), Chen (Kenny Lin), and Deng (Xuan Huang) do not mind so much that the foreign intruders won't state their purpose. They are more concerned by the monster paw recovered from their campsite. William notices that no one seems phased by the great, green claw he cut off of the attacking beast the night before. They are more concerned by what its presence foretells, which piques his interest enormously.

Tovar and William are thrown in chains and brought to the top of the wall to see what Lin and her army is so concerned about. From the valley below marches a horde of green reptilian monsters—Rhinoceros-sized foot soldiers working on behalf of a queen, cursed to rise every sixty years to remind the Chinese not to grow too greedy. The army is prepared for the first attack and comes away victorious, but not without a little help from the two mercenaries, who break free and join the defensive force, making an impressive enough show of their strength and skill that the Chinese bring them into their fold. William notices that they may have an ally yet in their quest for gunpowder in Sir Ballard (Willem Dafoe), the only other white face on the wall. But first they have to survive the increasingly vicious attacks from the monsters, who will stop at nothing to bring down the wall.

Eccentric epics like this have to work out a rhythm, and thankfully Zhang Yimou has a lot of experience orchestrating a thousand tiny moving parts. Unlike the average *Pirates of the Caribbean* movie, which can barely maintain a coherent grip on its characters for all the meaningless spectacle it has to orchestrate, *The Great Wall* has the expressive grandeur of a parade, and every odd, asymmetrical element just adds to the momentum. Zhang orchestrates the armies on the wall with his usual rigor and splendor, posing the many-hued uniforms of each commander's squad as if they were opposing color guard teams. Each new tactic they try out allows the director and his mammoth team to try out some new feat of art direction or sound design. There are warriors that swing from battlements like acrobats, arrows with flutes attached to them to allow warriors to hear when wounded creatures sneak up on them, and man-powered scissor-like contraptions posted along the wall, to name just a few dazzling techniques. Damon's strangely mannered performance, which would stick out like a sore thumb in a more conventional film, feels at home next to monsters and perfectly choreographed death marches. His voice, which sounds like a strange approximation of an Irish person trying and failing to do an American accent, is charmingly off from the get go but becomes ingratiating, like the rubbery CGI effects, by the second act break. Pascal, Jing, Dafoe and Lau all have the requisite roguish charisma to fit right into the swashbuckling and pyrotechnics.

It's Zhang's camera work and choreography that make the movie, oddball charms notwithstanding. The combat and pageantry that happens atop the wall and in the caves where the monsters live is an extension of the work he did for the Opening Ceremony. The blue-tinted cinematography and the whooshing, waltzing movement of the camera are intoxicating and easy to get lost in. The endless flow of colours blending and contrasting are reason enough to watch this film, even if it adds up to a marvelous, beautiful one-of-a-kind monster mash. That this much money went in and something this comprehensible and rich emerged is reason to celebrate.

Scout Tafoya

CREDITS

William: Matt Damon
Commander Lin Mae: Tian Jing
Tovar: Pedro Pascal
Ballard: Willem Dafoe
Peng Yong: Lu Han
Strategist Wang: Andy Lau
Origin: United States
Language: English, Mandarin Chinese, Ukrainian
Released: 2017
Production: Jon Jashni, Peter Loehr, Charles Roven, Thomas Tull; Atlas Entertainment, China Film Group Corp., Dentsu, Fuji Television Network, Kava Productions, Le Vision Pictures, Legendary East, Legendary Entertainment; released by Universal Pictures
Directed by: Yimou Zhang
Written by: Carlo Bernard; Doug Miro; Tony Gilroy
Cinematography by: Stuart Dryburgh; Xiaoding Zhao
Music by: Ramin Djawadi
Sound: Gwendolyn Yates Whittle
Music Supervisor: Peter Afterman; Margaret Yen
Editing: Mary Jo Markey; Craig Wood
Art Direction: Helen Jarvis
Costumes: Mayes C. Rubeo
Production Design: John Myhre
MPAA rating: PG-13
Running time: 103 minutes

REVIEWS

Collin, Robbie. *The Telegraph.* February 16, 2017.
Dargis, Manohla. *New York Times.* February 16, 2017.
Duralde, Alonso. *TheWrap.* February 17, 2017.
Ebiri, Bilge. *Village Voice.* February 17, 2017.
Lee, Maggie. *Variety.* December 15, 2016.
Rayns, Tony. *Sight & Sound.* April 2017.
Vishnevetsky, Ignatiy. *The A.V. Club.* February 16, 2017.
Watson, Keith. *Slant Magazine.* February 16, 2017.
Walsh, Katie. *Seattle Times.* February 16, 2017.
Zacharek, Stephanie. *Time.* February 16, 2017.

QUOTES

William: "I've been left for dead twice...it was bad luck."
Ballard: "For who?"
William: "The people who left me!"

TRIVIA

The filmmakers were denied permission to film on the actual Great Wall, so those locations were created digitally.

THE GREATEST SHOWMAN

Box Office: $128.3 Million

To put it mildly, *The Greatest Showman* is about as far from being a historically accurate depiction of the life of famed showman P.T. Barnum as one can possibly get without actually including Porgs in the supporting cast. While the real circumstances of who he was and what he did could indeed form the basis of a potentially fascinating and presumably bleak film, the true details of his life have instead been transformed here into a cheerfully over-the-top spectacle that combines heavily sanitized fact with outright fiction and even throws in songs from Benj Pasek and Justin Paul, the award-winning composers behind such hits as *La La Land* (2016) and the stage favorite "Dear Evan Handler," to boot. When it opened, many critics and commentators, presumably boosted by a quick visit to Barnum's Wikipedia entry, registered their outrage that a film—for presumably the first time in cinema history—would dare to play fast and loose with the historical record. What those complaints fail to consider is that by fudging the truth in the service of a better story and by stressing gaudy spectacle over grim reality, the filmmakers are doing the exact same thing that Barnum himself did a century or so earlier with his forays into the business of show and in that regard, it does a fairly accurate and oftentimes crazily entertaining job of recreating the spirit of the man and his legacy.

Following a wild opening number that introduces Barnum (Hugh Jackman) and his show in all their grandiose glory, the film backtracks to show us his hardscrabble early days as a poor child (Ellis Rubin) forced to make it on his own a young age. While struggling to survive, he meets and instantly falls in love with the well-bred Charity Hallett (Skylar Dunn), much to the chagrin of her snobbish father. Over the course of the song "A Million Dreams," we see them stay connected, despite her dad's best efforts, culminating in the now-adult Barnum and Charity (Michelle Williams) running off to get married and begin their own family. Although he vows to give his family the life of comfort and happiness that they deserve, he can only barely manage to support them with a dead-end job as a clerk in a shipping office and when even that falls through, all seems lost until he is seized with inspiration. Using a little bit of ingenuity and a lot of chicanery, he is able to secure a loan to purchase a museum in the middle of New York City dedicated to presenting exhibits of a decidedly unusual nature. At first, the public ignores his offerings in droves, leading Barnum to double down by offering a live presentation showcasing performers deemed to be freakish by the standards of the normal world—a midget he dubs General Tom Thumb (Sam Humphrey), a giant, and "bearded lady" Lettie Lutz (Keala Settle) among them. This may smack of exploitation, to be sure, but Barnum's defense against this argument is simple—because of their natural inclination to look askance at anything not considered "normal," people are always going to stare at them, so they might as well get paid for it.

His instincts prove to be correct and while the arbiters of good taste—represented here by a snobbish theater critic (Paul Sparks)—are aghast at his production, the curious crowds flock to see it in droves and Barnum finally becomes a success. Before long, Barnum takes on a business partner in Phillip Carlyle (Zac Efron), a well-bred playwright who decides to throw away his place in society (not to mention his inheritance) to join up with him, a notion that seems less crazy from his perspective when he first lays eyes on African-American trapeze artist Anne Wheeler (Zendaya) and falls instantly in love with her in defiance of the societal norms of the time. Having achieved massive success, Barnum now craves respectability and while on an overseas trip to Europe to present his troupe to Queen Victoria, he encounters celebrated singer Jenny Lind (Rebecca Ferguson), known to her adoring public as "the Swedish Nightingale," and decides to bring her across the ocean for her first tour of America. Although she proves to be a sensation in the States as well, the time and money spent taking her across the country threatens Barnum's personal and professional lives and he has to struggle to put them both back together again before he loses everything.

So, no, the version of Barnum's story presented in the screenplay by Jenny Bicks and Bill Condon does not exactly display much fidelity to the facts—in real life, for starters, Barnum's attitude towards his attractions was not quite as altruistic as it has been depicted here, key characters like Phillip and Anne never existed and while Barnum did indeed tour Jenny Lind in America, her romantic designs towards him did not happen. Instead, they have elected to mold it into a standard tale of an underdog who risks everything and winds up succeeding beyond his wildest dreams. This is not an especially bold or original approach but the funny thing about the film is that it actually kind of works to the point where it is indeed possible to push the more troubling real world concerns that are an inescapable part of Barnum's life and work aside and simply enjoy it on its admittedly more simplistic level, chiefly in the way that it tries to reposition Barnum and his circus as a celebration of true diversity in which people of all stripes are accepted just for being themselves. It is pure hokum, of course, but as such things go, it is well-handled hokum that has been put forth by debuting director Michael Gracey (with some reported post-production assistance from James Mangold, who receives an executive producer credit) with a lot of flash and style that enhances the proceedings without totally overwhelming them.

Since *The Greatest Showman*, as an original musical, does not have a familiar score on which to fall back on, the numbers, in order to succeed, have to pull off the hat trick of being inventively staged and energetically performed while at the same time convincing audiences that not only would the characters suddenly burst into song at any given moment, it is in fact the only thing that they could possibly do at that particular moment in time. For the most part, the production numbers here manage to pull all of that off with fairly glorious results, thanks in no small part to the incredibly catchy songs by Pasek and Paul and the inventive efforts of choreographer Ashley Wallen and cinematographer Seamus McGarvey, who create one exciting sequence after another ranging from the lyrical "A Million Dreams" (the aforementioned number chronicling the relationship between Barnum and Charity from childhood to marriage) to the high-energy Barnum-Phillip barroom duet "The Other Side" to "This Is Me," the big showstopper in which Lettie leads the other so-called "freaks" in a grand declaration that they will no longer stand for the second-class status that they have endured throughout their lives. The real standout, however, is "Rewrite the Stars," the big romantic duet between Phillip and Anne that is staged in an otherwise empty auditorium with her up in the air swinging from her trapeze and him climbing ropes in the hope of reaching her. Watching the two of them flying through the air, oftentimes just missing each other as one rises while the other falls, is a delight and when they finally do come together in midair, it is a swoon-worthy moment as exhilarating as any to appear in a musical since perhaps the "Elephant Love Medley" number from *Moulin Rouge* (2001).

Of course, *The Greatest Showman* has an advantage over most recent live-action musicals in that it has a cast that is for once actually well-stocked with people who really can sing and dance. Hugh Jackman, whose personal accolades include a Tony for his performance in *The Boy from Oz*, is pretty much the perfect choice to play Barnum—he is able to convey both Barnum's innate charm as well as the darker impulses that lead him to ignore those who truly care about him in his desperate quest to be accepted by the society types that once scorned him (especially his own father-in-law) while at the same time demonstrating the kind of singing and dancing chops that the old Arthur Freed unit at MGM would have killed to have utilized. Efron and Zendaya also have plenty of experience with singing and dancing as well and are able to sell their numbers while at the same time display a genuine romantic chemistry that helps to cut down on the potential schmaltz factor of their star-crossed-lovers subplot. The surprise of the cast, however, is Michelle Willams, who, to the best of my knowledge, has never really done much of anything of a musical nature before. You wouldn't know that from seeing her here, however, as she throws herself into her musical moments with the kind of utter fearlessness and abandon that mirrors her character's willingness to throw caution to the wind in order to support her husband. Already one of the best American actresses working today, it is thrilling to watch her display a new set of heretofore unsuspected talents.

Although the film begins to stumble a little bit in the second half with the conflicts involving Jenny Lind (though Ferguson is good in the role, especially in the way that she sells her lip-synching to the vocals of Loren Allred to such an extent that you can actually believe it is her singing), the only real problem with *The Greatest Showman*, at least in terms of its reception, is that, after years in development, it had the bad luck to debut not only a few months after the dissolution of the long-running circus that bore Barnum's name but at a moment when critics and commentators seemed to be going out of their way to find things to take offense at in order to demonstrate how woke they are on Twitter. As a result, the film has gotten a number of bad reviews that have dismissed it for not being accurate to the details of what really happened. Whatever its flaws, it is still a film that is jam-packed with any number of glories that will enrapture viewers of all ages willing to let themselves go and embrace its nuttiness. A musical like the live-action rendition of *Beauty and the Beast* (2017) may have been infinitely more successful from a box-office perspective but years from now, my guess is that it is *The Greatest Showman* that film fanatics will keep coming back to and celebrating.

Peter Sobczynski

CREDITS

P.T. Barnum: Hugh Jackman

Charity Barnum: Michelle Williams

Phillip Carlyle: Zac Efron

Anne Wheeler: Zendaya

Jenny Lind: Rebecca Ferguson

Origin: United States

Language: English

Released: 2017

Production: Laurence Mark, Jenno Topping, Peter Chernin; Chernin Entertainment, TSG Entertainment; released by Twentieth Century Fox Film Corp.

Directed by: Michael Gracey

Written by: Jenny Bicks; Bill Condon

Cinematography by: Seamus McGarvey

Music by: John Debney; Joseph Trapanese

Sound: Lewis Goldstein

Music Supervisor: Mark Wike

Editing: Tom Cross; Robert Duffy; Joe Hutshing; Michael McCusker; Jon Poll; Spencer Susser

Art Direction: Laura Ballinger

Costumes: Ellen Mirojnick

Production Design: Nathan Crowley
MPAA rating: PG
Running time: 105 minutes

REVIEWS

Burr, Ty. *Boston Globe*. December 20, 2017.
Chang, Justin. *Los Angeles Times*. December 20, 2017.
Gleiberman, Owen. *Variety*. December 20, 2017.
Lawson, Richard. *Vanity Fair*. December 20, 2017.
Merry, Stephanie. *Washington Post*. December 20, 2017.
Reed, Rex. *New York Observer*. December 21, 2017.
Rooney, David. *Hollywood Reporter*. December 20, 2017.
Yoshida, Emily. *New York Magazine/Vulture*. December 20, 2017.
Zacharek, Stephanie. *Time*. December 21, 2017.
Zinoman, Jason. *New York Times*. December 20, 2017.

QUOTES

Phillip Carlyle: "I can't just run off and join the circus."
P.T. Barnum: "Why not? You clearly have a flair for show business."
Phillip Carlyle: "There's show business?"
P.T. Barnum: "Mm-hmm."
Phillip Carlyle: "I never heard of it."
P.T. Barnum: "'Cause I just invented it."

TRIVIA

This has been a dream project for actor Hugh Jackman since 2009.

AWARDS

Golden Globes 2018: Song ("This Is Me")

Nominations:

Oscars 2017: Orig. Song Score and/or Adapt. ("This Is Me")
Golden Globes 2018: Actor--Mus./Comedy (Jackman), Film--Mus./Comedy

GUARDIANS OF THE GALAXY VOL. 2

You only get one chance to save the galaxy twice.
—Movie tagline

Box Office: $389.8 Million

James Gunn's *Guardians of the Galaxy* injected some much-needed personality into the Marvel Cinematic Universe. The brand's house style, all bright colors, bright lights, bright, snappy dialogue delivered by handsome actors with unerring comic timing, surrounded by largely homogenous action sequences with no real stakes, sorely needed a punch-spiking. Turns out a former Troma wunderkind was just the man for the job. Sure, it curbed his gore-happy, amoral, uber-cynical horror theatrics in the name of conforming to Marvel's dictates, but his sense of humor survived. The film was lousy with ironic pop-culture references and once-ubiquitous radio filler. It turned the need for the movie to have a happy ending into a comment on the narratives it was co-opting, and in general, the kitsch appeal of turning decades-old graphic novels into mass-market blockbuster entertainment. It seems like pure chance that Superman, Spider-Man, and Captain America were finally taking hold in the culture, so Gunn embraced the absurdity of these old warhorses being trotted out as if they were cutting edge entertainment, and he did so by adopting a bunch of maniacal outcasts in the Marvel universe. The Guardians are not heroic by nature, just by dumb luck and due to a nose for opportunity.

The Guardians, it seems, were feted to have more adventures, thanks to Marvel's never-ceasing film factory outlook, but it's just a good thing Gunn cared enough about his misfit heroes to write them a sequel that didn't feel like a collection of studio notes. When we last left Peter Quill (Chris Pratt), the self-proclaimed Star Lord, and his crew—Gamora (Zoe Saldana), Drax the Destroyer (Dave Bautista), Groot (voice of Vin Diesel), and Rocket the Raccoon (voice of Bradley Cooper)—they had accidentally saved the galaxy from certain doom at the hands of alien terrorist Ronan (Lee Pace). Now, they have been hired by golden-hued alien race, the Sovereigns, to protect their expensive power source from a carnivorous alien in exchange for Gamora's criminal sister Nebula (Karen Gillan). Gamora wants to bring her to justice for her part in aiding Ronan in his quest for domination of the galaxy. Rocket seizes upon the confusion of the alien space battle and the prisoner trading ceremony to steal some of the Sovereigns' powerful batteries to sell on the black market. Their queen, Ayesha (Elizabeth Debicki), sends a fleet of drones to stop them, but they only manage to hobble Quill's ship and strand them on a forest planet called Berhert.

When they crash land, aid comes in the form of a slick, bearded space traveler called Ego (Kurt Russell) and his aid Mantis (Pom Klementieff). Ego is Quill's father and has been searching the galaxy for him. Ego had traveled to Earth and met Quill's mother (Laura Haddock) and fell for her but had to return to the stars before Peter was born. In fact, the only reason that Quill was left with the scavenger Yondu (Michael Rooker) was because Ego had asked the criminal to pick the boy up and deliver him back to his real daddy. Yondu took a shine to Quill and taught him how to be a thief and pirate and never returned him to Ego. Now Ego wants to finally be a dad to his Earth-born son. Quill leaves

Rocket and Groot to fix their broken ship and watch Nebula, and takes Gamora and Drax with him to Ego's home planet.

Yondu, for his part, is much the worse for wear since he parted with Quill. No one in the bounty hunter community trusts him because he did not kill Quill when he had the chance, and because of the true nature of his deal with Ego. No one knows, but Ego asked Yondu to do something more nefarious than just pick up his son from his home planet. When Ayesha comes to Yondu and offers him a bounty to pick up Rocket so she can punish him for stealing the batteries, he accepts it, hoping he has a chance to reunite with Quill.

Meanwhile, Ego explains to his son that he's a form of sentient planet who takes human form to better understand and communicate with other alien species. His goal was to find someone in whom he could implant his titanic DNA to help him feel less alone in the universe, or so he says. Mantis seems to know something about Ego she does not want to tell Drax and Gamora, though they sense there's something fishy about him and his planet. Peter is too excited at finally be reunited with his dad that he does not notice any of the same strangeness. But when a newly-freed Nebula arrives, followed by Ayesha's drones, Ego is forced to show his hand and accelerate his father-son bonding activity, which is naturally less benign than he made it out to be. All those years ago, Yondu was delivering children that Ego was spawning all over the galaxy, which his scavenger colleagues saw as child trafficking and ostracized him. Ego had children with thousands of species on thousands of planets looking for one that would share enough of his DNA to control the titanic forces that Ego contains on his planet. All those other children died trying to impress their father but Peter seems to be capable of possessing it without being destroyed, making him Ego's last hope. Ego wants to wipe the universe clean and reshape it in his own image, the only perfect organism he ever met. The guardians have to put aside their differences again if they want to contain the threat he poses.

James Gunn's style remains charmingly idiosyncratic while under the dictates of Marvel Studios. He's not allowed to be as callous, gory or cynical as his previous work shows he's more interested in being. Gunn even gave himself an in-between vehicle in the stunningly grim and violent *The Belko Experiment* (2017), which he wrote but did not direct. *Guardians of the Galaxy, Vol. 2* doubles down on the cuddly family vibe hinted at in the first installment, though it also allows itself some of Gunn's theatrical disrespect. A prison break scene in particular has a staggering body count, but because Gunn scores it to some of the gold coast soft rock that has become a staple of his *Guardians* movies, it never quite sinks to the level of ghoulishness it might if all you could hear were the screams of the dying. His charismatically carefree attitude towards mass murder occasionally veers into overly self-conscious territory (the film too frequently calls to mind the work of Quentin Tarantino for its own good), but the soft center makes up for the rough edges.

That center is aided immeasurably by the performances, and when it fails it's because the characterizations needed more work. Gamora and Nebula's destructive sisterhood quarrels are deeply compelling as we learn how Nebula grew to be the half-cyborg like creation she is, while Gamora remained an almost perfect physical specimen. Saldana has proven easily defeated by a lot of dramatic work in films, but the level of emoting required by the character of Gamora fits her like a glove. Next to Gillan's Nebula, however, she does not stand a chance. Gillan is doing a lot of tremendous work under all the blue paint and prosthesis, communicating that her desire to hurt others is a way to distract from her interior scars. Even her voice, though electronically modified, carries the weight of years of sadness and neglect. Their dynamic is the strongest in the film. The relationships elsewhere suffer from dramatic imbalance. Chris Pratt has not yet figured out how to convey sadness or anger that isn't just his usual Golden Retriever-style eagerness with the wind knocked out of his sails. He does not express melancholy so much as he is just more obviously not happy any longer. This pulls the guts out of the film's climactic scene, leaving the emotional heavy lifting to be done by a henchman played by Sean Gunn, who was barely a character in the preceding two hours. Michael Rooker is unsurprisingly capable of picking up the slack as the heartbroken Yondu, trying to come to terms with his fatherly feelings for Quill and his growing disillusionment with a lifestyle that has gotten the better of him. Kurt Russell makes for a fascinating counterpoint to Rooker and not just because he's finally playing the villain and Rooker the hero for once. Russell's dynamism, his imperviousness to criticism, his million-dollar smile, hint at the way we wound up with movie idols like Pratt in the first place, while Rooker's presence is a reminder that without color, without a gritty foil, even the prettiest hero is not worth rooting for.

Cooper's characterization of Rocket as a kind of Joe Pesci-esque scrapper feels two decades old and the dialogue did not get any more clever this time out, so he remains comedic deadweight next to Bautista's ingenious portrayal of Drax. Hysterical and guileless, he fits perfectly with the throwback vibe of so much of *Guardians of the Galaxy Vol. 2*. Even Bautista's first career as a pro-wrestler feels aligned with the fetishization of 1980s culture, hinting at star turns taken by the likes of

Rowdy Roddy Piper and André the Giant. The film's stylistic debt to the likes of *Flash Gordon* (1980) and *Krull* (1983), with its mix of futuristic and antique technology and art direction (Pac-Man arcade games are a recurring motif), is most fully realized in the mammoth painted body of Bautista, who laughs a little too loud at his own jokes and is only just discovering sarcasm. His muscled naiveté continues to be the heart and soul of these films, the most enjoyably erratic of the Marvel universe.

Scout Tafoya

CREDITS

Peter Quill/Star-Lord: Chris Pratt
Gamora: Zoe Saldana
Drax: Dave Bautista
Baby Groot: Vin Diesel
Rocket Raccoon: Bradley Cooper
Ego: Kurt Russell
Origin: United States
Language: English
Released: 2017
Production: Kevin Feige; Marvel Studios; released by Walt Disney Pictures
Directed by: James Gunn
Written by: James Gunn
Cinematography by: Henry Braham
Music by: Tyler Bates
Sound: David Acord; Addison Teague
Music Supervisor: Dave Jordan
Editing: Fred Raskin; Craig Wood
Art Direction: Ramsey Avery
Costumes: Judianna Makovsky
Production Design: Scott Chambliss
MPAA rating: PG-13
Running time: 136 minutes

REVIEWS

Burr, Ty. *Boston Globe.* May 3, 2017.
Cole, Jake. *Slant Magazine.* May 2, 2017.
Dargis, Manohla. *New York Times.* May 4, 2017.
Duralde, Alonso. *TheWrap.* April 24, 2017.
Grierson, Tim. *Screen International.* April 24, 2017.
Hewitt, Chris. *Empire.* April 24, 2017.
Huddleston, Tom. *Time Out London.* April 24, 2017.
Turan, Kenneth. *Los Angeles Times.* May 3, 2017.
Tyrkus, Mike. *CinemaNerdz.com.* May 6, 2017.
Vishnevetsky, Ignatiy. *The A.V. Club.* May 2, 2017.
Zacharek, Stephanie. *Time.* April 24, 2017.

QUOTES

Yondu: "He may have been your father, Quill, but he wasn't your daddy."

TRIVIA

Dave Bautista's Drax makeup took only ninety minutes to apply, down from four hours for the first film. However, he would have to sit in a sauna at the end of the day to get all of the makeup off.

AWARDS

Nominations:

Oscars 2017: Visual FX

H

HAPPY DEATH DAY

Get up. Live your day. Get killed. Again.
—Movie tagline

Box Office: $55.7 Million

Film has a storied history with narratives about time loops from Chris Marker's canonical ode to memory, *La Jetée* (1962), to *Groundhog Day* (1993), one of the most well-regarded comedies of all time. But, in recent years, the subject has become less of a novel foundation than a playground for genre experiments. This past year alone brought the release of time loop riffs on young adult romances, raunchy low-brow comedies, high-brow dissections of relationships, and Christopher Landon's teen slasher trifle, *Happy Death Day*.

It's unclear exactly what caused this boon, especially when you consider that the most high-profile recent play on this gimmick, *Edge of Tomorrow* (2014), was eventually a success, but initially underperformed domestically. But the sub-genre's popularity makes its own kind of thematic sense. The time loop format aligns neatly with our most pervasive current cultural conversations, namely the effects of trauma and cycles of regret. It's hard to think of a better, more emotionally and direct method to examine someone's regrets and fears than forcing them to relive the same day over and over. And that's exactly what makes *Happy Death Day* so frustrating. All the pieces are there for a satisfying story, but the film never takes advantage of them.

The loop, in this case, wraps around the life in a day of Theresa "Tree" Gelbman (Jessica Rothe), a sorority girl at Bayfield University who is forced to repeatedly relive the day that she was mysteriously murdered by an assailant in a creepy bucktooth baby mask. For most of the first act, Tree is forced into this perfunctory routine of life/death until she becomes aware of what's happening. The only constant of her day is waking up in the dorm room of Carter Davis (Israel Broussard), an overly sweet and unconvincing geek, whom she clearly only noticed with beer goggles on.

Still, despite being initially brushed aside like a gnat, Tree, soon turns to Carter to help unpack why she's stuck in time. Even knowing that this set up needs to happen, the character's realization is far too slow. Landon's direction nonetheless, does a deft job of highlighting the series of details that Tree passes during the course of this day that she can't escape. As the day keeps repeating, these moments become a domino effect; whether it's an awkward stare from a mysterious student or the coincidence of passing a frat hazing event that goes wrong exactly as she walks by. Landon stages some early fun here, indulging in some juvenile sight gags, and making Tree a sort of conductor of the passage of time.

That entertainment is short lived though as the film falls into its own rut. Tree is at least refreshingly different from the expected heroine. She's a stereotypical mean girl, equally cold and manipulative—and clearly patterned after bullies in teen genre standbys like *Heathers* (1988) and *Mean Girls* (2004). Rothe's performance significantly complicates this caricature. It's to the actress' credit that her performance subtly reveals that her cool girl facade is a cloak for deeply repressed grief and growing numbness. Landon and writer Scott Lobdell have deep empathy for her character, even as she does her damnedest to be as unlikable for as long as possible.

The same positivity can't be echoed for the other character work, which ranges from dull to abhorrent. Watching Tree's arc is undeniably entertaining—particularly when her frustration about dying over and over manifests as nihilism—but the company she keeps is miserable. Carter is innocuous, but Tree's "friends" are a rotating group of backstabbers and slut-shamers who snipe at each other with overwritten one-liners, while the men are little more than walking representations of hormones.

At times, those cardboard thin characterizations feel like a homage to meta horror films like the *Scream* series or big budget sleaze like the 2000s reboots of *Friday the 13th* and *The Texas Chainsaw Massacre*. But this film isn't interested in the ritualistic murders of virgins, stoners, and jocks. Instead, these characterizations less like a subversion than a transposition of stock archetypes for the purpose of an uncluttered narrative. One of the last scenes in particular is so gallingly tone deaf in relation to a girl power message that it almost casts the whole film's supposed self-awareness in an entirely different light.

More problematically, *Happy Death Day* is a horror movie that's badly in need of tension or stakes. Recent years have challenged the myth that PG-13 horror movies will be automatically neutered (look no further than last year's excellent *Get Out* as Exhibit A of how to a make an intense, gripping horror film that doesn't require gallons of blood being spilt), but *Happy Death Day* is hopelessly blunted by its own premise. Admittedly, stakes are hard to communicate when there's no worry about consequence. And the film does an okay job bringing out the pain Tree feels, mostly through a montage of brutal deaths with the carnage carefully edited out to show the passage of time. But it's not enough to hide that the movie is going through the motions until it can deploy a new piece of information that can trigger a capricious tonal change. That transparency is rarely more evident than when a twist that could have changed the entire emotional resonance of the movie is quickly ignored to allow for a scenery change and the appearance of artificial urgency.

The final takeaway of *Happy Death Day* is less about its own merits than the continued sturdiness of its premise, and how much room there is still left to explore stories told through this method. If only Landon's film had been less enamored with its own self-referential slickness, it might have seen that it had a great character at its center.

Michael Snydel

CREDITS

Tree Gelbman: Jessica Rothe
Carter Davis: Israel Broussard
Lori Spengler: Ruby Modine
Gregory Butler: Charles Aitken
Stephanie Butler: Laura Clifton
Origin: United States
Language: English
Released: 2017
Production: Jason Blum; Blumhouse Productions, LLC., Digital Riot Media, Vesuvius Productions; released by Universal Pictures
Directed by: Christopher Landon
Written by: Scott Lobdell
Cinematography by: Toby Oliver
Music by: Bear McCreary
Sound: Trevor Gates
Music Supervisor: Andrea von Foerster
Editing: Gregory Plotkin
Art Direction: Michelle Harmon
Costumes: Meagan McLaughlin
Production Design: Cece Destefano
MPAA rating: PG-13
Running time: 96 minutes

REVIEWS

Catsoulis, Jeanette. *New York Times.* October 12, 2017.
Dowd, A.A. *The A.V. Club.* October 11, 2017.
Erbland, Kate. *IndieWire.* October 11, 2017.
Gilchrist, Todd *TheWrap.* October 11, 2017.
Robey, Tim. *The Telegraph.* October 19, 2017.
Tallerico, Brian. *RogerEbert.com.* October 13, 2017.
Tiffany, Kaitlyn. *The Verge.* October 11, 2017.
Ward, Sarah. *Screen International.* October 11, 2017.
Watson, Keith. *Slant Magazine.* October 11, 2017.
White, Danielle. *Austin Chronicle.* October 13, 2017.

QUOTES

Lori Spengler: "How do you know this?"
Tree Gelbman: "Because you already killed me once."
Lori Spengler: "Well I guess I'll just have to kill you all over again."

TRIVIA

The original mascot and mask designed by Tony Gardner for the film's killer was a pig, a motif that had already been done in the *Saw* films.

HAPPY END

Box Office: $197,697

Director Michael Haneke's latest examination of disaffection, *Happy End*, reunites Isabelle Huppert and

Jean-Louis Trintignant as daughter and father again after playing characters with the relationship in Haneke's *Amour* (2012). These two, however, are not the only elements retreaded in the newer film. The story of *Amour* comes up in confessional conversation and the misanthropic obsessions of the filmmaker are as inescapable, as his detached style, all failing to coalesce into anything justifying its existence.

Differentiation is not necessarily a filmmaker's duty, but when the pet themes of an auteur threaten to derail narrative for the sake of covered ground, exhaustion sets in on an audience. This exhaustion is seemingly shared by the filmmaker, whose film trods heavily towards its conclusion with the wordy weight of dense conversations slowing the often-elegant camerawork of cinematographer Christian Berger. These conversations are held mostly within the Laurent family, though their topics vary widely from construction business dealings to the morality of euthanasia.

The audience is introduced to the family through the hazy telephoto lens of a smartphone camera. The video, narrated by a series of on-screen text messages by the thirteen-year-old Eve (Fantine Harduin), sets a tone of ominous familiarity with domestic monotony that removes the audience a step further away—not just through the detached commentary, but the additional screen of viewership. A sociopathic little girl living with her mother and living through social media is itself a performance for an audience that is and isn't the one watching the film. Eve performs for her social media audience just as Harduin performs for the film audience. It is voyeurism to a much higher level than typical cinema is used to; it is psychotic behavior writ viral through the psychology of performativity.

So, when Eve poisons her divorced, depressed mother, it is no surprise. It is her acting through a proxy—this social media performance—and thus does not register to her as a criminal, violent act. She is tired of her mother's complaints, so she ends them. She is shuffled off to go live with her father (Mathieu Kassovitz) and their extended family—the patriarch grandfather grappling with dementia (Trintignant), the businesswoman aunt (Huppert), the stepmother (Laura Verlinden), and their two servants (Hassam Ghancy and Nabiha Akkari). Eve's troubled cousin Pierre (Franz Rogowski) crashes his way through a few cameos, but is more of a symbol than a character since his sole purpose in the film is to catalyze incident.

This is not due to Rogowski, as much of the acting is relegated to this role. Huppert, who stunned in *Elle* (2016), spends her time wandering the halls of her family's mansion or navigating the labyrinth of legal conversations after an accident on one of her construction sites. No character is directly implicated in any of the actions of the film, each separated by one or two degrees of technological or bureaucratic safety. The film implies that this smug separation has carried on to the younger generation that lives vicariously through the internet. Eve watches YouTube vloggers and films moments of her own life which make the film curious about her lack of empathy and implicate her internet use as the cause of its strange, detached development.

A distrust of technology comes out in other ways. The unrelenting focus on long e-mail typing scenes, scenes that are like watching laptop updates of James Joyce's vulgar love letters, sit the audience down and flash the fluorescent LCD of the future until it becomes just as vulgar. These writing segments that take place on a computer's desktop simply aren't evocative or inventive like the spectacular, form-bending piece of cinema manipulation that is *Unfriended* (2014). Instead, the scenes play up the dullness in comparison to the oversexed content of the e-mails, which might be humorous if it weren't so tedious.

The rest of the camerawork, besides a few of Berger's beautifully planned tracking shots, is similarly stoic. The camera lingers and waits, watching like a prowler from a safe distance—often starting with things in middle distance, then continuing to spy as the action wanders to the background. The ogling camera builds an indecisive tension that does not know whether to expect something to leap out or for its creepy loitering to be the sole generator of spectatorial strangeness.

Detached watching is a plot point too, as the construction firm's accident killed a worker and the family's Alzheimer's afflicted grandfather attempts again and again to end his own life. He drives off on his own, escaping his comfortable compound, only to botch his car accident and become wheelchair-bound. There is plenty of quiet loss on display (an old man losing his mind, a girl losing her humanity, a boy losing his self-worth, a father losing his daughter), but all are constantly undercut by bombastic overtures to symbolism. Random interludes here and there, like a drunkenly acrobatic karaoke performance of Sia's "Chandelier," create scattershot imagery that doesn't seem to be building to anything or sustaining a rhythm other than interruption.

Focusing too long on the depressed schemes of the young and old and too briefly on the distractions they and their relatives flee to, puzzling out the connections between scenes is never as satisfying as Haneke's omission-prone script expects. Skipping over the gut-punches is disaffective, but not worth more than a moment of bemusement because of the structural simplicity. Each scene's slowness pads in extra time for problem-solving and processing, but if it is clear from the start, there is no satisfaction in treading water.

Haneke has done this and done it better, not just treading water, but slowly sinking into it. There is some admirable tongue-in-cheek artistic grandstanding reminiscent of the kind in the art museum send-up *The Square* (2017). The servants are referred to as slaves to embarrass their employers; a wedding is crashed with a group of immigrants assumed to be unwelcome. There's none of the absurdism present in *The Square* though, just the interminable dryness that never quite grants the audience a punchline oasis. Instead, the wanderings are wordy, dull, and as arid as staring at the lengthy shots make one's eyes.

Euthanasia is grappled with and debated in so many words, but *Happy End* is mostly about people's lack of empathy when they have a degree or two of separation—be it a screen (TV or internet) or a socioeconomic line (the class and racial divide in the film, which is inelegantly handled)—from what this film determines to be the "real" world. Death by one's own hand or death as a mercy can be construed as a self-administered finale to the performance of life, but as far as *Happy End* is concerned, the Haneke morality on display damns anyone not engaging with their humanity correctly. While festooned with stylistic baubles and a tired tempo, the film's main argument consists of damning a generation of people recording life—all through a medium designed to do just that.

Jacob Oller

CREDITS

Anne Laurent: Isabelle Huppert
Georges Laurent: Jean-Louis Trintignant
Thomas Laurent: Mathieu Kassovitz
Eve Laurent: Fantine Harduin
Pierre Laurent: Franz Rogowski
Origin: United States
Language: French, English
Released: 2017
Production: Margaret Menegoz; ARTE, France 3 Cinema, Les Films du Losange, Wega-Film, Westdeutscher Rundfunk, X-Filme Creative Pool, Arte France Cinema; released by Sony Pictures Classics
Directed by: Michael Haneke
Written by: Michael Haneke
Cinematography by: Christian Berger
Editing: Monika Willi
Art Direction: Anthony Neale
MPAA rating: R
Running time: 107 minutes

REVIEWS

Chambers, Bill. *Film Freak Central.* September 21, 2017.
Croll, Ben. *TheWrap.* May 26, 2017.
Dowd, A.A. *The A.V. Club.* May 24, 2017.
Debruge, Peter. *Variety.* May 22, 2017.
Ebiri, Bilge. *Village Voice.* May 25, 2017.
Kohn, Eric. *IndieWire.* May 24, 2017.
Shannon, Gary. *The Young Folks.* October 23, 2017.
Strauss, Bob. *Los Angeles Daily News.* November 10, 2017.
Yoshida, Emily. *Vulture.* May 24, 2017.
Young, Deborah. *Hollywood Reporter.* May 22, 2017.

TRIVIA

This film was Austria's official submission to the Foreign Language Film Award of the 90th Annual Academy Awards.

THE HERO

Box Office: $4.1 Million

Brett Haley's *The Hero* gets a great deal of mileage from beginning to end by presenting the world with an actor who easily fascinates, whether it is when he does voiceover with that iconic baritone voice or just lays back and smokes weed. There is a charm in seeing Sam Elliott, who has been long overdue for such a lead role, presented as a regular person, while reflecting on his own career as a type of genre fixture. It is all the more a plain shame, then, that co-writer/director Haley gets in the way of this, with his story not so much winking about the importance of Elliott, but overtly telling audiences to appreciate him before he dies.

In the movie, Elliott plays a former movie star named Lee Hayden, who lives alone with bottles of whiskey and has become estranged from his wife Valarie (Katharine Ross), his daughter (Lucy Hayden), and the movie business. There was a big hit forty years ago, of which this film gets the title. Since then, he has enjoyed obscurity, picking up checks for commercial voiceover work (making for an equally funny and sad character introduction) and lingering in the minds of a niche audience that adores him.

Lee gets a diagnosis early into the movie that most characters seem to get when they are about to be celebrated—he has cancer, something that he doesn't communicate with his wife or daughter. Instead, when he does talk to them, he communicates with an on-brand Elliott twinkle in his eye that he wants to make a movie, a hopeful proposition and also something that causes a different type of worry in his estranged loved ones. Further keeping himself separated from the world, he even tells this lie to his friend and pot dealer, a former co-star named Jeremy (Nick Offerman, who makes for a couple of giddy moments while looking completely zonked out). In particular, he tells Jeremy that he has a dream he wants to make into a film, which Jeremy responds to with cynicism. But Lee counters thoughtfully, or perhaps with too much Haley behind it: "Movies are other people's dreams."

Lee experiences his real-life dream when he meets a friend of Jeremy's named Charlotte (Laura Prepon), a much younger stand-up comedienne who becomes more than amused by the older gentleman, as fantasy movies such as *The Hero* so readily depict. When Lee is asked to receive a lifetime achievement award from a western society—a humble but enthusiastic group of fans of Lee's, who share their own cute inferiority—Lee brings along Charlotte, which leads to a moment that goes viral, in turn giving Lee some newfound relevancy in the world. He receives movie deals. He is a star again.

Haley's movie, written with affection for his previous male lead in the 2015 film *I'll See You in My Dreams*, is marred by its lack of tact when referencing the impact of Elliott in real life. Elliott's scene in which he gives the award acceptance speech as Lee hits right on the head and then some, as if Haley is demanding the audience remember this self-eulogy. There are plenty of moments in which the reverence for Elliott is nearly obnoxious, as if becoming a type of propaganda that a viewer of *The Hero* would already appreciate. In turn, it threatens to make Elliott uninteresting.

There is a lack of poetry here that takes away from the impact of other emotional moments. In an initially promising scene, Lee grows emotionally attached to a monologue in a sci-fi movie that will inevitably be accompanied by CGI and loud music, weeping during his audition. But true to Haley's tact, or lack thereof, another scene quickly follows of Lee performing the monologue, this time for Jeremy, with the same emotional goal. By the end of the film, as Lee and Charlotte ebb and flow with their fling-turned-romance, Prepon is even shown reading actual poetry to him, as a type of grand emotional finale.

Elliott's performance in the movie remains appropriately compelling. Of all the actors who have appeared in almost 100 films, his is a mug, mustache, and voice that always has added something special to each project, almost redefining the limits of a character actor overall. To see all of that reflected in Lee, in quiet moments or scenes that seem to hint at his persona offscreen, can make the movie a bit of a thrill, especially if one is a fan. But Elliott himself proves that he can leave such a large impression while working with limited resources. Haley knows he can continue the magnetic nature of Elliott on camera, but does not provide him enough to work with. When Elliott is shown often in reflection, whether dreaming of the movie that will celebrate him or looking off onto a beach, the overall feeling is shallower than it should be with such a great title actor.

Nick Allen

CREDITS

Lee Hayden: Sam Elliott
Charlotte Dylan: Laura Prepon
Jeremy Frost: Nick Offerman
Lucy Hayden: Krysten Ritter
Valarie Hayden: Katharine Ross
Origin: United States
Language: English
Released: 2017
Production: Sam Bisbee, Houston King, Erik Rommesmo; Houston King Productions, Northern Lights Films, Park Pictures; released by The Orchard
Directed by: Brett Haley
Written by: Brett Haley; Marc Basch
Cinematography by: Rob Givens
Music by: Keegan DeWitt
Sound: Nicholas Schenck
Music Supervisor: Joe Rudge
Editing: Brett Haley
Costumes: Alana Morshead
Production Design: Eric J. Archer
MPAA rating: R
Running time: 93 minutes

REVIEWS

Catsoulis, Jeannette. *New York Times*. June 8, 2017.
Chang, Justin. *Los Angeles Times*. June 8, 2017.
D'Anglo, Mike. *The A.V. Club*. June 7, 2017.
Debruge, Peter. *Variety*. January 22, 2017.
Hornaday, Ann. *Washington Post*. June 15, 2017.
Jones, J.R. *Chicago Reader*. June 15, 2017.
Lemire, Christy. *RogerEbert.com*. June 9, 2017.
MacDonald, Moira. *Seattle Times*. June 20, 2017.
Walsh, Katie. *The Playlist*. January 22, 2017.
Zacharek, Stephanie. *Time*. June 8, 2017.

QUOTES

Lee Hayden: "Movies are other people's dreams."

TRIVIA

Sam Elliott and Nick Offerman starred together in several episodes of *Parks and Recreation* with Elliott playing Ron Dunn, the Eagleton counterpart of Offerman's character Ron Swanson.

THE HITMAN'S BODYGUARD

The world's top protection agent has a new client—his worst enemy.
—Movie tagline

Box Office: $75.5 Million

The Hitman's Bodyguard is a film that so desperately wants to be noticed and liked for being a hard-edged, R-rated, action-comedy buddy film, but it too often wears its desperation on its sleeve. The desire for this kind of notoriety (which has become harder and harder to achieve with each passing year) was part of a trend in the summer of 2017 with films like *Baby Driver* and *Atomic Blonde*, both of which took action sequences to heightened levels of comic absurdity and ultra-violence. *The Hitman's Bodyguard* would like to see itself placed alongside those films and, occasionally, it does work just fine as an action film. There are a few well-staged and finely-executed sequences here. Ultimately, though, the less-than-confident mid-August release date signaled that even the film's big studio distributor knew it had something a little too familiar on its hands.

If nothing else, though, Patrick Hughes' film distinguishes itself for taking place in Europe and not America. The story concerns a former protection agent named Michael Bryce (Ryan Reynolds) assigned to act as a singular secret service to dignitaries. A botched job that causes the death of a Japanese arms dealer results in Michael slumming it two years later as a freelance bodyguard who still uses his training from the CIA to kill anyone who gets in his way. His ex-girlfriend, Amelia (Elodie Yung), still works for Interpol and broke up with him during that two-year period. He lists her as "Pure Evil" on his phone when she calls. She now has a job for him: To keep a killer named Darius Kincaid (Samuel L. Jackson) alive long enough for him to testify against a corrupt and murderous president named Vladislav Dukhovich (Gary Oldman). Michael reluctantly takes the job, knowing that Darius is a guy who has been trying to kill him for years.

Darius has been wanted in a few countries for several years. He is a hitman who has dozens of killings to his credit. His wife, Sonia (Salma Hayek), sits in prison in Amsterdam for the same reasons. Darius has made a deal with the government that he will testify against Dukhovich if his wife is set free. They take him up on his offer, but during the prison transfer, Darius breaks free from the authorities and eventually winds up with Amelia, who puts he and Michael together. This gets the buddy-comedy aspect of the film going and it is not hard to see the trajectory that will take place soon thereafter. If Michael can keep Darius alive for the next couple days while several Interpol agents, and assassins hired by Dukhovich, try to find him and kill him, Michael will be given elite status as a protection agent again and his failings in his past will be put to rest.

As the buddy comedy goes on, Michael and Darius start out as enemies targeting the same faceless, gun-toting bad guys who are firing at them. As they spend more time together, of course, they slowly realize they need each other. The usual buddy-comedy tropes take place. They bond over their shared love of a song. One tries to double-cross the other by attempting escape, only to be foiled. They lose their car during an action scene, which leaves them on foot for a while. They willingly separate themselves due to a disagreement. They find they have a commonality in their past that they never realized. They bicker and argue and bicker and argue. Meanwhile, Interpol tries to get Sonia to help them locate Darius, but she refuses.

Screenwriter Tom O'Connor tailors his script after these tropes without much in the way of freshness. Luckily, the casting of Reynolds and Jackson makes this film go down a little easier. Their rapport can be fun to watch at times, but often, there seems to be a backstage game going on as to how many times they can get Jackson to say "mother****er" in one film. Likewise, O'Connor seems to be trying to break the record for the amount of expository flashbacks one can cram into a script. It is almost as if one can hear O'Connor and Hughes saying to themselves, "as long as Jackson is doing the narrating on the flashback, à la *The Hateful Eight* (2016), it will work like gangbusters!" It does not. Forcing an ironic use of Lionel Richie's song "Hello" into an ultra-violent action scene is also not as innovative or original as the filmmakers think it is. Still, Reynolds and Jackson do have their moments, even if they are just phoning in performances they have already given in a few other films before this.

There is also the problem of the film's visual palette. This is an odd-looking movie that can never quite decide what film stock or frame rate to use. Seemingly at random, cinematographer Jules O'Loughlin applies a smear across the frame, as though someone just wiped the lens with a dirty rag. It might have worked if it were just used for the flashback scenes. That at least would be consistent. Weirdly, it happens a few times within whole scenes. Then there are other moments during action scenes when the frame rate is changed, but again, randomly. There are other shots as well that look bleached-out and one unforgivably bad shot of a CGI boat going down the Gondolas during an otherwise well-done chase scene. Credit is due, though, to the crew for never once resorting to slow-motion during the action, an effect that mostly just ends up making a mediocre film that much longer.

The Hitman's Bodyguard is forgettable, but not unwatchable. Reynolds and Jackson are having fun and Oldman is typically over-the-top as the Russian on trial. It just owes a little too much to every kind of film before it. At one point, Reynolds and Jackson steal a car. The score at this point borrows heavily from Danny Elfman's spirited music from the great buddy comedy *Midnight Run* (1988). It is clearly a nod to that film and a wink from the filmmakers. Then, the car comes to a complete crash, in a comedic moment that was a good idea as an abrupt ending to an obvious (a little too obvious) tribute. The scene is rendered a complete throw-away. It also sums up this movie perfectly. It wants to be thought of as a throwback to the classic buddy-comedy elements while embracing the violent, modern-day trend of a high body-count and can-you-top-this action. Ultimately, it crashes, becomes forgotten, and the audience, like the characters in the car, just move onto the next thing.

Collin Souter

CREDITS

Michael Bryce: Ryan Reynolds
Amelia Roussel: Elodie Yung
Seifert: Richard E. Grant
Vladislav Dukhovich: Gary Oldman
Professor Asimov: Rod Hallett
Origin: United States
Language: English, French, Russian, Japanese
Released: 2017
Production: David Ellison, Mark Gill, Dana Goldberg, Matthew O'Toole, John Thompson, Les Weldon; Bodyguard Productions, Campbell Grobman Films, Cristal Pictures, East Light Media, Millennium Films, Nu Boyana Film Studios, Skydance Media; released by Summit Entertainment
Directed by: Patrick Hughes
Written by: Tom O'Connor
Cinematography by: Jules O'Loughlin
Music by: Atli Orvarsson
Sound: Dominic Gibbs
Music Supervisor: Selena Arizanovic
Editing: Jake Roberts
Art Direction: Tim Blake
Costumes: Stephanie Collie
Production Design: Russell de Rozario
MPAA rating: R
Running time: 118 minutes

REVIEWS

Douglas, Edward. *Film Journal International.* August 11, 2017.
Ehrlich, David. *IndieWire.* August 15, 2017.
Feeney, Mark. *Boston Globe.* August 17, 2017.
LaSalle, Mick. *San Francisco Chronicle.* August 16, 2017.
Scherstuhl, Alan. *Village Voice.* August 15, 2017.
Scott, A.O. *New York Times.* August 16, 2017.
Vishnevetsky, Ignatiy. *The A.V. Club.* August 17, 2017.
Walsh, Katie. *Tribune News Service.* August 16, 2017.
Whitty, Stephen. *Newark Star-Ledger.* August 16, 2017.
Worthington, Clint. *Consequence of Sound.* August 17, 2017.

QUOTES

Michael Bryce: "You've got a speck of blood on your...everywhere."

TRIVIA

Actor Samuel L. Jackson speaks one-hundred and twenty-two expletives throughout the course of the film.

HOME AGAIN

Starting over is not for beginners.
—Movie tagline

Box Office: $27 Million

With even a little self-awareness, *Home Again* might have contained some light-meta wisdom in a *Ruby Sparks* (2012)-meets-*Mamma Mia!* (2008) story of a woman who grew up around movies only to realize she later sought the temptations and trappings of her family's cinematic situations. Think of the complex screwball potential of a separated mother of two seriously wrestling with her broken marriage and changing relationship with her daughters while also developing bonds with three fully-created young men she has invited into her house to fulfill an unexamined need to live like a movie character. At the very least, she would learn that people have more dimension than they are given in most lighthearted onscreen romps, and things do not always settle gently into place.

Yet it is not especially surprising that *Home Again*, the debut from writer-director Hallie Meyers-Shyer, contains none of the minimal imagination that would have sharpened her premise. The daughter of filmmakers Nancy Meyers (*The Intern* [2015]) and Charles Shyer (*Father of the Bride* [1991]), Meyers-Shyer aspires to crowd-pleasing fluff but settles for a vague approximation of cutesy, like someone came up with a joke about what kind of movie Nancy Meyers and Charles Shyer's daughter would make and she took it as a serious suggestion. That is to say that virtually all of *Home Again* screams of both convention and contrivance, as Alice (Reese Witherspoon), containing no rough edges concerning her recent separation from her husband Austen (Michael Sheen) and her consequential move from New York, meets a trio of budding filmmakers at a bar and winds up allowing the three young men to stay with her and her two young daughters. Because clearly all ambitious twenty-somethings in Los Angeles are great with children and extremely trustworthy, this impulsive arrangement, fueled by the guys' fondness for Alice's legendary director/father and actress/mother (Candice Bergen), generates only the mildest of conflict, mostly driven by Alice's relatively benign relationship with Harry (Pico Alexander).

Like a remake of *This is 40* (2012), the first scene of *Home Again* takes place in a bathroom, on Alice's 40th birthday. But instead of Judd Apatow's film immediately addressing the anxiety and loneliness that emerges as interpersonal dynamics change over time, Meyers-Shyer depicts Alice crying into a mirror, then putting on a happy face as Isabel (Lola Flannery) and Rosie (Eden Grace Redfield) present signs acknowledging her special day. Alice asks, "Who wants pancakes?" and there is not the sense of a busy parent without the time to properly address her needs and disappointments so much as a film that cannot handle more than one feeling at a time.

This is why *Home Again* unfolds in the most straightforward, underwhelming manner possible, even as George (Jon Rudnitsky), the writer of Harry's South by Southwest buzz-generating short film, develops feelings for Alice. "I am not in love with Alice; I just love a lot of things about her, like her face and her personality," George says, in one of the film's very, very few good lines. Hopefully the charm provided by Rudnitsky, who was booted from *Saturday Night Live* almost before viewers realized he was there, will one day find a bigger role in a better movie. Of the three young men (which also includes Nat Wolff as Teddy, Harry's little brother and the actor of the trio), George seems most like an actual person, but Meyers-Shyer refuses to engage tough questions about the fallout of any feelings between the people in this house, whether it is the kids or the adults.

Most of the time, the film seems trapped in a drowsy state of blankness, from Isabel noting that all kids are on anti-depressants (this line of dialogue was likely written several years ago, much like the decision to have Austen pursuing a new version of the now-old-news Sam Smith or showcasing a bar blasting LMFAO's no-longer-ubiquitous "Party Rock Anthem") to nothing coming at all from the fact that Alice's long-divorced parents had a wide age difference. Meyers-Shyer has nothing to say about what type of people are or are not compatible, or the long-lasting impact of Alice's dad telling her on every birthday, "The future is yours." This is not a movie about a woman turning forty and confronting hard truths about the life she imagined compared to the life she has. It is merely an opportunity to wait around for her to remind herself why her estranged husband (who is in the music industry, another common element with *This is 40*) is a doofus and why taking the safest route possible in her personal life will yield the most mundane resolution possible. That way everyone goes home having indulged only in a fantasy and not actually having thought about the details of what is supposed to make the story worth telling in the first place.

All this mildness is why Witherspoon floats indifferently through the movie, and why financial concerns never take shape among universally white, privileged characters. That would require stakes and intelligence, where *Home Again* is far more interested in mediocre shenanigans like Harry telling Alice "You're so maternal, you should be a mom" before throwing up, an obnoxious social influencer (Lake Bell) being rude so Alice can tell her off and the inevitable collision of big family events and big career events. Only someone who has never seen a movie before will find drama in the decision-making involved.

In the midst of a lot of jingle-jangle music and approximately 500 dinner party montages, however, is one quite funny scene. Harry, George, and Teddy meet with a producer (Reid Scott) with ideas like a found-footage love story, or moving an intimate story set in Brooklyn to the South, adding a dance sequence and making it more like *American Sniper* (2014). That is a funny bit about creative vision and sacrifices to get a project made. Maybe if Meyers-Shyer had the slightest bit of originality or input other than the softest elements of her parents' work, she would realize her perception of cozy is actually a dusty old pillow in the dumpster.

Matt Pais

CREDITS

Alice Kinney: Reese Witherspoon
Austen: Michael Sheen
Zoey: Lake Bell
Teddy: Nat Wolff
Lillian Stewart: Candice Bergen
Origin: United States
Language: English
Released: 2017
Production: Nancy Meyers, Erika Olde; Black Bicycle Entertainment; released by Open Road Films
Directed by: Hallie Meyers-Shyer
Written by: Hallie Meyers-Shyer
Cinematography by: Dean Cundey
Music by: John Debney

Sound: Kami Asgar; Erin Oakley
Music Supervisor: Linda Cohen
Editing: David Bilow
Art Direction: Brianna Gorton
Costumes: Kate Brien Kitz
Production Design: Ellen Brill
MPAA rating: PG-13
Running time: 97 minutes

REVIEWS

Dargis, Manohla. *New York Times*. September 6, 2017.
Duralde, Alonso. *TheWrap*. September 5, 2017.
Erbland, Kate. *IndieWire*. September 5, 2017.
Frosch, Jon. *The Hollywood Reporter*. September 5, 2017.
Rife, Katie. *The A.V. Club*. September 7, 2017.
Roeper, Richard. *Chicago Sun-Times*. September 7, 2017.
Russo, Tom. *Boston Globe*. September 6, 2017.
Scott, Mike. *New Orleans Times-Picayune*. September 7, 2017.
Smith, Anna. *Time Out New York*. September 5, 2017.
Wilkinson, Alissa. *Vox*. September 7, 2017.

TRIVIA

At one point, actress Rose Byrne was attached to star in this film.

HOSTILES

We are all hostiles.
—Movie tagline

Box Office: $14.1 Million

Scott Cooper makes movies about macho men destroyed by corrupt systems or outdated definitions of masculinity. His latest, *Hostiles,* owes a great deal to the films of John Ford, but it's Cooper's skill with the ensemble that keeps it working to overcome some pretty egregious revisionism regarding this country's relationship with Native Americans. Most damagingly, this is the kind of film in which people act one way or have a certain history until the film demands they change for the sake of the screenplay. It's a film that's too often stumbling over its own feet and those of history, both the real kind and the films that have handled this kind of material more interestingly in the past. And yet, there's an occasional decision by one of the talented members of the ensemble or a nice composition by the great cinematographer Masanobu Takayanagi (*The Grey* [2011]) to make it palatable.

Hostiles opens in 1892 with a brutal massacre, which sets a tone for a world in which horrific violence can suddenly erupt that permeates all 133 minutes of the film that follows. Wesley Quaid (Scott Shepherd) lives with his wife, Rosalie (Rosamund Pike), and children in a small home that is beset upon by Comanches. They kill Wesley and his children as Rosalie flees to the cover of the trees nearby. Watching running children being shot in the back in a film's opening scene and seeing a man scalped before he's shot makes a statement—this is a violent, cruel, horrible place to live, a place where death could come on any average day.

Cut to a man who has seen his own share of carnage, Captain Joseph Blocker (Christian Bale), who arrives at Fort Berringer in New Mexico after rounding up an escaped Apache family. One gets the sense that in 1892, men in this part of the country have seen years and years of battles between Native Americans and the white men who believe they are owed as much right to this land they have found as the people they have found on it. Bale is convincing as a man whose eyes convey decades of brutal death. He has killed and seen his colleagues killed. And one of those colleagues, an old bearded friend named Thomas Metz (Rory Cochrane) appears to be near his breaking point. These are not fresh-faced men to the fight—these are grizzled, bitter soldiers who have been warped by the violence that has defined their existence.

Blocker is handed a life-changing assignment when he's told by Colonel Biggs (Stephen Lang) that he will be the head officer for orders that have come straight from the President. He's to accompany a dying Cheyenne War Chief named Yellow Hawk (Wes Studi) and his family back to their tribal land in Montana. At first, Blocker refuses to serve as protection for a former enemy, but he's told he has no choice. The mission changes drastically when they come upon the charred remains of the Quaid house from the opening scene, and pick up the only survivor, Rosalie, as a new traveling companion, and, of course, eventual love interest for Blocker.

Hostiles has an undeniably episodic structure to it as Blocker and his party encounter different hurdles on their journey, but it's a film that almost embraces what could be called a languid pace. There are a number of dialogue-heavy scenes around campfires about carnage seen and unknowable futures. Several of these scenes succumb to screenwriter's contrivances, feeling like scripted exchanges more than natural, organic developments. Everyone gets so philosophical as they age in the Old West. It's Cooper echoing films like *The Searchers* (1956) or Clint Eastwood's *Unforgiven* (1992)—movies that sought to deconstruct and analyze some of the Western tropes—but that kind of thing is much harder than it looks. *Hostiles* too often comes off as pretentious and over-written, consciously grabbing for some kind of cinematic importance that it can't quite reach.

It's saved from total disaster by a string of smart decisions by its cast—and credit to Cooper's work with ensemble, something he also displayed in *Black Mass* (2015). In particular, Bale gives his typical all to a part that could have been showy and scenery-chewing, but with which he goes mostly internal. He captures the world weariness of a man so exhausted that he's started to question some of his life decisions and perceptions about the Native Americans he has helped massacre. There are a number of great actors in small roles, including Ben Foster, Jesse Plemons, Timothée Chalamet, Bill Camp, and Peter Mullan. Sadly, Cooper does not give Pike quite enough to do, although she does as much as possible with the little she's been given.

A final interesting thing to consider is that *Hostiles* feels like the kind of movie that will not really be made that often in the very near future. It's the kind of budget level—rumored around $50 million—that's just increasingly difficult to get made when everything is either indie or Marvel. The filmmakers who used to make mid-budget films for adults are increasingly going to television or streaming services. And the budget for *Hostiles* proved to be a major problem point in its sale at the Toronto International Film Festival, as most distributors were scared of being able to make it back. It's impressive, and a testament to the genre draw and that of Bale, that the small company Entertainment Studios was able to get the film all the way to #3 on the box office charts and could eventually make back that budget, but *Hostiles* still feels like something of a relic, the kind of movie that will be harder to make in the era of Moviepass and Netflix. As much as it is an elegy to a changing West, the film itself feels like a product of a bygone era of filmmaking. Well, maybe not as long as Scott Cooper still has stories about men to tell.

Brian Tallerico

CREDITS

Wesley Quaid: Scott Shepherd
Rosalie Quaid: Rosamund Pike
Buffalo Man: David Midthunder
Captain Joseph J. Blocker: Christian Bale
Master Sergeant Thomas Metz: Rory Cochrane
Origin: United States
Language: English
Released: 2017
Production: Ken Kao, John Lesher, Scott Cooper; Le Grisbi Productions, Waypoint Entertainment; released by Entertainment Studios Motion Pictures
Directed by: Scott Cooper
Written by: Scott Cooper
Cinematography by: Masanobu Takayanagi
Music by: Max Richter
Editing: Tom Cross
Art Direction: Elliott Glick
Costumes: Jenny Eagan
Production Design: Donald Graham Burt
MPAA rating: R
Running time: 133 minutes

REVIEWS

Bahr, Lindsey. *The Associated Press*. January 11, 2018.
Burr, Ty. *Boston Globe*. January 4, 2018.
Cheshire, Godfrey. *RogerEbert.com*. December 22, 2017.
Laffly, Tomris. *Time Out*. December 21, 2017.
McCarthy, Todd. *Hollywood Reporter*. September 3, 2017.
Mobarak, Jared. *The Film Stage*. December 20, 2017.
Phillips, Michael. *Chicago Tribune*. January 4, 2018.
Scott, A.O. *New York Times*. December 21, 2017.
Vishnevestky, Ignatiy. *The A.V. Club*. December 14, 2017.
Yoshida, Emily. *New York Magazine*. December 15, 2017.

QUOTES

Rosalie Quaid: "Sometimes I envy the finality of death. The certainty. And I have to drive those thoughts away when I wake."

TRIVIA

Actress Rosamund Pike revealed in an interview that she and actor Christian Bale barely spoke during filming outside of shooting their scenes, saying that Bale "would keep a distance. Our characters in [the film] are quite dysfunctional but have this profound connection that we let happen without ever really talking about it."

THE HOUSE

If you can't beat the house, be...the House.
—Movie tagline

Box Office: $25.6 Million

Since leaving *Saturday Night Live* (SNL) and paying his dues in any number of goofy supporting turns in other SNL veteran's movies, Will Ferrell has become one of the most reliable comic presences out there. The crafting of Ron Burgundy in *Anchorman* (2004) started a string of collaborations with Adam McKay—including *Talladega Nights* (2006), *Step Brothers* (2008), and *The Other Guys* (2010)—that have become part of the same quotable lexicon that the previous generation delighted from the likes of John Belushi, Chevy Chase, Bill Murray, Dan Aykroyd, and Harold Ramis. Every one of them had their bumps in the road with shoddy material and ideas that just failed to connect to that subjective tissue which produces laughs. Television adaptations like *Land of the Lost* (2009) and *Bewitched* (2005) have certainly been an Achilles heel for Farrell, but no project on his résumé has felt so hopelessly dead on arrival than the version of *The House*.

Scott and Kate Johansen (Will Ferrell & Amy Poehler) are emerging empty nesters. Their daughter, Alex (Ryan Simpkins), has just been accepted into college and they could not be prouder. However, it turns out that what is empty is their nest egg and they do not know how to tell their only child they cannot afford it. Their neighbor, Frank (Jason Mantzoukas), is also going through a rough patch financially as well as emotionally having separated from his wife (Michaela Watkins). All he has to look forward to is the Vegas trip they had already planned to go together on; an excursion that sparks a grand solution to all of their problems.

Why travel to Nevada if you can bring Las Vegas to the suburbs? Specifically, the basement of the Johansens. Within moments of the crazy suggestion, tables have been setup and their close friends are being recruited for the underground casino. Money begins to roll in; more than enough to cover Alex's education and then some. Only the power flash begins to take hold of the couple and too much of a good thing becomes much harder to shut down. The longer it goes on, the more attention it attracts, particularly from an ambitious city councilor (Nick Kroll) and the local mob who are not seeing their percentage of the profit.

Comedies often begin with a foundation leading into the discovery of what can be mined for humor. Even one-joke premises tend to have the courage of their convictions to drive home singular punchlines. Bookended with two jokes about sexual assault in the first five minutes (talk about putting your audience on tilt early) and later an actual murder that results in the film's funniest scene, it's a wonder just what everyone found humorous about this idea. There is no true story in their midst to present a heightened reality, therefore it leaves the door open to explore the behavior of bored suburbanites. Settled down into an existence of complacency, its inhabitants begin lashing out on their innermost desire for risk, vices, and dreams of class jumping.

Instead of satire though, debut director Andrew Jay Cohen opts for straight parody and everyone appears lost in recognizing the difference. One of the problems of just going for easy callbacks to *Casino* (1995) is that the best of it was already seen in *Jane Austen's Mafia* (1998). Certainly, that is one of the weaker of the solo efforts by the master team of Zucker/Abrahams/Zucker which reveals just how little creativity exists in this screenplay. Its centerpiece sequence involving a cheater recalls the hammer comeuppance from Scorsese's film. They throw in a vice to double down on the reference for good measure. For triple they opine, "We gotta send a message. Like DeNiro in *Casino*." It might lead to a pressure cooker of dark comedy if everyone could not see the joke coming a mile away.

Neighborly squabbles and stroking suppressed male egos do not advance as comedy if the characters are first introduced as combatants before the first bet is placed. The devolving moral standards of the protagonists also have nowhere to go when their mental faculties are already in question. Frankly put, the Johnsons are not normal. But certainly not abnormal enough to be funny. Will Ferrell and Amy Poehler are too smart—even when playing dumb—for anyone to believe or, more importantly, sympathize with their plight as written. Here is a couple that lives in a beautiful suburban home. The recurring joke of Scott being a remedial student when it comes to mathematics calls into question how he could acquire—at the very worst—an upper middle-class lifestyle, let alone be so blinded to the costs associated with higher learning. This is not a family struggling to do right by their child. This is a systemic representation of the well-off throwing a pity party for themselves and tossing the bill of false hope to those who have less. Look at how we just stumbled into grittier territory for satire and comedic possibilities.

With a running time of just 80 minutes there is a choppiness on display in *The House* suggesting a lot of trims were made to allow less proximity between the jokes they felt were working. The shenanigans of *Ocean's Thirteen* (2007)—complex though they may be—had more fun with the possibilities of turning the odds against those that are already fixed against the players. The title alone is a vague enough moniker that could imply any number of institutions but this is a film that would rather play the penny slots and wait for its free drinks than sit in the high stakes room and risk everything.

Erik Childress

CREDITS

Scott Johansen: Will Ferrell

Kate Johansen: Amy Poehler

Frank: Jason Mantzoukas

Alex Johansen: Ryan Simpkins

Bob: Nick Kroll

Origin: United States

Language: English

Released: 2017

Production: Adam McKay, Joseph Drake, Jessica Elbaum, Nathan Kahane, Will Ferrell, Andrew Jay Cohen, Brendan O'Brien; Gary Sanchez Productions, Good Universe, New Line Cinema L.L.C., Village Roadshow Pictures; released by Warner Bros. Pictures
Directed by: Andrew Jay Cohen
Written by: Andrew Jay Cohen; Brendan O'Brien
Cinematography by: Jas Shelton
Music by: Andrew Feltenstein; John Nau
Sound: Michael J. Benavente; Elliott Koretz
Music Supervisor: Manish Raval; Tom Wolfe
Editing: Evan Henke; Michael L. Sale
Art Direction: Elliott Glick
Costumes: Christopher Oroza
Production Design: Clayton Hartley
MPAA rating: R
Running time: 88 minutes

REVIEWS

DeFore, John. *Hollywood Reporter*. June 30, 2017.
Duralde, Alonso. *TheWrap*. June 29, 2017.
Famurewa, Jimi. *Empire Magazine*. July 3, 2017.
Johanson, MaryAnn. *Flick Filosopher*. July 3, 2017.
Lemire, Christy. *RogerEbert.com*. June 30, 2017.
Nusair, David. *Reel Film Reviews*. July 21, 2017.
Orndorf, Brian. *Blu-Ray.com*. June 30, 2017.
Roeper, Richard. *Chicago Sun-Times*. June 30, 2017.
Scott, A.O. *New York Times*. July 1, 2017.
Snider, Eric D. *EricDSnider.com*. July 12, 2017.

TRIVIA

Mariah Carey was originally supposed to have a cameo in the movie, however her scenes were never filmed. Will Farrell recalled that Carey showed up four hours late to the shoot, then didn't want to do the scene she had agreed to.

HOW TO BE A LATIN LOVER

Age is a number, sexy is forever.
—Movie tagline

Box Office: $32.1 Million

After a successful career in Mexico as an actor/writer/director, Eugenio Derbez makes his Hollywood lead role debut with the film *How to Be a Latin Lover*, a comedy of many broad emotions and an unjust amount of laughs. Also marking the directorial debut of David Wain collaborator Kevin Marino, the film boasts a great amount of talent but has a dispiriting focus on cheaper jokes, wooing audiences with Derbez only so much.

Derbez plays Maximo, a gigolo, who, at the beginning of the movie, has settled down with a much older, rich woman. After a funny montage that shows how lazy he has become (listlessly traveling through his mansion on hoverboards, making maids clean up his coffee spills), he is soon kicked out of the house when she finds another lover, a car salesman played by Michael Cera. This puts him into a place that he has not been in for decades, jobless and without a rich older woman to take care of him, providing an excellent arrested development metaphor.

Directionless, Maximo crashes at the apartment belonging to his sister Sara (Salma Hayek) where he starts to become an influence on her wide-eyed, impressionable young son Hugo (Raphael Alejandro). This is where Derbez's interesting character, and the film's unique sense of humor that involves men trying to seduce elderly women, starts to fall apart: Maximo decides that if he can teach Hugo how to talk to women, he can get Hugo invited to a schoolmate crush's party, so that Maximo can try to woo the girl's rich grandmother (Raquel Welch). This leads to a couple of amusing passages in which Maximo tries to school Hugo in the twisted ways of talking to women (which are taken literally and with mixed results by Hugo), but also a movie that becomes overlong. As Maximo struggles to make money on his own, there's also a limp narrative thread with a couple of car wrap ad macho men (Rob Riggle and Rob Huebel), who terrorize Maximo after the former gigolo initially puts a strip club advertisement on Sara's car, but takes it off. Maximo's sporadic run-ins with these dopes make for clear plot machination, adding little to the story but extra conflicts.

Desiring to be a type of crowd-pleaser that plays many notes, *How to Be a Latin Lover* has a stubborn running time of almost two hours, which would be less of a chore were there more going on in the story. Instead, it feels like the movie invests more in feelings than order, leading to numerous heart-to-heart moments (with Hayek, Bell, and later even Rob Lowe, who plays a gigolo friend of Maximo's) but sporadic comedy rhythm. It is particularly fitting that the movie ends with a parade, with costumed people from all walks of life bopping through Los Angeles to "No Soy Tieste," as the movie yearns to be a party more than anything else.

Director Ken Marino does not bring much to the story in terms of filmmaking flavor, taking a more standard approach to the script that does not have nearly enough great gags as it thinks. His most unique sense of authorship in his directorial debut here is that he has brought many of his funny faces from his series *Burning Love,* which had a similar tone to making fun of vain love by parodying the ABC series *The Bachelor.* In this case, Marino gets a slightly less conventional comedic edge by working with people who do not normally have such big parts in studio projects, including the likes of Rob Corddry as a no-nonsense limo driver, and the aforementioned roles by Cera, Riggle, and Huebel. The strongest all-star of this batch is Kristen Bell, who plays an overly excited frozen yogurt employee who wears many scars from her many rescue cats, but has a sweet albeit pointed monologue where she tells Maximo that even though the cats hurt her, they are her family.

The movie offers a dispiriting juxtaposition between the talent and material: Derbez is clearly more nuanced than the material he is working with, even if he does endorse the film's repeated gags or easy jokes. His take on parodying the gigolo is a clear achievement in rendering the unlikable character into a sympathetic one: Maximo is not a hard worker or even a true lover, and little more than a predator on rich elderly women. But Derbez provides an incredibly grounded version of this character, gently balancing the goofiness of Maximo's pursuits while never forgetting the inherent darkness. It is quite a testament that he can sell a complicated character, and yet a reminder that Marino's film does not give him enough to work with.

How to Be a Latin Lover proves to be a decent start for Derbez, although at the American box office it was not quite the anticipated hit. While it may not succeed as a strong comedy, it does create a type of brand for him. He is working in a different environment, where movies are less led by their leading star power than by the pitch themselves, but he has enough talent clearly that this could be just the beginning. Derbez has the chops to be a great international entertainer, but that will be more evident once he gets better projects.

Nick Allen

CREDITS

Maximo: Eugenio Derbez
Sara: Salma Hayek
Rick: Rob Lowe
Cindy: Kristen Bell
Hugo: Raphael Alejandro
Origin: United States
Language: English, Spanish
Released: 2017
Production: Ben Odell, Eugenio Derbez; 3Pas Studios; released by Pantelion Films
Directed by: Ken Marino
Written by: Chris Spain; Jon Zack
Cinematography by: John Bailey
Music by: Craig Wedren
Sound: Will Riley
Music Supervisor: Howard Paar
Editing: John Daigle
Art Direction: Alex Gaines; Thomas P. Wilkins
Costumes: Molly Grundman
Production Design: Marcia Hinds
MPAA rating: PG-13
Running time: 115 minutes

REVIEWS

Cordova, Randy. *Arizona Republic*. April 27, 2017.
Estrada, Erick. *Cinegarage*. May 5, 2017.
Kenny, Glenn. *New York Times*. April 28, 2017.
Leydon, Joe. *Variety*. April 28, 2017.
Myers, Kimber. *Los Angeles Times*. April 28, 2017.
Pahle, Rebecca. *Pajiba*. May 5, 2017.
Puig, Claudia. *TheWrap*. April 28, 2017.
Rechtshaffen, Michael. *Hollywood Reporter*. May 1, 2017.
Vishnevetsky, Ignatiy. *The A.V. Club*. April 28, 2017.
Wloszczyna, Susan. *RogerEbert.com*. April 28, 2017.

QUOTES

Maximo: "I can teach you to use your skills of seduction to get what you want."
Hugo: "When do we start?"

TRIVIA

This is the first American movie to be released simultaneously in its original language and dubbed to Spanish.

I

I AM NOT YOUR NEGRO

In "Remember This House" Raoul Peck envisions the book James Baldwin never finished—a radical narration about race in America, through the lives and assassinations of three of his friends: Martin Luther King Jr., Medgar Evers, and Malcolm X, using only the writer's original words.

—Movie tagline

Box Office: $7.1 Million

There are artistic works of cinematic nonfiction that might be deemed revelatory in expected fashion. For an example of such a characterization, consider a movie like the Oscar®-nominated *Last Days in Vietnam* (2014). Even the poorest student of American history would likely be aware that the United States fought a long war in Vietnam, and that it ended in messy and ignominious fashion in the mid-1970s. The revelations of director Rory Kennedy's movie, then, which chronicles the fall of Saigon in APril 1975, unfold in a manner that conforms with what one might reasonably surmise to be some of the lessons of said time period. Via firsthand accounts, primary footage, new interviews, and other details, the film breathes multidimensionality into the moral quandary then facing American soldiers and diplomats—whether to obey the orders of the Ford Administration and evacuate only American citizens, or save the lives of as many South Vietnamese collaborators (sure to be incarcerated, or worse, by the Viet Cong) as possible.

In contrast, though, there are documentary films which illuminate hitherto unknown or under-appreciated subjects, and also contextualize their work in new ways, connecting them to present-day issues and events. Stacking philosophical insight and enlightenment upon intellectual revelation, these films might be called unexpectedly revelatory. Such is the description of Haitian-born director Raoul Peck's *I Am Not Your Negro*, a layered, elegiac broadside against moral apathy standing on the shoulders of American writer and social critic James Baldwin. At once a ruminative dirge as well as a bristling, vitally indignant call to arms, Peck's inventively structured nonfiction film is an exploration of 20th-century American racism—and the insidious shadow it now casts forward, into this still-young century.

Following its premiere at the 2016 Toronto Film Festival, Magnolia Pictures acquired theatrical rights to the movie and released it the following February. On the strength of near-universal critical praise (the movie was nominated for Best Documentary Feature at the 89th Academy Awards®, and was the winner of the Los Angeles Film Critics Association Award in the same category), *I Am Not Your Negro* would ride a four-month theatrical run to an eventual $7.1 million in domestic box office receipts.

At the time of his death from stomach cancer in late 1987, Baldwin had circled back around to a partial manuscript, *Remember This House*, stemming from an unfinished writing assignment in the late 1970s which focused on his personal recollections of slain civil rights leaders Medgar Evers; Martin Luther King, Jr.; and Malcolm X. It is this work, narrated by Samuel L. Jackson with a measured brilliance which runs counter to his more overtly theatrical instincts, that forms the spine of Peck's film.

I Am Not Your Negro opens in 1957, at a time when Baldwin was returning to the United States from life abroad in France. Filled with a mixture of hatred, pity, and shame at witnessing photos over the increasingly nasty and violent battle over school integration, Baldwin waxes rhapsodic about what he had missed about America: the way, he wrote, "when a dark face opens, the light seems to go everywhere—the light that had produced me." Other evocative passages in the film include Baldwin's memories of films from his youth, including Clinton Rosemond as a cowering African-American janitor who reminded him of his father in *They Won't Forget* (1937).

Eschewing contemporary interviewees to extol the virtues and brilliance of its subject (and by extension his viewpoints), Peck instead uses a more jazzy, indirect and, at times, impressionistic tack. Working with editor Alexandra Strauss, he juxtaposes clips from Baldwin's appearances on *The Dick Cavett Show* with voiceover and a wide range of other archival material, including images of racial inequity still fresh in the minds of viewers—from the videotaped beating of Rodney King to photos of Trayvon Martin, the Ferguson protests and more. The result is an artistic endeavor that feels less like a movie, and more like a cinematic essay.

Baldwin's personal connections to Evers, King, and Malcolm X give *I Am Not Your Negro* an intimacy that, remarkably, does not dim its sociological perspicacity one whit. This is a film which gives consideration and voice to a fuller range of the African-American experience than many Civil Rights Era movies accommodate. But it also has disarming personal anecdotes that ground it. Perhaps most jarring is Baldwin's recollection of splitting up with a white female acquaintance, leaving parties five minutes apart, taking separate routes to the metro and sitting apart on the train—all because she would be safer walking the streets at night without him.

I Am Not Your Negro is also notable for the stories it does not tell, and the details on which it does not dwell. It does not mention what is perhaps Baldwin's best-known book, 1953's semi-autobiographical *Go Tell It On the Mountain*. And while it does address his sexuality (Baldwin was gay), it does so in only incidental fashion—an FBI memorandum classifying him as a subversive figure. Instead, Peck's film presses onward, showing Baldwin making unified-theory arguments that attempt to put Americans of all colors in the same headspace with regards to conversations about race. This streamlining and lack of preciousness greatly benefit the movie, allowing it to connect on an emotional and spiritual level, rather than merely an intellectual one.

I Am Not Your Negro is a movie about the Civil Rights movement and racism both personal and institutional, yes, but it is also about much more than that. This is the surprise of its revelations. Peck's film is an admonition to mainstream culture, as well as an explanation and explication of how rhetoric uncomfortable to some Caucasian-Americans, from Malcolm X to Black Lives Matter, in fact simply corroborates the everyday reality of a large segment of minority communities. *I Am Not Your Negro* asks viewers to consider that not everything faced can be changed, but nothing can be changed until it is faced. Meanwhile, Baldwin's thesis—that people, in general, cannot bear very much reality—is born out in the mangled horizon of today's American political landscape.

Brent Simon

CREDITS

Narrator: Samuel L. Jackson
Himself (archive footage): James Baldwin
Himself (archive footage): Dick Cavett
Origin: United States
Language: English
Released: 2017
Production: Rémi Grellety, Hébert Peck, Raoul Peck; Velvet Film; released by Magnolia Pictures
Directed by: Raoul Peck
Written by: James Baldwin
Music by: Alexei Aigui
Editing: Alexandra Strauss
MPAA rating: PG-13
Running time: 95 minutes

REVIEWS

Baumgarten, Marjorie. *Austin Chronicle*. February 3, 2017.
Burr, Ty. *Boston Globe*. February 2, 2017.
Duralde, Alonso. *TheWrap*. February 3, 2017.
Gleiberman, Owen. *Variety*. October 3, 2016.
Hornaday, Ann. *Washington Post*. February 2, 2017.
Morgenstern, Joe. *Wall Street Journal*. February 2, 2017.
O'Hehir, Andrew. *Salon*. February 7, 2017.
Scott, A.O. *New York Times*. February 2, 2017.
Turan, Kenneth. *Los Angeles Times*. December 8, 2016.
Verniere, James. *Boston Herald*. February 3, 2017.

QUOTES

James Baldwin: "The story of the Negro in America is the story of America, and it is not a pretty story."

TRIVIA

The word "negro" is used seventy-eight times in the film.

AWARDS

British Acad. 2017: Feature Doc.

Nominations:

Oscars 2016: Feature Doc.

Directors Guild 2016: Documentary Director (Peck)

Ind. Spirit 2017: Feature Doc.

I, TONYA

Box Office: $19.5 Million

Craig Gillespie's *I, Tonya* serves multiple purposes, and accomplishes almost all of its goals successfully. On the one hand, it is designed to retell a story that most people only vaguely remember with new information often ignored by the talk show circuit and tabloid news industry that turned its title character into a punchline. It is also designed to show viewers the fluidity of true crime stories, playing with contradictory interviews that recalls the ways the Coen brothers mocked the very genre with their true-not-true masterpiece *Fargo* (1996) (and the film mimics their dark humor as well). Most of all, it is an actor's showcase, putting two excellent performers front and center in a way that practically guaranteed them Oscar® nominations (which they both received). As a complete package, it's flawed—it's a bit too long, relies on some obvious beats, and is a bit hypocritical when it tries to turn the blame on an audience it encouraged to laugh an hour earlier—but as all of the above—actor's showcase, commentary on the nature of true story filmmaking, and redemption for Tonya Harding—it works.

The structure of *I, Tonya* is key to its success, alternating fake interview footage of the major players with their life stories. So, characters like Tonya Harding and Jeff Gillooly speak directly the camera, narrating their own tragic histories, and sometimes even contradicting each other. The message of Steven Rogers's script isn't so much "here's what really happened" as "no one knows for sure, especially those of you who believed all the tabloids and rumors." Rogers has taken some flack for playing a bit loose with history according to some who covered the Tonya Harding story, but that misses the point of the film to a degree.

I, Tonya opens with a young Tonya Harding in 1970s Portland, Oregon, being taken for ice skating training by her mother LaVona Golden (Allison Janney), a profane, chain-smoking, abusive monster of a person. As played by Janney, LaVona is an instantly iconic movie mother—the actress spits curse words and vile insults at her daughter in a way that few performers could conceivably top. She hits every syllable of every swear word. Some have accused the performance of being a bit one-note, but it's the kind of scene-stealing note that wins performers awards, and she's the frontrunner for the Oscar® for Best Supporting Actress as of the writing of this review.

LaVona hires a reluctant trainer named Diane Rawlinson (Julianne Nicholson), and Tonya Harding (now played by Margot Robbie) matures into a promising skater, despite being held back by her low income and arguably lower social skills. *I, Tonya* portrays the skating world as one that always looked down on Harding, even as she began to display as much natural skill for the sport as anyone in it. Judges do not give her the scores she deserves, and Harding channels the outrage at the unjust treatment into her skating—performing even better when she's angry.

When she's very young, Harding meets Jeff Gillooly, played memorably by Sebastian Stan, probably best known as Bucky Barnes from the Marvel Cinematic Universe. Gillooly is portrayed as an abusive dope, the kind of low-IQ moron who lashes out at a woman when it appears she may be accomplishing more in life than he is. His best friend, Shawn Eckhardt (Paul Walter Hauser), is even dumber than he is, and the two end up involved in a violent incident that would make international news. First, Tonya has her routine disrupted by a death threat, and so Jeff has the idea to do something similar to Tonya's rival, Nancy Kerrigan. Shawn takes it too far, hiring a couple or moronic crooks to actually beat up Kerrigan, which led to her getting hit in the knee with a baton.

As presented in *I, Tonya,* Harding herself had no idea what was going to happen to Kerrigan—and some have disputed this assertion—but was embroiled in the case when Jeff said she knew more than she was admitting. This lead to an Obstruction of Justice charge and a judge banned Harding from skating for life. The final act of *I, Tonya* presents Harding's fall from fame, and points a finger at viewers for not caring enough about the truth and believing the tabloid spin, even suggesting that the public abused her as much as Gillooly. This is a bit of a stretch, but Robbie grounds the character emotionally in a way that sells the tragedy of Harding's skill going to waste.

To be fair, the movie doesn't work at all without what Robbie brings to it in nearly every scene. It is as a committed and daring a turn as any in 2017, and earned the performer her first Oscar® nomination. She gives her all to every scene, but one of the most memorable of the year in any film is just the look on her face as she wipes the make-up off in the mirror after everything has fallen apart. She tries to smile, but the emotion overtakes her. Robbie is completely believable in a movie that's full of exaggerated storytelling choices and frenetic editing. She is the human throughline through the chaos.

Sometimes, it feels like the movie is working against her. Gillespie uses music like a sledgehammer, pushing classic rock choices designed to underline what's happening in the film, whether it's "Witchy Woman" by The Eagles for LaVona or "Romeo and Juliet" by Dire Straits as Jeff and Tonya are beginning their relationship. They are defiant in their lack of subtlety, but they also add an energy to the film that it would have lacked otherwise. And, to be honest, figure skating routines are rarely known for their out-of-left-field music choices. The editing in *I, Tonya* also crosses the yellow line of perhaps calling too much attention to itself. It's undeniably accomplished but in a way that lacks any subtlety or nuance.

Perhaps the story of Tonya Harding indeed demands a lack of subtlety or nuance. To counter the story that was presented by shows like *Hard Copy* (and Bobby Cannavale gives a great supporting turn as a reporter for a show like that one), Gillespie and his team have to pull out all the stops to reclaim Harding's story. It's not the patient, subtle skating routines that win gold medals. And, in a sense, their film is not unlike Harding's notorious triple axel, a move that almost no one else has done in a figure skating competition, and made her instantly famous in the skating world when she landed it. Like that move, *I, Tonya* needed to push farther, be more daring, and break the rules. And, much to everyone's surprise, the film sticks the landing.

Brian Tallerico

CREDITS

Tonya Harding: Margot Robbie
Jeff Gillooly: Sebastian Stan
LaVona Golden: Allison Janney
Nancy Kerrigan: Caitlin Carver
Hard Copy producer: Bobby Cannavale
Origin: United States
Language: English
Released: 2017
Production: Tom Ackerley, Bryan Unkeless, Margot Robbie, Steven Rogers; Clubhouse Pictures, Lucky Chap Entertainment; released by 30West
Directed by: Craig Gillespie
Written by: Steven Rogers
Cinematography by: Nicolas Karakatsanis
Music by: Peter Nashel
Sound: Dave Paterson
Music Supervisor: Susan Jacobs; Jen Moss
Editing: Tatiana S. Riegel
Art Direction: Andi Crumbley
Costumes: Jennifer Johnson
Production Design: Jade Healy
MPAA rating: R
Running time: 119 minutes

REVIEWS

LaSalle, Mick. *San Francisco Chronicle*. December 19. 2017.
Lemire, Christy. *RogerEbert.com*. December 7, 2017.
Phillips, Michael. *Chicago Tribune*. December 21, 2017.
Roeper, Richard. *Chicago Sun-Times*. December 21, 2017.
Rothkopf, Joshua. *Time Out*. December 7, 2017.
Shoemaker, Allison. *Consequence of Sound*. December 8, 2017.
Stewart, Sara. *New York Post*. December 6, 2017.
Wilkinson, Alissa. *Vox*. December 9, 2017.
Wolfe, April. *Village Voice*. December 7, 2017.

QUOTES

Tonya Harding: "I mean, come on! What kind of friggin' person bashes in their friend's knee? Who would do that to a friend?"

TRIVIA

Actress Margot Robbie trained with choreographer Sarah Kawahara to prepare for her role.

AWARDS

Oscars 2017: Actress--Supporting (Janney)
British Acad. 2017: Actress--Supporting (Janney)
Golden Globes 2018: Actress--Supporting (Janney)
Ind. Spirit 2018: Actress--Supporting (Janney), Film Editing
Screen Actors Guild 2017: Actress--Supporting (Janney)

Nominations:

Oscars 2017: Actress (Robbie), Film Editing
British Acad. 2017: Actress (Robbie), Costume Des., Makeup, Orig. Screenplay
Golden Globes 2018: Actress--Mus./Comedy (Robbie), Film--Mus./Comedy
Ind. Spirit 2018: Actress (Robbie)
Screen Actors Guild 2017: Actress (Robbie)
Writers Guild 2017: Orig. Screenplay

IN THE FADE
(Aus dem Nichts)

Box Office: $142,269

Fatih Akin's award-winning *In the Fade* feels like a film that started with an author conceiving its "shocking" ending and then working backwards from there.

(To be fair, the author here may not be the filmmaker but the source material writer, Hark Bohm). Its closing scene, whether it's authorial or a product of the screenwriter, is angry and incendiary, illustrating the cycle of violence that the world currently seems to be speeding up with every generation. And its strength comes largely from the grounded, fiery performance from Diane Kruger, who won an acting award for her work here at Cannes. Sadly, the narrative build-up, despite Kruger's great work, is flatly directed and boring. The Akin who riveted viewers with films like *Head-On* (2004) and *The Edge of Heaven* (2007)—his two masterpieces—appears to have lost his passion for the form, as there's no other way to explain why the courtroom drama that makes up the bulk of this film looks so much like a *Law & Order* episode, and plays out with a similar lack of subtlety. It's a film about anger and injustice that should have had a visual language that matched its protagonist's fury, but it just can't produce.

German Katja (Kruger) is married to a Kurdish man named Nuri (Numan Acar), and the two have a son named Rocco (Rafael Santana). Nuri used to be a drug dealer, but he's gone straight since the birth of their son. They live in Hamburg, and Katja drops the child off at his office one afternoon, returning later that same day to see the road blocked off by police cars. She's told that a mail bomb went off in the street outside the office and both her husband and son are dead. After processing unimaginable grief, Katja remembers that she saw a woman outside the office, and the two even interacted when Katja realized the woman had not chained her bicycle. She wonders if that woman had something to do with the bombing and informs the police about the encounter.

At first, the authorities presume that the bombing was retaliation related to Nuri's former life in the drug trade, and it looks like they may write it off as such, basically ending the investigation. Katja knows this is unlikely, suggesting that perhaps her husband's ethnicity had something to do with his murder, and Akin's anger over so many recent racially-motivated murders in Europe is palpable. Over the last few years, as events like Brexit has shown, Europe remains deeply divided along racial lines. And, at least on some level, *In the Fade* feels like a response to those growing chasms.

Because, of course, Katja is right. A young neo-Nazi couple named André (Ulrich Brandhoff) and Edda (Hanna Hilsdorf) are arrested and put on trial. The proceedings do not go well as Katja's own drug use calls her testimony into question and enough doubt is raised as to whether or not the couple are responsible that they could get off. There's very little tension to these scenes, and the result is essentially a plodding courtroom drama without even the suspense of guilt or innocence. Akin portrays the couple's defense attorney, played by Johannes Krisch, with such malevolence that it approaches parody, and the result is like seeing a train wreck in very slow motion. It's clear that justice will not be served by the legal system, so viewers are merely forced to watch the broken process unfold. Again, Kruger's growing anger keeps it together, but just barely, and not in a way that makes for an overall satisfactory experience.

By the final act of *In the Fade,* viewers are more likely to feel manipulated rather than moved. We have gone through Hell with Katja, watched her on the verge of no longer wanting to live and losing everything that really matters to her. How could it possibly end in a satisfying manner? And so Akin literally blows it up, choosing the cycle of violence over forgiveness or redemption. It's designed to shock, especially for the viewers who may have fallen asleep during the courtroom stuff. It's a film that lacks the courage of its convictions, ending in a way designed to get viewers talking but that feels like a cheap twist given what's come before. One is tempted to say that Akin wrote himself into a corner and was unlikely to find a way out that did not feel manipulative, but that would imply that the ending isn't the only reason he made the film in the first place.

Brian Tallerico

CREDITS

Katja Sekerci: Diane Kruger
Danilo/lawyer/Nuri's friend: Denis Moschitto
Nuri/husband: Numan Acar
Birgit: Samia Muriel Chancrin
Haberbeck/defender lawyer: Johannes Krisch
Origin: United States
Language: German, Greek, English
Released: 2017
Production: Ann-Kristin Hofmann, Nurhan Sekerci-Porst, Herman Weigel, Fatih Akin; Bombero International, Corazon International, Macassar Productions, Pathé, Warner Bros. Pictures; released by Magnolia Pictures
Directed by: Fatih Akin
Written by: Fatih Akin; Hark Bohm
Cinematography by: Rainer Klausmann
Music by: Joshua Homme
Sound: Kai Storck
Music Supervisor: Pia Hoffmann
Editing: Andrew Bird
Art Direction: Seth Turner
Costumes: Katrin Aschendorf
Production Design: Tamo Kunz
MPAA rating: R
Running time: 106 minutes

REVIEWS

Bowen, Chuck. *Slant Magazine.* December 18, 2017.
Bradshaw, Peter. *The Guardian.* May 26, 2017.
D'Angelo, Mike. *The A.V. Club.* December 19, 2017.
Edelstein, David. *New York Magazine.* December 27, 2017.
Grozdanovic, Nikola. *The Playlist.* May 26, 2017.
Ide, Wendy. *Screen International.* May 26, 2017.
Meyer, Carla. *San Francisco Chronicle.* January 10, 2018.
Morgenstern, Joe. *Wall Street Journal.* December 29, 2017.
Phipps, Keith. *Uproxx.* January 3, 2018.
Scott, A.O. *New York Times.* December 26, 2017.

QUOTES

Katja Sekerci [attacking Edda in court]: "Look at me, you ****! I'll kill you!"

TRIVIA

This film was the official submission of Germany for the "Best Foreign Language Film" category of the 90th Academy Awards in 2018.

AWARDS

Golden Globes 2018: Foreign Film

AN INCONVENIENT SEQUEL: TRUTH TO POWER

Fight like your world depends on it.
—Movie tagline

Box Office: $3.5 Million

Davis Guggenheim's documentary *An Inconvenient Truth* (2006) helped push the topic of global warming further into the mainstream. The film followed Al Gore as he gave his slideshow presentations about the effects of global warming on the planet and what people, businesses, and corporations can do to combat it. The film served as a wake-up call to those who had turned a blind eye to environmental activists of all kinds since the early days of Greenpeace. The message could be ignored no longer, yet since the film's release, the subject has only gained more traction politically among the deniers and the corporations who have something to lose in the fight to transition to renewable energy. Meanwhile, the planet has only been getting warmer since 2006. While one single film might not be able to change the world, Gore has yet to settle down and let someone else take over the struggle for understanding between political parties.

Perhaps it was inevitable that there would be *An Inconvenient Sequel: Truth to Power*, a follow-up documentary that, again, follows Gore as he tries to make his voice heard among deaf ears. Gore has more fire in him now. His anger toward those who needlessly oppose him can be seen and felt as he gets more ramped-up during his presentations. Progress has not moved fast enough and the Trump administration will undoubtedly only make Gore's uphill battles that much harder to climb. Of course, the fact that there is a battle to begin with is what exists at the heart of *An Inconvenient Sequel: Truth to Power* as it covers the biggest floods of the last decade and the Climate Conference that took place in Paris in 2015 among the world leaders who, for the most part, believe that the threat of climate change is real and that drastic changes need to be made to ensure the continued survival of the planet.

The film starts out with footage of Gore at a Senate hearing in 2007 trying to answer a question, but getting shot down trying to expand on a single-word answer. Finally, when he is afforded the opportunity to speak, he states that he would love to talk about this without cameras and flashing lights so that he could take the theater away from the whole discussion. Unfortunately, the reality is that Gore needs the cameras and the media to pay attention so that the activism can reach and inspire a bigger audience. At one point, the film backtracks to Gore's first training session at his farm in Tennessee in 2006 where fifty people showed up and learned how to communicate properly about global warming to people who want to learn. He says that these were humble beginnings, but he has grown encouraged by the number of activists that has grown since then.

There are more pressing matters that come up, though. The governor of Florida will not talk to scientists, even when the city of Miami grapples with its worst flood in decades and which remains at the highest risk of flooding due to rising sea levels. The most criticized moment from the first film had to do with Gore's prediction that the World Trade Center memorial would get flooded because of the rising sea level in that area. In 2012, his prediction came true. The Attorney General in New York is investigating consumer fraud by companies who profit from climate change denial. In Syria, along with the deadly civil war that persists (and grows deadlier) today, farmers experienced their worst drought from 2006-10. Gore's biggest challenge occurs later in the film when India holds out against joining the rest of the world in the fight against climate change because of what it will do to their fragile economy. Gore goes out of his way to broker a deal so that the economics align with India's struggles.

An Inconvenient Sequel: Truth To Power was directed by Bonni Cohen and Jon Shenk. Their film differs from the first mainly in the way that it feels more like a film than Guggenheim's, if only because it cuts back quite a bit on the amount of footage devoted to Gore and his slideshows. This film sees Gore as more of a traveller and frustrated activist than someone who stands in front of an audience and delivers talking points. *An Inconvenient Truth* did win the Academy Award for Best Documentary (although it is often mistakenly reported that Gore took home the award, when all he did was give the acceptance speech), but not because of the craft of filmmaking. It won because Gore's message resonated and many felt that the message superseded the quality of Guggenheim's limited visual palette (Guggenheim, for the most part, filmed the presentation while cutting away to Gore's life story and Presidential election loss).

Cohen and Shenk's film has more moments of verité in it, but the film still feels slight and plagued by too many missed opportunities. While Cohen and Shenk clearly believe Gore's message and data should be at the forefront, Gore is rarely seen talking to anyone on the other side of the political aisle and engaging in a debate. The film's highlight is when he stops in Georgetown, Texas, the reddest town in one of the Union's reddest States, and visits with the very conservative governor, whose town is on track to be the first in Texas to be 100

renewable energy, demonstrating that climate change has no business being a political talking point. Toward the end of the film, Gore is seen getting on an elevator at Trump Tower to address newly-elected President Trump about climate change, but nothing else is mentioned about it. Most people who see the film will already be on Gore's side. The film would have even more of an impact if there had been more of a debate element to it, with Gore trying to convince the non-converted more overtly.

Collin Souter

CREDITS

Himself: Al Gore
Himself: George W. Bush
Himself: John Kerry
Herself: Angela Merkel
Himself: Vladimir Putin
Origin: United States
Language: English, French
Released: 2017
Production: Richard Berge, Jeff Skoll, Diane Weyermann; Actual Films, Participant Media L.L.C.; released by Paramount Pictures Corp.
Directed by: Bonni Cohen; Jon Shenk
Cinematography by: Jon Shenk
Music by: Jeff Beal
Editing: Don Bernier; Colin Nusbaum
MPAA rating: PG
Running time: 98 minutes

REVIEWS

Allen, Nick. *RogerEbert.com*. January 26, 2017.
Dowd, A.A. *The A.V. Club*. January 22, 2017.
Ebiri, Bilge. *Village Voice*. January 25, 2017.
Guzman, Rafer. *Newsday*. July 28, 2017.
Kenigsberg, Kenneth. *New York Times*. July 27, 2017.
Mayer, Dominick. *Consequence of Sound*. January 26, 2017.
Meyer, Robinson. *The Atlantic*. July 28, 2017.
Morgenstern. Joe. *Wall Street Journal*. July 27, 2017.
Pahle, Rebecca. *Film Journal International*. July 27, 2017.
Weitzman, Elizabeth. *TheWrap*. July 26, 2017.

QUOTES

Al Gore: "In order to address the environmental crisis, we're going to have to spend some time fixing the democracy crisis."

TRIVIA

The film received two standing ovations at the 2017 Sundance Film Festival.

AWARDS

Nominations:

British Acad. 2017: Feature Doc.

INGRID GOES WEST

She'll follow you.
—Movie tagline

Box Office: $3 Million

In an early scene from *Ingrid Goes West*, the central character played by Aubrey Plaza watches the great Howard Hawks's newspaper comedy, *His Girl Friday* (1939). This moment is particularly apt given the blithely unpredictable and elastic Plaza conjures the great screen actresses of the classic studio era like Rosalind Russell or Carole Lombard.

Plaza infuses her work with wit, grace, and sexually subversive underpinning. With her high cheekbones, dark eyes, and beguiling look, she projects a magnetic, lithe quality. She is a great deal more than just a beautiful face. Plaza is quick, fast, and always alert. Her film work is an abject study in the difficulties of finding material that fully utilizes and deepens her expressive capabilities. Since her striking early appearance in Judd Apatow's *Funny People* (2009), Plaza has stood apart with her brazen, droll delivery and stylized, kinky body movements. The straight or convention never suits her. She is at her best as an agent of chaos, a rambunctious id who unnerves everything around her.

The movie is the first narrative feature from Matt Spicer, who also wrote the script with David Branson Smith. The movie is confused and inchoate about what it wants to say, about the specific moment, but it is clearly a work of its time, expressing its particular idiom, of avatars, digital media, and how the very nature of human and social discourse has been fundamentally altered. Ingrid is conceived of monstrous self-regard, someone who violates most social or emotional boundaries. Even in her studied calculation, Plaza makes the character deeply recognizable, her pathos shaping moments of empathy and shrewd observation as part of a plaintive desire to connect.

Ingrid Thorburn, newly bereft following the death of her mother, catches that Hawks film not at a revival theater but on television at a group home, where she is carrying out her court-mandated therapy session after she crashed a wedding and pepper sprayed the bride who declined to invite her. After she inherits $60,000 from her mother's estate, Ingrid decamps her quietly desperate Pennsylvania hometown for the radiant light and ecstatic possibilities of southern California.

She quickly and deftly insinuates herself into the inner circle of a beautiful young photographer and Instagram influencer named Taylor Sloane (Elizabeth Olsen). She lives in Venice with her attractive young husband, Ezra (Wyatt Russell), an aspiring painter. Since the story's early sections play off themes of seduction and infatuation, Spicer and the cinematographer Bryce Fortner append the silky Instagram post or curated feed to the bright and glittering pop design. Armed with cash and the acute desire to fetishize her social and personal transactions, Ingrid operates in a privileged aura.

The darker implications of the material are clear. The two actresses bring an intoxicating zest to the movie's opening movement. Everything is an act of appropriation, of style, meaning and values. "We tell ourselves stories in order to live," is the opening line of the title essay of Joan Didion's *The White Album* (1979), Taylor's favorite book that Ingrid quickly adopts as her own. Spicer is investing a modern reading—the permeability of social networks—to a contemporary equivalent. His story traffics in the visual representations most significantly explored by Alfred Hitchcock, especially the idea of transference. In *Ingrid Goes West*, the idea reaches its apotheosis at the scene at the Joshua Tree, where Ingrid and Taylor pose for a photograph at the side of a road, their identities do not just blur together they become mirror images.

Ingrid's construction, or fable of invention, is not meant to last or survive a deeper inspection. The arrival of Nicky (Billy Magnussen), Taylor's amoral brother, marks the first serious threat to her artificial construct. A hedonist and thrill seeker, Nicky quickly proves himself a wholly different class of psychopath. He immediately seizes on and grows suspicious of Ingrid. The satirical thrusts and harsh judgment of the characters is pretty severe, at times. It is barbed, but never toxic or cheap caricature.

The storytelling is more discursive, even oblique. The most successful parts are concerned less about the central story than the supplemental material on the edges, particularly the detailed and lively work by the terrific actor O'Shea Jackson, Jr., who plays Ingrid's love interest. He is originally introduced as her landlord when she turns up seeking an apartment. Increasingly, she becomes dependent on him, like the use of his truck, or to play out the role of her boyfriend. The son of the rapper and actor Ice Cube, who played his own father as a young man in *Straight Outta Compton* (2015), Jackson displays a quiet ease and authority. As Dan he is a soft-spoken geek with a Batman fixation.

When Ingrid drafts him in order to carry out her own subterfuge, he becomes a willing accomplice, for complex and different reasons. Their attraction and developing friendship is authentic and lively. Spicer makes a serious mistake in the movie's final third as Ingrid's sanity and self-control begin to implode. Nicky is the instigator after he tries to blackmail her. Part of what is confusing and uncertain is that Ingrid remains fixated on the young couple even as she becomes a witness to their less than appealing characteristics. Sloane is increasingly seen as a kind of cipher and Wyatt an embittered drunk.

As narrative, *Ingrid Goes West* is unsettled. The movie has its unaccountable qualities, the realization is that this kind of gloss on a digital update of *Single White Female* (1992) should be crudely unwatchable. Even with its jagged and unsatisfying parts, Plaza makes *Ingrid Goes West* a deeply creditable experience. The emotional disintegration of her character is hard to watch. The skill and fearlessness the actress exhibits makes it impossible to turn away. The larger inquiry into her mental health seems of secondary concern. Ingrid is the protagonist of her own story and no longer the passive outsider shunned to the margins.

The filmmakers lose some nerve at the end. The movie acknowledges but does not quite address the deeper consequences. The script is too antic in the final third. That is typical of a lot of first films. Spicer shows promise and excitement as a director who links images well together, and also conveys a natural and intuitive ability with actors, giving them the freedom, range, and unpredictability to behave in unaccustomed manner. Elizabeth Olsen has the less showy part, but there is a charge in the brittleness and fatuousness of the character. Wyatt Russell has the same talent, for the underplayed moments.

Spicer wisely never loses sight of the movie's reason to exist. Aubrey Plaza is a whirl, a force of nature that is plugged in and never afraid to dance on the edge. She is always charged, and ready for the next adventure.

Patrick Z. McGavin

CREDITS

Ingrid Thorburn: Aubrey Plaza
Taylor Sloane: Elizabeth Olsen
Dan Pinto: O'Shea Jackson, Jr.
Ezra O'Keefe: Wyatt Russell
Nicky Sloane: Billy Magnussen
Origin: United States
Language: English
Released: 2017
Production: Adam Mirels, Robert Mirels, Jared Goldman, Tim White, Trevor White, Aubrey Plaza; 141 Entertainment, Mighty Engine, Star Thrower Entertainment; released by Neon
Directed by: Matt Spicer
Written by: Matt Spicer; David Branson Smith
Cinematography by: Bryce Fortner
Music by: Jonathan Sadoff; Nick Thorburn
Sound: Lon Bender
Music Supervisor: Marguerite Phillips
Editing: Jack Price
Art Direction: Chris Scharffenberg
Costumes: Natalie O'Brien
Production Design: Susie Mancini
MPAA rating: R
Running time: 98 minutes

REVIEWS

Anderson, John. *Wall Street Journal.* August 10, 2017.
Ebiri, Bilge. *Village Voice.* August 9, 2017.
Feeney, Mark. *Boston Globe.* August 24, 2017.
Goodykoontz, Bill. *Arizona Republic.* August 24, 2017.
Kenigsberg, Ben. *New York Times.* August 9, 2017.
Kupecki, Josh. *Austin Chronicle.* August 16, 2017.
LaSalle, Mick. *San Francisco Chronicle.* August 17, 2017.
Macdonald, Moira. *Seattle Times.* August 23, 2017.
Rife, Katie. *The A.V. Club.* August 9, 2017.
Yamato, Jen. *Los Angeles Times.* August 10, 2017.

QUOTES

Ingrid Thorburn: "Talk about something cool, like food or clothes or Joan Didion."

TRIVIA

Like his character in the film, actor Wyatt Russell does not participate in social media in real-life, which is ironic, given the theme of the film.

AWARDS

Nominations:

Ind. Spirit 2018: First Screenplay

IT

You'll float too.
—Movie tagline
It takes many forms.
—Movie tagline

Box Office: $327.5 Million

When Stephen King's novel *It* was first adapted as a miniseries in 1990, the time-alternating story hopped back and forth between the same characters as children in 1960 and as adults thirty years later, which to viewers at the time, would have been the present. The new film adaptation of the story, directed by Andy Muschietti, moves the timeline up significantly, to the time between 1988-89. The change in timeline alters the thematic heft of the story and its embrace of its decade imbues it with the kind of homey mise-en-scène needed to craft comfort around the scares. *It* is one of the few excellent adaptations of King, whose combination of supernatural terror and childhood innocence has proven difficult for cinema to capture.

Capturing the picturesque small town of Derry, which houses a horrible secret, is an operation delicately handled through ensemble. The gaggle of children, reminiscent of the close relationship and accurate pubescent dialogue of *Stand By Me* (1986), endure their share of childhood torments that serve as introductory scenes. The first, a bit of a prologue, introduces the horror and kinship that will fuel the film.

Stuttering Bill Denbrough (played by Jaeden Lieberher with an innocent, righteous sense of good) folds and waxes a paper boat for his little brother Georgie

(Jackson Robert Scott, aptly adorable) to play with in their neighborhood's rainy gutters. The scene captures a brotherly intimacy, finding closeness not just between the boys, but in the very act of creation. Hands and wax are in warmly-lit close-up, contrasted to the cold blues of the basement which stored the latter. The delicate, unknown fears of childhood and the safety that comes just as easily are just next door in the same home. When Georgie is taken by Pennywise (Bill Skarsgård) the clown, a beast lurking in the city's sewer, the reality of this closeness is all too disturbing.

A year later, Bill and his friends exit school for the summer to a world of bullies, sunshine, bicycles, and more missing children. Derry's population drops precipitously, yet nobody seems to mind beyond the countless "Missing" posters. Irresponsible adults are just as prevalent in the film as precocious children. These kids, which are shown more and more (thanks to some savvy editing) as unwitting innocents in a town built to house and execute them, come introduced in long takes walking through hallways. Then, they get their individual moments of depth that serve to further another point of the story: fear strikes when alone.

In the so-called "Loser's Club" are Richie (Finn Wolfhard, brazen and insufferable), a profane motor-mouth; Mike (Chosen Jacobs), a stoic orphan; Eddie (the wonderfully overwrought Jack Dylan Grazer), a hypochondriac; Stan (Wyatt Oleff), a Jewish pragmatist; and Ben (Jeremy Ray Taylor), the overweight new kid. The boys are all defined well, never blending personalities or roles. The only one not done justice is Stan, whose character brings one of the scariest augmentations of Pennywise (who we find transforms into that which strikes fear into the hearts of its victims) but not much else. Joining them is the put-upon Beverly (the film's breakout star, Sophia Lillis) whose burgeoning puberty attracts abuse at school and at home. The kids are bonded through individual trauma caused by "It," shot in gloriously inventive and terrifying ways by *Oldboy* cinematographer Chung-hoon Chung, a supernatural take on the natural community-building of the bullied.

This community, created just as well by the conversational nature of the script as the intimacy with which the film is directed, makes the horror all the more effective. The rapport between the young cast and the assault upon them by an increasingly Lovecraftian series of beasts and visions emphasizes how the creative visual effects push the boundaries and limits of normalcy until they burst, spewing sewage. The headstrong Lillis, whose every wink, gaze, and gesture imply a secret shared between her and the audience, becomes the focal point of the film not just for her ability, but her character's femininity. Surrounded by boys, she becomes the group's shared crush and their binding force when she is captured by Pennywise. Alternatively, Skarsgård is the creeping necrosis of fear and death, creeping up on the children like the inevitable passage of time. His movements and line deliveries are inhuman, both voice and body modulated in uncanny, disconcerting ways that have his physicality to thank as much as the virtuosic makeup work. The battle between these two forces—togetherness and fearsome nihilism—adds depth to a film whose story has quite literally been told before.

Yet some of the film's best material is specific to itself. While the fear of strangers, oddities, and unknown sources of bodily fluid hangs over this new 1980s version of *It*, making the historical mistreatment and fear of HIV a visceral flashback, there are also many quips and filmmaking choices that saturate the production in the decade. *It*'s nostalgia is not ironic nor rose-tinted, which its R-rating insures, but a redefinition of the era. When the children face Pennywise, it attempts to pull them apart and set them against each other, angling them towards the individualism that defined the decade's decadence and excess. The kids, rejecting this, demonstrate more than just childhood friendship. It's a revolt. The film has more 1980s heavy metal angst than 1950s facade, and it is all the stronger for placing its audience in the midst of the period's fears, strengths, and culture.

Jacob Oller

CREDITS

Pennywise: Bill Skarsgård
Bill Denbrough: Jaeden Lieberher
Ben Hanscom: Jeremy Ray Taylor
Beverly Marsh: Sophia Lillis
Richie Tozier: Finn Wolfhard
Origin: United States
Language: English
Released: 2017
Production: Seth Grahame-Smith, David Katzenberg, Roy Lee, Dan Lin, Barbara Muschietti; KatzSmith Productions, Lin Pictures, RatPac-Dune Entertainment, Vertigo Entertainment; released by New Line Cinema L.L.C.
Directed by: Andy Muschietti
Written by: Chase Palmer; Cary Fukunaga; Gary Dauberman
Cinematography by: Chung-hoon Chung
Music by: Benjamin Wallfisch
Sound: Victor Ray Ennis
Music Supervisor: Dana Sano
Editing: Jason Ballantine
Art Direction: Peter Grundy
Costumes: Janie Bryant
Production Design: Claude Pare
MPAA rating: R
Running time: 135 minutes

REVIEWS

Bahr, Lindsey. *Associated Press.* September 6, 2017.
Barker, Andrew. *Variety.* September 5, 2017.
Callahan, Dan. *TheWrap.* September 6, 2017.
Hertz, Barry. *Globe and Mail.* September 6, 2017.
Kohn, Eric. *IndieWire.* September 5, 2017.
Phillips, Michael. *Chicago Tribune.* September 6, 2017.
Rife, Katie. *The A.V. Club.* September 6, 2017.
Scott, A.O. *New York Times.* September 6, 2017.
Truitt, Brian. *USA Today.* September 6, 2017.
Whitty, Stephen. *Newark Star-Ledger.* September 6, 2017.

QUOTES

Ben Hanscom: "Derry is not like any town I've been in before. They did a study once and, it turns out, people die or disappear at six times the national average. And that's just grown ups. Kids are worse. Way, way worse."

TRIVIA

Actor Bill Skarsgard has admitted that he was so into his performance as Pennywise that he would had nightmares during and after production.

IT COMES AT NIGHT

Box Office: $14 Million

The superlative apocalyptic horror film, *It Comes at Night,* moves between the nightmarish dreams of its characters and the real-life day-to-day nightmares that inspire them so deftly that it also manages to do the one thing so many horror films fail at: creating believable characters who seem driven by real-life choices and traits. As accustomed as our culture has become to narratives involving survivalism and the decay of society, *It Comes at Night* takes those themes to a new level, concentrating on two families pushed to the absolute edge, while utilizing arch film craft to accomplish that narrative goal.

A plague has killed off much of mankind. Paul (Joel Edgerton) and Sarah (Carmen Ejogo), together with their teenage son Travis (Kelvin Harrison Jr.), have managed to avoid succumbing to sickness by isolating themselves in the forest. But when Bud (David Pendleton), Sarah's father, becomes sick, it is apparent that seclusion can only buy so much safety. Forced to kill Bud and burn his body in order to avoid infection, Paul adopts ever more stringent rules for their day-to-day life. The very next night, the family captures a man breaking into the house. After making sure the stranger is healthy, Paul interrogates him. The stranger says his name is Will (Christopher Abbott). Thinking the house was unoccupied, he broke into it to search for fresh water for his own family. Sarah convinces Paul to go with Will, pick up his family, and bring them back to the house to share resources.

Upon return, Paul relates his rules to Will and his wife Kim (Riley Keough), and a sense of fragile community is born between the two families. But noises in the woods and inconsistencies in Will's stories hammer at Paul's trust. Travis, meanwhile, has been deeply shaken by the death of his grandfather. When not haunted by horrific waking nightmares, he begins to find himself questioning his parents and being bothered by an unwelcome attraction to Kim. After waking late in the night, Travis discovers Will's young son Andrew asleep on the floor downstairs and the door to the outside opened. He tells his parents, and Paul becomes convinced that the possibility of contagion means the families should quarantine themselves in their own rooms to make sure no one is sick. The mystery of the open door is thusly left open.

Soon, Travis hears Kim begging Will to take them away. Faced with the possibility that Will and Kim could give away his own family's location to marauders, Paul confronts the couple only to be taken hostage. Rescued by Sarah, Paul forces Will, Kim, and Andrew out into the woods where he and Sarah shoot them as they try to flee. Travis, shell-shocked, has returned to the house where he begins vomiting blood into the sink, a sure sign that the sickness has begun. Later, after Travis has died, Paul and Sarah, infected, sit silently across from each other.

Writer/director Trey Edward Shults shows that his strong debut, *Krisha* (2015) was absolutely a portent of great things to come. His writing and direction here breathe fresh intensity into time-worn concepts. Most powerful is the revelation of evil in the real world and the way it invades even the most sacred human institutions. The film never really flirts with the idea of the supernatural. Comparison to other films here is a worthwhile enterprise if only to point out the things at which *It Comes at Night* excels. As in *28 Days Later...* (2002), human savagery is treated as an effective monster contributing as much to the isolation of the main characters as the plague that has them holed up in the house. Like recent efforts *10 Cloverfield Lane* (2016) or *They Look Like People* (2015), this is a film that effectively builds the tension created by its claustrophobic atmosphere to an absolute fever pitch. Finally, it resembles *Night of the Living Dead* (1968) in the way that it deals with race. Paul and Sarah are an interracial couple, yet the relevance of that is treated almost as an afterthought as if to say, as *Night of the Living Dead* does, that such distinctions must lose their urgency in the face of catastrophe if survival is the desired outcome. Especially if that survival is of one's sense of humanity.

The casting is all about ensemble and the energy between the players is palpable. Joel Edgerton makes many smart acting choices as family patriarch Paul, a character struggling to hang onto his humanity despite the need for deadly force. Riley Keough is all steely-eyed tension, wound tight, and heart broken. Kelvin Harrison Jr. as Travis has the hardest job. The script forces him through a wide variety of emotional and psychological states almost always in the service of barely discernible motivations. He is pulled, in many directions but clearly devoted to his family and the values that have kept them alive and held them close. It is his relationship with Paul which more sharply outlines the concerns the film has about race.

Prior to Roger Corman's *Panic in the Year Zero* (1962), apocalyptic cinema almost entirely focused on spectacle and large scale destruction. But Corman's low budget needs to focus on one families' desperate struggle for survival as they seek shelter during an atomic war certainly re-focused the genre on character arcs. *It Comes at Night* is not only a stark return to the non-supernatural type of apocalypse narrative that Corman envisioned. It is a timeless story of a time that must never come.

Dave Canfield

CREDITS

Paul: Joel Edgerton
Will: Christopher Abbott
Sarah: Carmen Ejogo
Kim: Riley Keough
Travis: Kelvin Harrison, Jr.

Origin: United States
Language: English
Released: 2017
Production: David Kaplan, Andrea Roa; Animal Kingdom; released by A24 Films LLC
Directed by: Trey Edward Shults
Written by: Trey Edward Shults
Cinematography by: Drew Daniels
Music by: Brian McOmber
Sound: Damian Volpe
Editing: Trey Edward Shults; Matthew Hannam
Art Direction: Naomi Munro
Costumes: Meghan Kasperlik
Production Design: Karen Murphy
MPAA rating: R
Running time: 91 minutes

REVIEWS

Bahr, Lindsey. *Associated Press*. June 6, 2017.
Burr, Ty. *Boston Globe*. June 8, 2017.
Chang, Justin. *Los Angeles Times*. June 8, 2017.
Covert, Colin. *Minneapolis Star Tribune*. June 8, 2017.
Edelstein, David. *New York Magazine/Vulture*. June 9, 2017.
Linden, Shari. *Hollywood Reporter*. May 31, 2017.
Rothkopf, Joshua. *Time Out*. June 7, 2017.
Scott, A.O. *New York Times*. June 8, 2017.
Sims, David. *The Atlantic*. June 9, 2017.
Walsh, Katie. *Tribune News Service*. June 7, 2017.

QUOTES

Paul: "You can't trust anyone but family."

TRIVIA

The painting featured at the beginning of the film is titled "The Triumph of Death."

J

JANE

Box Office: $1.6 Million

To make a documentary about the life and work of primatologist Jane Goodall, at least on the surface, sounds like a slam dunk proposition. After all, her groundbreaking research radically changed our basic knowledge of primate behavior and made her one of the most respected and beloved scientific minds of her time and her personal story of overcoming the sexist attitudes that greeted her in the early part of her career from those unwilling to accept her at first based solely on her gender is just as fascinating. The trouble with that, however, is that such a film runs the risk on becoming little more than an exercise in hagiography with little of real substance to offer. In putting together *Jane*, filmmaker Brett Morgen, whose previous subjects have included Robert Evans (*The Kid Stays in the Picture* [2002]), the trial of the Chicago 10 (*Chicago 10* [2007]), the Rolling Stones (*Crossfire Hurricane* [2012]), and Kurt Cobain (*Cobain: Montage of Heck* [2015]), manages to avoid that problem with an ace up his sleeve that transforms his film into something that is just as fascinating and compelling as the woman at its center.

In present-day remarks, Goodall talks about how she dreamed since childhood of one day going to Africa in order to observe its wildlife, a crazy dream under most circumstances but one practically unheard of for a young middle-class British woman to even think of contemplating. As luck would have it, she would become the secretary to noted Kenyan paleoanthropologist/archaeologist Louis Leakey, who would have the idea of placing her in the Gombe Stream National Park in Tanzania to observe the behavior of chimpanzees from as close of a vantage point as possible. At the time, Goodall was only 26 with no real formal training or education regarding the subject to speak of but in Leakey's eyes, this constituted an advantage in that her findings would theoretically not be influenced in any way by the dominant scientific theories of the time.

For several months, Goodall quietly observed the chimps from the sidelines and then found herself slowly being allowed by them to come in for a closer look as to how they lived and interacted. In doing so, her observations confirmed Leakey's then-radical theories regarding chimpanzee behavior by revealing that they were far closer to humans than had previously been suggested in terms of social and emotional behaviors. By the time that wildlife filmmaker Hugo van Lawick arrived to get a visual record of her work, useful for both scientific and fundraising purposes, her own interactions with them were of an unprecedented scale to the point where they began to accept her as one of them. While all this was going on, Goodall and van Lawick gradually found themselves falling in love, marrying in 1964 and having a child—actions that had the side benefits of allowing her to recognize additional parallels between the parent/child interactions in the chimp world and her own experiences as a mother. Although she would eventually leave Gombe, her work became known around the world and she would become an internationally celebrated activist who used her fame to campaign for the cause of wildlife conservation and preservation.

If *Jane* had merely consisted of Goodall sitting in front of a camera regaling stories about her life and career, it probably would have been a highly watchable movie in its own right—Goodall is an undeniably compelling presence and it is a joy to listen to her talk about her accomplishments in a manner that manages to be both erudite and accessible. However, Morgen was lucky enough to have access to over 100 hours of the 16MM color film footage that van Lawick shot of Goodall in Gombe that was long thought to be lost. As a result, viewers get to actually see the interactions that she observed and participated in so that they are able to witness the theories of the correlation between chimp and human emotional behavior play out before their eyes, ranging from mating habits to a brutal shift in the power dynamics of the community that leaves even Goodall shaken as a result. The raw footage is of itself absolutely fascinating and Morgen and co-editors Joe Beshenkovsky and Will Znidaric have molded it into a compelling narrative that is further bolstered by the modern-day interview footage (shot by Ellen Kuras) and an occasionally busy, but mostly effective, score by Phillip Glass. The old footage is also interesting on another level because as we watch Goodall deepening her relationship with the chimps, we are also more or less watching her relationship with van Lawick deepen as well—even if one did not know the details of their off-screen relationship, his adoration towards her can be detected in virtually every frame he shoots of her. (Alas, it would not last and the two would divorce in 1974).

There are only two problems of note with *Jane* (three, depending on your tolerance for the musical stylings of Glass), though neither one is especially damaging. Since the footage of Goodall in the wild comprises the bulk of the film, it is that period that gets the most attention, which might frustrate some viewers hoping for a more soup-to-nuts treatment of her life. Additionally, there is the sense during the contemporary interview footage that Morgen has become smitten with her as well and is therefore loathe to ask her any tougher questions about her work or the struggles that she presumedly had making a name for herself in a male-dominated industry. Those quibbles aside, this is a documentary that combines an undeniably compelling subject of whom it is almost impossible not to feel an enormous amount of admiration and eye-opening archival material into a film that is both spellbinding and endearing in equal measure. In a year in which many of the biggest and most significant movies of the year were ones centered on female heroes, *Jane* contains perhaps the mightiest and most admirable one of them all.

Peter Sobczynski

CREDITS

Herself: Jane Goodall
Origin: United States
Language: English
Released: 2017
Production: Brett Morgen, Bryan Burk, Tony Gerber, James A. Smith; National Geographic Studios, Public Road Productions; released by Abramorama Films
Directed by: Brett Morgen
Written by: Brett Morgen
Cinematography by: Ellen Kuras
Music by: Philip Glass
Sound: Warren Shaw
Editing: Joe Beshenkovsky
MPAA rating: PG
Running time: 90 minutes

REVIEWS

Edelstein, David. *New York Magazine/Vulture*. October 20, 2017.
Erbland, Kate. *IndieWire*. September 15, 2017.
Harvey, Dennis. *Variety*. September 19, 2017.
Horton, Robert. *Seattle Weekly*. December 1, 2017.
Kenigsberg, Ben. *New York Times*. October 18, 2017.
Linden, Sheri. *Los Angeles Times*. October 19, 2017.
Nicholson, Amy. *Uproxx*. October 20, 2017.
Padua, Pat. *Washington Post*. October 26, 2017.
Rooney, David. *Hollywood Reporter*. September 11, 2017.
Wolfe, April. *Village Voice*. October 18, 2017.

AWARDS

Writers Guild 2017: Documentary Screenplay
Nominations:
British Acad. 2017: Feature Doc.

JIGSAW

A new game begins.
—Movie tagline

Box Office: $38.1 Million

The Spierig Brothers, as Michael and Peter Spierig are professionally known, are definitely filmmakers to watch, but their latest film barely warrants watching at all. *Jigsaw* adds little to the franchise that spawned it other than better cinematography. It certainly fails to generate the same sense of danger that *Saw* (2004) did when it kicked everything off. Instead, the film, which has a few nice moments and will probably be enjoyed by franchise fans, plays like a dim reminder of the times when so-called torture porn could still elicit moralistic outrage and genre-fan glee.

Just before being shot by Police Detective Halloran (Callum Keith Rennie), Edgar Munsen (Josiah Black) triggers a death machine designed by the long-deceased John Kramer aka Jigsaw (Tobin Bell). As five people listen, a tape recording offers them the opportunity to shed blood for their sins, and the chains they are attached to begin drawing them towards a group of buzzsaws. Four survive by allowing themselves to be cut, but the fifth, unconscious, appears to be drawn to his death.

The opening sequence is effective and starts the film off exactly the way fans expect. Lots of gore and a simple introduction to the characters and convoluted plot that follows. Those characters include Carly (Brittany Allen), tough guy Ryan (Paul Braunstein), Anna (Laura Vandervoort), and Mitch (Mandela Van Peebles). How they relate to one another is treated as narrative fodder that allows for the various moral tests, traps, and elaborate kills that have spawned, at this count, eight films.

The "Saw" films have long used police officers as foils and *Jigsaw* is no different. Halloran and Hunt (Clé Bennett) exist not just as investigators but as those who must be investigated, reinforcing the series prerogative that suggests no character in a "Saw" film ultimately escapes judgement. Likewise forensic pathologists Logan (Matt Passmore) and Eleanor (Hannah Emily Anderson).

This film does have a different look and feel than previous entries. Not only do the Spierigs have a solid eye for gore but they bring atmosphere with a lighter palette. The wicked are, literally, dragged kicking and screaming into the light for punishment for a change although there are plenty of dark rooms and hallways on the journey. The tone of the film too, is a little lighter with occasional nods being given to past entries and characters. The character of Eleanor is a nice meta-touch. A "fan" of Jigsaw, who has even replicated his various traps, she provides an opportunity, however scant, for real-life true crime junkies to reflect on their macabre interests.

The Spierig Brothers are notable for never having made a bad film before now. *Undead* (2003) was an energetic indie exploiter and *Daybreakers* (2009) was awfully pretty to look at, managing to create an interesting future world to boot. *Predestination* (2014) breathed some life into the time travel genre. But *Jigsaw* seems more like a light bit of exercise.

The film's special effects are as effective as they need to be, but are not anything special. There are faces melted by acid, amputated limbs, spiral shredding screws, saws, and stabbing implements galore. But watching the effects of these is still less painful than observing the way the plot twists and turns in an effort to justify the idea of rebooting a franchise that ended just fine more than seven years ago. It should be remembered that the idea of Jigsaw being a moralist was offered up as an unlikely surprise at the end of the first film. Over the course of the franchise, it became primary and had been played with endlessly by better writers than Pete Goldfinger or Josh Stolberg, whose feature work includes *Piranha 3D* (2010), *Piranha 3DD* (2012), and *Sorority Row* (2009). That being said, this is far from the worst entry in the series.

Saw is often credited with kicking off the so-called torture porn horror sub genre. There is some fairness to that observation. *Hostel* (2005) came out a year later, but neither *Hostel*, nor any of the films that followed, were as good. That original film exists in rarified company with other extreme films that manage to be simultaneously funny and disturbing. Director James Wan and his co-writer and star Leigh Whannell brought an undeniable intensity and nail-biting suspense that they have since carried over to other projects with great success. *Jigsaw* is the only project the Spierig Brothers have directed without also writing. Fun movie no doubt. But even more fun is the sense one gets from it that even with merely okay material the Spierigs are amply able to entertain.

Dave Canfield

CREDITS

Logan Nelson: Matt Passmore
Jigsaw/John Kramer: Tobin Bell
Detective Halloran: Callum Keith Rennie
Eleanor Bonneville: Hannah Emily Anderson
Detective Keith Hunt: Cle Bennett
Origin: United States
Language: English
Released: 2017
Production: Mark Burg, Gregg Hoffman, Oren Koules; A Bigger Boat, Serendipity Productions, Twisted Pictures; released by Lionsgate
Directed by: Michael Spierig; Peter Spierig
Written by: Peter Goldfinger; Josh Stolberg
Cinematography by: Ben Nott
Music by: Charlie Clouser
Sound: Mark Gingras
Editing: Kevin Greutert
Art Direction: Greg Chown
Costumes: Steven Wright
Production Design: Anthony Cowley
MPAA rating: R
Running time: 92 minutes

REVIEWS

Gingold, Michael. *Time Out*. October 27, 2017.

Gleiberman, Owen. *Variety.* October 27, 2017.
Gullickson, Brad. *Film School Rejects.* October 27, 2017.
Hassenger, Jesse. *The A.V. Club.*October 28, 2017.
Marsh, James. *South China Morning Post.* October 25, 2017.
Newman, Kim. *Screen International.* October 30, 2017.
Rozsa, Matthew. *Salon.com.* October 29, 2017.
Snider, Eric D. *EricDSnider.com.* October 27, 2017.
Turner, Kyle. *TheWrap.* October 26, 2017.
Wilson, Staci Layne. *Dread Central.* October 26, 2017.

QUOTES

John Kramer: "Failure to make the right choice could result in death."

TRIVIA

This is the first film in the series since the first in the series that does not feature an opening death trap.

JOHN WICK: CHAPTER 2

Never stab the devil in the back.
—Movie tagline

Box Office: $92 Million

John Wick (2014) was one of the most unexpected pleasant surprises in recent cinematic history. The film hit theaters in 2014 with nothing but relatively small pre-release buzz and an engaging trailer that provoked a lot of incredulous reactions. Was Keanu Reeves really starring in a movie about a hitman who goes on a revenge spree because someone killed his dog? People could not decide if the premise was too ridiculous or just ridiculous enough, but, when the film was released, it quickly became the cult action hit of the year, almost tripling its budget at the box office.

Due credit goes to directors Chad Stahelski and David Leitch who turned what could have been a by-the-numbers assassin film into a truly stylish, bombastic experience. In the same way that the Wachowskis entranced audiences with the unexpected visual language of their action scenes in *The Matrix* (1999), *John Wick* won over fans of the genre with its impossibly-choreographed gun sequences intertwined in long, uncut action beats that let audiences marvel at the physicality of Reeves and his stunt team. The film was such a success that a sequel was inevitable and, for the most part, *John Wick: Chapter 2* does a solid job of building on the foundation of the original. (This installment was directed solely by Chad Stahelski, though it did also bring back screenwriter, Derek Kolstad.)

The biggest flaw of *John Wick: Chapter 2* is that it does not have the laser-focused narrative intensity of the first chapter. The original film was all about a legendary former hitman going after the criminals who disturbed his morose professional retirement. Like most revenge movies, it had a very simple structure (which worked)—want revenge, seek revenge, get revenge. However, *John Wick: Chapter 2* is, by necessity, a more narratively complex film, which is not entirely a good thing. It's not as pure and primal as the original. It's craftier, it's more ambitious, but it's also harder to find the emotional core of the story this time. Reeves's Wick continues to be an action icon of almost unrivaled ability, but, in this chapter, his intentions are harder to suss out and identify with. Chapter 2 presents a Wick who is not driven by revenge anymore. Instead, he's trapped in an almost mythical hitman purgatory and, as he struggles to find his direction, the audience too struggles to connect with his purpose.

That does not mean that *John Wick: Chapter 2* isn't fun. It is, spectacularly so at some points, but one can feel the heavy lifting that the filmmakers had to do to construct layers of retroactive continuity around Wick and his world. (One also gets the sense that, after the success of the original, the studio immediately encouraged the screenwriter to construct a whole film universe.) While the little flourishes of world-building in the original—the gold coins, the hotel for hitmen—were welcome bits of personality thrown in amongst the carnage, Kolstad overcompensates in Chapter 2 by expanding those brief, cool asides into major plot elements.

Though it is easy to overlook the overall sweatiness of the storytelling in Chapter 2 when Chad Stahelski and his production team put together a truly epic action sequence—and the movie features more than one. The film opens with Wick finishing up one last detail of his mission from the first chapter (reminding us that the criminals both killed his dog and stole his car). After he puts his business to rest, following an exhilarating car chase and shoot-out at a cab company, Wick tries to return to the suburbs and retire, only to find himself confronted by the suave international gangster Santino D'Antonio (Riccardo Scamarcio). We learn that part of the conditions of Wick's original retirement was that he agreed to a "marker" (a blood-oath promise) held by Santino. Since Wick so openly came out of retirement in Chapter 1, Santino decides to call in his marker and tells Wick to kill his sister Gianna (Claudia Gerini), who is Santino's rival for a seat at "The High Table"—the rulers of the criminal hierarchy of the cinematic Wick-i-verse.

When Wick refuses, Santino blows up Wick's home and strong-arms the forlorn hitman into taking the assignment. (This contributes to the overall narrative malaise in Chapter 2. The first movie was about a man questing to achieve a very direct goal, while this installment is all about a trapped hitman trying to wriggle his way out of an unending series of professional commitments.) Hoping to finally put his obligation to Santino to rest, Wick travels to Rome and plays the role of assassin. However, things quickly go wrong and, following some beautiful and relentless shoot-outs—where the effectiveness of Wick's Kevlar-lined suit strains credulity—Wick finds himself on the run, having attracted the ire of the entire international hitman community, most notably, his old colleague Cassian (Common).

Reeves's performance as Wick continues to be a remarkable physical achievement—he sells the hitman's virtuosity with guns in a wonderfully fluid fashion—though the character does hit some roadblocks in this second chapter. While he barreled through the first movie on righteous indignation alone, Chapter 2 presents a Wick who keeps making questionable decisions. To a certain extent, it makes him more human, but it also makes him less mythical. He's less the Baba Yaga in this sequel and more of a desperate man who is unsure how to survive. It's not a particularly satisfying direction for the character, but Reeves still finds ways to make Wick the coolest gunslinger in recent memory. (Apologies to Idris Elba.)

A lot of credit for that also needs to go to Kevin Kavanaugh's production design and the art direction by Cristina Onori, Saverio Sammali, and Chris Shriver. *John Wick: Chapter 2* is a gorgeous movie, even better looking than the original, and the design team does a breathtaking job of turning cities like Rome and New York into near-mythological landscapes for the baroque, almost biblical battles for Wick's soul that Stahelski choreographs throughout the movie.

Is *John Wick: Chapter 2* as satisfying as the original film? No. But it does continue to showcase all of the best qualities of the first movie, while making some earnest efforts to expand the film's storytelling world. While not all of those efforts pay off, this sequel does present some truly excellent cinematic mayhem and some world-building that's interesting enough to hold your attention for the inevitable third chapter.

Tom Burns

CREDITS

John Wick: Keanu Reeves
Cassian: Common
Bowery King: Laurence Fishburne
Santino D'Antonio: Riccardo Scamarcio
Ares: Ruby Rose
Origin: United States
Language: English
Released: 2017
Production: Basil Iwanyk, Erica Lee; 87Eleven, Lionsgate, TIK Films, Thunder Road Pictures; released by Summit Entertainment
Directed by: Chad Stahelski
Written by: Derek Kolstad
Cinematography by: Dan Laustsen
Music by: Tyler Bates; Joel J. Richard
Sound: Mark P. Stoeckinger
Music Supervisor: John Houlihan
Editing: Evan Schiff
Art Direction: Saverio Sammali; Chris Shriver
Costumes: Luca Mosca
Production Design: Kevin Kavanaugh
MPAA rating: R
Running time: 122 minutes

REVIEWS

Baumgarten, Marjorie. *Austin Chronicle*. February 8, 2017.
Debruge, Peter. *Variety*. February 6, 2017.
Hewitt, Chris. *Empire*. February 6, 2017.
Huddleston, Tom. *Time Out London*. February 6, 2017.
Kohn, Eric. *IndieWire*. February 6, 2017.
Lowe, Justin. *Hollywood Reporter*. February 6, 2017.
Mottram, James. *Total Film*. February 16, 2017.
Nashawaty, Chris. *Entertainment Weekly*. February 6, 2017.
Neish, Jamie. *CineVue*. February 7, 2017.
Vishnevetsky, Ignatiy. *The A.V. Club*. February 8, 2017.

QUOTES

John Wick: "You wanted me back...I'm back!"

TRIVIA

Chad Stahelski was also Keanu Reeves' stunt double in the *Matrix* trilogy.

JUMANJI: WELCOME TO THE JUNGLE

The game has evolved.
—Movie tagline

Box Office: $339.9 Million

Two years after the success of *Jurassic Park* (1993) and six years before he would helm the third film in that franchise, Joe Johnston took on an adaptation of Chris Van Allsburg's *Jumanji* (1995). At the time it did not come close to matching the enormous success of

Spielberg's film—though it was relatively profitable—nor might anyone have imagined we might be holding the films in relative context over two decades later. The nostalgia for what may have been a passable fantasy adventure comedy has no doubt been spurred on by the tragic passing of its beloved star, Robin Williams, and the opportunity to capitalize on that might seem like a coldly calculated enterprise. The good news is that the makers of the sequel show enough respect to the source material and Williams's memory as to not leave a sour taste in our own. The bad news is that the least interesting aspect of this sporadically charming movie is the actual Jumanji itself.

Diving right back into the closing events of the original film the mythical Jumanji board game is found on the very beach where we last saw it. Adapting to the gaming preferences of the time it transforms itself into a video game platform—with a cartridge resembling the more 1980s-like Atari 2600 games—and another unsuspecting kid is sucked into its universe. Flash-forward two decades later where meek-ish Spencer Gilpin (Alex Wolff) is caught helping school jock Anthony "Fridge" Johnson (Ser'Darius Blain) do his homework. They join popular Bethany Walker (Madison Iseman) and shy anti-gym activist, Martha Kaply (Morgan Turner) in detention where they are told to clean out the school basement. Guess what they find?

After picking their game characters, they are pulled into its jungle world and find themselves occupying the bodies of the avatars they have chosen. Spencer is now the jacked Dr. Smolder Bravestone (Dwayne Johnson) who has the benefit of having not a single weakness. Anthony has become a mini-fridge in zoologist Franklin "Mouse" Finbar (Kevin Hart). Martha morphs into striking martial arts expert, Ruby Roundhouse (Karen Gillan) complete in short shorts and a bare midriff. Finally, the vain Bethany looks in the water to see rotund cartographer Sheldon "Shelly" Oberon (Jack Black). To win the game and earn their escape they must obtain a jewel and return it to the eye of a giant jaguar statue or find themselves trapped in Jumanji forever, or at least as long as their three lives last them.

The things most remembered about Johnston's film were the crazy use of special effects. Though a bit dated today, the idea of letting a jungle and its inhabitants loose on an unsuspecting town led to some fantastical imagery of a house ensconced in vines and rhinos and elephants stampeding through the streets. Going directly into the jungle with the benefit of video game logistics should have been a cornucopia of ideas and challenges for the four credited screenwriters. Instead, this is where the film gets bogged down by its special effects instead of creating new wonders for the viewers. Outwitting a snake in one key scene aside, the screenplay is severely lacking in its own curiosity about the limitless possibilities for these characters to explore their new powers. Each get a list of skill sets and weaknesses, but in the heyday of such adventures in the 1980s those traits would be woven in rather than presented to us as a complete list. Waiting for venom and cake to pose threats while motorcycles and helicopters attempt to ramp up colorless set pieces provides a thought that the writers have not actively participated in games of any era.

Where the movie is saved moment-to-moment is through the interaction of its cast or, at least, their new avatars. Dwayne Johnson and Kevin Hart attempted a rapport playing against type in the laugh-free *Central Intelligence* (2016) but do a much better job here with the "who you are now vs. who you want to be" theme. Hart's usual screeching theatrics are still on display, but it is often balanced by the others. Black never overplays the opportunity to move and talk like a teenage girl even if the writers uncomfortably force him to make gags about his newfound appendage. Though Johnson has charm to spare and his willingness for self-deprecation only accentuates that, Gillan frequently steals the show here. Known primarily as one of Doctor Who's companions and for her role as the vengeful Nebula in the *Guardians of the Galaxy* series, Gillan shows remarkable comic chops in an extended sequence where her introverted real-world character must learn how to flirt. Undeniably it is a little odd for a family adventure film (even with a PG-13 rating) to have a teenager (even in the body of a 30-year-old) flaunt her attributes towards grimy, older henchmen (even if they are fictional game figures) but Gillan kills it in these moments and only opens a desire to see more comic opportunities for her.

Allsburg already had a spiritual sequel to *Jumanji* with *Zathura: A Space Adventure* (2005) directed by Jon Favreau, who had not quite yet mastered (in his third film) the blending of storytelling and a cadre of special effects. Director Jake Kasdan in his seventh effort that has included films both great (*Zero Effect* [1998], *Walk Hard: The Dewey Cox Story* [2007]) and lackluster (*Bad Teacher* [2011], *Sex Tape* [2014]) has never approached the kind of effects work and action beats this film needs to be successful. Good with actors and improv, sure, but there is nothing jazzy enough about the race to the end of the game to stoke the previous Jumanji generation into convincing the new one that it's any sort of classic they will be revisiting in another twenty years. "It's a lot easier to be brave when you have lives to spare," says one character who could just as easily be talking about the difference in viewing films through the varied lens of youth and adulthood. The nostalgic inclinations of that period may be producing a lot of money by sucking in the new guard with disappointments like *Tron: Legacy* (2010) and *Jurassic World* (2015) but those that grow out of them can still hold out hope that a reboot of David Cronenberg's *eXistenZ* (1999) might happen for them someday. And if not, they can always revisit the original for a couple hours.

Erik Childress

CREDITS

Spencer: Dwayne "The Rock" Johnson
Fridge: Kevin Hart
Bethany: Jack Black
Martha: Karen Gillan
Nigel: Rhys Darby
Origin: United States
Language: English
Released: 2017
Production: William Teitler, Matt Tolmach; Radar Pictures Inc., Seven Bucks Productions, Sony Pictures Entertainment Inc.; released by Columbia Pictures
Directed by: Jake Kasdan
Written by: Chris McKenna; Erik Sommers; Scott Rosenberg; Jeff Pinkner
Cinematography by: Gyula Pados
Music by: Henry Jackman
Sound: Joel Shryack; Julian Slater
Music Supervisor: Manish Raval; Tom Wolfe
Editing: Steve Edwards; Mark Helfrich
Art Direction: Steve Cooper; Hugo Santiago
Costumes: Laura Jean Shannon
Production Design: Owen Paterson
MPAA rating: PG-13
Running time: 119 minutes

REVIEWS

Berardinelli, James. *ReelViews.* December 20, 2017.
Edelstein, David. *New York Magazine/Vulture.* December 21, 2017.
Gronvall, Andrea. *Chicago Reader.* December 21, 2017.
Johanson, MaryAnn. *Flick Filosopher.* December 19, 2017.
Judy, Jim. *ScreenIt.* December 22, 2017.
Kenny, Glenn. *New York Times.* December 19, 2017.
Nicholson, Amy. *Uproxx.* December 20, 2017.
Seitz, Matt Zoller. *RogerEbert.com.* December 20, 2017.
Snider, Eric D. *EricDSnider.com.* December 21, 2017.
Verniere, James. *Boston Herald.* December 20, 2017.

QUOTES

Martha (sarcastically): "Are you gonna help, or are you too pretty?"
Bethany (serious): "I'm too pretty."

TRIVIA

The film's "African" jungle setting was actually shot in Hawaii.

JUST GETTING STARTED

Box Office: $6.1 Million

There was a time when Ron Shelton was American middlebrow filmmaking's answer to Howard Hawks. His ambling, easy, wry, sweaty, chummy dramas were a consistent delight and easier than first grade math to watch. *Bull Durham* (1988) and *White Man Can't Jump* (1992) are regarded as minor classic low-stakes sports movies and *Tin Cup* (1996), *Dark Blue* (2002), and *Cobb* (1994) all have their defenders. He took a step back from the limelight, directing little projects and writing big-budget movies, for the better part of a decade and his long-awaited return may unfortunately prove to be his last movie. Unfortunately, because even if the reviews for the truly, sadly terrible *Just Getting Started* were not enough to kill any director's career stone dead there doesn't seem to be much left of Shelton's talent to salvage.

Marguerite (Glenne Headly) is watching television in her imprisoned mobster husband's mansion in New Jersey when she makes a startling discovery. In a commercial for a Palm Springs retirement community called Villa Capri she spies the familiar face of Duke Diver (Morgan Freeman), the attorney who turned state's evidence and whose testimony subsequently landed her husband in jail. She calls her dimwit son and tells him to fly out to Palm Springs and kill Duke. Diver has been rather living it up since his day in court. He's become the king regent of his little retirement community, in charge of decoration spending and public outreach, a team of flunkies (Joe Pantoliano, George Wallace, and Graham Beckel) at his disposal, and a harem of randy older ladies (Jane Seymour, Elizabeth Ashley, and Sheryl Lee Ralph) ready to jump his bones whenever he has a spare few seconds and Viagra in his system. Everything's coming up roses for Duke until three mysterious figures enter his life. The first is Leo (Tommy Lee Jones), the retired world-traveling military man with a poet's soul who charms away his women and beats him at poker, challenging Duke's dominance in the home. The second is Suzie (Rene Russo), a bombshell sent from Villa Capri's corporate overlord to reign in Duke's spending and wrest back control of the everyday operations from the old codger. The third is Marguerite's son Salvador (Tasos Hernandez) who keeps planting clumsy death traps into which Duke keeps accidentally refusing to fall. An exploding golf cart, a snake hiding in Duke's luggage, and, finally, stray bullets convince Duke he has to come clean to Leo about the man trying to kill him, forcing them to put aside their petty rivalry, and their war of attrition in their courtship of Suzie. Both men have developed strong feelings for her and try increasingly elaborate ways of winning her heart, including hiring Johnny Mathis to play the home's annual holiday party.

There is a laundry list of problems with the sadistically low energy and low stakes *Just Getting Started.* More than 75

of the dialogue was plainly added in post-production, changing dynamic, direction, and volume every few seconds. To get around whatever feat of laziness or accidental disaster that caused the sound issues in the first place, Shelton frequently uses takes where the actors are not facing the camera or cuts away to external action in wider shots to mask the fact that he has no clean take of actors actually speaking to each other. Despite clearly not having the energy or patience to do so, Shelton films a series of perversely boring car chases in the third act. Jones and Freeman are not any more invested, barely mustering mild concern on their faces during the action sequences, let alone genuine fright or excitement. They are both bored and lost, Freeman in particular giving what must be the only bad performance of his career as a frequently drunk, blustery coot with a wily libido. Jones has taken the acceptable route and checked out without losing his dignity to the milieu of failure and sleepiness. Russo is flummoxed by the underwritten part she's been handed, and so throws every trick she can think of, most of them bad physical comedy tactics, to bring something to the table. She soundly fails and it's deeply upsetting. The script is an offensive collection of tropes, stock situations, and clichés, none of which Shelton has any interest in dusting off before he tosses them in front of the audience and waits for their applause. With an audience over 90 he might get it, but even that seems charitable. The film is not so much about retirement as it is an accurate simulation of life as a retiree. No one runs when they can walk, no one tells jokes you haven't heard, and no one seems in much of a hurry to do much more than brag to score meaningless points with other residents. A shamelessly arrogant, depressingly artless and worryingly listless film designed to fill time on movie channels and sucker people out of their money on streaming services, there is simply no way that anyone would ever watch this movie twice.

Scout Tafoya

CREDITS

Margarite: Glenne Headly
Suzie: Rene Russo
Duke: Morgan Freeman
Delilah: Jane Seymour
Leo: Tommy Lee Jones
Origin: United States
Language: English
Released: 2017
Production: Bill Gerber, Steve Richards; Endurance Media, Entertainment One, Gerber Pictures; released by Broad Green Pictures
Directed by: Ron Shelton
Written by: Ron Shelton
Cinematography by: Barry Peterson
Music by: Alex Wurman
Sound: Xander Lott
Music Supervisor: Laura Katz
Editing: Paul Seydor
Art Direction: Derek Jensen
Costumes: Carol Oditz
Production Design: Guy Barnes
MPAA rating: PG-13
Running time: 91 minutes

REVIEWS

Callahan, Dan. *TheWrap.* December 8, 2017.
Farber, Steohen. *Hollywood Reporter.* December 8, 2017.
Leydon, Joe. *Variety.* December 8, 2017.
Moore, Roger. *Movie Nation.* December 9, 2017.
Myers, Kimber. *Los Angeles Times.* December 8, 2017.
Savlov, Marc. *Austin Chronicle.* December 13, 2017.
Scott, A.O. *New York Times.* December 12, 2017.
Vishnevetsky, Ignatiy. *The A.V. Club.* December 9, 2017.
Wloszczyna, Susan. *RogerEbert.com.* December 9, 2017.
Zwecker, Bill. *Chicago Sun-Times.* December 8, 2017.

TRIVIA

This film features the final performance by actress Glenne Headly, who died on June 8, 2017.

JUSTICE LEAGUE

Unite,
—Movie tagline
Justice for all.
—Movie tagline
Unite the League.
—Movie tagline
You can't save the world alone.
—Movie tagline

Box Office: $228.1 Million

It should have come as no surprise that the DC movie franchise would look to Joss Whedon for its first team-centric installment. After all, Whedon more or less invented the formula for such an exercise when he wrote and directed *The Avengers* (2012) for Marvel's own "cinematic universe," and the DC Comics branch of superheroes has been trying to catch up with its competition ever since. Their recent movies, mainly *Man of Steel* (2013) and *Batman v Superman: Dawn of Justice* (2016) (and, to a lesser extent, the outright failure that was the villainous-team movie *Suicide Squad* [2016]), have been in such a rush to create this extended universe of heroes and villains that the results have lacked much personality—save for a crushingly dour tone and an apocalyptic sense of purpose.

There was a bright spot in 2017's *Wonder Woman*, which took the most promising element and sole strength of *Batman v Superman*—Gal Gadot's sincere and genuinely charismatic interpretation of the Amazon warrior—and created a rarity in superhero movies: an origin story that not only understood the core of the character but also created a narrative that made the character's essence its own core. The Patty Jenkins-directed film offered the DC universe of cinematic superheroes its first glimmer of hope.

It has, then, been a relatively short but seemingly lengthy road—filled with far more valleys than its singular peak, which accounts for why the trek has felt so long—to director Zack Snyder's *Justice League*. After turning Superman into a mere shadow of the character's iconic glory (in the filmmaker's *Man of Steel* and *Batman v Superman*) and making the entirety of the DC movie universe a very cynical place, Snyder clearly wants to hit a reset button with this entry.

That is where Whedon, who co-wrote the screenplay with Chris Terrio (and, after a tragedy in Snyder's family, reportedly took over directorial duties for reshoots), comes into play. Whedon's knack for finding the humor in even the most grandiose characters and over-the-top scenarios is in full play here. This is a massive change for these movies, and to an extent, it is also a welcome one.

No longer is Batman (Ben Affleck) a cruel and heartless vigilante with a twisted sense of justice, as firmly established in his most recent appearance in the DC/Snyder universe. He can crack a joke every so often, even if he does not seem to know it. When asked what his superpower is, the Dark Knight's alter ego Bruce Wayne simply offers, "I'm rich."

For the most part, the new characters are introduced with fixed personalities, too. Barry Allen (Ezra Miller), who goes by the Flash when he is stopping crime in his native Central City, is an awkward young man who understands the absurdity of the notion of superheroes. He serves as the movie's running joke (no pun intended), offering a commentary on the ridiculous aspects and played as the new guy finding his way in a scenario that is far beyond his current skills. Just before going into battle for the first time, Barry/the Flash admits that he actually has never fought anyone before; usually, he just pushes bad guys while running really, really fast.

Arthur Curry (Jason Momoa), better known as Aquaman, is a rough-and-tumble, heavy-metal god of the sea. He is presented as something of an adrenaline junkie, who saves people, less for the glory, more for the thrill and the free alcoholic beverages that come from the thankful patrons of a local tavern somewhere in Scandinavia.

The final new character is Victor Stone (Ray Fisher), aka Cyborg, a half-man, half-cyborg who was once a young, star football player, until an almost certainly fatal car accident prompted his father (played by Joe Morton) to experiment on his son in order to save the young man's life. Victor/Cyborg is more in the vein of the series' semi-tragic superheroes, whose origin story and internal conflicts are taken seriously. The clever aspect of the character comes from how his artificial intelligence continuously updates without Victor's knowledge—meaning that he is constantly imbued with new abilities. He does not realize this fact until those new powers manifest themselves in combat.

Lest anyone forget, Gadot's Diana Prince/Wonder Woman does, indeed, return. There is little more to say about the character that was not already established by *Batman v Superman* and her solo outing, except that she continues to serve as the brightest spot in these movies. Her re-introduction here sees her defeating a band of terrorists and saving a group of hostages by deflecting automatic gunfire.

All of the characters, with their various strengths (both their respective abilities and their capacity for playing off each other in the non-action-oriented sequences) and potentials, are in place. This is a promising start. The plot is set in the shadow of Superman's (Henry Cavill) death at the end of Snyder's previous installment. Bruce is convinced that an otherworldly threat is coming, and he wants to assemble a team of superheroes, known as "meta-humans" in the franchise's parlance, to face that threat.

The otherworld force is Steppenwolf, a particularly unconvincing computer-generated creation, who is voiced by Ciarán Hinds and has an army of flying, insect-like creatures. Steppenwolf falls squarely into the terrain of the generic comic-book villain. His motives are set on global domination. His methods involve a trio of science-fiction MacGuffins—boxes that possess power and that, when united, possess even more power. He must collect these boxes from their hidden places around the world, and the newly formed team of heroes must stop him before he does.

One can sense Whedon and Terrio's intentions with this rudimentary plot. It exists as an excuse to put together the eponymous team, and as such, its primary goal is to be as miniscule a distraction as possible. The focus is on the members of the team, yet even so, the generic plot and villain remain a gamble, which does not pay out to the extent that the filmmakers believe it will. The characters and their interactions have to work on their own, as well as compensate for the fact that the reason for their union is so transparently frivolous and inconsequential.

As appealing as these characters may be in theory or in practice, that is a significant burden to place on them—half of whom, after Superman's inevitable return, are being introduced to this franchise for the first time (their brief appearance in those email attachments in *Batman v Superman* surely cannot count as proper introductions). In addition to the story and villain issues, the movie also has to deal with narrative threads that end up feeling like housecleaning duties. There is Superman's resurrection, treated as a sort of exorcism performed on the character. After a massive battle with his future allies, Superman's demons have disappeared.

It has been a long time—perhaps during his first flying sequence in *Man of Steel*—since this iteration of Superman smiled, and Cavill is finally presented with the opportunity to play the icon with the kind of sincerity that one expects from the character. This also means reunions with his fiancée Lois Lane (Amy Adams, who, having been reduced to little more than a damsel in distress in her previous outings as the character, is now mostly reduced to a shell of grief) and his mother Martha (Diane Lane), yet those moments must be hastened. After all, there is a villain to fight—in action sequences that continue Snyder's trend of favoring perpetual, sometimes incomprehensible motion over a sense of place and cohesion. A brawl in a sewer is not helped by the dimness of the surroundings, and the climactic battle in a mostly abandoned city is so busy with superhero business that the already-low stakes are not helped in any way.

Compared to the other entries in this series, the movie is short. There is a surprising amount of ground to cover here, and it is somewhat refreshing that Whedon and Terrio avoid becoming too bogged down within inner and inter-character conflicts that had been established by the previous installments. The movie moves but does not feel rushed. Its primary aim is a near-complete about-face on what has come before it. There is no denying that such a decision is the correct one. The filmmakers simply overestimate how much ground their steps in the right direction will cover.

Mark Dujsik

CREDITS

Batman/Bruce Wayne: Ben Affleck

Superman/Clark Kent: Henry Cavill

Lois Lane: Amy Adams

Wonder Woman/Diana Prince: Gal Gadot

The Flash/Barry Allen: Ezra Miller

Origin: United States

Language: English, Irish, Russian, Icelandic

Released: 2017

Production: Jon Berg, Geoff Johns, Charles Roven, Deborah Snyder; Atlas Entertainment, Cruel & Unusual Films, DC Entertainment, Lensbern Productions, RatPac-Dune Entertainment; released by Warner Bros. Pictures

Directed by: Zack Snyder

Written by: Chris Terrio; Joss Whedon

Cinematography by: Fabian Wagner

Music by: Danny Elfman

Sound: Chuck Michael

Music Supervisor: Karen Elliott

Editing: David Brenner; Richard Pearson; Martin Walsh

Art Direction: Christian Huband; Helen Jarvis

Costumes: Michael Wilkinson

Production Design: Patrick Tatopoulos

MPAA rating: PG-13

Running time: 120 minutes

REVIEWS

Berardinelli, James. *ReelViews*. November 15, 2017.

Cole, Jake. *Slant Magazine*. November 15, 2017.

Dargis, Manohla. *New York Times*. November 15, 2017.

Ebiri, Bilge. *Village Voice*. November 15, 2017.

Larsen, Josh. *LarsenOnFilm*. November 15, 2017.

Robinson, Tasha. *Verge*. November 15, 2017.

Sobczynski, Peter. *EFilmCritic.com*. November 16, 2017.

Vishnevetsky, Ignatiy. *The A.V. Club*. November 15, 2017.

Walsh, Katie. *Chicago Tribune*. November 15, 2017.

Zacharek, Stephanie. *Time*. November 15, 2017.

QUOTES

Barry Allen: "What are your superpowers again?"

Bruce Wayne: "I'm rich."

TRIVIA

The film was released on the same day the animated television series *Justice League* first aired sixteen years earlier.

K

KEDI

A cat meowing at your feet, looking up at you, is life smiling at you...
—Movie tagline

Box Office: $2.8 Million

The Internet is obviously an amazing invention, contribution and deep wellspring of free, easily accessible knowledge. It's also inexplicably given rise to an enormous amount of widely consumed cat-centric information including videos, memes, photos, groups, and countless other ways to share everything imaginable about everyone's apparently favorite furry friend. Documentary filmmaker Ceyda Torun has wisely set her eyes on this cat "niche" to deliver the often charming but ultimately dull documentary *Kedi,* which focuses on the overabundance of felines on the streets of Istanbul. While fans of cats in any and every iteration will likely swoon over the adorable nature of the film, the experience becomes a somewhat tedious and redundant look at what is probably more of a nuisance than the film lets on.

Hundreds of thousands of cats freely roam the streets of Istanbul. While many "earn their keep" by getting rid of mice and rats, most spend their days mooching food of any kind from humans as well as reproducing at an alarming rate. Throughout the film, viewers meet and briefly follow seven of these street-smart felines as well as the many Turks who feel compelled to feed, house, and care for the adorable street urchins at their own expense. This can get pretty pricy as cat fights, sickness, and the harsh realities of homelessness add up. Again, cat lovers will swoon over the cute shots and stories of each cat and their individual personalities, yet the human stories of relating to cats become monotonous and not terribly insightful as at least four people reiterate that cats are a lot like people in many ways. Other than that insight, *Kedi* offers few others.

Kedi introduces viewers to Sari, an orange and white cat who is also a new mother. She is a hustler for food and is not afraid to beg or steal in order to fulfill her needs. Sari hangs around various shops in town to get food, water or attention before returning to her starving litter of kittens. While it is impressive how Sari has managed to stake out a life for herself and her new family, the cat also reminds viewers that these animals could really care less about anything but their own needs and desires as she wanders in and out of people's lives, taking what she's given and then moving on.

Where *Kedi* is most successful is in the rich and gorgeous photography of Istanbul. The film lays out several impressive aerial shots as well as utilizing a kind of "cat's eye view cam" as a cameraperson follows various cats while holding the camera low to the ground as if they were themselves a cat. These shots are fun, particularly when they steadily dash through crowded marketplaces. There's also some interesting people interviewed in the film including a sailor who relays a rather tall sounding tale of his brand-new boat sinking in a storm. Just as he thinks all is lost, he discovers a nearby cat (not surprising as there are cats everywhere in Istanbul) that leads him to a wallet with just enough cash to repair his boat.

Yet other stories throughout *Kedi* are redundant tales of cats giving life and purpose to formerly forlorn people who now spend countless hours a week as well as untold amounts of money walking around the city feeding the feral felines. Many times, these kindhearted folks also take the animals to the veterinarian at their own expense, all the while joking of an insurmountable vet bill that will likely never get paid off. While indeed very kind and caring, it's a bit of a Sisyphean task that makes one wonder just how bad these people had it before they decided to try and help the hundreds of thousands of hungry cats in their town. Yet it's the variety of cats who are the stars of the film.

Some cats like the loving, affable Bengü seem to genuinely enjoy human companionship and love. Always in the mood for a scratch or a deep brushing, Bengü seems like the kind of cat that would like a permanent home but keeps on wandering just the same. Other featured cats like Psikopat leave a trail of anger, jealousy, and scratch marks on whoever or whatever dares cross her path. Perhaps it's a tribute to the accepting nature the Turkish people have for their overabundance of feral cats but it's a bit baffling why people smile and shake their head at this crazy cat who herself has been the source of many cats needing medical help.

There's a fairly uncomfortable scene in Quentin Tarantino's *Inglorious Basterds* [2009] where the "Jew Hunter," Colonel Hans Landa (Cristoph Waltz), talks about how squirrels can just as easily carry the same diseases and plagues as rats. Yet people love squirrels and thus they are readily accepted as cute and not worthy of scorn. Landa also then makes an unsavory comparison to the Jewish people which is absolutely not the point here. Rather, it's that the same could easily be said for the hundreds of thousands of feral cats freely roaming the streets of Istanbul, reproducing at a frightening rate, mooching food and tearing each other apart over cloudy territorial issues. Granted, no cats have thus been discovered carrying diseases humans can catch but *Kedi* spends so much time lovingly filming these little scamps and the people helping them survive, it completely glosses over the fact that this many cats roaming freely in a city could also be considered a fairly large nuisance. As such, *Kedi* overly worships cats and thus becomes a feature length film version of any number of YouTube videos.

Don R. Lewis

CREDITS

Himself: Bülent Üstün
Origin: United States
Language: Turkish
Released: 2017
Production: Ceyda Torun, Charlie Wuppermann; Termite Films; released by Oscilloscope Films
Directed by: Ceyda Torun
Cinematography by: Alp Korfali; Charlie Wuppermann
Music by: Kira Fontana
Editing: Mo Stoebe
MPAA rating: Unrated
Running time: 80 minutes

REVIEWS

Ebiri, Bilge. *Village Voice.* February 7, 2017.
Johnson, G. Allen. *San Francisco Chronicle.* March 2, 2017.
Kenny, Glenn. *New York Times.* February 9, 2017.
Kohn, Eric. *IndieWire.* February 10, 2017.
Larson, Vanessa H. *Washington Post.* February 23, 2017.
Nicholson, Amy. *MTV News.* February 16, 2017.
O'Malley, Sheila. *RogerEbert.com.* February 10, 2017.
Rainer, Peter. *Christian Science Monitor.* February 17, 2017.
Watson, Keith. *Slant Magazine.* February 4, 2017.
Zacharek, Stephanie. *Time.* February 9, 2017.

TRIVIA

The cat-level action cam was mounted on a remote control toy car.

THE KILLING OF A SACRED DEER

Box Office: $2.3 Million

The work of Greek-born director Yorgos Lanthimos might best be characterized as cinema as psychological study—not only for the probing, off-center, and slightly bemused nature of his choices of narrative focus, but also for the manner in which his movies evoke the disconcerting feeling of being a test subject in a college-level Psych 101 graduate student experiment, where the full range of variables, and indeed the very aim of said evaluation, is not known.

In his previous movies like *Dogtooth* (2009), *Alps* (2011), and *The Lobster* (2015), Lanthimos has plumbed tragedy and death for dark comedy. For his second English-language film, Lanthimos again uses a deadpan tone and oblique narrative connections to explore a slow spread of interpersonal cruelty. Played early on for reactions that land somewhere between uncomfortable laughs and arched-brow confusion, before eventually taking a full-on swan dive into darker territory, *The Killing of a Sacred Deer* is an allegorical exploration of the long shadow of consequences and the terrible choices fate sometimes foists upon us—a cinematic slice of very primal, core emotions, served purposefully roiled and happy to provoke.

In advance of its world premiere at the Cannes Film Festival (where it would win the Best Screenplay Award), distributor A24 picked up North American rights to *The Killing of a Sacred Deer*—its title a metaphorical nod to the tale of King Agamemnon, ordered to sacrifice his daughter Iphigenia as punishment for offending the goddess Artemis. Opening theatrically in October by way of a platform-release strategy that topped out at just under 240 theaters, the film netted a domestic box office total of $2.1 million—somewhat of a surprise, given the presence of Colin Farrell and Nicole Kidman, and the $9 million gross of *The Lobster*.

The story centers on Dr. Steven Murphy (Farrell), a seemingly successful heart surgeon who lives in the suburbs with his ophthalmologist wife, Anna (Kidman), and their two children, 14-year-old Kim (Raffey Cassidy) and 11-year-old Bob (Sunny Suljic). After finishing surgery one day, Steven meets up at a diner with Martin (Barry Keoghan), a socially maladjusted teenage boy who for unclear reasons seems to regard him as a mentor.

After Steven reveals privately to Anna that Martin's father died in a car crash 10 years earlier, she suggests inviting him over to dinner. Martin does, and later returns the favor by insisting that Steven come eat with him and his mother (Alicia Silverstone), a scenario which ends awkwardly when she tries to foist herself upon Steven. Not long after, Martin's demands on Steven's time grow increasingly more frequent and desperate.

A mysterious illness then befalls Bob, rendering him unable to move. It turns out Steven operated on Martin's father, and was unable to save him. Holding Steven responsible for his death, Martin tells him that he has placed a curse on the entire Murphy family—the four specific stages of which he enumerates. The only thing that will break the curse is if Steven "balances" the death by killing one of his own family members. Naturally, Steven initially regards this as balderdash, but quickly comes to have second thoughts as elements of Martin's prophecies are born out.

There are other twists and narrative alleyways best left undiscussed, but any discussion or analysis of *The Killing of a Sacred Deer* is wise to focus equally if not more on the feelings it elicits than the plot itself. Even its detractors would likely have difficulty denying that the film evinces the feeling and atmospheric grip of a masterful auteur. If not quite Hitchcockian, both the movie's conceit and its self-conscious construction at least conjure visions of a psychological thriller that Brian De Palma might have directed in his heyday—except minus any mainstream commercial instinct to generate or pay off suspense. While utterly singular and unique in the broadest strokes, there is enough overlap, especially in its final hour, that *The Killing of a Sacred Deer* could play on a double bill alongside *Funny Games* (1997/2007), *The Gift* (2015), *mother!* (2017), or any number of other exactingly constructed movies in which a socially awkward interloper imposes disorder or worse onto the well-ordered lives of a white-collar family. Part of the dark genius of the film is that it arrives in this genre space at all—a development that seems both surprising and oddly sensible, given all the unease it generates.

Working again with his frequent screenwriting collaborator Efthymis Filippou, Lanthimos conjures a dispassionate, severe and at times almost sterile environment (one can safely assume no coincidence, given Steven's occupation), tidily rendered by production designer Jade Healy and art directer Daniel Baker. Cinematographer Thimios Bakatakis trades in high-angle compositions and wide establishing shots, which Lanthimos and editor Yorgos Mavropsaridis hold for long takes. The cumulative effect—particularly in the film's first act, but also in professional and medical settings—is often that of a somewhat clinical cinematic opera, which is not surprising given that compositions from Schubert, Bach, and other classical composers are forcefully used to summon a generally foreboding mood.

The Killing of a Sacred Deer again showcases Lanthimos' interest in the divergence between spoken language and what we mean or accept it to be. In *Dogtooth*, absurdism met malevolence in the form of a story about parents who keep their three children in a fenced-in compound and teach them incorrect words for objects, among other forms of abuse. In his latest film, Lanthimos has his stars deploy narcotized line readings, stripped free of normal cadence or inflection that might make the dialogue sound like part of a normal human conversation. The results sound stilted, and often—especially with Farrell's Steven—like an actor running lines in rehearsal rather than giving a performance. It takes some getting used to. But in utilizing this technique, Lanthimos targets the banality of conversational small talk, and highlights the differences between what characters are saying and thinking, or revealing in their actions.

If there is a lot to unpack thematically, there is no debate about the revelation of the film, 25-year-old Irish actor Keoghan, who also costarred in *Dunkirk* (2017). Physically resembling a younger brother of Joel Edgerton by way of Miles Teller, Keoghan has the same type of steely, dead-eyed charisma as Michael Shannon—an ability to unnerve a viewer in quiet, unique, non-hackneyed ways, coming from the inside out. Is Martin, as the film presents him, a real teenager, a physically manifested and weaponized outgrowth of Steven's guilty conscious, or perhaps some other avatar? There is nothing necessarily supernatural about the movie (at least as rendered on screen), but neither does Lanthimos' framing of the story rule out any of these readings. Keoghan negotiates the hairpin behavioral turns required of his character while retaining the same eerie essence throughout.

At the center of the film, though, are Farrell and Kidman—two stars who do not typically get enough credit for the ongoing adventurousness of their screen choices. Their willingness to submit to Lanthimos' vision, in wholesale fashion, as well as their ability to mine the subtlety and subtext of scenes, is what ultimately gives *The Killing of a Sacred Deer* its woozy lift.

Love or loathe him, there are few filmmakers working today with as distinctive and interesting an imprint as Lanthimos. In piecemeal fashion, from scene to scene, he can conjure the free-floating psychological horror of Roman Polanski, the emotional mercilessness of Lars von Trier or the chilly, almost mathematical technical precision of Stanley Kubrick. And yet his work is also singular and distinctive, open to multiple and wide-ranging interpretations. *The Killing of a Sacred Deer* is not in any way a conventional masterpiece—in fact, it may leave the same viewer wowed after one watch and cold after another, or vice versa. It is, however, unforgettable. And modern independent cinema could use more films like that, and more films from Lanthimos.

Brent Simon

CREDITS

Anna Murphy: Nicole Kidman
Dr. Steven Murphy: Colin Farrell
Martin: Barry Keoghan
Martin's Mother: Alicia Silverstone
Kim Murphy: Raffey Cassidy
Origin: United States
Language: English
Released: 2017
Production: Ed Guiney, Yorgos Lanthimos; Element Pictures, Film 4; released by A24 Films LLC
Directed by: Yorgos Lanthimos
Written by: Yorgos Lanthimos; Efthymis Filippou
Cinematography by: Thimios Bakatakis
Sound: Johnnie Burn
Music Supervisor: Sarah Giles; Nick Payne
Editing: Yorgos Mavropsaridis
Art Direction: Daniel Baker
Costumes: Nancy Steiner
Production Design: Jade Healy
MPAA rating: R
Running time: 120 minutes

REVIEWS

Abrams, Simon. *Slant Magazine*. May 22, 2017.
Burr, Ty. *Boston Globe*. October 26, 2017.
Chang, Justin. *Los Angeles Times*. October 19, 2017.
Lawson, Richard. *Vanity Fair*. May 22, 2017.
McDonald, Moira. *Seattle Times*. October 26, 2017.
O'Sullivan, Michael. *Washington Post*. October 26, 2017.
Phillips, Michael. *Chicago Tribune*. October 26, 2017.
Rooney, David. *Hollywood Reporter*. May 22, 2017.
Wilkinson, Alissa. *Vox*. May 31, 2017.
Wilson, Calvin. *St. Louis Post-Dispatch*. November 9, 2017.

QUOTES

Surgeon: "A surgeon never kills a patient. An anesthesiologist can kill a patient. But a surgeon never can."

TRIVIA

The heart surgery scenes depicted in the film are real. They were filmed during an actual operation on a real patient who was undergoing quadruple bypass surgery.

AWARDS

Nominations:

Ind. Spirit 2018: Actor--Supporting (Keoghan), Cinematog.

KING ARTHUR: LEGEND OF THE SWORD

From myth to legend.
—Movie tagline

Raised on the streets. Born to be king.
—Movie tagline

From nothing comes a King
—Movie tagline

Take back the kingdom.
—Movie tagline

Temptation blackens the heart.
—Movie tagline

From the stone to the throne.
—Movie tagline

Box Office: $39.2 Million

Over the course of *King Arthur: Legend of the Sword*, screenwriters Joby Harold, Guy Ritchie (who also directed), and Lionel Wigram try to reimagine and redefine Arthurian legend multiple times. As a result, there is no consistency to this movie, which alternates between big-budget spectacle, the origin story of a well-known hero, and an intentionally rambling attempt to undercut the previous two modes of storytelling.

Clearly emboldened by his popular and more-or-less effective efforts to modernize and reinterpret another British icon (namely Sherlock Holmes, in the clever, energetic *Sherlock Holmes* [2009] and the lesser *Sherlock Holmes: A Game of Shadows* [2011]), Ritchie has set his sights on another franchise-friendly staple of British lore. The version of King Arthur presented by the director and his fellow screenwriters is a potentially intriguing one for the first 20 minutes or so, until it becomes apparent that the screenplay has no idea whether it wants to embrace the Arthurian myths or to destroy them. The film's idea of a middle ground is to give the audience everything it expects from the Arthur legend—oftentimes without any narrative rationale for those story elements (The Lady of the Lake, for example, twice appears as a parenthetical thought)—and to set those mythical components against a central story that does not need them.

That is the most prevalent confusion of the screenplay, although Ritchie's style does not help matters at all in the more grounded parts of the story. It is obvious that Ritchie wants the tale of Arthur (Charlie Hunnam), an orphan of an unknown, but royal background who becomes a political revolutionary, to possess a degree of realism. The movie's interpretation of that aim is to turn the character into a street-wise thug and thief, raised in a brothel in Londinium, protective of his wards, trained in fighting by a local martial arts master named George (Tom Wu), and stealing money in order to save enough to escape his life.

All of this is, in general, fine enough. Ritchie, though, uses this backdrop—as well as later scenes involving Arthur teaming up with rebels who will later become his Knights of the Round Table—as an excuse for comic sequences, founded on quick editing, unreliable storytelling, and pauses of such length that one could be forgiven for wondering if the actors have forgotten their lines. The jokey nature of these sequences—such as Arthur lying to a king's guard about the robbery of a visiting Viking and a later adventure in a place filled with monsters—is supposed to undercut the grandness of Arthurian legend. Instead, Ritchie and editor James Herbert's hyperactive back-and-forth in time and intent (The fighting and evasion of the monsters is one mode, while the explanation of the place is another) is too jarring to work as comedy or adventure—let alone both.

They also, quite simply, do not fit in the bigger picture of the story, which, despite the screenplay's constant diversions, is more of a mythical mindset than a real one. The prologue—easily the movie's most effective sequence, if only because Ritchie takes an elliptical approach to telling it (The blanks are unnecessarily and repeatedly filled later)—fully embraces myth.

Arthur's father Uther (Eric Bana) is engaged in a war with an evil wizard. (By the way, Merlin is mentioned and briefly seen, although his role is replaced by a woman wizard, played by Astrid Bergès-Frisbey.) The battle at Camelot is gigantic in scale—the wizard has enlisted the aid of enormous elephants—and over-the-top in its approach. Beyond establishing a method and tone with which the movie later fights, the prologue sets up the plot: Uther is betrayed by his brother Vortigern (Jude Law, playing the dastardly villain with admirable but, perhaps, misguided restraint), who makes a murderous deal with an evil presence in a cavern below Camelot, kills his brother, and takes the throne.

Eventually, Arthur pulls the sword Excalibur from the stone, making him a threat to Vortigern. Bedivere (Djimon Hounsou), an Uther loyalist, recruits the outlaw into a band of men who hide in the forest and use guerilla-style tactics to undermine the rule of the usurper. At this point, one begins to wonder whether the screenwriters have mistaken one piece of British folklore for another or if they have run out of ideas about how to alter the established story in any, original way. Surely, the movie's depiction of an Excalibur wielding Arthur, who fights and moves in a way that is reminiscent of a video game (with the camera whipping around the hero as he battles foes at changing speeds), is clearer evidence of that lack of ideas.

The central problem is that Ritchie and the other screenwriters cannot decide which Arthur they want—the mythical one or something different. They cannot even decide what that "something different" should be, so with *King Arthur: Legend of the Sword*, they have made an Arthur story with the superficial trappings of Arthurian legend and a hodgepodge of other, familiar, and repeatedly changing notions of what the character and his story could be.

Mark Dujsik

CREDITS

Arthur: Charlie Hunnam

Vortigern: Jude Law

The Mage: Astrid Berges-Frisbey

Bedivere: Djimon Hounsou

Uther: Eric Bana

Origin: United States

Language: English

Released: 2017

Production: Steve Clark-Hall, Akiva Goldsman, Tory Tunnell, Guy Ritchie, Joby Harold, Lionel Wigram; RatPac-Dune Entertainment, Safehouse Pictures, Village Roadshow Pictures, Weed Road Pictures, Wigram Productions; released by Warner Bros. Pictures

Directed by: Guy Ritchie
Written by: Guy Ritchie; Joby Harold; Lionel Wigram
Cinematography by: John Mathieson
Music by: Daniel Pemberton
Sound: Dominic Gibbs
Music Supervisor: Karen Elliott
Editing: James Herbert
Art Direction: Denis Schnegg
Costumes: Annie Symons
Production Design: Gemma Jackson
MPAA rating: PG-13
Running time: 126 minutes

REVIEWS

Chang, Justin. *Los Angeles Times*. May 11, 2017.
Cole, Jake. *Slant Magazine*. May 10, 2017.
Dargis, Manohla. *New York Times*. May 11, 2017.
Macdonald, Moira. *Seattle Times*. May 10, 2017.
Morgenstern, Joe. *Wall Street Journal*. May 11, 2017.
Phillips, Michael. *Chicago Tribune*. May 9, 2017.
Robinson, Tasha. *Verge*. May 13, 2017.
Seitz, Matt Zoller. *RogerEbert.com*. May 12, 2017.
Vishnevetsky, Ignatiy. *The A.V. Club*. May 9, 2017.
Zacharek, Stephanie. *Time*. May 11, 2017.

QUOTES

King Arthur: "Why have enemies when you can have friends?"

TRIVIA

The film was intended to be the first installment of a six-film series.

KINGSMAN: THE GOLDEN CIRCLE

Reports of my death have been greatly exaggerated.
—Movie tagline

Box Office: $100.2 Million

As nonsensical, big-budget spectacles filled with mindless explosions, incoherent plotting and not even a glancing nod to anything remotely resembling an authentically human feeling or experience go, *Kingsman: The Secret Service* (2014) was about as bad as they come—a nasty, sexist, mean-spirited, and smug wallow through a virtual catalogue of every bad impulse and creatively bankrupt decision that makes up the majority of the jumbo-sized and pea-brained live-action cartoons masquerading as mass entertainment these days. That said, the basic concept of the film—a deliberate throwback to the cheeky style of the James Bond films before they started getting all serious that also included all of the nudity and gore that the Bond films have ritualistically shied away from over the years—has a certain giddy appeal to it. And so there was perhaps hope that, having gotten through all the boring establishing material setting up the concept in the first one, the filmmakers might be able to work out the kinks (deliberate and otherwise) and make it into the cheerfully over-the-top guilty pleasure that it clearly wants to be. Alas, it only takes a few minutes of the extended opening sequence of *Kingsman: The Golden Circle* to realize that not only have things not improved, they have actually deteriorated to heretofore unknown depths and, to make matters worse, it still has more than two bloated hours of running time to go.

For those with enough joy and peace in life to have managed to successfully avoid the first film, the Kingsman are a private British intelligence service whose headquarters are an old-fashioned tailoring shop that is a front for the latest in high-tech gadgetry that allow the Kingsman—all of whom assume the names of the Knights of the Round Table as their secret identities—to fight the forces of evil. That endeavor is made slightly more complicated early on when the organization suffers a surprise attack that destroys their headquarters and kills all of the Kingsman except for Eggsy (Taron Egerton) and technical wizard Merlin (Mark Strong). The two soon find themselves on the way to Kentucky to visit a venerable bourbon distillery that is revealed to be the secret headquarters for their American equivalent, a group called the Statesmen that is led by the venerable Champ (Jeff Bridges)—short for champagne—and includes the likes of Tequila (Channing Tatum), Whiskey (Pedro Pascal), and Ginger Ale (Halle Berry. Also, there is Harry (Colin Firth), Eggsy's presumed dead mentor who is suffering from amnesia and has no recollection of his life as a Kingsman. Together, the two groups attempt to get to the bottom of who would attack the Kingsman and why while at the same time trying to figure out how to bring Harry back completely.

The bad guy in all of this is Poppy (Julianne Moore), a relentlessly cheerful and peppy sort who is also the most powerful, successful, and ruthless drug dealer in the world—the kind who would force one underling to shove another head first into a giant meat grinder and then make and serve him a burger made of that very same meat without ever breaking the gooney grin on her face. (This bit is pretty much stolen in full from the bizarre Michael Ritchie crime film *Prime Cut* [1972].) Unfortunately for her, since her business is illegal, she is forced into seclusion in her remote jungle stronghold, which she has personally designed to resemble the world's largest Ed Debevic's thanks to a fascination with 1950s nostalgia, while plotting a way for her business acumen to be properly celebrated at last. Her master plan is to secretly lace her own drugs with a poison that will soon lead to paralysis and death for the hundreds of millions of users who have unknowingly ingested it. Of course, she also has an antidote that she will happily release as soon as the U.S. President (Bruce Greenwood) signs an executive order legalizing all drugs and thereby legitimizing her business. While those negotiations go on, Eggsy, Merlin, a newly revived Harry (oh, you knew that was coming), and their new Statesmen cohorts race against time to stop Poppy and retrieve the antidote in the nick of time.

Kingsman: The Golden Circle marks the third collaboration, following *Kick-Ass* (2010) and the previous *Kingsman* film, between director Matthew Vaughn, co-writer Jane Goldman, and Mark Millar, the co-creator of the comic books that the two franchises are based on, and if there is mercy in the world for film fans, they will hopefully now break up for good and follow their separate paths because they clearly seem to bring out the worst in each other. As was the case in those previous exercises, they are not concerned with telling a story that makes any amount of sense even by the standards of overtly goofy spy extravaganzas.

Astoundingly, this film required the participation of no fewer than five Oscar winners in key roles that will not be included in any career highlight reels. Then again, with the exception of Mark Strong, who is once again the only element of the film that kind of works, nobody else in the cast makes much of an impression either. As our nominal hero, Egerton is a bore who contributes little more than looking good in impeccably tailored suits while Firth, as his mentor, looks like a guy caught in the throes of a contract loophole forcing him to appear in a film that he does not want to make. Of the American contingent, Bridges only appears in a couple of scenes in what has become his acting default position since winning the Oscar—something resembling a cross between Yosemite Sam and Anthony Hopkins in *Legends of the Fall* (1994) after the stroke—while Tatum's even briefer turn barely rates as a cameo. Berry gets more screen time but has nothing to do while Moore turns in a career-low performance so awful and so utterly miscalculated in every possible way that the mere sight of her will be enough to make viewers flinch after a certain point.

Kingsman: The Golden Circle is a case of cinematic malpractice so thorough that dispirited and exhausted moviegoers will stagger out of it not wanting to see another movie again for a very long time. The only thing more depressing than the fact that something this charmless and ugly could attract so many talented people to sign on is the possibility that it could do well enough with viewers to inspire a third installment.

Peter Sobczynski

CREDITS

Harry Hart: Colin Firth
Poppy: Julianne Moore
Eggsy: Taron Egerton
Merlin: Mark Strong
Ginger: Halle Berry
Himself: Sir Elton John
Tequila: Channing Tatum
Champ: Jeff Bridges
Origin: United States
Language: English, Italian, Swedish
Released: 2017
Production: David Reid, Adam Bohling, Matthew Vaughn; Maru Films, Shangri-La Entertainment, TSG Entertainment; released by Twentieth Century Fox Film Corp.
Directed by: Matthew Vaughn
Written by: Matthew Vaughn; Jane Goldman
Cinematography by: George Richmond
Music by: Henry Jackman; Matthew Margeson
Sound: Matthew Collinge; Danny Sheehan
Music Supervisor: Ian Neil
Editing: Eddie Hamilton
Art Direction: Grant Armstrong
Costumes: Arianne Phillips
Production Design: Darren Gilford
MPAA rating: R
Running time: 141 minutes

REVIEWS

Abele, Robert. *TheWrap*. September 19, 2017.
Catsoulis, Jeanette. *New York Times*. September 20, 2017.
Chang, Justin. *Los Angeles Times*. September 21, 2017.
Cole, Jake. *Slant Magazine*. September 20, 2017.
Davis, Steve. *Austin Chronicle*. September 21, 2017.
DeBruge, Peter. *Variety*. September 18, 2017.
Ebiri, Bilge. *Village Voice*. September 18, 2017.
Kenny, Glenn. *RogerEbert.com*. September 20, 2017.
McCarthy, Todd. *Hollywood Reporter*. September 18, 2017.
Zacharek, Stephanie. *Time*. September 21, 2017.

QUOTES

Elton John: "Now go on and save the world."
Harry Hart: "If I save the world, will you get me two tickets to your next concert?"

Elton John: "Darling, if you save the world, I'll get you a backstage pass."

TRIVIA

The robot dogs, Bennie and Jet, are a reference to Elton John's song "Bennie and the Jets."

KONG: SKULL ISLAND

All hail the king.
—Movie tagline

Box Office: $168.1 Million

The *King Kong* movies are popular works loaded with deeper significance. They capture a mood. The original (1933), by the deft and brilliant Merian C. Cooper and Ernest Schoedsack, achieved instant notoriety with its iconic image of the titular ape majestically astride the Empire State Building. Willis O'Brien performed the legendary stop-action animation, creating visual effects that felt disarming, direct, and terrifying. What was truly liberating was the subtext, the startling Freudian sexuality and social disruption, signified by the pervasive doom of the Depression.

Peter Jackson's visually spectacular and accomplished update in 2005 was overlong, but still conveyed tremendous sweep, daring, and adventure. Jack Black's flamboyant producer was a droll self-portrait of Merian C. Cooper—one of the great figures of American cinema who made very idiosyncratic and distinctive films of his own and became a crucial collaborator on many of the masterpieces of John Ford.

The new iteration, *Kong: Skull Island*, directed by Jordan Vogt-Roberts, shows how completely contemporary movies recycle the myths, stories, and iconography of the past. (You have to get to the very end to understand the movie's complete reason for being.) The hybrid model works simultaneously as "monster movie," adventure tale, serial thriller, and jaundiced critique of American jingoism. Vogt-Roberts capably weaves together the Kong myth with pop art, eco-politics, and movie-mad culture in playing off the demands of the genre (thrills and destruction) sharply interwoven with some offbeat humor and visual flair. Gareth Edwards' *Godzilla* (2014) is the modern template.

Vogt-Roberts appears a counterintuitive choice to direct this kind of movie given his only previous feature, *The Kings of Summer* (2013), about teenage outsiders, was very intimately designed. In the post George Lucas/Steven Spielberg/James Cameron landscape, the contemporary event film is now the province of stunt coordinators, effects specialists, and computer artists. Directors like Vogt-Roberts are sought after to make the disparate pieces work emotionally. Curiously, the parts of this film that seemingly play to the director's strength—character development and dramatic shaping—are its weakest aspects.

The movie opens with a fantastic prologue, "set somewhere over the South Pacific," in 1944, with two fighter pilots forced to crash land on an island outpost after their planes are crippled in mid-air. The American fighter and his Japanese counterpart circle each other like gunfighters in a Western as their duet becomes a tense, hand-to-hand combat contested over a sleek Samurai sword. This tense encounter is interrupted by the appearance of a fantastic and terrifying presence.

The proper story, set in 1973, unfolds on a different battleground of street theater and massive social protest. "Mark my words, there will never be a more screwed up time in Washington," says mysterious operative Bill Randa (John Goodman). Richard Nixon has just delivered his "peace with honor" speech, announcing the withdrawal of American military forces from Vietnam.

With his protégé Houston Brooks (Corey Hawkins), Randa has turned up to solicit financial backing for an expedition to map out a mysterious uncharted atoll considered vital to American security interests. The Western motif is extended in the opening movement as the action shifts to Saigon and Randa assembles his team: Conrad (Tom Hiddleston), a British Special Forces trained tracker; the elite Vietnam helicopter squadron led by Lt. Col. Packard (Samuel L. Jackson); and the beautiful, skilled combat photographer, Mason Weaver (Brie Larson), avid to expose the secrecy of the operation.

The layering of Western and war movie archetypes allows for variations, like the platoon movie, embodied by the bluster and funny camaraderie in the exchanges between the gruff lifer Cole (Shea Whigham) and the more open-eyed Mills (Jason Mitchell). The tightly wound Packard is the movie's Ahab, a warrior with a single-minded pursuit, a quest designed to either purify him or kill him. "We didn't lose the war," he tells the photographer. "We abandoned it."

Joseph Conrad's brilliant short novel, *Heart of Darkness* (1899), has fascinated American filmmakers from Orson Welles to Francis Ford Coppola. Coppola's brilliant and surreal *Apocalypse Now* (1979) transposed Conrad's story to Vietnam. Vogt-Roberts and the three credited writers make the connection explicit by naming two of the characters after its author and narrator. Visually, *Kong: Skull Island* works out detailed riffs on *Apocalypse Now*. It is a dangerous perspective, of course, inviting unfair and unrealistic comparisons to a significant work of art. The strategy pays off in unexpected ways, pointing toward a different way to approach the material, fully acknowledging how the past informs and subverts the familiar.

The first major set piece has the teams of scientists, mission operatives, and military personnel grouped in a helicopter attack formation as they unleash the geological explosives necessary to chart the island. Vogt-Roberts patterns the movement on the remarkable helicopter assault sequence on a Vietnamese village in the Coppola film. Like Godzilla, which materialized from the radioactive fallout of the nuclear payload at Hiroshima, this example of unfiltered American militarism issues its own awakening as an aggrieved and terrified Kong annihilates most of the squadron.

Amid the terrifying noise, confusion, explosions, and carnage, the survivors are scattered throughout the island in smaller teams. Conrad, Mason, and a couple of the airmen make up one improvised attachment separate from another group composed primarily of Packard and Randa. "Monsters exist," Randa admits, staring down the gun Packard points at him. Randa admits he is part of the secret Monarch organization, and reveals the true purpose of the mission was assessing the wider threat.

The movie veers between these different mission objectives, a survival and rescue operation organized by Conrad and Mason in linking up with a resupply team and a revenge quest by Packard. The drama plays off this elemental conflict, sharpened by Vogt-Roberts through visual contrast and colorful humor introduced in the form of Marlow (John C. Reilly), the American pilot first seen in the prologue who is revealed to have been stranded there. He is a cross between the blitzed out photographer of Dennis Hopper and Marlon Brando's rogue colonel Kurtz from *Apocalypse Now*. He is a nativist who has adopted the customs of the indigenous tribe. Kong, he explains, is the protectorate against the malicious Skull Crawlers, a genocidal brand of reptilian creatures. They are truly terrifying beasts, with velociraptor necks and fiendishly elongated tongues who wiped out Kong's ancestral line.

Packard, of course, views Kong as an extension of the North Vietnamese, an implacable and evil force that must be extinguished. Coppola famously said his movie was not about Vietnam, it was Vietnam. The war is now reconceived as a new parable, like Cameron's *Aliens* (1986). There is little depth or characterization in the players, but that seems almost the point. The movie is more about human perseverance against impossible odds. The physical is privileged over the psychological or emotional complicated.

The two leads, Larson and Hiddleston, forsake depth with élan and style, demonstrating a kinetic grace under pressure that holds the larger enterprise together. The ideas and motifs are impressively played out. Conrad wields the Samurai sword in battle against a devilish band of winged creatures, the Pterosaurs. Another emotionally important personal object, Conrad's lighter, plays a crucial strategic importance. Larson is also liberated, sexy, and stylish but also a throwback who asserts her own authority, toughness, and verve in moments of extreme duress. Her beauty and sensuality conjures Fay Wray from the original. In one of loveliest images of the film, after the force of an explosion throws her into the river and her body plunging deeper and deeper, the massive hand of Kong gracefully pulls her to safety.

The human stakes, especially Packard's increasingly hateful pursuit against Kong, are secondary to the more elemental and complex battle staged between Kong and the wrathful Skull crawler. Vogt-Roberts reveals impressive formal command, detailing the fighting characteristic and habits of each creature—Kong's pure strength and power played out against the stealth, slippery tactics of his adversary—that builds to a sharp and telling denouement. Larry Fong's cinematography is crisp and smooth and captures the quickness, tension, and raw power.

This is big, large-scale moviemaking. Vogt-Roberts issues his own personal touches. Sometimes he goes too far, his humor too broad or sentimental, especially with the figure of Marlow. The scale and approach always feels sufficient and appropriate. The coda opens up new possibilities, wonder and surprise. This new incarnation pays telling tribute to the past. Smart and evocative, *Kong: Skull Island* makes its own way and points to thrilling directions going forward.

Patrick Z. McGavin

CREDITS

James Conrad: Tom Hiddleston
Preston Packard: Samuel L. Jackson
Mason Weaver: Brie Larson
Hank Marlow: John C. Reilly
Bill Randa: John Goodman
Origin: United States
Language: English
Released: 2017
Production: Alex Garcia, Jon Jashni, Mary Parent, Thomas Tull; Legendary Entertainment, Tencent Pictures; released by Warner Bros. Entertainment Inc.
Directed by: Jordan Vogt-Roberts
Written by: Dan Gilroy; Max Borenstein; Derek Connolly
Cinematography by: Larry Fong

Music by: Henry Jackman
Sound: Al Nelson; Steve Slanec
Music Supervisor: Peter Afterman; Margaret Yen
Editing: Richard Pearson
Art Direction: Bill Booth; Doug Meerdink
Costumes: Mary E. Vogt
Production Design: Stefan Dechant
MPAA rating: PG-13
Running time: 118 minutes

REVIEWS

Burr, Ty. *Boston Globe*. March 8, 2017.
Dowd, A.A. *The A.V. Club*. March 7, 2017.
Ebiri, Bilge. *Village Voice*. March 2, 2017.
Gleiberman, Owen. *Variety*. March 2, 2017.
Hornaday, Ann. *Washington Post*. March 9, 2017.
McCarthy, Todd. *Hollywood Reporter*. March 2, 2017.
Nicholson, Amy. *MTV News*. March 11, 2017.
Phillips, Michael. *Chicago Tribune*. March 8, 2017.
Rainer, Peter. *Christian Science Monitor*. March 10, 2017.
Zacharek, Stephanie. *Time*. March 9, 2017.

QUOTES

Captain James Conrad: "An uncharted island? Let me list all they ways you gonna die. Rain, heat, mud, disease carrying flies and mosquitoes. Sure you could load up on the Atabrine for the malaria...but what about the other bacteria? And we haven't even started on the things that want to eat you alive."

TRIVIA

Some sets were built at Kualoa Ranch, Hawaii, near the same filming locations used for *Jurassic World* (2015).

AWARDS

Nominations:

Oscars 2017: Visual FX

L

LADY BIRD

Time to fly.
—Movie tagline

Box Office: $42 Million

The stunning directorial debut of the true female heiress of the mumblecore movement, Greta Gerwig, *Lady Bird* works as well as it does because of Gerwig's sophisticated application of the style's strengths into the more polished setting of conventional indie filmmaking. An endearing, self-deprecating writer/actress, Gerwig semi-autobiographically transfers all her past precociousness into the vessel of Lady Bird (Saoirse Ronan), who stars as the rebellious Catholic high schooler at the heart of the coming of age story. Lady Bird is on the cusp of graduation, college, and escape from all the familiarities she feels as cages. Sacramento in the early 2000s is not the sexiest place in the world for a high school senior, which the film makes apparent as it lobs softball after softball at the San Francisco second-stringer, and neither is Lady Bird's socio-economic status.

The meticulous sets capture lower middle-class in the cramped-yet-comfortable way that only seems to embarrass those living in it. They, especially when juxtaposed against the private school and its wealthier attendees, create needless shame and describe the family's life, in which Lady Bird butts heads with her hard-earning mother (Laurie Metcalf). Metcalf brings a salty-sweet tumultuousness that comes inherent when a performance feels like a real person rather than simply lines on the page. Her love is exhausted, revealing the prickles all parents work so hard to conceal, but that keeps her far, far away from the simplicity of melodrama. Her care is not doting and their fights are not abusive. Instead, her actions are hesitant, imperfect, and ultimately well-meaning—but most importantly, they all build out two psychologies (her's and that of her daughter) for the scripting price of one.

Striking only upon later consideration, the efficiency with which the script (also by Gerwig) develops the interpersonal and geosocial relationships in the film is astonishing. Lady Bird's unreliable point of view sees herself as living a second-rate life in a second-rate city. When Sacramento is not the butt of the joke, Catholic school is being held up to the unfair standard of a New York City liberal arts college. Lady Bird perpetrates small rebellions against patient nuns (one played particularly well by Lois Smith) and goes along with the rituals, crushes, and costumes of the life—all while daydreaming of something else. It does not have to be more, but it does have to be different. This is not necessarily escapism, but the stretching and expanding of horizons like someone particularly eager to break out of their chrysalis.

Lady Bird's cocoon is comprised of her dissatisfaction with her overbearing mother's demands, her selection of unpopular friends, her lack of a boyfriend, and her creative unfulfillment. Its familiarity comes honed on the whetstone of detail to cut deeper and leave more impact. These are high school struggles, slight as they may be, that are painted authentically and humorously by Gerwig's deft dialogue and steadily-helming hand.

Each is treated with the abject seriousness one would expect from its teen protagonist and is undercut not by a smarmy pomposity, but by the knowing gaze of the camera (managed by cinematographer Sam Levy) that implies all the loving humor of one who has seen it all before. Love is framed with a low-key fantasy, while its destruction comes in a flurry of messy and cramped spaces and framings—both emulating how one would remember each situation when looking back. The wonders of the world (both Sacramento neighborhoods and New York City are shot with unassuming beauty that is never the focus of scenes, but always present. All of this comes together as a veil lying over the film's reality like a layer of dust. Without showing a calendar, it is unmistakably someone's past, waiting to be reclaimed, as teenagers are notoriously incapable of appreciating things in their own time. Some of this insight comes from Gerwig's directorial style—she gave the crew her old high school yearbooks, photos, and journals, and took them on a tour of her hometown—while some comes from the clever editing of Nick Houy, who never lingers too long to make a joke seem mean or a reaction shot seem overly-judgemental.

Gerwig's influence over her cast helps create the same lived-in effect. Tracy Letts, as Lady Bird's father, gives the light touch of sentimentality and vulnerability to both parts of the parental side of the central family relationship. His career difficulties and soft-spoken mumble mesh perfectly with the sometimes hard-edged Metcalf to create the two distinct sets of psychological ingredients from which Lady Bird's personality springs. She is also formed, tangentially, by her relationship to her best friend and the high school community.

An outsider, as the majority paradoxically defines themselves during that age, she finds the chance for expression in her school theatre program. The needling specificity of the circumstance and its treatment capture the delicate everything-and-nothing of teen life. Lady Bird auditions for a play and falls for the lead (Lucas Hedges). They are in love as quickly as it all falls apart. She wants to lose her virginity and finds the cool, disaffected guy (Timothée Chalamet) who seems perfect until that too ends. Each set-up has the momentum of climax and the denouement of one of life's stumbling blocks—each a reminder of the past importance of events that will only be valued as funny memories.

Lady Bird crashes onto the soul as a wave of memories, soaking its victims in nostalgic bittersweetness without resorting to sepia or over-romanticism. The unrelenting realism is stocked with enough punchlines that it has you laughing until the end, when you realize each guffaw has been a body blow preparing you for the emotional knockout. A perfect mother-daughter date film, *Lady Bird* so thoroughly explores a relationship shared by many that those who have not experienced it still feel pangs of recognition.

Ronan's impressive performance (and her back-and-forth with Metcalf) is one of the year's best and gives an open portrayal of an otherwise often closed-off period in life down to the acne. The relationship between mother and daughter is so often relegated to the criminal or abusive in cinema that the complex give-and-take between the hardworking, sacrificing nag and the ignorant, ungrateful, still-loving teen is a giant step forward in creating resonating, lasting film pairings. That both move towards the finale making mistakes (that the movie assures us matter, but are not irreversible) is indicative of *Lady Bird*'s dedication to optimistic realism and its beautiful insistence that people are just layers of their experiences, containing all the impulses and multitudes implied by their pasts.

Jacob Oller

CREDITS

Christine "Lady Bird" McPherson: Saoirse Ronan
Kyle Scheible: Timothée Chalamet
Jenna Walton: Odeya Rush
Marion McPherson: Laurie Metcalf
Darlene: Kathryn Newton
Origin: United States
Language: English
Released: 2017
Production: Eli Bush, Evelyn O'Neill, Scott Rudin; Entertainment 360, IAC Films, Scott Rudin Productions; released by A24 Films LLC
Directed by: Greta Gerwig
Written by: Greta Gerwig
Cinematography by: Sam Levy
Music by: Jon Brion
Sound: Paul Hsu
Music Supervisor: Michael Hill
Editing: Nick Houy
Costumes: April Napier
Production Design: Chris Jones
MPAA rating: R
Running time: 94 minutes

REVIEWS

Burr, Ty. *Boston Globe*. November 9, 2017.
Dowd, A.A. *The A.V. Club*. September 10, 2017.
Debruge, Peter. *Variety*. September 4, 2017.
Hornaday, Ann. *Washington Post*. November 9, 2017.
Greenblatt, Leah. *Entertainment Weekly*. November 2, 2017.
Kohn, Eric. *IndieWire*. September 5, 2017.
McCarthy, Todd. *Hollywood Reporter*. September 6, 2017.
Scott, A.O. *New York Times*. October 31, 2017.
Wloszczyna, Susan. *RogerEbert.com*. November 9, 2017.
Zarum, Lara. *Village Voice*. October 26, 2017.

QUOTES

Christine McPherson: "I hate California, I want to go to the east coast. I want to go where culture is like, New York, or Connecticut, or New Hampshire."

TRIVIA

This film opened the Special Presentations section at the 2017 Toronto International Film Festival where it received a standing ovation.

AWARDS

Golden Globes 2018: Film--Mus./Comedy, Film--Mus./Comedy (Ronan)

Ind. Spirit 2018: Screenplay

Nominations:

Oscars 2017: Actress (Ronan), Actress--Supporting (Metcalf), Director (Gerwig), Film, Orig. Screenplay

British Acad. 2017: Actress (Ronan), Actress--Supporting (Metcalf), Orig. Screenplay

Directors Guild 2017: Director (Gerwig)

Golden Globes 018: Screenplay

Golden Globes 2018: Actress--Supporting (Metcalf)

Ind. Spirit 2018: Actress (Ronan), Actress--Supporting (Metcalf), Film

Screen Actors Guild 2017: Actress (Ronan), Actress--Supporting (Metcalf), Cast

Writers Guild 2017: Orig. Screenplay

LADY MACBETH

Box Office: $1.1 Million

The character of Lady Macbeth has long fascinated for her malleability as a presence in one of the greatest works of theater ever written. She is considered just left of center and perhaps responsible for the tragedy that befalls the "hero." Is she already mad or is she driven mad by her guilt, and if so, guilt over what? Telling her husband to murder a king, or not doing anything to stop him? These questions have found their way into several parallel works, such as *Lady Macbeth of the Mtsensk District* by Nikolai Leskov, which was in turn adapted into an opera and two films. The latest of these is William Oldroyd's superb and beguiling *Lady Macbeth*, in which screenwriter Alice Birch transposes the action to rural England in the middle of Queen Victoria's reign.

In 1865, young Katherine (Florence Pugh) is married off to Alexander (Paul Hilton), a land owner with a vicious, antisocial demeanor. She tries to find her place in the house and in her husband's life, but he won't touch her, think of her sexually, or include her in his business dealings with other local landlords and merchants. She begins acting out to get his attention and as retribution for his cold, violent treatment of her, earning her further ire from Alexander and his equally nasty father Boris (Christopher Fairbank). When Alexander and Boris both leave on business matters, Katherine gets the run of the estate for a few days without supervision and makes a startling discovery. The housemaid Anna (Naomi Ackie) is being assaulted and chastised by a group of unkempt laborers in her husband's employ. She frees Anna and reprimands the men, but not before sharing an uncertain moment with Sebastian (Cosmo Jarvis), their ringleader.

Days pass and Katherine finds herself fixated on Sebastian, who slowly begins making trips further inside the grounds of the estate and finally into Katherine's bedroom. She so enjoys her new reclamation of her sexual identity that when Boris returns to the house ahead of Alexander, she doesn't feel much like conforming to the old Puritan's definition of a good wife. She so goads him one morning that he has a heart attack and Katherine deliberately waits too long to send Anna to fetch a doctor. It's a short while before Alexander comes home and demands answers, finding Katherine in no more modest a mood than did his father. Katherine's new found freedom seems to be limitless until she runs into one snag too many. After her husband goes "missing," a woman named Agnes (Golda Rosheuvel) arrives with a young boy (Anton Palmer) in tow who she claims was sired by Alexander. Katherine hadn't planned on this, but life without responsibility had been going so well and she doesn't feel it should end so soon just because of a mistake her husband made.

Oldroyd and Birch have some troubling but not inaccurate things to say about class and race that make their version of Lady Macbeth very much a product of the modern zeitgeist. Alexander's dalliance with a black woman and the entire household's taking advantage of the black servant show a white upper class thrashing wildly in the confines of responsibility they have not earned and do not want. Alexander and Boris seem completely unmoved by their position; they simply carry on being the landlords and masters of their house because this is the way of the world. Their treatment of both Anna and Katherine smacks of the perfunctory. Alexander doesn't want to be wed to anyone—he's practically asexual—let alone someone so willful as Katherine. He wants her to be as invisible as the servants, which she refuses to be. But of course the second Katherine discovers power over the men in her life, she takes on all their negative qualities too, namely her taking advantage of the workers and servants of the house. Sebastian is the tool she uses to rediscover her femininity, but he quickly falls right back into his role as a working class cog, whose advice she doesn't seek or want. He loses his agency and becomes her servant, because he believes in the charade that her freedom is the same as hers because they've slept together. And Anna, who silently watches the machinations of the rich whites around her, is punished worst of all for no reason, which is an accurate reflection of the way the wealthiest white powers will always treat a black working class.

The film's craft matches its thematic ambitions as splendidly. The performances are uniformly great, burying worlds of pain under gruff, silent exteriors. Florence Pugh is especially revelatory, using a tiny, sharky smirk to show what little of a broiling rage she can afford to make public. Their mutual repression sparks so much that when major violence happens behind closed doors or during cutaways, it reads like mercy. Watching these characters live with each other is violence enough, let alone when they decide to become physically violent. Oldroyd and photographer Ari Wegner handily capture the majestic but forbidding windswept heaths surrounding the estate where the major action transpires. The landscape's greens and blues (as well as the beautiful costumes by Holly Waddington) are tampered by the eternal rain and gray skies that hover over everything, seemingly keeping the world itself as repressed as the characters themselves. The film, modest in scope and consisting of only a few major characters, communicates how effortlessly hundreds of years of injustice can be passed down through generations. It takes only a few people to see that unfair systems remain in place and the wrong people suffer. The corrupting influence of power and the bone chilling winds around Katherine's home seem eternal, no matter the intentions of those who pass through.

Scout Tafoya

CREDITS

Katherine: Florence Pugh
Sebastian: Cosmo Jarvis
Alexander: Paul Hilton
Anna: Naomi Ackie
Boris: Christopher Fairbank
Origin: United States
Language: English
Released: 2017
Production: Fodhla Cronin O'Reilly; BBC Films, British Film Institute, Creative England, Sixty Six Pictures, iFeatures; released by Roadside Attractions
Directed by: William Oldroyd
Written by: Alice Birch
Cinematography by: Ari Wegner
Music by: Dan Jones
Editing: Nick Emerson
Art Direction: Thalia Ecclestone
Costumes: Holly Waddington
Production Design: Jacqueline Abrahams
MPAA rating: R
Running time: 89 minutes

REVIEWS

Burr, Ty. *Boston Globe*. July 19, 2017.
Clarke, Cath. *Time Out London*. April 25, 2017.
Dargis, Manohla. *New York Times*. July 13, 2017.
Lodge, Guy. *Variety*. September 9, 2016.
Phillips, Michael. *Chicago Tribune*. July 20 2017.
Puig, Claudia. *TheWrap*. July 13, 2017.
Rife, Katie. *The A.V. Club*. July 12, 2017.
Robey, Tim. *The Telegraph*. April 29, 2017.
Turan, Kenneth. *Los Angeles Times*. July 13, 2017.
Warren, Bradley. *The Playlist*. September 17, 2017.

TRIVIA

Only three musical passages are feature in the score of this film.

AWARDS

Nominations:

Ind. Spirit 2018: Foreign Film

LANDLINE

1995. When people were harder to reach.
—Movie tagline

Box Office: $940,854

After successfully tackling the comedy and drama within a comedian getting an abortion in *Obvious Child* (2014), noteworthy filmmaker Gillian Robespierre ventures to the dysfunctional New York City family dramedy with her sophomore project, *Landline*. The film is often at odds with the many similar productions that have come before it, taking on narrative interests akin to directors like Noah Baumbach or Lynn Shelton, but Robespierre is able to let a unique empathy shine when articulating characters who would be cast out in a world that treated subjects, such as monogamy, as black-and-white matters.

With credit to Robespierre and her collaborator Elisabeth Holm (of whom they both worked on the story with Tom Bean), *Landline* does not provide a typical image of a dysfunctional family. For one, the quartet is shown to have the ability to communicate with each other, through openly dark humor and sarcasm at the dinner table, with no one left out. Second, the story follows two sisters (as opposed to the usual brothers), Jenny Slate's anxious Dana and Abby Quinn's angsty Ali, as they take what they have learned from their parents (John Turturro's laid-back Alan and Edie Falco's comparably more uptight wife/mother Pat) into how they treat others.

Landline captures this quartet, of which one can imagine have had many great previous bonding experiences razing each other, in a state of crisis. Ali is going through a relatively common coming-of-age arc, in which she discovers sex with a friend named Jed (Marquis Rodriguez), but also dips into the dangerous world of casually using drugs like heroin and sneaking out at night. Meanwhile, in the middle of a five-year relationship with the possibly too-dopey Ben (Jay Duplass), Slate's character begins a tryst with a college friend named Nate (Finn Wittrock). This is mirrored by the uncertain actions of wannabe playwright Alan, who is discovered by Ali to have written lustful poems on the family computer, and not for their mother. When Dana moves back home, where Pat deals with her own uncertainties in age (she is gravely underdeveloped), the two sisters seek to spy on Alan in the city, which makes for a lightly amusing scene of amateur espionage.

But as the storyline with Alan and his affair unfolds, this becomes a story with more on its mind than comedy, or a twist about who the father could be sleeping with, or if Ben will find out that Dana has been cheating on him. Playing out better with its dramatic scenes of these curious but unflashy New Yorkers confronting each other, *Landline* is about these people openly addressing the pain they create for themselves, and coming to terms with the ideas of choosing one person, even when matters of the heart have more in mind. This storytelling interest makes for a handful of scenes that push *Landline* beyond its ordinary impulses, while setting up the likes of Slate and Turturro to have effective, climactic acting moments that are as strong as they are natural.

There is an experimental air to *Landline* that keeps it lively, even when the story drags without enough stakes. For one, the script works with the limits of empathy towards its selfish characters, whether in their actions towards loved ones (as in the case of Dana and Alan's mirroring infidelities) or in how Ali acts with others. Like the most interesting of stories about monogamy, *Landline* wisely believes selfish acts do not simplify a human being.

The other lively quality to the film is its 1990s setting, which does not entirely have a sense of purpose, but it does provide the story some edge along with a distinct visual trait given its sitcom-like atmosphere. Leaning on the reference within its specific title, the film takes place in a time before messages were able to be read on personal phones, via text. Some modern movies avoid the fact of texting in order to have characters talk face to face, and *Landline* seems to use its era as an explanation for so many of its heart-to-hearts.

Thankfully, Robespierre does not lean too much on the specific decade decision, especially regarding sight and sound. The production design by Kelly McGehee covers Ali's bedroom walls with a welcoming museum of 1990s alternative rock, and a scene with her investigating a boxy Macintosh computer creates a tinge of nostalgia. But Robespierre avoids the obvious soundtrack cues or overly tacky slang nudges to the era, even extending that lack of over sentimentality to using a contemporary song by Angel Olsen for the third act montage where everyone ponders what they have wrought. "All my life I thought I'd change," Olsen sings. It is biting food for thought that works for this pondering film and its inhabitants, regardless of the era.

Nick Allen

CREDITS

Dana: Jenny Slate
Pat: Edie Falco
Ali: Abby Quinn
Alan: John Turturro
Ben: Jay Duplass
Origin: United States
Language: English
Released: 2017
Production: Russell Levine, Gigi Pritzker, Elisabeth Holm; OddLot Entertainment, Route One Entertainment; released by Magnolia Pictures
Directed by: Gillian Robespierre
Written by: Gillian Robespierre; Elisabeth Holm
Cinematography by: Chris Teague
Music by: Chris Bordeaux; Jordan Cohen; Clyde Lawrence
Sound: Damian Volpe
Music Supervisor: Linda Cohen
Editing: Casey Brooks
Art Direction: Gonzalo Cordoba
Costumes: Elisabeth Vastola
Production Design: Kelly McGehee
MPAA rating: R
Running time: 97 minutes

REVIEWS

Brody, Richard. *New Yorker*. July 24, 2017.

Burr, Ty. *Boston Globe*. July 27, 2017.
Chang, Justin. *Los Angeles Times*. January 21, 2017.
Hornaday, Ann. *Washington Post*. July 27, 2017.
Linden, Sheri. *Los Angeles Times*. July 20, 2017.
MacAron, Alexandra. *Women's Voices for Change*. December 1, 2017.
Scott, A.O. *New York Times*. July 20, 2017.
Walsh, Katie. *Tribune News Service*. August 11, 2017.
Yoshida, Emily. *New York Magazine/Vulture*. July 21, 2017.
Zacharek, Stephanie. *Time*. July 20, 2017.

QUOTES

Jed: "You wanna get high and watch *Zelig*?"

TRIVIA

For the look of the characters' outfits, costume designer Liz Vastola took inspiration from the television show *Seinfeld* to achieve an accurate depiction of 1990s fashion.

LAST FLAG FLYING

Their last mission wasn't on the battlefield.
—Movie tagline

Box Office: $965,481

To call Richard Linklater's *Last Flag Flying* a sequel to the Hal Ashby favorite *The Last Detail* (1973) is not entirely accurate. Linklater's film is based on a 2005 novel by Darryl Ponicsan (who shares screenplay credit with Linklater) that was a direct sequel to his 1970 book that inspired Ashby's celebrated screen version three years later. However, the film does not share the exact same characters as those played so indelibly in the earlier film by Jack Nicholson, Otis Young, and Randy Quaid, nor does it quite continue its specific storyline. However, much in the manner of *Everybody Wants Some!!* (2016), Linklater's so-called "spiritual sequel" to his own cult classic *Dazed and Confused* (1993), it does share any number of thematic and emotional concerns that unite it with its predecessor while still working as its own separate entity. The end result is a quietly powerful drama (though one not without moments of humor here and there) that takes an understated, effective approach to its material.

Set in 2003 during the early years of America's wars in Iraq and Afghanistan, the film opens with a man quietly entering a dive in Virginia and sitting down at the bar practically unnoticed. This is Larry "Doc" Shepherd (Steve Carell) and it soon transpires that the bar is run, for lack of a better term, by Sal Nealon (Bryan Cranston), who served with Doc in the Marines during Vietnam. After talking over old times, the two decide to go and look up another guy from their unit, Richard Mueller (Laurence Fishburne), and are surprised to discover that the one-time hell-raiser has turned his life around and is now married and working as a pastor at his local church. That is not the only surprise in store as Doc now reveals the real reason why he has brought the three of them together again after so many years. His only son, Larry, has been killed serving in Iraq, and, with no one else in his life—his wife having recently passed away as well—he would like the other two to accompany him up to Washington, D.C. to meet Larry's body when it arrives at Dover Air Force base, and bring him to his eventual burial at Arlington National Cemetery. Sal is all in, and, after some initial reluctance, Mueller agrees to go as well. The three set off on their trip while uneasily trying to come to terms with the ways in which each other has changed—or not changed, in Sal's case—since they were last together.

When they arrive at Dover, Doc insists on seeing Larry's body and while he is doing that, Sal and Mueller talk with Larry's friend and fellow soldier, Charlie (J. Quinton Johnson), who was there when Larry was killed and reveals to them that the circumstances surrounding his death were far from the heroic narrative being spun by military brass. Sal insists that Doc, now reeling from the sight of his son's remains, be made aware of the truth and as a result of all this, Doc decides against the burial at Arlington—he now insists on taking Larry's body himself back to his hometown of Portsmouth, New Hampshire to be buried next to his mother instead. The military finally agrees to this but insists that Charlie goes along with them in order to keep tabs on what is happening. As they head to New Hampshire, with detours along the way in New York City and Boston, the three now-united friends find themselves trying to come to terms with a shared dark-secret regarding their own military service while at the same time preparing for Larry's funeral.

On paper, the notion of trying to do a follow-up, straightforward or otherwise, to something like *The Last Detail* seems dubious at best. That was one of those rare films in which all the right elements—the cast, the director, and the dramatically potent and hilariously profane screenplay by Robert Towne—aligned beautifully in ways that defied conventional wisdom. It didn't really contain much in the way of an elaborately detailed narrative structure, but the end result nevertheless said far more about the subjects of duty, patriotism, and personal ideals than most films that tackled those subjects overtly. By comparison, *Last Flag Flying* has a narrative that feels far more structured than its predecessor with the various twists and turns in the journey taken by Doc, Sal, and Mueller sometimes taking on a preordained feel, ranging from the back and forth between Sal and Mueller about the respective paths that their lives have taken to the parallels that eventually arise between the way that the military lied about Larry's death and a Vietnam-era incident in which a dying comrade suffered needlessly because the three squandered Doc's supply of morphine on themselves—an incident that landed Doc in the brig for a couple of years while the others got off. In lesser hands, this could have all resulted in a perfectly adequate but ultimately forgettable work that would have been remembered primarily for its connection with the earlier film.

Linklater is most certainly not "lesser hands," however, and his efforts help the material transcend the potential limitations of the premise through his typically solid and idiosyncratic filmmaking style. Some moments in the first section of the story are a bit heavy-handed and there is the sense that Linklater is struggling to find a balance between the necessities of the narrative and the byplay between the three central characters as they have their emotionally fraught reunion that he is clearly more interested in observing. As the film goes on, however, he eventually finds a groove that suggests what Ashby accomplished decades earlier without slavishly copying it. He does an excellent job of subtly reminding viewers of where America was at in 2003, from the need to see the death of every soldier as an act of glorious heroism instead of an anguishing waste to the jitters amongst the population that, in one of the funniest bits, land Sal and Mueller in hot water with the Department of Homeland Security when they attempt to rent a U-Haul van to transport Larry's body. As for the more overtly heart-rending moments, Linklater takes a more restrained approach in ways that connect with viewers far more successfully than the expected histrionics. Take the scene in which the guys go to visit the aging mother (Cicely Tyson) of the comrade whose death they feel partly responsible for—instead of milking it for melodrama, he stages it in a quieter and more realistic manner that only makes it all the more devastating. Hell, even though this marks his first true stab at the hallowed "road movie" genre, Linklater refuses to play by the expected rules—the conveyances are not especially fancy, the landscape is uninspired and the weather is always grey and rainy.

As for the performances, they are generally strong, though a bit of a mixed bag at times. The weakest of the bunch is delivered by Cranston, who is more or less playing the character essayed by Jack Nicholson in *The Last Detail* and who at times seems to be delivering an overly self-conscious Nicholson impression in lieu of a performance. To be fair, he gets better as the film progresses, but it is the closest that the film comes to a jarringly off-key note. Fishburne is stuck with the least developed of the three characters (despite having presumably gone through the most changes of the trio) but his strong and sturdy presence helps to counterbalance Cranston during his occasional drifts into histrionics—it is easy to believe in both his currently enlightened and faith-based view of the world and in the wild past that he seems to be constantly repenting for in one way or another. The best performance—the best thing in the film itself next to Linklater's direction—is the one contributed by Carell as Doc. Although still primarily known as a comedic actor, Carell has demonstrated his considerable dramatic chops as well in his performances in such films as *Little Miss Sunshine* (2006), *Foxcatcher* (2014), and *Battle of the Sexes* (2017). But nothing that he has done so far along those line comes close to touching his work here. His Doc is a portrait of quiet devastation—a man who has invested his entire life in the Marines and the ideals that they espouse and who has been left with nothing as a result. As he tries to grapple with his conflicted feelings towards the military and what it means to him, it is impossible not to feel for Doc thanks to Carell's keenly nuanced turn leading to a climactic moment involving the reading of a letter that might have inspired eye rolls from other actors but which proves to be both utterly devastating and strangely cathartic here.

Last Flag Flying may not have the one-of-a-kind feel of some of Linklater's more unique projects, such as the *Before Sunrise* trilogy (1995-2013) and *Boyhood* (2014) and its stubborn determination to play things emotionally close to the bone instead of inflating situations for a more crowd-pleasing dramatic effect may be a turn-off for audiences that increasingly require that their films tell them exactly what they should be thinking and feeling at any given moment. And yet, this is a beautifully made and undeniably effective work that explores the enduring legacies of America's involvement in Vietnam and Iraq and how they continue to affect those touched by them decades after the fact in ways both large and small. Whether one looks at it as a continuation of *The Last Detail* or as its own separate thing, this is a film to treasure.

Peter Sobczynski

CREDITS

Sal Nealon: Bryan Cranston
Reverend Richard Mueller: Laurence Fishburne
Larry "Doc" Shepherd: Steve Carell
Washington: J. Quinton Johnson
Ruth: Deanna Reed-Foster
Origin: United States
Language: English
Released: 2017

Production: Ginger Sledge, John Sloss, Richard Linklater; Big Indie Pictures, Cinetic Media L.L.C., Detour Filmproduction, Lionsgate; released by Amazon Studios
Directed by: Richard Linklater
Written by: Richard Linklater; Darryl Ponicsan
Cinematography by: Shane F. Kelly
Music by: Graham Reynolds
Sound: Tom Hammond
Editing: Sandra Adair
Art Direction: Gregory A. Weimerskirch
Costumes: Kari Perkins
Production Design: Bruce Curtis
MPAA rating: R
Running time: 125 minutes

REVIEWS

Chang, Justin. *Los Angeles Times*. November 2, 2017.
Ebiri, Bilge. *Village Voice*. October 31, 2017.
Edelstein, David. *New York Magazine/Vulture*. September 28, 2017.
Gleiberman, Owen. *Variety*. September 28, 2017.
Lane, Anthony. *New Yorker*. October 30, 2017.
Morgenstern, Joe. *Wall Street Journal*. November 2, 2017.
Reed, Rex. *New York Observer*. November 6, 2017.
Rooney, David. *Hollywood Reporter*. September 29, 2017.
Scott, A.O. *New York Times*. November 2, 2017.
Stevens, Dana. *Slate*. September 28, 2017.

QUOTES

Larry "Doc" Shepherd: "I'm not going to bury a marine. I'm just going to bury my son."

TRIVIA

The film is a spiritual sequel to *The Last Detail* (1973) and was filmed around Pittsburgh, Pennsylvania.

THE LAST WORD

An unexpected friendship that begins at the end
—Movie tagline

Box Office: $1.8 Million

As many of Hollywood's greatest stars begin to fade, so do they find themselves in fictional vehicles where their lead presence alone is meant to be worth the price of admission. This has been the case with the likes of the Lily Tomlin project *Grandma* (2015), Sam Elliott's *The Hero* (2017), and now, *The Last Word*, a weepy indie that celebrates Shirley MacLaine as a type of superhero. In this movie, she gets to do it all: cuss a lot, blow the minds of various young people, befriend a token African-American girl, and leave such an impression that her character's inevitable funeral is a crowd-pleasing moment itself. MacLaine's performance only becomes significant because it is the work of the legendary Shirley MacLaine.

Scripted by Stuart Ross Fink, the story concerns the life of Harriet Laurer (MacLaine), who feels the rattle of death's door, and starts to march towards it when she tries to kill herself. When that fails in an opening sequence that instills a true sense of loneliness, Harriet realizes that she must ensure her legacy as a person, even though it is hammered into viewers' heads that she has isolated her family and friends by her own volition. In an inspired twist on the idea of trying to change one's story, Harriet enlists the help of a young obituary writer named Anne (Amanda Seyfried, a game presence). An old soul, Anne takes on the task of researching Harriet's life and trying to construct a piece that will make Harriet look good, which most of all serves for exposition with actors like Philip Baker Hall (playing Harriet's ex-husband) painting a picture of Harriet's antagonism.

From here, the story takes on storylines of flashiness and very low stakes, but which are engineered to make MacLaine look cool by questionable standards. In one strand, a joke about Harriet creating some impact on the future generation by interacting with at-risk youth becomes a giant red flag, when this self-aware cliché then leads to a stereotype, with the token usage of a young African American girl named Brenda (AnnJewel Lee Dixon). As sweet as her presence is, in spite of the preciously flat line-readings, Brenda becomes a definitive token as a sidekick to Harriet, an attribute that corrodes the light-hearted intentions of the movie. Brenda is not afforded a background, instead she is grotesquely cosmetic.

Along with these two stories, Harriet is also shown entering back into the world, namely through realizing her dream as a disc jockey. This is the type of stubbornly out-of-fashion screenplay that features a young character like Seyfried's exclaiming how much she loves a certain radio station, so naturally it leads to Harriet lugging her vinyls and talking her way into a spot in the morning. As the radio station manager Robin Sands (Thomas Sadoski) looks on dumbfounded, she proclaims that her ear listening to decades of radio and song sequencing guarantees that she would be a good fit for the job. This leads to a montage of Harriet running the DJ booth like it were old hat, one of the more glaring conceits in the movie and not as much fun as Pellington's flighty montage (replete with Brenda and Harriet smiling and dancing) makes it out to be.

And yet, there is more. The missing piece to Anne's story about Harriet is Harriet's estranged daughter,

Elizabeth, who lives just a road trip and a bonding sequence away, according to the logic of this story. Emotional stakes still fail to arise in the process.

There is an almost admirable quality to the amount of crowd-pleasing clichés that Fink's script uses like a checklist. It's not enough that it has a wise, curmudgeonly older person showing a young one the ways, it has to feature a road trip, and even a sassy sidekick who errs on the side of racist screenwriting, in spite of whatever lighthearted intentions. For good measure, the media of the movie also concerns relics: records, radio stations, and newspapers that hire obituary writers seemingly fresh out of journalism school. All of it is brandished like the McDonald's product placement during the aforementioned road trip, in which the golden arches logo is treated with the defining tact of being recognized by the audience and nothing else.

The proceedings receive some nice dressing with the cinematography of Eric Koretz, who often uses framing as a type of way to make standard moments, or shots, more expressive than what is on the page. It does not change the vacuousness of the story, but it does provide a context of some artistry, even as Pellington hits every beat right on time, and takes a for-hire approach to a tale that wants to be all-inspiring and loved.

In the scheme of movies that look like *The Last Word* there have been worse. It is sad, though, that a story would settle on such standards, especially with the talents of MacLaine and Seyfried involved. Both of them have more to say than this movie's limited emotional vocabulary.

Nick Allen

CREDITS

Harriet Lauler: Shirley MacLaine
Anne Sherman: Amanda Seyfried
Brenda: AnnJewel Lee Dixon
Robin Sands: Thomas Sadoski
Edward: Philip Baker Hall
Origin: United States
Language: English
Released: 2017
Production: Kirk D'Amico, Anne-Marie Mackay, Mark Pellington; Franklin Street, Myriad Pictures, Parkside Pictures, Wondros; released by Bleecker Street Media
Directed by: Mark Pellington
Written by: Stuart Ross Fink
Cinematography by: Eric Koretz
Music by: Nathan Matthew David
Sound: Stanley Kastner
Editing: Julia Wong
Art Direction: Douglas Cumming
Costumes: Alix Hester
Production Design: Richard Hoover
MPAA rating: R
Running time: 108 minutes

REVIEWS

Abele, Robert. *Los Angeles Times*. March 2, 2017.
Dargis, Manohla. *New York Times*. March 2, 2017.
Duralde, Alonso. *TheWrap*. March 2, 2017.
Howell, Peter. *Toronto Star*. March 10, 2017.
Jones. J.R. *Chicago Reader*. March 9, 2017.
Keough, Peter. *Boston Globe*. March 9, 2017.
Lapin, Andrew. *NPR*. March 2, 2017.
Roeper, Richard. *Chicago Sun-Times*. March 9, 2017.
Vishnevetsky, Ignatiy. *The A.V. Club*. March 7, 2017.
Wolfe, April. *L.A. Weekly*. March 2, 2017.

QUOTES

Anne: "She puts the bitch in obituary."

TRIVIA

Veteran British actress Millicent Martin enjoys a quick cameo as Margaret Dumont, which was more than likely a tribute to the legendary character actress with whom MacLaine appeared in *What a Way to Go!* (1964).

LBJ

Box Office: $2.5 Million

Director Rob Reiner is responsible for a truly great film about the American presidency—*The American President* (1995). It's a wonderful piece of optimistic pop-patriotism with fantastic performances and a whip-smart script by Aaron Sorkin. Unfortunately, Reiner is also responsible for another film about another American President, *LBJ,* that fails to find any life or insight in one of the most tumultuous times in modern American history. *LBJ* definitely doesn't have the scale of Reiner's past political films—*A Few Good Men* (1992), *The American President*, or *The Ghosts of Mississippi* (1996)—but the problem with *LBJ* does not have anything to do with its budget. The problem is that the film does not really have anything to say.

It's hard not to place the lion's share of the blame on the uninspired screenplay by Joey Hartstone. The true story of Lyndon Baines Johnson's rise to the office of President has enough real-life drama that, in theory, it seems like an easy choice for a stirring political biopic. (Jay Roach's HBO adaptation of Robert Schenkkan play

All the Way [2016] presented a much more compelling portrait of LBJ.) However, every choice that Hartstone and Reiner make in *LBJ* seems to limit Johnson's story in unfortunate ways. They not only focus on an exceedingly narrow aspect of Johnson's overall life, but they also offer few insights on the slice of life they have chosen to highlight.

The narrative of Reiner's *LBJ* revolves around Johnson's run for the Democratic nomination for the 1960 U.S. Presidental election, his losing the nomination to the young upstart John F. Kennedy, and his reluctant acceptance of the role of Kennedy's Vice President. The film opens with a book-ending sequence, set in Dallas on that fateful day in 1963, letting the audience know that the film will also detail how Johnson dealt with Kennedy's eventual assassination. While that timeline has some fertile historical moments to mine for a narrative, Reiner's film feels surprisingly light on drama.

The blame for that rests largely on Hartstone's inch-deep, pop psychology analysis of Johnson's motivations. It has to be said that the strongest aspect of Reiner's *LBJ* is the cast. Woody Harrelson's performance is ornery, passionate, and full of enough charm that you can understand why Johnson could be elected president, even though the script keeps stressing how boring he is compared to Kennedy. Jennifer Jason Leigh brings an equal level of energy to her performance as Lady Bird Johnson, but, unfortunately, Reiner makes the misguided decision to bury his two leads under a metric ton of prosthetics.

It's understandable that a director would want the actors in his historical biopic to resemble the real-life people they're playing—and Harrelson does not have the natural resemblance to Johnson that *All the Way*'s Bryan Cranston had—but the make-up department simply went too far with their designs for LBJ and Lady Bird. Why would you hire two talents like Harrelson and Leigh and cover the most expressive parts of their bodies with ten pounds of latex? The make-up choices don't sell the illusion that we're really watching the president and his wife—instead, they distract from the admirable performances that both actors are delivering.

Richard Jenkins also deserves particular praise for his fortunately prosthetic-free performance as Senator Richard Russell, Johnson's early Southern ally, who later turns on him for supporting Kennedy's more progressive policies. Jenkins is the closest thing the movie has to a villain, and he brings a wonderful sense of menace as the film's representation of America's anti-civil-rights movement.

The big issue with *LBJ* is that the movie takes these impressive actors and historical circumstances and uses them to tell a story about Lyndon Johnson that feels as reductive as an elementary school biography. Throughout the movie, the script only makes two real claims about Johnson's character—that Johnson was a workhorse who could get things done and that Johnson could never understand why the American people didn't love him. The entire narrative is based around those two fortune-cookie-level insights, and it repeats them over and over and over again.

Reiner presents scene after scene of Johnson rolling up his sleeves and making calls—contrasted against the apparently all-flash Kennedy—and Johnson sitting sadly by himself, while Lady Bird wonders, "Why don't they love him?" It's an insultingly shallow depiction of such complex individuals, and the film constantly goes back to that dried-up psychological well rather than contextualizing Johnson's career or the time period in any real way. When Johnson finally becomes President, his embrace of civil rights legislation seemingly comes from out of nowhere. Reiner never takes the time to establish why Johnson would take up an initiative supported by Kennedy. Instead, the screenwriter just shoehorns in a scene where Johnson out-of-the-blue tells a story about his African-American cook to explain why he's suddenly rejecting Senator Russell's demands for him to drop any civil rights bills.

That moment isn't earned, and it blatantly paints Johnson as a civil rights hero without showing how he eventually got there. *LBJ* ends on that note—the idea that Johnson is an idealistic hero—without addressing any of the controversies of his own presidency, including Vietnam and the long and dangerous path to the actual Civil Rights Act of 1964. *The American President* also sold us a narrative about a romanticized president as a hero, but that was acceptable because it was fiction. In *LBJ*, Rob Reiner takes a true story that's more complex and interesting than any political fiction ever could be and distills it down into a bland, uninspired, and emotionally untrue American fable. LBJ, despite all of his flaws, deserved better.

Tom Burns

CREDITS

Lyndon B. Johnson: Woody Harrelson
Lady Bird Johnson: Jennifer Jason Leigh
Walter Jenkins: C. Thomas Howell
Ralph Yarborough: Bill Pullman
John F. Kennedy: Jeffrey Donovan
Origin: United States
Language: English
Released: 2017

Production: Matthew George, Liz Glotzer, Tim White, Trevor White, Michael R. Williams, Rob Reiner; Acacia Filmed Entertainment, Castle Rock Entertainment Inc., Parkside Pictures, Savvy Media Holdings, Star Thrower Entertainment; released by Electric Entertainment

Directed by: Rob Reiner

Written by: Joey Hartstone

Cinematography by: Barry Markowitz

Music by: Marc Shaiman

Sound: Lon Bender

Editing: Bob Joyce

Art Direction: Jaymes Hinkle

Costumes: Dan Moore

Production Design: Christopher R. DeMuri

MPAA rating: R

Running time: 98 minutes

REVIEWS

Cheshire, Godfrey. *RogerEbert.com*. November 3, 2017.
Dargis, Manohla. *New York Times*. November 2, 2017.
Goody, Bill. *Arizona Republic*. November 2, 2017.
LaSalle, Mick. *San Francisco Chronicle*. November 2, 2017.
Phillips, Michael. *Chicago Tribune*. November 2, 2017.
Rechtshaffen, Michael. *Los Angeles Times*. November 2, 2017.
Reed, Rex. *Observer*. November 7, 2017.
Roeper, Richard. *Chicago Sun-Times*. November 2, 2017.
Stewart, Sara. *New York Post*. November 3, 2017.
Vishnevetsky, Ignatiy. *The A.V. Club*. November 2, 2017.

QUOTES

Lyndon B. Johnson: "Power is where power goes."

TRIVIA

In an interview with Jimmy Kimmel, Woody Harrelson said he called Bryan Cranston and asked for advice for the role, Bryan Cranston was also shooting his own LBJ movie All the Way (2016) at around the same time. And Cranston did help him by giving advice and putting Harrelson in touch with people who knew LBJ.

LEAP!

(Ballerina)

Never give up on your dreams.
—Movie tagline

Box Office: $24.7 Million

On the surface, at least, *Leap!* (2017) would seem to offer viewers something slightly different—it tells a relatively straightforward story about people with no talking animals or elaborate musical numbers to be had and the late-19th century Paris setting is certainly unique. Unfortunately, these promising details are undone by a storyline that is as derivative as can be and the boneheaded decision to paper the soundtrack with a number of chirpy pop anthems that have been crassly included in the presumed hopes of scoring a soundtrack deal despite not fitting at all with the material at hand.

Stuck in an orphanage is Britanny, young Felicie (Elle Fanning) who yearns to one day make it to Paris to pursue her dream of becoming a famous dancer with the Paris Opera Ballet. Along with best friend Victor (Nat Wolff), she finally escapes the orphanage and the two soon make it to the City of Lights. Once there, she is taken in by washerwoman Odette (Carly Rae Jepsen) and helps her with the cleaning of the lavish house belonging to the rich and loathsome Regine (Kate McKinnon) and her horrible and wildly-spoiled daughter Camille (Maddie Ziegler). After being humiliated by Camille, Felicie acquires a letter to her informing her of her admittance to study with the Paris Opera Ballet and impulsively decides to go there herself while pretending to be Camille.

The problem, of course, is that Felicie has no actual ballet training to speak of, a fact that is apparent to company director Merante (Terrence Scammell) and when he announces that there will be a series of elimination auditions with the last dancer standing getting the role of Clara in the ballet's upcoming production of *The Nutcracker*, he all but announces that Felicie will be the first to go. However, through a combination of dumb luck and aggressive training under the tutelage of Odette, who herself was a great dancer whose promising career was squelched by an injury that left her lame, Felicie begins to improve enough that it appears that she might win the role and achieve her dream after all. Of course, it is at just that moment that Regine and Camille discover the deception and all seems lost for her, though this occurs at a point where there is still enough time on the clock for everything to still break Felicie's way after all.

Not surprisingly, the story devised by Carol Noble, Laurent Zeitoun, and Eric Summer (the latter also serving as co-director with Eric Warin) does not exactly break new ground in any way—it is the typical underdog narrative with plenty of montages and inspirational talk about "Being Yourself" and "Sticking to Your Dreams" and dotted with a few references to classic dance films of the past such as *The Red Shoes* (1948) and *Flashdance* (1983). (Although presumably unintentional, the climax in which old crone Regine tries to violently eliminate Felicie with a wrench and a sledgehammer seems to take its cue from such darker examples of the genre as *Suspiria* (1977) and *Black Swan* (2010).) The visual style of the film, on the other hand, is far more interesting—

although the character designs are fairly undistinguished, the film does a nice job of evoking 1880s-era Paris, complete with the half-finished Eiffel Tower looming over everything and a final chase through the scaffolding surrounding the under-construction Statue of Liberty. Admittedly, the film could have pushed this aspect a little further—it doesn't really explore any of its settings other than the opera house—but it does help to distinguish it from most recent animated features.

Where the film fails—brutally—is in its strange unwillingness to commit to the time period that is the one aspect that really distinguishes it from other animated features. Some of the anachronisms—such as the decidedly modern outfit that Felicie wears throughout—are minor enough that they can be ignored or forgiven. However, the musical cues are so bizarre that they cannot help but prove distracting. Considering the time period and the focus of the story, one might naturally expect to hear classical music on the soundtrack. Apparently, that was deemed to be too alienating for the kids and the soundtrack is instead dominated by pop anthems from the likes of Jepsen, Sia, and Demi Lovato; and, while those songs are perfectly adequate examples of contemporary pop music, they obviously do not fit the milieu. Some of this could have been forgiven as a necessary marketing move, but it becomes truly ridiculous at the finale when Felicie achieves her dream of dancing in *The Nutcracker*. But the music is yet another anthem. Considering that the target audience for this film is presumably young ballet fans, would it have been so bad to throw on a few bits of Tchaikovsky and save Carly or Demi or whoever for the end credits?

Although admittedly better than the genuinely loathsome likes of *The Emoji Movie* (2017), *Leap!* is just a big "meh" of a movie—the kind of middling effort that will distract children for 90 minutes without ever coming close to exciting or enthralling them. Clearly some effort went into trying to make the film more palatable for American audiences—Wolff actually re-recorded the Victor part (originally played by Dane DeHaan) for the domestic market and the contributions from McKinnon and Mel Brooks were made late in the game as well—but without a compelling central story to work from, it was all for naught. For a film that spends so much time talking about the importance of taking risks, *Leap!* is curiously unwilling to do that itself.

Peter Sobczynski

CREDITS

Voice of Felicie: Elle Fanning
Voice of Victor: Nat Wolff
Voice of Odette: Carly Rae Jepsen
Voice of Camille: Maddie Ziegler
Voice of Regine: Julie Khaner
Origin: United States
Language: English
Released: 2016
Production: Valerie d'Auteuil, Nicolas Duval-Adassovsky, Andre Rouleau, Yann Zenou, Laurent Zeitoun; Caramel Film, M6 Films, Main Journey, Quad Productions; released by The Weinstein Company
Directed by: Eric Summer; Eric Warin
Written by: Eric Summer; Carol Noble; Laurent Zeitoun
Cinematography by: Jerrica Cleland
Music by: Klaus Badelt
Sound: Paulette Victor-Lifton
Music Supervisor: Rebecca Delannet; Astrid Gomez-Montoya; Robyn Klein
Editing: Yvann Thibaudeau
MPAA rating: PG
Running time: 89 minutes

REVIEWS

Bahr, Lindsey. *Associated Press*. August 23, 2017.
Guzman, Rafer. *Newsday*. August 24, 2017.
Hassenger, Jesse. *The A.V. Club*. August 24, 217.
Jaworowski, Ken. *New York Times*. August 24, 2017.
Lodge, Guy. *Variety*. March 25, 2017.
Orndorf, Brian. *Blu-Ray.com*. August 24, 2017.
Truitt, Brian. *USA Today*. August 23, 2017.
VanDenburgh, Barbara. *Arizona Republic*. August 24, 2017.
Walsh, Katie. *Tribune News Service*. August 24, 2017.
Watson, Keith. *Slant Magazine*. August 20, 2017.

QUOTES

Victor [referring to his crudely built wings]: "I call them 'chicken wings'!"
Felicie [frustrated]: "Chickens don't fly!"

TRIVIA

Actor Nat Wolff replaced Dane DeHaan as the voice of Victor in the American release of the film.

THE LEGO BATMAN MOVIE

Always be yourself. Unless you can be Batman.
—Movie tagline

Box Office: $175.8 Million

The LEGO Batman Movie is a spin-off of 2014's *The LEGO Movie*, a film that Fox Business Channel referred to as "anti-corporation." Never mind that despite all its cleverness, *The LEGO Movie* was still a huge toy commercial that grossed $500 million worldwide. If children were being indoctrinated with a hatred of CEOs, as FBC incredulously claimed, they were also being conditioned to beg their parents to buy LEGO products. The latter is by far the greater of the two "evils," for disdain is free but LEGO merchandise is not. The ultimate job of the original film and its successor is to press into service as many LEGO products as possible to advance and reconcile the plot. It's a cynical ploy, to be sure, but it hardly negates the enjoyment generated by these movies. There's a heaping helping of cleverness served as a side order with the blatant marketing scheme.

The LEGO Batman Movie takes Will Arnett's memorable, hilarious Batman from *The LEGO Movie* and gives him the spotlight. Arnett's excellent vocal work, modeled after the gravelly-voiced Batman of director Christopher Nolan's trilogy, teeters precariously on the verge of parody. His job is not to take the piss out of Christian Bale's portrayal. Rather, he just makes the Dark Knight lighter and looser. This Batman thinks he is honoring the self-serious darkness first poured into his character by Frank Miller's *The Dark Knight Returns*, but, in actuality, he's harkening back to the earlier era where superhero movies could simply be fun. Before it devolves into the confusing climactic battle that's par for the course in every recent superhero movie, *The LEGO Batman Movie* evokes giddy memories of the Alexander and Ilya Salkind Superman films starring Christopher Reeve.

"All important movies start with a black screen," Batman tells viewers as we stare at a blank screen that has not yet borne witness to the Warner Bros. logo. "And music," he continues as Lorne Balfe's score rises within earshot, "edgy music that would make a parent or a studio executive nervous." Considering how many Warner Bros.-owned properties are on full display throughout *The LEGO Batman Movie*, one need not worry about the nerves of any higher-ups at the studio. Before fadeout, villainous characters from *Lord of the Rings* and the *Harry Potter* series, along with other DC characters like the Justice League, will all have something to do with the story. Plus, lip service and more are paid to Warner Bros. films like *Suicide Squad* and *Batman v. Superman*. The corporate force is strong with this one, which might strain viewer tolerance.

Though his Batman is rooted in the Nolan era, director Chris McKay does not shy away from earlier incarnations of his lead character. There are delectable shout-outs that extend as far back as the all-time best version of Batman—Adam West's beloved Batusi-dancing superhero from the mid-1960s television series. McKay also rights a series wrong by having Billy Dee Williams—the Harvey Dent of Burton's 1989 version of *Batman*—portray Dent's alter-ego Two-Face in this film instead of Tommy Lee Jones, who portrayed him in *Batman Forever* (1995). And lest one forgets, *The LEGO Batman Movie* presents the third cinematic iteration of the battle between Batman and the Joker.

As with every one of Batman's prior incarnations, Arnett's version is an egomaniac. In his latest battle with the Joker (voice of Zach Galifianakis), Batman swings into action while heavy metal shouting a song about himself. "Stop him before he starts singing!" pleads the Joker to no avail. After Batman plows through a litany of his arch-rivals, including well-known entities like the Riddler plus some obscure ones that the Joker dares us to Google for accuracy, Batman stares down an even tougher psychological battle. Batman immediately short-circuits in response to the Joker's claim that he is Batman's greatest nemesis and that the two need each other. Not only does Batman dis the Joker by saying his greatest foe is Superman, he twists the knife in his emotionally needy nemesis' back. "I don't need anyone!" growls Batman.

Of course, he will be proven wrong, but before that happens, the film shows Batman's lonely life. Outside of his talking computer and his butler/surrogate father Alfred (voice of Ralph Fiennes), Batman has nothing to keep him company but lobster thermidor dinners and a version of Harry Nilsson's classic "One" accompanying his home life on the soundtrack. Batman's only true joy comes whenever Commissioner Gordon flicks the switch on the Bat Signal, which he does so often one wonders why Gotham has a police force at all. Batman's loneliness will be forcibly soothed when Bruce Wayne accidentally adopts young orphan Dick Grayson (voice of Michael Cera), the future sidekick Robin.

Speaking of children: "I love you more than my own children!" yells one Gotham City resident as Batman bathes in the usual adulation he's afforded after every battle. Batman responds by pulling out a gun that shoots out tons of Batman-related products and memorabilia. (That gun is a visual representation of the film itself, come to think of it.) But with Commissioner Gordon retiring, Batman may soon be a man without a country. The new Commish is Barbara Gordon (voice of Rosario Dawson) aka Batgirl. Unlike her father, she prefers crime-fighting to be a group effort rather than dependent on the temperamental whims of the town vigilante. "It takes a village, not a Batman!" she says, before noting that "Gotham City is still the most crime-ridden city despite Batman's efforts." The film hints that this is very much by Batman's design; earlier, he let the Joker walk rather than take him to jail.

Meanwhile, the Joker, along with his hottie girlfriend Harley Quinn (voice of Jenny Slate), hatches a plan to force Batman to admit that, in the words of Jerry Maguire, "you complete me." The Joker and all the other criminals of Gotham City turn themselves in to Commissioner Barbara Gordon voluntarily, leaving Batman nothing to do. In anger, Batman decides to send the Joker to the Phantom Zone, a secure prison in the sky that normally gets its prisoners from Superman. Batman's hatred of Superman (voiced by a very funny Channing Tatum) leads him to use the orphan he never really wanted to assist in stealing the Phantom Zone Gun from Superman's Fortress of Solitude. Upon completion of the mission, Batman feels a new sensation when looking at the successful Robin. "That is called pride," the Bat Computer tells him.

Eventually, Batman has to learn to trust Barbara, Robin, and Alfred as members of his crime-fighting team, and to finally admit that the Joker is the Steve Wozniak to his Steve Jobs. He also learns to accept the son who shares more in common with him than he had realized. *The LEGO Batman Movie* visually brings this point home when Robin's family selfie heartbreakingly mimics the picture young Bruce Wayne took of his family just before his parents were killed.

These emotional scenes are surprisingly effective, even when they are smack-dab in the middle of the aforementioned confusing climactic battle. Why every superhero movie, good and bad, Marvel and DC, must end with this type of city-destroying nonsense is beyond comprehension. At least, amidst all the chaos, one can see clearly and distinctly every character that has a tie to Warner Bros. or LEGO (or both). "You can't be a hero if all you care about is yourself," Barbara tells Batman. And a film cannot sell toys if the kids cannot see them onscreen, either.

Odie Henderson

CREDITS

Batman/Bruce Wayne: Will Arnett
The Joker: Zach Galifianakis
Robin/Dick Grayson: Michael Cera
Batgirl/Barbara Gordon: Rosario Dawson
Alfred Pennyworth: Ralph Fiennes
Origin: United States
Language: English
Released: 2017
Production: Roy Lee, Dan Lin, Phil Lord, Chris(topher) Miller; DC Entertainment, Lego System A/S, Lin Pictures, Lord Miller, Vertigo Entertainment, Warner Bros. Animation; released by Warner Bros. Entertainment Inc.
Directed by: Chris McKay
Written by: Seth Grahame-Smith; Chris McKenna; Erik Sommers; Jared Stern; John Whittington
Music by: Lorne Balfe
Sound: Wayne Pashley
Editing: David Burrows; John Venzon; Matt Villa
Production Design: Grant Freckelton
MPAA rating: PG
Running time: 104 minutes

REVIEWS

Berardinelli, James. *ReelViews.* February 9, 2017.
Cole, Jake. *Slant Magazine.* February 5, 2017.
Dargis, Manohla. *New York Times.* February 8, 2017.
Duralde, Alonso. *TheWrap.* February 4, 2017.
Ebiri, Bilge. *Village Voice.* February 7, 2017.
Kuntzman, Gersh. *New York Daily News.* February 6, 2017.
Phillips, Michael. *Chicago Tribune.* February 9, 2017.
Rose, Steve. *The Guardian.* February 4, 2017.
Russo, Tom. *Boston Globe.* February 9, 2017.
Zacharek, Stephanie. *Time.* February 9, 2017.

QUOTES

Robin: "My name's Richard Grayson, but all the kids at the orphanage call me Dick."
Batman: "Well, children can be cruel."

TRIVIA

Batman's line in the opening action scene, "You want to get nuts? Let's get nuts!" is a reference to *Batman* (1989) where Bruce Wayne (Michael Keaton) says this to the Joker (Jack Nicholson).

THE LEGO NINJAGO MOVIE

Find your inner piece.
—Movie tagline

Box Office: $59.3 Million

Unlike the prior entries in the LEGO Movie series, *The LEGO Ninjago Movie* has precedent in a 2011 television series that coincided with the toy store release of numerous LEGO sets. The film version, which was written by eight people, including the show's writers, deviates from the source material enough that prior knowledge is unnecessary. Also unnecessary is *The LEGO Ninjago Movie* itself. While *The LEGO Movie* (2014) and *The LEGO Batman Movie* (2017) never hid their intention to sell toys, they managed to include other elements that made these feature length commercials imaginative, watchable fun. No such extras enliven *The*

LEGO Ninjago Movie. It's a rehash of the first movie mixed with an unholy mishmash of Japanese staples like *Voltron* and *Godzilla.*

Somebody at LEGO Movie headquarters has serious Daddy issues, because all three of the aforementioned LEGO films deal with fathers and sons or father figures and adopted sons. While these relationships populate a great portion of storytelling since time immemorial, *The LEGO Ninjago Movie* does nothing new with them. In fact, neither the father nor the son here is particularly interesting. The Dad, Lord Garmadon (voice of Justin Theroux) is a selfish prick who spends every day destroying the town of Ninjago where his son, Lloyd lives. Lloyd (voice of Dave Franco) is an unbearably whiny kid who needs therapy because his Dad's reign of terror makes Lloyd the least liked kid in town. Instead of laying on a shrink's couch, Lloyd finds solace as part of the Secret Ninja Force that battles Lord Garmadon every time he shows up.

Lord Garmadon has no idea that one of the battling machines his nemesis uses contains his son, not that he would actually give a damn. When he accidentally butt-dials Lloyd on Lloyd's birthday, he feigns ignorance, opting instead to attack Ninjago as a birthday gift. When he's defeated, he fires his Shark Army and sets out to make a machine that the Secret Ninja Force can't defeat on its own. They will need the "Ultimate Weapon" to combat Lord Garmadon's newest creation.

It's here that Master Wu, the Secret Ninja Force's mentor and Lloyd's uncle, shows up to discuss the "Ultimate Weapon" and why it must never be used. Master Wu is voiced by martial arts legend Jackie Chan, who appears in the film's live-action opening segment. That segment is a rather garish ripoff of *Gremlins* (1984), with a young boy stumbling into a store filled with Asian relics and mysticism. One almost expects Master Wu to try selling the kid a Mogwai in exchange for a smokeless ashtray. Instead, Master Wu spins the yarn that becomes *The LEGO Ninjago Movie.*

Back in the animated world, Lloyd finds the "Ultimate Weapon" and fires it, unleashing the film's one great idea. The weapon is a laser pointer, which, in true Toho Studios fashion, calls from the depths a giant monster named Meowthra. Meowthra is played by a real cat, whose size is enough to cause more damage to Ninjago than Lord Garmadon ever could. Meowthra's agent should demand a standalone movie for its client. Ninety minutes of a cat stomping on LEGOs would undoubtedly break the Internet and earn billions at the box office.

Unfortunately, Lord Garmadon gets the "Ultimate Weapon" and points it at the Secret Ninja Force's equipment. Meowthra predictably destroys their machines before Lloyd breaks the "Ultimate Weapon." After this defeat, Master Wu tells his team about the "Ultimate, Ultimate Weapon" which must be used to defeat Meowthra. They will need to get through the Forest of Dangers, the Canyon of Death, and the Temple of Fragile Foundations to obtain this weapon. Lord Garmadon secretly tags along in the hopes of obtaining even more power, but he's soon discovered and defeated by Master Wu.

Wu tells Lloyd he must find and use inner peace. He also tells Lloyd that his unique power is Green. Unlike the other ninjas, whose powers are fire, ice, and other tangible, comprehensible items, Green makes no sense to Lloyd, and before he can ask how to find inner peace, Master Wu falls off a cliff, leaving Garmadon as the crew's de facto leader. None of the Secret Ninja Force is happy about that, especially when Garmadon's recently fired army of sharks shows up for revenge.

Of course Lloyd and his Dad will bond, and after much explanation, cooperation, and battling with Meowthra, the two will come to a beautiful understanding while defeating poor Meowthra. *The LEGO Ninjago Movie* goes through these paces with a minimal amount of creativity. There's no memorable voice acting like Will Arnett in the first two LEGO films, nor interesting supporting characters despite having a multi-cultural cast of talented actors providing the voices. The movie also lacks the often-stunning visuals of its predecessors. In fact, at times, it's downright ugly to watch.

When the film finally returns to its live-action wraparound section, the shop owner offers to teach his young customer how to be a ninja. Since Meowthra is present in the store, and has a penchant for attacking its owner, one expects that it will be the big boss this kid will eventually face if Warner Bros. ever decides to make *The LEGO Meowthra Movie.* Hopefully, that will feel less like a cynical cash grab than *The LEGO Ninjago Movie.*

Odie Henderson

CREDITS

Master Wu: Jackie Chan (Voice)

Lloyd: Dave Franco (Voice)

Garmadon: Justin Theroux (Voice)

Cole: Fred Armisen (Voice)

Nya: Abbi Jacobson (Voice)

Origin: United States

Language: English

Released: 2017

Production: Maryann Garger, Roy Lee, Dan Lin, Phil Lord, Chris McKay, Christopher Miller; LEGO Systems A/S, Lin

Pictures, Lord Miller, RatPac-Dune Entertainment, Vertigo Entertainment, Warner Bros. Animation; released by Warner Bros. Pictures

Directed by: Charlie Bean; Paul Fisher; Bob Logan

Written by: Paul Fisher; Bob Logan; William Wheeler; Tom Wheeler; Jared Stern; John Whittington

Music by: Mark Mothersbaugh

Sound: Wayne Pashley

Music Supervisor: Kier Lehman

Editing: David Burrows; Garret Elkins; Ryan Folsey; Julie Rogers; John Venzon

Art Direction: Felicity Coonan; Charlie Revai

Production Design: Annie Beauchamp; Kim Taylor

MPAA rating: PG

Running time: 101 minutes

REVIEWS

Barker, Andrew. *Variety*. September 20, 2017.

Berardinelli, James. *Reelviews*. September 21, 2017.

Lee, Benjamin. *The Guardian*. September 20, 2017.

Lemiere, Christy. *RogerEbert.com*. September 21, 2017.

O'Sullivan, Michael. *Washington Post*. September 21, 2017.

Scott, A.O. *New York Times*. September 20, 2017.

Scotti, Ariel. *New York Daily News*. September 20, 2017.

Smith, Neil. *Total Film*. October 9, 2017.

Walsh, Katie. *Chicago Tribune*. September 21, 2017.

Weitzman, Elizabeth. *TheWrap*. September 20, 2017.

QUOTES

Sensei Wu: "Are you ready to risk your life for Ninjago?"

TRIVIA

Both Kumail Nanjiani and Michael Pena previously worked together on *Hell and Back* (2015).

THE LEISURE SEEKER

The title for the English-language debut of Italian director Paolo Virzì may refer to the vintage camper its characters use on their road trip down the Eastern seaboard, but the film's leisurely paced, hackneyed narrative is so stalled-out that it will leave most viewers seeking comfort instead in their own wandering imaginations, despite the presence and best efforts of screen legends Helen Mirren and Donald Sutherland.

After its world premiere at the Venice Film Festival, subsequent festival stopovers in both Toronto and Los Angeles (the latter for AFI Fest), and a quickie awards-qualifying theatrical run (for which Mirren was tossed a sigh-inducing Golden Globe®-nomination for her efforts, in the Best Actress, Musical or Comedy category), distributor Sony Pictures Classics bumped the wide release of *The Leisure Seeker* to 2018, where its commercial prospects seem limited to a very slim and particular art house demographic.

Set in the summer of 2016, the story centers on John and Ella Spencer (Sutherland and Mirren), a married couple of more than five decades. Faced at this point in their lives with more caregiving than they care to accept, John and Ella take leave of their Boston suburb and head south on one last journey together in their 1975 Winnebago Indian, to visit Ernest Hemingway's home in Key West, Florida. The complicating factor? John, a former high school English teacher, is suffering from Alzheimer's Disease, which rather understandably colors the opinions of the couple's adult children, Jane (Janel Moloney) and Will (Christian McKay), when they find out about their parents' unannounced excursion. Along the way, as Ella tries to navigate John's fragmented relationship with time and memory, the pair bicker, laugh, argue, and reconnect, in circular fashion.

What could be an interesting spin on cinematic road trip conventions, given its principal collaborators ("An Italian, a Brit, and a Canadian set off in search of America...") instead turns into little more than a wearying catalogue of episodic events—the result less a juggling of disparate tones than not having a firm editorial hand. At 112 minutes but feeling even longer, *The Leisure Seeker* vastly overstays its welcome. The sporadic appearance of John's obsession with Ella's old boyfriend, Dan (Dick Gregory), is eventually paid off, in a roundabout type of way; but while this plot thread achieves a sort of symmetry with one related to the Spencers' neighbor, Lillian (Dana Ivey), the film's constant return to the hand-wringing consternation of Jane and Will feels like an utter waste of time.

In adapting Michael Zadoorian's book of the same name, Virzì and screenwriting collaborators Francesco Piccolo, Francesca Archibugi, and Stephen Amidon change John's occupation and reorient both the departure and destination points; in the novel, the Spencers lived outside of Detroit, and decide to head west to Disneyland, just south of Los Angeles. These changes would seem to indicate a more literate and intellectually ambitious exploration of the difficulties of aging with dignity. But even the ideas that on paper read as good, or at least conceptually interesting—like John and Ella, already stumbling through an America that in many ways they can scarcely recognize, stumbling upon a Donald Trump rally—come across as misfires in execution.

The portions that most effectively connect on an emotional level relate to John's realization of his deteriorating condition ("Oh, my stupid empty head," he pitifully moans at one point), and how Ella, who arranges slide shows of old family photos as a brain exercise, cycles through different ways of trying to coax the man she loves back out of the unreliable shell he now inhabits. In a moment both amusing and heartbreaking, for example, John forgets that they are arguing, and smiles at his wife. Ella, however, forcefully returns to the argument—clearly desperate for the deeper and more sincere connection it provides, if somewhat knowingly not any legitimate catharsis. That is a truly incredible moment. However, scenes like this abut, and are eventually outnumbered at least two-to-one by, bad scenes, in which a string of buffoonish and/or familiar scenarios (redneck robbers) get acted out.

On the technical side, cinematographer Luca Bigazzi conveys a certain freewheeling energy, using wide shots and an abundance of natural lighting to breathe life into frames. And costume designer Massimo Cantini Parrini delivers smart, evocative work, capturing the characters' personalities in the small details of their clothing—the remnants of John's ingrained academic persona in his natty tweed jacket, and loosely-tied neckties and scarves, contrasted with Ella's more bubbly, Southern belle persona, characterized by brightly colored print blouses and bejeweled glasses.

The chief selling point of the movie remains its two stars, who deliver very professional, engaging performances that nevertheless lean more toward the functional than the intertwined. While their sheer craft allows for moments of fitful connection, *The Leisure Seeker* exudes a somewhat managed feeling, lacking any of the poignancy or sincere chemistry, for example, between Robert Redford and Jane Fonda in the somewhat similarly themed *Our Souls at Night* (2017).

Virzì seems content to let his performers follow their initial instincts, and his lack of an edifying, unifying vision is most evident in the fumbling direction of McKay, Moloney, and other supporting characters. *The Leisure Seeker* is not offensively bad—there is enough material here for a compelling short film. Unfortunately, as perhaps with many a cross-country drive with the wrong company, it goes on for simply far too long, churning through yawningly familiar landscapes.

Brent Simon

CREDITS

John Spencer: Donald Sutherland
Ella Spencer: Dame Helen Mirren
Jennifer Ward: Kirsty Mitchell
Jane Spencer: Janel Moloney
Will Spencer: Christian McKay
Origin: United States
Language: English
Released: 2017
Production: Marco Cohen, Fabrizio Donvito, Benedetto Habib, Marty Eli Schwartz; BAC Films Ltd., Indiana Production Company, RAI Cinema; released by Sony Pictures Classics
Directed by: Paolo Virzi
Written by: Paolo Virzi; Stephen Amidon; Francesca Archibugi; Francesco Piccolo
Cinematography by: Luca Bigazzi
Music by: Carlo Virzi
Editing: Jacopo Quadri
Art Direction: Justin O'Neal Miller
Costumes: Massimo Cantini Parrini
Production Design: Richard A. Wright
MPAA rating: R
Running time: 112 minutes

REVIEWS

Abele, Robert. *Los Angeles Times*. December 14, 2017.
Bleasdale, John. *CineVue*. September 3, 2017.
Brooks, Xan. *The Guardian*. September 3, 2017.
Collin, Robbie. *The Telegraph*. September 4, 2017.
Halligan, Fionnuala. *Screen International*. September 3, 2017.
Horwitz, Simi. *Film Journal International*. December 18, 2017.
Lemire, Christy. *RogerEbert.com*. December 15, 2017.
Rife, Katie. *The A.V. Club*. December 14, 2017.
Weissberg, Jay. *Variety*. September 3, 2017.
Young, Deborah. *Hollywood Reporter*. September 3, 2017.

TRIVIA

This film reunited director Paolo Virzì with producers Fabrizio Donvito, Benedetto Habib, and Marco Cohen from the Indiana Production Company.

AWARDS

Nominations:

Golden Globes 2018: Actress--Mus./Comedy (Mirren)

LEMON

Box Office: $29,258

Rising director Janicza Bravo tells stories about lonely failures, isolated by the fault of their own anxieties or social shortcomings. Her previous shorts, like *Gregory Go Boom* and *Pauline Alone*, (starring Michael

Cera and Gaby Hoffmann, respectively), are the type of compelling snippets into discordant lives that make a viewer want to focus on every word a character says, and chew on every detail by its writer/director.

Her debut feature, *Lemon,* is assuredly a movie from her incredibly exciting directorial vision. It tells of a man named Isaac (Brett Gelman, co-writer), who is designed to look like any type of wholesale character from a mopey indie movie made in the last 20 years: glasses, bearded, balding. In a perhaps subconscious nod to Paul Thomas Anderson's *Punch-Drunk Love* (2002), which also captures a different side of Los Angeles with anamorphic lenses, Isaac is often wearing drab suits, as if a costume for the maturity that he seems to only have by his age number.

Isaac's life has become a plateau in nearly every sense. Starting with the dissolution of his ten-year relationship with Ramona (Judy Greer), who leaves him at the beginning of the movie and appears in bizarre flashbacks to their most painful conversations. He faces even more disappointment in his life with his acting career, which fails to materialize beyond a few strange gigs like modeling for adult diapers. Isaac's failure is thrown back at him in his work as an acting coach, as he watches a beloved student named Alex (Michael Cera, perfectly ridiculous) earn a massive gig and brush off Isaac's friendship. Isaac's jealousy towards Alex quickly materializes to bullying him when Alex comes to the apartment, pointing a knife in his face. And before that instance, in an extremely funny sequence, Isaac writes an egregious racial slur on the side of Alex's vehicle.

Tone is a crucial aspect to the strange, cringeworthy pieces of this story, which are told with precise dialogue and filmmaking. Joi McMillon cuts the movie to be unpredictable with its jarring edits or extended sequences; a score by Heather Christian provides warbling clarinets and organs underneath everything, which gives them a nervous, offbeat energy that is perfect for the power Bravo is going for. Following her background in directing antagonistic theater productions, *Lemon* thrives with the most uncomfortable sequences, uninterested in providing stability in any sense.

And yet with all of this, there is a magnificent heart within this script that makes it a type of nonpareil love story. Isaac finds some type of warmth in the world from a hairdresser named Cleo (Nia Long), which reflects the true-life interracial relationship that director Bravo has with her co-writer and star, Gelman. For reasons that the movie does not really explain, nor does it need to, she takes a liking to him, despite his babyish antics, his naïveté towards cultures that are not his own, etc. A scene in which he meets members of her family continues the cringeworthy comedy that makes the film so special, especially as Isaac comes off like an anti-woke white liberal, explaining racial inequality to people of color. Isaac is plainly unlikable, and yet the discomfort makes it all so sweet. With such sincerity at its core, *Lemon* is a beautiful embodiment of the common notion that misery loves company.

But as *Lemon* shows in extended sequences the juxtaposing families that Isaac and Cleo come from, and always slingshots back to Isaac's way of trying to understand the world through his own privilege, the movie is far more than a regular tale of love possibly curing a case of arrested development. This is one of those rare comedies that directly engages a dumb white male's place in the world. It is a constant part of Isaac's interactions, whether with with a woman in his acting class that he constantly undermines (which makes for a hilarious running gag) or with Cleo. It makes for great comedy too, in which the ugliness of this character is played beyond his pathetic state of arrested development and into his place in society. As a key component to the story, Gelman's flailing, narcissistic, ridiculous performance is sincere to the dark comedy of Isaac while portraying him as the ultimate clown of privilege.

In a year involving the mainstream successes of *Get Out* (directed Jordan Peele) and *Wonder Woman* (directed by Patty Jenkins), American cinema has slowly been inching towards a representation of both filmmakers and characters outside of the common white pale perspective. *Lemon* deserves to be mentioned in the same film history book paragraphs as those films, despite its smaller size and limited theatrical release, due to the way it engages entitlement from the inside, confronting audiences with a critical image of being a white man in 2017. With Bravo maintaining her growing brilliance from start to finish, *Lemon* becomes an excellent balance of meaningful, pertinent comedy and an invigorating impulse to be so very strange.

Nick Allen

CREDITS

Isaac: Brett Gelman

Ramona: Judy Greer

Alex: Michael Cera

Ruthie: Shiri Appleby

Howard: Fred Melamed

Origin: United States

Language: English

Released: 2017

Production: David Bernon, Paul Bernon, Houston King, Sam Slater, Han West; Burn Later Productions, Cryk Productions, Killer Films; released by Magnolia Pictures

Directed by: Janicza Bravo
Written by: Brett Gelman; Janicza Bravo
Cinematography by: Jason McCormick
Music by: Heather Christian
Music Supervisor: Tiffany Anders
Editing: Joi McMillon
Art Direction: Ali Rubinfeld
Costumes: Ariel Goodman-Weston
Production Design: Grace Alie
MPAA rating: Unrated
Running time: 83 minutes

REVIEWS

Anderson, John. *Wall Street Journal.* August 17, 2017.
Bender, Abbey. *Village Voice.* August 23, 2017.
Kenigsberg, Ben. *New York Times.* August 23, 2017.
Kohn, Eric. *IndieWire.* January 25, 2017.
McCarthy, Todd. *Hollywood Reporter.* January 24, 2017.
O'Malley, Sheila. *RogerEbert.com.* August 18, 2017.
Turner, Kyle. *TheWrap.* August 10, 2017.
Vishnevetsky, Ignatiy. *The A.V. Club.* August 16, 2017.
Walsh, Katie. *Los Angeles Times.* August 17, 2017.
Yoshida, Emily. *New York Magazine/Vulture.* August 16, 2017.

TRIVIA

Writer/director Janicza Bravo and writer/actor Brett Gelman are married in real life. When the movie premiered, their families, who are portrayed as being dysfunctional, hadn't seen the film yet.

LIFE

We were better off alone.
—Movie tagline

Be careful what you search for.
—Movie tagline

Box Office: $30.2 Million

In the last couple of weeks leading up to the theatrical release of the space-based horror thriller *Life*, a bizarre theory took the Internet by storm positing that the film was actually a secret prequel to a proposed solo feature centered on the comic book character Venom, a destructive alien force that had previously been seen onscreen in *Spider-Man 3* (2007). The proof behind these assertions was shaky at best—the existence of the Venom project had just been announced a couple of weeks earlier, both films were under the aegis of Sony and the trailers for *Life* contained a couple of seconds of stock footage culled from *Spider-Man 3*—and the whole thing made zero sense the moment that anyone actually thought about it for more than a couple of seconds. But the notion did catch on with moviegoers right up until it officially opened and they realized that it was all nonsense, albeit nonsense that almost certainly added a few million more to its box-office take. (The filmmakers, no doubt seeing dollar signs, were certainly willing to play along, offering coy responses when asked about the prequel reports in pre-release interviews.) Unfortunately, despite the dumbness of this entire saga, it actually proves to be the most interesting thing about *Life,* as the end product is little more than an exceptionally blatant rip-off of the likes of *Alien* (1979) that will prove to be of interest only to those who derive some form of entertainment from watching smart actors trying to make their way through a screenplay that requires them to act as if they have bacon bits for brains at every turn of the plot.

In the not-too-distant future, the six-person crew of the International Space Station—commander Ekaterina Golokina (Olga Dihovichnaya), doctor David Jordan (Jake Gyllenhaal), systems analyst Sho Murakami (Hiroyuki Sanada), technician Rory Adams (Ryan Reynolds), exobiologist Hugh Derry (Ariyon Bakare), and CDC observer Miranda North (Rebecca Ferguson)—intercept an unmanned probe containing soil samples from Mars. Following this extended opening sequence, which has been put together in a way suggesting that it was done in one take, Henry examines the samples for signs of life and amazingly discovers a single-cell organism living in a state of suspended animation. Not realizing that he is in a crummy monster movie, he figures out how to awaken it and news of the discovery, which a grade school class names Calvin, captures the imagination of the world. It turns out that there is more to Calvin than meets the eye—not only is he growing larger, his organic structure operates in a way that suggests that each one of his cells can simultaneously be all muscle, all brain, and all eye.

Before long, Calvin, who seems docile at first, takes advantage of a momentary lapse of attention on Hugh's part to make the first of numerous violent moves. The crew quickly realizes that they are up against something dangerous and do everything that they can to try to outwit and kill the intruder. Luckily for Calvin, the combination of his intelligence and organic ingenuity and the unrelenting idiocy of the humans on board allow him to go around picking them off one by one in increasingly goopy ways. His big *coup de grace* comes when he fixes it so that the space station begins heading on an unstoppable trip back to Earth and the remaining crew members have to figure out a way to dispose of the intergalactic hitchhiker once and for all before he can wreak havoc on Earth.

The opening scene of *Life*—an extended bit that takes us on a tour of the International Space Station and introduces us to all the human characters in what is meant to suggest one long unbroken shot—is easily the best part of the film, if only because the blatant aping of the opening of *Gravity* (2013) at least feels slightly fresher than the liberal borrowings from *Alien* and its ilk that make up the rest of the film. Of course, the problem with *Life* is not that it borrows so heavily from the Ridley Scott classic but that it does so in such a clumsy and uninteresting manner. In that film, for example, even though the screenplay did not spend much time on backstories for its characters, viewers nevertheless got a sense of who they were and how they related to each other that ensured that once the creature began picking them off, there would be some degree of rooting interest in their survival and a sense of loss when things inevitably, and messily went sideways. Here, on the other hand, the characters, presumably to save precious space for their extended time in space, have each been afforded one notable character trait each—one is disabled, one has just become a father and is eager to return home to see his newborn child, one is a sarcastic wiseacre in the manner of most characters essayed by Ryan Reynolds—and as a result, it is impossible to care at all as they begin getting bumped off by Calvin. Even Calvin is kind of a bore—despite that aforementioned suggestion that he can somehow be all brain, muscle, and eye at the same time, his design is so forgettable that most will be hard-pressed to remember what he looks like whenever he slithers off-screen.

Director Daniel Espinoza is unable to do much with the painfully derivative screenplay by Rhett Reese & Paul Wernick to build any recognizable degree of tension and is therefore content to go for a series of cheap shocks in which the raw terror and tension that he is theoretically striving for is undercut by constantly having the characters, even in moments of extreme peril, referring to their antagonist by its new nickname. (If the name "Calvin" does not strike you as inherently amusing when you sit down to watch this film, it certainly will by its conclusion.) A decent cast has been assembled but they are all hobbled by a script that requires them to act like idiots throughout in order to keep the story moving along instead of acting sensibly and blowing themselves and the ship up in order to ensure Calvin does not make it to Earth—considering that the Gyllenhaal character is so disenchanted with life on Earth that he would do anything rather than return home, it seems like a potential source of tension has just been tossed away. Worst of all is the climax, a bit of dramatic misdirection that is handled so badly that what might have resulted in an amusing bit of jet-black humor instead comes off as stupid and sad.

Life was clearly not cheap to produce but considering the feebleness of the end results (which hit theaters about six weeks before the infinitely more ambitious and successful *Alien: Covenant* [2017]), one comes away from it wondering why those involved bothered with it at all. It isn't scary, it isn't visionary, and even the gross-outs are of an exceptionally perfunctory manner. Considering that it must have been apparent early on that this film just wasn't clicking, it must have taken a Herculean effort on the part of all involved with its production just to return to the set day after day. Other than the whole Venom kerfuffle, the only intriguing thing about *Life* is its title and that is only because one has to admire the amount of chutzpah required to name a film after something that it contains so little of itself.

Peter Sobczynski

CREDITS

David Jordan: Jake Gyllenhaal
Miranda North: Rebecca Ferguson
Rory Adams: Ryan Reynolds
Sho Murakami: Hiroyuki (Henry) Sanada
Ekaterina Golovkina: Olga Dihovichnaya
Hugh Derry: Ariyon Bakare
Origin: United States
Language: English, Chinese, Japanese
Released: 2017
Production: Bonnie Curtis, David Ellison, Dana Goldberg, Julie Lynn; LStar Capital, Skydance Media; released by Columbia Pictures
Directed by: Daniel Espinosa
Written by: Rhett Reese; Paul Wernick
Cinematography by: Seamus McGarvey
Music by: Jon Ekstrand
Sound: Per Hallberg
Editing: Mary Jo Markey; Frances Parker
Art Direction: Steven Lawrence
Costumes: Jenny Beavan
Production Design: Nigel Phelps
MPAA rating: R
Running time: 104 minutes

REVIEWS

Debruge, Peter. *Variety.* March 19, 2017.
DeFore, John. *Hollywood Reporter.* March 20, 2017.
Graham, Adam. *Detroit News.* March 24, 2017.
Kenigsberg, Ben. *New York Times.* March 23, 2017.
Klimek, Chris. *NPR.* March 23, 2017.
Morgenstern, Joe. *Wall Street Journal.* March 24, 2017.
Poritsky, Jonathan. *IndieWire.* March 23, 2017.

Reed, Rex. *New York Observer*. March 23, 2017.
Turan, Kenneth. *Los Angeles Times*. March 24, 2017.
Zacharek, Stephanie. *Time*. March 23, 2017.

QUOTES

Rory Adams: "This is some *Re-Animator* s**t."
Ekaterina Golovkina: "That's a very obscure reference."
Hugh Derry: "Not for a nerd."
Rory Adams: "Not if you're a nerd."

TRIVIA

Actor Ryan Reynolds was originally supposed to play the main character but scheduling conflicts with *The Hitman's Bodyguard* (2017) forced him to take on a supporting role instead.

THE LITTLE HOURS

Box Office: $1.6 Million

Raunchy comedies rarely cop to such well-regarded sources: *The Little Hours* claims its basis lies within Giovanni Boccaccio's 14th-century novella collection *The Decameron*, which makes its structure, bawdiness, and characterizations all feel appropriately pithy. A series of incidents involving three libidinous nuns—Alessandra, Genevra, and Fernanda (Alison Brie, Kate Micucci, and Aubrey Plaza, respectively)—and sexy farmhand-on-the-run Massetto (played by Dave Franco in full "romance novel cover" mode), *The Little Hours* finds writer/director Jeff Baena (who minored in Medieval and Renaissance Studies at NYU) delighting in updating *The Decameron*'s light and witty stories, helped by the fact that Boccaccio's language was opposed to the flowery erudition of most of the period's texts. That translates to a very vulgar (and funny) movie both indebted to and different than a wide spectrum of vulgar nun and nunsploitation movies that have spanned porn, hauntings, and thrillers promising both nude nuns and big guns.

Though the connective tissue keeping the film's story together often requires its thin characters to improvise or otherwise overstretch themselves from sketch to sketch—emphasizing their relative shallowness as short-story subjects—the medieval absurdity at the heart of the comedy always lands. Each vignette keeps the "swearing holy woman" gag fresh, partially due to the care Baena takes to situate us in a very specific time period (the filming took place in real castles from the era and the score/costuming feels spot-on) and partially thanks to the comic chemistry between its cast.

The Little Hours' plot as a whole is instigated by Massetto's unfortunate cuckolding of the blunt, boring, and politically-minded Lord Bruno (Nick Offerman, somewhere between his stoic Ron Swanson from *Parks and Recreation* and a *Game of Thrones* throne-chaser), followed by his escape to a convent. Once there, he must act deaf and dumb so there's no fuss about the young stud—whose shirt is almost always open—hanging around a temptation-averse nunnery. That the aversion was secretly perversion all along fits perfectly in line with contemporary culture's views of religious oppression.

Criticizing the practices of the church and satirizing the practice of families donating daughters to convents in lieu of a tithe, the film always bows to its women who persevere through the tightest subjugation. Establishing historical (and, analogically, modern) constraints for these women happens quickly and naturally, allowing the nuns' misbehavior to become an immediate punchline.

As for the nuns themselves, Alessandra is the spoiled newcomer and Genevra a sheltered believer, with Brie and (especially) Micucci bringing a raging energy to their roles, which is particularly impressive considering that all but their faces are hidden away by habits for most of the film. When Brie reveals her hair and her neck, it's incredibly sexualized due entirely to the success of the film's ascetic aesthetic.

Meanwhile, Fernanda is simply Aubrey Plaza. Plaza's schtick is the least interesting (though it still works) because it's so squarely in line with her acting persona. It's like if Alec Baldwin turned up as a smooth-talking textile merchant. Fernanda is the witchiest member of the convent, mysteriously running off to the woods in the middle of the night or getting drunk and frisky with her friend Marta (Jemima Kirke). The interplay of the nuns' sexualities (Fernanda's bisexuality spilling over to her nunmates) becomes some of the film's strongest material, altering Micucci and Plaza's relationship with one-sided experimental longing that mixes humor and impotency in a bittersweet aperitif, leaving us hungry for the film's surprisingly sentimental payoffs.

One of these affecting moments comes from John C. Reilly and Molly Shannon as romantically entwined church higher-ups. Both actors are at places in their careers where they are always in danger of stealing movies from everyone around them, but in *The Little Hours* their silliness feels appropriately low-key against the bombastic profanity of the foregrounded nuns. They swear like each dirty word is a personal "Hail Mary," pouring out in response to each sinful event or strict policy. The R-rating here is not an indicator of exploitation, but an opportunity to showcase a neverending cycle of expletives as institutional rebellion.

This notion is only emphasized more when the local bishop (Fred Armisen) rolls through town to discover that the realities of the idealized religious life must necessarily flaunt its expectations thanks to the pressures inherent in its enforcement. While the film can sometimes feel narratively sparse, the combination of this defiant juxtaposition, its diligently-defined historical context, and some perfectly-pitched nastiness casts *The Little Hours* into the midnight movie heavens.

Jacob Oller

CREDITS

Alessandra: Alison Brie
Massetto: Dave Franco
Ginerva: Kate Micucci
Fernanda: Aubrey Plaza
Father Tommasso: John C. Reilly
Origin: United States
Language: English
Released: 2017
Production: Elizabeth Destro, Aubrey Plaza; Bow and Arrow Entertainment, Concourse Media, Destro Films, Dublab Media, Exhibit, Foton Pictures, Productivity Media, StarStream Media; released by Gunpowder & Sky
Directed by: Jeff Baena
Written by: Jeff Baena
Cinematography by: Quyen Tran
Music by: Dan Romer
Sound: Christopher Barnett
Music Supervisor: Zach Cowie
Editing: Ryan Brown
Art Direction: Andrew Katz
Costumes: Natalie O'Brien
Production Design: Susie Mancini
MPAA rating: R
Running time: 90 minutes

REVIEWS

Bailey, Jason. *Flavorwire.* January 30, 2017.
Borders, Meredith. *Birth.Movies.Death.* January 20, 2017.
Bowen, Chuck. *Slant Magazine.* June 29, 2017.
Chang, Justin. *Los Angeles Times.* January 21, 2017.
Dowd, A.A. *The A.V. Club.* June 29, 2017.
Hornaday, Ann. *Washington Post.* July 6, 2017.
Phillips, Michael. *Chicago Tribune.* July 12, 2017.
Sims, David. *The Atlantic.* July 11, 2017.
Walsh, Katie. *Los Angeles Times.* June 30, 2017.
Wolfe, April. *L.A. Weekly.* June 26, 2017.

QUOTES

Lord Bruno: "One of you sluts thinks he's quite the jester."

TRIVIA

The screenplay is based on the first tale of the third day from *The Decameron* (1971).

LOGAN

His time has come.
—Movie tagline

Box Office: $226.3 Million

The final entry in Hugh Jackman's star-making run as the mutant character Wolverine in the superhuman X-Men series, *Logan*, named for the character's alter-ego, does more than any other superhero film thus far: it allows its hero to be human. Wolverine is the most iconic cinematic X-Man, with his extendable Adamantium claws, veiny muscularity, and distinctive muttonchops. Director James Mangold already worked on fleshing out the character with his 2013 entry *The Wolverine*, which *Logan* continues after a large time jump ages its more vulnerable antihero.

Knowledge of the character's history is not essential to appreciate the film, but it is certainly a work that draws on a rich variety of sources. From its cinematic visual touchpoints of the slice-and-dice Freddy Krueger or Han from *Enter the Dragon* (1973) to the comic-book source material to which it consistently winks, all the way to the more sweeping aesthetic and narrative references of 1953's Western *Shane*, *Logan* does not quite feel like a superhero movie. Unlike those typically superficial, plastic affairs, it soaks its audience in with a sense of history and artistic depth. Jackman has played this character for over seventeen years. His performance of the character brought the actor fame and pushed the character to the head of the series. Both broke each other out, deeply becoming each other for the moviegoing public at large thanks to the freshness of Jackman and superheroes to popular America.

The Canadian superhero finds himself on the Mexican border, driving a limo in a world that's moved beyond mutant heroes and has found solace in mutant scapegoats. Logan drifts and drives. He's dirty, sad, beat. He cares for an aged Professor X (Patrick Stewart, softened by a pathos riddled with degenerative mental disease) in a secret desert lair staffed with the lone other mutant in his world, an albino tracker (Stephen Merchant) not unlike the Native Americans of the Western cinematic idiom. When he meets a pursued young mutant, the first in years and years, named Laura (the incredible breakout Dafne Keen), the group must flee on a cross-country race through farmhouses and casinos to a promised land found in no holier text than a comic book. The professor's telepathic abilities suffer schizophrenic outbreaks thanks to his sickness, endangering the protagonists from within while those chasing them provide the fire on their heels.

A family develops between the Professor, Logan, and the girl he learns is his daughter/clone, formerly designated as X-23. Jackman relishes his evolving role that, in *Logan,* allows him to give his finest performance by granting a well-familiar character two complex, unfamiliar relationships. The loner is always more interesting when he's forced into relationships. Whether this means the drifting tough of 1953's *Shane* (that the trio watch in a hotel room before a bloody, time-disrupted showdown) or the begrudged father figure role, it's a side never seen. *Logan* gives Jackman two sides of paternalism: one guarding X-23 and one care-taking the dying Professor X. He's easing one generation out while welcoming the next.

Despite his resistance to wearing a costume fancier than jeans and a leather jacket or a dirtied suit, Logan flaunts a dirty panache stitched into the simple fabrics he wears. Daniel Orlandi's costuming and cinematographer John Mathieson's framing, of the man either backlit and softly deified or up-close and wrinkled like a Dust Bowl Okie, contribute to the film's dusty aesthetic, quintessentially American in its heroism.

All these attributes are unassuming alternatives to the clownish pomp of someone like Superman or Batman. Wolverine's plots are similarly simple. He runs, he looks for the truth, he protects. These are steady, grounded drives that echo the animalistic instincts running through his mutated genes. This is why he fits in so well with a simple farming family that hosts the group midway through the movie. He's got no great notions of being a superhero. His is a levelheadedness that cuts through fluffy, grand-speechifying rhetoric with Adamantium claws.

Logan comes to terms with himself alongside us, reveling in a final film of R-rated violence (one of the first of its superhero kind). The violence simultaneously unleashes the bloody pent-up fantasies generated by years of bloodless, inconsequential PG-13 slaughter while impressing upon the audience (and Laura) the lessons of the West. "There's no living with a killing," Shane tells his child companion. Logan's growling, bulldozing mania translates the moral changes of violence into physicality. He lunges, tears, and batters opponents with the whirling rage of someone with nothing left to lose and seemingly no way to suffer loss. Berserking necessarily takes an emotional toll.

Laura shares his powers (claws, superhuman healing, anger), supplemented with bladed feet and a knack for gymnastics. She has a grace that time and suffering have deadened in Logan. She still delights in the violence as a challenge, an expression, a revenge. Seeing the pair fight together (or later, in an inspired bit of symbolism, Logan's youth) reminds us that unstylized, gritty, upsetting violence still has purpose in cinema. It is a bridge between ages, a brutal highway that every hardened commuter warns newcomers away from. This seriousness permeates the film, making clear that superhero films are not just gags, primary colors, and cameos. They have the power to tap into a cultural consciousness with a memory and a power to use that memory to describe aging, loss, and regret with the poignancy of a revisited childhood.

Logan pushes the character farther than any cinematic superhero has ever gone or, maybe, will ever go—his end. Closure is something that Mangold has the luxury to provide and Jackman has the privilege to enact. The villains are faceless corporate cruelty, technologically-advanced greed run wild. The promise of a tragic end also includes a slight possibility of redemption—or at least a final imparted lesson. Losses punch like comic books cannot, just like the violence given blood, bone, and bite that stunning special effects push beyond that of the page. This film rewrites what superhero films can be—as most are simple action/adventures that tell a quarter of a larger, franchised story—and refines what some would call a genre into something more like noir, which is a set of tones, content, and style that can be mapped in different ways across genre. Superhero movies should entertain while they make us think and, like the lightly veiled allegory that these mutants are, inspire us like all good comic book heroes should. *Logan* succeeds with the lived-in gravitas, grumpiness, and begrudging kindness that makes it feel all the more real.

Jacob Oller

CREDITS

Logan: Hugh Jackman

Charles Xavier / Professor X: Patrick Stewart

Laura: Dafne Keen

Pierce: Boyd Holbrook

Caliban: Stephen Merchant

Origin: United States

Language: English, Spanish

Released: 2017

Production: Simon Kinberg, Hutch Parker, Lauren Shuler Donner; Donners' Company, Kinberg Genre, Marvel Entertainment L.L.C., TSG Entertainment; released by Twentieth Century Fox Film Corp.

Directed by: James Mangold

Written by: James Mangold; Scott Frank; Michael Green

Cinematography by: John Mathieson

Music by: Marco Beltrami

Music Supervisor: Ted Caplan
Editing: Michael McCusker; Dirk Westervelt
Art Direction: Chris Farmer
Production Design: Francois Audouy
MPAA rating: R
Running time: 137 minutes

REVIEWS

Chaw, Walter. *Film Freak Central.* March 28, 2017.
Dargis, Manohla. *New York Times.* March 2, 2017.
Kiang, Jessica. *BBC News.* March 3, 2017.
Nicholson, Amy. *MTV News.* March 2, 2017.
Patches, Matt. *Thrillist.* April 11, 2017.
Sims, David. *The Atlantic.* March 8, 2017.
Travers, Peter. *Rolling Stone.* March 9, 2017.
Turan, Kenneth. *Los Angeles Times.* March 2, 2017.
Walsh, Katey. *Tribune News Service.* March 6, 2017.
White, Armond. *National Review.* March 3, 2017.

QUOTES

Logan: "Nature made me a freak. Man made me a weapon. And God made it last too long."

TRIVIA

Sir Patrick Stewart lost twenty-one pounds to resprise his role of Charles Xavier as elderly and sick. Stewart claimed that he has had a steady weight since he was a teenager and had never deliberately lost weight before. Hugh Jackman genuinely held Stewart in all the scenes featuring Wolverine carrying Professor Xavier.

AWARDS

Nominations:

Oscars 2017: Adapt. Screenplay
Writers Guild 2017: Adapt. Screenplay

LOGAN LUCKY

See how the other half steals.
—Movie tagline

Box Office: $27.8 Million

It turns out that Steven Soderbergh's retirement from directing was blessedly short-lived. Sure, given his prodigious output over most of his career, the fact that he didn't headline a film between 2013's *Behind the Candleabra* and 2017's *Logan Lucky* arguably robbed the film world of more product than if another director had taken a typical four-year break, but Soderbergh came roaring back with two films in a nine-month span (*Logan Lucky* and the horror film *Unsane* [2018]) as well as a 2018 television series/app called *Mosaic,* which aired on both HBO and in a mobile form that allowed users to guide the story themselves. For his cinematic return in the summer of 2017, Soderbergh produced a film that felt like an offspring of his most beloved franchise, the "Ocean's" films. In fact, at one point, a character within the film even refers to the heist at its center as "Ocean's Seven-Eleven," and a speech given by a sports announcer about a veteran coming back to his career after some time off could have been about Soderbergh himself. And, to be fair, there are a few lurches in tone here that could be chocked up to rust being shaking off the frame of Soderbergh's ability; however, minor Soderbergh is still major filmmaking.

The touch that Soderbergh has lost none of for the bulk of this film is his remarkable economy of visual language. It never feels like he's setting up more shots than he needs to, conveying so much with simple cuts and compositions. There's an almost imperceptible rhythm to his films, and it's the reason this clever, subtle film works as well it does, bouncing from location to location and from detail to detail regarding a complex heist but never once feeling overly complicated or losing its easygoing tone. It's the kind of filmmaking that so many take for granted, very rarely showy and yet as technically accomplished as flashier directors like David Fincher or Michael Mann. Soderbergh is a craftsman who doesn't draw attention to his craft. It's what has made him one of the most essential filmmakers of the last quarter-century.

The title of Soderbergh's latest, written by "Rebecca Blunt"—widely believed to be a pseudonym for, in all likelihood, Jules Asner (Soderbergh's wife), or possibly Soderbergh himself, or mutual friend John Henson—is meant to be ironic, as the Logans believe they are anything but lucky. As the film opens, Jimmy Logan (Channing Tatum) is facing another blow of bad luck when he's fired from his job after a supervisor notices him limping (and doesn't want to risk the insurance liability). Drowning his sorrows at the local bar, Duck Tape, tended by his brother Clyde (Adam Driver), the siblings get into a fight with an obnoxious race car driver named Max Chilblain (Seth MacFarlane) and a pair of his lackeys, lighting the energy-drinking jerk's car on fire. It's time for the Logans to change their own luck.

And Jimmy knows just how to do it. The job he was just fired from was working under a massive NASCAR raceway, and he happened to see how the money is transported at such an impressive venture from concession stand cashiers to a vault through pneumatic tubes. He knows how easy it will be to blow open one of those tubes and, basically, just suck the money out. But they will need an explosives expert. Enter the scene-stealing

Joe Bang (Daniel Craig), who just happens to be "in-car-cer-ate-ted" at a nearby prison. With the help of Bang's brothers, Fish (Jack Quaid) and Sam (Brian Gleeson), the Logans, including sister Mellie (Riley Keough), are going to help break Joe Bang out of prison for a day, commit the redneck heist, and then put him back behind bars. Katherine Waterston, Sebastian Stan, Katie Holmes, and Hilary Swank all appear in supporting roles.

Of course, the bulk of *Logan Lucky* consists of the race day heist itself and it's a model of directorial pacing and tone management. Without the sizzle of something like *Ocean's Eleven* (2001), Soderbergh nonetheless never loses hold of each of his moving parts, whether it's Mellie racing down the freeway, the hysterical prison riot that serves as cover for Joe and Clyde's excursion, or the peak of the job itself, *Logan Lucky* hums along like, well, one of the well-tuned cars on the NASCAR track above. It helps a great deal of course that Soderbergh once again shoots his own film—under the pseudonym Peter Andrews—and edits his own film—under the pseudonym Mary Ann Bernard. One half wonders if he didn't really do the score and possibly catered for the film as well.

There are a few beats, particularly in the final act when Swank shows up to investigate the heist (with a partner played by the always-welcome Macon Blair), in which one can arguably see Soderbergh's perfectionism falter. The movies goes on a scene or two longer than it needs to, and them somehow feels like it wraps up too quickly. There's just something a bit off about the final half-hour, especially when compared to the clockwork precision of the preceding 90 minutes. But Soderbergh has more than accomplished what he set out to do by that point, and it's not like the closing scenes are flawed enough to sink the copious goodwill built up by what's come before. Ultimately, *Logan Lucky* is the kind of incredibly fun film that makes one sad upon completion because you have to leave these characters behind, but so well-done that you almost believe Jimmy Logan, Mellie Logan, and Joe Bang are out there somewhere in the real world, drinking beer, having fun, and hopefully getting the lucky break they deserve.

Brian Tallerico

CREDITS

Jimmy Logan: Channing Tatum
Sadie Logan: Farrah Mackenzie
Cal: Jim O'Heir
Mellie Logan: Riley Keough
Bobbie Jo Chapman: Katie Holmes
Origin: United States
Language: English
Released: 2017
Production: Reid Carolin, Gregory Jacobs, Mark Johnson, Channing Tatum; Free Association, Trans-Radial Pictures; released by Bleecker Street Media
Directed by: Steven Soderbergh
Written by: Rebecca Blunt
Cinematography by: Steven Soderbergh
Music by: David Holmes
Music Supervisor: Season Kent
Editing: Steven Soderbergh
Costumes: Ellen Mirojnick
Production Design: Howard Cummings
MPAA rating: PG-13
Running time: 118 minutes

REVIEWS

Hassenger, Jesse. *The A.V. Club*. August 15, 2017.
Roeper, Richard. *Chicago Sun-Times*. August 16, 2017.
Rothkopf, Joshua. *Time Out*. August 17, 2017.
Scott, A.O. *New York Times*. August 16, 2017.
Seitz, Matt Zoller. *RogerEbert.com*. August 17, 2017.
Taylor, Drew. *The Playlist*. July 24, 2017.
Turan, Kenneth. *Los Angeles Times*. August 17, 2017.
Welch, Alex. *IGN*. July 27, 2017.
Wilkinson, Alissa. *Vox*. August 17, 2017.
Zacharek, Stephanie. *Time*. August 17, 2017.

QUOTES

Joe Bang: "Is it twenty or is it thirty? We are dealing with science here!"

TRIVIA

The state trooper who pulls over the elderly lady is former NASCAR driver Carl Edwards.

LONG STRANGE TRIP

The untold story of the Grateful Dead.
—Movie tagline

Box Office: $351,957

For anyone who was lucky enough to see the Grateful Dead in concert at some point during their 30 years of existence, *Long Strange Trip*, Amir Bar-Lev's documentary on the group's long and storied history will have an oddly comforting and familiar feel to it. Instead of presenting a clear and concise collection of the key moments from throughout their career as a way of explaining who they were and what they meant in the manner of so many other music documentaries, he has presented their tale in a manner not unlike one of their fabled shows thanks to its extreme length (it clocks in at just under four hours) and a deceptively rambling structure that seems to be going off in all directions without rhyme or reason only to eventually pull itself back together with surprising force and power. While it may not be enough to sway any of the group's detractors, those with no working knowledge of the band and its wild past but with a willingness to accept their offbeat mystique are likely to find it fascinating as well.

Utilizing loads of rarely-seen footage taken from the Dead's voluminous archives and new interviews with the surviving founding members of the group, a few key insiders and notable fans, the film charts the group from its earliest days as a sort of house band for San Francisco's Haight-Ashbury district in the mid-1960s whose denizens sparked to their unique sound, a blend of folk, rock, bluegrass, jazz, blues, and avant-garde sounds that continue to defy easy explanation. This sound would land the group record deals but while their studio work would yield the occasional classic, such as the 1970 double-header *American Beauty* and *Workingman's Dead* and *Blues for Allah* (1975), it was the stage where the group—consisting of lead guitarist Jerry Garcia, rhythm guitarist Bob Weir, bassist Phil Leah, drummers Mickey Hart and Bill Kreutzmann, and harmonica-blowing force of nature Ron "Pigpen" McKernan as well as a number of additional musicians that would come and go over the years due to death or burnout among the other members—really came to life as they used their repertoire, a mixture of spacey originals and well-chosen covers, as an excuse for long, free-flowing jams that took both the audience and the group (which famously never used a set list for their shows) to unexpected places. Although mainstream acceptance would take a long time, the group became a cult sensation amongst fans who would go so far as to follow the band on the road to experience as many of their shows as possible, even recording them (with the group's permission) and trading the tapes with fellow so-called Deadheads.

Bar-Lev relates their story via a series of discrete sections that focus on certain key aspects of the group and their impact while at the same time providing a broadly chronological overview of their history. The closest thing to a consistent throughline on display is the one focusing on Garcia, the group's most notable member and the one who most seemed to represent the ideals of love, fun, and good music that they stood for. As the film opens, we see an old interview clip in which he talks about his first encounter with the movie that would go on to have a strangely profound effect on his life—*Abbott and Costello Meet Frankenstein* (1948)—in the way that it suggested how much fun the bizarre could be, especially in comparison to the things deemed "normal" by polite society. This was an attitude that he constantly conveyed throughout his life and work and it gave him a fanbase that literally looked upon him as a kind of deity. For someone with a mistrust of authority in all forms, such worship was profoundly disturbing—especially after the fluke success of their only Top 10 hit, 1987's "Touch of Grey" enlarged their audience to the point where the group could only play in the biggest and most impersonal stadiums—and it helped push him into problems involving drugs and his health that are chronicled during the final sections of the film and which would eventually lead to his death in 1995.

Bar-Lev weaves all of the material, new and old, together in an impressive manner and while the extreme length means that there are a few dull moments here and there (another aspect that the film has in common with an actual Dead concert), there are plenty of highlights as well. One-time tour manager Sam Cutler tells some fascinating stories about life on the road with the group in the early Seventies as they were developing their unique approach to live performances. As a way of representing the devotion and near-obsessiveness of the Deadheads, longtime fan Al Franken offers a complex explanation as to why one particular live performance of the group's 1980 song "Althea" ranks above all others to his ears. Depending on your point of view, the soundtrack is either a dream or a nightmare but if you fall into the former camp, the film is an embarrassment of riches as it highlights Dead favorites ranging from up-tempo rockers like "Uncle John's Band," "Playing in the Band," and a cover of "Not Fade Away" to the tear-jerking ballad "Stella Blue" to offbeat tunes like "Dark Star" and "Eyes of the World" that would serve as frameworks for extended jam sessions filled with musical improvisations that sometimes fell apart and other times led listeners to ecstasy. There are so many examples of the group's oeuvre on hand that one can almost—*almost*—forgive the film for somehow not including the great "Franklin's Tower" in the mix.

The only real flaw to *Long Strange Trip* is that the structure of the film does not allow for any full concert performances of the songs that would allow viewers to actually see the various interactions between the group members and get more of a sense of how the magic came together. Since there are plenty of visual records of their concerts out there, ranging from bootleg videos of old concerts on YouTube to the Dead's own grand cinematic experiment, *The Grateful Dead Movie* (1977), this is not as damaging a problem as one might think. Fans may also quibble about how some aspects of the group's history that they find particularly fascinating failed to make the final cut. (There is precious little mention of the group's infamous 1987 tour that found them playing alongside Bob Dylan, a combination that never quite jelled as one might have hoped.) Nevertheless, this is a strong and largely fascinating warts-and-all (with both the group and their fans being taken to task at times for their bad behavior and self-absorbed attitudes) look at a genuinely unique cultural phenomenon made by someone who understands it innately and who has the ability to convey what made them so special to those not already in the fold. They used to say "There is nothing like a Grateful Dead concert" and indeed, when it comes to rock music documentaries, there is nothing quite like *Long Strange Trip*.

Peter Sobczynski

CREDITS

Origin: United States

Language: English

Released: 2017

Production: Nicholas Koskoff, Alex Blavatnik, Ken Dornstein, Eric Eisner, Justin Kreutzmann; Activist Artists Management, Double E Pictures, Sikelia Productions; released by Amazon Studios

Directed by: Amir Bar-Lev

Cinematography by: Nelson Hume

Music Supervisor: David M. Lemieux; Kyle McKeveny; Joe Rudge

Editing: Keith Fraase; John W. Walter

MPAA rating: R

Running time: 418 minutes

REVIEWS

Anderson, John. *Wall Street Journal.* May 25, 2017.
Campbell, Jon. *Village Voice.* May 25, 2017.
Dalton, Stephen. *Hollywood Reporter.* April 26, 2017.
Fear, David. *Rolling Stone.* May 3, 2017.
Gilbert, Matthew. *Boston Globe.* May 31, 2017.
Gleiberman, Owen. *Variety.* March 18, 2017.
Gold, Daniel M. *New York Times.* May 25, 2017.
Hoffman, Jordan. *Vanity Fair.* January 26, 2017.
Linden, Sheri. *Los Angeles Times.* May 25, 2017.
Wheeler, Brad. *Globe and Mail.* April 26, 2017.

QUOTES

Sam Cutler: "The Grateful Dead are dumb. They make fabulous music, wonderful, amazing music. When it came to business decisions, stupid."

THE LOST CITY OF Z

In 1925, Percy Fawcett ventured into the Amazon in search of a myth. What he discovered became legendary.
—Movie tagline

Box Office: $8.6 Million

The Lost City of Z is the story of one man's unwavering passion and how, as it becomes obsession, this passion eats away at him—and everything around him—that isn't his one need. The pulpiness of a British man exploring a jungle is not that of cartoons, but of tragic noir novels where the pessimistic protagonist understands how completely captured he is by the horizontal bars of his environment and the vertical bars of his own desires. This is a cage we can all understand, even if it still boggles the mind that *The Lost City of Z* is based on real events.

Writer/director James Gray's film is based on the 2009 book of the same name by David Grann, which documents the idealistic explorations of South America by geographer Percy Fawcett (Charlie Hunnam) after his recruitment by the Royal Geographical Society. Fawcett is a military man skilled at survival and stifled in the political game of peacetime military service. When the Amazon calls, he answers. There is purpose in the jungle—even more than he initially expects. Fawcett, at first encouraged by his wife Nina (Sienna Miller) to seek balance between ambition and satisfaction, finds the dangers of the jungle intellectually, physically, and spiritually alluring. These temptations tilt what little balance there was in a routine life and make returning home to civilization's comforts anything but comforting.

Gray has taken a classical adventure story and segmented it expertly, so that each chapter feels inescapably grown from the last, as if there were no other choice but the narrative unfolding on screen. It is not a story about a man losing himself in the jungle, but of a man whose perspective was so broadened that, before he found it, it seemed like he had never yet begun to live. These feelings are carried on the back of Gray's direction, which turns a beautifully-structured script into a symphony with all the creeping progress of a vine through the undergrowth. The first expedition, with Fawcett and his aide-de-camp Henry Costin (Robert Pattinson), is one of hints, whispers, and small successes that only whet the appetites of the Englishmen hungry to make their mark on history. It is one of intoxicating splendor and the equally intoxicating illnesses of unpreparedly taking too much pleasure at once. They are feverish and hopeless, but find clues and survive.

Upon his first return, the alternative is felt. His loving wife and his adorable, ever-growing stable of children only imprison Fawcett further, with the help of some peak photography. Cinematographer Darius Khondji's uptight boardrooms and cramped brown British homes are as claustrophobic as his leafy greens and humid mysteries are seemingly endless and expansive. There's a boyish verve for exploration inherent in all aspects of the film that slowly realizes that it is in fact boyishness, but never counts that as a bad thing—instead coming to realize that its excitable immaturity is beautiful and poignant all at once. *The Lost City of Z*'s soft visuals are that of Stanley Kubrick's tragic yet lovable *Barry Lyndon* (1975) in a jungle, full of beautiful delusions of grandeur.

This is where Hunnam's performance finds its greatest strengths. Hunnam's adeptness at being a stubborn, long-suffering wannabe-intellectual isn't just apt for the character, it's thematically additive for the film. His unquenched thirst for adventure and knowledge masks an insatiable hunger for personal glory that leads to his ruin. Fawcett strains against his military surrounding yet is never accepted by the scholars either. He is caught between masculine glory and a genuine yearn for progress—a progress that goes against the racial beliefs of the time.

That's because Fawcett has found evidence, and heard rumbles from natives, that there is a city (or ruins of a city) in the Amazon that has existed long before conquistadors. This goes against the European ideas of the history of civilization and is widely mocked, as is Fawcett. But finding this Lost City of Z becomes a tangible quest for a man for whom intangibilities mean everything. He's drawn back to it, time and time again like the gravitational pull summoning the tide, not just to prove his theories correct about the natives and their history which would debunk centuries of European racist anthropological theory but to prove himself worthy of the important destiny he feels he deserves. His return to domesticity in between his jungle adventures (even when these adventures become more and more treacherous) hampers him—until his son (Tom Holland) has grown to the age where he can resent his father's absence.

This resentment is coupled with the outbreak of war, which is the film's historical thesis on men writ large. Where else can larger social ideals and the need for personal recognition be conflated, confused, and intermingled with such deadly consequences, and on such scale? It makes returning to the jungle seem almost safe and inviting by comparison. The natives they find are as complex and short of mythic as the jungle's various natural perils, which helps ground every part of the adventure in smokey, slow-burn realism. A hallucinogenic father-son encounter with the former gives a somehow more satisfying end to a mysterious true tale than any attempts at cut-and-dry closure, which allows Gray to create the legend of Percy Fawcett that Fawcett himself so desperately wanted to live.

Jacob Oller

CREDITS

Percy Fawcett: Charlie Hunnam
Henry Costin: Robert Pattinson
Nina Fawcett: Sienna Miller
Jack Fawcett: Tom Holland
Arthur Manley: Edward Ashley
Origin: United States
Language: English, Spanish, Portuguese, German
Released: 2017
Production: Dede Gardner, Dale Armin Johnson, Anthony Katagas, Jeremy Kleiner, James Gray; Keep Your Head, MICA Entertainment, MadRiver Pictures, Plan B Entertainment; released by Bleecker Street Media
Directed by: James Gray
Written by: James Gray
Cinematography by: Darius Khondji
Music by: Christopher Spelman
Music Supervisor: George Drakoulias
Editing: John Axelrad; Lee Haugen
Art Direction: Fiona Gavin
Costumes: Sonia Grande
Production Design: Jean-Vincent Puzos
MPAA rating: PG-13
Running time: 141 minutes

REVIEWS

Brody, Richard. *New Yorker*. April 17, 2017.
Burr, Ty. *Boston Globe*. April 20, 2017.
Chang, Justin. *Los Angeles Times*. April 14, 2017.
Dargis, Manohla. *New York Times*. April 13, 2017.
Ebiri, Bilge. *Village Voice*. April 11, 2017.
Merry, Stephanie. *Washington Post*. April 20, 2017.
Nicholson, Amy. *MTV*. April 12, 2017.
Tobias, Scott. *NPR*. April 13, 2017.
Vishnevetsky, Ignatiy. *The A.V. Club*. April 13, 2017.
Zacharek, Stephanie. *Time*. April 13, 2017.

QUOTES

James Murray: "You don't care about us, you don't even care about going home. You only care about your lost city."

TRIVIA

Director James Gray wrote to Francis Ford Coppola, who directed *Apocalypse Now* (1979), asking for advice on shooting in the jungle. Coppola's reply was "Don't go." When Coppola was planning *Apocalypse Now*, he received the same advice from Roger Corman.

LOST IN PARIS

(Paris pieds nus)

Box Office: $691,597

Dominique Abel and Fiona Gordon were born the same year, are both rail thin, have the same strange body language and they both love physical and film comedy. They made several shorts together before moving onto feature films with *L'iceberg* (2005), *Rumba* (2008), and *The Fairy* (2011). Their movies are the very definition of quirky and their latest, the little seen *Lost in Paris* is as good a distillation of their style and essence as performers and filmmakers as anything. It also showcases why their cinephilia-laden idiosyncrasies have failed to take off despite their overly cute filmmaking and performances. *Lost in Paris* is so heavy-handed and aggressive in its quirk it barely gives you a moment to consider that there ought to be more to a movie than twee, mannered glee.

Fiona (Fiona Gordon) lives in a snowy Canadian town working a clerking job at a small office when a letter arrives from her aunt Martha (Emmanuelle Riva), who left long ago to live in Paris. She still loves her adopted home but she's going to be forced out of her home and into a retirement community because her brain function has begun decreasing (she's introduced delivering the letter into a trash bin by mistake). So Fiona departs for the City of Light to meet up with her aunt for the first time in decades and help her figure out what the next stage in her life should be. The problem is that Fiona is no more attuned to the world around her than her dotty aunt. Within minutes of arriving she becomes lost, loses her bags in the Seine, has her phone accidentally stolen and thrown into a trash can, and has no place to stay. She's misinformed that Martha has died and so prepares for a funeral, but thanks to her new friendship with an eccentric homeless man named Dom (Dominique Abel), a series of bizarre events and investigations leads to her pry open her aunt's coffin and find it empty. So where has Aunt Martha gone off to? She's been gallivanting around Paris, hooking up with old acquaintances and meeting new ones like Dom. If Fiona has any hope of finding her aunt, she's going to have to think a little crazier and let go of her inhibitions, which becomes easier when Dom admits to having feelings for her that she finds herself less and less reluctant to return.

Abel and Gordon have a few very obvious touchstones. Their films and performances mix the elasticity of Looney Tunes, the high-stakes gymnastics of silent-era filmmakers Charlie Chaplin and Harold Lloyd, the precise framing and physicality of French auteur Jacques Tati, and the bold colors and charmed French lives presented by director Jean-Pierre Jeunet. Which is a longer way of saying that their films are entirely too silly and stylized for their own good. The story of *Lost in Paris* is entirely weightless, an excuse to move from one set-piece to another which wouldn't be a flaw, per se, except that their set-pieces and physical comedy aren't impressive or distinct enough to justify even this meager a running time. They've taken after Tati's shuffling, ambling style of stumbling into high-stakes blunders and causing havoc, but as they can't deliberately use the ruined luncheons and restaurants of *Mon Oncle* (1958) or *Playtime* (1967), they have to invent more preposterous circumstances for their humorous escalations. Sneaking into a funeral home or outwitting the police in a park are neither universal nor outlandish enough.

Gordon's character is a series of nervous tics, defined by her refusal to let anything new or exciting into her life, which doesn't make her easy to spend time with. Abel's character is even more threadbare, an obnoxious cinematic homeless person who's supposed charm is meant to disguise his poverty. Homelessness is just one more eccentric trait here, like his cross-dressing after discovering Fiona's discarded suitcase. The film has nothing to say about homelessness, which wouldn't be a problem, except that it ends with Fiona and Dom falling in love, apparently solving both his itinerancy and her lack of possessions and/or permanent residency. Maybe it's asking too much for a comedy to solve its marginal problems, but these questions should also never be on a viewer's mind. The film's only saving grace is the presence of French New Wave legend Riva, who's been making classic movies since the 1950s and who passed away before the film's release in the United States. Riva makes the most of a terribly underwritten part and is so effortlessly graceful and effervescent that it's a shame she didn't make more comedies in her lifetime. From the obnoxious score to the use of Paris as a non-stop carnival, *Lost in Paris* commits many crimes against craft and subtlety, and soft-pedals Riva's apparent dementia and Abel's homelessness, but no film with Riva can be a complete waste of time.

Scout Tafoya

CREDITS

Fiona: Fiona Gordon

Dom: Dominique Abel

Martha: Emmanuelle Riva

Duncan: Pierre Richard

Bob le Mountie: Frederic Meert

Origin: United States

Language: French, English

Released: 2017

Production: Charles Gillibert, Fiona Gordon, Dominique Abel, Cristie Molia; BE TV, CG Cinéma, Proximus SA, Scope Pictures, VOO; released by Oscilloscope Films

Directed by: Fiona Gordon; Dominique Abel

Written by: Fiona Gordon; Dominique Abel

Cinematography by: Claire Childeric; Jean-Christophe Leforestier

Editing: Sandrine Deegen
Costumes: Claire Dubien
Production Design: Nicolas Girault
MPAA rating: Unrated
Running time: 83 minutes

REVIEWS

Bowen, Chuck. *Slant.* June 14, 2017.
Chang, Justin. *Los Angeles Times.* July 6, 2017.
Debruge, Peter. *Variety.* May 17, 2017.
Fink, John. *The Film Stage.* June 15, 2017.
Kenigsberg, Ben. *New York Times.* June 15, 2017.
Kohn, Eric. *IndieWire.* May 22, 2017.
McCarthy, Todd. *Hollywood Reporter.* May 22 2017.
Morgenstern, Joe. *Wall Street Journal.* June 15, 2017.
Padua, Pat. *Washington Post.* July 13, 2017.
Donadoni, Serena. *Village Voice.* June 15, 2017.

TRIVIA

Actress Emmanuelle Riva died just under two months before the film was released in France.

THE LOVERS

A love so strong it can survive marriage.
—Movie tagline

Box Office: $2.2 Million

The movies by the American filmmaker Azazel Jacobs feature a beautiful and gloriously rich sideways or screwball syntax. His characters float and breathe in their own worlds, wired to alternate rhythms patterned on the circuitous and offbeat. The idea of his characters moving in a straight line is personally anathema.

Jacobs is an heir to a vital artistic tradition as the child of two key figures in the American avant-garde. His father is the great American experimental filmmaker Ken Jacobs, director of the groundbreaking *Star Spangled to Death* (2004). His mother is the painter and artist Flo Jacobs. Family has been central to his art, and a big part of studying his growth and development is watching the fascinating ways he has integrated personal details into his art. Azazel Jacobs is his own man with an assured style and fully considered personality.

The director's breakthrough feature *Momma's Man* (2008), observant and trenchant, concerned a young man overwhelmed by the demands of a wife and young child who retreats to the safe and protective space of his parents' spacious New York loft. Ken and Flo Jacobs played the parents, shot almost entirely in their own loft, enriching the emotional details and ratcheting the personal tension and anguish to a revealing and comically uncomfortable depth.

The director's follow-up film, *Terri* (2011), the first of his features he did not originate or write, was another rueful and quietly subversive work undercutting the typical rhythm of the coming of age film. In the director's discerning touch, Jacobs subtly showed how the protagonist's exchanges with a sympathetic assistant principal allow this introverted young outsider bereft of privilege or popularity to gain the right measure of definition and personality.

Six years after his last feature, Jacobs's *The Lovers* is another melancholy work of attenuated moods and sorrow that navigates the complex and wildly unpredictable in considering the nature of love and attraction, desire and rebirth as the movie dramatically charts the fissures and elastic shape of a marriage seemingly on the verge of collapse.

The central middle-age couple, Michael (Tracy Letts) and Mary (Debra Winger), occupy an emotional dead zone in their suburban Los Angeles split level ranch house. Each partner is wholly disconnected from the other. The early scenes between the two establish the almost cruel avoidance the two carry out. Michael sits in a nearly empty room, his face lit by the glare of a too-loud television. He is shown ostracized, emotionally isolated and his every attempt at natural or relaxed conversation feels insistently strained, awkward or banal. With his clean and orderly images, Jacobs draws out that stillness and strange quietness in showing the depth of their acrimony.

The apathy extends to their jobs as well. Both work in impersonal cubicle spaces, Michael as a zoning planner and Mary as an executive. Neither summons a great deal of excitement or initiative. Typically late, Michael strolls in nonchalantly and avoids his superiors. Mary seems perpetually out of time, always making plans only to cancel as her accepting colleague, Susan (Lesley Fera), learns to shrug it off.

The only time either feels the least bit free or satisfied emerges through their secret lives as each has taken on a lover: Lucy (Melora Walters), a tightly-wound ballet dancer and teacher for Michael and Robert (Aidan Gillen), a British novelist Mary is seeing. Now the affairs have reached the tipping point with each paramour applying pressure on the couple to disband their marriage. Michael and Mary appear ready to take the plunge.

Jacobs excels at upsetting the familiar, and this movie takes a thrilling detour just as the couple is seemingly about to acknowledge the futility of carrying on. Just as the two are about to carry out their dutiful and bleak morning routine, a strange, unaccountable, almost accidental private erotic moment proves transporting.

The surprise lights a spark of recognition, a charge of glee and almost animal need that has stayed suppressed for too long.

The reckoning turns instead into a volatile and wholly passionate sexual revival as the two turn their world upside down with their startling reversal. Michael and Mary are suddenly besotted with each other, concocting new rationale to avoid their outside lovers. In Jacobs' delicate and assured touch, *The Lovers* turns wholly unexpected and taps into a different realm of feeling, action and release, what the writer Stanley Cavell called the "comedy of remarriage," the kind of mysterious, sensual comedy of manners found in many of the great works of the classic studio era, like *The Awful Truth* (1937), *The Philadelphia Story* (1940), and *His Girl Friday* (1940).

At its best, *The Lovers* is a gracious and unrelenting study of a marriage, with its volatile swings and harsh self-analysis. Jacobs is neither a Puritan nor judgmental. He is more concerned with studying behavior and consequence. As Michael and Mary attempt to work through their complicated emotions, the movie locates something personal and necessary, the desire for a wholly different kind of surrender.

The narrative complications mirror the slippery fate of the characters. Lucy, for instance, the most combative of the four principals, senses Michael's sudden distance and throws down the gauntlet to assert her own value and importance. Two confrontations by the suddenly aggrieved parties, Lucy turning up at Mary's house or Robert intercepting Michael at the supermarket, lead to the movie's big third act confrontation.

The couple's son, Joel (Tyler Ross), turns up at the house for a Thanksgiving dinner with his new girlfriend, Erin (Jessica Sula), and promptly vents his fury and rage at what he sees as the fundamental dishonesty of his parents' marriage. Until now the film was mostly muted and internalized, the characters' trapped by their own passivity. Joel's entrance clears the decks and ends with overturned furniture and a hole punched in the wall.

The scene makes an impact, though not necessarily a revealing or satisfying one. The emotions are understandable yet off-note, an overreaction to a film that worked assiduously to find its own tone and style. Jacobs perhaps feared his film was too monotonous, but he goes too far and this is the one glaring mistake in a film that otherwise captures a quiet sadness and panic.

The actors are terrific. In the midst of his late career resurgence, Letts gives a physical, tense performance, of mood and heartbreak, gallant but also foolishness. Late in the film, when he sits down at the piano and bangs out, slightly off tune but with conviction, a number from his youth, the moment crystallizes his sense of regret and compromise. Winger has her first lead role in a long time, and she mediates that wealth of experience with both aplomb and a deeper sense of bitterness, summoning a prickly outrage and bruising wariness.

The photography, by Tobias Datum, is uncluttered and direct, closely aligned to the characters' feelings. Mandy Hoffman's score is also lovely and unforced. The movie's final moments are bittersweet and disruptive, indicative of a movie where nothing quite goes according to plan. The free-for-all is exhilarating.

Patrick Z. McGavin

CREDITS

Mary: Debra Winger
Michael: Tracy Letts
Lucy: Melora Walters
Robert: Aidan Gillen
Erin: Jessica Sula
Origin: United States
Language: English
Released: 2017
Production: Ben LeClair, Chris Stinson; released by A24 Films LLC
Directed by: Azazel Jacobs
Written by: Azazel Jacobs
Cinematography by: Tobias Datum
Music by: Mandy Hoffman
Sound: Alexandra Fehrman
Music Supervisor: Dan Wilcox
Editing: Darrin Navarro
Art Direction: Celine Diano
Costumes: Diaz Jacobs
Production Design: Sue Tebbutt
MPAA rating: R
Running time: 97 minutes

REVIEWS

Anderson, Melissa. *Village Voice*. May 3, 2017.
Burr, Ty. *Boston Globe*. May 10, 2017.
Callahan, Dan. *TheWrap*. April 28, 2017.
Catsoulis, Jeannette. *New York Times*. May 4, 2017.
Chang, Justin. *Los Angeles Times*. May 4, 2017.
Edelstein, David. *New York Magazine*. May 8, 2017.
Hornaday, Ann. *Washington Post*. May 11, 2017.
Kenny, Glenn. *RogerEbert.com*. May 5, 2017.
Vishnevetsky, Ignatiy. *The A.V. Club*. May 3, 2017.
Zacharek, Stephanie. *Time*. May 8, 2017.

QUOTES

Erin: "So, when you met Mary, you were a musician?"

Michael: "A long, long time ago."
Erin: "Oh."
Michael: "I sold her a bill of goods."
Erin: "Well, we all change."
Michael: "Yeah. It's too bad."

TRIVIA

Although playing characters of the same age, actress Debra Winger is actually over ten years older than co-star Tracy Letts.

AWARDS

Nominations:

Ind. Spirit 2018: Screenplay

LOWRIDERS

Box Office: $6.3 Million

Ricardo de Montreuil's *Lowriders* ruins a fascinating subcultural milieu and some terrific actors with the outrageously ridiculous architecture of its shopworn plot. Drama requires conflict for depth and nuance. Here it plays more like a perverse tyranny, imposed here to enliven it, it achieves the opposite effect, making painfully obvious the film's lack of authenticity or originality.

Everything flattens to the point of absurdity. What should be a fast, direct, and unpretentious movie about East Los Angeles car culture is reduced to an Oedipal tale, a perverse melodrama about damaged masculinity and wounded pride. The movie becomes too much of everything. Rather than challenge cultural presuppositions, *Lowriders* wallows in them. What it should illustrate dramatically the movie announces, with a heavy hand, betraying any kind of emotional plausibility.

The title refers to an intricately tricked out car, typically adorned in bright and exciting colors with elaborately designed murals, customized by a specialized hydraulic system that very stylishly either lowers or raises the car at the flip of a switch. This subculture began in Mexico and flourished in the émigré Latino communities in Los Angeles after World War II.

Like bikers, the swaggering, colorful, and self-expressive nature of the work has a political dimension. Because the car body rides lower than the wheel rims, the style has drawn the official censure of public officials, who have ostensibly outlawed its "official" practice.

The movie's young hero and narrator, Danny (Gabriel Chavarria), is drawn to the rebellious and transgressive part of the culture. He is a graffiti artist with a distinctive signature and a talent for getting into tough spots, like the distinctive architecture and overpasses that provide a dramatic platform for his work. "The whole city is my canvas," he says. He is sweet, though also a little restless, drawn to vicarious thrills and acting out with his friend Chuy (Tony Revolori).

After he receives a mysterious message that prompts him to carry out a dangerous late night tagging, Danny is chased by the cops and arrested along with Chuy. That impulsive action draws the wrath of Miguel (Demián Bichir), Danny's defiantly proud and stern father. The older man has little sympathy for this kind of extracurricular actions. Miguel owns a car repair shop and directs a local car club that performs in street shows. His prized possession, "Green Poison," is a stylishly high-end renegade Chevrolet Impala he runs on the lucrative cash circuit.

The film's early scenes show a certain promise and excitement, an intermingling of the loose and rhapsodic, suggesting a documentary verisimilitude that endows the cars with a funky mixture of the cool and outrageous. (The drivers make them do ridiculous and physically defiant acts.) These contained moments have a particular flair and thrill. Making his English-language debut, Montreuil understands the innate appeal and fascination of the subject matter. Unfortunately the mechanics of the plot take over, and the director cannot really bring anything new or distinctive to his story.

The script, by Elgin James and Cheo Hodari Coker, is episodic and crude, marked by too much harsh psychology and crude portraiture. Miguel is a recovering alcoholic with a supportive new wife, Gloria (Eva Longoria). The story turns on a prodigal return. Francisco (Theo Rossi), or "Ghost," is Danny's charismatic older brother who was recently released following an eight-year prison sentence. The mother of the brothers died years earlier, a traumatic action that initiated Ghost's downward slide.

The plot pivots between Danny's conflicted loyalty to his hard-working and imperfect father and his developing attraction to the amoral cool and unpredictable energy of his older brother. (Danny's friend Chuy also becomes a pawn in the triangle in a way that does the movie few favors.) A love interest is also introduced through the beautiful photographer (Melissa Benoist) who is drawn to Danny's raw, developing artistic sensibility.

The film's disparate parts—love story, cultural study, family drama—collide off each other, in an increasingly strained and absurdist manner. The script is also constantly at war with itself, fatally unsure of its direction, tone, or point of view. The movie goes off the rails in the middle passages. After the father upstages the two boys by winning the coveted street competition held at Elysian Park, Ghost retaliates with a particularly poorly thought out and psychologically murky revenge plot that leaves Miguel nearly dead from the altercation.

Anybody still with the movie at this point is likely to be flabbergasted by the leaps of logic. The underlying grievances and torment of Ghost toward his father is particularly unrevealing. The whole movie floats in a place that feels unbound by logic or consequence. Everything is unreal or underdeveloped. *Lowriders* is a peculiar beast, a movie that wants to be fast and kinetic and lively but one that too often settles for the sentimental.

The movie is too bloodless and torpid to ever feel dramatically persuasive. Part of the problem is the conception of Danny is too blank and dramatically unshaded to overcome the inherent weakness of the material. Chavarria is an appealing actor who projects a certain warmth and subtle ease. His character needs greater torment, guilt, and range but it never arrives. Likewise, Bichir is a great actor, but the part is standard issue. Rossi gives the most intense and expressive performance. He has a great face that goes either way, sharp and playful or a darker thread of menace.

The setting and subject at least suggests the fleeting promise of a sharp and good-looking movie. *Lowriders* fails at the basic level of craft and style. In the most dejected note, *Lowriders* is visually drab and rarely takes advantage of the local color, landscapes or imagery.

The only time the colors actually pop comes at the very end, during the closing credits. Finally unbound to the story and wholly free, these final images are a reminder of what was lost in the process. Like *The Fast and Furious* (2001), the cars are more memorable than the characters.

Patrick Z. McGavin

CREDITS

Danny: Gabriel Chavarria
Miguel Alvarez: Demian Bichir
Francisco "Ghost" Alvarez: Theo Rossi
Chuy: Tony Revolori
Lorelei: Melissa Benoist
Origin: United States
Language: English
Released: 2017
Production: Jason Blum, Brian Grazer; Blumhouse Productions, LLC., Imagine Entertainment; released by Universal Pictures
Directed by: Ricardo de Montreuil
Written by: Elgin James; Cheo Hodari Coker
Cinematography by: Andres Sanchez
Music by: Bryan Senti
Sound: Paul Hackner
Music Supervisor: John Bissell
Editing: Billy Fox; Kiran Pallegadda
Art Direction: Hunter Brown; Eve McCarney
Costumes: Mirren Gordon-Crozier
Production Design: Melanie Jones
MPAA rating: PG-13
Running time: 98 minutes

REVIEWS

Abele, Robert. *Los Angeles Times*. May 11, 2017.
Barker, Andrew. *Variety.*. June 3, 2017.
D'Angelo, Mike. *The A.V. Club* . May 11, 2017.
Lemire, Christy. *RogerEbert.com*. May 12, 2017.
Linden, Sheri. *Hollywood Reporter*. April 29, 2017.
Genzlinger, Neil. *New York Times*. May 10, 2017.
Guzman, Rafer. *Newsday*. May 12, 2017.
Scherstuhl, Alan. *Village Voice*. May 11, 2017.
Walsh, Katie. *Chicago Tribune*. May 11, 2017.
Weitzman, Elizabeth. *TheWrap*. May 11, 2017.

TRIVIA

Actress Lily Collins was originally set to star in the film but had to drop out due to scheduling conflicts.

LUCKY

Box Office: $955,925

Wim Wenders' modern classic *Paris, Texas* (1984) opens with panoramic images of desert landscape silhouetted against stylized, vertiginous rock formations. The camera suddenly moves in on a close up of Travis, the movie's enigmatic central character. In *Lucky*, a first feature directed by the actor John Carroll Lynch, the film opens with echoing visual grammar, the pungent, lived-in southwestern border landscape arrayed against the evocative mountain ridges and peaks.

The camera also quickly settles on a face—craggy, beaten down, and mysterious. The two films are mighty different in scale, emotional range, and ambition. The face is the essential link, a natural given it is one and the same, belonging to the great American actor Harry Dean Stanton. In Wenders' film, that visage is forlorn, hidden, and scruffy with a beard. As the movie opens out into a search through the past, that face becomes a landscape sculpted by a haunted suggestiveness. In *Lucky*, the face is more gaunt, serene, and transient. Moving through time and space, that face conveys a multitude of experience, life, wonder, heartbreak, and sorrow.

The story of Harry Dean Stanton is inextricably connected to the post-classic period of narrative American cinema. After spending much of his first working decade as an actor developing his style in television, Stanton became a key avatar in the New American Cinema through his work with actors like Jack Nicholson and Warren Oates, the producer and filmmaker Roger Corman, and directors like Monte Hellman, Thomas McGuane, Francis Ford Coppola, and Arthur Penn. Stanton worked in his own idiom, wary, sly, and offbeat, like his collaborations with Hellman, a wanted cowboy in *Ride in the Whirlwind* (1966), a hitchhiker in *Two-Lane Blacktop* (1971), or as a dapper gambler in *Cockfighter* (1974).

Harry Dean Stanton died, at the age of 91, on September 15, 2017. In a career lasting some six decades and hundreds of parts, Stanton only had two truly lead roles, in *Paris, Texas* and now, *Lucky*. If *Paris, Texas* marked a particular high-water point in the actor's career, *Lucky* is a fitting elegy, an ecstatic reminder of his range and soulful depth, the acuity and intelligence, and the unpredictability. Stanton was the character actor par excellence. *Lucky* demonstrates repeatedly another quality about the actor, a lyrical generosity, of how even in this rare moment in the spotlight, he was more than willing to cede the stage.

Like Stanton, John Carroll Lynch is a brilliant character actor. It no doubt explains the deeper sense of kinship. He is a much different style of actor. He is big and brawny, and his face is more wide open. He is at his most exciting and thrilling when he subverts his stolid, agreeable persona, a pitch black glee in playing Marge's husband in the Coen Brothers' *Fargo* (1996), or a malevolent underplaying as the most cunning suspect in David Fincher's *Zodiac* (2007). The new movie is a showcase for actors, of the life, the culture, and the milieu. Lynch has also worked with his share of great directors, but this film taps into the art and subtlety of performance, of inflection, vocal rhythms, and physical movement in expressing the most fundamental of emotions, love, sadness, anger, and regret. *Lucky* is restrained and plaintive, clearly composed in the direct and natural lighting of cinematographer Tim Suhrstedt.

In *Paris, Texas*, the playwright Sam Shepard conceived the character of Travis and braided him, psychologically, with his usual thematic preoccupations, the wayward or absent father, the dreamer in flight from his own past. With *Lucky*, any sense of discovery is nullified by the character's prickly self-determination. He floats to his own rhythms. In the Wenders film, Travis was emptied out and the narrative tracked his definition and shape.

In *Lucky*, the lead figure is solitary and self-contained. The screenwriters, Logan Sparks and Drago Sumonja, in their first produced script, wrote the film with Stanton in mind. The writers even fused parts of the actor's own biography to shape the role. Like his eponymous protagonist, Stanton grew up in Kentucky and served in the Navy during World War II. The script, stealthy, is also a work of concision. *Lucky* plays like an Eastern European village comedy, a virtually plotless work, constructed out of anecdotes and diversions given a buoyancy and shape in the lilting, imaginative voices of the various players.

Lucky lives, alone, in a modestly apportioned frame house in an unnamed Arizona desert town. Structurally the movie is shaped around his daily ritual, beginning with his early yoga exercises and his mornings spent, in leisurely idyll, at a diner having breakfast and assiduously working out a crossword puzzle. The cantankerous Lucky is never afraid to unload his philosophical musings, trading banter with the cook, Joe (Barry Shabaka Henley) and warmer exchanges with his preferred waitress, Loretta (Yvonne Huff). His acrimonious personality is also on view, evident by the harsh epithet he unfurls every time he walks by one particular street establishment. He also demonstrates a more tender side, most clearly expressed in his elegant interactions with the owner of a small grocery store, Bibi (Bertila Damas).

In the best sense, *Lucky* is a hangout movie. It's like a Nelson Algren novel, giving voice to the idiosyncratic, eccentric, and those who live on the colorful margins. The film locates some of its purest, unfiltered moments at the bar where Lucky ends his daily rounds. He works out a series of duets and often sharp-tongued back and forth with the regulars, the proprietor, Elaine (Beth Grant); her husband Paulie (James Darren); and his close friend, Howard (played with an insider's glee by the filmmaker David Lynch, with whom Stanton worked on many films). The bar is a performance space, a platform for soliloquies and sad tales, like Paulie's story of how his wife saved him from the cruelty of a small-time con life and dissolution or Howard's pain at the disappearance of his pet tortoise. John Carroll Lynch obviously understands the cadence and vocal patterns, and these vignettes have a bounce and flourish.

Lucky's orderly existence is suddenly thrown asunder one moment when the flashing digital clock on his coffee maker causes him to momentarily lose consciousness and occasions a visit to his doctor, (Ed Begley, Jr.). The moment sets up a natural conflict, the indefatigable Lucky who refuses to give up his pack a day cigarette habit or his drinking, and the realistic doctor who counsels him about biological inevitability and his encroaching mortality.

From this moment *Lucky* splits from the small, private moments of recognition and wonder giving way to meditation on aging and mortality. In one of the best scenes of the film, Loretta, the waitress, pays Lucky a surprise visit at his home to inquire about his health, and the two end up sharing a marijuana joint. The taciturn, withholding Lucky suddenly opens up, but his intimate revelation jars Loretta, making her deeply uncomfortable, underlining his reluctance to talk about his past.

Lucky's argumentative and difficult side has limitations, like a moment at the bar when he tears too aggressively into a life insurance salesman, Bobby (Ron Livingston). *Lucky* is never afraid to ruin the mood, but the movie never goes too far to humanize the man out of proportion. It's a portrait of a man, lonely and occasionally angry but also given to moments of breathtaking clarity and surprise. The actors weave it together, like an arabesque. They inhabit the roles, clear and naturally. David Lynch is the one exception. Even though his grandeur and emphatic delivery is disruptive and sometimes peculiar, it underscores the kind of cluttered, lived-in quality of the overall film.

Harry Dean Stanton's performance is a marvel of tact, underplaying, and withholding. It is also funky and nervy, like the way he performs with ease wearing just his cowboy boots and skivvies or the private moments of watching game shows at home on his couch. Stanton is always projecting intelligence and feeling, an uncompromising man moving to his own beat and patterns. *Lucky* is a movie of pieces, but they congeal. The movie builds beautifully toward two outstanding moments, an eerie and sharp exchange between Lucky and a Marine (Tom Skerritt) who also saw action in the Pacific theater, talking about fragility and perseverance in the face of madness.

As a character Lucky remains lucid and grounded. He is also a dreamer, and it is natural to wonder at times whether or not he slips into or out of reveries, dreams, hallucinations or flashbacks. The past is rarely addressed, but a shocking abrupt action or moment suggests a much more open and varied background. For all that is unknown and curious about the character, *Lucky* remains consistently engrossing through what is left unspoken. The mysterious qualities are invigorating and enveloping. Late in the film, when he launches into a wonderful rendition of the Spanish-language standard, "Volver, Volver," at a young boy's party, Lucky says all that is necessary as he unearths previously unexpressed depths. He has arrived at his own state of grace.

Patrick Z. McGavin

CREDITS

Lucky: Harry Dean Stanton

Howard: David Lynch

Bobby Lawrence: Ron Livingston

Dr. Christian Kneedler: Ed Begley, Jr.

Fred: Tom Skerritt

Origin: United States

Language: English

Released: 2017

Production: Ira Steven Behr, Danielle Renfrew, Greg Gilreath, Adam Hendricks, Richard Kahan, John H. Lang, Logan Sparks, Drago Sumonja; Divide/Conquer, Superlative Films; released by Magnolia Pictures

Directed by: John Carroll Lynch

Written by: Logan Sparks; Drago Sumonja

Cinematography by: Tim Suhrstedt

Music by: Elvis Kuehn

Music Supervisor: Mikki Itzigsohn; Lauren Marie Mikus

Editing: Robert Gajic

Costumes: Lisa Norcia

Production Design: Almitra Corey

MPAA rating: Unrated

Running time: 98 minutes

REVIEWS

Addlego, Walter. *San Francisco Chronicle.* October 4, 2017.

Brody, Richard. *New Yorker.* September 25, 2017.

Burr, Ty. *Boston Globe.* October 4, 2017.

Catsoulis, Jeannette. *New York Times.* September 28, 2017.

Chang, Justin. *Los Angeles Times.* September 28, 2017.

Phillips, Michael. *Chicago Tribune.* October 6, 2017.

Rothkopf, Joshua. *Time Out New York.* September 29, 2017.

Scherstuhl, Alan. *Village Voice.* October 5, 2017.

Seitz, Matt Zoller. *RogerEbert.com.* September 29, 2017.

Zacharek, Stephanie. *Time.* September 28, 2017.

QUOTES

Lucky: "There's a difference between lonely and being alone."

TRIVIA

This film reunited actors Harry Dean Stanton and Tom Skerritt thirty-eight years since they appeared together in *Alien* (1979).

M

THE MAN WHO INVENTED CHRISTMAS

Box Office: $5.7 Million

For all the positives *The Man Who Invented Christmas* has going for it—including a classic, well-known story, a solid cast, and an overall effervescent pizazz—it's quite odd that this *Shakespeare in Love*-esque (1998) imagining of how and why Charles Dickens wrote *A Christmas Carol* is so forgettable. That's not to say *The Man Who Invented Christmas* is a particularly bad film, but that it isn't likely to become a go-to holiday movie viewing film as time marches on. Alas, not every artist can be a Charles Dickens, who made art that has persisted for generations.

As *The Man Who Invented Christmas* opens, we see Dickens (Dan Stevens) trying to find a quiet place to work. His large house is under expensive renovation and his cadre of children clamor for his attention. This is a clever way to open the film as it lends a sense of pacing that remains imbued in the film throughout its 105-minute running-time. While Dickens does indeed seem to be enjoying the fruits of his labor with a large, happy household complete with maids and nannies to help, it is soon revealed that Dickens might be falling victim to keeping up appearances without the financial means to back it all up.

Upon meeting with his publishers, Dickens and his best-friend/manager John Forster (an amicable Justin Edwards) try to play off the recent poor sales of Dickens's latest novels, *The Old Curiosity Shop* and *Barnaby Ridge.* His travelogue *American Notes* also failed to dazzle, and the fact these titles also don't ring a bell to those who aren't huge Dickens fans drives home the point that the man is struggling following bestsellers *Oliver Twist* and *Nicholas Nickleby,* which are clearly household bookshelf mainstays, even nearly two centuries later. The coffers are running low, and Dickens knows it, but he's also a bit creatively blocked, likely due to his newfound success creating many more distractions. As if things were not tough enough, Dickens' shiftless, money-mooching father John (Jonathan Pryce) reemerges in England looking to not only get handouts based on his famous son but also to borrow more money. Indeed, even in the Merry Olde England of the mid-1800s, more money equals more problems.

Back to the wall, Dickens decides the only way forward out of his writer's block and dwindling finances is the same way he got rich and famous: writing. Thus, he pitches an idea he seemingly pulls out of thin air, a tale about Christmas, which, unbeknownst to modern audiences, isn't a popular holiday at all in 1843. In fact, Christmas trees are a bit of a new trend and the day is barely recognized at all so this idea falls flat to his publishers. Yet stubborn and a bit cocky (much like his father, a notion which gets driven home relentlessly throughout), Dickens feels he not only has the best idea he's even had but that he will publish the book himself, thus doubling-down on the idea he just concocted, Dickens also claims he will get the book written, illustrated, and out to the masses in time for the coming Christmas holiday, which is a mere month and a half away. From here, Dickens and audiences are off in a race against time as Dickens seeks to crank out *A*

Christmas Carol in order to solve all of his problems, which, incidentally, he kind of created himself.

Again, *The Man Who Invented Christmas* is a perfectly fine film but not much more than that. Stevens plays Dickens with a fun, kind of mad professor sensibility, and Stevens feels allowed to perform free from audience expectations as not much is known about Dickens by most moviegoers. It's also apparently factually correct that Dickens would often use real people for inspiration for his fictional characters and that happens throughout *The Man Who Invented Christmas.* A good example here is when a local curmudgeon Dickens comes across serves as inspiration for Ebenezer Scrooge (a wonderfully cranky Christopher Plummer), who then regularly appears in Dickens's home, giving him lines he feeds directly onto the page. The relationship between always-struggling patriarch John Dickens serving as the fire Charles Dickens has to succeed is also woven into the film, but it does tend to get a bit heavy-handed the third or fourth time it's noted.

Overall, *The Man Who Invented Christmas* is a clever biopic by way of origin story about one of the world's greatest and most beloved authors. Stevens as Dickens is a lot of fun and his kind of maniacal performance serves to liven up what, on paper could have been a fairly stuffy affair. All of the women in the film are vastly underused as well as clichéd, but, sadly, that seems to be the norm of late. And while *The Man Who Invented Christmas* is a family safe, holiday film, it's just something that kind of floats in and out of the cinematic ether, like a ghost of biopics past. Not good, not bad, but not terribly memorable either.

Don R. Lewis

CREDITS

Charles Dickens: Dan Stevens
Ebenezer Scrooge: Christopher Plummer
John Dickens: Jonathan Pryce
Leech: Simon Callow
Mrs. Fisk: Miriam Margolyes
Origin: United States
Language: English
Released: 2017
Production: Niv Fichman, Vadim Jean, Robert Mickelson, Susan Mullen, Ian Sharples; Mazur/Kaplan Company, Parallel Films, Rhombus Media, The Mob Film Co.; released by Bleecker Street Media
Directed by: Bharat Nalluri
Written by: Susan Coyne
Cinematography by: Ben Smithard
Music by: Mychael Danna
Sound: David McCallum
Editing: Stephen O'Connell; Jamie Pearson
Art Direction: Neill Treacy
Costumes: Leonie Prendergast
Production Design: Paki Smith
MPAA rating: PG
Running time: 104 minutes

REVIEWS

Duralde, Alonso. *TheWrap.* October 29, 2017.
Grierson, Tim. *Screen International.* October 29, 2017.
Henderson, Eric. *Slant Magazine.* November 21, 2017.
Jolin, Dan. *Empire.* December 4, 2017.
Lengel, Kerry. *Arizona Republic.* November 23, 2017.
Roeper, Richard. *Chicago Sun-Times.* November 22, 2017.
Rothkopf, Joshua. *Time Out.* November 23, 2017.
Taylor, Kate. *The Globe and Mail (Toronto).* November 24, 2017.
White, Danielle. *Austin Chronicle.* November 22, 2017.
Yoshida, Emily. *New York Magazine.* November 24, 2017.

TRIVIA

At 87 years of age, Christopher Plummer is the oldest actor to ever play Scrooge.

MARJORIE PRIME

Box Office: $180,608

Michael Almereyda's beautiful, allusive science-fiction drama *Marjorie Prime* begins with some shimmering and ecstatic water imagery followed by a medium-length reverse angle shot of a woman standing on the sundeck of a beach house as she gazes over the vastness of the ocean. Water is the movie's dominant visual motif, contemplative, mysterious, and marked by plaintive sorrow and regret.

For more than three decades, Almereyda has been an indispensable though criminally underrated figure in the independent American cinema. He makes steely, idiosyncratic and exciting movies on very low-budgets, and he has never had a popular breakthrough. His strongest films radiate a searching and restless intelligence, like his off-center and hilarious debut *Twister* (1989), the sinuous black and white vampire movie, *Nadja* (1996), made in collaboration with David Lynch, or his coolly passionate modern dress Shakespeare adaptation, *Hamlet* (2000).

He is also a serious and deeply informed student of film and film culture (he studied with the great American film critic turned painter Manny Farber). In addition to his narrative features, Almereyda has also made some terrific documentaries, on artists ranging from Sam Shepard to John Ashbery, exploring the very nature of creativity, drive, and originality. His new work is very much of a piece with his previous feature, *Experimenter* (2015), his exciting and breathtaking deconstruction on the life and practices of the behavioral theorist Stanley Milgram.

His new movie is an adaptation of Jordan Harrison's play of the same name from 2014. The story is futuristic, set around 2050, though the underpinning of science fiction is subtly rendered and much more unsettling in its social satire and the moral implications of its ideas. Despite the narrative importance of augmented reality, artificial intelligence and computer software programming, the movie is not about technology. It is about individuals, the past, and the desire to construct and shape those memories into something recuperative and meaningful.

Structurally, the movie is composed in three dominant movements. The form is deceptively straightforward, the action drawn out through a series of conversations. Like Harold Pinter or Edward Albee, the talk is mannered, oblique, curious, and sometimes unnervingly funny. Everybody is a player. "I feel like I am performing," is one of the first lines spoken. The woman shown at the start, Marjorie (Lois Smith), is an 85-year old widow who lives in the gorgeous beach house.

Her character is introduced, in conversation, with a handsome and mysterious man, identified as Walter (Jon Hamm). The nature of their exchanges creates a quietly transfixing tone and rhythm. She clearly needs a jolt of remembrance to carry her along, and his detached, odd vocal delivery only adds to the intrigue and dramatic suspense.

"I remember," he says, cryptically, as they share private reveries about events from more than fifty years earlier. The strangely passive voice and calculated behavior make clear that Walter is a so-called "Prime," a 3D hologram, or digital simulacrum of Marjorie's late husband. He is a kind of digital emanation, or projection, used to help her adapt and cope with her dementia.

Marjorie lives at the beach house with her daughter, Tess (Geena Davis) and her husband, Jon (Tim Robbins). The technology, which Tess discards as "grotesque," has only opened up old wounds and bitter grievances. Jon is more open and supportive, believing it a more graceful and soothing way for one to acknowledge their own mortality. Jon subsequently becomes the conduit for Walter's programming, helping him absorb important details Walter, about his work and his personality, to ensure a more fluid and spontaneous form of communication. "You didn't get prettier as you aged," Jon warns.

The film is never static or passive. Almereyda and his gifted young cinematographer, Sean Price Williams, create some thrilling and sharp visual rhyming in faces, or bodies framed against the imposing architecture. The language and images escalate and build off each other, giving psychological density and shape to physical surroundings, like another pensive moment with Marjorie in silhouette inside a deep-lined cathedral space that opens into her outside garden.

The water imagery, and its different permutations, as rain, the ocean, or most tenderly, a swimming pool, where Marjorie, in an evocative flashback, recalls the blissed moment when Walter proposed to her. "You are still too old for me," her younger iteration (Hannah Gross) says. Lois Smith originated the part of Marjorie in the two major theater productions, in Los Angeles and New York. She brings a wistful quality, but also something vital and lustful to the part. Her character was a great violinist until arthritis incapacitated her.

Time is both compressed and expanded, a fade out lasts days or a couple of years, particularly in a lyrical montage of photographs during one important bridging action about halfway through the film. Tess quotes William James, saying, "When you remember something, you are remembering the memory." The movie's conflict is shaped by the act of forgetting, of disavowal, in this case the emotional specifics and pain involving the death of a young man. *Marjorie Prime* allegorizes a present where a pain and loss hover over like a primordial menace. Any distance has been removed, the sorrow and intensity is undeniable.

Since the characters are artists, *Marjorie Prime* is filled with references, of high and low, from *Casablanca* (1941) to *My Best Friend's Wedding* (1997) to Mozart, Gertrude Stein, and Bob Dylan. The pieces are brilliantly fused together and Almereyda connects the feelings and emotions, showing the anguish, loneliness or heartbreak in a way that is quite devastating, like a still and quiet moment with Tess at a piano as she breaks into a few soft and intricate strains of Dylan's "I Shall Be Released."

The brilliant British musician Mica Levi composed the film's score, and her work here is much less abrasive and atonal than her work on Jonathan Glazer's *Under the Skin* (2014) or Pablo Larrain's *Jackie* (2016). Almereyda has brought together both brilliant technical collaborators and fantastic actors and synthesized their talents to help deepen them. Robbins, for instance, who has always used his height and size to great emotional effect, to hold back or push in, gives another of his wrenching and subtle performances. When he does break out, like slowly getting drunk and lashing out at Walter, the moment is chilling.

Davis gives the fullest and most complex screen performance of recent memory. When Tess vents her rage, like expressing her frustration at her estranged relationship with her daughter, it is neither cathartic nor easy. Like the best science fiction, *Marjorie Prime* is a potent reminder of imperfection, an abject lesson in the sacrifices of what it means to be human.

Patrick Z. McGavin

CREDITS

Young Marjorie: Hannah Gross
Walter: Jon Hamm
Tess: Geena Davis
Jon: Tim Robbins
Marjorie: Lois Smith
Origin: United States
Language: English
Released: 2017
Production: Uri Singer, Michael Almereyda; BB Film Productions, Passage Pictures; released by FilmRise
Directed by: Michael Almereyda
Written by: Michael Almereyda
Cinematography by: Sean Price Williams
Music by: Mica Levi
Music Supervisor: Lucy Bright; Jonathan Finegold
Editing: Kathryn J. Schubert
Costumes: Kama K. Royz
Production Design: Javiera Varas
MPAA rating: Unrated
Running time: 99 minutes

REVIEWS

Anderson, John. *Wall Street Journal.*. August 17, 2017.
Bowen, Chuck. *Slant Magazine.* August 14, 2017.
Chang, Justin. *Los Angeles Times.* August 17, 2017.
Edelstein, David. *New York Magazine.* August 16, 2017.
Kenny, Glenn. *New York Times.* August 17, 2017.
King, Danny. *Village Voice.* August 16, 2017.
Hornaday, Ann. *Washington Post.* August 31, 2017.
Rainer, Peter. *Christian Science Monitor.* August 24, 2017.
Rothkopf, Josh. *Time Out New York.* August 17, 2017.
Vishnevetsky, Ignatiy *The A.V. Club.* August 17, 2017.

TRIVIA

The film was made in thirteen days, with the actors working twelve of them.

AWARDS

Nominations:

Ind. Spirit 2018: Actor--Supporting (Smith)

MARSHALL

His name means justice.
—Movie tagline

Live hard. Fight harder.
—Movie tagline

Box Office: $10.1 Million

Director Reginald Hudlin thinks so highly of late civil rights great Thurgood Marshall, who loomed large in life and rose to be the first African American on the U.S. Supreme Court, that he says he has emphatically envisioned Marshall suitably situated way up there on Mount Rushmore, a black man who set legal precedents carved shoulder to shoulder with that illustrious quartet of white presidents. Hudlin apparently deems the addition of Marshall's face upon that of the mountain to be appropriate because he too forever changed the face of America. Yet, the filmmaker stressed that he did not want to depict someone loftily out of reach. While Marshall is now remembered the way, he was during his career-culminating stint on the highest court in the land, Hudlin wanted to persuasively turn back the clock to when this vitally-important figure possessed powerfully-impressive vitality. It is much the same as the manner in which Mount Vernon decided in recent years to create life-like, younger figurines of a certain guy already upon the aforementioned South Dakota landmark, depictions of the Father of our Country that exude vigor in stark contrast to that indelible image of a remote-rather-than-relatable, aged icon who stares out daily from dollars.

To garner as many of those as possible, Hudlin said he was determined to avoid making the kind of film that he has always abhorred: an "It's good for you!" history lesson delivered via an insufficiently-palatable "medicine movie" at which audiences might well turn up their noses. The director was determined that everything in his film about Marshall (Chadwick Boseman) would go down as pleasurably as possible, not a stolidly-elevating, exhaustive and exhausting cradle-to-grave movie that might slowly but surely make viewers begin to yearn for the latter, but instead a solidly-entertaining presentation that is both rousing and relevant. The director largely succeeds, but, to be totally truthful, one must add that his film often does so by disappointingly veering from veracity.

Perhaps that is fitting, since the real-life case chronicled here features both a defendant and supposed victim who are ultimately shown to have finessed the facts. This was early in Marshall's valiant legal career with the National Association for the Advancement of Colored People (NAACP), litigation lurid and incendiary enough in both 1941 and 2017 to make eyes widen with intrigue rather than glaze over from boredom. Unlike Marshall's later, time-honored triumph arguing against the concept of "separate-but-equal" in Brown v. Board of Education, viewers know little about this case and its outcome, allowing for the development of suspense.

White and wealthy Connecticut socialite Eleanor Strubing (Kate Hudson) alleged that Joseph Spell (Sterling K. Brown), the black chauffer-butler employed on the estate she shared with her husband (a former Princeton football star), had animalistically attacked her one night, repeatedly raping her before flinging her, bound and gagged, off a bridge into the freezing water below. Spell, no choir boy, initially insisted that he had never laid even a hand upon her, but quickly found himself all but tried and convicted in the titillating tabloid press coverage. This led to the baseless, better-safe-than sorry dismissals of numerous black household servants who had little chance of making a living in any other way. Showing that prejudice did not solely flourish on Southern soil, more than a few whipped-up Yankees raucously yelled for Spell to be put in his place—on the end of a lynching rope.

Arriving in town to save said neck was Marshall, then just in his early thirties. The film's succinct title makes him sound like a straight-shooting Western hero with an equally-unwavering determination that the rule of law would prevail, that Spell would be found innocent based on the facts and not have prejudgment based on pigmentation lead to a conviction based on color. There was no shortage of hurdles: the jury was all alabaster; the judge (James Cromwell) was an old pal of the man who begot the virulently-bigoted prosecutor (Dan Stevens); and, since Marshall was not a member of the state's bar, the case would be actually argued in court by a well-respected local attorney: Sam Friedman (Josh Gad), a Jew knowing a thing or two about intolerance who conscientiously answered the NAACP's call in the face of career-jeopardizing public displeasure and despite having extensive experience in civil rather than criminal matters. To continue the previously-used analogy about Marshall, it was like taking away the lawman's most potent weapon—his stirring, persuasive courtroom eloquence—with a stern warning from the bench that shooting off his mouth would have serious consequences.

Thus, Boseman understandably spoke of his initial disappointment at the curious choice of this case, essentially being asked to play a lion of litigators without the chance of dramatically emitting the man's righteous roar. (Introductory flashes and a moment on the courthouse steps provided the somewhat-frustrated thespian with consoling oratorical outlets.) Nevertheless, his Marshall winds up being like Gad's Friedman in the scene where the latter is gagged in the manner that Strubing claimed to have been: he has no trouble grabbing everyone's attention anyway. Boseman, who has spent a great deal of previous screen time playing other real-life prominent African Americans, does a fine job of capturing this one's high-mindedness, strategic smarts, dauntless drive, intrepid confidence, and devilish, often sarcastic sense of humor. Hudlin savvily sold his film as a "superhero origin story," presenting a toned, fun-loving legend-in-the-making. This incarnation of Marshall bursts forth from a phone booth at one point like Clark Kent becoming the Man of Steel, only what is being expressed here is not potency but pain (that his dedication to a great cause is keeping him so frustratingly far from his miscarrying wife).

Unfortunately, Hudlin had reportedly insisted on a reworking of the script by lawyer Michael Koskoff and his screenwriter son Jacob (then bearing the less-focused title "The Trial of Joseph Spell") that would further raise Marshall up by downplaying and downsizing Friedman. Thus, this dynamic duo is decidedly one-sided: Friedman is not much good without Marshall. Marshall's recounting in one scene of how he had excruciatingly lost one testicle may have made some audience members squirm, but, especially for those in the know, so did the semi-emasculation of Friedman here, inaccurately turning him into a nervous, nebbishy puppet who is virtually nothing without Marshall giving him a strong, steady hand, or an almost-empty vessel without the input of a co-counsel who is overflowing with acumen, assurance, and sometimes rather off-putting condescension. "I wanted a real contrast," Hudlin admitted, noting that the untrue-to-life casting of the comparatively-less-pulchritudinous Gad only increased the desired odd couple juxtaposition. The script invents parallel prejudiced attacks that result in the bonding of the similarly-put-upon black man and Jew. The damage done to either is nothing compared to that resulting from the film's smack down of the factual Friedman.

In one scene showing the interpersonal interactions between the two principals (largely screenwriter-imagined), Marshall both literally and figuratively looks down on Friedman and drops a couple F-bombs upon him. Sadly, there are too many other moments in which this well-acted, absorbing film comes uncomfortably close to dismissively doing the same. (*Marshall* only grossed about three-quarters of its $12 million production budget despite generally-favorable reviews.) In trying so hard to raise an already-monumental man to Rushmorian heights, the real Friedman—who, by all first-hand accounts, was an admirably able and gutsy, committed, and ultimately-indispensable man in his own right—unjustly ended up far below, all-but-obliterated under the rubble resulting from this screen sculpting of his eminent courtroom compatriot.

David L. Boxerbaum

CREDITS

Thurgood Marshall: Chadwick Boseman
Sam Friedman: Josh Gad
Eleanor Strubing: Kate Hudson
Joseph Spell: Sterling K. Brown
Loren Willis: Dan Stevens
Judge Foster: James Cromwell
Michael Koskoff
Origin: United States
Language: English
Released: 2017
Production: Jonathan Sanger, Paula Wagner, Reginald Hudlin; Cheestnut Ridge Productions, China Wit Media, Starlight Media, Super Hero Films; released by Open Road Films
Directed by: Reginald Hudlin
Written by: Jacob Koskoff
Cinematography by: Newton Thomas (Tom) Sigel
Music by: Marcus Miller
Sound: Craig Mann
Music Supervisor: Mary Ramos
Editing: Tom McArdle
Costumes: Ruth E. Carter
Production Design: Richard Hoover
MPAA rating: PG-13
Running time: 118 minutes

REVIEWS

Brody, Richard. *New Yorker*. October 11, 2017.
Coggan, Devan. *Entertainment Weekly*. October 14 2017.
Dargis, Manohla. *New York Times*. October 12, 2017.
Debruge, Peter. *Variety*. October 4, 2017.
Keough, Peter. *Boston Globe*. October 11, 2017.
McCarthy, Todd. *Hollywood Reporter*. October 11, 2017.
Morgenstern, Joe. *Wall Street Journal*. October 12, 2017.
Phillips, Michael. *Chicago Tribune*. October 12, 2017.
Roeper, Richard. *Chicago Sun-Times*. October 16, 2017.
Turan, Kenneth. *Los Angeles Times*. October 12, 2017.

TRIVIA

This is the fourth biographical figure played by Chadwick Boseman. He has also starred in film playing James Brown, Jackie Robinson, and Floyd Little.

AWARDS

Nominations:

Oscars 2017: Orig. Song Score and/or Adapt. ("Stand Up for Something")

MAUDIE

Without love, there is no purpose.
—Movie tagline

Box Office: $6.2 Million

Nobody expected much from Maud Lewis, née Dowley—least of all, perhaps, Lewis herself. Since she did not expect much from her own life, *Maudie* argues that hers was a good one. The film follows the course of Lewis' life in such a way that anyone watching the story would not expect much, either. Sherry White's screenplay is sly in its simplicity. By the end of the film, one has a genuine appreciation for Lewis' accomplishments, a real sense of how she lived, and a sincere feeling of sympathy for the man who becomes her husband, despite how poorly he treats her at the beginning of their relationship.

Maud is played by Sally Hawkins in a performance that matches the understated nature of the narrative and director Aisling Walsh's filmmaking approach. The real Lewis suffered from rheumatoid arthritis from a young age. The film begins with Maud in her thirties, having become accustomed to her condition as much as a person can. Hawkins does not play the pain or the severe physical limitations of the character. Instead, she treats every motion—no matter how pronounced or small—with a display of delicacy.

From the first moment the film's Maud picks up a paintbrush, it is apparent that the act of dabbing the brush in paint and bringing it to a canvass—whether it is an actual canvass, a piece of paper, or a wall—is a struggle. That struggle, though, is not at the heart of the character in Hawkins' performance. There is a deliberateness of movement here, which suggests something beyond a physical challenge. In a subtle but very thoughtful way, Hawkins communicates that Maud's painting may be laborious, given her condition, but also that it is a labor born of passion and love.

The story begins with Maud living with her aunt Ida (Gabrielle Rose), a stern woman who treats her niece as both a maid and a burden. After the death of her parents, Maud has nowhere else to live, and her brother Charles (Zachary Bennett) has sold the family's home without asking for Maud's advice or opinion on the matter. As an act of revolt, Maud answers an advertisement from Everett Lewis (Ethan Hawke), a local fish peddler who lives in Marshalltown, Nova Scotia—about five miles from Ida's home in Digby. Because she never learned to drive, Maud walks everywhere.

At first, Everett is skeptical of Maud's abilities. He ultimately agrees to take her on as a temporary worker, and in his crammed, two-story home, the two have to a share the only bed upstairs.

Everett is even more stern and cold than Ida. His way with Maud is harsh, uncaring, and, at times, violent. (When she "dares" to speak to one of his colleagues in a too-familiar manner, Everett slaps her across the face.) Hawke's performance is shaky near the beginning of the film. Juggling an accent and the difficulty of playing a character who is almost entirely unsympathetic, Hawke comes across as a bit stilted, especially compared to Hawkins' more natural approach to her performance.

There is a major shift, though, in the relationship between Maud and Everett as time passes, and with it, there is also a significant change in Hawke's performance. Maud begins as a servant and subservient to Everett. As she proves herself in the house's daily chores, Everett becomes calmer, quieter, and less prone to offering instructions. Maud begins painting flowers and birds on the walls and windows of Everett's house, and later, she says that she did not stop this practice because Everett never told her to do so.

So much of this relationship and its transition into something deeper is unspoken. Maud's paintings become popular, thanks to the patronage of Sandra (Kari Matchett), a nearby woman of means from New York City who is one of Everett's customers. She enjoys Maud's simple paintings, and eventually, Maud begins selling postcards of her art to the local general store. The owner (played by Lawrence Barry) argues that his kid could have painted them. Everett becomes defensive and sticks up for Maud: "But he didn't. Maud did."

This is a story of unanticipated fame, with Maud's many customers coming to include then-Vice President Richard Nixon, yet White and Walsh have as much concern about that fame as Maud and Everett—which is to say none. The house becomes a store for Maud's artwork, with only a simple sign announcing that paintings are for sale there. Maud convinces Everett that the two should marry, if only because they essentially have been living as husband and wife since the day she started working for him. Maud paints. Everett continues with his work and begins collecting the money, which is not used for anything special.

Theirs is a simple life, and the film respects that way of living enough simply to observe these two characters, as Maud becomes more sure of herself and Everett comes to realize that whatever success he may possess is only on account of his wife (There is a sweet moment when Maud shows her husband his name in the newspaper, and he comes about as close to expressing gratitude as he is capable). They do not speak much to each other, and they definitely do not express anything resembling romantic love. The love story here is conveyed through action: Maud requests a screen door to let some air into the house, and as against the idea as he is, Everett complies without complaint. After Maud learns that her brother sold her baby, whom she believed had died, Everett secretly finds his wife's daughter and brings her to her now-adult child.

The film communicates the bond between these characters in the way that they do. Their affection for each other may be unspoken—at the end of her life, Maud must say what her husband does not, and by following Everett's silent but obvious grief, the film's final moments confirm her statement—yet *Maudie* knows that words mean little. It is through their actions that these characters love.

Mark Dujsik

CREDITS

Everett Lewis: Ethan Hawke
Maud Lewis: Sally Hawkins
Sandra: Kari Matchett
Charles Dowley: Zachary Bennett
Aunt Ida: Gabrielle Rose
Origin: United States
Language: English
Released: 2017
Production: Bob Cooper, Susan Mullen, Mary Sexton, Mary Young Leckie; H Is 4 Productions, Landscape Entertainment, Painted House Films, Parallel Film Productions, Rink Rat Productions, Screen Door, Small Shack Productions, Solo Productions, Storyscape Entertainment; released by Sony Pictures Classics
Directed by: Aisling Walsh
Written by: Sherry White
Cinematography by: Guy Godfree
Music by: Michael Timmins
Sound: Steve Munro
Music Supervisor: Wayne Warren
Editing: Stephen O'Connell
Art Direction: Owen Power
Costumes: Trysha Bakker
Production Design: John Hand
MPAA rating: PG-13
Running time: 115 minutes

REVIEWS

Abele, Robert. *Los Angeles Times.* June 15, 2017.
Dargis, Manohla. *New York Times.* June 15, 2017.

Fujishima, Kenji. *Paste.* June 15, 2017.
Gire, Dann. *Daily Herald.* June 23, 2017.
Macdonald, Moira. *Seattle Times.* July 6, 2017.
Morgenstern, Joe. *Wall Street Journal.* June 15, 2017.
O'Sullivan, Michael. *Washington Post.* June 22, 2017.
Phillips, Michael. *Chicago Tribune.* June 22, 2017.
Thompson, Gary. *Philadelphia Daily News.* June 27, 2017.
Vishnevetsky, Ignatiy. *The A.V. Club.* June 14, 2017.

QUOTES

Maud Lewis: "Do you want me here or don't you? 'Cause I'll walk out right now!"

TRIVIA

Sean Bean was originally cast as Everett Lewis, but was then replaced by Ethan Hawke.

MEGAN LEAVEY

Box Office: $13.4 Million

A feel-good tearjerker that delivers in a pleasingly unadorned manner on what could, in the hands of lesser talented and in-lockstep collaborators, become predictable narrative beats, *Megan Leavey* tells the true story of a stubborn, emotionally disconnected Marine and her special bond with a Military Police K9 Unit dog who helps her save the lives of several of her fellow soldiers. Marked by a strong lead performance from Kate Mara and a refusal to sand down the edges of its characters to something smoothe and boring, this independently produced drama highlights an ironic yet special fact—that sometimes it takes an animal to bring out the best of someone's humanity.

Offered up as summer counter programming by distributor Bleecker Street, *Megan Leavey* debuted in eighth place its opening weekend. It finished its theatrical run with just under $13 million—not bad for a movie with no huge stars, but many woofs short of the $64 million domestic haul (and additional $130 million internationally) of the canine-lionizing surprise global hit *A Dog's Purpose*, from earlier in the year.

The film opens in upstate New York, where Mara's somewhat shiftless title character has trouble holding down a job, still wrapped up as she is in grief over the drug-related death of a friend. An obviously strained and conflicted adolescence with her mother Jackie (Edie Falco) and stepfather Jim (Will Patton) has left Megan emotionally walled-off and adrift. In need of structure and with few other prospects, she joins the Marines, and faces a bit of the expected doubt during her basic training, given her slight stature and lack of focus.

Things change when Megan becomes interested in joining the canine unit, however. She is paired with a German shepherd named Rex, who is to be trained to sniff out improvised explosive devices and clear houses of any similarly dangerous substances. Rex is at first combative and aggressive, but Megan slowly wins his trust and proves herself uniquely qualified for this risky yet important work. Deployed to Iraq, she and Rex serve with honor and distinction. When an IED cuts short Megan's deployment, separating her from Rex and briefly sending her home, she lapses back into depression. When Rex is then ruled medically incapable of further service, Megan dives into a labyrinthine and uphill bureaucratic battle to try to win custody of him from the United States military.

The narrative feature debut of director Gabriela Cowperthwaite, who revealed enormous reservoirs of sympathy and compassion with her critically lauded captive-killer-whale documentary *Blackfish* (2013), *Megan Leavey* exhibits a similarly discerning and affecting sense of the innate bond between animals and humans. In collaboration with cinematographer Lorenzo Senatore, Cowperthwaite works in a naturalistic yet unfussy style; together they establish differentiated color palettes for the movie's Stateside and Iraq settings, but mostly eschew close-ups and instead utilize a through-line of evocatively framed medium compositions to communicate Megan's isolation.

Screenwriters Pamela Gray, Annie Mumolo, and Tim Lovestedt also do a fairly good job of striking a balance between the dichotomous demands of Leavey's real-life story, with one foot apiece in the military and civilian worlds. The more obvious film would have pushed past the perfunctory portions of Megan's training and bonding with Rex, in order to focus mainly on the life-and-death stakes of her war service. And that, obviously and truly, is part of what will interest viewers. But *Megan Leavey*, thankfully and illuminatingly, has a less masculinized vision of its story, and that is what makes it compelling.

The film actually works as a more unusual and atypical slice of working-class portraiture—its military backdrop interestingly and convincingly sketched, but somewhat incidental—in which a young woman psychologically steels herself, and finds the ground beneath her feet. As much as Megan's legal battle for Rex drives the film's third act, the most interesting arc in *Megan Leavey* has to do with its protagonist's emotional blossoming. In showing that animals can act as somewhat of a mirror, reflecting back to people some of the negative and counterproductive behavioral, communication, and problem-solving approaches they may be employing in their lives, the film movingly depicts a more intimate and personal awakening—promulgating the value of a purpose-driven life, and positing that we can triumph over circumstances that initially seem beyond our control.

As Leavey's military superior, Common is a bit too telegraphed in his gruffness, which makes his later emoting all the more cringe-inducing. This weak link aside, however, the film's casting and acting is otherwise uniformly excellent. Mara is fantastic as Megan; her performance is akin to a closed fist, slowly unclenching. She shows you the character's woundedness, distrust, and emotional withdrawal without ever overselling any of her reactions or catharses. Especially effective are Megan's scenes with her biological father Bob (Bradley Whitford), who tries to temper his frustration with practical advice. Similarly excellent are Megan's scenes with fellow K9 Unit Corporal Matt Morales (Roman Rodriguez). Hearteningly, the movie asks you to sincerely invest in a romance that is for a reason and season rather than perhaps something more grandiose, and for life. As such, it feels more realistic, and properly scaled.

There are some familiar and predictable narrative hurdles in *Megan Leavey*, it is true. But it is rendered with assurance and intelligence, and at its core it tells an engaging story of perseverance.

Brent Simon

CREDITS

Megan Leavey: Kate Mara
Andrew Dean: Tom Felton
Matt Morales: Ramon Rodriguez
Bob: Bradley Whitford
Jackie Leavey: Edie Falco
Origin: United States
Language: English
Released: 2017
Production: Mickey Liddell, Jennifer Monroe, Pete Shilaimon; Calle Cruzada, LD Entertainment; released by Bleecker Street Media
Directed by: Gabriela Cowperthwaite
Written by: Pamela Gray; Annie Mumolo; Tim Lovestedt
Cinematography by: Lorenzo Senatore
Music by: Mark Isham
Sound: Karen Baker Landers; Martyn Zub
Music Supervisor: Julianne Jordan
Editing: Peter McNulty
Art Direction: Eduardo Hidalgo
Costumes: David Tabbert
Production Design: Ed Verreaux
MPAA rating: PG-13
Running time: 116 minutes

REVIEWS

Abele, Robert. *Los Angeles Times*. June 9, 2017.
Genzlinger, Neil. *New York Times*. June 8, 2017.
Graham, Adam. *Detroit News*. June 8, 2017.
LaSalle, Mick. *San Francisco Chronicle*. June 6, 2017.
Linden, Sheri. *Hollywood Reporter*. May 30, 2017.
O'Malley, Sheila. *RogerEbert.com*. June 9, 2017.
Persall, Steve. *Tampa Bay Times*. June 6, 2017.
Savlov, Marc. *Austin Chronicle*. June 9, 2017.
Schager, Nick. *Variety*. May 30, 2017.
Whitty, Stephen. *Newark Star-Ledger*. June 9, 2017.

QUOTES

Gunny Martin: "They're not even dogs anymore. They're warriors, and they come back with all the same issues we do."

TRIVIA

Both actress Kate Mara and the real-life Megan Leavey were born in 1983 and grew up in the suburbs of New York City.

MENASHE

There's nothing Orthodox about him.
—Movie tagline

Box Office: $1.7 Million

The documentary impulse is central to the history of narrative filmmaking art. From early examples like *Workers Leaving the Lumière Factory* (1895), by the pioneering French brothers Auguste and Pierre Lumière, the movies have privileged action or movement, drawing on the filmed image to document a particular kind of social behavior.

Sharp and revealing, the movie *Menashe* feels like primitive art. Part of it is deliberately opaque and unreachable. It is the kind of movie that invites scrutiny, an opening to a kind of vanished world. Watching it makes the viewer feel like somebody cast perennially on the outside and tasked with decoding the insular and forbidding religious and social order. The mysteriousness is enveloping and pulls the viewer in.

The director, Joshua Z. Weinstein, a cinematographer and documentary filmmaker making his first narrative film, is curious, fair, and inscrutable. He honors his characters and acknowledges their humanity, vulnerability, and anguish. He never cheapens the material. The movie is colored with a vitality and strangeness. It also has a prickly side, a rough-edged aspect that makes for a harrowing and occasionally uncomfortable experience. *Menashe* also features some moments of lyricism that are absolutely breathtaking.

The movie is set in the ultra-Orthodox Hasidic community in the Borough Park neighborhood of Brooklyn. Like F.W. Murnau's *Sunrise* (1927), *Menashe* is that strangest and loveliest of objects, a foreign film made in America. The movie is spoken almost entirely in Yiddish, the common language of millions of Ashkenazi Eastern European Jews that dates to the 12th century. The Holocaust, the Jewish Diaspora. and cultural modernization has reduced the language's contemporary practitioners to the hundreds of thousands. Yiddish film, theater. and music are central to identity and meaning of the Jewish experience.

As critic and scholar J. Hoberman, the author of the superb cultural history *Bridge of Light* (1991), has pointed out, Yiddish cinema is drawn from a deep artistic and cultural tradition. Edgar G. Ulmer, the great American director who made the fantastic *Detour* (1945), directed four Yiddish-language films. The Coen Brothers memorably and brilliantly played off the themes of guilt, memory, and time for their fantastic Yiddish-language prologue in *A Serious Man* (2009).

Weinstein wrote *Menashe* with Alex Lipschultz and Musa Syeed. A secular Jew who does not speak the language, the director wrote the script in English and worked closely on the set with a translator. The film adroitly blurs most formal distinctions between fiction and nonfiction. The movie is captured more than performed. A significant part of the plot is inspired by the life and experiences of Menashe Lustig, a voluble and likeable man who inhabits the central character with remarkable sensitivity, nuance and sureness.

The story takes place over a period of about a week, and the lean and compressed time frame sharpens the film's dramatic conflict. A supermarket clerk and recent widower, Menashe, is embroiled in a custody battle involving his young son, Rieven (Ruben Niborski). The boy is living with Menashe's brother-in-law, the coldly disapproving Eizik (Yoel Weisshaus), who cites religious law dictating that the child must be raised in a two-parent home. A prosperous real estate developer, Eizik is clearly contemptuous of Menashe, not just because of his more restrictive class origins, but for the way he typically flouts the religious and social customs, like refusing to wear the traditional heavy black coats.

Despite the wider family discord, a natural bond between father and son exists, clear from their first encounter as Menashe sees the child walking down the street from the inside of the store van he is driving. Menashe might be slovenly, of limited means, a solitary dreamer who increasingly lives inside his own head. The boy, with his bright, alert eyes, responds to him emotionally.

As much as he loves his son, Menashe longs for a freedom and spontaneity. In one of the film's best scenes, a date with another widower, he basically insults her, telling her, "You are not my type." Acknowledging he must find a new wife or relinquish custody of his son, Menashe works out a truce through his rabbi (Meyer Schwartz). Asserting his authority, Menashe insists on holding the memorial service for his wife at his small apartment. The rabbi grants him custody for a week, or until the ceremony.

These middle passages of the father and son's reconciliation, through marked by a certain tension or strife, are glorious. Weinstein streaks the moments in sorrow and pain, but he also visually rhymes the large and unruly Menashe with the child. At times the physical closeness, locked inside his tiny apartment, feels like entrapment. In other moments, when they share an ice cream or just lose themselves in the vast space of the stockroom at the supermarket, it is lilting, even transporting. Chronically short of money and constantly seeking loans, Menashe is hardly the ideal parent, given to offering his son cake and soda for breakfast. The slapstick scenes, like Menashe ruining the Gefilte fish when he improperly secures the back door of the van, is not played for ridicule though an act of forgiveness and deepening humanity.

An amateur comedian who has made some highly interesting videos of his own, Lustig is a combustible and highly likeable presence who freely mixes the deadpan with a bracing, off-center timing. He gives full vent to the agonizing and inevitable conflict between religious observance and personal freedom. There is a priceless moment, at a private gathering, where Menashe allows himself a private reverie and goes free with his movements and the boy, no doubt negatively influenced by his uncle's cruel judgment, admonishes him for "getting drunk." The pain that washes over Menashe registers with a real kick.

Visually the movie shifts brilliantly from panoramic street scenes predicated on distance and observation to closer and more intimate interiors, revealing in deft portraiture and subtle detail, the social codes, religious acts, and behavioral customs of Hasidic life. *Menashe* is about celebrating and honoring that culture while also subtly criticizing it.

The movie opens and closes with these jaunty and electric street scenes as the figure of Menashe takes greater definition. As a social document, *Menashe* is not intended to edify or inform. The viewer is a witness who must intuit a great deal to fully understand the man, his sly banter with his customers, or his more conflicted contact with his manager. Weinstein, who also photographed the film with Yoni Brook, works out fascinating visual patterns in those two modes, the street scenes and the intimate exchanges.

In the most jolting scene, the only performed in English, Menashe reveals to his two Latino co-workers about his arranged marriage and admits to the absence of love or emotional attraction in their relationship. *Menashe* is not a work of great depth and subtlety. The movie is small, direct, and telling. It is about finding the beauty in disappointment and loss. The ending might feel like a compromise or surrender, but it occasions a very particular state of grace.

Patrick Z. McGavin

CREDITS

Menashe: Menashe Lustig
Rieven: Ruben Niborski
Fischel: Yoel Weisshaus
Rabbi: Meyer Schwartz
Origin: United States
Language: Yiddish, English
Released: 2017
Production: Traci Carlson, Daniel Finkelman, Joshua Z Weinstein, Alex Lipschultz, Yoni Brook; Autumn Productions, Maiden Voyage Pictures, Shtick Film, Sparks Productions, Where's Eve?; released by A24 Films LLC
Directed by: Joshua Z Weinstein
Written by: Joshua Z Weinstein; Alex Lipschultz; Musa Syeed
Cinematography by: Joshua Z Weinstein; Yoni Brook
Music by: Aaron Martin; Dag Rosenqvist
Sound: Ian Stynes
Editing: Scott Cummings
MPAA rating: PG
Running time: 82 minutes

REVIEWS

Crump, Andrew. *Paste Magazine..* August 3, 2017.
Felsenthal, Daniel. *Village Voice.* July 27, 2017.
Greenblatt, Leah. *Entertainment Weekly.* July 27, 2017.
Jaworowski, Ken. *New York Times.* July 27, 2017.
Keough, Peter. *Boston Globe.* August 16, 2017.
Murray, Noel. *The A.V. Club.* July 26, 2017.
Phillips, Michael. *Chicago Tribune..* August 10, 2017.
Rothkopf, Josh. *Time Out New York.* July 28, 2017.
Turan, Kenneth. *Los Angeles Times.* July 27, 2017.
Zilberman, Alan. *Washington Post.* August 10, 2017.

TRIVIA

Director Joshua Z. Weinstein, who is neither a member of a Haredi community nor a speaker of Yiddish, used a translator on set.

THE MEYEROWITZ STORIES (NEW AND SELECTED)

Noah Baumbach's best films often feel like they are also his most personal films. There's the unique college-set take on intellectuals in *Kicking and Screaming* (1995), the look at divorce through the eyes of children impacted by it in *The Squid and the Whale* (2005), and the funny take on aging in *While We're Young* (2014). Arguably his best film feels like it works from a similarly personal undercurrent as it examines siblings, aging parents, and that moment when people realize that life may not turn out exactly as they expected. *The Meyerowitz Stories (New and Selected)* is a heartfelt masterpiece, anchored by some of the best performances Baumbach has directed and a keen understanding of how families communicate with one another...or, more accurately, don't.

Arranged almost as a series of short stories, reflecting its unique title, Baumbach's film alternates protagonists and perspectives, often shifting at unexpected times. It opens through the eyes of Danny Meyerowitz, played by Adam Sandler, doing the best work of his career since at least *Punch-Drunk Love* (2002), and arguably ever. Danny is in a bit of a rut, but he seems like one of those guys who would not admit such a thing to himself. Almost riffing on the man-child characters he's played before in broad comedies, Sandler finds ways to capture arrested development that feel true and honest. There are millions of guys like Danny out there, relatively happy but carrying increasingly heavy baggage from life's mistakes and random cruelties.

Danny is separated from his wife and now living with his father Harold (Dustin Hoffman), a retired Bard College art professor and frustrated sculptor. One gets the impression early on that Harold Meyerowitz is the kind of guy who has long been more obsessed with his own accomplishments and failures than those of his children. He constantly talks about his own legacy and career, to the point that one feels like he's barely a parent to Danny, although he gives lip service to such a thing and sings old songs with him that Danny wrote. Harold is also on his third marriage to Maureen (Emma Thompson), who may have a bit of a drinking problem. The opening "story" really just introduces us to these fascinating, well-drawn characters, a group which also includes Danny's artistic daughter Eliza (Grace Van Patten), who makes the kind of truly horrible college student films that only artistic college students can make. We also learn that Harold and Maureen are considering selling their townhouse, but Danny does not like the potential change. And we learn that Danny has a sister named Jean (Elizabeth Marvel) and a brother named Matthew (Ben Stiller). Danny accompanies his father to a show at the Museum of Modern Art that celebrates one of Harold's peers, L.J. Shapiro (Judd Hirsch). Harold cannot remotely hide his jealousy and flees the scene.

The second story also ends with a running Harold—it's a theme—after he has lunch with Matthew, at which his financial advisor son offers to help him sell their Manhattan home. Harold is clearly the kind of person who is not eager to age or change, and he acts out like a child, first ordering more expensive items when he finds out his son is paying and then nearly starting a fight with the person at the table next to them. After wrongly thinking he's been robbed, Harold and Matthew visit Matthew's mother Julia (Candice Bergen). She makes both of them uncomfortable and they flee.

This is all wonderful character set-up for the true brilliance of *The Meyerowitz Stories,* which comes when Harold is bedridden in a hospital after suffering a chronic subdural hematoma. His children are forced to deal with the possibility of a dying patriarch, which brings out their own insecurities and troubled histories. It culminates in a brilliant fight scene between Danny and Matthew, and a pair of speeches by the two at a Bard faculty group show.

It sounds clichéd, but there's an incredible amount of truth in Baumbach's screenplay for *The Meyerowitz Stories,* one that really understands every theme with which it's playing, including family, aging, intellectualism, artists, and sibling rivalry. It is a complex, emotional, resonant piece of work from line to line and scene to scene. It's one of the best scripts of 2017 and should have been a much bigger part of the awards season conversation. Just the way it clips from scene to scene without calling attention to how smart it truly is, allowing its characters to bloom and grow and feel three-dimensional without becoming mouthpieces for the writer. It's not a flashy script, but it's a brilliant one.

Baumbach's direction here is some of the most confident of his career. Scenes will sometimes get cut off mid-line, in odd places, as if we are reading short stories and skipped a page. And yet Baumbach's filmmaking is so strong that it never creates a herky-jerky rhythm. On the contrary, we fill in the gaps from story to story and scene to scene. And Baumbach's work with his cast is as good as he's ever been. As mentioned, Sandler's work is phenomenal, but he's not alone—Stiller, Marvel, Hoffman, and Thompson are all fantastic.

The Meyerowitz Stories (New and Selected) made a splash at Cannes in May of 2017 by virtue of the company that made it—Netflix. There was controversy when some of the jurors and power players at Cannes suggested that the film, and Bong Joon-ho's *Okja* (2017), should not be allowed in competition because they were never going to play theatrically in France. Of course, most people will tell you this is like trying to plug a breaking dam with a pinky finger, but it does feel like Netflix has yet to earn the artistic credit that it should, as evidenced by the underrated status of *Okja, Mudbound* (2017), and arguably the best Netflix film to date, *The Meyerowitz Stories (New and Selected).*

Brian Tallerico

CREDITS

Danny: Adam Sandler
Eliza Meyerowitz: Grace Van Patten
Harold: Dustin Hoffman
Jean Meyerowitz: Elizabeth Marvel
Maureen: Emma Thompson
Origin: United States
Language: English
Released: 2017
Production: Eli Bush, Scott Rudin, Lila Yacoub, Noah Baumbach; Gilded Halfwing, IAC Films; released by Netflix Inc.
Directed by: Noah Baumbach
Written by: Noah Baumbach
Cinematography by: Robbie Ryan
Music by: Randy Newman
Sound: Paul Hsu
Editing: Jennifer Lame
Art Direction: Nicolas Locke
Costumes: Joseph G. Aulisi
Production Design: Gerald Sullivan
MPAA rating: PG-13
Running time: 112 minutes

REVIEWS

Burr, Ty. *Boston Globe.* October 11, 2017.
Dowd, A.A. *The A.V. Club.* October 11, 2017.
Ebiri, Bilge. *Village Voice.* June 21, 2017.
Grierson, Tim. *Screen International.* May 23, 2017.
Henderson, Odie. *RogerEbert.com.* October 13, 2017.
Kenny, Glenn. *New York Times.* October 11, 2017.
Roeper, Richard. *Chicago Sun-Times.* October 16, 2017.
Roffman, Michael. *Consequence of Sound.* October 3, 2017.
Turan, Kenneth. *Los Angeles Times.* October 11, 2017.
Yoshida, Emily. *New York Magazine.* May 23, 2017.

TRIVIA

This is the first time in over twenty years that Ben Stiller and Adam Sandler have worked together in a movie since they appeared together in *Happy Gilmore* (1996).

THE MIDWIFE
(Sage femme)

Box Office: $603,582

Catherine Deneuve is, without a doubt, one of the true living cinema icons of all time—the kind of performer whose mere presence in a film, however fleeting, can help make a good movie into a great one and a thoroughly mediocre effort into something that is ultimately worth watching, at least during the scenes in which she is on-screen. Practically from the get-go, it is apparent that *The Midwife,* the latest film from writer/director Martin Provost, whose previous efforts have included the biopics *Séraphine* (2008) and *Violette* (2013), is an example of the latter. On its own, it is a fairly meh drama that does not exactly step terribly wrong, per se, but never quite makes the case as to why it should exist or why anyone watching it should stick it out to the end. However, whenever Deneuve turns up, she bestows some of the magic that has transfixed moviegoers throughout the world for more than a half-century. While the end result probably will not feature heavily in any Lifetime Achievement Award tribute reels, she helps to make the film better than it really has any right to be.

The film's title refers to Claire (Catherine Frot), who works as a midwife in a small-scale local medical clinic that is in the process of being taken over by a larger hospital featuring the latest technological advances but little in the way of humanity. Although filled with warmth and compassion in her professional capacity, she spends her personal life a step removed from the world around her with the only real relationship that she seems to have outside the workplace being one with her son (Quentin Dolmaire), who has just informed her of his plans to drop out of medical school in order to become a midwife himself. There is a guy, Paul (Olivier Gourmet), who seems nice and who is clearly sweet on her but she just as clearly could not be less interested in him.

With a life as tidy and organized as Claire's, it is only a matter of time before someone comes in to turn things upside down for her and that person is Béatrice (Deneuve), who is the kind of woman that might have once been referred to as a broad—she drinks, smokes, gambles, eats unhealthily, and lives way beyond her already meager means. Béatrice is not an unknown figure to Claire—she was, in fact, the former mistress of her beloved father until she left him abruptly for greener pastures and has returned after so many years in order to make amends to them both. Since Claire's father committed suicide soon after the dumping, an act that she believes was caused by the breakup, she understandably has no interest at all in reconnecting with Béatrice but when the woman informs her that she is alone, broke, and dying of brain cancer, she finds herself compelled, against her better judgement, to take on the role of caretaker for the woman who affected her life so profoundly. In news that may or may not constitute a spoiler, the two wind up bonding against all odds as Claire finds herself unexpectedly opening herself up to new possibilities in her life for once.

In many respects, *The Midwife* is not a particularly good movie. Provost's screenplay is an unwieldy mixture of plot twists straight out of a middling soap opera and stabs at social realism in the style of the Dardenne Brothers (Jean-Pierre and Luc), a blend of elements that the Dardennes themselves could not quite pull off in *The Unknown Girl* (2016). The main story is overwhelmingly sentimental without ever being truly affecting and the various subplots trucked in to beef things up do not add much either—the tentative romance between Claire and Paul is a non-starter, the stuff about the buyout of the clinic where she works does not seem to have been thought through very well (especially with the high-tech hospital, which is presumably meant to represent the French medical establishment, looking as if *Coma* (1978) is playing out in another wing) and the stuff involving her son feeling like a slow and softheaded version of the scabrous mother-son relationship shown in Paul Verhoeven's *Elle* (2016).

And yet, all of these flaws are forgotten, or at least temporarily overlooked, during the scenes in which Deneuve takes hold of the screen. Acting as though she is channeling her inner Gena Rowlands, she blasts her way through the film by perfectly embodying both Béatrice's unabashed public attitude that she is still all that and a bag of *chips de pomp de terre* and her private realization that she is long past her shelf date and has absolutely nothing to show for her cheerfully hedonistic lifestyle. She is enormous fun to watch throughout and also manages to handle the shift to the more saccharine material with more delicacy than the film itself does. Not exactly a shrinking violet of an actress herself, Frot is content to work in a quieter key and mostly cede the screen to her co-star but she gets a few moments of her own to show some fire as well. Best of all, the scenes in which the two are allowed to just go head to head with each other—they play off of each other so beautifully that one wishes that Provost had just abandoned the film proper and elected to instead make a documentary of the two just having lunch.

The Midwife is a largely forgettable work that is so blandly innocuous at times that it almost feels like it is its own unnecessary and dramatically denuded remake. And yet, as an excuse to genuflect at the shrine of the divine Deneuve (whose presence is presumably the only reason that the film made the trip stateside in the first place), it more or less gets the job done. No, it will not make anyone forget her stunning and justifiably celebrated collaborations over the years wth the likes of Jacques Demy, Roman Polanski, Luis Buñuel, or even Peter Hyams anytime soon. As a reminder of her undimmed star power and acting talents, however, it will do well enough until the next time that a more worthy showcase for them happens along.

Peter Sobczynski

CREDITS

Beatrice Sobo dite Sobolevski: Catherine Deneuve
Claire Breton: Catherine Frot
Paul Baron: Olivier Gourmet
Simon: Quentin Dolmaire
Rolande: Mylene Demongeot
Origin: United States
Language: French
Released: 2017
Production: Olivier Delbosc; Curiosa Films, France 3 Cinema, Versus Production; released by Music Box Films
Directed by: Martin Provost
Written by: Martin Provost
Cinematography by: Yves Cape
Music by: Gregoire Hetzel
Editing: Albertine Lastera
Costumes: Bethsabee Dreyfus
Production Design: Thierry Francois
MPAA rating: Unrated
Running time: 117 minutes

REVIEWS

Adams, Thelma. *New York Observer.* July 14, 2017.
Callahan, Dan. *TheWrap.* July 19, 2017.
Chang, Justin. *Los Angeles Times.* July 20, 2017.
Croll, Ben. *IndieWire.* February 17, 2017.
Gleiberman, Owen. *Variety.* February 14, 2017.
Kenney, Glenn. *New York Times.* July 20, 2017.
Kim, Kristen Yoonsoo. *Village Voice.* July 19, 2017.
Mintzer, Jordan. *Hollywood Reporter.* February 14, 2017.
Morgenstern, Joe. *Wall Street Journal.* July 20, 2017.
O'Sullivan, Michael. *Washington Post.* July 27, 2017.

TRIVIA

Actress Catherine Frot actually delivered five babies during filming.

MOLLY'S GAME

Box Office: $26.1 Million

In both an opening and climactic scene of *Molly's Game*, Molly Bloom (Jessica Chastain) moves very quickly (on skis and ice skates, respectively), confident in her abilities, only to fall on her face. It seems like a screenwriter as savvy and acclaimed as Aaron Sorkin would recognize the irony of an entire movie suffering the same fate. Yet the film, the directorial debut from the Oscar-winning writer (*The Social Network* [2010]), makes some rather un-Sorkin-like mistakes even as it hinges on linguistic ping pong that could never be attributed to anyone else.

With rare exception, the drama, an adaptation of the real-life Bloom's book about her path from Olympic hopeful to millionaire organizer of an extremely high-profile poker game to defendant in a federal indictment, never slows down enough to get its footing. Sorkin is no stranger to stuffing in the most-possible information; the aforementioned, award-winning script famously ran far longer than a standard two-hour movie could accommodate, solved by the rhythm of Sorkin's language and director David Fincher's ability to harness the remarkable speed with which the characters in that far superior film speak. In *Molly's Game*, which steals its predecessor's structure of bouncing between past events and the present legal proceedings that result, Sorkin's effort to cram in everything he can results in the most basic errors of Screenwriting 101: an over-reliance on voiceover and an inclination to tell rather than show.

The examples are too many to count, so to name just a few: even when dealing with something as obvious as a guy setting up a card table or Molly putting out a cheese platter, Molly explains what is happening in voiceover. That is also how she asserts that she never became romantically or sexually involved with any of the players in the game, though as multiple players (Justin Kirk, Chris O'Dowd) express their affections for her—to say nothing of the countless others who send suggestive texts, which Molly later tries to hide from prosecutors in an effort to protect the guys' families—there is never a sense of if any of them provided even the slightest bit of temptation. (While in interviews Sorkin has worn Molly's lack of love interest as a badge of honor, the film's refusal to acknowledge how she spends her time outside of the games she organizes comes off not as a win for gender equality but as a refusal to give the main character a full life and sexual agency.) When a strong player (Bill Camp) loses his cool and others show up to seek revenge for their losses, the emotions are only described, without seeing or feeling a sense of what these people have gone through. The same applies late in the film when Molly describes the suicide of a player she brought into her game; if Sorkin thinks making a quick passing reference to a death viewers did not previously know about will provide gravitas to his incessant narration and clipped dialogue, he is mistaken.

That said, the writer's strengths are often seen through characters with an absence of emotion rather than the effort to harness it sincerely. So when *Molly's Game* pauses for a heart to heart between Molly and her demanding father (Kevin Costner), his repeated utterance of "They're going to suffer," in reference to the man who beat her up, just presents as a filmmaker unsure how to capture a dad's sorrow and helplessness rather than an honest moment between estranged family members. (This comes after a painful depiction of him mansplaining her problems that does no favors to accusations that Sorkin struggles to write compelling, lead female characters.) Likewise, Molly insisting on her commitment to preserving her "good name" with her attorney, Charlie Jaffey (Idris Elba, given too much exposition and questionable speechifying), would play entirely false if Chastain were not so strong in the role. Setting aside its limitations, this is intended to be a story about an ambitious young woman whose injury on the slopes sparked a need to assert her abilities in a different, but also risky way, and Chastain's blend of toughness and goodness provides the heart of the film: that Molly was a relative innocent surrounded by players who were not always so clean.

Yet that is another place where Sorkin, a perfectly competent visual stylist even if his emphasis on voiceover minimizes the work he would have to do to stage scenes between actors and develop his story on screen, trips over himself. Molly appears extremely hard-working and smart, but her limited vetting of the increasingly criminal participants in the game is attributed to a drug problem that is barely seen. References to her loneliness come only with a quick shot of her lying in bed in a dark room, rather than an understanding of what she may have done, even in a low moment, to combat that loneliness. (She says she fell into a hole so deep it felt like she could go fracking, one of many mediocre, writerly turns of phrase that are far below the filmmaker's talents.) Sorkin really struggles to do more than one thing at a time in *Molly's Game*, creating a perpetual, shallow briskness that transitions from entertaining to dull as it grows more and more redundant.

The goal is a portrait of how easily a winner can lose, and the many factors that result in someone recovering from defeat or falling behind permanently. So it is all the more frustrating how little thought Sorkin gives to Molly's motivations as she steals the poker game from her former boss (Jeremy Strong) and eventually moves it from Los Angeles to New York after a falling out with a formerly favored player (Michael Cera in peak jerk mode). It is at best puzzling and, at worst, woefully underwritten when Molly seems to not have considered the possible nefarious doings of her ultra-rich players and pays a physical and legal price as a result. It is unclear how she could be so oblivious to get in over her head this way, especially when she is hardly shown pursuing and living some kind of luxurious life. When she eventually does not even have enough money for a hot dog, the attempt at depicting a fall from grace forgets how little has been seen of her life when not overseeing the game.

Even in a story about a job that becomes all-consuming, there must remain an idea of what else the person has or wants. In *Molly's Game*, Molly never gets to color outside the lines or even fill them in, Sorkin too busy playing against himself and losing.

Matt Pais

CREDITS

Molly Bloom: Jessica Chastain
Charlie Jaffey: Idris Elba
Larry Bloom: Kevin Costner
Player X: Michael Cera
Dean Keith: Jeremy Strong
Origin: United States
Language: English
Released: 2017
Production: Mark Gordon, Matt Jackson, Amy Pascal; Entertainment One Films Canada Inc., Huayi Brothers Pictures, Pascal Pictures, The Mark Gordon Co.; released by STX Entertainment
Directed by: Aaron Sorkin
Written by: Aaron Sorkin
Cinematography by: Charlotte Bruus Christensen
Music by: Daniel Pemberton
Sound: Michael J. Benavente; David McCallum
Music Supervisor: Carlton Kaller; Sean Mulligan
Editing: Alan Baumgarten; Elliot Graham; Josh Schaeffer
Costumes: Susan Lyall
Production Design: David Wasco
MPAA rating: R
Running time: 140 minutes

REVIEWS

Bishop, Bryan. *The Verge*. September 16, 2017.
Cole, Jake. *Slant Magazine*. September 10, 2017.
D'Angelo, Mike. *The A.V. Club*. December 15, 2017.
Debruge, Peter. *Variety*. September 16, 2017.
Ehrlich, David. *IndieWire*. September 16, 2017.
Ide, Wendy. *Screen International*. September 16, 2017.
Kurchak, Sarah. *Consequence of Sound*. September 12, 2017.
Lee, Benjamin. *The Guardian*. September 16, 2017.
McCarthy, Todd. *Hollywood Reporter*. September 16, 2017.
Wilkinson, Alissa. *Vox*. September 16, 2017.

TRIVIA

Molly Bloom reportedly told the director Aaron Sorkin that she wanted Jessica Chastain to portray her in the film.

AWARDS

Nominations:

Oscars 2017: Adapt. Screenplay

British Acad. 2017: Adapt. Screenplay

Golden Globes 2018: Actress--Drama (Chastain), Screenplay, Screenplay (Sorkin)

Writers Guild 2017: Adapt. Screenplay

MONSTER TRUCKS

On January 13, meet Creech.
—Movie tagline

Box Office: $33.4 Million

When *Monster Trucks* arrived in theaters, it did so after the kind of poisonous advanced word that suggested a disaster for the ages was in the making. It was originally slated to open in May 2015 and found itself bouncing in and out of the release calendar for nearly two years. Then it was revealed in the press that the initial idea for the film came from the son of Paramount's then-president Adam Goodman, who was all of four years old at the time. Finally, and perhaps most damaging, several months before it opened, Paramount announced a $115 million write-down that was soon revealed to be based on the amount of money they projected to lose on the film when it finally came out. With bad buzz like that, the only real hopes that *Monster Trucks* had were to either turn out to be a family film masterpiece along the lines of *E.T.* (1982) or, barring that, be something more along the lines of the infamous *E.T.* knockoff *MAC & Me* (1988)—a film so astonishingly, jaw-droppingly awful that it became a perversely entertaining gem in spite of itself. Okay, perhaps equaling *E.T.* was a bit of a pipe dream but *Monster Trucks* cannot even succeed at being a memorably awful film. It is a thoroughly mediocre slab of hard-sell whimsy that might temporarily satisfy very young and very easily entertained children but which contains virtually nothing of note for any viewer whose age is in the high single digits and above.

The film is set in a small North Dakota town that is totally dominated by a fairly evil oil company called Terravex. They have just stumbled upon a massive underground oil reserve just outside of town but standing between the company and the oil is a heretofore unknown and undisturbed ecosystem that appears to have something living in it. Saying "Nuts" to that, the Terravex boss (Rob Lowe) orders the drilling to continue and during the disaster that follows, three blobby creatures are released into our world. One is quickly recaptured and a second is found soon after but the third escapes and eventually finds its way to a junkyard, the perfect hideout for a creature whose favorite food appears to be pure, unadulterated oil.

This junkyard also happens to be where teen grease monkey Tripp (Lucas Till) spends all of his time trying to get a broken-down Dodge truck working. Tripp and the creature, whom he dubs Creech, eventually meet and become friends. To make things even better, at least from Tripp's perspective, when Creech stuffs himself under the hood of his friend's dilapidated truck, he can not only make it run but do wild things like drive up walls and race upon rooftops. This is all fun and games for a while but eventually Tripp realizes that Creech has a home that he needs to return to and when he learns that the Terravex weasels, in order to cover up their discovery so as not to lose out on all the oil, plan on destroying Creech and the other creatures, he and a couple of human friends—classmate crush object Meredith (Jane Levy) and a Terravex scientist with a recently developed conscience (Thomas Lennon)—plot to rescue them from the oil company's clutches and take them back to their home by deploying a plan that involves a lot of stunts involving monster trucks doing wild and unexpected things.

The conceit of *Monster Trucks* might be inane, but the film itself did not necessarily have to be. There have been any number of movies over the years involving the friendships between kids and fantastical creatures and a number of them, such as *E.T.*, *The Iron Giant* (1999), and the recent remake of *Pete's Dragon* (2016), have turned out to be thoroughly entertaining and surprisingly touching as well. Of course, in those cases, the films contained smart and compelling storylines, instantly relatable and likable characters, and relationships between the central characters that were instantly and completely convincing. *Monster Trucks* may have intended to include those elements but, to judge from the final product, the filmmakers included so many bits of product placement for Dodge and wacky car crashes that they simply did not have room for anything else. The screenplay by Derek Connolly is a limp affair that is too contrived to work as a straightforwardly good movie and far too boring to work as camp. None of the characters are of interest—Tripp is never particularly likable (and the fact that the actor playing him appears to be several years past his high school days does not help matters at all), Creech is simply a manic cartoon with no convincing emotional qualities and the others are essentially ciphers who come on only to further some plot development. (The way in which the film wastes the talents of Jane Levy on a nothing part is practically criminal.) Most fatally, there is never a single moment when the friendship between Tripp and Creech is ever even slightly convincing.

Little kids may get a mild kick out of *Monster Trucks* in the same way that they do with Pixar's substandard *Cars* films—they will enjoy seeing the trucks driving fast and crashing into things and they may even get a kick out of the cartoonish Creech as well. For everyone else, it will come across as a boring bit of nothing that fills the screen with random bit of color and noise for 90 minutes or so and does absolutely nothing else of notice or value. The best family films are the ones that not only entertain viewers of all ages but inspire younger moviegoers to understand the power of imagination and perhaps develop an interest in storytelling themselves. *Monster Trucks,* on the other hand, does none of that for kids watching it, though it may inspire adult viewers to try to figure out how to ban Take Your Child to Work days for good to help prevent something like it from ever happening again.

By: Peter Sobczynski

CREDITS

Tripp: Lucas Till
Meredith: Jane Levy
Jim Dowd: Thomas Lennon
Sheriff Rick: Barry Pepper
Reece Tenneson: Rob Lowe
Origin: United States
Language: English
Released: 2016
Production: Denis L. Stewart, Mary Parent; Disruption Entertainment, Nickelodeon Movies; released by Paramount Pictures Corp.
Directed by: Chris Wedge
Written by: Derek Connolly; Matthew Robinson; Jonathan Aibel; Glenn Berger
Cinematography by: Don Burgess
Music by: David Sardy
Sound: Douglas Murray; Addison Teague
Editing: Conrad Buff, IV
Art Direction: Chris Beach; David Clarke; Andrew Li
Costumes: Tish Monaghan
Production Design: Andrew Menzies
MPAA rating: PG
Running time: 104 minutes

REVIEWS

Barnard, Linda. *Toronto Star.* January 12, 2017.
Davis, Steve. *Austin Chronicle.* January 15, 2017.
Deburge, Peter. *Variety.* December 25, 2016.
Gonzalez, Ed. *Slant Magazine.* January 12, 2017.
Lewis, David. *San Francisco Chronicle.* January 12, 2017.
Orndorf, Brian. *Blu-ray.com.* January 12, 2017.
Rechtshaffen, Michael. *Hollywood Reporter.* December 29, 2016.
Walsh, Katie. *Los Angeles Times.* January 13, 2017.
Webster, Andy. *New York Times.* January 12, 2017.
Zilberman, Alan. *Washington Post.* January 12, 2017.

QUOTES

Reece Tenneson: "I'm not into hurting people. [Nods to Burke] That's his job."

TRIVIA

Jane Levy starred in *Evil Dead* (2013) and Samara Weaving starred in the first season of *Ash vs Evil Dead* (2015).

MOTHER!

Seeing is believing.
—Movie tagline

Box Office: $17.8 Million

The film *mother!* looks into the creative mind and finds a sociopath more than willing to crumple up the real world like a failed sketch and start all over again. The implications of that should shake any creative person to their core. But *mother!* is designed to unhinge viewers with sight and sound as well, as it leads them to that unsettling conclusion. Some will reject Darren Aronofsky's new film outright as too obvious, obnoxious, or even patently offensive. It may be fair to say Aronofsky has made a self-indulgent film, but in no way is it a boring one. For many, *mother!* is liable to be wildly entertaining, deeply insightful and, at times, almost too horrible to contemplate.

In the ruins of a large home ravaged by fire, Him (Javier Bardem) fixes a crystal onto a pedestal causing the building to magically restore itself and a character named Mother (Jennifer Lawrence) to materialize in a bedroom. Mother wakes, calls for Him and, begins walking around, plagued by disturbing visions including a heart beating inside the walls of the house. The outside is calm, inviting, a beautiful day.

Soon, a knock at the door reveals Man (Ed Harris), a sickly stranger asking if he can stay for a while. Him is enthusiastic, but Mother much less so. During one of Man's many coughing fits, Mother notices a wound in Man's side, though Him tries to cover it. Tensions rise further when Woman (Michelle Pfeiffer), Man's wife, arrives and Him pressures Mother to accept their presence, explaining that they are fans of his writing, and that Man is dying. The pair are certainly tactless, particularly Woman, who drinks constantly and nitpicks at almost everything Mother says. When Man and Woman enter Him's forbidden room and break the crystal, greatly upsetting Him, Mother attempts to throw them out.

Before they can leave, the couple's sons arrive. Oldest Son (Domhnall Gleeson) is angry about Man's will, which leaves everything to Younger Brother (Brian Gleeson). A fight ensues that leaves Younger Brother mortally wounded. Older Brother flees as his parents and Him take Younger Brother to get help. Left behind, Mother begins cleaning up the blood which has eaten a hole in the floor. She investigates the basement and finds a hidden door behind which is furnace oil tank. Upstairs, a large crowd has come for Younger Brother's wake. As their numbers grow they turn into an unruly mob causing a pipe to burst.

Having kicked everyone out, Mother angrily confronts Him about feeling ignored and overwhelmed by his adoring fans. They have sex, and the next morning she tells him she is pregnant. A period of happiness ensues during which Him overcomes a creative block allowing him to write his masterpiece. Mother is deeply moved by it and soon every copy of it is sold out. In celebration, she prepares a dinner for Him only to be overwhelmed once more by a group of unruly fans forcing her to barricade the door. The crowd grows to enormous size and breaks into the house. People begin stealing things and a cult forms around Him as his publisher, the Herald (Kristen Wiig) attempts to guide the chaos. Mother is terror stricken. The military shows up, rituals begin, people are slaughtered, and still the crowd grows.

Triggered into labor, Mother and Him escape to his study. After the baby is born a strange quiet descends over the house and Him tells Mother that the crowd wants to see their baby. Horrified, she refuses but Him waits until she sleeps. The baby is killed by the crowd and when Mother wakes up she discovers the mangled body and is nearly beaten to death by the crowd herself as she lashes out in revenge. Him stops them but Mother, completely unhinged goes to the basement and, despite Him's pleas, causes the furnace to explode killing everyone trapped in the house. As she lies dying in his arms, Him asks her for whatever love she has left and when she agrees, tears open her chest, tears her heart open, and removes yet another crystal. Him is then seen to place the crystal back on the pedestal in the ruins of the house which changes back into the beautiful manse. A new Mother also rises from the sheets as the sun rises and calls his name.

Mother! is certainly a film that offers rewards to those who have their own history with the biblical narrative of creation. But it is no simple allegory. Aronofsky has created a film designed to encourage passionate conversation on a number of topics. The nature of God comes into question as do the ideas of original sin and sacrifice. The creative mind itself and what it is willing to give up in order to achieve perfection is explored in chilling detail. Gender identifications come under scrutiny. *Mother!* is, if nothing else, a film that requires multiple viewings for anyone interested in any of these.

As an entertainment though, the film is a torrential assault, a roller coaster ride through a gore-soaked haunted house where the best viewers are likely able to try to keep up with what is going on around them. *Mother!* is so profoundly hallucinatory it invites comparisons to Terry Gilliam, David Lynch, or Alejandro Jodorowsky but the difference is that Aronofsky is not dealing in the inscrutable. Everything in *mother!* is disturbingly familiar and presented on ten, almost as if the camera had been thrown into the set's crowded rooms only to be caught and momentarily directed by Aronofsky before careening out of control once again

The film is perfectly cast. Javier Bardem makes of Him a soft-eyed deification that viewers will want to trust, but who can inspire fear in the blink of an eye. He seems justified in all he does until the consequences of his actions become so overwhelming the only question left is where faith lies. To trust Him may mean unbearable suffering. Jennifer Lawrence has never seemed as fragile as she does here. Her character fights for autonomy, to be loved, for her baby, for her home, to the point of exhaustion. Mother is no saint. At times the character seems deeply selfish but even this will be debated by those who are intent on developing the thread of feminism here. But she is ultimately at the mercy of Him and the forces he unleashes. Ed Harris and Michelle Pfeiffer are sheer perfection as Man and Woman bringing true fragility to parts that could have come off as simply boorish.

Aronofsky also engages in some very canny casting for the film's smaller roles. Kristen Wiig is perfect, if unexpected, in the role of the Herald, a person with a marketing plan where her heart should be. The underused Stephen McHattie brings a trademark level of intensity to the role of the Zealot.

The marketing of *mother!* as a horror film seems appropriate though it probably dissuaded some from viewing. The real shame of it is that one of the major accomplishments of Aronofsky's film is the way it transcends genre, creating something that seems to embrace elements of the creation story that have never been placed in the forefront prior. Imagine someone screaming out the book of Genesis, unblinking, lit only by a candle. Better yet, imagine being the one who screams in that dimly lit room only to realize that a mirror image screams back. The existential cry would almost be funny if the echo would just stop haunting the air, crying out for rebirth.

Dave Canfield

CREDITS

Mother: Jennifer Lawrence
Him: Javier Bardem
Man: Ed Harris
Woman: Michelle Pfeiffer
Oldest Son: Domhnall Gleeson
Origin: United States
Language: English
Released: 2017
Production: Scott Franklin, Ari Handel, Darren Aronofsky; Protozoa Pictures; released by Paramount Pictures Corp.
Directed by: Darren Aronofsky
Written by: Darren Aronofsky
Cinematography by: Matthew Libatique
Sound: Craig Henighan; Jill Purdy
Editing: Andrew Weisblum
Art Direction: Isabelle Guay
Costumes: Danny Glicker
Production Design: Philip Messina
MPAA rating: R
Running time: 121 minutes

REVIEWS

Anderson, John. *Wall Street Journal*. September 14, 2017.
Chang, Justin. *Los Angeles Times*. September 14, 2017.
Howell, Peter. *Toronto Star*. September 14, 2017.
MacDonald, Moira. *Seattle Times*. September 15, 2017.
Orr, Christopher. *The Atlantic*. September 15, 2017.
Scott, A.O. *New York Times*. September 13, 2017.
Stewart, Sara. *New York Post*. September 14, 2017.
Travers, Peter. *Rolling Stone*. September 13, 2017.
Vishnevetsky, Ignatiy. *The A.V. Club*. September 13, 2017.
Walsh, Katie. *Tribune News Service*. September 15, 2017.

QUOTES

Mother: "What are you?"
HIM: "Me? I am I. And you? You are home."

TRIVIA

Director Darren Aronofsky has said that the exclamation point in the title of the film is a reference to the story's final thirty minutes.

AWARDS

Nominations:

Golden Raspberries 2017: Worst Actor (Bardem), Worst Actress (Lawrence)

THE MOUNTAIN BETWEEN US

What if your life depended on a stranger?
—Movie tagline

Box Office: $30.3 Million

The "survival drama" is classically defined by characters trapped out of their element left to unfamiliar devices and extreme measures to get back to the life or loved ones waiting for them. Often when stories thrust attractive people into the same dire circumstances it is inevitable that their proximity will spark newfound feelings that culminate in the allusion that survival means a happily ever after. Hany Abu-Assad's *The Mountain Between Us* can never pretend that it is not headed for a big kiss between its stranded couple, but its failure to project either the horror of its situation or the potential beauty of its endurance makes its purpose phony.

Ben Bass (Idris Elba) and Alex Martin (Kate Winslet) have the same problem. Their flight has been canceled and each have important commitments on the other side of their landing. Ben is a doctor with a life-saving surgery the next morning and Alex, a photographer, is getting married. Instead of waiting around with the other suckers—who, given the odds, probably contain at least one or two other passengers with pressing obligations in their own lives—Alex suggests chartering a private plane. In one of the airport hangars, they meet Walter (Beau Bridges), who agrees to get them to their destination. He just was not planning on the stroke that would hit him mid-flight and right in the middle of a mountain range.

Miraculously, the only casualty of the crash is Walter. Even his dog survives. As does Alex who spends some time unconscious, enough for Ben to survey their limited rations, realize there's no phone signal, and tend to her injured leg. When she awakens, she is less patient of the wait-for-a-rescue scenario. One of the film's more comical moments is an attempt by Ben to signal a commercial aircraft with a flare gun. He wants to be more pragmatic about their predicament realizing that every step into the snowy nether land is one further from shelter and one more closer to death. Alex is persistent in getting them to try though, thus beginning a hike that is neither particularly scenic nor gripping.

Courting the bare minimum of drama of average individuals thrust into a barren landscape should be very simplistic at the early drafts of the story. Alex quickly lays out the schoolhouse logic of how long one can go without food and water. The rest should come naturally and with a little creativity in raising the stakes the makings of a good survival yarn fall into place. These two have a distinct advantage though that mutes any such peril. For one, there's a doctor in the house. And Alex, given her photojournalist credentials has likely been in situations where the elements were hardly ideal. She may not have been laid up with a cougar bearing down on her, but at least there were two flares to spare. Dinner is served.

Not every film can sell the kind of exasperation felt in Lawrence and Gasim's trek through the Nefud in *Lawrence of Arabia* (1962). Whatever was described on the pages of Charles Martin's book is not translated into something that absorbs an audience into a "what would I do" scenario. We would walk. And keep walking. The dog runs. And when the dog is out of sight, there are occasional ten second lapses into dread that something, anything, may be lost in this whole ordeal. Ben's mystery patient is never thought of again, even as a passing regret, leaving one to believe that either any doctor could fill in just as easily or the surgery was not as dire as we may have assumed.

With the terrain more inconvenient than immediately treacherous, it is left to the characters themselves to provide the drama. This proves to be just as disappointing. Alex can hardly put up a front of interest in her would-be-spouse; the casting of whom is practically an inside joke about the blandness of their engagement. Thankfully, there's an Idris Elba in the house. Literally, because they actually find a house. Here Alex has more time to wrestle with the agonizing decision to listen to the full voicemail from Ben's wife on his phone. The outcome will come as no surprise to anyone who has witnessed the awkward outrage of meddling into another's privacy or those who already worked out why he doesn't talk about her. If there's nothing back in civilization worth getting back for then surely the build-up to caring for each other would inspire enough of an instinct to drive them. Instead, it hardly amounts to a hill of beans, let alone a mountain.

The Grey (2011) had wolves as well as Alex's fiancé. *The Edge* (1997) had a bear to team up the men possibly destined to kill each other before getting out alive. *Cast Away* (2000) had a volleyball that earned hope and tears faster than Ben and Alex ever could. These are films rich in the survival film tradition of problem solving and obstacle course set pieces. On a different plain, *Speed* (1994) gently mocked the accelerated two-hour journey from strangers to lovers. "Relationships that start under intense circumstances, they never last," as spoken by Sandra Bullock in that film is tested here in a snicker-worthy epilogue that takes a hard turn from harsh reality to joyful hokum. So, by the end, even the mountain itself wants to distance itself for being credited as the primary wedge between two characters this screenplay had no intention of damaging permanently. Unlike the people who may have really needed them.

Erik Childress

CREDITS

Ben Bass: Idris Elba
Alex Martin: Kate Winslet
Walter: Beau Bridges
Mark: Dermot Mulroney
Pamela: Linda Sorensen
Origin: United States
Language: English
Released: 2017
Production: Peter Chernin, Dylan Clark, David Ready, Jenno Topping; Chernin Entertainment; released by Twentieth Century Fox Film Corp.
Directed by: Harry Abu-Assad
Written by: J. Mills Goodloe; Chris Weitz
Cinematography by: Mandy Walker
Music by: Ramin Djawadi
Sound: Mildred Iatrou; Ai-Ling Lee
Editing: Lee Percy
Art Direction: James Steuart
Costumes: Renee Ehrlich Kalfus
Production Design: Patrice Vermette
MPAA rating: PG-13
Running time: 100 minutes

REVIEWS

Berardinelli, James. *ReelViews.* October 6, 2017.
Erhlich, David. *IndieWire.* September 28, 2017.
Gronvall, Andrea. *Chicago Reader.* October 5, 2017.
Hornaday, Ann. *Washington Post.* October 5, 2017.
Jenkins, Mark. *NPR.* October 5, 2017.
LaSalle, Mick. *San Francisco Chronicle.* October 4, 2017.
Roeper, Richard. *Chicago Sun-Times.* October 6, 2017.
Russo, Tom. *Boston Globe.* October 5, 2017.
Turan, Kenneth. *Los Angeles Times.* October 5, 2017.
Vishnevetsky, Ignatiy. *ReelViews.* October 3, 2017.

QUOTES

Ben Bass: "If we stay here we're safe. If we leave, search and rescue, they're less likely to find us."

Alex Martin: "Look, I don't want to die up here because you're too scared to take a risk. We have to do something."

TRIVIA

Margot Robbie was originally attached to play Ashley Knox, but dropped out after Michael Fassbender left the project.

MUDBOUND

Few moments in the American cinema are as meaningful as seeing the artistic progression of a gifted young filmmaker. Dee Rees made an auspicious fiction feature debut with *Pariah* (2011), an autobiographically shaded piece about a black teenager's sexual coming of age. She brought emotional depth and a lyrical style to an outré subject of young women finding their liberation in the underground black culture of Brooklyn. The movie closed with its young protagonist, Alike (Adepero Oduye), delivering a piercing self assertion: "I'm not running. I'm choosing."

The movie was small, though significant. *Pariah* was compact, urgent, and beautiful to look at and think about. The director's second theatrical feature, *Mudbound*, shares those same affinities, and the beauty here is that the director is working on a much larger canvas but she never surrenders her distinctive touch. The new movie is a knockout, beautiful, exciting, tender, and terrifying. About the only meaningful complaint is that Rees is probably too ambitious for her own good, and some of the story threads unnecessarily dangle or characters float off on the periphery. Otherwise these are pretty minor qualms about such a striking achievement.

Rees has a novelist's feel for objects and landscape and a painter's eye for composition and color. She balances those sensibilities beautifully. Her literate, visually spellbinding adaptation of the same-titled novel (2008) by Hillary Jordan retains the panoramic density and multiplicity of voices of the original. She wields those qualities to the immediacy and breadth of the movies. The resulting power is cumulative and enthralling.

All directors must mediate the differences of language, soundtrack, and imagery. *Mudbound* is never less than a work of cinema. Rees adapted the script with Virgil Williams. She also worked closely with the editor, Mako Kamitsuna, in developing an elastic rhythm that plays off and accommodates the mellifluent range of voices. The movie has the shape of a dance, starting at the end and moving backward in time and space in creating a fluid collage style that colors its themes and ideas through a dizzying weave of contrasts and echoes. The movie is about faces, bodies and movement, of torment and release. Even in its quiet moments *Mudbound* is never less than active and it pulsates with feeling and excitement.

The movie is also a deeply Southern work, conjuring the novels of William Faulkner and short fiction of Flannery O'Connor, the raw and hard scrabble music of the Mississippi Delta and the evocative dust bowl photography of Dorothea Lange. The movie covers a lot of ground, the late period Depression South, the European theater and American home front during World War II, and the complex returning home for those soldiers who witnessed a country transformed socially and racially.

Bradley Young shot *Pariah* in a swirl of diagonal lines and voluptuous and silky colors. Rachel Morrison is the cinematographer of the new film, and her work is extraordinary. Right away Rees and Morrison imaginatively link character with history, grounding the people to the unforgiving and brutal landscape. A dominant theme is immediately established. *Mudbound* is about a reckoning, of ideas and beliefs, and action, behavior and mood are quickly understood to carry tangible consequences. The movie opens on a note of sharp discord. Two brothers, Henry (Jason Clarke) and Jamie McAllan (Garrett Hedlund), trying to dig a gravesite and bury their father on their Mississippi farm are interrupted by an apocalyptic rainstorm.

The whole enterprise appears ridiculous, even life-threatening. The moment also crystallizes deeper wounds, underscoring the two brothers' very different attitudes about their father. Another family, the Jackson clan, Hap (Rob Morgan) and his wife, Florence (Mary J. Bilge), black sharecroppers, turn up with their children and most of their possessions strapped to their truck. The cryptic remarks between Henry and Hap hint at some recent raw trauma. Henry asks for assistance with his father's burial, a request that Hap clearly resents though feels powerless to turn down.

This virtuoso opening establishes the foundation of the film, of themes, motifs, and style: the two families bound together though clearly separated by race and class; of past and present; of community and place. Rees deftly introduces most of the primary characters. The opening sets the tone, a peculiar and entrancing mood. The movie's intricate flashback structure feels organic and deeply intuitive in laying out character and story. "When I think of the farm, I think of mud," Henry's wife, Laura McAllan (Carey Mulligan), says. Laura's line, spoken in voiceover, announces another crucial storytelling element, of voice, speech, and shifting perspectives. Like Faulkner's *The Sound and the Fury* (1929), *Mudbound* toggles among multiple narrators, their rhyming internal monologues giving full range to joys, fears and ecstasies of the particular speakers.

The courtship of Henry and Laura dominates the first movement. "I was a 31-year old virgin," Laura says at the time she met Henry, a Memphis engineer. The two are not very compatible in temperament or taste. Laura is an aesthete, trained to be a teacher and a talented amateur pianist. She overlooks her objections. Henry liberated her from a regimented and socially restricted life, and she was grateful at the chance of escape and renewal. Laura's sharp personal differences with Henry are only accented when she meets his younger brother Jamie, the more dashing and naturally outgoing. A budding playwright, Jamie quotes Shakespeare with Laura, displaying an ease and confidence. He is also, on the basis of a swanky party the three attend, a suave ladykiller.

Laura's orderly existence as a young wife and mother with two young daughters is forever altered by Henry's announcement he has purchased a farm in Mississippi. Henry is clearly drawn to the land, with its promise of independence, solitude and freedom. He makes the trek with his family, including his father, Pappy (Jonathan Banks). Their new life puts them in immediate contact with the Jackson family, farm tenants who also dream of acquiring their own land. These early farm passages, detailing the extraordinary sacrifice, physical work and effort needed to plant the crops, are streaked in a primal intensity.

The Japanese attack at Pearl Harbor initiates the next major movement. Jamie, who has come down to work the farm, enlists in the Air Force and becomes a B-24 bomber pilot. Ronsel (Jason Mitchell), the Jackson's oldest son, is drafted as a tank commander in the famed 761st Battalion. With its claustrophobic and intense combat footage mostly viewed from inside the cockpit of Jamie's bomber, *Mudbound* changes registers completely and conveys a palpable sense of breakdown, violence, and disruption. Rees shows a thrilling and dynamic sense of space and restricted point of view.

Rees subtly contrasts the existential crisis in Europe with the more plaintive, direct struggles at home. As her romantic ardor with Henry cools, Laura quickly and skillfully adapts to the demands of farm life. Rees sharply delineates the power dynamics, of class, race, and sex, in these sections, demonstrating just how complex and pervasive race especially touches on every small action or colors every incident. When Florence, a midwife, comes to the aid of Laura's daughters when they develop whooping cough, she is prized for her talent and competence. After Hap suffers a gruesome leg injury, Henry exploits it to his own advantage.

The movie's third movement is its most jarring, dealing with the emotional, political, and cultural ramifications of the returning soldiers. "Home at last, home at last," Ronsel sings to himself. The pernicious life he fled, the soul-crushing institutional racism of Jim Crow, remains very much in place, a harsh lesson learned during an ugly confrontation with Pappy at a town store. *Mudbound* achieves a cruel and heartbreaking synthesis in tracking the furtive friendship of Jamie and Ronsel. Ronsel liberated Europe only to return home a second-class citizen. Jamie stared down death and returned a different kind of prisoner, suffering from post-traumatic stress disorder and his dependence on alcohol to blunt the pain.

At different points, six different narrators tell their stories. Rees is very good at individuating those voices. *Mudbound* is an exceptional work of emphasis. Rees is always attuned to differences of expression and tone, an observational clarity and off-handed humor in documenting the harshness of life on the farm or the more accelerated and intense rhythm involving the combat footage or in the most searing passage, a mournful and horrifying act of violence.

At times the movie is almost too much of a good thing, and Rees struggles to balance all the parts. A subplot involving another white family that works the farm makes for a messy fit. Laura's voice dominates and then she recedes into the background. Otherwise one strains to find the flaws.

By its conclusion, *Mudbound* is a strikingly coherent work. Rees's visual penchant for action and movement is the most revealing aspect. Her talent with actors is the most natural and carries over from her earlier work. Every single part feels right, lived in, complex and unmannered: Laura's grace and toughness, Henry's stubbornness and resilience, Florence's faith and salvation, Hap's honor and fortitude, Jamie's sacrifice and pain, and Ronsel's power and dignity. Even Pappy, a monster in many regards, in his abject racism toward Ronsel and cruelty toward Jamie, is a character of sinew and fiber, a dark emblem of hate who projectsd something irrational, almost unaccountable.

In making a film of symmetries, Dee Rees has not forsaken the ugliness and the pain. *Mudbound* is not a work of rounded corners and elegance. It is messy, confusing, horrifying, and finally, unforgettable.

Patrick Z. McGavin

CREDITS

Jamie McAllan: Garrett Hedlund
Laura McAllan: Carey Mulligan
Henry McAllan: Jason Clarke
Hap Jackson: Rob Morgan
Pappy McAllan: Jonathan Banks
Florence Jackson: Mary J. Blige
Origin: United States
Language: English
Released: 2017
Production: Carl Effenson, Sally Jo Effenson, Cassian Elwes, Charles King, Christopher Lemole, Kim Roth, Tim Zajaros; Armory Films, ArtImage Entertainment, Black Bear Pictures, Elevated Films, MACRO, MMC Joule Films, Zeal Media; released by Netflix
Directed by: Dee Rees
Written by: Dee Rees; Virgil Williams
Cinematography by: Rachel Morrison
Music by: Tamar-kali

Sound: Damian Volpe
Editing: Mako Kamitsuna
Art Direction: Arthur Jongewaard; Michael T. Boyd
Production Design: David J. Bomba
MPAA rating: R
Running time: 134 minutes

REVIEWS

Brody, Richard. *New Yorker*. November 16, 2017.
Burr, Ty. *Boston Globe*. November 16, 2017.
Chang, Justin. *Los Angeles Times*. November 16, 2017.
Dowd, A.A. *The A.V. Club*. November 15, 2017.
Hornaday, Ann. *Washington Post*. November 16, 2017.
Nashawaty, Chris. *Entertainment Weekly*. November 16, 2017.
Phillips, Michael. *Chicago Tribune*. November 16, 2017.
Scott, A.O. *New York Times*. November 16, 2017.
Yoshida, Emily. *New York Magazine*. November 16, 2017.
Zacharek, Stephanie. *Time*. November 20, 2017.

QUOTES

Ronsel Jackson: "Over there, I was a liberator. People lined up in the streets waiting for us. Throwing flowers and cheering. And here, I'm just another nigger pushing a plow."

TRIVIA

This is the second film featuring Garrett Hedlund and Carey Mulligan playing alongside each other, the first was *Inside Llewyn Davis* (2013).

AWARDS

Nominations:

Oscars 2017: Actor--Supporting (Blige), Adapt. Screenplay, Cinematog., Orig. Song Score and/or Adapt. ("Mighty River")
Golden Globes 2018: Actress--Supporting (Blige), Song ("Mighty River")
Screen Actors Guild 2017: Actress--Supporting (Blige), Cast
Writers Guild 2017: Adapt. Screenplay

THE MUMMY

Welcome to a new world of gods and monsters.
—Movie tagline
Ancient evil returns.
—Movie tagline

Box Office: $80.2 Million

The enormous success of the Marvel Cinematic Universe over the past decade has, like a dazzling and exotic new boy or girl who moves into town senior year and suddenly upturns the social strata of their high school, left Hollywood studios in a daze consisting of equal parts titillation and jealousy. Having foresight, Disney purchased Marvel Entertainment for $4 billion at the end of 2009. In the years since, they have reaped the rewards.

Slower off the starting block, other studios' answers have typically put results before the process. Warner Bros.' shared universe for its DC Comics characters, for example, aimed for lucre over any cohesive narrative plan, and has experienced all sorts of missteps before righting the ship critically and commercially with *Wonder Woman* (2017). Paramount, meanwhile, has convened a writers room not only for various *Transformers* spin-offs, but also for other Hasboro properties.

Then there is Universal, which has in its back catalogue a rich history of monster movies dating back to the 1920s, featuring characters like Frankenstein's Monster, the Wolf Man, Dracula, the Invisible Man, the Creature from the Black Lagoon, and more. Eying the billions of dollars being raked in by one of their competitors, Universal set out to create its own shared world for these characters, dubbed the "Dark Universe." Directed by Alex Kurtzman and starring Tom Cruise, *The Mummy* is the first of these offerings. Decidedly lacking in menace, cathartic release, or even a unified tone, however, the film mainly comes across as a case study in corporate cinematic second-guessing—so concerned with a scrupulous protection of the status quo that it tells a story which evaporates even as the credits roll.

The Mummy debuted to $31.7 million in its opening weekend, good for second place behind holdover *Wonder Woman*. Pummeled by critics (it clocked in at 16 percent fresh on Rotten Tomatoes), it finished its theatrical run with only $80 million domestically, though it was a much bigger hit internationally, where it grossed $313 million (including over $91 million in China).

The film opens with crusading knights burying a ruby in a tomb with one of their fallen comrades, and said tomb being unearthed in the present day by construction workers. A foreboding flashback then shows ancient Egyptian princess Ahmanet (Sofia Boutella) wreaking vengeance after being passed over for the throne by her father. Once captured, she is buried alive in mummified form.

Flashing forward to present day, military tomb raiders Nick Morton (Cruise) and Chris Vail (Jake Johnson) accidentally uncover Ahmanet's crypt when they call in an airstrike. Archeologist Jenny Halsey (Annabelle Wallis) arrives on the scene, but the eventual transport-plane extrication of Ahmanet's sarcophagus goes awry when Chris becomes possessed by Ahmanet, forcing Nick to shoot him dead. The plane crashes, with seemingly only Jenny escaping alive, via parachute.

Nick soon awakens in a morgue, however, and is visited by visions of Chris. It seems the latter has been zombified and the former cursed by Ahmanet—a fact later confirmed by Dr. Henry Jekyll (Russell Crowe), who identifies Jenny as an operative and himself as the head of Prodigium, a secret organization whose mission is to "recognize, contain, examine, and destroy evil." With a reanimated Ahmanet becoming more and more powerful, a disoriented Nick teams up with Jenny to try to fend off her evil plans.

The Mummy does not suffer from a paucity of ideas, necessarily. With a screenplay credited to David Koepp, Christopher McQuarrie, and Dylan Kussman and a story separately credited to Kurtzman, Jon Spaihts, and Jenny Lumet, the movie arrives with all the ample surgical scars of a cobbled-together, new Hollywood mega-production. Parts of the movie seem to augur a metaphysical exploration ("Evil is a shadow outside our world, continuously grasping for a way to come in," says Jekyll, after an obligatory appearance by his violent alter ego Mr. Hyde), while most of the film of course takes a mystical bent—even though Ahmanet's powers are frustratingly vague. Other portions of *The Mummy* flirt more with the romantic adventure genre with a light sprinkling of horror.

In the end, though, none of these ideas are particularly well-developed. As such, the film lurches to and fro. It serves up discrete and somewhat unconvincing special effects sequences (e.g. Nick being overrun by a swarm of CGI rats), as well as brawny fisticuffs where it is not always entirely clear why certain characters are fighting. In general, in lieu of character-motivated behavior and reaction, the movie feels like it is working its way down a checklist of phobias and action sequences that it believes viewers want to see.

Kurtzman, who with Roberto Orci penned entries in the *Transformers* and rebooted *Star Trek* franchises, came to know Cruise as a co-writer on *Mission: Impossible III* (2006). While he made his directorial debut with *People Like Us* (2012), this film represents a massive step up in scale, and despite Kurtzman's doubtless familiarity and comfort level with big-budget sets, he evinces no clear, unifying visual aesthetic for *The Mummy*. Except for the punch of a couple set pieces, the movie feels just about as generic and personality-free as a blockbuster could possibly be, down to a drab color palette and production design. Kurtzman is aided (or saved, if you prefer) in scene-to-scene fashion by a bit of superb technical craftsmanship—most notably visceral editing by Paul Hirsch, Gina Hirsch, and Andrew Mondshein, who help turn the zero-gravity airplane crash into the movie's indisputable high point.

Regrettably, it must also be said that *The Mummy* is weighed down by movie star casting. When *Iron Man* (2008) was made, Robert Downey, Jr. was not one of the biggest names in the world; in fact, he was only four years removed from Mel Gibson personally underwriting liability insurance so that he could work. One of the few remaining actors who can guarantee a sizable international opening, Cruise is a capable performer who works tirelessly to "plus" his movies, and offer audiences something fresh that they have not seen before. He does that again in *The Mummy* with its aforementioned airplane crash sequence, which he convinced McQuarrie to borrow from their next planned *Mission: Impossible* sequel.

The character of Nick Morton, however, is ill-fitting for Cruise. His performance, and specifically his desire to always have his leading men remain liked and in some element of control, contribute mightily to the film's misdialed tone. He ably captures Nick's self-regard and devil-may-care anti-authority streak, but the character is a louche who requires 15 to 25 percent harder depression on the "a-hole" pedal. The offscreen image protection of Cruise, the movie star, seems to bleed over into his portrayal of Nick, setting up boundaries and robbing it of any true wildness or rich, unhinged mania.

Other performances equally miss the mark. Johnson's comic relief comes across as irksome and unwelcome, and Wallis—unfortunately saddled with a clichéd subplot about her character having previously had a one-night stand with Nick—seems undone by conflicting direction, caught between screwball exasperation and something more naturalistic.

Apparently set on splitting the difference between Marvel and DC's respective worldviews and tones, *The Mummy* is a cautious, corporate-vetted piece of entertainment with so many fingerprints on it that it has no discernible set of its own. If Universal is serious about making its Dark Universe work, it needs to empower filmmakers to tell stories that matter—not that feel like cinematic curations of unopened "IP" collectibles.

Brent Simon

CREDITS

Nick Morton: Tom Cruise
Dr. Henry Jekyll: Russell Crowe
Jenny Halsey: Annabelle Wallis
Ahmanet: Sofia Boutella
Chris Vail: Jake Johnson
Origin: United States
Language: English, Egyptian
Released: 2017
Production: Genevieve Hofmeyr, Sarah Bradshaw, Sean Daniel, Chris Morgan, Alex Kurtzman; Dark Universe, Dentsu, Perfect World Pictures, Secret Hideout; released by Universal Pictures Inc.

Directed by: Alex Kurtzman
Written by: David Koepp; Christopher McQuarrie; Dylan Kussman
Cinematography by: Ben Seresin
Music by: Brian Tyler
Sound: Daniel Laurie; Christopher Scarabosio
Editing: Gina Hirsch; Paul Hirsch; Andrew Mondshein
Art Direction: Frank Walsh; Penny Rose
Production Design: Jon Hutman; Dominic Watkins
MPAA rating: PG-13
Running time: 120 minutes

REVIEWS

Adams, Thelma. *New York Observer.* June 9, 2017.
DeFore, John. *Hollywood Reporter.* June 7, 2017.
Ebiri, Bilge. *Village Voice.* June 7, 2017.
Gleiberman, Owen. *Variety.* June 7, 2017.
Goodykoontz, Bill. *Arizona Republic.* June 7, 2017.
Nashawaty, Chris. *Entertainment Weekly.* June 7, 2017.
Persall, Steve. *Tampa Bay Times.* June 7, 2017.
Rainer, Peter. *Christian Science Monitor.* June 9, 2017.
Robinson, Tasha. *The Verge.* June 7, 2017.
Whitty, Stephen. *Newark Star-Ledger.* June 7, 2017.

QUOTES

Dr. Henry Jekyll: "Welcome to a new world of gods and monsters."

TRIVIA

The zero gravity scene took sixty-four takes and was shot over two days in a falling plane. It has been reported that a lot of the crew got nauseous filming the scene, except for the main stars, Tom Cruise and Annabelle Wallis.

AWARDS

Golden Raspberries 2017: Worst Actor (Cruise)

Nominations:

Golden Raspberries 2017: Worst Director (Kurtzman), Worst Picture, Worst Remake/Sequel, Worst Screenplay, Worst Support. Actor (Crowe), Worst Support. Actress (Boutella)

MURDER ON THE ORIENT EXPRESS

Everyone is a suspect.
—Movie tagline

Box Office: $102.5 Million

Any filmmaker attempting to adapt Agatha Christie's 1934 whodunnit bestseller *Murder on the Orient Express* faces two insurmountable challenges—trying to make the enterprise exciting to the millions of people familiar with the various twists and turns of the plot leading up to one of the most well-known "surprise" endings of all time, while also making the entire thing interesting to audiences who might not otherwise be interested in watching a brilliant detective solving a murder using nothing but his wit. Never one to shy away from such a challenge, filmmaker Kenneth Branagh has stepped up to the plate to not only direct an elaborately produced adaptation of the piece but to star in it as well, leading a cast made up of a number of famous and award-winning faces. Alas, despite his herculean (pun intended) efforts, the resulting film is a weird misfire that is handsomely mounted but utterly empty beneath its glimmering surface, and one which inexplicably adds a leaden touch to proceedings that should be kept as light as possible if they are to succeed.

The titular conveyance sets off to shuttle a full load of colorful types from Istanbul to London. The passenger list includes Caroline Hubbard (Michelle Pfeiffer), a glamorous widow on the hunt for a new husband; Edward Ratchett (Johnny Depp), a shady art dealer who is accompanied by his valet (Derek Jacobi) and accountant (Josh Gad); Pilar (Penélope Cruz), a deeply religious missionary trying to atone for some unspoken past tragedy; Dr. Arbuthnot (Leslie Odom Jr.), a doctor who is rushing to London to attend to a patient and seems oddly familiar with governess Mary Debenham (Daisy Ridley); Gerhard Hardman (Willem Dafoe), an Austrian scientist and outspoken racist; and Marquez (Manuel Garcia-Rulfo), an eager-to-please salesman. Royalty is represented by the imperious Princess Dragomiroff (Judi Dench)—who is accompanied by her servant (Olivia Colman)—and the mysterious Count and Countess Andrenyi (Sergei Polunin and Lucy Boynton). Finally, there is Bouc (Tom Bateman), a representative of the train company, and the conductor, Pierre Michel (Marwan Kenzari). Suffice it to say, by the time the sun rises on the second day of the journey, one of the above mentioned turns up dead—murdered in their compartment, a victim of multiple stab wounds.

With no obvious suspects or clues to be had, it would take no less than the world's greatest detective to figure out who did it and, more importantly, why. Luckily, that person, legendary Belgian sleuth Hercule Poirot (Branagh) happens to be on the train as well, called away from a planned holiday by news regarding a case in London. With the train derailed by a convenient avalanche, Poirot decides to put his deductive skills to the test by investigating the scant clues left behind and interviewing the passengers in order to see who among them might have had a motive for wanting the victim dead. While most of the passengers appear to be strangers on the surface, Poirot soon uncovers that a number of them have connections to a world-famous unsolved mystery involving the kidnapping and murder of an American child not unlike the case of the Lindbergh baby. With the pressure of time upon him, Poirot must sift through all the information presented to figure out what is true and what is a lie, and ultimately determine who, indeed, is gulty in a group where literally anybody could legitimately be seen as a primary suspect.

Although there are a few tweaks to the material here and there, Branagh and screenwriter Michael Green have pretty much stuck to the basic parameters of Christie's novel, but it does not require the services of the greatest detective in the world to understand why this particular iteration never quite works. It has been produced with immaculate care with Haris Zambarloukos's impressive 70mm cinematography taking in every gleaming surface of Jim Clay's Art Deco-inspired production design. It also kicks off strongly with a lively and amusingly staged prologue set in Jerusalem that introduces viewers to Poirot, his matchless combination of fastidiousness and intuition, and, of course, that astonishing mustache, as he solves a case in which the suspects are a priest, a rabbi, and an imam. The trouble is that once the action shifts to the train, what was once effervescent—or at least as effervescent as Branagh is likely to get—becomes leaden and oppressive. The 1974 version of the source material was not exactly a masterpiece of filmmaking, but director Sidney Lumet approached the proceedings with a welcome (and rare for him) degree of wit and style that helped keep things moving. Branagh inexplicably goes in the exact opposite direction with a take that is far too serious and solemn for the material at hand that just does not fit with the cheerful preposterousness of the story being told. (This version is about 15 minutes shorter than Lumet's but somehow feels longer.)

Branagh is a man who is not afraid to add his own artistic two cents to someone else's work if the inspiration strikes. Here, for the most part, he sticks almost religiously to the original story, rendering the entire endeavor all but pointless to anyone who already knows its particulars. He even manages to bungle the most seemingly foolproof scene of them all, the climax in which Poirot gathers all the suspects and announces who among them is guilty—aside from an amusing *Last Supper*-like staging of those being interrogated, the entire sequence lands with a bewildering thud.

The cast is talented but they never manage to jell into a true ensemble. On the one hand, Pfeiffer is terrific as the widow and pretty much steals the scene whenever she appears, and Ridley is also good as the governess with a secret. On the other hand, it seems as if Depp has forgotten how to act without the overt affectations that have dominated his most recent performances to the point where he just seems kind of bored with the whole enterprise—watching him act against Branagh, the only thing you get from him is the sense that he wishes that he got to wear the wacko mustache. As for the rest, they wind up getting lost in the jumble of people jockeying for position, something that one might have thought impossible when including the likes of such players as Dench, Jacobi, Dafoe, and even Cruz, barely registering in the same role that won Ingrid Bergman her third Oscar. As Poirot, Branagh has a few amusing moments here and there (there is a priceless bit where we see him sleeping with a leather guard that is protecting his precious mustache) but his take pales in comparison to those offered in the past by the likes of Albert Finney and Peter Ustinov on the big screen and David Suchet on television.

Murder on the Orient Express is not a disaster by any means, but it is a curiously muted affair that feels more like a museum piece than anything else. Despite all the talent on hand, it just never comes alive in any meaningful way, either to fans of Poirot or those who look at the snowbound location, the locked-room mystery in need of solving, and the heroic facial hair and determine that it is a pastiche of Quentin Tarantino's *The Hateful Eight* (2015), right down to the use of 70mm cameras, rather than the other way around. This is especially frustrating when you consider just how well Branagh handled Christie-like material earlier in his career in the wonderful *Dead Again* (1991). There are a few pleasures to be had here and it is nice in a time when every other film seems to be a superhero epic to see so many resources on both sides of the camera being deployed in the service of a period whodunnit. However, when all is said and done, the failure of *Murder on the Orient Express* to fully work despite everything in its favor proves to be a bigger mystery than anything seen on the screen.

Peter Sobczynski

CREDITS

Hercule Poirot: Kenneth Branagh

Miss Mary Debenham: Daisy Ridley
Leslie Odom, Jr.

Biniamino Marquez: Manuel Garcia-Rulfo
Penelope Cruz

Origin: United States

Language: English

Released: 2017

Production: Mark Gordon, Judy Hofflund, Simon Kinberg, Michael Schaefer, Ridley Scott, Kenneth Branagh; Genre Films, Kinberg Genre, Latina Pictures; released by Twentieth Century Fox Film Corp.

Directed by: Kenneth Branagh
Written by: Michael Green
Cinematography by: Haris Zambarloukos
Music by: Patrick Doyle
Sound: James Mather
Music Supervisor: Maggie Rodford
Editing: Mick Audsley
Art Direction: Dominic Masters
Costumes: Alexandra Byrne
Production Design: Jim Clay
MPAA rating: PG-13
Running time: 114 minutes

REVIEWS

Chang, Justin. *Los Angeles Times.* November 9, 2017.
Debruge, Peter. *Variety.* November 2, 2017.
Ehrlich, David. *indieWire.* November 7, 2017.
Kenney, Glenn. *New York Times.* November 8, 2017.
Maher, Kevin. *Times (U.K.).* November 2, 2017.
McCarthy, Todd. *Hollywood Reporter.* November 2, 2017.
Merry, Stephanie. *Washington Post.* November 8, 2017.
Smith, Anna. *Time Out.* November 3, 2017.
Taylor, Ella. *NPR.* November 9, 2017.
White, Armond. *National Review.* November 10, 2017.

QUOTES

Hercule Poirot: "I see evil on this train."

TRIVIA

Actress Michelle Pfeiffer sings "Never Forget," a song co-written by composer Patrick Doyle and director/star Kenneth Branagh, over the film's closing credits.

MY COUSIN RACHEL

Box Office: $2.7 Million

Paranoia is a rich vein to mine cinematically, because it only takes a hint of something sinister to turn the ordinary malevolent. Alfred Hitchcock did this beautifully throughout his career, especially when adapting stories by the author Daphne du Maurier. *The Birds* (1963), *Jamaica Inn* (1939), and 1940's Best Picture winner *Rebecca* all showed what a master director could do with du Maurier's tales of upper crust lives rent asunder by suspicion and chaos. It turns out it's not just anyone who can turn her prose into high art, however, as Roger Michell's adaptation of her 1951 novel *My Cousin Rachel* can attest. Michell, a reliable purveyor of largely successful light romantic comedies, has no idea what to do with the many currents of possible intrigue running through the story. He cranks up the heavenly light on the gorgeous scenery and turns it down for drawing rooms. It's all very handsome but what he fails to make much of a meal of is the age-old idea that the ones we love may be out to kill us.

Philip (Sam Claflin) is orphaned at a young age and raised by his cousin Ambrose (Deano Bugatti) in Cornwall, England. His life is about as sunny as can be expected for a young man, and indeed trouble only darkens his door when his cousin falls in love with his widowed cousin Rachel (Rachel Weisz). Not long after their meeting, they wed and then Ambrose takes ill and dies. This sets young Philip's mind racing with ill thoughts. He doesn't know how but he's certain that Rachel had something to do with Ambrose's death. She's due for a visit soon and he plans to get to the bottom of it, even though his guardian and godfather Kendall (Iain Glen) and his daughter Louise (Holliday Grainger), who may harbor some affection for Philip, think he's overreacting out of understandable grief.

Rachel arrives very late at night and throws a monkey wrench in Philip's interrogation plan simply by looking so bewitching and acting so civil and charming. He sits down with her and talks and then the following day continues talking to her, and soon he's forgotten all about his suspicions. Indeed, the only thing he feels towards her is growing infatuation. They're soon in love and making plans, some that could threaten to upset the balance of Philip's estate. He tries to give her his valuables in order to make arrangements to wed her, but when she discovers this, she panics because it would interfere with the amount of money she receives simply for being a widow. She begins to chafe under his pressure to become his wife, even recoiling from his advances, and just as suddenly he falls ill. Rachel cares for him for months but their future remains uncertain, and as Philip's condition worsens under his paramour's care, he once again wonders whether she had anything to do with Ambrose's death.

It's possible there was an interesting way to treat the growing suspicion that makes up the subtextual backbone of *My Cousin Rachel*, but Roger Michell is either unequal to, or uninterested in, that particular task. He's content to whisk through one lovely, if slightly mysterious parlor or solarium after another watching the smiles of his leads ebb and flow depending on the demands of the source novel's plot. His interests, based on his work making the charming likes of *Morning Glory* (2010), *Le Week-End* (2013), and *Venus* (2006), are not in anything more complex than prickly personalities rubbing against each other like sandpaper until the edges are smoothed. Certainly there is quite a bit of that in

My Cousin Rachel, but when there's a potential murder that needs to be solved, the pleasantries and light flirting are by comparison boring.

It's also unhelpful that Claflin and Weisz don't have much chemistry and there are no stakes attached to their courtship. The will-they won't-they story is really all there is, as the idea of Rachel as a poisoning villainess never finds any kind of purchase in the rest of the story. Philip is always a step behind everyone else's appraisal of his actions, it hardly ever matters whether Rachel is guilty. It makes no difference ultimately whether she's guilty or not, because so little rests on the truth of the situation.

Michell does fine work photographing the countryside where all this flat intrigue transpires, but it's never good to encourage viewers to want to stare past the actors to get a better glimpse of trees and cliff-side vistas. As with Michell's other well-appointed thriller, the financial sector tug-of-war *Changing Lanes* (2002), Michell is better at lighting rooms than ratcheting up tension. He leaves the audience to fill in the blanks of the story while he focuses on the handsome faces and the little bits of malice hiding behind gentle eyes. Especially when placed next to the challenging pleasures of this year's other aristocratic fever dream *Lady Macbeth,* which plays with the same ideas and reaps much richer rewards, *My Cousin Rachel* functions as little more than a way to bring tourists to its rich filming locales.

Scout Tafoya

CREDITS

Rachel: Rachel Weisz
Philip: Sam Claflin
Louise: Holliday Grainger
Kendall: Iain Glen
Couch: Simon Russell Beale
Origin: United States
Language: English, Italian
Released: 2017
Production: Kevin Loader; Free Range Films; released by Fox Searchlight Pictures
Directed by: Roger Michell
Written by: Roger Michell
Cinematography by: Mike Eley
Music by: Rael Jones
Sound: Danny Sheehan
Editing: Kristina Hetherington
Costumes: Dinah Collin
Production Design: Alice Normington
MPAA rating: PG-13
Running time: 106 minutes

REVIEWS

Burr, Ty. *Boston Globe.* June 7 2017.
Clarke, Cath. *Time Out London.* July 5, 2017.
Dargis, Manohla. *New York Times.* June 8, 2017.
Debruge, Peter *Variety.* June 2, 2017.
Duralde, Alonso. *TheWrap.* June 2, 2017.
Jagernauth, Kevin. *The Playlist.* June 7, 2017.
Phillips, Michael. *Chicago Tribune.* June 8, 2017.
Robey, Tim. *The Telegraph.* June 8, 2017.
Turan, Kenneth. *Los Angeles Times.* June 8, 2017.
Vishnevetsky, Ignatiy. *The A.V. Club.* June 7, 2017.

QUOTES

Philip: "Whatever it cost my cousin in pain and suffering before he died I will return with full measure upon the woman that caused it."

TRIVIA

The country estate house used for filming was inherited by Bamber Gascoigne following the death of his aunt, Mary Innes-Ker, Duchess of Roxburghe, on July 2, 2014.

MY ENTIRE HIGH SCHOOL SINKING INTO THE SEA

Box Office: $68,883

My Entire High School Sinking Into the Sea starts with a promising title that conjures all sorts of imagery, ranging from the abstract to the metaphorical to the comically absurd. Everyone, at some point, has wished that their high school would just sink into a body of water, never to be heard from again, taking all the peer pressure, mean-spirited cliques, and algebra tests with it. This animated comic fantasy delights in the idea of taking a disaster movie scenario and combining the conventions of that genre with the teen angst comedy/dramas of decades past. In a brisk 75 minutes, it accomplishes more or less what it sets out to do, but with all the effort put into the animation, one wonders what could have transpired here if there were more thought or wit put into it. It is a mixed bag, for sure, one that tries to get a lot of attention for a lot of different reasons.

The story focuses on Tides High School's lower-on-the-food-chain students, Dash (voiced by Jason Schwartzman) and Assaf (voiced by Reggie Watts), both sophomores, who both write for the school paper. Dash feels more confident now that he has moved up to sophomore status. He leads his more nervous best friend to the back of the bus as a way of changing their social standing. "This is going to be a big year for our hero and his faithful sidekick," Dash says. For the paper's first issue, they write a Survival Guide to high school, but the article does not prove successful or popular. Dash may be a little too proud of his status, though. Later on, he gets kicked off the paper by his editor, Verti (voiced by Maya Rudolph), for writing a negative piece about Assaf.

Principal Grimm (voiced by Thomas Jay Ryan) is none too pleased with Dash either, but Dash does come off as incredibly annoying, so no one can blame anyone for not taking a liking to him. Later on, though, Dash happens upon some old files that indicate the high school's physical structure may not be up to code. If an earthquake strikes, the school could be in danger of falling into the sea and killing everyone. Dash tries to get the word out about this, but because he no longer has access to the school paper, he cannot get anyone's attention. Then, as often happens in disaster films, the earthquake hits and all the warning signs about the school's negligence come to pass. The high school sits atop a plot of land that breaks off and drifts into the sea.

As water slowly starts to seep in, students make their way to the upper levels. They end up at the cafeteria where a lunch lady named Lorraine (voiced by Susan Sarandon) becomes an unlikely hero. One of the more popular girls in school, Mary (voiced by Lena Dunham), tries to make crucial decisions based on how many people will follow her. Dash, Assaf, Verti, Mary, and Lorraine eventually break from the masses and head into the depths of the school to try and get people to a safer spot while also looking for more students who might be in danger. Not all goes well. One student gets eaten by a shark and there are plenty of moments where someone almost drowns. Of course, the most popular kid in school has his own idea of how things should be and that turns out to be another kind of disaster.

It is interesting to note that the writer and director of this film, Dash Shaw, shares the namesake of its main character, typical of many autobiographical comics. Shaw is playing with many reference points in popular culture and throwing them all in a colorful cartoon blender. Unfortunately, as much as Dash may be the hero here, he is a thoroughly unengaging character and it becomes hard to root for him. Fortunately, Shaw has surrounded him with much more likeable characters who have many more heroic feats than him. The cast Shaw has assembled to voice these characters is very appealing, particularly Sarandon, who is an inspired choice to play the gruff lunch lady. Dunham also has fun with her role as a perky would-be popular girl.

My Entire High School Sinking Into the Sea, though, looks more like a creative showcase for Shaw as an animator than as a storyteller. The entire film is crammed with collages, flashes, abstract backgrounds, and psychedelic flourishes that it becomes more of a feast for the eyes than anything else. Every single shot or cut has an element of animation that was not there before, which can be delightful one minute and a distraction the next. There is certainly something to be said about the ambition here as there are few animated films quite like this one, but the look of the film is often at odds with how the audience is meant to feel. The human characters have a flatness to them that makes it hard to fully engage with them. Given the *Scooby-Doo* like nature of the last half of the film (particularly the long shots of the characters running in silhouette), perhaps that is intentional.

So, there is as much to be frustrated with as there is to admire here. By the end of the very brisk running time, the sight of the characters dancing like the characters in *The Charlie Brown Christmas Special* should tell the viewer everything they need to know. This is a labor of love from someone who has great admiration for the animation of yesteryear, disaster movies, teen angst movies, comic books, and the late-night offerings on the Cartoon Network. Nothing wrong with that, of course, but hopefully, in future efforts, Dash won't sell his characters short and will give the audience a main character who is worth knowing and has more interesting features to look at. With this film, Shaw comes off like the cinematography student at film school who has great ideas for shots, but cannot construct a worthy story or characters to hang them together with. He shows great promise, but still has much to learn at school.

Collin Souter

CREDITS

Voice of Dash: Jason Schwartzman

Voice of Mary: Lena Dunham

Voice of Assaf: Reggie Watts

Voice of Verti: Maya Rudolph

Lunch Lady Lorraine: Susan Sarandon

Origin: United States

Language: English

Released: 2017

Production: Kyle Martin, Craig Zobel; Electric Chinoland, Low Spark Films, Washington Square Films; released by GKIDS

Directed by: Dash Shaw

Written by: Dash Shaw

Music by: Rani Sharone

Sound: Ryan M. Price
Editing: Alex Abrahams; Lance Edmands
MPAA rating: PG-13
Running time: 75 minutes

REVIEWS

Burr, Ty. *Boston Globe*. May 4, 2017.
Connelly, Sherilyn. *Village Voice*. April 12, 2017.
Covert, Colin. *Minneapolis Star Tribune*. May 4, 2017.
Jones, J.R. *Chicago Reader*. May 4, 2017.
Kenny, Glenn. *New York Times*. April 13, 2017.
Lamanna, Dean. *Film Threat*. May 18, 2017.
MacDonald, Moira. *Seattle Times*. April 20, 2017.
Murthi, Vikram. *RogerEbert.com*. April 17, 2017.
O'Sullivan, Michael. *Washington Post*. May 4, 2017.
VanDenburgh, Barbara. *Arizona Republic*. April 27, 2017.

TRIVIA

Director Dash Shaw has known actor Jason Schwartzman for many years due to their mutual love of comic books. They met after Dash's comic book called, "Bottomless Belly Button" came out and they have always kept in touch.

MY LIFE AS A ZUCCHINI
(Ma vie de Courgette)

Box Office: $309,766

Adult subject matter in animation aimed at kids is practically a requirement these days. The last two decades of Pixar's output alone have specialized in making movies that appeal to every demographic from toddlers to the elderly. That does not mean it's not exhilarating when a film makes difficult subjects like abuse and mental illness not only feel lived-in and incisive, but also charming and breezy. Based on Gilles Paris' novel, *Autobiographie d'une Cougarette*, the Swiss-French claymation film, *My Life as a Zucchini*, (2017) tells a minimal but fastidiously constructed story bursting with affection for its characters, and touched with just a bit of magical realism.

Adapted by indie darling, Céline Sciamma—the auteur behind the exceptional coming-of-age films *Girlhood* (2014) and Tomboy (2011)—and co-written with director Claude Barras, *My Life as a Zucchini* follows the life of a damaged orphan growing up in a group home. Comparable in tenor and sensitivity to the punishingly bittersweet *Mary and Max* (2009), the film sketches out a series of eccentrics who are introduced, but not defined through their misfortunes.

Distributed by GKids, *My Life as a Zucchini* continues the company's tradition of visually spectacular animation. Closest in presentation to early Laika output and Henry Selick's work with its coarse and deliberately chunky character designs, the faces have at once a Play-Doh primitivity and an inborn melancholy. The animation is anything but clunky though, instead placing these designs against the almost Monet-like impressionism of the washed backgrounds, creating a fluid textural contrast that echoes the film's deft intermingling of contradicting tones.

From the first scene, that design sense makes a dark story more palpable. The film begins with emphatic grimness as the barely decade old Icare (Erick Abbate) enters his frigid home and sneaks past his alcoholic mother up to his bedroom. Whatever happy days she once had have been replaced by long days in front of a television lamenting why Icare's father left. Even minutes in, Barras offers a glimpse of his visual instincts. The camera does not intrude on the scene, but it stays fixed just long enough for a brief look at Icare's expression: a numb stare highlighted by dinner plate eyes that communicate a frightening familiarity to the scene.

Building a tower from a stockade of empty beer cans like they're Lincoln Logs, it's only a moment before his mom stomps upstairs in a drunken rage. Cut to black, a loud thud, and a title dissolve, and Icare is being driven away from his childhood home to an orphanage in the back of Raymond's (Nick Offerman) car. Arriving at the orphanage, Icare takes on a new identity, "Zucchini," a symbolic gesture of the few memorable moments with his mother—a person who he heartbreakingly summates to a case worker with "she really liked to drink, she makes good mashed potatoes, and we sometimes got along."

And yet despite these introductory scenes, this is not a film that's mired in flamboyant despair. It's speckled with wince-worthy scenes like a clever montage that goes through each orphan's plight—these kids have experienced everything from living with debilitating mental illness to witnessing parents' suicides—but those details are key to communicating the stakes of these kids' daily existences and understanding why they alternate between prickliness and holding tight to each other.

The early orphanage scenes veer the closest to genre cliché as Zucchini acclimates to the day-to-day and deals with bullying from another boy, Simon (Romy Beckman), who tries to goad him into admitting what happened to his mother—a revelation that is obvious but still treated with care. Simon could have easily been a villain in a less human film, but he's treated with uncharacteristic diplomacy. It's an implicit reminder that he's just another kid who was born into an unfair situation, and has adapted by acting more guarded and aggressively.

Enjoyable as those early scenes are, they are transparently set-up for the arrival of Camille (Ness Krell), a spunky young girl who Zucchini immediately takes to, and most readily evokes the off-kilter French New Wave influence of the film with her starry-eyed charm and gallows humor. As a serious friendship blooms between them, and Zucchini finds his place among the other kids, the film likewise finds an indelible groove while also revealing its limitations. At barely over an hour, the biggest problem of *My Life as a Zucchini* is that it's just too short to support all of its interests.

The meat of the film is devoted to Zucchini and Camille bonding over trauma and the bright comedy of these kids goofing off with each other, but there's also a good amount of screen time spent on an undercooked ongoing story involving foiling Camille's abusive aunt Ida (Amy Sedaris), who wants to take in Camille in order to receive a monthly stipend check from the government. And while it fares far better, there's also time for a heartwarming sub-story involving the aforementioned Raymond, a lonely and kind police officer, who semi-regularly comes to the orphanage to check in with Zucchini. But both of these tangents are just evidence that the script needs to spend more time with these characters.

Still, this is a minor issue and a testament to the strength of the overall movie from the writing to the striking aesthetic to the vocal performances. Even as an ephemeral experience, *My Life as a Zucchini* is a film filled with both little grace notes and casually stunning moments. A sequence barely lasting thirty seconds in an amusement park puts most blockbuster animated films to shame with the sheer amount of bespoke elements in the scene. But that's the magic of this film. It's over in a flash, but it's the rare experience that manages to feel both unassuming and lyrical at the same time.

Michael Snydel

CREDITS

Mr. Paul: Will Forte (Voice)
Raymond: Nick Offerman (Voice)
Rosy: Ellen Page (Voice)
Aunt Ida: Amy Sedaris (Voice)
Zucchini: Erick Abbate (Voice)
Origin: France, Switzerland
Language: English, French
Released: 2016
Production: Marc Bonny, Armelle Glorennec, Pauline Gygax, Max Karli, Kate Merkt, Michel Merkt; Blue Spirit Animation, Gébéka Films, KNM, Rita Productions; released by GKIDS
Directed by: Claude Barras
Written by: Claude Barras; Celine Sciamma; Germano Zullo; Morgan Navarro
Cinematography by: David Toutevoix
Music by: Sophie Hunger
Editing: Valentin Rotelli
Art Direction: Ludovic Chemarin
Costumes: Christel Grandchamp; Vanessa Riera
MPAA rating: PG-13
Running time: 70 minutes

REVIEWS

Connelly, Sherilyn. *The Village Voice*. February 22, 2017.
D'Angelo, Mike. *The A.V. Club*. February 22, 2017.
Debruge, Peter. *Variety*. May 15, 2016.
Ide, Wendy. *Sight and Sound Magazine*. February 17, 2017.
Kenny, Glenn. *RogerEbert.com*. February 24, 2017.
Pahle, Rebecca. *Film Journal International*. February 23, 2017.
Rothkopf, Joshua. *TimeOut New York*. February 17, 2017.
Sicinski, Michael. *Movie Mezzanine*. February 17, 2017.
Yoshida, Emily. *Vulture*. February 23, 2017.
Zacharek, Stephanie. *Time*. February 16, 2017.

QUOTES

Raymond: "Your mum is no longer there, I care."
Courgette: "My name is Courgette!"
Raymond: "Courgette--did your mum call you that? My name is Raymond."
Courgette: "Did your mum call you that?"

TRIVIA

This was the official submission of Switzerland for the Best Foreign Language Film category of the 89th Academy Awards in 2017.

AWARDS

Nominations:
Oscars 2016: Animated Film
British Acad. 2017: Animated Film
Golden Globes 2017: Animated Film

MY LITTLE PONY: THE MOVIE

Friendship comes in many colors.
—Movie tagline
Discover a different breed of hero.
—Movie tagline

Box Office: $21.9 Million

Feature-length films of popular children's shows are nothing new and the rebooted *My Little Pony* animated show seems like a solid program to bring to the big screen. The "My Little Pony" franchise started in the 1980s as a toy line from Hasbro before becoming a popular cartoon. The rebooted show is sassy, colorful, and fun and as such, it's really quite shocking that the feature film is such a derivative bore. Also surprising is how lazy an effort *My Little Pony: The Movie* is once one looks at the star-studded cast pulled together to make the big screen adaptation.

As *My Little Pony: The Movie* opens, the audience learns that there's a "Friendship Festival" being planned for the horse and pony-populated "Ponyville." As is the case with pretty much every plot point in the "My Little Pony" universe, friendship is key. In fact, each main pony character represents a specific trait of a good friend. There's the ever-honest Applejack and the loyal Rainbow Dash (both voiced by Ashleigh Ball), the kind Fluttershy and comical Pinkie Pie (both voiced by Andrea Libman), the generous Rarity (voiced by Tabitha St. Germain), and perhaps the most popular little pony, Twilight Sparkle (voiced by Tara Strong), who possesses magical powers. Not only are these six ponies best friends forever, they're also precisely crafted characters designed to play perfect foil to one another creating tension and friction before always neatly resolving conflicts because, at the end of the day, they're all friends. It's a simple, positive message for kids that fails miserably upon transfer to a longer running-time.

Since there would not be much of a movie if there was not some drama, no sooner have guests started arriving for the "Friendship Festival" than a dark cloud covers Ponyville, and an evil broken-horned unicorn pony named Tempest Shadow (voiced by Emily Blunt) storms in and encases the leaders of Ponyville in black rock in order to steal their powers. It's up to Twilight Sparkle and "The Mane Six" to save the day by escaping and journeying to find a mysterious "Queen of the Hippogriffs" on Mount Eris who holds a pearl that can save their land. So, off we go on a very standard heroes journey that becomes a mish-mash of odd animation choices and a strange, almost meandering mix of animal characters, some of which are actually fairly racist. While yes, it does seem odd and a bit of a stretch to pull the race card on *My Little Pony: The Movie*, it's also hard to ignore the fact that two of the characters the ponies meet on their journey are voiced by African-American actors who in turn portray some pretty old stereotypes that draw attention to themselves by how awkwardly they're handled.

Once on the road to Mount Eris, the ponies meet a sly, grifter cat named Capper (voiced by African-American actor Taye Diggs). After charming the ponies with a song, he quickly sells them out to Tempest Shadow who is in hot pursuit. This, in and of itself, is fairly harmless, but Diggs heavily plays up stereotypical African-American slang and when he's revealed to be an untrustworthy hustler, the race flag shimmies up the flagpole. Soon the ponies escape before meeting a band of birds who used to be pirates who have an airship the ponies stow away upon. Don't ask. These pirate birds soon reveal that they are basically slaves to the evil overlord the Storm King (voiced by Liev Schreiber) and the ponies also learn that new archenemy Tempest Storm is also at the Storm King's beck and call. Thus the second act neatly sets up an impending showdown between the ponies, Tempest Shadow and the Storm King that will inevitably show the ponies victorious in act three.

Soon the ponies reach Mount Eris but the Queen of the Hippogriffs is nowhere to be found. Instead, they journey underwater where they find a tribe of Merponies (i.e. pony mermaids) lead but a lazy, egotistical Queen Novo (voiced by the other aforementioned African-American lead actor, Uzo Aduba) who wants to do nothing more but be pampered upon her throne as she lazily dismisses the ponies. Again, such a classic, racist stereotype as an African-American who is lazy and doesn't want to work simply cannot slip by unnoticed and the character and characterization is more than a bit troubling.

Still, the journey and drudge that is *My Little Pony: The Movie* slogs onward as the ponies soon discover the Merponies were in fact the Hippogriff's but they went undercover to avoid the wrath of the Storm King and after much ballyhoo, they get the pearl from Queen Novo. Since again, friendship is the main plot point when it comes to all things *My Little Pony*, onetime enemies like Capper and the pirate birds come to the aid of the ponies as they have a final showdown with the nasty Tempest Shadow as well as the Storm King. Since this is an animated movie aimed at children in the five-to-eight-year-old range, one can probably guess how it all turns out. But still, predictability is no excuse for the fact that a film based on a decent and highly popular television cartoon is incredibly boring. Perhaps 30-odd minutes of *My Little Pony* is the recommended daily allowance as much more may cause headaches.

Don R. Lewis

CREDITS

Voice of Queen Novo: Uzo Aduba
Voice of Applejack/Rainbow Dash: Ashleigh Ball
Voice of Tempest Shadow/Fizzlepop Berrytwist: Emily Blunt
Voice of Princess Skystar: Kristin Chenoweth

Voice of Capper: Taye Diggs
Origin: United States
Language: English
Released: 2017
Production: Haven Alexander, Stephen Davis, Brian Goldner, Marcia Gwendolyn Jones; Allspark Pictures, DHX Media Ltd., Hasbro Studios; released by Lionsgate
Directed by: Jayson Thiessen
Written by: Meghan McCarthy; Rita Hsiao; Michael Vogel
Cinematography by: Anthony Di Ninno
Music by: Daniel Ingram
Editing: Braden Oberson
Art Direction: Rebecca Dart
MPAA rating: PG
Running time: 99 minutes

REVIEWS

Bibbiani, William. *IGN*. October 5, 2017.
Davis, Steve. *Austin Chronicle*. October 4, 2017.
Hartlaub, Peter. *San Francisco Chronicle*. October 5, 2017.
Lemire, Christy. *RogerEbert.com*. October 6, 2017.
Nicholson, Amy. *Variety*. October 5, 2017.
Rechtshaffen, Michael. *Hollywood Reporter*. October 5, 2017.
VanDenburgh, Barbara. *Arizona Republic*. October 5, 2017.
Weitzman, Elizabeth. *TheWrap*. October 5, 2017.
Walsh, Katie. *Seattle Times*. October 5, 2017.
Watson, Keith. *Slant Magazine*. October 5, 2017.

QUOTES

Grubber: "I know you're disappointed, but I've got one word for you: 'Spongecake.'"

TRIVIA

Actor Liev Schreiber accepted the role of the film's main antagonist, the Storm King, because he wanted to appear in a film he would be able to take his children to see, given the violent, adult-oriented films he usually appears in.

N

NOCTURAMA

Box Office: $29,342

Though many reference points were vouchsafed by critics around its premiere, there is no other film that moves or feels quite like Bertrand Bonello's *Nocturama.* It does show traces of influences, ranging from George A. Romero's *Dawn of the Dead* (1978), with its mall setting and satirical capitalist indulgences, to Gus Van Sant's school-shooting docudrama *Elephant* (2003), with its shocking violence and reliance on unsettling long takes. It also resembles, in its scenes of Parisian youths having political dialogues in cafés as they careen towards an uncertain, dark future, the works of Jacques Rivette and Jean Eustache. All of these references do help situate the film in a certain viewer's mind, the decisions made behind the camera and in the screenplay remain singular. This film, ostensibly about junior terrorists trying to unseat government and financial institutions of Paris through acts of violence, is about the unknowable minds of people formed by political currents but who haven't yet become whole humans in response to them. These children don't really understand what they are taking part in, they just know they want to have some influence on the world.

A group of teenagers (Finnegan Oldfield, Vincent Rottiers, Hamza Meziani, Manal Issa, Martin Petit-Guyot, Jamil McCraven, Rabah Nait Oufella, Laure Valentinelli, Ilias Le Doré, and Robin Goldbronn) are introduced moving across Paris via subway cars, stalking buildings, meeting each other momentarily, then breaking apart again. They recruit, discuss an upcoming action, prepare explosives, talk about their politics, and rehearse their motions, keeping close eyes on the many parts of the plan. They even go so far as to start shooting people who stand in the way of their plan. Then, finally, the moment arrives, and they detonate bombs placed in French government property and banking firms and set fire to a golden statue of Joan of Arc. The whole crew retreats to a giant mall to wait out the manhunt the police form to ferret them out. They begin to celebrate, taking full advantage of every comfort and extravagance in the mall, but the police do eventually find out where they are, leaving them defenseless and ill-equipped to handle the ensuing raid.

Bonello has in recent years taken to film increasingly decadent lifestyles, finding only the melancholy of death and the inherent, though by no means stressed, emptiness of wealth as a counterpoint. In *House of Pleasures* (2011) and *Saint Laurent* (2014), both excellent, he looked at the drives of pampered servants, prostitutes serving an absurdly wealthy and frequently callous upper-class male clientele in the former, and designer Yves Saint Laurent serving fashion to an increasingly beleaguered and unknowable French elite in the latter. The protagonists in both use drink, sex and drugs to numb their sense of existential dread, though it doesn't always work. The numbness cannot be contained in *Nocturama*, it's on the sullen faces of every terrorist from the first moments to the last. They are aware of their insignificance, of their belonging to a wave of voiceless teenagers whose opinions are discounted by the financial and legislative bodies running the country. Bonello literalizes this by frequently cutting out the sound of their voices and hands, as in a shot of one of the teenagers locked out of the mall, screaming to be let in, his voice replaced by the sound of helicopters mobilized to search for him and his crew. Whatever their motivations for the crime, which it's hinted are malformed, blunted and largely taken without question from the most vocal members of their group, the noise of society will always drown them out.

When it becomes clear that the movie is about powerlessness, a lot of Bonello's filmmaking decisions begin to make logical sense, instead of seeming merely coolly energetic. He has traded in his usual decadence for hard, propulsive purpose. By showing his heroes at first as constantly in motion, with a vicious lack of social grace, their fervent, unformed zealotry written across their frowning faces, Bonello shows their potential for destruction, their eagerness to be heard and make *some* kind of difference. After the action, when they believe they have made their statement, they unwind. The teenagers do eventually start to make sense when they are in the mall trying on stolen clothes and dancing to loud music, becoming the kids they have been pretending not to be for the duration of the first act. They begin to blend in with the mannequins littering the mall, only coming alive when they start dancing, which makes them look like figures in music videos. Everything from their politics to their fashion is second hand. They watch their own crimes on television, hungry for recognition and some form of fame, proof that they exist, because they can't make sense of their lives divorced of context provided by media. They talk about hitting larger targets next time to make an even bigger splash on TV, as they're watched all the while by security cameras. Their lives are in thrall to the idea of surveillance, making this a very modern vision of terrorism and a savvy exploration of youth.

Unlike the feral teens of Sofia Coppola's *The Bling Ring* (2013), the kids in *Nocturama* understand that they are playing in a field of narrative superstructures designed by powerful men who have deliberately robbed most young people of purpose beyond the few acceptable careers available to the educated, but they wrongly believe they have found a way to combat them. They sink into their roles as consumers as soon as they are given the chance, wowed by their own power, stupefied by material goods, overcome by the police state, and powerless to prevent their actions from being co-opted and rewritten by the media. They are terrifying in their dedication to their chaotic mission, but all in all, just as impotent as the other people who surround them on the subway in the first scenes. Everyone's going to the same destination and "civilization" is unmoved. Films this bleakly political and intelligent are not made with such rigorous, beautiful craft all that frequently, keeping *Nocturama* a rarity and a pristine, haunting object of 21st-century evolution, of kids waiting to become ghosts, their secondhand ideas lost in gunfire and loud music.

Scout Tafoya

CREDITS

David: Finnegan Oldfield
Greg: Vincent Rottiers
Yacine: Hazma Meziani
Sabrina: Manal Issa
Andre: Martin Petitguyot
Origin: United States
Language: French
Released: 2017
Production: Alice Girard, Edouard Weil; My New Picture, Pandora Filmproduktion, Rectangle Productions, Scope Pictures, WPR/Arte, Wild Bunch, Arte France Cinema; released by Grasshopper Film
Directed by: Bertrand Bonello
Written by: Bertrand Bonello
Cinematography by: Leo Hinstin
Music by: Bertrand Bonello
Music Supervisor: Pascal Mayer
Production Design: Katia Wyszkop
MPAA rating: Unrated
Running time: 130 minutes

REVIEWS

Abrams, Simon. *RogerEbert.com*. August 11, 2017.
Anderson, Melissa. *The Village Voice*. August 10, 2017.
Chang, Justin. *Los Angeles Times*. August 14, 2017.
Dillard, Clayton. *Slant Magazine*. August 6, 2017.
Lyttleton, Oliver. *The Playlist*. October 14, 2016.
Mintzer, Jordan. *Hollywood Reporter*. September 8, 2016.
Phillips, Michael. *Chicago Tribune* . September 7, 2017.
Pianezza, Pamela. *Variety*. September 8, 2016.
Scott, A.O. *New York Times*. August 10, 2017.
Vishnevetsky, Ignatiy. *The A.V. Club*. August 10, 2017.

TRIVIA

The film's metro scenes were shot guerrilla-style.

NORMAN

(Norman: The Moderate Rise and Tragic Fall of a New York Fixer)

The moderate rise and tragic fall of a New York fixer.
—Movie tagline

Box Office: $3.8 Million

A long shot shortly into *Norman: The Moderate Rise and Tragic Fall of a New York Fixer,* a compelling, compassionate character study shows part of the Big Apple's impressive skyline, a sight that is quickly supplanted by a closeup glimpse from behind someone indefatigably determined to worm his way into things until he finally finds himself at the center of it all. This rear view instantly elicits a desire for the man to turn around and more fully reveal himself to the audience, something that happens moments later in the literal sense and then gradually (but never completely) thereafter in the figurative until the bittersweet ends of both the film and its titular persistent protagonist. Thanks to Richard Gere's winning, nuanced portrayal, it is affecting as this sometimes-vexatious loser endlessly endeavors against all odds to get in touch with someone who will validate him by association, perhaps enabling him to stand tall like those notable skyscrapers, because one senses that deep down within this Manhattan macher is a level of self-worth even lower than the subway.

The term "long shot" certainly seems to also apply to the chance of Norman Oppenheimer, the nobody operator, becoming a real somebody. It is surely not coincidental that the film has this strenuous striver spend much of the film literally out in the cold, nor that the first businessman (Dan Stevens) he hopes will warm to him winds up peeved in Central Park when a morning jog is interrupted by Norman's smiling "stalking": whether running or not when they encounter him, most people, it appears, end up feeling like doing so away from him. However, it is not someone wearing athletic shoes but high-fashion formal ones that enables Norman to get his own foot in the door, the pair oh-so-purposefully purchased by him for visiting Israeli Deputy Minister of Trade Micha Eshel (charismatic Lior Ashkenazi). Norman stands alone on the outside, looking in after following Eshel to a store selling the choicest of chocolates, but it is plain that he too hungers for some of the sweeter things in life.

Further along on Madison Avenue is a meet-cute in which this duo about to become fateful friends is framed together by a boutique's storefront window during the initial moments of shoe schmoozing that are presented like a silent short subject. Norman turns on the charm as he makes contact in multiple senses of the word: affably shaking hands, patting Eshel's shoulder and back, and leading him by the arm toward the entrance, all aiming to quickly foster a feeling of familiarity. Once inside, it is Norman and not any employee who insistently inveigles Eshel to buy what is being put forth, the high-pressure tactics appropriately and repeatedly reflected in a triptych mirror as he keeps looking for just the right angle toward the forging of a mutually-beneficial bond. The two seem to fit as nicely as the shoes, and so it seems worth it to Norman to pay the eye-popping $1,192.18. Neither man foresees that this transaction will eventually cost them both a great deal more.

Far from merely being an aimlessly-"Wandering Jew," Norman's trodding of the streets through much of the film is always targeted. Rather casually acquainted with the truth and with questionable claims of closeness to many key New York movers and shakers, he can now finagle an invitation for himself if accompanied by rising pol Eshel (who he enthuses is "a very, very close friend of mine") to an exclusive dinner in the home of a deep-pocketed power broker (Josh Charles). The seats lined up on either side of the elegantly-set table bring to mind an image that the film's Israeli (but American-born) writer/director Joseph Cedar said he had kept in his own throughout production: with the stopping and starting throughout of Jun Miyake's whimsical score, it is like Norman is continuously involved in a game of musical chairs, "trying his best to push his way to the right spot at the right time so he can get a seat...It's when the music stops that he's stuck." The iciest of silences ends things when Eshel unfortunately fails to appear, and thus Norman, although primed to play, is asked to disappear back out into the cozy-by-comparison winter's night.

However, three years later, Norman suddenly finds himself being shown respect instead of the door when Eshel becomes Israel's Prime Minister and magnanimously rewards his kind, generous, footwear-providing acquaintance with the title of Honorary Ambassador to American Jewry. It is poignant to perceive Norman's initial trepidation in a receiving line as his ego teeters on the brink: was Eshel about to draw a blank and leave him mortified in front of a throng of onlookers that included the ambivalently-appreciative nephew (Michael Sheen) he finally may have a chance to impress? As Eshel embraces Norman and calls him "my friend," a shot over the former's shoulder reveals how unaccustomed the latter is to people being happy to see him, rather dazed but deeply gratified as he soaks in being a celebrated center of attention. Cedar slows and even freezes elements of the mise-en-scène to emphasize Norman's savoring of this momentous moment. Another of the film's many interestingly-presented sequences follows, in which a sea of grinning faces expectantly wave their cards at this man acutely-awash with approval, requesting in unison a call that most would have previously refused. Now, in the grand scheme of things, VIPs aim to utilize him as indispensable connective tissue—instead of the disposable kind.

When Norman had been compared to a man frantically trying to get noticed by a passing ship as he treds water, this man with the ever-optimistic facade had said that he would be okay as long as his head remained above water. However, as the film's full title telegraphs, this well-meaning character who succinctly and seemingly sincerely states "I'm just here to help" cannot help himself when it comes to overstepping, overstating, overcomplicating, and overpromising: soon in over his head, he ultimately goes under. (Late scenes exhibiting the man's obliviousness on the way to oblivion are heartrending.) However, as he does, Norman intriguingly and rather touchingly creates ripples that spread far and wide and set many things right. One notes how his own recognition of being the key to these meaningful successes apparently wound up being worth more to Norman than the outward recognition he is shown to have bypassed with his anonymous donation of expertly-wangled millions to save the synagogue led by Rabbi Blumenthal (Steve Buscemi). Norman's attempt to prove his prowess at wheeling and dealing in order to make everyone happy and happy with him (both of which, in turn, seem to make him happy) has brought Eshel to the brink of political demise, and so Norman chooses to silence himself the night before what would be a damning deposition under oath. (Charlotte Gainsbourg is mesmerizing as a contrivedly-encountered Israeli investigator.) Thus, able to stay in office, Eshel signs a treaty that could save countless lives. Norman's final act takes place in that of the film, which starts with a title card reading "The Price of Peace." The machinations of this macher have led to his paying the ultimate one, seemingly finding serenity as he submerges in the knowledge that for once he was indeed the indispensable man. Gere is the same to Cedar's uniformly-well-cast, well-received first feature in which English predominates. One might say that the sixty-seven-year-old actor is, like Norman, doing his very best work late in life.

David L. Boxerbaum

CREDITS

Norman Oppenheimer: Richard Gere
Micha Eshel: Lior Ashkenazi
Philip Cohen: Michael Sheen
Rabbi Blumenthal: Steve Buscemi
Arthur Taub: Josh Charles
Origin: United States
Language: English, Hebrew
Released: 2017
Production: Miranda Bailey, Lawrence Inglee, David Mandil, Oren Moverman, Eyal Rimmon, Gideon Tadmor; Blackbird, Cold Iron Pictures, Movie Plus Productions, Oppenheimer Strategies, Tadmor; released by Sony Pictures Classics
Directed by: Joseph Cedar
Written by: Joseph Cedar
Cinematography by: Yaron Scharf
Music by: Jun Miyake
Sound: Niv Adiri
Editing: Brian A. Kates
Art Direction: Barbra Matis
Costumes: Michelle Matland
Production Design: Kalina Ivanov; Arad Sawat
MPAA rating: R
Running time: 118 minutes

REVIEWS

Brody, Richard. *New Yorker*. April 13, 2017.
Burr, Ty. *Boston Globe*. April 27, 2017.
Debruge, Peter. *Variety*. September 6, 2016.
Hornaday, Ann. *Washington Post*. May 4, 2017.
McCarthy, Todd. *Hollywood Reporter*. September 16, 2016.
Nashawaty, Chris. *Entertainment Weekly*. April 13, 2017.
Phillips, Michael. *Chicago Tribune*. April 20, 2017.
Rainer, Peter. *Christian Science Monitor*. April 14, 2017.
Roper, Richard. *Chicago Sun-Times*. April 20, 2017.
Scott, A.O. *New York Times*. April 13, 2017.

QUOTES

Norman Oppenheimer: "There are two kinds of moguls. First kind is like a big ocean liner ship. Makes a lot of waves, a lot of noise, everybody sees it coming from miles away. Like Jo Wilf. I think your boss, Minister Maor, is actually, in his close circle of friends, of course. And then there is Arthur. Well, Arthur is more like a nuclear submarine. He's quiet, he's fast, he's young. Extremely sophisticated."

TRIVIA

Half of the film was shot in New York City and the other half in Jerusalem, Israel.

NOVITIATE

Box Office: $577,501

It's so disheartening to see a film in which a talented ensemble never comes together because a director fails to get them all on the same page. There are individual elements of *Novitiate* that are undeniably strong, particularly a few of the supporting performances and the veracity of the film's setting. It also tells a story that should feel timely in the way it captures an era of radical change in belief and women's roles, two issues as prominent as ever in the cultural conversation of 2017. And yet these elements—a performance here (especially one in particular), a design choice there, a screenwriting decision or two—fail to cohere into an experience that satisfies overall. In a sense, that's the greatest role of the director—bringing the various puzzle pieces together into one visionary image—and it's all the more depressing when one can see the movie that could have been if someone had bothered to make them fit.

The title of Margaret Betts's film refers to the time in a young lady's life when she is in training to become a nun. And this particular novitiate takes place in 1964, a tumultuous time for the Catholic faith known historically as "Vatican II." More formally known as the Second Vatican Council, Vatican II was an ecumenical council that took place at St. Peter's Basilica in the Vatican, under Pope Paul VI. These major discussions of the tenets of the faith take place very rarely (it's the most recent on record), and often lead to radical changes. Vatican II led to dozens of changes in Catholic institutions around the world, some of them minor, some of them major. And these worldwide changes underlie the themes and issues of the very personal story at the heart of *Novitiate.*

That story is the one of Cathleen Harris (Margaret Qualley), a young woman who basically reveals her love for God. Perhaps the most interesting part of Betts's script is the way in which she captures a woman's willingness to devote her entire life to God as more of a relationship than a career decision. Cathleen is in love with God, and she's willing to sacrifice material goods and carnal needs to attest that love. There have been dozens of crisis-of-faith films but *Novitiate* is conceptually interesting in that it's not really Cathleen's faith that's questioned but tested by a cruel headmistress and system that does not really support someone like Cathleen, challenging her commitment instead of embracing it. She has faith. It's keeping it that becomes difficult.

And Cathleen is constantly challenged, mostly by a Reverend Mother Marie St. Clair (Melissa Leo), who feels her control being taken away by Vatican II and lashes out at the young women in front of her, including Sister Cathleen, Sister Evelyn (Morgan Saylor), Sister Emily (Liana Liberato), Sister Margaret (Ashley Bell), and others. She also fights with a younger nun named Sister Mary Grace (Dianna Agron), who feels more like a representation of the future of the Catholic church while Mother Marie stubbornly tries to hold on to the past. As Cathleen's mother Nora (a phenomenal Julianne Nicholson) remains startled and confused over the path her daughter is taking, the young lady is mentally and psychologically abused by a church and its leader who refuses to change.

It's not that far off-base to call *Novitiate* "Full Metal Habit" in that it exists as a story about a very different kind of basic training with a cruel taskmaster who pushes her charges to the breaking point. A (too) large portion of the midsection of the film consists of confessional scenes with the Reverend Mother in which the woman's viciousness and emotional warfare is on full display. In a circle, the fragile young ladies reveal their deepest and darkest histories and desires, breaking down in increasingly disturbing ways. These scenes start to break at the truthfulness of the film overall, feeling downright sadistic in their presentation. To be blunt, they are sensational and manipulative, and less of them would have made the point without the overkill.

The same could be said for Leo's performance, one that earned some surprising praise on the festival circuit, but stands among the most overcooked and overdone of 2017 in any film. To say she chews scenery here would be an understatement, and it's especially striking to watch her do so opposite performers who have clearly been directed to give more subtle, delicate performances. Agron, Qualley, and Nicholson are, bluntly, in a different film than Leo—a much better, more interesting film that trusts its audience and does not choose to spoon feed them with cartoonish line readings. Leo is a caricature of a twisted, cruel nun, and that decision leaves a black hole at the center of *Novitiate,* into which the other, more interesting characters get sucked.

It's easy to see *Novitiate* gaining life in the future after one or more of its young stars becomes a household name, something that could easily happen to the talented Agron, Liberato, or Qualley. And Betts herself will almost surely bounce back with a more interesting project next time. That's presuming she does not cast an actress who wrests the film away from her again and simply runs off with it as Melissa Leo does here.

Brian Tallerico

CREDITS

Sister Mary Grace: Dianna Agron
Sister Cathleen: Margaret Qualley
Sister Emily: Liana Liberato
Nora Harris: Julianne Nicholson
Sister Candace: Eline Powell
Reverend Mother: Melissa Leo
Origin: United States
Language: English
Released: 2017
Production: Carole Peterman, Celine Rattray, Trudie Styler; Maven Pictures, Novitiate Productions; released by Sony Pictures Classics
Directed by: Margaret Betts
Written by: Margaret Betts
Cinematography by: Kat Westergaard
Music by: Christopher Stark
Sound: Ruy Garcia
Music Supervisor: Tyler Bradley Walker

Editing: Susan E. Morse
Costumes: Vanessa Porter
Production Design: John Sanders
MPAA rating: R
Running time: 123 minutes

REVIEWS

D'Angelo, Mike. *The A.V. Club.* October 25, 2017.
Ebiri, Bilge. *Village Voice.* October 24, 2017.
Edelstein, David. *New York Magazine.* October 27, 2017.
Fink, John. *The Film Stage.* August 11, 2017.
Goldberg, Peter. *Slant Magazine.* October 24, 2017.
Moore, Roger. *Movie Nation.* October 17, 2017.
O'Sullivan, Michael. *Washington Post.* November 2, 2017.
Scott, A.O. *New York Times.* October 26, 2017.
Weitzman, Elizabeth. *TheWrap.* October 26, 2017.
Wilkinson, Alissa. *Vox.* October 26, 2017.

TRIVIA

Actors Margaret Qualley and Chris Zylka previously worked together in the HBO series *The Leftovers.*

THE NUT JOB 2: NUTTY BY NATURE

Get ready. Get set. Get nuts!
—Movie tagline

Box Office: $28.4 Million

Sometimes a movie sequel comes along that begs the question "Who asked for this movie?" The answer to that query is usually a greedy movie studio, especially if the film is of the animated variety. Children are a reliable market, one that's far less discerning than the unlucky parents who are forced to accompany them to the theater. One must also take into box-office account stoners and those seeking nostalgia in its various forms. Something mediocre can still be a hit if it has an all-star voice cast of actors who once populated a viewer's childhood. Regardless, a hit is a hit, and if a movie is a hit, Hollywood will undoubtedly attempt to replicate it.

This still does not explain, nor quantify *The Nut Job 2: Nutty by Nature,* the sequel to *The Nut Job* (2014). That film made $120 million worldwide, hardly a figure that would justify a $40 million sequel. In the crowded market of franchises like *Despicable Me, Ice Age,* and the output of Disney/Pixar, the call for a sequel here was practically non-existent. Still, Universal chose to roll the dice on the slapstick-filled adventures of Surly Squirrel (voice of Will Arnett) and his woodland creature crew. Once again, these characters are pitted against a human hell-bent on the destruction of their habitat.

Much of the voice talent believed in the series enough to return (or perhaps they were just contractually obligated), but none of the original filmmakers were so inclined. *The Nut Job 2: Nutty by Nature* has instead been entrusted to director Cal Brunker and his co-writer Bob Barlen. This duo does something unprecedented: they create a scene in a PG-rated movie that is so disgusting that it would make Dario Argento retch.

More on that revolting development later. *Nutty by Nature* opens in the nut shop that figured so prominently in the first film. Surly and his brethren live in the now-abandoned location, which is filled with enough contraband to feed all the rodents from nearby Liberty Park. The animation in this sequence is haphazard; the camera moves almost randomly from one spot to another as characters eat, joke, and execute poorly staged slapstick. A sense of setting and geography is conspicuously absent throughout the film, even when Brunker is paying specific homage to movies like Steven Spielberg's *1941* (1979). Perhaps the most lovingly rendered and assured shot in *Nutty by Nature* is the blatant product placement of Blue Diamond brand canned nuts.

In the nut shop, Surly is joined by, among others, Precious the Dog (voice of Maya Rudolph), Jimmy the hedgehog (voice of Gabriel Iglesias), a mute rat named Buddy, and a mole named Mole (voice of Jeff Dunham). Annie the squirrel (voice of Katherine Heigl) is also back as the voice of reason. She is concerned that the easy gluttony of the nut shop has dulled the foraging instincts of the animals. True to his moniker, Surly acts surly toward his potential love interest, mocking her concern while a nut-eating contest goes on in the background.

"What would happen if the nut shop suddenly didn't exist?" Annie asks Surly as they venture back to their respective homes in Liberty Park. Of course, the nut shop explodes immediately after Annie brings this up. Panic ensues when the animals realize they must fend for themselves, but Liberty Park can still provide sustenance if they're willing to revert to their primitive natures.

Unfortunately for the heroes, Liberty Park is about to be converted into a deathtrap of an amusement park by Mayor Muldoon (voice of Bobby Moynihan). Muldoon is so corrupt that his license plate says "MBEZLIN," but *Nutty by Nature* never makes it clear how a public official would financially benefit from the construction of an amusement park. Muldoon sends his incompetent wrecking crew to dig up the park and displace the animals, but the animals fight back to the strains of Steppenwolf's "Born to Be Wild." In temporary defeat, Muldoon vows revenge against Surly and company.

Mayor Muldoon has a Veruca Salt-like daughter, Heather (voice of Isabela Moner), whose petulant demands terrify her father. Heather's dog, Frankie (voice of Bobby Carnivale) figures in that aforementioned gross-out scene. While trying to woo Precious, Frankie regurgitates his dinner and attempts to feed it to her. When she declines, Frankie eats his own vomit, which causes Precious to throw up. Frankie not only eats her barf, he describes each morsel of it. This is what passes for romance in this abysmal cartoon.

The common theme of acceptance of the Other is represented by an army of martial-arts expert "city mice" led by Mr. Feng (voice of Jackie Chan). Mr. Feng is adorably animated and beats to a pulp anyone who points out this detail. At first, the mice don't take to kindly to "park folk" like Surly, but by the finale they've become allies against Muldoon and his amusement park. "Born to Be Wild" makes a return appearance here, proving that Steppenwolf should be pickier about who gets to use their classic rock staple.

The Nut Job 2: Nutty by Nature does nothing new, nor does it have characters even the youngest children will find interesting. Arnett, so great as a grumbly Batman in the LEGO movies, phones in his performance while sounding suspiciously like Seth Rogen. Though Heigl brings some conviction to her line readings, Annie is far too often seen as a wet blanket who won't let the male leads have any fun. And Jackie Chan is mildly amusing despite being completely extraneous to the overall plot. This story would have gone down the same way with or without Mr. Feng. And it would have been dull and unsatisfying either way.

Odie Henderson

CREDITS

Voice of Surly: Will Arnett
Voice of Andie: Katherine Heigl
Voice of Precious: Maya Rudolph
Voice of Frankie: Bobby Cannavale
Voice of Mr. Feng: Jackie Chan
Origin: United States
Language: English
Released: 2017
Production: Lili Ma, Sung-hwan Kim, Youngki Lee, Jonghan Kim, Harry Linden, Bob Barlen; DC Digital Content Comics, Lotte Entertainment, Red Rover International, ToonBox Entertainment; released by Open Road Films
Directed by: Callan Brunker
Written by: Callan Brunker; Bob Barlen; Scott Bindley
Music by: Heitor Pereira
Editing: Paul Hunter
Art Direction: Andrew Woodhouse
MPAA rating: PG
Running time: 91 minutes

REVIEWS

Castillo, Monica. *New York Times*. August 11, 2017.
Collin, Robbie. *The Telegraph*. August 24, 2017.
Fragoso, Sam. *TheWrap*. August 10, 2017.
Gleiberman, Owen. *Variety*. August 10, 2017.
McCahill, Mike. *The Guardian*. August 10, 2017.
Moore, Roger. *Movie Nation*. August 9, 2017.
O'Hara, Helen. *Empire*. August 14, 2017.
Savlov, Mark. *Austin Chronicle*. August 9, 2017.
Walsh, Katie. *Los Angeles Times*. August 10, 2017.
Watson, Keith. *Slant Magazine*. August 10, 2017.

QUOTES

Mr. Feng [after punching another character]: "Don't...call...me...cute!"

TRIVIA

The poster of the gang in the acorn is a homage to the poster for *Monty Python and the Holy Grail*.

O

OKJA

Joon-ho Bong (writing and directing here as Bong Joon Ho) makes movies like on one else. He tears apart traditional genres like the monster movie (*The Host* [2006]) or the post-apocalyptic thriller (*Snowpiercer* [2013]) and then reassembles them in a way that's distinctly fresh and singularly his own. With each film, he seems to be honing his already remarkable abilities, and his *Okja* is arguably his most ambitious work to date, challenging viewers with its daring construction, exaggerated performances, and almost cartoonish sense of humor. It is a film that is alternately thrilling, hilarious, and moving. It contains the filmmaker's most confrontational message about the way the world should work but never feels preachy. It is a masterful genre hybrid that's part sci-fi and part slapstick comedy, and proof that Bong's unpredictability is what makes him so essential.

Okja opens in 2007 as Lucy Mirando (Tilda Swinton) becomes CEO of the world-controlling Mirando Corporation in place of her crueler twin sister Nancy (also Swinton). Lucy promises a kinder Mirando Corporation, and reveals that they have been working on a breed of super pig, and 26 of them have been sent to farmers around the world. For a decade, each farmer will care for their animal, and one will be crowned the best in 2017.

Cut to South Korea, where a young girl named Mija (Seo-Hyun Ahn) has been living with her grandfather and super pig, Okja, a marvelous CGI creation. Okja is bigger than life and arguably more of a pet to Mija than livestock. She spends her days with the lovable swine, and Bong takes a great deal of time in this opening act setting up their relationship and peaceful off-the-grid life in South Korea. It will serve in stark contrast to where Mija and Okja end up once Mirando spokesperson Dr. Johnny Wilcox (Jake Gyllenhaal) climbs the steep mountain to their home and declares Okja the winning super pig. This means Okja will be taken to New York City for a major publicity event, and then, well, who knows? But Mija isn't having it.

Okja's first stop is in Seoul, and that's where Bong stages one of the most impressive sequences of his career, a series of scenes that's basically an escape movie for a giant pig. Chased by armed officials through an underground mall, Okja and Mija end up on a truck back to captivity when it's intercepted by members of the Animal Liberation Front, who tell Mija that they want to use the pig for a sting, to blow the lid off what Mirando is doing. They're going to put a recording device in Okja's ear and allow her to be recaptured.

Footage of Okja and Mija escaping in Seoul has gone viral, forcing Lucy to pay to bring the young girl to New York to show the world that everyone is on the same page. Okja is taken to a lab in New Jersey, and here is where Bong allows his film to get truly dark, as he reveals what the doctor and the people at Mirando are doing to these animals, forcibly breeding them and taking off chunks of their flesh for taste tests. The Animal Liberation Front (ALF) learns of this and infighting ensues as to what to do next.

In New York, Bong one-ups his Seoul sequence at a parade during which everything goes haywire. The ALF and Mija rescue Okja, revealing the video of what's been happening in the labs to the other super pigs, although

Bong offers no easy resolutions regarding animal cruelty or corporate malfeasance. The final act of his film is undeniably dark, although the closing images allow for hope that people can do better.

The cautionary tale against animal cruelty aspect of this film will surely appeal to some people who agree with that message, but *Okja* is such an entertaining film that it transcends typically preachy filmmaking. It's a movie made by a master craftsman, in which every detail of design, performance, and composition has been very carefully considered. The cinematography by the legendary Darius Khondji (*Se7en* [1995], *Midnight in Paris* [2011]) is vibrant and alive, whether in the hills of South Korea or the streets of New York and Seoul. *Okja* looks gorgeous, and reminds one how accomplished Bong is visually.

The filmmaker has also done something that not a lot of foreign-born directors can do, which is pull off the transition to directing English-speaking actors. Some criticized Gyllenhaal and Swinton's completely out-there performances—Gyllenhaal's practically approaches caricature—but it's a film about a giant super pig, and so it needed giant performances to match its title character. Also, there's far more subtle work that counters Gyllenhaal from Paul Dano, Steven Yeun, Lily Collins, and Shirley Henderson.

Okja garnered a bit of controversy when it premiered in competition at the Cannes Film Festival after already being acquired by Netflix. Filmgoers and jury members along the Riviera were hesitant to include the films of the streaming service alongside movies that were going theatrical, but this is just a typical resistance to change. Netflix had their best year ever in 2017, and while it would have been nice for more viewers to have seen *Okja* in theaters to appreciate its craft, it's nice that people can see it at all.

Brian Tallerico

CREDITS

Lucy Mirando / Nancy Mirando: Tilda Swinton
Jay: Paul Dano
Mija: Seo-Hyun Ahn
Hee Bong: Hee-Bong Byun
K: Steven Yeun
Origin: United States
Language: English, Korean, Spanish
Released: 2017
Production: Jeremy Kleiner, Ted Sarandos, Dooho Choi, Dede Gardner, Lewis Taewan Kim, Woo-sik Seo, Joon-ho Bong; Kate Street Picture Co., Lewis Pictures, Plan B Entertainment; released by Netflix
Directed by: Joon-ho Bong
Written by: Joon-ho Bong; Jon Ronson
Cinematography by: Darius Khondji
Sound: Tae-young Choi
Music Supervisor: Jemma Burns
Editing: Meeyeon Han; Yang Jinmo; Jin-mo Yang
Costumes: Se-yeon Choi; Catherine George; Choi Seyeon
Production Design: Ha-jun Lee; Kevin Thompson
MPAA rating: Unrated
Running time: 120 minutes

REVIEWS

Bradshaw, Peter. *The Guardian*. May 19, 2017.
Burr, Ty. *Boston Globe*. June 28, 2017.
Kiang, Jessica. *The Playlist*. May 19, 2017.
Kohn, Eric. *IndieWire*. May 19, 2017.
Lane, Anthony. *The New Yorker*. July 3, 2017.
Olsen, Mark. *Los Angeles Times*. June 27, 2017.
Scott, A.O. *New York Times*. June 27, 2017.
Seitz, Matt Zoller. *RogerEbert.com*. June 29, 2017.
Wilkinson, Alissa. *Vox*. May 23, 2017.
Yoshida, Emily. *New York Magazine*. May 19, 2017.

QUOTES

Jay: "Translations are sacred."

TRIVIA

Okja's face design was modeled after a manatee.

THE ONLY LIVING BOY IN NEW YORK

Box Office: $624,332

Films focused on the problems of bourgeois white people are currently subject to a well-earned backlash. In fact, the typically "quaint" problems facing the upper class in general society are receiving heaping handfuls of "push back" across the globe as publicly griped about issues such as poor customer service, bad restaurants, and lousy cell service truly pale in comparison to people, say, in countries facing genocide, massive deadly earthquakes, disease, or a lack of drinkable water. As a result, Marc Webb's *The Only Living Boy in New York* painted a target on its cinematic chest by simply daring to come into existence. While the film is indeed not great, it's certainly not worthy of the heaps of hate hurled upon it by critics and filmgoers alike. Yet, it's also a prime example of a typical story of what the social media spectrum deems "#whitepeopleproblems" in which spoiled, broken, and wealthy people get themselves into all sorts of entanglements while slurping down cocktails at chic restaurants after attending fancy art gallery openings.

The Only Living Boy in New York tells the story of Thomas Webb (Callum Turner), a typically-rendered, lost, millennial wannabe something who's chosen to take his lumps by living in a run-down apartment somewhere in Manhattan. It's also alluded to that his parents pay his rent, but, still, the apartment is very yucky. It barely has paint and sports no visible furniture. Thomas is also heartbroken as his love for Mimi (Kiersey Clemons) is unrequited, and, like most young men in the throes of such pain, he sees no way to escape the unending shredding of his heart. Thomas's parents, wealthy book publisher Ethan (Pierce Brosnan) and woman-on-the-constant-edge-of-a-nervous-breakdown Judith (Cynthia Nixon) just want Thomas to move home and maybe join the family business but Thomas wants more out of life. What he truly wants is unclear, but after a characteristically stuffy dinner with his parents' rich, artsy friends, viewers learn that Thomas does not want that lifestyle. The fact that the topic of dinner conversation becoming about the once vibrant, creative, and dangerous New York City being lost because of wealthy and scared people exactly like the bourgeois friends gathered in this scene is completely lost on everyone onscreen. Still, Thomas needs real direction in life and he soon finds it from new nosy-yet-world-wise neighbor W.F. Gerald (Jeff Bridges).

From the moment they first encounter one another in the stairwell of their expensive yet grimy apartment building, Thomas and W.F. hit it off like long-lost family members. W.F. wants to know everything about this aimless kid and correctly senses Thomas is at a loss in life. W.F. even expertly sniffs out that a woman may be at the root of his dour attitude. Before long, the two are quaffing wine and smoking pot and Thomas is soon pushing boundaries both in his life and with Mimi under the sensei-like advice of his elderly, newfound friend. On a night out on the town (a town that holds well over eight million people, by the way) Mimi and Thomas see Thomas's father canoodling with a woman (Kate Beckinsale) who isn't Thomas's mother and yet another dreary, conflicting problem plops into Thomas's lap: Who is this mystery woman Ethan is having an affair with and what should Thomas do to with this information? Since Thomas is an adult and knows his mother is mentally fragile, a wise thing to do would be to either leave it alone or confront his father. Yet, this would make *The Only Living Boy in New York* a fairly short film devoid of any attempt at conflict. Thus, Thomas does just about the dumbest thing he can do and starts his own affair with this mystery woman who turns out to be a beautiful yet damaged book editor named Johanna.

Again, *The Only Living Boy in New York* isn't a terrible film, however, it does fail in a few key areas which ultimately doom it. For one, it's incredibly difficult to care about any of the characters. While, life is tough and heartbreak stinks, these people will still be wealthy socialites, who, at the end of this latest situation, will have every opportunity to land back on their feet. Secondly, it's never clear why Johanna would want anything at all to do with her lover's son, let alone starting a sexual relationship with him. Thomas is a brooding, boring, dorky kid while Johanna is a gorgeous, intelligent, and worldly woman. The two have zero chemistry and such a plot device is merely a dully-lit fuse, set to go off in a predictable third act. Another issue gets at the idea of "writing what you know" versus being inclusive and thoughtful about representations of all sorts of people in society, especially in a film set in a city known as "the world's melting pot." To be fair, Thomas's initial love interest Mimi is cast as a woman of African-American descent but the lack of any other characters other than caucasion ones is striking and ludicrous.

In fact, it's a rather funny analogy to look at the career of *The Only Living Boy in New York* screenwriter Allan Loeb alongside the whiteness and problems wealthy white people in this film face. Loeb, himself a white male, has been a constantly working screenwriter since his barely mediocre debut film *Things We Lost in the Fire* (2007). Since then, he's written such dreck as *Wall Street: Money Never Sleeps* (2010), *The Dilemma* (2011), a trio of trash in 2012 with *Rock of Ages*, *Here Comes the Boom,* and the Miley Cyrus vehicle *So Undercover* and, likely the most recent film to receive as much grief as *The Only Living Boy in New York*, the horrendous *Collateral Beauty* (2016). One must wonder how a man with such a poor track record has had a film he wrote reach the big screen every year except 2009. Then again, maybe one doesn't need wonder; the struggle for some isn't real.

Don R. Lewis

CREDITS

Thomas Webb: Callum Turner
W.F. Gerald: Jeff Bridges
Johanna: Kate Beckinsale
Ethan Webb: Pierce Brosnan
Judith Webb: Cynthia Nixon
Origin: United States

Language: English
Released: 2017
Production: Albert Berger, Ron Yerxa; Amazon Studios, Big Indie Pictures, BonaFide Productions; released by Roadside Attractions
Directed by: Marc Webb
Written by: Allan Loeb
Cinematography by: Stuart Dryburgh
Music by: Ron Simonsen
Sound: Ron Bochar
Music Supervisor: Meghan Currier
Editing: Tim Streeto
Costumes: Michelle Matland
MPAA rating: R
Running time: 89 minutes

REVIEWS

Catsoulis, Jeannette. *New York Times.* August 10, 2017.
Ebiri, Bilge. *Village Voice.* August 9, 2017.
Ehrlich, David. *IndieWire.* August 5, 2017.
Gleiberman, Owen. *Variety.* August 5, 2017.
Kenny, Glenn. *RogerEbert.com.* August 11, 2017.
Moore, Roger. *Movie Nation.* August 17, 2017.
O'Sullivan, Michael. *Washington Post.* August 10, 2017.
Travers, Peter. *Rolling Stone.* August 10, 2017.
Whipp, Glenn. *Los Angeles Times.* August 10, 2017.
Wilson, Calvin. *St. Louis Post-Dispatch.* August 24, 2017.

TRIVIA

The title is taken from the title of a song by Simon & Garkunkel.

ONLY THE BRAVE

It's not what stands in front of you, it's who stands beside you.
—Movie tagline

Box Office: $18.3 Million

There's a reason more films about firefighters are not made and/or remembered in the same way movies about cops or even ambulance drivers are. There's an accepted notion of what audiences want to see from public servants of this nature. Cops carry guns and come into contact with crime, drugs, sex, and every other kind of vile human behavior. Police corruption is well-documented and thus an acceptable plot device for a film. Firefighters are in the picture for whatever the emergency is for the span of hours and do not hang around for the aftermath. They put the fires out and move on. So how do you spin compelling drama from men whose careers are spent waiting for the next disaster. The answer that director Joseph Kosinski came up with in his film *Only the Brave* was to revel in the all-American lifestyle of these men, then heroically kill them. As this is based on a true story, their fate does not count as a spoiler (their deaths are the only plot point mentioned on the film's Wikipedia page), but it also does not count as much of a deus ex machina, either.

Eric Marsh (Josh Brolin) is the superintendent of a beta team of firefighters in Prescott, Arizona. Marsh and his crew are tired of cleaning up after the teams on the frontlines of the fires, called Hotshots. He and his friend, mentor, and father-in-law Duane Steinbrink (Jeff Bridges) decide to put their best foot forward and work on the Mayor to convince him to help put money into getting the Prescott crew certified as hotshots, a first for a municipal fire fighting crew. Their decision to undergo the rigorous process coincides with the hiring of their latest recruit, local screw-up Brendan McDonough (Miles Teller). McDonough, a recovering drug addict whose ex-girlfriend just gave birth to a daughter, needs to turn himself around in a hurry if he has any chance of being included in his daughter's life. Marsh, himself a secretly recovering addict, sees something of himself in Brendan, and so rockets between giving him an especially hard time and being fatherly toward him, because he hasn't come to terms with what his own recovery means. Marsh's wife Amanda (Jennifer Connelly) wants desperately to crack Eric's hard shell, especially regarding his addiction, because she wants to start a family and Eric will not even have that conversation with her as long as he still fears his destructive past.

That's about as much plot as this film has to offer, though it spins its wheels in a dramatic enough fashion. It watches rapt as Brendan tries to turn into both a good firefighter and a good father, Eric tries to become a better husband and father to his crew, and fellow hotshot Chris MacKenzie (Taylor Kitsch) fall in and out of love, time and again. We watch the firefighters from Granite Mountain fight a handful of fires until they get the call from Yarnell, Arizona, which turns out to be their last fire. The flames consume all but Brendan McDonough, leaving nineteen grieving families in their wake. The strangest thing about the film's treatment of the tragedy is that right up until the moment they die, the film treats these boys as true blue American good old boys. They drink beer, listen to Metallica, play borderline homoerotic pranks on one another, compare masculine feats, have cookouts, raise their kids, and talk about girls. The film idolizes their vision of easy blue-collar living, turning them into minor deities as they sit on a hillside drinking in the sight of scorched trees falling off cliffs into a smoky abyss below, as if controlling the fire and conjuring it from thin air carried the same majestic, awe-inspiring power. But then the fire kills them for what has to be no reason, dramatically and scientifically, swatting the movie's borderline religious portrait of these strapping white workers out of the sky and back onto the ground.

If the purpose of the film is to ground the heroic notion of firefighters as some mythic breed of patriot to which mere mortals could never relate, then why treat their passing so unceremoniously? It comes like a sucker punch, not because we have gotten to know their families—in general we haven't—but because the film has made no room for their inevitable deaths in its tone. Eric Marsh's lifelong battle with addiction and fire, which are deliberately and bluntly intermingled, are given the kind of old school Western gravitas usually reserved for Clint Eastwood characters. He stares it down like an old gunfighter, talking to it and dreaming of it. When it kills him, it's naturally an indifferent sort of event because fire has no feelings and doesn't hold a grudge. It just burns, turning Marsh' heroic struggle painfully impotent and meaningless. It leaves only a crying wife and a mission to turn his boys into Hotshots a hollow joke. It's never stops being incredibly strange that this movie, that so loves and respects its hulking demigod heroes, accidentally proves that their idea to become a hotshot crew was a terrible, tragic mistake. When the film ends, leaving a gymnasium full of crying women and children, the message one is left with isn't one of resolution or community, but of the hubris of men who couldn't get safer jobs so their wives wouldn't have to raise their children alone. The movie may not have set out to make a movie that was a cautionary tale about not becoming a fire fighter, but that's absolutely how it plays out. A handful of good performances, competent bordering on good cinematography, and an unpretentious sense of place and family dynamics can't rescue the film from itself. *Only the Brave* has no idea how to tell the story it thinks it's telling, and doesn't know it's telling the story that it is.

Scout Tafoya

CREDITS

Eric Marsh: Josh Brolin
Brendan McDonough: Miles Teller
Duane Steinbrink: Jeff Bridges
Amanda Marsh: Jennifer Connelly
Jesse Steed: James Badge Dale
Origin: United States
Language: English
Released: 2017
Production: Lorenzo di Bonaventura, Erik Howsam, Thad Luckinbill, Trent Luckinbill, Michael Menchel, Dawn Ostroff, Molly Smith, Jeremy Steckler; Black Label Media, Conde Nast Entertainment, Di Bonaventura Pictures; released by Columbia Pictures
Directed by: Joseph Kosinski
Written by: Ken Nolan; Eric Warren Singer
Cinematography by: Claudio Miranda
Music by: Joseph Trapanese
Sound: Bjorn Ole Schroeder
Music Supervisor: Jonathan Watkins
Editing: Billy Fox
Costumes: Louise Mingenbach
Production Design: Kevin Kavanaugh
MPAA rating: PG-13
Running time: 133 minutes

REVIEWS

Ashton, Will. *The Playlist*. October 20, 2017.
Debruge, Peter. *Variety* October 10, 2017.
Duralde, Alonso. *TheWrap*. October 11, 2017.
Ebiri, Bilge. *Village Voice*. October 11, 2017.
Hassenger, Jesse. *The A.V. Club*. October 17, 2017.
Merry, Stephanie. *Washington Post* October 19, 2017.
Russo, Tom. *Boston Globe*. October 18, 2017.
Smith, Derek. *Slant Magazine*. October 12, 2017.
Turan, Kenneth. *Los Angeles Times*. October 19, 2017.
Webster, Andy. *New York Times*. October 19, 2017.

TRIVIA

This is the first time actors Josh Brolin and Jeff Bridges have worked with each other since *True Grit* (2010).

THE OTHER SIDE OF HOPE

(Toivon Tuolla Puolen)

Box Office: $181,322

Following the success of the universally-adored 2011 film *Le Havre*, Finland's favorite son Aki Kaurismäki has returned to the well of communities affected by immigration. The second film in what is meant to eventually be a trilogy on the subject, *The Other Side of Hope* follows two dreamers whose paths improbably connect when they both leave their normal lives in order to find something better. The one looks for freedom, the other for his sister, but both ultimately want to just be at peace.

The stunning opening sequence introduces our heroes wordlessly. Syrian refugee Khaled (Sherwan Haji) comes to Helsinki in secret in the cargo hold of a coal barge. Still covered in soot, he flees into the night and crosses the path of Waldemar (Sakari Kuosmanen), who is first seen silently putting his wedding ring and keys on his kitchen table for his wife (Kaija Pakarinen) to see, packing his bags and driving off. Both men don't make much of the other's appearance in their lives at first, but they will come to mean a great deal to one another. The next morning, Khaled cleans himself up and then turns himself in. He's put in a refugee processing camp and befriends an Iraqi named Mazdak (Simon Hussein Al-Bazoon), and tries to get the lay of the land. As he tells both Mazdak and the authorities, he's seeking asylum in Finland, but he's really looking for his sister, from whom he was separated during their flight from Syria. He's been through much of Europe looking for signs of her and he thinks he's got a good chance of finding her here. Finland denies his request, so he escapes the facility to continue his search on the streets.

Waldemar continues what looks like his downward spiral when he quits his job as a shirt salesman and heads to a poker game with all the money he has left. He improbably wins the whole pot and with his winnings, follows a friend's (Kati Outinen) advice and buys a bar. The place comes with three skeptical employees (played by Ilkka Koivula, Janne Hyytiäinen, and Nuppu Koivu), who at first don't like the direction the new boss wants to take the place. But, once they get to know him and see that he's not averse to paying them in advance and clearly cares about their well-being, they soften towards him and the place picks up. Soon they have live music and a healthy crowd of regulars. That's about when Khaled and Waldemar meet properly. Living on the street having made an enemy of local neo-Nazis, Khaled looks to be in bad shape when Waldemar discovers him hiding out by his restaurant's dumpster. Waldemar and his workers clean him up, get him new clothes and eventually agree to take him on as an employee. The five get along so well that they eventually help to get Khaled residency papers. All that's missing from his life now is some sign of his sister, which comes when Mazdak gets word that she might be in Finland after all.

Aki Kaurismäki's style is instantly recognizable to disciples of world cinema. The aggressive front lighting and soft backlighting, the freshly and splendidly painted walls, characters given to directly addressing the camera during conversations, bursts of music performed by bands or musicians who have been organically worked into the story, and an indefatigable sense of human decency all delineate his work from every other director. Like Jonathan Demme, another director who loved to put musicians in his features, there's joy to be found in the lowest depths of the human experience, and even the highest highs are a little melancholy and lonely. *The Other Side of Hope* is one of the Finnish master's finest and gentlest works. Kaurismäki takes immense pleasure showing the little tells that these hard-seeming characters subtly reveal they're decency and openness. Waldemar at first seems like a pretty cool customer, but a beautiful sight gag involving his employees lining up outside his office to ask for their salaries in advance, a request he's clearly going to grant to each of them though he's loathe to admit it, reveals he's hiding a heart of gold.

That Kaurismäki decided to make a movie about the Syrian refugee crisis is commendable enough, but his love and respect for Khaled is heartbreaking. Introduced covered head to toe in another country's export and forced to shower in a public restroom to find his face again under all the coal dust, it's plain that Khaled has been through more than most of the Fins he encounters when he arrives in Helsinki. It's only Waldemar who ensures that whatever his life's path from here on out, Khaled's going to be able to call someplace home, even if Kaurismäki is only too aware that Finland is still an oft-inhospitable place. The intrusion of neo-nazis into the story is a believable yet still jarring clue that he does listen to the tides of the real world crashing against the door of his carefully manicured cinematic fantasies. Just because he uses distancing mechanisms learned from Rainer Werner Fassbinder and Bertolt Brecht, doesn't mean that he's isolated himself from the actual toll of hatred and violence. This is a real story of the need for community and empathy, told with the grace and quiet of a fairy tale.

Scout Tafoya

CREDITS

Oikeussalin viranomainen: Ville Virtanen
Huligaani bussipysakilla: Dome Karukoski
Vaatekaupan omistaja: Kati Outinen
Melartin: Tommi Korpela
Wikstrom: Sakari Kuosmanen
Origin: United States
Language: Finnish, English, Arabic, Swedish
Released: 2017
Production: Aki Kaurismaki; Oy Bufo Ab, Sputnik; released by Janus Films
Directed by: Aki Kaurismaki
Written by: Aki Kaurismaki
Cinematography by: Timo Salminen
Editing: Samu Heikkila
Art Direction: Markku Patila
Costumes: Tiina Kaukanen
MPAA rating: Unrated
Running time: 100 minutes

REVIEWS

Brody, Richard. *New Yorker*. November 30, 2017.
Calhoun, Dave. *Time Out London*. May 22, 2017.
Grierson, Tim. *Paste Magazine*. December 21, 2017.
Keough, Peter. *Boston Globe*. December 6, 2017.
Kiang, Jessica. *The Playlist*. February 19, 2017.
Robey, Tim *The Telegraph*. February 17, 2017.
Scott, A.O. *New York Times*. November 30, 2017.
Semley, John. *The Globe & Mail*. December 7, 2017.
Turan, Kenneth. *Los Angeles Times*. November, 30, 2017.
Vishnevetsky, Ignatiy. *The A.V. Club*. November 30, 2017.

QUOTES

Khaled: "I don't understand humor."

TRIVIA

Prior to the film's release, director-producer Aki Kaurismäki and his long-time set decorator Markku Pätilä got into dispute on how the credits are listed in the Finnish titled version as all set related credits, which almost led to a delay in the film's release schedule. But, the court ruled that there is no need to ban the film and that the issues regarding the rights on the film's set design will be determined later—assuming the parties cannot reach a settlement outside of court.

P

PARIS CAN WAIT

(Bonjour Anne)

Take a break and go on a journey through the French countryside.
—Movie tagline

Box Office: $5.6 Million

Paris Can Wait represents Eleanor Coppola's directorial debut as a narrative filmmaker. She is perhaps most famous for being the wife of Francis Ford Coppola. The documentary *Hearts Of Darkness: a Filmmaker's Apocalypse* (1991)—which consists largely of home movie footage she shot while on location with Francis and the rest of their family—is essential viewing for any film lover. Since the film's release, her list of directing and producing credits consists mostly of other documentaries about her husband's films, as well as some behind-the-scenes work on her daughter Sofia's *Marie Antoinette* (2006). At age 79, Eleanor Coppola stepped behind the camera for a narrative film that clearly has a love of country as well as a love of being financially free within that country to explore everything on a whim. Whether or not viewers will be able to relate to such a luxury never seems to matter.

The film stars Diane Lane as Anne, the wife of a hugely successful movie producer named Michael (Alec Baldwin), whose current project is going over-budget and needs his attention. The two of them have just attended the Cannes Film Festival and want to enjoy the rest of their time in France on holiday, but Michael needs to get control of his project. A private jet arrives to take them to Budapest, but because Anne is having problems with her ears and does not want to deal with the air pressure of the small cabin, she decides to take a roadtrip to Paris where she will meet Michael when he has finished dealing with his film. She takes a ride with Jacques (Arnaud Viard), an old friend who knows his way around France, wine, and anything else related to food. He also happens to be unmarried and a bit older than Anne.

The plan is to head straight to Paris over the course of a couple days, but Jacques has a one-track mind when it comes to savoring everything the countryside has to offer, particularly when he is with a woman such as Anne, for whom he clearly has an attraction. When their car (rather conveniently) breaks down outside of Province, he wastes no time in getting out a blanket, some wine and cheese and making a picnic out of it, much to her confusion about his sense of responsibility. Something else seems a bit off about Jacques. When they go to restaurants, he orders just about everything off the menu in an effort to educate her on the bountifulness of French cuisine. When the bill comes, however, he requests that she pay for it and he will reimburse her as soon as possible. During the day, they visit cathedrals, a fabric museum and other wondrous sights, all while Anne insists they keep going so she can meet Michael in Paris on time.

Anne seems alternately perplexed and charmed by Jacques's inability to take a hint that she wants to keep this road trip moving toward its planned destination. Along the way, though, they have many personal conversations about marriage, sex, and the differing attitudes between the French and Americans on such subjects. When she asks about his failed marriage, though, he seems reluctant to divulge too much. She, on the other hand, over the course of a couple days, talks about how she used to own a shop and how she lost her infant son with her first husband and the pain of that ordeal. He seems interested, but ultimately, he is trying to win her heart, if only for a short period of time. At one point, he disappears while she picks something up in a gas station shop and comes back later with a car full of flowers for her.

Coppola also wrote the film and while one wonders how much in the way of autobiography is at play here, there appears to be more of an interest in making this a travelogue than a deeply nuanced and involved character study. Lane's Anne has a superficiality to her that the screenplay never overcomes. Even during the more serious mentions of her lost child, Anne comes off as shallow and the scene itself feels like an afterthought. This is especially true of Jacques, who knows a lot about food and clearly has a deep interest in Anne, but he never comes across as anything other than a relentless womanizer. His loneliness is never fully explored. Instead, Coppola spends too much time showing off France and its cuisine while the viewer struggles to invest in or care about these people. The film's basic premise is not unlike Michael Winterbottom's *The Trip* films, with Steve Coogan and Rob Brydon playing themselves and scuttling across Italy or England sampling the cuisine, except Winterbottom's characters had more personality and even more depth.

Here, the viewer just waits impatiently hoping for *Paris Can Wait* to take off. Laura Karpman's score keeps trying to underscore the idea that something comedic is happening even though the opposite is more often true. While one wants to champion Coppola for stepping up and directing a feature-length project this late in her career, the result is a film that is hard to love and even harder to connect with, even though the storyline has enough surface-level tension to be interesting. Jacques's repetitive advances and Anne's deflections grow tedious after a while and, although the countryside and the food look exquisite, the audience will spend more time thinking about where to eat afterwards than they will wondering if Jacques will break through her defenses. As a travelogue of France, *Paris Can Wait* works, but as an actual narrative, it has a long way to go.

Collin Souter

CREDITS

Anne: Diane Lane
Michael: Alec Baldwin
Jacques: Arnaud Viard
Gardien de musée: Cedric Monnet
Carol: Elodie Navarre
Origin: United States
Language: English, French
Released: 2017
Production: Fred Roos, Eleanor Coppola; A+E Studios, American Zoetrope, Corner Piece Capital, Lifetime Films; released by Sony Pictures Classics
Directed by: Eleanor Coppola
Written by: Eleanor Coppola
Cinematography by: Crystel Fournier
Music by: Laura Karpman
Editing: Glen Scantlebury
Costumes: Milena Canonero
Production Design: Anne Seibel
MPAA rating: PG
Running time: 92 minutes

REVIEWS

Burr, Ty. *Boston Globe.* May 25, 2017.
Graham, Adam. *Detroit News.* June 9, 2017.
Hassenger, Jesse. *The A.V. Club.* May 9, 2017.
Hornaday, Ann. *Washington Post.* May 18, 2017.
LaSalle, Mick. *San Francisco Chronicle.* May 18, 2017.
McDonald, Moira. *Seattle Times.* May 31, 2017.
Porter, Ryan. *Toronto Star.* May 25, 2017.
Walsh, Katie. *Los Angeles Times.* May 11, 2017.
Wloszczyna, Susan. *RogerEbert.com.* May 12, 2017.
Wolfe, April. *L.A. Weekly.* May 12, 2017.

TRIVIA

This was Eleanor Coppola's narrative feature film debut at the age of 80, making her one of the oldest first-time narrative feature film directors ever.

PATTI CAKE$

Box Office: $800,148

Sometimes movies that premiere at the Sundance Film Festival are noticeable almost by their scent. There's a telltale hint to them, their calculated quirkiness like the vanilla flavoring overpowering some cheap wines after too long in oak barrels. This happens to the rap coming-of-age tale *Patti Cake$*, which would be overwhelmed by its quirks if it were not constructed of them. An overweight white bartender, security worker, caterer, and aspiring battle rapper, Patricia (Danielle Macdonald) seeks the escape from New Jersey and her family (singer/burnout mother Barb, played by Bridget Everett, and wheelchair-bound grandmother, played by Cathy Moriarty) that fame and fortune could provide her. Her family is as suffocating as her class, conspiring together to suppress her art with their cynicism and need.

The most interesting part of this played-out tale is that its musical genre—even within the greater genre of motivational musician movies—fits so well with its themes. Rap—at least the rap Patricia is interested in—is built upon bravado and escapism. While the film's musical stylings and music video effects are more in line with first-time writer/director Geremy Jasper's childhood favorites Run-D.M.C. and the Beastie Boys, Patricia's lyrics hit harder than their relatively benign fare. Her rhymes taken from the school of "eye for an eye," dishing out plenty of insults for every depreciating verse in true rap feud style. Macdonald, charismatic even in her musical inexperience, spits well only to be let down by the film around her. The film's brief brushes with the dream imagery and stylistic edge one might expect from such an eccentric music film only make its narrative shortcomings more disappointing.

The dramedy cannot distance itself from the familiar ground tread by the superior *8 Mile* (2002) no matter how often it returns to the shallow differentiation of its portly female rapper. Music—rap in particular and the entertainment industry in general—is already toxic and abusive towards those women whom it deems desirable. If one is not skinny and beautiful with the right proportions, they are either moved behind the camera or into another industry. *Patti Cake$*, with the opportunity to say something about body image health in the entertainment world—in fact, setting the audience up to expect that—shies away from its own casting choice.

The story takes its star's disadvantages in this patriarchal structure and does even less with them than it does with its acknowledged problem of a white girl idolizing and (as her black rap idol later accuses her of in the film) scavenging a musical culture that was developed as a means of expression for a very different community. There are barriers between appropriation, appreciation, and contribution, but this uncomplicated film is not interested in giving them anything but cursory glances. *Patti Cake$* brushes past too many thorny, complicated topics to avoid its plot being snagged on one or two.

Instead, the film focuses on the ragtag group of friends and musicians Patricia (going by stage names Patti Cake$ and Killa P at different times) assembles to reach her dream of stardom. This crew, collectively known as PBNJ, helps Patti move from parking lot rap battles to recording singles and playing shows. There's her only friend Jheri (Siddharth Dhananjay), who operates as both hype man and R&B wannabe. Second is Basterd (Mamoudou Athie), who functions as a black metal Magical Negro thanks to his underwritten character and penchant for solving Patti's every problem. Patti speaks to Basterd (whose real name is Bob, the juxtaposition of normalcy and rebellion being one of film's sparse jokes) like a child, her tone altering to a patronizing coo—sometimes mid-scene—whenever he's addressed. Making this dynamic even odder, a romance springs up between the two (almost directly after Patti is lambasted by her idol), giving her the black approval of her art previously denied to her, now tainted further by an unearned sexual underpinning.

The only hint that Jasper has any potential as a scribe is Barb. The mother-daughter relationship between her and Patti is the only successful narrative component in a playlist of clichés thanks to the realistic combination of embarrassing interactions, sniping comments, and well-buried affection. Macdonald and Everett play off their characters' loneliness so well that their familial ties grow naturally.

These moments are all too brief as the movie favors its humor and music. The overplayed central track (a throwback to self-titled movie singles that explain the plot) grows out of a montage of melded styles where each of the overly-quirky characters bring something to the table. This track attempts to function as Patti and her cohorts' ticket to stardom and a punchline, while having neither the musical quality or deadpan cringe needed to walk that tightrope. The lyrics are wordplay for the sake of wordplay while Jheri's auto-tuned crooning creates such dissonance with Basterd's guitar riffs that the mash-up grates on the ears. That they also roped Patti's raspy-voiced grandmother into the proceedings is just an eccentric bridge too far.

The only way this unlikely scenario and its unlikely success would ever take place is if it happened in a music video director's first attempt at narrative filmmaking. While Jasper creates a few decent aesthetic riffs on the rap life and the class struggle that often accompanies it, Macdonald's star turn isn't enough to carry a movie that cannot think beyond its simple passion. *Patti Cake$*'s failure to engage in anything but its least interesting implications is as boring as its climactic concert.

Jacob Oller

CREDITS

Patti: Danielle Macdonald

Barb: Bridget Everett

Jheri: Siddharth Dhananjay

Basterd: Mamoudou Athie

Nana: Cathy Moriarty

Origin: United States

Language: English

Released: 2017

Production: Chris Columbus, Michael Gottwald, Dan Janvey, Noah Stahl, Daniela Taplin Lundberg, Rodrigo Teixeira; RT Features, Stay Gold Features, The Department of Motion Pictures; released by Fox Searchlight Pictures

Directed by: Geremy Jasper

Written by: Geremy Jasper

Cinematography by: Federico Cesca
Music by: Geremy Jasper; Jason Binnick
Sound: Ryan Bilia
Music Supervisor: Joe Rudge
Editing: Brad Turner
Art Direction: Heather Yancey
Costumes: Miyako Bellizzi
Production Design: Meredith Lippincott
MPAA rating: R
Running time: 109 minutes

REVIEWS

Allen, Nick. *RogerEbert.com*. January 25, 2017.
Anderson, Melissa. *Village Voice*. August 15, 2017.
Baumgarten, Marjorie. *Austin Chronicle*. August 24, 2017.
Brody, Richard. *New Yorker*. August 14, 2017.
Dowd, A.A. *The A.V. Club*. January 24, 2017.
Kohn, Eric. *IndieWire*. January 25, 2017.
McCarthy, Todd. *The Hollywood Reporter*. January 24, 2017.
Nashawaty, Chris. *Entertainment Weekly*. August 17, 2017.
Phipps, Keith. *Uproxx*. August 16, 2017.
Zacharek, Stephanie. *Time*. August 17, 2017.

QUOTES

Patti (to Barb): "Act your age."
Barb (to Patti): "Act your race."

TRIVIA

Australian actress Danielle Macdonald had to learn to rap and master a New Jersey accent for her role in the film.

PERSONAL SHOPPER

Box Office: $1.3 Million

Controversial French director Olivier Assayas's *Personal Shopper* opens with a woman moving her way through a giant, empty house. Immediately, a tone is set. The space around looks big, almost as if it has a life of its own. It is not unlike the mansions that are so definitive in the horror genre like those from *Rebecca* (1940) to *Crimson Peak* (2015). Later, at night, she hears what sounds like a door, and struggles to open a pair of doors to the outside. Assayas introduces a sound behind her that could be wind or something moving, and she turns almost to camera. She says the name, "Lewis?" Is this a ghost story? It most certainly is, but it's not like any other in recent memory.

The woman is Maureen (Kristen Stewart), the personal shopper for a celebrity named Kyra (Nora von Waldstatten). Lewis is her brother, who has recently passed away, but whom Maureen is convinced still lingers in this world. Maureen identifies as a "medium," someone who believes they can communicate with the supernatural world. And her brother Lewis identified as one as well. The siblings promised each other that the first to die from the congenital heart condition they shared would send back a sign to the living sibling. And so, Maureen is waiting in Paris for her sign.

While she's doing so, she's going about her work as a personal shopper to the stars, finding just the right outfits for the high-maintenance model named Kyra. Assayas captures Maureen in a variety of relatively mundane activities like clothes shopping, speaking to her boyfriend on Skype, or travelling the city. She becomes interested in an exhibition by an artist who claimed a close connection with the spiritual world. Throughout all of these relatively simple scenes, Assayas is playing with tone and theme. Maureen is shopping for someone who is not there, sometimes even trying on her clothes in a way that feels almost ethereal. Most of all, *Personal Shopper* is a uniquely solitary film. Much of it consists of only Maureen, surrounded by people but not communicating with most of them, not even sharing the same space with her boss. In her world, she's almost a ghost herself.

While going to pick up some garments from Kyra to return, she runs into Kyra's boyfriend Ingo (Lars Eidinger). It's clearly an important scene as Maureen does not have dialogue exchanges at length with really anyone else in the film. Here we learn that Kyra is planning to break up with Ingo after two years, and he's not happy about that. After another night in the house that opens the film, in which Assayas really lays his cards on the table regarding whether or not this is a ghost story—faucets turn on and apparitions fly around the house—Maureen starts getting mysterious text messages.

The text messages are where *Personal Shopper* either loses or hooks a viewer. It's a daring move by Assayas to make Stewart's biggest co-star in the film a smartphone, but that's essentially what unfolds. Shaken and vulnerable from what she witnessed the night before, Maureen immediately bites at the idea that the mysterious messages are coming from Lewis—a ghost with an iPhone. Stewart is incredible in these scenes, whether it's a worried look or a shaking finger as she texts. Whomever is on the other end starts to toy with Maureen—and viewers with any sense of whodunit investigative skills should begin to question whether or not it's actually Ingo and not Lewis on the other end.

This theory gains strength after *Personal Shopper* takes its most stunning turn. Following a visit to a fancy hotel room booked in her name and pre-paid in cash,

Maureen goes to drop off some jewelry at Kyra's apartment, only to find that she has been murdered. She's questioned, and a mystery unfolds. Who killed Kyra and why are they framing Maureen? From here, *Personal Shopper* gets even more open to interpretation, especially after a controversial scene in which Maureen goes to a hotel room to meet with her unknown texter and Assayas starts to truly play with point of view, including sliding his camera through elevators and doors with seemingly no human presence. Has Lewis come to protect Maureen? Is Maureen herself now dead?

While *Personal Shopper* lit message boards on fire with theories about its ending and meanings, it's not really a film that's meant to be unpacked and solved like an M. Night Shyamalan movie. It is the product of a filmmaker working in a thematic, emotional register more than a literal one. It is about grief, and the sense that there is something greater and more complex going on in the world around us. It is also a remarkably technical accomplishment in that it's the kind of film that flows and moves in ways that never call attention to its style but would not work at all without the skill of cinematographer Yorick Le Saux (a regular for Françoise Ozon, Luca Guadagnino, and Assayas) and editor Marion Monnier (who also cut Assayas's brilliant *Clouds of Sils Maria* [2014]). *Personal Shopper* is a beautiful film about beautiful people, but it has an ethereal ebb and flow to it that's hard to put into words, truly an impressive cinematic accomplishment.

Most of all, *Personal Shopper* should put an end to any remaining stigma that remains in the perception of Kristen Stewart's acting ability since the *Twilight* years. By now, it's clear that the sullen, mediocre performances in those films that made the actress easy to impersonate on *Saturday Night Live* were due to the fact that Stewart did not care about the material and was there to fulfill a contractual obligation. She has been truly spectacular in recent years, including *Clouds of Sils Maria* (2014), *Still Alice* (2014), *Certain Women* (2016), and *Café Society* (2016). Her work here is her best to date, indicating how much great work there is likely to come in her career. She's emotionally complex and yet grounded at the same time, selling the truth of a role that could have been silly in the wrong hands. We believe Maureen's arc because Stewart makes us believe. She's good enough to make you believe in ghosts.

Brian Tallerico

CREDITS

Maureen Cartwright: Kristen Stewart
Ingo: Lars Eidinger
Lara: Sigrid Bouaziz
Erwin: Anders Danielsen Lie
Gary: Ty Olwin
Origin: United States
Language: English, French, Swedish
Released: 2017
Production: Charles Gillibert; CG Cinéma; released by IFC Films
Directed by: Olivier Assayas
Written by: Olivier Assayas
Cinematography by: Yorick Le Saux
Sound: Nicolas Moreau
Editing: Marion Monnier
Costumes: Jurgen Doering
Production Design: Francois-Renaud Labarthe
MPAA rating: R
Running time: 105 minutes

REVIEWS

Anderson, Melissa. *Village Voice.* March 9, 2017.
Bradshaw, Peter. *The Guardian.* May 20, 2016.
Burr, Ty. *Boston Globe.* March 23, 2017.
Lane, Anthony. *New Yorker.* March 13, 2017.
Lodge, Guy. *Time Out London.* May 20, 2016.
Roeper, Richard. *Chicago Sun-Times.* March 16, 2017.
Scott, A.O. *New York Times.* March 9, 2017.
Sobczynski, Peter. *RogerEbert.com.* March 10, 2017.
Vishnevetsky, Ignatiy. *The A.V. Club.* March 9, 2017.
Zacharek, Stephanie. *Time.* March 9, 2017.

QUOTES

Ingo: "Well, how's within that, that the soul...continues to exist...after death?"

Maureen Cartwright: "I don't even know if I believe in that. But Lewis did. And I, I have to give his, spirit, whatever you wanna call it, a chance to prove him right."

TRIVIA

Writer/director Olivier Assayas describes this film as a companion piece of sorts to *Clouds of Sils Maria* (2014). In both films, actress Kristen Stewart plays a woman on the cusp of wealth and celebrity.

PHANTOM THREAD

Box Office: $11.4 Million

Paul Thomas Anderson's masterful *Phantom Thread* is a film about obsession, co-dependence, and living with a superficial creator. It is about a man who sees women as little more than fitting models, on which to hang his perfect, fashion creations, at least until he realizes that weakness adds a different color to the pattern of their relationship. It is a stunning piece of work, one of those films in which every angle, cut, line, and a multitude of other decisions were very carefully considered. In other words, it's made by someone who is arguably even more of a perfectionist than his protagonist.

Said protagonist is 1950s British fashion designer Reynolds Woodcock, played by Daniel Day-Lewis in what is reportedly his final performance as an actor, and easily one of the best turns in an already-legendary career. For his work here, Day-Lewis received his sixth Oscar® nomination, having won three in the past (*My Left Foot* [1989], *There Will Be Blood* [2007], and *Lincoln* [2012])—the only actor in history to have won three times for leading actor. Day-Lewis imbues Woodcock with a striking balance of perfectionism and vulnerability. He's the kind of creator who demands solitude to do his best work yet also needs people around for emotional stability. At least, he needs them around until he can no longer find a use for them, like a fashion trend that he's no longer willing to design.

That's basically how *Phantom Thread* opens, introducing us to Woodcock as he discards the latest model with whom he has been cohabitating, via the help of the only constant in his life, his sister/assistant Cyril (Lesley Manville). She manages not only the day-to-day operations of the House of Woodcock as an industry but deals with the whims and rages of her high maintenance brother. Anderson defines his title early on, revealing that Woodcock's mother taught him how to stitch hidden messages into the linings of the dresses he makes. There's something ethereal and hidden underneath the surface of all this beauty.

It's the awkward beauty of a waitress named Alma (Vicky Krieps) that instantly attracts Woodcock as she nearly stumbles across the restaurant he happens into one day after debuting a new piece for one of his clients. He flirts with her in a very Paul Thomas Anderson way, by ordering a complex breakfast meal and being impressed when she gets it right without writing any details down. He asks her out, and she accepts, and it appears that Alma will go through a routine that Anderson implies Woodcock has gone through several times before. As with so many creative types, Woodcock's fashion designs will always take precedence over his romantic life, and he starts to find ways to be annoyed by Alma, from the way she butters her toast to the way she makes a romantic dinner that does not conform precisely to his tastes.

At this point, Woodcock likely expects Alma to go the way of all the other women who once served his needs, but this year's model has something else in mind. She poisons Woodcock with some mushrooms she found outside the house, and it sends Woodcock to death's door. In one of the film's key scenes, Woodcock is laying in bed, hallucinating a vision of his mother at the other end of the room. He speaks to her, and then Alma comes in to help take care of him. Alma has replaced, in a sense, the nurturing aspect of another woman whom Woodcock obsessively misses. He learns that there's something other than physical companionship that can be given to him by another woman, and he asks her to marry him when he recovers. However, there are dark games of co-dependence left to play in this tale.

Of course, it's difficult not to consider the reported perfectionism of Anderson and Day-Lewis when looking at why *Phantom Thread* is such an accomplished piece of filmmaking. They are the kind of creators who do not make any decisions rashly or lightly, and here they are making a film about someone who is similarly dedicated to their craft. The result is a film that feels multi-layered, working as a fascinating character study with no further subtext to consider, or as a commentary on the life of a creator and the people who have to be around him. It's a mindblowing experience, the kind that rolls around in the viewer's head for days and weeks after seeing it, as images are recalled, and themes return to memory. It's a film that often feels like it's unfolding like a dream and has a similar power as one reflects on it the way one remembers something imagined.

Anderson has been drawing brilliant performances from actors for a generation now, whether it's Julianne Moore in *Boogie Nights* (1997), Tom Cruise in *Magnolia* (1999), Adam Sandler in *Punch-Drunk Love* (2002), Daniel Day-Lewis in *There Will Be Blood,* or Joaquin Phoenix and Philip Seymour Hoffman in *The Master* (2012). For most people who work with him, their performances in his films will be part of any lifetime achievement clip reel. And everyone in *Phantom Thread* can say the same. Seeing Day-Lewis play something relatively close to modern period here (most of his career consists of older, more stately period pieces) reminds one how playful and fun he can be with the right material. His Reynolds Woodcock relishes every word he says, almost over-pronunciating like some self-proclaimed intellectuals tend to do, but it's a performance that really exists in the eyes, whether they are looking at Alma with disdain or need. Newcomer Vicky Krieps completely holds her own opposite Day-Lewis, and Manville nearly steals the film, to such a degree that she landed a very-surprising Best Supporting Actress Oscar® nomination.

Ultimately, *Phantom Thread* became Anderson's second-most nominated film (after *There Will Be Blood*), which was very shocking given its late-year release and relatively difficult storytelling. This is not an easy movie to understand or appreciate, yet voters fell under its gorgeous spell, also nominating its costume design by Mark Bridges and the breathtaking score by Jonny Greenwood, which is one of the best of the modern era. Like the film itself, it weaves in and out of styles, feeling classical and new in consecutive beats. And, like the film, it haunts the viewer, returning as a melody echoing in the back of one's mind, a creative phantom reminding one of its themes and brilliance, sewn secretly into memory forever.

Brian Tallerico

CREDITS

Alma: Vicky Krieps

Reynolds Woodcock: Daniel Day-Lewis

Cyril: Lesley Manville

Biddy: Sue Clark

Nana: Joan Brown

Origin: United States

Language: English

Released: 2017

Production: Megan Ellison, Daniel Lupi, JoAnne Sellar, Paul Thomas Anderson; Annapurna Pictures, Ghoulardi Film Co., Perfect World Pictures; released by Focus Features L.L.C.

Directed by: Paul Thomas Anderson

Written by: Paul Thomas Anderson

Cinematography by: Paul Thomas Anderson

Music by: Jonny Greenwood

Sound: Matthew Wood

Editing: Dylan Tichenor

Art Direction: Denis Schnegg

Costumes: Mark Bridges

Production Design: Mark Tildesley

MPAA rating: R

Running time: 130 minutes

REVIEWS

Bowen, Chuck. *Slant Magazine.* December 7, 2017.

Bradshaw, Peter. *The Guardian.* December 7, 2017.

Burr, Ty. *Boston Globe.* January 11, 2018.

Chang, Justin. *Los Angeles Times.* December 24, 2017.

Ebiri, Bilge. *Village Voice.* December 20, 2017.

Kenny, Glenn. *RogerEbert.com.* December 19, 2017.

McCarthy, Todd. *Hollywood Reporter.* December 7, 2017.

Phipps, Keith. *Uproxx.* December 7, 2017.

Rothkopf, Joshua. *Time Out.* December 19, 2017.

Scott, A.O. *New York Times.* December 24, 2017.

QUOTES

Reynolds Woodcock: "Kiss me, my girl, before I'm sick."

TRIVIA

This is the first time Daniel Day-Lewis has used his natural English accent in a film since *Stars and Bars* in 1988.

AWARDS

Oscars 2017: Costume Des.

British Acad. 2017: Costume Des.

Nominations:

Oscars 2017: Actor (Day-Lewis), Actress--Supporting (Manville), Director (Anderson), Film, Orig. Score

British Acad. 2017: Actor (Day-Lewis), Orig. Score, Support. Actress (Manville)

Golden Globes 2018: Actor--Drama (Day-Lewis), Orig. Score, Orig. Score (Greenwood)

PHOENIX FORGOTTEN

Based on shocking untold true events.
—Movie tagline

Box Office: $3.6 Million

It is difficult to tell if screenwriters T.S. Nowlin and Justin Barber started with the framing story of *Phoenix Forgotten*, with the mystery being investigated within that framing narrative, or with some cohesive whole in mind. The primary reason for wondering is that it feels as if there are two separate entities at work here. The first, which takes place over the course of the first fifty minutes or so, examines an incident that one would expect to be the basis for a horror movie, with the distance of time and from the perspective of someone whose life was irrevocably altered by the mysterious event. The second, to which the final thirty minutes of the movie is exclusively devoted, is exactly the sort of generic found-footage horror movie that Nowlin and Barber have avoided until then.

The split between the two narratives is tough to reconcile. One is somewhat thoughtful and compassionate about loss—its effects and the inability for people to come to terms with a loss that has no rational explanation.

The other goes through the usual motions, and since the lengthy sequence is unceremoniously dropped in at a point when the framing story is just building up tension, the expected beats that lead up to the chaos of the climax land with a thud. Just when there is an expectation that the big mystery will be revealed, the movie decides to take its time, providing scenes of characters wandering the desert with no real goal in mind, talking about nothing in particular, and hinting at conflict between them without ever delving into it.

Those three characters are far more sympathetic in the first section of the movie, when they only exist as an idea. The movie is not really about Josh (Luke Spencer Roberts), Ashley (Chelsea Lopez), and Mark (Justin Matthew)—three teenagers who disappeared after a trip to the desert outside of Phoenix, Arizona. The story is set twenty years after their disappearance, as Sophie (Florence Hartigan), Josh's younger sister, returns home (with an unseen friend who operates the camera) to make a documentary about her brother, his two friends, and the families that they left behind when whatever happened to them happened. There is little to know about the trio of missing teens, except that they were fairly ordinary, were curious about strange lights that started appearing in the sky, and went missing while investigating the cause of those lights.

Their disappearance serves as a catalyst for Nowlin and Barber to explore how this loss, via some unexplained occurrence, has affected the people who knew and loved them. Sophie interviews an assortment of relatives—her now-divorced parents (played by Clint Jordan and Cyd Strittmatter), Ashley's parents (played by Jeanine Jackson and David Carrera), and Mark's older brother Dan (Matt Biedel)—as well as some experts on the investigation and amateurs on theories about the lights in the sky, which prompted the doomed trip to the desert. Barber, who also directed the movie, intercuts these interviews with fake yet convincing footage of home videos and news reports.

There is nothing particularly deep about the movie's examination of grief. After years of movies that have taken a similar faux-documentary approach to horror stories of the supernatural, though, it is refreshing to see one that has more on its mind than easy jump-scares and other cheap tactics. One could not be blamed for feeling a bit duped by the movie. (This, perhaps, might be part of the reason it was released in theaters with little marketing support or audience attention, since it does not even play as a horror movie until the final act.) Still, the first section creates a credible aura of mystery and dread for what might have happened to those teenagers, even as it treats the aftermath with more sincerity and severity than one might expect.

The shift to the typical found-footage horror material is sudden, as Sophie conveniently discovers a missing tape that fills in the gaps of the police investigation's timeline. That tape follows Josh, Ashley, and Mark on the night of their disappearance, and Berber inserts it into the finale of the movie without interruption.

It comes across as an entirely different narrative, complete with a slow build-up to learning about whatever caused the lights, and the segment immediately undermines the momentum that Sophie's investigation has been generating. To be frank, it feels as if this was the movie that the filmmakers intended to make. Upon realizing that there simply was not enough material for a full feature, they created the far more involving framing narrative as an afterthought.

The final thirty minutes is filled with just about every pitfall and cliché to which this subgenre has fallen victim: sketchy characters, unconvincingly improvised dialogue, shaky camerawork obscuring more than it reveals, a plot that revolves around the characters becoming lost, and a climax that attempts to make up for the earlier slowness with a lot of noise and some visual trickery. *Phoenix Forgotten* could have been different. The movie tries, for certain, to stand out from the crowd. Apparently, the temptation to be the same is too strong.

Mark Dujsik

CREDITS

Sophie: Florence Hartigan
Josh Bishop: Luke Spencer Roberts
Ashley Foster: Chelsea Lopez
Mark Abrams: Justin Matthews
Steve: Clint Jordan
Origin: United States
Language: English
Released: 2017
Production: Wes Ball, Mark Canton, Ridley Scott, Courtney Solomon, T.S. Nowlin; Cinelou Films, Scott Free Productions; released by Freestyle Releasing
Directed by: Justin Barber
Written by: Justin Barber; T.S. Nowlin
Cinematography by: Jay Keitel
Music by: Mondo Boys
Music Supervisor: Monica Zierhut; Zach Seivers
Editing: Joshua Rosenfield
Costumes: Aggie Guerard Rodgers
Production Design: Todd Fjelsted
MPAA rating: PG-13
Running time: 87 minutes

REVIEWS

D'Angelo, Mike. *The A.V. Club*. April 21, 2017.
Goodykoontz, Bill. *Arizona Republic*. April 21, 2017.
Leydon, Joe. *Variety*. April 21, 2017.
Lowe, Justin. *Hollywood Reporter*. April 22, 2017.
Moore, Roger. *Movie Nation*. April 25, 2017.
Orndorf, Brian. *Blu-ray.com*. April 21, 2017.
Righetti, Jamie. *Film School Rejects*. April 21, 2017.
Savlov, Marc. *Austin Chronicle*. April 28, 2017.
Terry, Josh. *Deseret News*. April 24, 2017.
Vaux, Rob. *Sci-Fi Movie Page*. April 22, 2017.

TRIVIA

To simulate the look of lo-fi analog footage which would have existed in 1997 (the film's time period), after the special effects were added, footage was copied to actual VHS tapes which were then re-digitized before final editing. The analog defects are therefore real and not simulated. This also had the added benefit of making the CGI effects look more integrated with the original footage.

PIRATES OF THE CARIBBEAN: DEAD MEN TELL NO TALES

All pirates must die.
—Movie tagline

Box Office: $172.6 Million

The premise was laughed at in 2003. Was Disney really making a feature film based on one of their theme park rides? It turned out to be one of the most entertaining tentpole films of that year and certainly the most surprising. Five Oscar nominations followed, including one for Johnny Depp's inspired characterization of the now immortal Jack Sparrow. The success that resulted only ensured that a sequel would soon be in production, a fact that turned into back-to-back completion of a trilogy whose epic nature soon invited greater skepticism and a thinning of patience. Gore Verbinski concluded his role after *Dead Man's Chest* (2006) and *At World's End* (2007) but the franchise continued. "Lived on" would be too much of a stretch with Rob Marshall's *On Stranger Tides* (2011) and it hardly fits Joachim Rønning & Espen Sandberg's fifth entry, *Pirates of the Caribbean: Dead Men Tell No Tales*, either. Though a slight improvement, the latest film is just further evidence that this series is a shell of its former self, now a full realization of that early skepticism about turning a theme park ride into a feature-length movie.

Will Turner (Orlando Bloom), last seen in the third film, was cursed to live out his days as a barnacle magnet on the Flying Dutchman; one day ashore for every ten years at sea. For the last nine years, Will's son, Henry (Brenton Thwaites) has been searching for the Trident of Poseidon as it can be used to reverse the curse. Along his travels, his ship is attacked by the charred remains of Captain Salazar (Javier Bardem) and his crew. They were once the most fearsome pirate hunters on the water and had nearly succeeded in wiping them all out. That is until he came upon a young Jack Sparrow (Depp, with a little CGI rendering) whose quick thinking steered them into the Devil's Triangle, where they have also been cursed to remain undead. Salazar vows revenge and asks Henry to deliver his message if he ever crosses paths with the famed pirate.

Captain Sparrow is currently found sleeping one off in the middle of a heist with his crew. During their getaway he meets another escapee, Carina Smyth (Kaya Scodelario), who has been sentenced for witchcraft. Through a series of contrived meetings and reunions, Henry, Carina, Jack, and his once-abandoned crew setoff together to find the trident. Thanks to a drunken lapse in judgment by Sparrow, Salazar has been set free from his physical imprisonment and gains an ally in Captain Barbossa (Geoffrey Rush, in extensive makeup suggesting a character decaying in real time), who agrees to help hunt Jack down if the lives of his own crew are spared.

Also spared is an audience who have felt weighed down by extended running times in this series. *Dead Men Tell No Tales* can indeed stand out as the shortest film of the lot, but it scarcely takes advantage of being a good ol' fashioned in-and-out adventure. The advantage of being just another one-off tale in the book of Jack Sparrow is that the film can focus on its primary McGuffin rather than expand upon relationships or its own mythology. Jeff Nathanson's screenplay loses course all too often by having to develop new characters, fresh backstories, and then trying to shoehorn in a connected revelation that is too late to elicit any substantial emotional reaction. *Dead Man's Chest* playfully shuffled three treasured components (a compass, a key, and the chest) and had fun with who needed what the most. This film has one—the trident—and it can barely muster up the anticipation for its big unveiling.

Perhaps most damagingly, the luster of the Sparrow character has unfortunately worn off over time. Depp has played oddball characters going back to *Edward Scissorhands* (1990), but the added popularity that came with his inspired interpretation of Sparrow made each subsequent attempt at one-upping it less interesting. The good-hearted scoundrel was smarter than he ever let on, but when the writing becomes about the characterization rather than what makes him tick, he becomes almost a bore. Thankfully for Depp he is placed frequently next to the blank slate of Brenton Thwaites, who is so hopefully bland that he barely seems to care.

At least there is a sense the franchise is still able to recognize what seemed to be widely overlooked in the original trilogy and that is the role for women in this world. No longer just part of the wench sale of the Disney ride, a woman managed to have a central role with an arc of real growth and power. Keira Knightley's Elizabeth Swan went from just another damsel in an arranged marriage being literally suffocated by her wardrobe to becoming an elected pirate leader. Though Golshifteh Farahani's black magic adviser to Barbossa seemingly disappears after a couple brief scenes, the standout by default (at least when Bardem is not present) becomes Scodelario's Carina. The actress does not possess the same kind of fierceness that Knightley was able to portray amidst all the action and special effects but, again, next to Thwaites, is able to communicate a confidence lacking in most of the narrative. It is thereby unfortunate that though Carina is clearly written as the smartest character in the film, when she is not being labeled a literal "witch," she is subjected to a running joke about the difference between her chosen field of horology and the world's oldest profession.

Joachim Rønning & Espen Sandberg received some attention for the lackluster WWII thriller, *Max Manus: Man of War* (2008), but it was likely *Kon-Tiki* (2012) their recreation of Thor Heyerdal's raft trip that got them this gig. *Pirates of the Caribbean: Dead Men Tell No Tales* is a film that needed more than just filmmakers who have familiarity with water. They do introduce a couple of fun flourishes like Sparrow's time in a revolving guillotine and dipping once again into their *Kon-Tiki* shark attack wheelhouse, but more elaborate set pieces probably looked better on the page than on the screen. In the hands of Gore Verbinski, the dragging of an entire bank through town would have fallen right in line with the Indiana Jones-like theatrics he brought to the action in each film. Rønning & Sandberg give it all the ingenuity of a mobile home on a trailer hitch attached to a moving walkway. There are too many myths and legends for the Pirates films to die a slow death through a lack of vision and a misunderstanding of what made those first three films tick. Depp could even have coasted through them as a supporting link while an injection of fresh blood kept the excitement level above life support. Even the film's memorable score, originated by Klaus Bedalt and expanded upon by Hans Zimmer, does not rally the same rousing feeling that it once did. Perhaps Disney can have a fresh start by ironically remembering what a great adventure is again rather than just a product when "Jungle Cruise" finally gets off the ground.

Erik Childress

CREDITS

Captain Jack Sparrow: Johnny Depp
Will Turner: Orlando Bloom
Carina Smyth: Kaya Scodelario
Captain Salazar: Javier Bardem
Captain Hector Barbossa: Geoffrey Rush
Origin: United States
Language: English
Released: 2017
Production: Jerry Bruckheimer; Infinitum Films, Jerry Bruckheimer Films; released by Walt Disney Pictures
Directed by: Joachim Ronning; Espen Sandberg
Written by: Jeff Nathanson
Cinematography by: Paul Cameron
Music by: Geoff Zanelli
Sound: Christopher Boyes; Jack Whittaker
Editing: Roger Barton; Leigh Folsom-Boyd
Art Direction: Ian Gracie
Costumes: Penny Rose
Production Design: Nigel Phelps
MPAA rating: PG-13
Running time: 129 minutes

REVIEWS

Berardinelli, James. *ReelViews*. May 26, 2017.
Douglas, Edward. *The Weekend Warrior*. May 26, 2017.
Edelstein, David. *New York Magazine/Vulture*. May 25, 2017.
Morgenstern, Joe. *Wall Street Journal*. May 25, 2017.
Nordine, Michael. *IndieWire*. May 22, 2017.
Ranson, Kevin A. *Moviecrypt.com*. May 30, 2017.
Roeper, Richard. *Chicago Sun-Times*. May 24, 2017.
Scott, A.O. *New York Times*. May 25, 2017.
Snider, Eric D. *EricDSnider.com*. May 25, 2017.
Walsh, Katie. *Los Angeles Times*. May 26, 2017.

QUOTES

Captain Jack Sparrow: "I once knew a Spaniard named...something in Spanish."

TRIVIA

Although this movie was initially claimed to be the last one in the series, a sixth installment was announced shortly after this was released.

AWARDS

Nominations:

Golden Raspberries 2017: Worst Actor (Depp), Worst Support. Actor (Bardem)

PITCH PERFECT 3

Last call, pitches.
—Movie tagline

Box Office: $102.9 Million

At one point during the original *Pitch Perfect* (2012), budding a cappella singer/music producer Beca (Anna Kendrick) is wooed by a suitor who tries to win her heart with his insistence that *The Breakfast Club* (1985) contains the best ending in the history of cinema. This is a highly debatable assertion but even those who do not exactly venerate that film can at least agree that it "had" an ending, which is more than can be said about the *Pitch Perfect* franchise. That will become painfully obvious to anyone who endures *Pitch Perfect 3,* a blatant cash-grab sequel that may cram in any number of mashed-up pop favorites on the soundtrack but which displays such a shocking lack of creativity, humor, or basic entertainment value that it makes *The Hangover: Part III* (2013) seem fresh and vital by comparison.

The original *Pitch Perfect* followed spunky rebel Beca as she fell in with a misfit all-girl a cappella group at college called the Belas and helped them win the big national competition at the feel-good finale. This was not a particularly great movie by any means (including a couple of stabs at gross-out humor that crossed the line from amusing to the merely disgusting) but the combination of its goofball energy, the likable presences of Kendrick and Rebel Wilson, who had her big breakthrough as Fat Amy, the most outrageous member of the group, and the spirited musical performances helped to make it a surprise hit in theaters and an instant slumber party perennial when it arrived on DVD. Although there was nothing to the story that warranted a continuation, those grosses ensured the release of *Pitch Perfect 2* (2015) a film that was bigger, louder, and dumber than its predecessor in every imaginable way. However, the massive fan base for the original not only guaranteed that it would become a hugely profitable hit as well but also meant that a third installment would soon be on the way.

And yet, despite its existence being a foregone conclusion, *Pitch Perfect 3* is so devoid of inspiration or purpose (other than the financial one) that there is the sense that screenwriters Kay Cannon (who wrote the two previous films) and Mike White (whose other 2017 credits have run the gamut from *Beatriz at Dinner* to *The Emoji Movie*) somehow flaked on the assignment and wound up slapping the script together during the weekend before the commencement of principal photography. This time around, Beca and her former cohorts are long out of college and flailing about in their personal and professional lives when a reunion somehow leads to them getting a slot on a USO tour in Europe with other unknown performers that include a rapper, a country group, and an all-female rock group named Evermoist. (The leader of Evermoist is played by Ruby Rose, who seems to have been cast in virtually every sequel to come out in 2017.) Of course, it would not be a *Pitch Perfect* movie without a competition, and so it transpires that DJ Khaled (playing himself), who is headlining the tour, will select one of the groups to open for him and presumably be launched to instant fame and fortune.

Even by the less-than-august standards of most pointless sequels, *Pitch Perfect 3* is amazingly lazy and off-key. Watching the Bellas once again starting at the bottom and overcoming adversity to win the big competition for a third straight time is now profoundly uninteresting, and the potentially interesting USO angle is squandered by a depiction of a tour that presumably bears no resemblance to the reality of such things. What is even deadlier is that the Bellas themselves are strangely unlikable and irritating this time around and therefore impossible to root for. Early on, there is one of the franchise's patented "riff-off" scenes involving the stringing together of a number of songs that can change on a single word. This time around, instead of all the various groups going against each other, the other three end up blending their divergent musical approaches together while the Bellas bitch and whine about how they aren't following the rules. As for Kendrick and Wilson, they fail to perk things up either—the former goes through her paces as through trying to stifle a yawn while the latter officially makes the transition from cheekily outrageous to the simply annoying.

Fat Amy also figures in the worst element of a film that is chock-full of such things. After arriving in Europe, she finds herself being pursued by a mysterious man who turns out to be her estranged father, a wealthy bounder and generally shady character—imagine a cross between Rupert Murdoch and Robert Durst—who wants to mend fences with his daughter and start anew. At first, she wants nothing to do with him, but soon succumbs to his line of patter before discovering the real reason behind his sudden interest in her—it turns out she has a heretofore unknown trust fund worth $180,000,000—and leading to developments that include the kidnapping of the other Bellas and a rescue mission filled with the decimation of dozens of henchmen and exploding yachts. Not only does this particular plot development come out of nowhere and add up to absolutely nothing (even if it does allow a break for the Bellas to entertain/distract their captors with a performance of Britney Spears's "Toxic") but it also presents viewers with the sorry sight of the great John Lithgow embarrassing both himself and the audience with one of the very worst performances of his career as Fat Amy's dad.

The only time *Pitch Perfect 3* even vaguely comes alive is during the musical performances, but, even there, the charm that they once possessed has now been replaced by a kind of rigid professionalism—the Bellas seem less like a group of underdogs united by their love of song than a highly polished and long-running Vegas act more concerned with precision than inspiration. The only truly good news to come out of this film is the insistence that it is indeed the conclusion of a franchise that frankly never really required even one sequel in the first place.

Peter Sobczynski

CREDITS

Beca: Anna Kendrick
Fat Amy: Rebel Wilson
Chloe: Brittany Snow
Aubrey: Anna Camp
Emily: Hailee Steinfeld
Origin: United States
Language: English
Released: 2017
Production: Paul Brooks, Max Handelman, Elizabeth Banks; Gold Circle Films, Perfect World Pictures; released by Universal Pictures
Directed by: Trish Sie
Written by: Kay Cannon; Mike White
Cinematography by: Matthew Clark
Music by: Christopher Lennertz
Sound: Kami Asgar; Erin Oakley
Editing: Craig Alpert; Colin Patton
Costumes: Salvador Perez, Jr.
Production Design: Toby Corbett
MPAA rating: PG-13
Running time: 93 minutes

REVIEWS

Bugbee, Teo. *New York Times*. December 20, 2017.
Callahan, Dan. *TheWrap*. December 19, 2017.
Chang, Justin. *Los Angeles Times*. December 21, 2017.
Gleiberman, Owen. *Variety*. December 19, 2017.
Larsen, Richard. *Slant Magazine*. December 19, 2017.
Russo, Tom. *Boston Globe*. December 21, 2017.
Scheck, Frank. *Hollywood Reporter*. December 19, 2017.
Scherstuhl, Alan. *Village Voice*. December 19, 2017.
White, Danielle. *Austin Chronicle*. December 21, 2017.
Yoshida, Emily. *New York Magazine/Vulture*. December 19, 2017.

PORTO

Box Office: $13,784

Movies are alchemical with a direct and cumulative power that capture an expressive and complex range of emotions, like desire, pain, or regret. The power also develops from the simplicity and elegance of its ideas. Jean-Luc Godard famously said all you needed to make a movie was a guy, a girl, and a gun. That expresses the essence of movies in freely mixing the spontaneous and freeform with more subtle emotional associations.

A first feature by Gabe Klinger, a Brazilian-born, Chicago-raised writer, critic, and curator, *Porto* ruminates on memory and time. At once fragmentary and evanescent, the story explores the tumultuous consequences of a brief, incandescent love affair. Klinger has called the movie a "novella," indicative of its delicate self-containment. The movie is intimate, quiet and deliberately restricted. The telling is ambitious and layered, especially in how it elides, stretches, and pushes forward time to fit a mood, a state of being.

Klinger's first film, the documentary *Double Play* (2013), was a thoughtful, probing, and fascinating study in passion and film culture exploring the friendship of two very different filmmakers—the gifted independent Richard Linklater and the radical experimentalist James Benning. The imprints of those two directors are felt here. The story of an affair between a cocksure, solitary American expatriate and a beautiful French archeologist and student in the Portuguese port city conjures Linklater's *Before Sunrise* (1995). The beguiling use of physical spaces evokes Benning's superb *Landscape Suicide* (1987). Klinger also acknowledges the Portuguese master Manoel de Oliveira (1908-2015), who lived in the city for nearly ninety years. Oliveira made his own intoxicating memory piece, *Porto of My Childhood* (2001), that Klinger's movie pays tribute.

Klinger works hard and purposely to develop his own ideas and not simply reproduce a series of quotations from other films. The result is far from perfect or clean though the aching, muffled qualities carry a jolt. Klinger wrote the script with Larry Gross, a versatile writer who has worked with directors like Walter Hill, Clint Eastwood, and Wayne Wang. The movie opens in an ecstatic reverie, with Jake (Anton Yelchin) and Mati (Lucie Lucas), intimately arranged in bed, and Jake poetically giving full voice to a passionate feeling of thrill and wonder.

These different sections, or chapters, are built out of the particular or shared experiences of the main characters. The three-part structure is built on overlap, or repetition. The first two sections, named after each principal, play off subtle variations in examining the same material from different points of view, sometimes amplified or filled in with greater detail. The pair first see each other at an archeological dig site in the countryside and notice each other again on a return train to the city. The crucial connection is made at a café later that night. Klinger executes a gliding camera movement that envelops the two. Jake, a natural wanderer, projects a nervous intensity that attracts Mati, who has pursued a more linear direction of academic excellence and professional achievement.

Klinger edited the film with Géraldine Mangenot. The movie circles and floats and dances to its own rhythms. That proves necessary given how the film takes leaps of faith with regard to character and psychological plausibility. The setup, a brief encounter between a man and woman, is fairly direct. The telling is anything but straightforward. In meditating on memory, the movie's fractured syntax creates its own nervous, at times, unsettling rhythms. For instance, in Jake's section, the movie flashes forward, presenting an even more haggard and abrasive version that proves a fairly damning portrait, like being drunk and abusive as he harasses a woman.

The moral trajectory of *Porto* is unusual in that Jake's behavior is wincing, at times deeply uncomfortable. During one particularly ugly incident in the street outside of Mati's apartment, his actions are downright appalling and establish a pattern of behavior, of blithe male entitlement, that hangs ominously over the rest of the film. *Porto* seems ultimately about instability. The whole film is built on an idea destined not to last. The more pragmatic and clear-eyed Mati understands that. Jake, who lives for experience and moments, is desperate to hold onto a possibility that has no chance of lasting. The profound differences, of circumstance, culture and class, clearly elude him. Jake has an awkward and tense three-way interaction with Mati and her partner, João (Paulo Calatré), her Portuguese professor, that only deepens Jake's disengagement from reality.

This is a movie of echoing themes about longing, pain, and disappointment. Mati's section features the strongest scene in the film, a charged and touching moment set in Paris with her mother (Françoise Lebrun). Mati asks whether her mother still feels moments of sexual need. "It's always present," the older woman says. "We're often disappointed, and then you're lonely." Mati experiences a much fuller range of experiences of marriage and the birth of her daughter. Like Jake, she is unmoored by a bruising sense of incompletion.

The third section is a synthesis. The allusions and remembrances of the first two sections give way to something purer though also bracing. The build up to the sexual encounter also plays out unexpectedly, with moments of downtime, like a three-minute take of Jake unloading boxes from her car. The whole movie hangs on the moment, a sense of rapture that haunts Jake and perhaps a moment of recklessness that unnerves Mati.

Klinger and his very talented cinematographer Wyatt Garfield play with different aspect ratios and film formats, creating a rapt visual correlative of memory. The conditional future is rendered in the more ephemeral Super-8 and 16mm stocks and composed in a very tight frame. The moments between Jake and Mati play out in a radiant, deep and stable 35mm widescreen.

It is a movie suffused in darkness and sorrow, and not just because of what unfolds on screen. *Porto* marked the final lead performance of the skilled and deeply capable Anton Yelchin, who was killed in a freak accident. This was not an actor who ever played it safe or conventional. He inhabited his parts and brought an intensity and edge even in this case animating far from heroic qualities. Jake is solipsistic, even misogynistic, and he is never afraid to illuminate those darker edges. In her first largely English-language role, Lucie Lucas is also terrific, inscrutable and unyielding, a woman always pushing herself forward for new experiences or states of grace.

Patrick Z. McGavin

CREDITS

Jake Kleeman: Anton Yelchin
Mati Vargnier: Lucie Lucas
Joao Monteiro Oliveira: Paulo Calatre
Mother: Francoise Lebrun
Blanca: Florie Auclerc
Origin: United States
Language: English, Portuguese, French
Released: 2017
Production: Rodrigo Areias, Sonia Buchman, Nicolas De La Mothe, Todd Remis, Julie Snyder, Gabe Klinger; Bando à Parte, Double Play Films, Gladys Glover, Salem Street Entertainment; released by Kino Lorber
Directed by: Gabe Klinger
Written by: Gabe Klinger; Larry Gross
Cinematography by: Wyatt Garfield
Music Supervisor: Daniel Vila
Editing: Gabe Klinger; Geraldine Mangenot
Costumes: Susana Abreu
Production Design: Ricardo Preto
MPAA rating: Unrated
Running time: 76 minutes

REVIEWS

Abele, Robert. *Los Angeles Times*. November 22, 2017.
Catsoulis, Jeannette. *New York Times*. November 16, 2017.
Farber, Stephen. *Hollywood Reporter*. March 14, 2017.
Gibbs, Ed. *The Guardian*. September 20, 2016.
Hassenger, Jesse. *The A.V. Club*. November 14, 2017.
Lodge, Guy. *Variety*. September 21, 2017.
Lund, Carson. *Slant Magazine*. November 9, 2017.
Seitz, Matt Zoller. *RogerEbert.com*. November 17, 2017.

Whittaker, Richard. *Austin Chronicle*. March 14, 2017.
Wolfe, April. *Village Voice*. November 16, 2017.

TRIVIA

As originally conceived, the film was supposed to be set in Athens. However, when financing for a shoot in Greece collapsed during pre-production, filming (and the story) was forced to move across the Mediterranean to Portugal.

THE POST

Box Office: $60.5 Million

Over the last decade or so, Steven Spielberg has largely shifted away from the slick genre entertainment that he built his legacy as one of Hollywood's most successful filmmakers on, and the ones that he has done, such as the execrable *The Adventures of Tin Tin* (2011) and *The BFG* (2016), have suggested a growing disenchantment with a kind of storytelling that he could do in his sleep (and may well have in the case of the aforementioned films). His real interest appears to be in presenting more adult-oriented dramas illustrating key events or eras in our collective history with the same kind of cinematic craft that he once utilized in the service of giant sharks and aliens. With his latest effort, *The Post*, he has completed a loose triptych of films, following *Lincoln* (2012) and *Bridge of Spies* (2015) that use the minute detail that went into the creation of watershed moments—the passage of the 13th Amendment abolishing slavery and the negotiations between the United States and the U.S.S.R to secure the release of captured pilot Francis Gary Powers—as a way of exploring, celebrating, and reclaiming the democratic notions upon which America was based. The difference between it and those previous films is that it has also been overtly crafted to serve as a commentary on a number of current political and social issues as well and, as a result, there is a sense of urgency and immediacy to the proceedings that not only prevents it from coming across merely as a well-appointed museum piece but also gives it a surprising degree of tension for a story whose outcome is presumably known to most members of the audience before the opening logos hit the screen.

The film concerns itself with the publication of the so-called "Pentagon Papers," a secret report commissioned by Secretary of Defense Robert McNamara (Bruce Greenwood) chronicling decades of U.S. involvement in Vietnam that demonstrated that government officials had systematically lied to the public and Congress about the possibility of military victory in the region. One of the people charged with helping to compile the report, military analyst Daniel Ellsberg (Matthew Rhys), was against the war and decided to make the information it contained known to all by making a copy of it and leaking it to the *New York Times* in 1971, much to the outrage of the Nixon White House and the consternation of *Washington Post* editor Ben Bradlee (Tom Hanks), who resents once again being scooped in his own city by the competition in New York. Through the efforts of beat reporter Ben Bagdikian (Bob Odenkirk), the *Post* acquires its own copy of the documents as well but by that time, the White House has obtained a court order preventing the *Times* from printing any more excerpts. This is a perfect opportunity for the *Post* to enter the fray as well by continuing where the *Times* left off. The only hitches are that the papers are all out of order and need to be collated immediately for any of it to make sense and the inescapable fact that by publishing them, the *Post* could potentially end up in the same legal hot water as the *Times*.

For an old school newspaperman like Bradlee, the idea to publish is a no-brainer, consequences be damned. For the actual publisher of the paper, Katherine Graham (Meryl Streep), the stakes are a little different. Having taken over the running of the paper following the suicide of her husband (even though it was her family who owned the paper, it was her husband that her father had appointed publisher years earlier), though still not taken particularly seriously, even by the members of her otherwise all-male board of directors, Graham hopes to expand the scope and influence of the paper (which was at the time basically a highly regarded metropolitan newspaper that had not yet reached the national prominence it would soon attain) by taking it public. Inevitably, it is at the very moment when the deal is almost, but not quite, finalized that the Pentagon Papers arrive and publishing the material could cause the deal to fall through, offering an even greater threat to the paper's existence than the White House pressure. To make things even more complicated for her—and to illustrate just how closely entwined the political and the personal can get in Washington, D.C., she runs in the same social circles as the likes of McNamara and to publish would likely destroy all those relationships as well.

Although the story it tells takes place in 1971, the issues brought up by *The Post* are timely enough that it is the rare period piece that has a genuine ripped-from-the-headlines feel to it. It is being released, of course, during the first year of a presidential administration that has, at times, been more hostile to the notion of a free press than Nixon ever dreamed of being and which has tried to sow distrust in the press wherever possible by designating any reports that they disagree with—practically everything not bearing the imprimatur of Fox News—as "fake news." At the same time, the ever-expanding wave of shocking accusations of systemic sexual harassment against women finds a parallel as well in its recounting of Graham and her attempts to be taken seriously in an industry where a woman in power was seen more as an easily overlooked novelty than anything else. (Even she is not particularly sure of herself at times—early on, we see her practicing exactly what she is going to say at a board meeting, only to get flustered and clam up at the last second while a male colleague ends up speaking on her behalf.) With an opportunity like no other to cinematically capture the zeitgeist, it is no wonder that Spielberg elected to fast-track Liz Hannah's screenplay in early 2017 and, following a rewrite by Josh Singer, launched it into production a few weeks later, while still doing post-production work on his latest fantasy epic *Ready Player One* (2018) and still having it out by the end of year, making it his first feature film of the Trump era.

Working on overlapping productions is nothing new for the seemingly inexhaustible Spielberg but in the past, it has led to some films that have been executed in such a mechanically workman-like manner that they feel as if they were untouched by human hands. *The Post*, on the other hand, has been made with such seemingly effortless skill that it seems impossible that it could have been put together in such a short amount of time. Although viewers with at least some working knowledge of the "Pentagon Papers" story will probably have an easier time getting into the story, Spielberg sets up and lays out both the complicated narrative and the vast cast of characters in a clean and efficient manner that gets newcomers up to speed while still keeping things lively for more historically inclined viewers. Although the script does not go to the extremes that such antecedents as *All the President's Men* (1976) and *Zodiac* (2007) did in their depiction of journalists obsessively pursuing the truth, there is never the sense that the film is trying to sweeten the material up to make it more palatable. (That said, there are a couple of clunky late-inning speeches attesting to the wonderfulness of Katherine Graham that slow things down, but the damage they do is minor.) Working with his usual crew—including cinematographer Janusz Kaminski, editors Michael Kahn and Sarah Broshar, production designer Rick Carter and composer John Williams—Spielberg has created an uncommonly stylish work that is always interesting to look at, an especially impressive achievement when you consider that virtually all of the film consists of people in rooms merely talking to one another. There is not a boring scene to be had and one climactic moment—Graham descending the stairs outside the Supreme Court into a crowd of women—is admittedly shameless but at the same time so stirring that even the biggest cynics would find it hard not to be moved by it.

And yet, while the film may look stately and elegant as can be, it moves with the rat-a-tat pace of an old Warner Brothers film from the Thirties and the headlong rush it develops is enough to get even the viewers who know all the details of the historical record swept up in its rush. Much of this is due to the absolutely killer cast that Spielberg has brought together, headlined by Hanks and Streep in what is, astonishingly enough, their first on-screen collaboration. Although working in the shadow of Jason Robards's indelible turn as Ben Bradlee in *All the President's Men*, Hanks nevertheless manages to make the role into a delight that is all his own without ever coming across as too insufferably noble for his own good. Streep, in her liveliest performance in a long time, is equally good as Graham—she is surprisingly convincing as the more timid and fluttering person in the early scenes and when she finally begins to assert herself in the later ones, she pretty much brings down the house as she brings down the hammer. Besides those previously mentioned, the supporting cast includes the likes of Tracy Letts, Bradley Whitford, Carrie Coon, David Cross, Alison Brie, and Jesse Plemons and they all turn in stiring work, though the supporting MVP is Odenkirk, who has one of the most thrillingly acted scenes in the entire film and it consists of nothing more than him and a bank of pay phones. (And yes, although they do not really share any scenes together, the presence of Odenkirk and Cross means that the film also serves as a wholly unexpected *Mr. Show* reunion.)

The Post is one of the best of Steven Spielberg's late career surge, a film that works both as an eye-opening look at recent American history and its current-day parallels and as an utterly engrossing and supremely entertaining example of the kind of adult-oriented cinema that used to be far more commonplace than it is these days. Most importantly, it stands as a much-needed celebration of the newspaper industry and freedom of the press in the face of mounting opposition to both of those concepts in recent days. He presents the basic mechanics that once went into the production of a daily newspaper with the kind of breathless excitement that he once deployed to present the most fantastical of sights. However, this is not merely some kind of nostalgic fetishization for the machinery of old because he is just as enamored with the purpose served by such mechanics—to keep the population informed as to what is going on in the world—and it is a feeling that audiences will feel acutely. With some films, one comes out of them with the sudden urge to purchase the soundtrack album. With *The Post*, viewers will come out of it with the sudden urge to take out a subscription to the actual *Post*.

Peter Sobczynski

CREDITS

Kay Graham: Meryl Streep
Ben Bradlee: Tom Hanks
Tony Bradlee: Sarah Paulson
Ben Bagdikian: Bob Odenkirk
Fritz Beebe: Tracy Letts
Origin: United States
Language: English
Released: 2017
Production: Kristie Macosko Krieger, Amy Pascal, Steven Spielberg; Amblin Entertainment, DreamWorks L.L.C., Participant Media L.L.C., Pascal Pictures, Star Thrower Entertainment; released by Twentieth Century Fox Film Corp.
Directed by: Steven Spielberg
Written by: Liz Hannah; Josh Singer
Cinematography by: Janusz Kaminski
Music by: John Williams
Sound: Brian Chumney; Robert Hymns
Editing: Sarah Broshar; Michael Kahn
Art Direction: Kim Jennings; Deborah Jensen
Costumes: Ann Roth
Production Design: Rick Carter
MPAA rating: PG-13
Running time: 115 minutes

REVIEWS

Dargis, Manohla. *New York Times.* December 21, 2017.
Duralde, Alonso. *TheWrap.* December 6, 2017.
Ebiri, Bilge. *Village Voice.* December 6, 2017.
Gleiberman, Owen. *Variety.* December 6, 2017.
Hornaday, Ann. *Washington Post.* December 7, 2017.
Kaplan, Fred. *Slate.* December 6, 2017.
Lane, Anthony. *New Yorker.* December 11, 2017.
Lawson, Richard. *Vanity Fair.* December 16, 2017.
McCarthy, Todd. *Hollywood Reporter.* December 6, 2017.
Turan, Kenneth. *Los Angeles Times.* December 21, 2017.

TRIVIA

Was filmed after director Steven Spielberg's *Ready Player One* (2018).

AWARDS

Nominations:
Oscars 2017: Actress (Streep), Film
Golden Globes 2018: Actor--Drama (Hanks), Actress--Drama (Streep), Director (Spielberg), Film--Drama, Orig. Score, Screenplay

POWER RANGERS
(Saban's Power Rangers)

It's morphin time!
—Movie tagline

Box Office: $85.4 Million

It's always difficult to change the public face of a brand after its reached ubiquity. When DC Comics relaunched its *Batman* film series with 2005's *Batman Begins*, it successfully wiped clean a slate that had become tainted by the cartoonish and near-unanimously reviled *Batman and Robin* (1997). By going dark and humane, they turned a comic book creation into as believable a flesh and blood character as was possible. The film, for all its heart and stabs at realism, set a dangerous precedent as everything from Archie comics to Transformers toys have been given glossy, dark, miserable updates. The gritty reboot has taken American media by storm and its latest victim is a line of action figures that gave rise to a small TV empire. The Power Rangers went from toys to the stars of a series about a bunch of mismatched teens who had to fight giant monsters (not dissimilar to the "kaiju" that Godzilla used to tackle) at the beck and call of a series of increasingly hammy villains. The show worked well enough entertaining kids after school, but the reason it endured was the interchangeable nature of the heroes, villains, conflicts, and themes. Giving it a gritty reboot seemed like a perverse choice and a shameless cash-grab by a money hungry studio, but thankfully it's less insufferably dark than it could have been.

The 2017 *Power Rangers* movie begins by establishing its heavy bonafides right away by showing an alien planet in ruins after an attack from Rita Repulsa (Elizabeth Banks), a kind of space warlord in a fetish costume. One of the lifeforms she is conquering is able to hide an energy source before he's killed. The purpose of the source is not immediately clear until decades later when a group of Earth teenagers stumble upon it. Jason (Dacre Montgomery) is a star football player who blows his big chance at a career when a prank involving a school mascot goes awry. At detention, he meets Billy (RJ Cyler), an awkward, autistic kid in need of defending from school bullies, and Kimberly (Naomi Scott), a rebel with a self-destructive streak. They both encourage him in their own way to keep following his instincts and fail as proudly as he wants.

Billy bribes Jason into hanging out with him by offering him the use of his deceased father's car and by hotwiring the delinquent's ankle bracelet so he can leave town without his parole officer knowing. Billy has an odd plan for them to spend their first afternoon as friends: going to a mine to look at bizarre objects, something he and his father used to do. It just so happens that Kimberly, as well as two other misfits, Trini (Becky G.) and Zack (Ludi Lin), are present when Billy detonates some explosives and uncovers an odd stone formation in the mine. Jason and Zach start chipping away pieces of it but, before they uncover its purpose, the authorities chase them off the scene. They appear to all die in a car crash but wake up the following day unscathed, sleeping next to the colorful pieces of stone they chipped off the rock formation. Those stone pieces happen to be the energy source the alien from the opening stashed away before his demise. The stones appear to give the kids superhuman strength and speed and it's a good thing, too, because a fishing trawler has just uncovered the still-breathing body of Rita Repulsa and she immediately sets about trying to destroy the planet.

The wisest choice that the corporate thinktank who devised this movie made was letting the film be lighthearted and brisk, even if the temptation to go gritty was overwhelming. Yes, there is undue heaviness littered throughout, starting with the opening scenes of planetary destruction. The sequence looks to be as indebted to *Saving Private Ryan* (1998) as it does Zack Snyder, but seconds later Jason's prank with a cow and a joke about accidentally milking its genitals knock the film off its high horse. It's an interesting strategy—undercutting its own self-seriousness before it becomes a crutch—but it continually makes the movie feel like a series of marketing decisions instead of an organically told story. By the time an alien god face (voiced by Bryan Cranston) and his wise-cracking robot sidekick (voiced by Bill Hader) arrive to say that the fate of the universe is in the hands of teenagers, all pretentions towards seriousness have been thrown out the window. The visions of burnt bodies and destroyed cities (borrowed from *Man of Steel* [2013]) that follow are disgustingly calculated and have no place in such a frothy concoction. Its overwhelming, unrelenting preciousness is never far away, so any time the film tries to bring up its supposed life or death stakes, it feels desperately disingenuous.

Not that it's unsuccessful as a silly little comedy about some teenagers who suddenly discover they can move at the speed of sound and bound over canyons. Director Dean Israelite and his cast do fine work with the film's twitchy witticisms. Israelite's visuals owe an incalculable debt to Alfonso Cuarón. His camera is never at rest, constantly showing off during heavily and carefully choreographed long takes. The famous 360-degree tracking shot in Cuarón's *Children of Men* (2006), is borrowed here for a shot of Jason fleeing the police following his stunt with the cow, crashing his car in the process. His visuals have Cuarón's bleached, high contrast hyper-realism and his reliance on little details in the margins—like a brilliant comedy aside involving a van full of nuns almost crushed by the Rangers' robot. His "style," borrowed though it may be, is endemic of the film's strengths and weaknesses. Moment to moment, the film can be thrilling and finds sublime notes, whether in watching the kids discover their newfound abilities during death-defying stunts or wading gracefully through water for long stretches of time. Those visuals just cannot cover up the film's utter lack of substance or purpose.

Scout Tafoya

CREDITS

Jason Lee Scott/The Red Ranger: Dacre Montgomery
Kimberly Hart/The Pink Ranger: Naomi Scott
Billy Cranston/The Blue Ranger: R.J. Cyler
Zack Taylor/The Black Ranger: Ludi Lin
Trini Kwan/The Yellow Ranger: Becky G
Rita Repulsa: Elizabeth Banks
Origin: United States
Language: English
Released: 2017
Production: Marty Bowen, Brian Casentini, Wyck Godfrey, Haim Saban; Saban Films, TIK Films, Temple Hill Entertainment, Toei Company Ltd., Videocine Prods.; released by Lionsgate
Directed by: Dean Israelite
Written by: John Gatins
Cinematography by: Matthew Lloyd
Music by: Brian Tyler
Sound: Joe Dzuban
Music Supervisor: Season Kent
Editing: Martin Bernfeld; Dody Dorn
Costumes: Kelli Jones
Production Design: Andrew Menzies
MPAA rating: PG-13
Running time: 124 minutes

REVIEWS

Duralde, Alonso. *TheWrap.* March 20, 2017.
Chang, Justin. *Los Angeles Times.* March 23, 2017.
Collin, Robbie. *The Telegraph.* March 22, 2017.
Grierson, Tim. *Screen International.* Marc 20, 2017.
Keough, Peter. *Boston Globe.* March 23, 2017.
Seitz, Matt Zoller. *RogerEbert.com.* March 23, 2017.
Vishnevetsky, Ignatiy. *The A.V. Club.* March 23, 2017.
Watson, Keith. *Slant Magazine.* March 23, 2017.
Yoshida, Emily. *New York Magazine.* March 27, 2017.
Yu, Danny. *Time Out New York.* March 24, 2017.

QUOTES

Trini: "Me and four kids found a spaceship buried underground. I'm pretty sure I'm a superhero."

TRIVIA

The Angel Grove High logo in the film is the same one used in *Mighty Morphin Power Rangers* (1993).

PROFESSOR MARSTON AND THE WONDER WOMEN

Meet the women behind the man behind the woman.
—Movie tagline

Ever wonder?
—Movie tagline

Box Office: $1.6 Million

When Patty Jenkins's *Wonder Woman* became the surprise blockbuster hit of summer 2017, it proved that female driven comic book movies could succeed as well as or better than those directed by men. The movie, arguably, sanitized the character of Wonder Woman, removing her bi-sexual flirtation with bondage and her more ambiguously sexual character in favor of a kind of a doe-eyed heterosexuality in the hands of Jenkins and actress Gal Gadot. Thankfully Angela Robinson's *Professor Marston and the Wonder Women,* by far the more compelling movie, was waiting in the wings to benefit from the public's renewed interest in the character. Depending on who you talk to, the film plays fast and loose with the facts of Marston's life, but it's undeniably more thrilling than another mushy CGI action movie in the Zach Snyder-coined DC Universe house style.

We meet William Moulton Marston (Luke Evans) in 1947, months before his death due to skin cancer. He's meeting with the head of the Child Study Association of America (Connie Britton) and a few of her colleagues to discuss the raunchier aspects of his beloved creation, the DC Comics hero Wonder Woman. Martston reflects on his life and the twists and turns that led him to this chair being chastised for his life and his livelihood. Marston was a down-on-his-luck Harvard educated psychology professor before Wonder Woman ever entered his life. He and his wife Elizabeth (Rebecca Hall) tag-team their classes at Harvard and Radcliffe waiting for their success in publishing. The dean of the college won't approve Elizabeth's doctorate, leaving her forever in her husband's shadow, despite having an even fiercer intellect and a more objective method of studying than the emotionally transparent Bill. Their lives change forever the day they meet prospective teaching assistant Olive Byrne (Bella Heathcote), niece of world-renowned feminist scholar Margaret Sanger. They want Olive to help them in both William's study of an idea he calls DISC (Dominance, Inducement, Submission, Compliance) Theory of human behavior, and on their joint research on a functioning lie detector, something that hadn't yet been perfected. After Elizabeth fails to chase off Olive by warning her not to try to sleep with William, they start spending long nocturnal sessions researching both the lie detector and the rituals of Olive's sorority sisters, whom William believes will give him some insight into the female mind. It's during these sessions that a mutual attraction develops between the three hungry academics, one that they don't quite know how to reconcile. They try to keep things platonic, but after a blow-up with her fiancée (Chris Conroy), Olive decides that she's tired of keeping her feelings a secret.

Their affair turns to scandal before long and they are chased out of both college and their New England home. The trio resettles in Rye, New York in order to find a home for themselves and the baby Olive is carrying, concocting a lie to explain their unusual arrangement. Before long, they have three children between the two mothers and a fourth on the way. Elizabeth works more steadily than William during this period as he tries to write books that will sell and fuel him intellectually. Another chance meeting sets his life on a new course. One day he happens upon a lingerie shop run by Charles Guyette (JJ Feild), and discovers in the pornographic pictures the French shopkeeper pedals, a real-life display of his DISC Theory. He sees in the erotic posing of the women each step of his theory acted out in reality. This gives him an idea to somehow merge the pornography with his ideas about human behavior in a populist fashion. But first he needs a vessel. He brings Olive and Elizabeth to a live bondage display and though the more uptight Elizabeth is disgusted, Olive takes to the rope and corsets, and suddenly William's imagination is alive with possibilities. He creates a comic book hero to rival Superman, a woman wearing fetish gear who uses bondage to get the truth out of villains. This has the added bonus of bringing in extra money for the family and reigniting Elizabeth, William, and Olive's playful sex lives. Both come to a screeching halt when outsiders figure out what the Marstons are up to, privately and publicly.

Robinson's screenplay apparently turned a lot of the Marstons's lives into straight-up fiction in order to make the story flow a little more like a classic biopic, which is perfectly fine, because the story she wound up telling is both entertaining and an illustration of Marston's theories regarding the Wonder Woman comic. It takes its ideas about boundary crossing art and slides it into a palatable, erotic adult contemporary romantic drama, the sort of thing Merchant Ivory used to win Oscars® for producing. It's naked, if palatable eroticism is needed in order to strengthen the conviction of it's through line regarding what the public learns through ostensibly salacious material. After all, it counts as a brave gesture these days to make a film that stumps for bisexual marriage and kinky sexuality as both a viable form of entertainment and a way to teach empathy. By exposing children to the idea that no form of sexual social behavior is wrong, that it's heroic to express yourself, then the bar for "normal" behavior moves to the left and fewer children are afraid of their own sexuality. That's the kind of victory Marston was attempting to win against the steely board out to judge both his comic book and his life. If the film needed to sensationalize and add a few white lies to get there, while still remaining true to the spirit of Marston, then it feels like an acceptable invention. Add to that excellent performances from the chain-smoking neurotic Hall at her best, Evans's perfectly utilized masculine tenderness and a script that makes great use of unspoken sexual tension and the fun of academic discourse and you have an adult drama that's as sexy as it is elucidating. The film is no masterpiece but it sure blows a chaste *Wonder Woman* movie out of the water.

Scout Tafoya

CREDITS

William Moulton Marston: Luke Evans
Elizabeth Marston: Rebecca Hall
Olive Byrne: Bella Heathcote
Josette Frank: Connie Britton
Charles Guyette: J.J. Feild
Origin: United States
Language: English
Released: 2017
Production: Terry Leonard, Amy Redford; Boxspring Entertainment, Opposite Field Pictures, Stage 6 Films, Topple Productions; released by Annapurna Pictures
Directed by: Angela Robinson
Written by: Angela Robinson
Cinematography by: Bryce Fortner
Music by: Tom Howe
Sound: Trevor Gates
Music Supervisor: Howard Paar
Editing: Jeffrey Werner
Costumes: Donna Maloney
Production Design: Carl Sprague
MPAA rating: R
Running time: 108 minutes

REVIEWS

Bradshaw, Peter. *The Guardian*. September 16, 2017.
Brody, Richard. *New Yorker* October 11, 2017.
Burr, Ty *Boston Globe* October 11, 2017.
Chang, Justin. *Los Angeles Times*. October 12, 2017.
Dargis, Manohla. *New York Times*. October 12, 2017.
Jagernauth, Kevin. *The Playlist*. September 18, 2016.
Kang, Inkoo. *TheWrap*. October 12, 2017.
Matousek, Mark. *Slant Magazine*. October 11, 2017.
Rife, Katie. *The A.V. Club*. October 11, 2017.
Wolfe, April. *Village Voice*. October 12, 2017.

QUOTES

Elizabeth Marston: "He respects me. He loves me. And he's never boring."

TRIVIA

William Marston's granddaughter, Christie Marston, has publicly stated that her family "completely rejects any claims made in the film and in no way support this work of fiction."

THE PROMISE

Empires fall. Love survives.
—Movie tagline

Box Office: $8.2 Million

The history of genocide has typically focused almost solely on the Holocaust. There have been numeroud books, films, and scholarly articles detailing the reasons that Hitler and his Nazi regime are indelibly etched on world consciousness. But it's fair to say that social consciousness worldwide has finally started to unbury its head from the sand and look around at the widespread mistreatment of a variety of peoples across the globe outside of World War II. Writer/director Terry George successfully brought depictions of the Rwanda genocide to light in *Hotel Rwanda* (2004) and now he's chosen to give the Armenian genocide the same attention in *The Promise,* with mixed results.

Films about lesser-known genocides are nothing new and some standouts include the aforementioned *Hotel Rwanda,* as well as *The Killing Fields,* (1984) which detailed massive human rights violations by the Khmer Rouge in Cambodia; *The Last King of Scotland* (2006), which delved into the abusive dictatorship of Idi Amin and his cruel rein in Uganda; *The Act of Killing* (2012), which is a brilliant-yet-eerie documentary about the U.S.-sanctioned massacre of Indonesian citizens; and, of course, *Schindler's List* (1993), among countless other films about the Holocaust. While all of these aforementioned works are notable and highly thought of, it's difficult to put a finger on just what makes them superior to *The Promise*, which has all the right elements yet somehow does not harness the struggle, pain, or gravitas of the depicted scenario.

The Promise opens on a young Armenian medical student hopeful named Mikael Boghosian (Oscar Isaac), who treats the ill in his village with tinctures and mixes that, while often do the job, are not true medicine. Mikael expresses his want to attend medical school via an opening monologue but explains that money has always been an issue. Thus, an arranged marriage to the lovely Maral (Angela Sarafyan), who comes from a somewhat wealthy family, could not be more well-timed—the dowry provided as a nest egg can be used for medical school. No sooner is the engagement announced than Mikael is off to Constantinople to get that medical degree with Maral's family savings to pay the way.

Upon arrival, Mikael shows he is a good-hearted man, willing to see the decency in everyone as he befriends the flaky Emre (Marwan Kenzari), who comes from a wealthy and well-respected Turkish family. While the reason these two hit it off so well is never quite clear, they become fast friends and are soon partying away the night in fancy nightclubs. One of these clubs is where they run across Emre's acquaintance, Chris Myers (Christian Bale), an American journalist who is also a bad drunk, and his lovely girlfriend Ana (Charlotte Le Bon). Thus the stage is set for the fall of the Ottoman Empire set against the forthcoming Armenian genocide with a love triangle thrown in for good measure as Mikael and Ana soon fall for one another amidst rising tensions and impending violence.

As act two starts, all the proper elements are in place for what should be a compelling, heartstring-pulling, award-winning epic for the cinematic ages. Sadly, *The Promise* never grabs hold of the audience and instead comes across as a bit derivative of other genocide films. A film about an overlooked massacre of over one million people with brilliant actors and a well-respected writer should not feel like "just another genocide movie" but that's really the best way to describe *The Promise*.

While there are indeed heavy, memorable moments (mostly via Isaacs' brilliant portrayal of a torn man who finds his belief in peoples' better nature challenged), the film gets bogged down in politics, and Bale's intense character gets lost for minutes at a time as the camera sticks with Mikael, who, by the third act, finds himself caught between the love of his wife and the passion he has for Ana, as well as trying to survive murderous Turkish thugs. While adding a love story to a war film is nothing new, *The Promise* suffers for it as it feels weirdly shoved in, and Le Bon, who may be competent and lovely, just does not have the screen presence to play opposite Isaac and Bale. As a result, *The Promise* comes off as somewhat messy, often times boring and is unclear in terms of whether it is a love story or a war movie. It ends up being neither.

Don R. Lewis

CREDITS

Mikael Boghosian: Oscar Isaac
Ana Khesarian: Charlotte Le Bon
Chris Myers: Christian Bale
Reverend Dikran Antreassian: Daniel Gimenez Cacho
Marta Boghosian: Shohreh Aghdashloo
Origin: United States
Language: English, Armenian, German, French
Released: 2017
Production: Eric Esrailian, William Horberg, Mike Medavoy; Babieka, Survival Pictures, Wonderful Films; released by Open Road Films
Directed by: Terry George
Written by: Terry George; Robin Swicord
Cinematography by: Javier Aguirresarobe
Music by: Gabriel Yared
Sound: Paul Hsu; Philip Stockton
Editing: Steven Rosenblum
Art Direction: Didac Bono
Costumes: Pierre-Yves Gayraud
Production Design: Benjamin Fernandez
MPAA rating: PG-13
Running time: 133 minutes

REVIEWS

Abele, Robert. *TheWrap*. April 18, 2017.
Baumgarten, Marjorie. *Austin Chronicle*. April 20, 2017.
Berardinelli, James. *Reel Views*. April 20, 2017.
Fujishima, Kenji. *Slant Magazine*. April 17, 2017.
Greenblatt, Leah. *Entertainment Weekly*. April 20, 2017.
Jagernauth, Kevin. *The Playlist*. September 17, 2017.
Kenny, Glenn. *RogerEbert.com*. April 21, 2017.
Lowry, Andrew. *Empire*. April 24, 2017.
Roeper, Richard. *Chicago Sun-Times*. April 20, 2017.
Walsh, Katie. *Los Angeles Times*. April 20, 2017.

QUOTES

Ana: "Our revenge will be to survive."

TRIVIA

The film was shot in seventy-two days across twenty locations throughout Spain, Malta, Portugal, and New York.

Q

A QUIET PASSION

Box Office: $1.9 Million

With a resume that has always emphasized strong female characters and which has already seen him tackling the works of such esteemed writers as John Kennedy Toole (*The Neon Bible* [1995]), Edith Wharton (*The House of Mirth* [2000]), and Lewis Grassic Gibbon (*Sunset Song* [2015]), acclaimed British filmmaker Terence Davies would seem, on paper at least, to be the ideal candidate to make the first major cinematic exploration of the life of celebrated poet Emily Dickinson. And yet, while *A Quiet Passion* has clearly been made with all due respect and the best of intentions, the end result is a curious mishmash that mixes together all the usual clichés of the literary biopic genre with odd tonal shifts that are more jarring than edifying.

Unlike a good number of recent films of this ilk, which have elected to concentrate on a key aspect in the life of their subject instead of trying to telescope everything about them into a conventional feature running time, *A Quiet Passion* follows Dickinson from the age of about 17, when she was a spirited student at Mount Holyoke, much to the consternation of her teachers and fellow students, to her death at 55 from kidney disease in the house where she would spend virtually all of her life after leaving school. At her Massachusetts home, Emily (played in the early school scenes by Emma Bell and as an adult by Cynthia Nixon) is surrounded by her family—a stern father (Keith Carradine), a depressive mother (Joanna Bacon), cheerful sister Vinnie (Jennifer Ehle), and obnoxious brother Austin (Duncan Duff)—and her lone close friend, Vryling Buffam (Catherine Bailey). Although appalled by his daughter's rebellious attitude, Emily's father nevertheless respects her intelligence and gift with words and, upon her suggestion, allows her to write poetry every day between the hours of 3 and 6 A.M. It is through this that she was able to channel her otherwise unfulfilled emotions and develop her unique literary voice that would eventually lead to her being deemed one of America's greatest poets, despite the fact that of the nearly 2,000 poems she wrote in her lifetime, only seven were said to have been in print at the time of her passing.

Dickinson's literary genius cannot be denied, but her suitability as the subject of a biographical film is questionable at best. The thing that made her so extraordinary—her utterly original poetic voice—is not the kind of element that translates particularly well into cinematic terms while the other well-known aspects of her life, such as her increasing reclusiveness, are not exactly the stuff of gripping drama. In attempting to navigate these seemingly insoluble problems, Davies has employed a number of approaches that are uneven at best. On the bright side, he resists the urge to "explain" Emily and her poetic gifts in any overt way and elects instead to tell her story more or less as a spare chamber piece that is a better fit for how we see her as a person than the lavishly appointed museum piece take that others might have employed. On the other hand, Davies's attempt to counteract the prevailing view of Dickinson as some kind of mousy and repressed recluse and convey her often underrated wit takes a strange turn for much of the middle section as he begins having her and her family and friends trading rat-a-tat barbs and bon mots that feel less like Dickinson and more like outtakes from Whit Stillman's *Love & Friendship* (2016).

The biggest problem with *A Quiet Passion* is that Davies never really demonstrates what it was about Dickinson's life and work that inspired him to try to bring it to the screen. There are moments when he begins to give us glimpses of both the person and the artist—such as when she develops a crush on a local minister (Eric Loren) who is perhaps the only person yet to fully appreciate her poetry but who is, alas, married or when she learns that a publisher has arbitrarily messed with her intricate punctuation in order to make it easier to read—but almost as soon as they start up, they are summarily abandoned. As for the poems, we hear a number of them being read but since Dickinson's poetry is better served when one reads it as opposed to listening to it—the better to appreciate the aforementioned punctuation and to allow for repeated readings to allow her dense wording and meaning to sink in—they just come across as mere words. (This is especially disappointing when one considers how deftly Davies handled the equally difficult dialogue in *Sunset Song* so as to make it accessible without losing the music of the language.) As for Nixon, her performance is just fine but it is just that—she never quite inhabits the role in a way that might truly illustrate what it was that made Dickinson tick. (By comparison, Jennifer Ehle, as Emily's sister, brings such life to her comparatively briefer turn that you cannot help but speculate what the film might have been like if she had played the lead instead.)

A Quiet Passion is not a particularly good movie but it is not necessarily a bad or lazy one either—it has clearly been made with a lot of care and the technical aspects, such as the lovely contributions by cinematographer Florian Hoffmeister (who previously worked with Davies on *The Deep Blue Sea* [2011]), are all done with care without going overboard in the manner of many other historical biopics. And yet, the film never comes together as Davies presents a portrait of a complex woman and groundbreaking writer that never seems to have a full grasp on what it was that made her so special or why her work continues to resonate to this very day. If this film had worked, it most likely would have inspired viewers to want to seek out and delve into the works of Dickinson themselves—either for the first time or, more likely, as a refresher. Instead, watching *A Quiet Passion* is more likely to inspire moviegoers to want to seek out and delve into a better movie.

Peter Sobczynski

CREDITS

Emily Dickinson: Cynthia Nixon
Vinnie Dickinson: Jennifer Ehle
Austin Dickinson: Duncan Duff
Father: Keith Carradine
Mother: Joanna Bacon
Origin: United States
Language: English
Released: 2017
Production: Roy Boulter, Sol Papadopoulos; Hurricane Films, WeatherVane Productions; released by Music Box Films
Directed by: Terence Davies
Written by: Terence Davies
Cinematography by: Florian Hoffmeister
Sound: Srdjan Kurpjel
Music Supervisor: Ian Neil
Editing: Pia Di Ciaula
Costumes: Catherine Marchand
Production Design: Merijn Sep
MPAA rating: PG-13
Running time: 125 minutes

REVIEWS

Anderson, Melissa. *Village Voice*. April 11, 2017.
Brody, Richard. *New Yorker*. October 5, 2016.
Chang, Justin. *Los Angeles Times*. April 20, 2017.
Klawans, Stuart. *The Nation*. March 28, 2017.
Lodge, Guy. *Variety*. February 15, 2016.
Merry, Stephanie. *Washington Post*. May 11, 2017.
Scott, A.O. *New York Times*. April 13, 2017.
Taylor, Ella. *NPR*. April 13, 2017.
White, Armond. *National Review*. May 1, 2017.
Young, Deborah. *Hollywood Reporter*. February 15, 2016.

QUOTES

Emily Dickinson: "Poems are my solace for the eternity which surrounds us all."

TRIVIA

Director Terence Davies first met Cynthia Nixon when auditioning actresses for a comedy film that ultimately never got made. He never forgot her and Nixon's resemblance to Emily Dickinson is what clinched her being cast in this film.

R

RAW

(Grave)

What are you hungry for?
—Movie tagline

Box Office: $514,870

Raw opens on an empty road, lined with trees. It could lead anywhere. Where it leads the viewer is harrowing indeed. Writer/director Julia Ducournau moves from images of car accidents and college hazing, chaotic makeshift dance clubs, and veterinary medicine with a sure command of the grotesque. But, ultimately, her film revels in flesh. Flesh dances, ripples, shines with sweat, and is consumed. Fans of body horror are liable to revel too. *Raw* is rich in film-craft and could support any number of viewings and different analysis. But only the truly adventurous will find themselves wanting to see it again.

Justine (Garance Marillier) has joined her sister Alexia (Ella Rumpf) at veterinary school. But the hazing is brutal. Among the many hardships, Justine, a strict vegetarian, is splattered with blood and required to eat a raw rabbit kidney leaving her with a horrific rash for which a doctor prescribes skin creme. Her shy personality begins to change as well. A chance encounter with the scene of a car accident leaves her with an unstoppable urge to devour raw meat. Later she throws up a ball of hair. After a night of drinking, While Alexia is using some scissors to remove a stuck piece of paper from her leg, Justine kicks her, cutting off her sister's finger. While waiting for the ambulance Justine begins eating the finger just as Alexia recovers consciousness. At the hospital, Alexia blames the family dog, covering for her sister in front of their parents.

Soon after, Alexia takes Justine to a remote stretch of road and causes an accident by suddenly lying down in front of an oncoming car. Horrified, Justine runs to her sister's aid but Alexia has already made her way over to the wrecked car and begins eating one of the people inside. Even after this, Justine's hunger for flesh grows, along with her sex drive, which leads to an intense one-night stand with her gay roommate that she can only fully consummate by biting deeply into her own arm to provoke a climax. Later, at a party, she gets blackout drunk and discovers footage the next day showing her paraded around by her sister like a dog, snapping at the exposed flesh of a corpse in the college morgue. A fight on the campus square ensues where the two bite each other mercilessly before limping off to tend each other's wounds. As hazing week draws to a close, Justine wakes up to find her roommate dead in their bed, his leg eaten down to the bone. Panicking, she goes into the next room and discovers Alexia, in an almost trance-like post feeding state and briefly contemplates killing her before choosing to wash her off.

Julia Ducournau has crafted an unusually complex and compelling screenplay considering how many other excellent films have used monstrousness as a metaphor for coming of age. But unlike *Teen Wolf* (1985), *Ginger Snaps* (2000), or *When Animals Dream* (2014), her monsters are, outwardly at least, completely human. Marillier and Rumpf have fantastic chemistry as the sisters and *Raw* leans into that instead of bothering to explain exactly what motivates their cannibalism. In fact, the film portrays the society they live in as cannibalistic as well. There are no answers anywhere for these dark urges. The intense and degrading hazing, the wild drunken parties, disaffected teachers and parents without answers, all contribute to the girl's inward mania as they try to find footing. The truly monstrous thing *Raw* suggests, is that here are no easy answers anywhere for the dark urges that make up an undeniable part of the human experience. To be human is to be constantly tempted and, ultimately, to stand or fall alone.

Special effects makeup makes an impact here that can't be overstated. *Raw* is more than shocking. It seems utterly realistic. There is no hyperbole in suggesting that *Raw* has something to nauseate everyone. Fetal mutants in formaldehyde, fecal veterinary procedures, and a host of raw flesh consumption seem absolutely real as presented. The score is an effective mix of ambient noise, surprisingly poignant guitars, and alternately pensive and sharp driving keyboards all used to underscore the needs of the moment but balanced enough to never be distracting. *Raw* ends on a jaw-dropping, if not altogether surprising image, that hammers home its point about the need of the individual to find a way to own their own darkness. But, ironically, that same image says a lot about the nature of love and family, suggesting that people can be defined by more than just their darkness.

Dave Canfield

CREDITS

Justine: Garance Marillier
Alexia: Ella Rumpf
Adrien: Rabah Nait Oufella
Le pere: Laurent Lucas
La mere: Joana Preiss
Origin: United States
Language: French
Released: 2017
Production: Jean des Forêts; Ezekiel Film Production, Petit Film, Rouge International; released by Focus World
Directed by: Julia Ducournau
Written by: Julia Ducournau
Cinematography by: Ruben Impens
Music by: Jim Williams
Sound: Severin Favriau
Music Supervisor: Guillaume Baurez
Editing: Jean-Christophe Bouzy
Art Direction: Laurie Colson
Costumes: Elise Ancion
Production Design: Laurie Colson
MPAA rating: R
Running time: 99 minutes

REVIEWS

Adams, Thelma. *New York Observer*. March 10, 2017.
Bray, Catherine. *Variety*. September 29, 2016.
Catsoulis, Jeannette. *New York Times*. March 9, 2017.
Chang, Justin. *Los Angeles Times*. March 9, 2016.
Clarke, Cath *Time Out*. March 15, 2017.
Howell, Peter. *Toronto Star*. April 27, 2017.
Keough, Peter. *Boston Globe*. March 16, 2017.
Lane, Anthony. *New Yorker*. March 6, 2017.
MacDonald, Moira. *Seattle Times*. March 29, 2017.
Mintzer, Jordan. *Hollywood Reporter*. September 29, 2016.

QUOTES

Le père: "Your mum was tough at first. Kept saying I was her best friend at school. It drove me nuts! It's not like she had a boyfriend. Just me. And then we had our first kiss. And I understood."

TRIVIA

Over thirty people walked out of the theater when this movie was shown in Sweden.

REBEL IN THE RYE

Don't ever tell anybody anything. If you do, you start missing everybody.
—Movie tagline

Box Office: $378,294

Danny Strong's barely serviceable and frequently irritating J.D. Salinger biopic, *Rebel in the Rye*, fails on multiple fronts, but the film's most glaring misstep is its embodiment of the fraudulence that its subject spent his life's work pushing back against. Best known as the author of *The Catcher In the Rye*, Salinger is responsible for the creation of the poster child of chip-on-the-shoulder adolescent rebellion, Holden Caulfield. But the seminal author's most prominent legacy isn't limited to that character, but a lifelong obsession with what that character represents—a plea for authenticity and a hatred of phonies.

That megalomaniacal worldview is fertile ground for a biopic, especially when folding in the modern view of Caulfield as a standard bearer rather than an outsider. But Strong's screenplay, adapted from Kenneth Slawenski's biography, *J.D. Salinger: A Life* treats the supposedly revolutionary author with the same straight-faced, hollow reverence of any other humdrum figure. As played by Nicholas Hoult, Salinger is defined by a repeated insistence that he's different than anyone else (multiple early scenes consist of the author complaining about the tin-eared prose of his contemporaries with deadening obviousness). But both Hoult's portrayal and the structure stumble into every cradle to the grave trope imaginable, aggressively signposting every coming revelation and hump with weening, self-congratulatory narration.

Forgettable, self-worshipping biopics are a disease in Hollywood, but *Rebel In the Rye* feels particularly frustrating for its lack of self-awareness. It doesn't diminish Salinger's body of work, but his writing takes on a different tenor in this millennium when Caulfield's mere existence has influenced every overly precocious male protagonist from the last century. Finding a balance between contemporary resonance and period influence is always sticky, but this film doesn't even try to communicate that relationship, instead presenting it without comment.

Compared to idiosyncratic outliers like Mike Leigh's *Mr. Turner* (2014) or Terence Davies's *A Quiet Passion* (2016), a film that reveled in twisting Emily Dickinson's sad sack image, this portrait is less characteristically prickly or challenging than merely finicky. It feels at once the result of unintended compromises and an exaggeration of thin material to give the appearance of grand revelations.

With the technical acumen of a History Channel miniseries (dingy lighting and flat staging that chokes even the most atmospheric compositions) and far less verisimilitude, Strong's film spends the first hour hopscotching back and forth between Salinger's post-World War II stint in a military hospital and his early unpublished days as a libertine who both scoffs at and desperately pleads for validation from his superiors. As an amateur, he trawls the bars, first becoming entranced with a famous playwright's socialite daughter, Oona O'Neill (Zoey Deutch at her most manic pixie), and then entering into an equally unsatisfying love affair with his own creative uncertainty.

Salinger is a classic writerly stereotype, a troublemaker toiling in obscurity in the shadow of a successful, uncreative family. And the film supplies the expected archetypes in spades. The woefully underused Hope Davis brings bland encouragement as Salinger's mother, while Victor Garber really leans into the staleness of the material as the tough love father. The smorgasbord of tropes finds its apotheosis in Whit Burnett, Salinger's professor, initially reluctant mentor, and friend who's played with slick ease by Kevin Spacey.

The problem with the back and forth structure is that it's less about giving thematic resonance to those early scenes than the path of most resistance to a number of moldy insights. As Salinger, Hoult is at once a dead ringer for the author's known hyperactive egocentricity, and too convincingly pouty. He's abrasive in a way that feels fidgety, but unrevealing. And as a nascent paranoia emerges, it becomes another clunky layer that never integrates into a natural part of the character.

The post-war hospital material is equally tedious, but comes closest to communicating the anxiety of being a famous writer and the author's uphill struggle with alcoholism. Unfortunately, these scenes are still constructed with a repeated bluntness. Director of photography Kramer Morgenthau stages at least a dozen variations of stolid shots of Hoult smoking in front of windows to signify his depression. The film briefly finds a pulse with the addition of Dorothy (Sarah Paulson), an agent who sees great things in Salinger's future, but her presence is too brief to keep the momentum going. Pulling her best impression of Rosalind Russell's brassy tommy gun patter, Paulson brings a sense of feeling and urgency to the screen that all but disappears as soon as she leaves again.

And that's before Salinger's flailing gives way to a patchy, interminable third act where the author begins his infamous reclusion from society, finding enlightenment in zen buddhism and saying things like "writing has become my religion" without a shred of irony. Admittedly, this was always going to be a hard turn to feel organic, but delivered with po-faced seriousness and prefaced by the equivalent of a meditation training montage, it borders on self-parody. It's the final nail in the coffin rendering what should be a moving end to an arc as little more than a summary of shopworn epiphanies and neat resolutions.

As a figure riddled with thorny contradictions and unresolved questions, Salinger was never going to be an easy subject to satisfyingly make a movie about. It's too bad then that *Rebel in the Rye* is so concerned with its own wittiness and easy conclusions that it shortchanges the complexities of Salinger and his legacy in the process.

Michael Snydel

CREDITS

J.D. Salinger: Nicholas Hoult
Whit Burnett: Kevin Spacey
Oona O'Neill: Zoey Deutch
Claire Douglas: Lucy Boynton
Dorothy Olding: Sarah Paulson
Origin: United States
Language: English
Released: 2017
Production: Bruce Cohen, Thad Luckinbill, Trent Luckinbill, Jason Shuman, Molly Smith, Danny Strong; Black Label Media, West Madison Entertainment; released by IFC Films

Directed by: Danny Strong
Written by: Danny Strong
Cinematography by: Kramer Morgenthau
Music by: Bear McCreary
Sound: Robert Hein
Music Supervisor: Jonathan Watkins
Editing: Joseph Krings
Art Direction: Maki Takenouchi
Costumes: Deborah Lynn Scott
Production Design: Dina Goldman
MPAA rating: PG-13
Running time: 106 minutes

REVIEWS

Burr, Ty. *Boston Globe*. September 14, 2017.
D'Angelo, Mike. *The A.V. Club*. September 5, 2017.
Dujsik, Mark. *Mark Reviews Movies*. September 14, 2017.
Erbland, Kate. *IndieWire*. January 26, 2017.
Hassannia, Tina. *National Post*. October 4, 2017.
Lodge, Guy. *Variety*. January 25, 2017.
Lund, Carson. *Slant Magazine*. September 5, 2017.
Oller, Jacob. *Paste Magazine*. September 15, 2017.
Ruimy, Jordan. *The Film Stage*. January 26, 2017.
Sims, David. *The Atlantic*. September 7, 2017.

TRIVIA

Actor Nicholas Hoult wore brown contact lenses for this role.

RESIDENT EVIL: THE FINAL CHAPTER

The beginning of the end.
—Movie tagline
Back to the Hive.
—Movie tagline
The end of all the destruction.
—Movie tagline
Evil comes home.
—Movie tagline
Evil will end.
—Movie tagline
*My name is Alice. This is the end of my story_*
—Movie tagline
It ends where it began.
—Movie tagline
Everything has led to this.
—Movie tagline
Fight to survive.
—Movie tagline
Finish the fight.
—Movie tagline
The journey ends.
—Movie tagline

Box Office: $26.8 Million

While many cinematic adaptations of video games are aimed at children, there has been a slow and steady flow of more adult-oriented game adaptations, especially of late. The films *Assassin's Creed* (2016), *Hitman: Agent 47* (2015), and *Warcraft* (2016) were all adapted from popular video games and all skewed towards more mature audiences yet flopped mightily at the box office. While the most obvious issue with these films is that they were just not very good, it's also incredibly tricky to take viewers who are in full control of the characters in the games they play and translate this personalized form of storytelling to the more singular vision of a film. Such is the issue with *Resident Evil: The Final Chapter*. Many times, the film gives the same feeling one gets watching someone else play a video game.

Since 2002, the *Resident Evil* movies have steadily rolled out about every a 2-5 years producing a total of six films in the small but mighty franchise. These films have dovetailed nicely with the zombie craze which appears to finally be fading from the pop culture skyline, yet they also have grown in popularity over the past fifteen years with each film earning a little more than its predecessor. However, if one is coming in late to the franchise or has very little idea what these films are about, *Resident Evil: The Final Chapter* is unable to stand on its own, and the result becomes a jumbled mess, akin to being handed a controller and thrown into a high level of a video game without any idea of how to play.

As the film opens, we hear Alice (Milla Jovovich), the main character of both the films and games, in a voiceover telling viewers all about the dreaded "T-Virus," which, while created as a cure for a sick child, quickly went viral in a very bad way causing mass extinction on earth. Of course, Alice is one of very few "good guys" in this bleak future and most remaining humans are up to no good, particularly Dr. Alexander Isaacs (Iain Glen), who, as it turns out, is pretty much the puppet master behind everything that's besot Alice for the past five films. Soon viewers are along for the bumpy ride with Alice and her newfound compatriots to seek out Isaacs in a place called "The Hive," and from there, this final chapter will be written.

As soon as the expository voiceover ends, audiences are immediately thrust into an awful-looking dystopian future where zombies spring up out of nowhere and swarm en masse but are nothing compared to a variety of gloomy CGI monsters that may also inexplicably pop up at any moment. Guiding us through this wicked world is Alice, the much put-upon heroine of the *Resident Evil* games and movies. While Jovovich possesses a certain gritty toughness, she's also incredibly beautiful and hardly ever seems out of sorts as the world explodes with violence all around her. Since the title of the film is *Resident Evil: The Final Chapter*, some closure is also bound to be found along the way.

Make no mistake, *Resident Evil: The Final Chapter* is not a good film. It looks cheap and is so frenetically paced it's nearly impossible to understand what's going on. Cinephiles love to nitpick Michael Bay for his over-indulgence of quick cuts and edits, but here director Paul W.S. Anderson gives Bay a run for his money. There are cuts within cuts in this film, and the only purpose they seem to serve is to keep a shabby story moving forwards toward a fairly predictable climax. The only really interesting question here is just how Alice became an expert in such a variety of skills such as parkour, gymnastics, hand-to-hand combat, and motorcycle stunt driving. Sure, she's been at the "surviving the apocalypse" game longer than most, but on-the-job training seems a bit dangerous when any number of creatures are trying to eat you alive. Still, fans of the *Resident Evil* franchise will not be dissuaded from seeing this film if they have been along for the ride throughout no matter how poorly made, silly, predictable, and boring this final installment reveals itself to be by the time the credits roll.

Don R. Lewis

CREDITS

Alice/Alicia Marcus: Milla Jovovich
Claire Redfield: Ali Larter
Dr. Isaacs: Iain Glen
Wesker: Shawn Roberts
Christian: William Levy
Origin: Australia, United States, Germany, France, United Kingdom, Japan, Canada, South Africa
Language: English, French, Portuguese, Spanish, Malay, Korean, Mandarin Chinese, Indonesian, Yue Chinese, Vietnamese, Thai
Released: 2016
Production: Jeremy Bolt, Samuel Hadida, Robert Kulzer, Paul W.S. Anderson; Constantin Film International, Davis Films, Impact Pictures; released by Screen Gems
Directed by: Paul W.S. Anderson
Written by: Paul W.S. Anderson
Cinematography by: Glen MacPherson
Music by: Paul Haslinger
Music Supervisor: Christoph Becker
Editing: Doobie White
Art Direction: Guy Potgieter
Costumes: Reza Levy
Production Design: Edward Thomas
MPAA rating: R
Running time: 106 minutes

REVIEWS

Adams, Thelma. *New York Observer*. January 28, 2017.
Collis, Clark. *Entertainment Weekly*. January 28, 2017.
Donato, Matt. *We Got This Covered*. January 28, 2017.
Kupecki, Josh. *Austin Chronicle*. February 1, 2017.
Leydon, Joe. *Variety*. January 27, 2017.
Moore, Roger. *Movie Nation*. January 27, 2017.
Myers, Kimber. *Los Angeles Times*. January 27, 2017.
Nordine, Michael. *TheWrap*. January 27, 2017.
Vestby, Ethan. *The Film Stage*. January 27, 2017.
Zwecker, Bill. *Chicago Sun-Times*. January 26, 2017.

QUOTES

Alice: "Sometimes I feel like this has been my whole life. Running. Killing."

TRIVIA

During production, stunt woman Olivia Jackson suffered a severe injury to her left arm after a motorcycle crash which ultimately resulted in arm being amputated.

RINGS

First you watch it. Then you die.
—Movie tagline

Box Office: $27.8 Million

Director Gore Verbinski did not have a particularly good year in 2017, at least not in the first half of the year. Not only did his directorial effort, the surreal paranoia thriller *A Cure for Wellness,* quickly disappear from theater screens after only a couple weeks, but one of his more successful films had its brand tarnished. Verbinski directed an Americanized remake of a Japanese horror film, *The Ring* (2002), and it ended up becoming one of the genre's most popular films at that time. It influenced many copycat films in the wake of its success, but it also spawned an unnecessary sequel and, in 2017, another one came out and did more harm to the original's reputation. Verbinski's film had been imitated and even parodied so many times since its release that another sequel just seemed like a lazy choice for a studio that needed a brand—not a film, but a brand, any brand—to safely fill out its release slate.

This is the first in the series since *The Ring Two* (2005), so naturally, the writers here feel the need to bring the audience back up to speed on the concept of the original. *Rings* opens with a hapless soul on an airplane who talks to a stranger sitting next to him about a video he watched that will kill anyone who watches it. Within minutes, the plane crashes, but not before hundreds of flies start swarming the area and the creepy girl born from black ooze manifests. Two years later, a college professor named Burke (Vincent D'Onofrio) buys a VHS player at a corner flea market, which contains the cassette that says "watch me." Of course he watches the video and then gets a phone call with a voice saying "seven days."

Cut to an impossibly good-looking teenage, suburban couple starting a new life. Holt (Alex Roe) is going to college. Julia (Matilda Lutz) is staying with her mother. Of course, Holt is going to the college where Burke teaches. Meanwhile, back home, Julia has nightmares about Holt killing her. They have been Skyping with each other since the move, but Julia stops hearing from Holt until one day, another student, Skye (Aimee Teegarden), is seen in Holt's room. She tells Julia that "she is coming and there is no escape." Julia decides to come out to the college and investigate further into Holt's whereabouts. She learns more about this mysterious tape as she digs deeper while conveniently overhearing many important conversations about where the tape came from, who made it and what should be done with it should it be watched.

Again, the audience needs reminding that when someone watches the tape, the viewer has seven days to make a copy of it and show it to someone else or die a horrible death. In this day and age, of course, VCRs are not in high supply, so Burke, rather stupidly, has the video digitized so he can study it. That has ramifications as well for any computer that has the file on it. Julia eventually finds Holt and they begin their own investigation as to where this video came from. Perhaps by destroying the source, they can end this whole ordeal. In an effort to save Holt, who has seen the video, Julia watches it and makes herself the next victim. They drive out to Sacramento Valley where the tape originated and where the girl in the tape was born.

The second half of the film finds these two going on a search for clues about the origin of the video and of course everybody in the town knows exactly what they are looking for and everyone knows what clues to give them and when to give them. It is all very arbitrary and lazy. The audience, instead of feeling any tension or fear, will be wondering to themselves how it is that nobody has investigated any of this until now, including the professor who appears to have files upon files of research notes and materials already. One of the townspeople says to Julia and Holt, "There's nothing about the girl that is worth being curious about." He is right. Eventually, of course, one of these townspeople becomes a MacGuffin that reveals itself later on, which will come as no surprise to anyone. Perhaps not surprisingly, the characters here are more props than fully-realized characters. They exist to advance the plot but never to interact with each other in any meaningful way or give the audience a reason to care about them.

Director F. Javier Gutiérrez tries to bring some kind of flair to the directing, but he mainly likes to go in for close-ups of items like hands and windshield wipers. That becomes about the only noticeable thing about his style. The cast fares no better as they look to be a collection of pretty faces straight out of a fashion magazine. The scares are set up and delivered in such a pedestrian way, there must be a checklist of shots out there somewhere that every director has to take with them for every shoot for a film such as this. The jump-scare that is just a cat, the creepy girl's head cracking sideways, the coughing up of black goo are just some of the items that must appear on that list. Throughout its running time, *Rings* just has an obligatory feel to it, a means to achieve a series of films that they can call a trilogy, when really it should have just been one film that was an effective remake of another film.

Collin Souter

CREDITS

Julia: Matilda Anna Ingrid Lutz

Holt: Alex Roe

Gabriel: Johnny Galecki

Burke: Vincent D'Onofrio

Skye: Aimee Teegarden

Origin: United States

Language: English

Released: 2017

Production: Laurie MacDonald, Walter F. Parkes; Macari/Edelstein, Parkes+MacDonald Image Nation, Vertigo Entertainment, Waddieish Claretrap; released by Paramount Pictures Corp.

Directed by: F. Javier Gutierrez

Written by: David Loucka; Jacob Aaron Estes; Akiva Goldsman

Cinematography by: Sharone Meir

Music by: Matthew Margeson

Sound: P.K. Hooker

Music Supervisor: Andrew Silver

Editing: Steve Mirkovich; Jeremiah O'Driscoll

Art Direction: Naaman Marshall

Costumes: Christopher Peterson

Production Design: Kevin Kavanaugh

MPAA rating: PG-13

Running time: 102 minutes

REVIEWS

Adams, Thelma. *New York Observer.* February 3, 2017.
Cruz, Lenika. *The Atlantic.* February 3, 2017.
Dowd, A.A. *The A.V. Club.* February 3, 2017.
Genzlinger, Neil. *New York Times.* February 3, 2017.
Howell, Peter. *Toronto Star.* February 3, 2017.
Robinson, Tasha. *The Verge.* February 3, 2017.
Slotek, Jim. *Toronto Sun.* February 3, 2017.
Tobias, Scott. *NPR.* February 3, 2017.
VanDenburgh, Barbara. *Arizona Republic.* February 3, 2017.
Wolfe, April. *L.A. Weekly.* February 28, 2017.

QUOTES

Burke: "You're here about the girl, the girl in the well."

TRIVIA

Before starring as Samara in this film, Bonnie Morgan was also featured in *The Ring Two* (2005) as Samara in the well-crawling sequence, though she was uncredited.

ROCK DOG

Chase your dreams. Watch your tail.
—Movie tagline

Box Office: $9.4 Million

The central story of *Rock Dog*, which is about an anthropomorphic Tibetan Mastiff who leaves his home in the mountains to pursue a career as a musician, is much better than it could have been, although its success has little to do with the dog at the center of that story. The shortcomings of the movie are mostly story-based, and they can be whittled down to a lack of faith in the story of the dog and his knotty relationship with a rock star, who happens to be a cat. There are multiple story threads here, and the others come across as material that has been created by a committee. (The end credits note nine people involved in the writing process, which provides some evidence as to that suspicion).

There is a fairly sturdy plot in the dog's quest to seek out the guidance of the cat, complete with its own trials and an antagonist who also happens to be the character whose help the hero is seeking. That dichotomy—between the student and the mentor, as well as within the rock-star cat himself—is far more involving than a generic subplot with a stock villain that becomes the foundation of the movie's third act. In that subplot, a pack of wolves is plotting to invade the dog's sanctuary home in order to capture and eat the sheep that Bodi (voice of Luke Wilson), the eponymous musically-inclined dog, has left in order to work on achieving his dreams.

The thinking behind this subplot seems to be that the computer-animated movie's target audience—kids, naturally—require clear-cut villains and a frantic, action-oriented climax to maintain their attention. This belief is a bit cynical, especially coming from a movie that, until the finale, mostly has promoted themes that are more aspirational and a view on music that suggests its capacity to dissuade or, at least, ease conflict. Here, music is both a means of completing oneself and of uniting others. That is the movie's philosophy until the climax of the story, at least, at which point music essentially becomes a weapon.

Bodi has lived in Snow Mountain for his entire life, growing up to learn about the dangers of wolves that have invaded this sanctuary for sheep and, one day, very well might invade again (the voice of Sam Elliott, playing a character named—to the groans of the adults in the audience—Fleetwood Yak, provides the narration of the back story). His father Khampa (voice of J.K. Simmons) banned loud noises, including the music that the sheep once loved, lest the sheep draw the wolves' attention (propaganda-style posters littered throughout the village warn of this looming threat).

Khampa wants his son to take over his position as the head guardian of the wolves one day, honing some kind of innate magic that the mastiff breed has mastered through the ages. Speaking of committee-based story points, the entire notion that the hero has magical abilities for no particular reason is near the top of that list.

One day, a passing plane drops a radio in the mountains, and upon finding it, Bodi discovers the appeal of rock-and-roll (a dreamy scene of him dancing to the first song he hears, with multi-colored streams of light punctuating his movements, effectively translates that feeling of revelation). He leaves for the city to seek the guidance of Angus Scattergood (voice of Eddie Izzard), a legend of rock. Meanwhile, Linnux (voice of Lewis Black), the leader of the wolf pack, sends a pair of henchmen (one is voiced by Kenan Thompson, and the other is silent) to follow Bodi, believing that capturing him will help in his plan to overtake the sanctuary.

Despite the title and the story's focus on Bodi (as well as Wilson's amiable vocal work), the real star of the movie is Izzard's work as the egotistical, deadline-pressured Angus. The mold of the character is nothing new, yet Izzard, adopting a semi-Cockney dialect and performing with an expertly toned sense of deadpan, provides the story with its one, key element of the unexpected. The screenplay, written by director Ash Brannon and Kurt Voelker (based on a graphic novel by Zheng Jun), clearly has an equal appreciation for the character and his apathetic-from-fame quirks. Secluded in a vast mansion (Angus' bed is about a hundred times too big for his slight body, and the grounds are protected by an electric fence and a hedge maze patrolled by larger version of mechanized cat toys), Angus stews over a bad case of writer's block, convinced of his greatness but unable to fulfill the minimum requirement to prove it.

That story eventually involves a case of plagiarism, which, apparently, is not enough in terms of conflict. Hence, the movie piles on unnecessary characters, such as Darma (voice of Mae Whitman), a bass-playing fox, and Germur (voice of Jorge Garcia), a drumming goat who is as much of a stoner as a kid's movie will allow, as fairly useless sidekicks. While there is some amusing material involving Linnux's henchmen (their traps to ensnare Bodi repeatedly backfire), those jokes are in service of a subplot that ultimately derails the movie's thematic and comic aims (it also forces Angus into the role of yet another inconsequential sidekick).

The relationship between Bodi and Angus, which leads to a spirited montage of them writing a song together, works, as does the movie's broadly satirical stab at the egocentric personality of a rock star lulled into complacency. *Rock Dog*, though, is too eager to match what it seems to believe is a set quota of kid-friendly material to go along with these elements.

Mark Dujsik

CREDITS

Khampa: J.K. Simmons
Bodi: Luke Wilson
Angus: Eddie Izzard
Linnux: Lewis Black
Riff: Kenan Thompson
Origin: United States
Language: English
Released: 2017
Production: Rob Feng, Joyce Lou, David B. Miller, Amber Wang; Dream Factory Group, Eracme Entertainment, Huayi Tencent Entertainment Company Ltd., Mandoo Pictures; released by Summit Premiere
Directed by: Ash Brannon
Written by: Ash Brannon
Music by: Rolfe Kent
Sound: Steven Ticknor
Music Supervisor: Liza Richardson
Editing: Ivan Bilancio; Ed Fuller
Art Direction: Christian Schellewald
Production Design: Elad Tibi
MPAA rating: PG
Running time: 90 minutes

REVIEWS

Abele, Robert. *TheWrap*. February 23, 2017.
Genzlinger, Neil. *New York Times*. February 23, 2017.
Hartlaub, Peter. *San Francisco Chronicle*. February 23, 2017.
Horwitz, Jane. *Washington Post*. February 23, 2017.
Kenny, Glenn. *RogerEbert.com*. February 24, 2017.
Rechtshaffen, Michael. *Hollywood Reporter*. February 24, 2017.
Russo, Tom. *Boston Globe*. February 23, 2017.
Thrower, Emma. *Empire*. June 7, 2017.
Vishnevetsky, Ignatiy. *The A.V. Club*. February 24, 2017.
Walsh, Katie. *Los Angeles Times*. February 23, 2017.

QUOTES

Angus Scattergood [lying on his back after being electrified by a fence, slammed into a sheet of glass, and flopping down on the road]: "I am completely paralyzed except for my mouth." [Then moves his arm and index finger.] "I am completely paralyzed except for my mouth...and my finger!"

TRIVIA

This is the second animated film where Eddie Izzard co-stars with a Wilson brother, the first being *Cars 2* where Izzard played Miles Axlerod and Owen Wilson played Lightning McQueen.

ROMAN J. ISRAEL, ESQ.

All rise.
—Movie tagline

Box Office: $11.9 Million

If one was to make a list of the most charismatic actors working today, it would be hard to imagine any iteration in which Denzel Washington was not in a place of high prominence. From the earliest days of his career, his searing magnetism, working in conjunction with his superlative skills as an actor, has made him into one of the most electrifying performers of his time. In *Roman J. Israel, Esq.*, Washington has been given one of the biggest challenges of his career—dial down the charisma factor to practically zero and play a character that most people will be find to be genuinely off-putting throughout. Because Washington is a supremely talented actor, he actually manages to pull off this considerable feat but is let down by a confused and meandering screenplay that does not really seem to know what to do with his efforts.

Washington plays the title character, a savant-like criminal defense attorney who has managed to maintain his 1970s-style idealism (along with his wardrobe and hairstyle) while working at a small law firm in Los Angeles. Because his brusque and oddball demeanor would put off any jury in an instant, it is his partner who does the actual work in court while he toils away behind the scenes to craft the defense strategies. His carefully calibrated world is shattered one day when his partner suffers a fatal heart attack and his family decides to close down the money-losing firm with the help of George Pierce (Colin Farrell), a former student of his partner who has become a slick, high-priced lawyer at one of the city's top firms. Recognizing Roman's unique gifts and imagining how much money his firm can derive from his work, George offers Roman a job. Roman refuses, more or less on principle, but then discovers that idealistic lawyers of a certain age without much in the way of people skills are not the hottest commodity on the job market. Even a local non-profit dedicated to social change is not interested in hiring him, and when the leader of the group (Carmen Ejogo) has Roman speak to the group about what to do when arrested while protesting, even they reject Roman and his old-school attitude for being insufficiently woke.

With nowhere else to go, Roman joins George's firm and begins toiling away, desperate to find a case to which he can apply his firebrand approach. He thinks he has one when he is assigned to look into the case of a young man (Niles Fitch) who is being charged with the murder of a convenience store clerk even though it was a still-at-large acquaintance who actually pulled the trigger. When Roman takes it upon himself to deal with the district attorney regarding a plea, he blows the talks for good and is nearly fired as a result. Assuming that he will be let go when his contract runs out, Roman decides to take matters into his own hand and, using the information that he gleaned from his client, hands over the ID of the real killer to the relatives of the victim in exchange for the $100,000 reward they are offering—a move that, while not technically illegal, is a deeply questionable move to make. With that money, he immediately remakes virtually every aspect of his life—he gets slick suits and a swank apartment and when he takes the social worker out for dinner, he eschews his usual peanut butter for four-star cuisine. Alas, the situation with the reward money comes back to haunt him in unexpected ways and forces Roman to have a confrontation between the person he has been and the one that he has quickly become.

In broad terms, *Roman J. Israel, Esq.* is a legal drama, but it is one that does not rely on wild courtroom confrontations in order to get its points across—there are only a couple of scenes that even enter a courtroom and they are as brief and anti-climactic as can be. This is an intriguing conceit on the part of writer-director Dan Gilroy, whose previous film was *Nightcrawler,* (2014) and the early scenes introducing Roman and his unique behavior are fairly promising. However, while it does not fit the parameters of a typical courtroom drama, it does not really replace those tropes with much of anything. Roman has the potential to be an interesting character, but the film doesn't really do much of anything with him. His grand moral and ethical shifts in character happen so quickly in both directions that it almost feels like parody, as if Gilroy were trying to do a legal variation of *Flowers for Algernon.* There are some interesting developments involving the side characters, especially regarding George and his own personal and professional evolution, but they never get a chance to go anywhere. Reportedly, Gilroy trimmed about 12 minutes from the film and restructured other parts in the immediate wake of its debut at the Toronto Film Festival, but the narrative flaws in the film are so pronounced that nothing short of a complete rewrite could have properly addressed them.

Washington is excellent in the way that he is able to successfully tamp down his innate charm and charisma to play someone who is almost completely lacking in the most basic social graces. From a technical perspective, his work is spot-on, but when it comes to making him a character worth basing an entire movie around, it comes up short. The trouble is that the script never gives viewers a chance to really know who Roman is or what really makes him tick—admittedly, part of this is because of the unique nature of the character he is playing, but part of it is due to the fact that he, when all is said and done, is more of a caricature than an actual three-dimensional character. The funny thing is that while Washington is doing all of his overt acting, Farrell manages to quietly and confidently steal every single scene that he appears in. When his character first appears, both the arc of the character and Farrell's approach to the part seem preordained and then we spend the rest of the film being pleasantly surprised on both counts. Although Farrell's role is clearly a supporting part, it proves to be engrossing enough to throw the entire film out of balance in the way that his character overshadows the putative center of the story.

Because *Roman J. Israel, Esq.* is an example of a style of filmmaking that has become increasingly rare these days—a mid-budget film aimed almost exclusively at an older audience—there is the temptation to cut it some slack regarding its failures. That said, the combination of a less-than-inspiring screenplay and a central character who plays more like a collection of tics than a believable person just ultimately does not work. It is not a total failure by any means but, unlike its title character, it proves itself to be far too willing to settle and move on instead of trying to do something riskier and potentially more rewarding.

Peter Sobczynski

CREDITS

Roman J. Israel, Esq.: Denzel Washington
George Pierce: Colin Farrell
Maya Alston: Carmen Ejogo
Vernita Wells: Lynda Gravatt
Lynn Jackson: Amanda Warren
Origin: United States
Language: English
Released: 2017
Production: Todd Black, Jennifer Fox, Denzel Washington; Bron Studios, Creative Wealth Media Finance, Cross Creek Pictures, Culture China-Image Nation Abu Dhabi Fund, Escape Artists, Imagination Abu Dhabi FZ, LStar Capital, MACRO, Topic; released by Columbia Pictures
Directed by: Dan Gilroy
Written by: Dan Gilroy
Cinematography by: Robert Elswit
Music by: James Newton Howard
Sound: Margit Pfeiffer
Editing: John Gilroy
Art Direction: Robert W. Joseph
Costumes: Francine Jamison-Tanchuck
Production Design: Kevin Kavanaugh
MPAA rating: PG-13
Running time: 122 minutes

REVIEWS

Crump, Andy. *Paste Magazine.* November 27, 2017.
Felperin, Leslie. *Hollywood Reporter.* September 11, 2017.
Gleiberman, Owen. *Variety.* September 11, 2017.
Hornaday, Ann. *Washington Post.* November 22, 2017.
Kenigsberg, Ben. *New York Times.* September 16, 2017.
Kohn, Eric. *IndieWire.* September 12, 2017.
Morgenstern, Joe. *Wall Street Journal.* November 16, 2017.
Scherstuhl, Alan. *Village Voice.* November 14, 2017.
Sragow, Michael. *Film Comment.* November 10, 2017.
Turan, Kenneth. *Los Angeles Times.* November 16, 2017.

TRIVIA

In this film, there is a visible gap between actor Denzel Washington's two front teeth that he hasn't sported since high school. The actor had the gap fixed after high school, but removed his dental caps for this role.

AWARDS

Nominations:

Oscars 2017: Actor (Washington)
Golden Globes 2018: Actor--Drama (Washington)
Screen Actors Guild 2017: Actor (Washington)

ROUGH NIGHT

Great friends. Terrible choices.
—Movie tagline

The best nights never go as planned.
—Movie tagline

The hangover will be the least of their problems.
—Movie tagline

Box Office: $22.1 Million

For decades, many in the entertainment industry have been of the mindset that women and comedy simply don't mix. Like many notions to come out of the entertainment industry, this was a profoundly stupid one. Nevertheless, it was one that persisted for a long time. Happily, the recent success of the Amy Schumer project *Trainwreck* (2015) seemed to indicate to Hollywood that not only could a thing such as a broad, bawdy female-centric comedy actually exist, it could also be a huge box-office hit that might inspire other such films to tap into a criminally underserved market that craves something more than the occasional *Sex and the City* spinoff. With its combination of female bonding and outrageous raunch, *Rough Night* is clearly hoping to score with that audience but fails so spectacularly—it is closer to an actual trainwreck than it is to *Trainwreck* the film—that it could set the causes of both feminism and comedy from a women's perspective back decades.

The film centers on four close friends and party animals from college who reunite for a bachelorette weekend in Miami. The bride-to-be is Jess (Scarlett Johansson), who is juggling both her impending nuptials to a fiancée (Paul. W. Downs) who is even more straitlaced than she is and a struggling campaign for state senate against a sexist pig competitor. The ringleader for the festivities is Alice (Jillian Bell), who proclaimed herself Jess's best friend back in school and is still determined to cling to that self-appointed designation. Blair (Zoë Kravitz) and Frankie (Ilana Glazer) were lovers back in the day but have since gone their separate ways—the former got married to a rich husband that she is in the process of divorcing while the latter is a rabble-rousing activist fighting all the injustices of the world. After settling down at the lavish glass-enclosed house where they will be staying, the four go out for the evening and are soon joined by a fifth person—Australian Pippa (Kate McKinnon), who became friends with Jess when she came to her country to study for a semester and who the jealous Alice sees as a threat to her position as best friend.

The evening soon turns into an orgy of booze, pot, and coke. And when they finally get back to the house, the others decide to hire a stripper for Jess. Alas, the rambunctious Alice causes an accident that leaves the stripper dead and they all wind up implicating themselves by trying to move the body away from all of the windows. Not wanting to go to prison, they decide that the best thing to do is to dump the body and be rid of it. This proves to be more difficult than anticipated thanks to the occasional intrusions of the horny next-door neighbors (Ty Burrell and Demi Moore) and the surprisingly resilient corpse. Meanwhile, having received a brief and garbled call from Jess suggesting that their engagement was off, her fiancée decides to fight for their relationship by arming himself with cases of Red Bull and adult diapers and driving all night to Miami to win her back.

Considering the level of talent on both sides of the camera—the film was directed and co-written by Lucia Aniello, who has directed numerous episodes of the acclaimed cable comedy series *Broad City*, which also features Glazer and Downs, the latter of whom also co-wrote *Rough Night*—one might have naturally expected a film that was, if not a groundbreaker along the lines of *Trainwreck* or *Broad City*, at least something that offered viewers a healthy amount of raunch as seen from a feminine perspective. Instead, the film is little more than a ripoff of the largely forgotten and deeply unpleasant dark comedy *Very Bad Things* (1998) that takes that film's basic premise—a rowdy bash for a bunch of friends celebrating the impending nuptials of one of them goes awry when they accidentally kill a stripper and try to cover up their crime—and removes the rampant and sneering misanthropy that marked the earlier movie. That may make *Rough Night* slightly more palatable to watch—you will not feel the need to take a *Silkwood*-style shower after it—but it fails to replace the nastiness with much of anything. Instead, the film is content to come across as little more than an extended *I Love Lucy* episode, albeit one with more cocaine, vibrators, and threesomes than usual, in which all the characters act as if their brains were replaced with bacon bits. Mind you, the idea of watching people trying to dispose of a body that they may have killed is not necessarily a bad idea for a comedy—Alfred Hitchcock took that concept and made it into one of his drollest movies with *The Trouble with Harry* (1955). Of course, that movie was filled with the kind of sly and subtle wit that could not be further from the increasingly obnoxious wackiness on display here. The end result feels more like the kind of thing that one could see being savaged mercilessly on *Broad City* than the product of some of the actual minds behind the show.

Although usually thought of as a more dramatic performer, Johansson has shown a flair for comedy in her numerous appearances on *Saturday Night Live* (*SNL*) but is mostly stuck in the straight woman part that offers her little to do except to constantly fret. As for Bell, she is supposed to play the clinging and overbearing friend with no life of her own but overdoes it so much that one starts involuntarily flinching whenever she appears on screen. Grazer and Kravitz wind up getting kind of lost amidst all the frenzy—they do generate a weird kind of chemistry as the former lovers reuniting and struggling to overlook the obvious spark that is still between them but the film has no idea of what to do with it. Even the great Kate McKinnon, who has single-handedly saved more than a few otherwise errant *SNL* sketches with the full force of her personality and comedic chops, is unable to come up with much for her character besides giving her the broadest Australian accent imaginable, one so broad, in fact, that you keep waiting for her to be exposed as a fraud who is pretending to be from Down Under just to impress Jess.

Rough Night is a bad movie but, more than that, it is just a waste. It is a waste of a premise that might have been transformed into a good and funny film. It is a waste of a cast that one might think would be incapable of delivering zero laughs but who are constantly stymied by weak material. It is a waste of a creative team that can seemingly do no wrong within the confines of a 30-minute cable show but which are all thumbs at presenting a feature-length narrative. It is a waste of time for anyone who assumed that this combination of talent could not possibly fail, only to find out that they certainly could. Worst of all, it is a waste of the potential for female-driven comedies that was sparked by *Trainwreck* that might have proved to be devastating if it was not for the arrival of *Girls Trip* (2017), another raunch fest that did manage to connect with critics and audiences alike in a way that *Rough Night* never manages to do.

Peter Sobczynski

CREDITS

Jess: Scarlett Johansson

Alice: Jillian Bell

Blair: Zoë Kravitz

Frankie: Ilana Glazer

Pippa: Kate McKinnon

Origin: United States

Language: English

Released: 2017

Production: Dave Becky, Matthew Tolmach, Lucia Aniello, Paul W. Downs; Paulilu Productions, Sony Pictures Entertainment Inc.; released by Columbia Pictures

Directed by: Lucia Aniello

Written by: Lucia Aniello; Paul W. Downs

Cinematography by: Sean Porter

Music by: Dominic Lewis

Sound: Kami Asgar

Editing: Craig Alpert

Art Direction: Ryan Heck

Costumes: Leah Katznelson
MPAA rating: R
Running time: 101 minutes

REVIEWS

Chang, Justin. *Los Angeles Times.* June 15, 2017.
Dargis, Manohla. *New York Times.* June 15, 2017.
Fujishima, Kenji. *Slant Magazine.* June 14, 2017.
Gleiberman, Owen. *Variety.* June 14, 2017.
Rooney, David. *Hollywood Reporter.* June 14, 2017.
Scherstuhl, Alan. *Village Voice.* June 14, 2017.
Stewart, Sara. *New York Post.* June 15, 2017.
Truitt, Brian. *USA Today.* June 14, 2017.
Yoshida, Emily. *New York Magazine/Vulture.* June 14, 2017.
Zacharek, Stephanie. *Time.* June 15, 2017.

QUOTES

Kiwi: "I have Australian dollars. They're stronger than US dollars."

TRIVIA

The film was originally entitled *Rock That Body,* before being renamed.

S

SAME KIND OF DIFFERENT AS ME

Box Office: $6.4 Million

A family drama with all the vim and distinction of an underhand, slow-toss softball game, *Same Kind of Different as Me* is a cloyingly sentimental, fuzzy and meandering cinematic exercise in feel-good affirmation. Based on a best-selling nonfiction book and a moderately interesting true story re-wrapped in so many bland, overlapping swatches of paper that it robs itself of anything interesting and distinguishing, the movie sacrifices nuance in favor of overly simplified conflict resolution and overt Christian proselytizing.

After acquiring it from Paramount Pictures, upstart faith-based distributor Pure Flix Entertainment released *Same Kind of Different as Me* on over 1,350 screens on October 20, 2017 where it slotted twelfth for its opening weekend, pulling in just under $2.6 million and finishing its domestic theatrical run with $6.4 million—far less than the somewhat similarly religiously-themed commercial breakout *Heaven Is for Real* (2014), which also starred Greg Kinnear, and grossed over $91 million.

Same Kind of Different as Me centers on Debbie and Ron Hall (Renée Zellweger and Kinnear), a wealthy Texas couple who have been married nearly two decades. After Debbie, who is still nursing wounds from an extramarital liaison confessed by her husband, has a dream in which she meets a wise man on a road who changes her life, she invites Ron to join her in volunteering at the inner-city homeless shelter. Ron, an international art dealer, would rather write a check than donate his time, but eventually relents.

There, dishing out lunches to the less fortunate, the pair befriend an ex-convict and itinerant farmer who calls himself Suicide (Djimon Hounsou), but is actually named Denver Moore. The victim of some terrible violence growing up, Denver is prone to violent acting out—the result of both mental illness and a marked distrust in humankind. Over time, however, he comes to accept Debbie and Ron's repeated offers of friendship, and helps to heal the divide not only between the two of them, but also between Ron and his alcoholic, socially retrograde father (Jon Voight).

With its white-savior approach to racism and prejudice, in which bigotry is called out by saintly, properly spiritual white people, *Same Kind of Different as Me* checks more than a couple boxes of older Caucasian demographic preference for storytelling featuring a minority character. The result is a movie that could slot comfortably alongside *The Legend of Bagger Vance* (2000) or *The Blind Side* (2009) on the cable channel of many a lily-white retirement home community room television.

Same Kind of Different as Me works best when it shunts its grander sociopolitical subtexts to the side, and simply lets its actors connect and play the scene. Second perhaps only to Steve Carell amongst his peers, Kinnear can channel the crinkly-eyed, sympathetic, and slightly wistful vibe of a sensitive guy who is self-aware of his shortcomings—all of which he pulls off with aplomb here in scenes after Ron is laid low. Zellweger, who returned to the big screen after a six-year absence with a big, $212 million-grossing hit in the form of *Bridget Jones's Baby* (2016), seems much more comfortable and relaxed here than in that puffed-up exercise in goading comedy. As a pair, Kinnear and Zellweger fit together, and are fun to watch.

Unfortunately, the film gives them too little of originality to do. The screenplay, written by the real-life Hall, in tandem with Alexander Foard and director Michael Carney, suffers from trite dialogue throughout. At just under two hours long, it drags unmercilessly—and is additionally done no favors by clunky staging that highlights meager production values. There is also a wrongheaded, overly indulgent framing device which shows Ron trying to write the very book on which the film is based.

Most problematically, however, the film fails to fully invest in Denver and Ron as equal narrators of, or even characters in, this story. Copious flashbacks to his younger years provide Hounsou the opportunity for a showcase reel's worth of solemn, world-weary voiceover narration. And he nails a number of these scenes, summoning an arresting grace and swallowed pain. But these moments are posed and artificial—long monologues, one literally delivered from a bully pulpit—and in that regard they come across not only as dramatically awkward, but they also slightly smack of condescension and fetishism.

Multi-ethnic friendships and indeed simply bearing witness to the stories of others not like us are both a wonderful thing, and can be used in real life as instruments of teaching—enabling practitioners to reach across divides and demonstrate to other loved ones the value of diversity. But in the two-dimensional *Same Kind of Different as Me*, it is a carbon copy of a carbon copy of a carbon copy of a story told before. Watching it, one yawns, and then quickly yearns for a different story.

Brent Simon

CREDITS

Ron Hall: Greg Kinnear
Deborah Hall: Renee Zellweger
Denver: Djimon Hounsou
Jon Voight
Regan Hall: Olivia Holt
Origin: United States
Language: English
Released: 2017
Production: Cale Boyter, Stephen D. Johnston, Darren Moorman, Mary Parent, Ron Hall; Disruption Entertainment, One October Films, Reserve Entertainment, Skodam Films; released by Paramount Pictures Corp.
Directed by: Michael Carney
Written by: Michael Carney; Alexander Foard; Ron Hall
Cinematography by: Don Burgess
Music by: John Paesano
Sound: Craig Mann
Editing: Eric A. Sears
Costumes: Alonzo Wilson
Production Design: William O. Hunter
MPAA rating: PG-13
Running time: 119 minutes

REVIEWS

Allen, Nick. *RogerEbert.com*. October 20, 2017.
Duncan, Ryan. *Crosswalk*. October 19, 2017.
Ives, David. *Aleteia*. October 20, 2017.
Kozlowski, Carl. *Pasadena Weekly*. October 19, 2017.
Nicholson, Amy. *Variety*. October 20, 2017.
Reed, Rex. *New York Observer*. October 23, 2017.
Uhlich, Keith. *Hollywood Reporter*. October 20, 2017.
Walsh, Katie. *Los Angeles Times*. October 20, 2017.
White, Dave. *TheWrap*. October 20, 2017.
Zwecker, Bill. *Chicago Sun-Times*. October 20, 2017.

QUOTES

Denver: "Whether we're rich or poor, or somewhere in between, we're all homeless, just working our way back home."

TRIVIA

Filmed in Canton, Mississippi, which the same place where *A Time To Kill* (1996) was filmed.

THE SENSE OF AN ENDING

Unravel the truth.
—Movie tagline

Box Office: $1.3 Million

Just two years after *45 Years* (2015) comes another movie co-starring Charlotte Rampling about echoes of the past and the secrets that exist between couples and friends. Unfortunately, where that earlier film heartbreakingly recognized how the nature of these inequalities mean that bonds can be much more fragile than anyone realizes or prefers to admit, *The Sense of an Ending* gets lost in delayed gratification, obscuring the intricacies of what did and did not happen. In place of those details is the monotonous and ultimately obvious recognition that allowing old memories to linger stands in the way of a person moving forward.

Adapting Julian Barnes's novel, writer Nick Payne and director Ritesh Batra alternate between past and present, neither one generating particular suspense or interest in answers. Tony (Jim Broadbent) embarks on a muted mini-investigation when he receives a letter indicating that an old friend's diary is being passed along to him but then never arrives, for reasons he very gradually discovers. As he tells his ex-wife, Margaret (Harriet Walter), stories about his youth she has never heard before, the film depicts Tony (played as a younger man by Billy Howle) and his relationship with Veronica (Freya Mavor), which apparently did not contain an especially strong physical or emotional connection. It suggests that the mark she left on his life was more a result of the chaos she inspired, which a blunt opening voiceover acknowledges is a pursuit of youth that older age prefers to avoid. In the flashback sequences, Veronica says it feels wrong to have sex with Tony only to say it feels right when they are broken up. There are not a lot of memorable moments between them beforehand, outside of Tony clearly taking to Veronica's mother, Sarah (Emily Mortimer). With limited screen time, Mortimer explodes the movie into places it never returns, her expressions and mannerisms revealing a complicated, curious, disappointed person who is far more interesting than her daughter.

Unfortunately, *The Sense of an Ending* declines this degree of consciousness from Tony, whose exasperation comes through in Broadbent's ever-expressive eyes but otherwise registers as naïve and narrowly drawn. Batra, both romanticizing suicide and allowing scenes to drag despite clearly hoping to build mystery, seemingly would like Tony to represent a tragic figure whose absence of closure resulted in a closed-off life, drifting through days while vaguely connected to the times that made a greater impact. In theory, that should devastate; after all, everyone only has so long, and not being present is a great way to feel like that time flew by even faster.

Tony's relationships with Margaret and his pregnant daughter, Susie (Michelle Dockery), do not follow through on a life lived in such a vacuum. Margaret suggests that Tony has created a shrine to Veronica, who introduced Tony to his first camera, by running a camera shop, but she has little investment in this observation, and Tony is far too passive to identify as someone whose denial is so strong it has rendered him numb to his own needs and regrets. As information drips out and the significance of multiple handwritten letters becomes clear, *The Sense of an Ending* strives for something profound about the speed with which a person arrives at both death and orgasm, but it cannot seem to source the confusion or people searching through the error of their ways. "How were we to know that our lives had already begun?" Tony asks in that aforementioned opening, commenting on young people's tendency to look ahead without appreciating the moment at hand.

The Sense of an Ending sticks to headlines, though, in teasing out the ultimately harmful decisions that these characters make, without seeming to understand how things might have been different. The film suffers from the same glassy-eyed nostalgia as Tony, reflective without illuminating. Tony eventually wishes he did not send a nasty letter, but it remains unclear if he learned anything from one of the sentiments within, which is that Victoria seems to have manipulated him and treated him poorly. Based on a late message that he sends to the older Victoria (played by Rampling), he still fails to connect any of the decisions and lessons in a meaningful, consistent way.

This presumption of feeling without actual, valuable content is reinforced by flashbacks in the classroom. Certainly the analyses of students often contain generalities, but plenty of purpose can come from knowing why someone feels a certain way and seeing how that influences their lives. Yet when Tony's friend Adrian (Joe Alwyn) makes comments about how the only accurate thing anyone can say about history is that "something happened" or that people may never know the truth about a student who took his own life, it makes him seem infatuated with the sound of his own voice while not saying anything particularly interesting. Based on how things unfold, it also seems Adrian does not really engage with anything he has said or heard.

That would be a sobering message: The extent to which people young and old get lost in their romantic missteps and fail to absorb the pre-existing elements that might point them in the right direction. *The Sense of an Ending* is too stiff to provide that much power, refusing to tune into its own message about the danger of people telling themselves their own life stories too slowly. What is off-screen, especially regarding Sarah, is far more compelling than what is on it, resulting in the need to appreciate small moments like the way Tony, as played by the inimitable Broadbent, says, "Lesbians, pregnant lesbians."

Matt Pais

CREDITS

Tony Webster: Jim Broadbent

Veronica Ford: Charlotte Rampling

Margaret Webster: Harriet Walter

Susie Webster: Michelle Dockery

Mr. Hunt: Matthew Goode

Origin: United States

Language: English

Released: 2017

Production: Ed Rubin, David M. Thompson; BBC Films, FilmNation Entertainment, Origin Pictures; released by CBS Films Inc.

Directed by: Ritesh Batra

Written by: Nick Payne

Cinematography by: Christopher Ross

Music by: Max Richter

Music Supervisor: Sarah Bridge

Editing: John F. Lyons

Art Direction: Max Klaentschi

Costumes: Odile Dicks-Mireaux

Production Design: Jacqueline Abrahams

MPAA rating: PG-13

Running time: 108 minutes

REVIEWS

Chang, Justin. *Los Angeles Times*. March 9, 2017.

D'Angelo, Mike. *The A.V. Club*. March 9, 2017.

Greene, Ray. *TheWrap*. January 16, 2017.

Greene, Steve. *IndieWire*. March 9, 2017.

Kenny, Glenn. *New York Times*. March 9, 2017.

Lemire, Christy. *RogerEbert.com*. March 10, 2017.

Persall, Steve. *Tampa Bay Times*. March 15, 2017.

Semerene, Diego. *Slant Magazine*. March 8, 2017.

Smith, Neil. *Total Film*. April 10, 2017.

Wolfe, April. *Village Voice*. March 19, 2017.

QUOTES

Tony Webster: "The longer life goes on, the fewer are those around to tell us our life is not our life. It is just a story we've told about our lives. A story about our lives told to others, but mainly to ourselves."

TRIVIA

At a festival screening in San Francisco, director Ritesh Batra said that he had tea with Julian Barnes, author of *The Sense of an Ending*, prior to filming. Batra was so nervous that he subsequently forgot most of their conversation, save for Barnes's parting line, spoken in jest: "Go ahead and betray me."

78/52: HITCHCOCK'S SHOWER SCENE

(78/52)

Seventy-eight shots and fifty-two cuts that changed cinema forever.
—Movie tagline

Box Office: $37,664

"What he did with the shower scene changed the language of cinema," says director Mick Garris about an hour into the documentary *78/52: Hitchcock's Shower Scene*. So much of cinema history hinges on that iconic scene at close to the center of Alfred Hitchcock's masterpiece *Psycho* (1960). It is notorious for a dozen things it did differently than nearly any scene that had come before, including its use of music, editing, and the narrative purpose it served in the film, transitioning the point of view from Janet Leigh's on-the-run heroine to Anthony Perkins's stuck-at-home sociopath. It also, largely through the clever marketing of its director, changed the way people watch movies. Viewers used to spend the day at the cinema, coming and going as they pleased—think of the phrase "I think this is where I came in"—but *Psycho* changed that as Hitchcock demanded that no one be seated after the film began. It turned the film into an event, and most of that event hinged on a murder in the shower. What other single scene could possibly justify an entire documentary about it?

To be fair, the title is a little misleading. While the majority of *78/52*—the title refers to the number of camera set-ups and cuts (editorial, not with Norman's knife) that exist in the three-minute scene—focuses on the unforgettable scene, it is placed within the context of film and American history. In fact, *78/52* makes a (mostly) persuasive case that the shower scene in *Psycho* was the culmination of 1950s culture that had started to distrust the American dream and presaged the tumultuous era of the 1960s that would follow. The film makes the case that this was no mere movie event, it was a turning point in American culture and the way people looked at and trusted (or distrusted) the world around them. We were no longer safe in our homes, our showers, or our lives. Some of the viewpoints about the importance of *Psycho* can sound a little hyperbolic, but the passion the interview subjects here have regarding the film is powerful.

There's also a wonderful—and the movie could have used more of it, actually—illustration of how the scene connects to the rest of Hitchcock's oeuvre and is foreshadowed in the film itself. There are wonderful connections to that scene within *Psycho* that even fans of the film probably didn't notice, such as the way the master director highlights a shower head over Marion (Leigh) in an early scene, the way the windshield wipers slash at the rain as she drives, or how Norman (Perkins) stutters as he mentions the bathroom. Even the painting that Norman removes to reveal his peeping-tom hole in the wall has thematic importance. And then there's the use of the word "mother" throughout the film, from Marion's office in early scenes to the legendary Mrs. Bates. And the film is well-connected in *78/52* to obsessions that resurface throughout Hitchcock's career, including, of course, his fascination with voyeurism.

Director Alexandre O. Phillippe assembled a unique crew of people to discuss the film and its crucial scene, including editors, composers, historians, directors, and fans of the film. Some of the most eloquent filmmakers alive, including the always-brilliant Guillermo del Toro and incredibly smart Danny Elfman, offer their analysis of the movie and the specific scene. At least half of the film breaks down the shower scene specifically—how it jumps stage line to disorient, how it unforgettably uses music, how each cut works together, how it plays with perspective, how it is a mini-masterpiece of its own. Some of the interview subjects are better than others (sorry, Eli Roth, and Peter Bogdanovich, comparing seeing *Psycho* for the first time to feeling raped is a bit, well, insensitive), but the love for the film is there in each of the sound bites.

People who don't already bow at the alter of the master of suspense are probably wondering how an entire feature film could be made that examines a single three-minute scene. There are times when *78/52* feels a little thin as a feature, and one would have liked a few more female voices commenting on Hitchcock's issues with women (although the wonderful director Karyn Kusama is a welcome presence). However, then someone like Elijah Wood or Richard Stanley starts gushing about the movie, and their love for it and knowledge about it becomes palpable. There are very few entire films much less single scenes that could justify a documentary about their existence. There are also very few films like *Psycho* or the shower scene that changed film forever.

Brian Tallerico

CREDITS

Himself: Alfred Hitchcock
Herself: Jamie Lee Curtis
Himself: Guillermo del Toro
Himself: Peter Bogdanovich
Himself: Danny Elfman
Origin: United States
Language: English
Released: 2017
Production: Kerry Deignan Roy; ARTE, Exhibit A Pictures, Milkhaus, Screen Division, Sensorshot Productions; released by IFC Midnight
Directed by: Alexandre O. Philippe
Written by: Alexandre O. Philippe
Cinematography by: Robert Muratore
Music by: Jon Hegel
Sound: Phillip Lloyd Hegel
Editing: Chad Herschberger
MPAA rating: Unrated
Running time: 91 minutes

REVIEWS

Cheshire, Godfrey. *RogerEbert.com*. October 13, 2017.
Davis, Steve. *Austin Chronicle*. October 25, 2017.
Dowd, A.A. *The A.V. Club*. October 12, 2017.
Ebiri, Bilge. *Village Voice*. October 12, 2017.
Jolin, Dan. *Empire*. November 6, 2017.
Kenigsberg, Ben. *New York Times*. October 12, 2017.
Nashawaty, Chris. *Entertainment Weekly*. October 13, 2017.
Phillips, Michael. *Chicago Tribune*. November 9, 2017.
Rothkopf, Joshua. *Time Out*. October 13, 2017.
Turan, Kenneth. *Los Angeles Times*. October 19, 2017.

TRIVIA

Marli Renfro, the body double for Janet Leigh in *Psycho*, was also an original *Playboy* bunny and was featured on the cover of the September 1960 issue of the magazine.

THE SHACK

You're never as alone as you think.
—Movie tagline

Box Office: $57.4 Million

The primary theology of *The Shack* is Christian, although the story's approach to that religious tradition comes from an angle of New Age philosophy, self-help books, and the crime drama. This is a mess of philosophy and theology, as well as narrative, which seems a minor point, relative to the philosophy. The entire story is little more than an excuse for characters such as God, Jesus, the Holy Spirit, and the personification of Wisdom to offer life lessons and answers to matters of faith to a character who has suffered in a way that no parent should. The point, it seems, is that, if this man—of all people—can accept and embrace the movie's teachings, then anyone can.

This character's acceptance of the movie's gospel—that a person can overcome any suffering if they just "let go and let God" (this movie's interpretation of the deity, naturally)—comes at a high price. It means that his youngest daughter must be abducted and killed by a serial child-murderer.

There are manipulative story devices, and then there is this cynical move by screenwriters John Fusco, Andrew Lanham, and Destin Cretton, who have adapted William P. Young's book of the same name (written in collaboration with Wayne Jacobsen and Brad Cummings).

It is not only a deceptive way to make the story look like one thing, only to switch goals at the end of the first act, but it also renders death and grief as meaningless in the big picture—of life and, especially, of this story.

Mackenzie "Mack" Phillips (Sam Worthington) is the father of the murdered girl, named Missy (Amelie Eve). Her abduction and the aftermath of her disappearance are shown in a lengthy flashback (after another flashback that implies Mack, as a child, poisoned his abusive, alcoholic father), which establishes Mack's uncertainty of faith (another example being he does not sing the hymns at church) and how adorably wise the soon-to-be murdered girl is. She is taken by the killer on a camping trip, after the canoe that Mack's other children, Kate (Megan Charpentier) and Josh (Gage Munroe), are in tips over. While reviving his son, Mack loses sight of Missy, whose body is never recovered (although, in an unlikely decision by the FBI, Mack is brought to the scene of the crime, where he howls at the sight of his daughter's clothes).

In the present day, some years later, Mack receives an unaddressed envelope with a note in the mailbox. It tells him to meet someone at the shack where Missy was killed and is signed "Papa"—his wife Nan's (Radha Mitchell) nickname for God. Despite the protests of his friend Willie (Tim McGraw), who unnecessarily narrates Mack's miraculous change from grief-stricken to faithful, Mack goes to the shack.

While there, a mysterious stranger leads him from snow-covered reality to a warm and sunny place in the woods. In this place, Mack meets Papa (Octavia Spencer, in a fine performance, in spite of the material, filled with compassion), Jesus (Avraham Aviv Alush), and Sarayu (Sumire), the personification of the Holy Spirit.

All of these characters speak in metaphor and analogy, offering trite words of wisdom in dulcet tones. Sarayu compares the condition of Mack's soul to an untended garden, while the two tend to an overgrown garden as a sappy song plays on the soundtrack (director Stuart Hazeldine does the manipulative-music trick again with an ethereal funeral for Missy, even after the movie has definitively shown that such a display is hollow in the grand design of a universe with an afterlife). Jesus shows Mack how to walk on water and gives him a glimpse of Missy in Heaven (the reason the funeral scene is unnecessary), while also decrying the concept of organized religion (an accurate characterization, although an unintentionally amusing one, too, given the movie's hodgepodge of philosophical influences).

Mack levels the biggest questions, of course, at Papa, the omnipotent, omnipresent, and omniscient creator of the universe who, in Mack's view, still allowed Missy to be murdered, despite all of that power and knowledge. The opportunities here for a thoughtful discussion of the age-old question ("Why does God allow bad things to happen, especially to good people?") are abundant. The movie dodges them entirely, a quality that even Mack points out by saying that Papa only speaks in riddles.

The deity does indeed—repetitive riddles, at that. So, too, does Sophia (Alice Braga), the personification of Wisdom, who gives Mack a chance to stand in judgement of humanity, in order to give him an opportunity to see how difficult Papa's job is. In the climax of that scene, the wisest of the wise forces the father to an arbitrary choice of deciding which of his surviving children will suffer eternal damnation, while the other enjoys the rewards of Heaven. No part of this scene makes any sense, even in the movie's confused theology.

The goal of *The Shack* clearly is to offer hope. Instead, the movie makes the argument that nothing in this world, or in life, matters except blind faith in a deity that does not have any answers, except that blind faith is the best way to live.

Mark Dujsik

CREDITS

Mack Phillips: Sam Worthington
Papa: Octavia Spencer
Willie: Tim McGraw
Nan Phillips: Radha Mitchell
Jesus: Avraham Aviv Alush
Origin: United States
Language: English
Released: 2017
Production: Brad Cummings, Gil Netter; Netter Productions, Summit Entertainment; released by Lionsgate
Directed by: Stuart Hazeldine
Written by: John Fusco; Andrew Lanham; Destin Daniel Cretton
Cinematography by: Declan Quinn
Music by: Aaron Zigman
Music Supervisor: Anastasia Brown
Editing: William Steinkamp
Art Direction: Gwen Margetson
Costumes: Stacy Caballero; Karin Nosella
Production Design: Joseph C. Nemec, III
MPAA rating: PG-13
Running time: 132 minutes

REVIEWS

Bentley, Rick. *Fresno Bee.* March 1, 2017.

Chang, Justin. *Los Angeles Times.* March 2, 2017.
Douglas, Edward. *New York Daily News.* March 2, 2017.
Genzlinger, Neil. *New York Times.* March 2, 2017.
Gleiberman, Owen. *Variety.* March 2, 2017.
Greydanus, Steven D. *National Catholic Register.* March 2, 2017.
Means, Sean P. *Salt Lake Tribune.* March 2, 2017.
Morgenstern, Joe. *Wall Street Journal.* March 2, 2017.
Sobczynski, Peter. *RogerEbert.com.* March 3, 2017.
Vishnevetsky, Ignatiy. *The A.V. Club.* March 2, 2017.

QUOTES

Papa: "Pain robs you of joy, and the capacity to love."

TRIVIA

The character that discusses Wisdom with Mack is named Sophia, which is the Greek word for wisdom.

THE SHAPE OF WATER

A fairy tale for troubled times.
—Movie tagline

Box Office: $39.2 Million

In a sense, Guillermo del Toro has been working towards *The Shape of Water,* his most acclaimed film to date, for his entire career. It contains echoes of several of his previous works, including the fantasy-meets-reality milieu of something like *Pan's Labyrinth* (2006), the political undercurrent of *The Devil's Backbone* (2001), and the sense of danger of his woefully-underrated *Crimson Peak* (2015). Most of all, it reflects the filmmaker's incredible craftsmanship, apparent in every decision of the production, storytelling, and visual composition. It is a beautiful, unforgettable piece of art that reminds us that film can still be magical.

The Shape of Water is set in Baltimore in 1962, and takes place primarily in two settings—a secret government laboratory and the apartment building occupied by a woman who works there, a cleaner named Elisa Esposito (Oscar®-nominated Sally Hawkins). Elisa is a mute—she has unique scars on her neck but no memory of how she got them or how she lost her ability to speak. She signs to friends and co-worker like her neighbor Giles (Oscar®-nominated Richard Jenkins) and her co-worker Zelda (Oscar®-nominated Octavia Spencer). She lives a life of routine, going to work at the same time every day and even setting a timer for her regular masturbation. But, everything changes when a government project lands at the lab.

Colonel Richard Strickland (Michael Shannon) accompanies a large tank into a holding room at the laboratory where Elisa and Zelda work. Elisa seems instantly interested and then quickly attracted to the creature in the tank, a being that could be called half-fish, half-man, and seems clearly inspired by *Creature from the Black Lagoon* (1954). Del Toro understands that part of the draw of the old-fashioned monster movie was sexual in nature—we are all fascinated by the "other," and Elisa finds herself drawn to another silent denizen of this planet, captured in a beautifully physical performance from regular Del Toro collaborator Doug Jones. Elisa plays music for the creature and brings it eggs, and the two become mutually fascinated with one another, communicating in ways that others cannot.

While Elisa displays kindness, Strickland goes the opposite route—using brute force to try to determine the creature's origins and strengths. Elisa learns that Strickland is going to kill and vivisect the creature to learn more about it, despite the protests of a scientist named Hoffstetler (Michael Stuhlbarg), who also happens to be a Russian spy. Working with Giles, Zelda, and Hoffstetler, Elisa breaks the fishman out of the laboratory, keeping him in her apartment, where the two fall deeper in love and we learn that the creature has the power to heal. But the creature is dying outside of the water tank, and the government wants him back. Can Elisa and her band of misfits help him escape for good?

Guillermo del Toro's political subtext is blatant but seems to have been surprisingly missed by a lot of people who wrote about *The Shape of Water* in purely fantasy genre terms. Sure, it's a monster movie, but the genre has always had political messages, and Del Toro's is right there in the plot—it will be the cleaners, disabled, gays, artists, scientists, and defectors who save us all from the corporate, capitalist machine. Shannon's Strickland is more than just a villain—he is the embodiment of a decaying (as his finger literally is) system that values fancy cars and power over everything else. In a sense, Strickland is the real monster of *The Shape of Water,* a heartless bureaucrat who's lost his soul.

However, and this is one of the reasons the film has been so wildly successful *The Shape of Water* is nowhere near as dark as the last paragraph suggests it could have been. It is a film that takes time for joy, dance, romance, and the good old-fashioned magic of movies. It is a perfectly balanced embodiment of the transportative power of fantasy filmmaking with Del Toro's refusal to sugarcoat its adult themes. Who else would actually allow Elisa and the fishman to consummate their relationship or let one of its romantic heroes literally eat a cat? Del Toro may have made one of his most accessible films here, but his quirky, dark sense of humor is still present, as is his refusal to dumb-down his themes or soften the fact that this is a film for adults.

As with everything Del Toro does, *The Shape of Water* is a technical masterpiece. Shot in Toronto, the film has a beautiful balance between feeling like it takes place in a fantasy world while also grounding itself in Cold War America. Elisa's apartment, the movie theater below it, the laboratory—these are all movie sets that are more than merely functional—they assist and enable the storytelling. Del Toro's palette of greens and blues captured by Dan Laustsen's camera add to the aquamarine fantasy in ways both beautiful and relatable. Laustsen earned his first Oscar® nomination, as did the production design team, editor Sidney Wolinsky, costume designer Luis Sequeira, and composer Alexandre Desplat, who does arguably his best work to date here, landing his amazing tenth Oscar® nomination in as many years.

Like most of Guillermo del Toro's films, *The Shape of Water* is a movie that will be around for generations. It feels both timeless and a commentary on the eras in which it was set and made. Del Toro uses his vast knowledge of filmmaking history and ability at his craft to not just present escapist fairy tales but to channel human concerns through them. His film is about finding your place in the world, doing what's right, and overcoming cruel, unchecked power. Fairy tales have always served as delivery devices for messages, and Del Toro's couldn't be timelier or more important. It is a reminder of so many reasons why people watch movies in the first place, and the true magic that can be uncovered in the best of them.

Brian Tallerico

CREDITS

Elisa Esposito: Sally Hawkins
Richard Strickland: Michael Shannon
Giles: Richard Jenkins
Zelda Fuller: Octavia Spencer
Dr. Robert Hoffstetler: Michael Stuhlbarg
Origin: United States
Language: English
Released: 2017
Production: J. Miles Dale, Guillermo del Toro; Bull Productions, Double Dare You, TSG Entertainment; released by Fox Searchlight Pictures
Directed by: Guillermo del Toro
Written by: Guillermo del Toro; Vanessa Taylor
Cinematography by: Dan Laustsen
Music by: Alexandre Desplat
Sound: Nathan Robitaille
Editing: Sidney Wolinsky
Art Direction: Nigel Churcher
Costumes: Luis Sequeira
Production Design: Paul Denham Austerberry
MPAA rating: R
Running time: 123 minutes

REVIEWS

Burr, Ty. *Boston Globe.* December 6, 2017.
Ebiri, Bilge. *Village Voice.* December 7, 2017.
Kiang, Jessica. *The Playlist.* August 31, 2017.
Lane, Anthony. *New Yorker.* December 4, 2017.
Lodge, Guy. *Variety.* August 31, 2017.
Phillips, Michael. *Chicago Tribune.* December 7, 2017.
Robinson, Tasha. *The Verge.* September 13, 2017.
Rooney, David. *Hollywood Reporter.* August 31, 2017.
Scott, A.O. *New York Times.* November 30, 2017.
Turan, Kenneth. *Los Angeles Times.* December 7, 2017.

QUOTES

Hoffstetler: "I don't want an intricate, beautiful thing destroyed!"

TRIVIA

Set during a real-life war and featuring magical elements; this was also the premise for Guillermo del Toro's *Pan's Labyrinth* (2006).

AWARDS

Oscars 2017: Director (del Toro), Film, Orig. Score, Production Design
British Acad. 2017: Director, Orig. Score, Production Design
British Acad. 2018: Director (del Toro)
Directors Guild 2017: Director (del Toro)
Golden Globes 2018: Director (del Toro), Orig. Score

Nominations:

Oscars 2017: Actress (Hawkins), Actress--Supporting (Jenkins), Actress--Supporting (Spencer), Cinematog., Costume Des., Film Editing, Orig. Screenplay, Sound, Sound FX Editing
British Acad. 2017: Actress (Hawkins), Actress--Supporting (Spencer), Cinematog., Costume Des., Film, Film Editing, Orig. Screenplay, Sound, Visual FX
Golden Globes 2018: Actor--Supporting (Jenkins), Actor--Supporting (Spencer), Actress--Drama (Hawkins), Film--Drama, Screenplay
Screen Actors Guild 2017: Actor--Supporting (Jenkins), Actress (Hawkins)
Writers Guild 2017: Orig. Screenplay

SLEEPLESS

Don't judge a cop by his cover.
—Movie tagline

Box Office: $20.8 Million

Baran bo Odar's *Sleepless* plays like a checklist of undercover cop movie clichés, all of them played out over the course of a single night in which secrets are easily revealed and everyone involved changes alliances just when things are about to get too messy for them. The tale involves seemingly dirty cops, straight-shooter internal affairs investigators, drug lords, middle-men, incompetent security guards and a wife and kid who have been kept on the sidelines by the main character for too long. It runs a brisk 95 minutes, which, for a movie like this, means the audience will not have to make much of an investment and will quickly forget about it once it finishes. What it lacks in imagination, it makes up for in brevity. The film's roster of talented actors helps save it from being completely disposable, but these people have all done better work in better films. Presumably, the title refers to the fact that everyone in the film is up all night trying figure to out where the drugs are, how the drugs were stolen, who is crooked and who killed who. The viewer will be way ahead of everyone.

It starts out with a pair of Las Vegas cops, Vincent (Jamie Foxx) and Sean (T.I.), who bungle a drug bust and end up taking the drugs home with them with the intent on making millions worth in sales down the road. Vincent has a teenage son, Thomas (Octavius J. Johnson), and an ex-wife, Dena (Gabrielle Union), and it is Vincent's turn to have his son with him for the weekend. That same day, Vincent and Sean get assigned to investigate the crime they just walked away from, much to the concern of internal affairs agents Bryant (Michelle Monaghan) and Dennison (David Harbour), who have had a bad feeling about Vincent for a long time.

Vincent and Sean do not know that, at first, the drugs they just stole are intended to be delivered to the biggest crime lord in Las Vegas, Novak (Scoot McNairy), who will be coming to collect them from Stan Rumbino (Dermot Mulroney), a casino owner who has no choice but to kidnap Vincent's son and hold him for ransom until Vincent brings the bag of drugs to him. Vincent hides half the stash in a men's room ceiling at the casino. Bryant, who has been tailing Vincent and Sean out of suspicion, witnesses this act and steals the drugs herself in an effort to bust both Novak and Vincent—a crime lord and a crooked cop in one night would be a major coup for her. Vincent will compromise anything he has to in order to get his son back and Bryant will stop at nothing to bust somebody for this drug trade.

The film spends most of its running time following Foxx desperately trying to get out of one situation after another. He has to dodge Novak, get the drugs back from Bryant, get his son back from Stan, keep his son from getting kidnapped again, don a couple disguises and assure his ex-wife that everything is fine every time she calls. Bryant becomes the second main character here. She gets fed up when her peers notice she has been in a fight, show concern for her and advise her to take it easy. Nobody would be saying that to one of the male agents. That is about all the viewer gets as far as character development goes with this film. Vincent has been a neglectful husband/father and Bryant gets too many looks of sympathy from her male co-workers.

A film like this could go a long way if it had a memorable villain, but *Sleepless* settles for a formulaic kind of heavy. Novak is introduced as a typically cold-blooded and merciless kingpin with slicked-back hair and tight clothing. He tortures those who get in his way by hanging them upside down and then leaving as his henchmen cut out the poor guy's tongue so he will never talk to anyone ever again. He is shorter in stature than everyone else in the film and that may be intentional, but it is the only noticeable thing about him. McNairy never finds much to do with him except fake an accent and stare menacingly. As Stan, Mulroney has been given a better role as the middleman in this situation. He would like to be at the top of the crime chain in this town, but he has to keep a front as a casino owner and take orders from Novak, who has a past with Stan, who knew his father.

Odar tries to keep everything moving at a breakneck pace. The film hits the ground running with a car chase that ends in a gunfight. Once the all-night storyline kicks in, Michael Kamm's score almost never ceases and gives the film a constant pulse. If nothing else, *Sleepless* moves quickly enough, but not so the viewer ever notices its derivativeness. The third act in Andrea Berloff's script (based on the film *Nuit Blanche* [2011]) ties everything together a little too nicely, so much so that even Dena's occupation as a nurse becomes a saving grace at just the right time. The film also has an obsession with throwing Foxx into an over-choreographed fist-fight every ten minutes to try and pad out the running time. It all concludes in a way that will not surprise anyone, except those who do not expect it to be open to a sequel.

Collin Souter

CREDITS

Vincent: Jamie Foxx
Bryant: Michelle Monaghan
Rubino: Dermot Mulroney
Dena: Gabrielle Union
Dennison: David Harbour
Origin: United States
Language: English, French, Spanish

Released: 2017
Production: Roy Lee, Adam Stone; FilmNation Entertainment, Riverstone Pictures, Vertigo Entertainment; released by Open Road Films
Directed by: Baran bo Odar
Written by: Andrea Berloff
Cinematography by: Mihai Malaimare, Jr.
Music by: Michael Kamm
Sound: Jussi Tegelman
Music Supervisor: Daryl Berg
Editing: Robert Rzesacz
Art Direction: Christopher Tandon
Costumes: Catherine George
Production Design: Tim Grimes
MPAA rating: R
Running time: 96 minutes

REVIEWS

Baumgarten, Marjorie. *Austin Chronicle.* January 19, 2017.
Chang, Justin. *Los Angeles Times.* January 13, 2017.
Duralde, Alonso. *TheWrap.* January 12, 2017.
Gleiberman, Owen. *Variety.* January 13, 2017.
Marks, Scott. *San Diego Reader.* January 16, 2017.
Nordine, Michael. *Village Voice.* January 25, 2017.
Scott, A.O. *New York Times.* January 13, 2017.
Schaefer, Stephen. *Boston Herald.* January 12, 2017.
Vishnevetsky, Ignatiy. *The A.V. Club.* January 17, 2017.
Zoller Seitz, Matt. *RogerEbert.com.* January 13, 2017.

QUOTES

Sean: "They said it was just gonna be a easy grab."
Vincent: "Well, it ain't no easy grab, they got T!"

TRIVIA

On the *Howard Stern Show* Jamie Foxx said that this is the hardest of his movies for him to watch, implying that he was not happy with the final product.

SLEIGHT

You can change the cards you're dealt.
—Movie tagline

Box Office: $4 Million

The "superhero" movie is perhaps the most successful film genre of the moment—though horror is probably still more profitable—but the genre's popularity has begun to take a creative toll. There has been such a glut of franchise-building, origin stories, and expanded cinematic universes over the past ten years that the stories are all beginning to run together. There is a uniformity to most major movies of this ilk that has simply de-saturated their uniqueness to the point where they are almost interchangeable.

This is why a movie like J.D. Dillard's *Sleight* carries such significance. It's an attempt to push the superhero genre out of its comfort zone. How does it accomplish this? By injecting some much-needed diversity into a traditional "capes and cowls" story. And that diversity is far-reaching. *Sleight* not only gets extra creative points for presenting a superhero origin story about a young person of color, written and directed by an African-American filmmaker, but it also works hard to push the standard superhero tale into other, more creatively fertile film genres as well.

Case in point, *Sleight* probably shares more creative DNA with Rick Famuyiwa's *Dope* (2015) or Boaz Yakin's *Fresh* (1994) than any Marvel film. That's even despite the fact that its protagonist, Bo (Jacob Latimore), could reasonably be described as a young Tony Stark, if Stark grew up with almost every socio-economic factor turned against him.

Teenaged Bo lives in a depressed area of Los Angeles and struggles to care for his young sister Tina (Storm Reid) after his parents' death. While he dreams of running away with his girlfriend Holly (Seychelle Gabriel), Bo keeps his family afloat with two very different jobs. He runs errands for aspiring drug dealer Angelo, played with a menacing charisma by the unlikely Dulé Hill. (Hill seems to relish the opportunity to add a little danger to his previously saintly on-screen persona, giving his performance an infectious charm.) And Bo performs street magic with an unnatural, almost mystical skill—an ability we quickly learn comes from a special electromagnet that technical wiz Bo developed during his time in high school.

This is where the superhero element comes into *Sleight*. Bo is, essentially, a street-level Iron Man or, at the very least, he's what would have happened if the characters in *Chronicle* (2012) had constructed their own superhuman abilities rather than acquired them through contact with some alien artifact. Dillard, to his great credit, makes Bo's homegrown magnet powers more interesting than implausible. They rarely pull one out of the story—which is more about a street hustler than a Superman—and Dillard and his cinematographer Ed Wu direct the street magic scenes with a verve and energy that puts the *Now You See Me* movies to shame.

Things quickly go south for Bo when Angelo's business gets threatened by Maurice (Mane Rich Andrew), a new force in the local drug trade. Recognizing hyper-competent Bo's abilities as a magician and pickpocket, Angelo tasks Bo with finding the illusive Maurice. Bo reluctantly agrees, kicking off a chain of events that ends with Angelo forcing Bo to get his hands dirty and Bo stealing from Angelo to finally escape the cycle of violence with Tina and Holly. This scheme backfires for Bo, leaving him desperate to pay back Angelo to save his family. He soon realizes that the only way he might be able to get the money and protect his loved ones is with the electromagnet strapped to his arm.

The story beats in *Sleight* are not particularly original. If you've seen a "crime gone wrong" movie before, you can predict the path of the story fairly easily, leaving the narrative feeling, well, "sleight" at parts. However, it is fascinating to see how Dillard takes those familiar storytelling tropes and associates them with the superhero genre. Bo's financial desperation and family ties give his story more emotional stakes than any "saving the world" plot in a Spider-Man or Iron Man movie. It's only when Dillard moves away from his "less is more" scenario that the movie's flaws become apparent.

While the majority of the film uses decidedly low-fi special effects—or shies away from opportunities to blatantly reveal Bo's abilities—*Sleight* ends with an extended sequence wherein Bo truly shows off his magnetic powers, a sequence that underwhelms to the extreme. On paper, it may have seemed like a solid idea for the film's climax, but in reality, it just delivers a series of unimpressive CGI moments that can't compare to the emotional thrills from the rest of the film.

In the end, *Sleight* is a good (but not great) look at how filmmakers will hopefully start adapting, re-mixing, and re-contextualizing standard superhero stories in the near future. More than anything, Dillard's film proves that comic book tropes can be elevated and refreshed if they are placed within stories about which people care. It might be hard to sympathize with an invulnerable hero trying to stop nanobots from consuming the planet, but if there are heroes who look like us, struggle like us, and use their fantastic situations to make their lives and the lives of their loved ones a little better—that's something worth believing in.

Tom Burns

CREDITS

Bo: Jacob Latimore
Holly: Seychelle Gabriel
Angelo: Dulé Hill
Tina: Storm Reid
Georgi: Sasheer Zamata
Origin: United States
Language: English
Released: 2017
Production: Eric B. Fleischman, Sean Tabibian, Alex Theurer; Diablo Entertainment; released by BH Tilt, High Top Releasing
Directed by: J.D. Dillard
Written by: J.D. Dillard; Alex Theurer
Cinematography by: Ed Wu
Music by: Charles Scott, IV
Sound: Kyle Schember
Editing: Joel Griffen
Art Direction: Megan Sunzeri
Costumes: Joanna David
Production Design: Susannah Honey
MPAA rating: R
Running time: 89 minutes

REVIEWS

Abele, Robert. *TheWrap*. April 27, 2017.
Debruge, Peter. *Variety*. April 28, 2017.
Dowd, A.A. *The A.V. Club*. April 28, 2017.
Franich, Darren. *Entertainment Weekly*. April 27, 2017.
Lowe, Justin. *Hollywood Reporter*. November 30, 2016.
Moore, Roger. *Movie Nation*. May 3, 2017.
Perez, Rodrigo. *The Playlist*. November 30, 2016.
Savlov, Marc. *Austin Chronicle*. May 3, 2017.
Walsh, Katie. *Chicago Tribune*. April 27, 2017.
Wolfe, April. *Village Voice*. April 26, 2017.
Yoshida, Emily. *Vulture*. April 28, 2017.

TRIVIA

The playing cards used in the film are Black Fontaines by Zach Mueller.

SMURFS: THE LOST VILLAGE

A whole new world awaits.
—Movie tagline

They were never alone.
—Movie tagline

Small is big.
—Movie tagline

New friendships are only an adventure away.
—Movie tagline

Box Office: $45 Million

The not-so-distant 1980s were indeed a halcyon time for Belgian cartoon characters the Smurfs. The tiny, blue elf-like creatures vaulted onto the pop culture landscape with a highly successful Saturday morning cartoon show which was easily parlayed into food products (Smurf cereal immediately comes to mind), toys, clothes, and various other pop culture touchstones like a massive balloon in the Macy's Thanksgiving Day

Parade. *The Smurfs* was a popular show because not only were the characters cute, they were easily expanded by merely trotting out a "new" character when things got slow. This was done by simply adding a hat or attitude to the basic Smurf character and a new favorite was born, easily pigeonholed into whatever trait they were given as a name. For example, at some point in the original series run, a farmer hat was placed on a Smurf's head, a sprig of wheat stuck in his mouth and, voilà, "Farmer Smurf" and any multitude of new storylines about farming, the environment and/or feeding the village. Yet almost as soon as the loveable Smurfs appeared on the scene, they vanished with nary a farewell. They returned off and on for several years in television and on DVD but it wasn't until 2011 when *The Smurfs* would hit the big screen in a film that blended live action with CGI animation.

Now the Smurfs are back with the fully computer animated *Smurfs: The Lost Village* which is a success on the congenial cuteness scale but, not much else. However, credit must be given to this latest Smurf film for answering an age-old question surrounding the little blue fellows: why is there only one female Smurf (Smurfette) in a village full of male Smurfs? While it's easy for any adult mind to go straight to the gutter with that question, it really is an intriguing one that speaks to male dominance in animation and comics as well as just plain old poor planning. While *Smurfs: The Lost Village* does its very best to bring the Smurfs franchise into these modern, inclusive times, it still cannot seem to do more than dip a toe in the water of feminism and never go deeper than a surface-level nod to the female gender.

For the uninitiated in regards to the basic Smurf plotline, *Smurfs: The Lost Village* starts off in the right place as the audience is reintroduced to the Smurfs idling away their days harvesting and eating Smurfberries as well as playing out their aforementioned designated personalities. Of course, there's a core group of characters always on-hand and they include Brainy Smurf (Danny Pudi), Clumsy Smurf (Jack McBrayer), Hefty Smurf (Joe Maganiello), and a whole of menagerie of Smurfs (including Table Eating Smurf which, was actually quite unexpected and funny) who won't figure much into this adventure. And, of course, there's Smurfette (Demi Lovato) who, since she is a female Smurf, wears high-heels and lives in her mushroom house that is mostly pink and adorned with hearts everywhere because, that's what every girl likes. All of these happy-go-lucky creatures are looked after by the benevolent, red-capped Papa Smurf (an actually excellent Mandy Patinkin) who makes sure all these diverse personalities get along as well as offering sage advice and major hand-wringing when bad choices are made.

Alas every simple, happy lifestyle must have an antagonist and that's where evil, half-wit wizard Gargamel (Rainn Wilson) and his smart cat Azrael come into play as their never-ending quest to destroy the Smurfs begins anew in in this latest installment. In this variation of a Smurf extinction plan, Gargamel creates small balls that will freeze the Smurfs. As Brainy, Hefty, Clumsy, and Smurfette once again escape Gargamel's half-baked plan, Smurfette tumbles down a hillside and ends up face to face with a set of eyes that look oddly familiar. As she makes her way back to the Smurf village, she convinces her compatriots that they must venture out to an area designated "Keep Out" by Papa Smurf to discover who's eyes she saw.

It's not much of a spoiler to say the eyes belong to a female Smurf who lives in a "lost village" full of rough and tumble female Smurfs who have names with matching attitudes like SmurfBlossom (Ellie Kemper); SmurfMelody (pop singer Meghan Trainor); gutsy SmurfStorm (Michelle Rodriguez); and their also benevolent, also red-capped leader SmurfWillow (Julie Roberts). At first the all-male Smurfs infringe on the lady Smurf village but soon a bond is formed to take on Gargamel who never met a Smurf he did not want to destroy and perhaps thinks he will have better luck in this newfound village.

Smurfs: The Lost Village is a fine animated cartoon for young children. It should also be given some credit for introducing more strong, female characters into the franchise, courtesy of a script by two female screenwriters, Stacey Harman and Pamela Ribon. Still, one can't help but feel this injection of girl power is handled somewhat poorly and in a very superficial way as each new Smurfette remains indelibly attached to a name or attitude which, in and of itself, cuts both ways as it does towards the male Smurfs as well. Story structure, character, plot, and storytelling has evolved so much since the Smurfs were created in the late 1950s, the franchise is already at a bit of a loss, similar to the early Disney characters like Mickey, Minnie, Donald, and Goofy that have struggled to find a place in modern pop culture as more than a cute, sentimental touchstone. There's just not a lot for Smurfs to do that other, more intriguing characters in franchises don't do better and with mediocre efforts like *Smurfs: The Lost Village*, the future of the Smurfs remains unclear.

Don R. Lewis

CREDITS

Smurfette: Demi Lovato (Voice)
Gargamel: Rainn Wilson (Voice)
Hefty Smurf: Joe Manganiello (Voice)

Clumsy Smurf: Jack McBrayer (Voice)
Brainy Smurf: Danny Pudi (Voice)
Origin: United States
Language: English
Released: 2017
Production: Mary Ellen Bauder Andrews, Jordan Kerner; Kerner Entertainment Company, Sony Pictures Animation; released by Columbia Pictures
Directed by: Kelly Asbury
Written by: Stacey Harman; Pamela Ribon
Music by: Christopher Lennertz
Sound: Robert L. Sephton
Editing: Bret Marnell
Art Direction: Dean Gordon; Marcelo Vignali
Production Design: Noelle Triaureau
MPAA rating: PG
Running time: 90 minutes

REVIEWS

Duralde, Alonso *TheWrap*. March 26, 2017.
Ehrlich, David. *IndieWire*. April 6, 2017.
Harley, Kevin. *Total Film*. April 9, 2017.
Moore, Roger. *Movie Nation*. April 4, 2017.
Padua, Pat. *Washington Post*. April 6, 2017.
Russo, Tom. *Boston Globe*. April 6, 2017.
Savlov, Marc. *Austin Chronicle*. April 5, 2017.
VanDenburgh, Barbara. *Arizona Republic*. April 6, 2017.
Walsh, Katie. *Los Angeles Times*. April 6, 2017.
Watson, Keith. *Slant Magazine*. April 2, 2017.

QUOTES

Farmer Smurf: "Smurfette is part Smurf and part Ette. So all we have to do is find out what an Ette is."

TRIVIA

The original title of this film was *Get Smurfy*.

SNATCHED

This is the closest they've been in years.
—Movie tagline

Mess with me, mess with my mother.
—Movie tagline

Box Office: $45.9 Million

Snatched is the type of studio project made explicitly for opening weekend audiences, despite the enduring talent brought on board. Released on Mother's Day Weekend (a selling point especially on official advertising), this abysmal comedy from grade-A entertainers (Amy Schumer, Goldie Hawn, and writer Katie Dippold) relies on the expectations brought by those names and egregiously underwhelms them in the process. As a type of non-party for viewers wanting to see a mother and daughter bond over wacky adventures, *Snatched* is little more than a sloppy mix of lazy comic filmmaking and general poor taste.

The premise for the story is innocent enough, and also kind of funny: a recently dumped woman named Emily (Amy Schumer) convinces her agoraphobic, single mother Linda (Goldie Hawn) to go on a trip to Ecuador meant for Emily and her now-ex boyfriend (Randall Park). Once there, the two women have different ideas of what they want from the nonrefundable trip: Emily wants to party, explore, and take good selfies; Linda wants to read her novellas in the shade, staying within the confines of the resort.

One night at said resort, Emily meets a handsome stranger named James (Tom Bateman), who quickly woos her and offers to take her outside the resort for some capoeira. The next morning, Emily convinces the very reluctant Linda to go with James and her on a journey throughout the countryside, which quickly turns into something insidious: the two women are kidnapped by members of a local cartel. They soon break free, after Emily accidentally kills the cartel leader's son, and find themselves in the neighboring country of Colombia, with no hope of getting back to safety.

The energy that could have arisen from this type of adventure, in which the two women are on the run through a foreign land with evil forces chasing them, is not taken advantage of by the story which gravely lacks tension. The chemistry between Schumer and Hawn during these wacky moments, which trace more as odd than funny, lacks the zip one might expect from two such comedic talents being paired together.

Instead, the story works with a revolving door of sometimes funny supporting actors: Christopher Meloni's portrays a sociopathic adventuring American whose interests in being their hero are limited; Ike Barinholtz plays Linda's nincompoop son who resorts to bugging an appropriately irritated federal agent (played by Bashir Salahuddin) into trying to get someone to rescue his family members. The most memorable appearances might be from Wanda Sykes and Joan Cusack, as a couple of intense women also staying at the resort who provide some strong arm heroism in the third act.

The narrative structure that has been provided by Katie Dippold, (*The Heat* [2013], co-writer of *Ghostbusters* [2016]—both directed by Paul Feig) is a mess, when viewed as something that wants audiences to laugh or to make them feel something. Jokes are both obvious from a mile away and simply dumped into the script, like when Emily slowly reveals to her captors that her ATM pin number is one, two, three, four; or numerous jokes that have the punchline of Emily being a trashy person. For good measure, a whole sequence is devoted to Schumer's character having a Cronenberg-esque tapeworm inside of her, which leads to an unpleasant, over-labored sequence where local doctors try to remove it. Later emotional beats, in which these two women find themselves emotionally closer due to the experience, feel like they pander to the audience instead of enhancing the story.

Perhaps most disappointing, Dippold's script is very passive with the ethics of its loaded pitch, in which white American tourists venture to South America and are put on an adventure that is due to their privilege and naïveté towards local culture. As the story goes on, the script becomes more focused with villainizing the region (of which Hawaii was used as a stand-in) and creating a rescue mission. The bad people in this story do not feel like more than a blip to the cultural radar. Meanwhile, the adventure that Schumer and Hawn are thrown into does not have the desired innocence that could make this movie fun in the plainest sense possible.

After making a splash with the 2015 Judd Apatow vehicle *Trainwreck,* Schumer struggles to bring her comic persona to this movie, while also honoring the title of her 2017 book, *The Girl with the Lower Back Tattoo.* Her character becomes plainly unlikable when working with images of the Ugly American, in part because Dippold's story never seems like a parody of the type of people that Schumer and Hawn are playing. Schumer has no choice but to lean into her character's tedious traits, and becomes memorable only for being so shallow. It is too early in her film career for Schumer to play such a tired character.

Snatched does mark the first role for Hawn in so many years, but it is essentially a throwaway part. Her casting manages to both overshadow the project and then make it a collective disappointment, playing a character of a few limited quirks, leading to a performance of scant comedy. In this case, as welcome as Hawn's presence is back on the silver screen, a less assuming talent might have done better with the role.

The movie is the latest from director Jonathan Levine, who started with notice in indies like *The Wackness* (2008) or *50/50* (2011), but has developed a very bland taste with his mainstream comedies. Like his previous effort to create a type of tentpole with grade-A talent, *The Night Before* (2015), *Snatched* lacks any distinct vision and is instead steered by whatever glimmers of hope can be provided by a supporting cast. Levine's contribution to his intriguing premises is to create a party, with overhead shots of beautiful locations and raucous slapstick-y sequences, but he has approximately zero edge throughout. Under the gaze of Levine, *Snatched* soon exemplifies studio comedies at their worst: bad jokes, shallow storytelling, ironic hip-hop music cues, and vacuous personality.

Nick Allen

CREDITS

Emily Middleton: Amy Schumer
Linda Middleton: Goldie Hawn
Barb: Joan Cusack
Jeffrey Middleton: Ike Barinholtz
Ruth: Wanda Sykes
Origin: United States
Language: English
Released: 2017
Production: Peter Chernin, Paul Feig, Jessie Henderson, Jenno Topping; Chernin Entertainment, Feigco Entertainment; released by Twentieth Century Fox Film Corp.
Directed by: Jonathan Levine
Written by: Katie Dippold
Cinematography by: Florian Ballhaus
Music by: Chris Bacon; Theodore Shapiro
Sound: Warren Hendriks
Music Supervisor: Gabe Hilfer
Editing: Zene Baker; Melissa Bretherton
Art Direction: Kevin Constant
Costumes: Leesa Evans
Production Design: Mark Ricker
MPAA rating: R
Running time: 90 minutes

REVIEWS

Anderson, Melissa. *Village Voice.* May 10, 2017.
Erbland, Kate. *IndieWire.* May 11, 2017.
Garber, Megan. *The Atlantic.* May 12, 2017.
Hornaday, Ann. *Washington Post.* May 11, 2017.
Lemire, Christy. *RogerEbert.com.* May 11, 2017.
MacDonald, Moira. *Seattle Times.* May 10, 2017.
Rowe, Amy. *New York Daily News.* May 19, 2017.
Vishnevetsky, Ignatiy. *The A.V. Club.* May 10, 2017.
Walsh, Katie. *Tribune News Service.* May 11, 2017.
Willmore, Alison. *Buzzfeed News.* May 12, 2017.

QUOTES

Emily Middleton: "Let's go out tonight. Hair, makeup, boobs...we're going out!"
Linda Middleton: "Emily, I am not going out at night."
Emily Middleton: "Everything shouldn't be so scary."

Ruth: "Oh, it damn well should. One in four tourists are kidnapped."

Emily Middleton: "Not true."

TRIVIA

The studio originally didn't want Goldie Hawn for the film, but co-star/producer Amy Schumer insisted and even threatened to leave the project if Hawn wasn't cast.

AWARDS

Nominations:

Golden Raspberries 2017: Worst Support. Actress (Hawn)

THE SNOWMAN

Soon the first snow will come, and then he will kill again.
—Movie tagline

Soon the first snow will fall, and the hunt for a killer begins.
—Movie tagline

Mister Police. You Could have Saved Her. I Gave You All The Clues.
—Movie tagline

Box Office: $6.7 Million

Someday, *The Snowman* is going to be studied in classrooms for reasons that almost have nothing to do with what's on the screen. From the film's marketing campaign to the director's own pre-release admition that the final product was problematic, there was an instant infamy that must have led to a giddy indulgence in exasperating every one of its flaws no matter how odd or misguided. Almost as if people wanted to solve a mystery as to how so many talented people could get caught up in something deemed so nonsensical. Though nobody should confuse *The Snowman* with a good movie nor some underappreciated masterpiece that think pieces will attempt to convince them of in ten years or so, it is easy to get caught up in the moment when piling on is encouraged. A simpler perspective at the end of its sluggish two hours might suggest that these same talented people tried to thaw the familiarity off a standard and very tedious pot-boiler and simply came up short.

Harry Hole (Michael Fassbender) is a well-regarded Norwegian detective despite his penchant for the bottle. Katrine Bratt (Rebecca Ferguson) is a fellow detective who, not unlike another newcomer in an Americanized remake of a Norwegian crime thriller, *Insomnia* (2002), has studied Hole's cases. They are teamed up to investigate the disappearance of a woman (Genevieve O'Reilly) who has left behind a husband and a young daughter. Also left behind is a snowman which looks disapprovingly at their house. On the case at another department is Detective Rafto (Val Kilmer) whose water bottle full of vodka suggests an even bigger problem than Harry's. Then again, he is the first to find an actual body.

Like many fictional serial killers, this one chooses to toy with the lead investigator. Although few do so before they even become the lead investigator. That might have been clue number one to the legendary Hole, but he is not nearly as invested in it as his new partner is. Katrine has her sights on the politician (J.K. Simmons) trying to bring the Winter Olympics to Oslo as well as his connection to Doctor Vetlesen (David Dencik) who may know more about the victims than the police do. Harry is less combative in his approach to detecting and, when not drinking, maintains a friendship with Rakel (Charlotte Gainsbourg), an ex-girlfriend of his; her teenage son, Oleg (Michael Yates); and even her new beau, Mathias (Jonas Karlsson). But wait, is there not a string of murders to solve?

Director Tomas Alfredson has admitted through interviews that the film's production was rushed. So rushed, in fact, that they neglected (or maybe just forgot) to shoot at least 15 percent of the finished script. Perhaps this is why there seems to be huge narrative gaps in characters's behavior and a fundamental lack of detail that may have aided in our appreciation of their perceived brilliance. The film's marketing played off the killer's preferred mode of communication; a handwritten letter with the drawing of a snowman underneath. "Mister Police, you could have saved her. I gave you all the clues," a note that does not appear in the finished film but actually sounds like a note relayed from novelist Jo Nesbø watching his seventh book in the Hole series get butchered in its first outing.

Given several changes to the novel's outcome by a trio of screenwriters, putting the pieces of the final product together was hard enough. Throw in the missing connective tissue that was never put in front of a camera, and it is even more daunting. Why is Katrine delivering a seemingly innocent young woman to the lecherous doctor? Why is an actress of Chloë Sevigny's talent brought in for just two scenes; one as a victim and the other as her twin sister only to never be heard of again? What is the killer's fascination with the song "Popcorn" by Hot Butter? The answers to these and other questions only further our own theories that maybe these protagonists are not the ones we would want on the case if a member of our family was in danger.

It is easy to point at Alfredson for a lack of leadership in keeping this whole mess together. On the other hand this is a filmmaker whose previous efforts include the magnificent vampire tale, *Let the Right One In* (2008) and the feature adaptation of John le Carré's *Tinker Tailor Soldier Spy* (2011). Since those were two films in genres whose familiarities can test even the most fervent proponents, it stands to reason that maybe, just maybe, Alfredson was making an effort to turn a routine detective novel into the kind of style over substance that David Fincher brought to a similarly stale narrative in *The Girl with the Dragon Tattoo* (2011). Again, it doesn't work but certainly not for a lack of trying.

Enter Thelma Schoonmaker, the three-time Oscar® winner who has edited pictures almost exclusively for Martin Scorsese over the years. (He was once attached to direct back in 2013, but is now only credited as an executive producer.) The film's prologue sets up a potentially intriguing thematic shift. Moviegoers unfamiliar with Harry's backstory could just as easily attribute a rough childhood and a suicidal mother as personal motivation to pursue certain cases. Especially when Schoonmaker immediately cuts to Harry passed out in the cold. Ever more curious in sowing the seeds of confusion is the decision to include Kilmer's portion of the story as running concurrently with Harry and Katrine's. It is revealed soon enough that these were flashbacks, but Kilmer, perhaps recognizing how little impact his character has on the story, goes almost full-blown Dr. Moreau by taunting his fellow officers, using his vodka thermos as an extended appendage. To say that he lost his head there might be giving Schoonmaker too much credit for cinematic foreshadowing.

Alfredson was clearly shooting for mood and instead wrought tedium. His impressive cast may have been excited to work with him but none of it shows on screen. Ferguson shows none of the confident mystique she brought to *Mission: Impossible—Rogue Nation* (2015). Simmons is reduced to just another red herring using his power to curry sexual favors. But it is Fassbender who appears lost in a whiteout of internal conflicts and complete indifference. His behavior only looks measured compared to his all-too-eager partner and even in his good cop routine still needs a victim's relative to provide the single connective thread that would have stood out to anyone who had ever read an Encyclopedia Brown mystery. Too bad that name was taken, Harry Hole. *The Snowman,* unfortunately, may end up a legend in its own brief moment and no magic hat can be used to save it. No director's cut can be crafted since the additional footage does not exist and it is too blandly odd to have future midnight audiences get engaged enough to throw carrots and coffee beans at the screen. Most movies would kill to be remembered for such a fleeting moment, but not even a note from Santa that reads "I am very sorry for what I did" would keep this from being forgotten by the next season. Nor would it clue Harry in that Mr. Claus might be responsible for the crime.

Erik Childress

CREDITS

Harry Hole: Michael Fassbender
Katrine Bratt: Rebecca Ferguson
Rakel: Charlotte Gainsbourg
Rafto: Val Kilmer
Arve Stop: J.K. Simmons
Origin: Sweden, United Kingdom, United States
Language: English
Released: 2017
Production: Tim Bevan, Eric Fellner, Peter Gustafsson, Robyn Slovo; Another Park Film, Perfect World Pictures, Working Title Films; released by Universal Pictures Inc.
Directed by: Tomas Alfredson
Written by: Peter Straughan; Hossein Amini; Soren Sveistrup
Cinematography by: Dion Beebe
Music by: Marco Beltrami
Music Supervisor: Emma Cronly
Editing: Thelma Schoonmaker; Claire Simpson
Production Design: Maria Djurkovic
MPAA rating: R
Running time: 119 minutes

REVIEWS

Bell, Josh. *Las Vegas Weekly.* October 21, 2017.
Berardinelli, James. *ReelViews.* October 21, 2017.
Edelstein, David. *New York Magazine/Vulture.* October 20, 2017.
Gire, Dann. *Daily Herald.* October 19, 2017.
Putman, Dustin. *TheFrightFile.com.* October 26, 2017.
Snider, Eric D. *ReelViews.* October 24, 2017.
Tobias, Scott. *NPR.* October 19, 2017.
Verniere, James. *Boston Herald.* October 20, 2017.
Wilkinson, Alissa. *Vox.* October 19, 2017.
Willmore, Allison. *BuzzFeed News.* October 26, 2017.

QUOTES

Katrine Bratt: "Cutting things up...that's what a child does to maintain order."

TRIVIA

Martin Scorsese was originally attached to direct this movie.

SONG TO SONG

Love. Obsession. Betrayal.
—Movie tagline

Box Office: $443,684

The life and art of Terrence Malick remains a startlingly open and elusive text. His remarkable first two features—*Badlands* (1973), a lyrical and violent version about young criminals on the run, and *Days of Heaven* (1978), a haunting work about doomed love in the Texas panhandle set during the American entry into World War I—combined breathtaking physical beauty with startling technique. Fusing his philosophical ideas and moral themes into a distinctive personal style, Malick worked closer to silent cinema in privileging landscape, physical gestures, and the expressiveness of the human face. His manner of working was also radically different, closer to the mode of a 19th century painter or poet, a painstaking and grueling perfectionist. On *Days of Heaven*, for instance, he shot thousands of feet of footage and spent more than two years editing the film.

The rise of the blockbuster corporate cinema appeared to have little regard for his kind of cinema. At the height of his artistic power, Malick withdrew from movies and ostensibly disappeared. Two decades passed before his third feature, *The Thin Red Line* (1998), adapted from James Jones's 1962 World War II novel. His absence was a profound stylistic protest. Rather than opening up his art, Malick turned even deeper inward. Like Orson Welles or Jean-Luc Godard, Malick gave up the chance of a popular audience in order to purify and deepen his art.

In Malick's refashioning of the material, Jones' story of a disparate group of American soldiers in the Pacific campaign became a reverie, of ecological and human destruction. His visually complex rhyming of image and sound proved gorgeous, free, and intuitive. His first two features had extensive off-screen narration, spoken by young women. *The Thin Red Line* introduced something different, grafting the modernist literary techniques of James Joyce, Ezra Pound, T. S. Eliot, and Virginia Woolf, particularly her novel, *The Waves* (1931), in forming a kind of private symphony, an overlapping series of internal monologues that linked the characters. Their interior consciousness, private reflections, and ruminations locate a collective voice that luxuriates in dreams, desires and fears.

Malick's fourth feature film, *The New World* (2005), using the relationship of John Smith (Colin Farrell) and Pocahontas (Q'orianka Kilcher) as a story of conquest and the contentious founding of the country, marked an important dividing line, the point where his work forsook most recognizable forms of narrative storytelling in favor of pure abstraction. The movie also opened up the first serious breach in critical thinking about the director, hardening into warring camps of enthusiasts and extreme skeptics about a vision of moviemaking that was either daring or folly.

Malick's *The Tree of Life* (2011), introducing a deeply autobiographical strain, only intensified the debate about the larger value and importance of the director's art, whether his work was bold and exciting or solipsistic and repetitive. The framing story with Sean Penn was the first time Malick worked in a contemporary setting; the movie itself was a fugue, a gliding and impressionistic assemblage of memories of his Texas childhood, growing up with a formidable father (Brad Pitt), beautiful mother (Jessica Chastain), and two brothers. During one charged sequence, the camera swirls and moves around Chastain, who performs her own kind of pirouette, until she takes flight, a moment of magic realism and ecstatic possibility.

In Malick's new film, *Song to Song*, his eighth feature, that desire to be wholly free and uninhibited, liberated from the known social boundaries, is the animating principle. To move, dance, and twirl is the ultimate act of self-assertion. It's the third work, with *To the Wonder* (2012) and *Knight of Cups* (2015), of a modern trilogy, the stories opaque and elliptical fragments littered across time and space, and left up to the watcher to intuit the meanings, connections and associations.

All of Malick's films are part of a unified whole, like chapters of a book. The love triangle of *Days of Heaven*, *The New World*, and *To the Wonder* is again a dominant narrative thread. The seeker, with its moral and spiritual framework, is another constant. Unlike *Knight of Cups*, which sought to work new angles on familiar forms, reframing part of *The Tree of Life* with the death of a brother opening old wounds between a father and surviving sons, *Song to Song* feels more organic, open, and better structured.

The spontaneity and discovery is also more naturally interwoven, a natural given the movie's backdrop is the vibrant music scene in the director's hometown of Austin, Texas. (Patti Smith, Iggy Pop, and the Red Hot Chili Peppers all make vivid appearances in the film.) Malick likes to pull the viewer in, glancing, sinuously, with little exposition or formation introduction, using time, action, and movement to tease out the different personal connections. Faye (Rooney Mara), lithe, beautiful, tremulous, is a young songwriter and guitarist eager to catch the wave. At a party, she is introduced to BV (Ryan Gosling) and the two immediately plunge into a full-throttled love affair.

Malick's elliptical and discontinuous style is wholly unburdened with any real linear shape. The movie slips in and out of the present tense. The scenes, short, fragmentary and discursive, achieve a peculiar rhythm of surrender and release, of ritual and performance, as the camera floats and whirls around a series of hangouts, parties, music festivals, and concerts. Cook (Michael Fassbender), the dramatic wild card, is a skilled, hypnotic music mogul with the resources and power to make a career. He is grooming BV for his breakthrough. The themes of pursuit and ambition have an almost maniacal glee, played out in one telling moment where Cook is trying to seduce by allowing him to try on his expensive Armani suit. In another moment, the two men and Faye take a private plane to Mexico for a drunken revelry.

Faye, it turns out, is also connected romantically with Cook, whom she has worked for as a receptionist since she was a teenager. As Faye oscillates between the two men, *Song to Song* becomes a kind of Faustian pact, the Machiavellian Cook orchestrating all manner of dramatic rises and tragic falls. This first section of the film, deeply elemental with its water imagery of rebirth, has a hushed and radiant glow, these beautiful people arrayed against the gleaming architecture, glass towers, and terraced swimming pools. Cook's magnetism, with his need for control and surrender, has a naturally punitive side and is played out in his interaction with Rhonda (Natalie Portman), a vulnerable teacher he sweeps off her feet and eventually marries.

As the different strands are pulled together, Malick enlarges rather than narrows his canvas. Conversation tends to be caught or overheard rather than dramatically played out in the expected dramaturgy. The characters push all the boundaries, the tension between their interior feelings and outside behavior yielding a particular release and abandon that proves either illuminating or destabilizing. The rawness of the moment, the volatility of attraction, upends all sense of trust or decorum, so BV falls in with the beautiful Amanda (Cate Blanchett) and Faye has an affair with the stunning French artist, Zoey (Bérénice Marlohe). Zoey has a terrific moment, stopping traffic just to strut and show off her new girlfriend, that underlines her private rapture.

In *Knight of Cups*, where Christian Bale played a Hollywood screenwriter, the movie was entombed by an empty virtuosity. The characters were so scattershot, their motivations and ideas too blank and unformed, there was little opportunity to get inside them psychologically. He has not wholly solved the problem here, but the actors, like Portman and Blanchett, who worked with Malick in *Knight of Cups*, come off her as much more solid and tenacious, making their fate all the more devastating.

Malick is fearless and unafraid to come off either absurd or ridiculous. At its most excessive, the film is more illustrated than directed, with its mélange of beautiful people, models, singers, and actresses and their perfect bone structure. Malick's style is going to naturally crowd out deserving performers, and the movie could have used a lot more of Portman's Rhonda. If some are frustrated by Malick's storytelling, it seems more galling that somebody so smart could be so insensitive or tone-deaf, about the casual misogyny or racism of the Mexican sequence.

Fassbender's Cook is a monster, cold and inviolate, but this tense, alive actor is wired in, his body taut and expressive, and his performance is an electrifying one. Gosling's role is more interior and conflicted, and the beats—jealousy and betrayal—are less explosive or dramatically illuminating. Mara is a beautiful woman, but she is also the most pliant character; there's a recurrent image of Cook, BV, and Zoey wrapping their arms around her stomach, as though they were avid to mold her.

The achievement is not the director's alone. Jack Fisk, the production designer who has also done seminal work for David Lynch and Paul Thomas Anderson, brings his own discerning eye. The great cinematographer Emmanuel Lubezki, who has photographed every Malick film since *The New World*, wields the camera with precision and flair. They work primarily in 35mm but also shoot in other formats, lower end video and Go Pro to better emphasize point of view.

Malick's style is unapologetic and argumentative. His movie is suffused with a natural beauty and wonder—cloud formations, pools of water, gradations of light—and it is in the faces where the images really sing and gain meaning. They help blot out some of the lingering ugliness. At a time of crushing sameness, *Song to Song* dares to stand alone.

Patrick Z. McGavin

CREDITS

BV: Ryan Gosling
Faye: Rooney Mara
Cook: Michael Fassbender
Rhonda: Natalie Portman
Amanda: Cate Blanchett
Origin: United States
Language: English
Released: 2017
Production: Nicolas Gonda, Sarah Green, Ken Kao; Buckeye Pictures, FilmNation Entertainment, Waypoint Entertainment; released by Broad Green Pictures
Directed by: Terrence Malick
Written by: Terrence Malick
Cinematography by: Emmanuel Lubezki
Sound: Joel Dougherty

Music Supervisor: Lauren Marie Mikus
Editing: Rehman Nizar Ali; Hank Corwin; Keith Fraase
Art Direction: Ruth De Jong
Costumes: Jacqueline West
Production Design: Jack Fisk
MPAA rating: R
Running time: 129 minutes

REVIEWS

Adams, Sam. *Slate.* March 23, 2017.
Burr, Ty. *Boston Globe.* March 23, 2017.
Hassenger, Jesse. *The A.V Club.* March 16, 2017.
Chang, Justin. *Los Angeles Times.* March 16, 2017.
Dargis, Manohla. *New York Times* . March 16, 2017.
Ebiri, Bilge. *Village Voice.* March 16, 2017.
Goodykoontz, Bill. *Arizona Republic.* March 23, 2017.
Hoffman, Jordan. *The Guardian.* March 12, 2017.
Hornaday, Ann. *Washington Post.* March 23, 2017.
Phillips, Michael. *Chicago Tribune.* March 23, 2017.

QUOTES

Patti Smith: "I never thought I would live long. You know, I'd be an artist and die young of tuberculosis or something, like Charlotte Brontë."

TRIVIA

Actor Michael Fassbender replaced Christian Bale role when Bale was forced to withdraw from the role due to *American Hustle* (2013).

THE SPACE BETWEEN US

He's running out of time.
—Movie tagline

Box Office: $7.9 Million

When Gary Oldman is standing in front of a NASA logo talking about depleted Earth resources and a childhood dream of living on Mars, at the open of *The Space Between Us*, the groundwork is laid for a story of survival and/or underdog triumph. His Nathaniel Shepherd hands the mission to a crew of six including flight commander, Sarah Elliot (Janet Montgomery), who begins vomiting soon into the trip. Only this is not caused by zero gravity, but from the life growing inside of her. After an entirely unconvincing conversation about whether to scrub the mission or carry the baby to term on the Red Planet, the decision for the latter costs Sarah her life. But Gardner Elliot is born.

For sixteen years, Gardner (Asa Butterfield) has been "raised in a bubble with scientists," making him quite the smart lad. He has even created a best friend in Centaur, a robot voiced by the film's own director, Peter Chelsom. Being at that age of rebellion, the boy has taken to being inquisitive about the world he has never known. That includes not only his birth mother and the unknown identity of his father, but his online chat pal, Tulsa (Britt Robertson), who feels just as much of an outsider as Gardner does with her revolving door of foster parents. With the help of his own maternal guardian, astronaut Kendra Wyndham (Carla Gugino), he prepares himself physically for a visit to the land of conception with the rigors of a gravitational pull.

Ambition is in rich supply in a tale that wants to begin like *The Martian* (2015) and then coast into a teenage version of *Starman* (1984). The difference being that both of those films were well-crafted science-fiction tales that began with intelligence and human emotion only to see both intersect on their journey. In the true story of the Apollo 13 mission, astronaut Ken Mattingly was scrapped three days prior to launch for mere exposure to measles (which he never contracted). The idea that some 45-plus years later (the story's precise timeline to present or future is never clear) the first manned-mission to Mars, a trip that could take up to nine months, would fail to identify a pregnancy is enough to make Neil DeGrasse Tyson pull his hair out.

Reducing the film's problems to a cautionary tale that the world could use more scientists just for film consultation alone would be a bit like criticizing *Star Wars* (1977) for hearing explosions in space. Then again this is a film where one hears a schoolteacher say, "And those are the highlights of the 19th century industrial revolution." CliffsNotes notwithstanding, everything about the narrative feels rushed; defined in a single moment where Gardner and Nathaniel ask each other questions but feel compelled to play it like a lightning round in the middle of a game of Musical Chairs. Escape, retreat, and repeat while two members of NASA basically chase Gardner around in hopes of either keeping him safe or his existence a secret. Again, the screenplay is never clear which takes priority but it does allow ample time for Oldman to appear as a crazy person for the rest of the film; shouting through fences, screaming from moving vehicles and harassing homeless teenage girls in the trunk of a car.

Oldman's embrace of desperate insanity does little to endear his character but it is at least bewildering enough to distract from all the holes in the film's storytelling. The biggest empty hole of it all though is the film's lead. A child actor may be able to get away with wide-eyed moxie and curiosity but as he continues towards a path into more complex situations and emotions, those skills must grow beyond the age of the body. Butterfield was shielded under the guise of a Scorsese picture in *Hugo* (2011), but through *Ender's Game* (2013) and *Miss Peregrine's Home for Peculiar Children* (2016) he has proven too often to be someone still in the awkward audition phase of his career who lacks the requisite motor skills to drive an audience to believe his reactions in such fantastical situations. Gardner may fashion himself an angel who has fallen to Earth to be with Tulsa, but Butterfield is so unconvincing in his curiosity for the mysteries of his new surroundings that the reach for any genuine romanticism is beyond more than just the stars.

The Man Who Fell to Earth (1976) this is not. It is barely *Mac and Me* (1988). Whatever happened from final draft to final edit, the screenplay credited to Allan Loeb barely imbues Gardner with the farsighted curiosity of *The Truman Show* (1998) in what lies beyond what he has called home all his life. His utter lack of chemistry with Tulsa can be summed up in the video of courtship rituals likely shared by Nicholas Sparks before sitting down with a bottle of wine and a medical glossary to write his next book. "He is suffering from an enlarged heart" (aka Osteogenssis Imperfecta) that cannot handle the atmosphere. A diagnosis like that is hardly the perfect time for a pop song, a shopping montage, and the fact that he is on his fifth greasy hamburger. Moments like these suggest the film is actively trolling viewers with its gleeful scientific ignorance, proving that the range to which *The Space Between Us* goes to divide itself between teenage dopamine and scientific truth can be measured in light years.

Erik Childress

CREDITS

Nathaniel Shepherd: Gary Oldman
Gardner Elliot: Asa Butterfield
Kendra Wyndham: Carla Gugino
Tulsa: Britt Robertson
Tom Chen: B.D. Wong
Origin: United States
Language: English
Released: 2017
Production: Richard Barton Lewis; Los Angeles Media Fund, Southpaw Entertainment; released by STX Entertainment
Directed by: Peter Chelsom
Written by: Allan Loeb
Cinematography by: Barry Peterson
Music by: Andrew Lockington
Sound: Todd Toon
Music Supervisor: Jason Markey
Editing: David Moritz
Art Direction: Domenic Silvestri
Costumes: Christopher Lawrence
Production Design: Kirk M. Petruccelli
MPAA rating: PG
Running time: 120 minutes

REVIEWS

Bell, Josh. *Las Vegas Weekly*. February 3, 2017.
Berardinelli, James. *ReelViews*. February 2, 2017.
Chang, Justin. *Los Angeles Times*. February 3, 2017.
Dowd, A.A. *The A.V. Club*. February 2, 2017.
Maltin, Leonard. *LeonardMaltin.com*. February 4, 2017.
Morgenstern, Joe. *Wall Street Journal*. February 3, 2017.
Nicholson, Amy. *MTV*. February 2, 2017.
Nusair, David. *Reel Film Reviews*. February 8, 2017.
Verniere, James. *Boston Herald*. February 3, 2017.
Whitty, Stephen. *Newark Star-Ledger*. February 3, 2017.

QUOTES

Sarah Elliot: "Courage is just fear that has said its prayers."

TRIVIA

In the scene where Gardener arrive on Earth, the space suit masks, worn by some of the scientists, are actually a brand of full-face snorkel masks.

SPIDER-MAN: HOMECOMING

Homework can wait. The city can't.
—Movie tagline

Box Office: $334.2 Million

If Marvel were the sort of corporation that needed to win over the public at large, their mantra or tag line could easily be "Marvel Listens, Marvel Cares." After all, The Marvel Movie Machine has led all other television, cinematic, and ancillary markets in terms of diversity by casting more women and people of color, as well as featuring more characters of unclear gender designation than any other major media conglomerate. Marvel's listens to what fans and consumers want from superhero franchise stories as well. An example of Marvel being present and invested in hearing from those buying their product has never been clearer than in *Spider-Man: Homecoming*, a near-perfect summer blockbuster that reignites, after long ambivalence, probably the easiest comic book character ever to bring to the big screen as well as a rare film that uses inclusivity as a plot twist.

Fox, the company who held the rights to Spider-Man on the big screen were simply doing it wrong with the character. From fogginess on how old Peter Parker (the man-behind-the-Spider-Man-mask) should be to downright blindness on not only what makes him tick but also how villains in the original comic books were specifically designed to be the antithesis of Parker himself, all conspired to make Fox look like a media company who wanted the buckets of cash from Spider-Man fans without doing the actual work of getting to know their cash cow. When Marvel took back the reigns on "Ole Web-Head" they immediately trotted out a near-perfect envisioning of how the property should be managed via a short cameo in *Captain America: Civil War* (2016) which, not coincidentally, is where *Spider-Man: Homecoming* begins.

Whereas the "inconsistent" Spider-Man films of the past decade and a half-felt content to make each of their reboot films an origin story, in *Spider-Man: Homecoming* Marvel immediately shows fans how much they listen by recognizing everyone already knows how Peter Parker got his spider-like powers. Furthermore, they also eschew the overdone storyline of Peter's father figure Uncle Ben reminding Peter that "with great power comes great responsibility" before being killed basically because Peter did not heed his words. Again, Marvel presents awareness that fans already know these story beats and they show faith in their audience by not forcing played out plot points down viewers throats in order to stick to a designated runtime or range of prescribed films. As a result, one feels ready to see what this Peter Parker/ Spider-Man is all about right when the gate opens, and this is where things get fun.

Spider-Man: Homecoming features a high-school age Peter Parker, who remains one thin thread away from being a complete social outcast. His science nerd tendencies make him a target for bullies and his inability to win the girl of his dreams have never been shown as well in a Spider-Man film. Yet, *Spider-Man: Homecoming* not only portrays Parker properly (young, smart, heart of gold, and a bit sassy) they also "dare" to cast a wide net of diverse actors to surround him including re-envisioning classic Parker bully nemesis Flash Thompson using an Indian actor (Tony Revolori, *The Grand Budapest Hotel* [2014]) and making Parker's love interest, Liz (Laura Harrier), African American. Yes, not only is his love interest not redheaded Mary Jane Watson, it's a woman of color. Although this is handled naturally, and without drawing self-congratulatory attention to itself.

So, *Spider-Man: Homecoming* gets Parker right, which is an obvious great first step but the film also nails its villain by casting Oscar nominee Michael Keaton (*Birdman* [2014]) as Adrian Toomes, a secondary Spidey villain also known as "The Vulture." While it's unclear if the filmmakers decided to cast Keaton as a thumb of the nose to the overly hyped and easily forgettable *Birdman,* which starred Keaton in the titular role and cleaned house at the Oscars (Best Picture, Best Director, Best Original Screenplay, Best Cinematography), it does not really matter as Keaton brings life to an everyman who gets tired of being pushed around by the "man." In reaction to this very real feeling in America today, Toomes decides to collect scavenged alien junk and, using mechanical know-how, turn that junk into dangerous weaponry. He makes himself a kind of vigilante, who is, of course, on a crash course towards a confrontation with Spider-Man.

As mentioned earlier, the played-out Uncle Ben storyline is completely gone. In its place is Iron Man himself, Tony Stark (Robert Downey Jr.), as a father figure trying to get Peter to become the hero they both think he can be. Peter's guardian Aunt May also gets a nice spin by not being a doddering old lady as in past films (and, the comics) and instead casting Marisa Tomei as an older, single, and comely Auntie. While *Spider-Man: Homecoming* does feature a few montages of Peter trying to learn how to master his abilities, the film even takes this in a different "origin" direction by letting Parker keep the fancy Spider-Man suit that was designed for him by Stark and given to him in the aforementioned *Captain America: Civil War.* This suit features almost as many gadgets as Stark's own Iron Man suit, including a kind of on-board Siri device that Parker connects with and names "Karen." The scenes of Parker navigating this new suit are truly clever and funny, and also add to a storyline about a young hero in training who thinks he's ready to be a grown-up hero, battle-tested and ready, but soon finds out that's not the case.

Peter Parker starts out in the Marvel comics as a smart kid given an extraordinary talent. The comics are so beloved because readers can grow with Parker (and, Spider-Man) and watch him struggle with real-life issues as well as those wrapped up in being Spidey. The previous cinematic efforts seemed to jump past all these struggles and go straight for adult love, adult relationships, and adult results. But this younger, spry story and character just works better as a whole. *Spider-Man: Homecoming* does indeed get intense and there are some spectacular scenes of Spider-Man trying to save the day while only a third prepared, but that's also why the film works. The audience believes that this young Spidey is in over his head and a happy ending is not necessarily a guarantee. As the third act expertly clicks into place, it becomes clearer that Spider-Man is exactly where he should be—in the loving arms of Marvel.

Don R. Lewis

CREDITS

Peter Parker/Spider-Man: Tom Holland
Adrian Toomes/Vulture: Michael Keaton
Tony Stark/Iron Man: Robert Downey, Jr.
May Parker: Marisa Tomei
Happy Hogan: Jon Favreau
Pepper Potts: Gwyneth Paltrow
Origin: United States
Language: English
Released: 2017
Production: Kevin Feige, Amy Pascal; Marvel Studios; released by Columbia Pictures
Directed by: Jon Watts
Written by: Jon Watts; Jonathan M. Goldstein; John Francis Daley; Christopher Ford; Chris McKenna; Erik Sommers
Cinematography by: Salvatore Totino
Music by: Michael Giacchino
Sound: Eric A. Norris; Steven Ticknor
Music Supervisor: Dave Jordan
Editing: Debbie Berman; Dan Lebental
Art Direction: Brad Ricker
Costumes: Louise Frogley
Production Design: Oliver Scholl
MPAA rating: PG-13
Running time: 133 minutes

REVIEWS

Abda-Santos, Alex. *Vox.* July 6, 2017.
Collin, Robbie. *The Telegraph.* June 30, 2017.
DeFore, John. *Hollywood Reporter.* June 29, 2017.
Graham, Jamie. *Total Film.* July 3, 2017.
Greenblatt, Leah. *Entertainment Weekly.* June 29, 2017.
LaSalle, Mick. *San Francisco Chronicle.* July 2, 2017.
Moore, Roger. *Movie Nation.* July 2, 2017.
Roffman, Michael. *Consequence of Sound.* June 29, 2017.
Stewart, Sara. *New York Post..* July 5, 2017.
Truitt, Brian. *USA Today.* June 26, 2017.

QUOTES

Peter Parker: "I'm sick of Mr. Stark treating me like a kid."
Ned Leeds: "But you are a kid."
Peter Parker: "Yeah, a kid who can stop a bus with his bare hands."

TRIVIA

Nick Fury was originally going to be Peter's mentor in the film, with Samuel L. Jackson reprising his role, but the decision was made to go with Tony Stark/Iron Man instead.

SPLIT

Kevin has twenty-three distinct personalities. The twenty-fourth is about to be unleashed.
—Movie tagline

Box Office: $138.3 Million

M. Night's Shyamalan's 2015 film *The Visit* was widely considered a return to form for the filmmaker *Time* once called "The Next Spielberg." After a few notable failures, including *The Happening* (2008) and *After Earth* (2013), *The Visit* brought the filmmaker back to his roots and made over $25 million in its opening weekend. But the question of whether or not that hit was a fluke or the start of a string of hits lingered in the air. Would Shyamalan return to the clunky filmmaking that marred the last decade or start another streak like the one that took him from *The Sixth Sense* (1999) to *Unbreakable* (2000) to *Signs* (2002)? It turns out that *The Visit* was no career aberration as his follow-up ended up as Shyamalan's biggest box office smash since *Signs. Split* set the box office on fire, sticking at number one for a stunning four weeks, and even garnering a few citations during the year-end push for awards, particularly for James McAvoy's tour de force lead performance. Sadly, the film fails to artistically live up to its box office success, frustrating as often as it is thrilling, and particularly disappointing when considered that it's all really designed as a surprise entry in a now-franchise.

Casey Cooke (Anya Taylor-Joy) seems like an average, quiet teenager, although she's a bit more reserved than most due to a dark secret in her past, one that Shyamalan will tease out rather manipulatively over the course of the film. Before that, she's just having an ordinary day with a couple of her friends, Claire (Haley Lu Richardson) and Marcia (Jessica Sula), although they seem to be kind of struggling to make the third wheel fit in on their trip to the mall. Everything changes for the trio when they get back into their car, thinking it's one of the girl's fathers there to pick them up but quickly discovering that the hooded shape behind the wheel is Kevin Wendell Crumb (McAvoy), a man with dissociative identity disorder (DID) that has resulted in at least 23 distinct personalities, and a possible 24th known only as "The Beast."

Kevin throws the girls into a locked room in his basement, and Shyamalan does his best work in *Split* just by letting McAvoy go wild for a few scenes. In these interactions, audiences are introduced to a few of the "people" living within Kevin, including "Barry" (the dominant, most "normal" personality for most of Kevin's life), "Dennis" (the OCD-stricken man who actually does the kidnapping), "Hedwig" (a 9-year-old boy), and "Patricia" (a matronly woman from England). While Kevin's doctor, Karen Fletcher (Betty Buckley) speaks of his two dozen personalities, she's most concerned about the one that all of his different identities seem to fear in equal measure, someone, or something, called "The Beast."

The bulk of *Split* is a cat-and-mouse game in which Casey tries to figure out how she can manipulate one of the personalities to save her and her friends. She soon realizes that the more-malevolent Dennis has taken a dominant role, and is preparing, with Patricia, for the arrival of The Beast. Casey befriends Hedwig in the hope that the young boy can find it in his heart to set them free. As the film unfolds, Shyamalan cuts to scenes with Dr. Fletcher and flashbacks that fill in Casey's background, revealing she was abused by her uncle. Both of these decisions drastically reduce the possible tension in the very structure of *Split*. It's as if Shyamalan did not trust his own skill to keep the suspense high enough if he trapped viewers in a madman's basement. Every time that the film leaves Casey's plight, the air comes out of it a bit, and the Fletcher character serves little purpose other than to over-explain to viewers the background of our villain, who would be a lot scarier were he explained less. There is a significantly better version of *Split* that never leaves Kevin's trap.

Split becomes something else entirely when "The Beast" actually arrives, and he's no mere serial killer. He actually possesses superhuman abilities, and he kills Dr. Fletcher before murdering Marcia and Claire. At this point, like so many Shyamalan films, *Split* becomes something other than how it began—turning from thriller into sci-fi/horror or arguably even superhero movie. It is essentially an origin story for a supervillain as Kevin/Dennis/Patricia/etc. eventually becomes known as "The Horde," who surprisingly spares Casey after seeing the scars of her former abuse on her body. The Beast wanted to rid the world of the "untouched," and so allows Casey to live because she is damaged. The development of yet another arc in which abuse becomes a strength instead of a weakness leaves a rather icky film over the final act, and Shyamalan's understanding of DID is superficial at best. The film earned some much-deserved criticism over the way it uses real mental illness as thriller fodder.

The thudding manipulation of the Casey arc and the disingenuous taste left by Kevin's illness would not have an impact if *Split* was simply better-made. It's not only the aforementioned tension breaks or the doctor character who exists purely to explain a villain's motives and background that disappoint—it's the final scenes which reveal this has all been a set-up/sequel to *Unbreakable*. As David Dunn (Bruce Willis), the protagonist from that far-superior film, shows up at a diner, audiences learn that The Horde and Mr. Glass exist in the same universe, confirmed by the announcement of *Glass,* to be released in 2019.

The one saving grace of *Split,* and the main reason it became such a box office hit, is the fearlessness of McAvoy. (Taylor-Joy and Richardson are not bad here, but the underwritten parts do not allow them to show too much of their increasingly impressive abilities. See *Thoroughbreds* [2017] and *Columbus* [2017] for that.) McAvoy is so riveting that it's often easy to let the flaws of the film fall by the wayside and just appreciate *Split* as an actor's showcase. It's just a shame that that showcase never feels centered in something worthy of its actor's efforts.

Brian Tallerico

CREDITS

Dennis/Patricia/Hedwig/The Beast/Kevin Wendell Crumb/Barry/Orwell/Jade: James McAvoy
Casey Cooke: Anya Taylor-Joy
Dr. Karen Fletcher: Betty Buckley
Claire Benoit: Haley Lu Richardson
Marcia: Jessica Sula
Origin: United States
Language: English, French, Spanish
Released: 2016
Production: Jason Blum, Marc Bienstock, M. Night Shyamalan; Blinding Edge Pictures, Blumhouse Productions, LLC.; released by Universal Pictures
Directed by: M. Night Shyamalan
Written by: M. Night Shyamalan
Cinematography by: Mike Gioulakis
Music by: West Dylan Thordson
Music Supervisor: Susan Jacobs
Editing: Luke Franco Ciarrocchi
Art Direction: Jesse Rosenthal
Costumes: Paco Delgado
Production Design: Mara Lepere-Schloop
MPAA rating: PG-13
Running time: 234 minutes

REVIEWS

Abele, Robert. *TheWrap.* January 19, 2017.
Edelstein, David. *New York Magazine.* January 24, 2017.
Kernion, Jette. *IndieWire.* September 17, 2016.
Lane, Anthony. *The New Yorker.* January 23, 2017.
Morgenstern, Joe. *Wall Street Journal.* January 19, 2017.
Scherstuhl, Alan. *Village Voice.* January 17, 2017.
Scott, A.O. *New York Times.* January 19, 2017.
Stewart, Sara. *New York Post.* January 18, 2017.
Willmore, Alison. *The Playlist.* January 19, 2017.
Zacharek, Stephanie. *Time.* January 19, 2017.

QUOTES

The Beast: "Those who have not been torn have no value in themselves and no place in this world! They are asleep!"

TRIVIA

Joaquin Phoenix was originally cast as the elad in this film, but when he could not reach a contract agreement, James McAvoy was cast instead.

THE SQUARE

Box Office: $1.4 Million

The talented Swedish writer and director Ruben Östlund is "filmmaker as performance artist." His deft sleight of hand is always about exposing the artifice and revealing a deeper truth, like the dazzling funhouse mirror sequence at the climax of Orson Welles's *The Lady from Shanghai* (1947). In turn, the damning and intimate portrait always unravels his characters.

In the director's breakthrough feature, *Force Majeure* (2014), a man's rational-though-questionable decision to think immediately of his own safety during a freak accident epitomizes his larger failure as a father and husband, a telling indictment of his narcissism, self-regard, and lack of nerve.

Östlund has a showy, even flamboyant tableau style, his observant and enveloping camera is always ready to pounce on a subject. His rigorous, deadpan style is meant as a test, a moral inquiry into the actions, behavior, and motivations of his characters. The audience is often implicated as well, and it is thrilling, even audacious at the director's use of dead space, awkward, long passages of deeply uncomfortable moments. It certainly takes the veil off.

The director's new film, *The Square,* is his boldest work to date, a rude, rollicking, and often frequently hilarious take down of what, for better or worse, might be called the current state of things. It's an art world satire, but often a great deal more, a peeling back of the false promise of a Scandinavian utopia, shrewdly and gleefully exposing all of its contradictions, inanities, and quintessential fakery.

The title refers to an exhibition, by a prominent Argentine artist, freshly installed at the X-Royal, a (fictitious) Stockholm museum. It is an illuminated exterior rectangular space with the title card declaring it a "sanctuary of trust and caring. Within its boundaries we all share equal rights and obligations." Over the movie's abundant two-and-a-half-hour running time, Östlund goes about ripping those sentiments to shreds.

The director also wrote the script, and the movie has a headlong, ferocious momentum, pinging from one absurd encounter to another and pausing at just the right moment to consider the darker implications of the material. The discursive plot comes together more in retrospect. Consistent with his own calling as a kind of expert puppet master or court jester, Östlund constructs the movie around three distinct acts of guerilla theater. The sharp and intuitive approach adroitly fuses the disparate parts.

The first episode introduces Christian (brilliantly played by the talented Danish actor Claes Bang), the chief curator of the X-Royal. Lanky and formidable, he radiates an aristocratic air and bemused entitlement. As Östlund later shrewdly demonstrates, everything about Christian is calculated and manufactured, like the way he carefully scripts a speech to make it seem spontaneous. At the film's start, in broad daylight walking to work, Christian is quickly humiliated by an elaborate ruse carried out by street hustlers. Believing that he has come to the aid of a young woman against a violently jealous boyfriend, Christian is instead shown as a hapless mark stripped of his wallet and cell phone.

His colleague, Michael (Christopher Læssø), tracks the phone to a rough, working-class apartment complex whose residents are primarily migrant workers and refugees. Christian drafts Michael into his ill-conceived plot of mass implication, callously having Michael drop an accusatory letter in each apartment mailbox that identifies them as the offending party and demanding the stolen possessions be returned. It works, up to a point, except the blowback occasioned by a persistent and angry young boy (Elijandro Edouard), who threatens to unleash chaos for Christian unless he apologizes for calling him a thief.

Christian's story grounds the film, but it splinters in other directions, with often disquieting and thrilling effects, especially in locating the brusque absurdity of the daily museum rituals, like a visiting American artist (Dominic West) whose interview about his work is profanely interrupted by a man who suffers from Tourette's syndrome. Östlund has the withering glare of a natural satirist, but he is not necessarily cruel or cold. Compositionally, the off-center framing and long take shots are jarringly deployed, like another hilarious moment, where a carefully mounted floor exhibition of gravel is accidentally vacuumed by a museum worker.

Two anarchic marketing consultants brought in by the museum to develop an advertising campaign for the new exhibition detonate the next guerilla campaign. Their callous and racist video, meant to send up the orderly and liberal values of the bourgeois gatekeepers, quickly goes viral and the distracted Christian ends up bearing the brunt of the horrifying professional consequences.

This leads to the third and most riveting and disquieting act of guerilla provocation. A stately gala dinner for the museum's donor class and cultural elite is undone by the sudden appearance of a different kind of intruder, a muscular and prehensile man named Oleg (Terry Notary). As he leaps from table to table, his swaggering, animalistic desires and sexual overtures produce from the shocked and terrified crowd a mixture of responses, from stunned apathy to, finally, a murderous rage.

Östlund has been criticized for the obviousness of his targets. The rhetorical flourishes of the art-world material is held up not as ridicule but emblematic of a deeper divide, of the vast difference between our highest ideas and principles and the crushing reality of how money, wealth, and class walls off the elite and powerful from hard and uncomfortable truths. The gala dinner sequence is powerful not just because of its sociological insights and its canny use of the bystander effect, but like Christian's being robbed or the viral marketing video, it forces a personal reckoning.

In the opening scene, a television interview between the curator and an American journalist (the superb Elisabeth Moss), Christian says the greatest difficulty is still money. *The Square* is all about the corruption of money. Again Östlund brings up obvious counterexamples, of beggars, migrants, and wailing children. The sanctuary promised by the movie's title is not about empowering and liberating the disenfranchised. It exists to inoculate the powerful from any sense of responsibility.

In *The Square,* Östlund uses time evocatively in drawing out character and incident. The movie has its longeurs, and sometimes the humor seems misplaced or off-rhythm. Östlund is very good at jarring others though less interested in any kind of self-exploration. His own story, especially being a divorced father with two girls, is mirrored in the conception of Christopher. The lead actor, Bang, brings both a solidity and sharp comic timing to the role. He is never afraid to bring out the smarmy side, like another discomfiting post-coitus sequence with Moss's American journalist.

Throughout, Östlund frames characters in distance through car windows and doors. What is ultimately most powerful, interesting and original is the way the characters in *The Square* are allowed no release or easy escape.

Patrick Z. McGavin

CREDITS

Christian: Claes Bang
Anne: Elisabeth Moss
Julian: Dominic West
Oleg: Terry Notary
Michael: Christopher Laesso
Origin: United States
Language: English, Swedish, Danish
Released: 2017
Production: Philippe Bober, Erik Hemmendorff; Arte France Cinema, Plattform Produktion; released by Magnolia Pictures
Directed by: Ruben Ostlund
Written by: Ruben Ostlund
Cinematography by: Fredrik Wenzel
Sound: Andreas Franck
Music Supervisor: Rasmus Thord
Editing: Ruben Ostlund; Jacob Secher Schulsinger
Costumes: Sofie Krunegard
Production Design: Josefin Asberg
MPAA rating: R
Running time: 142 minutes

REVIEWS

Chang, Justin. *Los Angeles Times.* October 26, 2017.
Dowd, A.A. *The A.V. Club.* October 26, 2017.
Ebiri, Bilge. *Village Voice.* October 23, 2017.
Gleiberman, Owen. *Variety.* May 25, 2017.
Kiang, Jessica. *Playlist.* May 25, 2017.
LaSalle, Mick. *San Francisco Chronicle.* November 9, 2017.
Morgenstern, Joe. *Wall Street Journal.* October 26, 2017.
Phipps, Keith. *Uproxx.* December 4, 2017.
Sims, David. *The Atlantic.* November 20, 2017.
Yoshida, Emily. *New York Magazine.* May 25, 2017.

QUOTES

Christian: "The Square is a sanctuary of trust and caring. Within it we all share equal rights and obligations."

TRIVIA

The incident where Christian's cell phone is stolen is based on a real-life experience of director Ruben Östlund, whose friend was robbed in a similar way.

AWARDS

Nominations:
Oscars 2017: Foreign Film
Golden Globes 2018: Foreign Film

THE STAR

It takes many tails to tell the greatest story ever.
—Movie tagline

Box Office: $40.8 Million

More interesting than anything that happens in the computer-animated family comedy *The Star* is a somewhat curious statement that comes at its conclusion, following the first portion of its end credits: "While having fun and taking some adventurous artistic license to tell this story, the filmmakers strived to remain true to the values and essence of the greatest story ever told."

Sounding like the result of a much-debated, exhaustively vetted corporate stab at preemptive apology and/or grading-on-a-curve persuasion, this declaration is unintentionally revealing about the compromises and different motivations that went into producing such a bland, shrug-inducing movie. *The Star*, you see, tells the story of the Nativity of Jesus—but in large measure from the perspective of animals surrounding the Virgin Mary. So, it presumably aims to lure evangelical Christian audiences for whom the Dove Family Award is a meaningful and trusted signifier of quality, while also shoehorning in enough back-and-forth banter between colorful critters to bait general audiences. The result, an achievement in clinically engineered mildness, is pleasing to no viewer seeking anything more than a video babysitter.

The Star's curious domestic release in mid-November—up against *Justice League* and the family drama *Wonder*, and just one week before Pixar's *Coco*—would seem to indicate that distributor Sony viewed the film as something of a niche-market legacy title, with a limited theatrical window and ancillary platforms its most likely path toward profitability. It would open to under $10 million, slotting sixth for its debut weekend, and end up grossing just over $34 million in the United States.

Coming in at a slim 79 minutes (minus end credits), *The Star* opens with a title card that establishes its setting as Nazareth, "nine months BC." Teenage Mary (voiced by Gina Rodriguez) is visited by an angel, who tells her she will bear the Messiah. A mouse named Abby (voiced by Kristin Chenoweth) overhears this conversation, and spreads word to other animals.

The movie then makes an awkward pivot in both perspective and timeline, leaping forward six months and introducing a miller's donkey, eventually dubbed Bo (voiced by Steven Yeun), who dreams of rising above his lot in life and joining a royal caravan. After Bo finally escapes captivity, and teams up with Dave (voiced by Keegan-Michael Key), a loquacious dove, the pair happen upon Mary and Joseph (voiced by Zachary Levi), who have just had their wedding dinner. Mary nurses Bo's wounded ankle, emotionally binding him to the couple, and stalling his plans to again set out on his own.

Meanwhile, after Mary and Joseph leave Nazareth for Bethlehem, King Herod (voiced by Christopher Plummer) hears word from three wisemen of a prophesied new king, and dispatches a soldier with two dogs, Thaddeus and Rufus (voiced by Ving Rhames and Gabriel Iglesias, respectively), to track down this threat to his rule. Bo then sets off, again with Dave, to warn Mary and Joseph. Along the way they meet a friendly sheep, Ruth (voiced by Aidy Bryant), who is similarly fascinated by the brightness of a new star in the sky. In the end, naturally, baby Jesus is born, surrounded by a beatific assortment of animals.

Several minutes in, one senses that *The Star* is merely a time-marking piece of placeholder entertainment, devoid of visual ambition, yes, but also any sort of particularly well-defined narrative perspective that would make it stand out. Director Timothy Reckart was nominated for a Best Animated Short Film Academy Award® for his stop-motion film *Head Over Heels* (2012), but *The Star* lacks any of the whimsicality or smart set-up and smooth pacing of that dialogue-free movie. Instead, working from a script by Carlos Kotkin, based on a story by Kotkin and Simon Moore, Reckart only engages in paint-by-number storytelling, awkwardly alternating between various groupings of characters who are given little to no reason (on-screen, at least) to be invested in the same cause.

Apart from a small handful of scatological jokes and a couple throwaway one-liners that offer up wan pop cultural references ("I love the smell of freshly ground grain in the morning," says Dave), *The Star* is mostly just a collection of very well-worn and familiar banter, stitched together with some clichéd scenes that advance the story geographically. If the movie was conceptually rigorous and committed to actually telling its story from the animals' point-of-view, that could be interesting. Instead the premise is applied three-quarters of the time, mixing in a bit of Mary and Joseph's story and leaving viewers to wonder what relevance a new Messiah has in the animal world, or even what exactly it means when Bo says, "Things are changing—that star means something, and I'm not going to be here forever."

The manner in which *The Star* tries to bridge the gap between the worlds of its human and animal characters certainly does not help. Early scenes establish that when animals are talking, humans merely hear noises appropriate to that specific species. But it is also dogs Thaddeus and Rufus who provide the main external threat in the film; they are proactive hunters of Mary, who extract information from Bo regarding her whereabouts. Even though they have a human handler, he never speaks, but apparently just waits in the background, out of frame, while dogs do the work with which he was tasked. Then, near its end, *The Star* ties the villainy of the dogs to their servitude, so when they are saved by Bo, they immediately recognize the error of their ways ("We're bad dogs"), apologize, and join in awestruck appreciation at the arrival of baby Jesus.

The movie boasts a deep roster of recognizable names—in addition to the previously mentioned cast members, other voice talent includes Tracy Morgan, Tyler Perry, Kris Kristofferson, Oprah Winfrey, Kelly Clarkson, popular televangelist Joel Osteen; and Mariah Carey, the latter of whom contributes an eponymous song to the movie's soundtrack. If the vocal performances are not especially memorable, they are at least of a piece, tonally; Reckart succeeds in taming the showier instincts of certain performers (Key, Morgan), resulting in a movie that at least possesses a modicum of modulated rather than manic energy.

The film's lack of stylistic sophistication is evidenced in its character work—with her matted hair, Mary comes across like a plastic children's toy—as well as the attention to background detail (or lack thereof). More grating is the nonsensical and unrealistic lighting design scheme in an important nighttime scene, in which animals are illuminated by a shining star as if key lit, despite no shadows existing elsewhere in the stable.

The film's music, mostly a selection of Christmas classics with R&B and pop inflections, is used in intrusive fashion, undercutting the introductions of various supporting characters; composer John Paesano's is scarcely better, also telling an audience what to feel about moments that have, more often than not, been under-sketched on a narrative level.

Rather senselessly, *The Star* tries to tell a specifically religious story while ignoring certain elements and also framing it in a way that, save two or three scenes, could be considered nonsectarian. Far from shining brightly, the result comes across as dreary and boring.

Brent Simon

CREDITS

Voice of Bo: Steven Yeun
Voice of Dave: Keegan Michael Key
Voice of Ruth: Aidy Bryant
Voice of Mary: Gina Rodriguez
Voice of Joseph: Zachary Levi
Origin: United States
Language: English
Released: 2017
Production: Jennifer Magee-Cook, Warren Franklin; Affirm Films; released by Columbia Pictures
Directed by: Timothy Reckart
Written by: Carlos Kotkin
Music by: John Paesano
Sound: Tim Chau
Editing: Pamela Ziegenhagen-Shefland
MPAA rating: PG
Running time: 86 minutes

REVIEWS

Debruge, Peter. *Variety.* November 16, 2017.
Duralde, Alonso. *TheWrap.* November 16, 2017.
Horwitz, Jane. *Washington Post.* November 16, 2017.
Linden, Sheri. *Hollywood Reporter.* November 16, 2017.
Means, Sean. *Salt Lake Tribune.* November 16, 2017.
Toumarkine, Doris. *Film Journal International.* November 16, 2017.
Vishnevetsky, Ignatiy. *The A.V. Club.* November 16, 2017.
Walsh, Katie. *Los Angeles Times.* November 16, 2017.
Watson, Keith. *Slant Magazine.* November 16, 2017.
Wloszczyna, Susan. *RogerEbert.com.* November 17, 2017.

TRIVIA

This is the second time that actor Christopher Plummer has played a character who could be referred to as King Herod. The first time was in *Jesus of Nazareth* (1977) when he played Herod Antipas, the son of this film's King Herod and the one of the people who presided over the trial of Jesus in the Easter story.

AWARDS

Nominations:

Golden Globes 2018: Song ("The Star")

STAR WARS: THE LAST JEDI

(Star Wars: Episode VIII—The Last Jedi)

Box Office: $611.5 Million

Writer/director Rian Johnson (previously best known for fare such as *The Brothers Bloom* [2008] and *Looper* [2012]) does with *Star Wars: The Last Jedi* what hasn't been done with the series in a very long time—he's made the saga epic again. Yes, J.J. Abrams brought the series back from the brink of death following George Lucas' prequels with *Star Wars: The Force Awakens* (2015), but with *The Last Jedi* Johnson takes the baton from Abrams and runs headlong into the series, never looking back (except for the adoring references and nods to earlier films). In fact, he did so well with this assignment, the powers that be have already brought him onboard to create an entirely new and separate trilogy of films set in the Star Wars universe.

The second installment of the third Star Wars trilogy, *The Last Jedi*, continues the Skywalker saga as Rey (Daisy Ridley), the unlikely hero from *The Force Awakens* begins training under the tutelage of Jedi Master Luke Skywalker (Mark Hamill) to hone her already evident powers. Meanwhile, the Resistance forces—including daring pilot Poe Dameron (Oscar Isaac) and former-Stormtrooper turned Resistance fighter Fin (John Boyega)—ready for battle against the re-invigorated militant forces of the First Order led by Kylo Ren (Adam Driver), who has grown even more powerful in the ways of the Force thanks to the teachings of his own master, the imposing and disfigured (a trait common among those in the Star Wars universe partial to the Dark Side) Supreme Leader Snoke (voiced by Andy Serkis). These multiple character arcs and plots all converge to culminate in an epic battle sequence that is reminiscent in scope of the classic samurai films of Akira Kurosawa.

While also a gifted filmmaker and storyteller, Johnson is clearly a fan of the series he is charged with continuing and this is evident in the reverence *The Last Jedi* affords its elder generation of heroes as both Hamill (as Skywalker) and the late Carrie Fisher (as Leia Organa) are allowed exquisite series-defining moments in a film that is remarkably strong in the emotional arena given its enormity and breadth. Another striking aspect of Johnson's approach to the material is, as Matt Zoller Seitz noted on *RogerEbert.com,* evident in the fact that the director somehow "manages to find a way to present the technology, mythology, and imagery [of the series] in a way that makes it feel new," all the while infusing the film with, what Manohla Dargis referred to in the *New York Times* as "visual wit and a human touch."

That "human touch" arrives mainly in the form of Kelly Marie Tran's Resistance fighter Rose, who teams up with Fin to search for a "master codebreaker" (played by Benicio Del Toro as a sort-of Han Solo surrogate) to help the Resistance defeat the First Order's devastating new weapon before it's used to eradicate the Resistance entirely. The pairing of these two is the emotional core and highlight of the film. Taken together with Ridley's ascension as Luke's protégé, these performances give *The Last Jedi* a gravitas that has been missing from the Star Wars galaxy since a long time ago. Via these interactions, we're also made aware of the "real" reason for Luke's self-imposed exile on Ahch-To and his reluctance to take on the training of Rey in the ways of the Force.

Although Rey is obviously the emotional core of the current trilogy, *The Last Jedi*'s focus is on Driver's ascension as "the" villain of the latest group of films. As, Brian Truitt wrote in *USA Today,* "as much as [*The*] *Force Awakens* was Ridley's," *The Last Jedi* belongs to Driver. Perhaps the next film in the sequence will shift the balance back to Ridley's Rey? Or, might there be another character lurking, just waiting to take up the mantle altogether? Regardless, Driver comes into his own here and effortlessly assumes the position of series villain.

Throughout the entire endeavor is Johnson's deft guiding hand and sprawling yet focused script. While the film's middle section may be a tad too long (the overall running time of *The Last Jedi* is two hours and thirty-two minutes—making it the longest film of the series to date, besting *Star Wars: Episode II—Attack of the Clones* [2002] by ten minutes), the film never plays as tedious. In fact, it shifts effortlessly from scene to scene and from character arc to character arc as each storyline is advanced to its own rewarding conclusion (of sorts).

Finally, the success of *The Last Jedi* relies upon the simple fact that it has made "Star Wars" indispensable, vital entertainment again. The film is, as the Zoller Seitz writes, "an earnest adventure full of passionate heroes and villains [as well as] a meditation on sequels and franchise properties." Ultimately, *Star Wars: The Last Jedi* is that rarest of cinematic commodities, the blockbuster film that succeeds in making you think while entertaining you all at the same time.

Michael J. Tyrkus

CREDITS

Luke Skywalker/Dobbu Scay: Mark Hamill
Leia Organa: Carrie Fisher
Kylo Ren: Adam Driver
Rey: Daisy Ridley
Finn: John Boyega
Origin: United States
Language: English
Released: 2017
Production: Ram Bergman, Leifur B. Dagfinnsson, Kathleen Kennedy; Lucasfilm Ltd., Ram Bergman Productions, Walt Disney Pictures; released by Walt Disney Studios Motion Pictures
Directed by: Rian Johnson
Written by: Rian Johnson
Cinematography by: Steve Yedlin
Music by: John Williams
Sound: Ren Klyce; Matthew Wood
Editing: Bob Ducsay
Art Direction: Todd Cherniawsky
Costumes: Michael Kaplan

Production Design: Rick Heinrichs
MPAA rating: PG-13
Running time: 152 minutes

REVIEWS

Dargis, Manohla. *New York Times.* December 12, 2017.
Dowd, A.A. *The A.V. Club.* December 12, 2017.
Graham, Adam. *Detroit News.* December 12, 2017.
Hornaday, Ann. *Washington Post.* December 12, 2017.
LaSalle, Mick. *San Francisco Chronicle.* December 12, 2017.
McCarthy, Todd. *Hollywood Reporter.* December 15, 2017.
Phillips, Michael. *Chicago Tribune.* December 12, 2017.
Roeper, Richard. *Chicago Sun-Times.* December 12, 2017.
Seitz, Matt Zoller. *RogerEbert.com.* December 12, 2017.
Truitt, Brian. *USA Today.* December 12, 2017.

QUOTES

Luke Skywalker: "This is not going to go the way you think!"

TRIVIA

Actor Mark Hamill told writer/director Rian Johnson after reading the script, "I pretty much fundamentally disagree with every choice you've made for this character. Now, having said that, I have gotten it off my chest, and my job now is to take what you've created and do my best to realize your vision."

AWARDS

Nominations:

Oscars 2017: Orig. Score, Sound, Sound FX Editing, Visual FX

British Acad. 2017: Sound, Visual FX

STEP

A real life story.
—Movie tagline

Box Office: $1.1 Million

Amanda Lipitz's *Step* has all the ingredients of a sports-related crowd pleaser. There's a team of underdogs in a hardscrabble city learning to work together to achieve one final shot at glory. There are familiar dramatic arcs for its main characters—a motley crew that includes the brainiac and the one struggling to beat the odds despite a troubled home life. Inspirational counselors and coaches will nurture the heroes, preparing them for competition and for life. The penultimate scene is a suspenseful contest of skill. And the film unfolds in a brisk 83 minutes, quite often feeling far too neatly designed to be anything but fiction.

Step, however, is no fiction. This is a documentary about the "Lethal Ladies of BLSYW," a step team of high school seniors looking for redemption at a statewide contest they've never been able to win. BLSYW is a predominantly African-American, all female charter school in Baltimore, and the "Lethal Ladies" are members of the institution's first graduating class. The school'd goal is to ensure that every single senior who walks across its stage in June will also be walking into college in September. The step team is not only a source of pride for the students but also a means of self-expression and a pleasant distraction from the sometimes harsh realities of working-class life.

Step follows three seniors: "Lethal Ladies" team founder Blessin Giraldo, Cori Grainger, and Tayla Solomon. Cori is the school's potential valedictorian whose dream is to go to Johns Hopkins University. Tayla is an average student with a no-nonsense corrections officer mother who won't stand for mediocre grades. Finally, Blessin's lack of attendance and low GPA has come back to haunt her in her final year, forcing her to play catch-up in order to land a spot in the New York City-area school she has chosen. Assisting each student is college advisor Paula Dofat, who guides her charges with a mixture of tough love, scholastic mentoring, and sisterly concern. Dofat shares most of her scenes with Blessin, who alternates between being committed to raising her GPA and cutting school due to her own fear of failure.

One would think that Lipitz, a Broadway producer, would ably handle the musical numbers. But the step routines are annoyingly protracted; fans of this style of performance will be disappointed and want more. The director proves far more adept at depicting the mother-daughter relationships of her subjects. Blessin's mother is open about her bouts with depression, which clearly affect her daughter (who may have also inherited the illness). Tayla's low-key demeanor bounces off her mother's more boisterous one. The introverted Cori's mother beams with pride whenever she looks at her daughter. Mrs. Grainger gets the film's best scene, a moment of unbridled joy when Cori earns a full ride to Johns Hopkins.

While the calculated stand-up-and-cheer structure of *Step* is undeniable and even welcome at times, it is also problematic. One can't help but feel that, to achieve that good time feeling, the film glosses over or omits numerous darker details. *Step* only skims the surface of the aftermath of Baltimore resident Freddy Gray's murder. The opening scene shows the Lethal Ladies discussing where they were when they heard about Gray, highlighting their complaints about how news outlets like CNN skewed coverage of protests. Since stepping is often tied to social commentary and activism, a deeper exploration of these issues would have only enriched the material.

Similarly, scenes featuring Blessin and her boyfriend feel judiciously edited to remove any drama. Viewers learn very little about him, and it's implied that his disapproval of Blessin's desire to leave Baltimore may be the catalyst for her inner conflicts. Since Blessin is the only one shown in a romantic relationship, one would assume he was included for reasons that weren't extraneous.

Step also misses an opportunity to further explore the general belief that, in order to be successful, one must put oneself into massive amounts of debt to obtain a degree. There's a fascinating line uttered by one of the school counselors about how "college got me out of Brooklyn." This idea could serve as one of the film's main themes, as all three Lethal Ladies share the same sentiment about Baltimore. They believe that a degree, no matter how costly, will help them achieve every parent's desire that their kids have better lives than they did. These tantalizing ideas are addressed only at a cursory level.

These complaints aside, *Step* will pay major dividends for those looking for an uplifting documentary. It is impossible to not root for these young women and to feel joy when they succeed. But one cannot escape the feeling that the filmmakers aimed to make this too perfect and tidy, and in doing so robbed viewers of a richer, deeper vein of emotional satisfaction.

Odie Henderson

CREDITS

Origin: United States

Language: English

Released: 2017

Production: Steven Cantor, Amanda Lipitz; Epiphany Story Lab, Impact Partners, Stick Figure Productions, Vulcan Productions; released by Fox Searchlight Pictures

Directed by: Amanda Lipitz

Cinematography by: Casey Regan

Music by: Laura Karpman; Raphael Saadiq

Sound: Jeff Seelye

Music Supervisor: Janet Billig Rich

Editing: Penelope Falk

MPAA rating: PG

Running time: 84 minutes

REVIEWS

Abele, Robert. *TheWrap*. August 1, 2017.

Berkshire, Geoff. *Variety*. February 22, 2017.

Greene, Steve. *IndieWire*. August 3, 2017.

Hornaday, Ann. *Washington Post*. August 3, 2017.

Kenny, Glenn. *New York Times*. August 3, 2017.

Rooney, David. *Hollywood Reporter*. January 21, 2017.

Turan, Kenneth. *Los Angeles Times*. August 3, 2017.

Watson, Keith. *Slant Magazine*. August 3, 2017.

Yoshida, Emily. *New York Magazine*. August 4, 2017.

Zacharek, Stephanie. *Time*. August 7, 2017.

QUOTES

Blessin Giraldo: "If you come together with a group of powerful women, the impact will be immense."

STRONGER

Strength defines us.
—Movie tagline

Box Office: $4.2 Million

The key takeaway of *Stronger* is that being afflicted with a sudden, unexpected disability does not necessarily change the fundamental character of a person. Movies about such characters often concentrate on how happy and fulfilled someone's life is before disease or injury strikes, and after that, it is the disability—and the disability alone—that defines that character, whether or not the movie intends that perspective.

John Pollono's screenplay firmly establishes that Jeff Bauman, played by Jake Gyllenhaal in the film, possesses plenty of problems before he is severely injured in the Boston Marathon bombing on April 15, 2013. In the early section of the film, he is content with a low-paying job at a wholesale store, still lives with his mother in a cramped apartment, is unreliable with regards to his job and his personal life, and, generally, seems incapable of committing to anything of significance. These issues likely would have continued to plague him if he had not been near the epicenter of one of the two bombs that killed three and injured over 250 people during the Boston Marathon. The central point of the film is that those issues do continue to be the primary things holding back Jeff, even after he loses both of his legs above the knee.

This is a unique but realistic perspective on matters. The injury is catastrophic, and the loss of his legs causes massive changes in the ways that Jeff has to go through life. At a certain point, though, those changes transform into a routine and it simply becomes the way that Jeff lives. There is something refreshing in seeing a cinematic portrayal of disability that does not pander in any way, does not suggest that the potential for a "normal" life is finished after experiencing a physical disability, and does not focus on the disability as the sum total of the character's problems. The film's interpretation of Jeff, which comes from Bauman's book of the same name (written with Bret Witter), is perfectly capable of living his life. The major obstacle is not the loss of his legs. It is something within him.

Jeff goes to the finish line of the marathon to see his on-again/off-again girlfriend Erin Hurley (Tatiana Maslany) finish the race. The couple is currently in one of their "off-again" phases, after Erin became frustrated with his constant tardiness or outright absence. Wanting to prove that he has changed, Jeff is almost on top of the first bomb when it detonates. Director David Gordon Green does not show the horror of the results until later in the film, focusing mostly on the confusion of family members and friends attempting to find their loved ones in the aftermath.

Jeff becomes something of a local and national hero from his hospital bed, helping the FBI with information about the bomber he saw. The status of "hero" is one that Jeff constantly rejects, ignoring questions from the press and admirers with a plastered-on smile and a thumbs-up. With both of his legs amputated above the knee (a doctor points out that the explosion, littered with pieces of metal and nails to cause more carnage, did most of the work), Jeff returns to the apartment he shares with his mother Patty (Miranda Richardson). With the family more concerned with the sudden fame that Jeff is receiving, Erin moves in to become his primary caregiver.

Gyllenhaal and especially Maslany's performances are notable in the way the two concentrate on their respective characters, not the circumstances in which those characters find themselves. Gyllenhaal's Jeff is a man clearly suffering from post traumatic stress disorder as well as survivor's guilt, yet he also becomes the same man who is more than content to leave his life as it was before the bombing. Maslany's Erin struggles with the thought that her newfound dedication to Jeff, as a caregiver and that returning to her role as his girlfriend, simply might be the result of her own sense of guilt, since he was only at the finish line for her. Even through all of this complexity, though, Maslany communicates a sense of empathy and basic decency. It takes a lot of stubbornness, complacency, and apathy from Jeff, who begins skipping his physical therapy sessions, for that empathetic core within Erin to finally crack.

Green is obviously drawn to such acts of kindness, empathy, and decency within this story, from the entirety of Erin's arc to smaller moments. Some of those include Jeff's boss (Danny McCarthy) at the big-box store arriving with a gift basket for his employee's extended family, as well as the good news that Jeff's insurance will cover the extensive costs of his medical bills, and a late, extended dialogue between Jeff and Carlos (Carlos Sanz), the cowboy hat-wearing man who saved Jeff's life after the bombing. In a film filled with pain and trauma, this quiet scene, in which the complete stranger explains why he ran toward the site of the explosion, points, not toward bravery, but toward how pain and trauma can be channeled for good.

Stronger is inspiring, not because of the film's situation or it's hollow sentiments about courage, but because it charts how Jeff overcomes himself, not his disability. It is also in how these simple and unthinking but profound acts of decency can change a life, as long as the person receiving those deeds is capable of realizing it and seeing such potential in him- or herself. That is Jeff's arc, and it is as precisely portrayed as his struggles to adjust to a life without his legs.

Green and Pollono have crafted a thoughtful examination of these characters, which elevates the film above the melodramatic approach it easily could have taken. Even in its final, climactic moment, *Stronger* eschews expectations. A lesser movie would turn Jeff's ultimate success, overcoming his disability with the aid of prosthetic legs, into a big moment. Here, instead, it is a quiet one, done in public yet witnessed by only two other people who understand what the moment means for Jeff and their own lives.

Mark Dujsik

CREDITS

Jeff Bauman: Jake Gyllenhaal
Erin Hurley: Tatiana Maslany
Patty Bauman: Miranda Richardson
Jeff Bauman, Sr.: Clancy Brown
Gail Hurley: Frankie Shaw
Origin: United States
Language: English
Released: 2017
Production: David Hoberman, Todd Lieberman, Michel Litvak, Scott Silver, Jake Gyllenhaal; Bold Films, Lionsgate, Mandeville Films, Nine Stories Productions; released by Roadside Attractions
Directed by: David Gordon Green
Written by: John Pollono
Cinematography by: Sean Bobbitt
Music by: Michael Brook
Sound: Todd Toon
Music Supervisor: Gabe Hilfer; Devoe Yates
Editing: Dylan Tichenor
Art Direction: Paul Richards

Costumes: Leah Katznelson; Kim Wilcox
Production Design: Stephen H. Carter
MPAA rating: R
Running time: 119 minutes

REVIEWS

Berardinelli, James. *ReelViews*. September 21, 2017.
Burr, Ty. *Boston Globe*. September 18, 2017.
Dowd, A.A. *The A.V. Club*. September 12, 2017.
Hartlaub, Peter. *San Francisco Chronicle*. September 21, 2017.
Kenny, Glenn. *New York Times*. September 21, 2017.
Orndorf, Brian. *Blu-Ray.com*. September 21, 2017.
Phillips, Michael. *Chicago Tribune*. September 21, 2017.
Tallerico, Brian. *RogerEbert.com*. September 22, 2017.
Thompson, Gary. *Philadelphia Daily News*. September 20, 2017.
Zacharek, Stephanie. *Time*. September 28, 2017.

TRIVIA

Jeff Bauman's former supervisor at Costco, Kevin, auditioned to portray himself in the movie. Although he was not chosen for the part, he does appear as an extra in more than one scene in the film.

SUBURBICON

A little slice of heaven.
—Movie tagline
Welcome to the neighborhood.
—Movie tagline

Box Office: $5.8 Million

The idea that *Suburbicon* is not just a bad movie but one of the most disappointing to emerge in 2017 may seem baffling to those who have yet to see it. To outsiders, the notion that a film combining the talents of George Clooney, Matt Damon, Julianne Moore (playing twins, no less), Oscar Isaac, and the Coen Brothers could be anything less than spectacular seems like an impossibility. In fact, it takes people of extraordinary talents to make a film this bad—they would be the only ones foolhardy enough to take material that clearly was not working and assume that they could put it over with the sheer force of their abilities. That is decidedly not the case and not only is the end result a film that does not work, it is impossible to understand how anyone could have possibly thought that it could have ever worked at all.

The film takes place in 1959 and is set amidst the well-manicured lawns of Suburbicon, a new-fangled planned community (one clearly modeled on Levittown) that offers, according to the mock promo reel that kicks things off, clean streets, good schools and friendly, diverse neighbors. Everything changes with the arrival of Suburbicon's first African-American family, Mr. and Mrs. Mayers (Leith M. Burke and Karimah Westbrook) and their young son Andy (Tony Espinosa). The presence of the newcomers does not engender much in the way of neighborly goodwill amongst the town's resident, and, before too long, high fencing is going up near their home, prices at the grocery store seem to skyrocket every time Mrs Mayers goes shopping, and, eventually, an ever-growing and increasingly threatening mob scene develops outside their home. The only person in the area who displays any trace kindness towards any of the Mayers is Nicky (Noah Jupe), a young boy who befriends Andy and takes him to play baseball in scenes that were apparently shot (featuring Josh Brolin as the boys' coach) but left on the cutting room floor.

While all this is going on, bad times invade the home that Nicky lives in with his parents, straight-arrow businessman Gardner (Matt Damon) and handicapped housewife Rose (Julianne Moore). One night, while Rose's twin sister, Margaret (also Moore) is visiting, two goons with some mysterious connection to Gardner arrive to tie up and chloroform the four of them and when Nicky wakes up in the hospital, he learns that his mother is dead. Immediately after the funeral, Margaret moves in, ostensibly to help out, and while Nicky is too young to fully grasp what is going on—even after catching them red-handed, so to speak—it is soon revealed that Gardner and Margaret have been having an affair and had Rose killed off in order to collect on her insurance policy. Their plan is not nearly as foolproof as Gardner and Rose think it is and soon attracts the attentions of a brilliant and eminently corruptible insurance company rep Bud Cooper (Oscar Issac) that soon lead to a number of unexpected and increasingly gory twists as Gardner desperately tries to keep one step ahead of the game, no matter the cost.

To fully understand why *Suburbicon* fails as badly as it does, it might help to understand the circumstances surrounding its existence. The screenplay was originally written by the Coens in 1986, just after they had their first success with their striking debut film, *Blood Simple* (1985). Because that film also dealt with murder, adultery, corrupt investigators, and copious amounts of bloodshed, they presumably did not have much interest in repeating themselves right out of the box and while they went on to one of the most striking and unique filmmaking careers of their era, *Suburbicon* wound up sitting on a shelf. Twenty years later, George Clooney acquired the script with an eye towards directing it and elected to, along with co-writer/producing partner Grant Heslov, take an idea they had been mulling over involving the first African-American family to move into Levittown and graft it onto the screenplay as a way of making it seem closer to the kind of socially conscious films, such as *Good Night, and Good Luck* (2005) and *The Ides of March* (2011) that he has gravitated more towards, both as an actor and as a filmmaker.

These two concepts, kept separate, might have resulted in two decent enough films but put together, especially when they are jammed together as uneasily as they are here, results in a disastrous clash of tones that takes them both down. The noir narrative is potentially intriguing but it is an area of storytelling that they have explored in the past with far better results (and there is the possibility that they may have raided this screenplay over the years for bits to put in other projects) and the sheer nastiness of the tone—in which virtually everyone save for Nicky is rotten to some degree—is so overwhelming that it seems a little much, even by the general standards of dark comedy.

Needless to say, the sardonic tone of these scenes is completely incompatible with the more earnest story involving the suffering of the Mayers at the hands of their vile neighbors. This plot thread is especially baffling because it does not seem as if Clooney and Heslov ever thought through what they wanted to say about them or their plight. They prefer to see them only as pious symbols of a shameful era and not as real people—neither Mr. nor Mrs. Mayers is ever afforded a first name and the former speaks maybe two lines total. Clooney presumably wanted to include this material to underscore the current and decidedly uneasy state of race relations in America today but can only accomplish this in the most grotesquely on-the-nose ways imaginable.

The only time that *Suburbicon* ever comes to life is when Isaac turns up as the sleazo insurance agent who pretty much knows right from the get-go that Gardner and Margaret are guilty of shady business and takes great pleasure in watching them as they try to outsmart him before he lowers the boom on them. The character itself may not be especially fresh—it is basically a variation of the role that Edward G. Robinson played in *Double Indemnity* (1944)—but he finds just the right angle to approach it, and his scenes genuinely shine as a result. Unfortunately, his character ends up giving up the ghost after only about ten minutes, and the film as a whole, which was already on the ropes long before then, quickly follows. Other than that, the only thing that *Suburbicon* has going for it is the fact that it is such a botch on every imaginable level that viewers are like to emerge from it feeling more baffled than enraged over what they have just experienced.

Peter Sobczynski

CREDITS

Gardner: Matt Damon
Rose, Margaret: Julianne Moore
Nicky: Noah Jupe
Sloan: Glenn Fleshler
Hightower: Jack Conley
Origin: United States
Language: English
Released: 2017
Production: Teddy Schwarzman, George Clooney, Grant Heslov; Black Bear Pictures, Dark Castle Entertainment, Huahua Media, Silver Pictures, Smokehouse Pictures; released by Paramount Pictures Corp.
Directed by: George Clooney
Written by: George Clooney; Joel Coen; Ethan Coen; Grant Heslov
Cinematography by: Robert Elswit
Music by: Alexandre Desplat
Sound: Oliver Tarney
Music Supervisor: Ian Neil
Editing: Stephen Mirrione
Art Direction: Christa Munro
Costumes: Jenny Eagan
Production Design: James D. Bissell
MPAA rating: R
Running time: 105 minutes

REVIEWS

Burr, Ty. *Boston Globe*. October 26, 2017.
Chang, Justin. *Los Angeles Times*. October 26, 2017.
Dargis, Manohla. *New York Times*. October 26, 2017.
Edelstein, David. *New York Magazine/Vulture*. September 10, 2017.
Gleiberman, Owen. *Variety*. September 2, 2017.
Hornaday, Ann. *Washington Post*. October 26, 2017.
Reed, Rex. *New York Observer*. October 30, 2017.
Rooney, David. *Hollywood Reporter*. September 2, 2017.
Truitt, Brian. *USA Today*. October 24, 2017.
Zacharek, Stephanie. *Time*. September 5, 2017.

QUOTES

Gardner: "I have to make decisions like what's best for the family."

TRIVIA

Actor Josh Brolin was cast in the movie as a baseball coach but his scenes ended up being removed after a test screening. Director George Clooney has admitted that these scenes deflated the tension from the film and felt badly about removing Brolin from the final cut as he considered his scenes some of the funniest in the entire picture.

SUPER DARK TIMES

Box Office: $33,109

Super Dark Times certainly agrees with the premise that "Guns don't kill people; people kill people." This bumper sticker philosophy implies that if we didn't have access to guns, our cavemen brains and violent natures would still compel us to murder each other with whatever we could get our hands on. A gun is just a tool, while it's innate in our delinquent species to wipe each other out. This is the philosophy held by the coming-of-age story that starts with an accidental death and keeps mounting larger and larger horrors upon its teenage friends.

Zach (Owen Campbell), Josh (Charlie Tahan), Daryl (Max Talisman), and Charlie (Sawyer Barth) are played with all the nascent vulgarity one should expect of early high school: eager to both impress and overcompensate in their search for dictional maturity. "Skittles are fucking delicious," Charlie says, carbon-dating the quartet between children and adults. Though their dynamic's accuracy is—like teen boys themselves—tiring to the point of grating and the skills of the actors vary wildly, the friendship is developed skillfully and naturally. Campbell, the lead, oscillates between milquetoast and overeager while Tahan's creepy potency emerges from quiet intensity.

Their relationship is no pastiche. There is only the unflinching pubescent mise-en-scène, of which *Super Dark Times* is a master, its landscape speckled with juvenile graffiti and parking lot shenanigans. Horniness and profanity are the language in which its poetry is written, the only language its characters know. That's why, when things go terribly wrong between the boys in the forest, when a samurai sword is involved in places it shouldn't be, we understand that the survivors have no idea how to cope. They can barely construct a sentence without a four-letter word.

Josh and Zach are at odds, like many best friends, even before this tragedy sets them off into their own horrible spirals though they keep their resentment bottled up. They both pine for Allison (Elizabeth Cappuccino, wonderful as a charming goofball who grows more serious and distant over time) but her affection lies with Zach, further complicating the mounting hormonal tempest within these stressed teens. And of course: the sword. Suburban baggage and self-importance come stuffed into it like no other weapon. It's the perfect device for a film simultaneously obsessed with and distracted from burgeoning toxic masculinity.

Super Dark Times, like many of its creepy modern kin, uses dream sequences and surreal natural imagery to great effect. Lynchian hallucinations play with our conceptions of speed and distance with such slow-burn dread, and cuts so quick, the film assumes its audience will be thinking about what they might have seen long after the fact. *Super Dark Times* is best when it sticks with this gamble. A sequence referencing Lars Von Trier's *Antichrist* is completely affecting, as is its opening scene capturing the death of a deer.

The deer is an unsettled, innocent creature (growing in popularity among these metaphors) whose only sin is resisting a world that simply isn't built for it. The implication is that perhaps people are similarly ill-fated. The boys' guilt boils over into suspicion and the resulting hypothesis appears like words traced on fogged glass: Maybe what happened in the woods wasn't an accident. First-time director Kevin Phillips shines most in his film's blackest moments. When he's bogged down in the high school lifestyle acting as connective tissue—parties, conversations with mom (Amy Hargreaves, striking in a bit part), phone calls and endlessly unsatisfying conversations between Zach and Allison—he loses track of what's important instead of plying the tension so well-established in earlier scenes.

Though beautifully shot by Eli Born as 1990s ultra-Americana, *Super Dark Times* never seems sure which way to direct its audience. The growing mystery between Josh and Zach is never quite clear enough in its intentions to be sinister, yet never implied enough to be foreboding. The film splits the difference, feeding the screen too much information too late, failing to build its crescendo of teen desire (for sex and violence) into a triumphant climax. Phillips simply tries to do too much. Without a focus on procedural details, the intensely confused and threatened masculinity of its characters, or its sublimely strange descent into pubescent madness, the film sputters. However, when it embraces and interrogates its darkness, the times it creates are super.

Jacob Oller

CREDITS

Zach: Owen Campbell
Josh: Charlie Tahan
Allison: Elizabeth Cappuccino
Daryl: Max Talisman
Charlie: Sawyer Barth
Origin: United States
Language: English
Released: 2017
Production: Edward Parks, Richard Peete, Jett Steiger; Neighborhood Watch, Om Films, Ways & Means; released by Netflix
Directed by: Kevin Phillips
Written by: Ben Collins; Luke Piotrowski
Cinematography by: Eli Born
Music by: Ben Frost
Sound: Colin Alexander
Music Supervisor: Earworm Music

Editing: Ed Yonaitis
Art Direction: Danny James Walton
Costumes: Stephani Lewis
Production Design: Jasmine E. Ballou
MPAA rating: Unrated
Running time: 100 minutes

REVIEWS

Beggs, Scott. *Nerdist.* July 20, 2017.
Fink, John. *The Film Stage.* April 30, 2017.
Frederick, Candice. *Reel Talk Online.* May 3, 2017.
Gingold, Michael. *Birth.Movies.Death.* March 15, 2017.
Halligan, Fionnuala. *Screen Daily.* March 15, 2017.
Kiang, Jessica. *The Playlist.* February 3, 2017.
Martin, Philip. *Arkansas Democrat-Gazette.* May 5, 2017.
Miska, Brad. *Bloody Disgusting.* April 21, 2017.
Weissberg, Jay. *Variety.* February 2, 2017.
Young, Neil. *Hollywood Reporter.* February 3, 2017.

T

T2 TRAINSPOTTING

Face your past. Choose your future.
—Movie tagline

Box Office: $2.4 Million

Ever since it premiered, people have been talking about the prospect of a sequel to *Trainspotting* (1996), the edgy cult sensation about a young Scottish junkie trying to pull himself together and get clean despite the influence of his user pals. The low-budget film became a cult sensation around the world, received a surprise Oscar® nomination, and jump-started the careers of filmmaker Danny Boyle and the soon-to-be-famous likes of Ewan McGregor, Robert Carlyle, Jonny Lee Miller, and Kelly MacDonald. For a while, it seemed as the falling out that occurred between Boyle and McGregor, stemming from the former's decision to skip over the latter and cast the red-hot Leonardo DiCaprio in the ultimately misguided screen adaptation of *The Beach* (2000), meant that the project was a no-go, but hopes rose after the two finally reconciled more than a decade later. In fact, a bigger problem surrounding any attempt to sequelize *Trainspotting* is that it was a film that so completely captured the cultural zeitgeist of the time in which it was made that it seemed impossible that a second film, no matter how well-intentioned, could possibly live up to its standards. And yet, against all odds, the cheekily titled *T2 Trainspotting* has finally arrived and not only that, pretty much the entire key members of the creative team on both side of the camera were roped back into service. The problem, however, is that it quickly becomes apparent that Boyle and company were so dedicated to simply getting a sequel to *Trainspotting* up and running despite seemingly insurmountable odds that they never quite got around to the theoretically equally important task of figuring out what they wanted such a thing to say.

In the first of numerous callbacks to the original film, *T2* once again opens with the sight of Mark Renton (McGregor) in mid-run, though the circumstances are somewhat different. The one-time junkie and reprobate is now a healthy and clean 46-year-old recent divorcee working in stock management in Amsterdam and when his run is interrupted this time, it is because of a cardiac episode. After his recovery, for reasons that the screenplay never quite makes clear, he decides to return to his former stomping grounds in Edinburgh for the first time since betraying his friends and making off with the money they made in a drug deal. Their reactions, to put it mildly, are mixed at best. Spud (Ewan Bremner) has changed the least—he is still struggling to quit heroin and is almost pathetically grateful to see his old friend again, even with their reunion occurring in the middle of his botched suicide attempt. Simon, a.k.a. Sick Boy (Miller) is now running his father's less-than-prosperous pub as well as a sideline gig running a sexual blackmail scam with sort-of girlfriend Veronika (Anjela Nedyalkova) while still nursing an intense grudge against his former friend. As for the hotheaded Begbie (Carlyle), he has just broken out of prison and is heading back to Edinburgh himself, not even realizing that the target of his murderous rage has also returned.

Simon also wants to destroy Renton but elects to go about it in a slightly more subtle manner. He plans to screw him over by getting him involved in a plan to transform a run-down building into a brothel—sorry, "spa"—that Veronika will run and then double-crossing him. However, this becomes a little complicated when the two former friends begin to reconnect while embarking on their scheme to scam a government funding program to get the funds for the project. For Renton, it becomes even more complicated when he finds himself in bed with Veronika, who makes no secret of her dissatisfaction with Simon. As for Begbie, he has returned, but when his attempts to bring his grown son into the criminal arts prove an abject failure—the kid would rather study hotel management—as is his ability to get an erection, he crosses over into full-blown psychosis that only grows larger when he meets up with Simon and discovers that Renton is around. As for Spud, he finds himself sitting on the sidelines for most of this but discovers a knack for chronicling everyone's misadventures on paper that could prove to be useful in the future.

The original *Trainspotting* was a one-of-a-kind cinematic cocktail that offered viewers an invigorating blend of stylish visuals, dark humor, charismatic performances, an instantly iconic soundtrack, and a genuine sense of anger aimed straight at a political system that offered its citizens, especially the younger ones, so little that becoming strung out on heroin could conceivably be seen as a viable lifestyle option. *T2* feels more like a piece of fan fiction that is content to rehash elements from the original without bringing much of anything that is fresh to the table. The screenplay by John Hodge, utilizing elements taken both from Irvine Welsh's original novel *Trainspotting* and its lesser-regarded sequel *Porno,* is a bit of a mess that offers poorly established character motivations, a rickety narrative construction that spends much of its time treading water until the climactic confrontation with Begbie, forced bits of shock humor ranging from projectile vomiting to a forced nude run through the countryside and numerous flashbacks and references to the previous film that range from the unsatisfying (such as Kelly MacDonald's appearance as Diane being limited to a single, decidedly non-essential scene) to the annoying (an updated version of Renton's famous "Choose Life" monologue that now incorporates slut shaming, reality TV, and social media in the most embarrassing manner imaginable). Boyle and cinematographer Anthony Dod Mantle try to cover up the story deficiencies with an array of visual tricks ranging from skewed angles to, at one low point, Snapchat filters, but the flashiness that seemed so alive and vibrant two decades ago now feels tired and gimmicky. Even the wall-to-wall soundtrack is kind of uninspired this time around with the only memorable musical moments being the ones where we hear snatches from tunes heard in the first film such as the Iggy Pop classic "Lust for Life."

And yet, at least for a little while, there is an undeniable charge in seeing the actors slipping back into their old roles—viewers who first encountered them twenty years ago will immediately find themselves flashing back to the Clinton era and taking stock of what has become of their own lives over the years. That charge cannot last forever, though, and when it does fade away, the actors are stuck with characters that are not nearly as finely drawn as they were the first time around. McGregor basically coasts through the film on his still-considerable charm but lacks the fire he previously brought to Renton. Miller and Bremmer come off better, possibly because they are not quite as ubiquitous and so seeing them again actually does mean something. Robert Carlyle, on the other hand, is stuck with a version of Begbie that ignores what made him so menacing in the first place—the hair-trigger temper that could switch from charming "bro" behavior to brutal violence in a flash—to make him a total psycho is much less interesting. As the sole significant new character, Nedyalkova is certainly a presence but, like the other women in the film such as Macdonald and Shirley Henderson, has been given precious little to do. The whole thing is like a reunion photo spread in *Entertainment Weekly* that has not quite come to life.

In the end, whether or not one likes *T2 Trainspotting* will depend on what one is expecting from it. If all a viewer wants is to see some old cinematic friends wreaking havoc on the big screen after a long absence, then it could prove to be at least reasonably satisfactory. However, viewers who would like to also have a compelling reason for their return will come away disappointed as this is one of those sequels that never quite makes a case for its own existence. Those people should probably put this movie to the side and choose life instead—or at the very least, a better movie.

Peter Sobczynski

CREDITS

Mark Renton: Ewan McGregor
Spud: Ewen Bremner
Sick Boy: Jonny Lee Miller
Begbie: Robert Carlyle
Diane: Kelly Macdonald
Origin: United States
Language: English, Bulgarian
Released: 2017
Production: Bernard Bellew, Christian Colson, Andrew Macdonald, Danny Boyle; Film 4, TriStar Pictures Inc.; released by Sony Pictures Releasing
Directed by: Danny Boyle
Written by: John Hodge

Cinematography by: Anthony Dod Mantle
Sound: Glenn Freemantle
Editing: Jon Harris
Art Direction: Patrick Rolfe
Costumes: Rachael Fleming; Steven Noble
Production Design: Patrick Rolfe; Mark Tildesley
MPAA rating: R
Running time: 117 minutes

REVIEWS

Catsoulis, Jeanette. *New York Times.* March 16, 2017.
Gray, Christopher. *Slant Magazine.* March 15, 2017.
Laws, Mike. *Village Voice.* March 10, 2017.
Lodge, Guy. *Variety.* March 2, 2017.
Solomons, Jason. *TheWrap.* January 19, 2017.
Thomas, June. *Slate.* March 13, 2017.
Tobias, Scott. *NPR.* March 16, 2017.
Turan, Kenneth. *Los Angeles Times.* March 16, 2017.
Young, Neil. *Hollywood Reporter.* January 19, 2017.
Zacharek, Stephanie. *Time.* March 16, 2017.

QUOTES

Renton: "I did steal the money, but they shouldn't have been surprised. I mean, we stole from all sorts of people. Shops, businesses, neighbours, family. Friends was just one more class of victim."

TRIVIA

Actor Jonny Lee Miller offered to shave his head to look older, but director Danny Boyle insisted that Sick Boy retain his iconic blond hair.

TABLE 19

You're invited to the wedding of the season.
—Movie tagline

Box Office: $3.6 Million

As domestic settings go for movies, weddings are a cornucopia of opportunities. All sorts of screwball wackiness can ensue if the single of dominoes fall during the most meticulously planned social event. There is drama and even sadness for those sitting on the outside wondering when it might be their time, the remembrance of a happier period or the cold water of mortality associated with giving a child away or speculating if you will even be in that position. Often it is stated that the wedding is the woman's day and cinema has acknowledged that with crafting romantic comedies both successful (*Four Weddings and a Funeral* [1994], *My Best Friend's Wedding* [1997]) and anything but (*27 Dresses* [2008], *Bride Wars* [2009]). Where Jeffrey Blitz's *Table 19* fits into the grand plan is anyone's guess, but it is clear that little planning went towards aligning the deckchairs on this sinking ship.

Eloise (Anna Kendrick) was once the maid of honor at her best friend's wedding. That was before she was dumped by her boyfriend, Teddy (Wyatt Russell), who also happens to be the bride's brother. Reluctantly, she accepts "with pleasure," as the invitation suggests, to attend, even as she sends it back partially burnt. When she arrives on the big day she discovers she has been relegated to Table 19 which she, as the one-time co-chair of the planning committee, knows is the one in the back reserved for people the lucky couple did not expect to attend.

This table also includes Jerry and Bina Kepp (Craig Robinson & Lisa Kudrow), a constantly bickering couple who own a restaurant. Renzo Eckberg (Tony Revolori) who is there to not only represent the true acquaintances of the wedding party, but as a desperate ploy by his parents to meet a girl. Jo Flanagan (June Squibb) is the bride's childhood nanny and Walter Thimble (Stephen Merchant) is the distant relative currently on parole for corporate embezzlement. What could this motley crew of complete opposites possibly talk about? It starts with a little gossip courtesy of Eloise's knowledge of the initial party planning but soon develops into personal grievances, alliances, and the kind of awkward encounters that begin to quickly disengage any empathy ever worth feeling towards any of these characters.

Blitz chooses to acknowledge early on that there are certain catastrophes people must expect whenever watching a fake wedding so he gets the whole cake destruction right out of the way. If that was the cue to just move the invitees of Table 19 away from the party perhaps something more genuine could have come of it all. Instead his insistence on keeping them in the vicinity with never so much as a wide-eyed reaction of shamed consequence towards the sugary symbol of happily ever after sums up exactly where this film is headed. Although Blitz's narrative appears caught up in some Christopher Nolan-esque warp where time slows down as the movie shifts gears so often in the first 45 minutes that the usual resolutions reserved for the climax appear laid out on the table and there is still half of a movie to contend with.

The way characters are established at the reception suggests Blitz is setting up some form of 1980s themed murder mystery party. Any film student in search of an editing degree could easily re-fashion a trailer suggesting as much. Robinson's Jerry has even brought a detective novel along which gives way to dialogue like "We could open our own ladies' detective agency" and "I just like being a good detective. It gives me something." A little something for the audience's effort of having to wade through armchair psychology would have been nice since all this suggests some grander meaning of a recurring theme. Instead it is just repetition in search of a motive. When a young girl is presented with a creepy dance request her table mate opines, "I thought we were going to be murdered there for a second." That may not pay off in the presumptive Miss-Scarlet-in-the-reception-hall-with-the-cake-knife but it should make most viewers wish they could switch tables.

The characters we are stuck with become defined by their singular malady whether it be physically or mentally self-inflicted and it is impossible to take any of their symptoms seriously. One minute they are making confessions to each other and the next they are walking out into the sunlight like zombies awoken by therapy. These are immensely talented comedic actors who can normally do more with a simple reaction shot than the checklist of conventions they must force feed here. The script barely seems to know the basic framework of how a reception progresses so to expect it to cram in 80 minutes of reconciliations en route to a happy ending is as wishful as the mythical consequences of catching the garter. When even after everyone associated with fronting the bill for this wedding has left, the band still sticks around on stage to play off the enlightened returnees of Table 19 for one final dance of forgiveness. It is enough to make even Ben and Elaine from *The Graduate* (1967) finally realize they made the right decision.

Erik Childress

CREDITS

Eloise McGarry: Anna Kendrick
Jerry Kepp: Craig Robinson
Jo Flanagan: June Squibb
Bina Kepp: Lisa Kudrow
Walter Thimble: Stephen Merchant
Renzo Eckberg: Tony Revolori
Origin: United States
Language: English
Released: 2017
Production: Dan Cohen, P. Jennifer Dana, Shawn Levy, Tom McNulty, Mark Roberts; 21 Laps Entertainment, 3311 Productions; released by Fox Searchlight Pictures
Directed by: Jeffrey Blitz
Written by: Jay Duplass; Mark Duplass
Cinematography by: Ben Richardson
Music by: John Swihart
Sound: Peter Brown
Music Supervisor: Andrea von Foerster
Editing: Yana Gorskaya
Art Direction: Brittany Hites
Costumes: Peggy Stamper
Production Design: Timothy David O'Brien
MPAA rating: PG-13
Running time: 87 minutes

REVIEWS

Bell, Josh. *Las Vegas Weekly*. March 2, 2017.
Chang, Justin. *Los Angeles Times*. March 2, 2017.
Clarke, Cath. *TimeOut*. April 3, 2017.
Erhlich, David. *IndieWire*. March 1, 2017.
Judy, Jim. *Screen It!*. March 3, 2017.
Orndorf, Brian. *Blu-ray.com*. March 2, 2017.
Roeper, Richard. *Chicago Sun-Times*. March 3, 2017.
Seitz, Matt Zoller. *RogerEbert.com*. March 3, 2017.
Snider, Eric D. *EricDSnider.com*. March 10, 2017.
Tobias, Scott. *NPR*. March 2, 2017.

QUOTES

Jerry Kepp: "I can smell the toilets from here, that's how well we know the bride and groom."

TRIVIA

This is the fourth collaboration between actress Anna Kendrick and cinematographer Ben Richardson.

A TAXI DRIVER

(Taeksi Woonjunsa)

Box Office: $1.5 Million

On its face, it does not seem as though Jang Hun's seriocomic *A Taxi Driver* has much to do with the more famous Martin Scorsese film *Taxi Driver* (1976), which makes the name something of a gamble. The connection is there, however, in the simple inversion of its lead character's moral philosophy after experience in the army. The title characters in both films have been left behind by society while they were serving that same society in the army, but in this case, life hasn't yet curdled the main character's outlook completely. Kim Man-seob, played by the great Korean actor Kang-ho Song, doesn't trust people, isn't doing a stellar job raising his daughter by himself, and is hanging onto his job for dear life, but he's basically a good person looking for a push in the right direction.

Kim Man-seob is based on the real taxi driver Kim Sa-bok, who in 1980 was asked by German journalist Jürgen "Peter" Hinzpeter (Thomas Kretschmann) to take him from Seoul, where he was covering Korean politics for the network ARD-NDR, to Gwangju. Peter hears from his contacts that something is going on in the city of Gwangju, but no reports have emerged from the area. The city's paper has been closed, as its editor fears reprisals from the soldiers who have occupied the region. Peter's thus the only hope of getting news of the city to the public. Gwangju was the subject of a student uprising in response to Major General Chun Doo-hwan seizing control of the government in a military coup. The military was called in to deal with student demonstrators and the roads in and out of the city were blocked. During this period, hundreds of Koreans were killed or injured. Peter only has an inkling about what's happening in the region and needs to get close enough to film it for broadcast on television. Kim doesn't like or trust the pushy German tourist in his cab, but he can't say no to the money, so they begrudgingly work together to sneak into the city. They convince the soldiers at the blockade that Peter's an exporter who will bring business to the country and needs to return to Gwangju to retrieve some important papers.

Gwangju looks deserted when they arrive, the streets full of trash and only a few people to be found anywhere. Kim and Peter find a truck full of student protestors led by young Jae-sik (Jun-yeol Ryu). Jae-Sik takes them around the city, showing them the people who've been oppressed by the military, who are willing to die in order to be counted in opposition to the brutal puppet government. Peter's coverage goes well enough until Kim's taxi experiences engine troubles and night falls and plain-clothes soldiers get wind of the foreign journalist inside the Gwangju city limits. The more Kim spends time with the people in the city, the more he sees he too has a moral obligation to help tell their story, especially when Jae-Sik does something stupidly heroic to ensure that he and Peter can escape with his footage.

A Taxi Driver suffers from too small a scale. The script's understanding of the Gwangju uprising is relegated to entirely too few people to get a sense of what really happened during the week of bloody reprisals. We only meet a few people who are living under the government's vicious rule and they all seem a little too saintly to be much more than obvious mouthpieces meant to slowly change Kim's way of thinking. It's admirable in theory, but the moral compass of a taxi driver can't seem like an overblown and inadequate center for a movie about an event that resulted in hundreds of deaths, injuries, and prison sentences. It could possibly be that the film's budget only allowed for a modest representation of the horrors of Gwangju, but the film just doesn't seem to understand the magnitude of what happened beyond what these two men saw. It's fair enough that a film stick with its chosen perspective, but it feels dramatically anemic that only these two frequently unpleasant men are our only windows into the tragedy. It's an all-too ordinary approach to an event that should register as more horrifying. Beginning the film as a comedy, complete with a galumphing, quirky score also feels like a misstep considering where the movie ends up.

The film does have many strengths. Jang Hun's direction emphasizes the faces of his characters, a nice shorthand way into a grand scale tragedy. He also shoots chaos and the military set pieces with conciseness and honesty. Kretschmann gives a serviceable performance as Peter, but as frequently happens when he's working for non-German directors, he tends to glower a little too much. The supporting cast is uniformly excellent, every actor making more of the underwritten characters. The real draw though, as usual for his movies, is Kang-ho Song. The script has him talking to himself in Korean for entirely too much of the movie, and it's to his credit that this almost never feels like the lazy imparting of inner life that should be done silently. The script doesn't trust us to make out Kim's character without having him talk to himself about everything that's happening, but Kang takes the sting out the insult by being so charming and authentically human throughout. He's carried less interesting and more didactic films than this, and his performance more than makes up for the film's deficiencies. The film will not replace Scorsese's *Taxi Driver* in the public consciousness anytime soon, but it's a worthy effort all the same.

Scout Tafoya

CREDITS

Man-seob Kim: Kang-ho Song
Peter: Thomas Kretschmann
Tae-sul/Hwang: Hae-jin Yoo
Jae-sik/Gu: Jun-yeol Ryu
Reporter Choi: Hyuk-kwon Park
Origin: United States
Language: Korean, German, English, Japanese
Released: 2017
Production: Eun-Kyung Park; The Lamp; released by Well Go USA Entertainment
Directed by: Hun Jang
Written by: Yu-na Eom
Production Design: Yi-jin Jeong; Hwa-seong Jo
MPAA rating: Unrated
Running time: 137 minutes

REVIEWS

Abrams, Simon. *RogerEbert.com*. August 11, 2017.

Bechervaise, Jordan. *Screen International.* August 10, 2017.
Hunter, Rob. *Film School Rejects.* September 1, 2017.
Lee, Maggie. *Variety.* August 16, 2017.
Linden, Sheri. *Hollywood Reporter.* August 16, 2017.
Moore, Roger. *Movie Nation.* August 12, 2017.
Noh, David. *Film Journal International.* August 11, 2017.
Rechtshaffen, Michael. *Los Angeles Times.* August 10, 2017.
VanDenburch, Barbara. *Arizona Republic.* August 11, 2017.
Webster, Andy. *New York Times.* August 10, 2017.

TRIVIA

This film was South Korea's submission to the Foreign Language Film Award of the 90th Annual Academy Awards.

THANK YOU FOR YOUR SERVICE

Box Office: $9.5 Million

Screenwriter Jason Hall created an all-American hit when he wrote a script about America's deadliest sniper, Chris Kyle, in an adaptation of his memoir. As directed by Clint Eastwood, *American Sniper* (2014) focused on the cost of being a hero, especially with the mythology projected upon those who kill but are still considered great. The story has contemporaries with other movies about modern heroes who endure other headline-topping tragedies, like Peter Berg's *Lone Survivor* (2013), or Michael Bay's *13 Hours* (2016). But Hall's directorial debut, *Thank You for Your Service*, takes a decidedly different approach to its storytelling and becomes a type of a non-fictional emotional disaster movie, albeit about soldiers simply coming home. These are not soldiers that made headlines like those of *American Sniper* or *Lone Survivor*, but neither is this a purely jingoistic veteran tribute.

As a debut director, Hall shows promise in telling a story that can get a large audience, but does not simplify their emotional journey through a heavy subject. In this case it is the real-life accounts of soldiers like Adam Schumann (Miles Teller) and Tausol "Solo" Aleti (Beulah Koale)—based from the book of the same name by David Finkel—who came back from war with physical and mental wounds to a system that did not provide them, and many other soldiers, the proper, quickest treatment. Schumann returns to a wife (Haley Bennett), their two children, and their quiet home, while images of a dead soldier sporadically haunt him; Solo resumes life with his girlfriend and a baby on the way, but remains damaged. Their friend Billy (Joe Cole) returns to America with them in the movie's first few minutes but after finding out that his girlfriend has left him along with his PTSD (Post-Traumatin Stress Disorder), kills himself. From the very beginning, Hall builds a stable, however simple sense of stakes to the story, in which the viewer most of all wants the characters to get proper help instead of succumbing to their trauma.

As the film tells this story of regular soldiers having to wait far too long to receive help, or unable to express the pain they are experiencing to their loved ones (as with the case of Schumann's arc in particular), Hall yearns for a non-political approach on veterans. While *American Sniper* complicated its commentary on mythology by offering plain jingoistic imagery, *Thank You for Your Service* provides little fanfare in its brief images of battle, and then places much of its anxieties on a very fallible veteran healthcare system that treats individual traumas with a slow assembly line. The movie does align with gun ownership and has a lifeless view of race given a subplot that involves Solo and drug dealing in the third act, but it remains compellingly bipartisan with the issue of PTSD and how to address it.

Teller has built an impressive resume in a relatively short time of playing men who can be as strong as they are flawed (*Bleed for This* [2016], *Whiplash* [2014]); he has a distinct ability to descend into the most crushing physical and emotional environments and reveal truth about men not in the business of weakness. Add his work in *Thank You for Your Service* to the top of that list, given the way that his emotional intensity is prevalent in the more peaceful moments (at home with his family, trying to restore some sort of balance) and in the heavily dramatic ones (a heartbreaking suicide attempt later in the film).

However, Cole is the actor who runs away with the film, presenting a man with equal scars and less of a control on it than Schumann. Cole's best work is often without dialogue, witnessing his inner turmoil as he becomes a hazard to himself and his pregnant partner. In a movie that is full of tragedy about how unstable these men are, Cole creates a particularly effective sadness in someone who cannot get help, or refuses to.

Thank You for Your Service is a movie of quiet and large moments. Its large moments often come with heavy hands, such as pivotal confrontations between Schumann and the widow of a fellow soldier (played by Amy Schumer), or a night-time hunting scene that tries to ratchet up tension from the soldiers's PTSD. In these instances, the film wears its mainstream interests on its sleeve, aware of the audience it can cultivate by mere subject alone.

With such strong emotional storytelling in these performances, the better passages are the ones that simply observe these characters, like watching Schumann at a roaring race car rally, absorbing the sounds of loud engines as a type of familiar environment, or later when he is dancing with his friends at a bar. For a movie that starts with a loud war sequence and has some melodramatic tendencies with dialogue, *Thank You for Your Service* gains an unexpected sensitivity by trusting in the atmosphere of its characters, understanding that capturing headspace is more than enough when cinematically discussing PTSD. While Hall seems to be torn between the way a Hollywood film would tell this story as opposed to a lower-budget indie, he gives the project a unique soul with his sincere interest in these people and the pain they share.

Nick Allen

CREDITS

Saskia Schumann: Haley Bennett
Billy Waller: Joe Cole
Adam Schumann: Miles Teller
Alea: Keisha Castle-Hughes
Amanda Doster: Amy Schumer
Origin: United States
Language: English
Released: 2017
Production: Jon Kilik; DreamWorks L.L.C., Dune Films, Reliance Entertainment; released by Universal Pictures
Directed by: Jason Hall
Written by: Jason Hall
Cinematography by: Roman Vasyanov
Music by: Thomas Newman
Music Supervisor: Susan Jacobs
Editing: Jay Cassidy; Dino Jonsater
Art Direction: Erik Polczwartek; Aziz Rafiq
Costumes: Hope Hanafin
Production Design: Keith P. Cunningham; John P. Goldsmith
MPAA rating: R
Running time: 109 minutes

REVIEWS

Carter, Philip. *Slate*. October 30, 2017.
Guzman, Rafer. *Newsday*. October 26, 2017.
Jones, J.R. *Chicago Reader*. November 9, 2017.
Kenigsberg, Ben. *New York Times*. October 26, 2017.
MacDonald, Moira. *Seattle Times*. October 25,2017.
Noveck, Jocelyn. *Associated Press*. October 26, 2017.
Puig, Claudia. *TheWrap*. October 25, 2017.
Scheck, Frank. *Hollywood Reporter*. October 24, 2017.
Walsh, Katie. *Tribune News Service*. October 26, 2017.
Yoshida, Emily. *New York Magazine/Vulture*. October 25, 2017.

QUOTES

Saskia Schumann: "I thought you were fine. You're lying to me, I found your VA questionnaire, everything's a lie! You're sick and I can't do anything if you don't f**king talk to me, Adam!"

Adam Schumann: "I have to be sick or I can't get my benefits."

TRIVIA

Amy Schumer donated the money she earned making this film to various veterans' foundations.

THEIR FINEST

In the fight for freedom everyone played a part.
—Movie tagline

The spirit of the nation is in her hands.
—Movie tagline

Box Office: $3.6 Million

Lone Scherfig's *Their Finest* shows how World War II propaganda filmmaking affected the British government and its citizens. Like Christopher Nolan's *Dunkirk* (2017) this excellent film uses the 1940 Dunkirk Evacuation as its subject. Though technically a defeat, the "Miracle at Dunkirk" became a major morale booster when regular British citizens used their boats to help retrieve over 300,000 Allied troops stranded by the Germans in France. Scherfig's melodramatic film-within-a-film depiction is a far less realistic take than Nolan's version, though both recreations serve to rouse and inspire the audience. Had the British government Nolan's technology and his budget in 1940, it might have turned out something that looked like *Dunkirk*.

The Dunkirk Evacuation strikes the most imaginative and creative chords in filmmakers. Nolan uses 70mm IMAX visuals, overwhelming sound design, and a narratively fractured timeline in his film. Ten years prior, director Joe Wright depicted Dunkirk in *Atonement* (2007) as a several minutes-long, unbroken take that is a master class in ostentatiousness. In similar fashion, *Their Finest*'s fictional screenwriters Catrin (Gemma Arterton) and Tom (Sam Claflin) constantly have to find clever ways to juice up or fix their heroic narrative. Their writing is often disrupted by filmmaking circumstances beyond their control, from the prima donna antics of famous actor Ambrose Hilliard (an excellent Bill Nighy) to disagreements about how heroic to make the female characters. And while Scherfig's rendition is in the cheap style befitting Tom and Catrin's budget, it is no less intriguing than the aforementioned flashier versions of the event.

One could argue that, because the British government wanted to equally engage female audiences with its propaganda war films, *Their Finest* has a tougher hand to play than the predominantly male prior incarnations of Wright and Nolan. Scherfig and her screenwriter, Gaby Chiappe (adapting Lissa Evans's novel *Their Finest Hour and a Half*) seem to say as much, though they do so in a sly, comic fashion. Catrin is hired to write what Tom calls "slop," that is, the dialogue for the female characters in the movies he's been tasked to churn out. She is also sent to interview the twin Starling sisters (Francesca and Lily Knight) who, against their father's wishes, took his boat from the harbor and, like their far more experienced compatriots, sailed toward the rescue mission at Dunkirk.

The Starlings become the subject of the latest cinematic effort, *The Nancy Starling,* a film named after their boat. Unbeknownst to anyone but Catrin, their story requires some serious dramatic license: The Starlings's boat broke down in the middle of the journey, and they only managed to obtain soldiers from another overloaded boat. Punching up the story is no sin—after all, this is propaganda—but Ministry of Information executives Phyl (Rachael Stirling) and Roger Swain (Richard E. Grant) take issue with too much dishonesty. If the women aren't heroes, the project must be scrapped. However, Catrin has some ideas on how to make the film heroic without sacrificing too much of the truth. Part of her solution is to add more slop.

So begins a series of rewrites and additions, most of which come from the government. When it's revealed that American audiences will see the film, the Ministry of War demands an American character be added. Since America wasn't yet involved in the war, this is a bending of facts far more absurd than anything Tom and Catrin wrote for the fictional version of the Starlings. As the American, Swain casts a Norweigan pilot named Carl Lundbeck (Jake Lacy) who's easy on the eyes but murder on the acting. Once again, Catrin comes to the rescue by convincing Ambrose Hilliard to help Lundbeck with his acting in exchange for more dramatic scenes himself.

The filmmaking process is depicted through the sometimes antagonistic but ultimately romantic relationship between Catrin and Tom. He's a bit of a sexist rogue not unlike many of the movie heroes of the era; she's spunky and resourceful, knowing which battles to fight and how strongly to fight them. The Welsh Catrin has a bit of early Kate Hepburn in her character, or perhaps Teresa Wright, who won an Oscar® for a film Catrin could have written had she gone Hollywood, the English drama, *Mrs. Miniver* (1942). Despite being a prime piece of wartime propaganda with loads of strong female performances and storylines, that Oscar®-winning Best Picture was probably too lavish to come from *Their Finest*'s film division. From the looks of *The Nancy Starling,* its closest real-world equivalent would have been Graham Greene's low budget mini-classic *Went the Day Well?* (1942).

Their Finest is a spiritual successor to the aforementioned films; it keeps focus on its female characters, making their lives as complex as the standard issue male characters who populate the majority of movies. Catrin has a backstory that features a painter husband who's envious of her scriptwriting. When she catches him in bed with another woman, she undergoes feelings of sadness and liberation in equal measure. As a result, her kiss-off line to her unfaithful partner is a bittersweet rebuke rather than full-on rage. And Phyl, a tough, refreshingly out lesbian, offers Catrin female camaraderie and wise advice when not scaring the pants off Tom with her bluntness.

Though this is a period drama with hints of romance and comedy, *Their Finest* never sugarcoats the fact that England is at war. The specter of violence and death hangs over the film like the sword of Damacles. An early, foreshadowing scene finds Catrin caught in a bombing of her neighborhood. She survives, and expresses relief when the bodies she sees strewn about turn out to be mannequins from a nearby store. Scherfig lulls the viewer into a false sense of security before revealing that one of the bodies is real. The moment is shocking.

The film also kills off likeable characters, but always lets the viewer have moments to grieve. Hilliard's amusing agent Sam Smith (Eddie Marsan) is killed in a bombing and Hilliard has to identify the body. Scherfig shows Smith's mangled remains, adding power to Hilliard's anguished reaction. Smith is replaced by his sister Sophie (Helen McCrory) who's even more shrewd than Sammy was. Her similar personality allows Hilliard to continue his decades-long association with his now-deceased agent by proxy. Establishing death as a supporting role makes the shocking, senseless demise of a major character play less like a cliché and more like operatic tragedy.

In a film that evokes so many other films from its timeframe, *Their Finest* saves its most relevant for its last sequence. A saddened Catrin, who has retreated from filmmaking after cheating death three times, goes to a theater to see the finished fruit of her and Tom's labors. The audience's reaction to the film evokes Preston Sturges's *Sullivan's Travels* (1941), though the communal emotional response is one of pride rather than laughter. Catrin learns how powerful and cathartic movies can be for a weary audience and she returns to her screenwriting duties. *Their Finest* has an inspirational ending that's profoundly effective, and actors who give their all to make it work so well.

Odie Henderson

CREDITS

Catrin Cole: Gemma Arterton
Tom Buckley: Sam Claflin
Ambrose Hilliard: Bill Nighy

Ellis Cole: Jack Huston
Raymond Parfitt: Paul Ritter
Origin: United States
Language: English, Hungarian, Polish, French
Released: 2017
Production: Finola Dwyer, Elizabeth Karlsen, Amanda Posey, Stephen Woolley; BBC Films, Pinewood Pictures, Welsh Government; released by STX Entertainment
Directed by: Lone Scherfig
Written by: Gaby Chiappe
Cinematography by: Sebastian Blenkov
Music by: Rachel Portman
Sound: Glenn Freemantle
Music Supervisor: Laura Katz
Editing: Lucia Zucchetti
Production Design: Alice Normington
MPAA rating: R
Running time: 117 minutes

REVIEWS

Berardinelli, James. *Reelview.* April 20, 2017.
Dargis, Manohla. *New York Times.* April 6, 2017.
Duralde, Alonso. *TheWrap.* April 5, 2017.
Fujishima, Kenji. *Slant Magazine.* April 2, 2017.
Huddleston, Tom. *Time Out London.* April 18, 2017.
Keough, Peter. *Boston Globe.* April 19, 2017.
Morgenstern, Joe. *Wall Street Journal.* April 6, 2017.
Murray, Noel. *The Playlist.* September 17, 2016.
Reed, Rex. *New York Observer.* April 11, 2017.
Turan, Kenneth. *Los Angeles Times.* April 6, 2017.

QUOTES

Gabriel Baker: "Wonderful! Authenticity, optimism, and a dog!"

TRIVIA

When Tom Buckley tells Catrin Cole, "Films are like life with the boring bits cut out," he is actually quoting Alfred Hitchcock.

THELMA

Box Office: $145,402

Born in Denmark, raised in Norway, Joachim Trier had resisted the icy tradition of Scandinavian cinema for the first decade of his career. His first three films, *Reprise* (2006), *Oslo, August 31* (2011), and *Louder Than Bombs* (2015) showed him developing a style more akin to an American novelist, replete with gorgeous, vivacious tangents that help us understand how he, his characters, and human beings in general, think and feel. He uses visual cues to send his characters through the sensuous corridors of memory and imagination, to understand why we end up in bad situations, bad relationships, and why it's easy to stay a lost dreamer rather than ever let our lives snap into place. Well, Trier has finally done a little snapping of his own. His newest film, the excellent sci-fi parable *Thelma* shows him focused on the internal pain of his hero with the same cold disharmony that used to animate Scandinavian legends like Ingmar Bergman and Carl Theodor Dreyer. Trier still lets his imagination run wild, but he's also more honed in on his title character's subjective experience than ever before.

Thelma (Eili Harboe) is a new student at a University in Oslo. Her parents Trond (Henrik Rafaelsen) and Unni (Ellen Dorrit Petersen) are reluctant to let her start this part of her life for reasons that her fellow students wouldn't understand. They call her constantly and take a keener than average interest in her dating and social calendar. Their religious conviction accounts for some of their cloying helicoptering, but there seems to be something more menacing in their over-parenting. It slides further into focus when Thelma has an attack in the school library. Her nose starts bleeding and she falls to the floor, the victim of an apparent seizure, but something stranger happens while she's writhing around on the floor. A flock of birds starts behaving erratically and some crash into the library windows, almost as if they have been compelled to by Thelma's seizure.

When Thelma has regained consciousness and doctors have pronounced her fit to leave, she returns to her schooling. She starts to see one of the witnesses to her attack, a gorgeous brunette named Anja (Kaya Wilkins), more and more in her classes, at the college's swimming pool, and at parties. She begins gently obsessing over Anja until one day they find themselves seated next to each other at the opera and their hands touch. Thelma tries to flee to avoid dealing with her feelings and how they conflict with her deeply held religious beliefs, but not before Anja finds her in the lobby of the opera house and kisses her. That throws Thelma's world into complete disarray. One hallucinatory episode at a party later and she's convinced she's done something terribly wrong. She goes to a doctor to see if she's got epilepsy or something else, but the tests come back negative. Something else happens, however, while she's undergoing the tests. In the throes of a full-blown meltdown, she has another round of hallucinations. The next morning Anja has disappeared. Her mother, her friends, no one knows where she's gone and Thelma begins to think she had some accidental hand in her friend's vanishing. She returns home to be with her parents, who have a few unsettling stories to tell her about her past and the source of her psychic anxieties.

Thelma could have devolved into easier genre fare at any point. The movie could have been a springboard for those hallucinations, allowing Trier to channel his inner Alejandro Jodorowsky or Stanley Kubrick circa *2001: A Space Odyssey* (1968) and make the film a non-stop feast of strange visual effects. He could have gone full bore into horror territory, seizing upon the similiarites the story has to Brian De Palma's horror touchstone *Carrie* (1976). Or he could have fallen back onto his stylistic devices and turned the movie into a more cerebral kind of science fiction tale. Any of those approaches would have softened his commitment to Thelma's humanity and trauma. The film never once wavers from her point of view, her abstract but relatable response to forbidden longings, her reluctant grappling with the impact of her long dormant abilities. In choosing to keep the film's temperament even without ever letting the potential for hysteria infect the mise-en-scène, he's keeping Thelma human, and her struggles understandable and relatable. She's not a supervillain, nor a superhero, she's just a teenaged girl who discovers she has powers that render a confusing time in her life even more terrible. Trier has tried and managed to make a film about a teenage girl that attempts to empathize with both the supernatural and the perfectly ordinary (if relatively horrifying, as hormone-fueled embarrassments tend to be) trials and tribulations Thelma faces.

Trier and co-writer Eskil Vogt place a similarly understated emphasis on the film's religious undercurrents. Like Mrs. White in *Carrie*, Thelma's parents at first seem socially hobbled by their steadfast beliefs, but there's more going on below the surface. They've committed not because they believe in the comfort provided by religion, but because it acts as a metaphorical and also a very real buffer against the potential terror their daughter is capable of inflicting on them and the world. It comes out that Thelma's religion was more or less a spontaneous gift, and when she adopted it, out went the emotional outbursts that led to her discovering her uncontrollable psychic abilities, only rediscovered when sexual urges supplant the confidence borne of her religious conviction. There's a subtle understanding of the tides of belief and the way they're meant to smooth out the fear we have before unanswerable questions that Trier and Vogt are wise to leave in the background. They let their images (courtesy of cinematographer Jakob Ihre, who conjures almost geometrically calculated scenes of frosty Norwegian landscapes and architecture) and Thelma's use of her powers speak louder than their ideas about religion, keeping the film more productively mysterious. When Thelma exits the picture, we have a pretty good idea what direction she wants to take her life, but everything we've just seen leaves the door open wide enough for potential catastrophe as soon as she's out of Trier's sight. That kind of open-endedness lets the film leave with its conviction intact.

Scout Tafoya

CREDITS

Thelma: Eili Harboe
Anja: Kaya Wilkins
Trond: Henrik Rafaelsen
Unni: Ellen Dorrit Petersen
Thelma at 6: Grethe Eltervag
Origin: United States
Language: Norwegian
Released: 2017
Production: Thomas Robsahm; Eurimages, Le Pacte, Motlys; released by The Orchard
Directed by: Joachim Trier
Written by: Joachim Trier; Eskil Vogt
Cinematography by: Jakob Ihre
Music by: Ola Flottum
Editing: Olivier Bugge Coutte
Costumes: Ellen Daehli Ystehede
Production Design: Roger Rosenberg
MPAA rating: Unrated
Running time: 116 minutes

REVIEWS

Barker, Andrew. *Variety* September 16, 2017.
Barton-Fumo, Margaret. *Film Comment*. November 3, 2017.
Bitel, Anton. *Village Voice*. October 3, 2017.
Cole, Jake. *Slant Magazine*. September 23, 2017.
Dowd, A.A. *The A.V. Club*. September 16, 2017.
Grierson, Tim. *Screen International* September 16, 2017.
Hayes, Britt. *Screen Crush*. September 23, 2017.
Perez, Rodrigo. *The Playlist*. September 16, 2017.
Rooney, David. *Hollywood Reporter*. September 16, 2017.
Vestby, Ethan. *The Film Stage*. September 16, 2017.

TRIVIA

Actress Eili Harboe attends the same university as her character Thelma does in the movie. She studies art history.

THOR: RAGNAROK

No Hammer. No Problem.
—Movie tagline
Thunder will reign.
—Movie tagline

Let the games begin.
—Movie tagline

Box Office: $313.7 Million

Many people feel that superheroes, as represented in comic books, television shows, and films are modern society's sort of "homage" to the Greek, Norse, and Roman Gods of yesteryear. While those ancient civilizations used these Gods and their stories as a way to teach humility, morality, and maybe even explain their place in the universe, modern day pop culture really tends to use superheroes as escapism. Still, the parallels are vast between ancient Gods and modern superheroes. While many superheroes often suffer the same moral and ultimately "human" drawbacks of their ancient God counterparts, they have much fancier costumes and are typically boiled down to stories of good versus evil. This preface is all a way to hold Thor, as portrayed via Marvel Comics, up to the light and note his existence in the way it first came to the fore, as the ancient Norse God of Thunder. And, that being said, the mere idea of making a Norse God into a comic book superhero is really pretty silly.

Yet, it's been working for Marvel Comics for decades and Thor's big screen adaptation (which debuted in *Thor* [2011] with charismatic muscle head Chris Hemsworth in the title role) was yet another Marvel Cinematic Universe victory as was the subsequent *Thor: The Dark World* (2013) and all of his appearances in *The Avengers* films thereafter. Which, one should remind viewers, is a team of made up superheroes in which he, an "actual" Norse God, willingly joined. All of this is to say, Thor should not work. It's a silly idea and a silly character (nice hammer) that somehow got lumped in with iconic comic book characters and is now well on it's way to an iconic cinematic legend. And as the curtain pulled back on *Thor: Ragnarok* this film too shouldn't work as it's helmed by quirky New Zealand native Taika Waititi who's never had a budget this big. Not to mention that few viewers if any have a clue as to what a "Ragnarok" is much less how to pronounce it. Still, *Thor: Ragnarok* is undoubtedly the funniest Marvel Cinematic Universe film to date and arguably one of if not the most purely entertaining.

Although *Thor: Ragnarok* is indeed a hoot, it stumbles a bit out of the blocks as it adheres to a somewhat irritating issue of many Marvel Comics Universe films: they are starting to feel routine in terms of how the stories unfold. A perilous battle opens nearly every film, which then leads to inevitable victory, personalities clash, and a longer form story unfolds before all coming together in a way that forms a jigsaw-like piece that fits expertly into the decades ahead crafted Marvel movie schedule that, judging by a recent press conference from Marvel owners Disney, will seemingly last forever.

In the case of the opening of *Thor: Ragnarok,* audiences meet Thor, who is trapped, hanging upside down as a captive of beastly Surtur (Clancy Brown), who's lifelong ambition is to destroy Thor's home world of Asgard and thus, put another notch on his world-dominating belt. The event which Surtur hopes to conjure to make this all happen is called "Ragnarok" so the confusing title is immediately spelled out for audiences. Since this would be a pretty short-lived film if the titular character were to die in act one, Thor soon escapes to the strains of Led Zepplin's rocking, epic, and fitting "Immigrant Song." While the scene is exciting and pitch perfect, it is also incredibly similar to opening scenes in other Marvel films of late including *Iron Man 2* (2010), which used AC/DC's "Shoot to Thrill" or, more recently, *Guardians of the Galaxy, Vol. 2* (2017), which soundtracked ELO's "Mr. Blue Sky" to kick off that sequel. From here, similar story beats set a familiar pace, yet the truly comical direction by Waititi make *Thor: Ragnarok* a film all its own which is very much a positive.

Previously, Thor films have essentially been "buddy pictures" where Thor is forced to work alongside, although frequently in friction with, his sly brother Loki (Tom Hiddleston) and this happens here, as well. Without giving too much away, Loki is up to his usual shenanigans (after all, he is the God of Mischief) and soon a long-lost sister named Hela (a deliciously scene-chewing Cate Blanchett) becomes the secret heir to the throne of Asgard. The bad news, aside from Thor and Loki discovering they aren't the rightful heirs and a vacated throne typically means only one thing, there's also much they do not know about the history of Asgard and much left unknown about father Odin (Anthony Hopkins). Also a drawback for the God-bros is the fact that sister Hela is the Goddess of Death and has no love for her good guy brothers. Thus, the two are, for lack of a better term, cast out to a somewhat post-apocalyptic planet called Sakaar which is overseen by a flaky, egomaniacal leader named simply Grandmaster (Jeff Goldblum).

Grandmaster keeps his poor constituents happy by featuring Gladiator-esque battles between the mightiest beings who have the misfortune of landing on Sakaar as bloody entertainment as a fine distraction for poor living conditions. And since every post-apocalyptic world needs to have a character who comes into play by selling "junk" in order to stay alive, enter Valkyrie (Tessa Thompson) who deems Thor a nice piece of junk and sells him to be a contestant in the Grandmaster's battles. No sooner has Thor got his dim wits about him then he's on stage, set to fight the greatest gladiator Sakaar has ever seen who, lo and behold, turns out to be The Hulk (Mark Ruffalo) who's been hiding on the planet (and, being treated as a God) since his departure at the end of *Avengers: Age of Ultron* (2015).

Thor: Ragnarok is a clever and funny entry into the yet-to-seriously-stumble Marvel Cinematic Universe. The characters here are diverse and well-defined and director Waititi (working off a script from Eric Pearson, Craig Kyle, and Christopher Yost) handles them all brilliantly as he sneakily takes apart the Loki/Thor buddy picture dynamic and reassembles it with a team consisting of pretty much everyone Thor meets on Sakaar. With great performances by Hemsworth, Hiddleston, and Blanchett, it's quite a pleasant surprise to see Tessa Thompson as the hard-drinking, battle-scarred (in more than one way) Valkyrie darn near steal the show. While she previously broke out as sassy yet heartfelt Bianca in Ryan Coogler's excellent *Creed* (2015), here she shows true star power and more than holds her own both in battle scenes and in more "dramedy" moments as well. While, in the end, *Thor: Ragnarok* does adhere to a fairly standardized Marvel blueprint, the great cast, solid comedy, and great eye of Waititi help mask this issue and almost make one forget this is a well-oiled, money-minting machine in action.

Don R. Lewis

CREDITS

Thor: Chris Hemsworth
Loki: Tom Hiddleston
Hela: Cate Blanchett
Heimdall: Idris Elba
Grandmaster: Jeff Goldblum
Origin: United States
Language: English
Released: 2017
Production: Kevin Feige; Marvel Studios; released by Walt Disney Studios Motion Pictures
Directed by: Taika Waititi
Written by: Eric Pearson; Craig Kyle; Christopher Yost
Cinematography by: Javier Aguirresarobe
Music by: Mark Mothersbaugh
Sound: Daniel Laurie; Shannon Mills
Music Supervisor: Dave Jordan
Editing: Zene Baker; Joel Negron
Costumes: Mayes C. Rubeo
Production Design: Dan Hennah; Ra Vincent
MPAA rating: PG-13
Running time: 130 minutes

REVIEWS

Bishop, Bryan. *The Verge.* October 19, 2017.
Chang, Justin. *Los Angeles Times.* November 3, 2017.
Dargis, Mahohla. *New York Times.* November 1, 2017.
DeBruge, Peter. *Variety.* October 19, 2017.
Ebiri, Bilge. *Village Voice.* October 29, 2017.
Kohn, Eric. *IndieWire.* October 19, 2017.
O'Sullivan, Michael. *Washington Post.* October 28, 2017.
Scotti, Ariel. *New York Daily News.* November 1, 2017.
Singer, Matt. *ScreenCrush.* October 19, 2017.
Webber, Rachel. *Total Film.* October 19, 2017.

QUOTES

Thor (addressing the Hulk): "So much has happened since I last saw you! I lost my hammer, like yesterday, so that's still fresh. Then I went on a journey of self-discovery. Then I met you."

TRIVIA

Thor's "friend from work" line about the Hulk was suggested to actor Chris Hemsworth by a Make-A-Wish child who paid a visit to the set on the day the scene was filmed.

THREE BILLBOARDS OUTSIDE EBBING, MISSOURI

Box Office: $38.1 Million

Martin McDonagh's *Three Billboards Outside Ebbing, Missouri* is the kind of film that one can feel becoming a classic when watching it. There is not a single wasted line of dialogue or a single character that has not been carefully thought out and fully explored, visually or verbally. The humor stings while often blindsiding the audience and the pace feels just right for a comedic crime drama that takes place in America's heartland. Every decision comes with a consequence and every consequence causes another unpredictable chain reaction of events. This is the kind of screenplay young, budding screenwriters hope to achieve one day and the kind any A-list actor will take a pay cut to be in, even if just for a small role. This quality of writing so rarely comes along, and yet its simplicity is part of its beauty and will help it endure far beyond the awards season hype.

The story takes place in a town that seems to have been untouched by time. One morning, gift shop owner Mildred Hayes (Frances McDormand) drives down a road nobody ever uses where three billboards have sat decaying over the decades from lack of use. She decides then and there to make better use of them by displaying three sentences in big bold letters against a red backdrop: "1. Raped while dying. 2. And still no arrests. 3. How come Chief Willoughby?" The billboards are first discovered by a hapless dolt of a police office, Dixon (Sam Rockwell), who informs said chief about them. Chief Willoughby (Woody Harrelson), completely caught off guard by the massive display of protest, does his best to reason with Mildred. The "raped while dying" billboard refers to Mildred's deceased daughter, who died about a year ago. There has been no progress on the case as to who did it. Sometimes, he tells her, there is nothing that can be found.

That is nowhere near good enough for Mildred, of course, who soon becomes a town pariah now that the media has taken notice and has given her story more attention. The townspeople are not without sympathy for Mildred's loss, but she happens to be going after a well-liked police chief who also happens to have pancreatic cancer. Unbeknownst to him, the whole town knows about it, including Mildred. After he quietly confesses to her of his illness, she says she has known for a while. "And you still put the billboards up?" he asks. "Yeah. It wouldn't do much good to put them up after you croak," she replies. The town priest tries to reason with her as well, but she sizes him up as someone who is guilty by association since much of the priesthood, as she sees it, has been known to molest children and then protect one another from consequence. Mildred does not take kindly to the judgment of others.

Her son, Robbie (Lucas Hedges), is not crazy about the idea of the billboards either, as he has been trying to wrap his head around his sister's tragic death for so many months. The billboards have become just a stinging reminder. Mildred's ex-husband, Charlie (John Hawkes), who has since started dating a 19-year-old, loses his temper over the idea of this stunt. Mildred does have some admirers, though. As long as she pays up for the rental of the billboard, she will always have a partner in crime in Red Welby (Caleb Landry Jones), the head of the advertising office in Ebbing. There is also the lovesick used car salesman, James (Peter Dinklage), who has been harboring a little crush on Mildred for a while now.

It is best not to give away any surprises here. If the above plot description makes the film sound like a downer, it is only because this set-up requires a bit of tragedy to emphasize the urgency behind the story. What follows beyond the exposition are many moments of comedic absurdity and memorable one-liners and comebacks. McDonagh has always had a flair for creating distinguished, colorful characters who float somewhere in the middle of morality and blind anger. *Three Billboards* explores where that anger takes these characters and it often comes up with an answer that feels right, even if the outcome has dire consequences. His screenplay uses humor as a means of relief. If the film were a hard-edged drama, many of the story turns would risk being obvious and possibly hollow. McDonagh is smart to know that using humor within tragedy helps the message enjoy a better, more fulfilling landing with the audience.

Nevertheless, this is McDonagh's angriest film so far, but it is also his most compassionate. Mildred stands for many women who have yet to see or receive any justice for rape, either of themselves or of loved ones and those in urban communities who have yet to see justice for murders against innocent, unarmed young men and women at the hands of the police force, many of whom never end up in prison for their actions. Yet, McDonagh sees the humanity within all of these characters, particularly in Willoughby and especially in Dixon, whose character arc feels earned and who becomes worthy of the audience's sympathies. McDonagh sees law enforcement not as the enemy, but as a collection of frustrated, sad individuals who wrestle with their incompetence and inner demons within the not-so-quiet confines of either their thankless job on the street (or at the desk) or homelife with the worst role models for parents.

This is also one of those rare films where nobody gives a stand-out performance because everyone here shines so brightly. It is hard to imagine anybody else besides McDormand playing this part. Her steely glare at anyone who dares cross her path with the intent to disrupt her plan is the face of someone who has had plenty of time to think about what she is doing, but who has also not lost the parental instinct to care for others. Her quiet moments by herself are among her strongest moments of her rich career. Harrelson also reminds the audience why he has become one of the most reliable and beloved actors of the last thirty or so years. He plays Willoughby as someone who hides so much that even the audience cannot detect his next action. There is anger, tragedy, humanity, and warmth all there in simple looks and line readings that only Harrelson could pull off in his own unique way.

Rockwell has the trickiest part, though, in that Dixon has to come off so unlikeable, yet loveable in his stupidity. Rockwell goes for more than one note, though, and Dixon becomes more fully fleshed out when he has no lines. Rockwell adds a nice physical touch to the performance as well, giving Dixon a bit of a gut and a bad back to deal with, possibly from sleeping on the same bed since he was a child (he lives with his mother). Hedges, as Mildred's son, has to keep his anger in check, but he also remembers the good times he had with his mom before the death of his sister. Their scenes alternate between anger and tenderness as there are still many unspoken words between them. Hawkes, Landry Jones, and Dinklage round out the cast nicely, as does a scene-stealing Samara Weaving, the 19-year-old animal lover who has a propensity for mis-reading the tension in every room she enters.

McDonagh has also surrounded himself with a top-notch group of people to bring this story to life. Ben Davis's cinematography is deceptively simple, while also pulling off a fantastic tracking shot during a pivotal and violent scene in the film. Davis also makes the town of Ebbing look timeless, as though stuck in a period piece, but without a specific period. The widescreen vistas of the hills and empty roads (the film was shot in Asheville, North Carolina) look beautiful and unforgiving all at once. Carter Burwell's score will sound familiar to fans of the Coen Brothers, particularly his work on *Miller's Crossing* (1990) and *Fargo* (1996). Burwell has always had a talent for finding the perfect sonic texture for every film in which he works and this is no exception.

This is McDonagh's best work so far, which is saying something after coming off *In Bruges* (2008) and *Seven Psychopaths* (2012), two films that showcased a remarkable talent for colorful characters, snappy dialogue, and a confidence behind the camera. *Three Billboards* is an important film for its time, yet it never feels full of itself. When the film fades out with the perfect closing line that only a writer of McDonagh's stature seems capable of pulling off (he is a renowned playwright), it comes with a feeling of being truly satisfied after a great film. There is nothing left to do but talk about it and remember all the favorite lines and unpredictable and uncomfortable moments. McDonagh may be an Englishman, but he had tapped into an American consciousness that few filmmakers of his generation have achieved. Its themes of blind anger causing irreparable damage may be universal, but has never felt more vital in America than in the year 2017.

Collin Souter

CREDITS

Mildred Hayes: Frances McDormand
Sheriff Bill Willoughby: Woody Harrelson
Officer Jason Dixon: Sam Rockwell
Anne Willoughby: Abbie Cornish
Robbie: Lucas Hedges
Origin: United States
Language: English
Released: 2017
Production: Graham Broadbent, Peter Czernin, Martin McDonagh; Blueprint Pictures, Film 4; released by Fox Searchlight Pictures
Directed by: Martin McDonagh
Written by: Martin McDonagh
Cinematography by: Ben Davis
Music by: Carter Burwell
Sound: Joakim Sundstrom
Music Supervisor: Karen Elliott
Editing: Jon Gregory
Art Direction: Jesse Rosenthal
Costumes: Merissa Lombardo
Production Design: Inbal Weinberg
MPAA rating: R
Running time: 115 minutes

REVIEWS

Braun, Liz. *Toronto Sun*. November 16, 2017.
Dargis, Manohla. *New York Times*. November 8, 2017.
Dowd, A.A. *The A.V. Club*. September 12, 2017.
Hornaday, Ann. *Washington Post*. November 16, 2017.
Howell, Peter. *Toronto Star*. November 16, 2017.
Lickona, Matthew. *San Diego Reader*. November 25, 2017.
MacDonald, Moira. *Seattle Times*. November 14, 2017.
Mayer, Dominick. *Consequence of Sound*. November 11, 2017.
Thompson, Gary. *Philadelphia Inquirer*. November 21, 2017.
Wolfe, April. *L.A. Weekly*. November 9, 2017.

QUOTES

Mildred Hayes: "My daughter Angela was murdered seven months ago, it seems to me the police department is too busy torturing black folk to solve actual crimes."

TRIVIA

The town where the movie was filmed is actually a small mountain town in western North Carolina called Sylva.

AWARDS

Oscars 2017: Actor--Supporting (Rockwell), Actress (McDormand)
British Acad. 2017: Actor--Supporting (Rockwell), Actress (McDormand), Film, Orig. Screenplay
Golden Globes 2018: Actor--Supporting (Rockwell), Actress--Drama (McDormand), Film--Drama, Screenplay
Ind. Spirit 2018: Actor--Supporting (Rockwell), Actress (McDormand)
Screen Actors Guild 2017: Actor--Supporting (Rockwell), Actress (McDormand), Cast

Nominations:

Oscars 2017: Actor--Supporting (Harrelson), Film, Film Editing, Orig. Score, Orig. Screenplay
British Acad. 2017: Actor--Supporting (Harrelson), Cinematog., Film Editing
British Acad. 2018: Director (McDonagh)
Directors Guild 2017: Director (McDonagh)
Golden Globes 2018: Director (McDonagh), Orig. Score

Ind. Spirit 2018: Screenplay
Screen Actors Guild 2017: Actor--Supporting (Harrelson)

TRANSFORMERS: THE LAST KNIGHT
(Transformers 5)

Rethink your heroes.
—Movie tagline
Every legend hides a secret.
—Movie tagline
There comes a moment when we are called upon to make a difference.
—Movie tagline
For one world to live, the other must die.
—Movie tagline
They have been here forever.
—Movie tagline

Box Office: $130.2 Million

By 2017, Michael Bay's *Transformers* franchise has become a regular summertime fixture, a tentpole studio product that many cinephiles the world over had come to dread. Every couple years, a new two-plus hour epic of mayhem and destruction would get released on more screens than every arthouse film from that same summer combined. When the first film was released in 2007, there existed some nostalgia for the Hasbro line of toys on which they were based so, despite the film being mediocre at best (and heavily marketed at worst), the film attracted a large audience and became the third highest grossing film of that year. The sequels that followed also did solid business, even surpassing the grosses of the original. Yet, despite the *Transformers* movies being a global hit worth over a billion dollars, there are no iconic lines of dialogue or images to cement its place in cinema history. They are quickly derided by many as being just noise.

It is hard to argue. Sitting through a *Transformers* movie is quite an endurance test. Bay's brand of overstuffed action and incoherence mixed with brain-dead screenwriting and occasional broad comedy has become a catch-all brand of how not to make a movie. Sure, one can argue that the box office grosses suggest otherwise, but did anyone really notice when the producers swiped Shia LaBeouf for Mark Wahlberg in the leading man role? Did anyone really miss Megan Fox after *Transformers: Revenge of the Fallen* (2009)? Most filmgoers could probably name one Transformer (Optimus Prime), but beyond that, the series has yet to create an enduring legacy beyond its bottom line. The films offer some special effects eye candy and brainless action for those who feel they do not deserve more.

Now, there are five films and *Transformers: The Last Knight* will hopefully be the final film as well. There is very little to distinguish this from the other four, except maybe that this one opens with a prologue that involves Arthurian legend, with Merlin (Stanley Tucci) walking around like a drunken buffoon. The film sets up the idea the the Transformers have existed on planet Earth since this time and have, at this point in history, hidden an artifact deep within a cave. Of course, this artifact will help save the planet from destruction during the present-day war between the Autobots and the Decepticons, but that will come up later. In the present day, the central human hero, Cade Yeager (Wahlberg), is in hiding in a junkyard repairing some of the Autobots. He now has an assistant named Jimmy (Jerrod Carmichael) and a young pre-teen girl who forces her way into his life.

Optimus Prime (voiced by Peter Cullen) has vanished in an effort to save the earth from other intergalactic hostiles. The biggest threat facing the planet comes in the form of Quintessa (Gemma Chan), a purely half-baked CGI creation that lacks any true menacing qualities to make her a memorable villain. Meanwhile, in England, Sir Edmund Burton (Anthony Hopkins) investigates the possibility of finding the hidden artifact that was established at the beginning of the film. He has so much information on the Transformers and their mythology, it is a wonder how the franchise managed to get through four films without making him look more useful. With him is Vivan Wembley (Laura Haddock), who is basically there to be pretty (Haddock plays what may as well just be called "the girl part").

Eventually, all these characters come together to help each other out and more mayhem ensues. Yeager may be in hiding, but he is still the main foster parent to the few remaining Transformers while the earth lays in ruin from the previous battles. He finds the talisman that is tied to the whole mythology of the Transformers, which goes on to explain (through poorly rendered flashbacks) that the secret of their existence here on earth have been kept by such people as Mozart and FDR. (Transformers were also responsible for killing Hitler. Never mind that, though.) Yeager and Wembley eventually meet each other and a forced love interest between them grows (more or less). Yeager has conflicts with his college-bound daughter, who has conveniently been written out of this film. Many of the other characters look as though they wish they could also be written out of the series as soon as possible.

Bay has never been an actor's director, of course. He specializes in action set-pieces, which he accomplished so well way back when he made *The Rock* (1996). That film benefitted greatly by a top-notch cast and a fun screenplay. Since then, Bay has yet to have such luck with material. *Transformers: The Last Knight* sees Hopkins and John Turturro spouting off expository dialogue (Turturro screams his into a phone, for the most part) and looking like they cannot wait for that paycheck to arrive in the mail. It is hard to imagine Hopkins actually sitting down and watching a film like this all the way through. Wahlberg fares no better in the leading man role. He spends much of the first half in the junkyard having conversations with CGI creations that clearly have an inadequate on-screen substitute with which Wahlberg can interact. He gives an unconvincing performance in these scenes, talking to nothing while nothing talks back.

And "nothing" is what amounts to the experience of watching *Transformers: The Last Knight*. There is action, but no suspense. There are CGI creatures, but nothing remotely human. There are attempts at humor, but no joy. Just a steady parade of explosions, slow-motion shots of forced heroism and a sinking feeling that the film will never end. It does, thankfully, and perhaps the weak reception at the U.S. box office will spell the end of this wholly forgettable and unnecessarily long franchise. The summer of 2017 saw a lot of reliable, money-making sequels dwindle after their first week of release. Of course, overseas money helps and there never seems to be any shortage of that here, but *Transformers: The Last Knight* underperformed substantially in the States where these things are born and bred, but never formed—or transformed—into anything worthwhile.

Collin Souter

CREDITS

Cade Yeager: Mark Wahlberg
Sir Edmund Burton: Anthony Hopkins
Colonel William Lennox: Josh Duhamel
Vivian Wembley: Laura Haddock
Santos: Santiago Cabrera
Origin: United States
Language: English
Released: 2017
Production: Ian Bryce, Tom DeSanto, Lorenzo di Bonaventura, Don Murphy; Hasbro Studios, Huahua Media; released by Paramount Pictures Corp.
Directed by: Michael Bay
Written by: Art Marcum; Matt Holloway; Ken Nolan
Cinematography by: Jonathan Sela
Music by: Steve Jablonsky
Sound: Ethan Van der Ryn
Editing: Roger Barton; Adam Gerstel; Debra Neil-Fisher; John Refoua; Mark Sanger; Calvin Wimmer
Art Direction: Jason Knox-Johnston
Costumes: Lisa Lovaas
Production Design: Jeffrey Beecroft
MPAA rating: PG-13
Running time: 149 minutes

REVIEWS

Bitel, Anton. *Sight and Sound*. July 14, 2017.
Braun, Liz. *Toronto Sun*. June 20, 2017.
Brody, Richard. *The New Yorker*. June 22, 2017.
Ebiri, Bilge. *Village Voice*. June 20, 2017.
Genzlinger, Neil. *New York Times*. June 20, 2017.
Keil, Matt. *Film Threat*. June 28, 2017.
Kohn, Eric. *IndieWire*. June 20, 2017.
Mayer, Dominick. *Consequence of Sound*. June 20, 2017.
Orr, Christopher. *The Atlantic*. July 8, 2017.
O'Sullivan, Michael. *Washington Post*. June 22, 2017.

QUOTES

Sir Edmund Burton: "One hundred billion trillion planets in the cosmos. You want to know, don't you, why they keep coming here?"

TRIVIA

With a budget of approximately $217 million, this is the most expensive Transformers film made to date.

AWARDS

Nominations:

Golden Raspberries 2017: Worst Director (Bay), Worst Picture, Worst Remake/Sequel, Worst Screenplay, Worst Support. Actor (Duhamel), Worst Support. Actor (Hopkins), Worst Support. Actor (Wahlberg), Worst Support. Actress (Haddock)

THE TRIP TO SPAIN

The two amigos are back.
—Movie tagline

Box Office: $1.2 Million

Until we are directly confronted with our own mortality, none of us really know how much time is left for our mortal coil. When Michael Winterbottom, Steve Coogan, and Rob Brydon took their initial road trip in search of the right copy for a food magazine, they probably had no idea it would develop into a trilogy of feature films. Though each "Trip" stems from a six-part television series, ironically it is the abbreviated approach to them in cinematic form that offers a greater context to their existence. This is not *My Dinner with Andre* (1981) but "My Many Meals With Rob" whittled down to the essentials, and during this humorous and introspective journey we may notice a little insight into our own.

Once again, the film begins with a phone call and an invitation to drive through the countryside and stop at restaurants where the food is announced upon serving. One look at his screaming baby and Brydon can't help but say yes. Having followed Coogan and Brydon from *The Trip* (2010) to *The Trip to Italy* (2014) at times it feels like a partnership of begrudging respect rather than an all-out friendship. Putting these two in a car together is an invitation for a casual quip to be received as an egotistical attempt at passive aggression. And as men of any age tend to do, they will not bow down in the face of a challenge of one upmanship.

Immortalized by one of the funniest scenes in any medium, the dynamic between the two men can be summed up by their dueling Michael Caine impressions in the first film. The juxtaposition of the older and younger Caine with his penchant for emotional outbursts or tranquility is not just hysterically funny and dead on but it also serves as an insight to the performers mimicking his on-screen personas. Brydon is more laid back and casually insistent over the adulation of reviewers who have propitiated his belief in his own skills. Coogan is more outspoken with his ego, perpetrated this time by how often he brings up his Oscar-nominated work on the screenplay for *Philomena* (2013). However, with that self-satisfaction comes an isolation that has always filled in the gaps between living the high life and feeling alone.

This has always been the quiet beating heart of the series; middle-aged men searching for some modicum of satisfaction with their personal lives and when they can't find it they turn to a satisfaction within themselves. The celebrity impersonations were lively asides for anyone not already focused on the displays and consumption of the food or the sights of the countryside. The sheer craftsmanship of not just the distinct vocal patterns but the situational conversations to which they would be inserted overshadowed the quieter moments which lacked in their dramatic depth compared to the heights of the comedy. For the third trip that element has been raised to an eleven-course meal where ten of them were desserts. No less than the likes of Al Pacino, David Bowie, John Hurt, Marlon Brando, Robert DeNiro, Michael Palin, and Woody Allen make vocal appearances here through Coogan and Brydon. But it is the frequency of their fascination with Mick Jagger and Roger Moore—who at one point engages in a discussion about the Moors—that nearly overloads what could be the grander purpose of this journey.

Over one meal, Brydon tells a story of overhearing David Bowie doing an interview. During it, the late singer recalls thinking about Brydon and how talented he was, but not remembering his name. It begins like an amusing anecdote but evolves into a more poignant recognition about legacy. Here is a legend, now a ghost from the past, expressing admiration for a fellow entertainer he cannot identify. Is Brydon's destiny to be just another "that guy who was in that thing" whose most notable contribution to comedy was the mimicry of more famous people? Is that why Coogan discusses following up arguing his most wide-reaching success in *Philomena* with the story of another parental figure searching for their offspring?

The Trip to Spain at times feels intent to give audiences what they remember and want they want more of from the previous two films. The clever interplay does end up providing some of the best laughs of the entire series. Though as delicious, sweet and palette-cleansing as they often are it has been in the past enough to consider pushing away from the table when the meat course is unveiled. That is not the case this time. Seven years can be a quick-moving eternity as our lives advance. Coogan looking out over vistas while trying to connect with his loved ones over a long-distance line may have seemed pretentious or half-hearted back then but now feels like a shared realization. The little pleasures are important, and laughter maybe even more so, but in our own trips through life who will love us enough to remember us? The answer cannot just be ourselves.

Erik Childress

CREDITS

Steve: Steve Coogan

Rob: Rob Brydon

Yolanda: Marta Barrio

Emma: Claire Keelan

Sally, Rob's wife: Rebecca Johnson

Origin: United States

Language: English

Released: 2017

Production: Josh Hyams, Stefano Negri, Melissa Parmenter; Revolution Films; released by IFC Films

Directed by: Michael Winterbottom

Cinematography by: James Clarke

Sound: Joakim Sundstrom

Editing: Mags Arnold; Paul Monaghan; Marc Richardson

MPAA rating: Unrated

Running time: 108 minutes

REVIEWS

Bramesco, Charles. *The Playlist*. April 24, 2017.

DeFore, John. *Hollywood Reporter*. April 25, 2017.
Dowd, A.A. *The A.V. Club*. August 14, 2017.
Feeney, Mark. *Boston Globe*. August 17, 2017.
Kenny, Glenn. *RogerEbert.com*. August 10, 2017.
Larsen, Josh. *LarsenOnFilm*. August 10, 2017.
Minow, Nell. *Movie Mom*. August 24, 2017.
Savadas, Elias. *Film International*. August 21, 2017.
Swietek, Frank. *One Guy's Opinion*. August 16, 2017.
Zacharek, Stephanie. *Time*. August 11, 2017.

QUOTES

Rob: "Do you know what the Welsh word for 'Carrot' is?"
Steve: "No."
Rob: "Moron."

TRIVIA

Actors Steve Coogan and Rob Brydon talk about the song "The Windmills of Your Mind" by Noel Harrison and it is played at the film's ending. A different version of this song by The King's Singers was played at the end of the final episode of *I'm Alan Partridge* (1997), where Alan goes to see the unsold copies of his autobiography being pulped.

TULIP FEVER

Box Office: $2.5 Million

Finally arriving in theaters after an extended and well-documented string of delays—produced in 2014, *Tulip Fever* had so many release dates announced and withdrawn over the next couple of years that some doubted it would actually see the light of day even after TV commercials began running—and on a Labor Day weekend that habitually sees the year's lowest box-office attendance figures. The film carries with it the stench of something far more pungent and off-putting than the fragrant bulb found in its title. And yet, even though *Tulip Fever* turns out to be as bad as expected, it is not bad in most of the expected ways. This is one of those films that flies off the rails in such weird ways that it almost inspires a certain morbid curiosity from viewers wondering if it was just the victim of years of post-production tinkering or if it was actually meant to be as odd and tonally suspect as it ultimately is.

Set against the backdrop of the period in the Dutch Golden Age when the mania among investors for the recently introduced tulip before the abrupt collapse of the market inspired what is generally considered to be history's first true economic bubble, the film stars Alicia Vikander as Sophia Sandvoort, a beautiful young orphan who has been essentially purchased from the orphanage where she has been raised to become the wife of powerful merchant Cornelius Sandvoort (Christoph Waltz). As these things go, Sophia has fared relatively well—Cornelius plainly loves and cares for his wife (thanks in no small part to a tragedy in his past), has a certain sense of humor himself and his world and is smart enough to recognize that the tulip rage cannot possibly last forever. Other than being a bit of a bore at times (albeit a well-meaning one), the only real cloud comes in the form of her seeming inability to produce the male heir that he so desperately wants (same tragedy as previously mentioned) but Cornelius is never cruel to Sophia because of this at any point.

However, a combination of vanity and a desire to leave something behind in the event that no child ever comes inspires him to commission a dual portrait of himself and Sophia and he ends up hiring struggling artist Jan van Loos (Dane DeHaan) to do the job. Since Jan is brash and dashing and looks vaguely like Leonardo DiCaprio, he and Sophia soon begin a passionate but clandestine affair—albeit one that is discovered almost immediately by Sophia's loyal housekeeper and friend Maria (Holliday Grainger), who is herself carrying on with ambitious fishmonger Willem (Jack O'Connell)—but despair of what they can do. When Willem, who has been secretly dabbling in the tulip market in order to make enough money to marry Maria, goes missing and Maria discovers she is pregnant, Sophia hits upon an insanely complex plan (one that begins with a fake pregnancy and speculation in the tulip market and grows exponentially) that will give her and Jan their freedom, Cornelius an heir and a better life for Maria's child than she could possibly provide. Somehow, this plot, which even Rube Goldberg might have deemed a tad too complex and unwieldy, goes askew and winds up threatening the happiness and well-being of everyone involved.

Tulip Fever may sound like an old fashioned bodice-ripper—if anyone involved actually kept their bodice on long enough for it to be ripped off—but it goes off the rails so quickly and in such bizarre ways that most viewers will be left scratching their heads instead of swooning. Rather than a straightforward period drama—or even the "erotic thriller" promised by the somewhat deceptive advertising—the film almost seems like it is trying to spoof this style of filmmaking even as it attempts to embody it. This is a film that theoretically wants to be taken seriously and yet also includes such risible sights as a wacky gynecologist (Tom Hollander), Christoph Waltz's O-face during the height (such as it is) of coitus (topped off with "God forgive me"), and a valuable tulip garden protected by a flock of attack geese. This all comes before the deployment of Sophia's cunning plan, a scheme that Lucy Ricardo herself might have attempted had the television censors been a little more permissive back in the day. Things get so silly that you almost wish that director Justin Chadwick and co-writers Deborah Moggach and Tom Stoppard could just throw in the towel altogether and go back in time to hand the entire project over to Mel Brooks in his prime, if only to hear Harvey Korman's version of Cornelius utter the deathless line "Are you in love with the fishmonger?" Whether the clashing tones are the result of attempts to fix an allegedly troubled project in post-production or are an accurate representation of Moggach's book, I cannot say, but the end result almost needs to be seen to be disbelieved.

And yet, the bigger problem with the film is the absolute failure of the central romantic relationship between the two young lovers at its core. Part of the reason this doesn't work is because there is never any sense that Sophia is suffering at all as Cornelius's wife—he shows nothing but affection for her and even though he may be conceived as a bore, the fact that he is played by Waltz—an actor incapable of delivering a boring line—makes him arguably the liveliest character on display. More problematic is the complete lack of chemistry between Vikander and DeHaan. Vikander is, of course, a wonderful actress but fails to invoke in Sophia any real sense of romantic excitement or even simple lust despite the amount of time the two characters spend between the sheets. DeHaan, on the other hand, is so remarkably unconvincing here that he seems less like the romantic lead and more like the creepy little weasel that the real romantic lead needs to defeat in order to save the day. You could actually take any two random members of the crazy-go-nuts cast assembled here (which also includes the likes of Matthew Morrison, Cara Delevingne, the perhaps-obvious Judi Dench and the perhaps-slightly-less-obvious Zach Galifianakis) and put them together and they would almost certainly produce a more convincing romantic spark than Vikander and DeHaan are able to muster up.

Tulip Fever is a film that never conjures any sense of passion or excitement despite all the huffing and puffing and bits of nudity on display. Even a narrative that completely dispensed with all the romantic silliness and focused exclusively on the fascinating story of the tulip-based economic boom and bust would have come across as far more exciting than anything seen here. The fact that it spent so many months sitting on a shelf and having one release date after another scuttled will not seem surprising at all to anyone who somehow manages to sit through the entire thing, though they may well question why it was finally allowed to slip out, however briefly, into theaters. Too weird to work as a conventional film and not weird enough to be interesting, *Tulip Fever* is, no pun intended, nothing but a dead bulb.

Peter Sobczynski

CREDITS

Sophia Sandvoort: Alicia Vikander
Jan van Loos: Dane DeHaan
Willem Brok: Jack O'Connell
Maria: Holliday Grainger
Dr. Sorgh: Tom Hollander
Origin: United States
Language: English
Released: 2017
Production: Alison Owen, Harvey Weinstein; Paramount Pictures Corp., Ruby Films, Worldview Entertainment; released by The Weinstein Company
Directed by: Justin Chadwick
Written by: Deborah Moggach; Tom Stoppard
Cinematography by: Eigil Bryld
Music by: Danny Elfman
Editing: Rick Russell
Art Direction: Bill Crutcher
Costumes: Michael O'Connor
Production Design: Simon Elliott
MPAA rating: R
Running time: 105 minutes

REVIEWS

Abele, Robert. *TheWrap*. September 1, 2017.
Cooper, Julia. *Globe and Mail*. September 1, 2017.
Debruge, Peter. *Variety*. September 1, 2017.
Eckland, Kate. *IndieWire*. September 1, 2017.
Guzman, Rafer. *Newsday*. September 1, 2017.
Kenigsberg, Ben. *New York Times*. September 1, 2017.
Linden, Sherri. *Hollywood Reporter*. September 1, 2017.
Myers, Kimber. *Los Angeles Times*. September 1, 2017.
Orndorf, Brian. *Blu-Ray.com*. September 1, 2017.
Reed, Rex. *New York Observer*. September 1, 2017.

QUOTES

Jan Van Loos: "I've come to paint a portrait."

TRIVIA

The film is set in the Netherlands with Dutch characters, but was entirely shot in the United Kingdom, with no Dutch actors.

U

UNDERWORLD: BLOOD WARS

Protect the bloodline.
—Movie tagline

Box Office: $30.4 Million

The fifth installment in the long-running *Underworld* series, *Underworld: Blood Wars,* feels like an attempt to reinvigorate a stubbornly anemic franchise. First-time director Anna Foerster is unavoidably hamstrung by rookie directorial jitters, subpar technical assets, and the convoluted backstory of the franchise, but she at least has the self-awareness to lean into the B-movie cheese of the source material, whether it's secret mountain societies with the power of resurrection or the pageantry of vampire nobility snidely tearing into each other.

Until this slight course correction, the most confounding aspect of this blockbuster action-horror franchise has been a dogged disregard for the most unique (and coincidentally) most cinematic qualities of its own vampire vs. werewolves mythology. *Blood Wars* at least tries to recognize its own dopiness in scenes where characters bite each other to transport into flashbacks. Contrast that with the rest of the series where the lead bloodsuckers rarely have the chance to bare fangs. If anything, the lion's share of the films have boiled down to extended stock sequences of blackcoat-clad bouncer rejects firing assault rifles.

That's certainly partly by design. Since the series' beginning in 2003, the *Underworld* franchise has never shirked from the shadow of more popular franchises, whether it be *The Matrix* (1999) or angsty 1990s superhero cult item *The Crow* (1994). And, by the same token, while the entirety of the *Underworld* series has been rooted in overly dense generational conflicts of taboo hybrids and hierarchal purity, lead character Selene's (Kate Beckinsale) most enduring characteristic has less to do with her identity as a superpowered vampire assassin than her familiar ensemble—a leather jacket and twin handguns that unavoidably recall Keanu Reeve's role as Neo in the *Matrix* films.

There's nothing inherently wrong with a well-wrought rehash, but the *Underworld* series has largely been one long slog, distinguished primarily by which prestige actor comes through to gnaw on the scenery as a big bad (past highlights have included a statuesque Bill Nighy and a stolidly sanctimonious Michael Sheen), and which McGuffin dominates the story. *Blood Wars* continues this tradition, bringing on a disappointingly tame and luxuriously-maned Tobias Menzies to glower as Lycanthrope freedom fighter Marius, and the return of Selene and Michael's (Scott Speedman) hybrid daughter, Eve, who exists strictly off-screen, but is nonetheless the subject of nearly every line of dialogue.

Threading in plotlines from throughout the series, *Blood Wars* feels both of a piece with the rest of the series and a fresh start, even including a stylized mini-recap for lapsed fans as an acknowledgement of passed time. It picks up where *Awakening* ended with Selene and the resurrected David (Theo James) on the run from both her former vampire allies (for killing previous vampire elders Markus and Viktor), and the Lycans, who are after her for the location of Eve, who may be the solution to the end of the Vampire/Lycan war. That immediacy is short-lived though as political chicanery brings Selene nearly immediately back to her former coven's hideout—a visually anonymous eastern European castle—with temporary clemency on the condition that she teach the remaining vampires who weren't wiped out in the genocide of *Awakening* how to fight.

If that summary feels too dense to read, it's just as messy in practice, even as Foerster tries valiantly to make these convolutions coherent, let alone interesting. *Game of Thrones* regular Charles Dance shows up to imbue dreary conversations about asylum with unearned gravitas, but it's entirely a perfunctory exercise in forcing Selene to bump heads with Semira (Laura Pulver), a deceptively kind and entertainingly domineering council member with megalomaniacal ambitions. Pulver wrings her scenes for all they're worth, but her evil plan is both overly complex and ultimately kind of boring, even as it involves everything from fake and real coups to drinking Selene's immortal blood.

As a whole, this first act is a poorly conceived mess, and the film feels just as aware of how unwieldy and sluggish the material feels, regularly abandoning Semira for glimpses of Marius' own schemes to capture Selene. Luckily, Selene and David quickly escape Semira and the film takes a long detour to a snowy mountain fortress where the members embark on spiritual walkabouts to a nether realm.

It dramatically perks up in these scenes with these sequences acting as a breather between all the battles shot with excessive speed ramping, and drawing room monologues. It's here that the script also becomes enamored with a prophecy involving David. Foerster's treatment of this interlude is entertainingly pulpy, even leading to a triumphant wardrobe change for Selene, but after extensive exposition about the coven's method of spiritual meditation, Foerster never even offers the necessary visual payoff. And while the atmospheric mountain fortress provides a welcome change of scenery, it only emphasizes the technical limitations of the budget and the realities of lighting an outside location draped in darkness.

Granted, the *Underworld* series has never had a sterling reputation for effects work. Even the earlier installments in the series were more half-hearted genuflections to the practical wizardry of pioneers like Rob Bottin or Rick Baker with werewolves' jaws cracking and extending into a snout than individually impressive effects transformations. But *Blood Wars* falls victim to the worst aspects of modern effects work, completely discarding the gooeyness and tactility that made watching monsters such campy entertainment. This generic futurism has extended into the prevailing visual aesthetic of the series, replacing the greasy, liquid slickness of earlier installments. These days, *Blood Wars* could easily be a cousin to young adult fare like the *Divergent* series rather than the late 1990s Nine Inch Nails music video grime of previous films.

By the time, *Blood Wars* limps to the end credits, and signals an inevitable sequel, it feels almost totally redundant, even as Beckinsale's practiced moodiness remains an evergreen appeal, and Foerster at least feels mostly in control of her vision. But, even by the standards of the previous films, impressively little has actually happened, let alone changed by the end of this mostly stale sequel. For once, the status quo feels less like a variation on the same idea than the beginning of a new chapter. Now, if only they can figure out what makes vampires and werewolves so fun in the first place.

Michael Snydel

CREDITS

Selene: Kate Beckinsale
David: Theo James
Marius: Tobias Menzies
Semira: Lara Pulver
Thomas: Charles Dance
Origin: United States
Language: English, French
Released: 2016
Production: David Kern, Gary Lucchesi, Tom Rosenberg, Len Wiseman; Lakeshore Entertainment, Sketch Films; released by Screen Gems
Directed by: Anna Foerster
Written by: Cory Goodman; Kyle Ward
Cinematography by: Karl Walter Lindenlaub
Music by: Michael Wandmacher
Sound: Michael Babcock
Music Supervisor: Eric Craig
Editing: Peter Amundson
Art Direction: Martin Vackar
Costumes: Bojana Nikitovic
Production Design: Ondrej Nekvasil
MPAA rating: R
Running time: 91 minutes

REVIEWS

Crump, Andy. *Paste Magazine*. January 13, 2017.
Gleiberman, Owen. *Variety*. January 6, 2017.
Kenigsberg, Ben. *New York Times*. January 6, 2017.
Mendelson, Scott. *Forbes*. January 6, 2017.
Myers, Kimber. *Los Angeles Times*. January 6, 2017.
Robey, Tim. *The Telegraph*. January 12, 2017.
Robinson, Tasha. *The Verge*. January 6, 2017.
Rothkopf, Joshua. *Time Out New York*. January 6, 2017.

Sobczynski, Peter. *RogerEbert.com.* January 6, 2017.
Vishnevetsky, Ignatiy. *The A.V. Club.* January 9, 2017.

QUOTES

Selene: "There is no beginning, there is no end. There is only becoming."

TRIVIA

On the wall in the castle there are several paintings of elder vampires including a rendering of Vlad the Impaler, also known as Dracula.

UNFORGETTABLE

When love ends, madness begins.
—Movie tagline

Box Office: $11.4 Million

The trailer for *Unforgettable* made it appear to be a deliberate and knowing throwback to all those Yuppie-in-Peril thrillers from the late 1980s and early 1990s in which a picture-perfect family unit had their idealized existence threatened by some malevolent outside interloper—maybe a spurned lover (as in *Fatal Attraction* [1987]) or a nanny with a grudge (like *The Hand That Rocks the Cradle* [1992])—until the outsider was violently dispatched in the last reel. The trouble with *Unforgettable* is that it feels as if none of the filmmakers ever actually saw any of those earlier films and are under the mistaken belief that they are presenting all the hoary clichés of the genre as if they have never been seen before. The end result is like one of those made-for-TV movies that Lifetime cranks out like sausages that manage to find the money to hire a higher caliber of actor than usual—based on the evidence supplied here, this was evidently accomplished by taking out most of the money that had been allotted to pay for a decent screenplay.

As the film opens, online writer Julia (Rosario Dawson) has traveled across the country to move in with her new fiancée, micro-brewery maven David (Geoff Stults), and his adorable young daughter, Lily (Isabella Kai Rice). Although Julia has the usual fears about fitting in and worrying about whether her soon-to-be stepdaughter will accept her or not, the real obstacle to her happiness is the presence of Tessa (Katherine Heigl), David's ex-wife and Lily's mother. A Type-A Plus personality, Tessa is an icy control freak whose drive for absolute perfection—clearly instilled by her equally uptight mother (Cheryl Ladd)—has driven her halfway around the bend and helped to lead to her divorce. At first, Tessa barely tolerates Julia, who she assumes is just a fling David is going through before coming to his senses and returning to her, and undermines her in all the usual ways—criticizing her cooking to her face and offering Lily expensive presents as a way of currying her favor over Julia's warmth and humanity—while Julia just quietly takes it all and David mindlessly insists that things will work themselves out. However, when Tessa's errant snooping at Julia's phone reveals news of the upcoming wedding, she goes the rest of the way round the bend and decides to get rid of her rival for good.

Some of her attempts are mundane enough—she anonymously sends flowers to Julia to make David think she is having an affair and using a minor mishap at a farmer's market to prove that Julia is not capable of caring for Lily. Things ramp up considerably when Tessa discovers that Julia has a dark secret—an abusive ex that she had a just-lapsed restraining order against—and, using a fake Facebook account (Julia having no Internet presence to speak of—as do so many online writers) and sexy photos stolen from Julia's phone, initiates contact with him and then sends him a care package including intimate items of Julia's that she broke in and stole. When things finally come to a head between the two, Tessa contacts the ex again and tells him where Julia lives which leads to a confrontation wherein he tries to rape Julia but she escapes after stabbing him in the leg. Having observed all of this, Tessa finishes the job on the ex, leading to Julia being accused of murder and having her secret exposed to David. Naturally, no one believes Julia and it falls on her shoulders to confront Tessa once and for all and have the catfight that the filmmakers have been promising throughout the entire film.

Unforgettable was co-written and directed by women (Christina Hodson and Denise Di Novi, respectively) but that does not keep it from being sexist, retrograde junk. Neither Julia nor Tessa are especially interesting, and, as a result, their battle of wills never amounts to much. There are times when *Unforgettable* feels like it was custom-made to drive the people behind the Bechdel Test absolutely insane. The whole thing is borderline appalling and one wonders what two smart and capable actresses like Dawson and Heigl could have possibly been thinking when they signed on. In fact, the only thing that keeps it from coming across as being as offensive as it really is deep down is that the whole enterprise is frankly too stupid to take its overt misogyny seriously.

Even if one puts all the film's misogynistic elements to the side and attempts to embrace it as the sort of trashy nonsense promised by the undeniably effective trailer, *Unforgettable* is still an across-the-board failure because it fails to succeed even by those standards. The film is clearly familiar with the sub-genre it is working in and knows what the expected ingredients are, but it is completely clueless as to how to effectively put them together. For example, it is to be expected that Julia will find it difficult to get people to believe that Tessa is as malevolent as she claims, but David so consistently refuses to believe any of her claims—even though he is fully aware of his ex's controlling nature and history of mental instability—that it almost seems at times as if he is gaslighting her instead of just being stupid. Furthermore, the notion of Tessa trying to make it seem as if Julia is carrying on with a former flame sounds plausible enough but to then make him a psychotic stalker and rapist spins it in a weirdly unpleasant direction from which the story never recovers.

A film that could only be more removed from the implications of its title if it were named "Best Movie of the Year," *Unforgettable* somehow manages to come across as both awesomely tasteless and incredibly boring. At least a film such as *Fatal Attraction*, despite its numerous flaws, was made with a certain style that allowed it to work on some basic fundamental level. This one, by comparison, shows only contempt for its audience virtually across the board with its dreadful screenplay, cardboard characters, and aggressively indifferent execution. If this film does not go down as one of the very worst films of 2017, it will only be because everyone who saw it will have completely and happily forgotten about it when it comes time to make those lists.

Peter Sobczynski

CREDITS

Tessa Connover: Katherine Heigl
Julia Banks: Rosario Dawson
David Connover: Geoff Stults
Ali: Whitney Cummings
Tessa's mother: Cheryl Ladd
Origin: United States
Language: English, French
Released: 2017
Production: Alison Greenspan, Ravi Mehta, Denise Di Novi; Di Novi Pictures; released by Warner Bros. Pictures
Directed by: Denise Di Novi
Written by: Christina Hodson; David Leslie Johnson
Cinematography by: Caleb Deschanel
Music by: Toby Chu
Sound: Jeremy Peirson
Music Supervisor: Kasey Truman
Editing: Frederic Thoraval
Art Direction: Christopher Dileo
Costumes: Marian Toy
Production Design: Nelson Coates
MPAA rating: R
Running time: 100 minutes

REVIEWS

Brown, Phil. *NOW Toronto.* April 21, 2017.
Clarke, Donald. *Irish Times.* April 21, 2017.
Debruge, Pete. *Variety.* April 20, 2017.
Genzlinger, Neil. *New York Times.* April 20, 2017.
Graham, Adam. *Detroit News.* April 21, 2017.
Greene, Steve. *IndieWire.* April 20, 2017.
Laffly, Tomris. *Time Out.* April 20, 2017.
Linden, Sheri. *Hollywood Reporter.* April 20, 2017.
Padua, Pat. *Washington Post.* April 20, 2017.
Walsh, Katie. *Los Angeles Times.* April 20, 2017.

TRIVIA

Amma Asante was initially set to direct this film, but left the project when Kerry Washington declined one of the lead roles. Producer Denise Di Novi then took over, making this her directorial debut.

AWARDS

Nominations:

Golden Raspberries 2017: Worst Actress (Heigl)

A UNITED KINGDOM

Box Office: $3.9 Million

A biographical interracial romantic drama based on a true story, *A United Kingdom* avoids the manufactured mawkishness of so many films of a similar ilk, anchored in particular by a wonderful performance from David Oyelowo. Directed by Amma Asante, the film enjoyed its world premiere at the 2016 Toronto Film Festival, where it was acquired for domestic distribution by Fox Searchlight Pictures. Released theatrically the following February, the film garnered good reviews (certified fresh on Rotten Tomatoes, with an 83 percent score), and eventually grossing $3.9 million in the United States to add to its $9.9 million international haul.

Adapted from Susan Williams' book *Colour Bar, A United Kingdom* blends together romance, history, and political intrigue, telling the true story of Seretse Khama (Oyelowo), a royal prince of Bechuanaland (now Botswana) who, in 1948, after being groomed to become the king of his nation, throws those plans into disarray. While completing his education in Great Britain, he meets and falls in love with Ruth Williams (Rosamund Pike), a white London office worker. Seretse tells Ruth of his status, and their whirlwind courtship ends in an engagement.

The union, though, is opposed by members of both families, including Seretse's respected uncle, Tshekedi

Khama (Vusi Kunene). Eventually, even entire governments weigh in. Great Britain, mostly embodied by diplomat Sir Ian Canning (Jack Davenport), is firmly opposed to any marriage, since they feel it will be seen as an endorsement of interracial coupling in what is still a British protectorate—plus an act of provocation against South Africa, who is set to implement a policy of apartheid. The country's business interests in the region inform this opinion. These pressures separate Seretse and Ruth for a while—at least geographically. But against considerable odds the determined duo stick together, and in doing so change the trajectory of their personal histories as well as the fate of a nation.

Asante, herself born in Great Britain to Ghanian parents, of course had a minor art house splash with *Belle* (2013), which told the story of the daughter of a white man and an enslaved African woman from the West Indies who, as a young woman, rises above her station and becomes involved in an important legal case. It is perhaps not a stretch, then, to note Asante's interest in and facility with stories that exist at the intersection of different cultures, and the tension such environments produce. She has a keen sense of pacing, again evidenced here, and an unflashy, deceptively laid back style that trains a viewer's focus on the performers.

The evocative cinematography of Sam McCurdy does a good job of using color and warmth to establish contrast of place, and the differing emotional temperatures of each setting. The moody British fog and grey tones of its streetscapes stand in marked difference to the amber, light brown, and orange color palettes of Africa, whose open savannas are captured with an inviting series of wide-angle shots.

Guy Hibbert's script is a little punchy in some of its speechifying. In his rebuke to his nephew, Tshekedi's reasoning is solid from the point-of-view of his character ("Your grandfather had no choice in outside rule," he tells Seretse, "but you bringing this woman here is demeaning to your people"). Yet it is delivered with a grandstanding directness that feels over-dialed, and aimed at hand-wringing, liberal-minded retirees in the audience as much as another character. There are a couple examples of this in the movie.

What is heartening, though, is that Asante's film takes the time to till the earth of opposition to Seretse and Ruth's union, and root these opinions in something more nuanced than blind bigotry or ignorance. Seretse's aunt and sister, for example, not only have doubts about Ruth being able to fully embody the proper matriarchal persona that their Bamangwato tribe requires, but they also have anger about the fact that the British, who have already exercised manipulative control of their land, have now seemingly managed to locate and deploy yet another implement of control. This is a legitimate concern, and treated as such.

A United Kingdom is a film of romantic pining and obstacles overcome, and not a movie to necessarily get down into the details of connection; as presented here, its love story feels somewhat preordained, so the film rushes through its courtship in order to get to a place where its characters are struggling to reunite and get on with their shared life together. To that end, the film's lead pairing matters tremendously. Oyelowo and Pike have a nice chemistry—and thankfully a much different relationship than in *Jack Reacher* (2012), where one of their characters actually electrocuted the other in an elevator.

Oyelowo does a good job of blending Seretse's accent—capturing not merely the affected, formal British accent from his studies in the United Kingdom, but also its African roots, and then smartly modulating that cadence further based on the nervousness or comfort level of certain circumstances (Seretse's breathy proposal to Ruth is enough to make one's heart pleasantly skip a beat). Pike, meanwhile, has a gift with communicating enigmatic emotional distance. Sometimes that can be poured into a character who is icy and dangerous, as with *Gone Girl* (2014), but here it is steered into the flip side of that persona—a steely fortitude.

For much of its 111-minute running time, the film's grander sociopolitical punch—the specific details about British interests in Bechuanaland uranium, gold, and other minerals—does not forcefully connect. But by the end of *A United Kingdom*, Asante has convincingly married the personal and political, and managed to sneakily tell an unheralded tale of national independence. It is a story worth seeking out.

Brent Simon

CREDITS

Seretse Khama: David Oyelowo
Ruth Williams: Rosamund Pike
Rufus Lancaster: Tom Felton
Sir Alistair Canning: Jack Davenport
Muriel Williams: Laura Carmichael
Origin: United States
Language: English
Released: 2017
Production: Brunson Green, Peter Heslop, Charlie Mason, Rick McCallum, Justin Moore-Lewy, David Oyelowo; BBC Films, British Film Institute, Film United, Harbinger Pictures, Ingenious Media Partners, Pathé, Perfect Weekend, Yoruba Saxon Productions; released by Fox Searchlight Pictures
Directed by: Amma Asante

Written by: Guy Hibbert
Cinematography by: Sam McCurdy
Music by: Patrick Doyle
Sound: James Mather
Editing: Jonathan Amos; Jon Gregory
Art Direction: Andrew Munro
Costumes: Jenny Beavan; Anushia Nieradzik
Production Design: Simon Bowles
MPAA rating: PG-13
Running time: 111 minutes

REVIEWS

Debruge, Peter. *Variety.* September 10, 2016.
Graham, Adam. *Detroit News.* February 23, 2017.
Heaton, Michael. *Cleveland Plain Dealer.* March 2, 2017.
Kenny, Glenn. *New York Times.* February 9, 2017.
Keough, Peter. *Boston Globe.* February 16, 2017.
LaSalle, Mick. *San Francisco Chronicle.* February 16, 2017.
McDonald, Moira. *Seattle Times.* February 23, 2017.
Simon, Jeff. *Buffalo News.* March 2, 2017.
Taylor, Ella. *NPR.* February 9, 2017.
Turan, Kenneth. *Los Angeles Times.* February 9, 2017.

QUOTES

Seretse Khama: "No man is free who is not master of himself."

TRIVIA

The house used in the film was the actual home of the real Ruth and Seretse.

THE UNKNOWN GIRL
(La fille inconnue)

Box Office: $150,549

Jean-Pierre and Luc Dardenne have a cinematic history filled with international acclaim. They are Cannes Festival darlings who have won the Palme d'Or twice, and their last film *Two Days, One Night* (2014) earned Marion Cotillard a deserved Oscar® nomination. While their films are not classified as thrillers or mysteries, the filmmakers still manage to infuse their works with suspenseful and tense moments. Their naturalistic style, straightforward storytelling, and hand-held camerawork are so well-known and revered that their oeuvre has become something of a genre itself. And like all genres, this one is ripe for both revision and mockery. *The Unknown Girl* (*La fille inconnue*) wants to take a revisionist approach by casting itself as an outright crime procedural-slash-mystery. Unfortunately, it plays as if the Dardennes were parodying themselves.

Dr. Jenny Davin (Adèle Haenel) is finishing up one of her shifts at a small clinic. She is currently facing a decision on whether to end her clinic tenure in favor of a fancier job. Davin seems competent and compassionate, making house calls to some of her regular patients in preparation for her exit from their care. Her bedside manner is so appealing that, in a beautiful scene reminiscent of the Dardennes at their best, a dying cancer patient sings her a farewell song he's written on her behalf. *The Unknown Girl* leans in on Davin's humility early on, so that when she ignores the buzzer pressing of a potential patient who has arrived after hours, it doesn't register as vindictive or lazy.

When the patient doesn't buzz more than once, Davin assumes there was no emergency and goes home. However, when the police arrive to ask for her security camera footage in the hopes of discovering a lead on a recent murder, Davin learns that the victim was the person she did not buzz in the night before. She is the unknown girl of the title, whom we only see fleetingly in Davin's security footage. She is an African woman who appears to be in distress, as if someone is chasing her. Whoever was in pursuit may be the person who cracked open her skull and left her for dead.

Since the body shows signs of struggle, the cops assume that the teenaged victim was a prostitute who met the wrong "client" and paid dearly. There's a business as usual approach to their investigation that strikes Davin as cold; since the victim had no identification, she'll be buried in an unmarked grave and likely forgotten. Though she prides herself on being able to overlook her emotions as a doctor, Davin cannot ignore the strong pull of guilt over these circumstances. When her conscience gets the better of her, Davin decides to open her own investigation to at least find the identity of the murdered woman.

Here's where *The Unknown Girl* starts to unravel in extreme fashion. The Dardennes are very good at teasing out the tensions that arise from their usual, more free-flowing stories. But procedurals require adhering to a stricter structure, and this screenplay builds a contraption that is laughably flimsy. Its central mystery is as complicated as a case on the Hanna-Barbera cartoon "Scooby-Doo." As Davin roams shady areas of town showing the picture of the deceased, every single lead she follows gets her closer to the truth. Not once does she chase a red herring or find herself at a dead end. As we meet the potential suspects, it becomes very easy to figure out exactly who the culprit is.

Even worse, Davin is no Jessica Fletcher nor Hercule Poirot. She's a rather boring detective who makes stupid horror movie-style mistakes that should result in her horrific demise. Even after she's violently warned to let the story die, Davin sashays into dangerous areas practically announcing her defiance to the potential killers. Her desire to get the answers that will hopefully absolve her plays less like a quest for justice and more like the demands of privileged entitlement.

Speaking of privilege, *The Unknown Girl* is way too coy to deal with its tougher implications head-on. By making the unknown girl a young African immigrant, the Dardennes think they are providing commentary on the sad plight of folks who emigrate to Belgium and become trapped in the underbelly of society, but their exploration is cursory at best. There are questions of colonialism and racism that could be addressed and explored via Davin's relentless snooping. However, the victim is merely a pawn here; her identity is coldly used to let White society off the hook. This is made explicit in a late scene where the victim's sister gives a graceful speech to Davin, one that is rather offensive in its content simply because the movie hasn't earned it. The filmmakers appear to be turning a blind eye to their own privilege with this sequence, and it makes *The Unknown Girl* unredeemable. It's a surprising misstep in an otherwise commendable career.

Odie Henderson

CREDITS

Jenny Davin: Adele Haenel
Julien: Olivier Bonnaud
La pere de Bryan: Jeremie Renier
Bryan: Louka Minnella
La mere de Bryan: Christelle Cornil
Origin: United States
Language: French
Released: 2017
Production: Denis Freyd, Jean-Pierre Dardenne, Luc Dardenne; Archipel 35, BE TV, France 2 Cinema, Les Films du Fleuve, Radio Television Belge Francophone, Savage Film, VOO; released by Sundance Selects
Directed by: Jean-Pierre Dardenne; Luc Dardenne
Written by: Jean-Pierre Dardenne; Luc Dardenne
Cinematography by: Alain Marcoen
Sound: Benoit De Clerck
Editing: Marie-Helene Dozo
Costumes: Maira Ramedhan-Levi
Production Design: Igor Gabriel
MPAA rating: Unrated
Running time: 113 minutes

REVIEWS

Bradshaw, Peter. *The Guardian.* May 19, 2016.
Calhoun, Dave. *Time Out London.* May 20, 2016.
Camia, Giovanni Marchini. *The Film Stage.* May 18, 2016.
Chang, Justin. *Los Angeles Times.* September 14, 2017.
Cole, Jake. *Slant Magazine.* September 13, 2016.
Dowd, A.A. *The A.V. Club.* September 6, 2017.
Lodge, Guy. *Variety.* May 19, 2016.
Robey, Tim. *The Telegraph.* December 1, 2016.
Scott, A.O. *New York Times.* September 7, 2017.
Sobczynski, Peter. *RogerEbert.com.* September 8, 2017.

QUOTES

Julien: "When I saw that kid having his fit, shaking all over...I saw myself when my dad hit me. All I got from him was beatings. I wanted to be a doctor to treat him or to treat myself, I don't know. Or to be a better doctor than ours who thought I bruised myself playing."

TRIVIA

Actress Adèle Haenel has been a fan of Jean-Pierre Dardenne and Luc Dardenne for a long time, citing *La Promesse* (1996) and *The Son* (2002) as her favorite among their works.

V

VALERIAN AND THE CITY OF A THOUSAND PLANETS

A universe without boundaries needs heroes without limits.
—Movie tagline

Box Office: $41.2 Million

Valerian and the City of a Thousand Planets is based on a legendary French graphic novel that served as inspiration for many essential (and perhaps non-essential) sci-fi fantasy creations, including *Star Wars* (1977), *Conan the Barbarian* (1982), and *Independence Day* (1996). Originally titled *Valérian* (and later *Valérian: Spatio-Temporal Agent* and then *Valérian and Laureline*), the series was first published in 1967 and told the story of two government agents who are assigned to stop time travelers from altering the order of the universe. It also encompassed various socio-political elements within the framework of a sci-fi adventure. The series has since been translated into numerous languages, has volumes of books and is considered one of the most important works to help shape modern science fiction. The series seemed ripe for some form of adaptation to the screen, which did occur via an animated series called *Time Jam: Valerian & Laureline*, but until now, a big-screen adaptation had yet to be made.

Perhaps unsurprisingly, Luc Besson got the ball rolling on turning this literary landmark into a large-scale spectacle for the 21st century, particularly on the 20th Anniversary of one of his most celebrated films, the futuristic sci-fi comedy *The Fifth Element* (1997), which itself borrowed many visual ideas from *Valérian*. That film could have been an "extended universe" for this series. They both have colorful, expansive backdrops, wild-looking background characters and a similar sense of humor. Besson's earlier film feels like a salute to *Valérian*, which makes him seem like an ideal choice to write and direct the long-overdue movie version. But was there an audience for it? It seemed like Besson's passion project was a case of being too late, in terms of relevance. Like *John Carter* (2012) before it, there seemed to be little interest for a film version of a sci-fi source that was decades old, no matter how influential.

The movie starts out with great promise, starting in the 20th century as David Bowie's "Space Oddity" invites the viewer in and Besson covers centuries of progress involving earthlings meeting with various beings from other worlds. The story then settles on the 28th century after the over-sized Alpha space station has been jettisoned from the earth's orbit, free to roam other galaxies. One of these planets is Mül, a tropical paradise inhabited by slender alien-like creatures whose home is invaded by large crashing ships that penetrate their atmosphere and destroy their homeland. One of these beings is left behind and sends a cosmic message to Valerian (Dane DeHaan), a government agent whose partner Laureline (Cara Delevingne) also happens to be his on-again, off-again girlfriend whom he eventually wants to marry, so long as he can erase the dozens of women who already exist in his "playlist."

Back to the sci-fi portion. Valerian and Laureline get assigned by their Defense Minister (Herbie Hancock) to track down a converter that belongs to the federation. The item (no more than a little black box) was taken by a ruthless gangster named Igon Siruss (voiced by John Goodman). In order to retrieve it, they must infiltrate a virtual shopping mall that takes place in a vast desert called Big Market. They are joined by other gunmen and military personnel who also use virtual reality simulations to shoot at anything dangerous and to alert Valerian of anything coming his way. They are also aided by their ship, Alex (voiced by Chloe Hollings), who basically has every answer for every question and can track Valerian and Laureline's every move.

Once the item is retrieved, the story shifts to the Alfa Space Station, where there is a radioactive threat to the ship and only the converter can destroy it. Under the leadership of Commander Arun Filitt (Clive Owen) and General Okto-Bar (Sam Spruell), the space station, which is comprised of many different societies, factions, and races, faces certain demise unless Valerian and Laureline can help track and destroy the virus. But, of course, there are internal conflicts that exist between the two leaders, and Valerian and Laureline get separated after a lengthy chase sequence. They spend much of the second act trying to find each other while running into various oddball characters along the way, including Jolly the Pimp (Ethan Hawke) and his multi-layered performer, Bubble (Rihanna). There is also a trio of creatures that look like upright gargoyle platypuses that provide even more comic relief and help to the heroes.

As stated before, Besson has made a film that is as much of a nod to himself as it is the original source. Just as *The Fifth Element* packed the frame with an endless array of visual ideas, *Valerian and the City of a Thousand Planets* lives up to its name in terms of visual concepts on screen per minute. It often feels overstuffed much in the same way George Lucas got carried away with his hyperactive visual landscapes for the *Star Wars* prequels. It is, at times, wondrous (especially in 3-D) and overwhelming. The crazy, cartoonish supporting performances also do not help matters much for the audience already struggling to stay engaged in the storyline. Although Hawke looks like he is having a great time being able to run wild and chew some scenery, his performance (and others like it) still comes off uninspired and is followed by a re-hash of Besson's musical interlude in *The Fifth Element* (that of the opera singer) with Rihanna stopping the narrative to dance her way into the story.

There is also the matter of DeHaan and Delevingne, who are supposed to have witty banter as a couple in a would-be relationship. They both appear too young to be the leads in a film like this and their chemistry is non-existent. That becomes the biggest problem of them all with a film like this. A viewer can certainly be on board with much of the goofiness on display here (and there is certainly plenty of that to go around), but without credible or interesting leads to be a guide, the journey can only take the audience so far. Besson clearly has a love for the source and its ideas, but he never figured out a way to parlay that into something tangible and concrete. *The Fifth Element* worked largely because of the screen presence of Bruce Willis, Milla Jovovovich, and Gary Oldman. Like Lucas before him, Besson, twenty years later, seems to have forgotten about the importance of the human element of space fantasy.

Collin Souter

CREDITS

Major Valerian: Dane DeHaan
Sergeant Laureline: Cara Delevingne
Commander Arun Filitt: Clive Owen
Bubble: Rihanna
Jolly the Pimp: Ethan Hawke
Origin: United States
Language: English, French
Released: 2017
Production: Virginie Besson-Silla, Luc Besson; EuropaCorp S.A., Fundamental Films, Gulf Film L.L.C., River Road Entertainment; released by STX Entertainment
Directed by: Luc Besson
Written by: Luc Besson
Cinematography by: Thierry Arbogast
Music by: Alexandre Desplat
Sound: Guillaume Bouchateau
Editing: Julien Rey
Costumes: Olivier Beriot
Production Design: Hugues Tissandier
MPAA rating: PG-13
Running time: 137 minutes

REVIEWS

Braun, Liz. *Toronto Sun*. July 20, 2017.
Brody, Richard. *The New Yorker*. July 17, 2017.
Chang, Justin. *Los Angeles Times*. July 20, 2017.
Colburn, Randall. *Consequence of Sound*. July 20, 2017.
Ebiri, Bilge. *Village Voice*. July 11, 2017.
Jones, J.R. *Chicago Reader*. July 20, 2017.
Morgenstern, Joe. *Wall Street Journal*. July 20, 2017.
Sims, David. *The Atlantic*. July 20, 2017.
Sobczynski, Peter. *RogerEbert.com*. July 20, 2017.
Whitty, Stephen. *Newark Star Ledger*. July 10, 2017.

QUOTES

Commander Arun Filitt: "A soldier will always choose death over humiliation."

TRIVIA

There are 2,734 special effect shots in this film, compared to only 188 in director Luc Besson's earlier film, *The Fifth Element* (1997).

VICTORIA & ABDUL

History's most unlikely friendship.
—Movie tagline

Box Office: $22.2 Million

A wan, simplistic exercise in cultural exoticism, *Victoria & Abdul* tells the true story of the improbable real-life relationship between Britain's Queen Victoria and an Indian-Muslim servant assigned to help celebrate her Golden Jubilee in 1887. A film that fetishizes the blithe, blinkered selfishness of its subjects, and portrays as astounding revelations of awakening the smallest hints of any broader self-awareness, *Victoria & Abdul* checks many of the boxes of conventional awards-season drama. But it hammers an unconvincing frame of progressivism around royalist colonialism, and additionally asks so little of its viewers that the sum total of its induced reactions can be tidily captured in three categories: emotional indifference, narcoleptic acquiescence, or general irritation.

Making all of this more distressing is the fact that the movie is directed by Stephen Frears, an accomplished filmmaker capable of much more nuance and social critique than this work, adapted from Shrabani Basu's novel of the same name, has any interest in exploring. Following its early September premiere at the Venice Film Festival, *Victoria & Abdul* opened theatrically later in September, attempting to catch the early autumnal wave of art house patrons hungry for adult dramas. Its domestic haul totaled in the mid-teens of millions of dollars, part of a cumulative box office gross of under $50 million.

The film opens in 1887, during which two commoners, Abdul Karim (Ali Fazal) and Mohammed (Adeel Akhtar), are selected from British-ruled India to travel to England and bequeath a token gift upon Queen Victoria (Judi Dench) as part of the celebration for the 50-year anniversary of her monarchal reign. The Queen then strikes up an unlikely friendship with Abdul. She asks him to teach her Urdu, and eventually anoints him as her "munshi," a title which involves the responsibilities of a secretary but also includes religious and cultural counseling.

Naturally, there are plenty of stuffy, upper-crust, British society types who are shocked—simply shocked!—by this turn of events, and the Queen's increasing penchant for independent thinking. Notable among these stand Sir Henry Ponsonby (Tim Pigott-Smith), the Queen's private secretary, and Victoria's son Bertie, the Prince of Wales (Eddie Izzard), who stands to ascend to the throne upon her death. As the Queen learns about mangoes and genocide from Abdul, Bertie and others work to undermine the pair's trust and relationship, through increasingly aggressive and contentious means.

In a certain fashion, *Victoria & Abdul* actually tells the story of two likeminded people, despite their many surface differences. Queen Victoria, of course, leads a sheltered life which actively discourages intellectual curiosity or self-examination. Abdul, though, is, in a way, every bit as narrow-minded and inconsiderate of others. He embraces the golden touch and good graces of the Queen very easily, with no questioning or seemingly significant reflection. And while Mohammed suffers, forced to remain in the country despite falling ill, as Abdul ascends, Frears' film never forces Abdul to consider Mohammed's point-of-view. Instead he only cheerfully scolds Mohammed that he is not recognizing the opportunity and privilege of their servitude.

The movie, however, is neither complex enough to recognize this odd parallel, nor smart enough to acknowledge and examine it. Screenwriter Lee Hall does not offer up a compelling reason, beyond a vague personal affinity and the fact that Abdul "is tall," for why the Queen suddenly decides to pull her head out of the sand, so to speak.

There is some early tonal gear-grinding, as the movie tries to strike a balance between character comedy and the type of speechifying fan-service that art house patrons of a "Dame Judi Dench film" would probably expect. (Talk of the Queen's bowel movements pops up a couple times.) Still, if there is a silver lining to this movie, it is that it once it surmounts these rough patches it at least allows the Queen, and the film itself, to have a sense of humor, which differentiates it a bit.

Dench is Dench, which is to say that she delivers an engaging and predictably nuanced turn, full of smart, humanizing choices. Though nominally billed in some arenas as a quasi-sequel to John Madden's *Mrs. Brown* (1997), which also starred Dench in the same matriarchal role, *Victoria & Abdul* in truth bears no substantive connective tissue to that movie. It takes place four years after the events from the end of that film, and if Dench probably made some actorly connections in terms of her performance, the movie in a macro sense fails, to its detriment, to really connect the Queen's relationship with Abdul to that of her friendship with Scottish servant John Brown—another relationship which was looked at askance by the Queen's family and advisors, eager to maintain the finely groomed nature of their own avenues of power-by-proxy.

The handsome Fazal, meanwhile, gives the type of pleasantly empty performance that unfortunately seems calculated to curry favor with older viewers who might be inclined to view the film as a genteel curio. With an idiot-grin personality and overly conciliatory tone, this Abdul rings less true as a sincere, multi-dimensional characterization than as merely a vessel for the type of polite, overly accommodating foreigner that Western viewers stereotypically wish to see.

Overall, *Victoria & Abdul* is the type of liberal, feel-good movie which posits that cross-cultural understanding is born of a single, golden-bullet encounter with someone "different," with no greater examination of conscience or potential complicity on the part of the member of a dominant and possibly oppressive culture. The real-life story of this unusual bond between a queen and a commoner from another country is doubtlessly an interesting one. Frears' film, however, presents a boring, unilluminating, and phony portrait of it.

Brent Simon

CREDITS

Queen Victoria: Dame Judi Dench
Abdul Karim: Ali Fazal
Sir Henry Ponsonby: Tim Pigott-Smith
Bertie, Prince of Wales: Eddie Izzard
Mohammed: Adeel Akhtar
Origin: United States
Language: English, Urdu, Hindi
Released: 2017
Production: Tim Bevan, Eric Fellner, Beeban Kidron, Tracey Seaward; BBC Films, Cross Street Films, Perfect World Pictures, Working Title Films Ltd.; released by Focus Features L.L.C.
Directed by: Stephen Frears
Written by: Lee Hall
Cinematography by: Danny Cohen
Music by: Thomas Newman
Sound: Becki Ponting
Music Supervisor: Karen Elliott
Editing: Melanie Oliver
Art Direction: Sarah Finlay; Adam Squires
Costumes: Consolata Boyle
Production Design: Alan MacDonald
MPAA rating: PG-13
Running time: 111 minutes

REVIEWS

Chang, Justin. *Los Angeles Times.* September 21, 2017.
Croll, Ben. *IndieWire.* September 5, 2017.
Duralde, Alonso. *TheWrap.* September 3, 2017.
Fujishima, Kenji. *Slant Magazine.* September 17, 2017.
Gleiberman, Owen. *Variety.* September 3, 2017.
Kenny, Glenn. *New York Times.* September 21, 2017.
Perez, Rodrigo. *The Playlist.* September 3, 2017.
Romney, Jonathan. *Screen International.* September 3, 2017.
Rooney, David. *Hollywood Reporter.* September 3, 2017.
Taylor, Ella. *NPR.* September 21, 2017.

TRIVIA

When filming began in September 2016, actress Judi Dench was one month older than the age that Queen Victoria was when she died.

AWARDS

Nominations:

Oscars 2017: Costume Des., Makeup
British Acad. 2017: Makeup
Golden Globes 2018: Actress--Mus./Comedy (Dench)
Screen Actors Guild 2017: Actress (Dench)

W

WAKEFIELD

What would your life be like without you?
—Movie tagline

Box Office: $262,599

It would be interesting to make every single person going through a mid-life crisis watch the film *Wakefield* if only to follow them for some months afterward. Seeing what people do after they get a glimpse of themselves in the movies is often a keen reminder of just how powerful a medium motion pictures can be. *Wakefield* plays like a perverse inversion of *It's a Wonderful Life* (1946), where George Bailey really does abandon his life and family, but, despite learning some valuable lessons, may not actually be a better person for it. Audiences are likely to be if they consider what they just watched.

In a film told almost entirely from his point of view, Howard Wakefield (Bryan Cranston) is a successful but unhappy man. His marriage is lifeless, except for the resentment caused by years of flirting he and wife Diana (Jennifer Garner) have used to try and maintain some semblance of a spark. When Howard gets back home late one night, he sees a raccoon and chases it into the garage attic. Suddenly, he realizes he has the perfect vantage point to watch his family eating dinner. But his enjoyment at his wife's annoyance stops when she throws his dinner in the trash. Deciding to wait for her to cool down, he falls asleep. He wakes up sure that his wife will never believe where he spent the night but while he waits for her to leave for work she tearfully calls the police to report him missing. However, his sympathy evaporates when his obnoxious mother-in-law Babs (Beverly D'Angelo) shows up to accuse him of having run off. When Diana does leave for work, he asks himself if she might be relieved at his disappearance, and, taking some food from the pantry, goes back to the garage.

His resentfulness not only allows Howard the ability to enjoy abandoning his responsibilities and watch his wife struggle to do the chores that were once his, but to fantasize about people blaming Diana for his disappearance. He spends his days spying on his family and friends, and grows to love his new lifestyle, abandoning his law practice and even the thought of spending the money he has in his wallet. Soon, he takes to foraging in the trash for food and secretly using a backyard shower that had been installed by his neighbor. Months go by, and his long hair and beard provide an effective enough disguise for Howard to pass unnoticed in town. His growing isolation gets him thinking about how he met his wife, stealing her away from a colleague (Jason O'Mara) through lies and manipulation. Wondering if he ever loved her at all, he also realizes how impossible it is for her to move on to another man under the present circumstances.

Cranston shines in the title role and is matched beautifully by Garner, although she is largely unheard for most of the film, merely seen through the eyes of her errant husband. The film can be forgiven for forcing the audience to adopt his self-absorbed point of view. Cranston goes straight for this role. Howard Wakefield is a heartbreaking character, a man with no sense left of what relationships are about and what it takes him to relearn that is daunting.

The film is an adaptation of a short story by E.L. Doctorow, which is, in turn, very loosely-based on a story of the same name by Nathaniel Hawthorne.

Director/writer Robin Swicord makes the wise choice to utilize flashbacks and voiceover to maintain the intimate point of view of her source material. The entire film hinges on whether Wakefield can take the audience on his journey and Swicord allows that to happen by taking a largely unsympathetic character and showcasing him through moments of humor, heartbreak and, ultimately, bravery. Of course, the film does leave ample room for another interpretation of Wakefield's actions. The ambiguity is palpable. Whether individual viewers feel Howard deserves one fate or the other may well change upon repeat viewings. Some may not feel he even deserves to have his story told. But Wakefield, both the film and the character, haunts, exposing the follies that only become apparent to men upon middle age and asking if hope for redemption is folly as well.

Dave Canfield

CREDITS

Howard Wakefield: Bryan Cranston
Diana Wakefield: Jennifer Garner
Babs: Beverly D'Angelo
Ben Jacobs: Ian Anthony Dale
Dirk Morrison: Jason O'Mara
Origin: United States
Language: English
Released: 2017
Production: Bonnie Curtis, Wendy Federman, Julie Lynn, Carl Moellenberg; Mockingbird Pictures; released by IFC Films
Directed by: Robin Swicord
Written by: Robin Swicord
Cinematography by: Andrei Bowden Schwartz
Music by: Aaron Zigman
Sound: Zach Seivers
Editing: Matt Maddox
Costumes: Kim H. Ngo
Production Design: Jeannine Oppewall
MPAA rating: R
Running time: 106 minutes

REVIEWS

Abele, Robert. *Los Angeles Times.* May 25, 2017.
Arriaga, Indra. *Anchorage Press.* July 14, 2017.
Debruge, Peter. *Variety.* September 6, 2016.
Jorgenson, Todd. *Cinemalogue.com.* May 26, 2017.
Nusair, David. *Reel Film Reviews.* September 17, 2016.
Scott, A.O. *New York Times.* May 17, 2017.
Scotti, Ariel. *New York Daily News.* May 18, 2017.
Sims, David. *The Atlantic.* June9, 2017.
Taylor, Ella. *NPR.* May 18, 2017.
Wilson, Calvin. *St. Louis Dispatch.* June 1, 2017.

QUOTES

Howard Wakefield: "People will say that I left my wife and I suppose, as a factual matter, I did, but where was the intentionality? I had no thought of deserting her."

TRIVIA

Was filmed in twenty days.

WALKING OUT

Survival runs in their blood.
—Movie tagline

Box Office: $101,947

Directors, and brothers, Alex and Andrew J. Smith deliver a very old-fashioned and effective survival drama in *Walking Out,* which premiered in Dramatic Competition at the Sundance Film Festival but did not make much of an impact when it was released theatrically. Time will likely catch up with this solid flick, the kind of movie that could play on cable regularly and garner a decent audience every time. What often happens to films like this is that modern audiences are looking for hooks or high concepts and a "boy and his father survive the woods" is not clever enough for the Twitter era. It's too bad because the leading men of this low-budget film bring their all to it, and the directors mostly know what to do with them.

Those two men are Matt Bomer (*Magic Mike* [2012]) and Josh Wiggins (*Hellion* [2014]), who play father and son Cal and David, respectively. David has not seen much of his father, spending most of his time living with his mother in Texas. Once a year, he goes to visit dear old dad in the middle of nowhere in Montana. The Smith brothers wisely do not waste too much time on set-up. Viewers do not need to know much more than the basics about Cal and David—they are not estranged but not close either; David is less of an outdoorsman than his dad. Like most 14-year-old boys, David kind of wants to just hang out in the cabin and play video games but Cal is more adventurous. He has been tracking a moose through the land nearby and he's going to make the majestic animal David's first kill on a snowy hunting trip.

Walking Out takes its time, for lack of a better phrase, "walking in." The Smith brothers clearly love the Big Sky Country landscape on which they are shooting, and allow the dynamic between Cal and David to develop organically. Cal is obviously attempting to impart some lessons, not only about hunting but life, to his son, trying to use every moment of this annual visit to its maximum, but Bomer and the Smiths are careful to keep the character from becoming an alpha male caricature.

When they find the aforementioned moose, everything goes wrong. It turns out that the animal has already been shot and abandoned by another hunter. And then they spot a dead bear cub, meaning that a mama bear is probably nearby. After a series of bad choices, Cal and David are both wounded. In fact, dad is so injured he can't really walk, and David will have to essentially carry him to safety.

From here, *Walking Out* becomes a survival two-hander. Lily Gladstone and Bill Pullman appear in cameos, the latter in flashback as Cal's father, but it is really a two-actor piece, and Bomer and Wiggins accept the acting weight of that structure. The scenery, shot by Todd McMullen, is gorgeous, but this film falls apart if either Wiggins or Bomer are unbelievable or exaggerated. They allow the moment to stay realistic and emotionally resonant. In fact, the film only falters when it leaves the pair for a series of flashbacks about another hunting trip from Cal's childhood, the one in which he killed his first moose. These scenes, which were not a part of the short story by David Quammen on which the film is based, feel pushed into the narrative, designed to make a short film into a feature, and they also serve the negative purpose of breaking the tension of Cal and David's predicament. It's the major decision that relays that the Smith brothers may have been concerned that their leading men couldn't carry the weight of the story. (Minor ones include an over-use of score and a bit of woodsman philosophy from Cal that doesn't sound quite genuine.)

Much like the nightmarish predicament at its center, *Walking Out* works best when it stays focused, and, as often as it threatens to succumb to its negative qualities, it never does. As the film builds to its obviously-inspirational ending, it achieves surprising emotional power, mostly through its performances. It's a cheesy thing to say about a movie, but they really don't make flicks like *Walking Out* that often anymore. (Even a survival horror drama like *The Revenant* (2015) relied on camera tricks like single-shots and the notorious stories about its shooting conditions.) *Walking Out* is a simple, well-told story. In an era of extreme marketing and twist endings and easter eggs, it's nice to be able to say that about a 2017 movie, and it's one of the reasons this movie feels likely to eventually find an audience. It just may take a bit longer of a cinematic walk to get to it.

Brian Tallerico

CREDITS

Cal: Matt Bomer
David: Josh Wiggins
Clyde: Bill Pullman
Young Cal: Alex Neustaedter
Lila: Lily Gladstone
Origin: United States
Language: English
Released: 2017
Production: Brunson Green, Laura Ivey; Harbinger Pictures; released by IFC Films
Directed by: Alex Smith; Andrew J. Smith
Written by: Alex Smith; Andrew J. Smith
Cinematography by: Todd McMullen
Music by: Ernst Reijseger
Sound: Zach Seivers
Editing: Michael Taylor
Art Direction: Chad Branham
Costumes: Nicola Dunn
Production Design: David Storm
MPAA rating: PG-13
Running time: 95 minutes

REVIEWS

Barker, Andrew. *Variety.* September 7, 2017.
Chang, Justin. *Los Angeles Times.* October 12, 2017.
DeFore, John. *Hollywood Reporter.* September 7, 2017.
Ebiri, Bilge. *Village Voice.* October 5, 2017.
Ehrlich, David. *IndieWire.* October 9, 2017.
Fear, David. *Rolling Stone.* October 7, 2017.
Jaworowski, Ken. *New York Times.* October 5, 2017.
Puig, Claudia. *TheWrap.* September 7, 2017.
Rothkopf, Joshua. *Time Out.* September 7, 2017.
Seitz, Matt Zoller. *RogerEbert.com.* October 6, 2017.

TRIVIA

According to the film's directors, actor Christian Bale was almost cast in the role of Cal but Bale ultimately decided against playing the part because he didn't want to spend time away from his family in a remote location so soon after the birth of his second child.

THE WALL

This isn't war. It's a game.
—Movie tagline

Box Office: $1.8 Million

The Iraq War has proven colossally difficult as a subject for film drama. There seems to be no way to completely remove American troops from the region a decade and a half after the first retaliatory strikes following 9/11. It wasn't fought for the reasons stated by the President of the United States and, unlike Vietnam, the real reasons came out in the middle of the fighting but that has not stopped or even stymied the conflict. Making three-act movies out of a war ostensibly fought over the greatest terror attack ever inflicted on the United States but really fought over corporate interests is not an enviable task. Where does one start and end when the story still seems to be unfolding? Veteran action director Doug Liman and screenwriter Dwain Worrell, however, have found a way to make something like sense of the utter senselessness of the setting and what it has come to represent in the American media. *The Wall* is a no-frills exercise in tension and confusion, like a one-act play or a low budget 1950s B-western, and in narrowing its focus to three guys alone in a desert, actually finds a proper mode of expression for this muddled conflict.

U.S. Army Staff Sergeant Shane Matthews (John Cena) and Sergeant Allen Isaac (Aaron Taylor-Johnson) have been looking at the corpses of a few American engineers at a construction site for hours. Matthews is tired of staring at the sight with the scope of his rifle. So, with Isaac, his spotter, watching his back, he descends from their vantage point on a hill to get a closer look. About a minute and a half into his reconnaissance, someone opens fire on the pair, hitting Matthews in the back and Isaac in the knee. Isaac's radio is damaged and he can only crawl to the relative safety of a makeshift wall. Isaac does not know how long Matthews has left before he succumbs to blood loss. When Matthews stops responding entirely, Isaac does not know if his sergeant is dead, playing possum, or merely unconscious. He gets on his radio and starts describing the situation to the first American voice (Laith Nakli) he hears. As he explains things the responses get increasingly fishy, less like something his superiors would tell him, and more like the words of someone who learned about the army from watching war movies. Isaac wises up and realizes that the voice on his radio belongs to the Iraqi sniper who's got him and Matthews pinned down a few hundred yards away.

Isaac does his best to keep the man talking to buy himself some time while he can think of a solution, but trapped behind the last piece of a bombed schoolhouse with nothing but his wits (what little he has), he is not swimming in options. The man on the other line has a lot of philosophical questions for Isaac, one of a thousand faceless white liberators littering the country he once knew. Isaac does not really understand the point of the interrogation and relies mostly on taunts, racism, and evasiveness to keep the sniper on the line while he tries to radio for back-up. He's fundamentally ill-equipped to do battle with the unseen enemy with whom he's now locked in a life-or-death struggle, his smarter commanding officers out of reach. The war has boiled down to two men with guns who cannot see or understand each other.

Liman pares back his muscular action filmmaking chops considerably to make this film. Compared to larger projects like the mammoth sci-fi war movie *Edge of Tomorrow* (2014) and the drug running picaresque *American Made* (2017), both starring Tom Cruise. *The Wall* is spare and almost micro-budgeted by comparison. Its biggest effect, a helicopter crash, is shown in pieces, in keeping with the small scale of the project. *The Wall*, like Liman's *Fair Game* (2010) about the Valerie Plame scandal, is about not knowing the perimeters of a war and not knowing your enemies. Isaac does not know what he's doing in Iraq and cannot explain himself in anything other than platitudes. Matthews, who, it's implied, could have handled himself in such a crisis, probably could have come up with the answers that the Iraqi sniper asks him and maybe even turned the situation around, but Liman wants us to see what happens when the least qualified and most aimless among us are forced to take responsibility for a nation. It was after all, the least qualified who started the conflict. Liman wants us to imagine what it would be like if George W. Bush was pinned down behind a bombed out schoolhouse, forced to explain his war to the person whose neighbors and children had been blown out of their homes. Isaac has the fervor of the true believer but absolutely no ideological intelligence.

Casting Cena and Taylor-Johnson was a master stroke. Cena's natural charisma and wrestler's physique make him seem like the perfect candidate to lead soldiers into battle. Losing his presence, turning him into one more piece of battlefield shrapnel, unseats the audience's expectation of a traditional narrative. Taylor-Johnson, an English actor affecting a pathetic-sounding southern accent, is miniature compared to Cena, and in every way represents a sort of last resort. He should not be in charge, hence his position as a spotter. Pitting him against the voice of a deadly, unseen force is not only a handy metaphor for the Iraq War but also a way to turn this war film into a kind of western without horses. The unforgiving desert landscape, the windswept outpost, the black hat deadshot just out of sight. Liman has gone back into the most poetically masculine genre for his grammar, and finds that it's no help for the modern cowboys in the Iraqi desert. The cavalry cannot ride to their rescue anymore, and even if they do, when and where does it all end? *The Wall* understands that war is an existential trap, a snake eating its own tale, and its perfectly distressing third act twist hits the reset button in the most distressing way possible.

Scout Tafoya

CREDITS

Isaac: Aaron Taylor-Johnson
Matthews: John Cena
Juba: Laith Nakli
Origin: United States
Language: English
Released: 2017
Production: David Bartis; Big Indie Pictures, Picrow; released by Amazon Studios
Directed by: Doug Liman
Written by: Dwain Worrell
Cinematography by: Roman Vasyanov
Sound: Mariusz Glabinski
Editing: Julia Bloch
Art Direction: Cassidy Shipley
Costumes: Cindy Evans
Production Design: Jeff Mann
MPAA rating: R
Running time: 90 minutes

REVIEWS

Ashton, Will. *The Playlist.* May 18, 2017.
Catsoulis, Jeannette. *New York Times.* May 11, 2017.
Debruge, Peter *Variety* April 28, 2017.
Dowd, A.A. *The A.V. Club.* May 15, 2017.
Phillips, Michael. *Chicago Tribune.* May 11, 2017.
Robey, Tim. *The Telegraph.* August 3, 2017.
Smith, Anna. *Time Out London.* July 25, 2017.
Russo, Tom. *Boston Globe.* May 10, 2017.
Turan, Kenneth. *Los Angeles Times.* May 11, 2017.
Worthington, Clint. *Consequence of Sound.* May 10, 2017.

QUOTES

Juba: "You Americans. You think you know it all. You think it's simple. That I am your enemy. But we are not so different, you and I."

TRIVIA

Former US Ranger Sniper and author of *The Reaper*, Nicholas Irving, was a technical advisor for the film.

WAR FOR THE PLANET OF THE APES

For freedom. For family. For the planet.
—Movie tagline

Box Office: $146.9 Million

Like it or not, the cinematic landscape, at least in terms of "blockbuster" movies, is heavily dominated by franchises. From the never-ending cycle of Marvel and DC Comics related properties to somewhat smaller yet equally as ubiquitous franchises like *The Fast and Furious* (2001-?) or the *Resident Evil* (2002-17) series, corporate media makers are all about movies with legs that can run to the bank for as many years as possible. Of course, mileage varies on each franchise in terms of quality but corporations are sticking to basic math when it comes to franchise films. This formula basically equates to: "If audiences turned out in droves for 'Part One,' they'll likely turn out in the same groupings for 'Part Two,' 'Three,'" and onward until the well goes dry. Yet as bloated summer blockbusters continue to hog screens around the world, the latest *Planet of the Apes* films (*Rise of the Planet of the Apes* [2011], *Dawn of the Planet of the Apes* [2014], and *War for the Planet of the Apes* [2017]) have steadily and somewhat quietly marched along to not only create incredibly entertaining, high quality films but also do very well at the box office. And, truth be told, this franchise is one tough sell. The fact that the films are very good let alone continually getting better is a cinematic miracle in and of itself.

The original *Planet of the Apes* franchise started in 1968 and pulled in audiences with its over-the-top performances and twist ending. The film spawned four sequels as well as two television shows (one live action, one animated) all to varying degrees of quality and success. The films then moved into cult status before Tim Burton's ill-fated attempt to bring the franchise back to pop culture consciousness with a *Planet of the Apes* (2001) reboot that was, frankly, ridiculous. Which really gets to the point. The *Planet of the Apes* are about Earth being overrun by intelligent, talking apes and as a result, humans are the subservient species. The original films were rather silly, kitschy, and somewhat tongue-in-cheek yet also provided sly social commentary, therefore adding some allegorical vitamins and minerals to what was otherwise cinematic junk food. When Burton tried to swim in these waters, millennial audiences just thought the movie was dumb—for good reason.

Thus, when it was more recently announced that the *Planet of the Apes* films were going to make another run at the box office, an audible sigh of indifference eased from the mouths of cinephiles. Yet as trailers began to impress and word that Andy Serkis, he himself a modern cinematic miracle (his performance as "Gollum" in the *Lord of the Rings* [2001-2003] trilogy has set the bar for motion-capture out of reach for all), was putting forth a near Oscar© worthy performance as lead ape "Caesar," attention and buzz became positive. Sure enough *Rise of the Planet of the Apes* delivered a modern cinematic rarity: an origin story that was not only compelling and unique but also opened the door for more anxiously awaited, skillfully crafted and ultimately greater films to follow though.

Rise of the Planet of the Apes detailed how Earth would eventually become a planet of apes and introduced audiences to Caesar—monkey patient zero for an illness that would soon wipe out most of the human species and give higher intelligence to apes. That illness is termed the "simian flu" and is inadvertently launched by humans who are, once again, messing with Mother Nature with disastrous results. For reasons unclear, yet ultimately for the best, Matt Reeves took over the subsequent two follow-up features, starting with the fantastic *Dawn of the Planet of the Apes* in which the dawning of an Earth (or at least, America as it's never made clear how far-reaching the simian flu has spread) in which talking apes are being fought back against by terrified humans. This is really where the films take on an intriguing allegory to war, racism, and privilege as the apes aren't really doing anything "wrong" but humans are scared and react, as humans typically do, towards things they do not understand, with harsh violence. Caesar becomes not only the leader of his simian brethren but also a cinematic hero for the ages.

When one attempts to explain just what a brilliant and nuanced character Caesar is and how emotionally gripping Serkis' performance is throughout these films, it sounds a little silly. It is a motion-captured, talking ape, who not only understands sign language and varied grunts from apes across a spectrum of intelligence, he also has amazing leadership skills and unparalleled empathy. On top of these character traits, he also exudes personal and existential conflict in nearly every scene. Caesar is an ape torn between trying to do right by his fellow apes and let them live a life of peace, but also not backing down when being unfairly bullied by humans. It simply cannot be understated how incredible Serkis' performance is in this role throughout the films. All of the inner torment of Caesar and outer conflict between ape and man comes to a head in *Dawn of the Planet of the Apes* and through some Machiavelli-by-way-of-the-Bible twists and turns, the stage is set for *War for the Planet of the Apes*.

As the film opens, a society of apes is trying to live in peace, yet they are constantly under attack from heavily-armed, militaristic humans. Once again, Caesar is the benevolent-yet-tormented and put-upon leader striving to create peace in a world becoming increasingly more scared and less peaceful. Caesar's hand is forced and as the title indicates, it's an all-out *War for the Planet of the Apes* in which common sense, fairness, and decency is thrown away for a last-ditch power grab by the humans led by maniacal Colonel McCullough (Woody Harrelson), who, through ghastly reasons soon revealed, has a personal vendetta against this new planet of the apes. Funnily enough, Harrelson's McCullough is really the only recognizable actor in the film and the movie stumbles a bit when he shows up. The film also manages to wedge in some much-needed comic relief via new cast addition "Bad Ape," a well-spoken if a bit daft monkey played by Steve Zahn.

While Serkis' performances throughout the films are indeed the backbone of the series, it's the deft nuances and deep screenwriting via Mark Bomback and Reeves himself that makes *War for the Planet of the Apes* such a winner. While Caesar had Christ-like tendencies in *Dawn of the Planet of the Apes*, he fully embodies the Christian leader here as humans beat him down in front of his followers in an attempt to usurp power and make the apes question his leadership ability and goals. They beat on Caesar, embarrass him, and hurt him deeply before stringing him up in an image meant to recall the Crucifixion, his crown of thorns a bucket of cold water in freezing, snowy weather. Forever conflicted, Serkis' Caesar tries time and again to take the high road only to be dragged down to the low one by those he trusts or, worse, has given a second chance. But, through it all, Caesar inspires his fellow apes to lay down their lives for him or, better, the movement.

Although they may lose battles, audiences know who's going to eventually win the war based on the title of the franchise. The fact one finds him- or herself rooting for the apes speaks volumes to the excellent writing and performances in these films as well. Yet for as strong as these parts of the films are (and indeed, they are strong) it's the impeccable world creating, scene-setting and direction by Matt Reeves that makes *Dawn of the Planet of the Apes* and *War for the Planet of the Apes* such strong films. They succeed on their own, and are setting a new standard when compared to other Young Adult franchises, animated follow-ups and ubiquitous superhero films that often feel churned out by a factory rather than human beings.

Don R. Lewis

CREDITS

Caesar: Andy Serkis
The Colonel: Woody Harrelson
Bad Ape: Steve Zahn
Maurice: Karin Konoval
Nova: Amiah Miller
Origin: United States
Language: English, Sign languages
Released: 2017
Production: Peter Chernin, Dylan Clark, Rick Jaffa, Amanda Silver; Chernin Entertainment; released by Twentieth Century Fox Film Corp.

Directed by: Matt Reeves
Written by: Matt Reeves; Mark Bomback
Cinematography by: Michael Seresin
Music by: Michael Giacchino
Sound: Will Files
Editing: William Hoy; Stan Salfas
Art Direction: Maya Shimoguchi
Costumes: Melissa Bruning
Production Design: James Chinlund
MPAA rating: PG-13
Running time: 140 minutes

REVIEWS

Chang, Justin. *Los Angeles Times*. July 12, 2017.
DeBruge, Peter. *Variety*. June 26, 2017.
Ebiri, Bilge. *Village Voice*. June 26, 2017.
Halligan, Fionnuala. *Screen International*. June 26, 2017.
Maytum, Matt. *Total Film*. June 26, 2017.
Moore, Roger. *Movie Nation*. July 3, 2017.
Savlov, Marc. *Austin Chronicle*. July 12, 2017.
Scott. A.O. *New York Times*. July 12, 2017.
Wilkinson, Alissa. *Vox*. July 13, 2017.
Zacharek, Stephanie. *Time*. June 29, 2017.

QUOTES

Caesar: "I did not start this war. I offered you peace. I showed you mercy. But now you're here. To finish us off...for good."

TRIVIA

The Overlook Hotel from *The Shining* (1980) makes an appearance in this film.

AWARDS

Nominations:

Oscars 2017: Visual FX
British Acad. 2017: Visual FX

THE WEDDING PLAN

(Laavor et hakir)

All she needs is a little faith.
—Movie tagline

Box Office: $1.4 Million

The remarkable Israeli film *Fill the Void* (2012) established the young American-born Israeli director Rama Burshtein as a truly exciting and distinctive voice in international cinema. In pondering the moral and personal ramifications of a young Orthodox Israeli woman of whether to marry her brother-in-law after her sister's tragic death, the director revealed a ferociously intelligent visual talent.

In her first feature Burshtein developed a layered and expressive visual design that dovetailed beautifully with her themes of restriction, anguish, and social exclusion. The visual rhyming—cloistered, restrictive, and intense—also sharpened the psychological and social undertow. Style and meaning fused naturally, and the director also showed a superb facility with actors.

The director's new film, *The Wedding Plan*, works in a much different register visually, though the themes and ideas correspond closely. The original English-language title, *Through the Wall*, makes the connection between the two films explicit. The tone and style of the new film are different. The rhythms are faster and colored by a more defiant and self-expressive edge. The colors are brighter and more buoyant. The new work is very much of a piece, drawing on the same intelligence and animated by the same driving social critique and cultural pessimism.

On the surface, the follow-up shows a lighter, more felicitous touch suggestive of a screwball-inflected farce framed by an Orthodox Israeli context. The story of another devout young woman who defiantly orchestrates a novel solution to being left alone, Burshtein has shrewdly, audaciously opened the material up in making it more accessible. She is concerned with very serious ideas—sacrifice, belonging, conviction—but her touch is subtle, even glancing. Without sacrificing or compromising the darker edges, she meticulously weaves them into the wider narrative.

It says something about her intuitive talents that she accomplishes this without being didactic or mannered. Just the opposite, Burshtein reveals an explosive and keen sense of humor. "Stop lying," a fortune, or truth, teller named Hulda (Odelia Moreh-Matalon), commands Michal (Noa Koler), a headstrong young woman who has come seeking her counsel. A 32-year-old independent Hasidic Jew, Michal has negotiated the maze entwining the intricate social and cultural Orthodox courting rituals for more than eleven years with no success in finding a suitable companion.

"I'm exhausted," she says. In this fantastic opening scene, the women size each other up through an elaborate food ritual, as the older woman carves out the "evil eye," of the fish with a scalpel and dispenses her own particular brand of wisdom. Hulda tells Michal her dreams of being loved and giving love are possible only if she is serious about her intentions. The woman's son, Shimi (Amos Tamam), even operates a wedding hall in Jerusalem. She can get her a discount.

Like the central character of *Fill the Void*, Michal is

trapped between the warring conflicts of tradition and modernity. She is a bit of a dreamer though also assertive and deeply proud. Her professional choices show off her independent streak. She works as the mobile operator of a petting zoo and performs at children's parties, making her effectively an actor. Her professional role also attests to her more uninhibited nature of someone not afraid to upend the social mores of a deeply conservative culture. Already a convert to the Orthodox sect, Michal is looked upon suspiciously. She remains enough of a true believer in the possibility of faith-based love.

A flash-forward of indeterminate length appears to vindicate Hulda's observation as Michal is shown going through the final preparations of her forthcoming wedding at a rehearsal space with her fiancé Gidi (Erez Drigues). She is elated though he appears strangely sullen, cold, and withdrawn. Prodded by her, Gidi delivers an exceptionally harsh put down and admits he does not love her. She remains implacable in the face of her social humiliation. She ends her engagement though steadfastly insists a wedding shall proceed, on the eighth day of Hanukkah, less than a month off. God, Michal declares, shall provide her with a husband for the occasion.

In *The Wedding Plan*, Burshtein deftly navigates between tragedy and farce. If the director orchestrates the disparate pieces, the intensely appealing and vibrant Koler holds them together and makes the parts really sing. This is her first significant lead role, and she is extraordinary. She inhabits the part with a steady conviction that remains unperturbed and remarkably unpredictable. Filled with a toughness and courage, she never wholly submits to panic or desperation. Michal even accepts the cruel absurdity of the situation, enduring a succession of wrong men, a pious man who refuses to look at her, and a deaf mute whose sign interpreter accompanies the couple to the restaurant.

That is not to say Michal is without doubt or not vulnerable to moments of intense worry. Her private doubts are manifested at her public wailing during a religious pilgrimage to the Ukraine. Her emotional plea for a sign from God materializes in the form of Yoss (Oz Zehavi), an impossibly great looking and charismatic pop singer. Their encounter is one of the strongest scenes in the film, a rush of emotions and feelings, at once sly and oblique, direct, and impassioned. The director and the actors are their best here, the language evasive and indirect, the feelings raw and vital.

The balance of the film plays out against this emotional backdrop, of longing and passion, independence and desire, thrust against the deeper imperatives of emotional suitability, commitment, and faith. The movie's against the clock countdown structure, as the wedding date gets nearer, only ups the ante. As the various men circle and float around her, Michal remains firmly committed to her ideas and beliefs. Her intransigence only makes her more desirable. As one of the men pivoting around her remarks, she is maddening but impossible to not think about.

The weaknesses are minor. *The Wedding Plan* lacks some of the concentration and tightness of *Fill the Void.* Some of the secondary characters, like Michal's mother or her sister, who is having her own relationship difficulties, are less successfully shaped into the wider story. The movie is almost too circumspect. The one significant issue never really addressed by the film is sex, suggesting that subject remains too taboo or untouchable to formally address in the ultra-Orthodox culture.

The closing parts are absolutely nerve shredding, at once giddy and exciting though also streaked in grief and possessed of a palpable uncertainty. By the end, the emotional plausibility is wholly irrelevant. After her breathtaking debut, Rama Burshtein works in a more open and recognizable style that still manages to shatter convention or expectation. Ultimately, *The Wedding Plan* is a jolt to the system, a comedy of religious and social mores that cuts deep and very hard.

Patrick Z. McGavin

CREDITS

Michal: Noa Koler
Shimi: Amos Tamam
Yos, rock star: Oz Zehavi
Sosh, Michal's mother: Irit Sheleg
Feggie: Ronny Merhavi
Origin: United States
Language: Hebrew
Released: 2017
Production: Assaf Amir; Norma Productions; released by Roadside Attractions
Directed by: Rama Burshtein
Written by: Rama Burshtein
Cinematography by: Amit Yasur
Music by: Roy Edri
Editing: Yael Hersonski
Art Direction: Uri Aminov
Costumes: Hava Levi Rozelsky
MPAA rating: PG
Running time: 110 minutes

REVIEWS

Baumgarten, Marjorie. *Austin Chronicle.* May 31, 2017.
Donadoni, Serena. *Village Voice.* May 11, 2017.

Dowd, A.A. *The A.V. Club.* May 10, 2017.
Goldstein, Gary. *Los Angeles Times.* May 18, 2017.
Johnson, G. Allen. *San Francisco Chronicle.* May 17, 2017.
Jenkins, Mark. *Washington Post.* May 25, 2017.
Kenigsberg, Ben. *New York Times.* May 11, 2017.
Keough, Peter. *New York Times.* August 17, 2017.
Morgenstern, Joe. *Wall Street Journal.*. May 11, 2017.
Rainer, Peter. *Christian Science Monitor.* May 12, 2017.
Tyrkus, Mike. *CinemaNerdz.com.* May 26, 2017.

TRIVIA

Actors Noa Koler and Amos Tamam played ex-spouses in the beloved Israeli TV show *Srugim.*

WHOSE STREETS?

Box Office: $182,799

One setback to the expansive accessibility of social media is the lack of a united voice. Timelines are unofficially created by witnesses to life events as soon as people can report them, but a focused narrative is lost. One of the many victories for Sabaah Folayan and Damon Davis's documentary *Whose Streets?* is that it provides a single perspective from seemingly endless amounts of Tweets, YouTube videos, and more. The documentary creates the image of a loving community divided and misrepresented, but united under the growing activism of Black Lives Matter.

By its construction, *Whose Streets?* is an act of justice. The events that followed in Ferguson, Missouri in August 2014, after the killing of Michael Brown by police officer Darren Wilson, were not given proper due by the rest of the world. Those who were not there do not really know what happened, especially if relying on news reports that favored sensationalism and baited racism in the process. To start, segments that often led with "a riot in Ferguson" left out the candlelight vigils and the peaceful protests that were the initial response to the tragedy. In the process they took away the humanity of a place and people, when that was the exact opposite response needed when such lives are in danger.

This movie tells the story of Ferguson from first-person perspectives—footage shot by people who were in the city after Michael Brown was killed, and when the militarized police came to further dehumanize its citizens. The police's military-level approach is all the more visceral when a flash grenade is captured on a shaky iPhone camera, or when explosions rip through the audio while showing people running away from police. Or footage of red dots appearing on Ferguson residents, a type of warning fit for a war zone. The found material, with its scope and intimacy, unforgettably captures the atmosphere, experience, the beauty of peace, and the fist-clenching rage.

Taking the form of an epic, *Whose Streets?* expands to five chapters, as told through the acts of various residents. It finds heroes in the likes of Brittany Ferrell, an activist who helps lead the cause for Black Lives Matter in Ferguson, and imparts that spirit onto her daughter. She is joined by residents such as David Whitt, a husband and father of four who protect a neighborhood memorial set up for Michael Brown, and also surveil police activity with his group CopWatch. And while the film gets a bit scattered when focusing on other subjects, other people are given screen-time, like hip-hop artist Tef Poe and activist Kayla Reed, are captured rallying people peacefully and forcefully in various moments of injustice.

The documentary makes a clear point to not interviewing any members of the police force or government, as many other projects with similar subject matters might. Through the lives of the aforementioned and others, *Whose Streets?* prominently belongs to its citizens, an important part of the documentary's perspective. The film also makes transparent its righteous outrage, which does not pretend that there is even an argument.

There is a particular intimacy into how Davis and Folayan capture these hearts and minds. The directors are not intrusive, given their perspective as insiders into the community, but their cameras rarely feel out of place. In a beautiful touch that any cinéma vérité worker could learn from, Davis and Folayan often interview people as they are driving, focused on the road but speaking their minds. The result is simple, yet effective, with the people of Ferguson seemingly sharing the ideas that have been in their brains for months if not years, divulged with the intimacy of a conversation happening with life in full action.

The movie is built on its frustrations and is unapologetic for them. Particularly by the end, it shows Brittany and other protestors blocking highway traffic, a particularly controversial act of defiance, and one that puts her in jail. But within the emotional arc of the movie, with its peacefulness juxtaposed with such clear injustice towards so many great people, it is only emboldened. Those who side with protestors seeing the film will be affirmed by such footage, but those against such acts will at the least see the passion behind it, if not be swayed to reconsider their views. *Whose Streets?* does not deal in empathy so much as it does in emotional truth and humanity.

Like very few other documentaries, *Whose Streets?* welcomes a viewer into a movement, presenting it while it is just starting. Davis and Folayan's film takes the shape of a righteous, vigorous epic about a community uniting over its pursuit for equality. Given the importance of Black Lives Matter and telling its story, this documentary is a landmark cinematic moment for the form and for history. It is an epic worthy of the Black Lives Matter movement, and of the most viewers possible.

Nick Allen

CREDITS

Origin: United States

Language: English

Released: 2017

Production: Sabaah Jordan, Jennifer MacArthur, Flannery Miller, Sabaah Folayan, Damon Davis; released by Magnolia Pictures

Directed by: Sabaah Folayan; Damon Davis

Cinematography by: Lucas Alvarado-Farrar

Music by: Samora Pinderhughes

Music Supervisor: Jasmine Martin

Editing: Christopher McNabb

MPAA rating: R

Running time: 90 minutes

REVIEWS

Burr, Ty. *Boston Globe*. September 7, 2017.

Fear. David. *Rolling Stone*. August 14, 2017.

Hornaday, Ann. *Washington Post*. August 10, 2017.

Lane, Anthony. *New Yorker*. July 31, 2017.

Linden, Sheri. *Los Angeles Times*. August 11, 2017.

Murray, Noel. *The A.V. Club*. August 10, 2017.

Phillips, Michael. *Chicago Tribune*. September 19, 2017.

Pickett, Leah. *Chicago Reader*. August 10, 2017.

Roeper, Richard. *Chicago Sun-Times*. August 11, 2017.

Zacharek, Stephanie. *Time*. August 10, 2017.

WILSON

He's a people person.
—Movie tagline

Box Office: $653,951

Writer/Director Craig Johnson has a soft spot for characters who are stuck in suspended animation in terms of personal growth and maturity. He first examined such stunted people in his excellent and awkward debut film *True Adolescents* (2009) in which a never-was rock star named Sam (Mark Duplass) realized his selfish actions weighed heavily on those around him. Johnson followed this up with the very well-received *The Skeleton Twins* (2014), which showed much growth from the filmmaker as his character-driven microscope zoomed in on brother/sister twins (played brilliantly by Bill Hader and Kristen Wiig) who, through tragedy, are finally able to shine a spotlight on a past that halted their growth into mature, responsible adults. Now, Johnson is back with the first feature film he's directed but did not write, and the results are mixed. While it would seem screenwriter Daniel Clowes (working from a graphic novel he wrote as source material) could scarcely be a more perfect match in terms of similar immature, self-defeating characters, the story arc and character transformation of title character Wilson (Woody Harrelson) never really feels earned. As a result, *Wilson* frequently plays like an episodic series of events connected by the ne'er-do-well lead character, who may or may not get his act together by the time the credits roll.

Wilson centers on a middle-aged jerk named Wilson (Harrelson). He lives alone with his dog, and, as viewers find out mere moments into the film, he only has one friend and that friend is moving out of state. Soon, Wilson receives more bad news in that his father has terminal cancer, and before audiences even have a chance to wonder if they want to see if Wilson get his life together, they're thrown into a film about a truly unlikable man and the pratfalls (all of which are self-imposed) that befall him at every turn. The overlying issue with *Wilson* is that things just "happen," and there's no lesson learning until the film has nearly reached its entire run time. By then, it's just too late to care.

Pushy, truculent characters who push away anyone who dare try to warm to them are nothing new yet there are typically a few bright spots of humanity for viewers to grasp in order to join these characters on their journey. In fact, all of Johnson's previous characters were imbued with at least one likable characteristic, making their frustrating personalities easier to take. The aforementioned Sam in *True Adolescents* is funny in an immature way and he also has empathy for his lonely nephew Oliver (Bret Loehr) which leads the two on an ill-fated camping trip. In *The Skeleton Twins,* the lead characters are beautifully, funnily, and tragically portrayed by comedic geniuses Bill Hader and Kristen Wiig and their performances give life and a connectivity to what could have easily been seen as just plain damaged, unlikable people. As such, when the story material in that film turns pitch black, viewers feel safe in the acting arms of Wiig and Hader and want to see redemption. Yet in *Wilson*, the titular character starts off at maximum "creep" and not until the third act does he start to maybe get a sense of how he affects those around him and by then, it's too late.

Among those sucked into Wilson's web of despair are former wife Pippi (an overwrought Laura Dern), who clearly had good reason to never expect nor want to see Wilson again; her sister Polly (Cheryl Hines), who has even more reason to despise him; and Claire (Isabella Amara), the child Pippi and Wilson never knew, who was thankfully given up for adoption. Wilson inserts himself into all of these people's lives in obnoxious ways and what makes *Wilson* even more difficult to parse is how characters sometimes like him, but then do not mere moments later. While that could be looked at as a unique way to develop a story or character, it again adds to the feeling the audience is being dragged through a series of events rather than guided on a cinematic experience.

Wilson is not without clever, funny moments. For as derisive as Wilson's personality is, there are still entertaining scenes where he understandably mocks what passes for acceptable behavior in modern-day America. It's also humorous that rather than audibly rant (although he does that too) Wilson typically takes his mocking of absurd behavior to the next level by directly confronting it and inserting himself into it. Throughout the film, viewers will find themselves wondering how Wilson has all his teeth and no facial bruising until he finally gets his comeuppance. But again, like much of the film, any lessons learned come much too late after a sense of true hatred for Wilson has formed and as such, emotional investment never takes hold.

Don R. Lewis

CREDITS

Wilson: Woody Harrelson
Pippi: Laura Dern
Polly: Cheryl Hines
Olsen: David Warshofsky
Claire: Isabella Amara
Origin: United States
Language: English
Released: 2017
Production: Jared Goldman, Mary Jane Skalski; Ad Hominem Enterprises; released by Fox Searchlight Pictures
Directed by: Craig Johnson
Written by: Daniel Clowes
Cinematography by: Frederick Elmes
Music by: Jon Brion
Music Supervisor: Marguerite Phillips
Editing: Paul Zucker
Costumes: Christopher Peterson
Production Design: Ethan Tobman
MPAA rating: R
Running time: 94 minutes

REVIEWS

Anderson, Melissa. *Village Voice.* March 21, 2017.
Fujishima, Kenji. *Slant Magazine.* March 20, 2017.
Grierson, Tim. *Screen International.* January 24, 2017.
Hernandez, Joseph. *We Got This Covered.* March 23, 2017.
Kohn, Eric. *IndieWire.* January 24, 2017.
MacDonald. Moira. *The Seattle Times.* March 23, 2017.
O'Sullivan, Michael. *Washington Post.* March 23, 2017.
Raup, Jordan. *The Film Stage.* January 26, 2017.
White, David. *New York Daily News.* March 23, 2017.
Wloszcyna, Susan. *RogerEbert.com.* March 24, 2017.

QUOTES

Wilson: "We all want people to love us for exactly who we are but that's not really possible in this world because we're just all too unbearable."

TRIVIA

Derek Cianfrance was at one point attached to direct the film before dropping out to direct *The Light Between Oceans* (2016) instead.

WIND RIVER

Nothing is harder to track than the truth.
—Movie tagline

Box Office: $33.8 Million

The American mythos of Cowboys and Indians has been both a successful aspect of American filmmaking and a burden. The notion that the American Cowboys can be seen as heroic saviors from the savage, merciless Indians is now seen as a racist trope of a bygone era. The media of yesteryear propagated that idea for decades and the images never really went far enough away to make up for the damage done. There was *Little Big Man* (1970), with Dustin Hoffman, which saw a white man caught between the two worlds, right up until Custer's Last Stand. Kevin Costner tried with his "white savior" epic *Dances with Wolves* (1990), a noble effort that, whatever flaws it might have, turned the mythology on its ear and made the "cowboys" the enemies. It was not until Chris Eyre's *Smoke Signals* (1998), based on the writings of Sherman Alexie, that the Indian Reservations became the setting for a major motion picture and cast a light on the plight of the contemporary Native American (even if it did skirt around a few issues). That film used humor to spoon-feed the audience its more serious subjects and the results were mixed, but mostly positive.

There were certainly other significant works that cast a different light that rendered the mythology of yesteryear all but dead. John Ford's *The Searchers* (and other Ford films) still enjoys anniversary screenings every five years or so, but that is about all that can be said for the genre in 2017, where racial and ethnic sensitivity and appropriation remain a major part of the cultural dialogue. Yet there are filmmakers who still return to the Reservations and find stories that resonate without resorting to White Saviorism or clichés. Kelly Reichardt's *Certain Women* (2016) told three stories—mostly from a white perspective—that served as metaphors for bad deals and isolation that remain a part of present-day life for Native Americans. Now, Taylor Sheridan's *Wind River* takes a standard police thriller and uses it to tell a story of just how forgotten the American Indian has become.

The film takes place in Wind River, a Reservation in Wyoming where brutal snowstorms arrive seemingly at random. A dead body of a woman is found within the tundra about three miles away from anything resembling civilization. How did she get there? Was she murdered at the spot? There are tracks, but not enough to indicate a direct conclusion. Nobody knows the land better than Cory Lambert (Jeremy Renner), a tracker who is recruited to help an FBI agent named Jane Banner (Elizabeth Olsen) figure out who committed the crime and how. Time is of the essence here because a snowstorm could come in and cover any tracks that might be helpful clues. Jane has to get over the culture shock, first and foremost, since she hails from Las Vegas and did not bring enough adequate winter gear to survive the landscape, much less the frostbite that occurs when travelling via snowmobile.

Cory's backstory is a familiar one. He has a Native-American ex-wife and they have a child together. They are all on good terms and on this particular weekend, Cory has custody of his son, Casey (Teo Briones), whom he teaches to ride a horse. "Like a cowboy, right dad?" he says. "Not exactly." Casey has to take a backseat when the case of the dead girl arrives. The head of the tribal police, Ben (Graham Greene), enlists Cory's help and Cory knows the weight of the case. He knows the parents of the dead woman, an 18-year-old named Natalie (Kelsey Asbille), and feels a deep sense of purpose to try and do whatever he can to figure out the cause of death and who might be responsible. Jane has to deal with the looks of skepticism from every Native American on the Reservation for her appearance and her general lack of familiarity of the landscape.

The investigation leads to a few dead ends. For bureaucratic reasons, the town doctor (Eric Lange) will not list the cause of death as murder, which means Jane cannot call it in to the authorities, despite the fact that there seems to be sufficient evidence to indicate that murder could very well have been the cause. Natalie's parents, Martin (Gil Birmingham) and Annie (Althea Sam), are too grief-stricken and isolated from their kids to know what could have precipitated this tragedy. Their son has succumbed to drug addiction and has no idea his sister has been killed. The more important matter for Martin seems to be Cory's purpose in all of this. "I'm a hunter," Cory tells him. "That's what I'm doing." Martin insists to Cory that whoever did this should pay dearly and without mercy.

This is Sheridan's follow-up to his Academy Award-nominated screenplay for *Hell and High Water* (2016), which similarly took a standard police procedural thriller and used it to examine a small pocket of America that has often been overlooked (in that case, West Texas) and used it to explore a bigger theme. Here, *Wind River* uses the story of this murder and has crafted a metaphor for the past and how white America must still atone for the sin of thievery, rape, and murder of Native Americans and their land. Sheridan does so without getting heavy-handed or obvious. The emotional core of the story never gets lost. In the end, the conceit of the piece remains about two wounded fathers who connect with each other even through tragedy and who can carry each other through the hardest times. This sense of loss makes Cory's ties to the land all the more fascinating and layered.

Wind River does not play well as a mystery, which will disappoint some people who are looking for a challenging whodunit. That is not a flaw, though. If the film has a major flaw, it is in Olsen's character, who comes off a little too naïve for this particular story. Sheridan is smart to not force any kind of romantic tension between her and Cory, though, and instead focuses on the land and its people. Ben Richardson's beautiful cinematography gives the film the proper mood with an unforgiving physical landscape. The haunting score by Nick Cave and Warren Ellis is laced with occasional chants of those who came before and still haunt this earth and those who inhabit it. Renner, again, remains one of those dependable actors who can convey a quiet, pensive, world-weary soul while remaining a likable and charismatic presence with whom the audience can connect. He is the perfect person to act as a bridge between the past and the present, which is what *Wind River* is all about.

Collin Souter

CREDITS

Cory Lambert: Jeremy Renner
Jane Banner: Elizabeth Olsen
Matt: Jon Bernthal
Chip: Martin Sensmeier

Wilma Lambert: Julia Jones
Origin: United States
Language: English
Released: 2017
Production: Elizabeth A. Bell, Peter Berg, Matthew George, Basil Iwanyk, Wayne L. Rogers; Acacia Filmed Entertainment, Film 44, Savvy Media Holdings, Thunder Road Pictures; released by Voltage Pictures
Written by: Taylor Sheridan
Cinematography by: Ben Richardson
Music by: Nick Cave; Warren Ellis
Sound: Alan Robert Murray
Editing: Taylor Sheridan; Gary D. Roach
Art Direction: Lauren Slatten
Costumes: Kari Perkins
Production Design: Neil Spisak
MPAA rating: R
Running time: 107 minutes

REVIEWS

Ebiri, Bilge. *Village Voice.* August 2, 2017.
Goodykoontz, Bill. *Arizona Republic.* August 10, 2017.
Hornaday, Ann. *Washington Post.* August 10, 2017.
Howell, Peter. *Toronto Star.* August 10, 2017.
Kenny, Glenn. *New York Times.* August 3, 2017.
Lemire, Christy. *RogerEbert.com.* August 5, 2017.
MacDonald, Moira. *Seattle Times.* August 9, 2017.
Mayer, Dominick. *Consequence of Sound.* August 11, 2017.
Morgenstern, Joe. *Wall Street Journal.* August 3, 2017.
Turan, Kenneth. *Los Angeles Times.* August 3, 2017.

QUOTES

Cory Lambert: "Luck don't live out here."

TRIVIA

Actress Elizabeth Olsen experienced a case of snow blindness while shooting this film.

WISH UPON

Be careful what you wish for.
—Movie tagline

Box Office: $14.3 Million

There are several directors that could be accused of building their careers off the backs of others, but how many have lined a résumé as exclusively as John R. Leonetti has producing fourth-rate sequels? A cinematographer by trade, he made his directorial debut with *Mortal Kombat: Annihilation* (1997). That was later followed by *The Butterfly Effect 2* (2006) which passed over theaters entirely in favor of home video exclusivity. After doing what may have been his best work ever shooting James Wan's *The Conjuring* (2013) he was hired to helm the prequel to that film's prologue in *Annabelle* (2014). Though his Charles Manson-inspired *Wolves at the Door* (2016) went the more-modern Video On Demand route, his first non-sequel/prequel project, *Wish Upon*, could have been his moment to finally show that he is more than just another director-for-hire. The ultimate result is a film even less original and poorly crafted than any of the films previously mentioned.

Clare Shannon (Joey King) witnessed her mom's suicide when she was just a kid. Since then, her dad (Ryan Phillippe) has turned into a professional scavenger seeking out scrap metal for restoration, sale, or personal use. She is active at school and has two loyal friends in Meredith (Sydney Park) and June (Shannon Purser). One day, dear ol' dad brings Clare an early birthday present as he calls it—a mysterious box with Chinese symbols that nobody can seem to open. Clare though, conveniently taking a Chinese class, reads the words "seven wishes."

While laying her hands on the box, she makes a wish directing harm at a school bully. "I hope she just rots," Clare says and the next morning the girl is horrified at what she finds under her clothes. Unfortunately for Clare is what she then finds under her house; the dog that her mom gave her is dead. Once realizing this might be more than just a coincidence—never mind the dead dog—she tries again asking for love, inheritance and popularity. Every time she is rewarded, but it takes her fellow Chinese classmate, Ryan (Ki Hong Lee), to make the connection that her wishes come at a price. Now she has her own fulfillment to grant and a similar fate could be waiting for her at the end of it.

Branding horror protagonists with the prospect of wheeling, dealing, and compromising their moral aptitude with supernatural forces is an age-old trope of horror. If not the Devil himself then a creature in the form of the Leprechaun or the Wishmaster is created to fill the void. Ancient Chinese secrets don't make for an intimidating manifestation aside from the usual ghostly powers embedded for cheap scares so the filmmakers have chosen to mash up the "Final Destination" series into a young adult version of *The Box* (2009). People of most ages have not seen—or outright rejected—Richard Kelly's uniquely bizarre adaptation of Richard Matheson's short story "Button, Button" so this film tries to lure teenagers into an easily digestible PG-13 tale that would rather passively titillate with familiarity than truly unnerve or even have some fun with it.

Barbara Marshall's screenplay flirts with the prospect of becoming horror's version of *Mean Girls* (2004)—

even if *Heathers* (1988) already qualified—with the outsider becoming destiny's queen, but that is heaping a load of credit on a narrative that has no imagination to speak of. Comedy, on the other hand, does become an unintended consequence. The aforementioned "Final Destination" franchise in its best moments was a showcase for a filmmakers's prowess with suspense and the macabre ways it would dispatch its victims. Marshall and Leonetti clearly have more faith in the strength of household garbage disposals than most consumers. Beyond that centerpiece's attempt to lay the groundwork for escalation, one victim slips on a rug, another (older) one slips in a bathtub, and a third gets on the wrong elevator. As a metaphysical debt collector, the invisible box force is efficient but as a showman it ranks somewhere below a three-year-old who leaves their toy cars and a banana peel on the floor.

It is unfair to blame the spirits within the box though. They are only let out seven times per each person who can read Chinese that the box comes across. So, you can't blame them for being restless. The protagonists and their relatives may have no control over them but Mr. Leonetti certainly did. Still he seems content in just going through the paces and letting each kill take its course to thin the herd of characters too dumb or bland to muster up any support for. Only Phillippe's arc from junkman to smooth jazz saxophonist is bizarre enough to command attention away from the film's comical image of the box chained up on the bed. Leonetti, ignoring the visual opportunity of the box breaking free of its shackles is a perfect metaphor for the film and an unfortunate one for his career.

Erik Childress

CREDITS

Clare Shannon: Joey King
Jonathan Shannon: Ryan Phillippe
Ryan Hui: Ki Hong Lee
June Acosta: Shannon Purser
Meredith McNeil: Sydney Park
Origin: United States
Language: English
Released: 2017
Production: Sherryl Clark; Broad Green Pictures, Busted Shark Productions; released by Orion Pictures
Directed by: John R. Leonetti
Written by: Barbara Marshall
Cinematography by: Michael Galbraith
Music by: tomandandy
Sound: Joe Dzuban; Gabriel J. Serrano
Music Supervisor: Alexandra Patsavas
Editing: Peck Prior
Art Direction: Andrea Kristof
Costumes: Antoinette Messam
Production Design: Bob Ziembicki
MPAA rating: PG-13
Running time: 90 minutes

REVIEWS

Bell, Josh. *Las Vegas Weekly*. July 13, 2017.
Catsoulis, Jeannette. *New York Times*. July 14, 2017.
Gire, Dann. *Daily Herald*. July 13, 2017.
Johanson, MaryAnn. *ReelViews*. July 14, 2017.
Judy, Jim. *Screen It*. July 13, 2017.
Kohn, Eric. *IndieWire*. July 13, 2017.
Marrs, Sarah. *Lainey Gossip*. October 13, 2017.
Oller, Jacob. *ReelViews*. July 13, 2017.
Schaefer, Stephen. *Boston Herald*. July 14, 2017.
Snider, Eric D. *ReelViews*. July 13, 2017.

QUOTES

Ryan Hui: "Hold up, you dig on multiverse?"

TRIVIA

A hotel/elevator scene was shot at Hilton Toronto/Markham Suites Conference Centre & Spa in November 2016 between 8:00 P.M. and 6:00 A.M.

THE WOMEN'S BALCONY
(Ismach Hatani)

Box Office: $1.2 Million

Emil Ben-Shimon's debut theatrical feature *The Women's Balcony* is a colorful and boisterous comedy of manners with a contentious spirit that touches on essential matters and sometimes innate conflicts of what it means to be Israeli, a woman, and Orthodox.

The movie was a monster commercial hit at home, reflective of its distinctive ensemble, excellent production values, and sharp writing. The movie also clearly touches a nerve, the cultural recognition pointing out longstanding generational or gender conflicts. It gives voice to the marginalized. The worst said about the film is that it is a little too eager to please. At its best, *The Women's Balcony* negotiates an insular world with verve, humor, and playful directness.

What is fascinating about the film is how precisely rendered is the cultural and social milieu. The movie takes place in Jerusalem, but it is not the cosmopolitan district of an elite global society but the virtual back alleys, cramped apartments, and vertical architecture of a wholly different setting. Modesty is the dominant mode of expression, touching all aspects of dress, appearance, and vocation. Visually, the point is made through the play of light and shadow, with a great deal of the action framed through tight prosceniums, like doorways and windows.

The movie limns a world of celebration and ritual, signaled by a dazzling and beautiful opening sequence as the congregants of a synagogue prepare for a bar mitzvah. Ben-Shimon comes out of television, but he demonstrates a fluid command of space and rhythm working with the excellent Kazak cinematographer Ziv Berkovich. The camera floats above the massing crowd of bodies and faces and reveals the intricately detailed lines of people, arranged like a musical number, as they carry gifts and food. The moment is flush with a buoyancy and lilt.

A crucial and thoughtless mistake, the forgetting of the symbolic candy, proves a dark omen. During the middle of the proceedings, a concrete stone latticework gives way and collapses. The structure was the gender-segregated balcony space that housed the women of the congregation. The accident has left the congregation bereft. The rabbi's wife is now comatose. The elderly rabbi, already frail, is further traumatized and exhibiting signs of dementia and mental breakdown.

Zion (Igal Naor), a shopkeeper whose grandson was the celebrant, now watches over the rabbi. Meeting at an improvised schoolroom for their mourning prayers, a group of men begin to discuss how to proceed with the necessary repairs and renovation of the synagogue. Jewish law mandates a quorum, of group of ten men, in order to conduct the services. The men invite a serious young man in traditional Hasidic clothes they see to participate. The man, David (Avraham Aviv Alush), a rabbi and teacher, returns with a group of his young seminary students.

Rabbi David seizes the void in leadership and quickly assumes control. He uses his clout to bypass permits and inspections and helps accelerate the reconstruction process. David is also a fundamentalist and literalist with a strict and unyielding point of view. "Thank the creator," he says. "I am only the messenger." He views the accident as a sign from God, and he utilizes the circumstances to impose his will. David carries a rapt hold over the mostly weak and compliant men, admonishing them to cover their wives, for instance.

This sets up the most interesting part of the movie. The script, by Shlomit Nehama, draws the women as much more forthright, intelligent, and complex figures. The cultural collision is something to see. Rabbi David destabilizes the sexual dynamics of the small-knit community. Much to his surprise, the women fight back. *The Women's Balcony* turns knottier, even confrontational, under the guile and steady leadership of Ettie (Evelin Hagoel), Zion's wife. She personifies an esprit de corps, implacable, tough-minded women who are devout though not deferential.

Much to their horror and shock, Rabbi David unveils the renovated space, their "balcony," is now wholly gone, literally wiped clean and the women are now dispatched to observe from an auxiliary space, or what one woman calls an "outhouse." Rabbi David is now an interloper who has upended all sense of decency. "Is that what a rabbi is supposed to do?" Ettie says, staring him down. "Enter a community of good people and fill them with fear."

In these riveting passages, *The Women's Balcony* is a battle of the sexes captured from the unique prism of an Orthodox Jewish community. Rabbi David claims there were insufficient funds to restore the balcony, and the women respond by organizing their own fund. He again upstages them by trying to divert that money for a rabbinical scroll. The power dynamics are not always clean cut. Rivalries emerge, not to mention fear and distrust, some of it directed at the central couple, Ettie and Zion. A lingering sense of suspicion pervades the film, represented by a young boy Zion occasionally watches over who is suddenly ordered to stay away.

As the women counterattack by effectively throwing their husbands out of their homes or mounting a protest at the rabbi's school, their call for equal treatment and dignity resonates. The movie's call for basic decency and fairness is a deeply compelling one. "Everyone should take care of his account with God," Ettie says.

It is a serious movie with a subversive side. The dominant subplot involves the quixotic attempts of Ettie's beautiful unmarried niece Yaffa (Yafit Asulin) to find a husband. In one hilarious early scene, that echoes Barry Levinson's *Diner* (1982), she must submit to a test by a prospective suitor. "Pass," she says to one particularly awkward query. In a deepening complication, she finds her soul mate but the young man is connected to Rabbi David.

The humor is biting though welcome. (The scene of the women chiseling down a contractor is worth the price of admission.) The humor provides a solidity and shape. The writer, Shlomit Nehama, has a wonderful ear for dialogue and one-liners. It would seem out of place given the subject matter. *The Women's Balcony* is better, more grounded and sharper, when it is at its most absurd. At times the more serious material is also the most didactic and doctrinaire. The movie comes to life in the asides, the comebacks, and the situational. The pain of recognition registers with authority.

Patrick Z. McGavin

CREDITS

Ettie: Evelin Hagoel
Zion: Igal Naor
Tikva: Orna Banai
Margalit: Einat Saruf
Rabbi David: Avraham Aviv Alush
Origin: United States
Language: Hebrew
Released: 2016
Production: Leon Edery, Moshe Edery, Osnat Handelsman-Keren, Talia Kleinhendler; Pie Films Inc.; released by Menemsha Films
Directed by: Emil Ben-Shimon
Written by: Shlomit Nehama
Cinematography by: Ziv Berkovich
Editing: Einat Glaser-Zarhin
Costumes: Rona Doron
MPAA rating: Unrated
Running time: 96 minutes

REVIEWS

Baumgarten, Marjorie. *Austin Chronicle*. July 19, 2017.
Cordova, Randy. *Arizona Republic*. June 8, 2017.
Herrington, Nicole. *New York Times*. May 25, 2017.
Hoffman, Jordan. *Village Voice*. May 25, 2017.
Keough, Peter. *Boston Globe*. July 5, 2017.
Lewis, David. *San Francisco Chronicle*. June 14, 2017.
Mobarak, Jared. *The Film Stage*. May 24, 2017.
O'Malley, Sheila. *RogerEbert.com*. May 26, 2017.
Padua, Pat. *Washington Post*. June 15, 2017.
Turan, Kenneth. *Los Angeles Times*. March 2, 2017.

WONDER

Are you ready to meet Auggie Pullman?
—Movie tagline

You can't try and blend in, When you were born to stand out.
—Movie tagline

Box Office: $130.6 Million

R.J. Palacio's debut novel *Wonder* became a *New York Times* #1 bestseller and soon went on to be a kind of "required reading" phenomenon at elementary and middle schools across the country. The tale of a boy with a disfigured face ("mandibulofacial dysostosis," or Treacher Collins syndrome) who, at the age of 10, finally sets foot into a mainstream elementary school, touched many hearts, young and old. Written from several characters' points of view, the book's story spans an entire school year. It successfully engaged young readers with its like-minded protagonists and gave older readers some keen insights into how kids and teenagers think about themselves and those around them. It also became a conversation starter with parents and educators who would use the novel to teach empathy and understanding to students. Could a movie version accomplish the same feat with those who had never read the source material?

That certainly seemed to be the goal here and director Stephen Chbosky was up to the task of bringing this celebrated work to the big screen without losing any of its substance. In the wrong hands, *Wonder* would have been a treacly, simplistic sap-fest with overbearing music and hamfisted sentiment. Thankfully, Chbosky and co-screenwriter Steven Conrad have successfully rendered an adaptation that never dumbs anything down. If anything, they have made improvements in certain areas while leaving plenty of reasons to still read the book. While much of the drama has been condensed, it never feels overly rushed or over-simplified. Adapting most books into a well-rounded screenplay is almost always a tall order, but Chbosky and his team have created a rarity—the effortless tearjerker.

The story begins just before the start of school as Auggie Pullman (Jacob Tremblay), age 10, finally enrolls in a public school where he will most definitely be looked at differently. Born with a severe facial disfigurement, Auggie has had twenty-six surgeries since birth and has been home-schooled all his life. His parents, Nate (Owen Wilson) and Isabel (Julia Roberts), are naturally very protective of him and have differing opinions as to whether this is the right time or even the right thing to do. Auggie is especially conflicted on the matter and considers the idea of wearing his astronaut helmet on the first day to avoid being seen, a helmet he has worn repeatedly in public since getting it. Instead, he faces the reality that the helmet would do more harm than good. On his first day, he is walked to the front gate by his parents and older sister, Via (Isabela Vidovic), who give him useful parting words of wisdom before turning him loose.

Auggie is not without friends on his first day. Prior to school starting, the principal, Mr. Tushman (Mandy Patinkin), made sure Auggie felt okay about his new surroundings by having three classmates introduce themselves and show Auggie around the school. Jack Will (Noah Jupe), Charlotte (Elle McKinnon), and Julian (Bryce Gheisar) give Auggie the tour, with slight trepidation. Only Julian has the nerve to break the ice and ask Auggie why he looks the way he looks, but only Jack seems like the kind of person who will be Auggie's friend for life. Auggie, of course, still gets long stares from other kids in the school, but manages to get different looks of disbelief in his science classes where he excels well beyond his years. Not all is well with his friend Jack, however, when Auggie overhears a conversation that convinces him that Jack may not be his friend after all.

Wonder takes after the book in telling it's story from multiple points of view. The other main character here is Via, Auggie's teenage sister. Via loves Auggie, of course, but feels set aside by her parents who have taken more of an interest in Auggie's well-being than hers. At the same time, Via's best friend since childhood (and family friend since before Auggie was born), Miranda (Danielle Rose Russell), has been distancing herself from Via lately and now runs with a new group of friends. As a means of retreat, Via tries out for the school play and ends up meeting a boy named Justin (Nadji Jeter) who takes an instant liking to her. But Miranda's absence has been felt by the whole family, none more so than Auggie who always thought of Miranda as another sister. When Via gets the role of Miranda's understudy for a role in *Our Town*, further complications ensue.

Chbosky and Conrad have a difficult task of adapting this book in a way that feels smooth for the uninitiated and loyal to the fans of the book. By incorporating this multi-perspective structure, *Wonder* achieves its goal of generating empathy for all the characters so that nobody here becomes just a prop to propel the narrative. The only shortcut from the book is the character of Julian, who ends up being Auggie's main bully as the school year goes on. A little more attention to his character would have been nice, but Chbosky and Conrad do a serviceable job of condensing his situation with just one scene. It gives the viewer just enough information to generate some audience sympathy, but one more scene would have made it even better. Still, the fact that Chbosky and Conrad maintained the device instead of taking the safe route of just making it about Auggie is a testament to the same kind of courage that Auggie had in going to a public school. It could have gone wrong in so many ways, but the result is worthy of applause.

None of it would work, of course, without the winning cast that has been assembled here. Roberts and Wilson have the right chemistry to play the parents, whose roles have been given more weight and depth than Palacio originally gave them (here, Nate is actually funny instead of the viewer just being told he is funny). As Via, Vidovic makes the role worthy of all the attention the film gives to her character. Unlike so many teenage roles these days, she has a believable presence and can get the viewer on board with her plight as well as Auggie's. Not an easy feat, really. In fact, all of the supporting roles here have been cast as though Chbosky and his team had a strict doctrine to only cast people who can convincingly play a teacher, a bully, a smart kid, an average kid, etc. Every kid looks their age and every teacher and faculty member has been written and acted as though plenty of research went into the part, a true rarity for films about schools and young students.

Of course, finally, there is Tremblay, who, at such a young age, has the difficult job of acting through his thick layers of make-up. Like the best actors, Tremblay can make the audience forget about the appearance and make the viewer focus solely on the story of the character. The make-up here is convincing and not overdone and Tremblay makes Auggie worth rooting for as a person and not just a tragic figure. He conveys Auggie's charm and brains without coming off as one of those annoyingly over-coached child actors, proving his breakout film, *Room* (2015), was no fluke. Likewise for Chbosky, who has made his first film since *The Perks of Being a Wallflower* (2012), another film about an outsider trying to fit in and a story that spans an entire school year. Both films have elevated their genres to a higher level simply by treating their characters as people, no matter their age or ailment.

Collin Souter

CREDITS

Auggie: Jacob Tremblay

Nate: Owen Wilson

Via: Izabela Vidovic

Isabel: Julia Roberts

Mr. Tushman: Mandy Patinkin

Origin: United States

Language: English

Released: 2017

Production: David Hoberman, Todd Lieberman; Mandeville Films, Participant Media L.L.C., Walden Media; released by Lionsgate

Directed by: Stephen Chbosky

Written by: Stephen Chbosky; Steve Conrad; Jack Thorne

Cinematography by: Don Burgess

Music by: Marcelo Zarvos

Sound: Perry Robertson; Scott Sanders

Music Supervisor: Alexandra Patsavas

Editing: Mark Livolsi

Art Direction: Kendelle Elliott

Costumes: Monique Prudhomme

Production Design: Kalina Ivanov

MPAA rating: PG
Running time: 113 minutes

REVIEWS

Covert, Colin. *Minneapolis Star-Tribune.* November 16, 2017.
Demara, Bruce. *Toronto Star.* November 16, 2017.
Ebiri, Bilge. *Village Voice.* November 20, 2017.
Edelstein, David. *Vulture.* November 17, 2017.
Feeney, Mark. *Boston Globe.* November 15, 2017.
Graham, Adam. *Detroit News.* November 17, 2017.
Jones, J.R. *Chicago Reader.* November 16, 2017.
Kenny, Glenn. *New York Times.* November 16, 2017.
Lemire, Christy. *RogerEbert.com.* November 17, 2017.
Turan, Kenneth. *Los Angeles Times.* November 15, 2017.

TRIVIA

This is the first time that actors Julia Roberts and Owen Wilson have worked together.

AWARDS

Nominations:
Oscars 2017: Makeup
British Acad. 2017: Makeup

WONDER WHEEL

Box Office: $1.4 Million

Wonder Wheel is Woody Allen's 49th directorial feature and his 51st screenplay made into a film. At this point, reviews of Allen's films and the films themselves have become somewhat interchangeable. When a director has had as much output as Allen has had over the past 50-plus years, inevitably, they will repeat themselves ad nauseum. This critique has been repeated so much about Allen's work, though, that it hardly matters anymore. Allen seems content with regurgitating the same material, but yet he still possesses an occasional zeal for playing with the form, either in story structure or in the visual presentation. With *Wonder Wheel,* Allen is certainly in all-too-familiar territory, but his most recent collaboration with cinematographer Vitorio Storaro (their second film together after *Café Society* [2016]) shows that he has not lost his flair for strong visuals and hiring the best cinematographers to bring his films to life.

In typical form, it all starts off with a jazz song, followed by a shot of Coney Island in the 1950s, followed by a young, male narrator (Justin Timberlake) explaining that he, while working as a lifeguard, is studying to be a writer majoring in European drama. "I love melodrama and larger than life characters," he says. This introduces the viewer to Carolina (Juno Temple), a young woman in her early twenties who is returning home to her father, Harold Humpty (Jim Belushi), a carousel operator who is now married to Ginny (Kate Winslet), a waitress at a crab restaurant. They have both been married before. Ginny has a young son named Richie (Jack Gore) from a previous marriage. The three live together off the pier in a home that has a fantastic view from just about every angle of the theme park.

Carolina's plight has to do with her gangster husband, who has just been caught by the cops. Two thugs come looking for Carolina, believing she gave her husband up to the police. She is in hiding and has not seen her father in five years. This set-up alone makes for rich drama by itself, but this being an Allen film, someone has to have an affair with someone else. Enter Mickey (Timberlake), who starts having said affair with Ginny, not knowing she is married at first. She eventually comes clean, but the affair continues. It is only a matter of time before Mickey and Carolina meet and start a romance of their own. They are closer in age and the future is theirs. Ginny is approaching forty, so her appeal is becoming more limited for Mickey as time goes on. Meanwhile, Ginny has to deal with her young son Richie, who cannot stop himself from setting anything and everything on fire.

Mickey's narration at the start promises the viewer that some melodrama will occur in this story. Allen may be trying to get ahead of his critics here, but *Wonder Wheel* is no more stylized in its acting or approach than anything else Allen has done. Perhaps at the outset, Allen wanted to create a kind of Tennessee Williams meets Douglas Sirk homage (the cinematography certainly works in its favor), but got cold feet or lost interest completely and just decided to let the actors do what came naturally. A wise choice in one respect (most of the acting is solid), but the film loses whatever personality it could have had to separate itself from the rest of Allen's recent work, which, at this point, has been mostly mediocre. Mickey also promises that Carolina will be a "larger than life character." She is not. She is the same directionless female character in her twenties that Allen has written at least ten times now.

Nevertheless, in spite of the familiarity on display here, there are a few things to admire in *Wonder Wheel.* Storaro's cinematography is the one thing that does bring Allen's film to a place of melodrama and theater. Storaro's colors are typically rich and vibrant, each scene having a theatricality to it that feels appropriate for what could easily be a stage play. Storaro, of course, worships the magic hour shots and *Wonder Wheel* is chock full of them, but that only represents a fraction of the gorgeous work being done here. There are many long scenes where the colors change as the tension rises and falls. Foreboding reds turn into deep blues and then back to natural colors as the scenes progress, making Coney Island a more purposeful presence than just a place where Allen can wax nostalgic once again (it is a recurring image throughout his films).

The best scenes are between Winslet and Belushi, who gives his best performance probably ever. These two characters are basically Danny Aiello and Mia Farrrow's characters from *The Purple Rose of Cairo* (1985) transported to the 1950s, but they try their best to rise above that convention and put as much flavor and nuance in their scenes as they can muster. Belushi has rarely been this good (a low bar, though), but Winslet remains a difficult character to warm up to and her performance becomes one-note after a while. The one actor who seems to be out of touch here is Timberlake, who looks as though he has only been given one take for all his scenes and he never quite masters it. That is not entirely his fault, of course, since Allen is notorious for not giving his actors direction or multiple takes. Still, his performance is at odds with everyone else. His narration is completely unnecessary and offers nothing, especially since he is not in every scene and cannot possibly know everything that is happening.

Wonder Wheel is neither one of Allen's worst films, nor one of his best. It falls squarely in the middle, along with about twenty or so of his other films. Like many of his recent works, it begs the question as to just what propels Allen to keep making films. If there is nothing new to say (and there certainly is nothing new here), what is the point, other than to just keep working? For *Wonder Wheel*, he clearly enjoys working with a new (for him) cinematographer. The rest is a mystery. It is a shame Allen never once tried directing a film he did not write. That would be the ultimate challenge and risk for him at this point in his accomplished career. These days, he has all the right people working for him, but he continues to work against himself.

Collin Souter

CREDITS

Humpty: Jim Belushi
Carolina: Juno Temple
Mickey: Justin Timberlake
Ginny: Kate Winslet
Ryan: Max Casella
Origin: United States
Language: English
Released: 2017
Production: Erika Aronson, Letty Aronson, Edward Walson; Gravier Productions, Perdido Productions; released by Amazon Studios
Directed by: Woody Allen
Written by: Woody Allen
Cinematography by: Vittorio Storaro
Sound: Robert Hein
Editing: Alisa Lepselter
Art Direction: Miguel Lopez-Castillo
Costumes: Suzy Benzinger
Production Design: Santo Loquasto
MPAA rating: PG-13
Running time: 101 minutes

REVIEWS

Callahan, Dan. *TheWrap*. October 13, 2017.
Chang, Justin. *Los Angeles Times*. November 30, 2017.
Cwick, Greg. *Slant Magazine*. October 14, 2017.
Edelstein, David. *Vulture*. October 14, 2017.
Guzman, Rafer. *Newsday*. November 30, 2017.
Kenny, Glenn. *RogerEbert.com*. November 29, 2017.
Kohn, Eric. *IndieWire*. October 13, 2017.
Gleiberman, Owen. *Variety*. October 13, 2017.
Rothkopf, Josh. *Time Out*. November 20, 2017.
Whitty Stephen. *New York Daily News*. November 27, 2017.

TRIVIA

The film was released on December 1, 2017, writer/director Woody Allen's 82nd birthday.

WONDER WOMAN

Power. Grace. Wisdom. Wonder.
—Movie tagline

Wonder. Power. Courage.
—Movie tagline

The future of justice begins with her.
—Movie tagline

Box Office: $412.6 Million

Elsewhere in this volume, in his review of *Justice League* (2017), Mark Dujsik perfectly posits that director Patty Jenkins' *Wonder Woman* (2017) offers fans of "the DC universe of cinematic superheroes its first glimmer of hope," with a far superior super hero film after a plethora of disappointing outings. This statement could not be more on point. The films of the DC universe, no doubt constructed in their current configurations to compete with those of rival Marvel have, to put it bluntly, been major disappointments, culminating in the bloated, bland team-up entry *Justice League*. However, as

Dujsik observed, the stand-alone adventure of the Amazonian warrior princess, Diana (aka Wonder Woman), interjected new-found life and actual fun into a series of films that seemed forever destined to languish in the wake of the Marvel Cinematic Universe.

Wonder Woman opens with a clever framing device set in modern-day Paris that finds Diana Prince (Gal Gadot) working in the antiquities department of the Louvre where she receives a package from Bruce Wayne (aka Batman) that suggests she has had at least one adventure before befriending Wayne and Clark Kent (aka Superman) to fight Doomsday back in *Batman v Superman: Dawn of Justice* (2016). The photo Wayne has sent then launches the narrative into the past, circa World War I to be precise, as Diana recalls battles fought and friends lost.

But first, we're introduced to a younger Diana living on an island called Themyscira. Diana's mother is Queen Hippolyta (Connie Nielsen) of the Amazons. Although she is being groomed to succeed her mother as a thoughtful leader, Diana secretly trains with her aunt, a fiery Amazon fighter named Antiope (Robin Wright). Once Diana's undeniable combat talents are established, the film skips ahead a few years to portray Diana as an adult (Gadot). It is at this point that a handsome pilot (Chris Pine) crashes offshore of the island and Diana rescues him. From the pilot, named Steve Trevor—who is, as A.O. Scott writes in the *New York Times*, "the living embodiment of the phrase 'not all men'"—Diana learns of the events of World War I and ultimately decides to leave the island to join the fight alongside Trevor and his rag-tag cadre of soldiers—thus becoming known as Wonder Woman to the world.

When first created, the character of Wonder Woman was, as A.A. Dowd points out in *The A.V. Club*, "dropped into the chaos of World War II, but [this film] rewinds back one world war, sending the character from a land with no men [instead] to no man's land, where she leads a motley band of brothers [the group is featured in the aforementioned photo delivered to Diana from Bruce Wayne] through the trenches." Diana, it seems, has become convinced that the god of war, Ares, is responsible for the evil that men are doing to one another throughout the world and determines that she must defeat him to restore peace among the peoples of the Earth. While that sounds like rather hefty material for what is ultimately supposed to be a comic-book film, there is never an overwhelming sense of doom that Zach Snyder's offerings to the DC universe have delivered. In fact, as Adam Graham points out in the *Detroit News*, *Wonder Woman* "dazzles in ways we're simply not used to from the DC Comics brand. This is a careful, considerate film that moves at its own pace and takes its time setting up its story and characters, and [this] pays off in a big way once the action gets rolling." Ty Burr concurred with these sentiments when he wrote in the *Boston Globe*, that the film is "the first of the recent wave of DC superhero movies to hold its weight rather than seem grim, glum, and self-serious."

Screenwriter Allan Heinberg—whose previous work consists of a variety of television dramas and comedies, including episodes of *Party of Five*, *Sex and the City*, and *Grey's Anatomy* (to name just a few)—does a surprisingly good job of infusing this super hero story with some actual dramatic heft. Sure, it may get a bit silly in a few parts, as most super hero films wont, but Jenkins never allows *Wonder Woman* to get too far off course and, as Ann Hornaday writes in the *Washington Post*, "injects all the right values...making [the film] swiftly moving, convincing, and legible—and often dazzling to look at." It also helps that the supporting actors rarely misstep during any of their performances.

Above them all though is Gadot, who is positively perfect as Diana/Wonder Woman. Her performance here is, as Moira Macdonald wrote in the *Seattle Times*, "a star making role." It's the kind of perfect performance that is, as Ty Burr notes, "eerily similar to...Christopher Reeve in...*Superman* (1978)." In short, she inhabits the role and it's easy as a viewer to get caught up in the whole thing and simply go along for the ride. Pine is similarly superbly cast as the proto-type hero Trevor, as are most of the companions our hero finds herself assorting with throughout the film.

Ultimately, *Wonder Woman* proves to be such a rousing success that you'll be hard-pressed not to agree with Peter Travers, who wrote in *Rolling Stone*, that "this big-screen outing for William Moulton Marston's creation... leaves the cornball 1970s TV series with Lynda Carter in the dust." It is easily the best of the current DC universe of films and perhaps that bodes well for the brand moving forward.

Michael J. Tyrkus

CREDITS

Diana/Wonder Woman: Gal Gadot
Steve Trevor: Chris Pine
Hippolyta: Connie Nielsen
Antiope: Robin Wright
Ludendorff: Danny Huston
Origin: United States
Language: English, German, Dutch
Released: 2017
Production: Charles Roven, Deborah Snyder, Zack Snyder, Richard Suckle; Atlas Entertainment, Cruel & Unusual Films, DC Entertainment, Tencent Pictures, WanDa Pictures; released by Warner Bros. Pictures

Directed by: Patty Jenkins
Written by: Allan Heinberg
Cinematography by: Matthew Jensen
Music by: Rupert Gregson-Williams
Sound: James Mather
Music Supervisor: Karen Elliott
Editing: Martin Walsh
Art Direction: Dominic Hyman
Costumes: Lindy Hemming
Production Design: Aline Bonetto
MPAA rating: PG-13
Running time: 141 minutes

REVIEWS

Barker, Andrew. *Variety.* May 29, 2017.
Burr, Ty. *Boston Globe.* May 31, 2017.
Dowd, A.A. *The A.V. Club.* May 31, 2017.
Graham, Adam. *Detroit News.* June 1, 2017.
Hornaday, Ann. *Washington Post.* May 31, 2017.
Macdonald, Moira. *Seattle Times.* June 1, 2017.
Phillips, Michael. *Chicago Tribune.* May 29, 2017.
Roeper, Richard. *Chicago Sun-Times.* May 30, 2017.
Scott, A.O. *New York Times.* May 31, 2017.
Travers, Peter. *Rolling Stone.* May 30, 2017.

QUOTES

Queen Hippolyta: "Be careful in the world of men, Diana. They do not deserve you."

TRIVIA

Gal Gadot was a part of re-shoots for the movie (including stunts) while being five months pregnant, so the crew created a costume which included a green screen around her belly, which was later removed during post-production.

WONDERSTRUCK

It's not what you look at that matters, it's what you see.
—Movie tagline

Box Office: $1.1 Million

When Martin Scorsese made *Hugo* (2011), it felt like a grand departure from his other work. Here was one of America's most esteemed directors taking a major detour from his usual examination of gangsters, New York history, and dark tales of anti-heroes and historical figures and, instead, making a kid-friendly 3-D fantasy film with robots, pratfalls, and wondrous special effects. Scorsese seemed to be tapping into his inner-Spielberg for the first time, and while many fans scoffed at that notion, *Hugo* itself turned out to be a true cinematic gift, not just for fans of the original source material, but for cinephiles who felt that 3-D had nothing to offer aside from being a promotional gimmick. The film felt like a labor of love for Scorsese, who clearly had an affection for the silent film era, upon which Brian Selznick's novel had been partly based. The moment when Georges Méliès' *A Trip to the Moon* (1902) comes to life in modern-day 3-D was one of the major cinematic high points of 2011.

Now comes Todd Haynes, no less respected and always open to taking risks, taking his turn in adapting a Selznick novel, *Wonderstruck,* to the screen, a novel every bit as multi-layered and full of leaps in logic as its predecessor. Again, supporters of Haynes' work seemed perplexed as to his decision to try his hand at making a film aimed at young people that ties itself together at the end so that everyone walks out happy. No ambiguity, no irony and no grand statements on the human condition. It is, like *Hugo*, a loving throwback to another era of filmmaking, but without doubling down on what Scorsese had already accomplished. It is a heartfelt and sentimental work that Haynes biggest admirers might not warm up to quite as much as the young fans of the novel. That disconnect is unfortunate, but probably inevitable.

When one looks at these two cinematic works, side by side, there is no telling who the auteur is behind either one of them, yet it appears the two films could have come from the same director. This is due in no small part to Selznick, whose books are ripe for the finest visual artists to try and adapt. When one opens one of his books, it becomes clear as to why it attracts directors such as Scorsese and Haynes. They are, in large part, storyboards, beautifully rendered in gorgeous, detailed pencil drawings. Page after page takes the viewer through what would probably be a dolly or crane shot, all allowing his story to be told visually, alternating between artful sketches and traditional written narrative. The books look massive, but can be finished in a day or two, giving young readers a sense of accomplishment from having finished something so thick, while also possibly inspiring them to become writers, sketch artists, or even filmmakers.

It also helps that the stories incorporate a little film history within them. With *Wonderstruck,* though, it is less in the foreground this time. The story takes place in two times and places. In 1977, young Ben (Oakes Fegley) lives with his Aunt and Uncle in Gunflint, Minnesota after the death of his mother. He never knew his father. One night, at his old house (which is conveniently located next door to his Aunt and Uncle's house), he finds some artifacts that indicate clues of his father's life. That same night, Ben gets struck by lightning, which renders him deaf. When he wakes in the hospital, he can no longer hear himself speak. Looking out the window of his hospital room, though, he sees a bus station. With the help of his cousin Janet (Morgan Turner) and some money stashed away that he found in his old house, Ben escapes, hops on a bus and heads for New York in search of a book store and the American Museum of Natural History.

The other half of *Wonderstruck* takes place in Hoboken, New Jersey in 1927 where a young deaf girl named Rose (Millicent Simmonds) lives with her domineering and unsympathetic father. She mostly stays secluded and locked in her room, but she escapes and takes refuge in a movie theater where she watches a film starring a renowned actress named Lillian Mayhew (Julianne Moore), who is actually her mother. With several newspaper clippings in hand, Rose escapes the confines of her unpleasant household and takes a ferry to New York, where she hopes to meet her mother and maybe even other family members. Her journey also takes her to the American Museum of Natural History.

The film then bounces back and forth between these two stories, which run parallel, of course, but only in terms of narrative similarities. When Ben is about to meet someone significant to his story, Rose does as well. Unlike Rose, though, Ben has an ally in his quest, a boy his age named Jamie (Jaden Michael), whose father is a security guard at the museum. Jamie hides Ben in one of the storage rooms where workers seldom enter. He brings Ben food every day and there are plenty of artifacts lying about that can lead to more clues. Ben's biggest find so far is a book called "Wonderstruck," which was written fifty years ago, about the history of museums and their curators.

The soul of the story, though, is the quest for belonging amid a feeling of isolation, a theme Haynes has explored in the past. While the quest here is more literal, it is not at the expense of risk-taking for Haynes and his team. Just as Selznick's books are half illustrated, half written, Haynes film honors that aesthetic by having Rose's story told as a black-and-white silent film. The flow between this device and the more traditional color storyline is not as jarring as one would expect, mainly because Ben's story is also told visually as much as possible. Ed Lachman's cinematography shifts between a sometimes grainy black-and-white to a darker shade of color where there is little in the way of unmotivated light. A pivotal scene where Ben tells Jamie of his predicament is kept in dark shadows so as not to paint too bright a picture of this moment.

The silent film portion of *Wonderstruck* would not work if Haynes had not employed an expressive and charming young actress to lead it. Simmonds is a real find and it goes to show how casting someone who actually has the ailment of the character (Simmonds is deaf in real life) can go a long way toward achieving authenticity. Simmonds beautifully expresses the pain, desperation and loneliness of someone lost in a world where there are many visual wonders, but few saviors for her existence. The other important element to this side of the story is composer Carter Burwell, who always seems to find the right sonic texture of every film score he composes (see just about every Coen Brothers film). He keeps the music cues delicate and vibrant, often in the same note.

The other side of the story does not fare quite as well. As good as *Wonderstruck* looks and as faithful as it is to the book, there is a sense that Haynes is out of his element a little too much in the opening scenes as well as some of the more dramatic scenes on Ben's side. There are scenes that could have benefitted from a couple more takes or a few more re-writes so that they ring a little truer and not as contrived. Early in the film, for example, Ben finds Janet dressed in his mother's clothes. He immediately has a fit about it. But because we know so little about Ben and because Fegley has been given a scene in which he has to suddenly act angry, that is what the viewer sees—someone acting angry. Fegley is a good child actor, as evidenced in his starring role in *Pete's Dragon* (2016), but Haynes seems to have no feel for scenes like this (and others in *Wonderstruck*), which is odd considering how much of an actor's director he has always been.

Still, one never gets the sense that Haynes is taking a break from being a unique storyteller or selling out to make a crowd pleaser. The silent film aspect alone helps the movie live up to its title and the final act is another Haynes creation that recalls, of all things, his breakthrough cult item *Superstar: The Karen Carpenter Story* (1988), utilizing a gimmick or stills, models, and dolls that makes sense for this story and is not just there for the sake of it. Haynes is even playful with the music. David Bowie's song "Space Oddity" becomes an important piece of the puzzle (at least in the book), but Haynes resists any urge to have the song blasting to underscore a pivotal moment. Likewise, instead of bringing in Burwell to give dramatic weight to an important encounter or even the final scene, he uses the soul/funk version of Strauss's "Also Sprach Zarathustra" (aka, the theme from *2001: A Space Odyssey* [1968]).

Such flourishes might not be enough for Haynes's most die-hard fans who are hoping for more in the way of complexity, experimentation, and ambiguity. *Wonderstruck* might be looked at as Hayne's biggest failure to date, yet it very much has a place in his filmography. Haynes is a humanist, always interested in finding a place in the world for his troubled, isolated protagonists.

That is no different here. While the book and the film *Wonderstruck* are filled with unbearable coincidences and contrived moments, one has to take into consideration that this was written with young people in mind, readers who don't often question such improbabilities. What is true of the book is true of the film and Haynes seems excited by that notion and runs with it. His audience might not be running with him, but it remains a thrill to see an artist such as this take the risk anyway.

Collin Souter

CREDITS

Ben: Oakes Fegley
Lillian Mayhew/Rose: Julianne Moore
Elaine: Michelle Williams
Rose: Millicent Simmonds
Older Walter: Tom Noonan
Origin: United States
Language: English
Released: 2017
Production: Pamela Koffler, John Sloss, Christine Vachon; Cinetic Media L.L.C., FilmNation Entertainment, Killer Films, Picrow; released by Amazon Studios
Directed by: Todd Haynes
Written by: Brian Selznick
Cinematography by: Edward Lachman
Music by: Carter Burwell
Music Supervisor: Randall Poster
Editing: Affonso Goncalves
Art Direction: Ryan Heck; Kim Jennings
Costumes: Sandy Powell
Production Design: Mark Friedberg
MPAA rating: PG
Running time: 117 minutes

REVIEWS

Dargis, Manohla. *New York Times.* October 19, 2017.
Dowd, A.A. *The A.V. Club.* May 18, 2017.
Ebiri, Belge. *Village Voice.* October 18, 2017.
Ehrlich, David. *IndieWire.* May 18, 2017.
Kaufman, Sophie Monks. *Sight and Sound.* May 24, 2017.
Lemire, Christy. *RogerEbert.com.* October 20, 2017.
Pond, Steve. *TheWrap.* May 26, 2017.
Stewart, Sara. *New York Post.* October 19, 2017.
Turan, Kenneth. *Los Angeles Times.* October 19, 2017.
Yoshida, Emily. *New York magazine.* May 18, 2017.

TRIVIA

Actress Millicent Simmonds sent a recording of her audition to director Todd Haynes, who in turn sent it to actress Julianne Moore, who instantly approved of casting the 14-year-old Simmonds.

WOODSHOCK

Box Office: $42,603

Following in the footsteps of Tom Ford, who turned from fashion to filmmaking with the excellent *A Single Man* (2009) and the deeply silly and pretentious *Nocturnal Animals* (2016), sister designers Kate and Laura Mulleavy have made their debut film. It's not surprising that the resulting product from the Rodarte founders is somewhere between both of Ford's films, nowhere near as profound as it imagines itself to be, but quite lovely and mesmerizing in places. Looking at times like an extended ad for a strange new clothing brand, the melancholy *Woodshock* is a study in loss of several stripes. Their hero experiences loss of self, loss of loved ones, loss of direction, loss of purpose, loss of desire, and loss of sense in the course of a curiously over-yet-understuffed 100 minutes. The film wants to go many places without ever leaving the small California town in which it transpires, but like its protagonist, can't decide on a direction.

Theresa (Kirsten Dunst) is a salesman at a specialty weed store. Her mother (Susan Traylor) is dying slowly and painfully of an illness, which gives her the idea to administer a fatal dose of a drug supplied by her boss Keith (Pilou Asbæk) to end her suffering. She goes through with it but can't seem to pick herself up off the ground after her mother passes, even though her mother agreed to the euthanasia plan. Theresa mopes around the house most of the time, confusing and enervating her working-class boyfriend Nick (Joe Cole). Keith tries to get her to be more social, to spend time at the shop, but when she does wind up going to parties, she mostly just keeps to herself. The only thing that snaps her out of her stupor, though not in the way Keith or Nick hope, is when a man named Ed (Steph DuVall) walks into the shop looking for her. Ed and Theresa have a history of some sort and Theresa is none too happy to see the old man. She stews for a few days after seeing him and then decides to poison him with the same drug she used to mercy kill her mother. The only problem is her friend Johnny (Jack Kilmer) stops in first and takes Ed's fatal dose by mistake.

Keith panics and tries to get Theresa to help him cover up the murder but Theresa is uninterested in helping him or anyone else. She takes to working on some abstruse construction project in the middle of the night. Is she sleepwalking, as she tells Nick, or is she trying to take out her frustrations with her situation in some strange way only she understands. Regardless, she makes herself a batch of weed, rolled into a handful of joints that are laced with a strong hallucinogen and starts burning through them as she sets about closing up loose ends. She pays vengeful visits to Keith and Ed as she begins having increasingly distressful visions of herself in the woods. The only question is whether she's actually performing these violent acts or merely hallucinating them.

The hallucinations are the most interesting part of *Woodshock,* and also why the film does not work as a feature. In order for a movie to build to a climactic bit of fourth-wall breaking visual showmanship in the vein of *2001: A Space Odyssey* (1968), the template for films with this structure, it needs to be able to support such an ending thematically as well as visually. *Woodshock* does not have much in the way of a story and its few strands never cohere to form a compelling whole. The death of Theresa's mother is only partially supported by the presence of Ed and her decision to kill him, except that it's never made explicit what Ed means to Theresa's overall story. He's an ominous figure, but he's too vague to work as the piece's villain, so he's a blank much like Johnny or Joe. Johnny's traitlessness doesn't harm the film because he's just a device to send Theresa into her tailspin. Joe's relative shapelessness as a character is more of a problem. He seems to tolerate Theresa more than he loves her, and they don't talk about anything of substance. Their relationship doesn't make much sense, but that could be because it's difficult to get a fix on Theresa as anything but a depressed accident waiting to happen. She starts and ends the film a nearly mute wreck, so depressed she's essentially catatonic. Identifying with her can only be done from the surface because her pain is defined by one event. No insight into her life before depression transformed her is given and the Mulleavy sisters use her pain as a vessel for their visual motifs, so they don't feel the need to apply rules or boundaries to it. She just is, moving through life like a sleepwalker, which makes for a few arresting visuals but not much of a character study. The practically achieved visual tricks are stunning and if the film were simply 25 minutes of double-exposed images of Dunst floating in a redwood forest, it would have made for an unforgettable short film. As a feature, there is not enough substance to make *Woodshock* the study of grief or the work of midnight movie imagination it tries to be.

Scout Tafoya

CREDITS

Theresa: Kirsten Dunst
Nick: Joe Cole
Keith: Pilou Asbaek
Ed: Steph Duvall
Johnny: Jack Kilmer
Origin: United States
Language: English
Released: 2017
Production: Michael Costigan, Ken Kao, Ben LeClair, K.K. Barrett; COTA Films, Waypoint Entertainment; released by A24 Films LLC
Directed by: Kate Mulleavy; Laura Mulleavy
Written by: Kate Mulleavy; Laura Mulleavy
Cinematography by: Peter Flinckenberg
Music by: Peter Raeburn
Sound: Per Sundstrom
Music Supervisor: Linda Cohen
Editing: Julia Bloch; Dino Jonsater
Art Direction: Celine Diano
Costumes: Kate Mulleavy; Laura Mulleavy; Christie Wittenborn
Production Design: K.K. Barrett
MPAA rating: R
Running time: 100 minutes

REVIEWS

Burr, Ty. *Boston Globe.* September 27, 2017.
Catsoulis, Jeannette. *Time Out London.* September 20, 2017.
Lemire, Christy. *RogerEbert.com.* September 23 2017.
Lodge, Guy *Variety.* September 12, 2017.
Rife, Katie. *The A.V. Club.* September 20, 2017.
Romney, Jonathan. *Screen International.* September 12, 2017.
Stewart, Henry. *Slant Magazine.* September 20, 2017.
White, Dave. *TheWrap.* September 22, 2017.
Yoshida, Emily. *New York Magazine.* September 22, 2017.
Zilberman, Alan. *Washington Post.* September 28, 2017.

TRIVIA

Some scenes were shot in the town of Arcata in Humboldt County, which is located in Northern California, where the Mulleavy sisters grew up.

THE WORK

Box Office: $5,853

Jairus McLeary and Gethin Aldous's *The Work* feels like a balm for a time in which empathy is in increasingly short supply. It allows for the idea that people who have committed horrible crimes are still human, still in need of emotional support, and still open to redemption. It is a simple and yet incredibly effective documentary about the way men who have both been wounded themselves and wounded others find ways to heal. It does not excuse these criminals for their crimes, but asks viewers to realize that these people are still human beings in need of empathy.

Since 2003, court videographer Jairus McLeary has been traveling from Illinois to the infamous Folsom

State Prison in Sacramento, California twice a year for what is basically men's group therapy. Prisoners break off into groups and talk about their pasts and their fears. The filmmakers do little to get in the way of what unfolds, which is a formal choice in and of itself. They make the viewers participants in the process, often placing the camera in a position in the circle in a way to make it feel like an observer in the group instead of an outsider.

As with any documentary like this, faces start to emerge from the crowd. As former Aryan Brothers, Crips, and Bloods look at each other nervously, walls start to fall. Although they do so with a pattern that something about the way men heal. In most instances of a truly notable breakthrough, a participant typically huffs and puffs and claims that this isn't possibly going to work for them. It's as if they have to verbalize their concern by trying to push away healing. They couldn't possibly fall for this therapy stuff as society and their lives have taught them to be "macho" and "masculine." *The Work* becomes a fascinating commentary on perceptions of masculinity as the film captures men going through the phases of them, thinking that any sort of emotional response will be perceived as a sign of weakness.

The filmmakers are also wise to start to focus on a few faces and stories instead of letting everyone blur into one story. The film settles primarily on three men and the three others who serve as their guides through a process that feels almost ancient at times. When true breakthroughs happen, sounds emerge from these men that almost do not sound human, as if demons are being released from deep inside. There's also something remarkable about watching people truly listen to one another. Men who have been through this process before often serve as support just by being there and looking the new participants square in the eyes.

Patterns of behavior and common histories start to emerge. Stories of fathers and sons become recurrent, but the film never becomes a work designed to excuse criminal behavior. In fact, the film rarely details why these men are even in prison. A lesser version of the film would have drawn a straight line from past to crime to healing but *The Work* realizes this is all more complex than that. And by not focusing on the crimes, the film avoids salacious details or easy moral judgement on the part of the viewer.

One has to wonder how much of what unfolds in *The Work* is at least a little performative. Of course, the prisoners knew they were being filmed and behavior is different in front of a camera. It's hard to say how that impacted their process. And we don't learn much about the entire process—like how people are chosen for this event. However, the film ends on the note that one hopes it would from the beginning, revealing via a title card how much this system has truly worked. Recidivism rates from those who participate in the program are lower than those who do not. In other words, empathy is effective. Redemption is possible. Healing can happen anywhere. And a film this powerful should be seen by everyone who has anything to do with our legal or prison system. It may actually impact policy and structure, and one hopes more programs like this pop up around the country, recognizing that therapy is a key a part of any civilized country's system of incarceration.

Brian Tallerico

CREDITS

Origin: United States

Language: English

Released: 2017

Production: Eon McLeary, Miles McLeary, Alice Henty, Angela Sostre, Jairus McLeary; Blanket Fort Media; released by Topic

Directed by: Jairus McLeary; Gethin Aldous

Cinematography by: Arturo Santamaria

Editing: Amy Foote

MPAA rating: Unrated

Running time: 89 minutes

REVIEWS

Abele, Robert. *TheWrap*. October 25, 2017.

Anderson, Matthew. *CineVue*. September 10, 2017.

Bowen, Chuck. *Slant Magazine*. October 23, 2017.

Catsoulis, Jeannette. *New York Times*. October 26, 2017.

Debruge, Peter. *Variety*. March 30, 2017.

Glasby, Matt. *Total Film*. September 6, 2017.

Goldstein, Gary. *Los Angeles Times*. October 26, 2017.

Kohn, Eric. *IndieWire*. March 16, 2017.

Linden, Sheri. *Hollywood Reporter*. March 16, 2017.

Murthi, Vikram. *RogerEbert.com*. October 26, 2017.

TRIVIA

This film was originally made in 2009.

WORMWOOD

The untold true story of the CIA, LSD experiments, and the death of a family man.
—Movie tagline

In 1953, a young boy named Eric Olson was told his father, Frank, had committed suicide by jumping from a hotel room window in New York late at night during Thanksgiving weekend. Eric was only nine years old when this happened. The Olson family went through life devastated, obviously, but also under the illusion that their patriarch had suffered a mental breakdown and decided to end it all by jumping straight through a window. A few questions lingered about this scenario. Did he really jump out? Seeing as there were no balconies at this hotel, in order to really jump out of this window, one would have to take a running leap and break through some pretty thick glass. Would that be possible? "Fell" from a window. "Jumped" from a window. Eric heard both of these words and spent the better part of his life trying to make sense of it all.

Then, in 1975, a *New York Times* reporter named Seymour Hersh broke a story about a report that detailed a CIA experiment involving LSD in 1953, in which Frank Olson had been the guinea pig. During that week in November, Frank had been summoned to Deep Creek Lake in Maryland by his superiors. Within this remote cabin, Frank drank from a glass of water that had been laced with a drug that the CIA might later use as a truth serum (if it worked). Ten days later, after experiencing bouts with depression, paranoia, and a general belief that he had said too much when under the influence, Frank took his own life. Or did he? Did he say too much? Was it possible he said incriminating things when under the influence of LSD? It is possible he may have been too much of a security risk for the agency and therefore had to be, for lack of a better term, let go?

Soon after the story broke in 1975, Eric Olson and his family had been invited to the White House by President Gerald Ford, who apologized for Frank Olson dying at the hands of an experiment run by the government. An apology from a President in this situation is a rare thing, which is why the Olsons warmed up to the administration's suggestion that the family try their case through Congress instead of going through the courts. Seemed like a good idea at the time until they had reached a settlement that turned out to be less than what they had expected. There had also been some language in the documents they received that barred them from ever talking about the case ever again. This was hush money and the Olsons were expected to take it and go away. Yet, over the next three decades, the case kept resurfacing, either through additional documents being discovered or those involved coming forward with new information.

Forty years after the original story broke, the Netflix series documentary *Wormwood* aired, directed by Errol Morris, whose most effective investigative piece, *The Thin Blue Line* (1988), helped set a man free from death row. Told over the course of six episodes, each one around 45-minutes long, *Wormwood* combs through layers of facts that don't add up while talking to the family's attorneys, Hersh and, mainly, Eric Olson himself, who will carry the burden and the weight of this investigation on his shoulders for the rest of his life. Much like *The Thin Blue Line*, the endgame for Morris is to instill a certain amount of distrust in the viewer of every fact that has been laid out, much like what Eric has been going through his whole life. The viewer binge-watches it, but Eric lives it.

Morris also goes many steps further in his reenactments, which has always been a staple in his work. The reenactment scenes here have been filmed and acted with an uncommon amount of artistry and gravitas. This device often comes off as a distraction and usually acted by unknowns who have been given poor direction. Here, Frank Olson is played by Peter Sarsgaard, who can convey all of Frank's pain and uncertainty without having to say much, giving the viewer even more of a reason to care for the victims in this story, even as Morris cuts away from him to a talking head interview. The reenactments alone could have made for an effective 90-minute movie with Sarsgaard and the rest of the cast assembled here. Morris and his crew frame each darkly-lit shot meticulously, creating a thriller with just the right amount of dread and sadness. The viewer knows the outcome of this story, but Sarsgaard and the rest of the cast (Tim Blake Nelson, Christian Camargo, Scott Shephard, and Bob Balaban, to name just a few) still manage to turn in performances that keep the viewer enrapt rather than distracted.

In a way, this is a return to form for Morris, who has crafted quite an ingenious thriller here in the way only he can produce. With a score by Paul Leonard-Morgan (which sounds very much like the kind of music Philip Glass would contribute), *Wormwood* has that same kind of rhythm and urgency to it that has been a trademark style for Morris throughout his career. Steven Hathaway's editing, likewise, has a fluidity that makes the daunting task of working in newsreel footage, talking head interviews, and beautifully crafted reenactments look effortless. There is also a playfulness that lets the viewer in on the process. Whenever Eric or anyone says a key phrase, it is repeated while showing virtually every camera angle in the room at the same time. Morris has the correct instinct for knowing when the audience's ears will perk up during an interview and knows when to underscore the moment.

Wormwood's dense story works well within the framework of a mini-series and Morris clearly feels comfortable with the format. No longer confined to a single two-hour movie structure, he is able to dig deep here, going so far as to investigate Eric's obsession with creating collages and how this story has many parallels to *Hamlet*. These are not sidebar indulgences, but further clues and layers into the story that might have otherwise had to have been cut out. Netflix had a huge success a couple years prior with their documentary series *Making a Murderer* (2015), which helped bring a death row case back to light and generated major public support to have two men exonerated. *Wormwood* likely will not have that same effect, but Netflix probably hoped for that same kind of addictive conversation starter. Time will tell if *Wormwood* becomes a key talking point with regards to conspiracy theories or government distrust, but it makes for an unforgettable viewing experience regardless.

Collin Souter

CREDITS

Frank Olson: Peter Sarsgaard
Dr. Robert Lashbrook: Christian Camargo
Himself: Eric Olson
Vincent Ruwet: Scott Shepherd
Sidney Gottlieb: Tim Blake Nelson
Origin: United States
Language: English
Released: 2017
Production: Sean Garrett Fogel, Tessa Treadway, Julie Ahlberg, Jesse Wann, Steven Hathaway; Fourth Floor Productions, Moxie Pictures; released by Netflix
Directed by: Errol Morris
Written by: Kieran Fitzgerald; Steven Hathaway; Molly Rokosz
Cinematography by: Ellen Kuras; Igor Martinovic
Music by: Paul Leonard-Morgan
Sound: Skip Lievsay
Music Supervisor: Susan Jacobs
Editing: Steven Hathaway
Art Direction: Anne Goelz; Eugenia Magann Haynes
Costumes: Catherine Riley; Jennifer Rogien
Production Design: Tommaso Ortino; Meredith Boswell
MPAA rating: Unrated
Running time: 241 minutes

REVIEWS

Ali, Lorraine. *Los Angeles Times*. December 14, 2017.
Gilbert, Matthew. *Boston Globe*. December 13, 2017.
Gilbert, Sophie. *The Atlantic*. December 18, 2017.
Kohn, Eric. *IndieWire*. December 13, 2017.
Murthi, Vikram. *The A.V. Club*. December 19, 2017.
Sachs, Ben. *Chicago Reader*. December 26, 2017.
Scott, A.O. *New York Times*. December 14, 2017.
Seitz, Matt Zoller. *Vulture*. December 14, 2017.
Stuever, Hank. *Washington Post*. December 14, 2017.
Syme, Rachel. *New Republic*. December 13, 2017.

TRIVIA

This story revolves around the story of a mid-1950s CIA experimentation program, code named "MK Ultra."

AWARDS

Nominations:

Directors Guild 2017: Documentary Director (Morris)

X-Z

XXX: RETURN OF XANDER CAGE

Kick some ass, get the girl, and try to look dope while you're doing it.
—Movie tagline

There are no more patriots, just rebels and tyrants.
—Movie tagline

Box Office: $44.9 Million

Few films of 2017 felt as truly international as *xXx: Return of Xander Cage*. The movie travels from Brazil to New York to the Dominican Republic to London to the Philippines to humble Detroit, Michigan with a cast just as global. A secret agent team composed of Xiang (Donnie Yen), Serena Unger (Deepika), and Talon (Tony Jaa), all generically well-versed in the leatherbound acrobatic martial arts that make up modern movie spycraft, steals a dangerous device with the power to down satellites. This is terrible news for anyone living in the world, which is directly underneath those orbiting satellites, so the CIA (led by a villainous Toni Collette) decides to bring back the wild, but effective "xXx Program" in order to retrieve the object. The third in the action-adventure series, this installment sees its original protagonist Cage (Vin Diesel) return from a self-imposed exile after faking his death in the first film of the series.

Though the machinations of the previous two films offer callbacks and minor fan services (like the strangely nostalgic appearance of a gaudy floor-length and fur-lined leather jacket received as a gift from a Russian crime lord) the real treat in the film is its willingness to shed modern film shackles of narrative importance for the gleeful rebellion of pure action. When Cage prepares to undertake his mission, he's so unimpressed with the military squares provided to him that he jettisons them out of the plane. He then recruits his own team of heavily-tattooed rebels, including Nicks (Kris Wu), Adele (Ruby Rose), and Tennyson (Rory McCann). All these characters are introduced with a Chinese-style freeze-frame (seen particularly in this year's *Railroad Tigers* [2017]) that includes comic bits of personal information, such as their favorite karaoke song or number of cars crashed.

Yes, of course "number of cars crashed" is a piece of comic information, at least in the *xXx* world. This is an imagining of action cinema not only as multiculturalist (especially with the self-described "ambiguous ethnic" Diesel as both protagonist and producer), but as violent celebration that sometimes dips into parody. Diesel's other action franchise with a new installment this year, *The Fast and the Furious*, takes a similar stance towards its action, but focuses primarily on large vehicular mayhem. Here, director D.J. Caruso finds plenty to enjoy in the pleasures of Yen's brutally technical martial arts and Diesel's contagious glee while controlling smaller, more personal means of transportation—whether that means skiing down a rainforest or riding a modified aquatic motorcycle into the barrel of a well-shaped wave.

That these actions are palatable rather than boring or unmotivated, is the strength of the film's sense of tone. There's a sense of humor about its own premise that permeates the movie and allows the technobabble to intermingle with the spy lingo in such a way that they bolster the following absurd action. The plot is full of betrayals, realignments, and globetrotting that all seem like the barest connective tissue. Thankfully, that's never the point, though the film can sometimes get bogged down in its own ridiculous rhetoric. The point comes when these neo-liberal, anarchist rebels continue to pull stunts, gunfight, and car chase for a greater good outside of the establishment. The kineticism and youthful creativity keep scenes so fresh that we're gaping instead of scratching our heads, but also drive home what an action hero might look like in a technologically-interlinked world. Some traditional action sequences may be well executed, like a gunfight in a tall stairwell that focuses on counting spent ammunition, but the crux of the film relies on the same virality as a popular internet video. This becomes the film's language, and its anxiety. The fear of a surveillance state is translated into both plot (with our orbiting communication technology used against us) and the futuristic aesthetic in the settings. The members of *xXx* may be indistinguishable characters, but they are all members of a completely identifiable generation.

Jacob Oller

CREDITS

Xander Cage: Vin Diesel
Xiang: Donnie Yen
Serena Unger: Deepika Padukone
Talon: Tony Jaa
Becky Claridge: Nina Dobrev
Origin: United States
Language: English, French, Portuguese, Spanish
Released: 2017
Production: Jeff Kirschenbaum, Joe Roth, Samantha Vincent, Vin Diesel; Huahua Media, Shanghai Film Group Corp; released by Paramount Pictures Corp.
Directed by: D.J. Caruso
Written by: F. Scott Frazier
Cinematography by: Russell Carpenter
Music by: Robert Lydecker; Brian Tyler
Sound: Karen Baker Landers
Editing: Vince Filippone; Jim Page
Art Direction: Aleksandra Marinkovich
Costumes: Kimberly Tillman
Production Design: Jon Billington
MPAA rating: PG-13
Running time: 96 minutes

REVIEWS

Crump, Andy. *Paste Magazine*. January 25, 2017.
Dry, Jude. *IndieWire*. January 24, 2017.
Duralde, Alonso. *TheWrap*. January 19, 2017.
Graham, Adam. *Detroit News*. January 20, 2017.
Huddleston, Tom. *Time Out*. January 23, 2017.
Kenny, Glenn. *RogerEbert.com*. January 21, 2017.
LaSalle, Mick. *San Francisco Chronicle*. January 20, 2017.
Pickett, Leah. *Chicago Reader*. January 26, 2017.
Rife, Katy. *The A.V. Club*. January 20, 2017.
Walsh, Katy. *Los Angeles Times*. January 19, 2017.

QUOTES

Darius Stone: "Rock, paper, scissors, grenade launcher."

TRIVIA

This film was originally going to be a direct sequel to the first film in the series, ignoring *xXx: State of the Union* (2005).

YOUR NAME

(Kimi no na wa.)

Box Office: $5 Million

American animation studios have been stuck creatively for so many years now that one often has to search outside the studio system to find true works of art. For every artistically successful Pixar, DreamWorks, or Laika film, there are dozens of forgettable, sitcom-level time-killers that serve more purpose as a 90-minute babysitter than a fulfilling cinematic experience (even for a silly comedy). Creative stagnation can be true of any animation studio in any country, though. Even the animated TV shows and movies that come out of Japan have a sameness about them that can be frustrating. So when a movie like *Your Name.* (its original title being *Kimi no na wa*) breaks out of the doldrums of anime and reaches a wide, appreciative audience in the United States, it should not be taken for granted. With a premise that will make any Young Adult novelist envious, *Your Name.* goes for greatness beyond just as a piece of animation, and succeeds.

The exposition necessary to tell this story seems daunting. Basically, there are two teenagers who live far from each other. Taki (voiced by Ryûnosuke Kamiki) lives in Tokyo and works nights as a waiter at a busy Tokyo restaurant. Mitsuha (voiced by Mone Kamishiraishi) lives in a small village called Itomori with her father (voiced by Kaito Ishikawa), sister Yotsuha (voiced by Kanon Tani), and grandmother (voiced by Sayaka Ohara). She yearns to escape the lifeless and seemingly uncultured small town and move to the big city. Both characters have the same problem. When they sleep, they inhabit the other person's life for an entire day.

Taki wakes up as Mitsuha and has to live her life not knowing anything about her. When he goes to sleep as Mitsuha, he wakes up as his normal self and has vague memories of the life he just led. The same is true for Mitsuha. She wakes up as Taki and has to live his life.

Their friends and family members seem perplexed about how sometimes Taki and Mitsuha cannot remember their odd behavior from the previous day. "It's like you had amnesia," they say, referring to how it appears they cannot remember what school they go to or where they work. Every other day, it seems, Mitsuha's sister Yotsuha catches Mitsuha touching her own breasts uncontrollably, when, in fact, it is Taki who is inhabiting her body and getting used to the feel of it. Taki, meanwhile, sometimes exhibits a more feminine side that his friends have never seen before. He suddenly has a knack for sewing and now, every so often, has an odd accent. When Taki's friends talk of going to a café, Taki is unusually excited about the idea because Mitsuha dreams of such a thing in her own small town where a trip to a café translates into getting an energy drink from a vending machine.

They wake up every day trying to sort all this out. They look at their smartphones every morning and find all kinds of activity on them that has disrupted their lives. Taki has a crush on one of his co-workers and Mitsuha, when inhabiting his body, has taken steps toward him getting a date with her. Eventually, once they both figure out what is happening with them and their dreams, they leave messages for each other in the form of notebook scribblings, notes in their phones, and messages written on their arms for each to see when they wake up the next day. They work out a system of rules and schedules so they can make this disposition as smooth as possible. One of their more amusing complications has to do with how much of Taki's money Mitsuha spends indulging in exotic foods at the café (exotic for her, anyway). He has to work extra hours to keep up with her habits.

The movie establishes its premise in a very succinct way. The difficult exposition is surprisingly very economical. Once these two characters find out that they are living each other's lives, the revelation is both funny and rewarding. It is done through a very skillfully edited and very energetic montage sequence, which in and of itself is a brave choice for such a pivotal moment in the film. By revealing this premise in that way, writer-director Makoto Shinkai shows great confidence and leaves the viewer with the feeling of great anticipation of what is going to happen next. The sequence is as much about the body-switching idea as it is about teenage self discovery and the pains of puberty. The moment of discovery happens early on and the movie takes a detour from farcical elements to something far more poetic and meaningful.

The body-switching stops and they make an attempt to meet each other, but they don't have all the information necessary to make the encounter happen. Also, there exists a comet in the sky that has everyone's attention, which would appear to be an unnecessary subplot, but turns out to be anything but. The comet breaks apart adding a further complication to their lives and their predicament. The movie miraculously does not crumble under the weight of all of the narrative threads that take place here. It remains lucid and easy to digest. Even the sidebar of Mitsuha's grandmother taking her grandchildren on a pilgrimage to see an old temple of the Gods and teaching them metaphors on sewing threads and their relation to time and space adds a spiritual element to the story that feels wholly natural and unforced.

Your Name. has a lot going on and it is to Shinkai's credit that the viewer can be carried along without experiencing any kind of tonal whiplash. While the movie has moments of high comedy, romantic tension, devastation, and fantasy, it never hits a false note. Shinkai rarely goes for obvious moments. For example, the first date sequence between Taki and his co-worker Okudera (voiced by Masami Nagasawa) has all the elements of a farce. Taki is going out on this date because Mitsuha said and did all the right things as him. Now, he is himself and has no idea what to do. Rather than play up all the comedic possibilities of everyone behaving idiotically, Shinkai instead focuses on the insecurity and the hopelessness of the situation in a very sensitive and meaningful way that makes it oddly dreamlike and kind of beautiful. Likewise, later in the film, at an incredibly crucial moment involving the two heroes, Shinkai injects humor at just the right time, completely pulling the rug out from under the audience, who will no doubt take pleasure in the surprise.

Like many of the best animators, Shinkai approaches this as a live-action film that happens to be animated. *Your Name.* has been designed in a way that shows Shinkai has a fondness for massive amounts of coverage in every scene. The cutaways are plentiful and give the movie a fluidity and urgency that is uncommon in animation. It is the kind of movie a director like Danny Boyle would be proud to have his name on, full of exhilarating fast-paced sequences that are a feast for the eyes and ears. Shinkai loves details and filling the screen with deep colors and striking imagery, even within the mundane. The recurring shot of the sliding doors never wears out its welcome and the rack focus shots are as exquisite as anything done in live action.

Some Western audiences might be put off with the amount of songs thrown into the mix. The lyrics, for the most part, come subtitled when the lack of dialogue allows for it. The device can be a bit much for some viewers to try and take it all in, particularly during the film's opening, but it is a common anime trope and one that this film uses wisely and in just the right amounts. The songs are the movie's least important element, though, and will not be remembered much beyond initial viewing. Thankfully, they neither really hurt nor help the film as a whole. The instrumental score by Radwimps is gorgeous, though, and never too intrusive. Shinkai has all the right instincts for when to use music and when to drop it.

Much of the second half of the film is focused on whether or not these two characters will meet, and the viewer always hopes that they do. The complications that keep them apart are enormous and impossible to predict. Even when the story takes on more apocalyptic matters in the second half, *Your Name.* never loses momentum or the sense of adventure and fun it established in the first half. Shinkai clearly loves these characters and wants to give his audience an emotionally satisfying payoff. His work is not widely known in the States, but *Your Name.* brought him his biggest audience yet and in a year that was not exactly rife with memorable animated films (though technically a 2016 film, it was released in the States in 2017). *Your Name.* has the kind of crowd-pleasing magic that could inspire a big American studio to do a live-action remake. If that day should come, it will be a tall order to replicate the kind of experience Shinkai has created for his audience, one that rewards in just about every way imaginable.

Collin Souter

CREDITS

Voice of Taki Tachibana: Ryunosuke Kamiki
Voice of Mitsuha Miyamizu: Mone Kamishiraishi
Voice of Katsuhiko Teshigawara: Ryo Narita
Voice of Sayaka Natori: Aoi Yuki
Voice of Tsukasa Fujii: Nobunaga Shimazaki
Origin: United States
Language: Japanese
Released: 2017
Production: Koichiro Ito, Genki Kawamura, Katsuhiro Takei; AMUSE Inc., CoMix Wave Films; released by FUNimation Entertainment
Directed by: Makoto Shinkai
Written by: Makoto Shinkai; Clark Cheng
Cinematography by: Makoto Shinkai
Music by: Radwimps
Editing: Makoto Shinkai
Art Direction: Akiko Majima; Takumi Tanji; Tasuku Watanabe
MPAA rating: PG
Running time: 106 minutes

REVIEWS

Chang, Justin. *Los Angeles Times.* April 6, 2017.
Connelly, Sherilyn. *Village Voice.* April 4, 2017.
Dargis, Manohla. *New York Times.* April 6, 2017.
Ehrlich, David. *IndieWire.* December 22, 2016.
Katz, Anita. *San Francisco Chronicle.* April 7, 2017.
Lickona, Matthew. *San Diego Reader.* April 7, 2017.
Mayer, Dominick. *Consequence of Sound.* April 7, 2017.
O'Sullivan, Michael. *Washington Post.* April 6, 2017.
Phipps, Keith. *Uproxx.* April 11, 2017.
Stables, Kate. *Sight and Sound.* November 18, 2016.

QUOTES

Hitoha Miyamizu: "Treasure the experience. Dreams fade away after you wake up."

TRIVIA

The meteor in the film is named Tiamat after the ancient Mesopotamian goddess of the ocean that represents female beauty, creation, and primordial chaos.

THE ZOOKEEPER'S WIFE

They gave all they had to save all they could.
—Movie tagline

In a nation gripped by fear one woman finds the power to resist.
—Movie tagline

Box Office: $17.6 Million

Though many films have been made about the German invasion of Poland before World War II and the Holocaust, the true story of the Warsaw Zoo harboring refugees is one that has yet to come to light. Trying to make an addition to the cinema about this horrific era, director Niki Caro's *The Zookeeper's Wife* also aims to woo audiences with a story that mixes the preciousness of animals with that of human beings, but does so with inconsistent dramatic sensibilities.

Based on the book by Diane Ackerman, this epic tells of how the owners of the Warsaw Zoo protected approximately 300 refugees during the German invasion. The movie starts in 1939 with an idea of peace, in which the Zabinskis operate their zoo like a neighborhood utopia, animals running around, tourists ready to enter as soon as the gates open. A maternal sense of mother/

wife Antonina (Jessica Chastain) is shown early on, when she saves a young baby elephant from death. While painting an image of a utopia, a menace starts to matriculate: the German's presence in Warsaw. And suddenly one day, they attack the city (and the zoo as well, in an early scene) and start putting Jewish people from Warsaw into ghettos.

Heroically, the Zabinskis elect to use their now-closed zoo as a place to hide people they smuggle from the ghettos, a type of service that they carry out for years, under the noses of German military personnel who move in and out of the zoo daily. The initial plan is to for husband Jan (Johan Heldenbergh) to travel to the ghetto, stow people in a truck carrying food scraps, and then eventually help them leave the city with new identities. Meanwhile, the Germans think that the place has merely become a pig farm run mostly by the Zabinskis.

To further add stakes to the situation, the film features tension between the Zabinskis and Daniel Brühl's Lutz Heck, who plays Hitler's lead zoologist. The dynamic makes for scenes in which Lutz tries to woo Antonina while she tries to keep her guests secret, in one case pressing up against him to distract him from the sounds of a refugee downstairs. These scenes make for the less thrilling parts of the movie, especially as Brühl plays the part with little dimension aside from his absurd ambitiousness to breed a type of bison, as to show Germany's power. As the lead face of this story's villainy, Brühl flattens out the proceedings, creating a type of tedious love triangle.

It is odd, and revealing, that the movie slacks when it comes to creating its sense of war, as it does in the beginning and in parts throughout. The pivotal attack on the Warsaw Zoo is particularly sloppy despite its narrative importance, using frantic jump cuts of animals or to create a sense of chaos unleashed upon a designated utopia. Later war scenes, with Jan going into battle with other people, lack the necessary cohesion for tension, even though they have the scope in its detailed production design. And throughout, is a strange calculation to the type of animal violence that is shown (animals being shot off-screen, or with very fake replacements) as if to not disgust the animal lovers who would want to see a film bearing this title.

The editing gets tangled up in a few instances when failing to explain the specific plots to get Jewish people out from the ghetto right in front of German officers, but the film excels at points when people emerge from hiding, and sit in a peaceful silence after hearing a music cue from Antonina's piano. A show-stopping moment occurs midway through the movie when Chastain has her acting power matched by a traumatized girl played by Shira Haas, as the two sit quietly in a cage. The movie gets its warmth from these passages, a quality it offers more uniquely than a harrowing tale of survival.

The Zookeeper's Wife does orchestrate some fleeting, gorgeous filmmaking moments towards the second half, such as a shot of luggage being burned in the foreground, as a freight train headed towards concentration camps is taken out from the station. There are also strong emotional passages with Antonina and Jan at home, trying to wrap their heads around the situation without losing emotional control. The movie is inconsistently beautiful, too much so, but it does make a case that its importance is more than just assumed period piece prestige.

One of the most sustainable elements of the film is the heavyweight performance of Chastain, where her imperfect Polish accent is about the only flaw. For such a demanding story, especially one that boasts numerous heartbreaking moments, Chastain is exquisite with each emotional beat. Caro is able to hold onto her face for moments that rely on Antonina's instantaneous reactions to something traumatic (thinking her young son has been shot, off-screen), and it continues the sporadic intimate power of the film. And in the movie's most assured moments, where characters are communicating through brief sentences or peaceful silence, Chastain creates a stoic, at-times fascinating presence. However inspiring the true story is, *The Zookeeper's Wife* as a film would not resonate as deeply without Chastain's expressiveness.

Nick Allen

CREDITS

Antonina Zabinski: Jessica Chastain

Lutz Heck: Daniel Brühl

Jan Zabinski: Johan Heldenbergh

Jerzyk: Michael McElhatton

Maurycy Fraenkel: Iddo Goldberg

Origin: United States

Language: English

Released: 2017

Production: Jeff Abberley, Diane Miller Levin, Jamie Patricof, Kim Zubick; Czech Anglo Productions, LD Entertainment, Rowe/Miller Productions, Scion Films; released by Focus Features L.L.C.

Directed by: Niki Caro

Written by: Angela Workman

Cinematography by: Andrij Parekh

Music by: Harry Gregson-Williams

Sound: Becky Sullivan

Music Supervisor: Gabe Hilfer

Editing: David Coulson
Costumes: Bina Daigeler
Production Design: Suzie Davies
MPAA rating: PG-13
Running time: 127 minutes

REVIEWS

Bahr, Lindsey. *Associated Press.* March 29, 2017.
Holden, Stephen. *New York Times.* March 29, 2017.
Jones, J.R. *Chicago Reader.* March 30, 2017.
MacDonald, Moira. *Seattle Times.* March 29, 2017.
Merry, Stephanie. *Washington Post.* March 30, 2017.
Morgenstern, Joe. *Wall Street Journal.* March 30, 2017.
Taylor, Kate. *Globe and Mail.* March 31, 2017.
Walsh, Katie. *Tribune News Service.* March 30, 2017.
Wolfe, April. *LA Weekly.* March 30, 2017.
Zuckerman, Esther. *The A.V. Club.* March 30, 2017.

QUOTES

Antonina Zabinski: "You can never tell who your enemies are, or who to trust. Maybe that's why I love animals so much. You look in their eyes, and you know exactly what's in their hearts. They're not like people."

TRIVIA

Between takes, actor Jessica Chastain claims she was taught "the nastiest German" swear words by he co-star Daniel Brühl.

List of Awards

Academy Awards

Film: *The Shape of Water*
Animated Film: *Coco*
Director: Guillermo del Toro (*The Shape of Water*)
Actor: Gary Oldman (*Darkest Hour*)
Actress: Frances McDormand (*Three Billboards Outside Ebbing, Missouri*)
Supporting Actor: Sam Rockwell (*Three Billboards Outside Ebbing, Missouri*)
Supporting Actress: Allison Janney (*I, Tonya*)
Original Screenplay: Jordan Peele (*Get Out*)
Adapted Screenplay: James Ivory (*Call Me by Your Name*)
Cinematography: Roger Deakins (*Blade Runner 2049*)
Editing: Lee Smith (*Dunkirk*)
Production Design: Paul D. Austerberry, Shane Vieau, Jeffrey A. Melvin (*The Shape of Water*)
Visual Effects: John Nelson, Gerd Nefzer, Paul Lambert, Richard R. Hoover (*Blade Runner 2049*)
Sound Mixing: Gregg Landaker, Gary Rizzo, Mark Weingarten (*Dunkirk*)
Sound Editing: Richard King, Alex Gibson (*Dunkirk*)
Makeup: Kazuhiro Tsuji, David Malinowski, Lucy Sibbick (*Darkest Hour*)
Costume Design: Mark Bridges (*Phantom Thread*)
Original Score: Alexandre Desplat (*The Shape of Water*)
Original Song: "Remember Me" (Kristen Anderson-Lopez, Robert Lopez *Coco*)
Foreign Language Film: *A Fantastic Woman*
Documentary, Feature: *Icarus*
Documentary, Short Subject: *Heaven is a Traffic Jam on the 405*
Short Film, Animated: *Dear Basketball*
Short Film, Live Action: *The Silent Child*

British Academy of Film & Television Awards

Film: *Three Billboards Outside Ebbing, Missouri*
Animated Film: *Coco*
Outstanding British Film: *Three Billboards Outside Ebbing, Missouri*
Foreign Film: Park Chan-wook, Syd Lim (*The Handmaiden*)
Documentary: Raoul Peck (*I Am Not Your Negro*)
Director: Guillermo del Toro (*The Shape of Water*)
Actor: Gary Oldman (*Darkest Hour*)
Actress: Frances McDormand (*Three Billboards Outside Ebbing, Missouri*)
Supporting Actor: Sam Rockwell (*Three Billboards Outside Ebbing, Missouri*)
Supporting Actress: Allison Janey (*I, Tonya*)
Original Screenplay: Martin McDonagh (*Three Billboards Outside Ebbing, Missouri*)
Adapted Screenplay: James Ivory (*Call Me by Your Name*)
Editing: Jonathan Amos, Paul Machliss (*Baby Driver*)
Cinematography: Roger Deakins (*Blade Runner 2049*)
Production Design: Paul Austerberry, Jeffrey A. Melvin, Shane Vieau (*The Shape of Water*)
Costume Design: Mark Bridges (*Phantom Thread*)
Makeup: David Malinowski, Ivana Primorac, Lucy Sibbick, Kazuhiro Tsuji (*Darkest Hour*)
Sound: Alex Gibson, Richard King, Gregg Landaker, Gary Rizzo, Mark Weingarten (*Dunkirk*)
Visual Effects: Richard R. Hoover, Paul Lambert, Gerd Nefzer, John Nelson (*Blade Runner 2049*)
Music: Alexandre Desplat (*The Shape of Water*)

Directors Guild of America Awards

Outstanding Directorial Achievement in Motion Pictures:

Guillermo del Toro (*The Shape of Water*)
Outstanding Directorial Achievement in Documentary: Matthew Heineman (*City of Ghosts*)
Outstanding Directorial Achievement of a First-Time Feature Film Director: Jordan Peele (*Get Out*)

Golden Globes

Film, Drama: *Three Billboards Outside Ebbing, Missouri*
Film, Musical or Comedy: *Lady Bird*
Animated Film: *Coco*
Director: Guillermo del Toro (*The Shape of Water*)
Actor, Drama: Gary Oldman (*Darkest Hour*)
Actor, Musical or Comedy: James Franco (*The Disaster Artist*)
Actress, Drama: Frances McDormand (*Three Billboards Outside Ebbing, Missouri*)
Actress, Musical or Comedy: Saoirse Ronan (*Lady Bird*)
Supporting Actor: Sam Rockwell (*Three Billboards Outside Ebbing, Missouri*)
Supporting Actress: Allison Janney (*I, Tonya*)
Screenplay: Martin McDonagh (*Three Billboards Outside Ebbing, Missouri*)
Score: Alexandre Desplat (*The Shape of Water*)
Song: "This Is Me" (Benj Pasek, Justin Paul *The Greatest Showman*)
Foreign Language Film: *In the Fade*

Golden Raspberry Awards

Worst Picture: *The Emoji Movie*
Worst Director: Tony Leondis (*The Emoji Movie*)
Worst Actor: Tom Cruise (*The Mummy*)
Worst Actress: Tyler Perry (*BOO! 2: A Medea Halloween*)
Worst Supporting Actor: Mel Gibson (*Daddy's Home 2*)
Worst Supporting Actress: Kim Basinger (*Fifty Shades Darker*)
Worst Screenplay: Tony Leondis, Eric Siegel, Mike White (*The Emoji Movie*)
Worst Screen Combo: Any two obnoxious emojis (*The Emoji Movie*)
Worst Prequel, Remake, Rip-Off or Sequel: (*Fifty Shades Darker*)

Independent Spirit Awards

Film: *Get Out*
Documentary: *Faces Places*
First Film: *Ingrid Goes West*
Director: Jordan Peele (*Get Out*)
Actor: Timothée Chalamet (*Call Me by Your Name*)
Actress: Frances McDormand (*Three Billboards Outside Ebbing, Missouri*)
Supporting Actor: Sam Rockwell (*Three Billboards Outside Ebbing, Missouri*)
Supporting Actress: Allison Janney (*I, Tonya*)
Screenplay: *Lady Bird*
First Screenplay: *The Big Sick*
Cinematography: Sayombhu Mukdeeprom *Call Me by Your Name*
Editing: Tatiana S. Riegel *I, Tonya*
Foreign Film: *A Fantastic Woman*
Robert Altman Award: *Mudbound*
John Cassavetes Award: *Life & Nothing More*
Someone to Watch Award: Justin Chon (*Gook*)
Truer than Fiction Award: Jonathan Olshefski *Quest*
Producers Award: Summer Shelton
Bonnie Award: Chloé Zhao

Screen Actors Guild Awards

Actor: Gary Oldman (*Darkest Hour*)
Actress: Frances McDormand (*Three Billboards Outside Ebbing, Missouri*)
Supporting Actor: Sam Rockwell (*Three Billboards Outside Ebbing, Missouri*)
Supporting Actress: Allison Janney (*I, Tonya*)
Ensemble Cast: *Three Billboards Outside Ebbing, Missouri*
Stunt Ensemble: *Wonder Woman*

Writers Guild of America Awards

Original Screenplay: Jordan Peele (*Get Out*)
Adapted Screenplay: James Ivory (*Call Me by Your Name*)
Documentary Screenplay: Brett Morgen (*Jane*)

Obituaries

Lola Albright (July 20, 1924-March 23, 2017). Film and television actress Lola Jean Albright was born in Akron, Ohio, to parents who were both gospel music singers. Singing is what would also break Albright into the film business by 1947, making her motion picture debut that year in the musical comedy *The Unfinished Dance*. Just two years later, Albright gained specific notice with her work opposite Kirk Douglas in the movie *Champion*. While she appeared in supporting roles in a fair share of smaller films, Albright earned more notice in 1961 for her work in the low-budget, black-and-white indie, *A Cold Wind in August*. This led to more work in bigger pictures, like an Elvis Presley musical in 1962 (*Kid Galahad*) and in *Joy House*, directed by Rene Clement. All the while working in film, Albright was the unusual actress to work in the medium of television in its earlier days, starting work on the small screen in 1951. Her most famous role came from playing Peter Gunn's love interest in the show named after the title character, a part that earned her an Emmy nomination in 1959. Her presence became so well-known on the show that it helped her music career, of which "Peter Gunn" composer Henry Mancini arranged her second album, and supported her with his orchestra. Albright officially retired from acting in the mid-1980s, and spent her time in Toluca Lake, California.

Richard Anderson (August 8, 1926-August 31, 2017). Richard Norman Anderson was born in Long Branch, New Jersey, with grandparents of Russian Jewish descent. After seeing a tour of duty during World War II, Anderson's career as an American actor began in 1950, when he was a contract player for MGM. He appeared in the likes of *The Student Prince* and *Forbidden Planet*, which led to further reputable work on television shows like *Perry Mason, I Spy, The Man from U.N.C.L.E., The Green Hornet, Bonanza,* and much more. Some of his most acclaimed television work came when he played Oscar Goldman in the second episode of *The Six Million Dollar Man,* portraying the character until the end of the series. In 2007, after a long list of credits in film and television, Anderson was honored with a Golden Palm Star on the Palm Springs Walk of Stars. Anderson died in Beverly Hills, California at the age of 91 from natural causes.

John G. Avildsen (December 21, 1935-June 16, 2017). John Guilbert Avildsen was born in Oak Park, Illinois to Ivy and Clarence John Avildsen. After an education that included the Hotchkiss School and New York University, Avildsen started out in the world of film directing by assisting the likes of Arthur Penn and Otto Preminger, making his own debut with the 1969 film *Turn on to Love*, which paved the way for his first hit, 1970's *Joe*. Avildsen's second film, 1973's *Save the Tiger*, received three Oscar® nominations and won one for Jack Lemmon with Best Actor. But his biggest triumph one could easily argue was the 1976 film Rocky, a critical, commercial and Oscar® success that won him Best Picture and Best Director. From there, Avildsen enjoyed a directorial career with movies of various sizes, like the 1981 comedy *Neighbors*, and his own franchise, *The Karate Kid*, directing all three of those films. Directing a movie almost every year after 1969 until 1992, his final film was 1999's *Inferno*, starring Jean-Claude Van Damme. Avildsen died at the age of 81 from pancreatic cancer.

Michael Ballhaus (August 5, 1935-April 12, 2017). Born in Berlin, Germany to the sons olfactory Lena Hutter and Oskar Ballhaus, Michael Ballhaus decided to take a career behind the camera as a cinematographer, especially with the support of family friend Max Ophuls. Ballhaus's first film in the role was with another director of note—Rainer Werner Fassbender—and it was the 1971 film, *Whity*. They would later collaborate on now-revered films like *The Bitter Tears of Petra von Kant* and *The Marriage of Maria Braun*. Ballhaus would then move onto American films, working with directors such as John Sayles (*Baby It's You*), Martin Scorsese (*After Hours*, *The Color of Money*, *The Last Temptation of Christ*, *Goodfellas*, and *The Age of Innocence* among others), Francis Ford Coppola (*Dracula*) and Barry Levinson (*Sleepers*). Three times, Ballhaus's stylish but efficient cinematographic approach earned him an Oscar®, but he never won the award. Ballhaus married Helga Betten in 1958, and they had a son who became a prestigious cinematographer himself, Florian Ballhaus. Michael Ballhaus died at age 81 on April 12, 2017.

Chuck Berry (October 18, 1926-March 18, 2017). Legendary American musician Charles Edward Anderson Berry was born in St. Louis, Missouri, where he developed interest in music at an early age. But it was until he was 1953 that the Chuck Berry as listeners know him was born, as Berry began performing blues with the Johnnie Johnson Trio at that time, influenced by the riff stylings of T-Bone Walker. His big break came in 1955 when he recorded one of his all-time biggest hits, "Maybelline," which set him off on a star path of more hit records and film appearances, popping up in movies like 1956's *Rock Rock Rock!* and 1959's *Go, Johnny, Go!*. His way of playing guitar became highly influential on how listeners defined and performed rock music, which was recognized in part by his induction to the Rock and Roll Hall of Fame in 1986. With songs like "Johnny B. Goode," "Rock and Roll Music" and others to his legacy, Berry passed away at the age of 90 in his home state of Missouri.

William Peter Blatty (January 7, 1928-January 12, 2017). Oscar®-winning writer and director William Peter Blatty has the unique legacy of winning awards acclaim using the horror genre. His interest in pain that was either human or supernatural started with his upbringing in New York City, living in a broken household and changing homes a reported 28 times during his childhood, under a deeply religious mother. The experiences would inform his first novel in 1960, *Which Way to Mecca, Jack?,* which led to comic novels in the following years. Blatty's skill with comedy led to collaborations with Blake Edwards, including films like *A Shot in the Dark, Gunn,* and *Darling Lili*. But in 1971, Blatty dove into the horror genre, penning a book titled *The Exorcist,* which he later adapted into a William Friedkin film that won him the Oscar® for Best Adapted Screenplay. With this experience, Blatty put his interest in cinematic storytelling into a now-cult classic, *The Ninth Configuration*, which was a commercial flop. A few years later, he adapted his own sequel to *The Exorcist, The Exorcist III,* which was based in part off his own novel, *Legion.* Afterward, Blatty would move away from the business and to the medium of novels and novellas, including stories like *Elsewhere, Dimiter,* and *Crazy.* But regardless of the medium, Blatty's work has made him a truly historical figure in the horror genre, whose influence will always be evident in the future writers to come. Blatty died of multiple myeloma at the age of 89.

Joseph Bologna (December 30, 1934-August 13, 2017). Born in Brooklyn, New York to an Italian-American family, Joseph Bologna made a career in film and television as a writer and an actor. After studying art history at Brown History and serving a tour as a Marine, Bologna transitioned to producing and directing commercials. This led to co-writing the comedy *Lovers and Other Strangers* with his wife Renee Taylor, which earned them an Academy Award® nomination for Best Adapted Screenplay. Working across genres and with big stars, Bologna continued to act throughout the decades, earning acclaim with the likes of 1982's *My Favorite Year,* and a Neil Simon romance *Chapter Two* (1979). Bologna worked in television as well up until he retired from acting in 2012. In 2017, he received the Night of 100 Stars Oscar® Gala Lifetime Achievement Award for his efforts to help save the Motion Picture Home and Hospital in 2012. Bologna died in Duarte, California, from pancreatic cancer at the age of 82.

Powers Boothe (June 1, 1948-May 14, 2017). Powers Allen Boothe was born in Snyder, Texas, a state background that would inform the toughness of many acting roles that would come throughout his long career. After a working through various Shakespearean productions in the 1970s, Boothe gained national attention for the first time playing Jim Jones in the television movie *Guyana Tragedy: The Story of Jim Jones,* a role that would earn him an Emmy, beating the likes of Henry Fonda and Jason Robards. Meanwhile, Boothe's film career was taking off, in tough films like *Southern Comfort, Red Dawn,* and *Extreme Prejudice*, where his stoic presence and tough voice made him a particularly memorable supporting presence. This charisma would carry over throughout his career, especially into roles that directly tapped into his strengths, like on the HBO series *Deadwood* or the two *Sin City* films. Booth married his college sweetheart, Pam Cole, in 1969 and remained married until his death, leaving behind two children, Parisse and Preston. After passing from effects of pancreatic cancer, Boothe was buried in Deadwood, Texas.

Brent Briscoe (May 21, 1961-October 18, 2017). Born in Moberly, Missouri, Brent Briscoe enjoyed a film career as an actor and screenwriter, which started at his pursuit of the theater after graduating from the University of Missouri. Briscoe moved to Los Angeles permanently after working with Billy Bob Thornton on the acclaimed film *Sling Blade*, and often worked with his college roommate Mark Fauser. Throughout his career, Briscoe appeared in films big and small, including the likes of *The Green Mile, Mulholland Drive, Spider-Man 2, The Dark Knight Rises*, and *Zombeavers*. In 2017, he had the role of Detective Dave Macklay in the highly-praised television series, *Twin Peaks.* Briscoe died from heart complications on October 18, 2017.

Glen Campbell (April 22, 1936-August 8, 2017). One of the biggest stars of country music, Glen Travis Campbell was a multi-hyphenate entertainer, known for his presence in television, film, on the stage and on the music charts. Growing up in Arkansas, his legacy started when he worked in a studio group known as "The Wrecking Crew," who accompanied the likes of The Beach Boys, Nat King Cole, Frank Sinatra, and Elvis Presley. Campbell soon broke out with his solo career, and had his first big hit in 1967 with "Gentle on My Mind." He expanded out of the music industry when he performed in the 1969 film *True Grit*, and even sung the Oscar®-nominated song of the same title. The recognition of his talents on-screen soon lead to him hosting his own variety show from 1969 to 1972, where he interviewed the likes of the Beatles, Johnny Cash, Willie Nelson, Linda Ronstadt, and more. When the series was canceled, Campbell continued to have a presence on television, appearing in television movie and specials, all the while gaining a prominent spot on the Billboard charts for songs like "Rhinestone Cowboy" and "Southern Nights." Campbell was inducted into the Country Hall of Fame in

2005, and worked in the industry until 2013, due to his conditions with Alzheimer's. Campbell's life journey was the subject of the 2014 documentary, *Glen Campbell: I'll Be Me*. Campbell died at the age of 81 in Nashville, Tennessee.

Bernie Casey (June 8, 1939-September 19, 2017). Bernard Terry Casey is the rare example of an athlete who successfully transitioned into life in front of television and film cameras, proving to be a man of many talents. Casey was originally a record-breaking track and field athlete, who was then drafted by the San Francisco 49ers, where he played the positions of halfback and flanker, leading to his best-known season for the Rams in 1967, the same year that he played in the all-star game known as the Pro Bowl. But such successes were only the beginning for someone like Casey, who started a film career in 1969 in *Guns of the Magnificent Seven*, a sequel to *The Magnificent Seven*. (In that same year, he published a book of paintings and poems, *Look at the People*.) He would then play opposite former NFL star Jim Jones in two crime dramas, and later had roles in movies as big as *Never Say Never Again*, *Revenge of the Nerds*, and *Spies Like Us*. He even played a version of himself in Keenen Ivory Wayans's 1988 film *I'm Gonna Git You Sucka*. Casey appeared in various film roles until 2007. He died on September 19 in Los Angeles after a stroke.

David Cassidy (April 12, 1950-November 21, 2017). David Bruce Cassidy was born in New York City, the son of actor Jack Cassidy and Evelyn Ward. David Cassidy would create his own musical legacy at a young age when he got the role of Keith Partridge on the television show *The Partridge Family*, a breakout that came after moving to Los Angeles and appearing in a few small series. Cassidy's work as a singer and actor on the show brought him immense fame at a young age, which made his early music career that of a teen idol, despite his constant interest in the music. With the success of his solo career, Cassidy became bigger than the Partridge Family, and focused on songwriting, recording and acting outside. In the 1980s, Cassidy returned to the theater performing that had gotten him his start, perfuming in London's West End and on Broadway. While his music carer picked up again with the 1990 single "Lyin' to Myself," he also continued acting on television, and made the rare appearance in movies, such as when he played Aaron Carter's manager in the 2005 film, *Poster*. Cassidy announced in 2017 that he was living with dementia, having previously been an outspoken supporter of Alzheimer's research in 2011. Cassidy died of liver failure at the age of 67 on November 21.

Mike Connors (August 15, 1925-January 26, 2017). Born Krekor Ohanian but professionally known as Mike Connors, the Armenian-American actor was perhaps best known for playing the private detective Joe Mannix in the CBS television series of that surname. Connors got into the acting business after director William Wellman famously noted the future-actor's expressive face, getting him set up on various shows, under the name of "Touch Connors." But his film career started in the early 1950s, first appearing in the 1952 movie *Sudden Fear*, and then having roles in the likes of 1956's *Swamp Women* and *The Ten Commandments*, of the same year. But while his film career would go on for decades in various projects, Connors' career took off with the success of the show *Mannix*, an opportunity that came to the actor after being seen on shows like *Gunsmoke, Perry Mason,* and *Tightrope!* Connors's last television appearance was on the show *Two and a Half Men*, playing a love interest to Holland Taylor. He passed away in Tarzana, California, at the age of 91.

Danielle Darrieux (May 1, 1917-October 17, 2017). Danielle Yvonne Marie Antoinette Darrieux did not plan to be an actress, which is all the more surprising given that her career would amount to 110 film appearances across eight decades. Originally, she was a cello player, who won a part in a musical (*Le Bal*), and her beauty, combined with her singing and dancing ability, was the start of a career in front of the camera. While she did appear in Hollywood movies early on in her career, like 1938's *The Rage of Paris*, Darrieux elected to work in the French film industry, even during the German occupation of World War II, a controversial decision. She was brought back to Hollywood by Joseph L. Mankiewicz, who got her to star in *5 Fingers*, co-starring James Mason. Darrieux's career would later include work in films such as *The Earrings of Madame de. . .* and *Lady Chatterley's Lover*. In 1985, after doing work across the globe as an actress and for different national film industries, Darrieux received an Honorary Cesar Award. Darrieux died at the age of 100, leaving behind a filmography of more than 100 films.

Jonathan Demme (February 22, 1944-April 26, 2017). Robert James Damme had a directorial career that spanned genres and various project sizes, but was nonetheless held together by a clear passion for cinematic storytelling and humanity itself. Born in Baldwin, New York, Demme then went on to graduate from the University of Florida before breaking into film directing with the help of B-movie guru Roger Corman. Demme earned a great deal of experience with these early pictures, which included 1971's *Angels Hard as They Come*, 1972's *The Hot Box*, and 1975's *Crazy Mama*. His first breakout was the 1980 film *Melvin and Howard*, which got Demme the gig of the 1984 Goldie Hawn and Kurt Russell vehicle *Swing Shift*, a project that didn't particularly connect with audiences or critics. An artistic reboot was in order, and it came in the shape of his unforgettable 1984 Talking Heads concert film *Stop Making Sense*, which led to unique directorial projects like 1986's *Something Wild* and 1987's Spalding Gray piece, *Swimming to Cambodia*. It was in 1991, however, when Demme made arguably his biggest film yet, a serial killer drama named *The Silence of the Lambs*, which garnered him an Oscar® for Best Director and Best Picture. Ever the unpredictable talent, his filmography then included the likes of AIDS drama *Philadelphia*, a Jimmy Carter documentary (*Man from Plains*) and a Dogme 95-influenced indie, *Rachel Getting Married*. One of Demme's last films was the Justin Timberlake concert film *Justin Timberlake + the Tennessee Kids*, which brought Demme's cinematic sense to Netflix. At the age of 73, Demme died from complications from esophageal cancer and heart disease, leaving behind a filmography and influence that will prove timeless across all of film.

Nelsan Ellis (November 30, 1977-July 8, 2017). Born in Harvey, Illinois, Nelsan Ellis started his artistic career with an acceptance to Juilliard School, which happened at the age of 22 after a brief time in the Marines. While at that school, Ellis wrote a semi-autobiographical play called *Ugly,* as influenced by his pregnant sister's murder at the hands of her husband. Ellis also earned a Bachelor of Fine Arts degree from Juilliard and met Rutina Wesley, who would work with Ellis on his big break, the television show *True Blood.* Appearing on the show from 2008 to 2014, Ellis made a presence as the character Lafayette Reynolds, which earned him a NAACP Image Award for Best Supporting Actor in 2011. On the silver screen, Ellis played the likes of Martin Luther King, Jr (in *The Butler*) and Bobby Byrd (James Brown biopic *Get On Up*). Ellis died at the age of 39 due to complications from alcohol withdrawal syndrome.

Miguel Ferrer (February 7, 1955-January 19, 2017). American actor Miguel Jose Ferrer was born into a life of talent, the son of Oscar®-winning actor Jose Ferrer and singer Rosemary Clooney. But Miguel's talents, with 124 acting credits to his name, were often those of a supporting actor who generated an overall unforgettable presence. Such a career began with television roles in the 1980s, playing the younger self of his father's character on *Magnum P.I.* But it was a villainous role in the 1987 Paul Verhoeven film *Robocop* that provided a breakthrough, and which led to numerous movies that used his tough glare and imposing presence, including *The Stand* and *Traffic.* Ferrer had a particularly classic role in David Lynch's *Twin Peaks* saga, appearing in both television iterations and in the film, *Twin Peaks: Fire Walk with Me.* His career throughout was splashed with voice-acting, television and film roles, and Ferrer was even nominated for a Grammy for his spoken word action for the album "Simba's Pride Read-Along," based off *The Lion King II.* Ferrer died from throat cancer at the age of 61 in his Los Angeles home.

June Foray (September 18, 1917-July 26, 2017). Anyone that has seen a popular American cartoon has heard the work of voice actress June Foray. Her lifelong passion for storytelling and character through her voice started in her hometown of Springfield, Massachusetts, where she was broadcast in a radio drama at the age of 12, and became a regular on the radio by the age of 15. Foray's skills with different voices and enunciation led her to various opportunities, including recording a number of children's albums for Capitol Records, voicing various characters in Disney shorts and features, voicing Cindy Lou Who in the iconic *How the Grinch Stole Christmas*, and working on Hanna-Barbera shows like *Tom and Jerry, Scooby-Doo, Where Are You!, The Flintstones*, and *The Rocky and Bullwinkle Show,* where she voiced the male character Rocky Squirrel. Throughout her prolific career, she was a proponent for the art of animation itself, and is credited with the idea of the Annie Awards, which specifically celebrates achievement; as a member of the Governors' board for the Academy of Motion Picture Arts & Sciences she was also able to help establish an Oscar® for Best Animated Feature. Foray died in Los Angeles, California at the age of 99.

Stephen Furst (May 8, 1954-June 16, 2017). Born Stephen Nelson Feuerstein, actor and director Stephen Furst enjoyed an artistic career throughout film and television, with perhaps his most famous role being that of Kent "Flounder" Durfman in the comedy *National Lampoon's Animal House.* He became a regular on the medical drama *St. Elsewhere* from 1983 to 1988, and had a role on *Babylon 5* from 1994 to 1998. Furst contributed to his respective mediums behind the camera as well, working as a director for low-budget movies like 2011's *Title to Murder*, and the children's movie *Baby Huey's Great Easter Adventure.* Furst also acted as a producer for films like *My Sister's Keeper*, directed by Nick Cassavetes. As the son of parents who both died of diabetes, Furst became a spokesperson for the American Diabetes Association, and co-authored the book *Confessions of a Couch Potato.* Furst died on June 16, 2017 from complications related to diabetes.

Dick Gregory (October 12, 1932-August 19, 2017). Multi-hyphenate entertainer and activist Dick Gregory was born in St. Louis, Missouri, the son of mother Lucille and father Presley. His skills of being a comedian and entertainer were first witnessed when he performed at talent shows while serving in the U.S. Army for two years. After returning to civilian life, Gregory was motivated to move to Chicago to join the new revolution of black comedians that included Nipsey Russell and Bill Cosby. He then became one of the first black comedians to perform for white audiences, which is when he met *Playboy* guru Hugh Hefner, who helped him get work at Chicago's Playboy Club, and later an appearance on *Tonight Starring Jack Paar.* Fitting to the career that would follow as an activist, Gregory only agreed to appearing on Jack Paar's show if he could talk after his set, which lead to a dialogue of the same spiritual vigor of his non-comedy, in which he became involved with the civil rights movement, protested the Vietnam War, and aligned with issues. Among an illustrious resume of protest acts, including hunger strikes, Gregory ran for Mayor of Chicago in 1967 against Richard J. Daley, and in the next year ran for President of the United States of America as a write-in candidate, which was discussed in his book vWrite Me In. It was later in his life that Gregory became more present on the silver and small screen, such as the 2002 film *The Hot Chick* and as a talking sun in the MTV series "Wonder Showzen." Gregory's last film role was in the 2018 film, *The Leisure Seeker*, opposite Helen Mirren and Donald Sutherland. Gregory passed away at the age of 84 in Washington, D.C.

Robert Guillaume (November 30, 1927-October 24, 2017). Born Robert Peter Williams, Robert Guillaume was an American actor who made much of his artistic presence on the stage and with television, especially on shows such as *Sports Night* and *Soap.* Born in St. Louis, Missouri, Guillaume adopted his surname as his stage name, which would be seen on Broadway for the first time in 1961 in the production of *Kwamina.* From then on, he would appear in other productions such as *Golden Boy, Tambourins to Glory,* and *Guys and Dolls,* which earned him a Tony Award nomination. He transitioned to television work through guest appearances on sitcoms like *Good Times, The Jeffersons, Sanford and Son,* and more, before becoming a regular on the ABC series *Soap,* of which he would continue his character work in the role of a butler named Benson into a spin-off series, *Benson.* In 1984, Guillaume received a star on the Hollywood Walk of Fame. Years later, Guillaume became known for doing voice acting for characters in television series and films, the most famous contribution possibly being his work as Rafiki in the Disney classic *The*

Lion King. He passed away in Los Angeles on October 24, 2017, due to prostate cancer.

Barbara Hale (April 18, 1922-January 26, 2017). Film and television actress Barbara Hale was born outside the city of Chicago in DeKalb, Illinois, where her interest in expression began to grow. While attending the Chicago Academy of Fine Arts with plans to be an artist, she started modeling to pay for her education, which led to a career move to Hollywood in 1943. Through the late 1940s she was under contract with RKO Pictures, with her first role being in the film *Gildersleeve's Bad Day*, released in 1943. But within a short time, Hale was sharing the screen with the likes of Frank Sinatra, Robert Mitchum and Robert Young. By 1951, she had top-billing with the title role in *Lorna Doone* and co-starred with James Stewart in a movie the same year called *The Jackpot*. Her last leading role was in the 1957 western *The Oklahoman*, starring opposite Joel McCrea; it was the same year that Hale took on her famous role as legal secretary Della Street in the television series *Perry Mason*, perhaps her most popular role, and one that helped her receive an Emmy in 1959 for Best Supporting Actress (Continuing Character) in a Dramatic Series. On February 8, 1960, Hale was recognized as a Star of Television on the Hollywood Walk of Fame. Hale died at the age of 94 on January 26, 2017 due to complications from chronic obstructive pulmonary disease.

Robert Hardy (October 29, 1925-August 3, 2017). British character actor Robert Hardy was born in the town of Cheltenham, and after serving in the Royal Air Force during World War II, he became an actor at the Shakespeare Memorial Theatre. His screen work began in 1951 on British television, and over the course of his 64-year career, he portrayed Prime Minister Winston Churchill in six separate television productions, earning a BAFTA nomination for his performance in the 1981 miniseries *Winston Churchill: The Wilderness Years*. Another BAFTA nomination came for his performance as the eccentric veterinarian Siegfried Farnon on the series *All Creatures Great and Small*. In film, Hardy appeared in *The Spy Who Came in from the Cold* (1965), played Sir John Middleton in Ang Lee's 1995 adaptation of *Sense and Sensibility*, and appeared in four of the *Harry Potter* movies as Cornelius Fudge, the Minister of Magic. Hardy died at the age of 91 at Denville Hall.

Richard Hatch (May 21, 1945-February 7, 2017). Best known for playing Captain Apollo on the original *Battlestar Galactica* (1978-1979), Santa Monica native Richard Hatch began working as a television actor in 1970. Making regular guest appearances on multiple shows, he replaced Michael Douglas on *The Streets of San Francisco (1972-1977) during the series's final season. The short-lived Battlestar Galactica*, for which he earned a Golden Globe nomination, would go on to consume much of Hatch's career, as the actor wrote novels set in the show's universe and attempted to reboot the series, while still maintaining his acting work. With writer/producer Ronald D. Moore's re-imagined version of the show (2004-2009), Hatch returned to that world as terrorist-turned-politician Thomas Zarek. While in hospice care for pancreatic cancer, Hatch died on February 7, 2017. He was 71.

Glenne Headly (March 13, 1955-June 8, 2017). Born in New London, Connecticut, and raised in San Francisco and New York City, Glenne Headly began her acting career on stage in Chicago, where she was part of the ensemble of the Steppenwolf Theatre. Her first film role was in Arthur Penn's *Four Friends* (1981), and her breakout role would come in *Dirty Rotten Scoundrels* (1988), in which she played the mark of confidence men played by Michael Caine and Steve Martin. Headly received Emmy nominations for her work on *Lonesome Dove* (1989) and *Bastard Out of Carolina* (1996), and her other film credits included *Mr. Holland's Opus* (1995), *Sgt. Bilko* (1996), and this year's *The Circle*. Headly died of complications from a pulmonary embolism at the age of 62 on June 8, 2017.

John Heard (March 7, 1946-July 21, 2017). John Heard arrived in movies as a leading man and became a prolific character actor on film and television over the course of his four-decade career. Born in Washington, D.C., Heard's first leading role was as Alex Cutter in *Cutter's Way* (1981). He followed this with starring roles in *Cat People* (1982) and *C.H.U.D.* (1984). His transition toward supporting roles would start in the late 1980s, with turns in *Big* (1988) and *Beaches* (1988), and in 1990, he played the forgetful father in *Home Alone* (reprising the role in the 1992 sequel), which arguably would become his most memorable role. He continued working in film and on television for the rest of his life, earning an Emmy nomination for his role as a corrupt and conscience-stricken police detective on *The Sopranos* (1999-2004). Heard died on July 21, 2017 of a heart attack at the age of 71.

Hugh Hefner (April 9, 1926-September 27, 2017). The playboy founder of *Playboy* was born and raised in Chicago, where he opened the magazine's first offices across the street from Holy Name Cathedral. Hugh Hefner, known to his friends as "Hef," was raised within a conservative, Midwestern family, but he made his career and fortune by publishing photos of nude women, starting with a photo spread of Marilyn Monroe in the magazine's first issue in 1953. He was also a publisher and editor-in-chief who sought controversy in the text of the magazine (for the people who read it for the articles), publishing interviews with Malcolm X and Martin Luther King, Jr. at the height of the Civil Rights Movement, while attacking "militant feminists" in other articles. Hefner briefly entered the world of movies by funding, through Playboy Enterprises, Roman Polanski's adaptation of *Macbeth* (1971). He appeared as himself in a variety of movies and television series, including a 1982 episode of *Laverne & Shirley*, a 1993 episode of *The Simpsons*, and a 2005 episode of *Curb Your Enthusiasm* that revolved around his trademark smoking jacket. Beginning in the 1970s, Hefner became involved in political and philanthropic work, while living in and partying at his Playboy Mansion in Los Angeles, where he died of cardiac arrest on September 27, 2017, aged 91. Hefner was buried next to Monroe, in a crypt he had purchased in 1992—a decision that, appropriately for the man, raised some controversy.

John Hillerman (December 20, 1932-November 9, 2017). After making a series of appearances in movies and television during the 1970s (from *The Last Picture Show* [1971], to *High Plains Drifters* [1973], to *Blazing Saddles* [1974], and to *Chinatown* [1974]), John Hillerman became best known for his role on *Magnum, P.I.* (1980-1988). For his performance as the English Johnathan Quayle Higgins III, the Texas-born Hillerman was nominated for four Emmy Awards, winning once. After the show concluded, the actor continued to work in television, retiring to Texas in 1999. At the age of 84, Hillerman died of cardiovascular disease on November 9, 2017.

Tobe Hooper (January 25, 1943-August 26, 2017). With *The Texas Chainsaw Massacre* (1974), Tobe Hooper helped to change the landscape of horror movies. The film, which Hooper directed, co-wrote, produced, and co-scored on a minimal budget, became an overnight sensation, garnering acclaim and controversy in equal measure. The Austin-born filmmaker began working as a college professor and documentary cameraman, making his first feature *Eggshells* in 1969. With the success of *The Texas Chainsaw Massacre*, Hooper went on to larger-budgeted horror fare, including *Eaten Alive* (1977), the television miniseries *Salem's Lot* (1979), and *The Funhouse* (1981). His greatest box-office success would arrive a year later with *Poltergeist*, after he was selected by co-writer/producer Steven Spielberg to helm the iconic haunted-house film (Debate about Spielberg's role on set, with some theorizing that he served as the film's stealth director, continues). Hooper went on to a three-picture deal with Cannon Films, resulting in *Lifeforce* (1985), *Invaders from Mars* (1986), and *The Texas Chainsaw Massacre 2*. Continuing to work within the genre he helped to redefine in film and on television until 2013, Hooper died at the age of 74 on August 26, 2017 of natural causes.

Rance Howard (November 17, 1928-November 25, 2017). Born into a farming family in Duncan, Oklahoma, Rance Howard became an actor and the patriarch of a notable Hollywood family. His first film credit came in 1956 with *Frontier Woman*, after which he continued to work in television. He appeared alongside his actor sons Ron and Clint on episodes of, respectively, *The Andy Griffith Show* (1960-68) and *Gentle Ben* (1967-69), and he acted on television and in films for the remainder of his life, appearing in a number of his son Ron's films, including *Cocoon* (1985), *Apollo 13* (1995), and *A Beautiful Mind* (2001). In addition to his sons, Howard's granddaughters Bryce Dallas Howard and Paige Howard also became actors. He died from heart failure on November 25, 2017 at the age of 89.

John Hurt (January 22, 1940-January 25, 2017). The much-lauded British actor was a significant presence throughout his 55-year career. The son of a Vicar and an engineer, Hurt began working on stage and television in 1962, with his first notable role arriving as Richard Rich in *A Man for All Seasons* (1966). He received the first of his seven BAFTA nominations for his performance in *10 Rillington Place* (1971). Hurt won the award for his performances in *The Naked Civil Servant* (1975), *Midnight Express* (1979), and *The Elephant Man* (1981), and he was nominated for Academy Awards® for his performances in the last two films. In between those two films, he appeared in Ridley Scott's *Alien* (1979) as the ill-fated Kane, whose death in the film's famous "chest-bursting" scene became a cultural milestone (Hurt would later parody the scene in Mel Brooks' *Spaceballs* [1987]). The actor also appeared as Caligula in the miniseries *I, Claudius (1976), but he primarily worked in film for the remainder of his career. He played the lead in the 1984 adaptation of George Orwell's Nineteen Eight-Four* and provided his recognizable voice for the animated films *The Lord of the Rings* (1978), *Watership Down* (1978), and *The Black Cauldron* (1985). Through his steady work, he became known to multiple generations of movie-goers, appearing in three of the *Harry Potter* films as wand-maker Garrick Ollivander and as Indiana Jones's mentor in *Indiana Jones and the Kingdom of the Crystal Skull* (2008). Amassing over 200 credits in film and television, the prolific actor died, aged 77, on January 25, 2017 of pancreatic cancer.

Clifton James (May 29, 1920-April 15, 2017). Character actor Clifton James was best known for playing Sheriff J.W. Pepper in the James Bond adventures *Live and Let Die* (1973) and *The Man with the Golden Gun* (1974), opposite Roger Moore, who also died this year. His acting career began in the 1950s, often playing military or police roles—a trend that would continue in films such as *The Last Detail* (1973), *Silver Streak* (1976), and *Superman II* (1980). A notable exception came in 1988, when he played Charles Comiskey, owner of the Chicago White Sox, in John Sayles's *Eight Men Out*. James would work with Sayles two more times in *Lone Star* (1996) and *Sunshine State* (2002). He died from complications of diabetes on April 15, 2017 at the age of 96.

Christine Kaufmann (January 11, 1945-March 28, 2017). Born in Nazi-annexed Austria, Christine Kaufmann was raised in Munich, becoming a ballerina for the Munich Opera. At the age of 7, she made her first film appearance in *The White Horse Inn* (1952). Seven years later, she was starring opposite Steve Reeves in *The Last Days of Pompeii* and, two years after that, opposite Kirk Douglas in *Town Without Pity*, for which she received a Golden Globe. A year later, in 1962, she appeared in *Taras Bulba* with Tony Curtis, who would become her husband from 1963 to 1968. She acted regularly throughout the 1980s in film and on television, also starting a cosmetic line and writing multiple books, including two autobiographies. On March 28, 2017, Kaufmann died in Munich at the age of 72 from leukemia.

Martin Landau (June 20, 1928-July 15, 2017). After working on television through the 1950s, Martin Landau first became known to audiences in Alfred Hitchcock's *North by Northwest*, one of three movies in which he appeared in 1959. He also appeared in *Cleopatra* (1963), *The Greatest Story Ever Told* (1965), and, opposite his fellow Actors Studio alum Steve McQueen, *Nevada Smith* (1965). The Brooklyn-born actor was cast as disguise expert Rollin Hand on *Mission: Impossible* (1966-1973) and went onto star in the short-lived series *Space: 1999* (1975-1977), while continuing to appear in movies. His career began reaching new heights in the late 1980s, when he received an Academy Award® nomination for his performance in Francis Ford Coppola's *Tucker: The Man and his Dream* (1988). The following year, Landau received a second Oscar® nomination for Woody Allen's *Crimes and Misdemeanors*, playing Judah Rosenthal, an ophthalmologist who faces a crisis of lack-of-conscience after having his mistress murdered. His Academy Award® came when he played a late-career Bela Lugosi, suffering from a debilitating addiction to opioids, in Tim Burton's *Ed Wood* (1994). Landau continued to work in film and on television, receiving Emmy nominations for guest appearances on *Without a Trace* (2002-2009) and *Entourage* (2004-2011) (adding to the three nominations he received for his work on *Mission: Impossible*), until his death on July 15, 2017. He was 89.

Jerry Lewis (March 16, 1926-August 20, 2017). At the age of five, Jerry Lewis began performing with his vaudeville parents in the Catskill Mountains (the "Borscht Belt"), then spent the next ten years honing his comedic craft, and started working the New York comedy circuit on his own. Lewis, born in Newark, New Jersey, came to prominence, though, as part of the duo Martin and Lewis—namely the straight-faced crooner Dean Martin and his own wacky self. The pair, who began collaborating in 1946, went from nightclubs, to radio, to television, and, ultimately, to the movies. They starred in a total of 16 movies together between 1949 and 1956, when their partnership ended. After the duo's disintegration, Lewis went on to a solo singing career at the Sands Hotel and Casino in Las Vegas, while continuing to work in film and on television. He turned to directing with *The Bellboy* (1960) and would direct himself in an additional dozen movies, including *The Ladies Man* (1961), *The Nutty Professor* (1963), and, in 1972, the completed but infamously unreleased *The Day the Clown Cried* (Lewis donated a copy to the Library of Congress, which is not allowed to publicly screen it before June of 2024). Starting in 1952, Lewis hosted telethons to raise money for the Muscular Dystrophy Associations of America (MDA), and from 1966 to 2010, he hosted an annual, all-day telethon for the cause, resulting in nearly $2.6 billion in donations. Lewis continued acting, notably in Martin Scorsese's *The King of Comedy* (1983) and most recently in *Max Rose* (2016). He died at the age of 91 on August 20, 2017 of cardiovascular disease.

Federico Luppi (February 23, 1936-October 20, 2017). A steadily working actor since 1964 in Argentina, Chile, Mexico, Spain, and the United States, Federico Luppi is best known for his work with director Guillermo del Toro. In 1993, he played the lead role in the filmmaker's debut feature *Cronos*, as an antique dealer who accidentally discovers a means to achieve immortality. Luppi also starred in Del Toro's *The Devil's Backbone* (2001), as a doctor running an orphanage, and appeared in *Pan's Labyrinth* (2006), as the King of the Underworld. He was nominated for two Goya Awards for his performances in two 1995 films, *Nadie hablará de nosotras cuando hayamos mureto* and *La ley de la frontera*, and directed his only feature film *Pasos* in 2005. Lupi died from complications of a subdural hematoma in Buenos Aires on October 20, 2017 at the age of 83.

Rose Marie (August 15, 1923-December 28, 2017). Rose Marie began working in the entertainment industry at the age of three and achieved fame as a singer at the age of five on the radio billed as "Baby Rose Marie." During her early career, she made multiple shorts and one feature film *International House* (1933), starring W.C. Fields. She toured lounges and nightclubs in major venues as a teenager and, in the 1950s, began working on television. She played Sally Rogers, a comedy writer, on *The Dick Van Dyke Show* (1961-1965) for the entirety of the show's run, receiving three Emmy nominations for the role, and had a starring role during the second and third seasons of *The Doris Day Show* (1968-1973). Her acting career continued in the 1990s, with guest appearances on *Murphy Brown* (1988-1998), *Wings* (1990-1997), and *Caroline in the City* (1995-1999). In her later years, she gained a following on social media, sharing stories of her career. Marie died of natural causes at the age of 94 on December 28, 2017 at her home in Van Nuys, California.

Dina Merrill (December 29, 1923-May 22, 2017). The daughter of a cereal heiress and a stockbroker, Dina Merrill was dubbed "Hollywood's new Grace Kelly" in 1959. Starting her acting career on stage, Merrill made her film debut in *Desk Set* (1957) with Spencer Tracy and Katharine Hepburn. Her notable credits include *Operation Petticoat* (1959), *Butterfield 8* (1960), and *The Player* (1992). On television, she made guest appearances on a variety of shows, including multiple game shows. She was appointed to the Board of Trustees of the John F. Kennedy Center for the Performing Arts and was a founding trustee of the Eugene O'Neill Theater. Suffering from dementia with Lewy bodies, Merrill died on May 22, 2017 at her East Hampton, New York, home at the age of 93.

Tomas Milian (March 3, 1933-March 22, 2017). After studying the "Method" with Lee Strasberg at the Actors Studio, Tomas Milian, who was born in Havana and became an American citizen, moved to Italy. While living there for 25 years, he had a successful career, performing in dramas (such as *The Agony and the Ecstasy* [1965]), Spaghetti Westerns, and crime films. Upon returning to the United States, Milian worked with Sidney Pollack (*Havana* [1990]), Oliver Stone (*JFK* [1991]), Steven Spielberg (*Amistad* [1997]), and Steven Soderbergh (*Traffic* [2000]). He died of a stroke at the age of 84 on March 22, 2017 at his Miami home.

Mary Tyler Moore (December 29, 1936-January 25, 2017). A comedy icon, Mary Tyler Moore was born in Brooklyn, New York the eldest of three children. At the age of eight, her family moved to Los Angeles, California, and at the age of 17, she began working as a dancer, making her first television appearance in commercials. Her first acting role, on *Richard Diamond, Private Detective* (1957-1960), did not show her face, but at the age of 24, she received her first break, playing Laura Petrie, the wife of star Dick Van Dyke's character, on *The Dick Van Dyke Show* (1961-1965). Moore received three Emmy nominations and two Emmy Awards for the role. She would receive seven Emmy nominations (winning three times) for her next show *The Mary Tyler Moore Show* (1970-1977), in which she played Mary Richards, the associate news producer at a Minneapolis television station. Moore also acted on Broadway and in film, co-starring in *Thoroughly Modern Millie* (1967) with Julie Andrews, *Change of Habit* (1969) with Elvis Presley, and in *Ordinary People* (1980), for which she was nominated for an Academy Award®. Her production company MTM Enterprises produced a variety of television shows, and Moore wrote two memoirs. Her philanthropic work included raising funds and awareness for Type I diabetes, with which she was diagnosed in 1969, as well as championing animals rights. At the age of 80, Moore died of cardiopulmonary arrest in Greenwich, Connecticut, on January 25, 2017.

Roger Moore (October 14, 1927-May 23, 2017). Roger Moore played British secret agent James Bond in seven films, more than any other actor to play the character in the official Eon Productions series. He attended the Royal Academy of Dramatic Art before being conscripted into the Royal Army Service Corps at the age of 18, later achieving the rank of captain. After working on British television and as a model, Moore came to the United States for some television jobs, before being signed to a contract with MGM in 1954. The contract lasted only two years, and early career success arrived playing the eponymous hero in the British television series *Ivanhoe* (1958-1959). He followed that with roles in two television Westerns, *The Alaskans* (1959-1960) and *Maverick* (1957-1962). Before Bond, Moore's first signature role was playing Simon Templar on *The Saint* (1962-1969), based on the books by Leslie Charteris. He was cast as Bond, after Sean Connery's second run at the character, in 1973's *Live and Let Die*, continuing to play the character in *The Man with the Golden Gun* (1974), *The Spy Who Loved Me* (1977), *Moonraker* (1979), *For Your Eyes Only* (1981), *Octopussy* (1983), and *A View to a Kill* (1985). In addition to acting after his stint as Bond, Moore became a UNICEF Goodwill Ambassador in 1991 and was knighted in 2003. He died of cancer on May 23, 2017 at his home in Crans-Montana, Switzerland, at the age of 89.

Erin Moran (October 18, 1960-April 22, 2017). Before being cast as Joanie Cunningham on *Happy Days* (1974-1984), Erin Moran began acting in television commercials at the age of five, before moving onto the show *Daktari* (1966-1969) and a role in the film *How Sweet It Is!* (1968) with Debbie Reynolds. At the age of 13, Moran was cast as Joanie and played the role until 1982, when she starred in the spin-off series *Joanie Loves Chachi* (1982-1983). Following those shows, she moved out of Los Angeles to the mountains of California, making occasional guest appearances on television. Along with three other cast members of *Happy Days*, Moran sued CBS for failure to pay merchandising revenues from the show. The suit was settled in 2012, by which point Moran had moved to Indiana. She died at the age of 56 of complications from throat cancer on April 22, 2017.

Jeanne Moreau (January 23, 1928-July 31, 2017). A star of the French New Wave, Jeanne Moreau worked with Louis Malle (on his directorial debut *Elevator to the Gallows* [1958], *The Lovers* [1959], and *Viva Maria!* [1967]) and with François Truffaut on his third film *Jules et Jim* (1962), for which she received a BAFTA nomination. Trained at the Paris Conservatory, Moreau started in the theater, and her career included working with other notable filmmakers, including Michelangelo Antonioni (*La notte* [1961] and *Beyond the Clouds* [1995]), Orson Welles (*The Trial [1962] and Chimes at Midnight* [1965]), and Luis Buñel (*Diary of a Chambermaid* [1964]). She also was a singer (performing with Frank Sinatra on one occasion) and a filmmaker, directing two features and a documentary. She died of natural causes on July 31, 2017 at the age of 89.

Charlie Murphy (July 12, 1959-April 12, 2017). Despite being the elder brother of one of the most famous comics in the world, stand-up comedian and actor Charlie Murphy took awhile to become famous, but he did as a writer and featured player on *Chappelle's Show* (2003-2006). Murphy was born in Brooklyn, and after 10-month jail sentence, he enlisted in the United States Navy, serving for six years. He appeared in his younger brother Eddie's sole directorial effort *Harlem Nights* (1989) and appeared in two films by Spike Lee (*Mo' Better Blues* [1990] and *Jungle Fever* [1991]), as well as playing the antagonistic night club owner in *CB4* (1993). Murphy's fame quickly rose from his appearances on Dave Chappelle's aforementioned sketch-comedy show, in which he narrated stories of his odd meetings with the likes of Rick James and Prince. Following the show, Murphy made appearances in film and on television. He died, aged 57, on April 12, 2017 from leukemia.

Jim Nabors (June 12, 1930-November 30, 2017). Born in Sylacauga, Alabama in 1930, Jim Nabors would achieve lasting fame as a singer and actor but he first found employment in the entertainment industry as an editor for a television station in Chattanooga. This led to a similar job with NBC in Los Angeles which then led him to The Horn, a Santa Monica nightclub where he performed a cabaret act that showcased his skills as both an actor and singer. He was discovered one night by comedian Bill Dana, who recruited him to appear on the short-lived *The Steve Allen Show.* He was later rediscovered in 1962 by Andy Griffith, who was in the audience and hired him to appear in an episode of the third season of *The Andy Griffith Show* playing an amiably scatterbrained gas station attendant inspired by one of the characters he played on stage. The character, Gomer Pyle, proved to be so popular with viewers that he became a regular on the long-running series and then went on two years later to star in the equally popular spin-off *Gomer Pyle, U.S.M.C.*. After that show left the air in 1969, Nabors became a familiar face on a number of television shows before electing to concentrate on live performances that allowed him to demonstrate his impressive singing talents. Although his only big screen work had been an uncredited bit in *Take Her, She's Mine* (1963), he spent part of the early 1980s working on a trio of films with good friend Burt Reynolds—an adaptation of the controversial stage musical *The Best Little Whorehouse in Texas* (1982) and the poorly received car crash epics *Stroker Ace* (1983) and *Cannonball Run II* (1984). Afterwards, he returned to live performances with appearances in dinner theater, cabaret shows in Las Vegas and an annual rendition of "Back Home Again in Indiana" preceding the running of the Indianapolis 500 until increasingly poor health (including a 1994 bout with hepatitis B that eventually led to a liver transplant) inspired him to retire from show business. He passed away at his home in Honolulu, Hawaii on November 30 at the age of 87.

Michael Nyqvist (November 8, 1960-June 27, 2017). Born in Stockholm, Sweden on November 8, 1960, Michael Nyqvist first became interested in acting when he took classes while spending his senior year of high school as an exchange student in Omaha, Nebraska. Upon returning to Sweden, Nyqvist first elected to study ballet but eventually gave that up and was eventually accepted into the Malmo Theatre Academy. His first major role came in 1997 when he was featured on the Swedish television series *Beck* and his big breakthrough came three years later with his acclaimed performance in Lukas Moodysson's *Together*, which earned him a nomination for the Swedish equivalent of the Best Actor Oscar®. He achieved international stardom by playing investigative writer Mikael Blomkvist in the Swedish screen adaptation of Steig Larsson's best-selling "Millennium" series—*The Girl with the Dragon Tattoo* (2009), *The Girl Who Played with Fire* (2009), and *The Girl Who Kicked the Hornet's Nest* (2009). He capitalized on his newfound fame by dividing his time between working in Hollywood, where he appeared in *Abduction* (2011), the massive hit *Mission Impossible—Ghost Protocol* (2011) and the cult favorite *John Wick* (2014), and Europe, where he was featured in films like *Europa Report* (2013), *The Girl in the Book* (2014), and the miniseries *Madiba* (2017). Nyqvist had completed work on *Hunter Killer* (2018) and *Radegund* (2018) and was filming *Kursk* (2018) when he died on June 27 from lung cancer at the age of 57.

Robert Osborne (May 3, 1932-March 6, 2017). Although he did not manage to break through in Hollywood as an actor as he intended, Robert Osborne would eventually become famous as one of the most respected and recognized chroniclers of motion picture history of his time. Born in Colfax, Washington in 1932, Osborne first found work in Hollywood as a contract player at Desilu Studios working under the tutelage of Lucille Ball herself. After appearances in a few television shows (including the 1962 pilot episode of *The Beverly Hillbillies*. Osborne, with the encouragement of Ball, began to focus instead on writing about film and published his first book, *Academy Awards Illustrated*, in 1965. Over the next few decades, he would work as a columnist for *The Hollywood Reporter*, win the National Film Book Award in 1979 for *50 Golden Years of Oscar* and serve as president of the Los Angeles Film Critics Association. In the 1980s, he moved to television, first as an entertainment reporter for KTTV in Los Angeles and then as the on-air host for the Showtime cable network. In 1994, he was hired by the newly-formed Turner Classic Movies channel to be the host for their evening broadcasts, a number of specials and, eventually, the weekly series *The Essentials* focusing on especially noteworthy titles. With his combination of folksy demeanor and encyclopedic knowledge of film, Osborne became a hugely popular personality throughout his long tenure with the network that ended with his 2016 retirement due to health problems that had been dogging him for a few years. He passed away from natural causes in his New York apartment on March 6, 2017.

Anita Pallenberg (April 6, 1942-June 13, 2017). Although best known for her romantic liaisons with Rolling Stones members Brian Jones and Keith Richards (having three children with the latter), style icon Anita Pallenberg also appeared in a number of notable appearances in movies throughout her career as a model/actress/artist/style icon. Born in Rome in 1942, Pallenberg left school at the age of 16 and hung with the party crowd before heading to New York to become part of Andy Warhol's Factory art collective. From there, she began modeling in Paris and worked throughout Europe and America as a model and stage actress before settling down in London and falling into the Stones orbit. She made her screen debut in *A Degree of Murder* (1967) and had a small role in the infamous sex farce *Candy* (1968) before making her first notable appearance as the Black Queen in the Roger Vadim cult favorite *Barbarella* (1968). Two years later, she appeared in the deeply controversial film *Performance* (1970) and while the hallucinatory tale of a gangster (James Fox) hiding out from enemies in an isolated mansion with a jaded rock star (Mick Jagger) and his two lovers (Pallenberg and Michele Breton) was held up for release for two years by Warner Brothers due to its then-shocking levels of sex, violence, and drug use, it has since gone on to be considered one of the key British films of the era. The next couple of decades were dogged by controversies ranging from drug busts to the questionable suicide of a 17-year-old boy in her bed who shot himself with a gun belonging to Richards. She eventually cleaned up and began making occasional appearances in films and on television in such things as *Love is the Devil* (1998), *Mister Lonely* (2007), *Cheri* (2009), and two films for director Abel Ferrara, *Go Go Tales* (2007) and *4:44 Last Day on Earth* (2011). Pallenberg died at the age of 75 on June 13 from complications from Hepatitis C.

Michael Parks (April 24, 1940-May 9, 2017). Known as much for his iconoclastic attitude as for his acting talents, Michael Parks did not achieve the stardom some had pegged him for but nevertheless carved out a career for himself as a dependable and entertaining character actor. Born Harry Samuel Parks in 1940 in Corona, California, he went through the usual array of menial jobs before deciding to give acting a try and, after being discovered on stage by actor/director Frank Silvera, soon began appearing on television shows like *The Untouchables*, *The Detectives*, and *Gunsmoke*; and films like *Wild Seed* (1965), *The Happening* (1967), and *The Bible: In the Beginning* (1966), where he played Adam for director John Huston. On the cusp of stardom, he was assigned by Universal Studios to appear in a remake of *Beau Geste* and when he refused, his contract with the studio was cancelled and his career stalled for a couple of years. Things picked up in 1969 when he won the lead in the series *Then Came Bronson*, in which he played a disillusioned reporter who roamed the country on his motorcycle and helped people he came across with their personal problems. Although it would go on to become a cult favorite, the combination of low ratings and Parks' conflicts with the producers led to its cancellation after only one season. For the next couple of decades, he popped up in a number of television shows and films such as *The Last Hard Man* (1976), *The Private Files of J. Edgar Hoover* (1979), and *The Return of Josey Wales* (1985) (which he also directed), recorded a half-dozen albums and ever tried to qualify as a runner in the 1972 Olympics. His career made an upswing in the nineties, first with a recurring role on *Twin Peaks* and then with his casting as a laconic sheriff in Robert Rodriguez's crime-vampire hybrid *From Dusk Til Dawn* (1996). Although his character did not survive that film, screenwriter Quentin Tarantino brought him and Parks back to appear in his two-part revenge epic *Kill Bill* (2003)—even giving him a second role as a Mexican crime kingpin in *Kill Bill Vol. 2* (2004)—and both Tarantino and Rodriguez employed the character in their separate halves of the two-part exploitation homage *Grindhouse* (2007). Parks also turned up in such films as *Niagara Niagara* (1997), *The Assassination of Jesse James by the Coward Robert*

Ford (2007), *Django Unchained* (2012), and *Argo* (2012); he also played rare lead roles for writer-director Kevin Smith as the leader of a murderous fundamentalist church in *Red State* (2011) and a reclusive old man who transforms a snarky podcaster into a human-walrus hybrid in the cult curiosity *Tusk* (2014). Parks died on May 9 at the age of 77 of undisclosed causes.

Bill Paxton (May 17, 1955-February 25, 2017). Of all the celebrity deaths to occur in 2017, one that hit film fans the hardest was that of actor-director Bill Paxton, partly because it was so unexpected (he died at the age of 61 of a stroke following heart surgery—his family has filed a wrongful death suit against the hospital) and partly because of the loss of such an immensely likable screen presence. Born in Fort Worth, Texas in 1955, Paxton got his start in the film industry as so many others had before him—toiling in the celluloid salt mines of Roger Corman's production company as a set decorator on such films as *Big Bad Mama* (1974, *Eat My Dust* (1976), and *Galaxy of Terror* (1981), the latter of which found him working alongside an ambitious Canadian by the name of James Cameron. Eventually, Paxton drifted into acting with small parts in films like *Stripes* (1981), *Mortuary* (1983), and *Streets of Fire* (1984) before working with Cameron on his low-budget sci-fi thriller *The Terminator* (1984). Over the next few years, he gained additional notice in films like Cameron's *Aliens* (1986), where he had a standout part as a Marine whose braggadocio dissolves into panic under alien attack, the cult vampire favorite *Near Dark* (1987) and *Predator 2* (1990) before achieving leading man status as a small town sheriff who is not as naive as he seems in the critically acclaimed drama *One False Move* (1992). After a few more years of entertaining turns in films such as *Trespass* (1992), *Tombstone* (1993), *Apollo 13* (1995), *Twister* (1996), and the Cameron collaborations *True Lies* (1994) and *Titanic* (1997), he gave what was arguably his best performance in Sam Raimi's drama *A Simple Plan* (1998) as an ordinary guy whose discovery of millions of dollars in illicit loot in the wreckage of a plane crash leads to paranoia and distrust that escalates in shocking ways. He made his directorial debut with *Frailty* (2001), a startlingly effective horror film about a man driven to murder by what he claims are the divine voices he hears in his head. Following a few more film performances, such as his funny turn as a faux-Jimmy Buffet in the horror spoof *Club Dread* (2004) and his follow-up directorial effort, *The Greatest Game Ever Played* (2005), he took on the role of a member of a polygamist community in the long-running HBO series *Big Love*. At the time of his passing, he had completed work on the film *The Circle* (2018) and was appearing in a television series adaptation of *Training Day* that left the air soon after his passing.

Tom Petty (October 20, 1950-October 2, 2017). Gainesville, Florida native Tom Petty achieved worldwide fame as one of the last true purveyors of old-fashioned rock music in a 40-year career that saw him record 13 albums with his longtime band the Heartbreakers, three as a solo artist, two as part of the supergroup The Traveling Wilburys and two as a member of a reconstituted version of his very first band, Mudcrutch. Over the years, his songs would find regular placement on the soundtracks of many movies—Cameron Crowe would make effective use of "Free Fallin" and "Learning to Fly" in *Jerry Maguire* (1996) and *Elizabethtown* (2005), respectively, and Jonathan Demme based memorable scenes in *The Silence of the Lambs* (1991) and *Ricki and the Flash* (2014) around "American Girl." Petty made some musical contributions to films of his own—he and the Heartbreakers backed up Bob Dylan on the theme song to *Band of the Hand* (1986) and he composed the music for *She's the One* (1996). Petty also made appearances in front of the camera from time to time—ranging from cameos in films like *FM* (1978) and *Made in Heaven* (1987) to vocal contributions to the animated television shows *King of the Hill*, where he had a recurring role, and *The Simpsons*. His most notable part came in *The Postman* (1997), where he plays the mayor of a small town in the post-apocalyptic future that Kevin Costner encounters on his journeyeven dottier, it is heavily implied that Petty is actually playing himself. On October 2, a day in which many were playing songs like "I Won't Back Down" in the wake of the massacre at a Las Vegas music festival, he died of what was later determined to be an overdose of prescription medication.

Tim Pigott-Smith (May 13, 1946-April 7, 2017). Born in Rugby, Warwickshire, England in 1946, Pigott-Smith trained as an actor at the Old Vic Theatre School. After working for years in smaller roles on television and stage and in such films as *Aces High* (1976), *Clash of the Titans* (1981), *Victory* (1981), he had his big breakthrough when he landed the key role of Indian Police Superintendent Ronald Merrick in the 1984 miniseries *The Jewel in the Crown* (1984), which went on to become a hit around the world and earned him the BAFTA-TV Award for Best Actor. While shooting the series, he composed a diary and published it alongside some poetry as *Out of India*. In subsequent years, he made numerous stage appearances, playing roles ranging from King Lear to former Enron head Ken Lay, wrote the children's books *The Dragon Tattoo* and *Shadow of Evil*, recorded a number of audiobooks that found him playing up to 22 different characters and turned up in such films as *The Remains of the Day* (1993), *Safe Conduct* (2002), *Bloody Sunday* (2002), *The Four Feathers* (2002), *Gangs of New York* (2002), *Alexander* (2004), *V For Vendetta* (2005), *Quantum of Solace* (2008), *RED 2* (2013), and *Jupiter Ascending* (2015). At the time of his death on April 7 at the age of 70, he had appearances in four films that would be released posthumously: *6 Days* (2017), *King Charles III* (2017), *Victoria & Abdul* (2017), and *The Little Vampire 3D* (2017).

Om Puri (October 18, 1950-January 6, 2017). Born in Ambala in 1950, Puri was raised in poverty and began working at the age of seven to help support his family and continued to work in odd jobs while simultaneously furthering his education. He then joined the National School of Drama in Delhi to study theater acting and from there joined the Film and Television Institute of India. He made his film debut in *Chor Chor Chhup* (1974) and over the next 40-odd years, would amass over 300 credits, including such films as *Ghashiram Kotwal* (1976), *Bhavni Bhavai* (1980), *Sadgati* (1981), *Disco Dancer* (1982), *Ghayal* (1990), *Maya Memsaab* (1991), *Maachis* (1996), *Gupt: The Hidden Truth* (1997), *Pyaar To Hona Hi Tha*

(1998), and *A.K. 47* (1999). After playing a small role in *Gandhi* (1982), Puri also began turning up in British and American productions, including *The Jewel in the Crown* (1985), *City of Joy* (1992), *Wolf* (1994), *The Ghost and the Darkness* (1996), *My Son, The Fanatic* (1997), *Such a Long Journey* (1998), *East is East* (1999), *The Mystic Masseur* (2001), *Code 46* (2003), *Charlie Wilson's War* (2007), and *The Hundred-Foot Journey* (2014). Puri died of a heart attack at his home in Mumbai at the age of 66, leaving two films, *Tubelight* (2017) and *Mr. Kabaadi* (2017), to be released posthumously.

Della Reese (July 6, 1931-November 19, 2017). Born Delloreese Patricia Early in Detroit, Michigan, Della Reese began singing with her church choir at the age of six and when she turned 13, she was hired by Mahalia Jackson to sing and tour with her gospel group. After leaving Wayne State University due to the death of her mother and the illness of her father, Reese eventually began singing in jazz clubs and signed her first recording contract in 1953, scoring a Top Twenty hit in 1957 with "And That Reminds Me." Over the next decade, she would record a string of albums in the jazz, R&B, and gospel genres, receiving three Grammy nominations along the way. In 1969, she became the host of her own talk show, *Della*, and while it was short-lived, it did lead to her becoming the first black woman to guest host *The Tonight Show* in 1970. Over the next couple of decades, she would be a familiar face on the small screen through guest appearances on a number of shows and made-for-television movies, a supporting role on the hit sitcom *Chico and the Man* and, most famously, her co-starring role as an angel in the long-running series *Touched by an Angel*, which earned her seven Image Awards for Lead Actress in a Drama Series during its 1994-2003 run. She made her big screen debut in the low-budget horror thriller *Psychic Killer* (1975) and next appeared fourteen years later opposite Eddie Murphy, Richard Pryor, and Redd Foxx in *Harlem Nights* (1989). From there, she made the occasional appearance in such films as *A Thin Line Between Love and Hate* (1996), *Dinosaur* (2000), *Beauty Shop* (2005), *Expecting Mary* (2010), and *Christmas Angel* (2012). Reese passed away in her Los Angeles home on November 19 at the age of 86.

Don Rickles (May 8, 1926-April 6, 2017). Although primarily known as a stand-up comedian specializing in hilarious and often outrageous insult humor, Don Rickles was also a regular presence in films and television and even developed an unexpected fan base among young children. Born in New York in 1926, Rickles served in the Navy during World War II and, after being honorably discharged in 1946, studied at the American Academy of Dramatic Arts. After only landing bit parts on television, he began performing stand-up comedy in clubs in New York, Los Angeles, and Miami. When his retorts to hecklers got a bigger response than his actual jokes, he shifted to performing as an insult comic. He soon became a popular performer in Las Vegas and turned up in episodes of such shows as *The Twilight Zone*, *The Addams Family*, *F Troop*, and *Gilligan's Island* before headlining his own shows, *The Don Rickles Show* (1968) and *CPO Sharkey* (1974). He made his first film appearance in *Run Silent, Run Deep* (1958), later turned up in the AIP classics *Muscle Beach Party* (1964), *Bikini Beach* (1964), *Pajama Party* (1964), and *Beach Blanket Bingo* (1965) and played a key role in the Clint Eastwood wartime action-comedy *Kelly's Heroes* (1970). After a two-decade hiatus from films, he returned in a supporting role as a Mob lawyer-turned-vampire in the horror comedy *Innocent Blood* (1992) and lent a taste of the real Las Vegas to Martin Scorsese's *Casino* (1995) in his role as an aide to casino operator Robert De Niro. His biggest film success would come when he provided the voice of Mr. Potato Head in the groundbreaking animated film *Toy Story* (1995), a job that would find him returning to the role for the sequels *Toy Story 2* (1999) and *Toy Story 3* (2010) and lead to appearances in other young-skewing films as *Dennis the Menace Strikes Again* (1998) and *Zookeeper* (2011). He was also the subject of *Mr Warmth* (1997), an acclaimed documentary from *Innocent Blood* director John Landis. He continued to make appearances on television and was still touring with his act when he passed away in his home in Beverly Hills from kidney failure on April 6 at the age of 90.

Emmanuelle Riva (February 24, 2027-January 27, 2017). Although Emmanuelle Riva would appear in more than 80 film and television credits in a career spanning seven decades, she is perhaps best known for one of her very first roles and one of her very last. Born Paulette Germaine Riva in 1927 in Chenimenil, France, she became interested in acting at a young age and, after growing up and working as a seamstress for several years, she applied to acting school in Paris at the age of 26, making her stage debut in a 1954 production of *Arms and the Man*. Her international breakthrough came when she was cast by Alain Resnais in the role of a French actress having a love affair with a Japanese architect in the controversial worldwide hit *Hiroshima, mon amour* (1959). Her work in that film earned her a BAFTA nomination for Best Foreign Actress in 1960 and launched a film career that would include the likes of *Kapo* (1960); *Leon Morin, Priest* (1961); *Therese Desqueyroux* (1962), which won her the Best Actress prize at the Venice Film Festival; *Three Colors: Blue* (1993); and *Venus Beauty Institute* (1999). Her other major film appearance came when she appeared in Michael Haneke's *Amour* (2012) as an elderly woman being cared for by her husband (Jean-Louis Trintignant) after suffering a series of increasingly debilitating strokes. Acclaimed throughout the world, she became, at the age of 86, the oldest woman nominated for the Best Actress Oscar® and she went on to win the BAFTA, Cesar, and Los Angeles Film Critics Association prizes for her performance. River passed away in Paris from cancer at the age of 90 on January 27.

Jean Rochefort (April 29, 1930-October 9, 2017). Although famous in his home country of France for an acting career spanning over five decades, Jean Rochefort is perhaps equally known in some circles for a film that he famously didn't get to make. Born in Paris in 1930, he enrolled at the Centre d'Art Dramtatique de la rue Blanche to study acting and, after performing his military service, began working as a theater actor and eventually started to find work in television and film as well. His first major role was in the drama *Hearth Fires* (1972). He would appear in such films as *The Tall Blonde Man with One Red Shoe* (1972), *The Clockmaker* (1973), *The Phantom of Liberty* (1974), and

The Return of the Tall Blonde Man with One Red Shoe (1974) before having a big hit with his leading performance in the comedy *An Elephant Can Be Extremely Deceptive* (1976). While continuing to work as an actor throughout the 1980s and 1990s, Rochefort's career grew in stature and expanded further when he was hired by Walt Disney Studios to narrate the French version of *Welcome to Pooh Corner* and ended up doing the dubbing for a number of their films. Having worked in France for nearly all of his career, Rochefort was set to have his big international breakthrough when he was cast by Terry Gilliam as Don Quixote in the filmmaker's long-gestating project *The Man Who Killed Don Quixote* but due to a number of setbacks, including Rochefort being stricken with a herniated disc, the production eventually collapsed after only a few days of filming. (The documentary *Lost in La Mancha* (2002) chronicled the history of the disastrous production.) After recovering, Rochefort returned to work with appearances in films like *Fanfan la tulipe* (2003), *L'enfer* (2005), *La clef* (2007), *Asterix et Obelix: Au Service de sa Majeste* (2012), *The Artist and the Model* (2012), and *Floride* (2015). He also contributed his voice to the animated film *April and the Twisted World* (2015). Rochefort passed away at the age of 87 on October 9.

George Romero (February 4, 1940-July 16, 2017). It is impossible to overestimate the impact that George Romero had on both the American independent filmmaking world in general and the horror genre in particular with his groundbreaking debut feature, *Night of the Living Dead* (1968), a film whose reverberations continue to be felt a half-century after its release. Born in the Bronx in 1940, Romero attended Carnegie Mellon University in Pittsburgh and, after graduation, formed a production company along with friends John Russo and Russell Streiner to make commercials and industrial films. Wanting to break into features and deciding that a low-budget horror film was the way to go, Romero came up with a screenplay about a sudden outbreak of the dead rising from the grave with a taste for human flesh and a few survivors attempting to fend off their ever-growing numbers. When it was released, those expecting the usual cheap junk were poleaxed by Romero's combination of dark humor, then-shocking levels of gore, and a story that mirrored the social concerns of the age, ranging from the exploding racial tensions to the horrors of Vietnam served up on the news each night, and which did not end happily ever after. The film eventually became a sleeper hit and a critical sensation but when it came time for a followup, Romero decided to shift gears for the anti-establishment romantic comedy *There's Always Vanilla* (1971) and the witch-themed feminists drama *Season of the Witch* (1972). Romero moved back into horror with the bio-terror story *The Crazies* (1973) and the haunting modern-day vampire tale *Martin* (1978). He then returned to the zombie genre with the bigger, bolder, bloodier, and (arguably) better *Dawn of the Dead* (1978). In the 1980s, he made *Knightriders* (1981), a straightforward drama centered on a Renaissance fair where the players ride motorcycles instead of horses; collaborated with fellow horror favorite Stephen King on the anthology film *Creepshow* (1982); returned to zombie land with the bleak *Day of the Dead* (1985); and directed the psychological thriller *Monkey Shines* (1988). For the next couple of decades, however, Romero hit a string of bad luck during which many projects that he planned fell through and the ones that he did get made—the Dario Argento collaboration *Two Evil Eyes* (1990), the King adaptation *The Dark Half* (1993), and the dark comedy *Bruiser* (2000)—suffered from poor distribution. Thanks to the resurgence of the zombie sub genre that he helped create, he was able to get studio financing for the long-gestating *Land of the Dead* (2005) and while it lacked the visceral aspect of his earlier films, the combination of gore and social satire was practically radical by major studio standards. He would stick with zombies for what would prove to be his last two features, the franchise reboot *Diary of the Dead* (2007), which presented a found-footage perspective to the beginning of the zombie outbreak as seen through the eyes of some aspiring horror filmmakers, and *Survival of the Dead* (2009), in which two long-quarreling families fought over what to do with the undead. Throughout the ups and downs of his career, he remained a fan favorite with enormous influence over subsequent generations of filmmakers. Romero passed away in Toronto, where he had relocated when it became too expensive to make his films in the Pittsburgh area, on July 16 at the age of 77 following a brief battle with lung cancer.

Peter Sallis (February 1, 1921-June 2, 2017). Although a familiar face to viewers of British television over the years, it would be the voice of actor Peter John Sallis that would make him beloved throughout the world. Born in Middlesex, England in 1921, Sallis joined the RAF after the outbreak of World War II and served as a radio mechanic and later as a teacher of radio procedures. He first took up acting while in the RAF and after the war, he enrolled in the Royal Academy of Dramatic Art. Following his first stage appearance in 1946, he appeared in a number of productions, most notably Orson Welles's famous 1955 show *Moby Dick—Rehearsed* and *Baker Street*, a 1964 musical based on Sherlock Holmes in which he played Dr. Watson. He also worked regularly in British television during this time and in 1973 landed the role of Norman Clegg in the series *Last of the Summer Wine*, a part he would play until the show left the air in 2010. He also worked in such films as *The Curse of the Werewolf* (1961), *The V.I.Ps* (1963), *The Mouse on the Moon* (1963), *Charlie Bubbles* (1967), and *Taste the Blood of Dracula* (1971). His most famous performance began to take root in 1983 when a student animator asked him to do the voice of an eccentric inventor with a passion for cheese for his newest film, a request Sallis granted in exchange for a donation to his favorite charity. The animator was Nick Park, the character was Wallace and the film was *Wallace and Gromit: A Grand Day Out* (1989) After the international success of that short, Sallis would play Wallace again in the award-winning shorts *The Wrong Trousers* (1993), *A Close Shave* (1995), and *A Matter of Loaf and Death* (2008) as well as the feature *Wallace & Gromit: The Curse of the Were-Rabbit* (2005), which earned him the Annie Award for Best Voice Acting in an Animated Feature. Around this time, his eyesight began to fail him and, following one more go-around as Wallace in the 2010 series

Wallace and Gromit's World of Invention, he retired due to his failing health. Sallis died on June 2 in Northwood, London at the age of 96.

Sam Shepard (November 5, 1943-July 27, 2017). One of the most celebrated playwrights of his generation, Sam Shepard also carved out an equally acclaimed second career as an actor. Born in Fort Sheridan, Illinois in 1943, he ended up in New York City after attending college and started working as part of the Off-Broadway scene in 1962, quickly earning a strong reputation for his stage plays. In addition to his work for the stage, he contributed to the screenplays of *Me & My Brother* (1968) and Michelangelo Antonioni's counter-cultural epic *Zabriskie Point* (1970) and then went on tour with Bob Dylan's Rolling Thunder Revue in 1975, eventually publishing a diary of the experience, *Rolling Thunder Logbook,* in 1978. That same year, his play *Buried Child* won the Pulitzer Prize and was nominated for five Tonys and Shepard received much acclaim for his performance in Terrence Malick's *Days of Heaven* (1978). Over the next few years, Shepard divided his time between writing plays and appearing in films such as *Resurrection* (1980); *Raggedy Man* (1981); *Frances* (1982), where he first met long-time lover Jessica Lange; and *The Right Stuff* (1983), where his performance as Chuck Yeager earned him a Best Supporting Actor Oscar® nomination. While still writing and directing for the stage, he co-wrote the award-winning *Paris, Texas* (1984), adapted his play *Fool for Love* (1985) for Robert Altman, and made his screen directing debut with *Far North* (1988). He was also a regular presence on the big screen as well with appearances in such films as *Country* (1984); *Crimes of the Heart* (1986); *Baby Boom* (1987); *Steel Magnolias* (1989); *The Pelican Brief* (1993); *All the Pretty Horses* (2000); *The Pledge* (2001); *Black Hawk Down* (2001); *The Notebook* (2004); *Don't Come Knocking* (2005), which he co-wrote with *Paris, Texas* collaborator Wim Wenders; *Fair Game* (2009); *August: Osage County* (2013); a recurring role on the cable series *Bloodline* (2014); and *Midnight Special* (2016). Shepard died on July 27 at his home in Kentucky from amyotrophic lateral sclerosis.

Harry Dean Stanton (July 14, 1926-September 15, 2017). Although he would only play a lead role in a film twice during his long career, Harry Dean Stanton nevertheless became an enormously popular character actor through indelible supporting turns that once led critic Roger Ebert to state that "no movie featuring either Harry Dean Stanton or M. Emmet Walsh in a supporting role can be altogether bad." Born in Kentucky in 1926, Stanton began to study acting at the Pasadena Playhouse in Pasadena, California before serving in the Navy during World War II. He made his screen debut with an unbilled bit part in Alfred Hitchcock's *The Wrong Man* (1957) and spent the next couple of decades playing supporting parts in such films as *Ride in the Whirlwind* (1966), *In the Heat of the Night* (1967), *Cool Hand Luke* (1967), *Kelly's Heroes* (1970), *Pat Garrett & Billy the Kid* (1973), *Dillinger* (1973), *The Godfather Part II* (1974), *The Missouri Breaks* (1976), *Straight Time* (1978), and *Wise Blood* (1979) before getting attention for playing a member of the ill-fated crew of the Nostromo in the sci-fi classic *Alien* (1979). After a few more years of scene-stealing supporting parts in *The Black Marble* (1980), *Private Benjamin* (1980), *Escape from New York* (1981), *One from the Heart* (1982), *Christine* (1983), and *Red Dawn* (1984) before landing his two most notable parts to date, first as a dissolute car repossessor teaching a punk kid the tricks of the trade in the cult classic *Repo Man* (1984) and then in his first true lead as a mysterious man who returns from a long and unexplained absence and attempts to reconnect with the wife and child that he left behind in the powerful *Paris, Texas* (1984). Although acclaimed for his performance in that film, he went back to supporting parts in a wide variety of films that included *Pretty in Pink* (1986), *The Last Temptation of Christ* (1988), *She's So Lovely* (1997, *Fear and Loathing in Las Vegas* (1998), *The Green Mile* (1999), *The Pledge* (2001), and *The Avengers* (2012). He also became a regular fixture in the films of David Lynch with appearances in *Wild at Heart* (1990), *Twin Peaks: Fire Walk With Me* (1992), *The Straight Story* (1999), *Inland Empire* (2006), and the television revival of *Twin Peaks* (2017). His life and career were also the subject of the documentary *Harry Dean Stanton: Partly Fiction* (2012). In what would prove to be one of his final roles, Stanton played only his second lead role in the indie drama *Lucky* (2017), in which he played a self-sufficient 90-year-old man who claims to be an atheist, but who is increasingly filled with unease about the possibility that death is indeed the end. Playing a character not too far removed from himself, Stanton was absolutely magnetic and when it was released, earned him some of the best reviews of his entire career. Just as *Lucky* was about to arrive in theaters, Stanton passed away in Los Angeles on September 15 at the age of 91.

George Steele (April 16, 1937-February 16, 2017). Born April 16, 1937 in Detroit, Michigan, William James Myers was working at Madison High School in Madison Heights, Michigan as a teacher and a football and wrestling coach when he decided to enter the local wrestling scene as a way of making extra money. Not wanting to expose his identity, he wore a mask in the ring and was identified only as The Student. The wild man persona he developed in the ring was popular enough to get him recruited by the World Wide Wrestling Federation in 1967 and after being told to get rid of the mask and the Student nickname, he began wrestling under the name George "The Animal" Steele. As the popularity of wrestling increased during the 1980s, he became one of the federation's most popular performers until he retired from the ring in 1988 after being diagnosed with Crohn's disease. He then began working for the WWF as an agent and made his big-screen debut in 1994 when he was hired to play another famous wrestler-turned-actor, Tor Johnson, in Tim Burton's acclaimed *Ed Wood* (1994). Although he received positive reviews for his work, he did not really pursue acting outside of small roles in a handful of obscure films such as *Blowfish* (1997), *Small Town Conspiracy* (2003), and *South of Heaven* (2008) and a Minolta television commercial opposite Tony Randall. On February 16, Steele died in a Florida hospital from kidney failure.

Seijun Suzuki (May 24, 1923-February 13, 2017). Although he spent a large portion of his filmmaking career making low-budget gangster movies within the Japanese studio system, Seijun Suzuki would develop a cult following throughout the world of fans entranced by the wild and unique cinematic style that he employed. Born in 1923 in Tokyo, Suzuki was recruited into the Japanese Army during World War II and, after the war, went to work as an assistant director with the Shochiku Company's Otuna Studios. He did not quite fit in there and in 1954, he went to work at the recently reopened Nikkatsu Studios and made his official directorial debut with *Victory is Mine* (1956). Over the next decade, he made more than 30 films and used the lax eye that the studio applied to its B-movie output to inject his films with weirdo humor, increasingly surreal narratives, and wild visuals stylings. Eventually, the studio ordered him to play it straight and reduced the budget for his next film. He responded with the crazy-cool *Tokyo Drifter* (1966), which transformed a crime potboiler into a one-of-a-kind head-spinner. Nikkatsu responded by cutting the budget for his next film even further and he responded with *Branded to Kill* (1967), an audacious crime movie spoof centered around Japan's #3 ranked hitman (who has a fetish for the scent of boiled rice) who is literally gunning for the #1 slot via a presumably impossible mission. The end result was arguably his masterpiece but led to his firing from Nikkatsu and a blacklisting from all the Japanese studios that lasted for more than a decade. He worked sporadically after that but his earlier works began to develop a cult following around the world with directors like Jim Jarmusch and Quentin Tarantino singing his praises. Among his later projects were *Pistol Opera* (2001), a loose sequel/remake of *Branded to Kill* that was just as strange as its predecessor and the romantic musical *Princess Raccoon* (2005). Following that film, he retired due to health reasons and passed away in Tokyo on February 13 at the age of 93 from pulmonary disease.

Jay Thomas (July 12, 1948-August 24, 2017). The people listed in these obituaries have numerous accomplishments to their credit but Jay Thomas is perhaps the only one to inspire a legitimate holiday tradition. Born in 1948, Thomas got his start working as a radio personality in New York beginning in 1976 and soon branched out into television as well, landing notable recurring roles in such popular shows as *Mork & Mindy*, *Cheers*, and *Murphy Brown*, where his performance as the on-off love interest of the title character earned him Emmy Awards in 1990 and 1991. While working in both radio and television, he made appearances in such films as *C.H.U.D.* (1984), *Legal Eagles* (1986), *Straight Talk* (1992), *Mr. Holland's Opus* (1995), *The Santa Clause 2* (2002), and *The Santa Clause 3: The Escape Clause* (2006). He is perhaps most beloved for his annual Christmastime appearances on *The Late Show with David Letterman*, which began in 1998 when he turned up during a segment in which the host and quarterback Vinny Testaverde were unsuccessfully trying to knock a meatball off the top of a Christmas tree with a football and hit it with one shot. Later, during his interview segment, he told a hilarious story from his early radio days involving a fender bender that occurred while he was driving actor Clayton Moore, still dressed in his Lone Ranger costume, from a promotional appearance. Until the show went off the air in 2015, Thomas would come back every Christmas to retell the story and once again try to hit the meatball. His final screen appearances were in the films *Underdogs* (2013) and *The Trials of Cate McCall* (2003) and in episodes of *Ray Donovan*. On August 24, he died in Santa Barbara, California from throat cancer at the age of 69.

Frank Vincent (April 15, 1937-September 13, 2017). Although he played a number of different roles throughout his career, Frank Vincent will forever be associated with the parts that he played in some of the most famous mobster movies of the contemporary era. Born in 1937 as Frank Vincent Gattuso Jr., the actor originally aspired to be a musician—he could play the trumpet, piano, and drums—but his career trajectory changed when he landed a part in the low-budget gangster movie *The Death Collector* (1976), in which he co-starred with fellow unknown actor Joe Pesci. Although not widely seen, one person who did see it was Robert De Niro, who brought it to the attention of Martin Scorsese, who was so impressed that he cast both Vincent and Pesci in *Raging Bull* (1980). Over the next decade he turned up, usually playing a mobster type, in such films as *Baby, It's You* (1983), *Easy Money* (1983), *The Pope of Greenwich Village* (1984), *Wise Guys* (1986), and *Do the Right Thing* (1989). His most notable film appearance came when he reunited with Scorsese, De Niro, and Pesci for the gangster classic *Goodfellas* (1990) as a recently paroled mobster whose relentless needling of Pesci's hothead character leads him to a spectacularly messy end. From there, he became a familiar presence in film and television through such projects as *Mortal Thoughts* (1991); *Jungle Fever* (1991); the Scorsese crime epic *Casino* (1995), where he got to deliver a brutal beatdown to Pesci as payback for *Goodfellas*; *She's the One* (1996); the television miniseries *Gotti* (1996); and *Cop Land* (1997). He played Aristotle Onassis in *Isn't She Great* (2000) and played a rare lead role in the indie drama *Chicago Overcoat* (2009). In 2006, he published the book *A Guy's Guide to Being a Man's Man* and continued to work in film, television, and video game voiceovers until his death on September 13 at the age of 80.

Selected Film Books of 2017

Baldwin, James and Raoul Peck. *I Am Not Your Negro: A Companion Edition to the Documentary Film Directed by Raoul Peck,* Vintage, 2017. Raoul Peck's award-winning film was comprised of footage set to the words of author James Baldwin about three assassinations: Medgar Evers, Malcolm X, and Martin Luther King. This tie-in edition of Baldwin's work includes 40 black-and-white images from Peck's film.

Batchelor, Bob. *Stan Lee: The Man Behind Marvel,* Rowman & Littlefield Publishers, 2017. Where would the Marvel Cinematic Universe and the modern blockbuster be without the work of Stan Lee? The first cradle to today biography of Stan Lee comes from a regular entertainment writer and looks at his work in the world of comics and the billion-dollar film industry that erupted from them.

Benjamin, Troy and Marc Sumerak. *Ghostbusters: Ectomobile,* Insight Editions, 2017. Every cult hit of a certain generation gets dozens of books and, believe it or not, this one examines, in great detail, the vehicle that drove the Ghostbusters around in the 1984 movie of the same name. It doesn't stop there. It also looks at variations on the car in *Ghostbusters II* (1989) and the 2016 remake. And it includes faux "commentary" by characters Ray Stantz, Peter Venkman, and Jillian Holtzmann.

Bergestrom, Signe and Michael Gracey. *The Art and Making of The Greatest Showman,* Weldon Owen, 2017. An art-book companion for the hit Fox film that includes not only the standard lavishly reproduced stills and behind-the-scenes anecdotes, but the lyrics to the songs from the movie, including the Oscar-nominated "This is Me" by Benj Pasek and Justin Paul.

Bernstein, Abbie. *Justice League: The Art of the Film,* Titan Books, 2017. The king (or Titan) of movie-tie in books tackles the WB/DC hit about the legendary superheroes who assemble to, of course, save the planet. It's standard coffee table fare with stills, concept art, sketches, and details about the making of the film starring Ben Affleck, Gal Gadot, and Henry Cavill.

Blauvelt, Christian. *Star Wars Made Easy: A Beginner's Guide to a Galaxy Far, Far Away,* DK, 2017. The Deputy Editor at BBC Culture dumbs down the Lucasverse for the people who may be new to the franchise that has grown even more popular with the recent films *The Force Awakens* (2015) and *The Last Jedi.* If one needs a refresher on what happened in the original or prequel trilogies or a guide to the characters, this is the place to start.

Bossert, David A. *Oswald the Lucky Rabbit: The Search for the Lost Disney Cartoons,* Disney Editions, 2017. Believe it or not, Mickey Mouse was not the first iconic character of the Disney company. That honor belongs to Oswald the Lucky Rabbit, created in 1927, and the star of over two dozen shorts for the company. When the rights to the character expired, Walt and company moved on to create Mickey, and a lot of the original Oswald work was lost. This book details the attempt to find those original shorts.

Bray, Adam and Cole Horton. *Star Wars: The Visual Encyclopedia,* DK, 2017. The machine that consists of books related to *Star Wars* continues with another visual tome, primarily for young viewers. It includes over 2,500 characters, creatures, items, and other things from the world of this famous George Lucas property, moving up through *The Force Awakens* (2015) and *Rogue One: A Star Wars Story* (2016).

Bricca, Jacob. *Documentary Editing: Principles & Practice,* Focal Press, 2017. An Assistant Professor at the University of Arizona's School of Theatre, Film and Television—and an editor of films, including *Lost in La Mancha* (2002)—offers his insight into the art of cutting together non-fiction films. The professor uses examples from over 100 films and presents a step-by-step guide.

Brown, Jeffrey. *Darth Vader and Family Coloring Book,* Chronicle Books, 2017. Author Jeffrey Brown has made a fortune reimagining classic *Star Wars* characters like Darth Vader and Princess Leia in a series of cartoonish, kiddie books like *Vader's Little Princess* and the artist appeals to his fan base with a coloring book in the same animated style as his other books.

Cummings, Whitney. *I'm Fine... And Other Lies,* G.P. Putnam's Sons, 2017. The stand-up comedian, roast specialist, writer, and actress does the comedic memoir thing, detailing her rise to fame and the mistakes she made along the way. Cummings has performed in comedy specials for HBO and Comedy Central, co-created CBS's *2 Broke Girls,* and directed her film debut, *The Female Brain* (2018).

DBG. *Art of Coloring: Tim Burton's The Nightmare Before Christmas: 100 Images to Inspire Creativity,* Disney Editions, 2017. The artwork of the beloved 1993 film directed by Henry Selick and produced by Tim Burton gets the coloring book for adults treatment in this clever little book that features the world of Jack Skellington and all of his spooky friends.

Degraff, Andrew and A.D. Jameson. *Cinemaps: An Atlas of 35 Great Movies,* Quirk Books, 2017. An acclaimed artist looks at the worlds of hit films and creates details, artistic maps of them, including *Back to the Future* (1985), *The Shining* (1980), *The Princess Bride* (1987), *King Kong* (1933), and a few dozen more. Each map is presented in detailed, 11x14 format, nearly suitable for framing.

Duncan, Paul. *David Bowie in The Man Who Fell to Earth,* TASCHEN, 2017. The kings of the coffee table art book tackle the 1976 sci-fi film starring the legendary musician. This hefty volume was released in conjunction with the 40th anniversary of the film and includes stills and behind-the-scenes images shot by unit photographer David James. It's a fitting tribute to a recently-lost legend.

Duncan, Paul. *The Pedro Almodovar Archives,* TASCHEN, 2017. The art book company's "Archives" series—which has chronicled the work of Stanley Kubrick, Charlie Chapin, Ingmar Bergman, and others in the past—turns to the filmography of the great Pedro Almodovar. Featuring the participation of the filmmaker himself, this includes behind-the-scenes images and personal details. Each film gets a detailed recounting.

Edwards, Gavin and R. Sikoryak. *The Tao of Bill Murray: Real-Life Stories of Joy, Enlightenment, and Party Crashing,* Random House, 2017. The Oscar-nominated TV and film star Bill Murray has developed quite an anecdotal reputation as an atypical celebrity in the manner in which he likes to interact with his fans, sometimes even crashing weddings and partying with them. This is an account of all of those wonderful stories being told at bars around the world about the time someone met Bill Murray.

Eyman, Scott. *Hank and Jim: The Fifty-Year Friendship of Henry Fonda and James Stewart,* Simon and Schuster, 2017. For nearly half the 20th century, Henry Fonda and James Stewart were two of the biggest stars in the world, but people may not know that they were also best friends. They got their start together as stage actors in New York, and were even roommates, both there and in Hollywood. This book chronicles their unique friendship.

Falconer, Daniel and K.M. Rice. *Middle-earth from Script to Screen: Building the World of The Lord of the Rings and The Hobbit,* Harper Design, 2017. An epic, in-depth look at the making of the six films by Peter Jackson, the trilogy based on *The Lord of the Rings* and the subsequent one based on *The Hobbit.* There have been volumes about all six films, but none look as comprehensively at the entire saga as this one.

Faris, Anna and Chris Pratt. *Unqualified,* Dutton, 2017. The star of *Scary Movie* and *The House Bunny* gets her turn behind the memoir microphone with a title that plays off that of her hit podcast, *Anna Faris is Unqualified.* The foreword by then-husband Chris Pratt is bittersweet given their late-2017 split.

Fisher, Joely. *Growing Up Fisher: Musings, Memories, and Misadventures,* William Morrow, 2017. Joely Fisher grew up in the gigantic shadows of her parents Eddie Fisher and Connie Stevens and her half-sister Carrie Fisher, but she found her way to her own acting career and two-decade marriage. She recounts how she got there and what her life has been like in this memoir.

Fitzmaurice, Simon. *It's Not Yet Dark: A Memoir,* Houghton Mifflin Harcourt, 2017. Also made into an inspirational documentary of the same name in 2017, this is the story of director Simon Fitzmaurice, who was diagnosed with Lou Gehrig's Disease in 2008 and given four years to live. He lost almost all motor function, but defied prognosis, living long enough to direct a feature film with only the ability to move his eyes. This is his story.

Gaines, Caseen and Brian and Wendy Froud. *The Dark Crystal: The Ultimate Visual History,* Insight Editions, 2017. Jim Henson and Frank Oz's 1982 fantasy flick has only gained in esteem and fan base in the 35 years since its release. This volume details the history of the making of the film comprehensively, using unseen interviews and new ones with the creative team behind the movie. It features never-before-seen concept art, notes, and sketches from the making of the film.

Gale, A Cengage Company. *VideoHound's Golden Movie Retriever 2018: The Complete Guide to Movies on VHS, DVD, and Hi-Def Formats,* Gale Research Inc., 2017. One of the few remaining annual volumes to actually attempt to chronicle every film ever made in capsule review form, featuring details about its release like MPAA rating and length, along with a 1-4 "bone" rating.

Gosling, Sharon. *Wonder Woman: The Art and Making of the Film,* Titan Books, 2017. Patty Jenkins' *Wonder Woman* (2017), staring Gal Gadot and Chris Pine, was one of the most beloved films of 2017, and so it gets the lavish coffee table book treatment with one of the best editions of the year. It's a gorgeous volume with sketches, storyboards, concept art, and other details about the filmmaking process that these books often ignore.

Greene, Joshua. *The Essential Marilyn Monroe by Milton H. Greene: Milton H. Greene: 50 Sessions,* Acc Art Books, 2017. Milton H. Greene was one of the most famous photographers of his era, and he became friends and business partners with the one-and-only Marilyn Monroe in the 1950s. The two worked together for only four years, but produced two feature films and over 5,000 photos, and some of the best, including ones that had never before been published, are assembled here.

Hanson, Helen. *Hollywood Soundscapes: Film Sound Style, Craft and Production in the Classical Era,* British Film Institute, 2017. Focusing on the early sound period of 1931 to the late studio period of 1946, this educational volume centers on the beginning of sound in film. The author is a Senior Lecturer in Film Studies at the University of Exeter.

Hart, Kevin and Neil Strauss. *I Can't Make This Up: Life Lessons,* Atria/37 INK, 2017. One of the most famous stand-up comedians of the 21st century and the star of films like *The Wedding Ringer* (2015), *Central Intelligence* (2016), and *Jumanji: Welcome to the Jungle* (2017) offers some humorous takes on his life and art.

Hasbro and Rebecca Dart. *The Art of My Little Pony: The Movie,* VIZ Media LLC, 2017. Fans of the colorful universe of Hasbro's *My Little Pony* are loyal enough to put an art tie-in volume such as this on their coffee table. This is your standard tie-in fare with concept sketches, notes, character designs, and artwork, accompanied by details about the making of the film from its director, screenwriter, and animators.

Henson, Taraji P. and Denene Millner. *Around the Way Girl: A Memoir,* Atria/37 INK, 2017. The Oscar-nominated star of *Hustle & Flow* (2005), *The Curious Case of Benjamin Button* (2008), and *Hidden Figures* (2016), among many others, gets the memoir treatment from growing up in Washington, DC to her current remarkable fame.

Hornaday, Ann. *Talking Pictures: How to Watch Movies,* Basic Books, 2017. Veteran film critic Ann Hornaday takes an interesting approach in this book, giving readers the vocabulary that most good critics have when it comes to dissecting cinema. What is good cinematography? Editing? Sound design? How do we talk about performance? It's a valuable resource for professional critics and amateur ones.

Horner, Doogie and J.J. Harrison. *A Die Hard Christmas: The Illustrated Holiday Classic,* Insight Editions, 2017. The popularity of 1988's *Die Hard* has only grown in the three decades since its release. It's gotten so popular that this riff on the classic "Night Before Christmas" was released as a sort of "kids' book for adults."

Insight Editions. *Harry Potter: A Cinematic Gallery: 80 Original Images to Color and Inspire,* Insight Editions, 2017. Adult coloring books have become something of a thing recently and here's another one, although it works for all ages. Assembled are detailed, elaborate images from the Harry Potter films, from the first to the last, several of which expand out to gatefolds that could even be suitable for framing with the right colorist.

Johnson, Mindy. *Ink & Paint: The Women of Walt Disney's Animation (Disney Editions Deluxe),* Disney Editions, 2017. The untold story of how much impact female animators had on the early days of the Walt Disney Company is finally put in print here by an expert on the company. These are the pioneers of the industry, many of whom have never gotten the credit they deserved until now.

Johnson, Patrick. *The Physics of Star Wars: The Science Behind a Galaxy Far, Far Away,* Adams Media, 2017. An assistant teaching professor at Georgetown University jumps into the Lucasfilm pool with this examination of the science in the sci-fi masterpieces that started with the story of Luke Skywalker. How close are we to actually realizing some of the things that were once just science fiction? And how accurate are the *Star Wars* films when it comes to physics?

Johnston, Jacob. *Marvel's Guardians of the Galaxy Vol. 2: The Art of the Movie,* Marvel, 2017. It's not a superhero movie without an art book and James Gunn's well-liked sequel gets the treatment with concept art, production stills, and comments from cast and crew, including Gunn and the visual artists who brought this movie to life.

Jones, Dylan. *David Bowie: A Life,* Crown Archetype, 2017. A massive biography (544 pages!) that examines the life of David Bowie from the cradle to the grave, using over 180 interviews with people who knew him as its foundation. It's an oral history of a genius, who changed popular music forever, and made his impact on film as well.

Jones, Stephen. *The Art of Horror Movies: An Illustrated History,* Applause Theatre & Cinema Books, 2017. The history of horror movies is captured not through words but through the art used to sell it, including posters, lobby cards, advertising, toys, and more. This clever volume also includes a foreword by director John Landis.

Jorgensen, Jay and Manoah Bowman. *Grace Kelly: Hollywood Dream Girl,* Dey Street Books, 2017. A visual biography of the legendary star from early appearances to her worldwide fame. Includes dozens of photographs, many from original negatives.

Kendrick, Anna. *Scrappy Little Nobody,* Touchstone, 2017. From her early days in Portland, Maine to her worldwide fame, Anna Kendrick does the autobiography, including discussion of her roles in *Twilight* (2008), *Up in the Air* (2009), *Pitch Perfect* (2012), and *Into the Woods* (2014).

Klastorin, Michael. *Close Encounters of the Third Kind: The Ultimate Visual History,* Harper Design, 2017. The 40th anniversary of the Steven Spielberg classic results in this tribute to the beloved film, including rare and never-before-seen imagery, along with photography, concept art, stoyboards, and more.

Kratter, Tia and John Lasseter. *The Color of Pixar,* Chronicle Books, 2017. The author has been a part of the Pixar team for 25 years and now manages Pixar University's art and film education classes. This is a collection of stills and examination of the use of color in the Pixar films.

Krefft, Vanda. *The Man Who Made the Movies: The Meteoric Rise and Tragic Fall of William Fox,* Harper, 2017. This massive volume (near 1,000 pages) chronicles the story of a pioneer, whom the book claims is as important as Steve Jobs and Walt Disney. You likely know the legacy of William Fox through the studio that still bears his name. This is his entire life story, culled from over ten years of research by the author.

Laurie, Greg and Marshall Terrill. *Steve McQueen: The Salvation of an American Icon,* American Icon Press, 2017. The author approaches the life of Steve McQueen from a religious background, interviewing his friends and family and discussing how the icon discovered Jesus Christ in his final days. He is the senior pastor of Harvest Christian Fellowship in California.

League, Tim and Brad Bird. *The Art of Mondo,* Insight Editions, 2017. Based in Austin, Texas, Mondo is an art company founded by people who love movies, and their posters and prints sell for hundreds of dollars. This allows people to collect the art without having to shell out for the originals.

Leong, Tim. *Star Wars Super Graphic: A Visual Guide to a Galaxy Far, Far Away,* Chronicle Books, 2017. The author is a graphic designer who presents the history and universe of *Star Wars* (1977) and its sequels in a new way, including visual graphics like flowcharts and pie graphs.

Lewis, Jenifer. *The Mother of Black Hollywood: A Memoir,* Amistad, 2017. Jenifer Lewis has more than 300 credited appearances in film and television, most recently as a major part of ABC's *Black-ish.* She does the autobiography thing here. She even gets into details on how her life was impacted by an undiagnosed mental illness, and how she overcame said illness.

Malone, Alicia. *Backwards and in Heels: The Past, Present and Future of Women Working in Film,* Mango Media, 2017. The author, a famous film reporter, looks at the role of women in Hollywood, including interviews with Geena Davis, Ava DuVernay, Octavia Spencer, America Ferrera, and more. Billed as an entry into "the complex world of women in film."

McDonald, Brian. *Invisible Ink: A Practical Guide to Building Stories that Resonate,* Talking Drum, 2017. The author has written for film, commercials, and comic books, and he has taught story structure at Pixar, Disney, and Lucasfilm. He brings his insight to this instructional volume.

McIntyre, Gina and Guillermo del Toro. *Guillermo del Toro's The Shape of Water: Creating a Fairy Tale from Troubled Times,* Insight Editions, 2017. The tie-in book and art volume for the Oscar-winning film for Best Director and Best Picture. It includes interviews with Del Toro and key actors and members of the creative team.

Media Lab Books and Editors of John Wayne Magazine. *John Wayne Cast Iron Official Cookbook,* Media Lab Books, 2017. The cult of fandom around John Wayne remains as large as ever, as proven by the fact that there's a cookbook based more on his public persona than anything that actually has to do with the real actor.

Media Lab Books and Editors of the Official John Wayne Magazine. *The John Wayne Code: Wit, Wisdom, and Timeless Advice,* Media Lab Books. John Wayne made around 150 movies, and there are probably now more books than that about him. At least this one includes advice and wisdom actually given by Wayne over the course of his life, including full-color photos and personal stories.

O'Sullivan, Mike. *Marvel Cinematic Universe Guidebook: The Good, The Bad, The Guardians,* Marvel, 2017. A tie-in volume that collects the stories of seven Marvel Cinematic Universe films, from *Captain America: The Winter Soldier* (2014) to *Doctor Strange* (2016). It offers recaps of the films along with fact sheets, production stills, and more details about their production.

Perry, Tyler. *Higher is Waiting,* Spiegel & Grau, 2017. The beloved director and creator of Madea goes the religious route with this book about his life and how he salvaged it by putting it in the hands of God. It is mostly a biography, but it is also billed as a "spiritual guidebook."

Peterson, Monique. *Harry Potter: The Wand Collection,* Insight Editions, 2017. The various wands used in the eight Harry Potter films, from Hermione Granger's to those of the Death Eaters, get detailed renderings and histories in the latest tie-in to this beloved series.

Rao, Sri. *Bollywood Kitchen: Home-Cooked Indian Meals Paired with Unforgettable Bollywood Films,* Houghton Mifflin Harcourt, 2017. The concept is so simple it's hard to believe someone didn't write it earlier—pair a recipe for a great Indian meal with a beloved Bollywood movie. Recipeces for brunch, kids meals, and cocktail parties are included as well.

Rea, Andrew. *Eat What You Watch: A Cookbook for Movie Lovers,* Dovetail, 2017. So many great films include great food, and this volume collects 40 of them to offer ways to literally recreate what you're seeing on-screen while you watch your favorite movies.

Rinzler, J.W. *Star Wars: The Blueprints,* Epic Ink, 2017. The world of *Star Wars* is more detailed than even hardcore fans realize and this volume collects the blueprints, photographs, and illustrations that go into creating this universe from technical drawing to finished products like the Millennium Falcon and Jabba the Hutt's throne room.

Rode, Alan K. *Michael Curtiz: A Life in Film,* University Press of Kentucky, 2017. He may not get the acclaim or love of his peers, but Michael Curtiz was one of the most formative voices in early Hollywood, directing films like *Casablanca* (1942) and *White Christmas* (1954). This exhaustive biography examines his entire life and career, including numerous affairs and children born out of wedlock.

Roussos, Eleni. *Marvel's Thor: Ragnarok—The Art of the Movie,* Marvel, 2017. Every Marvel movie gets an art book, and such is the case with the third Thor movie, starring Chris Hemsworth, Mark Ruffalo, Cate Blanchett, and Tessa Thompson. Concept art, behind-the-scenes photos, stills, interviews—this one checks all the boxes.

Roussos, Eleni. *Spider-Man: Homecoming—The Art of the Movie,* Marvel, 2017. See above. Another Marvel movie, another art book, this one for the latest adventure of Peter Parker, his first standalone in the Marvel universe. It even comes from the same author as the one about *Thor: Ragnarok* (2017) and works from the same model.

Ryan, Maureen. *Producer to Producer: A Step-by Step Guide to Low-Budget Independent Film Producing,* Michael Wiese Productions, 2017. The author is both a famous writer and the producer of James Marsh's *Man on Wire* (2009), which won the Oscar for Best Documentary. This is a step-by-step volume from pre-production meetings through post-production for those on a limited budget.

Salisbury, Mark. *Valerian and the City of a Thousand Planets: The Art of the Film,* Titan Books, 2017. Luc Besson's mega-budget sci-fi film was so complex that its universe could use a detailed art book more than most blockbusters, and this one fits the bill with information on the various alien species and how the filmmakers brought them to life.

Scheibli, James and Paul Scanlon. *Movie Quotes for All Occasions: Unforgettable Lines for Life's Biggest Moments,* Mango, 2017. The title pretty much says it all. Want the right quote for before the big game? At the end of a speech?

On a first date? This volume will help you find the right movie bon mot for all of your conversational needs.

Schoenberger, Nancy. *Wayne and Ford: The Films, the Friendship, and the Forging of an American Hero,* Nan A. Talese, 2017. Film history would not be the same without the collaborations between director John Ford and actor John Wayne. From the moment Ford really made him a star in 1939's *Stagecoach* through the dissolution of their friendship and working relationship in 1960, this book examines the incredible effect they had on the movies as a team.

Sermak, Kathryn and Danelle Morton. *Miss D and Me: Life with the Invincible Bette Davis,* Hachette Books, 2017. The author knew Bette Davis for a decade, first as an employee and then as a close friend, and she tells the story of the legendary star's final years. It's framed around a four-day road trip that the pair took near the end of her life.

Sexton, Jared. *Black Masculinity and the Cinema of Policing,* Palgrave Macmillan, 2017. A teacher of African-American Studies and Film and Media Studies at the University of California looks at the way black lives are captured in cinema, particularly in the way they capture (or fail to) the black male protagonist.

Sidibe, Gabourey. *This Is Just My Face: Try Not to Stare,* Mariner Books, 2017. The Oscar-nominated star of *Precious* (2009) does the autobiography thing, telling her story from life in Harlem to worldwide fame.

Silver, Alain and James Ursini. *Film Noir,* TASCHEN, 2017. There are dozens of books about the beloved genre of film noir, but few that have the art brand of TASCHEN, the king of coffee table books. This elaborate volume is dense with stills and posters, designed to capture the genre visually as much as through the written word. It also includes the writers' picks for the 50 best noirs.

Smith, Ian Haydn and Steven Jay Schneider. *1,001 Movies You Must See Before You Die,* Barron's Education Series, 2017. This series has become an annual event now and this is the seventh edition, now up to nearly 1,000 pages on films that the authors feel are essential to a cinema-loving life.

Solomon, Brian. *Godzilla FAQ: All That's Left to Know About the King of the Monsters,* Applause Theatre & Cinema Books, 2017. Since Godzilla's debut in 1954, he's become as iconic as any cinematic creation in history, and this volume captures every single detail about his history—both fictional and the production of the many films—in around 400 pages of monster insanity.

Stone, Matt and Dave Ekins. *McQueen's Motorcycles: Racing and Riding with the King of Cool,* Motorbooks, 2017. The former editor of a magazine called *Motor Trend* looks at how closely the imagery of actor Steve McQueen is tied to his love for motorcycles. McQueen didn't just make motorcycles cooler, he raced them and amassed a giant collection, much of which is detailed here in color photography.

Szostak, Phil and Lucasfilm LTD. *The Art of Star Wars: The Last Jedi,* Harry N. Abrams, 2017. A writer who has produced a number of books in the Lucasfilm universe produces the tie-in volume for *Star Wars: The Last Jedi* (2017) complete with concept art, costume sketches, storyboards, and more. The book also includes exclusive interviews.

Thwaite, Ann. *Goodbye Christopher Robin: A.A. Milne and the Making of Winnie-the-Pooh,* St. Martin's Griffin, 2017. A tie-in for the feature film starring Domhnall Gleeson, Margot Robbie, and Kelly Macdonald.

Titan Magazines. *Thor: Ragnarok The Official Movie Special,* Titan Comics, 2017. A thinner guide to the making of the Taika Waititi film than the Art-of book but one that still includes interviews and a gallery of images from the Marvel hit.

Titan. *Star Wars: The Last Jedi—The Official Collector's Edition,* Titan Comics, 2017. A guidebook to the #1 film of 2017 that includes characters, planets, ships, and more from the universe of the Rian Johnson sequel. There are also a handful of behind-the-scenes cast and crew shots.

Troyan, Michael and Jeffrey Paul Thompson. *Twentieth Century Fox: A Century of Entertainment,* Lyons Press, 2017. A look at the formation, impact, and history of Twentieth Century Fox from its inception in 1915 until 2015. It's the studio that made stars of Marilyn Monroe, Elvis Presley, James Dean, and so many more, and this volume uses the studio's archived and resources to tell its story.

Unkrich, Lee and Adrian Molins. *The Art of Coco,* Chronicle Books, 2017. The companion book to the Oscar-winning film for Best Animated Feature includes character sketches, artwork, storyboard, and more behind the Pixar hit.

Ward, Simon. *The Art and Making of Alien: Covenant,* Titan Books, 2017. The divisive Ridley Scott prequel gets the art-of tie-in with this great volume that shows the amount of detail that went into the creature and production design of this blockbuster film.

Windham, Ryder and Adam Bray. *Star Wars Stormtroopers: Beyond the Armor (Star Wars: Journey to Star Wars: The Last Jedi),* Harper Design, 2017. With a foreword by star John Boyega, this book chronicles the history of the iconic Stormtrooper characters from *A New Hope* (1977) through *The Last Jedi* (2017).

Director Index

Dominique Abel
Lost in Paris

Harry Abu-Assad
The Mountain Between Us

Fatih Akin (1973-)
In the Fade

Gethin Aldous
The Work

Tomas Alfredson (1965-)
The Snowman

Woody Allen (1935-)
Wonder Wheel

Michael Almereyda (1960-)
Marjorie Prime

Ana Lily Amirpour
The Bad Batch

Sean Anders
Daddy's Home 2

Paul Thomas Anderson (1970-)
Phantom Thread

Paul W.S. Anderson
Resident Evil: The Final Chapter

Peter Andrews (1963-)
See *Steven Soderbergh*

Lucia Aniello
Rough Night

Nikolaj Arcel
The Dark Tower

Darren Aronofsky (1969-)
mother!

Miguel Arteta (1965-)
Beatriz at Dinner

Amma Asante
A United Kingdom

Kelly Asbury (1960-)
Smurfs: The Lost Village

Olivier Assayas (1955-)
Personal Shopper

David Ayer (1972-)
Bright

Jeff Baena (1977-)
The Little Hours

Sean Baker
The Florida Project

Kyle Balda
Despicable Me 3

Amir Bar-Lev
Long Strange Trip

Justin Barber
Phoenix Forgotten

Claude Barras
My Life as a Zucchini

Ritesh Batra
The Sense of an Ending

Noah Baumbach (1969-)
The Meyerowitz Stories (New and Selected)

Michael Bay (1965-)
Transformers: The Last Knight

Charlie Bean
The LEGO Ninjago Movie

Emil Ben-Shimon
The Women's Balcony

Luc Besson (1959-)
Valerian and the City of a Thousand Planets

Margaret Betts
Novitiate

Kathryn Bigelow (1952-)
Detroit

Jeffrey Blitz (1969-)
Table 19

Baran bo Odar
Sleepless

Bertrand Bonello
Nocturama

Joon-ho Bong (1969-)
Okja

Benny Boom
All Eyez on Me

Laurent Bouzereau
Five Came Back

David Bowers (1970-)
Diary of a Wimpy Kid: The Long Haul

Danny Boyle (1956-)
T2 Trainspotting

Zach Braff (1975-)
Going in Style

Kenneth Branagh (1960-)
Murder on the Orient Express

Ash Brannon
Rock Dog

Janicza Bravo
Lemon

Callan Brunker
The Nut Job 2: Nutty by Nature

Rama Burshtein
The Wedding Plan

Martin Campbell (1940-)
The Foreigner

Robin Campillo
BPM (Beats Per Minute)

Michael Carney
Same Kind of Different as Me

Niki Caro (1967-)
The Zookeeper's Wife

D.J. Caruso (1965-)
xXx: Return of Xander Cage

Joseph Cedar
Norman

Justin Chadwick
Tulip Fever

Stephen Chbosky (1972-)
Wonder

Peter Chelsom (1956-)
The Space Between Us

George Clooney (1961-)
Suburbicon

Pierre Coffin
Despicable Me 3

Andrew Jay Cohen
The House

Bonni Cohen
An Inconvenient Sequel: Truth to Power

Bill Condon (1955-)
Beauty and the Beast

Scott Cooper (1970-)
Hostiles

Eleanor Coppola (1936-)
Paris Can Wait

Sofia Coppola (1971-)
The Beguiled

Gabriela Cowperthwaite
Megan Leavey

Eran Creevy (1976-)
Collide

Destin Daniel Cretton
The Glass Castle

Michael Cuesta (1963-)
American Assassin

Simon Curtis (1960-)
Goodbye Christopher Robin

Czar (1973-)
See *S. Craig Zahler*

Jean-Pierre Dardenne (1951-)
The Unknown Girl

Luc Dardenne (1954-)
The Unknown Girl

Terence Davies (1945-)
A Quiet Passion

Damon Davis
Whose Streets?

Jonathan Dayton (1957-)
Battle of the Sexes

Ricardo de Montreuil (1974-)
Lowriders

Guillermo del Toro (1964-)
The Shape of Water

Dean Devlin
Geostorm

Denise Di Novi
Unforgettable

J.D. Dillard
Sleight

Julia Ducournau (1983-)
Raw

Daniel Espinosa (1977-)
Life

Philippe Falardeau
Chuck

Valerie Faris (1958-)
Battle of the Sexes

Brian Fee
Cars 3

Paul Fisher
The LEGO Ninjago Movie

Anna Foerster
Underworld: Blood Wars

Sabaah Folayan
Whose Streets?

James Foley (1953-)
Fifty Shades Darker

Marc Forster (1969-)
All I See Is You

James Franco (1978-)
The Disaster Artist

Stephen Frears (1941-)
Victoria & Abdul

Stephen Gagham
Gold

Terry George
The Promise

Greta Gerwig (1983-)
Lady Bird

Craig Gillespie
I, Tonya

Dan Gilroy (1959-)
Roman J. Israel, Esq.

Fiona Gordon
Lost in Paris

Seth Gordon
Baywatch

Michael Gracey
The Greatest Showman

F. Gary Gray (1969-)
The Fate of the Furious

James Gray (1969-)
The Lost City of Z

David Gordon Green (1975-)
Stronger

Luca Guadagnino (1971-)
Call Me by Your Name

James Gunn (1970-)
Guardians of the Galaxy Vol. 2

F. Javier Gutierrez (1973-)
Rings

Brett Haley
The Hero

Jason Hall
Thank You for Your Service

Lasse Hallstrom (1946-)
A Dog's Purpose

John Lee Hancock (1956-)
The Founder

Michael Haneke (1942-)
Happy End

Todd Haynes (1961-)
Wonderstruck

Stuart Hazeldine
The Shack

Eliza Hittman
Beach Rats

Reginald Hudlin
Marshall

Patrick Hughes
The Hitman's Bodyguard

Dean Israelite
Power Rangers

Azazel Jacobs
The Lovers

Steve James (1955-)
Abacus: Small Enough to Jail

Hun Jang
A Taxi Driver

Geremy Jasper
Patti Cake$

Patty Jenkins (1971-)
Wonder Woman

Craig Johnson
Wilson

Rian Johnson (1973-)
Star Wars: The Last Jedi

Jake Kasdan (1975-)
Jumanji: Welcome to the Jungle

Aki Kaurismaki (1957-)
The Other Side of Hope

Richie Keen
Fist Fight

Gabe Klinger
Porto

Kogonada
Columbus

Hirokazu Kore-eda (1962-)
After the Storm

Joseph Kosinski (1974-)
Only the Brave

Alex Kurtzman (1973-)
The Mummy

Christopher Landon (1975-)
Happy Death Day

Yorgos Lanthimos
The Killing of a Sacred Deer

Malcolm Lee (1970-)
Girls Trip

David Leitch
Atomic Blonde

Sebastian Lelio
A Fantastic Woman

Tony Leondis (1967-)
The Emoji Movie

John R. Leonetti (1956-)
Wish Upon

David Leveaux (1957-)
The Exception

Jonathan Levine
Snatched

Doug Liman (1965-)
American Made
The Wall

Richard Linklater (1960-)
Last Flag Flying

Amanda Lipitz
Step

Zoe Lister-Jones (1982-)
Band Aid

Bob Logan
The LEGO Ninjago Movie

David Lowery
A Ghost Story

Sam Lowry (1963-)
***See** Steven Soderbergh*

Jon Lucas
A Bad Moms Christmas

John Carroll Lynch (1963-)
Lucky

Terrence Malick (1943-)
Song to Song

James Mangold (1964-)
Logan

Samuel Maoz
Foxtrot

Ken Marino (1968-)
How to Be a Latin Lover

Martin McDonagh (1970-)
Three Billboards Outside Ebbing, Missouri

Tom McGrath
The Boss Baby

Paul McGuigan (1963-)
Film Stars Don't Die in Liverpool

Chris McKay
The LEGO Batman Movie

Greg McLean
The Belko Experiment

Jairus McLeary
The Work

Stella Meghie
Everything, Everything

George Mendeluk (1948-)
Bitter Harvest

Hallie Meyers-Shyer (1987-)
Home Again

Roger Michell (1957-)
My Cousin Rachel

Takashi Miike (1960-)
Blade of the Immortal

Adriana Molina
Coco

Scott Moore
A Bad Moms Christmas

Brett Morgen
Jane

Errol Morris (1948-)
The B-Side: Elsa Dorfman's Portrait Photography
Wormwood

Jared Moshe
The Ballad of Lefty Brown

Oren Moverman
The Dinner

Kate Mulleavy
Woodshock

Laura Mulleavy
Woodshock

Cristian Mungiu (1968-)
Graduation

Andy Muschietti
It

Bharat Nalluri (1965-)
The Man Who Invented Christmas

Christopher Nolan (1970-)
Dunkirk

William Oldroyd
Lady Macbeth

Niels Arden Oplev (1961-)
Flatliners

Ruben Ostlund
The Square

Francois Ozon (1967-)
Frantz

Alexander Payne (1961-)
Downsizing

Raoul Peck (1953-)
I Am Not Your Negro

Jordan Peele (1979-)
Get Out

Mark Pellington (1962-)
The Last Word

Tyler Perry (1969-)
Boo 2! A Madea Halloween

Alexandre O. Philippe
78/52: Hitchcock's Shower Scene

Kevin Phillips
Super Dark Times

James Ponsoldt (1978-)
The Circle

Martin Provost
The Midwife

Timothy Reckart
The Star

Dee Rees
Mudbound

Matt Reeves (1966-)
War for the Planet of the Apes

Rob Reiner (1947-)
LBJ

Guy Ritchie (1968-)
King Arthur: Legend of the Sword

Johannes Roberts (1976-)
47 Meters Down

Gillian Robespierre
Landline

Angela Robinson (1971-)
Professor Marston and the Wonder Women

Joachim Ronning (1972-)
Pirates of the Caribbean: Dead Men Tell No Tales

Matt Ruskin
Crown Heights

Ry Russo-Young (1981-)
Before I Fall

Benny Safdie
Good Time

Joshua Safdie
Good Time

Carlos Saldanha (1968-)
Ferdinand

David F. Sandberg
Annabelle: Creation

Espen Sandberg (1971-)
Pirates of the Caribbean: Dead Men Tell No Tales

Rupert Sanders
Ghost in the Shell

Antonio Santini
Dina

Lone Scherfig (1959-)
Their Finest

Ridley Scott (1939-)
Alien: Covenant
All the Money in the World

Andy Serkis (1964-)
Breathe

Dash Shaw (1983-)
My Entire High School Sinking Into the Sea

Ron Shelton (1945-)
Just Getting Started

Jon Shenk
An Inconvenient Sequel: Truth to Power

Dax Shepard (1975-)
CHIPS

Lawrence Sher (1970-)
Father Figures

Makoto Shinkai
Your Name

Michael Showalter (1970-)
The Big Sick

Trey Edward Shults
It Comes at Night

M. Night Shyamalan (1970-)
Split

Daniel Sickles
Dina

Trish Sie
Pitch Perfect 3

Alex Smith
Walking Out

Andrew J. Smith
Walking Out

Zack Snyder (1966-)
Justice League

Steven Soderbergh (1963-)
Logan Lucky

David Soren
Captain Underpants: The First Epic Movie

Aaron Sorkin (1961-)
Molly's Game

Matt Spicer
Ingrid Goes West

Steven Spielberg (1947-)
The Post

Michael Spierig
Jigsaw

Peter Spierig
Jigsaw

Chad Stahelski
John Wick: Chapter 2

Danny Strong (1974-)
Rebel in the Rye

Eric Summer
Leap!

Robin Swicord (1952-)
Wakefield

Jonathan Teplitzky
Churchill

Jayson Thiessen
My Little Pony: The Movie

Stacy Title
The Bye Bye Man

Ceyda Torun
Kedi

Colin Trevorrow
The Book of Henry

Joachim Trier
Thelma

Nora Twomey
The Breadwinner

Lee Unkrich
Coco

Matthew Vaughn (1971-)
Kingsman: The Golden Circle

Gore Verbinski (1964-)
A Cure for Wellness

Simon Verhoeven
Friend Request

Nacho Vigalondo
Colossal

Denis Villeneuve (1967-)
Blade Runner 2049

Paolo Virzi
The Leisure Seeker

Jordan Vogt-Roberts
Kong: Skull Island

Taika Waititi
Thor: Ragnarok

Aisling Walsh
Maudie

Eric Warin
Leap!

Jon Watts
Spider-Man: Homecoming

Marc Webb
Gifted
The Only Living Boy in New York

Chris Wedge (1957-)
Monster Trucks

Joshua Z Weinstein
Menashe

Ben Wheatley
Free Fire

Mike White (1970-)
Brad's Status

Michael Winterbottom (1961-)
The Trip to Spain

Edgar Wright (1974-)
Baby Driver

Joe Wright (1972-)
Darkest Hour

S. Craig Zahler (1973-)
Brawl in Cell Block 99

Yimou Zhang (1951-)
The Great Wall

Screenwriter Index

Dominique Abel
Lost in Paris

Jonathan Aibel
Monster Trucks

Fatih Akin (1973-)
In the Fade

Matthew Aldrich
Coco

Woody Allen (1935-)
Wonder Wheel

Michael Almereyda (1960-)
Marjorie Prime

Stephen Amidon (1959-)
The Leisure Seeker

Hossein Amini (1966-)
The Snowman

Ana Lily Amirpour
The Bad Batch

Sean Anders
Daddy's Home 2

Paul Thomas Anderson (1970-)
Phantom Thread

Paul W.S. Anderson
Resident Evil: The Final Chapter

Lucia Aniello
Rough Night

Nikolaj Arcel
The Dark Tower

Francesca Archibugi
The Leisure Seeker

Anne Argula (1938-)
See Darryl Ponicsan

Darren Aronofsky (1969-)
mother!

Olivier Assayas (1955-)
Personal Shopper

Richard Bachynsky Hoover
Bitter Harvest

Jeff Baena (1977-)
The Little Hours

Steven Bagatourian
All Eyez on Me

Robert L. Baird
Ferdinand

Sean Baker
The Florida Project

James Baldwin (1924-1987)
I Am Not Your Negro

Matthew Ballen
Friend Request

Justin Barber
Phoenix Forgotten

Bob Barlen
The Nut Job 2: Nutty by Nature

Claude Barras
My Life as a Zucchini

Kenya Barris
Girls Trip

Marc Basch
The Hero

Noah Baumbach (1969-)
The Meyerowitz Stories (New and Selected)

Simon Beaufoy (1967-)
Battle of the Sexes

Glenn Berger
Monster Trucks

Chris Bergoch
The Florida Project

Andrea Berloff
Sleepless

Carlo Bernard
The Great Wall

Luc Besson (1959-)
Valerian and the City of a Thousand Planets

Margaret Betts
Novitiate

Jenny Bicks
The Greatest Showman

Scott Bindley
The Nut Job 2: Nutty by Nature

Alice Birch
Lady Macbeth

Rebecca Blunt
Logan Lucky

Mark Boal (1973-)
Detroit

Hark Bohm (1939-)
In the Fade

Mark Bomback (1971-)
War for the Planet of the Apes
Bertrand Bonello
Nocturama
Joon-ho Bong (1969-)
Okja
Max Borenstein
Kong: Skull Island
David Bowers (1970-)
Diary of a Wimpy Kid: The Long Haul
Frank Cottrell Boyce (1959-)
Goodbye Christopher Robin
Ash Brannon
Rock Dog
Janicza Bravo
Lemon
Callan Brunker
The Nut Job 2: Nutty by Nature
Simon Burke
The Exception
Rama Burshtein
The Wedding Plan
W. Bruce Cameron (1960-)
A Dog's Purpose
Robin Campillo
BPM (Beats Per Minute)
Kay Cannon
Pitch Perfect 3
Michael Carney
Same Kind of Different as Me
Joseph Cedar
Norman
Stephen Chbosky (1972-)
Beauty and the Beast
Wonder
Clark Cheng
Your Name
Gaby Chiappe
Their Finest
George Clooney (1961-)
Suburbicon
Daniel Clowes (1961-)
Wilson
Ethan Coen (1957-)
Suburbicon
Joel Coen (1954-)
Suburbicon
Andrew Jay Cohen
The House
Cheo Hodari Coker
Lowriders
Ben Collins
Super Dark Times
Bill Condon (1955-)
The Greatest Showman
Derek Connolly
Kong: Skull Island
Monster Trucks
Steve Conrad (1968-)
Wonder
Sean Conway
All I See Is You
Scott Cooper (1970-)
Hostiles
Brad Copeland
Ferdinand
Eleanor Coppola (1936-)
Paris Can Wait
Sofia Coppola (1971-)
The Beguiled
Susan Coyne
The Man Who Invented Christmas
Eran Creevy (1976-)
Collide
Destin Daniel Cretton
The Glass Castle
The Shack
Michael Cristofer (1945-)
Chuck
Czar (1973-)
***See** S. Craig Zahler*
John Francis Daley (1985-)
Spider-Man: Homecoming
Jean-Pierre Dardenne (1951-)
The Unknown Girl
Luc Dardenne (1954-)
The Unknown Girl
Gary Dauberman
Annabelle: Creation
It
Ken Daurio
Despicable Me 3
Terence Davies (1945-)
A Quiet Passion
Guillermo del Toro (1964-)
The Shape of Water
Dean Devlin
Geostorm
J.D. Dillard
Sleight
Katie Dippold
Snatched
Dr. and Mr. Haggis-On-Whey (1970-)
***See** Dave Eggers*
Anita Doron
The Breadwinner
Paul W. Downs
Rough Night
Julia Ducournau (1983-)
Raw
Jay Duplass (1973-)
Table 19
Mark Duplass (1976-)
Table 19
Dave Eggers (1970-)
The Circle
Deborah Ellis
The Breadwinner
Yu-na Eom
A Taxi Driver
Jacob Aaron Estes (1972-)
Rings
Hampton Fancher (1938-)
Blade Runner 2049
Tim Federle (1980-)
Ferdinand
Jeff Feuerzeig
Chuck
Efthymis Filippou
The Killing of a Sacred Deer
Michael Finch
American Assassin
Stuart Ross Fink
The Last Word
Paul Fisher
The LEGO Ninjago Movie
Kieran Fitzgerald
Wormwood
Tom Flynn (1980-)
Gifted
Alexander Foard
Same Kind of Different as Me
Maya Forbes
A Dog's Purpose
Christopher Ford
Spider-Man: Homecoming

Marc Forster (1969-)
All I See Is You

Scott Frank (1960-)
Logan

F. Scott Frazier
Collide
xXx: Return of Xander Cage

Cary Fukunaga (1977-)
It

John Fusco
The Shack

John Gatins
Power Rangers

Brett Gelman
Lemon

Terry George
The Promise

Greta Gerwig (1983-)
Lady Bird

Dan Gilroy (1959-)
Kong: Skull Island
Roman J. Israel, Esq.

Tony Gilroy (1956-)
The Great Wall

Peter Goldfinger
Jigsaw

Jane Goldman (1970-)
Kingsman: The Golden Circle

Akiva Goldsman (1962-)
The Dark Tower
Rings

Jonathan M. Goldstein (1969-)
Spider-Man: Homecoming

Eddie Gonzalez
All Eyez on Me

J. Mills Goodloe (1971-)
Everything, Everything
The Mountain Between Us

Cory Goodman
Underworld: Blood Wars

Emily V. Gordon (1979-)
The Big Sick

Fiona Gordon
Lost in Paris

Seth Grahame-Smith (1976-)
The LEGO Batman Movie

James Gray (1969-)
The Lost City of Z

Pamela Gray
Megan Leavey

Michael Green
Blade Runner 2049
Logan
Murder on the Orient Express

Seth Jared Greenberg (1976-)
***See** Seth Grahame-Smith*

Matt Greenhalgh
Film Stars Don't Die in Liverpool

Larry Gross (1953-)
Porto

James Gunn (1970-)
The Belko Experiment
Guardians of the Galaxy Vol. 2

Paul Guyot
Geostorm

Jeremy Haft (1972-)
All Eyez on Me

Brett Haley
The Hero

Jason Hall
Thank You for Your Service

Lee Hall
Victoria & Abdul

Ron Hall
Same Kind of Different as Me

Michael Haneke (1942-)
Happy End

Liz Hannah
The Post

Martin Hardy (1959-)
***See** Frank Cottrell Boyce*

Stacey Harman
Smurfs: The Lost Village

Joby Harold
King Arthur: Legend of the Sword

Dante Harper
Alien: Covenant

Mark Harris
Five Came Back

Joey Hartstone
LBJ

Steven Hathaway
Wormwood

Justin Haythe (1973-)
A Cure for Wellness

Allan Heinberg
Wonder Woman

Marshall Herskovitz (1952-)
American Assassin

Grant Heslov (1963-)
Suburbicon

Guy Hibbert
A United Kingdom

Eliza Hittman
Beach Rats

John Hodge (1964-)
T2 Trainspotting

Christina Hodson
Unforgettable

Matt Holloway
Transformers: The Last Knight

Elisabeth Holm
Landline

Rita Hsiao
My Little Pony: The Movie

Gregg Hurwitz
The Book of Henry

James Ivory (1928-)
Call Me by Your Name

Azazel Jacobs
The Lovers

Elgin James
Lowriders

Geremy Jasper
Patti Cake$

Anders Thomas Jensen (1972-)
The Dark Tower

David Leslie Johnson
Unforgettable

Rian Johnson (1973-)
Star Wars: The Last Jedi

Kurt Johnstad
Atomic Blonde

Amy Jump
Free Fire

Aki Kaurismaki (1957-)
The Other Side of Hope

Jeff Kinney
Diary of a Wimpy Kid: The Long Haul

Gabe Klinger
Porto

Philip Koch
Friend Request

David Koepp (1964-)
The Mummy

Kogonada
Columbus

Derek Kolstad
John Wick: Chapter 2

Hirokazu Kore-eda (1962-)
After the Storm

Jacob Koskoff
Marshall

Carlos Kotkin
The Star

Ehren Kruger (1972-)
Ghost in the Shell

Dylan Kussman (1971-)
The Mummy

Craig Kyle
Thor: Ragnarok

Max Landis (1985-)
Bright

Andrew Lanham
The Glass Castle
The Shack

Yorgos Lanthimos
The Killing of a Sacred Deer

Sebastian Lelio
A Fantastic Woman

Niall Leonard
Fifty Shades Darker

Tony Leondis (1967-)
The Emoji Movie

Richard Linklater (1960-)
Last Flag Flying

Alex Lipschultz
Menashe

Zoe Lister-Jones (1982-)
Band Aid

Scott Lobdell (1963-)
Happy Death Day

Allan Loeb
The Only Living Boy in New York
The Space Between Us

Bob Logan
The LEGO Ninjago Movie

John Logan (1961-)
Alien: Covenant

David Loucka
Rings

Tim Lovestedt
Megan Leavey

David Lowery
A Ghost Story

Jon Lucas
A Bad Moms Christmas

Maria Maggenti (1962-)
Before I Fall

Justin Malen
Father Figures

Terrence Malick (1943-)
Song to Song

James Mangold (1964-)
Logan

Samuel Maoz
Foxtrot

David Marconi
The Foreigner

Art Marcum
Transformers: The Last Knight

Barbara Marshall
Wish Upon

Patrick Massett
Gold

Gonzalo Maza
A Fantastic Woman

Anthony McCarten (1961-)
Darkest Hour

Anthony Peter Chanel Thomas Aquinas McCarten (1961-)
***See** Anthony McCarten*

Meghan McCarthy
My Little Pony: The Movie

Michael McCullers
The Boss Baby

Martin McDonagh (1970-)
Three Billboards Outside Ebbing, Missouri

Chris McKenna
Jumanji: Welcome to the Jungle
The LEGO Batman Movie
Spider-Man: Homecoming

Christopher McQuarrie (1968-)
The Mummy

Theodore Melfi
Going in Style

George Mendeluk (1948-)
Bitter Harvest

Hallie Meyers-Shyer (1987-)
Home Again

Roger Michell (1957-)
My Cousin Rachel

Cathryn Michon
A Dog's Purpose

Doug Miro
The Great Wall

Deborah Moggach (1948-)
Tulip Fever

Adriana Molina
Coco

Scott Moore
A Bad Moms Christmas

Chris Morgan
The Fate of the Furious

Brett Morgen
Jane

John Morris
Daddy's Home 2

Jared Moshe
The Ballad of Lefty Brown

Jamie Moss
Ghost in the Shell

Oren Moverman
The Dinner

Kate Mulleavy
Woodshock

Laura Mulleavy
Woodshock

Annie Mumolo
Megan Leavey

Cristian Mungiu (1968-)
Graduation

Keil Murray
Cars 3

Kumail Nanjiani (1978-)
The Big Sick

Jeff Nathanson
Pirates of the Caribbean: Dead Men Tell No Tales

Morgan Navarro
My Life as a Zucchini

Shlomit Nehama
The Women's Balcony

Scott Neustadter (1977-)
The Disaster Artist

William Nicholson (1948-)
Breathe

Carol Noble
Leap!

Christopher Nolan (1970-)
Dunkirk

Ken Nolan
Only the Brave
Transformers: The Last Knight

T.S. Nowlin
Phoenix Forgotten

Brendan O'Brien
The House

Tom O'Connor
The Hitman's Bodyguard

Tetsuya Oishi
Blade of the Immortal

Tracy Oliver
Girls Trip

Ruben Ostlund
The Square

Francois Ozon (1967-)
Frantz

Chase Palmer
It

Cinco Paul
Despicable Me 3

Alexander Payne (1961-)
Downsizing

Nick Payne
The Sense of an Ending

Eric Pearson
Thor: Ragnarok

Jordan Peele (1979-)
Get Out

Jonathan Penner (1962-)
The Bye Bye Man

Tyler Perry (1969-)
Boo 2! A Madea Halloween

Bob Peterson
Cars 3

Alexandre O. Philippe
78/52: Hitchcock's Shower Scene

Francesco Piccolo (1964-)
The Leisure Seeker

Jeff Pinkner
The Dark Tower
Jumanji: Welcome to the Jungle

Luke Piotrowski
Super Dark Times

John Pollono
Stronger

Darryl Ponicsan (1938-)
Last Flag Flying

James Ponsoldt (1978-)
The Circle

Martin Provost
The Midwife

Dee Rees
Mudbound

Rhett Reese
Life

Matt Reeves (1966-)
War for the Planet of the Apes

Pamela Ribon (1975-)
Smurfs: The Lost Village

Mike Rich (1959-)
Cars 3

Ernest Riera (1977-)
47 Meters Down

Ben Ripley
Flatliners

Guy Ritchie (1968-)
King Arthur: Legend of the Sword

Johannes Roberts (1976-)
47 Meters Down

Gillian Robespierre
Landline

Van Robichaux
Fist Fight

Angela Robinson (1971-)
Professor Marston and the Wonder Women

Matthew Robinson
Monster Trucks

Steven Rogers
I, Tonya

Molly Rokosz
Wormwood

Jon Ronson (1967-)
Okja

Scott Rosenberg (1963-)
Jumanji: Welcome to the Jungle

Matt Ruskin
Crown Heights

Benny Safdie
Good Time

Joshua Safdie
Good Time

David Scarpa
All the Money in the World

Stephen Schiff
American Assassin

Liev Schreiber (1967-)
Chuck

Celine Sciamma
My Life as a Zucchini

Brian Selznick (1966-)
Wonderstruck

Damian Shannon
Baywatch

Dash Shaw (1983-)
My Entire High School Sinking Into the Sea

Ron Shelton (1945-)
Just Getting Started

Dax Shepard (1975-)
CHIPS

Taylor Sheridan
Wind River

Makoto Shinkai
Your Name

Trey Edward Shults
It Comes at Night

M. Night Shyamalan (1970-)
Split

Eric Siegel
The Emoji Movie

Robert Siegel
The Founder

Eric Warren Singer
Only the Brave

Josh Singer
The Post

Alex Smith
Walking Out

Andrew J. Smith
Walking Out

David Branson Smith
Ingrid Goes West

Erik Sommers
Jumanji: Welcome to the Jungle
The LEGO Batman Movie
Spider-Man: Homecoming

Aaron Sorkin (1961-)
Molly's Game

Chris Spain
How to Be a Latin Lover

Logan Sparks
Lucky

Matt Spicer
Ingrid Goes West

Evan Spiliotopoulos
Beauty and the Beast

Gary Spinelli
American Made

Jerry Stahl (1953-)
Chuck
Jared Stern
The LEGO Batman Movie
The LEGO Ninjago Movie
Josh Stolberg (1971-)
Jigsaw
Nicholas Stoller
Captain Underpants: The First Epic Movie
Tom Stoppard (1937-)
Tulip Fever
Peter Straughan
The Snowman
Danny Strong (1974-)
Rebel in the Rye
Eric Summer
Leap!
Drago Sumonja
Lucky
Evan Susser
Fist Fight
Soren Sveistrup
The Snowman
Robin Swicord (1952-)
The Promise
Wakefield
Mark Swift
Baywatch
Musa Syeed
Menashe
Jim Taylor (1962-)
Downsizing
Vanessa Taylor
The Shape of Water
Chris Terrio
Justice League
Alex Theurer
Sleight
Lucy Thomas (1970-)
See *Dave Eggers*
Jack Thorne
Wonder
Joachim Trier
Thelma
Lee Unkrich
Coco
Simon Vaughan
Goodbye Christopher Robin
Matthew Vaughn (1971-)
Kingsman: The Golden Circle
Simon Verhoeven
Friend Request
Nacho Vigalondo
Colossal
Paolo Virzi
The Leisure Seeker
Michael Vogel
My Little Pony: The Movie
Eskil Vogt
Thelma
Alex von Tunzelmann (1977-)
Churchill
Kyle Ward
Underworld: Blood Wars
Jon Watts
Spider-Man: Homecoming
Michael H. Weber
The Disaster Artist
Joshua Z Weinstein
Menashe
Chris Weitz (1969-)
The Mountain Between Us
Audrey Wells (1960-)
A Dog's Purpose
Paul Wernick
Life
Ben Wheatley
Free Fire
Joss Whedon (1964-)
Justice League
Tom Wheeler
The LEGO Ninjago Movie
William Wheeler
Ghost in the Shell
The LEGO Ninjago Movie
Mike White (1970-)
Beatriz at Dinner
Brad's Status
The Emoji Movie
Pitch Perfect 3
Sherry White
Maudie
John Whittington
The LEGO Batman Movie
The LEGO Ninjago Movie
Lionel Wigram
King Arthur: Legend of the Sword
Virgil Williams
Mudbound
Wally Wolodarsky
A Dog's Purpose
Angela Workman
The Zookeeper's Wife
Dwain Worrell
The Wall
Edgar Wright (1974-)
Baby Driver
Christopher Yost (1973-)
Thor: Ragnarok
Jon Zack
How to Be a Latin Lover
S. Craig Zahler (1973-)
Brawl in Cell Block 99
Laurent Zeitoun
Leap!
John Zinman
Gold
Germano Zullo (1968-)
My Life as a Zucchini
Edward Zwick (1952-)
American Assassin

Cinematographer Index

Barry Ackroyd (1954-)
Detroit

Javier Aguirresarobe (1948-)
The Promise
Thor: Ragnarok

Maxime Alexandre (1971-)
Annabelle: Creation

Lucas Alvarado-Farrar
Whose Streets?

Mitchell Amundsen (1958-)
A Bad Moms Christmas
CHIPS

Paul Thomas Anderson (1970-)
Phantom Thread

Peter Andrews (1963-)
***See** Steven Soderbergh*

Thierry Arbogast (1957-)
Valerian and the City of a Thousand Planets

John Bailey (1942-)
How to Be a Latin Lover

Thimios Bakatakis
The Killing of a Sacred Deer

Benji Bakshi
Brawl in Cell Block 99

Florian Ballhaus (1965-)
Snatched

Bojan Bazelli (1957-)
A Cure for Wellness

Dion Beebe
The Snowman

Giora Bejach
Foxtrot

Christian Berger (1945-)
Happy End

Tom Bergmann
Abacus: Small Enough to Jail

Ziv Berkovich
The Women's Balcony

Luca Bigazzi (1958-)
The Leisure Seeker

Sebastian Blenkov
Their Finest

Sean Bobbitt
Stronger

Nicolas Bolduc
Chuck

Eli Born
Super Dark Times

Henry Braham (1965-)
Guardians of the Galaxy Vol. 2

Yoni Brook
Menashe

Eigil Bryld
Tulip Fever

Bobby Bukowski
The Dinner

Don Burgess (1956-)
Monster Trucks
Same Kind of Different as Me
Wonder

Brian Burgoyne
The Big Sick

Paul Cameron (1958-)
Pirates of the Caribbean: Dead Men Tell No Tales

Yves Cape (1960-)
The Midwife

Russell Carpenter (1950-)
xXx: Return of Xander Cage

Federico Cesca
Patti Cake$

Cesar Charlone (1958-)
American Made

Rodney Charters (1948-)
Going in Style

Enrique Chediak
American Assassin

Claire Childeric
Lost in Paris

Charlotte Bruus Christensen
Molly's Game

Elisha Christian
Columbus

Chung-hoon Chung (1970-)
It

Matthew Clark
Pitch Perfect 3

James Clarke
The Trip to Spain

Jerrica Cleland
Leap!

Danny Cohen
Victoria & Abdul

Dean Cundey (1946-)
Home Again

Drew Daniels
It Comes at Night

Tobias Datum
The Lovers

Ben Davis (1962-)
Three Billboards Outside Ebbing, Missouri

Roger Deakins (1949-)
Blade Runner 2049

Bruno Delbonnel (1957-)
Darkest Hour

Caleb Deschanel (1941-)
Unforgettable

Anthony Di Ninno
My Little Pony: The Movie

Stuart Dryburgh (1952-)
Gifted
The Great Wall
The Only Living Boy in New York

Benjamin Echazarreta
A Fantastic Woman

Eric Alan Edwards (1953-)
Fist Fight

Mike Eley
My Cousin Rachel

Frederick Elmes (1946-)
Wilson

Robert Elswit (1950-)
Gold
Roman J. Israel, Esq.
Suburbicon

Renato Falcao
Ferdinand

Michael Fimognari
Before I Fall

Peter Flinckenberg
Woodshock

Larry Fong
Kong: Skull Island

Bryce Fortner
Ingrid Goes West
Professor Marston and the Wonder Women

Crystel Fournier
Paris Can Wait

Michael Galbraith
Wish Upon

Greg Gardiner
Girls Trip

Wyatt Garfield
Beatriz at Dinner
Porto

Mike Gioulakis
Split

Rob Givens
The Hero

Guy Godfree
Maudie

Xavier Perez Grobet (1964-)
Brad's Status

Jess Hall
Ghost in the Shell

Joe Heim
Friend Request

David Higgs
Churchill

Leo Hinstin
Nocturama

Florian Hoffmeister (1970-)
A Quiet Passion

Nelson Hume
Long Strange Trip

Jakob Ihre
Thelma

Ruben Impens
Raw

Igor Jadue-Lillo
Everything, Everything

Matthew Jensen
Wonder Woman

Janusz Kaminski (1959-)
The Post

Nicolas Karakatsanis
I, Tonya

Jay Keitel
Phoenix Forgotten

Shane F. Kelly
Last Flag Flying

Darius Khondji (1955-)
The Lost City of Z
Okja

Sean Kirby
Five Came Back

Nobuyasu Kita
Blade of the Immortal

Rainer Klausmann (1949-)
In the Fade

James Kniest
The Bye Bye Man

Matthias Koenigwieser
All I See Is You

Eric Koretz
The Last Word

Alp Korfali
Kedi

Eric Kress (1962-)
Colossal
Flatliners

Ellen Kuras (1959-)
Jane
Wormwood

Ben Kutchins
Crown Heights

Edward Lachman (1948-)
Wonderstruck

Jeanne Lapoirie
BPM (Beats Per Minute)

Dan Laustsen (1954-)
John Wick: Chapter 2
The Shape of Water

Yorick Le Saux (1968-)
Personal Shopper

Philippe Le Sourd
The Beguiled

Jean-Christophe Leforestier
Lost in Paris

Sam Levy
Lady Bird

Matthew Libatique (1969-)
The Circle
mother!

Karl Walter Lindenlaub (1957-)
Underworld: Blood Wars

John Lindley
Father Figures

Matthew Lloyd
Power Rangers

Helene Louvart
Beach Rats

Sam Lowry (1963-)
See *Steven Soderbergh*

Emmanuel Lubezki (1964-)
Song to Song

Julio Macat (1959-)
Daddy's Home 2

Glen MacPherson (1957-)
Resident Evil: The Final Chapter

Mihai Malaimare, Jr.
Sleepless

Anthony Dod Mantle (1955-)
T2 Trainspotting

Alain Marcoen
The Unknown Girl

Barry Markowitz
LBJ

Pascal Marti
Frantz

Igor Martinovic
Wormwood

John Mathieson (1958-)
King Arthur: Legend of the Sword
Logan

Jason McCormick
Lemon

Sam McCurdy
A United Kingdom

David McFarland
The Ballad of Lefty Brown

Seamus McGarvey (1967-)
The Greatest Showman
Life

Todd McMullen
Walking Out

Glen McPherson (1957-)
***See** Glen MacPherson*

Sharone Meir
Rings

Peter Menzies, Jr.
All Eyez on Me

Douglas Milsome
Bitter Harvest

Claudio Miranda
Only the Brave

Kramer Morgenthau
Rebel in the Rye

Rachel Morrison
Mudbound

Sayombhu Mukdeeprom
Call Me by Your Name

Robert Muratore (1968-)
78/52: Hitchcock's Shower Scene

Ben Nott
Jigsaw

Toby Oliver
Get Out
Happy Death Day

Jules O'Loughlin
The Hitman's Bodyguard

Roman Osin (1961-)
The Exception

Gyula Pados (1969-)
Jumanji: Welcome to the Jungle

Andrew Droz Palermo
A Ghost Story

Tudor Vladimir Panduru
Graduation

Phedon Papamichael (1962-)
Downsizing

Andrij Parekh (1971-)
The Zookeeper's Wife

Brett Pawlak
The Glass Castle

Barry Peterson
Just Getting Started
The Space Between Us

Urszula Pontikos
Film Stars Don't Die in Liverpool

Bill Pope (1952-)
Baby Driver

Sean Porter
Rough Night

Declan Quinn (1957-)
The Shack

Casey Regan
Step

Ben Richardson
Table 19
Wind River

Robert Richardson
Breathe

Anthony B. Richmond (1942-)
Diary of a Wimpy Kid: The Long Haul

George Richmond
Kingsman: The Golden Circle

Laurie Rose
Free Fire

Christopher Ross
The Sense of an Ending

Robbie Ryan
The Meyerowitz Stories (New and Selected)

Timo Salminen (1952-)
The Other Side of Hope

Andres Sanchez
Lowriders

Linus Sandgren (1972-)
Battle of the Sexes

Luis David Sansans
The Belko Experiment

Arturo Santamaria
The Work

Roberto Schaefer
Geostorm

Yaron Scharf
Norman

Tobias A. Schliessler
Beauty and the Beast

Andrei Bowden Schwartz
Wakefield

John Schwartzman (1960-)
The Book of Henry
Fifty Shades Darker
The Founder

Jonathan Sela (1978-)
Atomic Blonde
Transformers: The Last Knight

Lorenzo Senatore (1974-)
Megan Leavey

Ben Seresin
The Mummy

Michael Seresin (1942-)
War for the Planet of the Apes

Jas Shelton
The House

Jon Shenk
An Inconvenient Sequel: Truth to Power

Makoto Shinkai
Your Name

Newton Thomas (Tom) Sigel (1961-)
Marshall

Mark Silk
47 Meters Down

Ben Smithard
Goodbye Christopher Robin
The Man Who Invented Christmas

Steven Soderbergh (1963-)
Logan Lucky

Hillary Spera
Band Aid

Terry Stacey
A Dog's Purpose

Eric Steelberg
Baywatch

Vittorio Storaro (1940-)
Wonder Wheel

Tim Suhrstedt
Lucky

Nathan Swingle
The B-Side: Elsa Dorfman's Portrait Photography

Nathan Allen Swingle
The B-Side: Elsa Dorfman's Portrait Photography

Masanobu Takayanagi
Hostiles

David Tattersall (1960-)
The Foreigner

Chris Teague
Landline

Salvatore Totino (1964-)
Spider-Man: Homecoming

David Toutevoix
My Life as a Zucchini

Quyen Tran
The Little Hours

Brandon Trost (1981-)
The Disaster Artist

Adam Uhl
Dina

Hoyte Van Hoytema (1971-)
Dunkirk

Roman Vasyanov
Bright
Thank You for Your Service
The Wall

Richard J. Vialet
Boo 2! A Madea Halloween

Rasmus Videbaek
The Dark Tower

Lyle Vincent
The Bad Batch

Fabian Wagner
Justice League

Mandy Walker (1963-)
The Mountain Between Us

Ari Wegner
Lady Macbeth

Joshua Z Weinstein
Menashe

Fredrik Wenzel
The Square

Kat Westergaard
Novitiate

Ed Wild
Collide

Sean Price Williams
Good Time
Marjorie Prime

Stephen Windon (1959-)
The Fate of the Furious

Dariusz Wolski (1956-)
Alien: Covenant
All the Money in the World

Ed Wu
Sleight

Charlie Wuppermann
Kedi

Yutaka Yamazaki
After the Storm

Amit Yasur
The Wedding Plan

Steve Yedlin
Star Wars: The Last Jedi

Alexis Zabe
The Florida Project

Haris Zambarloukos
Murder on the Orient Express

Xiaoding Zhao
The Great Wall

Editor Index

Alex Abrahams
My Entire High School Sinking Into the Sea

Sandra Adair
Last Flag Flying

Rehman Nizar Ali
Song to Song

Michel Aller
Annabelle: Creation

Craig Alpert
Pitch Perfect 3
Rough Night

Jonathan Amos
Baby Driver
A United Kingdom

Peter Amundson
Underworld: Blood Wars

Peter Andrews (1963-)
See *Steven Soderbergh*

Mags Arnold
The Trip to Spain

Mick Audsley
Murder on the Orient Express

John Axelrad
The Lost City of Z

Denis Bachter
Friend Request

Stuart Baird (1947-)
Bitter Harvest

Sean Baker
The Florida Project

Zene Baker
Snatched
Thor: Ragnarok

Jason Ballantine
It

Roger Barton
Pirates of the Caribbean: Dead Men Tell No Tales
Transformers: The Last Knight

Ben Baudhuin
Colossal

Alan Baumgarten
Molly's Game

Pete Beaudreau
A Cure for Wellness

Alan Edward Bell
The Dark Tower

Debbie Berman
Spider-Man: Homecoming

Martin Bernfeld
Power Rangers

Don Bernier
An Inconvenient Sequel: Truth to Power

Joe Beshenkovsky
Jane

Ivan Bilancio
Rock Dog

David Bilow
Home Again

Andrew Bird
In the Fade

Ken Blackwell
The Bye Bye Man

Julia Bloch
The Wall
Woodshock

Steve Bloom
Coco

Valerio Bonelli
Darkest Hour

Jean-Christophe Bouzy
Raw

Victoria Boydell
Goodbye Christopher Robin

David Brenner
Justice League

Melissa Bretherton
Snatched

Martin Brinkler
47 Meters Down

Aaron Brock
Bright

Ronald Bronstein
Good Time

Casey Brooks
Landline

Sarah Broshar
The Post

Ryan Brown
The Little Hours

Conrad Buff, IV
American Assassin
Monster Trucks

Olivier Bugge Coutte (1970-)
Thelma

David Burrows
The LEGO Batman Movie
The LEGO Ninjago Movie

Darragh Byrne
The Breadwinner

Robin Campillo
BPM (Beats Per Minute)

William Caparella
The Emoji Movie

Jay Cassidy
Thank You for Your Service

Angela Catanzaro
The Foreigner

Luke Franco Ciarrocchi
Split

Richard Comeau
Chuck

Hank Corwin
Song to Song

David Coulson
The Zookeeper's Wife

Joel Cox
All Eyez on Me

Tom Cross
The Greatest Showman
Hostiles

Libby Cuenin
Band Aid

Scott Cummings
Beach Rats
Menashe

John Daigle
How to Be a Latin Lover

Greg D'Auria
Brawl in Cell Block 99

Sandrine Deegen
Lost in Paris

Jay Deuby
Beatriz at Dinner

Pia Di Ciaula
A Quiet Passion

Claire Dodgson
Despicable Me 3

Luke Doolan
Colossal

Dody Dorn (1955-)
Power Rangers

Marie-Helene Dozo
The Unknown Girl

Bob Ducsay
Star Wars: The Last Jedi

Robert Duffy
The Greatest Showman

Lance Edmands
My Entire High School Sinking Into the Sea

Steve Edwards
Jumanji: Welcome to the Jungle

Garret Elkins
The LEGO Ninjago Movie

Tom Elkins
Flatliners

Peter S. Elliott
Baywatch

Nick Emerson
Film Stars Don't Die in Liverpool
Lady Macbeth

Penelope Falk
Step

John Farbrother
Abacus: Small Enough to Jail

Walter Fasano
Call Me by Your Name

Vince Filippone
xXx: Return of Xander Cage

Sarah Flack
The Beguiled

Ryan Folsey
The LEGO Ninjago Movie

Leigh Folsom-Boyd
Pirates of the Caribbean: Dead Men Tell No Tales

Amy Foote
The Work

Billy Fox
Lowriders
Only the Brave

Keith Fraase
Long Strange Trip
Song to Song

Richard Francis-Bruce
Fifty Shades Darker

Robert Frazen
The Founder

Matthew Freund
Fist Fight

Ed Fuller
Rock Dog

Robert Gajic
Lucky

Laure Gardette
Frantz

Nicolas Gaster
The Exception

Adam Gerstel
Transformers: The Last Knight

Terel Gibson
The Ballad of Lefty Brown

Chris Gill
Churchill
Collide

John Gilroy
Roman J. Israel, Esq.

Einat Glaser-Zarhin
The Women's Balcony

Dana E. Glauberman
Father Figures

William Goldenberg
Detroit

Affonso Goncalves
Wonderstruck

Yana Gorskaya
Table 19

Elliot Graham
Molly's Game

Paul Greenhouse
Crown Heights

Jon Gregory
Three Billboards Outside Ebbing, Missouri
A United Kingdom

Kevin Greutert
Jigsaw

Joel Griffen
Sleight

Brett Haley
The Hero

Alex Hall
The Dinner

Eddie Hamilton
Kingsman: The Golden Circle

Meeyeon Han
Okja

Matthew Hannam (1981-)
It Comes at Night

Jon Harris
T2 Trainspotting

Steven Hathaway
The B-Side: Elsa Dorfman's Portrait Photography
Wormwood

Lee Haugen
The Lost City of Z

Samu Heikkila (1971-)
The Other Side of Hope

Mark Helfrich
Jumanji: Welcome to the Jungle

Evan Henke
The House

James Herbert
King Arthur: Legend of the Sword

Chad Herschberger
78/52: Hitchcock's Shower Scene

Yael Hersonski
The Wedding Plan

Kristina Hetherington
My Cousin Rachel

Masahiro Hirakubo
Breathe

Gina Hirsch
The Mummy

Paul Hirsch
The Mummy

Harry Hitner
Ferdinand

Nick Houy
Lady Bird

William Hoy
War for the Planet of the Apes

Jason Hudak
Cars 3

Paul Hunter
The Nut Job 2: Nutty by Nature

Joe Hutshing
Crown Heights
The Greatest Showman

Yang Jinmo
Okja

Dino Jonsater (1969-)
Thank You for Your Service
Woodshock

Bob Joyce
LBJ

Amy Jump
Free Fire

Michael Kahn
The Post

Mako Kamitsuna
Mudbound

Brian A. Kates (1972-)
Norman

Virginia Katz
Beauty and the Beast

Myron Kerstein
Going in Style

Gabe Klinger
Porto

Kogonada
Columbus

Hirokazu Kore-eda (1962-)
After the Storm

Joseph Krings
Rebel in the Rye

Jennifer Lame
The Meyerowitz Stories (New and Selected)

Joe Landauer
Before I Fall

Matt(hew) Landon
Captain Underpants: The First Epic Movie

Lisa Lassek
The Circle

Albertine Lastera
The Midwife

Dan Lebental
CHIPS
Spider-Man: Homecoming

Chris Lebenzon
Geostorm

Stephanie Leger
BPM (Beats Per Minute)

Arik Leibovitch
Foxtrot

Robert Leighton
A Dog's Purpose

Alisa Lepselter
Wonder Wheel

Mark Livolsi
Wonder

David Lowery
A Ghost Story

Sam Lowry (1963-)
***See** Steven Soderbergh*

John F. Lyons
The Sense of an Ending

Paul Machliss
Baby Driver

Matt Maddox
Wakefield

Geraldine Mangenot
Porto

Mary Jo Markey
The Great Wall
Life

Bret Marnell
Smurfs: The Lost Village

Pamela Martin
Battle of the Sexes

Yorgos Mavropsaridis
The Killing of a Sacred Deer

Tom McArdle
Marshall

Michael McCusker
The Greatest Showman
Logan

Joi McMillon
Lemon

Christopher McNabb
Whose Streets?

Peter McNulty
Megan Leavey

Paul Millspaugh
Girls Trip

Steve Mirkovich
Rings

Stephen Mirrione
Suburbicon

Paul Monaghan
The Trip to Spain

Andrew Mondshein (1962-)
American Made
The Mummy

Marion Monnier
Personal Shopper

David Moritz
The Space Between Us

Susan E. Morse
Novitiate

Joe Murphy
Beach Rats

Robert Nassau
The Big Sick

Darrin Navarro
The Lovers

Joel Negron
Thor: Ragnarok

Debra Neil-Fisher
Transformers: The Last Knight

Guy Nemesh
Foxtrot

Colin Nusbaum
An Inconvenient Sequel: Truth to Power

Braden Oberson
My Little Pony: The Movie

Geoffrey O'Brien (1948-)
Bright

Stephen O'Connell
The Man Who Invented Christmas
Maudie

Jeremiah O'Driscoll
Rings

Alex O'Flinn
The Bad Batch

Melanie Oliver
Victoria & Abdul

Mircea Olteanu
Graduation

Ruben Ostlund
The Square

Jim Page
xXx: Return of Xander Cage

Kiran Pallegadda
Lowriders

Bill Pankow
Gifted

Frances Parker
Life

Colin Patton
Pitch Perfect 3

Jamie Pearson
The Man Who Invented Christmas

Richard Pearson
Justice League
Kong: Skull Island

Lee Percy (1953-)
The Mountain Between Us

Lance Pereira
A Cure for Wellness

Heather Persons
Brad's Status

Franklin Peterson
The Circle

Gregory Plotkin
Get Out
Happy Death Day

Jon Poll
The Greatest Showman

Jack Price
Ingrid Goes West

Peck Prior
Wish Upon

Jacopo Quadri
The Leisure Seeker

Fred Raskin
Guardians of the Galaxy Vol. 2

John Refoua
Geostorm
Transformers: The Last Knight

Julien Rey
Valerian and the City of a Thousand Planets

Billy Rich
Ghost in the Shell

Marc Richardson
The Trip to Spain

Nancy Richardson
Everything, Everything

Tatiana S. Riegel
I, Tonya

Gary D. Roach
Wind River

Jake Roberts (1977-)
The Hitman's Bodyguard

Julie Rogers
The LEGO Ninjago Movie

Elisabet Ronaldsdottir
Atomic Blonde

Ron Rosen
Geostorm

Steven Rosenblum
The Promise

Joshua Rosenfield
Phoenix Forgotten

Valentin Rotelli
My Life as a Zucchini

Anita Roth
BPM (Beats Per Minute)

Paul Rubell
The Fate of the Furious

Rick Russell
Tulip Fever

James Ryan
The Boss Baby

Robert Rzesacz
Sleepless

Benny Safdie
Good Time

Michael L. Sale
The House

Stan Salfas
War for the Planet of the Apes

Soledad Salfate
A Fantastic Woman

Nat Sanders
The Glass Castle

Mark Sanger
Transformers: The Last Knight

Pietro Scalia
Alien: Covenant

Glen Scantlebury
Paris Can Wait

Josh Schaeffer
Molly's Game

Evan Schiff
John Wick: Chapter 2

Thelma Schoonmaker
The Snowman

Stacey Schroeder
The Disaster Artist

Kathryn J. Schubert
Marjorie Prime

Jacob Secher Schulsinger
The Square

Eric A. Sears
Same Kind of Different as Me

Tom Seil
Friend Request

Larry Sexton
Boo 2! A Madea Halloween

Paul Seydor (1947-)
Just Getting Started

Taylor Sheridan
Wind River

Makoto Shinkai
Your Name

Trey Edward Shults
It Comes at Night

Claire Simpson
All the Money in the World
The Snowman

David E. Simpson
Abacus: Small Enough to Jail

Lee Smith (1960-)
Dunkirk

Neil Smith
Ghost in the Shell

Steven Soderbergh (1963-)
Logan Lucky

William Steinkamp
The Shack

Kevin Stitt
The Book of Henry

Mo Stoebe
Kedi

Alexandra Strauss
I Am Not Your Negro

Tim Streeto
The Only Living Boy in New York

Sofia Subercaseaux
Dina

Spencer Susser
The Greatest Showman

Lenka Svab
Bitter Harvest

Troy Takaki
Diary of a Wimpy Kid: The Long Haul

Michael Taylor
Walking Out

Kevin Tent
Downsizing

Yvann Thibaudeau
Leap!

James Thomas
A Bad Moms Christmas

Frederic Thoraval
Unforgettable

Dylan Tichenor (1968-)
Phantom Thread
Stronger

Michael Tronick
Bright

Brad Turner
Patti Cake$

Lee Unkrich
Coco

John Venzon
The LEGO Batman Movie
The LEGO Ninjago Movie

Matt Villa
The LEGO Batman Movie

Christian Wagner
The Fate of the Furious

Joe Walker
Blade Runner 2049

Martin Walsh
Justice League
Wonder Woman

John W. Walter
Long Strange Trip

Andrew Weisblum
mother!

Jeffrey Werner
Professor Marston and the Wonder Women

Dirk Westervelt
Logan

Ben Wheatley
Free Fire

Doobie White
Resident Evil: The Final Chapter

Brad Wilhite
Daddy's Home 2

Monika Willi
Happy End

Calvin Wimmer
Transformers: The Last Knight

Hughes Winborne
All I See Is You

Sidney Wolinsky
The Shape of Water

Julia Wong
The Belko Experiment
The Last Word

Craig Wood
The Great Wall
Guardians of the Galaxy Vol. 2

Kenji Yamashita
Blade of the Immortal

Jin-mo Yang
Okja

Ed Yonaitis
Super Dark Times

Harry Yoon
Detroit

Pamela Ziegenhagen-Shefland
The Star

Dan Zimmerman
The Dark Tower

Will Znidaric
Five Came Back

Lucia Zucchetti
Their Finest

Paul Zucker
Wilson

Art Director Index

Susanne Abel
Frantz

Uri Aminov
The Wedding Plan

Grant Armstrong
A Cure for Wellness
Kingsman: The Golden Circle

Ramsey Avery
Guardians of the Galaxy Vol. 2

Daniel Baker
The Killing of a Sacred Deer

Laura Ballinger
Going in Style
The Greatest Showman

Chris Beach
Monster Trucks

Greg Berry
Detroit

Tim Blake
The Hitman's Bodyguard

Rachel Block
Daddy's Home 2

Didac Bono
The Promise

Bill Booth
Kong: Skull Island

Michael T. Boyd
Mudbound

Chad Branham
Walking Out

Sean Brennan
The Bad Batch

Christopher Brown
Bright

Hunter Brown
Lowriders

Thomas Cardone
Ferdinand

Ryan L. Carlson
The Emoji Movie

Ludovic Chemarin
My Life as a Zucchini

Todd Cherniawsky
Star Wars: The Last Jedi

Michaela Cheyne
Flatliners

Greg Chown
Jigsaw

Nigel Churcher
Baby Driver
The Shape of Water

David Clarke
Everything, Everything
Monster Trucks

Laurie Colson
Raw

Kevin Constant
Snatched

Felicity Coonan
The LEGO Ninjago Movie

Steve Cooper
Jumanji: Welcome to the Jungle

Gonzalo Cordoba
Chuck
The Dinner
Landline

Chris Craine
Get Out

Andi Crumbley
I, Tonya

Bill Crutcher
Tulip Fever

Douglas Cumming
The Last Word

Elizabeth Cummings
American Made

Leanne Dare
Five Came Back

Rebecca Dart
My Little Pony: The Movie

Ruth De Jong
Song to Song

Jennifer Dehghan
The Beguiled

Nick Dent
The Foreigner

Celine Diano
The Lovers
Woodshock

Christopher Dileo
Unforgettable

Ciaran Duffy
The Breadwinner

Thalia Ecclestone
Lady Macbeth

Andy Eklund
The Big Sick

Eyal Elhadad
Foxtrot

Kendelle Elliott
Wonder

Kasra Farahani
Bright

Chris Farmer
Logan

Roberta Federico
Call Me by Your Name

Sarah Finlay
Victoria & Abdul

Roger Fires
Colossal

Tom Frohling
Baywatch

Alex Gaines
How to Be a Latin Lover

Jason Garner
Annabelle: Creation
The Bye Bye Man

Fiona Gavin
Churchill
The Lost City of Z

Elliott Glick
Hostiles
The House

Anne Goelz
Wormwood

Dean Gordon
Smurfs: The Lost Village

Brianna Gorton
Home Again

Nick Gottschalk
Darkest Hour

Ian Gracie
Alien: Covenant
Pirates of the Caribbean: Dead Men Tell No Tales

Matthew Gray
American Assassin

Peter Grundy
It

Isabelle Guay
mother!

Michelle Harmon
Happy Death Day

Adriaan Harsta
Columbus

Eugenia Magann Haynes
The B-Side: Elsa Dorfman's Portrait Photography
Wormwood

Ryan Heck
Rough Night
Wonderstruck

Eduardo Hidalgo
Megan Leavey

Jaymes Hinkle
LBJ

Brittany Hites
Table 19

Christian Huband
Justice League

Dominic Hyman
Wonder Woman

Paul Inglis
Blade Runner 2049

Kevin Ishioka
Dunkirk

Helen Jarvis
The Great Wall
Justice League

Kim Jennings
The Post
Wonderstruck

Deborah Jensen
The Post

Derek Jensen
Just Getting Started

Richard L. Johnson
Ghost in the Shell

Arthur Jongewaard
Mudbound

Robert W. Joseph
Roman J. Israel, Esq.

Andrew Katz
The Little Hours

Eggert Ketilsson
Dunkirk

Zsuzsa Kismarty-Lechner
Atomic Blonde

Max Klaentschi
The Sense of an Ending

Jason Knox-Johnston
Transformers: The Last Knight

Andrea Kristof
Wish Upon

Rejean Labrie
A Dog's Purpose

Steven Lawrence
Life

Nicolas Lepage
The Glass Castle

Andrew Li
Monster Trucks

Nicolas Locke
The Meyerowitz Stories (New and Selected)

Miguel Lopez-Castillo
Wonder Wheel

Akiko Majima
Your Name

Gwen Margetson
The Shack

Aleksandra Marinkovich
xXx: Return of Xander Cage

Naaman Marshall
Rings

Dominic Masters
Murder on the Orient Express

Barbra Matis
Norman

Eve McCarney
Lowriders

Doug Meerdink
Kong: Skull Island

Justin O'Neal Miller
The Leisure Seeker

Keiko Mitsumatsu
After the Storm

César Montoya
The Belko Experiment

Andrew Munro
A United Kingdom

Christa Munro
Suburbicon

Naomi Munro
It Comes at Night

Desma Murphy
The Fate of the Furious

Anthony Neale
Happy End

Peggy Oei
Five Came Back

Cristina Onori
All the Money in the World
Robyn Paiba
Collide
Markku Patila
The Other Side of Hope
Joshua Petersen
Crown Heights
David Pink
A Ghost Story
Erik Polczwartek
Thank You for Your Service
Nigel Pollock
Free Fire
Guy Potgieter
The Dark Tower
Resident Evil: The Final Chapter
Sarah M. Pott
The Circle
Owen Power
Maudie
Aziz Rafiq
Thank You for Your Service
Nick Ralbovsky
CHIPS
Charlie Revai
The LEGO Ninjago Movie
Reza Riahi
The Breadwinner
Paul Richards
Stronger
John Richardson
All Eyez on Me
Brad Ricker
The Dark Tower
Spider-Man: Homecoming
Gianpaolo Rifino
American Assassin
Rachel Rockstroh
The Disaster Artist
Patrick Rolfe
T2 Trainspotting
Penny Rose
The Mummy
Jesse Rosenthal
Split
Three Billboards Outside Ebbing, Missouri
Bradley Rubin
Bright
Ali Rubinfeld
Lemon
Zoe Sakellaropoulo
Brad's Status
Saverio Sammali
John Wick: Chapter 2
Hugo Santiago
Jumanji: Welcome to the Jungle
Chris Scharffenberg
Ingrid Goes West
Christian Schellewald
Rock Dog
Denis Schnegg
King Arthur: Legend of the Sword
Phantom Thread
Sebastian Schroder
The Circle
Maya Shimoguchi
War for the Planet of the Apes
Cassidy Shipley
The Wall
Chris Shriver
John Wick: Chapter 2
Domenic Silvestri
The Space Between Us
Lauren Slatten
Wind River
Francis Kiko Soeder
Foxtrot
Larry Spittle
A Dog's Purpose
Adam Squires
Victoria & Abdul
Jeremy Stanbridge
Fifty Shades Darker
James Steuart
The Mountain Between Us
Jason Baldwin Stewart (1974-)
Girls Trip
Megan Sunzeri
Sleight
Maki Takenouchi
Rebel in the Rye
Christopher Tandon
Sleepless
Takumi Tanji
Your Name
Neill Treacy
The Man Who Invented Christmas
Seth Turner
In the Fade
Martin Vackar
Underworld: Blood Wars
Marcelo Vignali
Smurfs: The Lost Village
Frank Walsh
The Mummy
Danny James Walton
Super Dark Times
Derek Wang
The Book of Henry
Tasuku Watanabe
Your Name
Tom Weaving
Film Stars Don't Die in Liverpool
Alexander Wei
Battle of the Sexes
Gregory A. Weimerskirch
Last Flag Flying
Thomas P. Wilkins
How to Be a Latin Lover
Max Wixom
Brawl in Cell Block 99
Andrew Woodhouse
The Nut Job 2: Nutty by Nature
Jeremy Woolsey
Father Figures
Heather Yancey
Patti Cake$
Kimberley Zaharko
Downsizing

Music Director Index

Michael Abels
Get Out

Joshua Adams
Abacus: Small Enough to Jail

Alexei Aigui
I Am Not Your Negro

Michael Andrews
The Big Sick
Daddy's Home 2

Chris Bacon
Snatched

Klaus Badelt (1968-)
Leap!

Lorne Balfe
Churchill
The Florida Project
Geostorm
Ghost in the Shell
The LEGO Batman Movie

Nathan Barr
Flatliners

Geoff Barrow
Free Fire

Tyler Bates
Atomic Blonde
The Belko Experiment
Guardians of the Galaxy Vol. 2
John Wick: Chapter 2

Jeff Beal (1963-)
An Inconvenient Sequel: Truth to Power

Christophe Beck (1972-)
American Made

Marco Beltrami (1966-)
Logan
The Snowman

Jason Binnick
Patti Cake$

Bertrand Bonello
Nocturama

Chris Bordeaux
Landline

Jon Brion (1963-)
Lady Bird
Wilson

Nicholas Britell
Battle of the Sexes

Michael Brook (1952-)
Stronger

Carter Burwell (1955-)
The Founder
Goodbye Christopher Robin
Three Billboards Outside Ebbing, Missouri
Wonderstruck

Nick Cave (1957-)
Wind River

Heather Christian
Lemon

Toby Chu
Unforgettable

Charlie Clouser (1963-)
Jigsaw

Jordan Cohen
Landline

Czar (1973-)
See *S. Craig Zahler*

Jeff Danna (1964-)
The Breadwinner

Mychael Danna (1958-)
The Breadwinner
The Man Who Invented Christmas

Nathan Matthew David
The Last Word

Mark De Gli Antoni (1962-)
Crown Heights

John Debney (1956-)
The Greatest Showman
Home Again

Alexandre Desplat (1961-)
The Shape of Water
Suburbicon
Valerian and the City of a Thousand Planets

Keegan DeWitt
The Hero

Ramin Djawadi (1974-)
The Great Wall
The Mountain Between Us

Patrick Doyle (1953-)
The Emoji Movie
Murder on the Orient Express
A United Kingdom

Roy Edri
The Wedding Plan
Fil Eisler
CHIPS
Jon Ekstrand
Life
Danny Elfman (1953-)
The Circle
Fifty Shades Darker
Justice League
Tulip Fever
Warren Ellis
Wind River
Koji Endo (1964-)
Blade of the Immortal
Ilan Eshkeri
Collide
The Exception
Andrew Feltenstein
The House
Ola Flottum
Thelma
Kira Fontana
Kedi
Ben Frost
Super Dark Times
Michael Giacchino (1967-)
The Book of Henry
Coco
Spider-Man: Homecoming
War for the Planet of the Apes
Philip Glass (1937-)
Jane
Gary Go
Friend Request
Ludwig Göransson (1984-)
Everything, Everything
Jonny Greenwood
Phantom Thread
Harry Gregson-Williams (1961-)
The Zookeeper's Wife
Rupert Gregson-Williams (1966-)
Wonder Woman
Hammock
Columbus
Daniel Hart
A Ghost Story
Paul Haslinger (1962-)
Resident Evil: The Final Chapter
Jon Hegel
78/52: Hitchcock's Shower Scene
Matthew Herbert
A Fantastic Woman
Jeff Herriott
Brawl in Cell Block 99
Gregoire Hetzel
The Midwife
Mandy Hoffman
The Lovers
Tom Holkenborg (1967-)
***See** Junkie XL*
David Holmes (1969-)
Logan Lucky
Joshua Homme (1973-)
In the Fade
James Newton Howard (1951-)
Detroit
Roman J. Israel, Esq.
Tom Howe
Professor Marston and the Wonder Women
Sophie Hunger
My Life as a Zucchini
Daniel Ingram
My Little Pony: The Movie
Mark Isham (1951-)
Megan Leavey
Steve Jablonsky (1970-)
Transformers: The Last Knight
Henry Jackman (1974-)
Jumanji: Welcome to the Jungle
Kingsman: The Golden Circle
Kong: Skull Island
Corey A. Jackson (1968-)
Chuck
Geremy Jasper
Patti Cake$
Dan Jones (1981-)
Lady Macbeth
Rael Jones
My Cousin Rachel
Junkie XL (1967-)
The Dark Tower
Michael Kamm
Sleepless
Laura Karpman
Paris Can Wait
Step
Rolfe Kent (1963-)
Downsizing
Rock Dog
Elvis Kuehn
Lucky
Jed Kurzel
Alien: Covenant
Clyde Lawrence
Landline
Ophir Leibovitch
Foxtrot
Christopher Lennertz (1972-)
A Bad Moms Christmas
Baywatch
Pitch Perfect 3
Smurfs: The Lost Village
Paul Leonard-Morgan
Wormwood
Nicholas Leone
Beach Rats
Mica Levi
Marjorie Prime
Dominic Lewis
Fist Fight
Rough Night
Andrew Lockington (1974-)
The Space Between Us
Daniel Lopatin
***See** Oneohtrix Point Never*
Lucius
Band Aid
Robert Lydecker
xXx: Return of Xander Cage
Clint Mansell (1963-)
Ghost in the Shell
Matthew Margeson
Kingsman: The Golden Circle
Rings
Dario Marianelli (1963-)
Darkest Hour
Jason Markey
The Foreigner
Aaron Martin
Menashe
Cliff Martinez (1954-)
The Foreigner
Steve Mazzaro
The Boss Baby
Bear McCreary (1979-)
Colossal
Happy Death Day
Rebel in the Rye
Brian McOmber
It Comes at Night

Alan Menken (1949-)
Beauty and the Beast

Marcus Miller (1959-)
Marshall

Jun Miyake
Norman

Mondo Boys
Phoenix Forgotten

Paul-Leonard Morgan
The B-Side: Elsa Dorfman's Portrait Photography

Mark Mothersbaugh (1950-)
Beatriz at Dinner
Brad's Status
The LEGO Ninjago Movie
Thor: Ragnarok

Peter Nashel
I, Tonya

John Nau
The House

David Newman (1954-)
Girls Trip

Randy Newman (1943-)
Cars 3
The Meyerowitz Stories (New and Selected)

Thomas Newman (1955-)
Thank You for Your Service
Victoria & Abdul

The Newton Brothers
The Bye Bye Man

Oneohtrix Point Never
Good Time

Atli Orvarsson
The Hitman's Bodyguard

John Paesano
All Eyez on Me
Same Kind of Different as Me
The Star

Daniel Pemberton
All the Money in the World
Gold
King Arthur: Legend of the Sword
Molly's Game

Heitor Pereira
The Nut Job 2: Nutty by Nature

Phoenix
The Beguiled

Samora Pinderhughes
Whose Streets?

Dave Porter
The Disaster Artist

Rachel Portman (1960-)
A Dog's Purpose
Their Finest

John Powell (1963-)
Ferdinand

Amit Poznansky (1974-)
Foxtrot

Steven Price
American Assassin
Baby Driver

Radwimps
Your Name

Peter Raeburn
Woodshock

J. Ralph (1975-)
Film Stars Don't Die in Liverpool

Arnaud Rebotini
BPM (Beats Per Minute)

Ernst Reijseger
Walking Out

Graham Reynolds (1971-)
Last Flag Flying

Joel J. Richard
John Wick: Chapter 2

Max Richter
Hostiles
The Sense of an Ending

Philippe Rombi (1968-)
Frantz

Dan Romer
The Little Hours

Dag Rosenqvist
Menashe

Raphael Saadiq
Step

Jonathan Sadoff
Ingrid Goes West

H. Scott Salinas
The Ballad of Lefty Brown

Ben Salisbury
Free Fire

David Sardy
Bright
Monster Trucks

Nitin Sawhney (1964-)
Breathe

Charles Scott, IV
Sleight

Bryan Senti
Lowriders

Marc Shaiman (1959-)
LBJ

Theodore Shapiro (1971-)
Captain Underpants: The First Epic Movie
Snatched

Rani Sharone
My Entire High School Sinking Into the Sea

Ed Shearmur (1966-)
Diary of a Wimpy Kid: The Long Haul

Shudder to Think
See *Craig Wedren*

Rob Simonsen (1978-)
Father Figures
Gifted
Going in Style

Ron Simonsen
The Only Living Boy in New York

Christopher Spelman
The Lost City of Z

Christopher Stark
Novitiate

Marc Streitenfeld
All I See Is You

John Swihart
Table 19

Tamar-kali
Mudbound

Adam Taylor
Before I Fall

Nick Thorburn
Ingrid Goes West

West Dylan Thordson
Split

Michael Timmins
Maudie

Martin Todsharow (1967-)
Friend Request

tomandandy
47 Meters Down
Wish Upon

Joseph Trapanese
The Greatest Showman
Only the Brave

Jeremy Turner
Five Came Back

Brian Tyler
The Fate of the Furious
The Mummy
Power Rangers
xXx: Return of Xander Cage

Carlo Virzi
The Leisure Seeker

Benjamin Wallfisch
Annabelle: Creation
Bitter Harvest
Blade Runner 2049
A Cure for Wellness
It

Michael Wandmacher (1967-)
Underworld: Blood Wars

Craig Wedren
How to Be a Latin Lover

Joel P. West
The Glass Castle

Philip White
Boo 2! A Madea Halloween

Jim Williams
Raw

John Williams (1932-)
The Post
Star Wars: The Last Jedi

Pharrell Williams (1973-)
Despicable Me 3

Alex Wurman (1966-)
Just Getting Started

Gabriel Yared (1949-)
The Promise

S. Craig Zahler (1973-)
Brawl in Cell Block 99

Geoff Zanelli (1974-)
Pirates of the Caribbean: Dead Men Tell No Tales

Marcelo Zarvos
Wonder

Aaron Zigman
The Shack
Wakefield

Hans Zimmer (1957-)
Blade Runner 2049
The Boss Baby
Dunkirk

Performer Index

Erick Abbate
My Life as a Zucchini (*V*)

Christopher Abbott
It Comes at Night

Barkhad Abdi
Good Time

Hiroshi Abe (1964-)
After the Storm

Dominique Abel
Lost in Paris

Austin Abrams (1996-)
Brad's Status

Numan Acar
In the Fade

Naomi Ackie
Lady Macbeth

Amy Adams (1974-)
Justice League

Sarah Adler
Foxtrot

Uzo Aduba
My Little Pony: The Movie

Ben Affleck (1972-)
Justice League

Casey Affleck (1975-)
A Ghost Story

Shohreh Aghdashloo (1952-)
The Promise

Dianna Agron (1986-)
Novitiate

Seo-Hyun Ahn (2004-)
Okja

Charles Aitken (1979-)
Happy Death Day

Adeel Akhtar
Victoria & Abdul

Raphael Alejandro (2007-)
How to Be a Latin Lover

Taylor Rae Almonte
The Dinner

Cristela Alonzo (1979-)
Cars 3 (*V*)

Avraham Aviv Alush (1982-)
The Shack
The Women's Balcony

Isabella Amara
Wilson

Ella Anderson
The Glass Castle

Hannah Emily Anderson
Jigsaw

Joseph Lee Anderson
The Ballad of Lefty Brown

Ann-Margret (1941-)
Going in Style

K.J. Apa
A Dog's Purpose

Shiri Appleby (1978-)
Lemon

Adria Arjona
The Belko Experiment

Alan Arkin (1934-)
Going in Style

Ana de Armas (1988-)
Blade Runner 2049

Fred Armisen (1966-)
Band Aid
The LEGO Ninjago Movie (*V*)

Will Arnett (1970-)
The LEGO Batman Movie
The Nut Job 2: Nutty by Nature

Gemma Arterton (1986-)
Their Finest

Pilou Asbaek (1982-)
Ghost in the Shell
Woodshock

Lior Ashkenazi (1969-)
Foxtrot
Norman

Edward Ashley
The Lost City of Z

Nnamdi Asomugha (1981-)
Crown Heights

Owen Asztalos
Diary of a Wimpy Kid: The Long Haul

Mamoudou Athie
Patti Cake$

Florie Auclerc
Porto

Joanna Bacon
A Quiet Passion

Ali Badshah
The Breadwinner

Ariyon Bakare (1971-)
Life

Kathy Baker (1950-)
The Ballad of Lefty Brown

Miles Christopher Bakshi
The Boss Baby

Alec Baldwin (1958-)
The Boss Baby
Paris Can Wait

James Baldwin (1924-1987)
I Am Not Your Negro

Christian Bale (1974-)
Hostiles
The Promise

Ashleigh Ball
My Little Pony: The Movie

Eric Bana (1968-)
King Arthur: Legend of the Sword

Orna Banai
The Women's Balcony

Claes Bang
The Square

Elizabeth Banks (1974-)
Power Rangers

Jonathan Banks (1947-)
Mudbound

Christine Baranski (1952-)
A Bad Moms Christmas

Javier Bardem (1969-)
mother!
Pirates of the Caribbean: Dead Men Tell No Tales

Ike Barinholtz (1977-)
Snatched

Samantha Barks
Bitter Harvest

Aneurin Barnard (1987-)
Bitter Harvest
Dunkirk

Marta Barrio
The Trip to Spain

Sawyer Barth
Super Dark Times

Kim Basinger (1953-)
Fifty Shades Darker

Dave Bautista (1969-)
Guardians of the Galaxy Vol. 2

Simon Russell Beale (1961-)
My Cousin Rachel

Gabrielle Beauvais (1972-)
***See** Gabrielle Union*

Kate Beckinsale (1973-)
The Only Living Boy in New York
Underworld: Blood Wars

Becky G (1997-)
Power Rangers

Paula Beer (1995-)
Frantz

Ed Begley, Jr. (1949-)
Lucky

Jamie Bell (1986-)
Film Stars Don't Die in Liverpool

Jillian Bell (1984-)
Fist Fight
Rough Night

Kristen Bell (1980-)
A Bad Moms Christmas
How to Be a Latin Lover

Lake Bell (1979-)
Home Again

Tobin Bell (1942-)
Jigsaw

Jim Belushi
Wonder Wheel

Annette Bening (1958-)
Film Stars Don't Die in Liverpool

Cle Bennett
Jigsaw

Haley Bennett (1988-)
Thank You for Your Service

Zachary Bennett (1980-)
Maudie

Melissa Benoist
Lowriders

Candice Bergen (1946-)
Home Again

Astrid Berges-Frisbey (1986-)
King Arthur: Legend of the Sword

Gael Garcia Bernal (1978-)
Coco

Jon Bernthal (1976-)
Wind River

Halle Berry (1968-)
Kingsman: The Golden Circle

Soma Bhatia
The Breadwinner

Demian Bichir (1963-)
Alien: Covenant
Lowriders

Juliette Binoche (1964-)
Ghost in the Shell

Nahuel Perez Biscayart
BPM (Beats Per Minute)

Jack Black (1969-)
Jumanji: Welcome to the Jungle

Lewis Black (1948-)
Rock Dog

Macon Blair
Gold

Marsha Stephanie Blake
Crown Heights

Cate Blanchett (1969-)
Song to Song
Thor: Ragnarok

Mary J. Blige (1971-)
Mudbound

Orlando Bloom (1977-)
Pirates of the Caribbean: Dead Men Tell No Tales

Marc Blucas (1972-)
Brawl in Cell Block 99

Emily Blunt (1983-)
My Little Pony: The Movie

Peter Bogdanovich (1939-)
78/52: Hitchcock's Shower Scene

Matt Bomer (1977-)
Walking Out

Cressida Bonas
The Bye Bye Man

Olivier Bonnaud
The Unknown Girl

Chadwick Boseman (1976-)
Marshall

Sigrid Bouaziz
Personal Shopper

Sofia Boutella (1982-)
The Mummy

John Boyega (1992-)
The Circle
Detroit
Star Wars: The Last Jedi

Lucy Boynton (1994-)
Rebel in the Rye

Richard Brake (1964-)
Bitter Harvest

Kenneth Branagh (1960-)
Murder on the Orient Express

Benjamin Bratt (1963-)
Coco
Ewen Bremner (1972-)
T2 Trainspotting
Beau Bridges (1941-)
The Mountain Between Us
Jeff Bridges (1949-)
Kingsman: The Golden Circle
The Only Living Boy in New York
Only the Brave
Alison Brie (1982-)
The Disaster Artist
The Little Hours
Connie Britton (1968-)
Beatriz at Dinner
Professor Marston and the Wonder Women
Jim Broadbent (1949-)
The Sense of an Ending
Adam Brody (1980-)
CHIPS
Josh Brolin (1968-)
Only the Brave
Pierce Brosnan (1953-)
The Foreigner
The Only Living Boy in New York
Israel Broussard (1994-)
Happy Death Day
Clancy Brown (1959-)
Stronger
Joan Brown
Phantom Thread
Sterling K. Brown
Marshall
Daniel Brühl (1978-)
The Zookeeper's Wife
Aidy Bryant
The Star
Rob Brydon (1965-)
The Trip to Spain
Betty Buckley (1947-)
Split
Lia Bugnar
Graduation
Steve Buscemi (1957-)
The Boss Baby
Norman
George W. Bush (1946-)
An Inconvenient Sequel: Truth to Power
Gerard Butler (1969-)
Geostorm
Asa Butterfield (1997-)
The Space Between Us
Hee-Bong Byun (1942-)
Okja
Santiago Cabrera (1978-)
Transformers: The Last Knight
Daniel Gimenez Cacho (1961-)
The Promise
Michael Caine (1933-)
Going in Style
Paulo Calatre
Porto
Simon Callow (1949-)
The Man Who Invented Christmas
Christian Camargo (1971-)
Wormwood
Anna Camp (1982-)
Pitch Perfect 3
Owen Campbell
Super Dark Times
Bobby Cannavale (1970-)
Ferdinand
I, Tonya
The Nut Job 2: Nutty by Nature
Elizabeth Cappuccino
Super Dark Times
Linda Cardellini (1975-)
Daddy's Home 2
The Founder
Steve Carell (1962-)
Battle of the Sexes
Despicable Me 3 (*V*)
Last Flag Flying
Robert Carlyle (1961-)
T2 Trainspotting
Laura Carmichael
A United Kingdom
Jennifer Carpenter (1979-)
Brawl in Cell Block 99
Keith Carradine (1949-)
A Quiet Passion
Jim Carrey (1962-)
The Bad Batch
Caitlin Carver
I, Tonya
Amira Casar (1971-)
Call Me by Your Name
Max Casella (1967-)
Wonder Wheel
Raffey Cassidy
The Killing of a Sacred Deer
Keisha Castle-Hughes (1990-)
Thank You for Your Service
Dick Cavett (1936-)
I Am Not Your Negro
Henry Cavill (1983-)
Justice League
John Cena (1977-)
Ferdinand
The Wall
McColm Cephas, Jr.
A Ghost Story
Michael Cera (1988-)
The LEGO Batman Movie
Lemon
Molly's Game
Timothée Chalamet
Call Me by Your Name
Lady Bird
Jackie Chan (1954-)
The Foreigner
The LEGO Ninjago Movie (*V*)
The Nut Job 2: Nutty by Nature
Samia Muriel Chancrin
In the Fade
Dean-Charles Chapman
Breathe
Josh Charles (1971-)
Norman
Jessica Chastain (1981-)
Molly's Game
The Zookeeper's Wife
Wes Chatham
All I See Is You
Hong Chau
Downsizing
Saara Chaudry
The Breadwinner
Gabriel Chavarria
Lowriders
Amari Cheatom
Crown Heights
Kristin Chenoweth (1968-)
My Little Pony: The Movie
Michael Chernus (1977-)
The Dinner

John Cho (1972-)
Columbus

Priyanka Chopra (1982-)
Baywatch

Enzo Cilenti (1974-)
Free Fire

Sam Claflin (1986-)
My Cousin Rachel
Their Finest

Sue Clark
Phantom Thread

Jason Clarke (1969-)
All I See Is You
Mudbound

Jemaine Clement (1974-)
Brad's Status

Kiersey Clemons
Flatliners

Laura Clifton
Happy Death Day

Rory Cochrane (1972-)
Hostiles

Joe Cole
Thank You for Your Service
Woodshock

Ellar Coltrane (1994-)
The Circle

Common (1972-)
John Wick: Chapter 2

Jack Conley
Suburbicon

Jennifer Connelly (1970-)
Only the Brave

Steve Coogan (1965-)
The Dinner
The Trip to Spain

Bradley Cooper (1975-)
Guardians of the Galaxy Vol. 2

Chris Cooper (1951-)
Cars 3 (*V*)

Francis Ford Coppola (1939-)
Five Came Back

James Corden (1978-)
The Emoji Movie (*V*)

Christelle Cornil (1977-)
The Unknown Girl

Abbie Cornish (1982-)
Geostorm
Three Billboards Outside Ebbing, Missouri

Chris Cornwell
Fist Fight

Miranda Cosgrove (1993-)
Despicable Me 3 (*V*)

Kevin Costner (1955-)
Molly's Game

Grover Coulson
A Ghost Story

Jai Courtney (1986-)
The Exception

Brian Cox (1946-)
Churchill

Bryan Cranston (1956-)
Last Flag Flying
Wakefield

James Cromwell (1940-)
Marshall

Russell Crowe (1964-)
The Mummy

Billy Crudup (1968-)
Alien: Covenant

Tom Cruise (1962-)
American Made
The Mummy

Penelope Cruz (1974-)
Murder on the Orient Express

Rory Culkin (1989-)
Columbus

Whitney Cummings (1982-)
Unforgettable

Jamie Lee Curtis (1958-)
78/52: Hitchcock's Shower Scene

Joan Cusack (1962-)
Snatched

R.J. Cyler (1995-)
Power Rangers

Alexandra Daddario (1986-)
Baywatch

Willem Dafoe (1955-)
The Florida Project
The Great Wall

Ian Anthony Dale (1978-)
Wakefield

James Badge Dale (1978-)
Only the Brave

Matt Damon (1970-)
Downsizing
The Great Wall
Suburbicon

Charles Dance (1946-)
Underworld: Blood Wars

Beverly D'Angelo (1951-)
Wakefield

Paul Dano (1984-)
Okja

Rhys Darby (1974-)
Jumanji: Welcome to the Jungle

Jack Davenport (1973-)
A United Kingdom

Seamus Davey-Fitzpatrick (1998-)
The Dinner

Cassi Davis (1964-)
Boo 2! A Madea Halloween

Geena Davis (1957-)
Marjorie Prime

Rosario Dawson (1979-)
The LEGO Batman Movie
Unforgettable

Charlie Day (1976-)
Fist Fight

Daniel Day-Lewis (1957-)
Phantom Thread

Ana de la Reguera (1977-)
Everything, Everything

Alycia Debnam-Carey (1993-)
Friend Request

Dane DeHaan (1986-)
A Cure for Wellness
Tulip Fever
Valerian and the City of a Thousand Planets

Guillermo del Toro (1964-)
Five Came Back
78/52: Hitchcock's Shower Scene

Cara Delevingne
Valerian and the City of a Thousand Planets

Mylene Demongeot (1935-)
The Midwife

Dame Judi Dench (1934-)
Victoria & Abdul

Catherine Deneuve (1943-)
The Midwife

Johnny Depp (1963-)
Pirates of the Caribbean: Dead Men Tell No Tales

Eugenio Derbez (1962-)
How to Be a Latin Lover

Laura Dern (1966-)
The Founder
Wilson

Zoey Deutch (1994-)
Before I Fall
Rebel in the Rye

Siddharth Dhananjay
Patti Cake$

Melonie Diaz (1984-)
The Belko Experiment

Harris Dickinson (1996-)
Beach Rats

Vin Diesel (1967-)
The Fate of the Furious
Guardians of the Galaxy Vol. 2
xXx: Return of Xander Cage

Taye Diggs (1971-)
My Little Pony: The Movie

Olga Dihovichnaya (1980-)
Life

Stephen (Dillon) Dillane (1956-)
Darkest Hour

AnnJewel Lee Dixon
The Last Word

Nina Dobrev (1989-)
Flatliners
xXx: Return of Xander Cage

Michelle Dockery (1981-)
The Sense of an Ending

Quentin Dolmaire
The Midwife

Vincent D'Onofrio (1959-)
Rings

Jeffrey Donovan (1968-)
LBJ

Elsa Dorfman
The B-Side: Elsa Dorfman's Portrait Photography

Jamie Dornan (1982-)
Fifty Shades Darker

Robert Downey, Jr. (1965-)
Spider-Man: Homecoming

Maria Dragus
Graduation

Adam Driver (1983-)
Star Wars: The Last Jedi

Jason Drucker
Diary of a Wimpy Kid: The Long Haul

Duncan Duff
A Quiet Passion

Josh Duhamel (1972-)
Transformers: The Last Knight

Faye Dunaway (1941-)
The Bye Bye Man

Lindsay Duncan (1950-)
Gifted

Lena Dunham (1986-)
My Entire High School Sinking Into the Sea

Kirsten Dunst (1982-)
The Beguiled
Woodshock

Jay Duplass (1973-)
Beatriz at Dinner
Landline

Richard Durden (1944-)
Churchill

Romain Duris (1974-)
All the Money in the World

Steph Duvall
Woodshock

Joel Edgerton (1974-)
Bright
It Comes at Night

Zac Efron (1987-)
Baywatch
The Greatest Showman

Taron Egerton (1989-)
Kingsman: The Golden Circle

Jennifer Ehle (1969-)
A Quiet Passion

Lars Eidinger
Personal Shopper

Carmen Ejogo (1973-)
It Comes at Night
Roman J. Israel, Esq.

Idris Elba (1972-)
The Dark Tower
Molly's Game
The Mountain Between Us
Thor: Ragnarok

Danny Elfman (1953-)
78/52: Hitchcock's Shower Scene

Ansel Elgort (1994-)
Baby Driver

Sam Elliott (1944-)
The Hero

Grethe Eltervag
Thelma

Yousef Erakat (1990-)
Boo 2! A Madea Halloween

Raul Esparza (1970-)
Ferdinand

Susie Essman (1955-)
Band Aid

Chris Evans (1981-)
Gifted

Luke Evans (1979-)
Beauty and the Beast
Professor Marston and the Wonder Women

Bridget Everett
Patti Cake$

Christopher Fairbank (1959-)
Lady Macbeth

Edie Falco (1963-)
Landline
Megan Leavey

Elle Fanning (1998-)
The Beguiled
Leap!

Anna Faris (1976-)
The Emoji Movie (*V*)

Colin Farrell (1976-)
The Beguiled
The Killing of a Sacred Deer
Roman J. Israel, Esq.

Michael Fassbender (1977-)
Alien: Covenant
The Snowman
Song to Song

Jon Favreau (1966-)
Spider-Man: Homecoming

Ali Fazal (1986-)
Victoria & Abdul

Ray Fearon
The Foreigner

Oakes Fegley
Wonderstruck

J.J. Feild (1978-)
Professor Marston and the Wonder Women

Tom Felton (1987-)
Megan Leavey
A United Kingdom

Rebecca Ferguson
The Greatest Showman
Life
The Snowman

Will Ferrell (1968-)
Daddy's Home 2
The House

Ralph Fiennes (1962-)
The LEGO Batman Movie

Nathan Fillion (1971-)
Cars 3 (*V*)

Colin Firth (1960-)
Kingsman: The Golden Circle

Jenna Fischer (1974-)
Brad's Status

Laurence Fishburne (1961-)
John Wick: Chapter 2
Last Flag Flying

Carrie Fisher (1956-2016)
Star Wars: The Last Jedi

Rory Fleck-Byrne
The Foreigner

Glenn Fleshler
Suburbicon

Nicole Flyus
Beach Rats

Peter Fonda (1940-)
The Ballad of Lefty Brown

Michelle Forbes (1965-)
Columbus

Harrison Ford (1884-1957)
Blade Runner 2049

Will Forte (1970-)
My Life as a Zucchini (*V*)

Jamie Foxx (1967-)
Baby Driver
Sleepless

Claire Foy (1984-)
Breathe

Dave Franco (1985-)
The Disaster Artist
The LEGO Ninjago Movie (*V*)
The Little Hours

James Franco (1978-)
The Disaster Artist

Lily Franky
***See** Riri Furanki*

Morgan Freeman (1937-)
Going in Style
Just Getting Started

Catherine Frot (1956-)
The Midwife

Lucy Fry
Bright

Sota Fukushi
Blade of the Immortal

Riri Furanki
After the Storm

Seychelle Gabriel (1991-)
Sleight

Josh Gad (1981-)
Beauty and the Beast
A Dog's Purpose (*V*)
Marshall

Gal Gadot (1985-)
Justice League
Wonder Woman

Jim Gaffigan (1966-)
Chuck

Dana Gaier
Despicable Me 3 (*V*)

Charlotte Gainsbourg (1972-)
The Snowman

Johnny Galecki (1975-)
Rings

Zach Galifianakis (1969-)
The LEGO Batman Movie

John Gallagher, Jr. (1984-)
The Belko Experiment

Manuel Garcia-Rulfo (1981-)
Murder on the Orient Express

Andrew Garfield (1983-)
Breathe

Jennifer Garner (1972-)
Wakefield

Esther Garrel (1991-)
Call Me by Your Name

Ben Gavin
The Dark Tower

Yani Gellman (1985-)
47 Meters Down

Brett Gelman
Lemon

Richard Gere (1949-)
Norman

Mel Gibson (1956-)
Daddy's Home 2

Tyrese Gibson (1978-)
The Fate of the Furious

Karen Gillan (1987-)
The Circle
Jumanji: Welcome to the Jungle

Aidan Gillen (1968-)
The Lovers

Lily Gladstone
Walking Out

Ilana Glazer (1987-)
Rough Night

Domhnall Gleeson (1983-)
American Made
Goodbye Christopher Robin
mother!

Iain Glen (1961-)
My Cousin Rachel
Resident Evil: The Final Chapter

Tom Glynn-Carney
Dunkirk

Luis Gnecco
A Fantastic Woman

Iddo Goldberg (1975-)
The Zookeeper's Wife

Jeff Goldblum (1952-)
Thor: Ragnarok

Tony Goldwyn (1960-)
The Belko Experiment

Rebecca Marie Gomez (1997-)
***See** Becky G*

Eiza González (1990-)
Baby Driver

Jane Goodall (1934-)
Jane

Matthew Goode (1978-)
The Sense of an Ending

John Goodman (1952-)
Atomic Blonde
Kong: Skull Island

Fiona Gordon
Lost in Paris

Al Gore (1948-)
An Inconvenient Sequel: Truth to Power

Jack Gore
Ferdinand

Ryan Gosling (1980-)
Blade Runner 2049
Song to Song

Mia Goth (1993-)
A Cure for Wellness

Olivier Gourmet (1963-)
The Midwife

McKenna Grace (2006-)
Gifted

Kat Graham (1989-)
All Eyez on Me

Stephen Graham (1973-)
Film Stars Don't Die in Liverpool

Holliday Grainger (1988-)
My Cousin Rachel
Tulip Fever

Richard E. Grant (1957-)
The Hitman's Bodyguard

Lynda Gravatt
Roman J. Israel, Esq.

Ari Graynor (1983-)
The Disaster Artist

Paul Greengrass (1955-)
Five Came Back

Brad Greenquist (1959-)
Annabelle: Creation

Judy Greer (1975-)
Lemon

Mary Grill
Father Figures

Hannah Gross
Marjorie Prime

Marie Gruber (1955-)
Frantz

Carla Gugino (1971-)
The Space Between Us

Noorin Gulamgaus
The Breadwinner

Danai Gurira (1978-)
All Eyez on Me

Jake Gyllenhaal (1980-)
Life
Stronger

Shira Haas
Foxtrot

Tiffany Haddish (1980-)
Girls Trip

Laura Haddock (1985-)
Transformers: The Last Knight

Adele Haenel
BPM (Beats Per Minute)
The Unknown Girl

Evelin Hagoel
The Women's Balcony

Kathryn Hahn (1973-)
A Bad Moms Christmas

Philip Baker Hall (1931-)
The Last Word

Rebecca Hall (1982-)
Professor Marston and the Wonder Women

Regina Hall (1970-)
Girls Trip

Rod Hallett
The Hitman's Bodyguard

Mark Hamill (1952-)
Star Wars: The Last Jedi

Jon Hamm (1971-)
Baby Driver
Marjorie Prime

Armie Hammer (1986-)
Call Me by Your Name
Cars 3 (*V*)
Free Fire

Lu Han (1990-)
The Great Wall

Tom Hanks (1956-)
The Circle
The Post

Ryan Hansen (1981-)
CHIPS

Eili Harboe
Thelma

David Harbour (1974-)
Sleepless

Fantine Harduin
Happy End

Hill Harper (1966-)
All Eyez on Me

Woody Harrelson (1962-)
The Glass Castle
LBJ
Three Billboards Outside Ebbing, Missouri
War for the Planet of the Apes
Wilson

Ed Harris (1950-)
mother!

Kelvin Harrison, Jr. (1994-)
It Comes at Night

Kevin Hart (1979-)
Captain Underpants: The First Epic Movie (*V*)
Jumanji: Welcome to the Jungle

Florence Hartigan
Phoenix Forgotten

Anne Hathaway (1982-)
Colossal

Zachary Haven
Father Figures

Ethan Hawke (1971-)
Maudie
Valerian and the City of a Thousand Planets

Sally Hawkins (1976-)
Maudie
The Shape of Water

Goldie Hawn (1945-)
Snatched

Salma Hayek (1966-)
Beatriz at Dinner
How to Be a Latin Lover

Dennis Haysbert (1954-)
The Dark Tower

Chandler Head
The Glass Castle

Glenne Headly (1955-2017)
Just Getting Started

Bella Heathcote (1987-)
Fifty Shades Darker
Professor Marston and the Wonder Women

Lucas Hedges
Three Billboards Outside Ebbing, Missouri

Garrett Hedlund (1984-)
Mudbound

Katherine Heigl (1978-)
The Nut Job 2: Nutty by Nature
Unforgettable

Johan Heldenbergh (1967-)
The Zookeeper's Wife

Ed Helms (1974-)
Captain Underpants: The First Epic Movie (*V*)
Father Figures

Chris Hemsworth (1983-)
Thor: Ragnarok

Christina Hendricks (1975-)
Fist Fight

Taylor Hickson (1997-)
Everything, Everything

Tom Hiddleston (1981-)
Kong: Skull Island
Thor: Ragnarok

Dulé Hill (1975-)
Sleight

Paul Hilton
Lady Macbeth

Cheryl Hines (1965-)
Wilson

Alfred Hitchcock (1899-1980)
78/52: Hitchcock's Shower Scene

Kate Hodge (1966-)
Beach Rats

Sylvia Hoeks
Blade Runner 2049

Dustin Hoffman (1937-)
The Meyerowitz Stories (New and Selected)
Stephen Hogan
The Foreigner
Boyd Holbrook (1981-)
Logan
Tom Holland (1996-)
The Lost City of Z
Spider-Man: Homecoming
Tom Hollander (1967-)
Tulip Fever
Katie Holmes (1978-)
Logan Lucky
Claire Holt (1988-)
47 Meters Down
Olivia Holt
Same Kind of Different as Me
Anthony Hopkins (1937-)
Collide
Transformers: The Last Knight
Nicholas Hoult (1989-)
Collide
Rebel in the Rye
Djimon Hounsou (1964-)
King Arthur: Legend of the Sword
Same Kind of Different as Me
Bryce Dallas Howard (1981-)
Gold
C. Thomas Howell (1966-)
LBJ
Kate Hudson (1979-)
Marshall
Neal Huff
Beach Rats
Charlie Hunnam (1980-)
King Arthur: Legend of the Sword
The Lost City of Z
Holly Hunter (1958-)
The Big Sick
Isabelle Huppert (1953-)
Happy End
Danny Huston (1962-)
Wonder Woman
Jack Huston (1982-)
Their Finest
An Seo Hyun (2004-)
See *Seo-Hyun Ahn*
Ice Cube (1969-)
Fist Fight
Hayato Ichihara (1987-)
Blade of the Immortal
Annie Ilonzeh (1983-)
All Eyez on Me
Max Irons (1985-)
Bitter Harvest
Oscar Isaac (1980-)
The Promise
Jason Isaacs (1963-)
A Cure for Wellness
Manal Issa
Nocturama
Danny Isserles
Foxtrot
Vlad Ivanov
Graduation
Eddie Izzard (1962-)
Rock Dog
Victoria & Abdul
Tony Jaa (1976-)
xXx: Return of Xander Cage
Hugh Jackman (1968-)
The Greatest Showman
Logan
O'Shea Jackson, Jr. (1991-)
Ingrid Goes West
Samuel L. Jackson (1948-)
I Am Not Your Negro
Kong: Skull Island
Abbi Jacobson (1984-)
The LEGO Ninjago Movie (*V*)
Lily James (1989-)
Baby Driver
Darkest Hour
The Exception
Theo James (1984-)
Underworld: Blood Wars
Allison Janney (1959-)
I, Tonya
Cosmo Jarvis
Lady Macbeth
Richard Jenkins (1947-)
The Shape of Water
Carly Rae Jepsen
Leap!
Tian Jing
The Great Wall
Scarlett Johansson (1984-)
Ghost in the Shell
Rough Night
Sir Elton John (1947-)
Kingsman: The Golden Circle
Aaron Johnson (1990-)
See *Aaron Taylor-Johnson*
Chris Johnson (1977-)
47 Meters Down
Dakota Johnson (1989-)
Fifty Shades Darker
Don Johnson (1949-)
Brawl in Cell Block 99
Dwayne 'The Rock' Johnson (1972-)
Baywatch
The Fate of the Furious
Jumanji: Welcome to the Jungle
Eric Johnson (1979-)
Fifty Shades Darker
J. Quinton Johnson
Last Flag Flying
Jake Johnson (1978-)
The Mummy
Rebecca Johnson
The Trip to Spain
Caleb Landry Jones (1989-)
American Made
Get Out
Doug Jones (1960-)
The Bye Bye Man
Felicity Jones (1983-)
Collide
Julia Jones (1981-)
Wind River
Toby Jones (1966-)
Atomic Blonde
Tommy Lee Jones (1946-)
Just Getting Started
Clint Jordan
Phoenix Forgotten
Milla Jovovich (1975-)
Resident Evil: The Final Chapter
Noah Jupe
Suburbicon
Jet Jurgensmeyer
Ferdinand
Daniel Kaluuya (1989-)
Get Out
Ryunosuke Kamiki (1993-)
Your Name

Mone Kamishiraishi
Your Name

Elena Kampouris (1997-)
Before I Fall

Dome Karukoski
The Other Side of Hope

Lawrence Kasdan (1949-)
Five Came Back

Mathieu Kassovitz (1967-)
Happy End

Zoe Kazan (1983-)
The Big Sick

Michael Keaton (1951-)
American Assassin
The Founder
Spider-Man: Homecoming

Claire Keelan
The Trip to Spain

Dafne Keen
Logan

Catherine Keener (1959-)
Get Out

Anna Kendrick (1985-)
Pitch Perfect 3
Table 19

Marwan Kenzari (1983-)
Collide

Barry Keoghan
The Killing of a Sacred Deer

Riley Keough (1989-)
It Comes at Night
Logan Lucky

John Kerry (1943-)
An Inconvenient Sequel: Truth to Power

Keegan Michael Key (1971-)
The Star

Julie Khaner (1957-)
Leap!

Anupam Kher (1955-)
The Big Sick

Nicole Kidman (1967-)
The Beguiled
The Killing of a Sacred Deer

Udo Kier (1944-)
Brawl in Cell Block 99

Kirin Kiki
After the Storm

Jack Kilmer
Woodshock

Val Kilmer (1959-)
The Snowman

Jimmy Kimmel (1967-)
The Boss Baby

Takuya Kimura
Blade of the Immortal

Joey King (1999-)
Going in Style
Wish Upon

Ben Kingsley (1943-)
Collide

Greg Kinnear (1963-)
Same Kind of Different as Me

Takeshi 'Beat' Kitano (1947-)
Ghost in the Shell

Taylor Kitsch (1981-)
American Assassin

Kevin Kline (1947-)
Beauty and the Beast

Satomi Kobayashi
After the Storm

Noa Koler
The Wedding Plan

Karin Konoval (1961-)
War for the Planet of the Apes

Tommi Korpela
The Other Side of Hope

Michael Koskoff
Marshall

John Krasinski (1979-)
Detroit

Zoë Kravitz (1988-)
Rough Night

Thomas Kretschmann (1962-)
A Taxi Driver

Vicky Krieps
Phantom Thread

Johannes Krisch
In the Fade

Nick Kroll (1978-)
Captain Underpants: The First Epic Movie (*V*)
The House

Diane Kruger (1976-)
In the Fade

Lisa Kudrow (1963-)
The Boss Baby
Table 19

Mila Kunis (1983-)
A Bad Moms Christmas

Sakari Kuosmanen (1956-)
The Other Side of Hope

Aline Kuppenheim
A Fantastic Woman

Cheryl Ladd (1951-)
Unforgettable

Christopher Laesso
The Square

Amy Landecker (1969-)
Beatriz at Dinner

Diane Lane (1965-)
Paris Can Wait

Anthony LaPaglia (1959-)
Annabelle: Creation

Alexandra Maria Lara (1978-)
Geostorm

Larry the Cable Guy (1963-)
Cars 3 (*V*)

Brie Larson (1989-)
Free Fire
The Glass Castle
Kong: Skull Island

Ali Larter (1976-)
Resident Evil: The Final Chapter

Rolf Lassgard (1955-)
Downsizing

Sanaa Lathan (1971-)
American Assassin

Jacob Latimore (1996-)
Sleight

Andy Lau (1961-)
The Great Wall

Oona Laurence (2002-)
The Beguiled

Lucien Laviscount
The Bye Bye Man

Jude Law (1972-)
King Arthur: Legend of the Sword

Kian Lawley (1995-)
Before I Fall

Jennifer Lawrence (1990-)
mother!

Alex Lawther
Goodbye Christopher Robin

Charlotte Le Bon (1986-)
The Promise

Francoise Lebrun
Porto

Ki Hong Lee
Wish Upon

Samara Lee
Annabelle: Creation

Adam LeFevre (1950-)
Gold

Jennifer Jason Leigh (1962-)
Good Time
LBJ

Thomas Lennon (1970-)
Monster Trucks

Melissa Leo (1960-)
Novitiate

Tracy Letts (1965-)
The Lovers
The Post

Zachary Levi (1980-)
The Star

Jane Levy (1989-)
Monster Trucks

William Levy
Resident Evil: The Final Chapter

Liana Liberato (1995-)
Novitiate

Anders Danielsen Lie (1979-)
Personal Shopper

Jaeden Lieberher (2003-)
The Book of Henry
It

Sophia Lillis (2002-)
It

Ludi Lin
Power Rangers

Peggy Lipton (1946-)
A Dog's Purpose

Zoe Lister-Jones (1982-)
Band Aid

John Lithgow (1945-)
Beatriz at Dinner
Daddy's Home 2

Blake Lively (1987-)
All I See Is You

Ron Livingston (1967-)
Lucky

Chelsea Lopez
Phoenix Forgotten

Demi Lovato (1992-)
Smurfs: The Lost Village (*V*)

Patrice Lovely
Boo 2! A Madea Halloween

Jack Lowden (1990-)
Dunkirk

Rob Lowe (1964-)
How to Be a Latin Lover
Monster Trucks

Laurent Lucas (1965-)
Raw

Lucie Lucas
Porto

Diego Luna (1979-)
Flatliners

Menashe Lustig
Menashe

Matilda Anna Ingrid Lutz
Rings

David Lynch (1946-)
Lucky

John Carroll Lynch (1963-)
The Founder

Danielle Macdonald
Patti Cake$

Kelly Macdonald (1976-)
T2 Trainspotting

Farrah Mackenzie
Logan Lucky

Shirley MacLaine (1934-)
The Last Word

Billy Magnussen (1985-)
Ingrid Goes West

Tobey Maguire (1975-)
The Boss Baby

Yoko Maki (1962-)
After the Storm

Aiden Malik
The Florida Project

Joe Manganiello (1976-)
Smurfs: The Lost Village (*V*)

Malina Manovici
Graduation

Jason Mantzoukas (1972-)
The House

Lesley Manville (1956-)
Phantom Thread

Kate Mara (1983-)
Megan Leavey

Rooney Mara (1985-)
A Ghost Story
Song to Song

Miriam Margolyes (1941-)
The Man Who Invented Christmas

Garance Marillier
Raw

Felix Maritaud
BPM (Beats Per Minute)

Brooke Markham
Friend Request

Eddie Marsan (1968-)
Atomic Blonde
The Exception

Elizabeth Marvel (1969-)
The Meyerowitz Stories (New and Selected)

Tatiana Maslany (1985-)
Stronger

Kari Matchett (1970-)
Maudie

Justin Matthews
Phoenix Forgotten

James McAvoy (1979-)
Atomic Blonde
Split

Jack McBrayer (1973-)
Smurfs: The Lost Village (*V*)

Danny McBride (1976-)
Alien: Covenant

Matthew McConaughey (1969-)
The Dark Tower
Gold

Kelly McDonald
Goodbye Christopher Robin

Frances McDormand (1957-)
Three Billboards Outside Ebbing, Missouri

Michael McElhatton (1963-)
The Zookeeper's Wife

John C. McGinley (1959-)
The Belko Experiment

Tim McGraw (1967-)
The Shack

Ewan McGregor (1971-)
Beauty and the Beast
T2 Trainspotting

Christian McKay (1973-)
The Leisure Seeker

Kate McKinnon (1984-)
Rough Night

Jessica McNamee (1986-)
CHIPS

Janet McTeer (1961-)
The Exception
Frederic Meert
Lost in Paris
Fred Melamed (1956-)
Lemon
Robert Jon Mello
Father Figures
Ben Mendelsohn (1969-)
Darkest Hour
Tobias Menzies (1974-)
Underworld: Blood Wars
Stephen Merchant (1974-)
Logan
Table 19
Ronny Merhavi
The Wedding Plan
Angela Merkel (1954-)
An Inconvenient Sequel: Truth to Power
Laurie Metcalf (1955-)
Lady Bird
Hazma Meziani
Nocturama
Kate Micucci (1980-)
The Little Hours
Thomas Middleditch (1982-)
Captain Underpants: The First Epic Movie (*V*)
David Midthunder
Hostiles
Amiah Miller
War for the Planet of the Apes
Ezra Miller (1992-)
Justice League
Jonny Lee Miller (1972-)
T2 Trainspotting
Logan Miller (1992-)
Before I Fall
Sienna Miller (1981-)
The Lost City of Z
T.J. Miller (1981-)
The Emoji Movie (*V*)
Louka Minnella
The Unknown Girl
Dame Helen Mirren (1945-)
The Leisure Seeker
Jason Mitchell
Detroit
Kirsty Mitchell (1974-)
The Leisure Seeker
Radha Mitchell (1973-)
The Shack
Matthew Modine (1959-)
47 Meters Down
Ruby Modine (1990-)
Happy Death Day
Janel Moloney (1969-)
The Leisure Seeker
Jason Momoa (1979-)
The Bad Batch
Michelle Monaghan (1976-)
Sleepless
Cedric Monnet
Paris Can Wait
Dacre Montgomery (1994-)
Power Rangers
Julianne Moore (1960-)
Kingsman: The Golden Circle
Suburbicon
Wonderstruck
Mandy Moore (1984-)
47 Meters Down
Natalie Morales
Battle of the Sexes
Brit Morgan (1987-)
Friend Request
Rob Morgan
Mudbound
Tracy Morgan (1968-)
Fist Fight
Cathy Moriarty (1960-)
Patti Cake$
Denis Moschitto
In the Fade
William Moseley (1987-)
Friend Request
Carrie-Anne Moss (1967-)
The Bye Bye Man
Elisabeth Moss (1982-)
Chuck
The Square
Carey Mulligan (1985-)
Mudbound
Dermot Mulroney (1963-)
The Mountain Between Us
Sleepless
Eloise Mumford (1986-)
Fifty Shades Darker
Cillian Murphy (1976-)
Free Fire
Laith Nakli (1969-)
The Wall
Ivo Nandi
A Cure for Wellness
Kumail Nanjiani (1978-)
The Big Sick
Fist Fight
Igal Naor
The Women's Balcony
Ryo Narita
Your Name
Elodie Navarre
Paris Can Wait
Shiva Negar
American Assassin
Tim Blake Nelson (1964-)
Wormwood
Alex Neustaedter
Walking Out
Kathryn Newton
Lady Bird
Ruben Niborski
Menashe
Julianne Nicholson (1971-)
Novitiate
Connie Nielsen (1965-)
Wonder Woman
Bill Nighy (1949-)
Their Finest
Pierre Niney (1989-)
Frantz
Cynthia Nixon (1966-)
The Only Living Boy in New York
A Quiet Passion
Tom Noonan (1951-)
Wonderstruck
Dean Norris (1963-)
The Book of Henry
James Norton (1985-)
Flatliners
Terry Notary
The Square
B.J. Novak (1979-)
The Founder
Dylan O'Brien (1991-)
American Assassin

Jack O'Connell (1990-)
Tulip Fever

Bob Odenkirk (1962-)
The Post

Leslie Odom, Jr.
Murder on the Orient Express

Nick Offerman (1970-)
The Founder
The Hero
My Life as a Zucchini (*V*)

Jim O'Heir
Logan Lucky

Finnegan Oldfield
Nocturama

Gary Oldman (1958-)
Darkest Hour
The Hitman's Bodyguard
The Space Between Us

Edward James Olmos (1947-)
Coco

Elizabeth Olsen (1989-)
Ingrid Goes West
Wind River

Eric Olson
Wormwood

Ty Olwin
Personal Shopper

Jason O'Mara (1972-)
Wakefield

Ahna O'Reilly (1985-)
All I See Is You

Miranda Otto (1967-)
Annabelle: Creation

Rabah Nait Oufella (1992-)
Raw

Kati Outinen (1961-)
The Other Side of Hope

Clive Owen (1964-)
Valerian and the City of a Thousand Planets

Dana Elaine Owens (1970-)
See *Queen Latifah*

David Oyelowo (1976-)
A United Kingdom

Deepika Padukone
xXx: Return of Xander Cage

Ellen Page (1987-)
Flatliners
My Life as a Zucchini (*V*)

Adam Pally (1982-)
Band Aid

Gwyneth Paltrow (1973-)
Spider-Man: Homecoming

Connor Paolo (1990-)
Friend Request

Hyuk-kwon Park
A Taxi Driver

Sydney Park (1997-)
Wish Upon

Trey Parker (1969-)
Despicable Me 3 (*V*)

Pedro Pascal (1975-)
The Great Wall

Matt Passmore (1972-)
Jigsaw

Mandy Patinkin (1952-)
Wonder

Robert Pattinson (1986-)
Good Time
The Lost City of Z

Natalie Paul
Crown Heights

Sarah Paulson (1974-)
The Post
Rebel in the Rye

Jordan Peele (1979-)
Captain Underpants: The First Epic Movie (*V*)

Michael Peña (1976-)
CHIPS

Barry Pepper (1970-)
Monster Trucks

Ron Perlman (1950-)
Chuck

Tyler Perry (1969-)
Boo 2! A Madea Halloween

Ellen Dorrit Petersen
Thelma

Martin Petitguyot
Nocturama

Michelle Pfeiffer (1958-)
mother!

Ryan Phillippe (1974-)
Wish Upon

Tim Pigott-Smith (1946-)
Victoria & Abdul

Rosamund Pike (1979-)
Hostiles
A United Kingdom

Chris Pine (1980-)
Wonder Woman

Jada Pinkett Smith (1971-)
Girls Trip

Michael Pitt (1981-)
Ghost in the Shell

Aubrey Plaza (1984-)
Ingrid Goes West
The Little Hours

Jesse Plemons (1988-)
American Made

Arthur Christopher Orme Plummer (1929-)
See *Christopher Plummer*

Charlie Plummer
All the Money in the World
The Dinner

Christopher Plummer (1929-)
All the Money in the World
The Exception
The Man Who Invented Christmas

Amy Poehler (1971-)
The House

Natalie Portman (1981-)
Song to Song

Parker Posey (1968-)
Columbus

Will Poulter (1993-)
Detroit

Eline Powell
Novitiate

Chris Pratt (1979-)
Guardians of the Galaxy Vol. 2

Joana Preiss
Raw

Laura Prepon (1980-)
The Hero

Brooklynn Prince
The Florida Project

Jonathan Pryce (1947-)
The Man Who Invented Christmas

Danny Pudi
Smurfs: The Lost Village (*V*)

Florence Pugh
Lady Macbeth

Bill Pullman (1953-)
The Ballad of Lefty Brown
LBJ
Walking Out

Lara Pulver (1980-)
Underworld: Blood Wars

Shannon Purser
Wish Upon

Vladimir Putin (1952-)
An Inconvenient Sequel: Truth to Power

Dennis Quaid (1954-)
A Dog's Purpose

Margaret Qualley
Novitiate

Queen Latifah (1970-)
Girls Trip

Abby Quinn
Landline

Henrik Rafaelsen
Thelma

Miranda Raison (1980-)
Breathe

Edgar Ramirez (1977-)
Bright
Gold

Charlotte Rampling (1946-)
The Sense of an Ending

Noomi Rapace (1979-)
Bright

John Ratzenberger (1947-)
Coco

Vanessa Redgrave (1937-)
Film Stars Don't Die in Liverpool

Deanna Reed-Foster
Last Flag Flying

Keanu Reeves (1964-)
The Bad Batch
John Wick: Chapter 2

Storm Reid
Sleight

John C. Reilly (1965-)
Kong: Skull Island
The Little Hours

Jeremie Renier (1981-)
The Unknown Girl

Jeremy Renner (1971-)
Wind River

Callum Keith Rennie (1960-)
Jigsaw

Retta
Father Figures

Tony Revolori (1996-)
Lowriders
Table 19

Francisco Reyes
A Fantastic Woman

Ryan Reynolds (1976-)
The Hitman's Bodyguard
Life

Giovanni Ribisi (1974-)
The Bad Batch

Pierre Richard (1934-)
Lost in Paris

Haley Lu Richardson (1995-)
Columbus
Split

Miranda Richardson (1958-)
Churchill
Stronger

Daisy Ridley (1992-)
Murder on the Orient Express
Star Wars: The Last Jedi

Diana Rigg (1938-)
Breathe

Rihanna
Valerian and the City of a Thousand Planets

Sam Riley (1980-)
Free Fire

Andrea Riseborough (1981-)
Battle of the Sexes

Krysten Ritter (1981-)
The Hero

Paul Ritter
Their Finest

Emmanuelle Riva (1927-)
Lost in Paris

Christopher Rivera
The Florida Project

Daniel Robb (1929-)
***See** Christopher Plummer*

Margot Robbie (1990-)
Goodbye Christopher Robin
I, Tonya

Tim Robbins (1958-)
Marjorie Prime

Julia Roberts (1967-)
Wonder

Luke Spencer Roberts
Phoenix Forgotten

Shawn Roberts (1984-)
Resident Evil: The Final Chapter

Britt Robertson (1990-)
A Dog's Purpose
The Space Between Us

Craig Robinson (1971-)
Table 19

Nick Robinson (1995-)
Everything, Everything

Rock, The (1972-)
***See** Dwayne 'The Rock' Johnson*

Sam Rockwell (1968-)
Three Billboards Outside Ebbing, Missouri

Gina Rodriguez
The Star

Michelle Rodriguez (1978-)
The Fate of the Furious

Ramon Rodriguez (1979-)
Megan Leavey

Alex Roe (1990-)
Rings

Seth Rogen (1982-)
The Disaster Artist

Franz Rogowski
Happy End

Kelly Rohrbach
Baywatch

Ray Romano (1957-)
The Big Sick

Saoirse Ronan (1994-)
Lady Bird

Anika Noni Rose (1972-)
Everything, Everything

Gabrielle Rose (1954-)
Maudie

Ruby Rose (1986-)
John Wick: Chapter 2

Katharine Ross (1940-)
The Hero

Yolonda Ross
The Bad Batch

Theo Rossi
Lowriders

Jessica Rothe (1987-)
Happy Death Day

Jessica A. Rothenberg (1987-)
***See** Jessica Rothe*

Vincent Rottiers (1986-)
Nocturama

Maya Rudolph (1972-)
The Emoji Movie (*V*)
My Entire High School Sinking Into the Sea
The Nut Job 2: Nutty by Nature

Ella Rumpf
Raw

Geoffrey Rush (1951-)
Pirates of the Caribbean: Dead Men Tell No Tales

Odeya Rush
Lady Bird

Kurt Russell (1951-)
Guardians of the Galaxy Vol. 2

Wyatt Russell (986-)
Ingrid Goes West

Rene Russo (1954-)
Just Getting Started

Jun-yeol Ryu
A Taxi Driver

Nicolas Saavedra
A Fantastic Woman

Laara Sadiq
The Breadwinner

Thomas Sadoski (1976-)
The Last Word

Benny Safdie
Good Time

Halston Sage (1993-)
Before I Fall

Zoe Saldana (1978-)
Guardians of the Galaxy Vol. 2

Hiroyuki (Henry) Sanada (1960-)
Life

Adam Sandler (1966-)
The Meyerowitz Stories (New and Selected)

Susan Sarandon (1946-)
A Bad Moms Christmas
My Entire High School Sinking Into the Sea

Peter Sarsgaard (1971-)
Wormwood

Einat Saruf
The Women's Balcony

Riccardo Scamarcio (1979-)
John Wick: Chapter 2

Adrian Schiller
A Cure for Wellness

Liev Schreiber (1967-)
Chuck

Amy Schumer (1981-)
Snatched
Thank You for Your Service

Meyer Schwartz
Menashe

Jason Schwartzman (1980-)
My Entire High School Sinking Into the Sea

Kaya Scodelario (1992-)
Pirates of the Caribbean: Dead Men Tell No Tales

Naomi Scott (1993-)
Power Rangers

Tom Everett Scott (1970-)
Diary of a Wimpy Kid: The Long Haul

Kristin Scott Thomas (1960-)
Darkest Hour

Amy Sedaris (1961-)
My Life as a Zucchini (*V*)

Martin Sensmeier
Wind River

Andy Serkis (1964-)
War for the Planet of the Apes

Chloe Sevigny (1974-)
Beatriz at Dinner

Amanda Seyfried (1985-)
The Last Word

Jane Seymour (1951-)
Just Getting Started

Michael Shannon (1974-)
The Shape of Water

Frankie Shaw
Stronger

Michael Sheen (1969-)
Brad's Status
Home Again
Norman

Irit Sheleg
The Wedding Plan

Dax Shepard (1975-)
CHIPS

Scott Shepherd
Hostiles
Wormwood

Nobunaga Shimazaki
Your Name

Demetrius Shipp, Jr.
All Eyez on Me

Yonathan Shiray
Foxtrot

Sarah Silverman (1970-)
Battle of the Sexes
The Book of Henry

Alicia Silverstone (1976-)
Diary of a Wimpy Kid: The Long Haul
The Killing of a Sacred Deer

Millicent Simmonds
Wonderstruck

J.K. Simmons (1955-)
Rock Dog
The Snowman

Hannah Simone (1980-)
Band Aid

Ryan Simpkins (1998-)
The House

Bill Skarsgård (1990-)
It

Tom Skerritt (1933-)
Lucky

Jenny Slate (1982-)
Gifted
Landline

John Slattery (1962-)
Churchill

Michael Smiley (1963-)
Free Fire

Algee Smith
Detroit

Lois Smith (1930-)
Marjorie Prime

Will Smith (1968-)
Bright

Brittany Snow (1986-)
Pitch Perfect 3

Kang-ho Song (1967-)
A Taxi Driver

Linda Sorensen (1942-)
The Mountain Between Us

Lodovico Sorret (1951-)
See *Tom Noonan*

Kevin Spacey (1959-)
Baby Driver
Rebel in the Rye

Michael Spears
The Ballad of Lefty Brown

Octavia Spencer (1970-)
Gifted
The Shack
The Shape of Water

Steven Spielberg (1947-)
Five Came Back

June Squibb (1929-)
Table 19

Terence Stamp (1938-)
Bitter Harvest

Sebastian Stan (1982-)
I, Tonya

Lakeith Stanfield (1991-)
Crown Heights

Harry Dean Stanton (1926-2017)
Lucky

Jason Statham (1967-)
The Fate of the Furious

Hailee Steinfeld (1996-)
Pitch Perfect 3

Amandla Stenberg (1998-)
Everything, Everything

Dan Stevens (1982-)
Beauty and the Beast
Colossal
The Man Who Invented Christmas
Marshall

Kristen Stewart (1990-)
Personal Shopper

Patrick Stewart (1940-)
Logan

Ben Stiller (1965-)
Brad's Status

Emma Stone (1988-)
Battle of the Sexes

Ernst Stötzner (1952-)
Frantz

Austin Stowell (1984-)
Colossal

Yvonne Strahovski (1982-)
All I See Is You

Meryl Streep (1949-)
The Post

Jeremy Strong (1978-)
Molly's Game

Mark Strong (1963-)
Kingsman: The Golden Circle

Michael Stuhlbarg (1968-)
Call Me by Your Name
The Shape of Water

Geoff Stults (1977-)
Unforgettable

Jim Sturgess (1978-)
Geostorm

Harry Styles
Dunkirk

Jason Sudeikis (1975-)
Colossal

Hana Sugisaki
Blade of the Immortal

Jessica Sula (1994-)
The Lovers
Split

Donald Sutherland (1935-)
The Leisure Seeker

Tilda Swinton (1960-)
Okja

Wanda Sykes (1964-)
Snatched

Charlie Tahan (1996-)
Super Dark Times

Beat Takeshi (1947-)
See *Takeshi 'Beat' Kitano*

Max Talisman
Super Dark Times

Amos Tamam
The Wedding Plan

Larenz Tate (1975-)
Girls Trip

Channing Tatum (1980-)
Kingsman: The Golden Circle
Logan Lucky

Jeremy Ray Taylor
It

Tom Taylor (2001-)
The Dark Tower

Aaron Taylor-Johnson (1990-)
The Wall

Anya Taylor-Joy
Split

Aimee Teegarden (1989-)
Rings

Miles Teller (1987-)
Only the Brave
Thank You for Your Service

Juno Temple (1989-)
Wonder Wheel

Charlize Theron (1975-)
Atomic Blonde

Justin Theroux (1971-)
The LEGO Ninjago Movie (*V*)

Emma Thompson (1959-)
The Meyerowitz Stories (New and Selected)

Kenan Thompson (1978-)
Rock Dog

Kenneisha Thompson
A Ghost Story

Lucas Till (1990-)
Monster Trucks

Will Tilston
Goodbye Christopher Robin

Justin Timberlake (1981-)
Wonder Wheel

Adrian Titieni
Graduation

Erika Toda (1988-)
Blade of the Immortal

Marisa Tomei (1964-)
Spider-Man: Homecoming

Mehdi Toure
BPM (Beats Per Minute)

Jacob Tremblay (2006-)
The Book of Henry
Wonder

Jean-Louis Trintignant (1930-)
Happy End

Callum Turner
The Only Living Boy in New York

John Turturro (1957-)
Landline

Tyrese (1978-)
See *Tyrese Gibson*

Alanna Ubach (1975-)
Coco

Gabrielle Union (1972-)
Sleepless

Bülent Üstün
Kedi

Arnaud Valois
BPM (Beats Per Minute)

Jane van Lawick-Goodall (1934-)
See *Jane Goodall*

Grace Van Patten
The Meyerowitz Stories (New and Selected)

Vince Vaughn (1970-)
Brawl in Cell Block 99

Daniela Vega
A Fantastic Woman

Arnaud Viard
Paris Can Wait

Izabela Vidovic
Wonder

Alicia Vikander (1988-)
Tulip Fever

Bria Vinaite
The Florida Project
Ville Virtanen
The Other Side of Hope
Jon Voight (1938-)
Same Kind of Different as Me
Johann von Bülow (1972-)
Frantz
Julian Wadham (1958-)
Churchill
Mark Wahlberg (1971-)
All the Money in the World
Daddy's Home 2
Transformers: The Last Knight
Annabelle Wallis (1984-)
The Mummy
Harriet Walter (1950-)
The Sense of an Ending
Julie Walters (1950-)
Film Stars Don't Die in Liverpool
Melora Walters (1960-)
The Lovers
Christoph Waltz (1956-)
Downsizing
Amanda Warren
Roman J. Israel, Esq.
David Warshofsky (1961-)
Wilson
Denzel Washington (1954-)
Roman J. Israel, Esq.
Suki Waterhouse (1992-)
The Bad Batch
Katherine Waterston (1980-)
Alien: Covenant
Emma Watson (1990-)
Beauty and the Beast
The Circle
Naomi Watts (1968-)
The Book of Henry
Chuck
The Glass Castle
Reggie Watts
My Entire High School Sinking Into the Sea
Taliah Webster
Good Time
Madeline Weinstein
Beach Rats
Yoel Weisshaus
Menashe
Rachel Weisz (1970-)
My Cousin Rachel
Dominic West (1969-)
The Square
Diamond White
Boo 2! A Madea Halloween
Fionn Whitehead
Dunkirk
Bradley Whitford (1959-)
Get Out
Megan Leavey
Daniel Lawrence Whitney (1963-)
***See** Larry the Cable Guy*
Josh Wiggins
Walking Out
Kristen Wiig (1973-)
Despicable Me 3 (*V*)
Downsizing
Kaya Wilkins
Thelma
Allison Williams (1988-)
Get Out
Michelle Williams (1980-)
All the Money in the World
The Greatest Showman
Wonderstruck
Luke Wilson (1971-)
Brad's Status
Rock Dog
Lulu Wilson
Annabelle: Creation
Owen Wilson (1968-)
Cars 3 (*V*)
Wonder
Rainn Wilson (1968-)
Smurfs: The Lost Village (*V*)
Rebel Wilson (1980-)
Pitch Perfect 3
Debra Winger (1955-)
The Lovers
Kate Winslet (1975-)
The Mountain Between Us
Wonder Wheel
Reese Witherspoon (1976-)
Home Again
Nat Wolff (1994-)
Home Again
Leap!
Finn Wolfhard
It
B.D. Wong (1960-)
The Space Between Us
Sam Worthington (1976-)
The Shack
Charlie Wright
Diary of a Wimpy Kid: The Long Haul
Robin Wright (1966-)
Blade Runner 2049
Wonder Woman
Sarah Wright (1983-)
American Made
Steven Wright (1955-)
The Emoji Movie (*V*)
Robin Wright Penn (1966-)
***See** Robin Wright*
Daniel Wu (1974-)
Geostorm
Anton Yelchin (1989-2016)
Porto
Donnie Yen (1963-)
xXx: Return of Xander Cage
Steven Yeun (1983-)
Okja
The Star
Hae-jin Yoo
A Taxi Driver
Aoi Yuki
Your Name
Elodie Yung (1981-)
The Hitman's Bodyguard
Steve Zahn (1967-)
War for the Planet of the Apes
Sasheer Zamata (1986-)
Sleight
Oz Zehavi
The Wedding Plan
Renee Zellweger (1969-)
Same Kind of Different as Me
Zendaya
The Greatest Showman
Maddie Ziegler
Leap!

Subject Index

Action-Adventure

American Assassin
Atomic Blonde
Baby Driver
Baywatch
Blade of the Immortal
Bright
Collide
Colossal
The Dark Tower
The Emoji Movie
The Fate of the Furious
The Foreigner
47 Meters Down
Geostorm
Ghost in the Shell
The Great Wall
John Wick: Chapter 2
Jumanji: Welcome to the Jungle
Justice League
King Arthur: Legend of the Sword
Kingsman: The Golden Circle
Kong: Skull Island
The LEGO Batman Movie
The LEGO Ninjago Movie
Logan
The Lost City of Z
The Mountain Between Us
The Mummy
My Little Pony: The Movie
Okja
Only the Brave
Pirates of the Caribbean: Dead Men Tell No Tales
Power Rangers
Snatched
The Space Between Us
Spider-Man: Homecoming
Thor: Ragnarok
Transformers: The Last Knight
Valerian and the City of a Thousand Planets
War for the Planet of the Apes
Wonder Woman

Action-Comedy

Free Fire
Guardians of the Galaxy Vol. 2
The Hitman's Bodyguard
Just Getting Started
The LEGO Batman Movie
Snatched

Adapted from a Book

All the Money in the World
American Assassin
Before I Fall
The Beguiled
The Boss Baby
Call Me by Your Name
Captain Underpants: The First Epic Movie
The Circle
The Dark Tower
Diary of a Wimpy Kid: The Long Haul
The Dinner
A Dog's Purpose
Everything, Everything
The Exception
Fifty Shades Darker
Film Stars Don't Die in Liverpool
The Foreigner
I Am Not Your Negro
It
The Little Hours
The Lost City of Z
The Mountain Between Us
Murder on the Orient Express
My Cousin Rachel
My Life as a Zucchini
The Shack
The Snowman
Stronger
A United Kingdom
Wonderstruck
The Zookeeper's Wife

Adapted from a Cartoon

Transformers: The Last Knight

Adapted from a Play

Frantz

Adapted from a Story

Wakefield

Adapted from Comics

Atomic Blonde
Ghost in the Shell

Guardians of the Galaxy Vol. 2
Kingsman: The Golden Circle
The LEGO Batman Movie
Logan
Spider-Man: Homecoming
Wilson
Wonder Woman

Adapted from Television
Baywatch
CHIPS
Power Rangers
Smurfs: The Lost Village

Adolescence
Beach Rats
Before I Fall
Call Me by Your Name
Lady Bird
Step

Adoption
My Life as a Zucchini
Wilson

Africa
Jane
A United Kingdom

African America
Detroit
I Am Not Your Negro
Mudbound
Roman J. Israel, Esq.

Aging
The Last Word
The Leisure Seeker

AIDS/HIV
BPM (Beats Per Minute)

Aircraft or Air Travel
American Made
The Mountain Between Us

Alcoholic Beverages
Rough Night

Alcoholism
The Glass Castle

Alien Beings
Alien: Covenant
Guardians of the Galaxy Vol. 2
Life
Transformers: The Last Knight

American Indians
Wind River

American Remakes of Asian Films
Ghost in the Shell

American South
The Beguiled

Animals
Ferdinand
Jane
Kedi
The Nut Job 2: Nutty by Nature
Okja
The Star

Animation & Cartoons
The Boss Baby
The Breadwinner
Captain Underpants: The First Epic Movie
Cars 3
Coco
Despicable Me 3
The Emoji Movie
Ferdinand
Leap!
The LEGO Batman Movie
The LEGO Ninjago Movie
My Entire High School Sinking Into the Sea
My Life as a Zucchini
My Little Pony: The Movie
The Nut Job 2: Nutty by Nature
Rock Dog
Smurfs: The Lost Village
The Star
Your Name

Archaeology
The Mummy

Architecture
Columbus

Arctic or Antarctic Regions
The Fate of the Furious
The Mountain Between Us
Wind River

Art or Artists
Lowriders
The Meyerowitz Stories (New and Selected)
The Square
Tulip Fever

Asia
All I See Is You
The Breadwinner
A Taxi Driver

Assassins or Assassination
John Wick: Chapter 2

Automobiles
Baby Driver
The Fate of the Furious

Automobiles—Racing
Cars 3
The Fate of the Furious
Logan Lucky

Bachelor Party
Rough Night

Beach Films
Baywatch

Behind the Scenes
78/52: Hitchcock's Shower Scene

Berlin
Atomic Blonde

Biography
All the Money in the World
American Made
The B-Side: Elsa Dorfman's Portrait Photography
Battle of the Sexes
Breathe

Chuck
Churchill
Crown Heights
Darkest Hour
The Disaster Artist
Film Stars Don't Die in Liverpool
The Founder
The Glass Castle
Goodbye Christopher Robin
The Greatest Showman
I, Tonya
Jane
LBJ
The Lost City of Z
The Man Who Invented Christmas
Marshall
Maudie
Megan Leavey
The Post
Professor Marston and the Wonder Women
A Quiet Passion
Rebel in the Rye
Stronger
Thank You for Your Service
A United Kingdom
Victoria & Abdul
Wormwood
The Zookeeper's Wife

Biography: Music
All Eyez on Me

Black Culture
Step
Whose Streets?

Blindness
All I See Is You

Bodyguards
Blade of the Immortal
The Hitman's Bodyguard

Books or Bookstores
The Man Who Invented Christmas

Boston
Free Fire

Boxing
Chuck

Business or Industry
The Founder
The Other Side of Hope

B/W and Color Combinations
Frantz
I Am Not Your Negro
Song to Song
Wonderstruck

Camelot
Transformers: The Last Knight

Camp or Camping
Boo 2! A Madea Halloween

Canada
Maudie

Cancer
The Hero
The Midwife

Cannibalism
The Bad Batch
Raw

Cats
Kedi
The LEGO Ninjago Movie

Child Abuse
The Book of Henry

Childhood
The Florida Project
Wonderstruck

Children
The Breadwinner
The Florida Project
Leap!
Wonder
Wonderstruck

China
The Great Wall

Christianity
Novitiate
The Shack

Christmas
A Bad Moms Christmas
Daddy's Home 2
The Man Who Invented Christmas
The Star

Circus
The Greatest Showman

Civil Rights
Detroit
I Am Not Your Negro
Marshall

Civil War
The Beguiled

Clothing or Fashion
Phantom Thread

Clowns
It

Cold War
Atomic Blonde

College
Brad's Status
Friend Request
Graduation
Happy Death Day
Raw

Coma
The Big Sick
Columbus

Comedy
A Bad Moms Christmas
Baywatch
Boo 2! A Madea Halloween
The Boss Baby
CHIPS
Daddy's Home 2
The Disaster Artist
Father Figures
Fist Fight
Get Out

Girls Trip
Going in Style
Happy Death Day
The House
How to Be a Latin Lover
Jumanji: Welcome to the Jungle
Kingsman: The Golden Circle
The LEGO Ninjago Movie
The Little Hours
Lost in Paris
Pitch Perfect 3
Rough Night
Table 19
Thor: Ragnarok
Three Billboards Outside Ebbing, Missouri
The Wedding Plan
Wilson

Comedy-Drama

American Made
Band Aid
Battle of the Sexes
Beatriz at Dinner
Brad's Status
Colossal
The Disaster Artist
Downsizing
Ingrid Goes West
Lady Bird
Landline
Last Flag Flying
The Last Word
The Leisure Seeker
Lemon
Logan Lucky
The Lovers
The Meyerowitz Stories (New and Selected)
My Entire High School Sinking Into the Sea
The Other Side of Hope
Paris Can Wait
The Square
Their Finest
The Trip to Spain
The Women's Balcony

Comic Books

Professor Marston and the Wonder Women

Coming of Age

Beach Rats
Call Me by Your Name
The Glass Castle
Lady Bird
The Women's Balcony

Computers

Friend Request

Courtroom Drama

The Hitman's Bodyguard
Marshall
Molly's Game

Crime Drama

Brawl in Cell Block 99
Crown Heights
Detroit
The Dinner
Good Time
Graduation
Murder on the Orient Express
The Snowman
Wind River

Crime or Criminals

Baby Driver
Baywatch
The Belko Experiment
Collide
Crown Heights
Ghost in the Shell
Going in Style
The House
Logan Lucky
Roman J. Israel, Esq.
Three Billboards Outside Ebbing, Missouri

Dance

Step

Dance--Ballet

Leap!

Dating

The Big Sick
Everything, Everything
Get Out
How to Be a Latin Lover
Song to Song

Deadly Viruses

BPM (Beats Per Minute)
It Comes at Night

Deafness

Wonderstruck

Death & the Afterlife

Annabelle: Creation
The Ballad of Lefty Brown
Before I Fall
The Book of Henry
BPM (Beats Per Minute)
Coco
A Fantastic Woman
A Ghost Story
Happy Death Day
In the Fade
Last Flag Flying
The Last Word
Personal Shopper
Rough Night
The Shack
Suburbicon

Demons or Wizards

Transformers: The Last Knight
Wish Upon

Deserts

The Bad Batch
The Mummy
The Wall

Detroit

Detroit

Disaster Films

Geostorm
An Inconvenient Sequel: Truth to Power
Only the Brave

Diseases or Illness

The Big Sick
Breathe
A Cure for Wellness

Divorce

How to Be a Latin Lover
Unforgettable

Doctors

A Cure for Wellness
The Killing of a Sacred Deer

Documentary Films

Abacus: Small Enough to Jail
The B-Side: Elsa Dorfman's Portrait Photography
Dina
Five Came Back
I Am Not Your Negro
An Inconvenient Sequel: Truth to Power
Jane
Kedi
Long Strange Trip
78/52: Hitchcock's Shower Scene
Step
Whose Streets?
The Work
Wormwood

Dogs

The Boss Baby
Megan Leavey
Rock Dog

Dragons

Super Dark Times

Drama

After the Storm
All Eyez on Me
All I See Is You
All the Money in the World
The Bad Batch
Beach Rats
Before I Fall
The Beguiled
Bitter Harvest
Blade of the Immortal
The Book of Henry
BPM (Beats Per Minute)
The Breadwinner
Breathe
Bright
Call Me by Your Name
Chuck
Churchill
Columbus
Darkest Hour
Detroit
Dunkirk
Everything, Everything
The Exception
A Fantastic Woman
Film Stars Don't Die in Liverpool
Flatliners
The Florida Project
The Founder
Foxtrot
Frantz
A Ghost Story
Gifted
The Glass Castle
The Greatest Showman
Happy End
The Hero
Hostiles
In the Fade
The Killing of a Sacred Deer
King Arthur: Legend of the Sword
Lady Macbeth
LBJ
Lowriders
Lucky
Marjorie Prime
Maudie
Megan Leavey
Menashe
The Midwife
Molly's Game
mother!
Mudbound
My Cousin Rachel
Nocturama
Norman
Novitiate
Okja
The Only Living Boy in New York
Only the Brave
Patti Cake$
Personal Shopper
Phantom Thread
Porto
The Post
A Quiet Passion
Raw
Rebel in the Rye
Roman J. Israel, Esq.
The Sense of an Ending
The Shack
The Shape of Water
Sleight
Song to Song
Stronger
Suburbicon
T2 Trainspotting
A Taxi Driver
Thank You for Your Service
Thelma
Tulip Fever
Unforgettable
A United Kingdom
The Unknown Girl
Victoria & Abdul
Wakefield
Walking Out
The Wall
Wonder
Wonder Wheel
Wonderstruck
Woodshock
Your Name
The Zookeeper's Wife

Dreams or Nightmares

Flatliners

Drug Abuse

T2 Trainspotting

Drugs

American Made
Collide
Long Strange Trip
Woodshock
Wormwood

Dystopian Themes

The Bad Batch

Earthquakes

My Entire High School Sinking Into the Sea

Ecology or Environment

An Inconvenient Sequel: Truth to Power

Education or Schooling

Captain Underpants: The First Epic Movie
Step
Wonder

Engagement

Unforgettable

Epic Battles
The Dark Tower
Fist Fight
Justice League
Star Wars: The Last Jedi
Transformers: The Last Knight

Ethics & Morals
The Circle
Graduation
Molly's Game

Existentialism
Brad's Status

Explorers or Exploration
Kong: Skull Island
The Lost City of Z
Smurfs: The Lost Village

Family
The Boss Baby
The Fate of the Furious
Ferdinand
Foxtrot
Landline
Lost in Paris
Lowriders
Marjorie Prime
The Meyerowitz Stories (New and Selected)
The Only Living Boy in New York
Patti Cake$
Wonder
Wonder Wheel

Family Comedy
Diary of a Wimpy Kid: The Long Haul

Family Drama
After the Storm
Goodbye Christopher Robin
Wakefield

Family Reunions
Despicable Me 3
Wilson

Family Viewing
Captain Underpants: The First Epic Movie
Cars 3
The LEGO Ninjago Movie
Smurfs: The Lost Village

Fantasy
Beauty and the Beast
Bright
A Ghost Story
The Great Wall
Justice League
The Mummy
Pirates of the Caribbean: Dead Men Tell No Tales
The Shack
The Shape of Water
Valerian and the City of a Thousand Planets
Your Name

Farms or Farming
Mudbound

Fathers
Brad's Status
Daddy's Home 2
Father Figures
The Foreigner
It Comes at Night
The Killing of a Sacred Deer
The LEGO Ninjago Movie
Menashe
The Meyerowitz Stories (New and Selected)
The Shack
Wilson

Fathers and Children
After the Storm
Columbus
Daddy's Home 2
Goodbye Christopher Robin
Graduation
The Hero
Suburbicon
Walking Out

Female Domestic Employees
Beatriz at Dinner
The Exception
Personal Shopper

Female Friends
Before I Fall
Rough Night

Feminism
Battle of the Sexes

Femme Fatales
Atomic Blonde

Film History
Chuck
Five Came Back
78/52: Hitchcock's Shower Scene

Filmmaking
The Disaster Artist
Five Came Back
78/52: Hitchcock's Shower Scene
Their Finest

Firemen
Only the Brave

Fires
Only the Brave

Flood
An Inconvenient Sequel: Truth to Power

Food Industry
The Founder
Okja

Foreign: Belgian
Graduation

Foreign: British
Breathe
Churchill
Goodbye Christopher Robin
The Killing of a Sacred Deer

Foreign: Canadian
Colossal

Foreign: Czech
The Zookeeper's Wife

Foreign: Finnish
The Other Side of Hope

Foreign: French
BPM (Beats Per Minute)
Frantz
Graduation
Happy End
My Life as a Zucchini
Raw

Foreign: German
Frantz
Friend Request

Foreign: Irish
The Killing of a Sacred Deer

Foreign: Japanese
After the Storm

Foreign: Korean
Okja
A Taxi Driver

Foreign: Romanian
Graduation

Foreign: Spanish
Colossal
The Promise

Foreign: Swiss
My Life as a Zucchini

Foreign: Turkish
Kedi

Forests or Trees
Smurfs: The Lost Village

France
BPM (Beats Per Minute)
Dunkirk
Frantz
Happy End
Leap!
The Midwife
Paris Can Wait
Raw
The Unknown Girl

Friends or Friendship
The Ballad of Lefty Brown
Captain Underpants: The First Epic Movie
Crown Heights
Friend Request
Girls Trip
The Last Word
Same Kind of Different as Me
Super Dark Times
T2 Trainspotting

Friendship
Crown Heights

Funerals
Foxtrot

Gambling
The House

Games
Jumanji: Welcome to the Jungle
Molly's Game

Gays or Lesbians
Beach Rats
BPM (Beats Per Minute)
Call Me by Your Name

Germany
Collide
Frantz
In the Fade

Ghosts or Spirits
Boo 2! A Madea Halloween
Friend Request
A Ghost Story
Personal Shopper
Pirates of the Caribbean: Dead Men Tell No Tales
Rings

Gifted Children
The Book of Henry
Brad's Status
Gifted

Golf
Just Getting Started

Great Britain
Darkest Hour
Kingsman: The Golden Circle
Lady Macbeth
The Man Who Invented Christmas
A United Kingdom

Grim Reaper
The Belko Experiment

Handicapped
Stronger

Heists
Baby Driver
Collide
Despicable Me 3
Going in Style
Logan Lucky

High School
Before I Fall
Fist Fight
Lady Bird
My Entire High School Sinking Into the Sea
Power Rangers
Spider-Man: Homecoming
Wish Upon

Holidays
Boo 2! A Madea Halloween

Homosexuality
Beach Rats
BPM (Beats Per Minute)
Call Me by Your Name
Thelma

Horror
Alien: Covenant
Annabelle: Creation
The Belko Experiment
A Cure for Wellness
Flatliners
47 Meters Down
Friend Request
Get Out
Happy Death Day
It
It Comes at Night
Jigsaw
The Killing of a Sacred Deer
Life
mother!
The Mummy
Phoenix Forgotten
Raw
Rings
78/52: Hitchcock's Shower Scene
Wish Upon

Horror Comedy
Boo 2! A Madea Halloween

Horses
My Little Pony: The Movie

Hospitals or Medicine
A Cure for Wellness
The Killing of a Sacred Deer
The Midwife
The Unknown Girl

Hotels or Motels
The Florida Project

Hunting
Walking Out
Wind River

Immigration
Happy End

Infants
The Boss Baby

Inteligence Service Agencies
American Assassin
Atomic Blonde
Kingsman: The Golden Circle
Molly's Game
Wormwood

International Relations
Darkest Hour
A United Kingdom

Interracial Affairs
The Big Sick
Crown Heights
Detroit
Get Out
I Am Not Your Negro
A United Kingdom

Islam
The Big Sick

Islands
Kong: Skull Island
Wonder Woman

Israel
Foxtrot
The Wedding Plan
The Women's Balcony

Italy
Call Me by Your Name

Japan
After the Storm
Blade of the Immortal
Ghost in the Shell
Your Name

Journalism
The Last Word
The Post
A Taxi Driver

Judaism
Menashe
The Women's Balcony

Jungle Stories
Jane
Jumanji: Welcome to the Jungle
The Lost City of Z
Snatched

Kidnappers or Kidnappings
All the Money in the World
Collide
Sleight
Snatched

Kings
King Arthur: Legend of the Sword
Transformers: The Last Knight

Law or Lawyers
Jigsaw
Just Getting Started
Marshall
Roman J. Israel, Esq.

Lifeguards
Baywatch

Little People
Downsizing

London
Churchill
The Foreigner
The Mummy
Phantom Thread
The Sense of an Ending
Their Finest
A United Kingdom
Victoria & Abdul

Loneliness
Wakefield
Wilson

Los Angeles
Beatriz at Dinner
Bright
The Disaster Artist
Five Came Back
Home Again
Ingrid Goes West
Lowriders

Mad Scientists
The Belko Experiment
A Cure for Wellness

Magic
Sleight

Male Domestic Employees
Victoria & Abdul

Marriage
All I See Is You
Band Aid
I, Tonya
Landline
The Leisure Seeker
The Lovers
Same Kind of Different as Me
Wakefield

May-December Romance
A Fantastic Woman
Film Stars Don't Die in Liverpool
Home Again
How to Be a Latin Lover

The Meaning of Life
Lucky

Medieval Era
The Great Wall
King Arthur: Legend of the Sword
The Little Hours
Transformers: The Last Knight

Men
Mudbound
The Work

Mental Health
Thank You for Your Service

Miami
Rough Night

Midlife Crisis
Brad's Status

Military: Army
Hostiles
Thank You for Your Service

Military: Foreign
Foxtrot

Military: Marines
Megan Leavey

Missing Persons
Blade Runner 2049
Lost in Paris
Phoenix Forgotten
Wakefield

Mistaken Identity
Captain Underpants: The First Epic Movie

Monkeys
Jane
War for the Planet of the Apes

Monsters
Colossal
The Great Wall

Mothers
A Bad Moms Christmas
Columbus
I, Tonya
Snatched
Three Billboards Outside Ebbing, Missouri
Unforgettable

Mountaineering
The Mountain Between Us

Mummies
The Mummy

Museums
The Square
Wonderstruck

Music
Baby Driver
Band Aid
Coco
Long Strange Trip
Pitch Perfect 3
Rock Dog
Song to Song

Music: Hip-Hop or Rap
All Eyez on Me
Patti Cake$

Musical
Beauty and the Beast
The Greatest Showman

Mystery & Suspense
Blade Runner 2049
The Circle
A Cure for Wellness
Get Out
Happy Death Day
The Killing of a Sacred Deer
mother!
Murder on the Orient Express
My Cousin Rachel
Personal Shopper
Phoenix Forgotten
The Sense of an Ending
Sleight
The Snowman
Suburbicon
Thelma
The Unknown Girl
Walking Out
Wind River

Mythology or Legend
King Arthur: Legend of the Sword
Transformers: The Last Knight
Wonder Woman

Native Americans
Hostiles
Wind River

New Jersey
Chuck
Patti Cake$

New Orleans
Girls Trip

New York City
Beach Rats
Crown Heights
Good Time
Menashe
Okja
The Only Living Boy in New York
Wonderstruck

Newspapers
The Last Word

Non-Linear Narratives
Dunkirk
Wonderstruck

Notable Death Scenes
All Eyez on Me

Nuns or Priests
The Little Hours
Novitiate

Obsessive Love
Tulip Fever

Ocean Dangers
47 Meters Down

Oceans
Everything, Everything
Pirates of the Caribbean: Dead Men Tell No Tales

Organ Transplantation
Ghost in the Shell

Organized Crime
Just Getting Started

Parenthood
Brad's Status
The Dinner
Gifted
Graduation
The House
Lady Bird
Menashe
Unforgettable

Paris
BPM (Beats Per Minute)
Lost in Paris
Nocturama
Personal Shopper

Parties
Beatriz at Dinner
Boo 2! A Madea Halloween
Rough Night

Period Piece
The Ballad of Lefty Brown
Battle of the Sexes
The Beguiled
Bitter Harvest
Blade of the Immortal
BPM (Beats Per Minute)
Chuck
Dunkirk
The Exception
Film Stars Don't Die in Liverpool
Frantz
Free Fire
Hostiles
Lady Macbeth
Landline
Leap!
The Man Who Invented Christmas
My Cousin Rachel
The Post
Professor Marston and the Wonder Women
The Promise
A Quiet Passion
Rebel in the Rye
A United Kingdom
Victoria & Abdul
Wonder Woman
Wonderstruck
The Zookeeper's Wife

Period Piece: 1920s
The Lost City of Z
Wonderstruck

Period Piece: 1950s
Annabelle: Creation
The Founder
Phantom Thread
Suburbicon
Wonder Wheel

Period Piece: 1960s
Detroit
I Am Not Your Negro
The Shape of Water

Period Piece: 1980s
Atomic Blonde
Call Me by Your Name
Crown Heights
It

Period Piece: Medieval Era
The Little Hours

Phones
The Emoji Movie

Photography or Photographers
The B-Side: Elsa Dorfman's Portrait Photography

Pigs
Okja

Pirates
Pirates of the Caribbean: Dead Men Tell No Tales

Poets or Poetry
A Quiet Passion

Poisons
My Cousin Rachel

Police
Bright
CHIPS
Detroit
Jigsaw
Whose Streets?

Politics & Government
BPM (Beats Per Minute)
LBJ
Norman

Politics or Government
An Inconvenient Sequel: Truth to Power
The Post

Post-Apocalypse
It Comes at Night
War for the Planet of the Apes

Poverty
The Florida Project

Presidency
LBJ

Princes or Princesses
The Mummy
Wonder Woman

Prison or Jail
Brawl in Cell Block 99
In the Fade
The Work

Queens
Victoria & Abdul

Race Against Time
All the Money in the World

Rape
Three Billboards Outside Ebbing, Missouri
Wind River

Religious Themes
Menashe
mother!
The Shack

Rescue Missions
The Book of Henry
Collide
Dunkirk
Okja

The Resistance
Whose Streets?

Reunions
Last Flag Flying
Pitch Perfect 3
T2 Trainspotting

Revenge
American Assassin
The Foreigner
In the Fade
John Wick: Chapter 2
The Killing of a Sacred Deer
My Cousin Rachel
Pirates of the Caribbean: Dead Men Tell No Tales

Road Trips
Diary of a Wimpy Kid: The Long Haul
Everything, Everything
Father Figures
The Leisure Seeker
Paris Can Wait
The Trip to Spain

Robots & Androids
Blade Runner 2049
Colossal
Ghost in the Shell
Star Wars: The Last Jedi
Transformers: The Last Knight

Romance
The Bad Batch
Beauty and the Beast
Bitter Harvest
Breathe
Call Me by Your Name
Dina
Everything, Everything
The Exception
A Fantastic Woman
Fifty Shades Darker
Film Stars Don't Die in Liverpool
Frantz
The Hero
The Leisure Seeker
The Lovers
Maudie
The Mountain Between Us
My Cousin Rachel
Paris Can Wait
Phantom Thread
Porto
Professor Marston and the Wonder Women
The Promise
The Shape of Water
Song to Song
The Space Between Us
Their Finest
Thelma
Tulip Fever
A United Kingdom
The Wedding Plan

Romantic Comedy
The Big Sick
Home Again

Royalty
King Arthur: Legend of the Sword
A United Kingdom
Victoria & Abdul

Russia/USSR
Bitter Harvest

Salespeople
The Founder

San Francisco
Long Strange Trip

Satire or Parody
Beatriz at Dinner
Downsizing

Science Fiction
Alien: Covenant
The Bad Batch
Blade Runner 2049
Colossal
The Dark Tower
Despicable Me 3
Downsizing
Flatliners
Geostorm
Ghost in the Shell
Guardians of the Galaxy Vol. 2
Kong: Skull Island
Life
Logan
Okja
Phoenix Forgotten
Power Rangers
Sleight
The Space Between Us
Star Wars: The Last Jedi
Transformers: The Last Knight
Valerian and the City of a Thousand Planets
War for the Planet of the Apes
Wonder Woman

Science or Scientists
An Inconvenient Sequel: Truth to Power
Jane
Wormwood

Scotland
T2 Trainspotting

Serial Killers
Jigsaw
The Snowman

Sex or Sexuality
The Beguiled
Fifty Shades Darker
Lady Macbeth
The Little Hours
Novitiate
Porto
Raw

Sexual Abuse
The Book of Henry

Sibling Rivalry
The Boss Baby
Despicable Me 3

Singles
Home Again

Skating
I, Tonya

Slice of Life
Lucky

South America
American Made
The Lost City of Z
Snatched

Space Exploration or Outer Space
Alien: Covenant
Guardians of the Galaxy Vol. 2
Life
The Space Between Us
Star Wars: The Last Jedi
Transformers: The Last Knight
Valerian and the City of a Thousand Planets

Spain
Ferdinand
The Trip to Spain

Spies and Espionage
American Assassin
Atomic Blonde
The Boss Baby
The Exception
Kingsman: The Golden Circle

Sports
Battle of the Sexes
Chuck
I, Tonya

Stalkers
Ingrid Goes West

Star Wars Saga
Star Wars: The Last Jedi

Stepparents
Unforgettable

Strippers
Rough Night

Submarines
The Fate of the Furious

Suburban Dystopia
Wakefield

Super Heroes
Captain Underpants: The First Epic Movie
Ghost in the Shell
Justice League
The LEGO Batman Movie
Logan
Power Rangers
Sleight
Spider-Man: Homecoming
Thor: Ragnarok

Survival
The Belko Experiment
Free Fire
The Mountain Between Us
Stronger

Teaching or Teachers
The Beguiled
Fist Fight

Teamwork
Captain Underpants: The First Epic Movie
Megan Leavey

Technology
The Circle
The Emoji Movie
Marjorie Prime

Tennis
Battle of the Sexes

Terrorism
American Assassin
The Fate of the Furious
The Foreigner
Nocturama
Stronger

Texas
LBJ
Song to Song

Thrillers
Alien: Covenant
American Assassin
Atomic Blonde
The Beguiled
The Belko Experiment
The Circle
Collide
The Dinner
The Fate of the Furious
Geostorm
Good Time
The Killing of a Sacred Deer
Life
Nocturama
Norman
Personal Shopper
The Snowman
Super Dark Times
Unforgettable
The Wall
Wind River
Woodshock

Time Travel
A Ghost Story

Torrid Love Scenes
Fifty Shades Darker
Lady Macbeth

Trains
Murder on the Orient Express

Transvestites or Transsexuals
A Fantastic Woman

True Crime
Crown Heights

True Stories
All Eyez on Me
Battle of the Sexes
The Big Sick
Chuck
Churchill
Dunkirk
The Founder
The Lost City of Z
Megan Leavey
The Promise
Same Kind of Different as Me
Stronger
A United Kingdom
Victoria & Abdul
The Zookeeper's Wife

Twins
Despicable Me 3
Father Figures
Personal Shopper

Vacations
Girls Trip
Snatched

Veterans
Last Flag Flying
Lucky
Mudbound

Veterinarians
Raw

War: General
Bitter Harvest
The Great Wall
Last Flag Flying
Megan Leavey
The Promise
Thank You for Your Service
The Wall
War for the Planet of the Apes

Weddings
Dina
Table 19
The Wedding Plan

Westerns
The Ballad of Lefty Brown
The Dark Tower
Hostiles

Wild Kingdom
47 Meters Down
Jane
Kong: Skull Island

Wilderness Areas
Jane
Walking Out

Women
The Beguiled
Girls Trip
Ingrid Goes West
Pitch Perfect 3
Rough Night
The Women's Balcony

Women of Substance
Atomic Blonde
Battle of the Sexes
Ghost in the Shell
Megan Leavey
Wonder Woman

World War One
Frantz
Wonder Woman

World War Two
Churchill
Darkest Hour
Dunkirk
The Exception
Five Came Back
Their Finest
The Zookeeper's Wife

Writers
I Am Not Your Negro
mother!

Zoos
The Zookeeper's Wife

Title Index

This cumulative index is an alphabetical list of all films covered in the volumes of the *Magill's Cinema Annual.* Film titles are indexed on a word-by-word basis, including articles and prepositions. English leading articles (A, An, The) are ignored, as are foreign leading articles (El, Il, La, Las, Le, Les, Los). Acronyms appear alphabetically as if regular words. Common abbreviations in titles file as if they are spelled out. Proper names in titles are alphabetized beginning with the individual's first name. Titles with numbers are alphabetized as if the numbers were spelled out. When numeric titles gather in close proximity to each other, the titles will be arranged in a low-to-high numeric sequence. Films reviewed in this volume are cited in bold; films reviewed in past volumes are cited with the *Annual* year in which the review was published. Original and alternate titles are cross-referenced to the American release title. Titles of retrospective films are followed by the year, in brackets, of their original release.

A

A corps perdu. *See* Straight for the Heart.

A. I.: Artificial Intelligence 2002

A la Mode (Fausto) 1995

A Lot Like Love 2006

A Ma Soeur. *See* Fat Girl.

A nos amours 1984

Abacus: Small Enough to Jail 2018

Abandon 2003

ABCD 2002

ABCs of Death, The 2014

Abduction 2012

Abgeschminkt! *See* Making Up!.

About a Boy 2003

About Adam 2002

About Elly 2016

About Last Night... 1986

About Last Night (2015) 2015

About Schmidt 2003

About Time 2014

Above the Law 1988

Above the Rim 1995

Abraham Lincoln: Vampire Hunter 2013

Abre Los Ojos. *See* Open Your Eyes.

Abrazos rotos, Los. *See* Broken Embraces.

Abril Despedacado. *See* Behind the Sun.

Absence of Malice 1981

Absolute Beginners 1986

Absolute Power 1997

Absolution 1988

Abyss, The 1989

Accepted 2007

Accidental Tourist, The 1988

Accompanist, The 1993

Accordeur de tremblements de terre, L'. *See* Piano Tuner of Earthquakes, The.

Accountant, The 2017

Accused, The 1988

Ace in the Hole [1951] 1986, 1991

Ace Ventura: Pet Detective 1995

Ace Ventura: When Nature Calls 1996

Aces: Iron Eagle III 1992

Acid House, The 2000

Acqua e sapone. *See* Water and Soap.

Across the Tracks 1991

Across the Universe 2008

Act of Killing, The 2014

Act of Valor 2013

Acting on Impulse 1995

Action Jackson 1988

Actress 1988

Adam 2010

Adam Sandler's 8 Crazy Nights 2003

Adam's Rib [1950] 1992

Adaptation 2003

Addams Family, The 1991

Addams Family Values 1993

Addicted 2015

Addicted to Love 1997
Addiction, The 1995
Addition, L'. *See* Patsy, The.
Adieu au Langage. *See* Goodbye to Language.
Adjo, Solidaritet. *See* Farewell Illusion.
Adjuster, The 1992
Adjustment Bureau, The 2012
Admission 2014
Adolescente, L' 1982
Adoration 2010
Adore 2014
Adult Beginners 2016
Adventureland 2010
Adventures in Babysitting 1987
Adventures of Baron Munchausen, The 1989
Adventures of Buckaroo Banzai, The 1984
Adventures of Elmo in Grouchland, The 2000
Adventures of Felix, The 2002
Adventures of Ford Fairlane, The 1990
Adventures of Huck Finn, The 1993
Adventures of Mark Twain, The 1986
Adventures of Milo and Otis, The 1989
Adventures of Pinocchio, The 1996
Adventures of Pluto Nash, The 2003
Adventures of Priscilla, Queen of the Desert, The 1995
Adventures of Rocky and Bullwinkle, The 2001
Adventures of Sebastian Cole, The, 2000
Adventures of Sharkboy and Lavagirl in 3-D, The 2006
Adventures of the American Rabbit, The 1986
Adventures of Tintin, The 2012
Advocate 1995
Aelita 1995
Aeon Flux 2006
Affair of Love, An 2001
Affair of the Necklace, The 2002
Affaire de Femmes, Une. *See* Story of Women.
Affaire de Gout, Un. *See* Matter of Taste, A.
Affengeil 1992
Affliction 1999
Afraid of the Dark 1992
Africa the Serengeti 1995
After Dark, My Sweet 1990
After Earth 2014
After Hours 1985
After Life 2000
After Midnight 1989
After the Rehearsal 1984
After the Storm 2018
After the Sunset 2005
After Tiller 2014
Afterglow 1979
After.life 2011
Afternoon Delight 2014
Against All Odds 1983
Against the Ropes 2005
Age Isn't Everything (Life in the Food Chain) 1995
Age of Adaline, The 2016
Age of Innocence, The 1993
Agent Cody Banks 2004
Agent Cody Banks 2: Destination London 2005
Agent on Ice 1986
Agnes Browne 2001
Agnes of God 1985
Agora 2011
Ai Weiwei: Never Sorry 2013
Aid 1988
Aileen: Life and Death of a Serial Killer 2005
Aileen Wuornos: The Selling of a Serial Killer 1995
Ain't Them Bodies Saints 2014
Air America 1990
Air Bud 1997
Air Bud: Golden Receiver 1999
Air Force One 1997
Air Guitar Nation 2008
Air I Breathe, The 2009
Air Up There, The 1995
Airborne 1993
Airheads 1995
Airplane II: The Sequel 1982
Ajami 2011
Akai Hashi no Shita no Nurui Mizo. *See* Warm Water Under a Red Bridge.
Akamreul boatda. *See* I Saw the Devil.
Akeelah and the Bee 2007
Akira Kurosawa's Dreams 1990
Al-Jenna-An. *See* Paradise Now.
Aladdin (Corbucci) 1987
Aladdin (Musker & Clements) 1992
Alamo, The 2005
Alamo Bay 1985
Alan and Naomi 1992
Alan Smithee Film, An 1999
Alarmist, The 1999
Alaska 1996
Albert Nobbs 2012
Alberto Express 1992
Albino Alligator 1997
Alchemist, The 1986
Alex & Emma 2004
Alex Cross 2013
Alexander 2005
Alexander and the Terrible, Horrible, No Good, Very Bad Day 2015
Alfie 2005
Alfred Hitchcock's Bon Voyage & Aventure Malgache. *See* Aventure Malgache.
Ali 2002
Alias Betty 2004
Alice (Allen) 1990
Alice (Svankmajer) 1988
Alice et Martin 2001
Alice in Wonderland 2011
Alice Through the Looking Glass 2017
Alien: Covenant 2018
Alien Nation 1988
Alien Predator 1987
Alien Resurrection 1997
Alien vs. Predator 2005

Aliens 1986

Alien3 1992

Aliens in the Attic 2010

Aliens vs. Predator: Requiem 2008

Alive 1993

Alive and Kicking 1997

All About My Mother 2000

All About Steve 2010

All About the Benjamins 2003

All Dogs Go to Heaven 1989

All Dogs Go to Heaven II 1996

All Eyez on Me 2018

All Good Things 2011

All I Desire [1953] 1987

All I See Is You 2018

All I Want for Christmas 1991

All is Lost 2014

All of Me 1984

All or Nothing 2003

All Over Me 1997

All Quiet on the Western Front [1930] 1985

All the King's Men 2007

All the Light in the Sky 2014

All the Little Animals 2000

All the Money in the World 2018

All the Pretty Horses 2001

All the Rage. *See* It's the Rage.

All the Real Girls 2004

All the Right Moves 1983

All the Vermeers in New York 1992

All's Fair 1989

All-American High 1987

Allan Quatermain and the Lost City of Gold 1987

Allegiant 2017

Alley Cat 1984

Allied 2017

Alligator Eyes 1990

Allnighter, The 1987

Almost an Angel 1990

Almost Christmas 2017

Almost Famous 2001

Almost Heroes 1999

Almost You 1985

Aloha 2016

Aloha Summer 1988

Alone. *See* Solas.

Alone in the Dark 2006

Alone with Her 2008

Along Came a Spider 2002

Along Came Polly 2005

Alpha and Omega 2011

Alpha Dog 2008

Alphabet City 1983

Alpine Fire 1987

Altars of the World [1976] 1985

Alvin and the Chipmunks 2008

Alvin and the Chipmunks: Chipwrecked 2012

Alvin and the Chipmunks: Road Chip 2016

Alvin and the Chipmunks: The Squeakquel 2010

Always (Jaglom) 1985

Always (Spielberg) 1989

Amadeus 1984, 1985

Amanda 1989

Amantes. *See* Lovers.

Amantes del Circulo Polar, Los. *See* Lovers of the Arctic Circle, The.

Amantes pasajeros, Los. *See* I'm So Excited.

Amants du Pont Neuf, Les 1995

Amateur 1995

Amateur, The 1982

Amazing Grace 2008

Amazing Grace and Chuck 1987

Amazing Panda Adventure, The 1995

Amazing Spider-Man, The 2013

Amazing Spider-Man 2, The 2015

Amazon Women on the Moon 1987

Ambition 1991

Amelia 2010

Amelie 2002

Amen 2004

America 1986

American, The 2011

American Anthem 1986

American Assassin 2018

American Beauty 2000

American Blue Note 1991

American Buffalo 1996

American Carol, An 2009

American Chai 2003

American Cyborg: Steel Warrior 1995

American Desi 2002

American Dream 1992

American Dreamer 1984

American Dreamz 2007

American Fabulous 1992

American Flyers 1985

American Friends 1993

American Gangster 2008

American Gothic 1988

American Haunting, An 2007

American Heart 1993

American History X 1999

American Honey 2017

American Hustle 2014

American in Paris, An [1951] 1985

American Justice 1986

American Made 2018

American Me 1992

American Movie 2000

American Ninja 1984, 1991

American Ninja 1985

American Ninja II 1987

American Ninja III 1989

American Outlaws 2002

American Pastoral 2017

American Pie 2000

American Pie 2 2002

American Pop 1981

American President, The 1995

American Psycho 2001

American Reunion 2013

American Rhapsody, An 2002

American Sniper 2015

American Stories 1989

American Splendor 2004

American Summer, An 1991

American Taboo 1984, 1991

American Tail, An 1986

American Tail: Fievel Goes West, An 1991

American Teen 2009
American Ultra 2016
American Wedding 2004
American Werewolf in London, An 1981
American Werewolf in Paris, An 1997
American Women. *See* The Closer You Get.
America's Sweethearts 2002
Ami de mon amie, L'. *See* Boyfriends and Girlfriends.
Amin: The Rise and Fall 1983
Amistad 1997
Amityville Horror, The 2006
Amityville II: The Possession 1981
Amityville 3-D 1983
Among Giants 2000
Among People 1988
Amongst Friends 1993
Amor brujo, El 1986
Amores Perros 2002
Amos and Andrew 1993
Amour 2013
Amour de Swann, Un. *See* Swann in Love.
Amours d'Astrée et de Céladon, Les. *See* Romance of Astree and Celadon, The.
Amreeka 2010
Amy 2016
Anaconda 1997
Analyze That 2003
Analyze This 2000
Anastasia 1997
Anchorman: The Legend of Ron Burgundy 2005
Anchorman 2: The Legend Continues 2014
Anchors Aweigh [1945] 1985
And God Created Woman 1988
...And God Spoke 1995
And Life Goes On (Zebdegi Edame Darad) 1995
And Nothing but the Truth 1984
And Now Ladies and Gentlemen 2004
And So It Goes 2015
And the Ship Sails On 1984
And You Thought Your Parents Were Weird 1991
And Your Mother Too. *See* Y tu mama tambien.
Andre 1995
Android 1984
Ane qui a bu la lune, L'. *See* Donkey Who Drank the Moon, The.
Angel at My Table, An 1991
Angel Baby 1997
Angel Dust 1987
Angel Dust (Ishii) 1997
Angel Eyes 2002
Angel Heart 1987
Angel 1984
Angel III 1988
Angel Town 1990
Angel-A 2008
Angela's Ashes 2000
Angelo My Love 1983
Angels & Demons 2010
Angels and Insects 1996
Angels in the Outfield 1995
Anger Management 2004
Angie 1995
Angriest Man in Brooklyn, The 2015
Angry Birds Movie, The 2017
Angry Harvest 1986
Anguish 1987
Angus 1995
Angustia. *See* Anguish.
Anima Mundi 1995
Animal, The 2002
Animal Behavior 1989
Animal Factory 2001
Animal Kingdom 2011
Animal Kingdom, The [1932] 1985
Animals 2016
Anna 1987
Anna and the King 2000
Anna Karamazova 1995
Anna Karenina 2013
Annabelle 2015
Annabelle: Creation 2018
Annapolis 2007
Anne Frank Remembered 1996
Annee des meduses, L' 1987
Annees sandwiches, Les. *See* Sandwich Years, The.
Annie 1982
Annie 2015
Annihilators, The 1986
Anniversary Party, The 2002
Anomalisa 2016
Anonymous 2012
Another Day in Paradise 2000
Another Earth 2012
Another 48 Hrs. 1990
Another Stakeout 1993
Another State of Mind 1984
Another Time, Another Place 1984
Another Woman 1988
Another Year 2011
Another You 1991
Anslag, De. *See* Assault, The.
Answer Man, The 2010
Ant Bully, The 2007
Antarctica (Kurahara) 1984
Antarctica (Weiley) 1992
Anthropoid 2017
Antichrist 2010
Antigone/Rites of Passion 1991
Antitrust 2002
Ant-Man 2016
Antonia and Jane 1991
Antonia's Line 1996
Antwone Fisher 2003
Antz 1999
Anvil! The Story of Anvil 2010
Any Given Sunday 2000
Any Man's Death 1990
Anything But Love 2004
Anything Else 2004
Anywhere But Here 2000
Apache [1954] 1981
Apartment, The [1960] 1986
Apartment Zero 1988
Apex 1995
Apocalypse Now Redux 2002
Apocalypto 2007
Apollo 18 2012

Apollo 13 1995
Apostle, The 1997
Appaloosa 2009
Apparition, The 2013
Apple, The 2000
Appointment with Death 1988
Apprentice to Murder 1988
Apres l'amour. *See* Love After Love.
Apres mai. *See* Something in the Air.
April and the Extraordinary World 2017
April Fool's Day 1986
April Is a Deadly Month 1987
Apt Pupil 1999
Aquamarine 2007
Arabian Knight, 1995
Arachnophobia 1990
Ararat 2003
Arashi Ga Oka 1988
Arbitrage 2013
Arch of Triumph [1948] 1983
Archangel 1995
Architecture of Doom, The 1992
Are We Done Yet? 2008
Are We Officially Dating? *See* That Awkward Moment.
Are We There Yet? 2006
Argent, L' 1984
Argo 2013
Aria 1988
Ariel 1990
Arlington Road 2000
Armageddon 1999
Armageddon, The. *See* Warlock.
Armed and Dangerous 1986
Armed Response 1986
Armee des ombres, L'. *See* Army of Shadows.
Armored 2010
Army in the Shadows. *See* Army of Shadows.
Army of Darkness 1993
Army of Shadows 2007
Around the Bend 2005
Around the World in 80 Days 2005
Arrangement, The [1969] 1985
Aristocrats, The 2006
Arrival 2017
Arrival, The 1996
Art Blakey 1988
Art Deco Detective 1995
Art of Cinematography, The. *See* Visions of Light.
Art of Getting By, The 2012
Art of War, The 2001
Art School Confidential 2007
Artemisia 1999
Arthur 1981
Arthur 2012
Arthur Christmas 2012
Arthur II 1988
Arthur and the Invisibles 2008
Arthur Newman 2014
Arthur's Hallowed Ground 1986
Article 99 1992
Artist, The 2012
As Above, So Below 2015
As Good As It Gets 1997
Ashes of Time Redux 2009
Ashik Kerib 1988
Ask the Dust 2007
Aspen Extreme 1993
Assassin, The 2016
Assassination 1987
Assassination of Jesse James by the Coward Robert Ford, The 2008
Assassination of Richard Nixon, The 2006
Assassination Tango 2004
Assassins 1995
Assasin's Creed 2017
Assault, The 1986
Assault of the Killer Bimbos 1988
Assault on Precinct 13 2006
Assignment, The, 1997
Associate, The 1996
Astonished 1989
Astro Boy 2010
Astronaut Farmer, The 2008
Astronaut's Wife, The 2000
Asya's Happiness 1988
Asylum 2006
At Any Price 2014
At Close Range 1986
At First Sight 2000
At Play in the Fields of the Lord 1991
Atame. *See* Tie Me Up! Tie Me Down!.
Atanarjuat, the Fast Runner 2002
A-Team, The 2011
Atentado, El. *See* Attack, The.
ATL 2007
Atlantic City 1981
Atlantis 1995
Atlantis: The Lost Empire 2002
Atlas Shrugged: Part 1 2012
Atlas Shrugged II: The Strike 2013
Atomic Blonde 2018
Atonement 2008
Atraves da Janela. *See* Through the Window.
Attack, The 2014
Attack the Block 2012
Attention Bandits. *See* Warning Bandits.
Au Revoir les Enfants 1987
Auf der anderen Seite. *See* Edge of Heaven, The.
August 1996
August: Osage County 2014
August Rush 2008
August 32nd on Earth 1999
Aura, The 2007
Aus dem Nichts. *See* In the Fade.
Austenland 2014
Austin Powers in Goldmember 2003
Austin Powers: International Man of Mystery, 1997
Austin Powers: The Spy Who Shagged Me 2000
Australia 2009
Author! Author! 1981
Author: The JT Leroy Story 2017
Auto Focus 2003
Autumn in New York 2001
Autumn Tale 2000
Avalon (Anderson) 1988
Avalon (Levinson) 1990

Avanti [1972] 1986
Avatar 2010
Avengers: Age of Ultron 2016
Avengers, The 1999
Avengers, The 2013
Avenging Angel 1985
Avenging Force 1986
Aventure Malgache 1995
Avenue Montaigne 2008
Aviator, The (Miller) 1985
Aviator, The (Scorsese) 2005
AvP. *See* Alien vs. Predator.
Awake 2008
Awakenings 1990
Away From Her 2008
Away We Go 2010
Awesome! I F***in' Shot That! 2007
Awfully Big Adventure, An 1995
Ayn Rand: A Sense of Life 1999
Ayneh. *See* The Mirror.

B

B. Monkey 2000
B-Side: Elsa Dorfman's Portrait Photography, The 2018
Ba Mua. *See* Three Seasons.
Baadassss! 2005
Baader Meinhoff Complex, The 2010
Babadook, The 2015
Babar 1989
Babe, The 1992
Babe: Pig in the City 1999
Babe, the Gallant Pig, 1995
Babel 2007
Babette's Feast 1987
Babies 2011
Baby 1985
Baby Boom 1987
Baby Boy 2002
Baby Driver 2018
Baby Geniuses 2000
Baby Mama 2009
Baby, It's You 1982
Baby's Day Out 1995
Babyfever 1995
Babylon A.D. 2009
Babymakers, The 2013
Babysitter's Club 1995
Bacalaureat. *See* Graduation.
Bacheha-Ye aseman. *See* The Children of Heaven.
Bachelor, The 2000
Bachelor Mother [1939] 1986
Bachelor Party 1984
Bachelorette 2013
Bachir Lazhar. *See* Monsieur Lazhar.
Back Door to Hell [1964] 1995
Back to School 1986
Back to the Beach 1987
Back to the Future 1985
Back to the Future Part II 1989
Back to the Future Part III 1990
Back-Up Plan, The 2011
Backbeat 1995
Backdraft 1991
Backfire 1987
Backstage 1988
Backstage at the Kirov 1984
Bad Batch, The 2018
Bad Behaviour 1993
Bad Blood 1989
Bad Boy, The 1985
Bad Boys 1982
Bad Boys 1995
Bad Boys 2 2004
Bad Company (Harris) 1995
Bad Company (Schumacher) 2003
Bad Dreams 1988
Bad Education 2005
Bad Girls 1995
Bad Guys 1986
Bad Influence 1990
Bad Lieutenant 1992
Bad Lieutenant: Port of Call New Orleans 2010
Bad Manners 1997
Bad Medicine 1985
Bad Moms 2017
Bad Moms Christmas, A 2018
Bad Moon 1996
Bad News Bears, The 2006
Bad Santa 2004
Bad Santa 2 2017
Bad Teacher 2012
Bad Words 2015
Bagdad Cafe 1988
Baggage Claim 2014
Bagman. *See* Casino Jack.
Bail Jumper 1990
Bait 2001
Baja Oklahoma 1988
Bakjwi. *See* Thirst.
Bal, Le 1984
Balance, La 1983
Ball of Fire 1987
Ballad of Jack and Rose, The 2006
Ballad of Lefty Brown, The 2018
Ballad of Little Jo, The 1993
Ballad of the Sad Cafe, The 1991
Ballast 2009
Ballerina. *See* Leap!
Ballistic: Ecks vs. Sever 2003
Balls of Fury 2008
Balto 1995
Balzac and the Little Chinese Seamstress 2006
Balzac et la petite tailleuse Chinois *See* Balzac and the Little Chinese Seamstress
Bamba, La 1987
Bambi [1942] 1984
Bamboozled 2001
Band Aid 2018
Band Called Death, A 2014
Band of the Hand 1986
Band Wagon, The [1953] 1981
Bande de Filles. *See* Girlhood.
Band's Visit, The 2009
Bandit Queen 1995
Bandits 1988
Bandits 2002
Bandslam 2010
Bandwagon 1997
Banger Sisters, The 2003
Bangkok Dangerous 2009
Bank Job, The 2009

Banlieue 13: Ultimatum. *See* District 13: Ultimatum.
B.A.P.s 1997
Bar Esperanza 1985
Bar Girls 1995
Baraka 1993
Baran 2002
Barb Wire 1996
Barbarian Invasions, The 2004
Barbarians, The 1987
Barbarosa 1982
Barbary Coast [1935] 1983
Barbershop 2003
Barbershop: The Next Cut 2017
Barbershop 2: Back in Business 2005
Barcelona 1995
Bare Knuckles. *See* Gladiator.
Barefoot Contessa, The [1954] 1981
Barfly 1987
Bari, Al. *See* Innocent, The.
Barjo 1993
Bark! 2003
Barney's Great Adventure 1999
Barney's Version 2011
Barnyard 2007
Bartleby 2003
Barton Fink 1991
BASEketball 1999
Bashu, the Little Stranger 1990
Basic 2004
Basic Instinct 1992
Basic Instinct 2 2007
Basileus Quartet 1984
Basket, The 2001
Basket Case II 1990
Basket Case III: The Progeny 1992
Basketball Diaries, The 1995
Basquiat 1996
Bastille 1985
Bat 21 1988
Batkid Begins 2016
Batman [1989] 1995
Batman and Robin 1997
Batman Begins 2006
Batman Forever 1995
Batman: Mask of the Phantasm 1993
Batman Returns 1992
Batman vs. Superman 2017
Bats 2000
Battement d'Aniles du Papillon, Le, *See* Happenstance.
Batteries Not Included 1987
Battle for Terra 2010
Battle in Seattle 2009
Battle: Los Angeles 2012
Battle of the Sexes 2018
Battle of Shaker Heights, The 2004
Battle of the Year 2014
Battlefield Earth 2001
Battleship 2013
Battlestruck 1982
Baule les Pins, La. *See* C'est la vie.
Baxter, The 2006
Bay, The 2013
Baywatch 2018
Be Cool 2006
Be Kind Rewind 2009
Beach 1985
Beach, The 2001
Beach Girls, The 1982
Beach Rats 2018
Beaches 1988
Bean 1997
Beans of Egypt, Maine, The 1995
Bears 2015
Beast, The 1988
Beast in the Heart, The. *See* Don't Tell.
Bear, The (Annaud) 1989
Bear, The (Sarafian) 1984
Beast Within, The 1982
Beastly 2012
Beastmaster, The 1982
Beastmaster II 1991
Beasts of No Nation 2016
Beasts of the Southern Wild 2013
Beat, The 1987
Beat Generation-An American Dream, The 1987
Beat Street 1984
Beating Heart, A 1992
Beating of the Butterfly's Wings, The *See* Happenstance.
Beatriz at Dinner 2018
Beats, Rhymes & Life: The Travels of a Tribe Called Quest 2012
Beau Mariage, Le 1982
Beau Pere 1981
Beau Travail 2001
Beaufort 2009
Beaumarchais: The Scoundrel 1997
Beautician and the Beast, The 1997
Beautiful 2001
Beautiful Boy 2012
Beautiful Creatures 2002
Beautiful Creatures 2014
Beautiful Dreamers 1991
Beautiful Girls 1996
Beautiful Mind 2002
Beautiful People 2001
Beautiful Planet, A 2017
Beautiful Thing 1996
Beauty and the Beast 1991
Beauty and the Beast 2018
Beauty Shop 2006
Beaver, The 2012
Beavis and Butt-head Do America 1996
Bebe's Kids 1992
Bebes. *See* Babies.
Because I Said So 2008
Because of Winn-Dixie 2006
Becky Sharp [1935] 1981
Becoming Colette 1992
Becoming Jane 2008
Bed and Breakfast 1992
Bed of Roses 1996
Bedazzled 2001
Bedroom Eyes 1986
Bedroom Window, The 1987
Bedtime for Bonzo [1951] 1983
Bedtime Stories 2009
Bee Movie 2008
Bee Season 2006
Beefcake 2000
Beerfest 2007
Beethoven 1992

Beethoven's Second 1993
Beetlejuice 1988
Before and After 1996
Before I Fall 2018
Before I Go to Sleep 2015
Before Midnight 2014
Before Night Falls 2001
Before Sunrise 1995
Before Sunset 2005
Before the Devil Knows You're Dead 2008
Before the Rain 1995
Before We Go 2016
Begin Again 2015
Beginners 2012
Begotten 1995
Beguiled, The [1971] 1982
Beguiled, The 2018
Behind Enemy Lines 2002
Behind the Sun 2002
Beijing Bicycle 2003
Being at Home with Claude 1993
Being Flynn 2013
Being Human 1995
Being John Malkovich 2000
Being Julia 2005
Bel Ami 2013
Belfast, Maine 2001
Believers, The 1987
Belizaire the Cajun 1986
Belko Experiment, The 2018
Bella Martha. *See* Mostly Martha.
Belle 2015
Belle Epoque 1995
Belle Noiseuse, La 1991
Bellflower 2012
Bellman and True 1988
Bells Are Ringing [1960] 1983
Belly of an Architect 1987
Beloved 2003
Beloved Rogue [1927] 1983
Below 2004
Benchwarmers, The 2007
Bend It Like Beckham 2004
Benefit of the Doubt 1993
Bengali Night, The 1988
Ben-Hur 2017
Benji: Off the Leash! 2005
Benji the Hunted 1987
Benny and Joon 1993
Bent 1997
Beowulf 2008
Beowulf & Grendel 2007
Berberian Sound Studio 2014
Berkeley in the Sixties 1990
Berlin Alexanderplatz 1983
Bernadette 1988
Bernie 2013
Berry Gordy's The Last Dragon 1985
Bert Rigby, You're a Fool 1989
Beshkempir: The Adopted Son 2000
Besieged 2000
Best Defense 1984
Best Exotic Marigold Hotel, The 2013
Best Friends 1982
Best in Show 2001
Best Intentions, The 1992
Best Laid Plans 2000
Best Little Whorehouse in Texas, The 1982
Best Man, The 1999
Best Man, The 2000
Best Man Holiday, The 2014
Best of Enemies 2016
Best of Me, The 2015
Best of the Best 1989
Best of the Best II 1993
Best of Times, The 1986
Best of Youth, The 2006
Best Revenge, The 1996
Best Seller 1987
Best Worst Movie 2011
Best Years of Our Lives, The [1946] 1981
Bestia nel cuore, La. *See* Don't Tell.
Betrayal 1983
Betrayed 1988
Betsy's Wedding 1990
Better Life, A 2012
Better Luck Tomorrow 2004
Better Off Dead 1985
Better Than Chocolate 2000
Better Than Sex 2002
Betty 1993
Betty Blue 1986
Between the Teeth 1995
Beverly Hillbillies, The 1993
Beverly Hills Brats 1989
Beverly Hills Chihuahua 2009
Beverly Hills Cop 1984
Beverly Hills Cop II 1987
Beverly Hills Cop III 1995
Beverly Hills Ninja 1997
Bewitched 2006
Beyond Borders 2004
Beyond Rangoon 1995
Beyond Reasonable Doubt 1983
Beyond Silence 1999
Beyond the Gates 2008
Beyond the Hills 2014
Beyond the Lights 2015
Beyond the Limit 1983
Beyond the Mat 2001
Beyond the Rocks 2006
Beyond the Sea 2005
Beyond Therapy 1987
BFG, The 2017
Bhaji on the Beach 1995
Bian Lian. *See* The King of Masks.
Bicentennial Man 2000
Big 1988
Big Bad Mama II 1988
Big Bad Wolves 2015
Big Bang, The 1990
Big Blue, The (Besson) 1988
Big Blue, The (Horn) 1988
Big Bounce, The 2005
Big Bully 1996
Big Business 1988
Big Chill, The 1983
Big Daddy 2000
Big Easy, The 1987
Big Eyes 2015
Big Fan 2010
Big Fat Liar 2003

Big Fish 2004
Big Game 2016
Big Girls Don't Cry, They Get Even 1992
Big Green, The 1995
Big Hero 6 2015
Big Hit, The 1999
Big Kahuna, The 2001
Big Lebowski, The 1999
Big Man on Campus 1989
Big Miracle 2013
Big Momma's House 2001
Big Momma's House 2 2007
Big Mommas: Like Father, Like Son 2012
Big Night 1996
Big One, The 1999
Big Picture, The 1989
Big Short, The 2016
Big Shots 1987
Big Sick, The 2018
Big Squeeze, The 1996
Big Tease, The 2001
Big Time 1988
Big Top Pee-Wee 1988
Big Town, The 1987
Big Trouble (Cassavetes) 1986
Big Trouble (Sonnenfeld) 2003
Big Trouble in Little China 1986
Big Wedding, The 2014
Big Year, The 2012
Biker Boyz 2004
Bikur Ha-Tizmoret. *See* Band's Visit, The.
Bill and Ted's Bogus Journey 1991
Bill and Ted's Excellent Adventure 1989
Billy Bathgate 1991
Bill Cunningham New York 2012
Billy Budd [1962] 1981
Billy Elliot 2001
Billy Lynn's Long Halftime Walk 2017
Billy Madison 1995
Billy's Hollywood Screen Kiss 1999
Biloxi Blues 1988
Bin-jip. *See* 3-Iron.
Bingo 1991
BINGO 2000
Bio-Dome 1996
Bir zamanlar Anadolu'da. *See* Once Upon a Time in Anatolia.
Bird 1988
Bird on a Wire 1990
Birdcage, The 1996
Birdman, or (The Unexpected Virtue of Ignorance) 2015
Birdy 1984
Birth 2005
Birth of a Nation, The [1915] 1982, 1992
Birth of a Nation, The 2017
Birthday Girl 2003
Bitter Harvest 2018
Bitter Moon 1995
Bittere Ernte. *See* Angry Harvest.
Biutiful 2011
Bix (1990) 1995
Bix (1991) 1995
Bizet's Carmen 1984
Black and White 2001
Black Beauty 1995
Black Book 2008
Black Cat, The (Fulci) 1984
Black Cat (Shin) 1993
Black Cat, White Cat 2000
Black Cauldron, The 1985
Black Christmas 2007
Black Dahlia, The 2007
Black Dog 1999
Black Dynamite 2010
Black Harvest 1995
Black Hawk Down 2002
Black Joy 1986
Black Knight 2002
Black Lizard 1995
Black Mask 2000
Black Mass 2016
Black Moon Rising 1986
Black Nativity 2014
Black or White 2016
Black Peter [1964] 1985
Black Rain (Imamura) 1990
Black Rain (Scott) 1989
Black Robe 1991
Black Sea 2016
Black Sheep 1996
Black Snake Moan 2008
Black Stallion Returns, The 1983
Black Swan 2011
Black Widow 1987
Blackboard Jungle [1955] 1986, 1992
Blackfish 2014
Blackhat 2016
Blackout 1988
Blackout. *See* I Like It Like That.
Blackthorn 2012
Blade 1999
Blade of the Immortal 2018
Blade II 2003
Blade Runner 1982
Blade Runner 2049 2018
Blade: Trinity 2005
Blades of Glory 2008
Blair Witch 2017
Blair Witch Project, The 2000
Blame It on Night 1984
Blame It on Rio 1984
Blame It on the Bellboy 1992
Blancanieves 2014
Blank Check 1995
Blankman 1995
Blassblaue Frauenschrift, Eine. *See* Woman's Pale Blue Handwriting, A.
Blast 'em 1995
Blast from the Past 2000
Blaze 1989
Bleed For This 2017
Bleeder, The. *See* Chuck.
Blended 2015
Bless Me, Ultima 2014
Bless the Child 2001
Bless Their Little Hearts 1991
Blessures Assassines, Les. *See* Murderous Maids.
Blind Date 1987
Blind Fairies *See* Ignorant Fairies

Blind Fury 1990
Blind Side, The 2010
Blind Swordsman: Zatoichi, The. *See* Zatoichi.
Blindness 2009
Bling Ring, The 2014
Blink 1995
Bliss 1986
Bliss 1997
Blob, The 1988
Blood and Chocolate 2008
Blood and Concrete 1991
Blood and Wine 1997
Blood Diamond 2007
Blood Diner 1987
Blood Father 2017
Blood, Guts, Bullets and Octane 2001
Blood in Blood Out 1995
Blood Money 1988
Blood of Heroes, The 1990
Blood Salvage 1990
Blood Simple 1985
Blood Wedding 1982
Blood Work 2003
Bloodfist 1989
Bloodhounds of Broadway 1989
BloodRayne 2007
Bloodsport 1988
Bloody Sunday 2003
Blow 2002
Blow Dry 2002
Blow Out 1981
Blown Away 1995
Blue (Jarman) 1995
Blue (Kieslowski) 1993
Blue Caprice 2014
Blue Car 2004
Blue Chips 1995
Blue City 1986
Blue Crush 2003
Blue Desert 1991
Blue Ice 1995
Blue Iguana, The 1988
Blue in the Face 1995
Blue is the Warmest Color 2014
Blue Jasmine 2014
Blue Kite, The 1995
Blue Like Jazz 2013
Blue Monkey 1987
Blue Ruin 2015
Blue Skies Again 1983
Blue Sky 1995
Blue Steel 1990
Blue Streak 2000
Blue Thunder 1983
Blue Valentine 2011
Blue Velvet 1986
Blue Villa, The 1995
Bluebeard's Eighth Wife [1938] 1986
Blues Brothers 2000 1999
Blues Lahofesh Hagadol. *See* Late Summer Blues.
Boat, The. *See* Boot, Das.
Boat is Full, The 1982
Boat That Rocked, The. *See* Pirate Radio.
Boat Trip 2004
Bob le Flambeur [1955] 1983
Bob Marley: Time Will Tell. *See* Time Will Tell.
Bob Roberts 1992
Bobby 2007
Bobby Jones: Stroke of Genius 2005
Bodies, Rest, and Motion 1993
Body, The 2002
Body and Soul 1982
Body Chemistry 1990
Body Double 1984
Body Heat 1981
Body Melt 1995
Body of Evidence 1993
Body of Lies 2009
Body Parts 1991
Body Rock 1984
Body Shots 2000
Body Slam 1987
Body Snatchers 1995
Bodyguard, The 1992
Bodyguards, The. *See* La Scorta.
Boesman & Lena 2001
Bogus 1996
Boheme, La [1926] 1982
Boiler Room 2001
Boiling Point 1993
Bolero (Derek) 1984
Bolero (Lelouch) 1982
Bollywood/Hollywood 2003
Bolt 2009
Bom Yeorum Gaeul Gyeoul Geurigo...Bom. *See* Spring, Summer, Autumn, Winter...And Spring.
Bon Plaisir, Le 1984
Bon Voyage 1995
Bon Voyage (Rappenaeau) 2005
Bone Collector, The 2000
Bonfire of the Vanities, The 1990
Bongwater 1999
Bonjour Anne. *See* Paris Can Wait.
Bonne Route. *See* Latcho Drom.
Boo! A Madea Halloween 2017
Boo 2! A Madea Halloween 2018
Boogeyman 2006
Boogie Nights 1997
Book of Eli, The 2011
Book of Henry, The 2018
Book of Life, The 2015
Book of Love 1991
Book of Shadows: Blair Witch 2 2001
Book Thief, The 2014
Boomerang 1992
Boondock Saints: All Saints Day, The 2010
Boost, The 1988
Boot, Das 1982
Boot Ist Voll, Das. *See* Boat Is Full, The.
Bootmen 2001
Booty Call 1997
Booye Kafoor, Atre Yas. *See* Smell of Camphor, Fragrance of Jasmine.
Bopha! 1993
Borat: Cultural Learnings of America for Make Benefit Glorious Nation of Kazakhstan 2007
Border, The 1982

Boricua's Bond 2001
Born American 1986
Born in East L.A. 1987
Born Into Brothels: Calcutta's Red Light Kids 2006
Born on the Fourth of July 1989
Born Romantic 2002
Born to Be a Star. *See* Bucky Larson: Born to Be a Star.
Born to Be Blue 2017
Born to Be Wild 1996
Born to Race 1988
Born Yesterday 1993
Borrowers, The 1999
Borstal Boy 2003
Bose Zellen. *See* Free Radicals.
Boss, The 2017
Boss Baby, The 2018
Bossa Nova 2001
Bostonians, The 1984
Bottle Rocket 1996
Bottle Shock 2009
Boum, La 1983
Bounce 2001
Bound 1996
Bound and Gagged 1993
Bound by Honor 1993
Bounty, The 1984
Bounty Hunter, The 2011
Bourne Identity, The 2003
Bourne Legacy, The 2013
Bourne Supremacy, The 2005
Bourne Ultimatum, The 2008
Bowfinger 2000
Box, The 2010
Box of Moonlight 1997
Boxer, The 1997
Boxer and Death, The 1988
Boxing Helena 1993
Boxtrolls, The 2015
Boy, The 2017
Boy and the Beast, The 2017
Boy in Blue, The 1986
Boy in the Striped Pajamas, The 2009
Boy Next Door, The 2016
Boy Who Could Fly, The 1986
Boy Who Cried Bitch, The 1991
Boyfriend School, The. *See* Don't Tell Her It's Me.
Boyfriends 1997
Boyfriends and Girlfriends 1988
Boyhood 2015
Boynton Beach Bereavement Club, The. *See* Boynton Beach Club, The.
Boynton Beach Club, The 2007
Boys 1996
Boys, The 1985
Boys and Girls 2001
Boys Are Back, The 2010
Boys Don't Cry 2000
Boys from Brazil, The [1978] 1985
Boys Next Door, The 1986
Boys on the Side 1995
Boyz N the Hood 1991
BPM (Beats Per Minute) 2018
Bra Boys 2009
Braddock 1988
Brad's Status 2018
Brady Bunch Movie, The 1995
Brady's Escape 1984
Brain Damage 1988
Brain Dead 1990
Brain Donors 1995
Brainstorm 1983
Bram Stoker's Dracula 1992
Branches of the Tree, The 1995
Brand New Day. *See* Love Happens.
Brand Upon the Brain! 2008
Brandon Teena Story, The 2000
Brassed Off 1997
Brat. *See* Brother.
Bratz 2008
Brave 2013
Brave One, The 2008
Brave Little Toaster, The 1987
Braveheart 1995
Brawl in Cell Block 99 2018
Brazil 1985
Breach 2008
Bread and Roses 2002
Bread and Salt 1995
Bread and Tulips 2002
Bread, My Sweet, The 2004
Breadwinner, The 2018
Break of Dawn 1988
Break-Up, The 2007
Breakdown 1997
Breakfast Club, The 1985
Breakfast of Champions 2000
Breakfast on Pluto 2006
Breakin' 1984
Breakin' All the Rules 2005
Breaking and Entering 2008
Breaking In 1989
Breaking the Rules 1992
Breaking the Sound Barrier. *See* Sound Barrier, The.
Breaking the Waves 1996
Breakin' II: Electric Boogaloo 1984
Breaking Up 1997
Breath of Life, A 1993
Breathe 2018
Breathing Room 1996
Breathless 1983
Brenda Starr 1992
Brendan and the Secret of Kells. *See* Secret of Kells, The.
Brewster McCloud [1970] 1985
Brewster's Millions 1985
Brian Wilson: I Just Wasn't Made for These Times 1995
Brick 2007
Brick Mansions 2015
Bride, The 1985
Bride and Prejudice 2006
Bride of Chucky 1999
Bride of Re-Animator 1991
Bride of the Wind 2002
Bride Wars 2010
Bride with White Hair, The 1995
Brideshead Revisited 2009
Bridesmaid, The 2007
Bridesmaids 2012
Bridge of San Luis Rey, The [1929] 1981
Bridge of San Luis Rey, The 2006

Bridge of Spies 2016
Bridge on the River Kwai, The [1957] 1990
Bridget Jones's Baby 2017
Bridge to Terabithia 2008
Bridges of Madison County, The 1995
Bridget Jones: The Edge of Reason 2005
Bridget Jones's Diary 2002
Brief Encounter [1946] 1990
Brief History of Time, A 1992
Bright 2018
Bright Angel 1991
Bright Lights, Big City 1988
Bright Star 2010
Bright Young Things 2005
Brighton Beach Memoirs 1986
Brimstone and Treacle 1982
Bring It On 2001
Bring on the Night 1985
Bringing Down the House 2004
Bringing Out the Dead 2000
Brittania Hospital 1983
Broadcast News 1987
Broadway Damage 1999
Broadway Danny Rose 1984
Brodre. *See* Brothers.
Brokeback Mountain 2006
Brokedown Palace 2000
Broken April. *See* Behind the Sun.
Broken Arrow 1996
Broken Blossoms [1919] 1984
Broken City 2014
Broken Embraces 2010
Broken English 1997
Broken Flowers 2006
Broken Hearts Club, The 2001
Broken Lizard's Club Dread. *See* Club Dread.
Broken Rainbow 1985
Broken Vessels 1999
Broken Wings 2005
Bronson 2010
Bronx Tale, A 1993
Bronze, The 2017
Brooklyn 2016
Brooklyn Castle 2013
Brooklyn's Finest 2011
Brother (Balabanov) 1999
Brother (Kitano) 2001
Brother Bear 2004
Brother from Another Planet, The 1984
Brother of Sleep 1996
Brotherhood of the Wolf 2003
Brothers 2006
Brothers 2010
Brothers, The 2002
Brothers Bloom, The 2010
Brothers Grimm, The 2006
Brothers Grimsby, The 2017
Brother's Keeper 1993
Brother's Kiss, A 1997
Brothers McMullen, The 1995
Brothers Solomon, The 2008
Brown Bunny, The 2005
Brown Sugar 2003
Browning Version, The 1995
Bruce Almighty 2004
Bruce Lee Story, The. *See* Dragon.
Brüno 2010
Bu-Su 1988
Bubba Ho-Tep 2004
Bubble 2007
Bubble Boy 2002
Buche, La [2000] 2001
Buck 2012
Bucket List, The 2009
Buckminster Fuller: Thinking Out Loud 1996
Bucky Larson: Born to Be a Star 2012
Buddy 1997
Buddy Boy 2001
Buddy Buddy 1981
Buddy System, The 1984
Buena Vista Social Club, The 2000
Buffalo 66 1999
Buffalo Soldiers 2004
Buffy the Vampire Slayer 1992
Bug 2008
Bug's Life, A 1999
Bugsy 1991
Building Bombs 1995
Bull Durham 1988
Bulldog Drummond [1929] 1982
Bullet to the Head 2014
Bulletproof (Carver) 1988
Bulletproof (Dickerson) 1996
Bulletproof Heart 1995
Bulletproof Monk 2004
Bullets Over Broadway 1995
Bullhead 2013
Bullies 1986
Bullshot 1985
Bully 2002
Bully 2013
Bully Project, The. *See* Bully.
Bulworth 1999
Bum Rap 1988
'Burbs, The 1989
Burglar 1987
Burglar, The 1988
Buried 2011
Buried on Sunday 1995
Burke and Hare 2012
Burke and Wills 1987
Burlesque 2011
Burn After Reading 2009
Burnin' Love 1987
Burning Plain, The 2010
Burning Secret 1988
Burnt 2016
Burnt by the Sun 1995
Bushwhacked 1995
Business of Fancydancing, The 2003
Business of Strangers, The 2002
Busted Up 1987
Buster 1988
But I'm a Cheerleader 2001
Butcher Boy, The 1999
Butcher's Wife, The 1991
Butler, The. *See* Lee Daniels' The Butler.
Butter 2013
Butterfield 8 [1960] 1993

Butterflies 1988
Butterfly 2003
Butterfly Effect 2005
Buy and Cell 1988
Buying Time 1989
By Design 1982
By the Sea 2016
By the Sword 1993
Bye Bye Blue Bird 2001
Bye Bye Blues 1990
Bye Bye, Love 1995
Bye Bye Man, The 2018
Byzantium 2014

C

Cabaret Balkan 2000
Cabeza de Vaca 1992
Cabin Boy 1988
Cabin Fever 2004
Cabin in the Woods, The 2013
Cabinet of Dr. Ramirez, The 1995
Cable Guy, The 1996
Cache 2007
Cactus 1986
Caddie [1976] 1982
Caddyshack II 1988
Cadence 1991
Cadillac Man 1990
Cadillac Records 2009
Cafe Ole 2001
Cafe Society 1997
Cafe Society 2017
Cage 1989
Cage aux folles III, La 1986
Cage/Cunningham 1995
Caged Fury 1984
Cairo Time 2011
Cake 2016
Cal 1984
Calendar 1995
Calendar Girl 1993
Calendar Girls 2004
Calhoun. *See* Nightstick.
Call, The 2014
Call Me 1988
Call Me by Your Name 2018
Calle 54 2002
Caller, The 1987
Calling the Shots 1988
Came a Hot Friday 1985
Cameraperson 2017
Cameron's Closet 1989
Camilla 1995
Camille Claudel 1988, 1989
Camorra 1986
Camp 2004
Camp at Thiaroye, The 1990
Camp Nowhere 1995
Campaign, The 2013
Campanadas a medianoche. *See* Falstaff.
Campus Man 1987
Can She Bake a Cherry Pie? 1983
Canadian Bacon 1995
Can't Buy Me Love 1987
Can't Hardly Wait 1999
Candy Mountain 1988
Candyman 1992
Candyman II: Farewell to the Flesh 1995
Cannery Row 1982
Cannonball Run II 1984
Canone Inverso. *See* Making Love.
Cantante, El 2008
Canyons, The 2014
Cape Fear 1991
Capitalism: A Love Story 2010
Capitano, Il 1995
Capote 2006
Captain America: Civil War 2017
Captain America: The First Avenger 2012
Captain Corelli's Mandolin 2002
Captain Fantastic 2017
Captain Phillips 2014
Captain Ron 1992
Captain Underpants: The First Epic Movie 2018
Captive 2016
Captive Hearts 1987
Captive in the Land, A 1995
Captives 1996
Captivity 2008
Capturing the Friedmans 2004
Car 54, Where Are You? 1995
Caramel 2009
Carandiru 2005
Caravaggio 1986
Cardinal, The [1963] 1986
Care Bears Adventure in Wonderland, The 1987
Care Bears Movie, The 1985
Care Bears Movie II 1986
Career Girls 1997
Career Opportunities 1991
Careful He Might Hear You 1984
Carlito's Way 1993
Carlos 2011
Carmen 1983
Carnage 2004
Carnage 2012
Carne, La 1995
Caro Diario 1995
Carol 2016
Carpenter, The 1988
Carpool 1996
Carrie 2014
Carried Away 1996
Carriers Are Waiting, The 2001
Carrington 1995
Cars 2007
Cars 3 2018
Cars 2 2012
Casa de los Babys 2004
Casa de mi Padre 2013
Casa in bilico, Una. *See* Tottering Lives.
Casanova 2006
Case 39 2011
Casino 1995
Casino Jack 2011
Casino Jack and the United States of Money 2011
Casino Royale 2007
Casper 1995
Cassandra's Dream 2009
Cast Away 2001

Castle, The 2000
Casual Sex? 1988
Casualties of War 1989
Cat on a Hot Tin Roof [1958] 1993
Cat People [1942] 1981, 1982
Catacombs 1988
Catch a Fire 2007
Catch and Release 2008
Catch Me If You Can 1989
Catch Me If You Can (Spielberg) 2003
Catch That Kid 2005
Catfish 2011
Catfish in Black Bean Sauce 2001
Cats & Dogs 2002
Cats & Dogs: The Revenge of Kitty Galore 2011
Cats Don't Dance 1997
Cat's Meow, The 2003
Cattle Annie and Little Britches 1981
Catwoman 2005
Caught 1996
Caught Up 1999
Calvary 2015
Camp X-Ray 2015
Can a Song Save Your Life? *See* Begin Again.
Captain America: The Winter Soldier 2015
Captive, The 2015
Cave, The 2006
Cave Girl 1985
Cave of Forgotten Dreams 2012
Caveman's Valentine, The 2002
CB4 1993
Cease Fire 1985
Cecil B. Demented 2001
Cedar Rapids 2012
Celebrity 1999
Celeste 1982
Celeste & Jesse Forever 2013
Celestial Clockwork 1996
Cell, The 2001
Cellular 2005
Celluloid Closet, The 1996
Celtic Pride 1996
Cement Garden, The 1995
Cemetery Club, The 1993
Cemetery Man 1996
Cemetery of Spendor 2017
Center of the Web 1992
Center of the World, The 2002
Center Stage 2001
Central do Brasil. *See* Central Station.
Central Intelligence 2017
Central Park Five, The 2013
Central Station 1999
Centurion 2011
Century 1995
Ceravani tanto Amati. *See* We All Loved Each Other So Much.
Cercle Rouge, Le 2004
Ceremonie, La 1996
Certain Fury 1985
Certain Regard, Un. *See* Hotel Terminus.
Certain Women 2017
Certified Copy 2012
Cesar Chavez 2015
C'est la vie 1990
Ceux qui m'aiment predont le train. *See* Those Who Love Me Can Take the Train.
Chac 2001
Chain of Desire 1993
Chain Reaction 1996
Chaindance. *See* Common Bonds.
Chained Heat 1983
Chairman of the Board 1999
Challenge, The 1982
Chamber, The 1996
Chambermaid of the Titanic, The 1999
Chameleon Street 1991
Champion [1949] 1991
Champions 1984
Chan Is Missing 1982
Chances Are 1989
Change-Up, The 2012
Changeling 2009
Changing Lanes 2003
Changing Times 2007
Chansons d'amour, Les. *See* Love Songs.
Chantilly Lace 1995
Chaos 2004
Chaos. *See* Ran.
Chaos Theory 2009
Chaplin 1992
Chappie 2016
Character 1999
Chariots of Fire 1981
Charlie and the Chocolate Factory 2006
Charlie Bartlett 2009
Charlie St. Cloud 2011
Charlie's Angels 2001
Charlie's Angels: Full Throttle 2004
Charlie Wilson's War 2008
Charlotte Gray 2003
Charlotte's Web 2007
Charm Discret de la Bourgeoisie, Le. *See* The Discreet Charm of the Bourgeoisie.
Chase, The 1995
Chasers 1995
Chasing Amy 1988
Chasing Liberty 2005
Chasing Mavericks 2013
Chasing Papi 2004
Chateau, The 2003
Chateau de ma mere, Le. *See* My Mother's Castle.
Chattahoochee 1990
Chattanooga Choo Choo 1984
Che 2010
Cheap Shots 1991
Cheap Thrills 2015
Cheaper by the Dozen 2004
Cheaper by the Dozen 2 2006
Cheatin' Hearts 1993
Check Is in the Mail, The 1986
Checking Out 1989
Cheech & Chong Still Smokin' 1983
Cheech & Chong's The Corsican Brothers 1984
Cheetah 1989
Chef 2015

Chef in Love, A 1997
Chelsea Walls 2003
Chere Inconnue. *See* I Sent a Letter to My Love.
Chéri 2010
Cherish 2003
Chernobyl Diaries 2013
Cherry Orchard, The 2003
Cherry Pink. *See* Just Looking.
Chevre, La. *See* Goat, The.
Chi bi. *See* Red Cliff.
Chicago 2003
Chicago Joe and the Showgirl 1990
Chicago 10 2009
Chicken Hawk: Men Who Love Boys 1995
Chicken Little 2006
Chicken Run 2001
Chico & Rita 2013
Chief Zabu 1988
Chihwaseon: Painted Fire 2003
Child 44 2016
Child, The 2007
Child's Play 1988
Child's Play II 1990
Child's Play III 1991
Children of a Lesser God 1986
Children of Heaven, The 2000
Children of Men 2007
Children of Nature 1995
Children of the Corn II 1993
Children of the Revolution 1997
Chile, la Memoria Obstinada. *See* Chile, Obstinate Memory.
Chile, Obstinate Memory 1999
Chill Factor 2000
Chilled in Miami. *See* New In Town.
Chimes at Midnight. *See* Falstaff.
China Cry 1990
China Girl 1987
China Moon 1995
China, My Sorrow 1995
China Syndrome, The [1979] 1988
Chinese Box 1999
Chinese Ghost Story II, A 1990
Chinese Ghost Story III, A 1991
Chipmunk Adventure, The 1987
Chi-raq 2016
CHIPS 2018
Chloe 2011
Chocolat (Denis) 1989
Chocolat (Hallstrom) 2001
Chocolate War, The 1988
Choice, The 2017
Choke 2009
Choke Canyon 1986
Choose Me 1984, 1985
Chopper 2002
Chopper Chicks in Zombie Town 1991
Chopping Mall 1986
Choristes, Les. *See* Chorus, The.
Chorus, The 2006
Chorus Line, A 1985
Chorus of Disapproval, A 1989
Chosen, The 1982
Christine 1983
Christine F. 1982
Christmas Carol, A 2010
Christmas Story, A 1983
Christmas Tale, A 2009
Christmas with the Kranks 2005
Christopher Columbus: The Discovery 1992
Chronicle 2013
Chronicles of Narnia: Prince Caspian, The 2009
Chronicles of Narnia: The Lion, the Witch and the Wardrobe, The 2006
Chronicles of Narnia: The Voyage of the Dawn Treader, The 2011
Chronicles of Riddick, The 2005
Chronos 1985
Chuck 2018
Chuck & Buck 2001
Chuck Berry: Hail! Hail! Rock 'n' Roll 1987
C.H.U.D. 1984
Chungking Express 1996
Chunhyang 2001
Churchill 2018
Chutney Popcorn 2001
Ciao, Professore! 1995
Cidade des homens. *See* City of Men.
Cider House Rules, The 2000
Cienaga, La 2002
Cinderella 2016
Cinderella Man 2006
Cinderella Story, A 2005
Cinema Paradiso 1989
Cinema Verite: Defining the Moment 2001
Circle, The 2002
Circle, The 2018
Circle of Deceit 1982
Circle of Friends 1995
Circuitry Man 1990
Cirque du Freak: The Vampire's Assistant 2010
Cirque du Soleil: Worlds Away 2013
Citadel 2013
Citizen Ruth 1996
Citizenfour 2015
Citta della donne, La. *See* City of Women.
City by the Sea 2003
City Girl, The 1984
City Hall 1996
City Heat 1984
City Limits 1985
City of Angels 1999
City of Ember 2009
City of Ghosts 2004
City of God 2004
City of Gold 2017
City of Hope 1991
City of Industry 1997
City Island 2011
City of Joy 1992
City of Lost Children 1996
City of Men 2009
City of Women 1981
City of Your Final Destination, The 2011
City Slickers 1991
City Slickers II: The Legend of Curly's Gold 1995
City Zero 1995

Civil Action, A, 1999
Civil Brand 2004
Claim, The 2002
Claire of the Moon 1993
Clan of the Cave Bear, The 1986
Clara's Heart 1988
Clash of the Titans 1981
Clash of the Titans 2011
Clash of the Titans 2. *See* Wrath of the Titans.
Class 1982
Class, The 2010
Class Act 1992
Class Action 1991
Class of 1984 1982
Class of 2000 1990
Class of Nuke 'em High 1986
Class of Nuke 'em High Part II 1991
Clay Pigeons 1999
Clean and Sober 1988
Clean Slate 1995
Clean Slate. *See* Coup de torchon.
Clear and Present Danger 1995
Clearcut 1992
Clearing, The 2005
Cleopatra [1963] 1993
Clerks 1995
Clerks II 2007
Click 2007
Client, The 1995
Client 9: The Rise and Fall of Eliot Spitzer 2011
Cliffhanger 1993
Clifford 1995
Clifford's Really Big Movie 2005
Climate for Killing, A 1995
Climates 2007
Cloak and Dagger 1984
Clock, The 1981
Clockers 1995
Clockstoppers 2003
Clockwatchers 1999
Clockwise 1986
Close My Eyes 1991
Close to Eden 1992
Close Your Eyes 2005
Closed Circuit 2014
Closer 2005
Closer You Get, The 2001
Closet, The 2002
Closet Land 1991
Cloud Atlas 2013
Clouds of Sils Maria 2016
Cloudy with a Chance of Meaballs 2010
Cloudy with a Chance of Meatballs 2 2014
Cloverfield 2009
Club, The 2017
Club Dread 2005
Club Earth. *See* Galactic Gigolo.
Club Paradise 1986
Clue 1985
Clueless 1995
Coach Carter 2006
Cobb 1995
Cobra 1986
Cobra Verde 1988
Coca-Cola Kid, The 1985
Cocaine Wars 1986
Cocktail 1988
Coco 2018
Coco avant Chanel. *See* Coco Before Chanel.
Coco Before Chanel 2010
Cocoon 1985
Cocoon: The Return 1988
Code 46 2005
Code Inconnu: Recit Incomplet de Divers Voyages. *See* Code Unknown.
Code Name: The Cleaner 2008
Code of Silence 1985
Code Unknown 2003
Coeur en hiver, Un 1993
Coeur qui bat, Un. *See* Beating Heart, A.
Coeurs. *See* Private Fears in Public Places.
Coffee & Cigarettes 2005
Cold Comfort 1989
Cold Comfort Farm 1995
Cold Creek Manor 2004
Cold Feet (Dornhelm) 1989
Cold Feet (Van Dusen) 1984
Cold Fever 1996
Cold Heaven 1992
Cold in July 2015
Cold Light of Day, The 2013
Cold Moon 1995
Cold Mountain 2004
Cold Souls 2010
Cold Steel 1987
Coldblooded 1995
Collapse 2010
Collateral 2005
Collateral Beauty 2017
Collateral Damage 2003
Collection, The 2013
Collector, The 2010
College Road Trip 2009
Collide 2018
Colombiana 2012
Colonel Chabert 1995
Colonel Redl 1985
Color Adjustment 1995
Color Me Kubrick 2008
Color of Money, The 1986
Color of Night 1995
Color Purple, The 1985
Colorado Territory [1949] 1985
Colors 1988
Colossal 2018
Colpo di Luna. *See* Moon Shadow.
Columbus 2018
Combat Shock 1986
Combination Platter 1995
Come and Get It [1936] 1981
Come Back to the Five and Dime Jimmy Dean, Jimmy Dean 1982
Come See the Paradise 1990
Come Undone 2002
Comebacks, The 2008
Comedian Harmoniest: Six Life Stories, The 1995
Comedy of Power 2008
Comfort and Joy 1984

Comfort of Strangers, The 1991
Comic Book Confidential 1988
Coming to America 1988
Commandments 1997
Commando 1985
Commando Squad 1987
Comme une image. *See* Look at Me.
Coming Home 2016
Commitments, The 1991
Committed 2001
Common Bonds 1995
Communion 1989
Como Agua Para Chocolate. *See* Like Water for Chocolate.
Compadres 2017
Company, The 2005
Company Business 1991
Company Man 2002
Company Men, The 2011
Company of Strangers, The. *See* Strangers in Good Company.
Company of Wolves, The 1985
Company You Keep, The 2014
Competition [1963] 1985
Complex World 1995
Compliance 2013
Complot, Le. *See* To Kill a Priest.
Compromising Positions 1985
Computer Chess 2014
Con Air 1997
Conan O'Brien Can't Stop 2012
Conan the Barbarian 1982
Conan the Barbarian 2012
Conan the Destroyer 1984
Conceiving Ada 2000
Concert, The 2011
Concussion 2014
Concussion 2016
Coneheads 1993
Confessions of a Dangerous Mind 2003
Confessions of a Shopaholic 2010
Confessions of a Teenage Drama Queen 2005
Confidence 2004
Confidences trop intimes. *See* Intimate Strangers.
Confidentially Yours 1984
Confusion of Genders 2004
Congo 1995
Congress, The 2015
Conjuring, The 2014
Conjuring 2, The 2017
Connection, The 2016
Connie and Carla 2005
Consenting Adults 1992
Conspiracy Theory 1997
Conspirator, The 2012
Conspirators of Pleasure 1997
Constant Gardener, The 2006
Constantine 2006
Consuming Passions 1988
Contact 1997
Contagion 2012
Conte d'Automne. *See* Autumn Tale.
Conte de Noël, Un. *See* Christmas Tale, A.
Conte de printemps. *See* Tale of Springtime, A.
Conte d'Hiver. *See* Tale of Winter, A.
Contender, The 2001
Continental Divide 1981
Contraband 2013
Control 2008
Control Room 2005
Convent, The 1995
Conviction 2011
Convicts 1991
Convincer, The. *See* Thin Ice.
Convoyeurs Attendent, Les. *See* The Carriers Are Waiting.
Coogan's Bluff [1968] 1982
Cook, the Thief, His Wife, and Her Lover, The 1990
Cookie 1989
Cookie's Fortune 2000
Cookout, The 2005
Cool as Ice 1991
Cool Dry Place, A 2000
Cool Runnings 1993
Cool School, The 2009
Cool World 1992
Cooler, The 2004
Cop 1987
Cop and a Half 1993
Cop Land 1997
Cop Out 2011
Copie conforme. *See* Certified Copy.
Cops and Robbersons 1995
Copycat 1995
Coraline 2010
Core, The 2004
Coriolanus 2012
Corky Romano 2002
Corporation, The 2005
Corpse Bride. *See* Tim Burton's Corpse Bride.
Corrina, Corrina 1995
Corruptor, The 2000
Cosi 1997
Cosi Ridevano. *See* Way We Laughed, The.
Cosmic Eye, The 1986
Cosmopolis 2013
Cotton Club, The 1984
Couch Trip, The 1988
Counselor, The 2014
Count of Monte Cristo, The 2003
Countdown to Zero 2011
Counterfeiters, The 2009
Country 1984
Country Bears, The 2003
Country Life 1995
Country of My Skull. *See* In My Country.
Country Strong 2011
Coup de foudre. *See* Entre nous.
Coup de torchon 1982
Coupe de Ville 1990
Couples Retreat 2010
Courage Mountain 1990
Courage of Lassie [1946] 1993
Courage Under Fire 1996
Courageous 2012
Courier, The 1988
Cours Toujours. *See* Dad On the Run.

Cousin Bette 1999
Cousin Bobby 1992
Cousins 1989
Cove, The 2010
Covenant, The 2007
Cover Girl 1985
Coverup 1988
Cowboy [1958] 1981
Cowboy Way, The 1995
Cowboys & Aliens 2012
Cowboys Don't Cry 1988
Coyote Ugly 2001
CQ 2003
Crabe Dans la Tete, Un. *See* Soft Shell Man.
Crack House 1989
Crack in the Mirror 1988
Crackdown. *See* To Die Standing.
Crackers 1984
Cradle 2 the Grave 2004
Cradle Will Rock 2000
Craft, The 1996
Crank 2007
Crank: High Voltage 2010
Crash (Cronenberg) 1997
Crash (Haggis) 2006
Crawlspace 1986
Crazies, The 2011
crazy/beautiful 2002
Crazy Family, The 1986
Crazy Heart 2010
Crazy in Alabama 2000
Crazy Love 2008
Crazy Moon 1988
Crazy People 1990
Crazy, Stupid, Love 2012
Creation 2011
Creator 1985
Creature 2012
Creature from the Black Lagoon, The [1954] 1981
Creed 2016
Creepozoids 1987
Creepshow 1982
Creepshow II 1987
Crew, The 2001
Crime + Punishment in Suburbia 2001
Crime of Father Amaro, The 2003
Crimes and Misdemeanors 1989
Crimes of Passion 1984
Crimes of the Heart 1986
Criminal 2005
Criminal 2017
Criminal Law 1988, 1989
Criminal Lovers 2004
Crimson Peak 2016
Crimson Tide 1995
Crisscross 1992
Critical Care 1997
Critical Condition 1987
Critters 1986
Critters II 1988
Crna macka, beli macor. *See* Black Cat, White Cat.
"Crocodile" Dundee 1986
"Crocodile" Dundee II 1988
"Crocodile" Dundee in Los Angeles 2002
Crocodile Hunter: Collision Course, The 2003
Cronos 1995
Croods, The 2014
Crooked Hearts 1991
Crooklyn 1995
Cropsey 2011
Cross Country 1983
Cross Creek 1983
Cross My Heart 1987
Crossed Tracks. *See* Roman de gare.
Crossing Delancey 1988
Crossing Guard, The 1995
Crossing Over 2010
Crossing the Bridge 1992
Crossover Dreams 1985
Crossroads 1986
Crossroads 2003
Crouching Tiger, Hidden Dragon 2001
Croupier [1997] 2001
Crow: City of Angels, The 1996
Crow, The 1995
Crown Heights 2018
Crucible, The 1996
Crude Oasis, The 1995
Cruel Intentions 2000
Cruel Story of Youth [1960] 1984
Crumb 1995
Crush (Maclean) 1993
Crush (McKay) 2003
Crush, The (Shapiro) 1993
Crusoe 1988
Cry Baby Killers, The [1957]
Cry Freedom 1987
Cry in the Dark, A 1988
Cry in the Wild, The 1990
Cry, the Beloved Country 1995
Cry Wolf [1947] 1986
Cry_Wolf 2006
Cry-Baby 1990
Crying Game, The 1992
Crystal Fairy & the Magical Cactus 2014
Crystal Heart 1987
Crystalstone 1988
Cuban Fury 2015
Cucaracha, La 2000
Cuckoo, The 2004
Cujo 1983
Cup, The 2001
Cup Final 1992
Curdled 1996
Cure, The 1995
Cure for Wellness, A 2018
Cure in Orange, The 1987
Curious Case of Benjamin Button, The 2009
Curious George 2007
Curly Sue 1991
Current Events 1990
Curse of the Golden Flower 2007
Curse of the Jade Scorpion, The 2002
Curse of the Pink Panther 1983
Cursed 2006
Curtains 1983
Cut and Run 1986

Cutthroat Island 1995
Cutting Edge, The 1992
Cyborg 1989
Cyclo 1996
Cyclone 1987
Cyrano de Bergerac 1990
Cyrus 2011
Czlowiek z Marmuru. *See* Man of Marble.
Czlowiek z Zelaza. *See* Man of Iron.

D

D Train, The 2016
Da 1988
Da Vinci Code, The 2007
Dabba. *See* Lunchbox, The.
Dad 1989
Dad On the Run 2002
Daddy and the Muscle Academy 1995
Daddy Day Camp 2008
Daddy Day Care 2004
Daddy Nostalgia 1991
Daddy's Boys 1988
Daddy's Dyin' 1990
Daddy's Home 2016
Daddy's Home 2 2018
Daddy's Little Girls 2008
Dadetown 1996
Daffy Duck's Quackbusters 1988
Dai zong shi, Yi. *See* Grandmaster, The.
Dakhtaran-e Khorshid. *See* Daughters of the Sun.
Dakota 1988
Dallas Buyers Club 2014
Damage 1992
Damned in the U.S.A. 1992
Damned United, The 2010
Damsels in Distress 2013
Dan in Real Life 2008
Dance Flick 2010
Dance Maker, The 2000
Dance of the Damned 1989
Dance with a Stranger 1985
Dance with Me 1999
Dancer in the Dark 2001
Dancer, Texas Pop. 81 1999
Dancer Upstairs, The 2004
Dancers 1987
Dances with Wolves 1990
Dancing at Lughnasa 1999
Dancing in the Dark 1986
Dangerous Beauty 1999
Dangerous Game (Ferrara) 1995
Dangerous Game (Hopkins) 1988
Dangerous Ground 1997
Dangerous Liaisons 1988
Dangerous Lives of Altar Boys, The 2003
Dangerous Love 1988
Dangerous Method, A 2012
Dangerous Minds 1995
Dangerous Moves 1985
Dangerous Woman, A 1993
Dangerously Close 1986
Daniel 1983
Danish Girl, The 2016
Danny Boy 1984
Danny Collins 2016
Danny Deckchair 2005
Danny the Dog. *See* Unleashed.
Dante's Peak 1997
Danton 1983
Danzon 1992
Darbareye Elly. *See* About Elly.
Daredevil 2004
Darfur Now 2008
Darjeeling Limited, The 2008
Dark Backward, The 1991
Dark Before Dawn 1988
Dark Blue 2004
Dark Blue World 2002
Dark City
Dark Crystal, The 1982
Dark Days 2001
Dark Eyes 1987
Dark Half, The 1993
Dark Horse 2013
Dark Knight, The 2009
Dark Knight Rises, The 2013
Dark Obsession 1991
Dark of the Night 1986
Dark Places 2016
Dark Shadows 2013
Dark Skies 2014
Dark Star [1975] 1985
Dark Tower, The 2018
Dark Water 2006
Dark Wind, The 1995
Darkest Hour 2018
Darkest Hour, The 2012
Darkman 1990
Darkness 2005
Darkness, The 2017
Darkness, Darkness. *See* South of Reno.
Darkness Falls 2004
Darling Companion 2013
D.A.R.Y.L. 1985
Date Movie 2007
Date Night 2011
Date with an Angel 1987
Daughter of the Nile 1988
Daughters of the Dust 1992
Daughters of the Sun 2001
Dauntaun Herozu. *See* Hope and Pain.
Dave 1993
Dave Chappelle's Block Party 2007
Dawn of the Dead 2005
Dawn of the Planet of the Apes 2015
Day After Tomorrow, The 2005
Day I Became a Woman, The 2002
Day in October, A 1992
Day of the Dead 1985
Day the Earth Stood Still, The 2009
Daybreakers 2011
Dayereh. *See* Circle, The.
Daylight 1996
Days of Glory 2008
Days of Thunder 1990
Days of Wine and Roses [1962] 1988
Daytrippers, The 1997
Dazed and Confused 1993
D.C. Cab 1983

De Eso No Se Habla. *See* I Don't Want to Talk About It.
De-Lovely 2005
De Palma 2017
De Poolse Bruid. *See* Polish Bride, The.
Dead, The 1987
Dead Again 1991
Dead Alive 1993
Dead Bang 1989
Dead Calm 1989
Dead Heat 1988
Dead Man 1996
Dead Man Down 2014
Dead Man on Campus 1999
Dead Man Walking 1995
Dead Man's Curve 2000
Dead Men Don't Wear Plaid 1982
Dead of Winter 1987
Dead Poets Society 1989
Dead Pool, The 1988
Dead Presidents 1995
Dead Ringers 1988
Dead Silence 2008
Dead Snow 2010
Dead Space 1991
Dead Women in Lingerie 1991
Dead Zone, The 1983
Dead-end Drive-in 1986
Deadfall 1995
Deadfall 2013
Deadline 1987
Deadly Eyes 1982
Deadly Friend 1986
Deadly Illusion 1987
Deadly Intent 1988
Deadpool 2017
Deal, The 2006
Deal of the Century 1983
Dealers 1989
Dear American 1987
Dear Diary. *See* Caro Diario.
Dear Frankie 2006
Dear God 1996
Dear John 2011
Dear White People 2015
Death and the Maiden 1995
Death at a Funeral 2008
Death at a Funeral 2011
Death Becomes Her 1992
Death Before Dishonor 1987
Death of a Soldier 1986
Death of an Angel 1986
Death of Mario Ricci, The 1985
Death of Mr. Lazarescu, The 2007
Death Proof. *See* Grindhouse.
Death Race 2009
Death Sentence 2008
Death to Smoochy 2003
Death Valley 1982
Death Warrant 1990
Death Wish II 1982
Death Wish III 1985
Death Wish IV 1987
Death Wish V: The Face of Death 1995
Deathtrap 1982
Deathstalker 1984
D.E.B.S. 2006
Debt, The 2012
Decade Under the Influence, A 2004
Decalogue, Parts 1 & 2, The [1988] 2001
Decalogue, Parts 3 & 4, The [1988] 2001
Decalogue, Parts 5 & 6, The [1988] 2001
Decalogue, Parts 7 & 8, The [1988] 2001
Decalogue, Parts 9 & 10, The [1988] 2001
Deceived 1991
Deceiver 1999
Deceivers, The 1988
December 1991
Deception 1993
Deception 2009
Deck the Halls 2007
Decline of the American Empire, The 1986
Decline of Western Civilization Part II, The 1988
Deconstructing Harry 1997
Deep Blue Sea 2000
Deep Blue Sea, The 2013
Deep Cover 1992
Deep Crimson 1997
Deep End, The 2002
Deep End of the Ocean 2000
Deep Impact 1999
Deep in the Heart 1984
Deep Rising 1999
Deepstar Six 1989
Deepwater Horizon 2017
Deer Hunter, The 1981
Def by Temptation 1990
Def-Con 4 1985
Def Jam's How to Be a Player 1997
Defending Your Life 1991
Defense Play 1988
Defenseless 1991
Defiance 2009
Defiant Ones, The [1958] 1992
Definitely, Maybe 2009
Defying Gravity 2000
Deja Vu 1999
Deja Vu 2007
Delicatessen 1992
Delirious 1991
Deliver Us from Eva 2004
Deliver Us From Evil 2015
Delivery Man 2014
Delta, The 1997
Delta Farce 2008
Delta Force, The 1986
Delta Force II 1990
Delta of Venus 1995
Delusion 1991
Demoiselle d'honneur, La. *See* Bridesmaid, The.
Demolition 2017
Demolition Man 1993
Demon 2017
Demonlover 2004
Demons 1986
Demons in the Garden 1984

Den Goda Viljan. *See* Best Intentions, The.

Denial 2017

Denise Calls Up 1996

Dennis the Menace 1993

Den skaldede frisor. *See* Love is All You Need.

Departed, The 2007

Departures 2010

Depuis Qu'Otar est Parti. *See* Since Otar Left…

Der Stand der Dinge. *See* State of Things, The.

Der Untergang. *See* Downfall.

Derailed 2006

Dernier Combat, Le 1984

Desa parecidos, Los. *See* Official Story, The.

Descendants, The 2012

Descent, The 2007

Desert Bloom 1986

Desert Blue 2000

Desert Hearts 1986

Desierto 2017

Designated Mourner, The 1997

Desire (Salt on Our Skin) 1995

Desire and Hell at Sunset Motel 1992

Desperado 1995

Desperate Hours 1990

Desperate Measures 1999

Desperate Remedies 1995

Desperately Seeking Susan 1985

Despicable Me 2011

Despicable Me 3 2018

Despicable Me 2 2014

Destinees Sentimentales. *See* Sentimental Destiny.

Destiny in Space 1995

Destiny Turns on the Radio 1995

Detachment 2013

Detective 1985

Deterrence 2001

Detour [1946] 1985

Detroit 2018

Detroit Rock City 2000

Deuce Bigalow: European Gigolo 2006

Duece Bigalow: Male Gigolo 2000

Deuces Wild 2003

Deux Jours, Une Nuit. *See* Two Days, One Night.

Devil 2011

Devil and Daniel Johnston, The 2007

Devil in a Blue Dress 1995

Devil Inside, The 2013

Devil Wears Prada, The 2007

Devil's Advocate, The 1997

Devil's Backbone, The 2002

Devil's Double, The 2012

Devil's Due 2015

Devil's Knot 2015

Devil's Own, The 1997

Devil's Rejects, The 2006

Devotion [1944] 1981

Dheepan 2017

Diabolique 1996

Diagonale du fou. *See* Dangerous Moves.

Dialogues with Madwomen 1995

Diamond Skulls. *See* Dark Obsession.

Diamond's Edge 1990

Diana 2014

Diarios de motocicleta. *See* Motorcycle Diaries, The.

Diary of a Hitman 1992

Diary of a Mad Black Woman 2006

Diary of a Mad Old Man 1987

Diary of a Seducer 1997

Diary of a Teenage Girl, The 2016

Diary of a Wimpy Kid 2011

Diary of a Wimpy Kid: Dog Days 2013

Diary of a Wimpy Kid: Rodrick Rules 2012

Diary of a Wimpy Kid: The Long Haul 2018

Diary of the Dead 2009

Dice Rules 1991

Dick 2000

Dick Tracy 1990

Dickie Roberts: Former Child Star 2004

Dictator, The 2013

Did You Hear About the Morgans? 2010

Die Another Day 2003

Die Fetten Jahre sind vorbei. *See* Edukators, The.

Die Hard 1988

Die Hard II 1990

Die Hard with a Vengeance 1995

Die Mommie Die! 2004

Die Story Von Monty Spinneratz. *See* A Rat's Story.

Dieu Est Grand, Je Suis Tout Petite. *See* God Is Great, I'm Not.

Different for Girls 1997

DIG! 2005

Digging for Fire 2016

Digging to China 1999

Diggstown 1992

Dilemma, The 2012

Dim Sum 1985

Dimanche a la Campagne, Un. *See* A Sunday in the Country.

Diminished Capacity 2009

Dina 2018

Diner 1982

Dinner, The 2018

Dinner for Schmucks 2011

Dinner Game, The 2000

Dinner Rush 2002

Dinosaur 2001

Dinosaur's Story, A. *See* We're Back.

Dirty Cop No Donut 2003

Dirty Dancing 1987

Dirty Dancing: Havana Nights 2005

Dirty Dishes 1983

Dirty Grandpa 2017

Dirty Harry [1971] 1982

Dirty Love 2006

Dirty Pretty Things 2004

Dirty Rotten Scoundrels 1988

Dirty Shame, A 2005

Dirty Work 1999

Disappearance of Alice Creed, The 2011

Disappearance of Eleanor Rigby, The 2015

Disappearance of Garcia Lorca, The 1997
Disappointments Room, The 2017
Disaster Artist, The 2018
Disaster Movie 2009
Disclosure 1995
Disconnect 2014
Discreet Charm of the Bourgeoisie, The [1972] 2001
Discrete, La 1992
Disgrace 2010
Dish, The 2002
Disney's A Christmas Carol. *See* Christmas Carol, A.
Disney's Planes. *See* Planes.
Disney's Teacher's Pet 2005
Disney's The Kid 2001
Disorder 2017
Disorderlies 1987
Disorganized Crime 1989
Disraeli [1929] 1981
Distant Harmony 1988
Distant Thunder 1988
Distant Voices, Still Lives 1988
Distinguished Gentleman, The 1992
District 9 2010
District 13: Ultimatum 2011
Distribution of Lead, The 1989
Disturbed 1990
Disturbia 2008
Disturbing Behavior 1999
Diva 1982
Divan 2005
Divergent 2015
Divided Love. *See* Maneuvers.
Divided We Fall 2002
Divine Intervention: A Chronicle of Love and Pain 2004
Divine Secrets of the Ya-Ya Sisterhood, The 2003
Diving Bell and the Butterfly, The 2008
Diving In 1990
Divo, Il 2010
Divorce, Le 2004
Divorcee, The [1930] 1981
Django Unchained 2013
Djomeh 2002
Do or Die 1995
Do the Right Thing 1989
Do You Believe? 2016
D.O.A. 1988
DOA: Dead or Alive 2008
Doc Hollywood 1991
Doc's Kingdom 1988
Docteur Petiot 1995
Doctor, The 1991
Doctor Strange 2017
Dr. Agaki 2000
Doctor and the Devils, The 1985
Dr. Bethune 1995
Dr. Butcher, M.D. 1982
Doctor Detroit 1983
Dr. Dolittle 1999
Dr. Dolittle 2 2002
Dr. Giggles 1992
Dr. Jekyll and Ms. Hyde 1995
Dr. Petiot. *See* Docteur Petiot.
Dr. Seuss' Horton Hears a Who! 2009
Dr. Seuss' How the Grinch Stole Christmas 2001
Dr. Seuss' The Cat in the Hat 2004
Dr. Seuss' The Lorax 2013
Dr. Sleep. *See* Close Your Eyes.
Dr. T and the Women 2001
Doctor Zhivago [1965] 1990
Do-Deca-Pentahlon, The 2013
Dodgeball: A True Underdog Story 2005
Dog of Flanders, A 2000
Dog Park 2000
Dogfight 1991
Dogma 2000
Dog's Purpose, A 2018
Dogtooth 2011
Dogville 2005
Doin' Time on Planet Earth 1988
Dolls 1987
Dolls 2006
Dolly Dearest 1992
Dolly In. *See* Travelling Avant.
Dolores Claiborne 1995
Dolphin Tale 2012
Dolphin Tale 2 2015
Dom Hemingway 2015
Domestic Disturbance 2002
Dominick and Eugene 1988
Dominion: Prequel to the Exorcist 2006
Domino 2006
Don Jon 2014
Don Jon's Addiction. *See* Don Jon.
Don Juan DeMarco 1995
Don Juan, My Love 1991
Don McKay 2011
Dona Herlinda and Her Son 1986
Donkey Who Drank the Moon, The 1988
Donna della luna, La. *See* Woman in the Moon.
Donnie Brasco 1997
Donnie Darko 2003
Donny's Boy. *See* That's My Boy.
Don't Be a Menace to South Central While Drinking Your Juice in the Hood 1996
Don't Be Afraid of the Dark 2012
Don't Breathe 2017
Don't Come Knocking 2007
Don't Cry, It's Only Thunder 1982
Don't Move 2006
Don't Say a Word 2002
Don't Tell 2007
Don't Tell Her It's Me 1990
Don't Tell Mom the Babysitter's Dead 1991
Don't Tempt Me! *See* No News from God.
Don't Touch the Axe. *See* Duchess of Langeais, The.
Doom 2006
Doom Generation, The 1995
Doomsday 2009
Door in the Floor, The 2005
Door to Door 1984
Doors, The 1991
Dopamine 2004
Dope 2016

Doppia ora, La. *See* Double Hour, The.
Dorm That Dripped Blood, The 1983
Dorothy and Alan at Norma Place 1981
Double, The 2012
Double, The 2015
Double Dragon 1995
Double Edge 1992
Double Happiness 1995
Double Hour, The 2012
Double Impact 1991
Double Indemnity [1944] 1981, 1986, 1987
Double Jeopardy 2000
Double Life of Veronique, The 1991
Double Take 2002
Double Team 1997
Double Threat 1993
Double Trouble 1992
Double Vie de Veronique, La. *See* Double Life of Veronique, The.
Doublure, La. *See* Valet, The.
Doubt 2009
Doug's First Movie 2000
Down and Out in Beverly Hills 1986
Down by Law 1986
Down in the Delta 1999
Down in the Valley 2007
Down Periscope 1996
Down Terrace 2011
Down the Hill. *See* Footnote.
Down to Earth 2002
Down to You 2001
Down Twisted 1987
Down With Love 2004
Downfall 2006
Downsizing 2018
Downtown 1990
Dracula. *See* Bram Stoker's Dracula.
Dracula: Dead and Loving It 1995
Dracula 2001. *See* Wes Craven Presents: Dracula 2001.
Dracula Untold 2015
Draft Day 2015
Drag Me to Hell 2010
Dragnet 1987
Dragon 1993
Dragon Chow 1988
Dragonball: Evolution 2010
Dragonfly 2003
Dragonheart 1996
Dragonslayer 1981
Draughtsman's Contract, The 1983
Dream a Little Dream 1989
Dream Demon 1988
Dream for an Insomniac 1999
Dream House 2012
Dream Lover (Kazan) 1986
Dream Lover (Pakula) 1995
Dream of Light 1995
Dream Team, The 1989
Dream With the Fishes 1997
Dreamcatcher 2004
Dreamchild 1985
Dreamer: Inspired by a True Story 2006
Dreamers, The 2005
Dreamgirls 2007
Dreamlife of Angels, The 2000
Dreams. *See* Akira Kurosawa's Dreams.
Dreams with Sharp Teeth 2009
Dreamscape 1984
Dredd 2013
Drei Sterne. *See* Mostly Martha.
Dresser, The 1983
Dressmaker, The 1988
Dressmaker, The 2017
Drifter, The 1988
Drifting 1984
Drillbit Taylor 2009
Drinking Buddies 2014
Drive 1992
Drive 2012
Drive Angry 2012
Drive Me Crazy 2000
Driven 2002
Driving Miss Daisy 1989
Drop, The 2015
Drole de Felix. *See* Adventures of Felix, The.
Drop Dead Fred 1991
Drop Dead Gorgeous 2000
DROP Squad 1995
Drop Zone 1995
Drowning by Numbers 1988
Drowning Mona 2001
Drug War 2014
Drugstore Cowboy 1989
Drumline 2003
Drunks 1997
Dry Cleaning 2000
Dry White Season, A 1989
D3: The Mighty Ducks 1996
Duchess, The 2009
Duchess of Langeais, The 2009
Duck Season 2007
Ducktales, the Movie 1990
Dude, Where's My Car? 2001
Dudes 1987
Dudley Do-Right 2000
Due Date 2011
Duel in the Sun [1946] 1982, 1989
Duet for One 1986
Duets 2001
DUFF, The 2016
D.U.I. 1987
Duke of Burgundy, The 2016
Dukes of Hazzard, The 2006
Dulcy [1923] 1981
Duma 2006
Dumb and Dumber 1995
Dumb and Dumber To 2015
Dumb and Dumberer: When Harry Met Lloyd 2004
Dummy 2004
Dune 1984
Dungeons & Dragons 2001
Dunkirk 2018
Dunston Checks In 1996
Duolou Tianshi. *See* Fallen Angels.
Duplex 2004
Duplicity 2010
Dust Devil: The Final Cut 1995

Dutch 1991
Duva satt pa en gren och funerade pa tillvaron, En. *See* Pigeon Sat on a Branch Reflecting on Existence, A.
Dying Gaul, The 2006
Dying Young 1991
Dylan Dog: Dead of Night 2012

E

E la nave va. *See* And the Ship Sails On.
Eagle, The 2012
Eagle Eye 2009
Eagle vs. Shark 2008
Earth 2001
Earth 2010
Earth Girls Are Easy 1989
Earth to Echo 2015
Earthling, The 1981
East, The 2014
East Is East 2001
East is Red, The 1995
Eastern Promises 2008
East-West 2002
Easy A 2011
Easy Money 1983
Easy Virtue 2010
Eat a Bowl of Tea 1989
Eat and Run 1986
Eat Drink Man Woman 1995
Eat Pray Love 2011
Eat the Rich 1988
Eating 1990
Eating Raoul 1982
Ebro Runs Dry, The 1993
Echo Park 1986
Echoes 1983
Echoes of Paradise 1989
Eclipse, The 2011
Ed 1996
Ed and His Dead Mother 1993
Ed Wood 1995
Eddie 1996
Eddie and the Cruisers 1983
Eddie and the Cruisers II 1989
Eddie the Eagle 2017
Eddie Macon's Run 1983
Eddie Murphy Raw 1987
Eden 1999
Eden 2016
Edes Emma, Draga Bobe: Vazlatok, Aktok. *See* Sweet Emma, Dear Bobe: Sketches, Nudes.
Edge, The 1997
Edge of Darkness 2011
Edge of Heaven, The 2009
Edge of Sanity 1989
Edge of Seventeen 2000
Edge of Seventeen, The 2017
Edge of Tomorrow 2015
Edith and Marcel 1984
Edith's Diary 1986
Ed's Next Move 1996
Edtv 2000
Educating Rita 1983
Education, An 2010
Education of Little Tree, The 1997
Edukators, The 2006
Edward Scissorhands 1990
Edward II 1992
Efficiency Expert, The 1992
Efter Repetitionen. *See* After the Rehearsal.
Egares, Les. *See* Strayed.
Eiga Joyu. *See* Actress.
8 1/2 Women 2001
Eight Below 2007
Eight Days a Week 2000
Eight Heads in a Duffle Bag 1997
Eight Legged Freaks 2003
Eight Men Out 1988
8 Mile 2003
Eight Million Ways to Die 1986
8MM 2000
8 Seconds 1995
8 Women 2003
Eighteen Again 1988
Eighth Day, The 1997
88 Minutes 2009
Eighty-Four Charing Cross Road 1987
Eighty-Four Charlie MoPic 1989
Eine Liebe in Deutchland. *See* Love in Germany, A.
Elaine Stritch: Shoot Me 2015
Election 2000
Electric Dreams 1984
Elektra 2006
Elephant 2004
Elegant Criminel, L' 1992
Elegy 2009
Elementary School, The 1995
Elena 2013
Eleni 1985
Eleni (2005). *See* Weeping Meadow.
11-11-11 2012
Elf 2004
Eliminators 1986
Elizabeth 1999
Elizabeth: The Golden Age 2008
Elizabethtown 2006
Ella Enchanted 2005
Elle 2017
Elling 2003
Elliot Fauman, Ph.D. 1990
Eloge de l'Amour. *See* In Praise of Love.
Elvira, Mistress of the Dark 1988
Elysium 2014
Elvis & Nixon 2017
Embalmer, The 2004
Embrace of the Serpent 2017
Emerald Forest, The 1985
Emile 2006
Eminent Domain 1991
Emma 1996
Emmanuelle 5 1987
Emoji Movie, The 2018
Emperor 2014
Emperor Waltz, The [1948] 1986
Emperor's Club, The 2003
Emperor's New Clothes, The 1987
Emperor's New Clothes, The (Taylor) 2003
Emperor's New Groove, The 2001
Emperor's Shadow 2000
Empire of the Sun 1987
Empire Records 1995

Empire Strikes Back, The [1983] 1997
Emploi du Temps, L. *See* Time Out.
Employee of the Month 2007
Emporte-Moi. *See* Set Me Free.
Empty Mirror, The 2000
Enchanted 2008
Enchanted April 1992
Enchanted Cottage, The [1945] 1981
Encino Man 1992
Encore. *See* One More.
End of Days 2000
End of Innocence, The 1990
End of Old Times, The 1992
End of the Affair 2000
End of the Line (Glenn) 1987
End of the Line (Russell) 1988
End of the Spear 2007
End of the Tour, The 2016
End of Violence, The 1997
End of Watch 2013
Endangered Species 1982
Ender's Game 2014
Endurance 2000
Enduring Love 2005
Endgame 1986
Endless Love 2015
Endless Summer II, The 1995
Enemies, A Love Story 1989
Enemy 2015
Enemy at the Gates 2002
Enemy Mine 1985
Enemy of the State 1999
Enemy Territory 1987
Enfant, L'. *See* Child, The.
English Patient, The 1996
Englishman Who Went Up a Hill But Came Down a Mountain, The 1995
Enid Is Sleeping. *See* Over Her Dead Body.
Enigma (Szwarc) 1983
Enigma (Apted) 2003
Enough 2003
Enough Said 2014
Enron: The Smartest Guys in the Room 2006
Enter the Ninja 1982
Enter the Void 2011
Entity, The 1983
Entourage 2016
Entrapment 2000
Entre les murs. *See* Class, The.
Entre nous 1984
Envy 2005
Epic 2014
Epic Movie 2008
Equalizer, The 2015
Equilibrium 2003
Equinox 1993
Equity 2017
Eragon 2007
Eraser 1996
Erendira 1984
Erik the Viking 1989
Erin Brockovich 2001
Ermo 1995
Ernest Goes to Camp 1987
Ernest Goes to Jail 1990
Ernest Rides Again 1993
Ernest Saves Christmas 1988
Ernest Scared Stupid 1991
Eros 2006
Erotique 1995
Escanaba in da Moonlight 2002
Escape Artist, The 1982
Escape from Alcatraz [1979] 1982
Escape from L.A. 1996
Escape from New York 1981
Escape From Planet Earth 2014
Escape from Safehaven 1989
Escape From Tomorrow 2014
Escape Plan 2014
Escape 2000 1983
Escobar: Paradise Lost 2016
Escort, The. *See* Scorta, La.
Especially on Sunday 1993
Esperame en el cielo. *See* Wait for Me in Heaven.
Espinazo de Diablo, El. *See* Devil's Backbone, The.
Est-Ouest. *See* East-West.
Esther Kahn 2003
Et maintenant on va ou? *See* Where Do We Go Now?
E.T.: The Extra-Terrestrial 1982
Etat sauvage, L' [1978] 1990
Ete prochain, L'. *See* Next Summer.
Eternal Sunshine of the Spotless Mind 2005
Eternity and a Day 2000
Ethan Frome 1993
Etoile du nord 1983
Eu Tu Eles. *See* Me You Them.
Eulogy 2005
Eulogy of Love. *See* In Praise of Love.
Eureka 1985
Eureka 2002
Europa 1995
Europa, Europa 1991
Europa Report 2014
Eurotrip 2005
Evan Almighty 2008
Eve of Destruction 1991
Evelyn 2003
Even Cowgirls Get the Blues 1995
Evening 2008
Evening Star 1996
Event Horizon 1997
Events Leading Up to My Death, The 1995
Ever After: A Cinderella Story 1999
Everest 2016
Everlasting Piece, An 2002
Everlasting Secret Family, The 1989
Every Breath 1995
Every Little Step 2010
Every Man for Himself [1979] 1981
Every Time We Say Goodbye 1986
Everybody Wants Some!! 2017
Everybody Wins 1990
Everybody's All-American 1988
Everybody's Famous! 2002
Everybody's Fine 1991
Everybody's Fine 2010
Everyone Says I Love You 1996
Everyone's Hero 2007

Everything, Everything 2018
Everything is Illuminated 2006
Everything Must Go 2012
Every Thing Will Be Fine 2016
Eve's Bayou 1997
Evil Dead 2014
Evil Dead, The 1983
Evil Dead II 1987
Evil That Men Do, The 1984
Evil Under the Sun 1982
Evil Woman. *See* Saving Silverman.
Evita 1996
Evolution 2002
Ex Machina 2016
Excalibur 1981
Exception, The 2018
Excess Baggage 1997
Exchange Lifeguards 1995
Execution Protocol, The 1995
Executive Decision 1996
Exiles, The 2009
eXistenZ 2000
Exit Through the Gift Shop 2011
Exit to Eden 1995
Exit Wounds 2002
Exodus: Gods and Kings 2015
Exorcism of Emily Rose, The 2006
Exorcist: The Beginning 2005
Exorcist III, The 1990
Exorcist, The [1973] 2001
Exotica 1995
Expendables, The 2011
Expendables 3, The 2015
Expendables 2, The 2013
Experience Preferred...but Not Essential 1983
Experimenter 2016
Explorers 1985
Exposed 1983
Express, The 2009
Extract 2010
Extramuros 1995
Extraordinary Measures 2011
Extreme Measures 1996
Extreme Ops 2003
Extreme Prejudice 1987
Extremely Loud and Incredibly Close 2012
Extremities 1986
Eye for an Eye, An 1996
Eye in the Sky 2017
Eye of God 1997
Eye of the Beholder 2001
Eye of the Needle 1981
Eye of the Tiger, The 1986
Eye, The 2009
Eyes of My Mother, The 2017
Eyes of Tammy Faye, The 2001
Eyes Wide Shut 2000

F

F/X 1986
F/X II 1991
Fabulous Baker Boys, The 1989
Fabulous Destiny of Amelie Poulain, The. *See* Amelie.
Face/Off 1997
Faces of Women 1987
Facing Windows 2005
Factory Girl 2008
Factotum 2007
Faculty, The 1999
Fading Gigolo 2015
Fahrenheit 9/11 2005
Failure to Launch 2007
Fair Game 1995
Fair Game 2011
Fairytale—A True Story 1997
Faithful 1996
Faithless 2002
Fakebook 1989
Falcon and the Snowman, The 1985
Fall 1997
Fallen 1999
Fallen Angels 1999
Falling, The. *See* Alien Predator.
Falling Down 1993
Falling from Grace 1992
Falling in Love 1984
Fälscher, Die. *See* Counterfeiters, The.
Falstaff [1966] 1982
Fame 2010
Family, The 1988
Family, The 2014
Family Business 1989
Family Fang, The 2017
Family Man 2001
Family Prayers 1993
Family Stone, The 2006
Family Thing, A 1996
Famine Within, The 1992
Fan, The 1996
Fanboys 2010
Fandango 1985
Fanny and Alexander 1983
Fanny och Alexander. *See* Fanny and Alexander.
Fantasies [1973] 1982
Fantastic Beasts and Where to Find Them 2017
Fantastic Four 2006
Fantastic Four 2016
Fantastic Four: Rise of the Silver Surfer 2008
Fantastic Mr. Fox 2010
Fantastic Woman, A 2018
Fantomes des Trois Madeleines, Les. *See* Three Madeleines, The.
Fantome D'henri Langlois, Le. *See* Henri Langlois: The Phantom of the Cinematheque.
Far and Away 1992
Far from Heaven 2003
Far from Home 1989
Far From Home: The Adventures of Yellow Dog 1995
Far from the Madding Crowd 2016
Far North 1988
Far Off Place, A 1993
Far Out Man 1990
Faraway, So Close 1993
Farewell Illusion 1986
Farewell My Concubine 1993
Farewell, My Queen 2013
Farewell to the King 1989
Fargo 1996
Farinelli 1995
Farmer and Chase 1997

Fast & Furious 2010
Fast & Furious 6 2014
Fast & Furious 7. *See* Furious 7.
Fast and the Furious, The 2002
Fast and the Furious: Tokyo Drift, The 2007
Fast, Cheap & Out of Control 1997
Fast Five 2012
Fast Food 1989
Fast Food, Fast Women 2002
Fast Forward 1985
Fast Talking 1986
Fast Times at Ridgemont High 1982
Faster 2011
Fat Albert 2005
Fat City [1972] 1983
Fat Girl 2002
Fat Guy Goes Nutzoid 1987
Fat Man and Little Boy 1989
Fatal Attraction 1987
Fatal Beauty 1987
Fatal Instinct 1993
Fate Ignoranti. *See* Ignorant Fairies.
Fate of the Furious, The 2018
Father 1995
Father Figures 2018
Father Hood 1993
Father of the Bride (Minnelli) [1950] 1993
Father of the Bride (Shyer) 1991
Father of the Bride Part II 1995
Fathers and Sons 1992
Father's Day 1997
Fault In Our Stars, The 2015
Faults 2016
Fausto. *See* A la Mode.
Fauteuils d'orchestre. *See* Avenue Montaigne.
Favor, The 1995
Favour, the Watch, and the Very Big Fish, The 1992
Fay Grim 2008
Fear 1988
Fear 1996
Fear and Loathing in Las Vegas 1999
Fear, Anxiety and Depression 1989
Fear of a Black Hat 1995
Feardotcom 2003
Fearless 1993
Fearless. *See* Jet Li's Fearless.
Feast of July 1995
Feast of Love 2008
Fed Up 2015
Federal Hill 1995
Fedora [1978] 1986
Feds 1988
Feed 1992
Feel the Heat 1987
Feeling Minnesota 1996
Felicia's Journey 2000
Felix 1988
Fellini: I'm a Born Liar 2004
Female Perversions 1997
Femme d'a Cote, La. *See* Woman Next Door, The.
Femme de Chambre du Titanic, La. *See* Chambermaid of the Titanic.
Femme de mon pote, La. *See* My Best Friend's Girl.
Femme Fatale 2003
Femme Nikita, La 1991
Femmes de personne 1986
Fences 2017
Ferdinand 2018
FernGully: The Last Rainforest 1992
Ferris Bueller's Day Off 1986
Festival Express 2005
Festival in Cannes 2003
Feud, The 1990
Fever 1988
Fever Pitch 1985
Fever Pitch 2000
Fever Pitch 2006
Few Days with Me, A 1988
Few Good Men, A 1992
Fido 2008
Field, The 1990
Field in England, A 2015
Field of Dreams 1989
Fierce Creatures 1997
15 Minutes 2002
Fifth Element, The 1997
Fifth Estate, The 2014
5th Wave, The 2017
50 First Dates 2005
51st State, The. *See* Formula 51.
54 1999
50/50 2012
Fifty-Fifty 1993
56 Up 2014
Fifty Shades Darker 2018
Fifty Shades of Black 2017
Fifty Shades of Grey 2016
Fifty-two Pick-up 1986
Fight Club 2000
Fighter 2002
Fighter, The 2011
Fighting 2010
Fighting Back 1982
Fighting Temptations, The 2004
Fill the Void 2014
Fille coupée en deux, La. *See* Girl Cut in Two, A.
Fille du RER, La. *See* Girl on the Train, The.
Fille inconnue, La. *See* Unknown Girl, The.
Filles ne Savent pas Nager, Les. *See* Girls Can't Swim.
Filly Brown 2014
Film Socialisme 2012
Film Stars Don't Die in Liverpool 2018
Film Unfinished, A 2011
Fils, Le. *See* Son, The.
Filth 2015
Filth and the Fury, The 2001
Fin aout debut septembre. *See* Late August, Early September.
Final Analysis 1992
Final Approach 1991
Final Cut 2005
Final Destination 2001
Final Destination, The 2010
Final Destination: Death Trip 3D. *See* Final Destination, The.
Final Destination 2 2004
Final Destination 3 2007

Final Destination 4. *See* Final Destination, The.
Final Destination 5 2012
Final Fantasy: The Spirits Within 2002
Final Friday, The. *See* Jason Goes to Hell.
Final Girls, The 2016
Final Option, The 1983
Final Sacrifice, The. *See* Children of the Corn II.
Final Season 1988
Final Season, The 2008
Find Me Guilty 2007
Finders Keepers 1984
Finding Dory 2017
Finding Forrester 2001
Finding Nemo 2004
Finding Neverland 2005
Finding Vivian Maier 2015
Fine Mess, A 1986
Fine Romance, A 1992
Finest Hours, The 2017
Finestra di Fronte, La. *See* Facing Windows.
Finzan 1995
Fiorile 1995
Fire and Ice (Bakshi) 1983
Fire and Ice (Bogner) 1987
Fire Birds 1990
Fire Down Below 1997
Fire from the Mountain 1987
Fire in Sky 1993
Fire This Time, The 1995
Fire Walk with Me. *See* Twin Peaks: Fire Walk with Me.
Fire with Fire 1986
Fired Up! 2010
Fireflies in the Garden 2012
Firefox 1982
Firehead 1991
Firelight 1999
Firemen's Bell, The [1967] 1985
Fireproof 2009
Firestorm 1999
Firewalker 1986
Firewall 2007
Fireworks 1999
Fires of Kuwait 1995
Firm, The 1993
First Blood 1982
First Daughter 2005
First Descent 2006
First Kid 1996
First Knight 1995
First Love, Last Rites 1999
First Monday in May, The 2017
First Monday in October 1981
First Name, Carmen 1984
First Position 2013
First Power, The 1990
First Saturday in May, The 2009
First Sunday 2009
First Wives Club, The 1996
Firstborn 1984
Fish Called Wanda, A 1988
Fish Tank 2011
Fisher King, The 1991
Fist Fight 2018
Fistfighter 1989
Fits, The 2017
Fitzcarraldo 1982
Five Came Back 2018
Five Corners 1987
Five Days One Summer 1982
Five Graves to Cairo [1943] 1986
Five Heartbeats, The 1991
(500) Days of Summer 2010
Five Minutes of Heaven 2010
Five Senses, The 2001
Five-Year Engagement, The 2013
Flags of Our Fathers 2007
Flame in My Heart, A 1987
Flaming Star [1960] 1982
Flamingo Kid, The 1984
Flamme dans mon coeur, Une. *See* Flame in My Heart, A.
Flanagan 1985
Flash of Genius 2009
Flash of Green, A 1985
Flashback 1990
Flashdance 1983
Flashpoint 1984
Flatliners 1990
Flatliners 2018
Flawless 2000
Flawless 2009
Flaxfield, The 1985
Fled 1996
Fleeing by Night 2004
Flesh and Blood 1985
Flesh and Bone 1993
Flesh Gordon Meets the Cosmic Cheerleaders 1995
Fleshburn 1984
Fletch 1985
Fletch Lives 1989
Flicka 2007
Flickan som lekte med elden. *See* Girl Who Played with Fire, The.
Flight 2013
Flight of the Innocent 1993
Flight of the Intruder 1991
Flight of the Navigator 1986
Flight of the Phoenix 2005
Flight of the Phoenix, The [1966] 1984
Flight of the Red Balloon 2009
Flight to Fury [1966]
Flightplan 2006
Flintstones, The 1995
Flipper 1996
Flipping 1997
Flirt 1996
Flirting 1992
Flirting with Disaster 1996
Florence Foster Jenkins 2017
Florida Project, The 2018
Floundering 1995
Flower of Evil, The 2004
Flower of My Secret, The 1996
Flowers in the Attic 1987
Flowing 1985
Flubber 1997
Fluffy Movie: Unity Through Laughter, The 2015
Fluke 1995

Flushed Away 2007
Fly, The 1986
Fly II, The 1989
Fly Away Home 1996
Fly by Night 1995
Fly Me to the Moon 2009
Flyboys 2007
Flying Duchman, The 1995
Flying Scotsman, The 2008
Focus 2016
Fog, The 2006
Fog of War: Eleven Lessons from the Life of Robert S. McNamara, The 2005
Folks 1992
Follow the Bitch 1999
Food, Inc. 2010
Food of the Gods II 1989
Fool for Love 1985
Foolish 2000
Fool's Gold 2009
Fools of Fortune 1990
Fools Rush In 1997
Footloose 1984
Footloose 2012
Footnote 2013
For a Good Time, Call... 2013
For a Lost Soldier 1993
For Colored Girls 2011
For Ever Mozart 1997
For Greater Glory 2013
For Keeps 1988
For Love of the Game 2000
For Love or Money 1993
For Me and My Gal [1942] 1985
For My Sister. *See* Fat Girl.
For Queen and Country 1988, 1989
For Richer or Poorer 1997
For Roseanna 1997
For Sasha 1992
For the Boys 1991
For the Moment 1996
For Your Consideration 2007
For Your Eyes Only 1981
Forbidden Choices. *See* Beans of Egypt, Maine, The.
Forbidden Dance, The 1990
Forbidden Kingdom, The 2009
Forbidden Quest 1995
Forbidden World 1982
Force Majeure 2015
Forced Vengeance 1982
Forces of Nature 2000
Foreign Affair, A [1948] 1986
Foreign Body 1986
Foreign Student 211
Foreigner, The 2018
Forest, The 2017
Forever 1995
Forever, Lulu 1987
Forever Mary 1991
Forever Young 1992
Forget Paris 1995
Forgetting Sarah Marshall 2009
Forgotten, The 2005
Formula 51 2003
Forrest Gump 1995
Forsaken, The 2002
Fort Apache [1948] 1983
Fort Apache, the Bronx 1981
Fortress 1993
Fortune Cookie, The [1966] 1986
40 Days and 40 Nights 2003
40 Year Old Virgin, The 2006
48 Hrs. 1982
45 Years 2016
47 Meters Down 2018
47 Ronin 2014
42 2014
Foster Daddy, Tora! 1981
Founder, The 2018
Fountain, The 2007
Four Adventures of Reinette and Mirabelle 1989
Four Brothers 2006
Four Christmases 2009
Four Days in September 1999
Four Feathers, The 2003
Four Friends 1981
Four Lions 2011
4 Little Girls 1997
4 luni, 3 saptâmani si 2 zile. *See* 4 Months, 3 Weeks and 2 Days.
4 Months, 3 Weeks and 2 Days 2009
Four Rooms 1995
Four Seasons, The 1981
Four Weddings and a Funeral 1995
1492: Conquest of Paradise 1992
1408 2008
Fourth Kind, The 2010
4th Man, The 1984
Fourth Protocol, The 1987
Fourth War, The 1990
Fox and the Hound, The 1981
Foxcatcher 2015
Foxfire 1996
Foxtrap 1986
Foxtrot 2018
Fracture 2008
Frailty 2003
Frances 1982
Frances Ha 2014
Frank 2015
Frank and Ollie 1995
Frank Miller's Sin City. *See* Sin City.
Frank Miller's Sin City: A Dame to Kill For. *See* Sin City: A Dame to Kill For.
Frankenhooker 1990
Frankenstein. *See* Mary Shelley's Frankenstein.
Frankenstein Unbound. *See* Roger Corman's Frankenstein Unbound.
Frankenweenie 2013
Frankie & Alice 2011
Frankie and Johnny 1991
Frankie Starlight 1995
Frantic 1988
Frantz 2018
Fraternity Vacation 1985
Frauds 1995
Freaked 1993
Freakonomics 2011
Freaky Friday 2004
Fred Claus 2008
Freddie as F.R.O.7 1992
Freddy Got Fingered 2002

Freddy vs. Jason 2004
Freddy's Dead 1991
Free and Easy 1989
Free Birds 2014
Free Enterprise 2000
Free Fire 2018
Free Radicals 2005
Free Ride 1986
Free State of Jones 2017
Free Willy 1993
Free Willy II: The Adventure Home 1995
Free Willy III: The Rescue 1997
Freebie, The 2011
Freedom On My Mind 1995
Freedom Writers 2008
Freedomland 2007
Freeheld 2016
Freejack 1992
Freeway 1988
Freeway 1996
Freeze—Die—Come to Life 1995
French, La. *See* Connection, The.
French Connection, The [1971] 1982
French Kiss 1995
French Lesson 1986
French Lieutenant's Woman, The 1981
French Twist 1996
Frequency 2001
Fresh 1995
Fresh Horses 1988
Freshman, The 1990
Freud [1962] 1983
Frida 2003
Friday 1995
Friday After Next 2003
Friday Night 2004
Friday Night Lights 2005
Friday the 13th 2010
Friday the 13th, Part III 1982
Friday the 13th, Part IV 1984
Friday the 13th, Part VI 1986
Friday the 13th Part VII 1988
Friday the 13th Part VIII 1989
Fried Green Tomatoes 1991
Friend of the Deceased, A 1999
Friend Request 2018
Friends & Lovers 2000
Friends With Benefits 2012
Friends with Kids 2013
Friends with Money 2007
Fright Night 1985
Fright Night 2012
Frighteners, The 1996
Fringe Dwellers, The 1987
From Beyond 1986
From Dusk Till Dawn 1996
From Hell 2002
From Hollywood to Deadwood 1988
From Paris With Love 2011
From Prada to Nada 2012
From Swastikas to Jim Crow 2001
From the Hip 1987
From Up on Poppy Hill 2014
Front, The [1976] 1985
Frosh: Nine Months in a Freshman Dorm 1995
Frost/Nixon 2009
Frozen 2011
Frozen 2014
Frozen Assets 1992
Frozen River 2009
Fruhlingssinfonie. *See* Spring Symphony.
Fruit Machine, The 1988
Fruitvale Station 2014
Fu-zung cen. *See* Hibiscus Town.
Fucking Amal. *See* Show Me Love.
Fugitive, The 1993
Full Blast 2001
Full Frontal 2003
Full Metal Jacket 1987
Full Monty, The 1997
Full Moon in Paris 1984
Full Moon in the Blue Water 1988
Full of It 2008
Fun Down There 1989
Fun Size 2013
Fun With Dick and Jane 2006
Funeral, The 1987
Funeral, The (Ferrara) 1996
Funny About Love 1990
Funny Bones 1995
Funny Farm (Clark) 1983
Funny Farm (Hill) 1988
Funny Games 2009
Funny People 2010
Furious 7 2016
Fury 2015
Furry Vengeance 2011
Further Adventures of Tennessee Buck, The 1988
Future, The 2012

G

Gabbeh 1997
Gabriela 1984
Gabrielle 2007
Gaby—A True Story 1987
Gadjo Dilo 1999
Gake no une no Ponyon. *See* Ponyo.
Galactic Gigolo 1988
Galaxy Quest 2000
Gallipoli 1981
Gallows, The 2016
Gambler, The 2000
Gambler, The 2015
Game, The 1989
Game, The 1997
Game Plan, The 2008
Game 6 2007
Gamer 2010
Gamin au velo, Le. *See* Kid with a Bike, The.
Gandhi 1982
Gang-Related 1997
Gangs of New York 2003
Gangster No. 1 2003
Gangster Squad 2014
Garage Days 2004
Garbage Pail Kids Movie, The 1987
Garbo Talks 1984
Garde a vue 1982
Garden, The 1995
Garden State 2005

Gardens of Stone 1987
Garfield 2005
Garfield: A Tail of Two Kitties 2007
Gas Food Lodging 1992
Gate, The 1987
Gate II 1992
Gatekeepers, The 2013
Gattaca 1997
Gaudi Afternoon 2002
Gay Divorcee, The [1934] 1981
Gegen die Wand. *See* Head-On.
Genealogies D' Un Crime. *See* Genealogies of a Crime.
Genealogies of a Crime 1999
General, The 1999
General's Daughter, The 2000
Genghis Blues 2000
Genius 2017
Gentilezza del tocco, La. *See* Gentle Touch, The.
Gentle Touch, The 1988
Gentlemen Broncos 2010
Gentlemen Don't Eat Poets 1997
Gentlemen's Agreement [1947] 1989
Genuine Risk 1990
George A. Romero's Diary of the Dead. *See* Diary of the Dead.
George A. Romero's Land of the Dead 2006
George Balanchine's The Nutcracker 1993
George of the Jungle 1997
George's Island 1991
Georgia 1988
Georgia 1995
Georgia Rule 2008
Geostorm 2018
Germinal 1993
Geronimo 1993
Gerry 2004
Get Back 1991
Get Bruce! 2000
Get Carter 2001
Get Crazy 1983
Get Hard 2016
Get Him to the Greek 2011
Get Low 2011
Get on the Bus 1996
Get On Up 2015
Get Out 2018
Get Over It! 2002
Get Real 2000
Get Rich or Die Tryin' 2006
Get Shorty 1995
Get Smart 2009
Getaway 2014
Getaway, The 1995
Geteilte Liebe. *See* Maneuvers.
Gett: The Trial of Viviane Amsalem 2016
Getting Away with Murder 1996
Getting Even 1986
Getting Even With Dad 1995
Getting It Right 1989
Getting to Know You 2001
Gettysburg 1993
G Force 2010
Ghare Bhaire. *See* Home and the World, The.
Ghost 1990
Ghost and the Darkness, The 1996
Ghost Dad 1990
Ghost Dog: The Way of the Samurai 2000
Ghost in the Shell 2018
Ghost in the Shell II: Innocence 2005
Ghosts of Girlfriends Past 2010
Ghost Rider 2008
Ghost Rider: Spirit of Vengeance 2013
Ghost Ship 2003
Ghost Story, A 2018
Ghost Writer, The 2011
Ghosts Can't Do It 1990
Ghosts of Mississippi 1996
Ghosts...of the Civil Dead 1988
Ghost Story 1981
Ghost Town 1988
Ghost Town 2009
Ghost World 2002
Ghosts of Mars. *See* John Carpenter's Ghosts of Mars.
Ghostbusters 1984
Ghostbusters 2017
Ghostbusters II 1989
G.I. Jane 1997
G.I. Joe: Retaliation 2014
G.I. Joe: The Rise of Cobra 2010
Giant [1956] 1993, 1996
Gift, The (Lang) 1983
Gift, The (Raimi) 2001
Gift, The 2016
Gift From Heaven, A 1995
Gifted 2018
Gig, The 1986
Gigli 2004
Gimme Shelter 2015
Gimme the Loot 2014
Ginger Ale Afternoon 1989
Ginger and Fred 1986
Ginger & Rosa 2014
Ginger Snaps 2002
Gingerbread Man, The 1999
Giornata speciale, Una. *See* Special Day, A.
Giovane Toscanini, II. *See* Young Toscanini.
Girl Cut in Two, A 2009
Girl from Paris, The 2004
Girl in a Swing, The 1988
Girl in the Picture, The 1986
Girl in Progress 2013
Girl, Interrupted 2000
Girl Next Door, The 2001
Girl Next Door, The (Greenfield) 2005
Girl on the Train, The 2011
Girl on the Train, The 2017
Girl Rising 2014
Girl 6 1996
Girl Talk 1988
Girl Who Kicked the Hornet's Nest, The 2011
Girl Who Played with Fire, The 2011
Girl with a Pearl Earring 2004
Girl with the Dragon Tattoo, The 2011

Girl with the Dragon Tattoo, The 2012

Girl with the Hungry Eyes, The 1995

Girl with the Red Hair, The 1983

Girlfight 2001

Girlfriend Experience, The 2010

Girlhood 2016

Girls Can't Swim 2003

Girls School Screamers 1986

Girls Town 1996

Girls Trip 2018

Give My Regards to Broad Street 1984

Giver, The 2015

Giving, The 1992

Gladiator (Herrington) 1992

Gladiator (Scott) 2001

Glamazon: A Different Kind of Girl 1995

Glamour 2002

Glaneurs et la Glaneuse, Les. *See* Gleaners and I, The.

Glass Castle, The 2018

Glass House, The 2002

Glass Menagerie, The 1987

Glass Shield, The 1995

Gleaming the Cube 1989

Gleaners and I, The 2002

Glee: The 3D Concert Movie 2012

Glengarry Glen Ross 1992

Glimmer Man, The 1996

Glitter 2002

Gloire de mon pere, La. *See* My Father's Glory.

Gloomy Sunday 2004

Gloria (Cassavetes) [1980] 1987

Gloria (Lumet) 2000

Gloria 2015

Glory 1989

Glory Road 2007

Gnomeo & Juliet 2012

Go 2000

Go Fish 1995

Go Now 1999

Goal! The Dream Begins 2007

Goat 2017

Goat, The 1985

Gobots 1986

God Bless America 2013

God Doesn't Believe in Us Anymore 1988

God Grew Tired of Us 2008

God Is Great, I'm Not 2003

God Is My Witness 1993

God Said "Ha"! 2000

Goddess of 1967, The 2003

Godfather, Part III, The 1990

Gods and Generals 2004

Gods and Monsters 1999

Gods Must Be Crazy, The 1984

Gods Must Be Crazy II, The 1990

God's Not Dead 2015

God's Not Dead 2 2017

God's Pocket 2015

God's Will 1989

Gods of Egypt 2017

Godsend 2005

Godzilla 1985 1985

Godzilla 1997

Godzilla 2000 2001

Godzilla 2015

Gohatto. *See* Taboo.

Goin' to Chicago 1991

Going All the Way 1997

Going Berserk 1983

Going in Style 2018

Going the Distance 2011

Going Undercover 1988

Goin' South 1978

Gold 2018

Gold Diggers: The Secret of Bear Mountain 1995

Golden Bowl, The 2002

Golden Child, The 1986

Golden Compass, The 2008

Golden Gate 1995

Golden Seal 1983

Goldeneye 1995

Gomorrah 2010

Gone 2013

Gone Baby Gone 2008

Gone Fishin' 1997

Gone Girl 2015

Gone in Sixty Seconds 2001

Gone With the Wind [1939] 1981, 1982, 1997

Gong fu. *See* Kung Fu Hustle.

Gonza the Spearman 1988

Good Boy! 2004

Good Burger 1997

Good Bye Cruel World 1984

Good Bye, Lenin! 2005

Good Day to Die Hard, A 2014

Good Deeds. *See* Tyler Perry's Good Deeds.

Good Dinosaur, The 2016

Good Evening, Mr. Wallenberg 1995

Good German, The 2007

Good Girl, The 2003

Good Hair 2010

Good Kill 2016

Good Luck Chuck 2008

Good Man in Africa, A 1995

Good Marriage, A. *See* Beau Mariage, Le.

Good Morning, Babylon 1987

Good Morning, Vietnam 1987

Good Mother, The 1988

Good Night, and Good Luck 2006

Good Old Fashioned Orgy, A 2012

Good Shepherd, The 2007

Good Son, The 1993

Good, the Bad, the Weird, The 2011

Good Thief, The 2004

Good Time 2018

Good Weather, But Stormy Late This Afternoon 1987

Good Will Hunting 1997

Good Woman, A 2007

Good Woman of Bangkok, The 1992

Good Work. *See* Beau Travail.

Good Year, A 2007

Goodbye, Children. *See* Au Revoir les Enfants.

Goodbye Christopher Robin 2018

Goodbye Lover 2000

Goodbye, New York 1985

Goodbye People, The 1986

Goodbye Solo 2010

Goodbye to Language 2015

GoodFellas 1990

Goods: Live Hard, Sell Hard, The 2010

Goods: The Don Ready Story, The. *See* Goods: Live Hard, Sell Hard, The.

Goofy Movie, A 1995

Goon 2013

Goonies, The 1985

Goosebumps 2016

Gordy 1995

Gorillas in the Mist 1988

Gorky Park 1983

Gorky Triology, The. *See* Among People.

Gosford Park 2002

Gospel 1984

Gospel According to Vic 1986

Gossip 2001

Gossip (Nutley) 2003

Gost 1988

Gotcha! 1985

Gothic 1987

Gothika 2004

Gout des Autres, Le. *See* Taste of Others, The.

Gouttes d'Eau sur Pierres Brulantes. *See* Water Drops on Burning Rocks.

Governess 1999

Goya in Bordeaux 2001

Grace Is Gone 2008

Grace of My Heart 1996

Grace Quigley 1985

Gracie 2008

Graduation 2018

Graffiti Bridge 1990

Gran Fiesta, La 1987

Gran Torino 2009

Grand Bleu, Le. *See* Big Blue, The (Besson).

Grand Budapest Hotel, The 2015

Grand Canyon 1991

Grand Canyon: The Hidden Secrets 1987

Grand Chemin, Le. *See* Grand Highway, The.

Grand Highway, The 1988

Grand Illusion, The 2000

Grand Isle 1995

Grand Piano 2015

Grand Seduction, The 2015

Grande bellezza, La. *See* Great Beauty, The.

Grande Cocomero, Il. *See* Great Pumpkin, The.

Grandfather, The 2000

Grandma 2016

Grandma's Boy 2007

Grandmaster, The 2014

Grandview, U.S.A. 1984

Grass Harp, The 1996

Grave. *See* Raw.

Gravesend 1997

Graveyard Shift. *See* Stephen King's Graveyard Shift.

Gravity 2014

Gray Matters 2008

Gray's Anatomy 1997

Grease [1978] 1997

Grease II 1982

Great Balls of Fire! 1989

Great Barrier Reef, The 1990

Great Beauty, The 2014

Great Buck Howard, The 2010

Great Day In Harlem, A 1995

Great Debaters, The 2008

Great Expectations 1999

Great Gatsby, The 2014

Great Mouse Detective, The 1986

Great Muppet Caper, The 1981

Great Outdoors, The 1988

Great Pumpkin, The 1993

Great Raid, The 2006

Great Wall, A 1986

Great Wall, The 2018

Great White Hype, The 1996

Greatest, The 2011

Greatest Game Ever Played, The 2006

Greatest Movie Ever Sold, The. *See* POM Wonderful Presents: The Greatest Movie Ever Sold.

Greatest Showman, The 2018

Greedy 1995

Green Card 1990

Green Desert 2001

Green Hornet, The 2012

Green Inferno, The 2016

Green Lantern 2012

Green Mile, The 2000

Green Room 2017

Green Zone 2011

Greenberg 2011

Greenfingers 2002

Greenhouse, The 1996

Gregory's Girl 1982

Gremlins 1984

Gremlins II 1990

Grey, The 2013

Grey Fox, The 1983

Grey Zone, The 2003

Greystoke 1984

Gridlock'd 1988

Grief 1995

Grievous Bodily Harm 1988

Grifters, The 1990

Grim Prairie Tales 1990

Grind 2004

Grindhouse 2008

Gringo 1985

Grizzly Man 2006

Grizzly Mountain 1997

Groomsmen, The 2007

Groove 2001

Gross Anatomy 1989

Grosse Fatigue 1995

Grosse Pointe Blank 1997

Ground Truth, The 2008

Ground Zero 1987, 1988

Groundhog Day 1993

Grown Ups 2011

Grown Ups 2 2014

Grudge, The 2005

Grudge 2, The 2007
Grumpier Old Men 1995
Grumpy Old Men 1993
Grudge Match 2014
Grune Wuste. *See* Green Desert.
Guard, The 2012
Guardian, The 1990
Guardian, The 2007
Guardians of the Galaxy 2015
Guardians of the Galaxy Vol. 2 2018
Guarding Tess 1995
Guatanamera 1997
Guelwaar 1995
Guerre du Feu, La. *See* Quest for Fire.
Guess Who 2006
Guess Who's Coming to Dinner? [1967] 1992
Guest, The 1984
Guest, The 2015
Guests of Hotel Astoria, The 1989
Gui lai. *See* Coming Home.
Guilt Trip, The 2013
Guilty as Charged 1992
Guilty as Sin 1993
Guilty by Suspicion 1991
Guinevere 2000
Gulliver's Travels 2011
Gummo 1997
Gun in Betty Lou's Handbag, The 1992
Gun Shy 2001
Gunbus. *See* Sky Bandits.
Guncrazy 1993
Gunfighter, The [1950] 1989
Gung Ho 1986
Gunman, The 2016
Gunmen 1995
Gunner Palace 2006
Guru, The 2004
Guy Named Joe, A [1943] 1981
Guy Thing, A 2004
Guys, The 2003
Gwendoline 1984
Gwoemul. *See* Host, The.
Gyakufunsha Kazoku. *See* Crazy Family, The.
Gymkata 1985

H

H. M. Pulham, Esq. [1941] 1981
Hable con Ella. *See* Talk to Her.
Hackers 1995
Hacksaw Ridge 2017
Hadesae: The Final Incident 1992
Hadley's Rebellion 1984
Haevnen. *See* In a Better World.
Hail, Caesar! 2017
Hail Mary 1985
Hairdresser's Husband, The 1992
Hairspray 1988
Hairspray 2008
Haizi wang. *See* King of the Children.
Hak hap. *See* Black Mask
Hak mau. *See* Black Cat.
Half-Baked 1999
Half Moon Street 1986
Half of Heaven 1988
Halfmoon 1996
Hall of Fire [1941] 1986
Halloween (Zombie) 2008
Halloween II 2010
Halloween III: Season of the Witch 1982
Halloween IV 1988
Halloween V 1989
Halloween VI: the Curse of Michael Myers 1995
Halloween H20 1999
Halloween: Resurrection 2003
Hall Pass 2012
Hamburger 1986
Hamburger Hill 1987
Hamlet (Zeffirelli) 1990
Hamlet (Branagh) 1996
Hamlet (Almereyda) 2001
Hamlet 2 2009
Hammett 1983
Hana-Bi. *See* Fireworks.
Hancock 2009
Hand That Rocks the Cradle, The 1992
Handful of Dust, A 1988
Handmaid's Tale, The 1990
Handmaiden, The 2017
Hands of Stone 2017
Hangfire 1991
Hanging Garden, The 1999
Hanging Up 2001
Hangin' with the Homeboys 1991
Hangover, The 2010
Hangover Part III, The 2014
Hangover Part II, The 2012
Hanky Panky 1982
Hanna 2012
Hanna K. 1983
Hannah and Her Sisters 1986
Hannah Arendt 2014
Hannah Montana: The Movie 2010
Hannibal 2002
Hannibal Rising 2008
Hanoi Hilton, The 1987
Hans Christian Andersen's Thumbelina 1995
Hansel and Gretel 1987
Hansel & Gretel: Witch Hunters 2014
Hanussen 1988, 1989
Happening, The 2009
Happenstance 2002
Happily Ever After 1993
Happily Ever After 2006
Happily N'Ever After 2008
Happiness 1999
Happy Accidents 2002
Happy Christmas 2015
Happy Death Day 2018
Happy End 2001
Happy End 2018
Happy Endings 2006
Happy Feet 2007
Happy Feet Two 2012
Happy '49 1987
Happy Gilmore 1996
Happy Hour 1987
Happy New Year 1987

Happy, Texas 2000
Happy Times 2003
Happy Together 1990
Happy Together 1997
Happy Valley 2015
Happy-Go-Lucky 2009
Happythankyoumoreplease 2012
Hard Candy 2007
Hard Choices 1986
Hard Core Logo 1999
Hard Eight 1997
Hard Hunted 1995
Hard Promises 1992
Hard Rain 1999
Hard Target 1993
Hard Ticket to Hawaii 1987
Hard Times 1988
Hard to Hold 1984
Hard to Kill 1990
Hard Traveling 1986
Hard Way, The (Badham) 1991
Hard Way, The (Sherman) 1984
Hard Word, The 2004
Hardball 2002
Hardbodies 1984
Hardbodies II 1986
Hardcore Henry 2017
Hardware 1990
Harlem Nights 1989
Harley Davidson and the Marlboro Man 1991
Harmonists, The 2000
Harold & Kumar Escape from Guantanamo Bay 2009
Harold & Kumar Go to White Castle 2005
Harriet Craig [1950] 1984
Harriet the Spy 1996
Harrison's Flowers 2003
Harry and Son 1984
Harry and the Hendersons 1987
Harry Brown 2011
Harry, He's Here to Help. *See* With a Friend Like Harry.
Harry Potter and the Chamber of Secrets 2003
Harry Potter and the Deathly Hallows: Part 1 2011
Harry Potter and the Deathly Hallows: Part 2 2012
Harry Potter and the Goblet of Fire 2006
Harry Potter and the Half-Blood Prince 2010
Harry Potter and the Order of the Phoenix 2008
Harry Potter and the Prisoner of Azkaban 2005
Harry Potter and the Sorcerer's Stone 2002
Harry, Un Ami Qui Vous Veut du Bien. *See* With a Friend Like Harry.
Hart's War 2003
Harvard Man 2003
Harvest, The 1995
Hasty Heart, The [1949] 1987
Hatchet Man, The [1932] 1982
Hatchet II 2011
Hateful Eight, The 2016
Hateship Loveship 2015
Hatouna Mehuheret. *See* Late Marriage.
Haunted Honeymoon 1986
Haunted House, A 2014
Haunted House 2, A 2015
Haunted Mansion, The 2004
Haunted Summer 1988
Haunting, The 2000
Haunting in Connecticut, The 2010
Hauru no ugoku shiro. *See* Howl's Moving Castle.
Haute tension. *See* High Tension.
Hav Plenty 1999
Havana 1990
Hawk, The 1995
Hawks 1988
Haywire 2013
He Got Game 1999
He Liu. *See* River, The.
He Loves Me...He Loves Me Not 2004
He Named Me Malala 2016
He Said, She Said 1991
Head Above Water 1997
Head in the Clouds 2005
Head Office 1986
Head of State 2004
Head On 2000
Head-On 2006
Head Over Heels 2002
Headhunters 2013
Heads or Tails 1983
Hear My Song 1991
Hear No Evil 1993
Hearat Shulayim. *See* Footnote.
Hearing Voices 1991
Heart 1987
Heart and Souls 1993
Heart Condition 1990
Heart in Winter, A. *See* Coeur en hiver, Un.
Heart Like a Wheel 1983
Heart of a Stag 1984
Heart of Dixie 1989
Heart of Midnight 1989
Heart of the Game, The 2007
Heartaches 1982
Heartbreak Hotel 1988
Heartbreak Kid, The [1972] 1986
Heartbreak Kid, The (Farrelly/Farrelly) 2008
Heartbreak Ridge 1986
Heartbreaker 1983
Heartbreakers 2002
Heartburn 1986
Heartland 1981
Hearts in Atlantis 2002
Hearts of Darkness: A Filmmaker's Apocalypse 1992
Hearts of Fire 1987
Heat 1987
Heat (Mann) 1995
Heat, The 2014
Heat and Dust 1984
Heat of Desire 1984
Heathcliff 1986
Heathers 1989
Heatwave 1983
Heaven (Keaton) 1987

Heaven (Tykwer) 2003
Heaven and Earth (Kadokawa) 1991
Heaven and Earth (Stone) 1993
Heaven Help Us 1985
Heaven Is for Real 2015
Heaven Knows What 2016
Heaven's Gate 1981
Heaven's Prisoners 1996
Heavenly Bodies 1984
Heavenly Creatures 1995
Heavenly Kid, The 1985
Heavy 1996
Heavyweights 1995
Hecate 1984
Hedwig and the Angry Inch 2002
Heidi Fleiss: Hollywood Madame 1996
Heights 2006
Heist, The 2002
Helas Pour Moi 1995
Held Up 2001
Hell High 1989
Hell or High Water 2017
Hell Ride 2009
Hellbent 1989
Hellbound 1988
Hellboy 2005
Hellboy II: The Golden Army 2009
Heller Wahn. *See* Sheer Madness.
Hellion 2015
Hello Again 1987
Hello, Dolly! [1969] 1986
Hello I Must Be Going 2013
Hello Mary Lou 1987
Hello, My Name is Doris 2017
Hellraiser 1987
Hellraiser III: Hell on Earth 1992
Hellraiser IV: Bloodline 1996
Help, The 2012
Henna 1991
Henri Langlois: The Phantom of the Cinematheque 2006
Henry 1990
Henry and June 1990
Henry IV 1985
Henry V 1989
Henry Fool 1999
Henry Poole in Here 2009
Her 2014
Her Alibi 1989
Her Name Is Lisa 1987
Herbes folles, Les. *See* Wild Grass.
Herbie: Fully Loaded 2006
Hercules 1983
Hercules 2015
Hercules II 1985
Herdsmen of the Sun 1995
Here Come the Littles 1985
Here Comes the Boom 2013
Here On Earth 2001
Hereafter 2011
Here's to Life 2002
Hero 1992
Hero 2004
Hero 2005
Hero and the Terror 1988
Hero, The 2018
Hesher 2012
He's Just Not That Into You 2010
He's My Girl 1987
Hey Arnold! The Movie 2003
Hexed 1993
Hibiscus Town 1988
Hidalgo 2005
Hidden. *See* Cache.
Hidden, The 1987
Hidden Agenda 1990
Hidden Hawaii 1995
Hidden Figures 2017
Hide and Seek 2006
Hideaway 1995
Hideous Kinky 2000
Hiding Out 1987
Hifazaat. *See* In Custody.
High Art 1999
High Crimes 2003
High Fidelity 2001
High Heels 1991
High Heels and Low Lives 2002
High Hopes 1988, 1989
High Lonesome: The Story of Bluegrass Music 258
High-Rise 2017
High Risk 1995
High Road to China 1983
High School 2013
High School High 1996
High School Musical 3: Senior Year 2009
High Season 1988
High Spirits 1988
High Tension 2006
High Tide 1987
Higher Ground 2012
Higher Learning 1995
Highlander 1986
Highlander 2: The Quickening 1991
Highlander 3: The Final Dimension 1995
Highlander: Endgame 2001
Highway Patrolman 1995
Highway 61 1992
Highway to Hell 1992
Hijacking, A 2014
Hijacking Hollywood
Hijo se la Novia, El. *See* Son of the Bride.
Hi-Lo Country, The 2000
Hilary and Jackie 1999
Hills Have Eyes, The 2007
Hills Have Eyes II, The 2008
Himmel uber Berlin, Der. *See* Wings of Desire.
Histories d'amerique. *See* American Stories.
History Boys, The 2007
History Is Made at Night [1937] 1983
History of Violence, A 2006
Hit, The 1985
Hit and Run 2013
Hit and Runway 2002
Hit List 1989
Hit the Dutchman 1995
Hitch 2006
Hitchcock 2013
Hitchcock/Truffaut 2016

Hitcher, The 1986

Hitcher, The (Meyers) 2008

Hitchhiker's Guide to the Galaxy, The 2006

Hitman 2008

Hitman, The 1991

Hitman: Agent 47 2016

Hitman's Bodyguard, The 2018

Hive, The. *See* Call, The.

Hoax, The 2008

Hobbit: An Unexpected Journey, The 2013

Hobbit: The Battle of the Five Armies, The 2015

Hobbit: The Desolation of Smaug, The 2014

Hobo with a Shotgun 2012

Hocus Pocus 1993

Hodejegerne. *See* Headhunters.

Hoffa 1992

Holcroft Covenant, The 1985

Hold Back the Dawn [1941] 1986

Hold Me, Thrill Me, Kiss Me 1993

Holes 2004

Holiday [1938] 1985

Holiday, The 2007

Holiday Inn [1942] 1981

Hollars, The 2017

Hollow Man 2001

Hollow Reed 1997

Hollywood Ending 2003

Hollywood Homicide 2004

Hollywood in Trouble 1986

Hollywood Mavericks 1990

Hollywood Shuffle 1987

Hollywood Vice Squad 1986

Hollywoodland 2007

Hologram For the King, A 2017

Holy Blood. *See* Santa Sangre.

Holy Innocents, The 1985

Holy Man 1999

Holy Motors 2013

Holy Rollers 2011

Holy Smoke 2000

Holy Tongue, The 2002

Hombre [1967] 1983

Home 2016

Home Again 2018

Home Alone 1990

Home Alone II: Lost in New York 1992

Home Alone III 1997

Home and the World, The 1985

Home at the End of the World, A 2005

Home for the Holidays 1995

Home Free All 1984

Home Fries 1999

Home Is Where the Heart Is 1987

Home of Our Own, A 1993

Home of the Brave 1986

Home on the Range 2005

Home Remedy 1987

Homeboy 1988

Homefront 2014

Homegrown 1999

Homer and Eddie 1990

Home Run 2014

Homesman, The 2015

Homeward Bound 1993

Homeward Bound II: Lost in San Francisco 1996

Homework 1982

Homework. *See* Art of Getting By, The.

Homicide 1991

Homme et une femme, Un. *See* Man and a Woman, A.

Hommes et des dieux, Des. *See* Of Gods and Men.

Hondo [1953] 1982

Honey 2004

Honey, I Blew Up the Kid 1992

Honey, I Shrunk the Kids 1989

Honeybunch 1988

Honeydripper 2008

Honeymoon Academy 1990

Honeymoon in Vegas 1992

Honeymooners, The 2006

Hong Gaoliang. *See* Red Sorghum.

Honky Tonk Freeway 1981

Honkytonk Man 1982

Honneponnetge. *See* Honeybunch.

Honor Betrayed. *See* Fear.

Honorable Mr. Wong, The. *See* Hatchet Man, The.

Honour of the House 2001

Hoodlum 1997

Hoodwinked 2007

Hoodwinked Too! Hood vs. Evil 2012

Hook 1991

Hoop Dreams 1995

Hoosiers 1986

Hoot 2007

Hop 2012

Hope and Glory 1987

Hope and Pain 1988

Hope Floats 1999

Hope Springs 2013

Horns 2015

Horrible Bosses 2012

Horrible Bosses 2 2015

Horror Show, The 1989

Hors de prix. *See* Priceless.

Hors la Vie 1995

Horse of Pride, The 1985

Horse Whisperer, The 1999

Horseman on the Roof, The 1996

Horton Hears a Who! *See* Dr. Seuss' Horton Hears a Who!

Host, The 2008

Host, The 2014

Hostage 2006

Hostel 2007

Hostel: Part II 2008

Hostiles 2018

Hot Chick, The 2003

Hot Dog...The Movie 1984

Hot Fuzz 2008

Hot Pursuit 1987

Hot Pursuit 2016

Hot Rod 2008

Hot Shots! 1991

Hot Shots! Part Deux 1993

Hot Spot, The 1990

Hot to Trot 1988

Hot Tub Time Machine 2011

Hot Tub Time Machine 2 2016
Hotel Colonial 1987
Hotel De Love 1997
Hotel for Dogs 2010
Hotel New Hampshire, The 1984
Hotel Rwanda 2005
Hotel Terminus 1988
Hotel Transylvania 2013
Hotel Transylvania 2 2016
Hotshot 1987
Hottest State, The 2008
Hound of the Baskervilles, The 1981
Hours, The 2003
Hours and Times, The 1992
House 1986
House, The 2018
House II 1987
House Arrest 1996
House at the End of the Street 2013
House Bunny, The 2009
House of Cards 1993
House of D 2006
House of Flying Daggers 2005
House of Fools 2004
House of Games 1987
House of Luk 2001
House of Mirth 2002
House of 1,000 Corpses 2004
House of Sand and Fog 2004
House of the Devil, The 2010
House of the Spirits, The 1995
House of Wax 2006
House of Yes, The 1997
House on Carroll Street, The 1988
House on Haunted Hill 2000
House on Limb, A. *See* Tottering Lives.
House on Sorority Row, The. *See* Sorority Row.
House Party 1990
House Party II 1991
House Party III 1995
House Where Evil Dwells, The 1982
Houseboat [1958] 1986
Houseguest 1995
Household Saints 1993
Householder, The 1984
Housekeeper, A 2004
Housekeeper, The 1987
Housekeeping 1987
Housesitter 1992
How Do You Know 2011
How I Got into College 1989
How I Killed My Father 2004
How I Live Now 2014
How She Move 2009
How Stella Got Her Groove Back 1999
How to Be a Latin Lover 2018
How to Be Single 2017
How to Deal 2004
How to Eat Fried Worms 2007
How to Get Ahead in Advertising 1989
How to Get the Man's Foot Outta Your Ass. *See* Baadassss!
How to Lose a Guy in 10 Days 2004
How to Lose Friends & Alienate People 2009
How to Make an American Quilt 1995
How to Make Love to a Negro Without Getting Tired 1990
How to Survive a Plague 2013
How to Train Your Dragon 2011
How to Train Your Dragon 2 2015
Howard the Duck 1986
Howard's End 1992
Howl 2011
Howling, The 1981
Howling III, The. *See* Marsupials, The.
Howl's Moving Castle 2006
Hsi Yen. *See* Wedding Banquet, The.
Hsimeng Jensheng. *See* Puppetmaster, The.
H2: Halloween 2. *See* Halloween II.
Hudson Hawk 1991
Hudsucker Proxy, The 1995
Hugh Hefner: Once Upon a Time 1992
Hugo 2012
Hugo Pool 1997
Huit Femmes. *See* 8 Women.
Hulk 2004
Human Centipede: First Sequence, The 2011
Human Centipede II (Full Sequence), The 2012
Human Nature 2003
Human Resources 2002
Human Shield, The 1992
Human Stain, The 2004
Humongous 1982
Humpday 2010
Hunchback of Notre Dame, The 1996
Hundred-Foot Journey, The 2015
Hungarian Fairy Tale, A 1989
Hunger, The 1983
Hunger Games, The 2013
Hunger Games: Catching Fire, The 2014
Hunger Games: Mockingjay—Part 1, The 2015
Hunger Games: Mockingjay—Part 2, The 2016
Hungry Feeling, A 1988
Hungry Hearts 2016
Hunk 1987
Hunt, The 2014
Hunt for Red October, The 1990
Hunt For the Wilderpeople 2017
Hunted, The 1995
Hunted, The 2004
Hunter, The 2013
Hunters of the Golden Cobra, The 1984
Hunting Ground, The 2016
Hunting Party, The 2008
Huntsman: Winter's War, The 2017
Huo Yuan Jia. *See* Jet Li's Fearless.
Hurt Locker, The 2010
Hurlyburly 1999
Hurricane, The 2000
Hurricane Streets 1999
Husbands and Wives 1992
Hush (Darby) 1999
Hush! (Hashiguchi) 2003

Hustle & Flow 2006
Hyde Park on Hudson 2013
Hyenas 1995
Hypnotic. *See* Close Your Eyes.
Hysteria 2013

I

I Am 2012
I Am David 2005
I Am Legend 2008
I Am Love 2011
I Am My Own Woman 1995
I Am Not Your Negro 2018
I Am Number Four 2012
I Am Sam 2002
I Can Do Bad All By Myself 2010
I Can't Sleep 1995
I Capture the Castle 2004
I Come in Peace 1990
I, Daniel Blake 2017
I Demoni. *See* Demons.
I Don't Buy Kisses Anymore 1992
I Don't Know How She Does It 2012
I Don't Want to Talk About It 1995
I Dreamed of Africa 2001
I, Frankenstein 2015
I Got the Hook-Up 1999
"I Hate Actors!" 1988
I Hate You, Dad. *See* That's My Boy.
I Heart Huckabees 2005
I Hope They Serve Beer in Hell 2010
I Know What You Did Last Summer 1997
I Know Where I'm Going [1945] 1982
I Know Who Killed Me 2008
I Like It Like That 1995
I Love Trouble 1995
I Love You 1982
I Love You, Beth Cooper 2010
I Love You, Don't Touch Me 1999
I Love You, I Love You Not 1997
I Love You, Man 2010
I Love You Phillip Morris 2011
I Love You to Death 1990
I, Madman 1989
I Married a Shadow 1983
I Now Pronounce You Chuck and Larry 2008
I Only Want You to Love Me 1995
I Origins 2015
I Ought to Be in Pictures 1982
I Remember Mama [1948] 1981
I, Robot 2005
I Saw the Devil 2012
I Saw the Light 2017
I Sent a Letter to My Love 1981
I Served the King of England 2009
I Shot Andy Warhol 1996
I Smile Back 2016
I Spit on Your Grave 2011
I Spy 2003
I Stand Alone 2000
I Still Know What You Did Last Summer 1999
I, the Jury 1982
I Think I Do 2000
I Think I Love My Wife 2008
I, Tonya 2018
I Want to Go Home 1989
I Want Someone to Eat Cheese With 2008
I Was a Teenage Zombie 1987
I Went Down 1999
I Wish 2013
I Woke Up Early the Day I Died 2000
Ice Age 2003
Ice Age: Collision Course 2017
Ice Age: Continental Drift 2013
Ice Age: Dawn of the Dinosaurs 2010
Ice Age: The Meltdown 2007
Ice Harvest, The 2006
Ice House 1989
Ice Pirates, The 1984
Ice Princess 2006
Ice Rink, The 2001
Ice Runner, The 1993
Ice Storm, The 1997
Iceman 1984
Iceman, The 2014
Icicle Thief, The 1990
Ida 2015
Ideal Husband, An 2000
Identical, The 2015
Identity 2004
Identity Crisis 1989
Identity Thief 2014
Ides of March, The 2012
Idiocracy 2007
Idiots, The [1999] 2001
Idle Hands 2000
Idlewild 2007
Iedereen Beroemd! *See* Everybody's Famous!
If I Stay 2015
If Looks Could Kill 1991
If Lucy Fell 1996
If You Could See What I Hear 1982
Igby Goes Down 2003
Ignorant Fairies 2002
Igor 2009
Iklimler. *See* Climates.
Il y a longtemps que je t'aime. *See* I've Loved You So Long.
Ill Testimone dello Sposo. *See* Best Man, The.
I'll Be Home for Christmas 1999
I'll Do Anything 1995
I'll See You in My Dreams 2016
I'll Sleep When I'm Dead 2005
Illtown 1999
Illuminata 2000
Illusionist, The 2007
Illusionist, The 2011
Illustrious Energy 1988
Ils se Marient et Eurent Beaucoup D'Enfants. *See* Happily Ever After.
I'm Dancing as Fast as I Can 1982
I'm Going Home 2003
I'm No Angel [1933] 1984
I'm Not There 2008
I'm Not Rappaport 1997
I'm So Excited 2014
I'm Still Here 2011
I'm the One That I Want 2001
Imagemaker, The 1986

Imaginarium of Doctor Parnassus, The 2010
Imaginary Crimes 1995
Imaginary Heroes 2006
Imagine 1988
Imagine Me & You 2007
Imagine That 2010
Imitation Game, The 2015
Immediate Family 1989
Immigrant, The 2015
Immortal Beloved 1995
Immortals 2012
Imperative 1985
Importance of Being Earnest, The 1995
Importance of Being Earnest, The (Parker) 2003
Imported Bridegroom, The 1991
Impossible, The 2013
Imposter, The 2013
Impostor 2003
Impostors 1999
Impromptu 1991
Impulse (Baker) 1984
Impulse (Locke) 1990
In a Better World 2012
In a Shallow Grave 1988
In a Valley of Violence 2017
In a World... 2014
In America 2004
In and Out 1997
In Bloom. *See* Life Before Her Eyes, The.
In Bruges 2009
In Country 1989
In Crowd, The 2001
In Custody 1995
In Dangerous Company 1988
In Darkness 2013
In Dreams 2000
In Fashion. *See* A la Mode.
In God's Hands 1999
In Good Company 2006
In Her Shoes 2006
In-Laws, The 2004
In Love and War 1997
In My Country 2006
In Our Hands 1983
In Praise of Love 2003
In Secret 2015
In the Army Now 1995
In the Bedroom 2002
In the Company of Men 1997
In the Cut 2004
In the Fade 2018
In the Heat of Passion 1992
In the Heat of the Night [1967] 1992
In the Heart of the Sea 2016
In the Land of Blood and Honey 2012
In the Land of the Deaf 1995
In the Land of Women 2008
In the Line of Fire 1993
In the Loop 2010
In the Mirror of Maya Deren 2004
In the Mood 1987
In the Mood for Love 2002
In the Mouth of Madness 1995
In the Name of the Father 1993
In the Name of the King: A Dungeon Seige Tale 2009
In the Realms of the Unreal 2006
In the Shadow of Kilimanjaro 1986
In the Shadow of the Moon 2008
In the Shadow of the Stars 1992
In the Soup 1992
In the Spirit 1990
In the Valley of Elah 2008
In This World 2004
In Time 2012
In Too Deep 2000
In Weiter Ferne, So Nah! *See* Faraway, So Close.
Incendies 2012
Inception 2011
Inchon 1982
Incident at Oglala 1992
Incident at Raven's Gate 1988
Incognito 1999
Inconvenient Sequel: Truth to Power, An 2018
Inconvenient Truth, An 2007
Incredible Burt Wonderstone, The 2014
Incredible Hulk, The 2009
Incredible Journey, The. *See* Homeward Bound.
Incredibles, The 2005
Incredibly True Adventures of Two Girls in Love, The 1995
Incubus, The 1982
Indecent Proposal 1993
Independence Day 1996
Independence Day: Resurgence 2017
Indian in the Cupboard, The 1995
Indian Runner, The 1991
Indian Summer 1993
Indiana Jones and the Kingdom of the Crystal Skull 2009
Indiana Jones and the Last Crusade 1989
Indiana Jones and the Temple of Doom 1984
Indigènes. *See* Days of Glory.
Indignation 2017
Indochine 1992
Inevitable Grace 1995
Infamous 2007
Infernal Affairs 2005
Inferno 2017
Infiltrator, The 2017
Infinitely Polar Bear 2016
Infinity 1991
Infinity (Broderick) 1996
Informer, The [1935] 1986
Informant!, The 2010
Informers, The 2010
Inglourious Basterds 2010
Ingrid Goes West 2018
Inherent Vice 2015
Inkheart 2010
Inkwell, The 1995
Inland Empire 2007
Inland Sea, The 1995
Inner Circle, The 1991
Innerspace 1987
Innkeepers, The 2013

Innocent, The 1988
Innocent, The 1995
Innocent Blood 1992
Innocent Man, An 1989
Innocent Sleep, The 1997
Innocents, The 2017
Innocents Abroad 1992
Inside I'm Dancing. *See* Rory O'Shea Was Here.
Inside Job 2011
Inside Llewyn Davis 2014
Inside Man 2007
Inside Monkey Zetterland 1993
Inside Out 2016
Insider, The 2000
Insidious 2012
Insidious: Chapter 2 2014
Insidious: Chapter 3 2016
Insignificance 1985
Insomnia (Skjoldbjaerg) 1999
Insomnia (Nolan) 2003
Inspector Gadget 2000
Instant Karma 1990
Instinct 2000
Insurgent 2016
Intacto 2004
Intermission 2005
Intern, The 2016
Internal Affairs 1990
International, The 2010
Internship, The 2014
Interpreter, The 2006
Interrogation, The 1990
Interrupters, The 2012
Intersection 1995
Interstellar 2015
Interview 2008
Interview, The 2015
Interview with the Vampire 1995
Intervista 1993
Intimacy 2002
Intimate Relations 1997
Intimate Strangers 2005
Into the Abyss 2012
Into the Blue 2006
Into the Night 1985
Into the Storm 2015
Into the Sun 1992
Into the West 1993
Into the Wild 2008
Into the Woods 2015
Intolerable Cruelty 2004
Intouchables, The 2013
Intruders 2013
Invaders from Mars 1986
Invasion! *See* Top of the Food Chain.
Invasion, The 2008
Invasion of the Body Snatchers [1956] 1982
Invasion U.S.A. 1985
Inventing the Abbotts 1997
Invention of Love 2001
Invention of Lying, The 2010
Invictus 2010
Invincible 2003
Invincible 2007
Invisible, The 2008
Invisible Circus 2002
Invisible Kid, The 1988
Invisible War, The 2013
Invitation, The 2017
Invitation au voyage 1983
Invitation to the Dance [1956] 1985
Io e Te. *See* Me and You.
Ip Man 3 2017
I.Q. 1995
Iris 2002
Iris 2016
Irma la Douce [1963] 1986
Irma Vep 1997
Iron Eagle 1986
Iron Eagle II 1988
Iron Giant, The 2000
Iron Lady, The 2012
Iron Man 2009
Iron Man 3 2014
Iron Man 2 2011
Iron Maze 1991
Iron Triangle, The 1989
Iron Will 1995
Ironweed 1987
Irrational Man 2016
Irreconcilable Differences 1984
Irreversible 2004
Is Anybody There? 2010
Ishtar 1987
Island, The 2006
Island of Dr. Moreau, The 1996
Ismach Hatani. *See* Women's Balcony, The.
Isn't She Great 2001
Istoriya As-Klyachimol. *See* Asya's Happiness.
It 2018
It Comes at Night 2018
It Could Happen to You 1995
It Couldn't Happen Here 1988
It Follows 2016
It Had to Be You 1989
It Happened One Night [1934] 1982
It Happened Tomorrow [1944] 1983
It Might Get Loud 2010
It Runs in the Family 2004
It Takes Two 1988
It Takes Two 1995
Italian for Beginners 2002
Italian Job, The 2004
Italiensk for Begyndere. *See* Italian for Beginners.
It's a Wonderful Life [1946] 1982
It's Alive III 1987
It's All About Love 2005
It's All Gone Pete Tong 2006
It's All True 1993
It's Complicated 2010
It's Kind of a Funny Story 2011
It's My Party 1996
It's Pat 1995
It's the Rage 2001
Ivan and Abraham 1995
I've Heard the Mermaids Singing 1987
I've Loved You So Long 2009

J

J. Edgar 2012

Jack 1996
Jack and His Friends 1993
Jack and Jill 2012
Jack and Sarah 1996
Jack Frost 1999
Jack Goes Boating 2011
Jack Reacher 2013
Jack Reacher: Never Go Back 2017
Jack Ryan: Shadow Recruit 2015
Jack the Bear 1993
Jack the Giant Slayer 2014
Jackal, The 1997
Jackass Number Two 2007
Jackass Presents: Bad Grandpa 2014
Jackass 3D 2011
Jacket, The 2006
Jackie 2017
Jackie Brown 1997
Jackie Chan's First Strike 1997
Jacknife 1989
Jackpot 2002
Jack's Back 1988
Jacob 1988
Jacob's Ladder 1990
Jacquot of Nantes 1993
Jade 1995
Jafar Panahi's Taxi 2016
Jagged Edge 1985
Jagten. *See* Hunt, The.
J'ai epouse une ombre. *See* I Married a Shadow.
Jailhouse Rock [1957] 1986
Jake Speed 1986
Jakob the Liar 2000
James and the Giant Peach 1996
James Cameron's Sanctum. *See* Sanctum.
James' Journey to Jerusalem 2005
James Joyce's Women 1985
James White 2016
Jamon, Jamon 1993
Jane 2018
Jane Austen Book Club, The 2008
Jane Eyre 1996
Jane Eyre 2012
Jane Got a Gun 2017
January Man, The 1989
Japanese Story 2005
Jarhead 2006
Jason Bourne 2017
Jason Goes to Hell 1993
Jason X 2003
Jason's Lyric 1995
Jawbreaker 2000
Jaws: The Revenge 1987
Jaws 3-D 1983
Jay and Silent Bob Strike Back 2002
Jazzman 1984
Je Rentre a la Maison. *See* I'm Going Home.
Je tu il elle [1974] 1985
Je vous salue, Marie. *See* Hail Mary.
Jean de Florette 1987
Jeanne Dielman, 23 Quai du Commerce, 1080 Bruxelles [1976] 1981
Jeepers Creepers 2002
Jeepers Creepers 2 2004
Jeff, Who Lives at Home 2013
Jefferson in Paris 1995
Jeffrey 1995
Jekyll and Hyde...Together Again 1982
Jem and the Holograms 2016
Jennifer Eight 1992
Jennifer's Body 2010
Jerky Boys 1995
Jerome 2001
Jerry Maguire 1996
Jersey Boys 2015
Jersey Girl 2005
Jerusalem 1996
Jessabelle 2015
Jesus of Montreal 1989
Jesus' Son 2000
Jet Lag 2004
Jet Li's Fearless 2007
Jetsons 1990
Jeune et Jolie. *See* Young and Beautiful.
Jewel of the Nile, The 1985
JFK 1991
Jigsaw 2018
Jigsaw Man, The 1984
Jim and Piraterna Blom. *See* Jim and the Pirates.
Jim and the Pirates 1987
Jiminy Glick in Lalawood 2006
Jimmy Hollywood 1995
Jimmy Neutron: Boy Genius 2002
Jimmy the Kid 1983
Jindabyne 2008
Jingle All the Way 1996
Jinxed 1982
Jiro Dreams of Sushi 2013
Jit 1995
Jo-Jo at the Gate of Lions 1995
Jo Jo Dancer, Your Life Is Calling 1986
Joan the Mad. *See* Mad Love.
Joan Rivers: A Piece of Work 2011
Jobs 2014
Jocks 1987
Jodaelye Nader az Simin. *See* Separation, A.
Jodorowsky's Dune 2015
Joe 2015
Joe Dirt 2002
Joe Gould's Secret 2001
Joe Somebody 2002
Joe the King 2000
Joe Versus the Volcano 1990
Joe's Apartment 1996
Joey 1985
Joey Takes a Cab 1991
John and the Missus 1987
John Carpenter's Ghosts of Mars 2002
John Carpenter's The Ward. *See* Ward, The.
John Carpenter's Vampires 1999
John Carter 2013
John Dies at the End 2014
John Grisham's the Rainmaker 1998
John Huston 1988
John Huston and the Dubliners 1987
John Q 2003
John Tucker Must Die 2007

John Wick: Chapter 2 2018
Johnny Be Good 1988
Johnny Dangerously 1984
Johnny English 2004
Johnny English Reborn 2012
Johnny Handsome 1989
Johnny Mnemonic 1995
Johnny Stecchino 1992
Johnny Suede 1992
johns 1997
Johnson Family Vacation 2005
Joke of Destiny, A 1984
Jonah Hex 2011
Jonas Brothers: The 3D Concert Experience 2010
Joneses, The 2011
Joseph Conrad's the Secret Agent 1996
Josh and S.A.M. 1993
Joshua 2008
Joshua Then and Now 1985
Josie and the Pussycats 2002
Journey into Fear [1943] 1985
Journey of August King 1995
Journey of Hope 1991
Journey of Love 1990
Journey of Natty Gann, The 1985
Journey to Spirit Island 1988
Journey to the Center of the Earth 2009
Journey 2: The Mysterious Island 2013
Joy 2016
Joy Luck Club, The 1993
Joy of Sex 1984
Joy Ride 2002
Joyeux Noel 2007
Joyful Noise 2013
Joysticks 1983
Ju Dou 1991
Juana la Loca. *See* Mad Love.
Judas Kiss 2000
Judas Project, The 1995
Jude 1996
Judge, The 2015
Judge Dredd 1995
Judgement in Berlin 1988
Judgement Night 1993
Judy Berlin 2001
Judy Moody and the Not Bummer Summer 2012
Juice 1992
Julia 2010
Julia Has Two Lovers 1991
Julian Po 1997
Julia's Eyes 2012
Julie & Julia 2010
Julien Donkey-Boy 2000
Julieta 2017
Jumanji 1995
Jumanji: Welcome to the Jungle 2018
Jument vapeur, La. *See* Dirty Dishes.
Jump Tomorrow 2002
Jumper 2009
Jumpin' at the Boneyard 1992
Jumpin' Jack Flash 1986
Jumpin' Night in the Garden of Eden, A 1988
Jumping the Broom 2012
Junebug 2006
Jungle Book 2017
Jungle Book, The 1995
Jungle Book 2, The 2004
Jungle Fever 1991
Jungle2Jungle 1997
Junior 1995
Juno 2008
Jupiter Ascending 2016
Jurassic Park 1993
Jurassic Park III 2002
Jurassic World 2016
Juror, The 1996
Jury Duty 1995
Jusan-nin no shikaku. *See* 13 Assassins.
Just a Kiss 2003
Just a Little Harmless Sex 2000
Just Another Girl on the I.R.T. 1993
Just Between Friends 1986
Just Cause 1995
Just Friends 2006
Just Getting Started 2018
Just Go with It 2012
Just Like a Woman 1995
Just Like Heaven 2006
Just Looking 2002
Just Married 2004
Just My Luck 2007
Just One of the Guys 1985
Just One Time 2002
Just the Ticket 2000
Just the Way You Are 1984
Just Visiting 2002
Just Wright 2011
Just Write 1999
Justice in the Coalfields 1996
Justice League 2018
Justin Bieber: Never Say Never 2012
Juwanna Mann 2003

K

K-9 1989
K-19: The Widowmaker 2003
K-PAX 2002
Kaboom 2012
Kadisbellan. *See* Slingshot, The.
Kadosh 2001
Kaena: The Prophecy 2005
Kafka 1991
Kahlil Gibran's The Prophet 2016
Kalifornia 1993
Kama Sutra: A Tale of Love 1997
Kamikaze Hearts 1995
Kamilla and the Thief 1988
Kandahar 2002
Kandyland 1988
Kangaroo 1987
Kangaroo Jack 2004
Kansas 1988
Kansas City 1996
Kapringen. *See* A Hijacking.
Karakter. *See* Character.
Karate Kid, The 1984
Karate Kid, The 2011
Karate Kid: Part II, The 1986
Karate Kid: Part III, The 1989

Kari-gurashi no Arietti. *See* Secret World of Arrietty, The.

Kate & Leopold 2002

Kate Plays Christine 2017

Katy Perry: Part of Me 2013

Kazaam 1996

Kaze tachinu. *See* Wind Rises, The.

Kazoku. *See* Where Spring Comes Late.

Keanu 2017

Kedi 2018

Keep, The 1983

Keep the River On Your Right: A Modern Cannibal Tale 2002

Keep the Lights On 2013

Keeping Mum 2007

Keeping Room, The 2016

Keeping the Faith 2001

Keeping Up with the Joneses 2017

Keeping Up with the Steins 2007

Kerouac, the Movie 1985

Kevin Hart: Let Me Explain 2014

Kevin Hart: What Now? 2017

Key Exchange 1985

Keys of the Kingdom, The [1944] 1989

Keys to Tulsa 1997

Khuda Gawah. *See* God Is My Witness.

Kick-Ass 2011

Kick-Ass 2 2014

Kickboxer 1989

Kickboxer II 1991

Kicked in the Head 1997

Kickin' It Old Skool 2008

Kicking and Screaming (Baumbach) 1995

Kicking & Screaming 2006

Kid, The. *See* Vie en Rose, La.

Kid & I, The 2006

Kid Brother, The 1987

Kid Colter 1985

Kid in King Arthur's Court, A 1995

Kid Stays in the Picture, The 2003

Kid with a Bike, The 2013

Kidnapped 1987

Kids 1995

Kids Are All Right, The 2011

Kids in the Hall: Brain Candy, The 1996

Kids in America. *See* Take Me Home Tonight.

Kika 1995

Kikujiro 2001

Kill Bill: Vol. 1 2004

Kill Bill: Vol. 2 2005

Kill List 2013

Kill Me Again 1989

Kill Me Later 2002

Kill the Irishman 2012

Kill the Messenger 2015

Kill Your Darlings 2014

Kill-Off, The 1990

Killer Elite 2012

Killer Image 1992

Killer Inside Me, The 2011

Killer Instinct 1995

Killer Joe 2013

Killer Klowns from Outer Space 1988

Killer of Sheep 2008

Killer Party 1986

Killers 2011

Killing Affair, A 1988

Klling Fields, The 1984

Killing Floor, The 1995

Killing of a Chinese Bookie, The [1976] 1986

Killing of a Sacred Deer, The 2018

Killing of John Lennon, The 2009

Killing Them Softly 2013

Killing Time 1999

Killing Time, The, 1987

Killing Zoe 1995

Killpoint 1984

Killshot 2010

Kimi no na wa. *See* Your Name.

Kindergarten Cop 1990

Kindred, The 1987

King, The 2007

King Arthur 2005

King Arthur: Legend of the Sword 2018

King and I, The 2000

King David 1985

King Is Alive, The 2002

King Is Dancing, The 2002

King James Version 1988

King Kong [1933] 1981

King Kong 2006

King Kong Lives 1986

King Lear 1987

King of Comedy, The 1983

King of Jazz [1930] 1985

King of Kong: A Fistful of Quarters, The 2008

King of Masks, The 2000

King of New York 1990

King of the Children 1988

King of the Hill 1993

King Ralph 1991

King Solomon's Mines 1985

Kingdom, Part 2, The 1999

Kingdom, The 1995

Kingdom, The 2008

Kingdom Come 2002

Kingdom of Heaven 2006

Kingpin 1996

Kings and Queen 2006

Kings of Summer, The 2014

King's Ransom 2006

King's Speech, The 2011

Kingsman: The Golden Circle 2018

Kingsman: The Secret Service 2016

Kinjite 1989

Kinky Boots 2007

Kinsey 2005

Kipperbang 1984

Kippur 2001

Kirk Cameron's Saving Christmas. *See* Saving Christmas.

Kiss Before Dying, A 1991

Kiss Daddy Good Night 1987

Kiss Kiss Bang Bang 2006

Kiss Me a Killer 1991

Kiss Me Goodbye 1982

Kiss Me, Guido 1997

Kiss Me, Stupid [1964] 1986

Kiss of Death 1995
Kiss of the Dragon 2002
Kiss of the Spider Woman 1985
Kiss or Kill 1997
Kiss, The 1988
Kiss the Girls 1997
Kissed 1997
Kisses 2011
Kissing a Fool 1999
Kissing Jessica Stein 2003
Kit Kittredge: An American Girl 2009
Kitchen Party 1999
Kitchen Stories 2005
Kitchen Toto, The 1987
Kite Runner, The 2008
Kitty and the Bagman 1983
Klynham Summer 1983
Knafayim Shvurot. *See* Broken Wings.
Knight of Cups 2017
Knight and Day 2011
Knight's Tale, A 2002
Knights of the City 1986
Knock Knock 2016
Knock Off 1999
Knockaround Guys 2003
Knocked Up 2008
Knowing 2010
Kokuriko-zaka kara. *See* From Up on Poppy Hill.
Kolya 1997
Kong: Skull Island 2018
Kongelig affaere, En. *See* Royal Affair, A.
Kon-Tiki 2014
Korczak 1991
Koyaanisqatsi 1983
Krampack. *See* Nico and Dani.
Krampus 2016
Krays, The 1990
Krieger und die Kaiserin, Der. *See* Princess and the Warrior, The.
Krippendorf's Tribe 1999
Krisha 2017
Krotki film o zabijaniu. *See* Thou Shalt Not Kill.
Krull 1983
Krush Groove 1985
K2 1992
Kubo and the Two Strings 2017
Kuffs 1992
Kull The Conqueror 1997
Kumiko the Treasure Hunter 2016
Kundun 1997
Kung Fu Hustle 2006
Kung Fu Panda 2009
Kung Fu Panda 2 2012
Kung Fu Panda 3 2017
Kuroi ame. *See* Black Rain.
Kurt and Courtney 1999
Kynodontas. *See* Dogtooth.

L

L. I.. E. 2002
L.627 1995
L.A. Confidential 1997
La La Land 2017
La Meglio Gioventu. *See* Best of Youth, The.
La Sorgente del fiume. *See* Weeping Meadow.
L.A. Story 1991
La Terre qui pleure. *See* Weeping Meadow.
Laavor et hakir. *See* Wedding Plan, The.
Laberinto del Fauno, El. *See* Pan's Labyrinth.
Labyrinth 1986
Labyrinth of Passion 1990
Ladder 49 2005
Ladies Club, The 1986
Ladies' Man, The 2001
Labor Day 2015
Ladri di saponette. *See* Icicle Thief, The.
Ladro Di Bambini, Il 1993
Lady, The 2013
Lady and the Duke, The 2003
Lady Beware 1987
Lady Bird 2018
Lady Chatterley 2008
Lady Eve, The [1941] 1987
Lady in the Van, The 2016
Lady in the Water 2007
Lady in White 1988
Lady Jane 1986
Lady Macbeth 2018
Lady Sings the Blues [1972] 1984
Ladybird, Ladybird 1995
Ladybugs 1992
Ladyhawke 1985
Ladykillers, The 2005
Lagaan: Once Upon a Time in India 2003
Laggies 2015
Lair of the White Worm, The 1988
Laissez-Passer. *See* Safe Conduct.
Lake House, The 2007
Lake Placid 2000
Lakeview Terrace 2009
Lambada 1990
L'america 1996
Lan Yu 2003
Land and Freedom 1995
Land Before Time, The 1988
Land Girls, The 1999
Land Ho! 2015
Land of Faraway 1988
Land of the Dead. *See* George A. Romero's Land of the Dead.
Land of the Lost 2010
Landline 2018
Landlord Blues 1988
Landscape in the Mist 1989
L'Anglaise et le Duc. *See* Lady and the Duke, The.
Lantana 2002
Lara Croft: Tomb Raider 2002
Lara Croft Tomb Raider: The Cradle of Life 2004
Larger Than Life 1996
Larry Crowne 2012
Larry the Cable Guy: Health Inspector 2007
Lars and the Real Girl 2008
Laserman, The 1988, 1990
Lassie 1995
Lassie 2007

Lassie Come Home [1943] 1993
Lassiter 1984
Last Act, The 1992
Last Action Hero 1993
Last Airbender, The 2011
Last American Virgin, The 1982
Last Boy Scout, The 1991
Last Call at Maud's 1993
Last Castle, The 2002
Last Chance Harvey 2010
Last Cigarette, The 2000
Last Dance, The 1996
Last Day of Winter, The 1987
Last Days 2006
Last Days in the Desert 2017
Last Days in Vietnam 2015
Last Days of Disco, The 1999
Last Emperor, The 1987
Last Exit to Brooklyn 1990
Last Exorcism, The 2011
Last Exorcism Part II, The 2014
Last Five Years, The 2016
Last Flag Flying 2018
Last Holiday 2007
Last House on the Left, The 2010
Last Hunter, The 1984
Last King of Scotland, The 2007
Last Kiss, The 2003
Last Kiss, The 2007
Last Legion, The 2008
Last Man Standing 1996
Last Mimzy, The 2008
Last Night 1999
Last of England, The 1988
Last of the Dogmen 1995
Last of the Finest, The 1990
Last of the Mohicans, The 1992
Last Orders 2003
Last Party, The 1993
Last Resort 1986
Last Resort 2002
Last Rites 1988
Last Samurai, The 2004
Last Seduction, The 1995
Last September, The 2001
Last Shot, The 2005
Last Song, The 2011
Last Stand, The 2014
Last Starfighter, The 1984
Last Station, The 2010
Last Straw, The 1987
Last Supper 1996
Last Temptation of Christ, The 1988
Last Time I Committed Suicide, The 1997
Last Time I Saw Paris, The [1954] 1993
Last Summer in the Hamptons 1995
Last Vegas 2014
Last Wedding 2003
Last Witch Hunter, The 2016
Last Word, The 2018
Lat den rätte komma in. *See* Let the Right One In.
Latcho Drom 1995
Late August, Early September 2000
Late Chrysanthemums [1954] 1985
Late for Dinner 1991
Late Marriage 2003
Late Quartet, A 2013
Late Summer Blues 1987
Latin Boys Go to Hell 1997
Latter Days 2005
L'Auberge Espagnole 2004
Laurel Canyon 2004
Law Abiding Citizen 2010
Law of Desire, The 1987
Law of Enclosures, The 2002
Lawn Dogs 1999
Lawless 2013
Lawless Heart 2004
Lawnmower Man, The 1992
Lawnmower Man 2: Beyond Cyberspace 1996
Lawrence of Arabia [1962] 1990
Laws of Attraction 2005
Laws of Gravity 1992
Layer Cake 2006
Lazarus Effect, The 2016
Lazer Team 2017
LBJ 2018
Le Week-End 2015
L' Ecole de la chair. *See* School of Flesh, The.
Leading Man, The 1999
League of Extraordinary Gentlemen, The 2004
League of Their Own, A 1992
Lean on Me 1989
Leap! 2018
Leap of Faith 1992
Leap Year 2011
Leatherface 1990
Leatherheads 2009
Leave It to Beaver 1997
Leave to Remain 1988
Leaves of Grass 2011
Leaving Las Vegas 1995
Leaving Normal 1992
Lebanon 2011
Lebedyne ozero. *See* Swan Lake.
Leben der Anderen, Das. *See* Lives of Others, The.
Lectrice, La. *See* Reader, The.
L'Ecume des Jours. *See* Mood Indigo.
Lee Daniels' The Butler 2014
Leela 2003
Left Behind 2015
Left Hand Side of the Fridge, The 2002
Legal Eagles 1986
Legally Blonde 2002
Legally Blonde 2: Red, White & Blonde 2004
Legend 1986
Legend 2016
Legend of Bagger Vance, The 2001
Legend of Billie Jean, The 1985
Legend of the Guardians: The Owls of Ga'Hoole 2011
Legend of Hercules, The 2015
Legend of 1900 2000
Legend of Rita, The 2002
Legend of Tarzan, The 2017
Legend of Wolf Mountain, The 1995
Legend of Zorro, The 2006
Legends 1995

Legends of the Fall 1995

Legends of Oz: Dorothy's Return 2015

Leggenda del Pianista Sull'oceano, La. *See* Legend of 1900.

Legion 2011

LEGO Batman Movie, The 2018

LEGO Movie, The 2015

LEGO Ninjago Movie, The 2018

Leisure Seeker, The 2018

Lemale et ha'halal. *See* Fill the Void.

Lemon 2018

Lemon Sisters, The 1990

Lemon Sky 1987

Lemony Snicket's A Series of Unfortunate Events 2005

Leo Tolstoy's Anna Karenina 1997

Leolo 1993

Leon the Pig Farmer 1995

Leonard Part VI 1987

Leopard Son, The 1996

Leprechaun 1993

Leprechaun II 1995

Les Miserables 2013

Les Patterson Saves the World 1987

Less Than Zero 1987

Let Him Have It 1991

Let It Come Down: The Life of Paul Bowles 2000

Let It Ride 1989

Let Me In 2011

Let the Right One In 2010

Let's Be Cops 2015

Let's Fall in Love. *See* New York in Short: The Shvitz and Let's Fall in Love.

Let's Get Lost 1988

Let's Make Friends. *See* I Love You, Man.

Let's Spend the Night Together 1983

Lethal Weapon 1987

Lethal Weapon 2 1989

Lethal Weapon 3 1992

Lethal Weapon 4 1999

Letter to Brezhnev 1986

Letters from Iwo Jima 2007

Letters to Juliet 2011

Leviathan 1989

Leviathan 2014

Leviathan 2015

Levity 2004

Levy and Goliath 1988

Ley del deseo, La. *See* Law of Desire, The.

L'heure d'été. *See* Summer Hours.

Liaison Pornographique, Une. *See* Affair of Love, An.

Liam 2002

Lianna 1983

Liar, Liar 1997

Liar's Moon 1982

Liberal Arts 2013

Libertine, The 2007

Liberty Heights 2000

Licence to Kill 1989

License to Drive 1988

License to Wed 2008

Lie Down With Dogs 1995

Liebestraum 1991

Lies 1986

Life 2000

Life 2016

Life 2018

Life, Above All 2012

Life After Beth 2015

Life After Love 2002

Life and Nothing But 1989

Life and Times of Allen Ginsberg, The 1995

Life and Times of Judge Roy Bean, The [1972] 1983

Life Aquatic with Steve Zissou, The 2005

Life as a House 2002

Life As We Know It 2011

Life Before Her Eyes, The 2009

Life Classes 1987

Life During Wartime 2011

Life in the Food Chain. *See* Age Isn't Everything.

Life in the Theater, A 1995

Life Is a Long Quiet River 1990

Life Is Beautiful 1999

Life Is Cheap 1989

Life Is Sweet 1991

Life Itself 2015

Life Less Ordinary, A 1997

Life Lessons. *See* New York Stories.

Life of Adele, The. *See* Blue is the Warmest Color.

Life of David Gale, The 2004

Life of Pi 2013

Life on a String 1992

Life on the Edge 1995

Life or Something Like It 2003

Life Stinks 1991

Life with Father [1947] 1993

Life with Mikey 1993

Life Without Zoe. *See* New York Stories.

Lifeforce 1985

Lift 2002

Light Ahead, The [1939] 1982

Light Between Oceans, The 2017

Light It Up 2000

Light Keeps Me Company 2001

Light of Day 1987

Light Sleeper 1992

Lighthorsemen, The 1987

Lightning in a Bottle 2005

Lightning Jack 1995

Lightship, The 1986

Lights Out 2017

Like Crazy 2012

Like Father Like Son 1987

Like Father, Like Son 2015

Like Mike 2003

Like Someone in Love 2014

Like Water for Chocolate 1993

Lili Marleen 1981

Lilies 1997

Lilies of the Field [1963] 1992

Lillian 1995

Lilo & Stitch 2003

Lily in Love 1985

Limbo 2000

Limey, The 2000

Limitless 2012

Limits of Control, The 2010
Lincoln 2013
Lincoln Lawyer, The 2012
L'inconnu du lac. *See* Stranger by the Lake.
Line One 1988
Lingua del Santo, La. *See* Holy Tongue, The.
Linguini Incident, The 1992
Linie Eins. *See* Line One.
Link 1986
L'instinct de mort. *See* Mesrine.
Lion 2017
Lion King, The 1995
Lionheart (Lettich) 1991
Lionheart (Shaffner) 1987
Lions for Lambs 2008
Liquid Dreams 1992
Liquid Sky 1983
Lisa 1990
Listen to Me 1989
Listen Up 1990
Listen Up Philip 2015
Little Big League 1995
Little Bit of Heaven, A 2013
Little Black Book 2005
Little Boy 2016
Little Buddha 1995
Little Children 2007
Little Devil, the 1988
Little Dorrit 1988
Little Drummer Girl, The 1984
Little Fockers 2011
Little Giants 1995
Little Hours, The 2018
Little Indian, Big City 1996
Little Jerk 1985
Little Man 2007
Little Man Tate 1991
Little Men 1999
Little Men 2017
Little Mermaid, The 1989
Little Miss Sunshine 2007
Little Monsters 1989
Little Nemo: Adventures in Slumberland 1992
Little Nicky 2001
Little Nikita 1988
Little Noises 1992
Little Odessa 1995
Little Prince, The 2017
Little Princess, A 1995
Little Rascals, The 1995
Little Secrets 1995
Little Secrets (Treu) 2003
Little Sex, A 1982
Little Shop of Horrors [1960] 1986
Little Stiff, A 1995
Little Sweetheart 1988
Little Thief, The 1989
Little Vampire, The 2001
Little Vegas 1990
Little Vera 1989
Little Voice 1999
Little Women [1933] 1982
Little Women 1995
Live By Night 2017
Live Die Repeat: Edge of Tomorrow. *See* Edge of Tomorrow.
Live Flesh 1999
Live Free or Die Hard 2008
Live Nude Girls 1995
Live Virgin 2001
Lives of Others, The 2008
Livin' Large 1991
Living Daylights, The 1987
Living End, The 1992
Living in Oblivion 1995
Living on Tokyo Time 1987
Living Out Loud 1999
Living Proof: HIV and the Pursuit of Happiness 1995
L'ivresse du pouvoir. *See* Comedy of Power.
Lizzie McGuire Movie, The 2004
Ljuset Haller Mig Sallskap. *See* Light Keeps Me Company.
Lo and Behold 2017
Lo sono l'amore. *See* I Am Love.
Loaded 1996
Lobster, The 2017
Local Hero 1983
Locke 2015
Lock, Stock, and Two Smoking Barrels 2000
Lock Up 1989
Lockout 2013
Locusts, The 1997
Lodz Ghetto 1989
Loft, The 2016
Logan 2018
Logan Lucky 2018
Lola 1982
Lola La Loca 1988
Lola Rennt. *See* Run, Lola, Run.
Lola Versus 2013
Lolita 1999
London Has Fallen 2017
London Kills Me 1992
Lone Ranger, The 2014
Lone Runner, The 1988
Lone Star 1996
Lone Survivor 2014
Lone Wolf McQuade 1983
Lonely Guy, The 1984
Lonely Hearts (Cox) 1983
Lonely Hearts (Lane) 1995
Lonely in America 1991
Lonely Lady, The 1983
Lonely Passion of Judith Hearne, The 1987
Lonesome Jim 2007
Long Day Closes, The 1993
Long Dimanche de Fiancailles, Un. *See* Very Long Engagement, A.
Long Good Friday, The 1982
Long Gray Line, The [1955] 1981
Long Kiss Goodnight, The 1996
Long Live the Lady! 1988
Long, Long Trailer, The [1954] 1986
Long Lost Friend, The. *See* Apprentice to Murder.
Long Strange Trip 2018
Long Walk Home, The 1990
Long Way Home, The 1999
Long Weekend, The 1990
Longest Ride, The 2016
Longest Yard, The 2006

Longshot, The 1986
Longshots, The 2009
Longtime Companion 1990
Look at Me 2006
Look of Silence, The 2016
Look Who's Talking 1989
Look Who's Talking Now 1993
Look Who's Talking Too 1990
Lookin' to Get Out 1982
Looking for Comedy in the Muslim World 2007
Looking for Richard 1996
Lookout, The 2008
Looney Tunes: Back in Action 2004
Loong Boonmee raluek chat. *See* Uncle Boonmee Who Can Recall His Past Lives.
Looper 2013
Loophole 1986
Loose Cannons 1990
Loose Connections 1988
Loose Screws 1986
L'ora di religione: Il sorriso di mia madre. *See* My Mother's Smile.
Lorax, The. *See* Dr. Seuss' The Lorax.
Lord of Illusions 1995
Lord of the Flies 1990
Lord of the Rings: The Fellowship of the Ring 2002
Lord of the Rings: The Return of the King 2004
Lord of the Rings: The Two Towers 2003
Lord of War 2006
Lords of Discipline, The 1983
Lords of Dogtown 2006
Lords of the Deep 1989
Lords of Salem, The 2014
Lore 2014
Lorenzo's Oil 1992
Loser 2001
Losers, The 2011
Losin' It 1983
Losing Isaiah 1995
Loss of a Teardrop Diamond, The 2010
Loss of Sexual Innocence 2000
Lost and Delirious 2002
Lost and Found 2000
Lost Angels 1989
Lost Boys, The 1987
Lost City, The 2007
Lost City of Z, The 2018
Lost Highway 1997
Lost in America 1985
Lost in La Mancha 2004
Lost in Paris 2018
Lost in Siberia 1991
Lost in Space 1999
Lost in Translation 2004
Lost in Yonkers. *See* Neil Simon's Lost in Yonkers.
Lost Moment, The [1947] 1982
Lost Prophet 1995
Lost River 2016
Lost Souls 2001
Lost Weekend, The [1945] 1986
Lost Words, The 1995
Lost World, The 1997
Lottery Ticket 2011
Lou, Pat, and Joe D 1988
Louder Than a Bomb 2012
Louder Than Bombs 2017
Louis Bluie 1985
Louis Prima: The Wildest 2001
Loulou 1981
Love Actually 2004
Love Affair 1995
Love After Love 1995
Love Always 1997
Love and a .45 1995
Love and Basketball 2001
Love and Death in Long Island 1999
Love & Friendship 2017
Love and Human Remains 1995
Love & Mercy 2016
Love and Murder 1991
Love and Other Catastrophes 1997
Love and Other Drugs 2011
Love & Sex 2001
Love at Large 1990
Love Child, The 1988
Love Child: A True Story 1982
Love Come Down 2002
Love Crimes 1992
Love Don't Cost a Thing 2004
Love Field 1992
Love Guru, The 2009
Love Happens 2010
Love in Germany, A 1984
Love in the Afternoon [1957] 1986
Love in the Time of Cholera 2008
Love in the Time of Money 2003
Love Is a Dog from Hell 1988
Love is All You Need 2014
Love Is Strange 2015
Love Is the Devil 1999
love jones 1997
Love/Juice 2001
Love Letter, The 2000
Love Letters 1984
Love Liza 2004
Love Potion #9 1992
Love Ranch 2011
Love Serenade 1997
Love Song for Bobby Long, A 2006
Love Songs 2009
Love Stinks 2000
Love Story, A. *See* Bound and Gagged.
Love Streams 1984
Love the Coopers 2016
Love the Hard Way 2004
Love, the Magician. *See* Amor brujo, El.
Love! Valour! Compassion! 1997
Love Walked In 1999
Love Without Pity 1991
Lovelace 2014
Loveless, The 1984, 1986
Lovelines 1984
Lovely & Amazing 2003
Lovely Bones, The 2010
Lover, The 1992
Loverboy 1989
Loverboy 2007
Lovers 1992

Lovers, The 2018
Lovers and the Despot, The 2017
Lovers of the Arctic Circle, The 2000
Lovers on the Bridge 2000
Love's a Bitch. *See* Amores Perros.
Love's Labour's Lost 2001
Loves of a Blonde [1965] 1985
Lovesick 1983
Loving 2017
Loving Jezebel 2001
Low Blow 1986
Low Down, The 2002
Low Down Dirty Shame, A 1995
Low Life, The 1996
Lowriders 2018
Lucas 1986
Lucia, Lucia 2004
Lucia y el Sexo. *See* Sex and Lucia.
Lucie Aubrac 2000
Luckiest Man in the World, The 1989
Lucky 2018
Lucky Break 2003
Lucky Number Slevin 2007
Lucky Numbers 2001
Lucky One, The 2013
Lucky Ones, The 2009
Lucky Them 2015
Lucky You 2008
Lucy 2015
Luftslottet som sprängdes. *See* Girl Who Kicked the Hornet's Nest, The.
L'Ultimo Bacio. *See* Last Kiss, The.
Luminous Motion 2001
Lumumba 2002
Lumumba: Death of a Prophet 1995
Luna Park 1995
Lunatic, The 1992
Lunatics: A Love Story 1992
Lunchbox, The 2015
Lune Froide. *See* Cold Moon.
Lunga vita alla signora! *See* Long Live the Lady!
Lurkers 1988
Lush Life 1995
Lust, Caution 2008
Lust for Life [1956] 1991
Lust in the Dust 1985
Luther 2004
Luzhin Defence, The 2002
Lymelife 2010

M

M. Butterfly 1993
Ma Femme Est une Actrice. *See* My Wife Is an Actress.
Ma vie de Courgette. *See* My Life as a Zucchini.
Ma Vie en Rose 1997
Mac 1993
Mac and Me 1988
Macaroni V 1988
MacArthur's Children 1985
Macbeth 2016
Maccheroni. *See* Macaroni.
MacGruber 2011
Machete 2011
Machete Kills 2014
Machine Gun Preacher 2012
Machinist, The 2005
Macht der Bilder, Die. *See* Wonderful, Horrible Life of Leni Riefenstahl, The.
Mack the Knife 1990
Macomber Affair, The [1947] 1982
Mad City 1997
Mad Dog and Glory 1993
Mad Dog Coll. *See* Killer Instinct.
Mad Dog Time 1996
Mad Love 1995
Mad Love 2003
Mad Max Beyond Thunderdome 1985
Mad Max: Fury Road 2016
Mad Money 2009
Madagascar 2006
Madagascar: Escape 2 Africa 2009
Madagascar Landing. *See* Aventure Malgache.
Madagascar Skin 1996
Madagascar 3: Europe's Most Wanted 2013
Madame Bovary 1991
Madame Sata 2004
Madame Sousatzka 1988
Made 2002
Made in America 1993
Made in Dagenham 2011
Made in Heaven 1987
Made of Honor 2009
Madea Christmas, A. *See* Tyler Perry's A Madea Christmas.
Madea Goes to Jail 2010
Madea's Family Reunion 2007
Madea's Witness Protection 2013
Madeline 1999
Madeo. *See* Mother.
Madhouse 1990
Madman 1983
Madness of King George, The 1995
Madness of Love. *See* Mad Love.
Maelstrom 2001
Mafia! 1999
Magdalene Sisters, The 2004
Maggie 2016
Maggie's Plan 2017
Magic Hunter 1996
Magic in the Moonlight 2015
Magic in the Water 1995
Magic Mike 2013
Magic Mike XXL 2016
Magic of Belle Isle, The 2013
Magic Trip: Ken Kesey's Search for a Kool Place 2012
Magnificent Seven, The 2017
Magnolia 2000
Magyar Stories 1988
Mahabharata, The 1990
Maid, The 2010
Maid in Manhattan 2003
Maid to Order 1987
Mail Order Wife 2006
Majestic, The 2002
Major and the Minor, The [1942] 1986
Major League 1989
Major League: Back to the Minors 1999

Major League II 1995
Major League III. *See* Major League: Back to the Minors.
Major Payne 1995
Make Way for Tomorrow [1937] 1981
Making Love (Hiller) 1982
Making Love (Tognazzi) 2002
Making Mr. Right 1987
Making the Grade 1984
Making Up! 1995
Makioka Sisters, The 1985
Mal d'aimer, Le. *See* Malady of Love, The.
Mala education, La. *See* Bad Education
Malady of Love, The 1987
Malcolm 1986
Malcolm X 1992
Maleficent 2015
Malena 2001
Malibu Bikini Shop, The 1987
Malibu's Most Wanted 2004
Malice 1993
Mallrats 1995
Malone 1987
Maltese Falcon, The [1941] 1983
Mama 2014
Mama, There's a Man in Your Bed 1990
Mamba 1988
Mambo Italiano 2004
Mambo Kings, The 1992
Mamma Mia! 2009
Mammoth 2010
Man, The 2006
Man and a Woman, A 1986
Man Apart, A 2004
Man Bites Dog 1993
Man Called Sarge, A 1990
Man cheng jin dai huang jin jia. *See* Curse of the Golden Flower.
Man from Elysian Fields, The 2003
Man from Snowy River, The 1982
Man from U.N.C.L.E., The 2016
Man Hunt [1941] 1984
Man I Love, The [1946] 1986
Man in Love, A 1987
Man in the Iron Mask, The 1999
Man in the Moon, The 1991
Man in Uniform, A 1995
Man Inside, The 1990
Man of Iron 1981
Man of Marble [1977] 1981
Man of No Importance, A 1995
Man of Steel 2014
Man of the Century 2000
Man of the House (Orr) 1995
Man of the House 2006
Man of the Year 1996
Man of the Year 2007
Man on a Ledge 2013
Man on Fire 2005
Man on the Moon 2000
Man on the Train, The 2004
Man Outside 1988
Män som hatar kvinnor. *See* Girl with the Dragon Tattoo, The.
Man Trouble 1992
Man Who Cried, The 2002
Man Who Fell to Earth, The [1975] 1982
Man Who Invented Christmas, The 2018
Man Who Knew Too Little, The 1997
Man Who Loved Women, The 1983
Man Who Wasn't There, The 1983
Man Who Wasn't There, The 2002
Man Who Would Be King, The [1975] 1983
Man with One Red Shoe, The 1985
Man with the Iron Fists, The 2013
Man with Three Coffins, The 1988
Man with Two Brains, The 1983
Man Without a Face, The 1993
Man Without a Past, The 2003
Man Without a World, The 1992
Man, Woman and Child 1983
Management 2010
Manchester by the Sea 2017
Manchurian Candidate, The 2005
Mandela: Long Walk to Freedom 2014
Manderlay 2007
Maneuvers 1988
Manglehorn 2016
Mangler, The 1995
Manhattan by Numbers 1995
Manhattan Murder Mystery 1993
Manhattan Project, The 1986
Manhunter 1986
Maniac 2014
Maniac Cop 1988
Manic 2004
Manifesto 1989
Manito 2004
Mannequin 1987
Mannequin Two 1991
Manny & Lo 1996
Manon des sources. *See* Manon of the Spring.
Manon of the Spring 1987
Man's Best Friend 1993
Mansfield Park 2000
Mao's Last Dancer 2011
Map of the Human Heart 1993
Mapantsula 1988
Maps to the Stars 2016
Mar Adentro. *See* Sea Inside, The.
Marc Pease Experience, The 2010
March of the Penguins 2006
Marci X 2004
Margaret 2012
Margaret's Museum 1997
Margarita Happy Hour 2003
Margin Call 2012
Margot at the Wedding 2008
Maria Full of Grace 2005
Maria's Lovers 1985
Mariachi, El 1993
Mariages 2003
Marie 1985
Marie Antoinette 2007
Marie Baie des Anges. *See* Marie from the Bay Angels.
Marie from the Bay Angels 1999
Marilyn Monroe 1987

Marine, The 2007

Marine Life 2001

Marius and Jeannette 1999

Marius et Jeannette: Un Conte de L'Estaque. *See* Marius and Jeannette.

Marjorie Prime 2018

Marked for Death 1990

Marlene 1986

Marley 2013

Marley & Me 2009

Marmaduke 2011

Marooned in Iraq 2004

Marquis 1995

Marriages. *See* Mariages.

Married Life 2009

Married to It 1993

Married to the Mob 1988

Marrying Man, The 1991

Mars Attacks! 1996

Mars Needs Moms 2012

Marshall 2018

Marsupials, The 1987

Martha and Ethel 1995

Martha and I 1995

Martha Marcy May Marlene 2012

Martha, Ruth, and Edie 1988

Martian, The 2016

Martian Child 2008

Martians Go Home 1990

Marusa No Onna. *See* Taxing Woman, A.

Marvel's The Avengers. *See* Avengers, The.

Marvin & Tige 1983

Marvin's Room 1996

Mary and Max 2010

Mary Reilly 1996

Mary Shelley's Frankenstein 1995

Masala 1993

Mask 1985

Mask, The 1995

Mask of the Phantasm. *See* Batman: Mask of the Phantasm.

Mask of Zorro, The 1999

Masked and Anonymous 2004

Masque of the Red Death 1989

Masquerade 1988

Mass Appeal 1985

Massa'ot James Be'eretz Hakodesh. *See* James' Journey to Jerusalem.

Master, The 2013

Master and Commander: The Far Side of the World 2004

Master of Disguise 2003

Master of the Crimson Armor. *See* Promise, The.

Masterminds 1997

Masterminds 2017

Masters of the Universe 1987

Matador, The 2007

Match Point 2006

Matchmaker, The 1997

Matchstick Men 2004

Material Girls 2007

Matewan 1987

Matilda 1996

Matinee 1993

Matrix, The 2000

Matrix Reloaded, The 2004

Matrix Revolutions, The 2004

Matter of Struggle, A 1985

Matter of Taste, A 2002

Maudie 2018

Maurice 1987

Maverick 1995

Max 2003

Max 2016

Max Dugan Returns 1983

Max Keeble's Big Move 2002

Max Payne 2009

Max Steel 2017

Maxie 1985

Maximum Overdrive 1986

Maximum Risk 1996

May Fools 1990

Maybe Baby 2002

Maybe...Maybe Not 1996

Maze Runner, The 2015

Maze Runner: The Scorch Trials 2016

McBain 1991

McFarland USA 2016

McHale's Navy 1997

Me and Earl and the Dying Girl 2016

Me and Isaac Newton 2001

Me and My Gal [1932] 1982

Me and Orson Welles 2010

Me and the Kid 1993

Me and Veronica 1995

Me and You 2015

Me and You and Everyone We Know 2006

Me Before You 2017

Me, Myself & Irene 2001

Me Myself I 2001

Me Without You 2003

Me You Them 2002

Mean Creek 2005

Mean Girls 2005

Mean Season, The 1985

Meatballs II 1984

Meatballs III 1987

Meatballs IV 1992

Mechanic, The 2012

Mechanic: Resurrection 2017

Medallion, The 2004

Meddler, The 2017

Medicine Man 1992

Mediterraneo 1992

Meek's Cutoff 2012

Meet Dave 2009

Meet Joe Black 1999

Meet John Doe [1941] 1982

Meet the Applegates 1991

Meet the Blacks 2017

Meet the Browns. *See* Tyler Perry's Meet the Browns.

Meet the Deedles 1999

Meet the Fockers 2005

Meet the Hollowheads 1989

Meet the Parents 2001

Meet the Robinsons 2008

Meet the Spartans 2009

Meet Wally Sparks 1997

Meeting Venus 1991

Megaforce 1982

Megamind 2011

Megan Leavey 2018
Mein Liebster Feind. *See* My Best Fiend.
Melancholia 2012
Melinda and Melinda 2006
Melvin and Howard 1981
Memento 2002
Memoirs of a Geisha 2006
Memoirs of a Madman 1995
Memoirs of a River 1992
Memoirs of an Invisible Man 1992
Memories of Me 1988
Memphis Belle 1990
Men 1986
Men 1999
Men at Work 1990
Men Don't Leave 1990
Men in Black 1997
Men in Black II 2003
Men in Black 3 2013
Men in Tights. *See* Robin Hood.
Men of Honor 2001
Men of Respect 1991
Men Who Stare at Goats, The 2010
Men with Brooms 2003
Men with Guns 1999
Men, Women & Children 2015
Menace II Society 1993
Ménage 1986
Menashe 2018
Men's Club, The 1986
Mephisto 1981
Mercenary Fighters 1988
Merchant of Venice, The 2006
Merci pour le Chocolat 2003
Mercury Rising 1999
Mermaid, The 2017
Mermaids 1990
Merry Christmas. *See* Joyeux Noel.
Merry Christmas, Mr. Lawrence 1983
Merry War, A 1999
Mesrine 2011
Mesrine: Killer Instinct. *See* Mesrine.
Mesrine: Public Enemy #1. *See* Mesrine.
Message in a Bottle 2000
Messenger, The 1987
Messenger, The 2010
Messenger: Joan of Arc, The 2000
Messenger of Death 1988
Messengers, The 2008
Metallica: Some Kind of Monster 2005
Metallica Through the Never 2014
Metalstorm: The Destruction of Jarred-Syn 1983
Metamorphosis: The Alien Factor 1995
Meteor Man, The 1993
Metro 1997
Metroland 2000
Metropolitan 1990
Mexican, The 2002
Meyerowitz Stories (New and Selected), The 2018
Mi Vida Loca 1995
Mia Eoniotita ke Mia Mers. *See* Eternity and a Day.
Miami Blues 1990
Miami Rhapsody 1995
Miami Vice 2007
Michael 1996
Michael Clayton 2008
Michael Collins 1996
Michael Jackson's This Is It 2010
Mickey Blue Eyes 2000
Micki & Maude 1984
Micmacs 2011
Microcosmos 1996
Midan, Al. *See* Square, The.
Middle Men 2011
Middle of Nowhere 2013
Middle School: The Worst Years of My Life 2017
Midnight (Leisen) 1986
Midnight (Vane) 1989
Midnight Clear, A 1992
Midnight Crossing 1988
Midnight in the Garden of Good and Evil 1997
Midnight in Paris 2012
Midnight Run 1988
Midnight Special 2017
Midsummer Night's Sex Comedy, A 1982
Midwife, The 2018
Midwinter's Tale, A 1996
Mies Vailla Menneisyytta. *See* Man Without a Past, The.
Mifune 2001
Mighty, The 1999
Mighty Aphrodite 1995
Mighty Ducks, The 1992
Mighty Heart, A 2008
Mighty Joe Young 1999
Mighty Macs, The 2012
Mighty Morphin Power Rangers: The Movie 1995
Mighty Quinn, The 1989
Mighty Wind, A 2004
Mike and Dave Need Wedding Dates 2017
Mike's Murder 1984
Mikey and Nicky 1984
Milagro Beanfield War, The 1988
Mildred Pierce [1945] 1986
Miles Ahead 2017
Miles from Home 1988
Milk 2009
Milk and Honey 1989
Milk & Honey 2006
Milk Money 1995
Millennium 1989
Millennium Mambo 2003
Miller's Crossing 1990
Million Dollar Arm 2015
Million Dollar Baby 2005
Million Dollar Hotel, The 2002
Million Dollar Mystery 1987
Million to Juan, A 1995
Million Ways to Die In the West, A 2015
Millions 2006
Mimic 1997
Mina Tannenbaum 1995
Mindhunters 2006
Mindwalk 1991
Minions 2016

Ministry of Vengeance 1989
Minner. *See* Men.
Minority Report 2003
Minotaur 1995
Minus Man, The 2000
Mio Viaggio in Italia. *See* My Voyage to Italy.
Miracle 2005
Miracle, The 1991
Miracle at St. Anna 2009
Miracle Mile 1988, 1989
Miracle on 34th Street 1995
Miracle Woman, The (1931) 1982
Miracles From Heaven 2017
Miral 2012
Mirror, The 2000
Mirror Has Two Faces, The 1996
Mirror Mirror 2013
Mirrors 2009
Misadventures of Mr. Wilt, The 1990
Mischief 1985
Miserables, The 1995
Miserables, The 1999
Misery 1990
Misfits, The [1961] 1983
Mishima 1985
Misma luna, La. *See* Under the Same Moon.
Misplaced 1995
Misplaced 1989
Miss Congeniality 2001
Miss Congeniality 2: Armed and Fabulous 2006
Miss Firecracker 1989
Miss March 2010
Miss Mary 1986
Miss Mona 1987
Miss...or Myth? 1987
Miss Peregrine's Home for Peculiar Children 2017
Miss Pettigrew Lives for a Day 2009
Miss Potter 2008
Miss Sloane 2017
Miss You Already 2016
Missing 1982, 1988
Missing, The 2004
Missing in Action, 1984
Missing in Action II 1985
Mission, The (Joffe) 1986
Mission, The (Sayyad) 1983
Mission: Impossible 1996
Mission: Impossible—Ghost Protocol 2012
Mission: Impossible Rogue Nation 2016
Mission: Impossible 2 2001
Mission: Impossible III 2007
Mission to Mars 2001
Missionary, The 1982
Mississippi Burning 1988
Mississippi Grind 2016
Mississippi Masala 1992
Mist, The 2008
Mr. and Mrs. Bridge 1990
Mr. & Mrs. Smith 2006
Mr. Baseball 1992
Mr. Bean's Holiday 2008
Mr. Brooks 2008
Mr. Death: The Rise and Fall of Fred A. Leuchter, Jr. 2000
Mr. Deeds 2003
Mr. Deeds Goes to Town [1936] 1982
Mr. Destiny 1990
Mr. Frost 1990
Mr. Holland's Opus 1995
Mr. Holmes 2016
Mr. Jealousy 1999
Mister Johnson 1991
Mr. Jones 1993
Mr. Love 1986
Mr. Magoo 1997
Mr. Magorium's Wonder Emporium 2008
Mr. Mom 1983
Mr. Nanny 1993
Mr. Nice Guy 1999
Mr. North 1988
Mr. Payback 1995
Mr. Peabody & Sherman 2015
Mr. Popper's Penguins 2012
Mr. Right 2017
Mister Roberts [1955] 1988
Mr. Saturday Night 1992
Mr. Smith Goes to Washington [1939] 1982
Mr. 3000 2005
Mr. Turner 2015
Mr. Wonderful 1993
Mr. Woodcock 2008
Mr. Write 1995
Mr. Wrong 1996
Mistress 1992
Mrs. Brown 1997
Mrs. Dalloway 1999
Mrs. Doubtfire 1993
Mrs. Henderson Presents 2006
Mrs. Palfrey at the Claremont 2007
Mrs. Parker and the Vicious Circle 1995
Mrs. Soffel 1984
Mrs. Winterbourne 1996
Mistress America 2016
Misunderstood 1984
Mit Liv som Hund. *See* My Life as a Dog.
Mitad del cielo, La. *See* Half of Heaven.
Mixed Blood 1985
Mixed Nuts 1995
Mo' Better Blues 1990
Mo' Money 1992
Moana 2017
Moartea domnului Lazarescu. *See* Death of Mr. Lazarescu, The.
Mobsters 1991
Mod Squad, The 2000
Modern Girls 1986
Modern Romance 1981
Moderns, The 1988
Mogan Do. *See* Infernal Affairs.
Mois d'avril sont meurtriers, Les. *See* April Is a Deadly Month.
Moitie Gauche du Frigo, La. *See* Left Hand Side of the Fridge, The.
Moll Flanders 1996
Molly 2000
Molly's Game 2018
Mom and Dad Save the World 1992

Môme, La. *See* Vie en Rose, La.
Mommie Dearest 1981
Moms' Night Out 2015
Mon bel Amour, Ma Dechirure. *See* My True Love, My Wound.
Mon meilleur ami. *See* My Best Friend.
Mona Lisa 1986
Mona Lisa Smile 2004
Mondays in the Sun 2004
Mondo New York 1988
Mondovino 2006
Money for Nothing 1993
Money Man 1995
Money Monster 2017
Money Pit, The 1986
Money Talks 1997
Money Train 1995
Money Tree, The 1992
Moneyball 2012
Mongol 2009
Mongolian Tale, A 1997
Monkey Kingdom 2016
Monkey Shines 1988
Monkey Trouble 1995
Monkeybone 2002
Monsieur Hire 1990
Monsieur Ibrahim 2004
Monsieur Lazhar 2013
Monsieur N 2006
Monsignor 1982
Monsoon Wedding 2003
Monster 2004
Monster, The 1996
Monster House 2007
Monster in a Box 1992
Monster Calls, A 2017
Monster-in-Law 2006
Monster in the Closet 1987
Monster Squad, The 1987
Monster Trucks 2018
Monsters 2011
Monster's Ball 2002
Monsters, Inc. 2002
Monsters University 2014
Monsters vs. Aliens 2010
Montana Run 1992
Monte Carlo 2012
Montenegro 1981
Month by the Lake, A 1995
Month in the Country, A 1987
Monty Python's The Meaning of Life 1983
Monument Ave. 1999
Monuments Men, The 2015
Mood Indigo 2015
Moolaade 2005
Moon 2010
Moon in the Gutter 1983
Moon Over Broadway 1999
Moon over Parador 1988
Moon Shadow [1995] 2001
Moonlight 2017
Moonlight and Valentino 1995
Moonlight Mile 2003
Moonlighting 1982
Moonrise Kingdom 2013
Moonstruck 1987
More Than A Game 2010
Morgan Stewart's Coming Home 1987
Moriarty. *See* Sherlock Holmes.
Morning After, The 1986
Morning Glory 1993
Morning Glory 2011
Morons from Outer Space 1985
Morris From America 2017
Mort de Mario Ricci, La. *See* Death of Mario Ricci, The.
Mortal Instruments: City of Bones, The 2014
Mortal Kombat 1995
Mortal Kombat II: Annihilation 1997
Mortal Thoughts 1991
Mortdecai 2016
Mortuary Academy 1988
Morvern Callar 2003
Mosca addio. *See* Moscow Farewell.
Moscow Farewell 1987
Moscow on the Hudson 1984
Mosquito Coast, The 1986
Most Dangerous Game, The [1932] 1985
Most Dangerous Man in America: Daniel Ellsberg and the Pentagon Papers, The 2011
Most Fertile Man in Ireland, The 2002
Most Violent Year, A 2015
Most Wanted 1997
Most Wanted Man, A 2015
Mostly Martha 2003
Mother 1996
Mother 2011
mother! 2018
Mother, The 2005
Mother and Child 2011
Mother Lode 1983
Mother Night 1996
Mother Teresa 1986
Motherhood 2010
Mothering Heart, The [1913] 1984
Mother's Boys 1995
Mother's Day 2017
Mothman Prophecies, The 2003
Motorama 1993
Motorcycle Diaries, The 2005
Moulin Rouge 2002
Mountain Between Us, The 2018
Mountain Gorillas 1995
Mountains May Depart 2017
Mountains of Moon 1990
Mountaintop Motel Massacre 1986
Mouse Hunt 1997
Mouth to Mouth 1997
Movers and Shakers 1985
Movie 43 2014
Moving 1988
Moving the Mountain 1995
Moving Violations 1985
MS One: Maximum Security. *See* Lockout.
Much Ado About Nothing 1993
Much Ado About Nothing 2014
Mud 2014
Mudbound 2018

Mugen no jünin. *See* Blade of the Immortal.
Mui du du Xanh. *See* Scent of Green Papaya, The.
Mujer Fantástica, Una. *See* Fantastic Woman, A.
Mujeres al borde de un ataque de nervios. *See* Women on the Verge of a Nervous Breakdown.
Mulan 1999
Mulholland Drive 2002
Mulholland Falls 1996
Multiplicity 1996
Mumford 2000
Mummy, The 2000
Mummy, The 2018
Mummy Returns, The 2002
Mummy: Tomb of the Dragon Emperor, The 2009
Munchie 1995
Munchies 1987
Munich 2006
Muppets, The 2012
Muppet Christmas Carol, The 1992
Muppets from Space 2000
Muppet Treasure Island 1996
Muppets Most Wanted 2015
Muppets Take Manhattan, The 1984
Mur, Le. *See* Wall, The.
Murder at 1600 1997
Murder by Numbers 2003
Murder in the First 1995
Murder on the Orient Express 2018
Murder One 1988
Murderball 2006
Murderous Maids 2003
Muriel's Wedding 1995
Murphy's Law 1986
Murphy's Romance 1985
Muscle Shoals 2014
Muse, The 2000
Muses Orphelines, Les. *See* Orphan Muses, The.
Museum Hours 2014
Music and Lyrics 2008
Music Box 1989
Music for the Movies: Bernard Herrmann 1995
Music From Another Room 1999
Music of Chance, The 1993
Music of the Heart 2000
Music Tells You, The 1995
Musime si Pomahat. *See* Divided We Fall.
Musketeer, The 2002
Must Love Dogs 2006
Mustang: The Hidden Kingdom 1995
Musuko. *See* My Sons.
Mutant on the Bounty 1989
Mute Witness 1995
Mutiny on the Bounty [1962] 1984
My African Adventure 1987
My All American 2016
My American Cousin 1986
My Apprenticeship. *See* Among People.
My Architect 2005
My Baby's Daddy 2005
My Beautiful Laundrette 1986
My Best Fiend 2000
My Best Friend 2008
My Best Friend Is a Vampire 1988
My Best Friend's Girl 1984
My Best Friend's Girl 2009
My Best Friend's Wedding 1997
My Big Fat Greek Wedding 2003
My Big Fat Greek Wedding 2 2017
My Blind Brother 2017
My Bloody Valentine 3D 2010
My Blue Heaven 1990
My Blueberry Nights 2009
My Boss's Daughter 2004
My Boyfriend's Back 1993
My Chauffeur 1986
My Cousin Rachel [1952] 1981
My Cousin Rachel 2018
My Cousin Vinny 1992
My Crazy Life. *See* Mi Vida Loca.
My Dark Lady 1987
My Demon Lover 1987
My Dinner with Andre 1981
My Entire High School Sinking Into the Sea 2018
My Family (Mi Familia) 1995
My Father Is Coming 1992
My Father, the Hero 1995
My Father's Angel 2002
My Father's Glory 1991
My Favorite Martian 2000
My Favorite Season 1996
My Favorite Year 1982
My Fellow Americans 1996
My First Mister 2002
My First Wife 1985
My Foolish Heart (1949) 1983
My Giant 1999
My Girl 1991
My Girl II 1995
My Golden Days 2017
My Heroes Have Always Been Cowboys 1991
My Idiot Brother. *See* Our Idiot Brother.
My Left Foot 1989
My Life 1993
My Life and Times with Antonin Artaud 1996
My Life as a Dog [1985] 1987
My Life as a Zucchini 2018
My Life in Pink. *See* Ma Vie en Rose.
My Life in Ruins 2010
My Life So Far 2000
My Life Without Me 2004
My Life's in Turnaround 1995
My Little Pony 1986
My Little Pony: The Movie 2018
My Mom's a Werewolf 1989
My Mother's Castle 1991
My Mother's Courage
My Mother's Smile 2006
My Name is Joe 2000
My Neighbor Totoro 1993
My New Gun 1992
My New Partner 1985
My Old Lady 2015
My One and Only 2010
My Other Husband 1985

My Own Private Idaho 1991
My Reputation [1946] 1984, 1986
My Science Project 1985
My Sister's Keeper 2010
My Son, My Son, What Have Ye Done 2011
My Son the Fanatic 2000
My Sons 1995
My Soul to Take 2011
My Stepmother Is an Alien 1988
My Summer of Love 2006
My Super Ex-Girlfriend 2007
My Sweet Little Village 1986
My True Love, My Wound 1987
My Tutor 1983
My Twentieth Century 1990
My Uncle's Legacy 1990
My Voyage to Italy 2003
My Week With Marilyn 2012
My Wife Is an Actress 2003
Mysterious Skin 2006
Mystery, Alaska 2000
Mystery Date 1991
Mystery of Alexina, The 1986
Mystery of Rampo 1995
Mystery of the Wax Museum [1933] 1986
Mystery Men 2000
Mystery Science Theater 3000: The Movie 1996
Mystery Train 1989
Mystic Masseur, The 2003
Mystic Pizza 1988
Mystic River 2004
Myth of Fingerprints, The 1998

N

Nacho Libre 2007
Nader and Simin, a Separation. *See* Separation, A.
Nadine 1987
Nadja 1995
Naked 1993
Naked Cage, The 1986
Naked Gun, The 1988
Naked Gun 2 1/2, The 1991
Naked Gun 33 1/3: The Final Insult 1995
Naked in New York 1995
Naked Lunch 1991
Name of the Rose, The 1986
Namesake, The 2008
Nana, La. *See* Maid, The.
Nancy Drew 2008
Nanny Diaries, The 2008
Nanny McPhee 2007
Nanny McPhee Returns 2011
Nanou 1988
Napoleon [1927] 1981
Napoleon 1997
Napoleon Dynamite 2005
Narc 2003
Narrow Margin 1990
Nasty Girl, The 1990
Nate and Hayes 1983
National Lampoon's Christmas Vacation 1989
National Lampoon's Class Reunion 1982
National Lampoon's European Vacation 1985
National Lampoon's Loaded Weapon I 1993
National Lampoon's Senior Trip 1995
National Lampoon's Vacation 1983
National Lampoon's Van Wilder 2003
National Security 2004
National Treasure 2005
National Treasure: Book of Secrets 2008
National Velvet [1944] 1993
Native Son 1986
Nativity Story, The 2007
Natural, The 1984
Natural Born Killers 1995
Navigator, The 1989
Navy SEALs 1990
Ne le dis à personne. *See* Tell No One.
Ne touchez pas la hache. *See* Duchess of Langeais, The.
Near Dark 1987
Nebo nashevo detstva. *See* Sky of Our Childhood, The.
Nebraska 2014
Necessary Roughness 1991
Ned Kelly 2005
Ned Rifle 2016
Need for Speed 2015
Needful Things 1993
Negotiator, The 1999
Neighborhood Watch. *See* Watch, The.
Neighbors 2015
Neighbors 2 2017
Neil Simon's Lost in Yonkers 1993
Neil Simon's The Odd Couple 2 1999
Neil Simon's The Slugger's Wife 1985
Neil Young: Heart of Gold 2007
Neil Young Journeys 2013
Nell 1995
Nell Gwyn [1934] 1983
Nelly & Mr. Arnaud 1996
Nemesis 1993
Nenette et Boni 1997
Neon Bible, The 1995
Neon Demon, The 2017
Neruda 2017
Nerve 2017
Nervous Ticks 1995
Nest, The. *See* Sisters.
Net, The 1995
Nettoyoge a Sec. *See* Dry Cleaning.
Never Again 2003
Never Back Down 2009
Never Been Kissed 2000
Never Cry Wolf 1983
Never Die Alone 2005
Never Let Me Go 2011
Never Say Never Again 1983
Never Talk to Strangers 1995
Never too Young to Die 1986
Neverending Story, The 1984
Neverending Story II, The 1991
New Adventures of Pippi Longstocking, The 1988

New Age, The 1995
New Babylon, The [1929] 1983
New Eve, The 2001
New Guy, The 2003
New In Town 2010
New Jack City 1991
New Jersey Drive 1995
New Kids, The 1985
New Life, A 1988
New Moon. *See* Twilight Saga: New Moon, The.
New Nightmare. *See* Wes Craven's New Nightmare.
New Rose Hotel 2000
New World, The 2006
New Year's Day 1989
New Year's Eve 2012
New York, I Love You 2010
New York in Short: The Shvitz and Let's Fall in Love 1995
New York Minute 2005
New York, New York [1977] 1983
New York Stories 1989
Newsies 1992
Newton Boys, The 1999
Next 2008
Next Best Thing, The 2001
Next Big Thing, The 2003
Next Day Air 2010
Next Friday 2001
Next Karate Kid, The 1995
Next of Kin 1989
Next Stop Greenwich Village [1976] 1984
Next Stop Wonderland 1999
Next Summer 1986
Next Three Days, The 2011
Next Year if All Goes Well 1983
Niagara Falls 1987
Niagara, Niagara 1999
Nice Girls Don't Explode 1987
Nice Guys, The 2017
Nicholas Nickleby 2003
Nick and Jane 1997
Nick & Norah's Infinite Playlist 2009
Nick of Time 1995
Nico and Dani 2002
Nico Icon 1996
Nie yin niang. *See* Assassin, The.
Niezwykla podroz Balthazara Kobera. *See* Tribulations of Balthasar Kober, The.
Night and Day 1995
Night and the City 1992
Night at the Museum 2007
Night at the Museum: Battle of the Smithsonian 2010
Night at the Museum: Secret of the Tomb 2015
Night at the Roxbury, A 1999
Night Before, The 2016
Night Catches Us 2011
Night Crossing 1982
Night Falls on Manhattan 1997
Night Friend 1988
Night Game 1989
Night in Heaven, A 1983
Night in the Life of Jimmy Reardon, A 1988
Night Listener, The 2007
'night, Mother 1986
Night Moves 2015
Night of the Comet 1984
Night of the Creeps 1986
Night of the Demons II 1995
Night of the Hunter, The [1955] 1982
Night of the Iguana, The [1964] 1983
Night of the Living Dead 1990
Night of the Pencils, The 1987
Night of the Shooting Stars, The 1983
Night on Earth 1992
Night Patrol 1985
Night Shift 1982
Night Song [1947] 1981
Night Visitor 1989
Night Watch 2007
Night We Never Met, The 1993
Nightbreed 1990
Nightcap. *See* Merci pour le Chocolat.
Nightcrawler 2015
Nightfall 1988
Nightflyers 1987
Nighthawks 1981
Nighthawks II. *See* Strip Jack Naked.
Nightmare at Shadow Woods 1987
Nightmare Before Christmas, The 1993
Nightmare on Elm Street, A 2011
Nightmare on Elm Street, A 1984
Nightmare on Elm Street: II, A 1985
Nightmare on Elm Street: III, A 1987
Nightmare on Elm Street: IV, A 1988
Nightmare on Elm Street: V, A 1989
Nightmare, The 2016
Nightmares III 1984
Nights in Rodanthe 2009
Nightsongs 1991
Nightstick 1987
Nightwatch 1999
Nil by Mouth 1999
Nim's Island 2009
9 2010
Nine 2010
9 1/2 Weeks 1986
9 Deaths of the Ninja 1985
Nine Lives 2017
Nine Months 1995
Nine Queens 2003
976-EVIL 1989
1918 1985
1969 1988
1990: The Bronx Warriors 1983
1991: The Year Punk Broke 1995
Ninety Days 1986
99 Homes 2016
Ninja Assassin 2010
Ninja Turf 1986
Ninotchka [1939] 1986
Ninth Gate, The 2001
9th Life of Louis Drax, The 2017
Nixon 1995
No 1999
No 2014
No Country for Old Men 2008

No End in Sight 2008
No Escape 1995
No Escape 2016
No Fear, No Die 1995
No Good Deed 2015
No Holds Barred 1989
No Looking Back 1999
No Man of Her Own [1949] 1986
No Man's Land 1987
No Man's Land 2002
No Mercy 1986
No News from God 2003
No Picnic 1987
No Reservations 2008
No Retreat, No Surrender 1986
No Retreat, No Surrender II 1989
No Secrets 1991
No Small Affair 1984
No Strings Attached 2012
No Such Thing 2003
No Way Out 1987, 1992
Noah 2015
Nobody Loves Me 1996
Nobody Walks 2013
Nobody's Fool (Benton) 1995
Nobody's Fool (Purcell) 1986
Nobody's Perfect 1990
Noce en Galilee. *See* Wedding in Galilee, A.
Noche de los lapices, La. *See* Night of the Pencils, The.
Nochnoi Dozor. *See* Night Watch.
Nocturama 2018
Nocturnal Animals 2017
Noel 2005
Noises Off 1992
Nomads 1986
Non ti muovere. *See* Don't Move.
Non-Stop 2015
Nora 2002
Norbit 2008
Nordwand. *See* North Face.
Norm of the North 2017
Normal Life 1996
Norman 2018
Norman: The Moderate Rise and Tragic Fall of a New York Fixer. *See* Norman.
Norte, El 1983
North 1995
North Country 2006
North Face 2011
North Shore 1987
North Star, The [1943] 1982
Northfork 2004
Nostalgia 1984
Nostradamus 1995
Not Another Teen Movie 2002
Not Easily Broken 2010
Not Fade Away 2013
Not for Publication 1984
Not of This Earth 1988
Not Quite Paradise 1986
Not Since Casanova 1988
Not Without My Daughter 1991
Notebook, The 2005
Notebook on Cities and Clothes 1992
Notes on a Scandal 2007
Nothing but Trouble 1991
Nothing in Common 1986
Nothing Personal 1997
Nothing to Lose 1997
Notorious 2010
Notorious Bettie Page, The 2007
Notte di San Lorenzo, La. *See* Night of the Shooting Stars, The.
Notting Hill 2000
Nouvelle Eve, The. *See* New Eve, The.
November 2006
November Man, The 2015
Novitiate 2018
Novocaine 2002
Now. *See* In Time.
Now and Then 1995
Now You See Me 2014
Now You See Me 2 2017
Nowhere 1997
Nowhere Boy 2011
Nowhere in Africa 2004
Nowhere to Hide 1987
Nowhere to Run 1993
Nowhereland. *See* Imagine That.
Nueve Reinas. *See* Nine Queens.
Nuit de Varennes, La [1982] 1983, 1984
Nuits Fauves, Les. *See* Savage Nights.
Nuits de la pleine lune, Les. *See* Full Moon In Paris.
Number One with a Bullet 1987
Number 23, The 2008
Nuns on the Run 1990
Nurse Betty 2001
Nut Job, The 2015
Nut Job 2: Nutty by Nature, The 2018
Nutcracker Prince, The 1990
Nutcracker, The 1986
Nutcracker, The. *See* George Balanchine's the Nutcracker.
Nuts 1987
Nutty Professor, The 1996
Nutty Professor 2: The Klumps 2001
Nymphomaniac, Volume 1 2015
Nymphomaniac: Volume II 2015

O

O 2002
O Brother, Where Art Thou? 2001
O' Despair. *See* Long Weekend, The.
Oak, The 1995
Oasis, The 1984
Obecna Skola. *See* Elementary School, The.
Oberst Redl. *See* Colonel Redl.
Object of Beauty, The 1991
Object of My Affection, The 1999
Oblivion 1995
Oblivion 2014
Observe and Report 2010
Obsessed 1988
Obsessed 2010
Obsluhoval jsem anglického krále. *See* I Served the King of England.
Obvious Child 2015
O.C. and Stiggs 1987
Oceans 2011

Ocean's Eleven 2002
Ocean's Thirteen 2008
Ocean's Twelve 2005
Oci Ciornie. *See* Dark Eyes.
October Baby 2013
October Sky 2000
Octopussy 1983
Oculus 2015
Odd Life of Timothy Green, The 2013
Odd Man Out [1947] 1985
Oedipus Rex 1995
Oedipus Rex [1967] 1984
Oedipus Wrecks. *See* New York Stories.
Of Gods and Men 2012
Of Human Bondage [1946] 1986
Of Love and Shadows 1996
Of Men and Mavericks. *See* Chasing Mavericks.
Of Mice and Men 1992
Of Unknown Origin 1983
Off Beat 1986
Off Limits 1988
Off the Menu: The Last Days of Chasen's 1999
Office Christmas Party 2017
Office Killer 1997
Office Party 1989
Office Space 2000
Officer and a Gentleman, An 1982
Official Story, The 1985
Offret. *See* Sacrifice, The.
Oh God, You Devil 1984
O'Hara's Wife 1982
Ojos de Julia, Los. *See* Julia's Eyes.
Okja 2018
Okuribito. *See* Departures.
Old Dogs 2010
Old Explorers 1991
Old Gringo 1989
Old Joy 2007
Old Lady Who Walked in the Sea, The 1995
Old School 2004
Oldboy 2006
Oldboy 2014
Oleanna 1995
Oliver and Company 1988
Oliver Twist 2006
Olivier Olivier 1993
Olympus Has Fallen 2014
Omen, The 2007
On Deadly Ground 1995
On Golden Pond 1981
On Guard! 2004
On the Edge 1986
On the Line 2002
On the Other Side. *See* Edge of Heaven, The.
On the Road 2013
On the Town [1949] 1985
On Valentine's Day 1986
Once 2008
Once Around 1991
Once Bitten 1985
Once More 1988
Once Were Warriors 1995
Once Upon a Crime 1992
Once Upon A Forest 1993
Once Upon a Time in America 1984
Once Upon a Time in Anatolia 2013
Once Upon a Time in Mexico 2004
Once Upon a Time in the Midlands 2004
Once Upon a Time...When We Were Colored 1996
Once We Were Dreamers 1987
Ondine 2011
One 2001
One, The 2002
One and a Two, A. *See* Yi Yi.
One Crazy Summer 1986
One Day 2012
One Day in September 2001
One Direction: This Is Us 2014
One False Move 1992
One Fine Day 1996
One Flew over the Cuckoo's Nest [1975] 1985, 1991
One for the Money 2013
One from the Heart 1982
One Good Cop 1991
One Hour Photo 2003
101 Dalmatians 1996
101 Reykjavik 2002
112th and Central 1993
120 battements par minute. *See* BPM (Beats Per Minute).
127 Hours 2011
102 Dalmatians 2001
187 1997
One I Love, The 2015
One Magic Christmas 1985
One Missed Call 2009
One More Saturday 1986
One More Tomorrow [1946] 1986
One Nation Under God 1995
One Night at McCool's 2002
One Night Stand 1997
One Shot. *See* Jack Reacher.
One Tough Cop 1999
One True Thing 1999
Onegin 2000
Ong Bak: The Beginning. *See* Ong Bak 2.
Ong Bak 2 2010
Onimaru. *See* Arashi Ga Oka.
Only Emptiness Remains 1985
Only God Forgives 2014
Only Living Boy in New York, The 2018
Only Lovers Left Alive 2015
Only the Brave 2018
Only the Lonely 1991
Only the Strong 1993
Only the Strong Survive 2004
Only Thrill, The 1999
Only When I Laugh 1981
Only You 1995
Only Yesterday 2017
Open Doors 1991
Open Range 2004
Open Season 2007
Open Water 2005
Open Your Eyes 2000
Opening Night 1988
Opera 1987

Operation Condor 1997
Operation Dumbo Drop 1995
Opportunists, The 2001
Opportunity Knocks 1990
Opposite of Sex, The 1999
Opposite Sex, The 1993
Orange County 2003
Orchestra Seats. *See* Avenue Montaigne.
Ordeal by Innocence 1985
Order, The 2004
Orfanato, El. *See* Orphanage, The.
Orgazmo 1999
Original Gangstas 1996
Original Kings of Comedy, The 2001
Original Sin 2002
Orlando 1993
Orphan 2010
Orphan Muses, The 2002
Orphanage, The 2009
Orphans 1987
Orphans of the Storm 1984
Osama 2005
Oscar 1991
Oscar & Lucinda 1997
Osmosis Jones 2002
Ososhiki. *See* Funeral, The.
Osterman Weekend, The 1983
Otac Na Sluzbenom Putu. *See* When Father Was Away on Business.
Otello 1986
Othello 1995
Other Boleyn Girl, The 2009
Other Guys, The 2011
Other People 2017
Other People's Money 1991
Other Side of the Door, The 2017
Other Side of Heaven, The 2003
Other Side of Hope, The 2018
Other Sister, The 2000
Other Voices, Other Rooms 1997
Other Woman, The 2015
Others, The 2002
Ouija 2015
Ouija 2 2017
Our Brand is Crisis 2016
Our Family Wedding 2011
Our Idiot Brother 2012
Our Kind of Traitor 2017
Our Lady of the Assassins 2002
Our Relations [1936] 1985
Our Song 2002
Out Cold 1989
Out for Justice 1991
Out in the World. *See* Among People.
Out of Africa 1985
Out of Bounds 1986
Out of Control 1985
Out of Life. *See* Hors la Vie.
Out of Order 1985
Out of Sight 1999
Out of Sync 1995
Out of the Dark 1989
Out of the Furnace 2014
Out of the Past [1947] 1991
Out of Time 2004
Out-of-Towners, The 2000
Out on a Limb 1992
Out to Sea 1997
Outbreak 1995
Outfoxed: Rupert Murdoch's War on Journalism 2005
Outing, The 1987
Outland 1981
Outrage 2010
Outrageous Fortune 1987
Outside Providence 2000
Outsiders, The 1983
Over Her Dead Body 1995
Over Her Dead Body 2009
Over the Edge [1979] 1987
Over the Hedge 2007
Over the Hill 1995
Over the Ocean 1995
Over the Top 1987
Overboard 1987
Overexposed 1990
Overnight, The 2016
Overnighters, The 2015
Overseas 1991
Owning Mahowny 2004
Ox, The 1992
Oxford, Blues 1984
Oxygen 2000
Oz the Great and Powerful 2014

P

P.O.W. the Escape 1986
P.S. 2005
Pacific Heights 1990
Pacific Rim 2014
Pacifier, The 2006
Package, The 1989
Pacte des Loups, Le. *See* Brotherhood of the Wolf.
Paddington 2016
Pagemaster, The 1995
Pain & Gain 2014
Paint Job, The 1995
Painted Desert, The 1995
Painted Veil, The 2008
Palais Royale 1988
Pale Rider 1985
Palindromes 2006
Pallbearer, The 1996
Palmetto 1999
Palo Alto 2015
Palombella Rossa. *See* Redwood Pigeon.
Palookaville 1996
Pan 2016
Panama Deception, The 1992
Pandorum 2010
Pane e Tulipani. *See* Bread and Tulips.
Panic 2001
Panic Room, The 2003
Pan's Labyrinth 2007
Panther 1995
Papa: Hemingway in Cuba 2017
Papa's Song 2001
Paparazzi 2005
Paper, The 1995
Paper Heart 2010
Paper Hearts 1995
Paper Mask 1991
Paper Towns 2016

Paper Wedding, A 1991
Paperback Romance 1997
Paperboy, The 2013
Paperhouse 1988
Paprika 2008
Paradise (Donoghue) 1991
Paradise (Gillard) 1982
Paradise Lost 1996
Paradise Lost. *See* Escobar: Paradise Lost.
Paradise Now 2006
Paradise Road 1997
Paranoia 2014
Paranoid Park 2009
Paranormal Activity 2010
Paranormal Activity 5: The Ghost Dimension 2016
Paranormal Activity 4 2013
Paranormal Activity 3 2012
Paranormal Activity: The Marked Ones 2015
Paranormal Activity 2 2011
ParaNorman 2013
Parasite 1982
Parde-ye akhar. *See* Last Act, The.
Parent Trap, The 1999
Parental Guidance 2013
Parenthood 1989
Parents 1989
Pariah 2012
Paris, I Love You. *See* Paris, je t'aime.
Paris, Texas 1984
Paris Blues [1961] 1992
Paris Can Wait 2018
Paris Is Burning 1991
Paris je t'aime 2008
Paris pieds nus. *See* Lost in Paris.
Parker 2014
Parsifal 1983
Parsley Days 2001
Parting Glances 1986
Partisans of Vilna 1986
Partners 1982
Party Animal 1985
Party Girl 1995
Party Line 1988
Party Monster 2004
Pascali's Island 1988
Pass the Ammo 1988
Passage, The 1988
Passage to India, A 1984, 1990
Passages 1995
Passed Away 1992
Passenger 57 1992
Passengers 2017
Passion (Duncan) 2001
Passion (Godard) 1983
Passion d'amore 1984
Passion Fish 1992
Passion in the Desert 1999
Passion of Martin, The 1991
Passion of Mind 2001
Passion of the Christ, The 2005
Passion Play 2012
Passion to Kill, A 1995
Passionada 2003
Past, The 2014
Pastime 1991
Patch Adams 1999
Patch of Blue, A [1965] 1986
Paterson 2017
Pathfinder 1990
Pathfinder 2008
Pathology 2009
Paths of Glory [1957] 1991
Patinoire, La. *See* Ice Rink, The.
Patriot, The 2001
Patriot Games 1992
Patriots Day 2017
Patsy, The 1985
Patti Cake$ 2018
Patti Rocks 1987
Patty Hearst 1988
Paul 2012
Paul Blart: Mall Cop 2010
Paul Blart: Mall Cop 2 2016
Paul Bowles: The Complete Outsider 1995
Paulie 1999
Pauline a la plage. *See* Pauline at the Beach.
Pauline and Paulette 2003
Pauline at the Beach 1983
Paura e amore. *See* Three Sisters.
Pavilion of Women 2002
Pawn Sacrifice 2016
Pay It Forward 2001
Payback 2000
Paycheck 2004
PCU 1995
Peace, Love, & Misunderstanding 2013
Peace, Propaganda & The Promised Land 2006
Peaceful Air of the West 1995
Peacemaker, The 1997
Peanuts Movie, The 2016
Pearl Harbor 2002
Pearl Jam Twenty 2012
Pebble and the Penguin, The 1995
Pecker 1999
Peeples 2014
Pee-wee's Big Adventure 1985
Peggy Sue Got Married 1986
Pelican Brief, The 1993
Pelle Erobreren. *See* Pelle the Conqueror.
Pelle the Conquered 1988
Pelle the Conqueror 1987
Penelope 2009
Penguins of Madagascar 2015
Penitent, The 1988
Penitentiary II 1982
Penitentiary III 1987
Penn and Teller Get Killed 1989
Pennies from Heaven 1981
People I Know 2004
People Like Us 2013
People on Sunday [1929] 1986
People Under the Stairs, The 1991
People vs. George Lucas, The 2012
People vs. Larry Flynt, The 1996
Pepi, Luci, Bom 1992
Percy Jackson & the Olympians: The Lightning Thief 2011
Percy Jackson: Sea of Monsters 2014
Perez Family, The 1995

Perfect 1985

Perfect Candidate, A 1996

Perfect Getaway, A 2010

Perfect Guy, The 2016

Perfect Host, The 2012

Perfect Man, The 2006

Perfect Match, The 1987

Perfect Match, The 2017

Perfect Model, The 1989

Perfect Murder, A 1999

Perfect Murder, The 1988

Perfect Score, The 2005

Perfect Son, The 2002

Perfect Storm, The 2001

Perfect Stranger 2008

Perfect Weapon, The 1991

Perfect World, A 1993

Perfectly Normal 1991

Perfume: The Story of a Murderer 2008

Perhaps Some Other Time 1992

Peril 1985

Peril en la demeure. *See* Peril.

Perks of Being a Wallflower, The 2013

Permanent Midnight 1999

Permanent Record 1988

Persepolis 2009

Personal Best 1982

Personal Choice 1989

Personal Services 1987

Personal Shopper 2018

Personal Velocity 2003

Personals, The 1983

Persuasion 1995

Pervola, Sporen in die Sneeuw. *See* Tracks in the Snow.

Pest, The 1997

Pet Sematary 1989

Pet Sematary II 1992

Pete Kelly's Blues [1955] 1982

Peter Ibbetson [1935] 1985

Peter Pan 2004

Peter Von Scholten 1987

Peter's Friends 1992

Pete's Dragon 2017

Petit, Con. *See* Little Jerk.

Petite Bande, Le 1984

Petite Veleuse, La. *See* Little Thief, The.

Peyote Road, The 1995

Phantasm II 1988

Phantom 2014

Phantom, The 1996

Phantom of the Opera, The (Little) 1989

Phantom of the Opera, The (Schumacher) 2005

Phantom Thread 2018

Phantoms 1999

Phar Lap 1984

Phat Beach 1996

Phat Girlz 2007

Phenomenon 1996

Philadelphia 1993

Philadelphia Experiment, The 1984

Philadelphia Experiment II, The 1995

Philomena 2014

Phobia 1988

Phoenix 2016

Phoenix Forgotten 2018

Phone Booth 2004

Phorpa. *See* Cup, The.

Physical Evidence 1989

Pi 1999

Piaf 1982

Pianist, The 2003

Pianiste, La. *See* Piano Teacher, The.

Piano, The 1993

Piano Piano Kid 1992

Piano Teacher, The 2003

Piano Tuner of Earthquakes, The 2007

Picasso Trigger 1988

Piccolo diavolo, II. *See* Little Devil, The.

Pick-Up Artist, The 1987

Pickle, The 1993

Picture Bride 1995

Picture Perfect 1997

Picture This: The Life and Times of Peter Bogdanovich in Archer City, Texas 1995

Pie in the Sky 1996

Pieces of April 2004

Piel que habito, La. *See* Skin I Live In, The.

Pigalle 1995

Pigeon Sat on a Branch Reflecting on Existence, A 2016

Piglet's Big Movie 2004

Pigs and Pearls. *See* Montenegro.

Pile ou face. *See* Heads or Tails.

Pillow Book, The 1997

Pimp, The 1987

Pineapple Express 2009

Pinero 2002

Pink Cadillac 1989

Pink Flamingos [1972] 1997

Pink Floyd the Wall 1982

Pink Nights 1991

Pink Panther, The 2007

Pink Panther 2, The 2010

Pinocchio 2003

Pinocchio and the Emperor of the Night 1987

Pipe Dream 2003

Piranha 3D 2011

Piranha 3DD 2013

Pirate, The [1948] 1985

Pirate Movie, The 1982

Pirate Radio 2010

Pirates! Band of Misfits, The 2013

Pirates of Penzance, The 1983

Pirates of the Caribbean: At World's End 2008

Pirates of the Caribbean: Dead Man's Chest 2007

Pirates of the Caribbean: Dead Men Tell No Tales 2018

Pirates of the Caribbean: On Stranger Tides 2012

Pirates of the Caribbean: The Curse of the Black Pearl 2004

Pirates Who Don't Do Anything: A VeggieTales Movie, The 2009

Pit and the Pendulum, The 1991

Pitch Black 2001

Pitch Black 2: Chronicles of Riddick. *See* Chronicles of Riddick, The.

Pitch Perfect 2013

Pitch Perfect 3 2018
Pitch Perfect 2 2016
Pixels 2016
Pixote 1981
Pizza Man 1991
Pizzicata 2000
Placard, Le. *See* Closet, The.
Place Beyond the Pines, The 2014
Place in the Sun, A [1951] 1993
Place in the World, A 1995
Places in the Heart 1984
Plague, The 1995
Plague Sower, The. *See* Breath of Life, A.
Plain Clothes 1988
Plan B 1997
Planes 2014
Planes: Fire & Rescue 2015
Planes, Trains and Automobiles 1987
Planet 51 2010
Planet of the Apes 2002
Planet Terror. *See* Grindhouse.
Platform 2004
Platoon Leader 1988
Play It to the Bone 2001
Play Misty for Me [1971] 1985
Playboys, The 1992
Player, The 1992
Players Club, The 1999
Playing by Heart 1999
Playing for Keeps 1986
Playing for Keeps 2013
Playing God 1997
Playing the Field. *See* Playing for Keeps.
Please Give 2011
Pleasantville 1999
Pledge, The 2002
Plemya. *See* Tribe, The.
Plenty 1985
Plot Against Harry, The 1990
Plouffe, Les 1985
Ploughman's Lunch, The 1984
Plump Fiction 1999
Plunkett and Macleane 2000
Pocahontas 1995
Poetic Justice 1993
Poetry 2012
Point Break 1991
Point Break 2016
Point of No Return 1993
Pointsman, The 1988
Poison 1991
Poison Ivy 1992
Pokayaniye. *See* Repentance.
Pola X 2001
Polar Express, The 2005
Police 1986
Police Academy 1984
Police Academy II 1985
Police Academy III 1986
Police Academy IV 1987
Police Academy V 1988
Police Academy VI 1989
Police, Adjective 2010
Polish Bride, The 2000
Polish Wedding 1999
Politist, Adj. *See* Police, Adjective.
Pollock 2001
Poltergeist 1982
Poltergeist 2016
Poltergeist II 1986
Poltergeist III 1988
POM Wonderful Presents: The Greatest Movie Ever Sold 2012
Pomme, La. *See* Apple, The.
Pompatus of Love, The 1996
Pompeii 2015
Ponette 1997
Pontiac Moon 1995
Ponyo 2010
Ponyo on the Cliff by the Sea. *See* Ponyo.
Pooh's Heffalump Movie 2006
Poolhall Junkies 2004
Pootie Tang 2002
Popcorn 1991
Pope Must Die, The 1991
Pope of Greenwich Village, The 1984
Popstar: Never Stop Never Stopping 2017
Porgy and Bess [1959] 1992
Porky's 1982
Porky's II: The Next Day 1983
Pornographic Affair, An. *See* Affair of Love, An.
Porte aperte. *See* Open Doors.
Porto 2018
Portrait Chinois 2000
Portrait of a Lady, The 1996
Poseidon 2007
Positive I.D. 1987
Posse 1993
Possession 2003
Possession, The 2013
Possible Worlds 2001
Post, The 2018
Post Coitum 1999
Post Coitum, Animal Triste. *See* Post Coitum.
Post Grad 2010
Post Grad Survival Guide, The. *See* Post Grad.
Post Tenebras Lux 2014
Postcards from America 1995
Postcards from the Edge 1990
Poster Boy 2007
Postman, The (Radford) 1995
Postman, The (Costner) 1997
Postman Always Rings Twice, The 1981
Potiche 2012
Pound Puppies and the Legend of Big Paw 1988
Poupees russes, Les. *See* Russian Dolls.
Poussière d'ange. *See* Angel Dust.
Powaqqatsi 1988
Powder 1995
Power 1986
Power, The 1984
Power of One, The 1992
Power Rangers 2018
Powwow Highway 1988
Practical Magic 1999
Prairie Home Companion, A 2007
Prancer 1989

Prayer for the Dying, A 1987
Prayer of the Rollerboys 1991
Preacher's Wife, The 1996
Precious: Based on the Novel 'Push' by Sapphire 2010
Predator 1987
Predator II 1990
Predators 2011
Prefontaine 1997
Prelude to a Kiss 1992
Premium Rush 2013
Premonition 2008
Prenom, Carmen. *See* First Name, Carmen.
Presidio, The 1988
Presque Rien. *See* Come Undone.
Prestige, The 2007
Presumed Innocent 1990
Pret-a-Porter. *See* Ready to Wear.
Pretty Baby [1978] 1984
Pretty in Pink 1986
Pretty Persuasion 2006
Pretty Woman 1990
Prettykill 1987
Prey for Rock and Roll 2004
Priatiel Pakoinika. *See* Friend of the Deceased, A.
Price Above Rubies, A 1999
Price of Glory 2001
Price of Milk 2002
Priceless 2009
Prick Up Your Ears 1987
Pride 2008
Pride 2015
Pride and Glory 2009
Pride and Prejudice 2006
Pride and Prejudice and Zombies 2017
Priest 1995
Priest 2012
Priest of Love 1981
Primal Fear 1996
Primary Colors 1999
Primary Motive 1995
Prime 2006
Prince and Me, The 2005
Prince Avalanche 2014
Prince of Darkness 1987
Prince of Egypt, The 1999
Prince of Pennsylvania, The 1988
Prince of Persia: The Sands of Time 2011
Prince of the City 1981
Prince of Tides, The 1991
Princess Academy, The 1987
Princess and the Frog, The 2010
Princess and the Goblin, The 1995
Princess and the Warrior, The 2002
Princess Bride, The 1987
Princess Caraboo 1995
Princess Diaries, The 2002
Princess Diaries 2, The 2005
Principal, The 1987
Principio da Incerteza, O. *See* Uncertainty Principle, The.
Prison 1988
Prisoners 2014
Prisoners of the Mountain 1998
Prisoners of the Sun 1991
Private Fears in Public Places 2008
Private Function, A 1985
Private Investigations 1987
Private Life of Sherlock Holmes, The [1970] 1986
Private Lives of Pippa Lee, The 2010
Private Parts 1997
Private School 1983
Private Worlds [1935] 1982
Prize Winner of Defiance, Ohio, The 2006
Prizzi's Honor 1985
Problem Child 1990
Problem Child II 1991
Producers, The 2006
Professional, The 1995
Professor Marston and the Wonder Women 2018
Program, The 1993
Programmed to Kill 1987
Project Almanac 2016
Project Greenlight's Stolen Summer. *See* Stolen Summer.
Project Nim 2012
Project X 1987
Project X 2013
Prom 2012
Prom Night 2009
Prom Night II. *See* Hello Mary Lou.
Promesse, La 1997
Prometheus 2013
Promise, The 1995
Promise, The 2007
Promise, The 2018
Promised Land 1988
Promised Land 2013
Promised Life, The 2005
Promotion, The 2009
Proof (Moorhouse) 1992
Proof 2006
Proof of Life 2001
Prophecy, The 1995
Prophet, A 2011
Proposal, The 2010
Proposition, The 1999
Proposition, The 2007
Proprietor, The 1996
Prospero's Books 1991
Protocol 1984
Przesluchanie. *See* Interrogation, The.
P.S. I Love You 2008
Psych-Out [1968] 1995
Psycho (Hitchcock) [1960] 1981
Psycho (Van Sant) 1999
Psycho II 1983
Psycho III 1986
Psycho Beach Party 2001
Puberty Blues 1983
Public Access 1995
Public Enemies 2010
Public Eye, The 1992
Puerto Rican Mambo (Not a Musical), The 1995
Pulp Fiction 1995
Pulse 2007
Pump Up the Volume 1990
Pumping Iron II 1985
Pumpkin 2003

Pumpkinhead 1988
Punch-Drunk Love 2003
Punchline 1988
Puncture 2012
Punisher, The 2005
Puppet Masters, The 1995
Puppetmaster, The 1995
Puppetoon Movie 1987
Puppies [1957] 1985
Pure Country 1992
Pure Luck 1991
Purgatory 1989
Purge, The 2014
Purge: Anarchy, The 2015
Purge: Election Year, The 2017
Purple Haze 1983
Purple Hearts 1984
Purple Noon [1960] 1996
Purple People Eaters, The 1988
Purple Rain 1984
Purple Rose of Cairo, The 1985
Pursuit of Happyness, The 2007
Push 2010
Pushing Tin 2000
Puss in Boots 2012
Pyramid, The 2015
Pyromaniac's Love Story, A 1995

Q

Q & A 1990
Qianxi Mambo. *See* Millennium mambo.
Qimsong. *See* Emperor's Shadow, The.
Qiu Ju Da Guansi. *See* Story of Qiu Ju, The.
Quantum of Solace 2009
Quarantine 2009
Quarrel, The 1992
Quartet 1981
Quartet 2013
Quatre Aventures de Reinette et Mirabelle. *See* Four Adventures of Reinette and Mirabelle.
Queen, The 2007
Queen City Rocker 1987
Queen Margot 1995
Queen of Diamonds 1995
Queen of Hearts 1989
Queen of Katwe 2017
Queen of the Damned 2003
Queen of Versailles, The 2013
Queens Logic 1991
Quelques Jours avec moi. *See* Few Days with Me, A.
Querelle 1983
Quest, The 1996
Quest for Camelot 1999
Quest for Fire 1982
Question of Silence, The 1984
Quick and the Dead, The 1995
Quick Change 1990
Quiet, The 2007
Quiet American, The 2003
Quiet Earth, The 1985
Quiet Man, The [1952] 1981
Quiet Ones, The 2015
Quiet Passion, A 2018
Quiet Room, The 1997
Quigley Down Under 1990
Quills 2001
Quitting 2003
Quiz Show 1995

R

Rabbit Hole 2011
Rabbit-Proof Fence 2003
Race 2017
Race for Glory 1989
Race the Sun 1996
Race to Witch Mountain 2010
Rachel Getting Married 2009
Rachel Papers, The 1989
Rachel River 1987
Racing Stripes 2006
Racing with the Moon 1984
Radio 2004
Radio Days 1987
Radio Flyer 1992
Radioland Murders 1995
Radium City 1987
Rage: Carrie 2 2000
Rage in Harlem, A 1991
Rage of Honor 1987
Raggedy Man 1981
Raggedy Rawney, The 1988
Raging Angels 1995
Raging Fury. *See* Hell High.
Ragtime 1981
Raid: Berandal, The. *See* Raid 2, The.
Raid: Redemption, The 2013
Raid 2, The 2015
Raiders of the Lost Ark 1981
Railway Man, The 2015
Rain 2003
Rain. *See* Baran.
Rain Killer, The 1990
Rain Man 1988
Rain Without Thunder 1993
Rainbow Brite and the Star Stealer 1985
Rainbow, The 1989
Raining Stones 1995
Raintree County [1957] 1993
Rainy Day Friends 1985
Raise the Red Lantern 1992
Raise Your Voice 2005
Raisin in the Sun, A [1961] 1992
Raising Arizona 1987
Raising Cain 1992
Raising Helen 2005
Raising Victor Vargas 2004
Rambling Rose 1991
Rambo 2009
Rambo: First Blood Part II 1985
Rambo III 1988
Ramona 1995
Ramona and Beezus 2011
Rampage 1987, 1992
Rampart 2012
Ran 1985
Random Hearts 2000
Rango 2012
Ransom 1996
Rapa Nui 1995
Rapid Fire 1992

Rappin' 1985
Rapture, The 1991
Raspad 1992
Rasputin [1975] 1985
Rat Race 2002
Ratatouille 2008
Ratboy 1986
Ratchet & Clank 2017
Rat's Tale, A 1999
Ratcatcher 2001
Rate It X 1986
Raven, The 2013
Ravenous 2000
Raw 2018
Raw Deal 1986
Rawhead Rex 1987
Ray 2005
Rayon vert, Le. *See* Summer.
Razorback 1985
Razor's Edge, The 1984
Re-Animator 1985
Read My Lips 2003
Reader, The 1988, 1989
Reader, The 2009
Ready to Rumble 2001
Ready to Wear 1995
Real Blonde, The 1999
Real Genius 1985
Real McCoy, The 1993
Real Men 1987
Real Steel 2012
Real Women Have Curves 2003
Reality 2014
Reality Bites 1995
Reaping, The 2008
Rear Window [1954] 2001
Reason to Believe, A 1995
Rebel 1986
Rebel in the Rye 2018
Rebelle. *See* War Witch.
Rebound 2006
[Rec] 2 2011
Reckless 1984
Reckless 1995
Reckless Kelly 1995
Reckoning, The 2005
Recruit, The 2004
Recruits 1986
Red 1995
RED 2011
Red Army 2016
Red Cliff 2010
Red Corner 1997
Red Dawn 1984
Red Dawn 2013
Red Dragon 2003
Red Eye 2006
Red Firecracker, Green Firecracker 1995
Red Heat 1988
Red Hill 2011
Red Hook Summer 2013
Red Lights 2013
Red Planet 2001
Red Riding Hood 2012
Red Riding Trilogy, The 2011
Red Riding: 1980. *See* Red Riding Trilogy, The.
Red Riding: 1983. *See* Red Riding Trilogy, The.
Red Riding: 1974. *See* Red Riding Trilogy, The.
Red Road 2008
Red Rock West 1995
Red Scorpion 1989
Red Sonja 1985
Red Sorghum 1988
Red State 2012
Red Surf 1990
Red Tails 2013
Red Turtle, The 2017
RED 2 2014
Red Violin, The 1999
Redbelt 2009
Redemption 2014
Redl Ezredes. *See* Colonel Redl.
Reds 1981
Redwood Pigeon 1995
Reefer and the Model 1988
Ref, The 1995
Reflecting Skin, The 1991
Reform School Girls 1986
Regarding Henry 1991
Regeneration 1999
Reign of Fire 2003
Reign Over Me 2008
Reindeer Games 2001
Reine Margot, La. *See* Queen Margot.
Rejuvenator, The 1988
Relatos Salvajes. *See* Wild Tales.
Relax, It's Just Sex 2000
Relentless 1989
Relic, The 1997
Religion Hour, The. *See* My Mother's Smile.
Religulous 2009
Reluctant Fundamentalist, The 2014
Remains of the Day, The 1993
Remember 2017
Remember Me 2011
Remember the Titans 2001
Remo Williams 1985
Renaissance Man 1995
Rendez-vous 1988
Rendezvous in Paris 1996
Rendition 2008
Renegades 1989
Renoir 2014
Reno 911!: Miami 2008
Rent 2006
Rent-a-Cop 1988
Rent Control 1984
Rented Lips 1988
Repentance 1987
Replacement Killers, The 1999
Replacements, The 2001
Repo Man 1984
Repo Men 2011
Repo! The Genetic Opera 2009
Repossessed 1990
Requiem for a Dream 2001
Requiem for Dominic 1991
Rescue, The 1988
Rescue Dawn 2008
Rescuers Down Under, The 1990
Reservation Road 2008

Reservoir Dogs 1992
Resident Alien: Quentin Crisp in America 1992
Resident Evil 2003
Resident Evil: Afterlife 2011
Resident Evil: Apocalypse 2005
Resident Evil: Extinction 2008
Resident Evil: Retribution 2013
Resident Evil: The Final Chapter 2018
Respiro 2004
Ressources Humaines. *See* Human Resources.
Restless 2012
Restless Natives 1986
Restoration 1995
Restrepo 2011
Results 2016
Resurrected, The 1995
Resurrecting the Champ 2008
Retour de Martin Guerre, Le. *See* Return of Martin Guerre, The.
Return, The 2007
Return of Horror High 1987
Return of Martin Guerre, The 1983
Return of Superfly, The 1990
Return of the Jedi 1983, 1997
Return of the Living Dead, The 1985
Return of the Living Dead II 1988
Return of the Living Dead III 1993
Return of the Musketeers, The 1989
Return of the Secaucus 7 1982
Return of the Soldier, The 1983
Return of the Swamp Thing, The 1989
Return to Me 2001
Return to Never Land 2003
Return to Oz 1985
Return to Paradise 1999
Return to Snowy River 1988
Return to the Blue Lagoon 1991
Reuben, Reuben 1983
Revenant, The 2016
Revenge 1990
Revenge of the Nerds 1984
Revenge of the Nerds II 1987
Revenge of the Ninja 1983
Reversal of Fortune 1990
Revolution 1985
Revolution! 1995
Revolution #9 2004
Revolutionary Road 2009
Rhapsody in August 1991
Rhinestone 1984
Rhyme & Reason 1998
Rhythm Thief 1995
Rich and Famous 1981
Rich Girl 1991
Rich in Love 1993
Rich Man's Wife 1996
Richard III 1995
Richard Pryor Here and Now 1983
Richard's Things 1981
Richie Rich 1995
Ricki and the Flash 2016
Ricochet 1991
Riddick 2014
Riddle of the Sands, The 1984
Ride 1999
Ride Along 2015
Ride Along 2 2017
Ride in the Whirlwind 1966
Ride to Wounded Knee 1995
Ride with the Devil 2000
Ridicule 1996
Riding Giants 2005
Riding in Cars with Boys 2002
Riding the Edge 1989
Rien ne va plus. *See* Swindle, The.
Riff-Raff 1993
Right Hand Man, The 1987
Right Stuff, The 1983
Righteous Kill 2009
Rikky and Pete 1988
Rimini Rimini 1987
Ring, The 2003
Ring Two, The 2006
Ringer, The 2006
Ringmaster 1999
Rings 2018
Rio 2012
Rio 2 2015
Riot in Cell Block 11 [1954] 1982
R.I.P.D. 2014
Ripe 1997
Ripoux, Les. *See* My New Partner.
Risen 2017
Rise of the Guardians 2013
Rise of the Planet of the Apes 2012
Rising Sun 1993
Risk 1995
Risky Business 1983
Rita, Sue and Bob Too 1987
Rite, The 2012
River, The (Rydell) 1984
River, The (Tsai) 2002
River of Death 1993
River Rat, The 1984
River Runs Through It, A 1992
River Wild, The 1995
Riverbend 1989
River's Edge 1987
Road, The 2010
Road Home, The 2002
Road House 1989
Road to El Dorado, The 2001
Road to Perdition 2003
Road to Wellville, The 1995
Road Trip 2001
Road Warrior, The 1982
Roadside Prophets 1992
Rob Roy 1995
Robert A. Heinlein's The Puppet Masters. *See* Puppet Masters, The.
Robin Hood 1991
Robin Hood 2011
Robin Hood: Men In Tights 1993
Robocop 1987
RoboCop 2015
Robocop II 1990
Robocop III 1993
Robot & Frank 2013
Robot Jox 1990
Robot Stories 2005
Robots 2006
Rock, The 1996

Rock-a-Doodle 1992
Rock Dog 2018
Rock 'n Roll Meller. *See* Hellbent.
Rock Hudson's Home Movies 1995
Rock of Ages 2013
Rock School 2006
Rock Star 2002
Rock the Boat 2000
Rock the Kasbah 2016
Rocker, The 2009
Rocket Gibraltar 1988
Rocket Man 1997
Rocket Science 2008
Rocketeer, The 1991
RocknRolla 2009
Rocky III 1982
Rocky IV 1985
Rocky V 1990
Rocky Balboa 2007
Roger and Me 1989
Roger Corman's Frankenstein Unbound 1990
Roger Dodger 2003
Rogue One: A Star Wars Story 2017
Roi Danse, Le. *See* King Is Dancing, The.
Rois et reine. *See* Kings and Queen.
Rok spokojnego slonca. *See* Year of the Quiet Sun, A.
Role Models 2009
Roll Bounce 2006
Rollerball 2003
Rollercoaster 2001
Rolling Stones at the Max 1991
Roman de gare 2009
Roman Holiday [1953] 1989
Roman J. Israel, Esq. 2018
Roman Polanski: Wanted and Desired 2009
Romance 2000
Romance of Astree and Celadon, The 2009
Romance of Book and Sword, The 1987
Romancing the Stone 1984
Romantic Comedy 1983
Romeo 1989
Romeo and Julia 1992
Romeo & Juliet 2014
Romeo is Bleeding 1995
Romeo Must Die 2001
Romper Stomper 1993
Romuald et Juliette. *See* Mama, There's a Man in Your Bed.
Romulus, My Father 2009
Romy & Michelle's High School Reunion 1997
Ronin 1999
Rooftops 1989
Rookie, The 1990
Rookie, The 2003
Rookie of the Year 1993
Room 2016
Room 237 2014
Room with a View, A 1986
Roommate, The 2012
Roommates 1995
Rory O'Shea Was Here 2006
Rosa Luxemburg 1987
Rosalie Goes Shopping 1990
Rosary Murders, The 1987
Rose Garden, The 1989
Rosencrantz and Guildenstern Are Dead 1991
Rosewater 2015
Rosewood 1997
Rosie 2000
Rouge of the North 1988
Rough Cut 1982
Rough Magic 1997
Rough Night 2018
Roughly Speaking [1945] 1982
Rouille et d'os, De. *See* Rust and Bone.
'Round Midnight 1986
Rounders 1999
Rover, The 2015
Rover Dangerfield 1991
Row of Crows, A. *See* Climate for Killing, A.
Roxanne 1987
Roy Rogers: King of the Cowboys 1995
Royal Affair, A 2013
Royal Tenenbaums, The 2002
Royal Wedding [1951] 1985
Rubin and Ed 1992
Ruby 1992
Ruby in Paradise 1993
Ruby Sparks 2013
Rudderless 2015
Rude Awakening 1989
Rudo y Cursi 2010
Rudy 1993
Rudyard Kipling's the Second Jungle Book 1997
Rugrats Go Wild! 2004
Rugrats in Paris: The Movie 2001
Rugrats Movie, The 1999
Ruins, The 2009
Rules of Attraction, The 2003
Rules of Engagement 2001
Rules Don't Apply 2017
Rum Diary, The 2012
Rumba, La. *See* Rumba, The.
Rumba, The 1987
Rumble Fish 1983
Rumble in the Bronx 1996
Rumor Has It... 2006
Rumpelstiltskin 1987
Run 1991
Run All Night 2016
Run, Fatboy, Run 2009
Run Lola Run 2000
Run of the Country, The 1995
Runaway Bride 2000
Runaway Jury 2004
Runaway Train 1985
Runaways, The 2011
Rundown, The 2004
Rundskop. *See* Bullhead.
Runestone, The 1992
Runner Runner 2014
Running Brave 1983
Running Free 2001
Running Hot 1984

Running Man, The 1987
Running on Empty 1988
Running Scared 1986
Running Scared 2007
Running with Scissors 2007
Rupert's Land 2001
Rush 1991
Rush 2014
Rush Hour 1999
Rush Hour 2 2002
Rush Hour 3 2008
Rushmore 1999
Russia House, The 1990
Russian Dolls 2007
Russia's Wonder Children 2001
Russkies 1987
Russlands Wunderkinder. *See* Russia's Wonder Children.
Rust and Bone 2013
Rustler's Rhapsody 1985
Rustling of Leaves, A 1990
Ruthless People 1986
RV 2007
Ryan's Daughter [1970] 1990

S

S.F.W. 1995
Sabotage 2015
Sabrina [1954] 1986
Sabrina 1995
Sacrament, The 2015
Sacrifice, The 1986
Saddest Music in the World, The 2005
Sade 2004
Safe 1995
Safe 2013
Safe Conduct 2003
Safe Haven 2014
Safe House 2013
Safe Journey. *See* Latcho Drom.
Safe Passage 1995
Safety Not Guaranteed 2013
Safety of Objects, The 2003
Sage femme. *See* Midwife, The.
Sahara 2006
Sahara (McLaglen) 1984
St. Elmo's Fire 1985
Saint, The 1997
Saint Clara 1997
Saint of Fort Washington, The 1993
St. Vincent 2015
Saison des Hommes, La. *See* Season of Men, The.
Salaam Bombay! 1988
Salesman, The 2017
Salinger 2014
Salmer fra Kjokkenet. *See* Kitchen Stories.
Salmon Fishing in the Yemen 2013
Salmonberries 1995
Salome's Last Dance 1988
Salsa 1988
Salt 2011
Salt of the Earth [1954] 1986
Salt of the Earth, The 2016
Salt on Our Skin. *See* Desire.
Salton Sea, The 2003
Saltwater 2002
Salvador 1986
Sam and Sarah 1991
Samantha 1995
Sam's Son 1984
Samba Traore 1995
Same Kind of Different as Me 2018
Same Old Song 2000
Sammy and Rosie Get Laid 1987
Samsara 2013
San Andreas 2016
Sanctum 2012
Sandlot, The 1993
Sandwich Years, The 1988
Sang for Martin, En. *See* Song for Martin, A.
Sans toit ni loi. *See* Vagabond.
Santa Claus 1985
Santa Clause, The 1995
Santa Clause 2, The 2003
Santa Clause 3: The Escape Clause, The 2007
Santa Fe 1988
Santa Sangre 1990
Sapphires, The 2014
Sara 1995
Saraband 2006
Sarafina! 1992
Satan 1995
Satisfaction 1988
Saturday Night at the Palace 1987
Saturday Night, Sunday Morning: The Travels of Gatemouth Moore 1995
Saul fia. *See* Son of Saul.
Sausage Party 2017
Sauve qui peut (La Vie). *See* Every Man for Himself.
Savage Beach 1989
Savage Island 1985
Savage Nights 1995
Savages 2013
Savages, The 2008
Savannah Smiles 1983
Save the Last Dance 2002
Save the Tiger [1973] 1988
Saved! 2005
Saving Christmas 2015
Saving Grace (Young) 1986
Saving Grace (Cole) 2001
Saving Mr. Banks 2014
Saving Private Ryan 1999
Saving Silverman 2002
Savior 1999
Saw 2005
Saw V 2009
Saw IV 2008
Saw VI 2010
Saw III 2007
Saw 3D: The Final Chapter 2011
Saw II 2006
Say Anything 1989
Say It Isn't So 2002
Say Yes 1986
Scandal 1989
Scandalous 1984
Scanner Darkly, A 2007
Scanners III: The Takeover 1995
Scaphandre et le papillon, Le. *See* Diving Bell and the Butterfly, The.

Scarface 1983
Scarlet Letter, The [1926] 1982, 1984
Scarlet Letter, The 1995
Scarlet Street [1946] 1982
Scary Movie 2001
Scary Movie 2 2002
Scary Movie 3 2004
Scary Movie 4 2007
Scary Movie 5 2014
Scavengers 1988
Scenes from a Mall 1991
Scenes from the Class Struggle in Beverly Hills 1989
Scent of a Woman 1992
Scent of Green Papaya, The (Mui du du Xanh) 1995
Scherzo del destino agguato dietro l'angelo come un brigante di strada. *See* Joke of Destiny, A.
Schindler's List 1993
Schizo 2006
Schizopolis 1997
School Daze 1988
School for Scoundrels 2007
School of Flesh, 432
School of Rock 2004
School Spirit 1985
School Ties 1992
Schtonk 1995
Schultze Gets the Blues 2006
Science des reves, La. *See* Science of Sleep, The.
Science of Sleep, The 2007
Scissors 1991
Scooby-Doo 2003
Scooby-Doo 2: Monsters Unleashed 2005
Scoop 2007
Scorched. *See* Incendies.
Scorchers 1995
Score, The 2002
Scorpion 1986
Scorpion King, The 2003
Scorta, La 1995
Scotland, PA 2003
Scott Pilgrim vs. the World 2011
Scout, The 1995
Scout's Guide to the Zombie Apocalypse 2016
Scream 1996
Scream 4 2012
Scream 2 1997
Scream 3 2001
Scream of Stone 1995
Screamers 1996
Screwed 2001
Scrooged 1988
Se, jie. *See* Lust, Caution.
Sea Inside, The 2005
Sea of Love 1989
Sea Wolves, The 1982
Seabiscuit 2004
Search and Destroy 1995
Search for Signs of Intelligent Life in the Universe, The 1991
Searching for Bobby Fischer 1993
Searching for Sugar Man 2013
Season of Dreams 1987
Season of Fear 1989
Season of Men, The 2003
Season of the Witch 2012
Seasons 1995
Second Best 1995
Second Best Exotic Marigold Hotel, The 2016
Second Chance, The 2007
Second Sight 1989
Second Skin 2003
Second Thoughts 1983
Secondhand Lions 2004
Secret Admirer 1985
Secret Garden, The 1993
Secret in Their Eyes, The 2011
Secret in Their Eyes 2016
Secret Life of Bees, The 2009
Secret Life of Pets, The 2017
Secret Life of Walter Mitty, The [1947] 1985
Secret Life of Walter Mitty, The 2014
Secret Lives of Dentists, The 2004
Secret Love, Hidden Faces. *See* Ju Dou.
Secret of Kells, The 2011
Secret of My Success, The 1987
Secret of NIMH, The 1982
Secret of Roan Inish, The 1995
Secret of the Sword, The 1985
Secret Places 1985
Secret Policeman's Third Ball, The 1987
Secret Window 2005
Secret World of Arrietty, The 2013
Secretariat 2011
Secretary 2003
Secreto de sus ojos, El. *See* Secret in Their Eyes, The.
Secrets 1984
Secrets & Lies 1996
Seduction, The 1982
See No Evil 2007
See No Evil, Hear No Evil 1989
See Spot Run 2002
See You in the Morning 1989
Seed of Chucky 2005
Seeing Other People 2005
Seeker: The Dark Is Rising, The 2008
Seeking a Friend for the End of the World 2013
Seeking Justice 2013
Segunda Piel. *See* Second Skin.
Selena 1998
Self Made Hero, A 1998
Self/Less 2016
Selma 2015
Semi-Pro 2009
S'en Fout la Mort. *See* No Fear, No Die.
Sender, The 1982
Senna 2012
Sensations 1988
Sense and Sensibility 1995
Sense of an Ending, The 2018
Sense of Freedom, A 1985
Senseless 1999
Sentimental Destiny 2002
Sentinel, The 2007
Separate Lies 2006
Separate Vacations 1986

Separation, A 2012
Seppan 1988
September 1987
September Dawn 2008
September Issue, The 2010
Serendipity 2002
Serenity 2006
Sgt. Bilko 1996
Seraphim Falls 2008
Serbuan maut. *See* Raid: Redemption, The.
Serena 2016
Serial Mom 1995
Series 7: The Contenders 2002
Serious Man, A 2010
Serpent and the Rainbow, The 1988
Servants of Twilight, The 1995
Serving Sara 2003
Sesame Street Presents: Follow That Bird 1985
Session 9 2002
Sessions, The 2013
Set It Off 1996
Set Me Free 2001
Seto uchi shonen yakyudan. *See* MacArthur's Children.
Seunlau Ngaklau. *See* Time and Tide.
Seven 1995
Seven Hours to Judgement 1988
Seven Men from Now [1956] 1987
Seven Minutes in Heaven 1986
Seven Pounds 2009
Seven Psychopaths 2013
Seven Women, Seven Sins 1987
Seven Year Itch, The [1955] 1986
Seven Years in Tibet 1998
17 Again 2010
Seventh Coin, The 1993
Seventh Sign, The 1988
Seventh Son 2016
78/52: Hitchcock's Shower Scene 2018
'71 2016
Severance 1989
Sex and Lucia 2003
Sex and the City: The Movie 2009
Sex and the City 2 2011
Sex Drive 2009
Sex, Drugs, and Democracy 1995
Sex, Drugs, Rock and Roll 1991
sex, lies and videotape 1989
Sex: The Annabel Chong Story 2001
Sex Tape 2015
Sexbomb 1989
Sexy Beast 2002
Seymour: An Introduction 2016
Shack, The 2018
Shades of Doubt 1995
Shadey 1987
Shadow, The 1995
Shadow Army, The. *See* Army of Shadows.
Shadow Conspiracy, The
Shadow Dancer 2014
Shadow Dancing 1988
Shadow Magic 2002
Shadow of the Raven 1990
Shadow of the Vampire 2001
Shadow of the Wolf 1993
Shadowboxer 2007
Shadowlands 1993
Shadows and Fog 1992
Shadrach 1999
Shaft 2001
Shag 1988
Shaggy Dog, The 2007
Shakedown 1988
Shakes the Clown 1992
Shakespeare in Love 1999
Shaking the Tree 1992
Shall We Dance? 1997
Shall We Dance? 2005
Shallow Grave 1995
Shallow Hal 2002
Shallows, The 2017
Shame 1988
Shame 2012
Shanghai Knights 2004
Shanghai Noon 2001
Shanghai Surprise 1986
Shanghai Triad 1995
Shaolin Soccer 2005
Shape of Things, The 2004
Shape of Water, The 2018
Shark Night 3D 2012
Shark Tale 2005
Sharky's Machine 1981
Sharma and Beyond 1986
Shatterbrain. *See* Resurrected, The.
Shattered 1991
Shattered Glass 2004
Shaun of the Dead 2005
Shaun the Sheep Movie 2016
Shaunglong Hui. *See* Twin Dragons.
Shawshank Redemption, The 1995
She Hate Me 2005
She Must Be Seeing Things 1987
Sherrybaby 2007
She-Devil 1989
Sheena 1984
Sheer Madness 1985
Shelf Life 1995
Sheltering Sky, The 1990
Sherlock Holmes [1922] 1982
Sherlock Holmes 2010
Sherlock Holmes: A Game of Shadows 2012
Sherman's March 1986
She's All That 2000
She's De Lovely. *See* De-Lovely.
She's Funny That Way 2016
She's Gotta Have It 1986
She's Having a Baby 1988
She's Out of Control 1989
She's Out of My League 2011
She's So Lovely 1997
She's the Man 2007
She's the One 1996
Shi. *See* Poetry.
Shiloh 2: Shiloh Season 2000
Shimian Maifu. *See* House of Flying Daggers.
Shine 1996
Shine a Light 2009
Shining, The [1980]
Shining Through 1992

Shipping News, The 2002
Shipwrecked 1991
Shiqisuide Danche. *See* Beijing Bicycle.
Shirley Valentine 1989
Shiza. *See* Shizo.
Shoah 1985
Shock to the System, A 1990
Shocker 1989
Shomerei Ha'saf. *See* Gatekeepers, The.
Shoot 'Em Up 2008
Shoot the Moon 1982
Shoot to Kill 1988
Shooter 2008
Shooting, The [1966] 1995
Shooting Dogs. *See* Beyond the Gates.
Shooting Fish 1999
Shooting Party, The 1985
Shootist, The [1976] 1982
Shopgirl 2006
Short Circuit 1986
Short Circuit II 1988
Short Cuts 1993
Short Film About Love, A 1995
Short Term 12 2014
Short Time 1990
Shorts: The Adventures of the Wishing Rock 2010
Shot, The 1996
Shout 1991
Show, The 1995
Show Me Love 2000
Show of Force, A 1990
Showdown in Little Tokyo 1991
Shower, The 2001
Showgirls 1995
Showtime 2003
Shrek 2002
Shrek Forever After 2011
Shrek the Third 2008
Shrek 2 2005
Shrimp on the Barbie, The 1990
Shutter 2009
Shutter Island 2011
Shvitz, The. *See* New York in Short: The Shvitz and Let's Fall in Love.
Shy People 1987
Siberiade 1982
Sibling Rivalry 1990
Sicario 2016
Sicilian, The 1987
Sick: The Life and Death of Bob Flanagan, Supermasochist 1997
Sicko 2008
Sid and Nancy 1986
Side by Side 2013
Side Effects 2014
Side Out 1990
Sidekicks 1993
Sidewalk Stories 1989
Sidewalks of New York, The 2002
Sideways 2005
Siege, The 1999
Siesta 1987
Sightseers 2014
Sign o' the Times 1987
Sign of the Cross, The [1932] 1984
Signal Seven 1986
Signal, The 2015
Signs 2003
Signs & Wonders 2002
Signs of Life 1989
Silence 2017
Silence, The 2001
Silence After the Shot, The. *See* Legend of Rita, The.
Silence at Bethany, The 1988
Silence of the Lambs, The 1991
Silence, The 2014
Silencer, The 1995
Silent Fall 1995
Silent Hill 2007
Silent Hill: Revelation 3D 2013
Silent Madness, The 1984
Silent House 2013
Silent Night 1988
Silent Night, Deadly Night 1984
Silent Night, Deadly Night II 1987
Silent Night, Deadly Night III 1989
Silent Rage 1982
Silent Tongue 1995
Silent Touch, The 1995
Silent Victim 1995
Silk Road, The 1992
Silkwood 1983
Silver City (Sayles) 2005
Silver City (Turkiewicz) 1985
Silver Linings Playbook 2013
Silverado 1985
Simon Birch 1999
Simon Magnus 2002
Simon the Magician 2001
Simone 2003
Simpatico 2000
Simple Men 1992
Simple Plan, A 1999
Simple Twist of Fate, A 1995
Simple Wish, A 1997
Simply Irresistible 2000
Simpsons Movie, The 2008
Sin City 2006
Sin City: A Dame to Kill For 2015
Sin Nombre 2010
Sin Noticias de Dios. *See* No News from God.
Sinbad: Legend of the Seven Seas 2004
Since Otar Left 2005
Sincerely Charlotte 1986
Sinful Life, A 1989
Sing 1989
Sing 2017
Sing Street 2017
Singin' in the Rain [1952] 1985
Singing Detective, The 2004
Singing the Blues in Red 1988
Single Man, A 2010
Single Moms' Club, The. *See* Tyler Perry's The Single Moms' Club.
Single Shot, A 2014
Single White Female 1992
Singles 1992
Sinister 2013
Sinister 2 2016
Sioux City 1995
Sirens 1995

Sister Act 1992
Sister Act II 1993
Sister, My Sister 1995
Sister, Sister 1987
Sisterhood of the Traveling Pants, The 2006
Sisterhood of the Traveling Pants 2, The 2009
Sisters 2016
Sisters. *See* Some Girls.
Sitcom 2000
Sitter, The 2012
Siu lam juk kau. *See* Shaolin Soccer.
Siulam Chukkau. *See* Shaolin Soccer.
Six Days, Seven Nights 1999
Six Days, Six Nights 1995
Six Degrees of Separation 1993
Six Pack 1982
Six-String Samurai 1999
Six Ways to Sunday 2000
Six Weeks 1982
16 Blocks 2007
Sixteen Candles 1984
Sixteen Days of Glory 1986
Sixth Day, The 2001
Sixth Man, The 1997
Sixth Sense, The 2000
Sixty Glorious Years [1938] 1983
'68 1987
Skeleton Key, The 2006
Skeleton Twins, The 2015
Ski Country 1984
Ski Patrol 1990
Skin Deep 1989
Skin I Live In, The 2012
Skins 2003
Skinwalkers 2008
Skipped Parts 2002
Skulls, The 2001
Sky Bandits 1986
Sky Blue 2006
Sky Captain and the World of Tomorrow 2005
Sky High 2006
Sky of Our Childhood, The 1988
Skyfall 2013
Skyline 1984
Skyline 2011
Slacker 1991
Slackers 2003
Slam 1997
Slam Dance 1987
Slap Shot [1977] 1981
Slapstick 1984
Slate, Wyn, and Me 1987
Slave Coast. *See* Cobra Verde.
Slave Girls from Beyond Infinity 1987
Slaves of New York 1989
Slaves to the Underground 1997
Slayground 1984
SLC Punk 2000
Sleazy Uncle, The 1991
Sleep With Me 1995
Sleepers 1996
Sleeping Beauty 2012
Sleeping with Other People 2016
Sleeping with the Enemy 1991
Sleepless 2018
Sleepless in Seattle 1993
Sleepover 2005
Sleepwalk with Me 2013
Sleepwalkers. *See* Stephen King's Sleepwalkers.
Sleepwalking 2009
Sleepy Hollow 2000
Sleepy Time Gal, The 2002
Sleight 2018
Sleuth 2008
Sliding Doors 1999
Sling Blade 1996
Slingshot, The 1995
Slipping Down Life, A 2005
Slither 2007
Sliver 1993
Slow Burn 2008
Slow West 2016
Slugs 1988
Slumdog Millionaire 2009
Slums of Beverly Hills 1999
Small Faces 1996
Small Soldiers 1999
Small Time Crooks 2001
Small Wonders 1996
Smart People 2009
Smash Palace 1982
Smashed 2013
Smell of Camphor, Fragrance of Jasmine 2001
Smile Like Yours, A 1997
Smiling Fish and Goat on Fire 2001
Smilla's Sense of Snow 1997
Smithereens 1982, 1985
Smoke 1995
Smoke Signals 1999
Smokey and the Bandit, Part 3 1983
Smokin' Aces 2008
Smoking/No Smoking [1995] 2001
Smooth Talk 1985
Smurfs, The 2012
Smurfs and the Magic Flute, The 1983
Smurfs: The Lost Village 2018
Smurfs 2, The 2014
Snake Eyes 1999
Snake Eyes. *See* Dangerous Game.
Snakes on a Plane 2007
Snapper, The 1993
Snatch 2002
Snatched 2018
Sneakers 1992
Sniper 1993
Snitch 2014
Snow Angels 2009
Snow Day 2001
Snow Dogs 2003
Snow Falling in Cedars 2000
Snow Flower and the Secret Fan 2012
Snow White. *See* Mirror Mirror.
Snow White and the Huntsman 2013
Snowden 2017
Snowman, The 2018
Snowpiercer 2015
Snows of Kilimanjaro, The [1952] 1982
S.O.B. 1981
So I Married an Axe Murderer 1993

Soapdish 1991
Sobibor, October 14, 1943, 4 p.m. 2002
Social Network, The 2011
Society 1992
Sofie 1993
Soft Fruit 2001
Soft Shell Man 2003
Softly Softly 1985
Sokhout. *See* Silence, The.
Sol del Membrillo, El. *See* Dream of Light.
Solarbabies 1986
Solaris 2003
Solas 2001
Soldier 1999
Soldier, The 1982
Soldier's Daughter Never Cries, A 1999
Soldier's Story, A 1984
Soldier's Tale, A 1988
Solid Gold Cadillac, The [1956] 1984
Solitary Man 2011
Solo 1996
Soloist, The 2010
Solomon and Gaenor 2001
Some Girls 1988
Some Kind of Hero 1982
Some Kind of Wonderful 1987
Some Like It Hot [1959] 1986, 1988
Some Mother's Son 1996
Someone Else's America 1996
Someone Like You 2002
Someone to Love 1987, 1988
Someone to Watch Over Me 1987
Somersault 2007
Something Borrowed 2012
Something in the Air 2014
Something New 2007
Something to Do with the Wall 1995
Something to Talk About 1995
Something Wicked This Way Comes 1983
Something Wild 1986
Something Within Me 1995
Something's Gotta Give 2004
Somewhere 2011
Sommersby 1993
Son, The 2003
Son of Darkness: To Die For II 1995
Son of God 2015
Son of No One, The 2012
Son of Rambow 2009
Son of Saul 2016
Son of the Bride 2003
Son of the Mask 2006
Son of the Pink Panther 1993
Son-in-Law 1993
Sonatine 1999
Song for Marion. *See* Unfinished Song.
Song for Martin 2003
Song to Song 2018
Songcatcher 2001
Songwriter 1984
Sonny 2003
Sonny Boy 1990
Sons 1989
Sons of Steel 1988
Son's Room, The 2002
Sontagsbarn. *See* Sunday's Children.
Sophie's Choice 1982
Sorcerer's Apprentice, The 2011
Sorority Babes in the Slimeball Bowl-o-Rama 1988
Sorority Boys 2003
Sorority House Massacre 1987
Sorority Row 2010
Soshite chichi ni naru. *See* Like Father, Like Son.
Sotto Sotto. *See* Softly Softly.
Soul Food 1997
Soul Kitchen 2011
Soul Man 1986
Soul Men 2009
Soul Plane 2005
Soul Power 2010
Soul Surfer 2012
Soul Survivors 2002
Sound Barrier, The [1952] 1984, 1990
Sound City 2014
Sound of My Voice, The 2013
Sound of Thunder, A 2006
Sour Grapes 1999
Source, The 2000
Source Code 2012
Soursweet 1988
Sous le Sable. *See* Under the Sand.
Sous le Soleil de Satan. *See* Under the Sun of Satan.
Sous Sol 1997
South Central 1992
South of Reno 1987
South Park: Bigger, Longer & Uncut 2000
Southbound 2017
Southern Comfort 1981
Southland Tales 2008
Southpaw 2016
Southside with You 2017
Souvenir 1988
Space Between Us, The 2018
Space Chimps 2009
Space Cowboys 2001
Space Jam 1996
Spaceballs 1987
Spacecamp 1986
Spaced Invaders 1990
Spacehunter: Adventures in the Forbidden Zone 1983
Spalding Gray's Monster in a Box. *See* Monster in a Box.
Spanglish 2005
Spanish Prisoner, The 1999
Spanking the Monkey 1995
Spare Parts 2016
Sparkle 2013
Spartacus [1960] 1991
Spartan 2005
Spawn 1997
Speaking in Strings 2000
Speaking Parts 1990
Special Day, A 1984
Special Effects 1986
Specialist, The 1995
Species 1995

Species 2 1999
Spectacular Now, The 2014
Specter of the Rose [1946] 1982
Spectre 2016
Speechless 1995
Speed 1995
Speed Racer 2009
Speed 2: Cruise Control 1997
Speed Zone 1989
Spellbinder 1988
Spellbound [1945] 1989
Sphere 1999
Spice World 1999
Spices 1989
Spider 2004
Spider-Man 2003
Spider-Man: Homecoming 2018
Spider-Man 3 2008
Spider-Man 2 2005
Spiderwick Chronicles, The 2009
Spies like Us 1985
Spike of Bensonhurst 1988
Spirit, The 2009
Spirit of '76, The 1991
Spirit of St. Louis, The [1957] 1986
Spirit: Stallion of the Cimarron 2003
Spirited Away 2004
Spitfire Grill, The 1996
Splash 1984
Splendor 2000
Splice 2011
Split 1991
Split 2018
Split Decisions 1988
Split Image 1982
Split Second 1992
Splitting Heirs 1993
Sponge Bob Square Pants Movie, The 2005
SpongeBob Movie: Sponge Out of Water, The 2016
Spoorloos. *See* Vanishing, The.
Spotlight 2016
Spread 2010
Spring 2016
Spring Break 1983
Spring Breakers 2014
Spring Forward [2000] 2001
Spring, Summer, Autumn, Winter...And Spring 2005
Spring Symphony 1986
Sprung 1997
Spun 2004
Spy 2016
Spy Game 2002
Spy Hard 1996
Spy Kids 2002
Spy Kids: All the Time in the World in 4D 2012
Spy Kids 2: The Island of Lost Dreams 2003
Spy Kids 3-D: Game Over 2004
Spy Next Door, The 2011
Squanto: A Warrior's Tale 1995
Square, The 2011
Square, The 2014
Square, The 2018
Square Dance 1987
Squeeze 1997
Squeeze, The 1987
Squid and the Whale, The 2006
Stacking. *See* Season of Dreams.
Stage Beauty 2005
Stake Land 2012
Stakeout 1987
Stakeout II. *See* Another Stakeout.
Stalag 17 [1953] 1986
Stand and Deliver 1988
Stand by Me 1986
Stand Up Guys 2014
Standard Operating Procedure 2009
Stander 2005
Standing in the Shadows of Motown 2003
Stanford Prison Experiment, The 2016
Stanley and Iris 1990
Stanley Kubrick: A Life in Pictures 2002
Stanno tutti bene. *See* Everybody's Fine.
Stanza de Figlio, La. *See* Son's Room, The.
Star, The 2018
Star Chamber, The 1983
Star 80 1983
Star Is Born, A [1954] 1983, 1985
Star Kid 1999
Star Maker, The 1996
Star Maps 1997
Star Trek 2010
Star Trek Beyond 2017
Star Trek Into Darkness 2014
Star Trek II: The Wrath of Khan 1982
Star Trek III: The Search for Spock 1984
Star Trek IV:The Voyage Home 1986
Star Trek V: The Final Frontier 1989
Star Trek VI: The Undiscovered Country 1991
Star Trek: First Contact 1996
Star Trek: Generations 1995
Star Trek: Insurrection 1999
Star Trek: Nemesis 2003
Star Trek: The Motion Picture [1979] 1986
Star Wars: Episode I—The Phantom Menace 2000
Star Wars: Episode II—Attack of the Clones 2003
Star Wars: Episode III—Revenge of the Sith 2006
Star Wars: Episode IV—A New Hope [1977] 1997
Star Wars: Episode VII—The Force Awakens. *See* Star Wars: The Force Awakens.
Star Wars: Episode VIII—The Last Jedi. *See* Star Wars: The Last Jedi.
Star Wars: The Clone Wars 2009
Star Wars: The Force Awakens 2016
Star Wars: The Last Jedi 2018
Starchaser 1985
Stardom 2001
Stardust 2008
Stardust Memories [1980] 1984
Stargate 1995
Starman 1984

Starred Up 2015
Stars and Bars 1988
Stars Fell on Henrietta, The 1995
Starship Troopers 1997
Starsky & Hutch 2005
Starstruck 1982
Starter for 10 2008
Startup.com 2002
State and Main 2001
State of Grace 1990
State of Play 2010
State of Things, The 1983
Statement, The 2004
Stateside 2005
Station, The 1992
Station Agent, The 2004
Stay 2006
Stay Alive 2007
Stay Tuned 1992
Staying Alive 1983
Staying Together 1989
Steal America 1992
Steal Big, Steal Little 1995
Stealing Beauty 1996
Stealing Harvard 2003
Stealing Heaven 1988
Stealing Home 1988
Stealth 2006
Steamboy 2006
Steaming 1986
Steel 1997
Steel Magnolias 1989
Steele Justice 1987
Stella 1990
Stella Dallas [1937] 1987
Step 2018
Step Brothers 2009
Step Into Liquid 2004
Step Up 2007
Step Up: All In 2015
Step Up Revolution 2013
Step Up 3D 2011
Step Up 2 the Streets 2009
Stepfather, The 1987
Stepfather, The 2010
Stepfather II 1989
Stepford Wives, The 2005
Stephanie Daley 2008
Stephen King's Cat's Eye 1985
Stephen King's Children of the Corn 1984
Stephen King's Graveyard Shift 1990
Stephen King's Silver Bullet 1985
Stephen King's Sleepwalkers 1992
Stephen King's The Night Flier 1999
Stephen King's Thinner 1996
Stepmom 1999
Stepping Out 1991
Steve Jobs 2016
Stick 1985
Stick, The 1988
Stick It 2007
Sticky Fingers 1988
Stigmata 2000
Still Alice 2015
Still Crazy 1999
Still Mine 2014
Still of the Night 1982
Stille Nach Dem Schuss, Die. *See* Legend of Rita, The.
Sting II, The 1983
Stir Crazy [1980] 1992
Stir of Echoes 2000
Stitches 1985
Stoker 2014
Stolen Life, A [1946] 1986
Stolen Summer 2003
Stomp the Yard 2008
Stone 2011
Stone Boy, The 1984
Stone Cold 1991
Stone Reader 2004
Stonewall 1996
Stonewall 2016
Stoning of Soraya M., The 2010
Stop Making Sense 1984
Stop! Or My Mom Will Shoot 1992
Stop-Loss 2009
Stories from the Kronen 1995
Stories We Tell 2014
Storks 2017
Stormy Monday 1988
Story of Qiu Ju, The 1993
Story of the Weeping Camel, The 2005
Story of Us, The 2000
Story of Women 1989
Story of Xinghau, The 1995
Storytelling 2003
Storyville 1992
Straight for the Heart 1990
Straight Out of Brooklyn 1991
Straight Outta Compton 2016
Straight Story, The 2000
Straight Talk 1992
Straight to Hell 1987
Strange Brew 1983
Strange Days 1995
Strange Invaders 1983
Strange Love of Martha Ivers, The [1946] 1991
Strange Magic 2016
Strange Wilderness 2009
Stranger, The 1987
Stranger Among Us, A 1992
Stranger by the Lake 2015
Stranger Is Watching, A 1982
Stranger Than Fiction 2007
Stranger than Paradise 1984, 1986
Strangers, The 2009
Stranger's Kiss 1984
Strangers in Good Company 1991
Strangers with Candy 2007
Strapless 1990
Straw Dogs 2012
Strawberry and Chocolate 1995
Strayed 2005
Streamers 1983
Street Fighter 1995
Street Fighter: The Legend of Chun-Li 2010
Street Kings 2009
Street Smart 1987
Street Story 1989
Street Trash 1987
Street Wars 1995

Streets 1990
Streets of Fire 1984
Streets of Gold 1986
Streetwalkin' 1985
Streetwise 1985
Strictly Ballroom 1993
Strictly Business 1991
Strictly Propaganda 1995
Strike It Rich 1990
Striking Distance 1993
Strip Jack Naked (Nighthawks II) 1995
Stripes 1981
Stripped to Kill 1987
Stripped to Kill 2 1989
Stripper 1986
Striptease 1996
Stroker Ace 1983
Stronger 2018
Stryker 1983
Stuart Little 2000
Stuart Little 2 2003
Stuart Saves His Family 1995
Stuck On You 2004
Student Confidential 1987
Stuff, The 1985
Stupids, The 1996
Submarine 2012
Substance of Fire, The 1996
Substitute, The 1996
Suburbans, The 2000
Suburban Commando 1991
Suburbia 1984
subUrbia 1997
Suburbicon 2018
Subway 1985
Subway to the Stars 1988
Such a Long Journey 2001
Sucker Punch 2012
Sudden Death 1985
Sudden Death 1995
Sudden Impact 1983
Sudden Manhattan 1997
Suddenly, Last Summer [1959] 1993
Suddenly Naked 2002
Suffragette 2016
Sugar 2010
Sugar & Spice 2002
Sugar Cane Alley 1984
Sugar Hill 1995
Sugar Town 2000
Sugarbaby 1985
Suicide Kings 1999
Suicide Squad 2017
Suitors, The 1989
Sukkar banat. *See* Caramel.
Sullivan's Pavilion 1987
Sully 2017
Sum of All Fears, The 2003
Sum of Us, The 1995
Summer 1986
Summer Camp Nightmare 1987
Summer Catch 2002
Summer Heat 1987
Summer Hours 2010
Summer House, The 1993
Summer Lovers 1982
Summer Night with Greek Profile, Almond Eyes, and Scent of Basil 1987
Summer of Sam 2000
Summer Palace 2009
Summer Rental 1985
Summer School 1987
Summer Stock [1950] 1985
Summer Story, A 1988
Summertime [1955] 1990
Sunchaser 1996
Sunday 1997
Sunday in the Country, A 1984
Sunday's Child 1989
Sunday's Children 1995
Sunset 1988
Sunset Boulevard [1950] 1986
Sunset Park 1996
Sunset Song 2017
Sunshine 2001
Sunshine (Boyle) 2008
Sunshine Cleaning 2010
Sunshine State 2003
Super 2012
Super, The 1991
Super Dark Times 2018
Super 8 2012
Super Mario Bros. 1993
Super Size Me 2005
Superbad 2008
Supercop 1997
Superfantagenio. *See* Aladdin.
Supergirl 1984
Superhero Movie 2009
Superman II 1981
Superman III 1983
Superman IV 1987
Superman Returns 2007
Supermensch: The Legend of Shep Gordon 2015
Supernova 2001
Superstar 1991
Superstar 2000
Superstition. *See* Gallows, The.
Sur 1988
Sur Mes Levres. *See* Read My Lips.
Sure Fire 1993
Sure Thing, The 1985
Surf II 1984
Surf Nazis Must Die 1987
Surf Ninjas 1993
Surf's Up 2008
Surfwise 2009
Surrender 1987
Surrogate, The. *See* Sessions, The.
Surrogates 2010
Surveillance 2010
Survival Quest 1990
Survival of the Dead 2011
Surviving Christmas 2005
Surviving the Game 1995
Surviving Picasso 1996
Survivors, The 1983
Suspect 1987
Suspect Zero 2005
Suspended Animation 2004
Suspicious River 2002
Suture 1995

S-VHS. *See* V/H/S/2
Swamp, The. *See* Cienaga, La.
Swamp Thing 1982
Swan Lake 1991
Swan Princess, The 1995
Swann in Love 1984
S.W.A.T. 2004
Sweeney Todd: The Demon Barber of Fleet Street 2008
Sweet and Lowdown 2000
Sweet Country 1987
Sweet Dreams 1985
Sweet Emma, Dear Bobe: Sketches, Nudes 1995
Sweet Hearts Dance 1988
Sweet Hereafter, The 1997
Sweet Home Alabama 2003
Sweet Liberty 1986
Sweet Lorraine 1987
Sweet Nothing 1996
Sweet November 2002
Sweet Revenge 1987
Sweet Sixteen 1984
Sweet Sixteen 2004
Sweet Talker 1991
Sweetest Thing, The 2003
Sweetgrass 2011
Sweetie 1990
Sweetwater 1988
Swept Away 2003
Swept from the Sea 1999
Swimfan 2003
Swimming Pool 2004
Swimming to Cambodia 1987
Swimming Upstream 2006
Swimming With Sharks 1995
Swindle, The 2000
Swing Kids 1993
Swing Shift 1984
Swing Vote 2009
Swingers 1996
Swiss Army Man 2017
Switch 1991
Switch, The 2011
Switchback 1997
Switching Channels 1988
Swoon 1992
Sword and the Sorcerer, The 1982
Swordfish 2002
Swordsman III. *See* East is Red, The.
Sydney White 2008
Sylvester V 1987
Sylvia 1985
Sylvia 2004
Synecdoche, New York 2009
Syriana 2006

T

T2 Trainspotting 2018
Table for Five 1983
Table 19 2018
Tabloid 2012
Taboo 2001
Tacones lejanos. *See* High Heels.
Tadpole 2003
Tadpole and the Whale 1988
Taeksi Woonjunsa. *See* Taxi Driver, A.
Tag 1982
Tai-pan 1986
Tailor of Panama, The 2002
Take a Letter, Darling [1942] 1984
Take Me Home Tonight 2012
Take Shelter 2012
Take the Lead 2007
Take This Waltz 2013
Take Two 1988
Taken 2010
Taken 3 2016
Taken 2 2013
Takers 2011
Taking Care of Business 1990
Taking Lives 2005
Taking of Beverly Hills, The 1991
Taking of Pelham 123, The 2010
Taking Off [1971] 1985
Taking Sides 2004
Taking Woodstock 2010
Tale of Despereaux, The 2009
Tale of Ruby Rose, The 1987
Tale of Springtime, A 1992
Tale of Winter, A 1995
Talented Mr. Ripley, The 2000
Tales from the Crypt: Bordello of Blood 1996
Tales from the Crypt Presents Demon Knight 1995
Tales from the Darkside 1990
Tales from the Hood 1995
Tales of Ordinary Madness 1983
Tales of the Grim Sleeper 2015
Talk 1995
Talk of Angels 1999
Talk Radio 1988
Talk to Her 2003
Talk to Me 2008
Talkin' Dirty After Dark 1991
Tall Guy, The 1990
Tall Tale: The Unbelievable Adventures of Pecos Bill 1995
Talladega Nights: The Ballad of Ricky Bobby 2007
Talons of the Eagle 1995
Talvisota 1989
Tamara Drewe 2011
Taming of the Shrew, The [1967] 1993
Tammy 2015
Tampopo 1987
Tangerine 2016
Tangled 2011
Tango and Cash 1989
Tango Bar 1988, 1989
Tango Lesson, The 1998
Tank 1984
Tank Girl 1995
Tao of Steve, The 2001
Tap 1989
Tape 2002
Tapeheads 1988
Taps 1981
Target 1985
Target 1996
Tarnation 2005
Tarzan 2000
Tarzan and the Lost City 1999

Tasogare Seibei. *See* Twilight Samurai, The.
Taste of Others, The 2002
Tatie Danielle 1991
Taxi 2005
Taxi. *See* Jafar Panahi's Taxi.
Taxi Blues 1991
Taxi Driver, A 2018
Taxi nach Kairo. *See* Taxi to Cairo.
Taxi Tehran. *See* Jafar Panahi's Taxi.
Taxi to Cairo 1988
Taxi to the Dark Side 2009
Taxi to the Toilet. *See* Taxi Zum Klo.
Taxi Zum Klo 1981
Taxing Woman, A 1988
Taxing Woman's Return, A 1989
Tea in the Harem 1986
Tea With Mussolini 2000
Teachers 1984
Teacher's Pet: The Movie. *See* Disney's Teacher's Pet.
Teaching Mrs. Tingle 2000
Team America: World Police 2005
Tears of the Sun 2004
Ted 2013
Ted 2 2016
Ted and Venus 1991
Teen Witch 1989
Teen Wolf 1985
Teenage Mutant Ninja Turtles 1990
Teenage Mutant Ninja Turtles (2007). *See* TMNT.
Teenage Mutant Ninja Turtles 2015
Teenage Mutant Ninja Turtles: Out of the Shadows 2017
Teenage Mutant Ninja Turtles II 1991
Teenage Mutant Ninja Turtles III 1993
Teeth 2009
Telephone, The 1988
Tell No One 2009
Telling Lies in America 1997
Témoins, Les. *See* Witnesses, The.
Temp, The 1993
Tempest 1982
Tempest, The 2011
Temporada de patos. *See* Duck Season.
Temps qui changent, Les. *See* Changing Times.
Temps qui reste, Les. *See* Time to Leave.
Temps Retrouve. *See* Time Regained.
Temptation: Confessions of a Marriage Counselor. *See* Tyler Perry's Temptation: Confessions of a Marriage Counselor.
Temptress Moon 1997
Ten 2004
10 Cloverfield Lane 2017
Ten Things I Hate About You 2000
10,000 B.C. 2009
10 to Midnight 1983
10 Years 2013
Tenacious D in the Pick of Destiny 2007
Tender Mercies 1983
Tenebrae. *See* Unsane.
Tenue de soiree. *See* Menage.
Tequila Sunrise 1988
Terminal, The 2005
Terminal Bliss 1992
Terminal Velocity 1995
Terminator, The 1984
Terminator Genisys 2016
Terminator Salvation 2010
Terminator 2 1991
Terminator 3: Rise of the Machines 2004
Termini Station 1991
Terminus. *See* End of the Line.
Terms of Endearment 1983
Terri 2012
Terror Within, The 1989
Terrorvision 1986
Tess 1981
Test of Love 1985
Testament 1983
Testament of Youth 2016
Testimony 1987
Tetro 2010
Tetsuo: The Iron Man 1992
Tex 1982, 1987
Texas Chainsaw 3D 2014
Texas Chainsaw Massacre, The (Nispel) 2004
Texas Chainsaw Massacre, Part II, The 1986
Texas Chainsaw Massacre: The Beginning, The 2007
Texas Comedy Massacre, The 1988
Texas Killing Fields 2012
Texas Rangers 2003
Texas Tenor: The Illinois Jacquet Story 1995
Texasville 1990
Thank You and Good Night 1992
Thank You for Smoking 2007
Thank You for Your Service 2018
Thanks for Sharing 2014
That Awkward Moment 2015
That Championship Season 1982
That Darn Cat 1997
That Night 1993
That Old Feeling 1997
That Sinking Feeling 1984
That Thing You Do! 1996
That Was Then...This Is Now 1985
That's Entertainment! III 1995
That's Life! 1986, 1988
That's My Boy 2013
The au harem d'Archi Ahmed, Le. *See* Tea in the Harem.
Their Finest 2018
Thelma 2018
Thelma and Louise 1991
Thelonious Monk 1988
Then She Found Me 2009
Theory of Everything, The 2015
Theory of Flight, The 1999
There Goes My Baby 1995
There Goes the Neighborhood 1995
There Will Be Blood 2008
There's Nothing Out There 1992
There's Something About Mary 1999
Therese. *See* In Secret.
Theremin: An Electronic Odyssey 1995

They All Laughed 1981
They Call Me Bruce 1982
They Drive by Night [1940] 1982
They Live 1988
They Live by Night [1949] 1981
They Might Be Giants [1971] 1982
They Still Call Me Bruce 1987
They Won't Believe Me [1947] 1987
They're Playing with Fire 1984
Thiassos, O. *See* Traveling Players, The.
Thief 1981
Thief, The 1999
Thief of Hearts 1984
Thieves 1996
Thin Blue Line, The 1988
Thin Ice 2013
Thin Line Between Love and Hate, A 1996
Thin Red Line, The 1999
Thing, The 1982
Thing, The 2012
Thing Called Love, The 1995
Things Are Tough All Over 1982
Things Change 1988
Things to Come 2017
Things to Do in Denver When You're Dead 1995
Things We Lost in the Fire 2008
Think Big 1990
Think Like a Man 2013
Think Like a Man Too 2015
Third Person 2015
Third World Cop 2001
Thirst 2010
Thirteen 2004
13 Assassins 2012
Thirteen Conversations About One Thing 2003
Thirteen Days 2001
Thirteen Ghosts 2003
13 Going On 30 2005
13 Hours 2017
Thirtieth Floor, The 2000
Thirtieth Warrior, The 2000
30 Days of Night 2008
30 Minutes or Less 2012
35 Shots of Rum 2011
Thirty Two Short Films About Glenn Gould 1995
Thirty-five Up 1992
37, 2 le Matin. *See* Betty Blue.
Thirty-six Fillette 1988
33, The 2016
This Boy's Life 1993
This Christmas 2008
This Is Elvis 1981
This Is 40 2013
This is My Father 2000
This is My Life 1992
This Is Spinal Tap 1984
This Is It. *See* Michael Jackson's This Is It.
This Is the End 2014
This Is Where I Leave You 2015
This Means War 2013
This Must Be the Place 2013
This Side of the Truth. *See* Invention of Lying, The.
This World, Then the Fireworks 1997
Thomas and the Magic Railroad 2001
Thomas Crown Affair, The 2000
Thomas in Love 2002
Thor 2012
Thor: Ragnarok 2018
Thor: The Dark World 2014
Those Who Love Me Can Take the Train 2000
Thou Shalt Not Kill 1988
Thousand Acres, A 1997
Thousand Pieces of Gold 1991
Thousand Words, A 2013
Thrashin' 1986
Three Amigos 1986
Three Billboards Outside Ebbing, Missouri 2018
Three Brothers 1982
Three Burials of Melquiades Estrada, The 2007
3 Days to Kill 2015
Three...Extremes 2006
3:15 1986
Three for the Road 1987
Three Fugitives 1989
300 2008
360 2013
300: Rise of an Empire 2015
3-Iron 2006
Three Kinds of Heat 1987
Three Kings 2000
Three Lives & Only One Death 1996
Three Madeleines, The 2001
Three Men and a Baby 1987
Three Men and a Cradle 1986
Three Men and a Little Lady 1990
Three Monkeys 2010
Three Musketeers, The 1993
Three Musketeers, The 2012
Three Ninjas Kick Back 1995
Three Ninjas 1992
Three O'Clock High 1987
Three of Hearts 1993
Three Seasons 2000
Three Sisters 1988
Three Stooges, The 2013
3 Strikes 2001
3:10 to Yuma 2008
3000 Miles to Graceland 2002
Three to Get Ready 1988
Three to Tango 2000
Three Wishes 1995
Threesome 1995
Threshold 1983
Through the Eyes of the Children. *See* 112th and Central.
Through the Olive Trees 1995
Through the Wire 1990
Through the Window 2001
Throw Momma from the Train 1987
Thumbelina. *See* Hans Christian Andersen's Thumbelina.
Thumbsucker 2006
Thunder Alley 1986
Thunderbirds 2005
Thunderheart 1992
THX 1138 [1971] 1984

Thy Kingdom Come...Thy Will Be Done 1988
Tian di ying xiong. *See* Warriors of Heaven and Earth.
Tian Yu. *See* Xiu Xiu: The Sent Down Girl.
Tian zhu ding. *See* Touch of Sin, A.
Ticket to Ride. *See* Post Grad.
Tickled 2017
Tideland 2007
Tie Me Up! Tie Me Down! 1990
Tie That Binds, The 1995
Tieta of Agreste 2000
Tiger Warsaw 1988
Tigerland 2002
Tiger's Tale, A 1987
Tigger Movie, The 2001
Tightrope 1984
Til' There Was You 1997
Till Human Voices Wake Us 2004
Tillman Story, The 2011
Tillsammans. *See* Together.
Tim and Eric's Billion Dollar Movie 2013
Tim Burton's Corpse Bride 2006
Timbuktu 2016
Time After Time 1983
Time and Tide 2002
Time Bandits 1981
Time Code 2001
Time for Drunken Horses, A 2001
Time Indefinite 1995
Time Machine, The (Pal) [1960] 1983
Time Machine, The (Wells) 2003
Time of Destiny, A 1988
Time of Favor 2002
Time of the Gypsies 1990
Time Out 2003
Time Out of Mind 2016
Time Regained 2001
Time to Die, A 1991
Time to Kill, A 1996
Time to Leave 2007
Time Traveler's Wife, The 2010
Time Will Tell 1992
Timebomb 1992
Timecop 1995
Timeline 2004
Timerider 1983
Timothy Leary's Dead 1997
Tin Cup 1996
Tin Men 1987
Tinker Tailor Soldier Spy 2012
Titan A.E. 2001
Titanic 1997
Tito and Me 1993
Titus 2000
TMNT 2008
To Be or Not to Be 1983
To Begin Again. *See* Volver a empezar.
To Die For 1989
To Die For 1995
To Die Standing (Crackdown) 1995
To Do List, The 2014
To Gillian on Her 37th Birthday 1996
To Kill a Mockingbird [1962] 1989
To Kill a Priest 1988
To Live 1995
To Live and Die in L.A. 1985, 1986
To Protect Mother Earth 1990
To Render a Life 1995
To Return. *See* Volver.
To Rome with Love 2013
To Sir with Love [1967] 1992
To Sleep with Anger 1990
To the Wonder 2014
To Wong Foo, Thanks for Everything! Julie Newmar 1995
Todo Sobre Mi Madre. *See* All About My Mother.
Together 2002
Together 2004
Toivon tuolla puolen. *See* Other Side of Hope, The.
Tokyo Pop 1988
Tokyo-Ga 1985
Tom and Huck 1995
Tom and Jerry 1993
Tom & Viv 1995
Tomb Raider. *See* Lara Croft: Tomb Raider.
Tomboy 1985
Tombstone 1993
Tomcats 2002
Tommy Boy 1995
Tomorrow [1972] 1983
Tomorrowland 2016
Tomorrow Never Dies 1997
Tomorrow's a Killer. *See* Prettykill.
Toni Erdmann 2017
Too Beautiful for You 1990
Too Hot to Handle [1938] 1983
Too Much 1987
Too Much Sleep 2002
Too Much Sun 1991
Too Outrageous! 1987
Too Scared to Scream 1985
Too Soon to Love [1960]
Tooth Fairy 2011
Tootsie 1982
Top Dog 1995
Top Five 2015
Top Gun 1986
Top of the Food Chain 2002
Top Secret 1984
Topio stin omichi. *See* Landscape in the Mist.
Topsy-Turvy 2000
Tora-San Goes to Viena 1989
Torajiro Kamone Uta. *See* Foster Daddy, Tora!
Torch Song Trilogy 1988
Torinoi lo, A. *See* Turin Horse, The.
Torment 1986
Torn Apart 1990
Torn Curtain [1966] 1984
Torque 2005
Torrents of Spring 1990
Tortilla Soup 2002
Total Eclipse 1995
Total Recall 1990
Total Recall 2013
Totally F***ed Up 1995
Toto le heros. *See* Toto the Hero.
Toto the Hero 1992

Tottering Lives 1988
Touch 1997
Touch and Go 1986
Touch of a Stranger 1990
Touch of Evil [1958] 1999
Touch of Larceny, A [1959] 1986
Touch of Sin, A 2014
Touch the Sound 2006
Touched with Fire 2017
Touching the Void 2005
Touchy Feely 2014
Tough Enough 1983
Tough Guys 1986
Tough Guys Don't Dance 1987
Tougher than Leather 1988
Touki-Bouki 1995
Tourist, The 2011
Tous les matins du monde 1992
Toward the Within 1995
Tower Heist 2012
Town, The 2011
Town and Country 2002
Town is Quiet, The 2002
Toxic Avenger, The 1986
Toxic Avenger, Part II, The 1989
Toxic Avenger, Part III, The 1989
Toy, The 1982
Toy Soldiers (Fisher) 1984
Toy Soldiers (Petrie) 1991
Toy Story 1995
Toy Story 3 2011
Toy Story 2 2000
Toys 1992
Trace, The 1984
Trance 2014
Traces of Red 1992
Track 1988
Tracks 2015
Tracks in the Snow 1986
Trade 2008
Trade Winds [1939] 1982
Trading Hearts 1988
Trading Mom 1995
Trading Places 1983
Traffic 2001
Tragedia di un umo ridiculo. *See* Tragedy of a Ridiculous Man.
Tragedy of a Ridiculous Man 1982
Trail of the Lonesome Pine, The. *See* Waiting for the Moon.
Trail of the Pink Panther 1982
Train de Vie. *See* Train of Life.
Train of Life 2000
Training Day 2002
Trainspotting 1996
Trainwreck 2016
Traitor 2009
Trancers 1985
Transamerica 2006
Transcendence 2015
Transformers 2008
Transformers, The 1986
Transformers: Age of Extinction 2015
Transformers: Dark of the Moon 2012
Transformers 4. *See* Transformers: Age of Extinction.
Transformers: Revenge of the Fallen 2010
Transformers: The Last Knight 2018
Transporter Refueled, The 2016
Transporter 3 2009
Transporter 2 2006
Transsiberian 2009
Transylvania 6-5000 1985
Trapped 2003
Trapped in Paradise 1995
Traps 1995
Traveling Players, The [1974] 1990
Traveller 1997
Travelling Avant 1987
Travelling North 1987
Traviata, La 1982
Tre fratelli. *See* Three Brothers.
Treasure Island 2001
Treasure of the Four Crowns 1983
Treasure of the Sierra Madre, The [1948] 1983
Treasure Planet 2003
Tree of Life, The 2012
Trees Lounge 1996
Trekkies 2000
Tremors 1990
Trenchcoat 1983
Trespass 1992
Trespass 2012
Trial, The 1995
Trial and Error 1997
Trial by Jury 1995
Tribe, The 2016
Tribulations of Balthasar Kober, The 1988
Trick 2000
Trick or Treat 1986
Trigger Effect, The 1996
Trilogia: To Livadi pou dakryzei. *See* Weeping Meadow.
Trilogy: After the Life, The 2005
Trilogy: An Amazing Couple, The 2005
Trilogy: On the Run, The 2005
Trilogy: Weeping Meadow, The. *See* Weeping Meadow.
Trip, The 2012
Trip to Bountiful, A [1953] 1982
Trip to Bountiful, The 1985
Trip to Italy, The 2015
Trip to Spain, The 2018
Triple 9 2017
Triplets of Belleville, The 2004
Trippin' 2000
Trishna 2013
Tristan & Isolde 2007
Tristram Shandy: A Cock and Bull Story 2007
Triumph of Love, The 2003
Triumph of the Spirit 1989
Trixie 2001
Trmavomodry Svet. *See* Dark Blue World.
Trois Couleurs: Blanc. *See* White.
Trois Couleurs: Bleu. *See* Blue.
Trois Couleurs: Rouge. *See* Red.
Trois Hommes et un couffin. *See* Three Men and a Cradle.
Trojan Eddie 1997
Trol Hunter, The. *See* Trollhunter.
Troll 1986

Trollhunter 2012

Trolljegeren. *See* Trollhunter.

Trolls 2017

Trolosa. *See* Faithless.

TRON 1982

TRON: Legacy 2011

Troop Beverly Hills 1989

Trop belle pour toi. *See* Too Beautiful for You.

Tropic Thunder 2009

Tropical Rainforest 1992

Trouble at the Royal Rose. *See* Trouble with Spies, The.

Trouble Bound 1995

Trouble in Mind 1985

Trouble with Dick, The 1987

Trouble with Spies, The 1987

Trouble with the Curve 2013

Troubles We've Seen: A History of Journalism in Wartime, The 2006

Troublesome Creek: A Midwestern 1997

Trout, The 1983

Troy 2005

Truce, The 1999

Trucker 2010

True Believer 1989

True Blood 1989

True Colors 1991

True Confessions 1981

True Crime 2000

True Grit 2011

True Heart Susie [1919] 1984

True Identity 1991

True Lies 1995

True Love 1989

True Romance 1993

True Stories 1986

True Story 2016

Truite, La. *See* Trout, The.

Truly, Madly, Deeply 1991

Truman Show, The 1999

Trumbo 2016

Trumpet of the Swan, The 2002

Trust 1991

Trust 2012

Trust Me 1989

Trust the Man 2007

Trusting Beatrice 1993

Truth 2016

Truth About Cats & Dogs, The 1996

Truth About Charlie, The 2003

Truth or Consequences: N.M., 1997

Truth or Dare 1991

Tsotsi 2007

Tuck Everlasting 2003

Tucker 1988

Tucker & Dale vs. Evil 2012

Tuff Turf 1985

Tulip Fever 2018

Tully 2004

Tumbleweeds 2000

Tune, The 1992

Tune in Tomorrow... 1990

Tunel, El. *See* Tunnel, The.

Tunnel, The 1988

Turandot Project, The 2002

Turbo 2014

Turbo: A Power Rangers Movie, 1997

Turbulence, 1997

Turin Horse, The 2013

Turist. *See* Force Majeure.

Turistas 2007

Turk 182 1985

Turn It Up 2001

Turner and Hooch 1989

Turning Paige 2003

Turtle Beach 1995

Turtle Diary 1985, 1986

Turtles are Back...In Time, The. *See* Teenage Mutant Ninja Turtles III.

Tusk 2015

Tuxedo, The 2003

TV Set, The 2008

Twelfth Night 1996

Twelve 2011

Twelve Monkeys 1995

Twelve O'Clock High [1949] 1989

12 Rounds 2010

12 Years a Slave 2014

Twenty Bucks 1993

20 Dates 2000

28 Weeks Later 2008

20 Feet from Stardom 2014

20th Century Women 2017

25th Hour 2003

24 Hour Party People 2003

24 Hours. *See* Trapped.

21 & Over 2014

21 Grams 2004

TwentyFourSeven 1999

24 Hour Woman 2000

28 Days 2001

28 Days Later 2004

28 Up 1985

2046 2006

Twenty-ninth Street 1991

Twenty-one 1991

21 Jump Street 2013

20,000 Days on Earth 2015

2012 2010

21 2009

27 Dresses 2009

22 Jump Street 2015

Twice Dead 1988

Twice in a Lifetime 1985

Twice upon a Time 1983

Twilight 1999

Twilight 2009

Twilight of the Cockroaches 1990

Twilight of the Ice Nymphs 1999

Twilight Saga: Breaking Dawn, Part 1, The 2012

Twilight Saga: Breaking Dawn, Part 2, The 2013

Twilight Saga: Eclipse, The 2011

Twilight Saga: New Moon, The 2010

Twilight Samurai, The 2005

Twilight Zone: The Movie 1983

Twin Dragons 2000

Twin Falls Idaho 2000

Twin Peaks: Fire Walk with Me 1992

Twin Town 1997

Twins 1988

Twist 1993

Twist and Shout 1986

Twisted 2005
Twisted Justice 1990
Twisted Obsession 1990
Twister 1990
Twister 1996
Two Bits 1995
Two Brothers 2005
Two Can Play That Game 2002
2 Days in New York 2013
2 Days in Paris 2008
2 Days in the Valley 1996
Two Days, One Night 2015
Two Evil Eyes 1991
Two Family House 2001
2 Fast 2 Furious 2004
Two for the Money 2006
Two Girls and a Guy 1999
2 Guns 2014
200 Cigarettes 2000
Two If By Sea 1996
Two Jakes, The 1990
Two Lovers 2010
Two Moon Junction 1988
Two Mothers. *See* Adore.
Two Much 1996
Two Ninas 2002
Two of a Kind 1983
Two Small Bodies 1995
2016 Obama's America 2013
2010 1984
Two Weeks Notice 2003
Twogether 1995
Tycoon 2004
Tyler Perry's A Madea Christmas 2014
Tyler Perry's Boo 2! A Madea Halloween. *See* Boo 2! A Madea Halloween.
Tyler Perry's Daddy's Little Girls. *See* Daddy's Little Girls.
Tyler Perry's Good Deeds 2013
Tyler Perry's I Can Do Bad All By Myself. *See* I Can Do Bad All By Myself.
Tyler Perry's Madea Goes to Jail. *See* Madea Goes to Jail.
Tyler Perry's Meet the Browns 2009
Tyler Perry's The Single Moms' Club 2015
Tyler Perry's Temptation: Confessions of a Marriage Counselor 2014
Tyler Perry's Why Did I Get Married?. *See* Why Did I Get Married?
Tyler Perry's Why Did I Get Married Too? *See* Why Did I Get Married Too?
Tyrannosaur 2012
Tyson 2010

U

U-571 2001
UFOria 1986
Ugly, The 1999
Ugly Truth, The 2010
UHF 1989
Ulee's Gold 1997
Ultraviolet 2007
Ulysses' Gaze 1995
Umi yori mo mada fukaku. *See* After the Storm.
Un Air de Famille 1999
Unaccompanied Minors 2007
Unbearable Lightness of Being, The 1988
Unbelievable Truth, The 1990
Unborn, The 1991
Unborn, The 2010
Unbreakable 2001
Unbroken 2015
Uncertainty Principle, The 2003
Uncle Boonmee Who Can Recall His Past Lives 2012
Uncle Buck 1989
Uncommon Valor 1983
Unconquering the Last Frontier 2002
Undead 2006
Undefeated 2013
Undefeated, The 2012
Under Cover 1987
Under Fire 1983
Under Hellgate Bridge 2002
Under Siege 1992
Under Siege II: Dark Territory 1995
Under Solen. *See* Under the Sun.
Under Suspicion (Moore) 1992
Under Suspicion (Hopkins) 2001
Under Suspicion. *See* Garde a vue.
Under the Boardwalk 1988
Under the Cherry Moon 1986
Under the City's Skin. *See* Under the Skin of the City.
Under the Donim Tree 1996
Under the Same Moon 2009
Under the Sand 2002
Under the Skin 1999
Under the Skin 2015
Under the Skin of the City 2003
Under the Sun 2002
Under the Sun of Satan 1987
Under the Tuscan Sun 2004
Under the Volcano III 1984
Underclassman 2006
Undercover Blues 1993
Undercover Brother 2003
Underdog 2008
Underground 1999
Underneath, The 1995
Undertow (Red) 1995
Undertow (Green) 2005
Underworld 1997
Underworld (Wiseman) 2004
Underworld: Awakening 2013
Underworld: Blood Wars 2018
Underworld: Evolution 2007
Underworld: Rise of the Lycans 2010
Undisputed 2003
Unexpected 2016
Unfaithful (Lyne) 2003
Unfaithful, The [1947] 1985
Unfaithfully Yours 1984
Unfinished Business 1986
Unfinished Business 2016
Unfinished Life, An 2006
Unfinished Piece for Piano Player, An [1977] 1982
Unfinished Song 2014
Unforgettable 1996
Unforgettable 2018
Unforgiven 1992

Unfriended 2016

Ungfruin Goda Og Husid. *See* Honour of the House.

Unheard Music, The 1986

Unholy, The 1988

Unhook the Stars 1996

Uninvited, The 2010

Union Square 2005

United Kingdom, A 2018

United 93 2007

United States of Leland 2005

Universal Soldier 1992

Universal Soldier: The Return 2000

Unknown 2012

Unknown Girl, The 2018

Unknown White Male 2007

Unlawful Entry 1992

Unleashed 2006

Unreasonable Man, An 2008

Unsane 1987

Unstoppable 2011

Unstrung Heroes 1995

Untamed Heart 1993

Until September 1984

Until the End of the World 1991

(Untitled) 2010

Untouchables, The 1987

Untraceable 2009

Unzipped 1995

Up 2010

Up at the Villa 2001

Up Close & Personal 1996

Up for Grabs 2006

Up in the Air 2010

Up the Creek 1984

Upside Down 2014

Upside of Anger, The 2006

Upstream Color 2014

Uptown Girls 2004

Uranus 1991

Urban Legend 1999

Urban Legends: Final Cut 2001

Urbania 2001

Ursula 1987

U.S. Marshals 1999

U.S. vs. John Lennon, The 2007

Used People 1992

Usual Suspects, The 1995

Utu 1984

U-Turn 1997

U2: Rattle and Hum 1988

V

V for Vendetta 2007

V. I. Warshawski 1991

V lyudyakh. *See* Among People.

Va Savoir 2002

Vacancy 2008

Vacation 2016

Vagabond 1986

Valentin 2005

Valentina 1983

Valentine 2002

Valentine's Day 2011

Valentino Returns 1989

Valentino: The Last Emperor 2010

Valerian and the City of a Thousand Planets 2018

Valet, The 2008

Valhalla Rising 2011

Valiant 2006

Valkyrie 2009

Valley Girl 1983

Valmont 1989

Vals Im Bashir. *See* Waltz with Bashir.

Vamp 1986

Vampire Academy 2015

Vampire in Brooklyn 1995

Vampire's Kiss 1989

Vampires Suck 2011

Van, The 1997

Van Gogh 1992

Van Helsing 2005

Vanilla Sky 2002

Vanishing, The (Sluizer) 1988

Vanishing, The (Sluizer) 1993

Vanishing on 7th Street 2012

Vanity Fair 2005

Vantage Point 2009

Vanya on 42nd Street 1995

Varsity Blues 2000

Vasectomy 1986

Vatican Tapes, The 2016

Vegas in Space 1993

Vegas Vacation 1997

Veillees d'armes. *See* Troubles We've Seen, The: A History of Journalism in Wartime.

Velocity of Gary, The 2000

Velvet Goldmine 1999

Vendetta 1986

Venice/Venice 1992

Venom 1982

Venus 2007

Venus a la Fourrure, La. *See* Venus in Fur.

Venus Beauty Institute 2001

Venus in Fur 2015

Vera Drake 2005

Verdict, The 1982

Vermont is for Lovers 1995

Verne Miller 1987

Veronica Guerin 2004

Veronica Mars 2015

Veronika Voss 1982

Very Annie Mary 2003

Very Long Engagement, A 2005

Vertical Limit 2001

Vertical Ray of the Sun, The 2002

Vertigo [1958] 1996

Very Bad Things 1999

Very Brady Sequel, A 1996

Very Good Girls 2015

Very Harold & Kumar 3D Christmas, A 2012

Very Thought of You, The 2000

Vesnicko ma strediskova. *See* My Sweet Little Village.

Veuve de Saint-Pierre, La. *See* Widow of Saint-Pierre, The.

V/H/S 2013

V/H/S/2 2014

Via Appia 1991

Viaggio d'amore. *See* Journey of Love.

Vibes 1988

Vice Squad 1982

Vice Versa 1988
Vicky Cristina Barcelona 2009
Victim [1961] 1984
Victor Frankenstein 2016
Victoria 2016
Victoria & Abdul 2018
Victor/Victoria 1982
Victory 1981
Victory. *See* Vincere.
Videodrome 1983
Vie Apres l'Amour, La. *See* Life After Love.
Vie continue, La 1982
Vie d'Adele, La. *See* Blue is the Warmest Color.
Vie de Boheme, La 1995
Vie en Rose, La 2008
Vie est rien d'autre, La. *See* Life and Nothing But.
Vie est un long fleuve tranquille, La. *See* Life Is a Long Quiet River.
Vie Promise, La. *See* Promised Life, The.
Vierde Man, De. *See* 4th Man, The.
View from the Top 2004
View to a Kill, A 1985
Village, The 2005
Village of the Damned 1995
Ville est Tranquille, La. *See* Town is Quiet, The.
Vince Vaughn's Wild West Comedy Show: 30 Days & 30 Nights—Hollywood to the Heartland 2009
Vincent and Theo 1990
Vincere 2011
Violets Are Blue 1986
Violins Came with the Americans, The 1987
Violon Rouge, Le. *See* Red Violin, The.
Viper 1988
Virgen de los Sicanos, La. *See* Our Lady of the Assassins.
Virgin Queen of St. Francis High, The 1987
Virgin Suicides, The 2001
Virtuosity 1995
Virus 2000
Vision Quest 1985
Visions of Light 1993
Visions of the Spirit 1988
Visit, The 2002
Visit, The 2016
Visiting Hours 1982
Visitor, The 2009
Visitor, The. *See* Ghost.
Vital Signs 1990
Volcano 1997
Volere, Volare 1992
Volunteers 1985
Volver 2007
Volver a empezar 1982
Vor. *See* Thief, The.
Vow, The 2013
Voyage du ballon rouge, Le. *See* Flight of the Red Balloon.
Voyager 1992
Voyages 2002
Voyeur 1995
Vroom 1988
Vulture, The 1985
Vzlomshik. *See* Burglar, The.

W

W. 2009
Wackness, The 2009
Waco: The Rules of Engagement 1997
Wag the Dog 1997
Wagner 1983
Wagons East! 1995
Wah-Wah 2007
Wailing, The 2017
Waist Deep 2007
Wait for Me in Heaven 1990
Wait Until Spring, Bandini 1990
Waiting... 2006
Waiting for Gavrilov 1983
Waiting for Guffman 1997
Waiting for 'Superman' 2011
Waiting for the Light 1990
Waiting for the Moon 1987
Waiting to Exhale 1995
Waitress 1982
Waitress (Shelly) 2008
Wakefield 2018
Waking Life 2002
Waking Ned Devine 1999
Waking the Dead 2001
Walk, The 2016
Walk Among the Tombstones, A 2015
Walk Hard: The Dewey Cox Story 2008
Walk in the Clouds, A 1995
Walk in the Woods, A 2016
Walk Like a Man 1987
Walk on the Moon, A 1987
Walk on the Moon, A (Goldwyn) 2000
Walk the Line 2006
Walk to Remember, A 2003
Walker 1987
Walking and Talking 1996
Walking After Midnight 1988
Walking Dead, The 1995
Walking Out 2018
Walking Tall 2005
Walking with Dinosaurs 3D 2014
Wall, The 1986
Wall, The 2018
Wall Street 1987
Wallace & Gromit: The Curse of the Were-Rabbit 2006
WALL-E 2009
Wall Street: Money Never Sleeps 2011
Waltz Across Texas 1983
Waltz with Bashir 2009
Wandafuru raifu. *See* After Life.
Wanderlust 2013
Wannsee Conference, The 1987
Wannseekonferenz, Die. *See* Wannsee Conference, The.
Wanted 2009
Wanted: Dead or Alive 1987
War 1988
War (Arwell) 2008
War, The 1995
War Against the Indians 1995

War and Love 1985
War at Home, The 1997
War Dogs 2017
War for the Planet of the Apes 2018
War Horse 2012
War, Inc. 2009
War of the Buttons 1995
War of the Roses, The 1989
War of the Worlds 2006
War Party 1988
War Room 2016
War Room, The 1993
War Tapes, The 2007
War Witch 2014
War Zone, The 2000
Ward, The 2012
Warcraft 2017
WarGames 1983
Warlock 1989, 1990
Warlock: The Armageddon 1993
Warm Bodies 2014
Warm Nights on a Slow Moving Train 1987
Warm Summer Rain 1989
Warm Water Under a Red Bridge 2002
Warning Bandits 1987
Warning Sign 1985
Warrior 2012
Warrior Queen 1987
Warriors of Heaven and Earth 2005
Warriors of Virtue 1997
Wash, The 1988
Washington Heights 2004
Washington Square 1997
Wassup Rockers 2007
Watch It 1993
Watch, The 2013
Watcher, The 2001
Watchers 1988
Watchmen 2010
Water 1986
Water 2007
Water and Soap 1985
Water Diviner, The 2016
Water Drops on Burning Rocks 2001
Water for Elephants 2012
Water Horse: Legend of the Deep, The 2008
Waterboy, The 1999
Waterdance, The 1992
Waterland 1992
Waterloo Bridge [1940] 1981
Waterworld 1995
Wave, The 2017
Wavelength 1983
Waxwork 1988
Way, The 2012
Way Back, The 2011
Way Down East [1920] 1984
Way of the Gun, The 2001
Way Way Back, The 2014
Way We Laughed, The 2002
Way We Were, The [1973] 1981
waydowntown 2001
Wayne's World 1992
Wayne's World II 1993
W.E. 2012
We All Loved Each Other So Much 1984
We Are Marshall 2007
We Are the Best! 2015
We Are What We Are 2014
We Are Your Friends 2016
We Bought a Zoo 2012
We Don't Live Here Anymore 2005
We Need to Talk About Kevin 2012
We Never Die 1993
We of the Never Never 1983
We Own the Night 2008
We the Living 1988
We Think the World of You 1988
We Were Soldiers 2003
Weather Man, The 2006
Weather Underground, The 2004
Wedding, A [1978] 1982
Wedding Banquet, The 1993
Wedding Bell Blues 1997
Wedding Crashers 2006
Wedding Date, The 2006
Wedding Gift, The 1995
Wedding in Galilee, A 1987
Wedding Plan, The 2018
Wedding Planner, The 2002
Wedding Ringer, The 2016
Wedding Singer, The 1999
Weeds 1987
Weekend at Bernie's 1989
Weekend at Bernie's II 1993
Weekend Pass 1984
Weekend Warriors 1986
Weekend with Barbara und Ingrid, A 1995
Weeping Meadow 2006
Weight of Water, The 2003
Weiner 2017
Weininger's Last Night 1995
Weird Science 1985
Weisse Band, Das. *See* White Ribbon, The.
Welcome Home 1989
Welcome Home Roscoe Jenkins 2009
Welcome Home, Roxy Carmichael 1990
Welcome in Vienna 1988
Welcome to Collinwood 2003
Welcome to Me 2016
Welcome to Mooseport 2005
Welcome to Sarajevo 1997
Welcome to the Dollhouse 1996
Welcome to the Rileys 2011
Welcome to Woop Woop 1999
Wendigo 2003
Wendy and Lucy 2009
We're Back 1993
We're No Angels [1955] (Curtiz) 1982
We're No Angels (Jordan) 1989
We're Talkin' Serious Merry 1992
We're the Millers 2014
Wes Craven Presents: Dracula 2000 2001
Wes Craven Presents: They 2003
Wes Craven's New Nightmare 1995
West Beirut 2000
West Beyrouth. *See* West Beirut.

West of Memphis 2013
Western 1999
Wet and Wild Summer. *See* Exchange Lifeguards.
Wet Hot American Summer 2002
Wetherby 1985
Wettest County in the World, The. *See* Lawless.
Whale Rider 2004
Whales of August, The 1987
What a Girl Wants 2004
What About Bob? 1991
What Dreams May Come 1999
What Happened to Kerouse? 1986
What Happened Was... 1995
What Happens in Vegas 2009
What If 2015
What Just Happened 2009
What Lies Beneath 2001
What Maisie Knew 2014
What Planet Are You From? 2001
What the (Bleep) Do We Know? 2005
What Time Is It There? 2002
What to Expect When You're Expecting 2013
What We Do in the Shadows 2016
What Women Want 2001
Whatever 1999
Whatever It Takes (Demchuk) 1986
Whatever It Takes (Raynr) 2001
Whatever Works 2010
What's Cooking? 2001
What's Eating Gilbert Grape 1993
What's Love Got To Do With It 1993
What's the Worst That Could Happen? 2002
What's Your Number? 2012
When a Man Loves a Woman 1995
When a Stranger Calls 2007
When Brendan Met Trudy 2002
When Did You Last See Your Father? 2009
When Father Was Away on Business 1985
When Harry Met Sally 1989
When in Rome 2011
When Love Comes 2000
When Nature Calls 1985
When Night is Falling 1995
When the Bough Breaks 2017
When the Cat's Away 1997
When the Game Stands Tall 2015
When the Party's Over 1993
When the Whales Came 1989
When the Wind Blows 1987
When We Were Kings 1997
When Will I Be Loved 2005
Where Angels Fear to Tread 1992
Where Are the Children? 1986
Where Do We Go Now? 2013
Where Spring Comes Late 1988
Where the Boys are '84 1984
Where the Day Takes You 1992
Where the Green Ants Dream 1985
Where the Heart Is (Boorman) 1990
Where the Heart Is (Williams) 2001
Where the Heart Roams 1987
Where the Money Is 2001
Where the Outback Ends 1988
Where the River Runs Black 1986
Where The Rivers Flow North 1995
Where the Truth Lies 2006
Where the Wild Things Are 2010
Where to Invade Next 2016
Wherever You Are 1988
While We're Young 2016
While You Were Sleeping 1995
Whip It 2010
Whiplash 2015
Whiskey Tango Foxtrot 2017
Whispers in the Dark 1992
Whistle Blower, The 1987
Whistleblower, The 2012
White 1995
White Badge 1995
White Balloon, The 1996
White Bird in a Blizzard 2015
White Boys 2000
White Chicks 2005
White Countess, The 2006
White Dog 1995
White Fang 1991
White Fang II: Myth of the White Wolf 1995
White Girl, The 1990
White God 2016
White House Down 2014
White Hunter, Black Heart 1990
White Man's Burden 1995
White Material 2011
White Men Can't Jump 1992
White Mischief 1988
White Nights 1985
White Noise 2006
White of the Eye 1987, 1988
White Oleander 2003
White Palace 1990
White Ribbon, The 2010
White Rose, The 1983
White Sands 1992
White Sister, The [1923] 1982
White Squall 1996
White Trash 1992
White Winter Heat 1987
Whiteout 2010
Who Framed Roger Rabbit 1988
Who Killed the Electric Car? 2007
Who Killed Vincent Chin? 1988
Who Knows? *See* Va Savoir.
Who Shot Pat? 1992
Whole Nine Yards, The 2001
Whole Ten Yards, The 2005
Whole Wide World, The 1997
Whoopee Boys, The 1986
Whore 1991
Who's Afraid of Virginia Wolf? [1966] 1993
Who's Harry Crumb? 1989
Who's That Girl 1987
Who's the Man? 1993
Whose Life Is It Anyway? 1981
Whose Streets? 2018
Why Did I Get Married? 2008
Why Did I Get Married Too? 2011
Why Do Fools Fall In Love 1999

Why Has Bodhi-Dharma Left for the East? 1995
Why Him? 2017
Why Me? 1990
Why We Fight 2007
Wicked Lady, The 1983
Wicked Stepmother 1989
Wicker Man, The [1974] 1985
Wicker Man, The 2007
Wicker Park 2005
Wide Awake 1999
Wide Sargasso Sea 1993
Widow of Saint-Pierre, The 2002
Widows' Peak 1995
Wiener-Dog 2017
Wife, The 1996
Wigstock: the Movie 1995
Wilbur Wants to Kill Himself 2005
Wild 2015
Wild, The 2007
Wild America 1997
Wild at Heart 1990
Wild Bill 1995
Wild Bunch, The [1969] 1995
Wild Duck, The 1985
Wild Geese II 1985
Wild Grass 2011
Wild Hearts Can't Be Broken 1991
Wild Hogs 2008
Wild Horses 1984
Wild Life, The 1984
Wild Life, The 2017
Wild Man Blues 1999
Wild Orchid 1990
Wild Orchid II: Two Shades of Blue 1992
Wild Pair, The 1987
Wild Parrots of Telegraph Hill, The 2006
Wild Reeds 1995
Wild Tales 2016
Wild Thing 1987
Wild Things 1999
Wild Thornberrrys Movie, The 2003
Wild West 1993
Wild West Comedy Show. *See* Vince Vaughn's Wild West Comedy Show: 30 Days & 30 Nights—Hollywood to the Heartland.
Wild Wild West 2000
Wildcats 1986
Wilde 1999
Wilder Napalm 1993
Wildfire 1988
Willard 2004
William Shakespeare's A Midsummer's Night Dream 2000
William Shakespeare's Romeo & Juliet 1996
William Shakespeare's The Merchant of Venice. *See* Merchant of Venice, The.
Willow 1988
Wilson 2018
Wilt. *See* Misadventures of Mr. Wilt, The.
Wimbledon 2005
Win. *See* Vincere.
Win a Date with Tad Hamilton 2005
Win Win 2012
Wind 1992
Wind, The [1928] 1984
Wind in the Willows, The 1997
Wind Rises, The 2014
Wind River 2018
Wind the Shakes the Barley, The 2008
Wind Will Carry Us, The 2001
Window Shopping 1995
Window to Paris 1995
Windtalkers 2003
Windy City 1984
Wing Commanders 2000
Winged Migration 2004
Wings of Desire 1988
Wings of the Dove 1997
Winner, The 1997
Winners, The 2000
Winners Take All 1987
Winnie the Pooh 2012
Winslow Boy, The 2000
Winter Guest, The 1997
Winter Meeting [1948] 1986
Winter of Our Dreams 1982
Winter on Fire: Ukraine's Fight for Freedom 2016
Winter Passing 2007
Winter People 1989
Winter Sleep 2015
Winter Solstice 2006
Winter Tan, A 1988
Winter War, The. *See* Talvison.
Winter's Bone 2011
Winter's Tale 2015
Wiping the Tears of Seven Generations 1995
Wired 1989
Wired to Kill 1986
Wirey Spindell 2001
Wisdom 1986
Wise Guys 1986
Wisecracks 1992
Wish I Was Here 2015
Wish Upon 2018
Wish You Were Here 1987
Wishmaster 1997
Witch, The 2017
Witchboard 1987
Witches, The 1990
Witches of Eastwick, The 1987
With a Friend Like Harry 2002
With Friends Like These... 2006
With Honors 1995
With Love to the Person Next to Me 1987
Withnail and I 1987
Without a Clue 1988
Without a Paddle 2005
Without a Trace 1983
Without Evidence 1996
Without Limits 1999
Without You I'm Nothing 1990
Witless Protection 2009
Witness 1985
Witness for the Prosecution 1986
Witness to a Killing 1987
Witnesses, The 2009
Wittgenstein 1995

Wizard, The 1989

Wizard of Loneliness, The 1988

Wizard of Oz, The [1939], 1999

Wo De Fu Qin Mu Qin. *See* Road Home, The.

Wo Die Gruenen Ameisen Traeumen. *See* Where the Green Ants Dream.

Wo Hu Zang Long. *See* Crouching Tiger, Hidden Dragon.

Wolf 1995

Wolf of Wall Street, The 2014

Wolfen 1981

Wolfman, The 2011

Wolfpack, The 2016

Wolverine, The 2014

Woman, Her Men, and Her Futon, A 1992

Woman, The 2012

Woman in Black, The 2013

Woman in Black 2: Angel of Death, The 2016

Woman in Flames, A 1984

Woman in Gold 2016

Woman in Red, The 1984

Woman in the Moon 1988

Woman in the Window, The [1944] 1982

Woman Next Door, The 1982

Woman on the Beach, The [1947] 1982

Woman's Pale Blue Handwriting, A 1988

Woman's Tale, A 1991

Wombling Free [1979] 1984

Women, The 2009

Women in Trouble 2010

Women on the Verge of a Nervous Breakdown 1988

Women's Affair 1988

Women's Balcony, The 2018

Wonder 2018

Wonder Boys 2001

Wonder Wheel 2018

Wonder Woman 2018

Wonderful Days. *See* Sky Blue.

Wonderful, Horrible Life of Leni Riefenstahl, The 1995

Wonderland (Saville) 1989

Wonderland (Winterbottom) 2001

Wonderland (Cox) 2004

Wonderstruck 2018

Won't Back Down 2013

Woo 1999

Wood, The 2000

Woodshock 2018

Woodsman, The 2005

Woodstock 1995

Wordplay 2007

Words, The 2013

Words and Pictures 2015

Work, The 2018

Working Girl 1988

Working Girls 1987

World According to Garp, The 1982

World and Time Enough 1996

World Apart, A 1988

World Gone Wild 1988

World Is Not Enough, The 2000

World of Henry Orient, The [1964] 1983

World Trade Center 2007

World Traveler 2003

World War Z 2014

World's End, The 2014

World's Fastest Indian, The 2007

World's Greatest Dad 2010

Wormwood 2018

Worth Winning 1989

Wraith, The 1986

Wrath of the Titans 2013

Wreck-It Ralph 2013

Wrestler, The 2009

Wrestling Ernest Hemingway 1993

Wristcutters: A Love Story 2008

Wrong Couples, The 1987

Wrong Guys, The 1988

Wrong Is Right 1982

Wrong Man, The 1995

Wrong Turn 2004

Wrongfully Accused 1999

Wu ji. *See* Promise, The.

Wu jian dao. *See* Infernal Affairs.

Wuthering Heights 2013

Wyatt Earp 1995

X

X. *See* Malcolm X.

X-Files, The 1999

X-Files: I Want to Believe, The 2009

X-Men, The 2001

X-Men: Apocalypse 2017

X-Men: Days of Future Past 2015

X-Men: First Class 2012

X-Men: The Last Stand 2007

X-Men Origins: Wolverine 2010

X2: X-Men United 2004

Xero. *See* Home Remedy.

Xiao cai feng. *See* Balzac and the Little Chinese Seamstress.

Xica [1976] 1982

Xica da Silva. *See* Xica.

Xingfu Shiguang. *See* Happy Times.

Xiu Xiu, The Sent Down Girl 2000

Xizao. *See* Shower, The.

XX/XY 2004

XXX 2003

XXX: Return of Xander Cage 2018

XXX: State of the Union 2006

Y

Y tu mama tambien 2003

Yaaba 1990

Yards, The 2001

Yari No Gonza Kasane Katabira. *See* Gonza the Spearman.

Yatgo Ho Yan. *See* Mr. Nice Guy.

Year My Voice Broke, The 1987, 1988

Year of Comet 1992

Year of Living Dangerously, The 1983

Year of the Dog 2008

Year of the Dragon 1985

Year of the Gun 1991

Year of the Horse 1997

Year of the Quiet Sun, A 1986

Year One 2010

Yearling, The [1946] 1989

Yella 2009

Yellowbeard 1983

Yen Family 1988, 1990

Yentl 1983

Yes 2006

Yes, Giorgio 1982

Yes Man 2009

Yesterday. *See* Quitting.

Yi Yi 2001

Yihe yuan. *See* Summer Palace.

Ying xiong. *See* Hero.

Yoga Hosers 2017

Yogi Bear 2011

Yol 1982

Yor: The Hunter from the Future 1983

You Again 2011

You, Me and Dupree 2007

You Can Count on Me 2001

You Can't Hurry Love 1988

You Don't Mess with the Zohan 2009

You Got Served 2005

You Kill Me 2008

You So Crazy 1995

You Talkin' to Me? 1987

You Toscanini 1988

You Will Meet a Tall Dark Stranger 2011

Young Adam 2005

Young Adult 2012

Young and Beautiful 2015

Young@Heart 2009

Young Dr. Kildare [1938] 1985

Young Doctors in Love 1982

Young Einstein 1988

Young Guns 1988

Young Guns II 1990

Young Messiah, The 2017

Young Ones 2015

Young Poisoner's Handbook, The 1996

Young Sherlock Holmes 1985

Young Soul Rebels 1991

Young Victoria, The 2010

Youngblood 1986

Your Friends & Neighbors 1999

Your Highness 2012

Your Name 2018

Your Sister's Sister 2013

You're Next 2014

Yours, Mine & Ours 2006

Youth 2016

Youth in Revolt 2011

Youth Without Youth 2008

You've Got Mail 1999

Yu-Gi-Oh! The Movie 2005

Z

Z for Zachariah 2016

Zack and Miri Make a Porno 2009

Zappa 1984

Zapped! 1982

Zathura 2006

Zatoichi 2005

Zebdegi Edame Darad. *See* And Life Goes On.

Zebrahead 1992

Zegen. *See* Pimp, The.

Zelary 2005

Zelig 1983

Zelly and Me 1988

Zentropa 1992

Zero Dark Thirty 2013

Zero Degrees Kelvin 1996

Zero Effect 1999

Zero Patience 1995

Zero Theorem, The 2015

Zeus and Roxanne 1997

Zhou Yu's Train 2005

Zir-e Poust-e Shahr. *See* Under the Skin of the City.

Zjoek 1987

Zodiac 2008

Zombie and the Ghost Train 1995

Zombie High 1987

Zombieland 2010

Zookeeper 2012

Zookeeper's Wife, The 2018

Zoolander 2002

Zoolander 2 2017

Zoom 2007

Zoot Suit 1981

Zootopia 2017

Zuotian. *See* Quitting.

Zus & Zo 2004

Zwartboek. *See* Black Book.